Cost Accounting

Cost Accounting

FOUNDATIONS AND EVOLUTIONS 7E

CECILY A. RAIBORN
Texas State University – San Marcos

MICHAEL R. KINNEY
Texas A&M University

SOUTH-WESTERN
CENGAGE Learning™

Australia • Brazil • Canada • Mexico • Singapore • Spain • United Kingdom • United States

SOUTH-WESTERN
CENGAGE Learning™

Cost Accounting: Foundations and Evolutions, Seventh Edition
Cecily A. Raiborn and Michael R. Kinney

VP/Editorial Director:
Jack W. Calhoun

Editor-in-Chief:
Rob Dewey

Acquisitions Editor:
Keith Chasse

Associate Developmental Editor:
Jessica Kempf

Marketing Manager:
Kristen Hurd

Associate Content Project Manager:
Scott Dillon

Marketing Communications Manager:
Libby Shipp

Managing Technology Project Manager:
Matt McKinney

Senior Manufacturing Coordinator:
Doug Wilke

Art Director:
Stacy Jenkins Shirley

Internal Designer:
Ke Design, Cincinnati

Production House:
Newgen–Austin

Library of Congress Control Number:
2007933039

For more information about our products, contact us at:

Cengage Learning Academic Resource Center
1-800-423-0563

South-Western Cengage Learning
5191 Natorp Boulevard
Mason, OH 45040
USA

Brief Contents

Contents

CHAPTER 8
The Master Budget 271

CHAPTER 9
Break-Even Point and
Cost-Volume-Profit Analysis 319

CHAPTER 10
Relevant Information for Decision Making 355

CHAPTER 11
Allocation of Joint Costs and
Accounting for By-Product/Scrap 399

Preface

Cost accounting is a dynamic discipline constantly responding to the needs of managers in a highly competitive and global business world. Managers need cost accounting tools to develop, implement, and evaluate strategy. Managers also need cost accounting methods to determine product costs for internal management and external financial reporting. The seventh edition of *Cost Accounting: Foundations and Evolutions* provides in-depth coverage of cost management concepts and procedures in a logically sequenced and student-friendly framework. This text encourages students to go beyond the numbers and think critically about business decisions.

A text is valuable only when students find the subject matter applicable to their business and personal lives. Through the use of a straightforward, readable approach, *Cost Accounting: Foundations and Evolutions* displays the real-world relevance of this topic to its readers.

Improvements in the Seventh Edition

Streamlined Approach

The seventh edition of *Cost Accounting: Foundations and Evolutions* has been reformatted in a way that conveys the importance of the material to students. Real-world examples and ethical coverage are now incorporated into the main text rather than contained within boxed features. This adds to each chapter's flow and readability and helps to close the gap between the real world and the classroom experience. The fictional companies used within the chapters have been based in part on actual companies and their activities; elimination of the boxed features, however, allows the reader to move more quickly through each chapter's substance.

End-of-Chapter Improvements

The end-of-chapter content has been enhanced in both quantity and quality. All end-of-chapter exercises and problems have been matched to the learning objectives for easy reference to the chapter content when completing the assignments. Furthermore, cost accounting instructors across the country identified weak exercises and problems in the sixth edition and those have been eliminated or improved to make them more useful to students. A number of problems with various degrees of difficulty have been added to each chapter to provide more assignment options for instructors. Problems pertaining to the service industry have been added where appropriate as well. In the solutions manual available to instructors, the degree of difficulty (easy, medium, and difficult) for each exercise and problem is noted.

Increased Coverage of Ethics

Due to the importance of ethics in today's business environment, more attention was given to the topic as it relates to cost accounting. A new end-of-chapter section titled *Potential Ethical Issues* brings awareness to the dilemmas one may encounter when applying the concepts of that chapter. Coverage of ethics is also expanded in the chapters where applicable and a new ethics icon alerts readers of this coverage. This same icon is used in the end-of-chapter materials to designate items that contain ethical situations.

The previous editions' features that users indicated were strengths of this cost textbook over its competitors were retained in the seventh edition. Hence, the comprehensive review module, solution strategies, demonstration problems, and end-of-chapter content have been continued and updated. These hallmark features make this text easy for students to read and understand as well as easy for faculty to teach.

Instructor Support Materials

A comprehensive instructor support package is provided for this text, including:

PowerPoint Lecture Slides. The PowerPoint slides provide valuable and informative outlines of the text information. The full-color, electronic presentations are ready to use in your classroom and provide the basis for a lecture. The PowerPoint Lecture Slides can be found at international.cengage .com.

ExamView Pro® Testing Software. This software is easy-to-use and it allows you to customize exams, practice tests, and tutorials. ExamView Pro software allows you to deliver these materials over a network, on the Web, or in printed form. The ExamView Pro Testing Software can be found at international.cengage.com.

Test Bank. The Test Bank is also available in Microsoft Word format. It contains thousands of multiple-choice, short exercise, and short discussion questions with related solutions. All test bank questions and solutions have been verified for accuracy. The Test Bank can be found at international .cengage.com.

Excel Spreadsheet Solutions. The Excel Spreadsheet Solutions provide instructors with solutions to the student spreadsheets created for designated end-of-chapter exercises and problems. Spreadsheet Solutions are available online at international.cengage.com.

Instructor's Manual. The Instructor's Manual is available online at international.cengage.com. The Instructor's Manual contains terminology glossaries for each chapter, lecture outline summaries, and chapter post-tests.

Solutions Manual. The seventh edition's Solutions Manual has been prepared by the authors and verified twice for accuracy. It contains solutions to all numerical end-of-chapter materials and many non-numerical items with discussion points provided for many of the features in the book. The Solutions Manual also includes a copy of the Student Check Figures.

Solution Transparency Acetates. Acetates are provided from the Solutions Manual for all numerical end-of-chapter materials.

Web Resources. This text's supporting Web site at international.cengage.com provides downloadable versions of key instructor supplements, as well as student features that enhance students' learning experience.

WebTutor Toolbox for WebCT and WebTutor Toolbox for Blackboard. These items provide instructors with the course management tools and multimedia assets that instructors need to facilitate online learning. (See Student Support Materials for learning features.)

Student Support Materials

Excel Spreadsheet Templates. This package allows students to solve selected and icon-designated end-of-chapter exercises and problems using Excel. Templates are available online at the text Web site or from the instructor.

Web Resources. This text's supporting Web site at international.cengage.com provides online quizzes, Excel templates to solve selected end-of-chapter problems, links to other cost accounting resources, updates on URL citations in the text, and more.

Acknowledgments

We would like to thank all the people who have helped us during the revision of this text. The constructive comments and suggestions made by the following reviewers were instrumental in developing, rewriting, reorganizing, and improving the quality, readability, and student orientation of *Cost Accounting: Foundations and Evolutions*.

Ron Stunda
Birmingham-Southern College

Herb Martin
Hope College

Ping Lin
California State University at Long Beach

James A. Rodwell
Davenport University

Allison G. Hubley
Davenport University

Emilia Chukwuma
Gallaudet University

J. David Fred
Indiana University at South Bend

Kenneth P. Sinclair
Lehigh University

Barbara Woods McElroy
Susquehanna University

Michael Haselkorn
Bentley College

Charles Wain
Babson College

Robert E. Holtfreter
Central Washington University

Adam Koch
Carnegie Mellon University

Barbara A. Durham
University of Central Florida

We are grateful for the materials from the Institute of Management Accountants, American Institute of CPAs, and various periodical publishers that have contributed significantly to making this text a truly useful learning tool for the students. The authors wish to thank all the people at Thomson/South-Western (especially Scott Dillon, content project manager, and Jessica Kempf, associate developmental editor) who have helped us on this project. Special thanks go to Jamie Armstrong, at Newgen–Austin Publishing and Data Services, for her time and effort on this edition. Dawn Newell, now a Masters of Accountancy graduate from Texas State University–San Marcos, provided excellent insight on ways to make the text more student-friendly and readable. Lastly, sincere gratitude goes to our families and friends who provided unending support and encouragement during this process.

Cecily Raiborn & Mike Kinney

Cost Accounting

1 Introduction to Cost Accounting

Objectives

After completing this chapter, you should be able to answer the following questions:

LO.1 What are the relationships among financial, management, and cost accounting?

LO.2 What are the sources of authoritative pronouncements for the practice of cost accounting?

LO.3 What are the sources of ethical standards for cost accountants?

LO.4 What is a mission statement, and why is it important to organizational strategy?

LO.5 What must accountants understand about an organization's structure and business environment to perform effectively in that organization?

LO.6 What is a value chain, and what are the major value chain functions?

LO.7 How is a balanced scorecard used to implement an organization's strategy?

LO.8 Why is ethical behavior so important in organizations?

Introduction

Starting a career as a junior auditor with the goal of becoming partner in a public accounting firm is the dream of many accounting majors. However, a career goal of becoming a chief financial officer or controller is equally viable, and the end result can be equally rewarding. This text presents tools and techniques used by cost and management accountants and provides problem-solving methods that are useful in achieving corporate goals. Such knowledge will prove valuable to a student who wants to become a Certified Public Accountant (CPA) and/or a Certified Management Accountant (CMA). The first part of this text presents the traditional methods of cost and management accounting that are the building blocks for generating information used to satisfy internal and external user needs. The second part of the text presents innovative cost and management accounting topics and methods.

LO.1
What are the relationships among financial, management, and cost accounting?

Comparison of Financial, Management, and Cost Accounting

Accounting is called the language of business. As such, accounting can be viewed as having different "dialects." The financial accounting "dialect" is often characterized as the primary focus of accounting. Financial accounting concentrates on the preparation and reporting of financial statements: the balance sheet, income statement, cash flow statement, and statement of changes in stockholders' equity. The second "dialect" of accounting is that of management and cost accounting. Management accounting is concerned with providing information to parties inside an organization so that they can plan, control operations, make decisions, and evaluate performance.[1]

Financial Accounting

The objective of financial accounting is to provide useful information to external parties, including investors and creditors. Financial accounting requires compliance with generally accepted accounting principles (GAAP), which are primarily issued by the Financial Accounting Standards Board (FASB) and the Securities and Exchange Commission (SEC). Financial accounting information is typically historical, quantitative, monetary, and verifiable. Such information usually reflects activities of the whole organization. Publicly held companies are required to have their financial statements audited by an independent auditing firm. Oversight of auditing standards for public companies is the responsibility of the Public Company Accounting Oversight Board (PCAOB). The PCAOB was created by the Sarbanes-Oxley Act of 2002 (SOX) because, in part, of perceived abuses of accounting information by corporate managers.

In the early 1900s, financial accounting was the dominant source of information for evaluating business operations. Companies often used return on investment (ROI) to allocate resources and evaluate divisional performance.[2] ROI is calculated as net income divided by total assets. Using a single measure such as ROI for decision making was considered reasonable when companies engaged in one type of activity, operated only domestically, were primarily labor intensive, and were managed and owned by a small number of people who were very familiar with the operating processes.

As the securities market grew, so did the demand for audited financial statements. Preparing financial reports was costly, and information technology was limited. Developing a management accounting system separate from the financial accounting system would have been cost prohibitive, particularly given the limited benefits that would have accrued to managers and owners who were intimately familiar with their company's singular operating activity. Collecting

---

[1] Other accounting "dialects," such as tax and auditing, are beyond the scope of this text.
[2] H. Thomas Johnson and Robert S. Kaplan, *Relevance Lost: The Rise and Fall of Management Accounting* (Boston, MA: Harvard Business School Press, 1987).

information and providing reports to management on a real-time basis would have been impossible in that era.

Management Accounting

Management accounting is used to gather the financial and nonfinancial information needed by internal users. Managers are concerned with fulfilling corporate goals, communicating and implementing strategy, and coordinating product design, production, and marketing while simultaneously running distinct business segments. Management accounting information commonly addresses individual or divisional concerns rather than those of the firm as a whole. Management accounting is not required to adhere to GAAP but provides both historical and forward-looking information for managers.

By the mid-1900s, managers were often no longer owners but, instead, individuals who had been selected for their positions because of their skills in accounting, finance, or law. These managers frequently lacked in-depth knowledge of a company's underlying operations and processes. Additionally, companies began operating in multiple states and countries, and manufacturing many products in a non-labor-intensive environment. Trying to manage by using only financial reporting information sometimes created dysfunctional behavior. Managers needed an accounting system that could help implement and monitor a company's goals in a globally competitive, multiple-product environment. Introduction of affordable information technology allowed management accounting to develop into a discipline separate from financial accounting. Thus, under these new circumstances, management accounting evolved to be independent of financial accounting. The primary differences between financial and management accounting are shown in Exhibit 1–1.

Cost Accounting

As illustrated in Exhibit 1–2, cost accounting can be seen as the intersection between financial and management accounting. Cost accounting information addresses the demands of both financial and management accounting by providing product cost information to (1) external parties (stockholders, creditors, and various regulatory bodies) for investment and credit decisions and (2) internal

EXHIBIT 1–1
Financial and Management Accounting Differences

	Financial Accounting	Management Accounting
Primary users	External	Internal
Primary organizational focus	Whole (aggregated)	Parts (segmented)
Information characteristics	Must be	May be
	• Historical	• Current or forecasted
	• Quantitative	• Quantitative or qualitative
	• Monetary	• Monetary or nonmonetary
	• Verifiable	• Timely and, at a minimum, reasonably estimated
Overriding criteria	Generally accepted accounting principles	Situational relevance (usefulness)
	Consistency	Benefits in excess of costs
	Verifiability	Flexibility
Recordkeeping	Formal	Combination of formal and informal

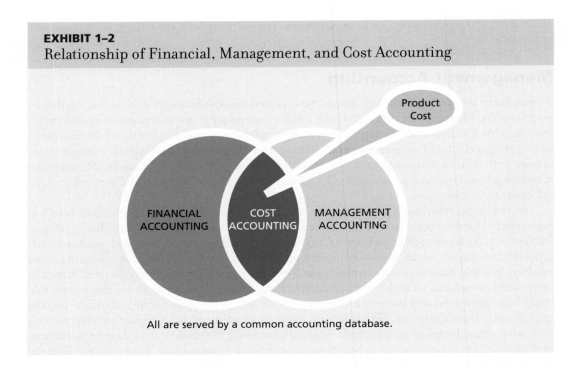

EXHIBIT 1–2
Relationship of Financial, Management, and Cost Accounting

All are served by a common accounting database.

managers for planning, controlling, decision making, and evaluating performance. Product cost information is developed in compliance with GAAP for financial reporting purposes. As such, **product cost** is the sum of the costs incurred within the factory to make one unit of product. But product cost information can also be developed outside of the constraints of GAAP to assist management in its needs for planning and controlling operations.

As companies grew and were organized across multiple locations, financial accounting became less appropriate for satisfying management's information needs. To prepare plans, evaluate performance, and make more complex decisions, management needed forward-looking information rather than only the historical data provided by financial accounting. The **upstream costs** (research, development, and product design) and **downstream costs** (marketing, distribution, and customer service) that companies incurred were becoming a larger percentage of total costs. When making pricing decisions, managers needed to add these upstream and downstream costs to the GAAP-determined product cost. The various types of costs associated with products are shown in Exhibit 1–3.

As companies expand their operations, managers must recognize that a single cost can no longer be computed for a product. For example, a company's Asian operations could be highly labor intensive, whereas North American operations could be highly capital intensive. Product costs cannot be easily compared between the two locations because their production processes are not similar. Such complications have resulted in the evolution of the cost accounting database, which includes more than simply financial accounting measures.

Cost Accounting Standards

LO.2
What are the sources of authoritative pronouncements for the practice of cost accounting?

Although internal accounting reports need not comply with the GAAP established by the FASB and the SEC, three important bodies (the Institute of Management Accountants, Society of Management Accountants of Canada, and Cost Accounting Standards Board) do issue cost accounting guidelines or standards.

The Institute of Management Accountants (IMA) is a voluntary membership organization of accountants, finance specialists, academics, and others. The IMA issues directives on the practice of management and cost accounting called Statements on Management Accounting (SMAs). SMAs are not legally binding standards, but they undergo a rigorous developmental and exposure process

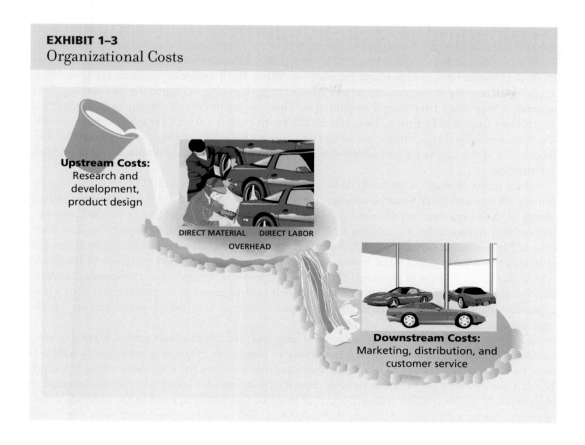

EXHIBIT 1–3
Organizational Costs

Upstream Costs:
Research and development, product design

DIRECT MATERIAL   DIRECT LABOR
OVERHEAD

Downstream Costs:
Marketing, distribution, and customer service

that ensures their wide support. The Society of Management Accountants of Canada, which is similar to the IMA, also issues guidelines on the practice of management accounting. These Management Accounting Guidelines (MAGs), like SMAs, are not mandatory for organizational accounting but are guidelines for high-quality accounting practices. Lastly, in 1970 the U.S. Congress established the Cost Accounting Standards Board (CASB), a public sector body, to issue uniform cost accounting standards for defense contractors and federal agencies. The CASB produced 20 cost accounting standards (one of which has been withdrawn) from its inception until it was terminated in 1980. The CASB was re-created in 1988 as an independent board of the Office of Federal Procurement Policy to help ensure uniformity and consistency in government contracting. CASB standards do not constitute a comprehensive set of rules, but compliance is required for companies bidding on or pricing cost-related contracts to the federal government. Hence, CASB standards are legally binding, whereas SMAs are not.

Although the IMA, Society of Management Accountants of Canada, and CASB have been instrumental in standards development, much of the body of knowledge and practice in management accounting has been provided by industry practice and by economic and finance theory. Thus, no "official" agency publishes generic management accounting standards for all companies, but there is wide acceptance of (and, therefore, authority for) the methods presented in this text.

Because accounting and other information is used to measure an organization's performance, managers may be tempted to manipulate the information to manage the perceptions of others about an organization's performance. A strong organizational commitment to ethical behavior can curb deceptive uses of information.

Professional Ethics

It is important that managers achieve their financial targets; such achievement should be accomplished by concentrating on acquiring a targeted market share and desired levels of customer satisfaction. However, executives at many companies have exhibited unethical behavior in trying to "make their numbers." Earnings management is any accounting method or practice used by

LO.3
What are the sources of ethical standards for cost accountants?

managers or accountants to deliberately "adjust" a company's profit amount to meet a predetermined internal or external target. Earnings management allows a company to meet earnings estimates, preserve a specific earnings trend, convert a loss to a profit, increase management compensation (tied to stock performance), or hide illegal transactions. When the boundaries of reason are exceeded in applying accounting principles, companies are said to be engaging in "aggressive" accounting. Such aggression may range from simply stretching the limits of legitimacy all the way to outright fraud. WorldCom (now MCI), Enron, Tyco, and HealthSouth are but a few of the many companies having managers who faced criminal penalties from acting unethically within the parameters of their jobs. Some of the aggressive accounting practices that have been exposed involved cost accounting information.

As a result of many large financial frauds, the U.S. Congress passed SOX to hold chief executive officers and chief financial officers (CEOs and CFOs) personally accountable for the accuracy of their organizations' financial reporting. In addition, the accounting profession promotes high ethical standards for accountants through several of its professional organizations. The Institute of Management Accountants administers the Certified Management Accountant Exam and publishes the *Statement of Ethical Professional Practice*. CMAs are required to adhere to the IMA's ethical standards. This set of standards (Exhibit 1–4) focuses on competence, confidentiality, integrity, and credibility. Adherence to these standards helps management accountants attain a high level of professionalism, thereby facilitating the development of trust from people inside and outside the organization.

Competence means that individuals will develop and maintain the skills needed to practice their profession. For instance, cost accountants working in companies involved in government contracts must be familiar with not only GAAP but also standards issued by the Cost Accounting Standards Board. Confidentiality means that individuals will refrain from disclosing company information to inappropriate parties (such as competitors) that could be specifically defined in the company's code of ethics. Acting with integrity means that individuals will not participate in activities that would discredit their company or profession. Having integrity precludes such behaviors as cost accountants accepting gifts from suppliers because such gifts could bias (or be perceived to bias) the accountants' ability to fairly evaluate the suppliers and their products. Credibility means that individuals will provide full, fair, and timely disclosure of all relevant information. For example, a cost accountant should not intentionally miscalculate product cost data to materially misstate a company's financial position or results of operations.

Cost and management accountants can face instances in which others in their organization act illegally or immorally; such activities could include financial fraud, theft, environmental violations, or employee discrimination. The accountants should evaluate the situation and, if appropriate, "blow the whistle" on the activities by disclosing them to appropriate persons or agencies. Federal laws, including SOX, provide for legal protection of whistle-blowers. The False Claims Act allows whistle-blowers to receive 15 to 30 percent of any settlement proceeds resulting from the identification of such activities related to fraud against the U.S. government. If managers fail to blow the whistle and knowingly provide false information in public financial reports, they can be severely punished. For example, if the chief financial or chief executive officer knowingly certifies false financial reports, he or she may be punished with a maximum penalty of a $5 million fine, 20 years in prison, or both under SOX.[3]

The IMA's code of ethical conduct also provides guidance on what to do when confronted with ethical issues. Accountants should document what (if any) regulations have been violated, research and record the appropriate actions that should have been taken, and provide evidence of violation of such actions. This information should be kept confidential but reported and discussed with a superior who is not involved in the situation—meaning that it could be necessary to communicate up the corporate ladder, even as far as the audit committee. It is important to document each communication and finding in the process. If accountants cannot resolve the matter, their only recourse could be to resign and consult a legal adviser before reporting the matter to regulatory authorities.

All accountants, regardless of geographical or organizational placement, should recognize their obligations to their profession and to professional ethics. Although the world of business is expanding globally, there are some aspects of business that are similar worldwide. ▲

---

[3]Utpal Bhattacharya, Peter Groznik, and Bruce Haslem, "Is CEO Certification Credible?" *Regulation* (Fall 2003), pp. 8–10.

EXHIBIT 1–4
Statement of Ethical Professional Practice

COMPETENCE

Each member has a responsibility to:
- Maintain an appropriate level of professional expertise by continually developing knowledge and skills.
- Perform professional duties in accordance with relevant laws, regulations, and technical standards.
- Provide decision support information and recommendations that are accurate, clear, concise, and timely.
- Recognize and communicate professional limitations or other constraints that would preclude responsible judgment or successful performance of an activity.

CONFIDENTIALITY

Each member has a responsibility to:
- Keep information confidential except when disclosure is authorized or legally required.
- Inform all relevant parties regarding appropriate use of confidential information. Monitor subordinates' activities to ensure compliance.
- Refrain from using confidential information for unethical or illegal advantage.

INTEGRITY

Each member has a responsibility to:
- Mitigate actual conflicts of interest. Regularly communicate with business associates to avoid apparent conflicts of interest. Advise all parties of potential conflicts.
- Refrain from engaging in any conduct that would prejudice carrying out duties ethically.
- Abstain from engaging in or supporting any activity that might discredit the profession.

CREDIBILITY

Each member has a responsibility to:
- Communicate information fairly and objectively.
- Disclose all relevant information that could reasonably be expected to influence an intended user's understanding of the reports, analyses, or recommendations.
- Disclose delays or deficiencies in information, timeliness, processing, or internal controls in conformance with organization policy and/or applicable law.

RESOLUTION OF ETHICAL CONFLICT

In applying the Standards of Ethical Professional Practice, you may encounter problems identifying unethical behavior or resolving an ethical conflict. When faced with ethical issues, you should follow your organization's established policies on the resolution of such conflict. If these policies do not resolve the ethical conflict, you should consider the following courses of action:
- Discuss the issue with your immediate supervisor except when it appears that the supervisor is involved. In that case, present the issue to the next level. If you cannot achieve a satisfactory resolution, submit the issue to the next management level. If your immediate superior is the chief executive officer or equivalent, the acceptable reviewing authority may be a group such as the audit committee, executive committee, board of directors, board of trustees, or owners. Contact with levels above the immediate superior should be initiated only with your superior's knowledge, assuming he or she is not involved. Communication of such problems to authorities or individuals not employed or engaged by the organization is not considered appropriate, unless your believe there is a clear violation of the law.
- Clarify relevant ethical issues by initiating a confidential discussion with an IMA Ethics Counselor or other impartial advisor to obtain a better understanding of possible courses of action.
- Consult your own attorney as to legal obligations and rights concerning the ethical conflict.

Source: Institute of Management Accountants, IMA Statement of Ethical Professional Practice (2000). Copyright by Institute of Management Accountants, Montvale, NJ, http://www.imanet.org/about_ethics _statement.asp.

Competing in a Global Environment

Most businesses participate in the global economy, which encompasses the international trade of goods and services, movement of labor, and flows of capital and information.[4] The world has essentially become smaller through improved technology and communication capabilities as well as trade agreements that promote international movement of goods and services among countries. Multinational corporation managers must achieve their organization's strategy within a global structure

---

[4]Paul Krugman, *Peddling Prosperity*, quoted by Alan Farmham in "Global—or Just Globaloney," *Fortune* (June 27, 1994), p. 98.

and under international regulations while exercising ethical behavior. One of the key responsibilities of top managers in organizing their businesses for global competition is the assignment of the authority and responsibilities to make decisions.

The cost accountant supplies information needed by both financial and management accountants. Although financial accounting must be prepared in compliance with GAAP, management accounting must be prepared in accordance with management needs. Managers need information that can be used in developing mission statements, implementing strategy, measuring and controlling the value chain and managers' performance, and setting balanced scorecard goals, objectives, and targets.

Organizational Strategy

LO.4
What is a mission statement, and why is it important to organizational strategy?

Each company should have a mission statement that expresses the purposes for which the organization exists, what the organization wants to accomplish, and how its products and services can uniquely meet its targeted customers' needs. Mission statements are generally modified over time to adapt to the ever-changing business environment. These statements are used to develop the organization's strategy or plan of how the firm will fulfill its goals and objectives by deploying its resources to create value for customers and shareholders.

Each organization is unique and, therefore, even organizations in the same industries have unique strategies that are feasible and likely to be successful. Exhibit 1–5 provides a model of the major factors that influence an organization's strategy. These factors include core competencies, organizational structure, management style and organizational culture, organizational constraints, and environmental constraints.

Organizational strategy should be designed to help the firm achieve an advantage over its competitors. For instance, in March 2007, Borders Group Inc. decided to end its alliance with Amazon .com and reopen its own e-commerce Web site in early 2008, to sell or franchise the majority of its overseas stores, and to close almost half of its U.S. Waldenbooks stores . . . all as a result of a change in its strategy to curtail lost book sales to discount and online chains.[5] Small organizations frequently

EXHIBIT 1–5
Factors Influencing Organizational Strategy

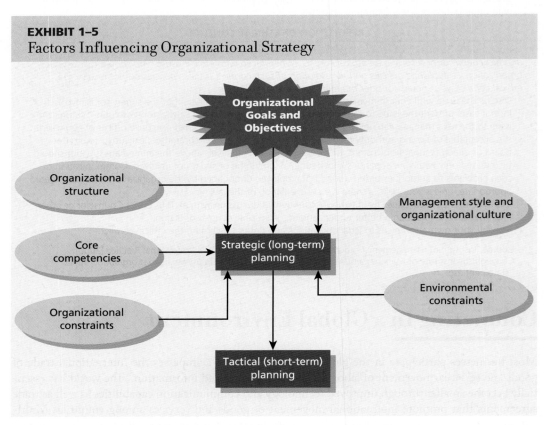

[5]Jeffrey Trachtenberg, "Borders Business Plan Gets a Rewrite," *Wall Street Journal* (March 22, 2007), p. B1.

develop only a single strategy whereas large organizations often design an overall entity strategy as well as individual strategies for each business unit (such as a division). Business unit strategies flow from the organization's overall strategy to ensure effective and efficient resource allocations that are compatible with corporate goals.

Deciding on a strategy is a difficult and often controversial process that should reflect the organization's core competencies. A core competency is any critical function or activity in which an organization seeks a higher proficiency than its competitors, making it the root of competitiveness and competitive advantage. "Core competencies are different for every organization; they are, so to speak, part of an organization's personality."[6] Technological innovation, engineering, product development, and after-sale service are examples of core competencies. The Japanese electronics industry is viewed as having a core competency in the miniaturization of electronics. Disney believes it has a core competency in entertainment. Toyota believes its core competencies are quality engineering and flexible, lean production work flow.

Managers are concerned with formulating strategy, and cost accountants are charged with providing management with the information necessary for assessing progress toward strategic achievement. Most companies employ either a "cost leadership" or a "product differentiation" strategy. Cost leadership refers to a company's ability to maintain its competitive edge by undercutting competitor prices. Successful cost leaders sustain a large market share by focusing almost exclusively on manufacturing products or providing services at a low cost. For example, Wal-Mart, the Honda Fit, and Bic pens compete in their markets based on prices. Product differentiation refers to a company's ability to offer superior quality products or more unique services than competitors; such products and services are, however, generally sold at premium prices. Neiman Marcus, the Mercedes-Benz G-Class, and Mont Blanc pens compete on quality and features. Successful companies generally focus on one strategy or the other; however, many firms focus on both strategies at the same time (possibly for different product lines), although one often dominates.

Cost accountants gather financial and nonfinancial information to help management achieve organizational strategy. Exhibit 1–6 provides a checklist of questions that help indicate whether an organization has a comprehensive strategy in place.

Organizational Structure

An organization is composed of people, resources other than people, and commitments that are acquired and arranged to achieve organizational strategies and goals. An organization normally evolves from its mission, strategies, goals, and managerial personalities. Organizational structure reflects the way in which authority and responsibility for making decisions are distributed in an organization. Authority refers to the right (usually by virtue of position or rank) to use resources to accomplish a task or achieve an objective. Responsibility is the obligation to accomplish a task or achieve an objective.

Every organization contains line and staff personnel, some of whom are in management positions. Line personnel work directly toward attaining organizational goals. Persons in these positions will be held responsible for achieving targeted balanced scorecard measures or budgeted operating income for their divisions or geographic regions. For example, after Kraft Foods Inc. was spun off from its parent company Altria Group Inc. in early 2007, international line managers were told to identify international acquisition targets (especially in Brazil, Mexico, Russia, and Ukraine) because a company "cannot run the world from . . . headquarters. . . . Operating decisions need to be made by local experts."[7]

Staff personnel give assistance and advice to line personnel. Thus, at Kraft Foods, the international line managers would likely develop teams of staff employees to gather financial, product, and distribution network information on various firms that might fit with Kraft's core business operations as a global food company. Relative to top accounting jobs, the treasurer and controller are staff positions. Treasurers are generally responsible for achieving short- and long-term financing, investing, and cash management goals. The controller is responsible for delivering financial reports in conformity with GAAP to management.

LO.5
What must accountants understand about an organization's structure and business environment to perform effectively in that organization?

[6]Peter F. Drucker, "The Information Executives Truly Need," *Harvard Business Review* (January–February 1995), p. 60.
[7]Julie Jargon, "Kraft Sets Path for Overseas Expansion," *Wall Street Journal* (March 22, 2007), p. B4.

EXHIBIT 1–6
Checklist of Strategy Questions

1. Who are your five most important competitors?

2. Is your firm more or less profitable than these firms?

3. Do you generally have higher or lower prices than these firms, for equivalent product/service offerings? Is this difference due mainly to the mix of customers, to different costs, or to different requirements for profit?

4. Do you have higher or lower costs relative to your main competitors? Where in the cost structure (for example, cost of raw materials, cost of product, cost of selling, cost of distributing, cost of advertising and marketing) are the differences most pronounced?

5. [What are] the different business segments which account for 80 percent of your profits? [You will probably find that you are in many more segments than you thought and that their profit variability is much greater than you thought.] If you cannot define the segments that constitute 80 percent of your total profits, you need to conduct a detailed product line profitability review.

6. In each of the business segments defined above, how large are you relative to the largest of your competitors? Are you gaining or losing relative market share?

7. In each of your important business segments, what are your customers' and potential customers' most important purchase criteria?

8. How do you and your main competitors in each segment rate on these purchase criteria?

9. What are the main strengths of the company as a whole, based on aggregating customers' views of your firm in the segments that comprise most of your profits? What other competencies do you believe the firm has, and why do they seem to be not appreciated by the market?

10. Which are your priority segments and where is it most important to the firm as a whole that you gain market share? How confident are you that you will achieve this, given that other firms may have targeted the same segments for market share gain? What is your competitive advantage in these segments and how sure are you that this advantage is real rather than imagined? (If you are not gaining relative market share, the advantage is probably illusory.)

Source: *The Financial Times Guide to Management and Finance* (London: Financial Times/Pearson Education Limited, 1994), p. 359.

A variety of organizational constraints may affect a firm's strategy options. In almost all instances, these hindrances are short term because they can be overcome by existing business opportunities. Three common organizational constraints involve monetary capital, intellectual capital, and technology. Although additional capital funding can almost always be acquired through borrowings or equity sales, management should decide whether (1) the capital can be obtained at a reasonable cost or (2) reallocation of current capital would be more effective and efficient. Intellectual capital encompasses all of the intangible assets contained in an organization: knowledge, skills, and information. Companies rely on their intellectual capital to create ideas for products or services, to train and develop employees, and to attract and retain customers. As to technology, companies must adopt emerging technologies to stay at the top of their industry and achieve a competitive advantage over competitors.

Going global, expanding core competencies, and investing in new technology are all decisions that require organizational change. An organization's ability to change depends heavily on its management style and organizational culture. Different managers exhibit different preferences in how to interact with the entity's stakeholders, especially employees. Management style is exhibited in decision-making processes, risk taking, willingness to encourage change, and employee development, among other issues. Typically, management style is also reflected in the culture of an organization: the basic manner in which the organization interacts with its business environment, the manner in which employees interact with each other and with management, and the underlying beliefs and attitudes held by employees about the organization. Culture has a significant role in determining whether the communication system tends to be formal or informal, whether authority is likely to be concentrated in management or distributed throughout the organization, and whether there are feelings of well-being or stress in organizational members.

Environmental constraints also impact organizational strategy. An environmental constraint is any limitation caused by external cultural, fiscal (such as taxation structures), legal/regulatory, or political situations and by the competitive market structures. Because these constraints cannot be directly controlled by an organization's management, these factors tend to be long-run rather than short-run influences.

Value Chain

LO.6
What is a value chain, and what are the major value chain functions?

The foundation of strategic management is the value chain, which is used to identify the processes that lead to cost leadership or product differentiation. The value chain is a set of value-adding functions or processes that convert inputs into products and services for company customers. Following are definitions contained in the generic value chain shown in Exhibit 1–7. Examples from General Motors are used to illustrate the functions within the value chain.

- Research and Development—experimenting to reduce costs or improve quality. GM can experiment with various paint formulas to produce the most lasting exterior paint finish.

- Design—developing alternative product, service, or process designs. In 1996, GM changed the Corvette design by moving the transmission to the back of the car; this change gave passengers more leg room. Many companies have redesigned plant layouts to reduce production time per unit of output.

- Supply—managing raw materials received from vendors. Companies often develop long-term alliances with suppliers to reduce costs and improve quality. Johnson Controls is the supplier for some General Motors cars' seating systems, electronics, instrument panels, overhead systems, floor consoles, door systems, and cargo management systems. The relationship is working well, given that Johnson Controls is considered one of GM's top suppliers almost every year. In many instances, suppliers become extensions of a company's upstream operations.

- Production—acquiring and assembling resources to manufacture a product or render a service. For GM, production reflects the acquisition of tires, metal, paint, fabric, glass, electronics, brakes, and other inputs and the assembly of those items into an automobile.

- Marketing—promoting a product or service to current and prospective customers. Promotion could involve developing a Super Bowl half-time commercial, placing automobiles on a showroom floor, designing a billboard advertisement, or recording a radio announcement to inform customers about the company's products or services.

- Distribution—delivering a product or service to a customer. GM uses trains and trucks to deliver automobiles to dealerships. Other companies could use airlines or couriers to distribute their products.

- Customer Service—supporting customers after the sale of a product or service. GM provides a 1-800 number for its customers to call if they have questions or need roadside service. Other companies may require customers to return a product if it needs repair.

After developing a strategy, company managers must communicate that strategy to all members in the value chain so that the strategy can be effectively implemented. The communication network needed for coordination between functions is designed in part with input from cost accountants who integrate the information needs of managers of each value chain function.

Balanced Scorecard

LO.7
How is a balanced scorecard used to implement an organization's strategy?

Accounting information is helpful to managers, as they can use it to measure dimensions of performance that are important to accomplishing strategic goals. In the past, management spent significant time analyzing historical financial data to assess whether organizational strategy was effective. Today, firms use a portfolio of information to determine not only how the organization has performed but also how it is likely to perform in the future. Historical financial data reflect lag indicators or outcomes that have resulted from past actions, such as installing a new production process or implementing a new software system. For example, an increase in operating profits (lag indicator) could occur after a new production process is installed. Unfortunately, lag indicators are often recognized and assessed too late to significantly improve current or future actions.

In contrast, lead indicators reflect future financial and nonfinancial outcomes (including opportunities and problems) and thereby help assess strategic progress and guide decision making

EXHIBIT 1–7
Components of a Value Chain

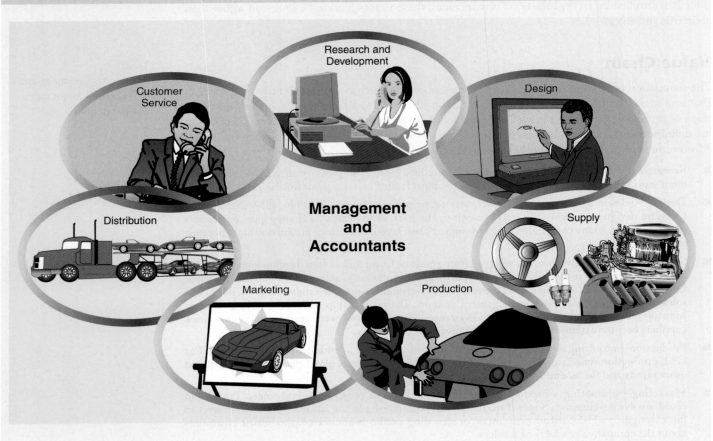

before lag indicators are known. For example, a lead indicator would be the percentage of employees trained on a new paperless accounting information system. The expectation is that the higher the percentage of employees trained to use the new accounting system, the more rapidly orders will be processed, the more satisfied customers will be with turnaround time after placing an order, and the more quickly profits will be realized from the system's increased efficiency over that of the old system. If an insufficient percentage of employees are trained (lead indicator) compared to the planned percentage of those to be trained, future profits (lag indicator) will decrease (or not increase as expected) because some customers will be unhappy with sales order turnaround time.

Lead and lag performance indicators can be developed for many dimensions of performance. Management often uses both lead and lag indicators in a balanced scorecard to assess strategy congruence. The **balanced scorecard (BSC)**, developed by Robert Kaplan (Harvard University) and David Norton (Renaissance Solutions Inc.), is a framework that restates an organization's strategy into clear and objective performance measures focused on customers, internal business processes, employees, and shareholders. Thus, the balanced scorecard provides a means by which actual business outcomes can be evaluated against performance targets.

The BSC includes long-term and short-term, internal and external, financial and nonfinancial measures to balance management's view and execution of strategy. As illustrated in Exhibit 1–8, this simplified BSC has four perspectives: learning and growth, internal business, customer value, and financial performance. Each of these perspectives has a unique set of goals and measures.

The **learning and growth perspective** focuses on using the organization's intellectual capital to adapt to changing customer needs or to influence new customers' needs and expectations through

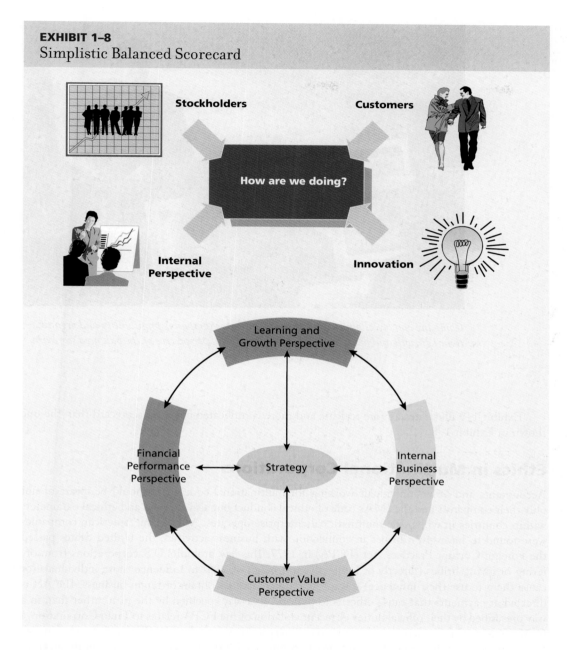

EXHIBIT 1–8
Simplistic Balanced Scorecard

product or service innovations. This perspective addresses whether a company can continue to progress and be seen by customers as adding value. The **internal business perspective** focuses on those things that the organization must do well to meet customer needs and expectations. This perspective concentrates on issues such as employee satisfaction, product quality control, and cost reduction. The **customer value perspective** addresses how well the organization is doing relative to important customer criteria such as speed (lead time), quality, service, and price (both purchase and after purchase). Customers must believe that, when a product or service is purchased, the price paid was worth the value received. Finally, the **financial performance perspective** addresses the concerns of stockholders and other stakeholders about profitability and organizational growth. A company could, for example, reduce costs by outsourcing its technologies to countries where labor costs are lower. For example, it has been estimated that an airline "with $10 billion in annual revenues could save about $100 million per year by outsourcing certain labor-intensive tasks (such as reservations, administration of loyalty plans, and customer care) to a region with lower labor costs and comparable or even higher-quality talent pools."[8]

[8]Vikash Daga and Noshir Kaka, "Taking Offshoring Beyond Labor Cost Savings," *CFO.com* (June 19, 2006).

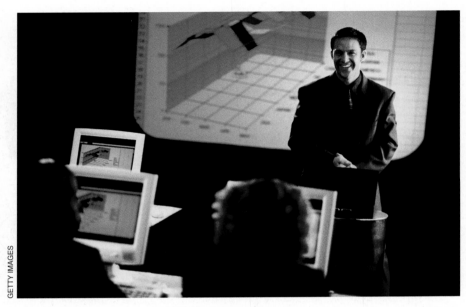

Company employees have a genuine interest in the company's profitability and organizational growth and are thus attuned to the financial perspective of the balanced scorecard.

Exhibit 1–9 illustrates a more realistic and more complicated balanced scorecard than the one shown in Exhibit 1–8.

Ethics in Multinational Corporations

LO.8
Why is ethical behavior so important in organizations?

Accountants and other individuals working for multinational companies should be aware of not only their company's and the IMA's code of ethical conduct but also the laws and ethical parameters within countries in which the multinational enterprise operates. After many American companies were found to have given bribes in connection with business activities, the United States passed the Foreign Corrupt Practices Act (FCPA) in 1977. This law prohibits U.S. corporations from offering or giving bribes (directly or indirectly) to foreign officials to influence those individuals (or cause them to use their influence) toward helping companies obtain or retain business. The Act is directed at payments that cause officials to perform in a way specified by the firm rather than in a way prescribed by their official duties. A recent violation of the FCPA relates to Titan Corporation, a California-based information and communications products provider. The SEC and the U.S. Justice Department filed suit against Titan relating to paying $3.5+ million to high officials of Benin from 1999 to 2001 as well as providing $2 million to the incumbent president's 2001 reelection campaign. Titan then falsified its financial statements to hide the bribes. In March 2005, Titan pled guilty under the FCPA and agreed to pay $28 million to settle the charges.[9]

In addition to the FCPA in the United States, the Organization of Economic Cooperation and Development (OECD) issued a document to combat bribery in early February 1999. This document "makes it a crime to offer, promise or give a bribe to a foreign public official in order to obtain or retain international business deals."[10] As of the end of 2005, the 36 countries in Exhibit 1–10 had signed this document, and the United States has modified the FCPA to conform to several of the document's provisions. Signing the OECD convention illustrates that companies globally are beginning to acknowledge that bribery should not be considered an appropriate means of doing business. ▲

---

[9] U.S. Securities and Exchange Commission, *Securities And Exchange Commission v. The Titan Corporation, Civil Action No. 05-0411* (D.D.C.) (JR) (filed March 1, 2005); http://www.sec.gov/litigation/litreleases/lr19107.htm.
[10] http://www.oecd.org.

EXHIBIT 1–9

Balanced Scorecard and Perspectives

Learning and Growth Perspective

Goals	Measures	
Technology leadership	Time to develop next generation	**TARGET**
Manufacturing learning	Process time to maturity	
Product focus	Percent of products that equals 80% of sales	
Time to market	New product introduction versus competition	

Internal Business Perspective

Goals	Measures	
Technology capability	Manufacturing ability versus competition's	**TARGET**
Manufacturing excellence	Cycle time	
	Unit cost	
	Yield	
Design productivity	Engineering efficiency	
New product introduction	Actual production schedule versus plan	

Customer Value Perspective

Goals	Measures	
New products	Percent of sales from new products	**TARGET**
	Percent of sales from proprietary products	
Responsive supply	On-time delivery (defined by customer)	
Preferred supplier	Share of key accounts' purchases	
Customer partnership	Number of cooperative engineering efforts	

Financial Performance Perspective

Goals	Measures	
Survive	Cash flow	**TARGET**
Succeed	Quarterly sales growth and operating income by division	
Prosper	Increased market share and return on equity (or investment)	

Source: Robert S. Kaplan and David P. Norton, "The Balanced Scorecard—Measures that Drive Performance," *Harvard Business Review* (January–February 1992), pp. 72–76. Copyright © 1992 by The Harvard Business School Publishing Corporation. All rights reserved.

EXHIBIT 1–10
Countries Signing the OECD Bribery Convention (as of November 24, 2005)

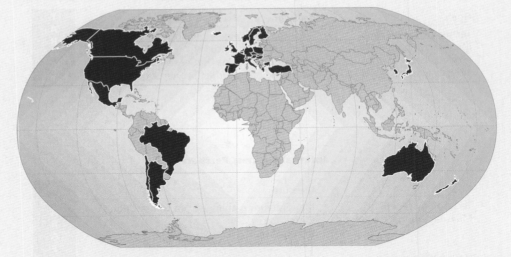

Argentina (2/01)	France (7/00)	New Zealand (6/01)
Australia (10/99)	Germany (11/98)	Norway (12/98)
Austria (5/99)	Greece (2/99)	Poland (9/00)
Belgium (7/99)	Hungary (12/98)	Portugal (11/00)
Brazil (8/00)	Iceland (8/98)	Slovak Republic (9/99)
Bulgaria (12/98)	Ireland (9/03)	Slovenia* (9/01)
Canada (12/98)	Italy (12/00)	Spain (1/00)
Chile (4/01)	Japan (10/98)	Sweden (6/99)
Czech Republic (1/00)	Korea (1/99)	Switzerland (5/00)
Denmark (9/00)	Luxembourg (3/01)	Turkey (7/00)
Estonia (11/04)	Mexico (5/99)	United Kingdom (12/98)
Finland (12/98)	Netherlands (1/01)	United States (12/98)

*Slovenia has not yet enacted full implementing legislation.

Source: OECD (Organisation for Economic Co-operation and Development) Convention on Combating Bribery of Foreign Public Officials in International Business Transactions: Ratification Status as of November 24, 2005, http://www.oecd.org/dataoecd/59/13/1898632.pdf. Copyright © 2005 OECD.

Comprehensive Review Module

Chapter Summary

1. Accounting

   • provides information to external parties (stock-holders, creditors, and various regulatory bodies) for investment and credit decisions.

   • helps estimate the cost of products made and of services provided by the organization.

   • provides information useful to internal managers who are responsible for planning, controlling, decision making, and evaluating performance.

2. The purposes of financial, management, and cost accounting are as follows:

   • financial accounting is designed to meet external information needs and to comply with generally accepted accounting principles;

- management accounting attempts to satisfy internal users' information needs; and

- cost accounting overlaps financial accounting and management accounting by providing product costing information for financial statements and quantitative, disaggregated, cost-based information that managers need to perform their responsibilities.

3. Generally accepted cost accounting standards

   - do not exist for companies that are not engaged in contracts with the federal government; however, the Statements on Management Accounting and Management Accounting Guidelines are well-researched suggestions related to high-quality management accounting practices.

   - are prepared by the Cost Accounting Standards Board for companies engaged in federal government cost/bidding contracts.

4. The organizational mission and strategy are important to cost accountants because they help to

   - establish appropriate measures of accomplishment.

   - develop, implement, and monitor the necessary information systems.

5. Two common corporate strategies are

   - cost leadership, which refers to maintaining a competitive edge by undercutting competitor prices, and

   - product differentiation, which refers to offering (generally at a premium price) superior quality products or more unique services than competitors.

6. Organizational strategy may be constrained by

   - monetary capital, intellectual capital, and/or technology.

   - external cultural, fiscal, legal/regulatory, or political situations.

   - competitive market structures.

7. The organizational structure

   - is composed of people, resources other than people, and commitments that are acquired and arranged relative to authority and responsibility to achieve the organizational mission, strategy, and goals.

   - is used by cost accountants to understand how information is communicated between managers and departments as well as the authority and responsibility of each manager.

   - has line personnel who seek to achieve the organizational mission and strategy through balanced scorecard targets.

   - has staff personnel, such as cost accountants, who seek to advise and assist line personnel.

   - is influenced by management style and organizational culture.

8. The value chain is a set of value-adding functions or processes that convert inputs into products and services for company customers, and organizations add value through the value chain functions of

   - research and development,

   - product design,

   - supply,

   - production,

   - marketing,

   - distribution, and

   - customer service.

9. A balanced scorecard

   - is a four-perspective measure of critical goals and targets needed to operationalize strategy.

   - measures success factors for learning and growth, internal business, customer satisfaction, and stockholder value.

   - includes financial and nonfinancial, internal and external, long-term and short-term, and lead and lag indicators.

10. Ethical behavior in organizations is addressed in part in the following items:

   - IMA's Statement of Ethical Professional Practice refers to issues of competence, confidentiality, integrity, and credibility.

   - Sarbanes-Oxley Act requires corporate CEOs and CFOs to sign off on the accuracy of financial reports.

   - False Claims Act provides for whistle-blowing protection related to frauds against the U.S. government.

   - Foreign Corrupt Practices Act prohibits U.S. corporations from offering or giving bribes to foreign officials to influence those individuals to help obtain or retain business.

Potential Ethical Issues

1. Using earnings management techniques to generate materially misleading financial statements
2. Achieving the strategy of "low-cost producer" at any cost
3. Retaliating against whistle-blowers within an organization
4. Developing a strategic alliance that would restrict fair trade (such as by fixing prices)
5. Engaging in bribery or other forms of corruption to obtain or retain business
6. Using accounting practices that are intended to hide illegal or improper managerial acts ▲

Key Terms

authority, **p. 9**

balanced scorecard (BSC), **p. 12**

competence, **p. 6**

confidentiality, **p. 6**

core competency, **p. 9**

cost accounting, **p. 3**

cost leadership, **p. 9**

credibility, **p. 6**

customer value perspective, **p. 13**

downstream costs, **p. 4**

earnings management, **p. 5**

environmental constraint, **p. 11**

financial performance perspective, **p. 13**

integrity, **p. 6**

intellectual capital, **p. 10**

internal business perspective, **p. 13**

lag indicator, **p. 11**

lead indicator, **p. 11**

learning and growth perspective, **p. 12**

line personnel, **p. 9**

mission statement, **p. 8**

organizational structure, **p. 9**

product cost, **p. 4**

product differentiation, **p. 9**

responsibility, **p. 9**

return on investment (ROI), **p. 2**

staff personnel, **p. 9**

strategy, **p. 8**

upstream costs, **p. 4**

value chain, **p. 11**

Questions

1. Flexibility is said to be the hallmark of modern management accounting, whereas standardization and consistency describe financial accounting. Explain why the focus of these two accounting systems differs.
2. Why is it more important to have legally binding cost accounting standards for defense contractors than it is for other entities?
3. Why would operating in a global (rather than a strictly domestic) marketplace create a need for additional information for management? Discuss some of the additional information managers would need and why such information would be valuable.
4. Why is a mission statement important to an organization?
5. What is organizational strategy? Why would each organization have a unique strategy or set of strategies?
6. What is a core competency, and how do core competencies impact the feasible set of alternative organizational strategies?
7. Why should businesses concern themselves about a clean environment when it might be substantially less expensive to pollute, thus helping them pursue a "low-cost producer" strategy and make their products cheaper for consumers? ▲
8. Differentiate between authority and responsibility. Can you have one without the other? Explain.
9. "If an organization can borrow money or sell stock, it does not have a capital constraint." Is this statement true or false? Discuss the rationale for your answer.

10. How does workplace diversity affect organizational culture? Include in your answer a discussion of both the potential benefits and the potential difficulties in having workers with diverse backgrounds.
11. How can a change in governmental laws or regulations create a strategic opportunity for an organization? Give an example.
12. What is the value chain of an organization, and how does it interface with strategy?
13. What is a balanced scorecard, and how is it more useful than ROI in implementing and monitoring strategy in a global economy?
14. What ethical issues might affect a U.S. or Canadian company considering opening a business in Russia? ▲

Exercises

15. **LO.1 (Interview)** Call a local company and set up an interview with the firm's cost or management accountant. Use the following questions as starting points for your interview.
    - What is your educational background?
    - What was your career path to attain this position?
    - What are your most recurring tasks?
    - What aspects of your job do you find to be the most fun? The most challenging?
    - What college courses do you think would be the most helpful in preparing a person for your job? Why were these courses chosen?
    a. Compare and contrast your interview answers with those of other students in the class.
    b. Which one or two items from the interview were of the most benefit to you? Why?
16. **LO.1 (Accounting information)** You are a partner in a local accounting firm that does financial planning and prepares tax returns, payroll, and financial reports for medium-size companies. Business is good, and your monthly financial statements show that your organization is consistently profitable. Cash flow is becoming a small problem, however, and you need to borrow from your bank. You have also been receiving customer complaints about time delays and price increases.
    a. What accounting information do you think is most important to take with you to discuss a possible loan with your banker?
    b. What accounting information do you think is most important for ascertaining the business activities of your accounting firm in regard to addressing time delays and price increases? What nonaccounting information is important?
    c. Can the information in parts (a) and (b) be gathered from the accounting records directly? Indirectly? If it is not from the accounting records at all, where would you obtain such information?
17. **LO.1 (Organizational accountants)** Use library and Internet resources to find how the jobs of management accountants have changed in the past ten years.
    a. Prepare a "then-versus-now" comparison.
    b. What five skills do you believe are the most important for management accountants to possess? Discuss the rationale for your choices. Do you think these skills have changed over the past ten years? Why or why not?

18. **LO.4 (Strategic information)** On the Web, select the financial reports of a multinational manufacturing company. Assume that you have just been offered a position as this company's CEO. Use the information in the annual report (or 10-K) to develop answers to each of the following questions that should help you make your acceptance decision.
    a. What is the company's mission?
    b. What is the company's strategy? Does it differ from the strategy the company had two years ago?
    c. What are the company's core competencies?
    d. What are the value chain processes for this company?
    e. What products does the company manufacture?
    f. What is the company's organizational structure? Prepare an organizational chart.
    g. What would be your top priorities for this company in the coming year?
    h. Based on your findings, would you accept this offer and why?

19. **LO.3 (Ethics)** In pursuing organizational strategy, cost and management accountants want to instill trust between themselves and their constituents, including other organizational members and the independent auditing firm. The IMA published a code of conduct for management accountants.
    a. List and explain each of the major guidelines of the IMA's code.

b. What steps should a management accountant who detects unethical behavior by his or her supervisor take before deciding to resign? ▲

20. **LO.4 (Strategy)** Choose a company that might use each of the following strategies relative to its competitors and discuss the benefits that might be realized from that strategy. Indicate the industry in which the company does business, the company's primary competitors, and whether a code of conduct or corporate governance appears on its Web site.
   a. Differentiation
   b. Cost leadership

21. **LO.4 (Mission statement)** Mission statements are intended to indicate what an organization does and why it exists. Some of them, however, are simply empty words with little or no substance used by few people to guide their activities.
   a. Does an organization really need a mission statement? If so, why?
   b. How could a mission statement help an organization in its pursuit of ethical behavior from employees?
   c. How could a mission statement help an organization in its pursuit of the production of high-quality products and the provision of high levels of customer service? ▲

22. **LO.4 (Strategy)** You are the manager of a small restaurant in your hometown.
   a. What information would you obtain for making the decision of whether to add quiche and spicy chicken wings to your menu?
   b. Why would each of the information items in part (a) be significant?

23. **LO.4 (Mission statement)** You have managed Missouri's Best Appliances franchises for 15 years and have 100 employees. Business has been profitable, but you are concerned that the Kansas City, Missouri, locations could soon experience a downturn in growth. You have decided to prepare for such an event by engaging in a higher level of strategic planning, beginning with a company mission statement.
   a. How does a mission statement add strength to the strategic planning process?
   b. Who should be involved in developing a mission statement and why?
   c. What factors should be considered in the development of a mission statement? Why are these factors important?
   d. Prepare a mission statement for Best Appliances and discuss how your mission statement will provide benefits to strategic planning.

24. **LO.4 (Strategy)** You are the manager of a large home improvement store. What are the five factors that you believe are most critical to the success of your organization? How would these factors influence your store's strategy?

25. **LO.4 (Mission statement)** Obtain a copy of the mission statement of your college or university. Draft a mission statement for this cost accounting class that supports the school's mission statement.
   a. How does your mission statement reflect the goals and objectives of the college mission statement?
   b. How can you measure the successful accomplishment of your college objectives?

26. **LO.8 (Ethics)** Intellectual capital is extremely important to the longevity of an organization. There are, however, "intellectual capital pirates" who make their livings from stealing.
   a. Assume you have made several popular music recordings that are being pirated overseas. Discuss your feelings about these intellectual capital pirates and what (if anything) should be done to them.
   b. Copying a copyrighted computer software program is also intellectual capital piracy. Do you perceive any difference between this type of copying and the copying of music recordings? Discuss the rationale for your answer. ▲

27. **LO.5 (Organizational constraints)** Three common organizational constraints involve monetary capital, intellectual capital, and technology. Additionally, the environment in which the organization operates may present one or more types of constraints: cultural, fiscal, legal/regulatory, or political.
   a. Discuss whether each of these constraints would be influential in the following types of organizations:
      1. City Hall in a major metropolitan city
      2. a franchised quick-copy business
      3. a newly opened firm of attorneys, all of whom recently graduated from law school
      4. an international oil exploration and production company
   b. For each of the previously listed organizations, discuss your perceptions of which of the constraints would be most critical and why.

28. **LO.4 (Strategy)** Select a major U.S. or non-U.S. manufacturing company. Use library, Internet, and other resources to answer as completely as possible the questions in Exhibit 1–6 about the manufacturer you have chosen.

29. **LO.8 (Ethics)** You have recently been elected President of the United States. One of your most popular positions is that you want to reduce the costs of doing business in the United States. When asked how you intended to accomplish this, you replied, "By seeking to repeal all laws that create unnecessary costs. Repealing such laws will be good not only for business but also for the consumer since product costs and, therefore, selling prices, will be reduced." Congress heard the message loud and clear and has decided to repeal all environmental protection laws.
    a. Discuss the short-term and long-term implications of such a policy.
    b. How would such a policy affect the global competitiveness of U.S. companies?
    c. What reactions would you expect to such a policy from (1) other industrialized nations and (2) developing countries? ▲

30. **LO.5 (Organizational structure)** Early this year, you started a financial planning services firm and now have 20 clients. Because of other obligations (including classes toward an advanced degree), you have hired three employees to help service the clients.
    a. What types of business activities would you empower these employees to handle and why?
    b. What types of business activities would you keep for yourself and why?

31. **LO.4 (Core competencies)** As a team, list the core competencies of your local public school district and explain why you believe these items to be core competencies. Make appointments with the principal of one of the high schools or the superintendent of the public school system and, without sharing your list, ask this individual what he or she believes the core competencies to be and why. Prepare a written or video presentation that summarizes, compares, and contrasts all of the competencies on your lists. Share copies of your presentation with the individuals whom you contacted.

32. **LO.6 (Value chain)** Strategic alliances represent an important value chain arrangement. In many organizations, suppliers are beginning to provide more and more input into customer activities.
    a. In the United States, when would a strategic alliance be considered illegal?
    b. What would you perceive to be the primary reasons for pursuing a strategic alliance?
    c. You are the manager of a catalog company that sells flowers and plants. With whom would you want to establish strategic alliances? What issues might you want to specify prior to engaging in the alliance?

33. **LO.5 (Value chain)** You are the management accountant for an automobile manufacturer. You've been asked to prepare a presentation that will illustrate the company's value chain.
    a. What activities or types of companies would you include in the upstream (supplier) part of the value chain?
    b. What internal activities would you include in the value chain?
    c. What activities or types of companies would you include in the downstream (distribution and retailing) part of the value chain?

34. **LO.8 (Ethics)** The Foreign Corrupt Practices Act (FCPA) prohibits U.S. firms from giving bribes to officials in foreign countries, although bribery is customary in some countries. Non-U.S. companies operating in foreign countries are not necessarily similarly restricted; thus, adherence to the FCPA could make competing with non-U.S. firms more difficult in foreign countries. Do you think bribery should be considered so ethically repugnant to Americans that companies are asked to forgo a foreign custom and, hence, the profits that could be obtained through observance of the custom? Prepare both a pro and a con position for your answer, assuming you will be asked to defend one position or the other. ▲

35. **LO.7 (Balanced scorecard)** You attended a conference on the balanced scorecard last week and your manager has asked you to prepare a short report on the following items.
    a. Why is a balanced scorecard used?
    b. What are the benefits of a balanced scorecard approach to measuring organizational performance?
    c. What are the disadvantages of using a balanced scorecard approach?

36. **LO.8 (Ethics)** You are a senior manager at MegaMac Inc. All senior managers and the board of directors are scheduled to meet next week to discuss some earnings management techniques that were found by the outside independent auditors. The CEO has asked you to be prepared to start the discussion by developing questions that should be addressed before responding to the auditors.
    a. Why would the CEO be concerned about earnings management? After all, it is the auditor who attests to the fair presentation of financial reporting.
    b. If the earnings management were deemed to be "abusive" and you decided to resign and blow the whistle, would you have any protection? Explain. ▲

37. **LO.8 (Ethics)** Accounting has a long history of being an ethical profession. In recent years, however, some companies have asked their accountants to help "manage earnings."

a. Who is more likely to be involved in managing earnings: the financial accountant or the management accountant? Why?

b. Do you believe that "managing earnings" is ethical? Discuss the rationale for your answer. ▲

38. LO.8 (Ethics) Use library and Internet resources to research the names and countries of the stock exchanges on which Toyota Motor Company lists. Write a short paper on the complexities relative to ethics of listing on stock exchanges across multiple countries. ▲

39. LO.8 (Ethics) "Few trends could so thoroughly undermine the very foundation of our free society," writes Milton Friedman in *Capitalism and Freedom* (Chicago: University of Chicago Press, 1962), "as the acceptance by corporate officials of a social responsibility other than to make as much money for their shareholders as possible."

a. Discuss your reactions to this quote from a legal standpoint.

b. Discuss your reactions to this quote from an ethical standpoint.

c. How would you resolve any ethical conflicts that exist between your two answers? ▲

2 | Cost Terminology and Cost Behaviors

Objectives

After completing this chapter, you should be able to answer the following questions:

LO.1 Why are costs associated with a cost object?

LO.2 What assumptions do accountants make about cost behavior, and why are these assumptions necessary?

LO.3 How are costs classified on the financial statements, and why are such classifications useful?

LO.4 How does the conversion process occur in manufacturing and service companies?

LO.5 What are the product cost categories, and what items comprise those categories?

LO.6 How is cost of goods manufactured calculated and used in preparing an income statement?

Introduction

No product can be produced without the incurrence of costs for material, labor, and overhead. At a minimum, no service can be produced without the incurrence of costs for labor and overhead; a cost for material may or may not be involved. Cost reflects the monetary measure of resources expended to attain an objective such as making a good or delivering a service. However, the term *cost* must be defined more specifically before "the cost" of a product or service can be determined and communicated to others. Thus, a clarifying adjective is generally used to specify the type of cost being considered. For example, an asset's balance sheet value is an unexpired cost, but the portion of an asset's value consumed or sacrificed during a period is an expense or expired cost, which is shown on the income statement.

To effectively communicate information, accountants must clearly understand the differences among the various types of costs, their computations, and their usage. This chapter provides the necessary terminology for understanding and communicating cost and management accounting information. The chapter also presents cost flows and the process of cost accumulation in a production environment.

Cost Terminology

A cost management system is a set of formal methods developed for planning and controlling an organization's cost-generating activities relative to its strategy, goals, and objectives. This system is designed to communicate all value chain functions about product costs, product profitability, cost management, strategy implementation, and management performance. Cost concepts and terms have been developed to facilitate this communication process. Some important types of costs are summarized in Exhibit 2–1.

LO.1
Why are costs associated with a cost object?

Association with Cost Object

A cost object is anything for which management wants to collect or accumulate costs. Production operations and product lines are common cost objects. For example, Toyota managers could define the company's Princeton, Indiana, plant as a cost object and request information about operating costs for a specific period; alternatively, Toyota managers could define the Tundra truck as the cost object and request its production cost during the same period. Collecting these costs in different ways can help management make decisions regarding the efficiency of operations at the Princeton plant or the cost management effectiveness in producing the Tundra.

Costs related to the making of a product or delivery of a service are appropriately labeled product or service costs. The costs associated with any cost object can be classified according to their relationship to the cost object.

Direct costs are conveniently and economically traceable to the cost object. If management requested cost data about the Tundra, direct costs would include tires, fiberglass, CD player, leather, paint, and production line labor. Although glue is used in the Tundra, tracing that material would not be cost effective because the cost amount is insignificant. In fact, the clerical and information-processing cost of tracing the glue cost would probably be significantly higher than either the glue cost or any benefits that management might obtain from the information. Thus, the cost of the glue used in each truck would not be classified as direct.

Indirect costs cannot be economically traced to the cost object but instead must be allocated to the cost object. The cost of glue used by Toyota to manufacture trucks is one example of an indirect cost. For another example, the Toyota plant in Princeton incurs property tax, janitorial maintenance, cost accounting, and building depreciation costs each period. Because many styles of Tundras as well as Sienna and Sequoia SUVs are produced in this plant, these costs are not economically traceable to the Tundra as a cost object. Additionally, it might not be important for Toyota managers to know how much janitorial labor cost is used to produce each kind of Tundra.

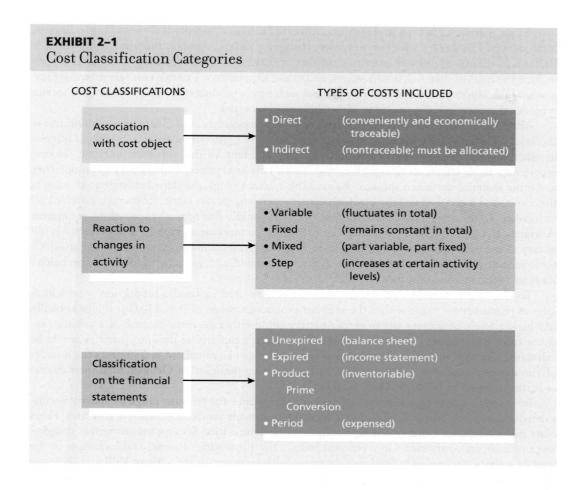

EXHIBIT 2–1
Cost Classification Categories

COST CLASSIFICATIONS   TYPES OF COSTS INCLUDED

Association with cost object
- Direct   (conveniently and economically traceable)
- Indirect   (nontraceable; must be allocated)

Reaction to changes in activity
- Variable   (fluctuates in total)
- Fixed   (remains constant in total)
- Mixed   (part variable, part fixed)
- Step   (increases at certain activity levels)

Classification on the financial statements
- Unexpired   (balance sheet)
- Expired   (income statement)
- Product   (inventoriable)
      Prime
      Conversion
- Period   (expensed)

Classification of a cost as direct or indirect depends on the specification of the cost object. For example, if the Princeton plant is specified as the cost object, then the plant's depreciation cost is directly traceable. However, if the cost object is specified as the Tundra, the plant's depreciation cost is not directly traceable, in which case the depreciation is classified as indirect and must be allocated to the cost object.

Reaction to Changes in Activity

LO.2
What assumptions do accountants make about cost behavior, and why are these assumptions necessary?

To manage costs, accountants must understand how the costs behave relative to changes in output volume. Accountants describe a cost's behavior pattern according to the way its total (rather than its unit) cost reacts to changes in a related activity measure. Every organizational cost will change if extreme shifts in activity levels occur or if enough time passes. However, a total cost can behave in a particular way for a given period relative to changes in an associated activity measure. Common activity measures include production volume, service and sales volumes, hours of machine time used, pounds of material moved, and number of purchase orders processed.

To properly identify, analyze, and use cost behavior information, a time frame must be specified to indicate how far into the future a cost should be examined and a particular range of activity must be assumed. For example, the purchase cost of each set of Tundra tires might be expected to increase by $25 next year but by $80 in the year 2012. When Toyota estimates production costs for next year, the $25 increase would be relevant, but the $80 increase would not be. The assumed range of activity that reflects the company's normal operating range is referred to as the relevant range. Within the relevant range, the two extreme cost behaviors are variable and fixed.

A cost that varies in total in direct proportion to changes in activity is a variable cost. Because total cost varies in direct proportion to activity changes, a variable cost is a constant amount per unit. Relative to volume of units of output or number of customers serviced, examples of variable costs include the costs of material, hourly wages, and sales commissions. Variable costs are extremely important to a company's total profitability because each time a product is produced or sold, or a service is rendered, a corresponding amount of variable cost is incurred.

Although accountants view variable costs as linear, economists view these costs as curvilinear as shown in Exhibit 2–2. The cost line slopes upward at a given rate until a range of activity is reached in which the average variable cost rate becomes fairly constant. Within this relevant range, the firm experiences stable effects on costs such as discounts on material prices, worker skill and productivity, and other material waste and spoilage. Beyond this relevant range, the slope becomes quite steep as the firm enters a range of activity in which certain operating factors cause the average variable cost to increase. In this range, the firm finds that costs rise rapidly due to worker crowding, equipment shortages, and other operating inefficiencies. Although the curvilinear graph is more correct, it is not as easy to use in planning or controlling costs. Accordingly, accountants choose the range in which these variable costs are assumed to behave as they are defined, and, as such, the assumed cost behavior is an approximation of reality.

To illustrate a variable cost, assume that the battery used in Tundra production costs $30 as long as purchases are made within the relevant production range of 0 to 130,000 trucks annually. (At higher levels of activity, the price per battery could either decrease because of a volume discount from the supplier or increase because the supplier's capacity to produce batteries would be exhausted.) Within this relevant range, total battery cost can be calculated as $30 times the number of Tundras produced. For instance, if 10,000 Tundras were produced in October, total variable cost of batteries would be $300,000 ($30 × 10,000).

In contrast, a cost that remains constant in total within the relevant range of activity is considered a fixed cost. Many fixed costs are incurred to provide production capacity to a firm. Fixed costs include salaries (as opposed to hourly wages), depreciation (computed using the straight-line method), and insurance. On a per-unit basis, a fixed cost varies inversely with changes in the level of activity: the per-unit fixed cost decreases with increases in the activity level and increases with decreases in the activity level. If a higher volume is achieved, then fixed costs per unit are lower.

To illustrate how to determine the total and unit amounts of a fixed cost, suppose that Toyota rents some of its Tundra manufacturing equipment for $12,000,000 per year. The equipment has a maximum annual output capacity of 150,000 Tundras. If Toyota expects to produce 120,000 Tundras per year, its annual equipment rental is a fixed cost of $12,000,000 and its equipment rental

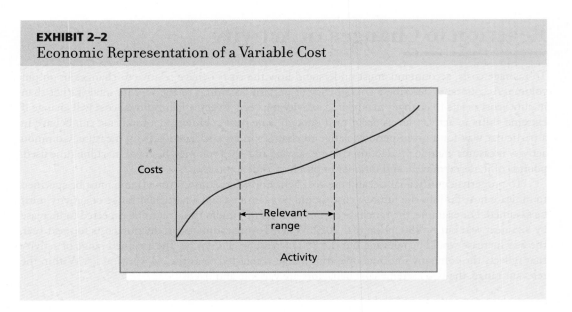

EXHIBIT 2–2
Economic Representation of a Variable Cost

expense per Tundra is $100 ($12,000,000 ÷ 120,000). However, if Toyota produces 125,000 Tundras in a year, total equipment rental expense remains at $12,000,000, but rental expense per truck decreases to $96 ($12,000,000 ÷ 125,000). In summary, total fixed equipment rental cost remains constant as the level of activity changes within the relevant range of production, but fixed cost per unit varies inversely from $100 to $96 as the level of Tundras produced increases from 120,000 to 125,000. The respective total cost and unit cost definitions for variable and fixed cost behaviors are presented in Exhibit 2–3.

In the long run, however, even fixed costs do not remain constant. Business volume will increase or decrease sufficiently that production capacity will be added or sold. Alternatively, management could decide to "trade" fixed and variable costs for one another. For example, a company installing new automated production equipment would incur an additional large fixed cost for depreciation but eliminate the variable cost of wages for hourly production workers.

Alternatively, if a company decides to outsource its data processing support function, the fixed costs of data processing equipment depreciation and personnel salaries can be traded for a variable cost that reflects transaction volume. Whether variable costs are traded for fixed costs or vice versa, a shift from one type of cost behavior to another type changes a company's basic cost structure and can have a significant impact on its profits.

Other costs exist that are not strictly variable or fixed. For example, a mixed cost has both a variable and a fixed component. On a per-unit basis, a mixed cost does not fluctuate in direct proportion to changes in activity, nor does it remain constant with changes in activity. An electric bill that is computed as a flat charge for basic service (the fixed component) plus a stated rate for each kilowatt hour of usage (the variable component) is an example of a mixed cost. Exhibit 2–4 shows a graph for a firm's electric bill, assuming a cost of $5,000 per month plus $0.018 per kilowatt hour (kWh) consumed. In a month when the firm uses 80,000 kWhs of electricity, the total electricity bill is $6,440 [$5,000 + ($0.018 × 80,000)]. If the firm uses 90,000 kWhs, the total electricity bill is $6,620 [$5,000 + ($0.018 × 90,000)].

Another type of cost shifts upward or downward when activity changes by a certain interval or "step." A step cost can be variable or fixed. Step variable costs have small steps; step fixed costs have large steps. For example, a water bill computed as $0.002 per gallon for up to 1,000 gallons, $0.003 per gallon for 1,001 to 2,000 gallons, and $0.005 per gallon for 2,001 to 3,000 gallons is a step variable cost. In contrast, the salary cost for airline reservations agents is a step fixed cost. Assume that each agent can serve a maximum of 1,000 customers per month and is paid $3,200 per month. If airline volume increases from 3,500 customers to 6,000 customers each month, the airline will need six reservations agents rather than four. Each additional 1,000 passengers will result in an additional step fixed cost of $3,200.

Understanding the types of behavior exhibited by costs is necessary to make valid estimates of total costs at various activity levels. Variable, fixed, and mixed costs are the typical types of cost

EXHIBIT 2–3
Comparative Total and Unit Cost Behavior Definitions

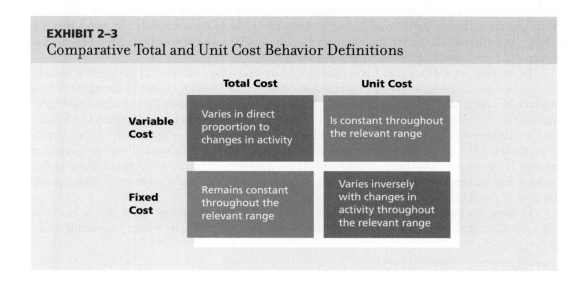

	Total Cost	Unit Cost
Variable Cost	Varies in direct proportion to changes in activity	Is constant throughout the relevant range
Fixed Cost	Remains constant throughout the relevant range	Varies inversely with changes in activity throughout the relevant range

EXHIBIT 2–4
Graph of a Mixed Cost

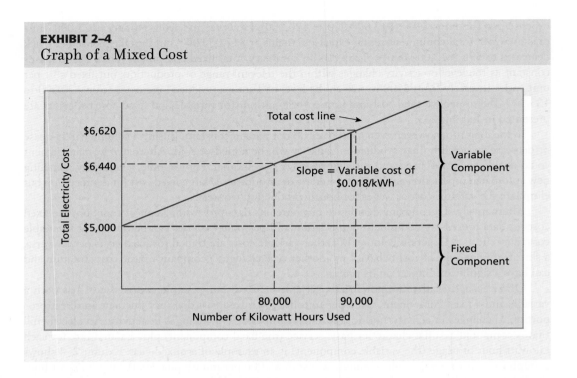

behavior encountered in business. Cost accountants generally separate mixed costs into their variable and fixed components so that the behavior of these costs is more readily apparent.[1] When step variable or step fixed costs exist, accountants must choose a specific relevant range of activity to use for analysis so that the step variable costs can be treated as variable and step fixed costs can be treated as fixed.

By separating mixed costs into their variable and fixed components and by specifying a time period and relevant range, cost accountants force all costs into either variable or fixed categories. Assuming a variable cost is constant per unit and a fixed cost is constant in total within the relevant range can be justified for two reasons. First, if the company operates only within the relevant range of activity, the assumed conditions approximate reality and, thus, the cost assumptions are appropriate. Second, selection of a constant per-unit variable cost and a constant total fixed cost provides a convenient, stable measurement for use in planning, controlling, and decision-making activities.

Accountants use predictors of cost changes to make these generalizations about variable and fixed costs. A predictor is an activity measure that, when changed, is accompanied by a consistent, observable change in a cost item. However, simply because the two items change together does not prove that the predictor causes the change in the other item. For instance, assume that every time you see a Tundra commercial during a sports event, the home team wins the game. If this is consistent, observable behavior, you can use a Tundra commercial to predict the winning team—but viewing the commercial does not cause the team to win!

In contrast, a predictor that has an absolute cause-and-effect relationship to a cost is called a cost driver. For example, production volume has a direct effect on the total cost of raw material used and can be said to "drive" that cost. Exhibit 2–5 plots production volume on the x-axis and raw material cost on the y-axis to show the linear cause-and-effect relationship between production volume and total raw material cost. This exhibit also illustrates the variable cost characteristic of raw material cost: the same amount of raw material cost is incurred for each unit produced. If the raw material is assumed to be engines and the units produced are assumed to be Tundras, this illustration shows that as total Tundra production rises, total engine cost also rises. Thus, Tundra production volume could be used to predict total engine cost.

In most situations, the cause-and-effect relationship between a driver and a cost is less clear than as illustrated by engines and truck production because multiple factors commonly cause

[1]Separation of mixed costs is discussed in Chapter 3.

EXHIBIT 2–5
Total Raw Material Cost Relative to Production Volume

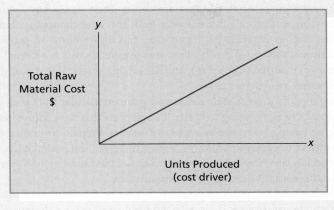

cost incurrence. For example, in addition to production volume, factors such as material quality, worker skill levels, and level of automation affect product spoilage cost. Although determining which factor actually caused a specific change in a spoilage cost can be difficult, any of these factors could be chosen to predict that cost if confidence exists about the factor's relationship with cost changes. To be used as a predictor, the factor and the cost need only change together in a reliable manner.

Traditionally, a single predictor has often been used to predict costs but accountants and managers are realizing that single predictors do not necessarily provide the most reliable forecasts. This realization has caused a movement toward activity-based costing (covered in Chapter 4), which uses multiple cost drivers to predict different costs. Production volume, for instance, would be a valid cost driver for the cost of the rearview mirrors attached to each Tundra produced, but distance to sales outlets would be a more realistic driver for Toyota's product shipping costs.

Classification on the Financial Statements

The balance sheet and income statement are two basic financial statements. The balance sheet is a statement of unexpired costs (assets) and liabilities and owners' capital; the income statement is a statement of revenues and expired costs (expenses and losses). The concept of matching revenues and expenses on the income statement is central to financial accounting. The matching concept provides a basis for deciding when an unexpired cost becomes an expired cost and is moved from an asset category to an expense or loss category.

Expenses and losses differ in that expenses are intentionally incurred in the process of generating revenues, but losses are unintentionally incurred in the context of business operations. Cost of goods sold and expired selling and administrative costs are examples of expenses. Costs incurred for damage from a fire, for abnormal production waste, and for the sale of a machine at below book value are examples of losses.

When a product is specified as the cost object, all costs can be classified as either product or period. Product costs are related to making or acquiring the products or providing the services that directly generate the revenues of an entity; period costs are related to business functions other than production, such as selling and administration.

Product costs are also called inventoriable costs and include direct costs (direct material and direct labor) and indirect costs (overhead). Precise classification of some costs into one of these categories can be difficult and requires judgment; however, the following definitions (with Tundra examples) are useful. Any material that can be easily and economically traced to a product is a

LO.3
How are costs classified on the financial statements, and why are such classifications useful?

direct material. Direct material includes raw material (sheet metal), purchased components from contract manufacturers (batteries), and manufactured subassemblies (engines and transmissions). **Direct labor** refers to the time spent by individuals who work specifically on manufacturing a product or performing a service. At Toyota's Princeton plant, the labor of people welding the parts to the frame is considered direct and their associated wages are direct labor costs. Any factory or production cost that is indirect to the product or service is overhead. This cost element includes Toyota factory supervisors' salaries as well as depreciation, insurance, and utility costs on production machinery, equipment, and facilities. The sum of direct labor and overhead costs is referred to as **conversion cost**—those costs that are incurred to convert materials into products. The sum of direct material and direct labor cost is referred to as **prime cost**.[2]

Period costs are generally more closely associated with a particular time period than with making or acquiring a product or performing a service. Period costs that have future benefit are classified as assets, whereas those having no future benefit are expenses. Prepaid insurance on an administration building represents an unexpired period cost; when the premium period ends, the insurance becomes an expired or period cost (insurance expense). Salaries paid to the sales force and depreciation on computers in the administrative area are also period costs.

One particularly important type of period cost is that of distribution. A **distribution cost** is any cost incurred to warehouse, transport, or deliver a product or service. Financial accounting rules prescribe that distribution costs be expensed as incurred. However, managers should remember that these costs relate directly to products and services and should not adopt an "out-of-sight, out-of-mind" attitude about these costs simply because of the way they are handled under generally accepted accounting principles (GAAP). Distribution costs must be considered in relationship to product/service volume, and these costs must be controlled for profitability to result from sales. Thus, even though distribution costs are not technically considered part of product cost, they can have a major impact on management decision making.

The Conversion Process

LO.4
How does the conversion process occur in manufacturing and service companies?

To some extent, all organizations convert or change inputs into outputs. Inputs typically consist of material, labor, and overhead. In general, product costs are incurred in the production (or conversion) area and period costs are incurred in all nonproduction (or nonconversion) areas.[3] Conversion process outputs are usually either products or services. See Exhibit 2–6 for a comparison of the conversion activities of different types of organizations. Note that many service companies engage in a high degree of conversion. Firms of professionals (such as accountants, architects, attorneys, engineers, and surveyors) convert labor and other resource inputs (material and overhead) into completed services (audit reports, building plans, contracts, blueprints, and property survey reports).

Firms that engage in only low or moderate degrees of conversion can conveniently expense insignificant costs of labor and overhead related to conversion. The clerical cost savings from expensing outweigh the value of any slightly improved information that might result from assigning such costs to products or services. For example, when employees open shipping containers, hang clothing on racks, and tag merchandise with sales tickets, a labor cost for conversion is incurred. However, retail clothing stores do not attach the stock workers' wages to inventory; such labor costs are treated as period costs and are expensed when they are incurred. The major distinction of retail firms relative to service and manufacturing firms is that retailers have much lower degrees of conversion than the other two types of firms.

In contrast, in high-conversion firms, the informational benefits gained from accumulating the material, labor, and overhead costs incurred to produce output significantly exceed clerical accumulation costs. For instance, immediately expensing the labor costs incurred for production employees working on a Tundra assembly line as a period cost would be inappropriate. Similarly, when constructing a house, certain types of costs are quite significant (see Exhibit 2–7). The exhibit indicates that the clerical cost of accumulating direct labor costs is only $165, or 0.33 percent of direct labor costs.

---

[2]In the past, direct material and direct labor cost represented the largest percentage of production cost. In the current automated production environment, direct labor cost has become a very low percentage of product cost and, thus, "prime cost" has lost much of its significance.
[3]It is less common but possible for a cost incurred outside the production area to be in direct support of production and, therefore, considered a product cost. An example of this situation is the salary of a product cost analyst who is based at corporate headquarters; this cost is part of overhead.

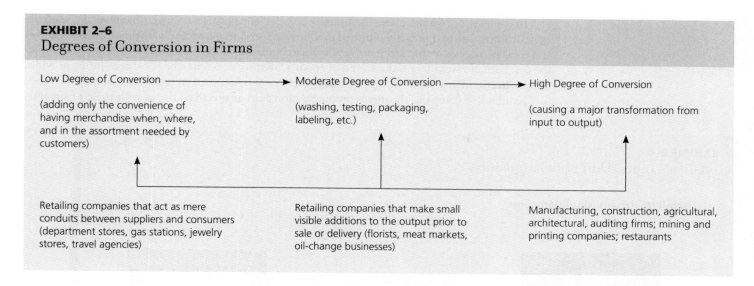

EXHIBIT 2–6
Degrees of Conversion in Firms

Low Degree of Conversion ⟶ Moderate Degree of Conversion ⟶ High Degree of Conversion

(adding only the convenience of having merchandise when, where, and in the assortment needed by customers)

(washing, testing, packaging, labeling, etc.)

(causing a major transformation from input to output)

Retailing companies that act as mere conduits between suppliers and consumers (department stores, gas stations, jewelry stores, travel agencies)

Retailing companies that make small visible additions to the output prior to sale or delivery (florists, meat markets, oil-change businesses)

Manufacturing, construction, agricultural, architectural, auditing firms; mining and printing companies; restaurants

Direct labor cost of $50,000 is accumulated as a separate component of product cost both because the amount is material and that cost requires management's cost-control attention. Furthermore, direct labor cost is inventoried as part of the cost of the construction job until the house is completed.

For convenience, a **manufacturer** is defined as any company engaged in a high degree of conversion of raw material input into a tangible output. Manufacturers typically use people and machines to convert raw material to output that has substance and can, if desired, be physically inspected. A **service company** refers to a firm engaged in a high or moderate degree of conversion using a significant amount of labor. A service company's output can be tangible (an architectural drawing) or intangible (insurance protection). Service firms can be either for-profit businesses or not-for-profit organizations.

Firms engaging in only low or moderate degrees of conversion ordinarily have only one inventory account (Merchandise Inventory). In contrast, manufacturers normally use three inventory accounts: (1) Raw Material Inventory, (2) Work in Process Inventory (for partially converted goods), and (3) Finished Goods Inventory. Service firms have an inventory account for the supplies used in the conversion process and could have a Work in Process Inventory account, but these firms do not normally have a Finished Goods Inventory account because services typically cannot be warehoused. If collection is yet to be made for a completed service engagement, the service firm has a receivable from its client instead of Finished Goods Inventory.

Retailers versus Manufacturers/Service Companies

Retail companies purchase goods in finished or almost finished condition; these goods typically need little, if any, conversion before being sold to customers. Costs associated with such inventory are usually easy to determine, as are the valuations for financial statement presentation.

EXHIBIT 2–7
Building Construction Costs

	Manufacturing Cost	Clerical Cost
Direct material	40%	34%
Manufacturing overhead	35	44
Direct labor	25	22
Total cost	$200,000	$750

In comparison, manufacturers and service companies engage in activities that involve the physical transformation of inputs into finished products and services, respectively. The materials or supplies and conversion costs of manufacturers and service companies must be assigned to output to determine the cost both of inventory produced and of goods sold or services rendered. Cost accounting provides the structure and process for assigning material and conversion costs to products and services.

Exhibit 2–8 compares the input–output relationships of a retail company with those of a manu-

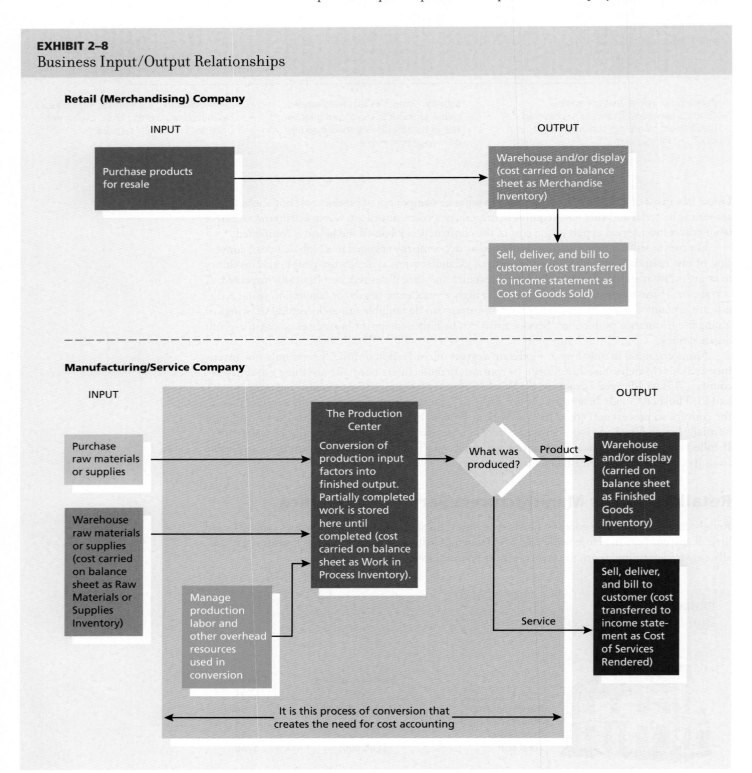

EXHIBIT 2–8
Business Input/Output Relationships

Retail (Merchandising) Company

INPUT

Purchase products for resale

OUTPUT

Warehouse and/or display (cost carried on balance sheet as Merchandise Inventory)

Sell, deliver, and bill to customer (cost transferred to income statement as Cost of Goods Sold)

Manufacturing/Service Company

INPUT

Purchase raw materials or supplies

Warehouse raw materials or supplies (cost carried on balance sheet as Raw Materials or Supplies Inventory)

Manage production labor and other overhead resources used in conversion

The Production Center

Conversion of production input factors into finished output. Partially completed work is stored here until completed (cost carried on balance sheet as Work in Process Inventory).

What was produced?

Product

Service

OUTPUT

Warehouse and/or display (carried on balance sheet as Finished Goods Inventory)

Sell, deliver, and bill to customer (cost transferred to income statement as Cost of Services Rendered)

It is this process of conversion that creates the need for cost accounting facturing/service company. This exhibit illustrates that the primary difference between retail companies and manufacturing/service companies is the absence or presence of the area labeled the "production center." In a production center, input factors, such as raw material, enter and are transformed and stored until the goods or services are completed. If the output is a product, it can be warehoused and/or displayed until it is sold. Service outputs are directly provided to the client commissioning the work. Retail companies normally incur very limited conversion time, effort, and cost compared to manufacturing or service companies. Thus, although a retailer could have a department (such as one that adds store name labels to goods) that might be viewed as a "mini" production center, most often retailers have no designated "production center."

Exhibit 2–9 depicts an accrual-based accounting system in which costs flow from the various inventory accounts on the balance sheet through (if necessary) the production center. The cost accumulation process begins when raw materials or supplies are placed into production. As work progresses on a product or service, costs are accumulated in the firm's accounting records. Accumulating costs in appropriate inventory accounts allows businesses to match the costs of buying or manufacturing a product or providing a service with the revenues generated when the goods or services are sold. At the point of sale, these product/service costs will flow from an inventory account to Cost of Goods Sold or Cost of Services Rendered on the income statement.

Manufacturers versus Service Companies

Several differences in accounting for conversion activities exist between a manufacturer and a service company. A manufacturer accounts for production costs using three inventory accounts. An accrual accounting system is essential for such organizations so that total production costs can be accumulated as goods flow through the manufacturing process. On the other hand, most service firms need only track their work in process (incomplete jobs). Such accounting is acceptable because service firms normally have few, if any, raw material costs other than supplies for work not started. Because services generally cannot be warehoused, costs of finished jobs are usually transferred immediately to the income statement to be matched against service revenue rather than being carried on the balance sheet in a Finished Goods Inventory account.

Despite the accounting differences among retailers, manufacturers, and service firms, each type of organization can use management and cost accounting concepts and techniques, although to a different degree. Managers in all firms engage in planning, controlling, evaluating performance, and making decisions. Thus, management accounting is appropriate for all firms. Cost accounting techniques are essential to all firms engaged in significant conversion activities. In most companies, a main focus of managers is finding ways to reduce costs without sacrificing quality or productivity; both management and cost accounting techniques are used extensively in this pursuit.

Stages of Production

The production or conversion process occurs in three stages: (1) work not started (raw material), (2) work started but not completed (work in process), and (3) work completed (finished goods). Costs are associated with each processing stage. The stages of production in a manufacturing firm and some costs associated with each stage are illustrated in Exhibit 2–9. In the first stage of processing, the costs incurred reflect the prices paid for raw materials and/or supplies. As work progresses through the second stage, accrual-based accounting requires that labor and overhead costs related to the conversion of raw materials or supplies be accumulated and attached to the goods. The total costs incurred in stages 1 and 2 equal the total production cost of finished goods in stage 3.

Cost accounting uses Raw Material, Work in Process, and Finished Goods inventory accounts to accumulate processing costs and assign them to the goods produced. The three inventory accounts relate to the three stages of production shown in Exhibit 2–9 and form a common database for cost, management, and financial accounting information.

In a service firm, the "work not started" stage of processing normally consists of the cost of supplies needed to perform the services (Supplies Inventory). When supplies are placed into work in process, labor and overhead are added to achieve finished results. Determining the cost of services

EXHIBIT 2–9
Stages and Costs of Production

(Stage 1)
WORK NOT STARTED
(Raw Material)

Hood   Roof

Door
(Direct material)

Primer

Clear coat

Color
(Indirect material)

Uniframe
(Direct material)

Adhesive   Screws
(Indirect material)

Chassis, drive train, and suspension
(Direct material)

Tires and wheels
(Direct material)

(Stage 2)
WORK IN PROCESS

(Direct labor)   (Electricity–part of overhead)

Inspection

(Stage 3)
FINISHED WORK

Warehouse

(Balance sheet)

(Total production cost $$$)

Cost of Goods Sold
(Income Statement)

provided is extremely important in both profit-oriented service businesses and not-for-profit enti-ties. For instance, architectural firms accumulate the costs incurred for designs and models of each project, and hospitals accumulate the cost of an X-ray, MRI, or outpatient surgery for each patient.

Components of Product Cost

Product costs are related to items that generate an entity's revenues. These costs can be separated into three components: direct material, direct labor, and production overhead.[4]

LO.5
What are the product cost categories, and what items comprise those categories?

Direct Material

Any readily identifiable part of a product is a direct material. Theoretically, direct material cost should include the cost of all materials used to manufacture a product or perform a service. However, some material costs are not conveniently or economically traceable. Such costs are treated and classified as indirect costs. For example, all of the items shown in stage 1 of Exhibit 2–9 are essential in produc-ing a Tundra truck. However, the cost of adhesive and screws could be neither easily traceable nor monetarily significant to Tundra's production cost. Thus, these costs can be classified and accounted for as indirect materials and included as part of overhead.

In a service business, direct materials are often insignificant or are not easily traced to a desig-nated cost object. For instance, the cost of the paper on which an architect prepares building plans is very small relative to the plans' overall value. Accordingly, even though the paper can easily be traced to the final product (the actual blueprints), paper cost is so insignificant that tracking it as a direct material cannot be justified.

Direct Labor

Direct labor refers to the effort of individuals who manufacture a product or perform a service. Direct labor could also be considered work that directly adds value to the final product or service. The welder on Toyota's production line, the chef preparing the meals at the local restaurant, and the hygienist at the dental clinic represent direct labor personnel.

Direct labor cost consists of the wages or salaries paid to direct labor personnel. Such wages and salaries must also be conveniently traceable to the product or service. Direct labor cost should include basic compensation, production efficiency bonuses, and the employer's share of Social Secu-rity and Medicare taxes. In addition, if a company's operations are relatively stable, direct labor cost should include all employer-paid insurance costs, holiday and vacation pay, and pension and other retirement benefits.[5]

As with materials, some labor costs that theoretically should be considered direct are treated as indirect. One reason for this treatment is that specifically tracing certain labor costs to produc-tion can be inefficient. For instance, fringe benefit costs should be treated as direct labor cost, but the time, effort, and clerical expense of tracing this cost might not justify the additional accuracy it would provide. Thus, the treatment of employee fringe benefits as indirect costs is often based on clerical cost efficiencies.

A second reason for not treating certain labor costs as direct is that doing so could result in erroneous information about product or service costs. Assume that the Eikner Corporation em-ploys 20 assembly department workers who are paid $12 per hour and time and a half ($18) for overtime. One week, the employees worked a total of 1,000 hours (including 200 hours of overtime) to complete all production orders. Of the total employee labor payroll of $13,200, only $12,000 (1,000 hours × $12 per hour) is classified as direct labor cost. The remaining $1,200 (200 hours × $6 per hour) is considered overhead. If the overtime cost were assigned to products made during the overtime hours, those products would have a labor cost 50 percent higher than items made during regular working hours. Because products are assigned to regular or overtime shifts randomly, the

---

[4]This definition of product cost is the traditional one and is referred to as absorption cost. Another product costing method, called variable costing, excludes the fixed overhead component. Absorption and variable costing are compared in Chapter 3.
[5]Institute of Management Accountants (formerly National Association of Accountants), *Statements on Management Accounting Number 4C: Definition and Measurement of Direct Labor Cost* (Montvale, N.J.: NAA, June 13, 1985), p. 4.

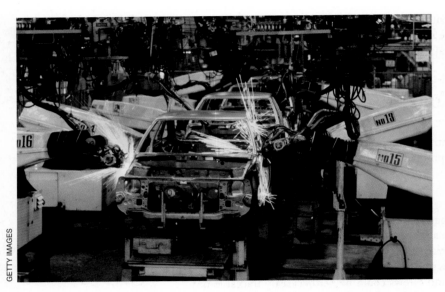

The direct labor cost saved by replacing humans with robots is partly made up in depreciation costs for these robots.

items completed during overtime hours should not be forced to bear overtime charges. Therefore, costs for overtime or shift premiums are usually considered overhead rather than direct labor cost and are allocated among all units.

On some occasions, however, costs such as overtime should not be considered overhead. If a customer requests a job to be scheduled during overtime hours or is in a rush and requests overtime to be worked, overtime or shift premiums should be considered direct labor cost and attached to the job that created the costs. Assume that on a Friday in July, McGinnis Company asked Eikner Corporation to deliver 100 units of product the following Monday. Because completion of the order would require workers to work overtime, Eikner Corporation would charge McGinnis Company a higher selling price for each unit and, additionally, the overtime costs should be included as part of the direct labor cost of the McGinnis Company order.

Because people historically performed the majority of conversion activity, direct labor once represented a large portion of total manufacturing cost. Now, in highly automated work environments, direct labor often represents only 10 to 15 percent of total manufacturing cost. Thus, managers often find that a substantial portion of direct labor cost has been replaced by the depreciation cost associated with robots and other fully automated machinery.

Overhead

Overhead is any factory or production cost that is indirect to manufacturing a product or providing a service. Accordingly, overhead does not include direct material and direct labor. Overhead does, however, include indirect material and indirect labor as well as all other costs incurred in the production area.[6] Automated and computerized technologies have made manufacturing more capital intensive. With direct labor becoming a progressively smaller proportion of product cost, overhead has become a progressively larger proportion, and such costs merit much more attention than they did in the past.

Overhead costs can be variable or fixed based on how they behave in response to changes in production volume or other activity measure. Variable overhead includes the costs of indirect material, indirect labor paid on an hourly basis (such as wages for forklift operators, material handlers, and other workers who support the production, assembly, and/or service process), lubricants used for machine maintenance, and the variable portion of factory utility charges. Depreciation calculated using either the units-of-production or service-life method is also a variable overhead cost; these depreciation methods reflect a decline in machine utility based on usage rather than time passage and are appropriate in an automated plant.

Fixed overhead includes costs such as straight-line depreciation on factory assets, factory license fees, and factory insurance and property taxes. Fixed indirect labor costs include salaries for production supervisors, shift superintendents, and plant managers. The fixed portion of factory mixed costs (such as maintenance and utilities) is also part of fixed overhead. Investments in new equipment can create significantly higher fixed overhead costs but can also improve product or service quality—and, thus, reduce another overhead cost, that of poor quality.

Quality costs are an important component of overhead cost. Quality is a managerial concern for two reasons. First, high-quality products and services enhance a company's ability to generate revenues and produce profits. Consumers want the best quality product for the money they spend.

---

[6]Another term used for overhead is *burden*. Although this is the term under which the definition appeared in *Statements on Management Accounting Number 2, Management Accounting Terminology*, the authors believe that this term is unacceptable because it connotes costs that are extra, unnecessary, or oppressive. Overhead costs are essential to the conversion process but simply cannot be traced directly to output.

Second, managers are concerned about production process quality because higher process quality leads to shorter production time and reduced costs for spoilage and rework. The level of customer satisfaction with a company's products and services is usually part of the customer perspective in the balanced scorecard.

Quality costs are usually referred to as being either costs of controlling quality or costs of failing to control quality. Control costs include prevention and appraisal costs. Prevention costs are incurred to improve quality by precluding product defects and improper processing from occurring. Amounts spent on implementing training programs, researching customer needs, and acquiring improved production equipment are prevention costs. Amounts incurred for monitoring or inspecting are called appraisal costs; these costs are incurred to find mistakes not eliminated through prevention.

Failure costs can be internal (such as scrap and rework) or external (such as product return costs caused by quality problems, warranty costs, and complaint department costs). Amounts spent for prevention costs minimize the costs incurred for appraisal and failure. Management techniques to improve quality are discussed in greater depth in Chapter 17.

Quality costs exhibit different types of cost behaviors. Some quality costs are variable in relation to the quantity of defective output, some are step fixed with increases at specific levels of defective output, and some are fixed for a specific time. For example, rework cost approaches zero if the quantity of defective output is also nearly zero. However, rework cost would be extremely large if the number of defective parts produced were high. In contrast, training expenditures are set by management and might not vary regardless of the quantity of defective output produced in a given period.

Accumulation and Allocation of Overhead

Direct material and direct labor are easily traced to a product or service. Overhead, on the other hand, must be accumulated over a period and allocated to the products manufactured or services rendered during that period. Cost allocation refers to the assignment of an indirect cost to one or more cost objects using some reasonable allocation base or driver. Cost allocations can be made over several time periods or within a single time period. For example, in financial accounting, a building's cost is allocated through depreciation charges over its useful or service life. This process is necessary to satisfy the matching principle. In cost accounting, production overhead costs are allocated within a period through the use of allocation bases or cost drivers to products or services. This process reflects application of the cost principle, which requires that all production or acquisition costs attach to the units produced, services rendered, or units purchased.

Overhead costs are allocated to cost objects for three reasons: (1) to determine the full cost of the cost object, (2) to motivate the manager in charge of the cost object to manage it efficiently, and (3) to compare alternative courses of action for management planning, controlling, and decision making.[7] The first reason relates to financial statement valuations. Under GAAP, the "full cost" of a cost object must include allocated production overhead. In contrast, the assignment of nonmanufacturing overhead costs to products is not normally allowed under GAAP.[8] The other two reasons for overhead allocations are related to internal purposes and, thus, no specific rules apply to the allocation process.

Regardless of why overhead is allocated, the method and basis of allocation should be rational and systematic so that the resulting information is useful for product costing and managerial purposes. Traditionally, the information generated for satisfying the "full cost" objective was also used for the second and third objectives. However, because the first purpose is externally focused and the others are internally focused, different methods can be used to provide different costs for different needs.

Overhead can be allocated to products or services in one of two ways. In an actual cost system, actual direct material and direct labor costs are accumulated in Work in Process (WIP) Inventory as the costs are incurred. Actual production overhead costs are accumulated separately in an Overhead Control account and are assigned to WIP Inventory at the end of a period or at completion of

---

[7]Institute of Management Accountants, *Statements on Management Accounting Number 4B: Allocation of Service and Administrative Costs* (Montvale, N.J.: NAA, June 13, 1985), pp. 9–10.
[8]Although potentially unacceptable for GAAP, certain nonmanufacturing overhead costs must be assigned to products for tax purposes.

production. Use of an actual cost system is generally considered to be difficult because all production overhead information must be available before any cost allocation can be made to products or services. For example, the cost of products and services produced in May could not be calculated until the May electricity bill is received in June.

An alternative to an actual cost system is a normal cost system, which combines actual direct material and direct labor costs with overhead that is assigned using a predetermined rate or rates. A predetermined overhead rate (or overhead application rate) is a charge per unit of activity that is used to allocate (or apply) overhead cost from the Overhead Control account to WIP Inventory for the period's production or services. Predetermined overhead rates are discussed in detail in Chapter 3.

Actual Cost System

Product costs can be accumulated using either a perpetual or a periodic inventory system. In a perpetual inventory system, all product costs flow through Work in Process Inventory to Finished Goods (FG) Inventory and, ultimately, to Cost of Goods Sold (CGS); this cost flow is diagrammed in Exhibit 2–10. The perpetual inventory system continuously provides current information for

EXHIBIT 2–10
Illustration of Perpetual Inventory Accounting System

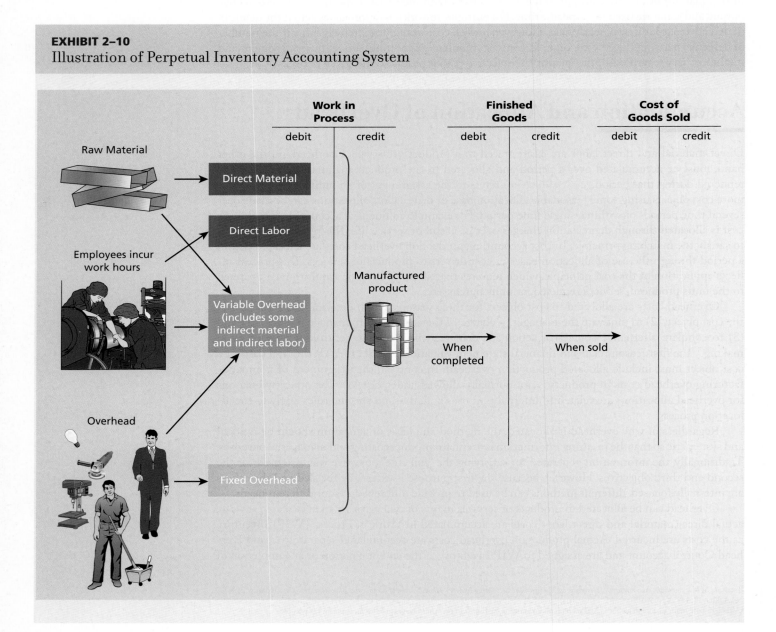

financial statement preparation and for inventory and cost control. Because the cost of maintaining a perpetual system has diminished significantly as computerized production, bar coding, and information processing have become more pervasive, this text assumes that all companies discussed use a perpetual system.

The Eikner Corporation is used to illustrate the flow of product costs in a manufacturing company's actual cost system. The April 1, 2008, inventory account balances for the company were as follows: Raw Material Inventory (all direct), $73,000; Work in Process Inventory, $145,000; and Finished Goods Inventory, $87,400. Eikner Corporation uses separate variable and fixed accounts to record overhead costs. In this illustration, actual overhead costs are used to allocate overhead to WIP Inventory. The journal entries in Exhibit 2–11 are keyed to the following transactions representing Eikner Corporation's activity for April.

EXHIBIT 2–11

Eikner Corporation—April 2008 Journal Entries

(1) Raw Material Inventory	280,000	
Accounts Payable		280,000
To record cost of raw material purchased on account		
(2) Work in Process Inventory	284,000	
Raw Material Inventory		284,000
To record raw material transferred to production		
(3) Work in Process Inventory	436,000	
Variable Overhead Control	94,000	
Salaries & Wages Payable		530,000
To accrue factory wages for direct and indirect labor		
(4) Fixed Overhead Control	20,000	
Salaries & Wages Payable		20,000
To accrue production supervisors' salaries		
(5) Variable Overhead Control	16,000	
Fixed Overhead Control	12,000	
Utilities Payable		28,000
To record mixed utility cost in its variable and fixed amounts		
(6) Variable Overhead Control	5,200	
Supplies Inventory		5,200
To record supplies used		
(7) Fixed Overhead Control	7,000	
Cash		7,000
To record payment for factory property taxes for the period		
(8) Fixed Overhead Control	56,880	
Accumulated Depreciation—Equipment		56,880
To record depreciation on factory assets for the period		
(9) Fixed Overhead Control	3,000	
Prepaid Insurance		3,000
To record expiration of prepaid insurance on factory assets		
(10) Work in Process Inventory	214,080	
Variable Overhead Control		115,200
Fixed Overhead Control		98,880
To record the assignment of actual overhead costs to WIP Inventory		
(11) Finished Goods Inventory	1,058,200	
Work in Process Inventory		1,058,200
To record the transfer of work completed during the period		
(12) Accounts Receivable	1,460,000	
Sales		1,460,000
To record sales price of goods sold on account during the period		
(13) Cost of Goods Sold	1,054,000	
Finished Goods Inventory		1,054,000
To record cost of goods sold for the period		

During the month, Eikner's purchasing agent bought $280,000 of direct material on account (entry 1), and the warehouse manager transferred $284,000 of direct material to the production area (entry 2). April's production wages totaled $530,000, of which $436,000 was for direct labor (entry 3). April salaries for the production supervisor were $20,000 (entry 4). April utility cost of $28,000 was accrued; an analysis of this cost indicated that $16,000 was variable and $12,000 was fixed (entry 5). Supplies costing $5,200 were removed from inventory and used in production (entry 6). Also, Eikner paid $7,000 for April's property taxes on the factory (entry 7), depreciated the factory assets $56,880 (entry 8), and recorded the expiration of $3,000 of prepaid insurance on the factory assets (entry 9). Entry 10 shows the assignment of actual overhead cost to WIP Inventory for April. During the month, $1,058,200 of goods were completed and transferred to FG Inventory (entry 11). Total April sales were $1,460,000 and these were all on account (entry 12); goods that were sold had a total cost of $1,054,000 (entry 13). An abbreviated presentation of the cost flows is shown in selected T-accounts in Exhibit 2–12.

Cost of Goods Manufactured and Sold

LO.6
How is cost of goods manufactured calculated and used in preparing an income statement?

The T-accounts in Exhibit 2–12 provide detailed information about the cost of material used, goods transferred from work in process, and goods sold. This information is needed to prepare financial statements. Because most managers cannot access the detailed accounting records, the flow of costs and calculation of important income statement amounts must be presented to them in a formalized manner. Therefore, a schedule of cost of goods manufactured is prepared as a preliminary step to the determination of cost of goods sold.[9] Cost of goods manufactured (CGM) is the total production cost of the goods that were completed and transferred to Finished Goods Inventory during the period. This amount is similar to the cost of net purchases in the cost of goods sold schedule for a retailer.

EXHIBIT 2–12
Selected T-Accounts for Eikner Corporation's April 2008 Production and Sales

Raw Material Inventory: Beg. bal. 73,000; (1) 280,000; (2) 284,000; End. bal. 69,000

Variable Overhead Control: (3) 94,000; (5) 16,000; (6) 5,200; (10) 115,200

Work in Process Inventory: Beg. bal. 145,000; (2) DM 284,000; (3) DL 436,000; (10) OH 214,080; (11) 1,058,200; End. bal. 20,880

Fixed Overhead Control: (4) 20,000; (5) 12,000; (7) 7,000; (8) 56,880; (9) 3,000; (10) 98,880

Finished Goods Inventory: Beg. bal. 87,400; (11) CGM 1,058,200; (13) CGS 1,054,000; End. bal. 91,600

Cost of Goods Sold: (13) CGS 1,054,000

[9]A service business prepares a schedule of cost of services rendered.

Formal schedules of cost of goods manufactured and cost of goods sold are presented in Exhibit 2–13 using the amounts shown in Exhibits 2–11 and 2–12. The schedule of cost of goods manufactured starts with the beginning balance of WIP Inventory and details all product cost components. The cost of material used in production during the period is equal to the beginning balance of Raw Material (RM) Inventory plus raw material purchased minus the ending balance of RM Inventory. If RM Inventory includes both direct and indirect materials, the cost of direct material used is assigned to WIP Inventory and the cost of indirect material used is included in variable overhead. Because direct labor cannot be warehoused, all charges for direct labor during the period are part of WIP Inventory. Variable and fixed overhead costs are added to direct material and direct labor costs to determine total manufacturing costs.

Beginning WIP Inventory cost is added to total current manufacturing costs to obtain a subtotal amount referred to as total cost to account for. The value of ending WIP Inventory is calculated (through techniques discussed in Chapters 5, 6, and 7) and subtracted from the subtotal to provide the CGM for the period. The schedule of cost of goods manufactured is usually prepared only as an internal schedule and is not provided to external parties.

EXHIBIT 2–13
Cost of Goods Manufactured and Cost of Goods Sold Schedules

EIKNER CORPORATION
Schedule of Cost of Goods Manufactured
For the Month Ended April 30, 2008

Beginning balance of Work in Process Inventory, 4/1/08			$ 145,000
Manufacturing costs for the period			
Raw Material Inventory (all direct)			
Beginning balance	$ 73,000		
Purchases of material	280,000		
Raw material available	$353,000		
Ending balance	(69,000)		
Total raw material used		$284,000	
Direct labor		436,000	
Variable overhead			
Indirect labor	$ 94,000		
Utilities	16,000		
Supplies	5,200	115,200	
Fixed overhead			
Supervisor's salary	$ 20,000		
Utilities	12,000		
Factory property taxes	7,000		
Factory asset depreciation	56,880		
Factory insurance	3,000	98,880	
Total current period manufacturing costs			934,080
Total costs to account for			$1,079,080
Ending balance of Work in Process Inventory, 4/30/08			(20,880)
Cost of goods manufactured			$1,058,200

EIKNER CORPORATION
Schedule of Cost of Goods Sold
For the Month Ended April 30, 2008

Beginning balance of Finished Goods Inventory, 4/1/08	$ 87,400
Cost of goods manufactured	1,058,200
Cost of goods available for sale	$1,145,600
Ending balance of Finished Goods Inventory, 4/30/08	(91,600)
Cost of goods sold	$1,054,000

In the schedule of cost of goods sold, the CGM is added to the beginning balance of FG Inventory to find the cost of goods available for sale during the period. Ending FG Inventory is calculated by multiplying a physical unit count times a unit cost. If a perpetual inventory system is used, the actual amount of ending FG Inventory can be compared to the amount shown in the accounting records; any differences can be attributed to losses that could have arisen from theft, breakage, evaporation, or accounting errors. Ending FG Inventory is subtracted from the cost of goods available for sale to determine the CGS.

Comprehensive Review Module

Chapter Summary

1. Costs are classified as

   - direct or indirect, depending on their relationship to a cost object.

   - variable, fixed, or mixed depending on their reaction to changes in a related activity level.

   - unexpired (assets) or expired (expenses or losses) depending on whether they have future value to the company.

   - product (inventoriable) or period (selling, administrative, and financing) depending on their association with the revenue-generating items sold by the company.

2. To estimate product cost within a relevant range of activity, accountants assume that

   - variable costs are constant per unit and will change in total in direct proportion to changes in activity.

   - fixed costs are constant in total and will vary inversely on a per-unit basis with changes in activity.

   - step costs are either variable or fixed, depending on the size of the changes (width of the steps) in cost that occur with changes in activity.

   - mixed costs fluctuate in total with changes in activity and can be separated into their variable and fixed components.

3. The conversion process differs among manufacturers, service companies, and retailers in that

   - manufacturers require extensive activity to convert raw material into finished goods; the primary costs in these companies are raw material, direct labor, and overhead; manufacturers use three inventory accounts (Raw Material, Work in Process, and Finished Goods).

   - service companies often require extensive activity to perform a service; the primary costs in these companies are direct labor and overhead; service companies may use Supplies Inventory and Work in Process Inventory accounts but typically have no Finished Goods Inventory.

   - retailers require little, if any, activity to make purchased goods ready for sale; the primary costs in these companies are purchase prices for goods and labor wages; retailers use a Merchandise Inventory account.

4. Three product cost categories are

   - direct material, which is the cost of any item that is physically and conveniently traceable to the product or service.

   - direct labor, which is the labor cost of the people whose work is physically and conveniently traceable to the product or service.

   - overhead, which is any cost incurred in the conversion (or production) area that is not direct material or direct labor; overhead includes indirect material and indirect labor costs.

5. Cost of goods manufactured

 • equals the costs that were in the conversion area at the beginning of the period plus production costs (direct material, direct labor, and overhead) incurred during the period minus the cost of incomplete goods that remain in the conversion area at the end of the period.

 • is shown on an internal management report called the schedule of cost of goods manufac-

tured; it is equivalent to the cost of goods purchased in a retail company.

 • is added to beginning Finished Goods Inventory to determine the cost of goods available (CGA) for sale for the period; CGA is reduced by ending Finished Goods Inventory to determine cost of goods sold on the income statement.

Potential Ethical Issues

1. Leaving expired costs on the balance sheet as assets, thereby causing an increase in net income

2. Treating period costs as product costs to inflate inventory assets and increase net income

3. Treating product costs as period costs to reduce the cost of goods manufactured and increase gross profit on the income statement, thereby making the conversion area appear more profitable than it actually was

4. Attaching the "random" costs of direct labor (such as overtime) to specific production units to inflate the cost of those units—especially if the buyer is required to pay for production cost plus a specified profit percentage

5. Overstating the cost of ending inventory accounts to reduce the cost of goods manufactured, reduce the cost of goods sold, and increase net income ▲

Solution Strategies

Product Cost

	Direct Material
+	Direct Labor
+	Overhead
=	Total Product Cost

Schedule of Cost of Goods Manufactured

Beginning balance of Work in Process Inventory		$XXX
Manufacturing costs for the period:		
Raw material (all direct):		
Beginning balance	$XXX	
Purchases of material	XXX	
Raw material available for use	$XXX	
Ending balance	(XXX)	
Direct material used		$XXX
Direct labor		XXX
Variable overhead		XXX
Fixed overhead		XXX
Total current period manufacturing costs		XXX
Total cost to account for		$XXX
Ending balance of Work in Process Inventory		(XXX)
Cost of goods manufactured		$XXX

Cost of Goods Sold

Beginning balance of Finished Goods Inventory	$XXX
Cost of goods manufactured	XXX
Cost of goods available for sale	$XXX
Ending balance of Finished Goods Inventory	(XXX)
Cost of goods sold	$XXX

Demonstration Problem

Salome Company had the following account balances as of August 1, 2008:

Raw Material (direct and indirect) Inventory	$20,300
Work in Process Inventory	7,000
Finished Goods Inventory	18,000

During August, the company incurred the following factory costs:

1. Purchased $164,000 of raw material on account.
2. Issued $180,000 of raw material, of which $134,000 was direct to the product.
3. Accrued factory payroll of $88,000; $62,000 was for direct labor and the rest was for supervisors' salaries.
4. Accrued utility costs of $7,000; of these costs, $1,600 were fixed.
5. Accrued property taxes on the factory in the amount of $2,000.
6. Recorded $1,600 of prepaid insurance on factory equipment that expired in August.
7. Depreciated (straight-line) factory equipment, $40,000.
8. Applied actual overhead to Work in Process Inventory.
9. Transferred goods costing $320,000 to Finished Goods Inventory.
10. Recorded total sales of $700,000; of these, $550,000 were on account.
11. Recorded cost of goods sold of $330,000.
12. Recorded selling and administrative costs of $280,000 (credit "Various accounts").

Required:

a. Journalize the transactions for August.
b. Post transactions to the general ledger accounts for Raw Material Inventory, Work in Process Inventory, Finished Goods Inventory, and Cost of Goods Sold.
c. Prepare a schedule of cost of goods manufactured for August using actual costing.
d. Prepare an income statement, including a detailed schedule of cost of goods sold.

Solution to Demonstration Problem

a.

(1)	Raw Material Inventory	164,000	
	Accounts Payable		164,000
	To record raw material purchased on account		
(2)	Work in Process Inventory	134,000	
	Variable Overhead Control	46,000	
	Raw Material Inventory		180,000
	To transfer direct and indirect materials to production		
(3)	Work in Process Inventory	62,000	
	Fixed Overhead Control	26,000	
	Salaries and Wages Payable		88,000
	To accrue factory wages and salaries		
(4)	Variable Overhead Control	5,400	
	Fixed Overhead Control	1,600	
	Utilities Payable		7,000
	To accrue factory utility expenses		

(5)	Fixed Overhead Control		2,000	
	Property Taxes Payable			2,000
	To accrue property tax			
(6)	Fixed Overhead Control		1,600	
	Prepaid Insurance			1,600
	To record expired insurance on factory equipment			
(7)	Fixed Overhead Control		40,000	
	Accumulated Depreciation—Factory Equipment			40,000
	To record depreciation on factory equipment			
(8)	Work in Process Inventory		122,600	
	Variable Overhead Control			51,400
	Fixed Overhead Control			71,200
	To assign actual overhead to WIP Inventory			
(9)	Finished Goods Inventory		320,000	
	Work in Process Inventory			320,000
	To record cost of goods manufactured			
(10)	Accounts Receivable		550,000	
	Cash		150,000	
	Sales			700,000
	To record sales on account and for cash			
(11)	Cost of Goods Sold		330,000	
	Finished Goods Inventory			330,000
	To record cost of goods sold for the period			
(12)	Selling & Administrative Expenses		280,000	
	Various accounts			280,000
	To record selling and administrative expenses			

b.

Raw Material Inventory

BB	20,300	(2)	180,000
(1)	164,000		
EB	4,300		

Work in Process Inventory

BB	7,000	(9)	320,000
(2)	134,000		
(3)	62,000		
(8)	122,600		
EB	5,600		

Finished Goods Inventory

BB	18,000	(11)	330,000
(9)	320,000		
EB	8,000		

Cost of Goods Sold

(11)		330,000	

where BB = beginning balance
      EB = ending balance

c.

SALOME COMPANY
Schedule of Cost of Goods Manufactured
For Month Ended August 31, 2008

Balance of Work in Process Inventory, 8/1/08		$ 7,000
Manufacturing costs for the period		
Raw material		
Beginning balance	$ 20,300	
Purchases of material	164,000	
Raw material available	$184,300	
Indirect material used	$46,000	
Ending balance	4,300	(50,300)
Total direct material used		$134,000
Direct labor		62,000
Variable overhead		51,400
Fixed overhead		71,200
Total current period manufacturing costs		318,600
Total cost to account for		$325,600
Balance of Work in Process Inventory, 8/31/08		(5,600)
Cost of goods manufactured[a]		$320,000

[a]Notice the similarity between the schedule of cost of goods manufactured and the Work in Process Inventory T-account.

d.

SALOME COMPANY
Income Statement
For the Month Ended August 31, 2008

Sales		$700,000
Cost of goods sold		
Finished goods, 8/1/08	$ 18,000	
Cost of goods manufactured	320,000	
Cost of goods available	$338,000	
Finished goods, 8/31/08	(8,000)	
Cost of goods sold		(330,000)
Gross margin		$370,000
Selling and administrative expenses		(280,000)
Income from operations		$ 90,000

Key Terms

actual cost system, *p. 37*

appraisal costs, *p. 37*

conversion cost, *p. 30*

cost, *p. 24*

cost allocation, *p. 37*

cost driver, *p. 28*

cost management system, *p. 24*

cost object, *p. 24*

cost of goods manufactured (CGM), *p. 40*

direct costs, *p. 24*

direct labor, *p. 30*

direct material, *p. 30*

distribution cost, *p. 30*

expired cost, *p. 24*

failure costs, *p. 37*

finished goods, *p. 33*

fixed cost, *p. 26*

indirect costs, *p. 24*

inventoriable costs, *p. 29*

manufacturer, *p. 31*

mixed cost, *p. 27*

normal cost system, *p. 38*

overhead, *p. 29*

period cost, *p. 29*

predetermined overhead rate, *p. 38*

predictor, *p. 28*

prevention cost, *p. 37*

prime cost, *p. 30*

product cost, *p. 29*

raw material, *p. 33*

relevant range, *p. 25*

service company, *p. 31*

step cost, *p. 27*

total cost to account for, *p. 41*

unexpired cost, *p. 24*

variable cost, *p. 26*

work in process, *p. 33*

Questions

1. Why must the word *cost* be accompanied by an adjective to be meaningful?
2. Relative to a cost object, what is the distinction between a direct cost and an indirect cost?
3. Why is it necessary for a company to specify a relevant range of activity when making assumptions about cost behavior?
4. How do cost drivers and predictors differ, and why is the distinction important?
5. What is the distinction between a product cost and a period cost?
6. What are conversion costs? Why are they called this?
7. In the past 10 to 15 years, which product cost category has been growing most rapidly? Why?

8. How does an actual costing system differ from a normal costing system? What advantages does a normal costing system offer?

9. What is meant by the term *cost of goods manufactured*? Why does this item appear on an income statement?

Exercises

10. **LO.1 (Association with cost object)** Following is a list of raw materials that might be used in the production of a laptop computer: touch pad and buttons, glue, network connector, battery, paper towels used by line employees, AC adapter, CD drive, motherboard, screws, paper towels, and oil for production machinery. The laptops are produced in the same building and using the same equipment that produces desktop computers and servers. Classify each raw material as direct or indirect when the cost object is the
    a. Laptop
    b. Computer production plant

11. **LO.1 (Association with cost object)** Morris & Assoc., owned by Cindy Morris, provides accounting services to clients. The firm has two accountants (Jo who performs basic accounting services, and Steve who performs tax services) and one office assistant. The assistant is paid on an hourly basis for the actual hours worked. One client the firm served during April was Vic Kennedy. During April 2008, the following labor time was incurred. Classify the labor time as direct or indirect based on whether the cost object is (1) Kennedy's services, (2) tax services provided, or (3) the accounting firm.
    a. Four hours of Jo's time in preparing Kennedy's financial statements
    b. Six hours of the assistant's time in copying Kennedy's tax materials
    c. Three hours of Cindy Morris' time playing golf with Kennedy
    d. Eight hours of continuing education paid for by the firm for Steve to attend a tax update seminar
    e. One hour of the assistant's time spent at lunch on the day that Kennedy's tax return was prepared
    f. Two hours of Jo's time spent with Kennedy and his banker discussing Kennedy's financial statements
    g. One-half hour of Steve's time spent talking to an IRS agent about a deduction taken on Kennedy's tax return
    h. Forty hours of janitorial wages
    i. Seven hours of Steve's time preparing Kennedy's tax return

12. **LO.1 (Association with cost object)** Witchita University's College of Business has five departments: Accounting, Economics, Finance, Management, and Marketing. Each department chairperson is responsible for the department's budget preparation. Indicate whether each of the following costs incurred in the Finance Department is direct or indirect to the department:
    a. Finance faculty salaries
    b. Finance chairperson's salary
    c. Cost of computer time of university server used by members of the department
    d. Cost of office assistant salaries (office assistants are shared by the entire college)
    e. Cost of travel by department faculty paid from externally generated funds contributed directly to the department
    f. Cost of equipment purchased by the department from allocated state funds
    g. Depreciation allocation of the college building cost for the number of offices used by department faculty
    h. Cost of periodicals/books purchased by the department
    i. Long-distance telephone calls made by finance faculty

13. **LO.2 (Predictors and cost drivers; team activity)** Therriott & Therriott CPAs often use factors that change in a consistent pattern with costs to explain or predict cost behavior.
    a. As a team of three or four, select factors to predict or explain the behavior of the following costs:
       1. Staff accountant's travel expenses
       2. Inventory of office supplies
       3. Laptops used to record audit findings
       4. Maintenance costs for the firm's lawn service
    b. Prepare a presentation of your chosen factors that also addresses whether the factors could be used as cost drivers in addition to cost predictors.

14. **LO.2 (Cost behavior)** Thomason Company manufactures playground basketballs. Costs are incurred in the production process for rubber material used to make the balls, a steel mesh material used in the balls, deprecia-

tion on the factory building, and utilities to run production machinery. Graph the most likely cost behavior for each of these costs and show what type of cost behavior is indicated by each cost.

15. **LO.2 (Cost behavior)** Flaherity Accounting Services pays $800 per month for a tax software license. In addition, variable charges average $6 for every tax return the firm prepares.
    a. Determine the total cost and the cost per unit if the firm expects to prepare the following number of tax returns in March 2008:
       1. 400
       2. 600
       3. 1,000
    b. Why does the cost per unit change in (1), (2), and (3) of part (a)?

16. **LO.2 (Cost behavior)** Merry Olde Games produces croquet sets. The company makes fixed monthly payments to the local utility based on prior year electrical usage. Any difference between actual and expected usage is paid in January of the year following usage. In February 2008, Merry Olde Games made 2,000 croquet sets and incurred the following costs:

Cardboard boxes (1 per set)	$ 1,000
Mallets (2 per set)	12,000
Croquet balls (6 per set)	9,000
Wire hoops (12 per set, including extras)	3,600
Total hourly wages for production workers	8,400
Supervisor's salary	2,600
Building and equipment rental	2,800
Utilities	1,300
Total	$40,700

    a. What was the per-unit cost of each croquet set component?
    b. What was the total cost per croquet set?
    c. Production for March 2008 is expected to be 2,500 croquet sets. What is the estimated cost per set for March?

17. **LO.2 (Cost behavior)** The next winner of *America's Idol* will perform at your fraternity's charity event for free at your school's basketball arena (25,000 person capacity) on January 28, 2009. The school is charging your fraternity $37,500 for the facilities and $10 for each ticket sold. The fraternity asks you, their only numbers-astute member, to determine how much to charge for each ticket. The group wants to make a profit of $6 per ticket sold. You assume that 15,000 tickets will be sold.
    a. What is the total cost incurred by the fraternity if 15,000 tickets are sold?
    b. What price per ticket must be charged for the fraternity to earn its desired profit margin?
    c. Suppose that on January 28, 2009, a major snowstorm hit your area, bringing in 36 inches of snow and ice. Only 5,000 tickets are sold because most students were going to buy their tickets at the door. What is the total profit or loss to the fraternity?
    d. What assumptions did you make about your calculations that should have been conveyed to the fraternity?
    e. Suppose instead that fair weather prevails and, by showtime, 20,000 concert tickets had been sold. What is the total profit or loss to the fraternity?

18. **LO.2 (Cost behavior)** Wisdom Company produces athletic caps. The company incurred the following costs to produce 6,000 caps last month:

Cardboard for the brims	$ 2,400
Cloth	6,000
Plastic for headbands	3,000
Straight-line depreciation	3,600
Supervisors' salaries	9,600
Utilities	1,800
Total	$26,400

    a. What did each cap component cost on a per-unit basis?
    b. What is the probable type of behavior that each of the costs exhibits?
    c. The company expects to produce 5,000 caps this month. Would you expect each type of cost to increase or decrease? Why? Why can't the total cost of 5,000 caps be determined?

19. **LO.2 & LO.3 (Cost behavior and classification)** Indicate whether each of the following items is a variable (V), fixed (F), or mixed (M) cost and whether it is a product/service (PT) or period (PD) cost. If some items have alternative answers, indicate the alternatives and the reasons for them.

  a. Wages of factory maintenance workers
  b. Wages of forklift operators who move finished goods from a central warehouse to the loading dock
  c. Insurance premiums paid on the headquarters of a manufacturing company
  d. Cost of labels attached to shirts made by a company
  e. Property taxes on a manufacturing plant
  f. Paper towels used in factory restrooms
  g. Salaries of office assistants in a law firm
  h. Freight costs of acquiring raw material from suppliers
  i. Computer paper used in an accounting firm
  j. Cost of wax to make candles
  k. Freight-in on a truckload of furniture purchased for resale

20. **LO.2 (Cost drivers)** Assume that Rymer Hospital performs the following activities in providing outpatient service:
  a. Verifying patient's insurance coverage
  b. Scheduling patient's arrival date and time
  c. Scheduling staff to prepare patient's surgery room
  d. Scheduling doctors and nurses to perform surgery
  e. Ordering patient tests
  f. Moving patient to laboratory to administer lab tests
  g. Moving patient to the operating room
  h. Administering anesthetic
  i. Performing surgery
  j. Moving patient to recovery room
  k. Discharging patient
  l. Billing patient's insurance company
  Assume that the patient is the cost object and determine the appropriate cost driver or drivers for each activity.

21. **LO.3 (Financial statement classification)** Brad Langley's Airboats purchased a $420,000 machine to make airboat hulls. The machine was expected to have a life of 10 years and a salvage value at time of disposition of $20,000. The company uses straight-line depreciation. During its first operating year, the machine produced 10,000 hulls, of which 8,500 were sold.
  a. What part of the $420,000 machine cost is expired?
  b. Where would each of the amounts related to this machine appear on the financial statements?

22. **LO.2 & LO.3 (Cost behavior and classification)** Classify each of the following costs incurred in manufacturing bicycles as variable (V), fixed (F), or mixed (M) cost (using number of units produced as the activity measure). Also indicate whether the cost is direct material (DM), direct labor (DL), or overhead (OH).
  a. Factory supervision
  b. Aluminum tubing
  c. Rims
  d. Emblem
  e. Gearbox
  f. Straight-line depreciation on paint machine
  g. Fenders
  h. Inventory clerk's salary
  i. Inspector's salary
  j. Handlebars
  k. Metal worker's wages
  l. Roller chain
  m. Spokes (assuming cost is considered significant)
  n. Paint (assuming cost is considered significant)

23. **LO.4 (Company type)** Indicate whether each of the following terms is associated with a manufacturing (Mfg.), a retailing or merchandising (Mer.), or a service (Ser.) company. There can be more than one correct answer for each term.
  a. Depreciation—factory equipment
  b. Prepaid rent
  c. Auditing fees expense
  d. Merchandise inventory

e. Sales salaries expense
f. Finished goods inventory
g. Cost of services rendered
h. Cost of goods sold
i. Direct labor wages

24. **LO.3 (Financial statement classification)** J. Delgado Company incurred the following costs in May 2008:

- Paid a six-month (May through October) premium for insurance of company headquarters, $18,600.
- Paid three months (May through July) of property taxes on its factory building, $15,000.
- Paid a $10,000 bonus to the company president for his performance during May 2008.
- Accrued $20,000 of utility costs, of which 40 percent was for the headquarters and the remainder was for the factory.

a. What expired period cost is associated with the May information?
b. What unexpired period cost is associated with the May information?
c. What product cost is associated with the May information?
d. Discuss why the product cost cannot be described specifically as expired or unexpired in this situation.

25. **LO.5 (Product cost classifications)** Dauterive Co. makes aluminum canoes. The company's June 2008 costs for material and labor were as follows:

Material costs	
Janitorial supplies	$ 300
Chrome rivets to assemble canoes	4,170
Sealant	310
Aluminum	361,000
Labor costs	
Janitorial wages	$ 7,000
Aluminum cutters	19,700
Salespeople salaries	12,250
Welders	52,000
Factory supervisor salaries	29,000

a. What is the direct material cost for June?
b. What is the direct labor cost for June?

26. **LO.4 (Degrees of conversion)** Indicate whether each of the following types of organizations is characterized by a high, low, or moderate degree of conversion.
a. Textbook publisher
b. Bakery in a grocery store
c. Convenience store
d. Christmas tree farm
e. Auto manufacturer
f. Cranberry farm
g. Custom print shop
h. Italian restaurant
i. Sporting goods retailer
j. Concert ticket seller

27. **LO.5 (Labor cost classification)** Tidy House produces a variety of household products. The firm operates 24 hours per day with three daily work shifts. The first-shift workers receive "regular pay." The second shift receives an 8 percent pay premium, and the third shift receives a 12 percent pay premium. In addition, when production is scheduled on weekends, the firm pays an overtime premium of 50 percent (based on the pay rate for first-shift employees). Labor premiums are included in overhead. The October 2008 factory payroll is as follows:

Total wages for October for 32,000 hours	$424,800
Normal hourly wage for first-shift employees	$12
Total regular hours worked, split evenly among the three shifts	28,000

a. How many overtime hours were worked in October?
b. How much of the total labor cost should be charged to direct labor? To overhead?
c. What amount of overhead was for second- and third-shift premiums? For overtime premiums?

28. LO.5 (Product cost classifications) Madden Inc. manufactures stainless steel knives. Following are factory costs incurred during 2008:

Material costs
Stainless steel	$400,000
Equipment oil and grease	3,000
Plastic for handles	2,800
Wood blocks for knife storage	12,400

Labor costs
Equipment operators	$250,000
Equipment mechanics	41,000
Factory supervisors	136,000

a. What is the direct material cost for 2008?
b. What is the direct labor cost for 2008?
c. What are the total indirect material and indirect labor costs for 2008?

29. LO.5 (Product cost classifications) In June 2008, Schneider Gardens incurred the following costs. One of several projects in process during the month was a landscaped terrace for Robin Jones. Relative to the Jones' landscaping job, classify each of the costs as direct material, direct labor, or overhead. The terrace required two days to design and one five-day work week to complete. Some costs may not fit entirely into a single classification; in such cases, and if possible, provide a systematic and rational method to allocate such costs.

Mulch purchased for the Jones' landscaping	$ 320
June depreciation on the company loader, driven by a gardener and used on the Jones' landscaping one day	200
Landscaping rock purchased for the Jones' landscaping	1,580
June salary of Z. Trumble, the landscape designer, who worked 20 days in June	3,000
Construction permit for the Jones' landscaping	95
June rent on Schneider Gardens offices, where Z. Trumble has an office which occupies 150 square feet of 3,000 square feet	2,400
June utility bills for Schneider Gardens	1,800
Gardeners' wages; all worked on the Jones' landscaping; gardeners work eight hours per day, five days per week; 20 working days in June	3,840
Plants and pots purchased for the Jones' landscaping	1,950

30. LO.5 (Labor cost classification) Old West Restaurant Supply operates in two shifts, paying a late-shift premium of 10 percent and an overtime premium of 75 percent. The May 2008 payroll follows:

Total wages for 6,000 hours	$48,000
Normal hourly employee wage	$8
Total regular hours worked, split evenly between the shifts	5,000

All overtime was worked by the early shift during May. Shift and overtime premiums are considered part of overhead rather than direct labor.
a. How many overtime hours were worked in May?
b. How much of the total labor cost should be charged to direct labor? To overhead?
c. What amount of overhead was for second-shift premiums? For overtime premiums?

31. LO.6 (CGM; CGS) Yashir Company had the following inventory balances at the beginning and end of August 2008:

	August 1	August 31
Raw Material Inventory	$ 48,000	$ 64,000
Work in Process Inventory	272,000	336,000
Finished Goods Inventory	124,000	96,000

All raw material is direct to the production process. The following information is also available about August manufacturing costs:

Cost of raw material used	$512,000
Direct labor cost	648,000
Manufacturing overhead	464,000

a. Calculate the cost of goods manufactured for August.
b. Determine the cost of goods sold for August.

32. LO.6 (Journal entries—service industry) Hopkins & Bruder CPAs incurred the following costs in performing audits during September 2008. The firm uses a Work in Process Inventory account for audit engagement costs and records overhead in fixed and variable overhead accounts. Prepare journal entries for each of the following transactions:

a. Used $1,000 of previously purchased supplies on audit engagements.
b. Paid $2,000 of partner travel expenses to an accounting conference.
c. Recorded $6,500 of depreciation on laptops used in audits.
d. Recorded $1,800,000 of depreciation on the Hopkins & Bruder Building, located in downtown New York; 10 percent of the space is used to house audit personnel.
e. Accrued audit partner salaries, $200,000.
f. Accrued remaining audit staff salaries, $150,000.
g. Paid credit card charges for travel costs for client engagements, $9,400.
h. Paid insurance on the downtown building, $17,300.
i. Accrued $3,400 of office assistant wages; the office assistant works only for the audit partners and staff.
j. Paid all accrued salaries and wages for the month.

33. LO.6 (CGM; CGS) The cost of goods sold in March 2008 for Raggae Rocks Co. was $2,300,000. March 31 Work in Process Inventory was 40 percent of the March 1 Work in Process Inventory. Overhead was 225 percent of direct labor cost. During March, $1,182,000 of direct material was purchased. Other March information follows:

Inventories	March 1	March 31
Direct Material	$ 30,000	$42,000
Work in Process	90,000	?
Finished Goods	125,000	24,000

a. Prepare a schedule of the cost of goods sold for March.
b. Prepare the March cost of goods manufactured schedule.
c. What was the amount of prime cost incurred in March?
d. What was the amount of conversion cost incurred in March?

34. LO.6 (CGM; CGS) It's Kinda China produces collectible pieces of art. The company's Raw Material Inventory account includes the costs of both direct and indirect materials. Account balances for the company at the beginning and end of July 2008 follow:

	July 1	July 31
Raw Material Inventory	$46,600	$34,800
Work in Process Inventory	73,200	60,000
Finished Goods Inventory	36,000	52,400

During the month, the company purchased $164,000 of raw material; direct material used during the period amounted to $128,000. Factory payroll costs for July were $197,000 of which 85 percent was related to direct labor. Overhead charges for depreciation, insurance, utilities, and maintenance totaled $150,000 for July.

a. Prepare a schedule of cost of goods manufactured.
b. Prepare a schedule of cost of goods sold.

35. LO.6 (Cost of services rendered) The following information is related to the Caspari Veterinary Clinic for April 2008, the firm's first month of operation:

Veterinarian salaries for April	$36,000
Assistants' salaries for April	12,600
Medical supplies purchased in April	4,800
Utilities for month (80 percent related to animal treatment)	2,700
Office salaries for April (20 percent related to animal treatment)	7,800
Medical supplies on hand at April 30	2,200
Depreciation on medical equipment for April	1,800
Building rental (70 percent related to animal treatment)	2,100

Compute the cost of services rendered.

Problems

36. LO.2 (Cost behavior) Premium Printers makes stationery sets of 100 percent rag content edged in 24 karat gold. In an average month, the firm produces 40,000 boxes of stationery; each box contains 100 pages of stationery and 80 envelopes. Production costs are incurred for paper, ink, glue, and boxes. The company manufactures this product in batches of 500 boxes of a specific stationery design. The following data have been extracted from the company's accounting records for June 2008:

Cost of paper for each batch	$ 5,000
Cost of ink and glue for each batch	500
Cost of 500 gold boxes for each batch	16,000
Direct labor for producing each batch	8,000
Cost of designing each batch	20,000

Overhead charges total $204,000 per month and are considered fully fixed for purposes of cost estimation.
  a. What is the cost per box of stationery based on average production volume?
  b. If sales volume increases to 60,000 boxes per month, what will be the cost per box (assuming that cost behavior patterns remain the same as in June)?
  c. If sales volume increases to 60,000 boxes per month but the firm does not want the cost per box to exceed its current level [based on part (a)], what amount can the company pay for design costs, assuming all other costs are the same as June levels?
  d. Assume that Premium Printers is now able to sell, on average, each box of stationery at a price of $150. If the company is able to increase its volume to 60,000 boxes per month, what sales price per box will generate the same gross margin that the firm is now achieving on 40,000 boxes per month?
  e. Would it be possible to lower total costs by producing more boxes per batch, even if the total volume of 40,000 is maintained? Explain.

37. **LO.1–LO.3 (Cost classifications)** Geoff Payne painted four houses during April 2008. For these jobs, he spent $1,200 on paint, $80 on mineral spirits, and $300 on brushes. He also bought two pairs of coveralls for $100 each; he wears coveralls only while he works. During the first week of April, Payne placed a $100 ad for his business in the classifieds. He hired an assistant for one of the painting jobs; the assistant was paid $25 per hour and worked 50 hours.

   Being a very methodical person, Payne kept detailed records of his mileage to and from each painting job. His average operating cost per mile for his van is $0.70. He found a $30 receipt in his van for a metropolitan map that he purchased in April. He uses the map as part of a contact file for referral work and for bids that he has made on potential jobs. He also had $30 in receipts for bridge tolls ($2 per trip) for a painting job he did across the river.

   Near the end of April, Payne decided to go camping, and he turned down a job on which he had bid $6,000. He called the homeowner long distance (at a cost of $3.20) to explain his reasons for declining the job.

   Using the following headings, indicate how to classify each of the April costs incurred by Payne. Assume that the cost object is a house-painting job.

Type of Cost	Variable	Fixed	Direct	Indirect	Period	Product

38. **LO.2 (Cost behavior)** Toni Rankin has been elected to handle the local Little Theater summer play. She is trying to determine the price to charge Little Theater members for attendance at this year's performance of *The Producers*. She has developed the following cost estimates associated with the play:
   - Cost of printing invitations will be $260 for 100 to 500; cost to print between 501 and 600 will be $280.
   - Cost of readying and operating the theater for three evenings will be $1,000 if attendance is 500 or less; this cost rises to $1,200 if attendance is above 500.
   - Postage to mail the invitations will be $0.40 each.
   - Cost of building stage sets will be $1,215.
   - Cost of printing up to 1,000 programs will be $250.
   - Cost of security will be $110 per night plus $30 per hour; five hours will be needed each night.
   - Cost to obtain script usage, $1,000.
   - Costumes will be donated by several local businesses.

The Little Theater has 200 members, and each member is allowed two guests. Ordinarily only 75 percent of the members attend the summer offering, each bringing the two allowed guests. The play will be presented from 8 to 11 P.M. each evening. Invitations are mailed to those members calling to say they plan to attend and also to each of the guests they specify. Rankin has asked you to help her by answering the following items.
  a. Indicate the type of cost behavior exhibited by each of the items Rankin needs to consider.
  b. If the ordinary attendance occurs, what will be the total cost of the summer production?
  c. If the ordinary attendance occurs, what will be the cost per person attending?

d. If 90 percent of the members attend and each invites two guests, what will be the total cost of the play? The cost per person? What primarily causes the difference in the cost per person?

39. LO.2 (Cost behavior; ethics) Celestial Delights prepares meals for several airlines, and sales average 300,000 meals per month. The significant costs of each meal prepared are for the meat, vegetables, and plastic trays and utensils; no desserts are provided because the airlines are concerned about cost control. The company prepares meals in batches of 1,000. The following data are shown in the company's accounting records for June 2008:

Cost of meat for 1,000 meals	$1,800
Cost of vegetables for 1,000 meals	720
Cost of plastic trays and utensils for 1,000 meals	240
Direct labor cost for 1,000 meals	1,900

Monthly overhead charges amount to $2,400,000 and are fully fixed. Company management has asked you to answer the following items.

a. What is the cost per meal based on average sales and June prices?

b. If sales increase to 400,000 meals per month, what will be the cost per meal (assuming that the cost behavior patterns remain the same as in June)?

c. Assume that sales increase to 400,000 meals per month. Celestial Delights wants the per-unit cost to remain the same as was computed in part (a). By how much can the company increase its per-unit spending for meat, assuming all other costs remain constant?

d. The company's major competitor has bid a price of $21.92 per meal to the airlines. The profit margin in the industry is 100 percent of total cost. If Celestial Delights is to retain the airlines' business, how many meals must the company produce each month to reach the bid price of the competitor and maintain the 100 percent profit margin? Assume June cost patterns will not change and meals must be produced in batches of 1,000.

e. Consider your answer to part (d). Under what circumstances might the manager for Celestial Delights retain the airlines' business but cause the company to be less profitable than it currently is? Show calculations. ▲

40. LO.2 (Cost drivers and predictors) Customers now demand a wide variety of "personalized" products and want those products delivered quickly. Factory automation is replacing the traditional labor-intensive production lines. Thus, product costs are determined when they are "on the drawing board" because, once they are designed, it is difficult to change the method of production or component materials of products.

a. Why is determining the cost to manufacture a product quite a different activity from determining how to control such costs?

b. Why has the advancement of technology made costs more difficult to control?

c. For many production costs, why should "number of units produced" not be considered a cost driver even though it is certainly a valid cost predictor?

41. LO.2 (Cost behavior) Braunfels Company's cost structure contains a number of different cost behavior patterns. Following are descriptions of several different costs; match these to the appropriate graphs. On each graph, the vertical axis represents cost and the horizontal axis represents level of activity or volume.

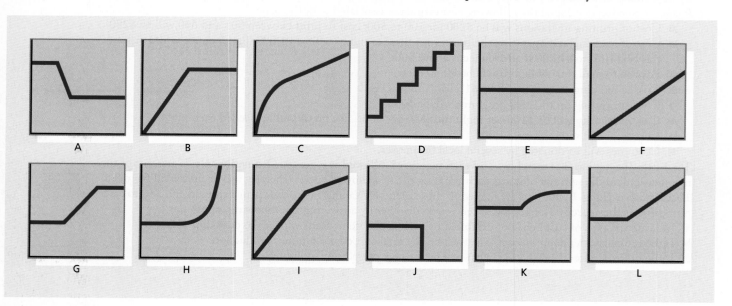

Identify, by letter, the graph that illustrates each of the following cost behavior patterns. Each graph can be used more than once.

1. Cost of raw material, where the cost decreases by $0.06 per unit for each of the first 150 units purchased, after which it remains constant at $2.75 per unit.
2. City water bill, which is computed as follows: first 750,000 gallons or less, $1,000 flat fee; next 15,000 gallons, $0.002 per gallon used; next 15,000 gallons, $0.005 per gallon used; next 15,000 gallons, $0.008 per gallon used; and so on.
3. Salaries of maintenance workers, assuming one maintenance worker is needed for every 1,000 hours or less of machine time.
4. Electricity bill—a flat fixed charge of $250 plus a variable cost after 150,000 kilowatt hours are used.
5. Depreciation of equipment using the straight-line method.
6. Rent on a machine that is billed at $1,000 for up to 500 hours of machine time. After 500 hours of machine time, an additional charge of $1 per hour is paid up to a maximum charge of $2,500 per period.
7. Rent on a factory building donated by the county; the agreement provides for a monthly rental of $100,000 less $1 for each labor hour worked in excess of 200,000 hours. However, a minimum rental payment of $20,000 must be made each month.
8. Cost of raw materials used.
9. Rent on a factory building donated by the city with an agreement providing for a fixed-fee payment unless 250,000 labor hours are worked, in which case no rent needs to be paid.

(AICPA adapted)

42. **LO.5 (Journal entries)** The following transactions were incurred by Dresser Industries during January 2008:
    1. Direct material issued to production, $350,000.
    2. Direct labor cost paid, 70,000 hours at $16 per hour.
    3. Indirect labor cost accrued, 15,500 hours at $10 per hour.
    4. Depreciation on factory assets recorded, $75,400.
    5. Supervisors' salaries paid, $28,000.
    6. Indirect material issued to production, $19,200.
    7. Goods costing $1,680,000 were completed and transferred to finished goods.
    a. Prepare journal entries for these transactions using a single overhead account for both variable and fixed overhead. The Raw Material Inventory account contains only direct material; indirect materials are included in Supplies Inventory.
    b. If Work in Process Inventory had a beginning balance of $24,500, what is its ending balance?

43. **LO.2 (Cost behavior; cost management; ethics)** An extremely important and expensive variable cost per employee is health care provided by the employer. This cost is expected to rise each year as more and more expensive technology is used on patients and as the costs of that technology are passed along through the insurance company to the employer.
    One simple way to reduce these variable costs is to reduce employee insurance coverage.
    a. Discuss the ethical implications of reducing employee health care coverage to reduce the variable costs incurred by the employer.
    b. Assume that you are an employer with 600 employees. You are forced to reduce some insurance benefits. Your coverage currently includes the following items: mental health coverage, long-term disability, convalescent facility care, nonemergency but medically necessary procedures, dependent coverage, and life insurance. Select the two you would eliminate or dramatically reduce and provide reasons for your selections.
    c. Prepare a plan that might allow you to "trade" some variable employee health care costs for a fixed or mixed cost. ▲

44. **LO.5 (Ethics)** You are the chief financial officer for a small manufacturing company that has applied for a bank loan. In speaking with the bank loan officer, you are told that two minimum criteria for granting loans are (1) a 40 percent gross margin and (2) income of at least 15 percent of sales. Looking at the last four months' income statements, you find that gross margin has been between 30 and 33 percent and income ranged from 18 to 24 percent of sales. You discuss these relationships with the company president, who suggests that some of the product costs included in Cost of Goods Sold be moved to the selling and administrative categories so that the income statement will conform to the bank's criteria.
    a. Which types of product costs might be most easily reassigned to period cost classifications?
    b. Because the president is not suggesting that any expenses be kept off the income statement, do you see any ethical problems with the request? Discuss the rationale for your answer.

c. Write a short memo to convince the banker to loan the company the funds in spite of its noncompliance with the specified loan criteria. ▲

45. LO.5 (Essay on direct labor) A portion of the costs incurred by business organizations is designated as direct labor cost. As used in practice, the term *direct labor cost* has a wide variety of meanings. Unless the meaning intended in a given context is clear, misunderstanding and confusion are likely to ensue. If a user does not understand the elements included in direct labor cost, erroneous interpretations of the numbers can occur and can result in poor management decisions. In addition to understanding the conceptual definition of direct labor cost, management accountants must understand how direct labor cost should be measured. Write a paper that discusses the following issues:

a. Distinguish between direct labor and indirect labor.

b. Discuss why some nonproductive labor time (such as coffee breaks, personal time) can be and often is treated as direct labor whereas other nonproductive time (such as downtime or training) is treated as indirect labor.

c. Following are labor cost elements that a company has classified as direct labor, manufacturing overhead, or either direct labor or manufacturing overhead, depending on the situation.

- ■ Direct labor: Included in the company's direct labor are cost production efficiency bonuses and certain benefits for direct labor workers such as FICA (employer's portion), group life insurance, vacation pay, and workers' compensation insurance.
- ■ Manufacturing overhead: Included in the company's overhead are costs for wage continuation plans in the event of illness, the company-sponsored cafeteria, the personnel department, and recreational facilities.
- ■ Direct labor or manufacturing overhead: Included in the "situational" category are maintenance expense, overtime premiums, and shift premiums.

Explain the rationale used by the company in classifying the cost elements in each of the three categories.

d. The two aspects of measuring direct labor costs are (1) the quantity of labor effort that is to be included, and (2) the unit price by which the labor quantity is multiplied to arrive at a labor cost. Why are these considered separate and distinct aspects of measuring labor cost?

(CMA adapted)

46. LO.5 & LO.6 (CGM; journal entries) Weatherguard manufactures mailboxes. The following data represent transactions and balances for December 2008, the company's first month of operations.

Purchased direct material on account	$124,000
Issued direct material to production	93,000
Accrued direct labor payroll	67,000
Paid factory rent	1,800
Accrued factory utilities	8,100
Recorded factory equipment depreciation	7,900
Paid supervisor salary	3,200
Ending Work in Process Inventory (6,000 units)	17,500
Ending Finished Goods Inventory (3,000 units)	?
Sales on account ($12 per unit)	324,000

As a consultant, you have been asked to address the following:

a. How many units were sold in December? How many units were completed?

b. What was the total cost of goods manufactured in December?

c. What was the per unit cost of goods manufactured in December?

d. Prepare the journal entries to record the flow of costs for December. Weatherguard uses a perpetual inventory system and a single Manufacturing Overhead Control account.

47. LO.5 & LO.6 (CGM; journal entries) Designer Rags makes evening dresses. The following information was gathered from the company records for 2008, the first year of company operations. Work in Process Inventory at the end of 2008 was $91,500.

Direct material purchased on account	$1,110,000
Direct material issued to production	894,000
Direct labor payroll accrued	645,000
Indirect labor payroll accrued	186,000
Prepaid factory insurance expired	6,000
Factory utilities paid	42,900
Depreciation on factory equipment recorded	65,100
Factory rent paid	252,000
Sales on account	2,862,000

The company's gross profit rate for the year was 35 percent.
a. Compute the cost of goods sold for 2008.
b. What was the total cost of goods manufactured for 2008?
c. If net income was $150,000, what were total selling and administrative expenses for the year?
d. Prepare journal entries to record the flow of costs for the year, assuming the company uses a perpetual inventory system and a single Manufacturing Overhead Control account.

48. **LO.6 (CGM; CGS)** Flex-Em began business in July 2008. The firm makes an exercise machine for home and gym use. Following are data taken from the firm's accounting records that pertain to its first month of operations.

Direct material purchased on account	$450,000
Direct material issued to production	424,000
Direct labor payroll accrued	236,000
Indirect labor payroll paid	90,600
Factory insurance expired	6,000
Factory utilities paid	17,800
Factory depreciation recorded	35,800
Ending Work in Process Inventory (96 units)	111,000
Ending Finished Goods Inventory (30 units)	91,200
Sales on account ($3,700 per unit)	740,000

a. How many units did the company sell in July 2008? How many units were completed that month?
b. Prepare a schedule of cost of goods manufactured for July 2008.
c. What was the per-unit cost of goods manufactured for the month?
d. What was the cost of goods sold in the first month of operations?
e. What was the gross margin for July 2008?

49. **LO.4–LO.6 (Cost flows; CGM; CGS)** For each of the following cases, compute the missing amounts.

	Case 1	Case 2	Case 3
Sales	$9,300	$?	$112,000
Direct material used	1,200	?	18,200
Direct labor	?	4,900	?
Prime cost	3,700	?	?
Conversion cost	4,800	8,200	49,300
Manufacturing overhead	?	?	17,200
Cost of goods manufactured	6,200	14,000	?
Beginning work in process inventory	500	900	5,600
Ending work in process inventory	?	1,200	4,200
Beginning finished goods inventory	?	1,900	7,600
Ending finished goods inventory	1,200	?	?
Cost of goods sold	?	12,200	72,200
Gross profit	3,500	?	?
Operating expenses	?	3,500	18,000
Net income	2,200	4,000	?

50. **LO.5 & LO.6 (Missing data)** Rocky Mount Company suffered major losses in a fire on June 18, 2008. In addition to destroying several buildings, the blaze destroyed the company's work in process inventory for an entire product line. Fortunately, the company was insured; however, it needs to substantiate the amount of the claim. To this end, the company has gathered the following information that pertains to production and sales of the affected product line:
1. The company's sales for the first 18 days of June amounted to $920,000. Normally, this product line generates a gross profit equal to 30 percent of sales.
2. Finished Goods Inventory was $116,000 on June 1 and $170,000 on June 18.
3. On June 1, Work in Process Inventory was $192,000.
4. During the first 18 days of June, the company incurred the following costs:

Direct material used	$304,000
Direct labor	176,000
Manufacturing overhead	168,000

a. Determine the value of Work in Process Inventory that was destroyed by the fire, assuming Rocky Mount Company uses an actual cost system.

b. What other information might the insurance company require? How would management determine or estimate this information?

51. LO.3 & LO.6 (Product and period costs; CGM; CGS) On August 1, 2008, Ross Corporation had the following account balances:

Raw Material Inventory (both direct and indirect)	$ 72,000
Work in Process Inventory	108,000
Finished Goods Inventory	24,000

During August, the following transactions took place.
1. Raw material was purchased on account, $570,000.
2. Direct material ($121,200) and indirect material ($15,000) were issued to production.
3. Factory payroll consisted of $180,000 for direct labor employees and $42,000 for indirect labor employees.
4. Office salaries totaled $144,600 for the month.
5. Utilities of $40,200 were accrued; 70 percent of the utilities cost is for the factory.
6. Depreciation of $60,000 was recorded on plant assets; 80 percent of the depreciation is related to factory machinery and equipment.
7. Rent of $66,000 was paid on the building. The factory occupies 60 percent of the building.
8. At the end of August, the Work in Process Inventory balance was $49,800.
9. At the end of August, the balance in Finished Goods Inventory was $53,400.

Ross Corporation uses an actual cost system and debits actual overhead costs incurred to Work in Process Inventory.

a. Determine the total amount of product cost (cost of goods manufactured) and period cost incurred during August 2008.
b. Compute the cost of goods sold for August 2008.

3 | Predetermined Overhead Rates, Flexible Budgets, and Absorption/Variable Costing

Objectives

After completing this chapter, you should be able to answer the following questions:

LO.1 Why and how are overhead costs allocated to products and services?

LO.2 What causes underapplied or overapplied overhead, and how is it treated at the end of a period?

LO.3 What impact do different capacity measures have on setting predetermined overhead rates?

LO.4 How are the high–low method and least squares regression analysis used in analyzing mixed costs?

LO.5 How do managers use flexible budgets to set predetermined overhead rates?

LO.6 How do absorption and variable costing differ?

LO.7 How do changes in sales or production levels affect net income computed under absorption and variable costing?

Introduction

Any cost of doing business that is not incurred for direct material or direct labor is overhead. Overhead costs are incurred both in the production area and in selling and administrative departments. Manufacturers traditionally considered direct material and direct labor as the primary production costs; similarly, a retailer's primary costs were for inventory and sales salaries. Historically, overhead was often an "additional" cost that was necessary but not of an exceptionally significant amount. However, many manufacturing firms have begun to heavily invest in automation, and many retailers have been pressured by customers to provide better customer service and more product variety. These changes have significantly increased the costs of manufacturing and nonmanufacturing overhead.

Regardless of where costs are incurred, a simple fact exists: for a company to be profitable, product or service selling prices must cover all costs. Direct material and labor costs can be easily traced to output and, as such, create few accounting difficulties. In contrast, indirect costs cannot be traced directly to separately distinguishable outputs.

Whereas Chapter 2 discusses and illustrates actual cost systems in which actual direct material, direct labor, and manufacturing overhead are assigned to products, this chapter discusses normal costing and its use of predetermined overhead rates to determine product cost. Separation of mixed costs into variable and fixed elements, flexible budgets, and various production capacity measures are also discussed.

In addition, this chapter discusses two methods of presenting information on financial statements: absorption and variable costing. Absorption costing is commonly used for external reporting; variable costing is commonly used for internal reporting. Each method uses the same basic data but structures and processes those data differently. Either method can be used in job order or process costing and with actual, normal, or standard costs.

Normal Costing and Predetermined Overhead

Normal costing is a costing system that is an alternative to actual costing. As shown in Exhibit 3–1, normal costing assigns actual direct material and direct labor to products but allocates manufacturing overhead (OH) to products using a predetermined rate. The overhead allocation can occur in real time as products are manufactured or as services are delivered. Many accounting procedures are based on allocations. Cost allocations can be made across time periods or within a single time period. For example, in financial accounting, a building's cost is allocated through depreciation charges over its useful life. This process is necessary for fulfilling the matching principle. In cost accounting, manufacturing OH costs are allocated to products or services within a period through the use of predictors or cost drivers. This process reflects the application of the cost principle, which requires that all production or acquisition costs attach to the units produced, services rendered, or units purchased.

EXHIBIT 3–1
Actual versus Normal Costing

	Actual Cost System	Normal Cost System
Direct material	Assigned to product/service	Assigned to product/service
Direct labor	Assigned to product/service	Assigned to product/service
Overhead	Assigned to product/service	Assigned to overhead (OH) control account; predetermined OH rate is used to allocate overhead to product/ service

There are four primary reasons for using predetermined overhead rates in product costing. First, a predetermined rate facilitates the assignment of overhead during a period as goods are produced or sold and services are rendered. Thus, a predetermined OH rate improves the timeliness of information.

Second, predetermined OH rates adjust for variations in actual overhead costs that are unrelated to fluctuations in activity. Overhead can vary monthly because of seasonal or calendar (days in a month) factors. For example, factory utility costs could be highest in summer because of the necessity to run air conditioning. If monthly production were constant and actual overhead were assigned to production, the increase in utilities would cause product cost per unit to be higher in summer than during the rest of the year. To illustrate, assume that a company produces 3,000 units of its sole product each month. Utility costs for April and July were $1,200 and $1,800, respectively. The average actual utility cost per unit would be $0.40 ($1,200 ÷ 3,000 units) in April but $0.60 ($1,800 ÷ 3,000) in July. Although this single cost difference is not necessarily significant, numerous differences of this type could cause a large distortion in unit cost.

Third, predetermined OH rates overcome the problem of fluctuations in activity levels that have no impact on fixed overhead costs. Even if total manufacturing overhead were the same for each period, changes in activity would cause a per-unit change in fixed overhead cost. For example, if a company incurred $600 of utility cost in both October and November but produced 3,750 units in October and 3,000 units in November, the average actual unit utility cost would be $0.16 ($600 ÷ 3,750 units) in October and $0.20 ($600 ÷ 3,000 units) in November. As mentioned earlier, many such overhead cost differences could create major variations in unit cost. By establishing a uniform annual predetermined OH rate for all units produced during the year, the problems illustrated in these examples are overcome.

Finally, using predetermined OH rates—especially when the bases for those rates truly reflect the drivers of costs—often allows managers to be more aware of individual product or product line profitability as well as the profitability of business with a particular customer or vendor. For instance, assume that a gift shop purchases a product that retails for $40 from Vendor X for $20. If the gift shop manager has determined that a reasonable OH rate per hour for vendor telephone conferences is $5 and that she often spends three hours on the phone with Vendor X because of customer complaints or shipping problems, the gift shop manager could decide that the $5 profit on the product [$40 selling price − ($20 product cost + $15 in overhead)] does not make it cost beneficial to continue working with Vendor X.

Formula for Predetermined Overhead Rate

With one exception, normal cost system journal entries are identical to those made in an actual cost system. In both systems, overhead is debited during the period to a manufacturing overhead account and credited to the various accounts that "created" the overhead costs. In an actual cost system, the total amount of actual overhead cost is then transferred from the overhead account to Work in Process (WIP) Inventory. Alternatively, in a normal cost system overhead cost is assigned to WIP Inventory through the use of a predetermined OH rate.

To calculate a predetermined OH rate, total budgeted overhead cost at a specific activity level is divided by the related activity level:

$$\text{Predetermined OH Rate} = \frac{\text{Total Budgeted OH Cost at a Specified Activity Level}}{\text{Volume of Specified Activity Level}}$$

Overhead cost and its related activity measure are typically budgeted for one year, although a longer or shorter period could be more appropriate in some organizations' production cycle. For example, a longer period is more appropriate in a company that constructs ships, bridges, or high-rise office buildings.

Companies should use an activity base that is logically related to actual overhead cost incurrence. Although production volume might be the first activity base considered, this base is reasonable only if the company manufactures one type of product or renders just one type of service. If a company makes multiple products or performs multiple services, production volumes cannot be summed to determine "activity" because of the heterogeneous nature of the items.

LO.1

Why and how are overhead costs allocated to products and services?

A construction company that builds bridges will likely budget overhead cost for a period longer than one year.

To effectively allocate overhead to heterogeneous products or services, a measure of activity that is common to all output must be selected. The activity base should be a cost driver that directly causes the incurrence of overhead costs. Direct labor hours and direct labor dollars are common activity measures; however, these bases could be deficient if a company is highly automated. Using any direct labor measure to allocate overhead costs in automated plants results in extremely high overhead rates because the costs are applied over a relatively small activity base. In automated plants, machine hours could be a more appropriate base for allocating overhead. Other possible measures include the number of purchase orders, product-related physical characteristics such as tons or gallons, number or amount of time of machine setups, number of parts, material handling time, product complexity, and number of product defects.

Applying Overhead to Production

Once calculated, the predetermined OH rate is used throughout the period to apply overhead to WIP Inventory using the predetermined rate and the actual level of activity. Thus, applied overhead is the dollar amount of overhead assigned to WIP Inventory using the activity measure that was selected to develop the application rate. Overhead can be applied when goods or services are transferred out of WIP Inventory or at the end of each month if financial statements are to be prepared. Or, under the real-time systems currently in use, overhead can be applied continuously as production occurs.

For convenience, both actual and applied overhead are recorded in a single general ledger account.[1] Debits to the account represent actual overhead costs, and credits represent applied overhead. Variable and fixed overhead may be recorded either in a single account or in separate accounts, although separate accounts provide better information to managers. Exhibit 3–2 presents the alternative overhead recording possibilities.

If variable and fixed overhead are applied using separate rates, the general ledger will have separate variable and fixed overhead accounts. Because overhead represents an ever-larger part of product cost in automated factories, the benefits of separating overhead according to its variable or fixed behavior is thought to be greater than the time and effort needed to make that separation. Separation of mixed costs is discussed later in this chapter.

Regardless of the number of predetermined OH rates used, actual overhead is debited to the general ledger overhead account and credited to the source of the overhead cost. Overhead is applied to WIP Inventory as production occurs, as measured by the activity identified in the denominator in the predetermined OH rate formula. Applied overhead is debited to WIP Inventory and credited to the overhead general ledger account.

Assume that Doggett Industries, a manufacturer of children's car seats, budgeted the following amounts for the current year: 50,000 machine hours, $375,000 of variable overhead costs, and $630,000 of fixed overhead costs. Doggett computes separate fixed and variable predetermined OH rates using machine hours as the allocation base. Thus, the company's variable and fixed rates are, respectively, $7.50 ($375,000 ÷ 50,000) and $12.60 ($630,000 ÷ 50,000) per machine hour. For the most recent month, the company worked 4,300 machine hours and incurred $31,385 of actual variable overhead costs and $55,970 of actual fixed overhead costs. Using the predetermined OH rates, Doggett would apply $32,250 (4,300 × $7.50) of variable overhead and $54,180 (4,300 ×

---

[1]Some companies may use separate overhead accounts for actual and applied overhead. In such cases, the actual overhead account has a debit balance and the applied overhead account has a credit balance. The applied overhead account is closed at the end of the year against the actual overhead account to determine the amount of underapplied or overapplied overhead.

EXHIBIT 3–2
Cost Accounting System Possibilities for Manufacturing Overhead

Single overhead account for variable and fixed overhead:

Manufacturing Overhead Control

Total actual OH incurred	Total OH applied
$VVFF	$AABB

Separate overhead accounts for variable and fixed overhead:

Manufacturing Variable Overhead (VOH) Control

Total actual VOH incurred	Total VOH applied
$VV	$AA

Manufacturing Fixed Overhead (FOH) Control

Total actual FOH incurred	Total FOH applied
$FF	$BB

$12.60) of fixed overhead to the month's production. Journal entries to record the actual and applied overhead for this example follow.

Variable Manufacturing Overhead	31,385	
Fixed Manufacturing Overhead	55,970	
Various accounts		87,355
To record actual manufacturing overhead		
Work in Process Inventory	86,430	
Variable Manufacturing Overhead		32,250
Fixed Manufacturing Overhead		54,180
To apply variable and fixed manufacturing overhead to WIP		

At year-end, total actual overhead will differ from total applied overhead. The difference is called underapplied or overapplied overhead. Underapplied overhead means that the overhead applied to WIP Inventory is less than the actual overhead incurred; overapplied overhead means that the overhead applied to WIP Inventory is more than actual overhead incurred. Underapplied or overapplied overhead must be closed at year-end because a single year's activity level was used to determine the predetermined OH rate(s).

Under- or overapplication is caused by two factors that can work independently or jointly. These two factors are cost differences and utilization differences. For example, if actual fixed overhead (FOH) cost differs from expected FOH cost, a fixed manufacturing overhead spending variance is created. If actual capacity utilization differs from expected utilization, a volume variance arises.[2] The independent effects of these differences (or for similar differences related to variable OH) are as follows:

> Actual FOH Cost > Expected FOH Cost = Underapplied FOH
> Actual FOH Cost < Expected FOH Cost = Overapplied FOH
> Actual Utilization > Expected Utilization = Overapplied FOH
> Actual Utilization < Expected Utilization = Underapplied FOH

In most cases, however, both cost and utilization differ from estimates. When this occurs, no generalizations can be made as to whether overhead will be underapplied or overapplied.

LO.2
What causes underapplied or overapplied overhead, and how is it treated at the end of a period?

Disposition of Underapplied and Overapplied Overhead

Overhead accounts are temporary accounts and, as such, are closed at period-end. Closing the accounts requires disposition of the underapplied or overapplied overhead. Disposition depends on the materiality of the amount involved. If the amount is immaterial, it is closed to Cost of Goods Sold.

[2]These variances are covered in depth in Chapter 7.

As shown in Exhibit 3–3, when overhead is underapplied (debit balance), an insufficient amount of overhead was applied to production and the closing process causes Cost of Goods Sold to increase. Alternatively, overapplied overhead (credit balance) reflects the fact that too much overhead was applied to production, so closing overapplied overhead causes Cost of Goods Sold to decrease.

To illustrate the closing process in the case that the underapplied or overapplied overhead is immaterial, assume that Doggett Industries incurred $383,000 and $657,000, respectively, of actual variable and fixed overhead costs during 2008. The company used 51,500 machine hours during the year, and, thus, applied variable overhead (VOH) was $386,250 (51,500 × $7.50) and applied FOH was $648,900 (51,500 × $12.60). At year-end, the Variable Manufacturing Overhead account has a credit, or overapplied, balance of $3,250 ($383,000 − $386,250), and the Fixed Manufacturing Overhead account has a debit, or underapplied, balance of $8,100 ($657,000 − $648,900). Each amount is immaterial, so the journal entries to close these amounts are:

Variable Manufacturing Overhead	3,250	
Cost of Goods Sold		3,250
To close overapplied VOH		
Cost of Goods Sold	8,100	
Fixed Manufacturing Overhead		8,100
To close underapplied FOH		

If the amount of applied overhead differs materially (significantly) from actual overhead costs, it should be prorated among the accounts in which applied overhead is recorded: Work in Process Inventory, Finished Goods Inventory, and Cost of Goods Sold. Proration of the underapplied or overapplied overhead makes the account balances conform more closely to actual historical cost as required by generally accepted accounting principles (GAAP) for external reporting. Exhibit 3–4 uses assumed data for Doggett Industries to illustrate proration of a material amount of overapplied fixed overhead to the accounts based on their year-end account balances.[3] If the overhead had been underapplied, the accounts debited and credited in the journal entry would be reversed.

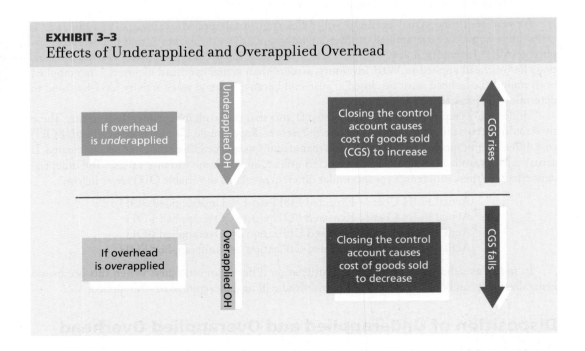

EXHIBIT 3–3
Effects of Underapplied and Overapplied Overhead

---

[3]Theoretically, underapplied or overapplied overhead should be allocated based on the amounts of applied overhead contained in each account rather than on total account balances. Use of total account balances could cause distortion because they contain direct material and direct labor costs that are not related to actual or applied overhead. In spite of this potential distortion, use of total balances is more common in practice for two reasons. First, the theoretical method is complex and requires detailed account analysis. Second, overhead tends to lose its identity after leaving Work in Process Inventory, thus making the determination of the amount of overhead in Finished Goods Inventory and Cost of Goods Sold account balances more difficult.

EXHIBIT 3–4

Proration of Overapplied Fixed Overhead

Fixed Manufacturing Overhead			Account Balances	
Actual FOH	$220,000		Work in Process Inventory	$ 45,640
Applied FOH	260,000		Finished Goods Inventory	78,240
Overapplied FOH	$ 40,000		Cost of Goods Sold	528,120

1. Add balances of accounts and determine proportional relationships:

Balance		Proportion	Percentage
Work in Process	$ 45,640	$45,640 ÷ $652,000	7
Finished Goods	78,240	$78,240 ÷ $652,000	12
Cost of Goods Sold	528,120	$528,120 ÷ $652,000	81
Total	$652,000		100

2. Multiply percentages by the overapplied overhead amount to determine the adjustment amount:

Account	%	×	Overapplied FOH	=	Adjustment Amount
Work in Process	7	×	$40,000	=	$ 2,800
Finished Goods	12	×	$40,000	=	$ 4,800
Cost of Goods Sold	81	×	$40,000	=	$32,400

3. Prepare the journal entry to close manufacturing overhead account and assign adjustment amount to appropriate accounts:

Fixed Manufacturing Overhead	40,000	
Work in Process Inventory		2,800
Finished Goods Inventory		4,800
Cost of Goods Sold		32,400
To close overapplied fixed overhead		

Alternative Capacity Measures

The two primary causes of underapplied or overapplied overhead are (1) a difference between budgeted and actual costs and (2) a difference in the activity level chosen to compute the predetermined OH rate and the actual activity level experienced. The activity level used in setting the predetermined OH rate generally reflects a consideration of organizational capacity.

The estimated maximum potential activity for a specified time is the **theoretical capacity**. This measure assumes that all production factors are operating perfectly. Theoretical capacity disregards realities such as machinery breakdowns and reduced or stopped plant operations on holidays. Choosing this activity level for setting a predetermined OH rate nearly guarantees a significant amount of underapplied overhead cost. The amount by which overhead is underapplied reflects the difference between actual capacity and theoretical capacity.

Reducing theoretical capacity by ongoing, regular operating interruptions (such as holidays, downtime, and start-up time) provides the **practical capacity** that could be achieved during regular working hours. Consideration of historical and estimated future production levels and the cyclical fluctuations provides a **normal capacity** measure that encompasses the firm's long-run (5 to 10 years) average activity and represents an attainable level of activity. Although it may generate substantial differences between actual and applied overhead in the short run, use of this capacity measure has been required under GAAP.[4]

LO.3
What impact do different capacity measures have on setting predetermined overhead rates?

---

[4]FASB Statement No. 151, titled *Inventory Costs*, was issued in November 2004. The statement indicates that some variation in production levels from period to period is expected and establishes the range of normal capacity. The range of normal capacity will vary based on business- and industry-specific factors. The actual level of production may be used if it approximates normal capacity. In periods of abnormally high production, the amount of fixed overhead allocated to each unit of production is decreased so that inventories are not measured above cost. The amount of fixed overhead allocated to each unit of production is not increased as a consequence of abnormally low production or idle plant.

Expected capacity is a short-run concept that represents the firm's anticipated activity level for the coming period based on projected product demand. Expected capacity level is determined during the budgeting process, which is discussed in Chapter 8. If actual results are close to budgeted results (in both dollars and volume), this measure should result in product costs that most closely reflect actual costs and, thus, generate an immaterial amount of underapplied or overapplied overhead. [5]

See Exhibit 3–5 for a visual representation of capacity measures. Although expected capacity is shown in this diagram as much smaller than practical capacity, it is possible for expected and practical capacity to be more equal—especially in a highly automated plant.

Regardless of the capacity level chosen for the denominator in calculating a predetermined OH rate, any mixed overhead costs must be separated into their variable and fixed components.

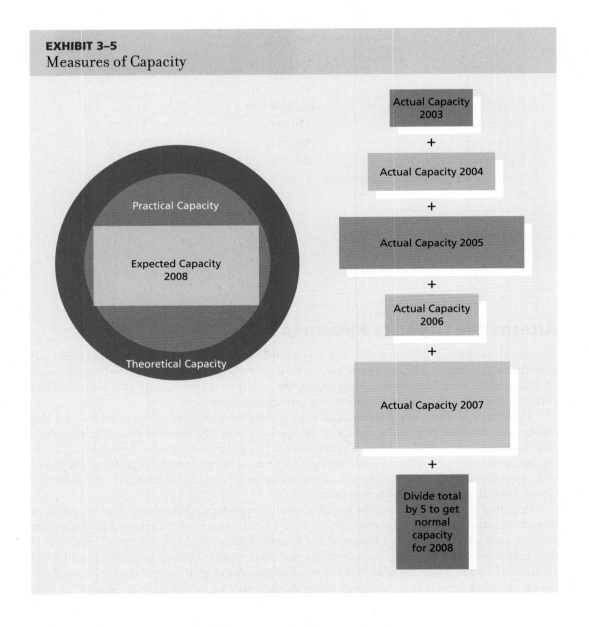

EXHIBIT 3–5
Measures of Capacity

[5]Except where otherwise noted in the text, expected capacity has been chosen as the basis to calculate the predetermined fixed manufacturing overhead rate because it is believed to be the most prevalent practice. This choice, however, may not be the most effective for planning and control purposes as is discussed further in Chapter 7 with regard to standard cost variances.

Separating Mixed Costs

As discussed in Chapter 2, a mixed cost contains both a variable and a fixed component. For example, a cell phone plan that has a flat charge for basic service (the fixed component) plus a stated rate for each minute of use (the variable component) creates a mixed cost. A mixed cost does not remain constant with changes in activity, nor does it fluctuate on a per-unit basis in direct proportion to changes in activity.

To simplify estimation of costs, accountants typically assume that costs are linear rather than curvilinear. Because of this assumption, the general formula for a straight line can be used to describe any type of cost within a relevant range of activity. The straight-line formula is

$$y = a + bX$$

where: y = total cost (dependent variable)
$\quad\quad a$ = fixed portion of total cost
$\quad\quad b$ = unit change of variable cost relative to unit changes in activity
$\quad\quad X$ = activity base to which y is being related (the predictor, cost driver, or independent variable)

If a cost is entirely variable, the a value in the formula is zero. If the cost is entirely fixed, the b value in the formula is zero. If a cost is mixed, it is necessary to determine formula values for both a and b. Two methods of determining these values—and thereby separating a mixed cost into its variable and fixed components—are the high–low method and regression analysis.

High–Low Method

The high–low method analyzes a mixed cost by first selecting the highest and lowest levels of activity in a data set if these two points are within the relevant range. Activity levels are used because activities cause costs to change, not vice versa. Occasionally, operations occur at a level outside the relevant range (a special rush order could require excess labor or machine time), or cost distortions occur within the relevant range (a leak in a water pipe goes unnoticed for a period of time). Such nonrepresentative or abnormal observations are called outliers and should be disregarded when analyzing a mixed cost.

Next, changes in activity and cost are determined by subtracting low values from high values. These changes are used to calculate the b (variable unit cost) value in the $y = a + bX$ formula as follows:

$$b = \frac{\text{Cost at High Activity Level} - \text{Cost at Low Activity Level}}{\text{High Activity Level} - \text{Low Activity Level}}$$

$$b = \frac{\text{Changes in Total Cost}}{\text{Changes in Activity Level}}$$

The b value is the unit variable cost per measure of activity. This value is multiplied by the activity level to determine the amount of total variable cost contained in the total cost at either the high or the low level of activity. The fixed portion of a mixed cost is found by subtracting total variable cost from total cost.

As the activity level changes, the change in total mixed cost equals the change in activity multiplied by the unit variable cost. By definition, the fixed cost element does not fluctuate with changes in activity.

Exhibit 3–6 illustrates the high–low method using machine hours and utility cost information for Doggett Industries. In November 2007, the company wants to determine its predetermined OH rate to use in calendar year 2008. Doggett gathered information for the prior 10 months' machine hours and utility costs. During 2007, the company's normal operating range of activity was

LO.4
How are the high–low method and least squares regression analysis used in analyzing mixed costs?

EXHIBIT 3–6

Analysis of Mixed Cost for Doggett Industries

The following machine hours and utility cost information is available:

Month	Machine Hours	Utility Cost
January	7,260	$2,960
February	8,850	3,410
March	4,800	1,920
April	9,000	3,500
May	11,000	3,900 *Outlier*
June	4,900	1,860
July	4,600	2,180
August	8,900	3,470
September	5,900	2,480
October	5,500	2,310

STEP 1: Select the highest and lowest levels of activity within the relevant range and obtain the costs associated with those levels. These levels and costs are 9,000 and 4,600 hours, and $3,500 and $2,180, respectively.

STEP 2: Calculate the change in cost compared to the change in activity.

	Machine Hours	Associated Total Cost
High activity	9,000	$3,500
Low activity	4,600	2,180
Changes	4,400	$1,320

STEP 3: Determine the relationship of cost change to activity change to find the variable cost element.

$$b = \$1,320 \div 4,400 \text{ MH} = \$0.30 \text{ per machine hour}$$

STEP 4: Compute total variable cost (TVC) at either level of activity.

High level of activity: TVC = $0.30(9,000) = $2,700
Low level of activity: TVC = $0.30(4,600) = $1,380

STEP 5: Subtract total variable cost from total cost at the associated level of activity to determine fixed cost.

High level of activity: $a = \$3,500 - \$2,700 = \$800$
Low level of activity: $a = \$2,180 - \$1,380 = \$800$

STEP 6: Substitute the fixed and variable cost values in the straight-line formula to get an equation that can be used to estimate total cost at any level of activity within the relevant range.

$$y = \$800 + \$0.30X$$

where X = machine hours

between 3,500 and 9,000 machine hours per month. Because it is substantially in excess of normal activity levels, the May observation is viewed as an outlier and should not be used in the analysis of utility cost.

One potential weakness of the high–low method is that outliers can inadvertently be used in the calculation. Estimates of future costs calculated from a line drawn using such points will not indicate actual costs and probably are not good predictions. A second weakness of this method is that it considers only two data points. A more precise method of analyzing mixed costs is least squares regression analysis.

Least Squares Regression Analysis

Least squares regression analysis is a statistical technique that analyzes the relationship between independent (causal) and dependent (effect) variables. The least squares method is used to develop an equation that predicts an unknown value of a dependent variable (cost) from the known values of one or more independent variables (activities that create costs). When multiple independent variables exist, least squares regression also helps to select the independent variable that is the best predictor of the dependent variable. For example, managers can use least squares to decide whether machine hours, direct labor hours, or pounds of material moved best explain and predict changes in a specific overhead cost. [6]

Simple regression analysis uses one independent variable to predict the dependent variable based on the $y = a + bX$ formula for a straight line. In multiple regression, two or more independent variables are used to predict the dependent variable. All text examples use simple regression and assume that a linear relationship exists between variables so that each one-unit change in the independent variable produces a constant unit change in the dependent variable. [7]

A regression line is any line that goes through the means (or averages) of the independent and dependent variables in a set of observations. As shown in Exhibit 3–7, numerous straight lines can be drawn through any set of data observations, but most of these lines would provide a poor fit to the data. Actual observation values are designated as y values; these points do not generally fall directly on a

EXHIBIT 3–7
Illustration of Least Squares Regression Line

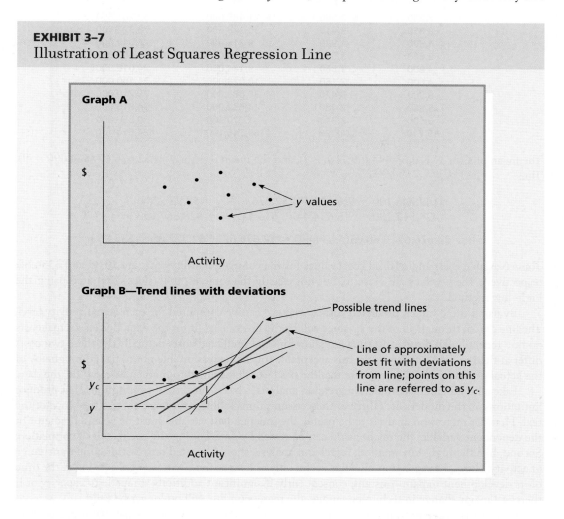

Graph A

$

y values

Activity

Graph B—Trend lines with deviations

Possible trend lines

$

y_c

Line of approximately best fit with deviations from line; points on this line are referred to as y_c.

y

Activity

[6]Further discussion of finding independent variable(s) that best predict the value of the dependent variable can be found in most textbooks on statistical methods treating regression analysis under the headings of dispersion, coefficient of correlation, coefficient of determination, or standard error of the estimate.

[7]Curvilinear relationships between variables also exist. For example, quality defects (dependent variable) tend to increase at an increasing rate in relationship to machinery age (independent variable).

regression line. The least squares method mathematically fits the best possible regression line to observed data points. The method fits this line by minimizing the sum of the squares of the vertical deviations between the actual observation points and the regression line. The regression line represents computed values for all activity levels, and the points on the regression line are designated as y_c values.

The regression line of best fit is found by predicting the a and b values in a straight-line formula using the actual activity and cost values (y values) from the observations. The equations necessary to compute b and a values using the method of least squares are as follows:[8]

$$b = \frac{\Sigma xy - n(\bar{x})(\bar{y})}{\Sigma x^2 - n(\bar{x})^2}$$

$$a = \bar{y} - b\bar{x}$$

where $\bar{x}$ = mean of the independent variable
$\bar{y}$ = mean of the dependent variable
n = number of observations

Using the machine hour and utility cost data for Doggett Industries (presented in Exhibit 3–6 and excluding the May outlier), the following calculations can be made:

x	y	xy	x²
7,260	$ 2,960	$ 21,489,600	52,707,600
8,850	3,410	30,178,500	78,322,500
4,800	1,920	9,216,000	23,040,000
9,000	3,500	31,500,000	81,000,000
4,900	1,860	9,114,000	24,010,000
4,600	2,180	10,028,000	21,160,000
8,900	3,470	30,883,000	79,210,000
5,900	2,480	14,632,000	34,810,000
5,500	2,310	12,705,00	30,250,000
59,710	$24,090	$169,746,100	424,510,100

The mean of x (or $\bar{x}$) is 6,634.44 (59,710 ÷ 9), and the mean of y (or $\bar{y}$) is $2,676.67 ($24,090 ÷ 9). Thus,

$$b = \frac{\$169,746,100 - 9(6,634.44)(\$2,676.67)}{424,510,100 - 9(6,634.44)(6,634.44)} = \frac{\$9,922,241}{\$28,367,953} = \underline{\underline{\$0.35}}$$

$$a = \$2,676.67 - \$0.35(6,634.44) = \$2,676.67 - \$2,322.05 = \underline{\underline{\$354.62}}$$

The b (variable cost) and a (fixed cost) values for the company's utility costs are $0.35 and $354.62, respectively. These values are close to, but not exactly the same as, the values computed using the high–low method.

By using these values, predicted costs (y_c values) can be computed for each actual activity level. The line drawn through all of the y_c values will be the line of best fit for the data. Because actual costs do not generally fall directly on the regression line and predicted costs naturally do, these two costs differ at their related activity levels. It is acceptable for the regression line not to pass through any of the actual observation points because the line has been determined to mathematically "fit" the data.

Like all mathematical models, regression analysis is based on certain assumptions that produce limitations on the model's use. Three of these assumptions follow; others are beyond the scope of the text. First, for regression analysis to be useful, the independent variable must be a valid predictor of the dependent variable; the relationship can be tested by determining the coefficient of correlation. Second, like the high–low method, regression analysis should be used only within a relevant range of activity. Third, the regression model is useful only as long as the circumstances existing at the time of its development remain constant; consequently, if significant additions are made to capacity or if there is a major change in technology usage, the regression line will no longer be valid.

Once a method has been selected and mixed overhead costs have been separated into fixed and variable components, a flexible budget can be developed to indicate the estimated amount of overhead at various levels of the denominator activity.

---

[8]These equations are derived from mathematical computations beyond the scope of this text but can be found in many statistics books. The symbol Σ means "the summation of."

Flexible Budgets

A **flexible budget** is a planning document that presents expected variable and fixed overhead costs at different activity levels. Activity levels shown on a flexible budget usually cover the contemplated range of activity for the upcoming period. If all activity levels are within the relevant range, costs at each successive level should equal the previous level plus a uniform monetary increment for each variable cost factor. The increment is equal to variable cost per unit of activity times the quantity of additional activity.

Expected cost information from the flexible budget is used for the numerator in computing the predetermined OH rate. See Exhibit 3–8 for a flexible overhead budget for Doggett Industries at selected levels of activity. All amounts have been assumed. Note that the variable overhead cost per machine hour (MH) does not change within the relevant range, but the fixed overhead cost per machine hour varies inversely with the level of activity. Given that the company selected 50,000 machine hours as the denominator level of annual activity, the variable and fixed predetermined OH rates were $7.50 and $12.60, respectively.

Plantwide versus Departmental Overhead Rates

Because most companies produce many different kinds of products, calculation of a plantwide predetermined OH rate generally does not provide the most useful information. Assume that Doggett Industries has two departments, Assembly and Finishing. Assembly is highly automated, but Finishing requires significant direct labor. As such, it is highly probable that machine hours would be the more viable overhead allocation base for Assembly, and direct labor hours would be the better allocation base for Finishing.

Exhibit 3–9 uses a single product (Part #AB79Z) to show the cost differences that can be created by using a plantwide predetermined OH rate. Production of this part requires 1 hour of machine time in Assembly and 5 hours of direct labor time in Finishing. The departmental cost amounts shown in Exhibit 3–9 have been assumed so that they will balance with information provided in Exhibit 3–8. Notice that the $20.10 plantwide OH rate using machine hours is the same total rate calculated in Exhibit 3–8: a variable rate of $7.50 per MH plus a fixed rate of $12.60 per MH. For purposes of this illustration, the use of separate variable and fixed OH rates is ignored.

LO.5
How do managers use flexible budgets to set predetermined overhead rates?

EXHIBIT 3–8

Flexible Overhead Budget for Doggett Industries

	Number of Machine Hours (MHs)				
	40,000	**45,000**	**50,000**	**55,000**	**75,000**
Variable OH (VOH)					
Indirect material	$ 60,000	$ 67,500	$ 75,000	$ 82,500	$112,500
Indirect labor	120,000	135,000	150,000	165,000	225,000
Utilities	14,000	15,750	17,500	19,250	26,250
Other	106,000	119,250	132,500	145,750	198,750
Total	$300,000	$337,500	$375,000	$412,500	$562,500
VOH rate per MH	$7.50	$7.50	$7.50	$7.50	$7.50
FOH					
Factory salaries	$215,000	$215,000	$215,000	$215,000	$215,000
Depreciation	300,000	300,000	300,000	300,000	300,000
Utilities	9,600	9,600	9,600	9,600	9,600
Other	105,400	105,400	105,400	105,400	105,400
Total	$630,000	$630,000	$630,000	$630,000	$630,000
FOH rate per MH	$15.75	$14.00	$12.60	$11.45	$8.40

EXHIBIT 3–9

Plantwide versus Departmental Predetermined OH Rate for Doggett Industries

	Plantwide	Assembly	Finishing
Budgeted annual overhead	$1,005,000	$724,500	$280,500
Budgeted annual direct labor hours (DLHs)	13,000	3,000	10,000
Budgeted annual machine hours (MHs)	50,000	45,000	5,000

Departmental overhead rates

   Assembly (automated): $724,500 ÷ 45,000 = $16.10 per MH

   Finishing (manual): $280,500 ÷ 10,000 = $28.05 per DLH

Plantwide overhead rates

   Using DLHs: $1,005,000 ÷ 13,000 = $77.31 per DLH

   Using MHs: $1,005,000 ÷ 50,000 = $20.10 per MH

Part #AB79Z

Overhead assigned using departmental rates

Assembly	1 MH × $16.10	$ 16.10
Finishing	5 DLHs × $28.05	140.25
Total		$156.35

Total overhead assigned using plantwide rates

Based on DLHs	5 DLHs × $77.31	$ 386.55
Based on MHs	1 MH × $20.10	20.10

Using assumed direct material and direct labor costs, the total cost of Part AB79Z is:

	Using Departmental OH Rates	Using a Plantwide Rate Based on DLHs	Using a Plantwide Rate Based on MHs
Direct material	$110.00	$110.00	$110.00
Direct labor	36.00	36.00	36.00
Overhead	156.35	386.55	20.10
Total cost	$302.35	$532.55	$166.10

    Exhibit 3–9 shows how product cost can change dramatically depending on the predetermined OH rate. A company with multiple departments that use significantly different types of work effort (such as automated vs. manual), as well as diverse materials that require considerably different processing times in those departments, should use separate departmental predetermined OH rates to attach overhead to products to derive the most rational product cost. Homogeneity is more likely to occur within a department than across departments; thus, separate departmental OH rates generally provide better information for management planning, control, and decision making than do plantwide OH rates. Computing departmental OH rates allows each department to select the most appropriate measure of activity (or cost driver) relative to its operations.

    Additionally, the use of variable and fixed categories within each department lets management understand how costs react to changes in activity. The use of variable and fixed categories also makes it easier to generate different reports for external and internal reporting purposes.

LO.6
How do absorption and variable costing differ?

Overview of Absorption and Variable Costing

In preparing financial reports, costs can be accumulated and presented in different ways. The choice of cost accumulation method determines which costs are recorded as part of product cost and which are considered period costs. In contrast, the choice of cost presentation method determines how costs are shown on external financial statements or internal management reports. Accumulation and presentation procedures are accomplished using one of two methods: absorption costing or variable costing. Each method structures or processes the same basic data differently, and either method can be used in job order or process costing and with actual, normal, or standard costs.

Absorption costing treats the costs of all manufacturing components (direct material, direct labor, variable overhead, and fixed overhead) as inventoriable, or product, costs in accordance with GAAP. Absorption costing is also known as full costing, and this method fits the product cost definition given in Chapter 2. Under absorption costing, costs incurred in the nonmanufacturing areas of the organization are considered period costs and are expensed in a manner that properly matches them with revenues. Exhibit 3–10 depicts the absorption costing model. In addition, absorption costing presents expenses on an income statement according to their functional classifications. A functional classification is a group of costs that were all incurred for the same principal purpose. Functional classifications generally include cost of goods sold, selling expense, and administrative expense.

In contrast, variable costing is a cost accumulation method that includes only direct material, direct labor, and variable overhead as product costs. This method treats fixed manufacturing overhead (FOH) as a period cost. Like absorption costing, variable costing treats costs incurred in the organization's selling and administrative areas as period costs. Variable costing income statements typically present expenses according to cost behavior (variable and fixed), although expenses can also be presented by functional classifications within the behavioral categories. Variable costing is also known as direct costing. See Exhibit 3–11 for the variable costing model.

Two differences exist between absorption and variable costing: one relates to cost accumulation and the other relates to cost presentation. The cost accumulation difference is that absorption

EXHIBIT 3–10
Absorption Costing Model

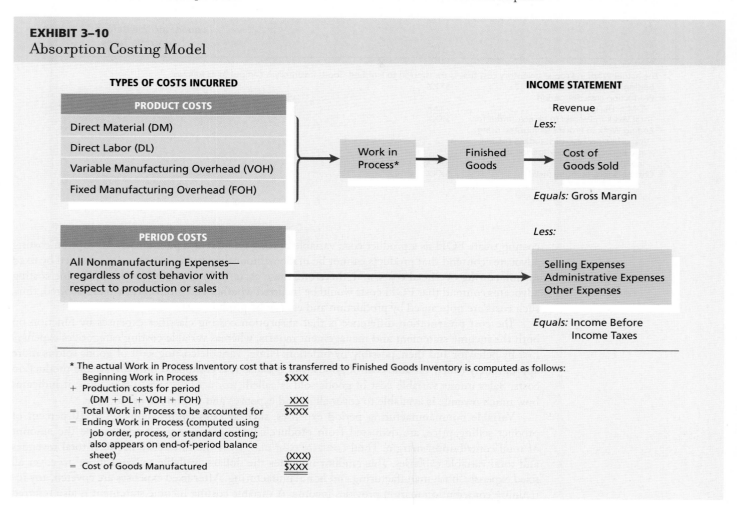

* The actual Work in Process Inventory cost that is transferred to Finished Goods Inventory is computed as follows:

Beginning Work in Process	$XXX
+ Production costs for period (DM + DL + VOH + FOH)	XXX
= Total Work in Process to be accounted for	$XXX
− Ending Work in Process (computed using job order, process, or standard costing; also appears on end-of-period balance sheet)	(XXX)
= Cost of Goods Manufactured	$XXX

EXHIBIT 3–11
Variable Costing Model

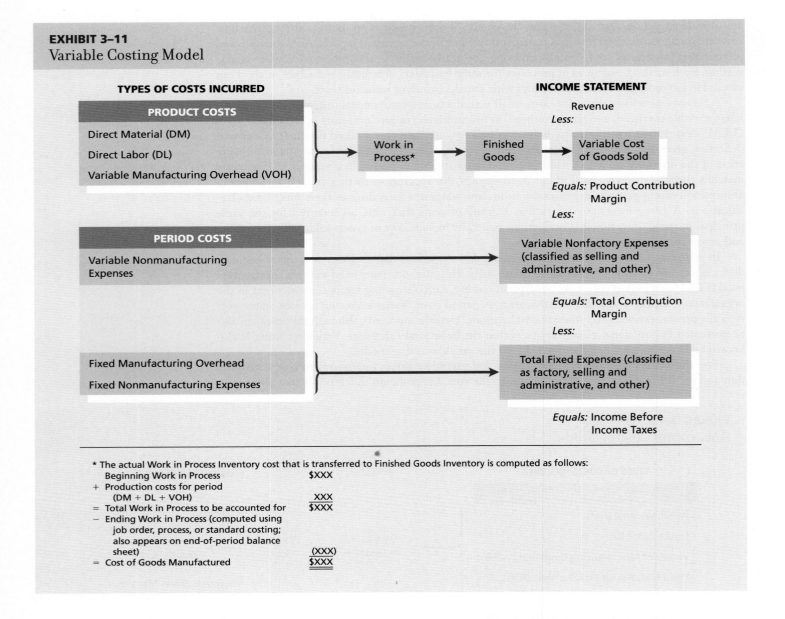

* The actual Work in Process Inventory cost that is transferred to Finished Goods Inventory is computed as follows:

Beginning Work in Process	$XXX
+ Production costs for period	
(DM + DL + VOH)	XXX
= Total Work in Process to be accounted for	$XXX
− Ending Work in Process (computed using job order, process, or standard costing; also appears on end-of-period balance sheet)	(XXX)
= Cost of Goods Manufactured	$XXX

costing treats FOH as a product cost; variable costing treats it as a period cost. Absorption costing advocates contend that products cannot be made without the production capacity provided by fixed manufacturing overhead costs, and, therefore, these costs "belong" to the product. Variable costing advocates contend that FOH costs would be incurred whether any products are manufactured; thus, such costs are not caused by production and cannot be product costs.

The cost presentation difference is that absorption costing classifies expenses by function on both the income statement and management reports, whereas variable costing categorizes expenses first by behavior and then, possibly, by function. Under variable costing, cost of goods sold is more appropriately called variable cost of goods sold because it is composed only of variable production costs. Sales minus variable cost of goods sold is called product contribution margin; it indicates how much revenue is available to cover all period expenses and to provide net income.

Variable nonmanufacturing period expenses, such as sales commissions set at 10 percent of product selling price, are deducted from product contribution margin to determine the amount of total contribution margin. Total contribution margin is the difference between total revenues and total variable expenses. This amount indicates the dollars available to "contribute" to cover all fixed expenses, both manufacturing and nonmanufacturing. After fixed expenses are covered, any remaining contribution margin provides income. A variable costing income statement is also referred

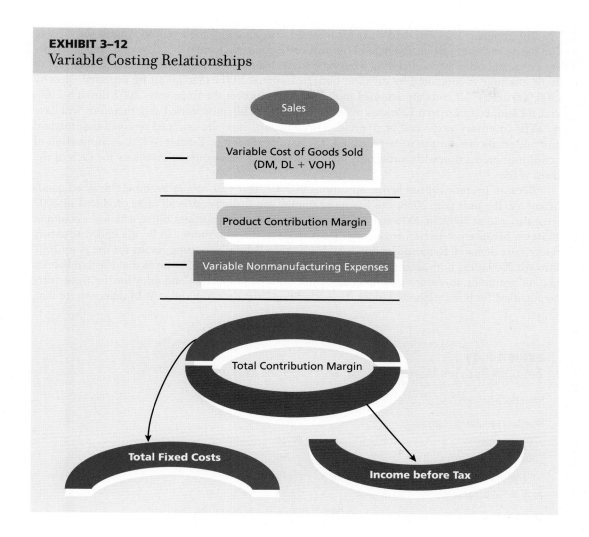

EXHIBIT 3–12
Variable Costing Relationships

to as a contribution income statement. See Exhibit 3–12 for a diagram of these variable costing relationships.

Major authoritative bodies of the accounting profession, such as the Financial Accounting Standards Board (FASB) and the Securities and Exchange Commission (SEC), require the use of absorption costing to prepare external financial statements. Absorption costing is also required for filing tax returns with the Internal Revenue Service. The accounting profession has, in effect, disallowed the use of variable costing as a generally accepted inventory method for external reporting purposes.

Because absorption costing classifies expenses by functional category, cost behavior (relative to changes in activity) cannot be observed from an absorption costing income statement or management report. Understanding cost behavior is extremely important for many managerial activities including budgeting, cost-volume-profit analysis, and relevant costing.[9] Thus, internal financial reports distinguishing costs by behavior are often prepared for use in management decision making and analysis. The next section provides a detailed illustration using both absorption and variable costing.

Absorption and Variable Costing Illustrations

Eastern Fabrics began operations in 2007 and has been hired by Doggett Industries to make car seat cushions. Product specifications are likely to be constant at least until model year 2010. Data for this product are used to compare absorption and variable costing procedures and presentations.

---

[9]These topics are covered in Chapters 8 (budgeting), 9 (cost-volume-profit analysis), and 10 (relevant costing).

The company uses standard costs for material and labor and predetermined rates for variable and fixed overhead.[10] See Exhibit 3–13 for unit production costs, annual budgeted nonmanufacturing costs, and other basic operating data for Eastern Fabrics. The predetermined fixed OH rate of $0.54 per unit is computed by dividing budgeted annual FOH ($162,000) by expected capacity (300,000 units). All costs are assumed to remain constant over the three years 2007 through 2009, and, for simplicity, Eastern Fabrics is assumed to complete all units started and, therefore, will have no WIP Inventory at the end of a period. Also, all actual costs are assumed to equal the standard and budgeted costs for the years presented. The bottom section of Exhibit 3–13 is a comparison of actual unit production with actual unit sales to determine the change in inventory for each of the three years.

Because Eastern Fabrics began operations in 2007, that year has no beginning finished goods inventory. The next year, 2008, also has no beginning inventory because all units produced in 2007 were also sold in 2007. In 2008 and 2009, production and sales quantities differ, which is a common situation because production frequently "leads" sales so that inventory can be stockpiled to satisfy future sales demand. Refer to Exhibit 3–14 for Eastern Fabrics' operating results for the years 2007 through 2009 using both absorption and variable costing. This example assumes that Eastern Fabrics had no beginning inventory and that cumulative units of production and sales for the three years are identical for both methods. Under these conditions, the data in Exhibit 3–14 demonstrate that,

EXHIBIT 3–13
Eastern Fabrics Basic Data for 2007, 2008, and 2009

Sales price per unit	$6.00
Standard variable cost per unit	
Direct material	$2.04
Direct labor	1.50
Variable manufacturing overhead	0.18
Total variable manufacturing cost per unit	$3.72

$$\text{Standard Fixed Factory Overhead Rate} = \frac{\text{Budgeted Annual Fixed Factory Overhead}}{\text{Budgeted Annual Capacity in Units}}$$

FOH rate = $162,000 ÷ 300,000 = $0.54

Total absorption cost per unit	
Standard variable manufacturing cost	$3.72
Standard fixed manufacturing overhead (SFOH)	0.54
Total absorption cost per unit	$4.26
Budgeted nonproduction expenses	
Variable selling expenses per unit	$ 0.24
Fixed selling and administrative expenses	$2,340

Total budgeted nonproduction expenses = ($0.24 per unit sold + $2,340)

	2007	2008	2009	Total
Actual units made	300,000	290,000	310,000	900,000
Actual unit sales	(300,000)	(270,000)	(330,000)	(900,000)
Change in Finished Goods Inventory	0	+ 20,000	(20,000)	0

[10]Actual costs can also be used under either absorption or variable costing. Standard costing was chosen for these illustrations because it makes the differences between the two methods more obvious. If actual costs had been used, production costs would vary each year, and such variations would obscure the distinct differences caused by the use of one method, rather than the other, over a period of time. Standard costs are also treated as constant over time to more clearly demonstrate the differences between absorption and variable costing and to reduce the complexity of the chapter explanations.

EXHIBIT 3–14

Eastern Fabrics Absorption and Variable Costing Income Statements for 2007, 2008, and 2009

ABSORPTION COSTING PRESENTATION

	2007	2008	2009	Total
Sales ($6 per unit)	$1,800,000	$1,620,000	$1,980,000	$5,400,000
Cost of goods sold (CGS) ($4.26 per unit)	(1,278,000)	(1,150,200)	(1,405,800)	(3,834,000)
Standard gross margin	$ 522,000	$ 469,800	$ 574,200	$1,566,000
Volume variance (U)	0	(5,400)	5,400	0
Adjusted gross margin	$ 522,000	$ 464,400	$ 579,600	$1,566,000
Selling and administrative expenses	(95,400)	(88,200)	(102,600)	(286,200)
Income before tax	$ 426,600	$ 376,200	$ 477,000	$1,279,800

VARIABLE COSTING PRESENTATION

	2007	2008	2009	Total
Sales ($6 per unit)	$1,800,000	$1,620,000	$1,980,000	$5,400,000
Variable CGS ($3.72 per unit)	(1,116,000)	(1,004,400)	(1,227,600)	(3,348,000)
Product contribution margin	$ 684,000	$ 615,600	$ 752,400	$2,052,000
Variable selling expenses ($0.24 × units sold)	(72,000)	(64,800)	(79,200)	(216,000)
Total contribution margin	$ 612,000	$ 550,800	$ 673,200	$1,836,000
Fixed expenses				
Manufacturing	$ 162,000	$ 162,000	$ 160,200	$ 486,000
Selling and administrative	23,400	23,400	23,400	70,200
Total fixed expenses	$ (185,400)	$ (185,400)	$ (185,400)	$ (556,200)
Income before tax	$ 426,600	$ 365,400	$ 487,800	$1,279,800
Differences in income before tax	$ 0	$ 10,800	$ (10,800)	$ 0

regardless of whether absorption or variable costing is used, the cumulative income before tax will be the same ($1,279,800). Also, as in 2007, for any year in which there is no change in inventory from the beginning to the end of the year, both methods will result in the same net income.

Actual production and operating costs have been assumed to equal the standard and budgeted costs for years 2007 through 2009. However, differences in actual and budgeted capacity utilization occurred for 2008 and 2009, which created a volume variance for each of those years under absorption costing. A **volume variance** reflects the monetary impact of a difference between the budgeted capacity used to determine the predetermined FOH rate and the actual capacity at which the company operates. Thus, for Eastern Fabrics, there is no volume variance for 2007 because 300,000 units were both budgeted and produced. For 2008, the volume variance is calculated as [$0.54 × (290,000 − 300,000)] or $5,400 unfavorable. For 2009, it is calculated as [$0.54 × (310,000 − 300,000)] or $5,400 favorable. Each of these amounts is considered immaterial and is shown as an adjustment to the year's gross margin. No volume variances are shown under variable costing because fixed manufacturing overhead is not applied to products using a budgeted capacity measure; the FOH is deducted in its entirety as a period expense.

The income statements in Exhibit 3–14 show that absorption and variable costing provide different income figures in some years. Comparing the two sets of statements indicates that the difference in income arises solely from the different treatment of fixed overhead. If no beginning or ending inventories exist, cumulative total income under both methods will be identical. Over the three-year period, Eastern Fabrics produced and sold 900,000 units. Thus, all the costs incurred (whether variable or fixed) are expensed in one year or another under either method. The income difference in each year is caused solely by the timing of the expensing of fixed manufacturing overhead.

In Exhibit 3–14, absorption costing income before tax for 2008 exceeds that of variable costing by $10,800. This difference is caused by the FOH assigned to the 20,000 units made but not sold ($0.54 × 20,000) and, thus, placed in inventory in 2008. Critics of absorption costing refer to this phenomenon as creating illusionary or phantom profits. **Phantom profits** are temporary absorption costing profits caused by producing more inventory than is sold. When previously produced inventory is sold, the phantom profits disappear. In contrast, variable costing expenses all FOH in the year it is incurred.

In 2009, inventory decreased by 20,000 units. This decrease, multiplied by the FOH rate of $0.54, explains the $10,800 by which 2009 absorption costing income falls short of variable costing income in Exhibit 3–14. For 2009, not only is all current year fixed manufacturing overhead expensed through Cost of Goods Sold, but also the $10,800 of FOH that was retained in 2008's ending inventory is shown in 2009's Cost of Goods Sold. Only 2009 fixed manufacturing overhead is shown on the 2009 variable costing income statement.

Comparison of the Two Approaches

LO.7
How do changes in sales or production levels affect net income computed under absorption and variable costing?

Whether absorption costing income is more or less than variable costing income depends on the relationship of production to sales. In all cases, to determine the effect on income, it must be assumed that variances from standard are immaterial and that unit product costs are constant over time. See Exhibit 3–15 for the possible relationships between production and sales levels and the effects of these relationships on income. These relationships are as follows:

EXHIBIT 3–15
Production/Sales Relationships and Effects on Income and Inventory

where P = Production and S = Sales
      AC = Absorption Costing and VC = Variable Costing

	Absorption vs. Variable Income Statement Income before Taxes	Absorption vs. Variable Balance Sheet Ending Inventory
P = S	AC = VC No difference from beginning inventory $FOH_{EI} - FOH_{BI} = 0$	No additional difference $FOH_{EI} = FOH_{BI}$
P > S (Stockpiling inventory)	AC > VC By amount of fixed OH in ending inventory minus fixed OH in beginning inventory $FOH_{EI} - FOH_{BI} = +$ amount	Ending inventory increased (by fixed OH in additional units because P > S) $FOH_{EI} > FOH_{BI}$
P < S (Reducing inventory)	AC < VC By amount of fixed OH released from balance sheet beginning inventory $FOH_{EI} - FOH_{BI} = -$ amount	Ending inventory difference reduced (by fixed OH from BI charged to cost of goods sold) $FOH_{EI} < FOH_{BI}$

*The effects of the relationships presented here are based on two qualifying assumptions:
  (1) that unit costs are constant over time
  (2) that any fixed cost variances from standard are written off when incurred rather than being prorated to inventory balances.

■ If production equals sales, absorption costing income will equal variable costing income.

■ If production is more than sales, absorption costing income is greater than variable costing income. This result occurs because some fixed manufacturing overhead cost is deferred as part of inventory cost on the balance sheet under absorption costing, whereas the total amount of fixed manufacturing overhead cost is expensed as a period cost under variable costing.

■ If production is less than sales, income under absorption costing is less than income under variable costing. In this case, absorption costing expenses all of the current period fixed manufacturing overhead costs and releases some fixed manufacturing overhead cost from the beginning inventory where it had been deferred from a prior period.

This process of deferring FOH costs into, and releasing FOH costs from, inventory makes it possible to manipulate income under absorption costing by adjusting levels of production relative to sales. For this reason, some people believe that variable costing is more useful for external purposes than absorption costing. For internal reporting, variable costing information provides managers information about the behavior of the various product and period costs. To plan, control, and make decisions, managers need to understand and be able to project how costs will change in reaction to changes in activity levels. Variable costing, through its emphasis on cost behavior, provides that necessary information.

Comprehensive Review Module

Chapter Summary

1. Manufacturing overhead costs are allocated to products to

   • eliminate the problems caused by delays in obtaining actual cost data.

   • make the overhead allocation process more effective.

   • allocate a uniform amount of overhead to goods or services based on related production efforts.

   • allow managers to be more aware of individual product or product line profitability as well as the profitability of doing business with a particular customer or vendor.

2. Underapplied (actual is more than applied) or overapplied (actual is less than applied) overhead is

   • caused by a difference between actual and budgeted OH costs and/or a difference between the actual and budgeted level of activity chosen to compute the predetermined OH rate.

   • closed at the end of each period (unless normal capacity is used for the denominator level of activity) to

   ➢ Cost of Goods Sold (CGS) if the amount of underapplied or overapplied overhead is immaterial (underapplied will cause CGS to increase, and overapplied will cause CGS to decrease)

   or

   ➢ Work in Process Inventory, Finished Goods Inventory, and Cost of Goods Sold (based on their proportional balances), if the amount of underapplied or overapplied overhead is material.

3. Capacity measures affect the setting of predetermined OH rates because the use of

   • expected capacity (the budgeted capacity for the upcoming year) will result in a predetermined OH rate that would probably be most closely related to an actual OH rate.

   • practical capacity (the capacity that allows for normal operating interruptions) will generally result in a predetermined OH rate that is substantially lower than an actual OH rate would be.

- normal capacity (the capacity that reflects a long-run average) can result in an OH rate that is higher or lower than an actual OH rate, depending on whether capacity has been over- or under-utilized during the years under consideration.

- theoretical capacity (the estimated maximum potential capacity) will result in a predetermined OH rate that is exceptionally lower than an actual OH rate; however, this rate reflects a company's true ability to use its capacity.

4. Mixed costs are separated into their variable and fixed components by

   - the high–low method, which considers the change in cost between the highest and lowest activity levels in the data set (excluding outliers) and determines a variable cost per unit based on that change; fixed cost is then determined by subtracting total variable cost at either the highest or the lowest activity level from total cost at that level.

   - regression analysis, which uses the costs and activity levels in the entire data set (excluding outliers) as input to mathematical formulas that allow the determination first of variable cost and, subsequently, of fixed cost.

5. Flexible budgets are used by managers to help set predetermined OH rates by

   - allowing managers to understand what manufacturing OH costs are incurred and what the behaviors (variable, fixed, or mixed) of those costs are.

   - allowing managers to separate mixed costs into their variable and fixed elements.

   - providing information on the budgeted costs to be incurred at various levels of activity.

   - providing the impacts on the predetermined fixed OH rate (or on a plantwide rate) from changing the denominator level of activity.

6. Absorption and variable costing differ in that

   - absorption costing

     ➤ includes all manufacturing costs, both variable and fixed, as product costs.

   ➤ presents nonmanufacturing costs on the income statement according to functional areas.

   - variable costing

     ➤ includes only the variable costs of production (direct material, direct labor, and variable manufacturing overhead) as product costs.

     ➤ presents both nonmanufacturing and manufacturing costs on the income statement according to cost behavior.

7. Differences between sales and production volume result in differences in income between absorption and variable costing because

   - absorption costing requires fixed costs to be written off as a function of the number of units sold;

     ➤ thus, if production volume is higher than sales volume, some fixed costs will be deferred in inventory at year-end, making net income higher than under variable costing.

     ➤ conversely, if sales volume is higher than production volume, the deferred fixed costs from previous periods will be written off as part of Cost of Goods Sold, making net income lower than under variable costing.

   - variable costing requires all fixed costs to be written off in the period incurred, regardless of when the related inventory is sold;

     ➤ thus, if production volume is higher than sales volume, all fixed manufacturing costs are expensed in the current period and are not deferred until the inventory is sold, making net income lower than under absorption costing.

     ➤ conversely, if sales volume is higher than production volume, only current period fixed manufacturing costs are expensed in the current period, making net income higher than under absorption costing.

Potential Ethical Issues

1. Using an inappropriately high, normal capacity activity level to compute the predetermined OH rate, thereby reducing product cost and increasing operating income upon the sale of inventory—given that the closing of the underapplied manufacturing OH account would be deferred for multiple periods

2. Producing significantly more inventory than is necessary to meet current and anticipated sales, thereby lowering the predetermined fixed OH rate per unit and inventory cost, while increasing reported operating income

3. Treating period costs as product costs rather than expenses to inflate inventory (assets) and increase reported net income

4. Manipulating sales around the end of an accounting period to shift revenues and expired product costs into the current period or into the following period

5. Choosing a method of OH allocation that distorts the "true" profitability of specific products or specific subunits ▲

Solution Strategies

Predetermined Overhead Rate

$$\text{Predetermined OH Rate} = \frac{\text{Total Budgeted OH Cost at a Specified Activity Level}}{\text{Volume of Specified Activity Level}}$$

(Can be separate variable and fixed rates or a combined rate)

High–Low Method

(Using assumed amounts)

	(Independent Variable) Activity	(Dependent Variable) Associated Total Cost	−	Total Variable Cost (Rate × Activity)	=	Total Fixed Cost
"High" level	14,000	$18,000	−	$11,200	=	$6,800
"Low" level	9,000	14,000	−	7,200	=	6,800
Differences	5,000	$ 4,000				

$0.80
variable cost per unit of activity

Least Squares Regression Analysis

The equations necessary to compute b and a values using the method of least squares are as follows:

$$b = \frac{\Sigma xy - n(\bar{x})(\bar{y})}{\Sigma x^2 - n(\bar{x})^2}$$

$$a = \bar{y} - b\bar{x}$$

where $\bar{x}$ = mean of the independent variable
$\bar{y}$ = mean of the dependent variable
n = number of observations

Underapplied and Overapplied Overhead

Manufacturing Overhead Control	XXX	
Various accounts		XXX
To record actual overhead costs		
Work in Process Inventory	YYY	
Manufacturing Overhead Control		YYY
To apply overhead to WIP		

A debit balance in Manufacturing Overhead at the end of the period is underapplied overhead; a credit balance is overapplied overhead. The debit or credit balance in the overhead account is closed at the end of the period to Cost of Goods Sold or prorated to Work in Process Inventory, Finished Goods Inventory, and Cost of Goods Sold.

Flexible Budget

To prepare a flexible budget,

1.   separate mixed costs into variable and fixed elements;

2.   determine the $a + bX$ cost formula for each item of the budget category (for example, all items creating manufacturing overhead);

3.   select several potential levels of activity within the relevant range; and

4.   use the cost formulas to determine the total cost expected at each of the selected levels of activity.

Absorption and Variable Costing

1.   Determine which method is being used (absorption or variable). The following abbreviations are used: VOH, variable manufacturing overhead; FOH, fixed manufacturing overhead; DM, direct material; DL, direct labor.

   a.   If absorption:

   - Determine the FOH application rate.

   - Determine the denominator capacity used in determining manufacturing FOH.

   - Determine whether production was equal to the denominator capacity. If not, a FOH volume variance must be properly assigned to CGS and, possibly, inventories.

   - Determine the cost per unit of product, which consists of (DM + DL + VOH + FOH).

   b.   If variable:

   - Determine the cost per unit of product, which consists of (DM + DL + VOH).

   - Determine the total fixed manufacturing OH and assign that amount to the income statement as a period expense.

2.   Determine the relationship of production to sales.

   a.   If production = sales, then absorption costing income = variable costing income.

   b.   If production > sales, then absorption costing income > variable costing income.

   c.   If production < sales, then absorption costing income < variable costing income.

3.   The dollar difference between absorption costing income and variable costing income equals (fixed predetermined OH rate × change in inventory units).

Demonstration Problem

La Mancha Company management uses predetermined VOH and FOH rates to apply overhead to its products. For 2007, the company budgeted production at 27,000 units, which would require 54,000 direct labor hours (DLHs) and 27,000 machine hours (MHs). At that level of production, total variable and fixed manufacturing overhead costs were expected to be $13,500 and $105,300, respectively. Variable overhead is applied to production using direct labor hours, and fixed overhead is applied using machine hours. During 2007, La Mancha Company produced 23,000 units and experienced the following operating statistics and costs: 46,000 direct labor hours; 23,000 machine hours; $11,980 actual variable manufacturing overhead; and $103,540 actual fixed manufacturing overhead. By the end of 2007, all 23,000 units that were produced were sold; thus, the company began 2008 with no beginning finished goods inventory.

In 2008 and 2009, La Mancha Company management decided to apply manufacturing overhead to products using units of production (rather than direct labor hours and machine hours). The company produced 25,000 and 20,000 units, respectively, in 2008 and 2009. La Mancha's budgeted and actual fixed manufacturing overhead for both years was $100,000. Production in each year was projected at 25,000 units. Variable production cost (including variable manufacturing overhead) is $3 per unit. The following absorption costing income statements and supporting information are available:

	2008	2009
Net sales (20,000 units and 22,000 units)	$300,000	$330,000
Cost of goods sold (a)	(140,000)	(154,000)
Volume variance (0 and 5,000 units × $4)	0	(20,000)
Gross margin	$160,000	$156,000
Operating expenses (b)	(82,500)	(88,500)
Income before tax	$ 77,500	$ 67,500

(a) Cost of goods sold

Beginning inventory	$ 0	$ 35,000
Cost of goods manufactured[a]	175,000	140,000
Goods available for sale	$175,000	$175,000
Ending inventory[b]	(35,000)	(21,000)
Cost of goods sold	$140,000	$154,000

[a]CGM
    25,000 units × $7 (of which $3 are variable) = $175,000
    20,000 units × $7 (of which $3 are variable) = $140,000
[b]EI
    25,000 − 20,000 = 5,000 units; 5,000 × $7 = $ 35,000
    5,000 + 20,000 − 22,000 = 3,000 units; 3,000 × $7 = $ 21,000

(b) Analysis of operating expenses

Variable	$ 50,000	$ 55,000
Fixed	32,500	33,500
Total	$ 82,500	$ 88,500

Required:

a. Determine the predetermined variable and fixed overhead rates for 2007, and calculate how much underapplied or overapplied overhead existed at the end of that year.

b. Recast the 2008 and 2009 income statements on a variable costing basis.

c. Reconcile income for 2008 and 2009 between absorption and variable costing.

Solution to Demonstration Problem

a. VOH rate = $13,500 ÷ 54,000 DLHs = $0.25 per DLH
    FOH rate = $105,300 ÷ 27,000 MHs = $3.90 per MH

Actual VOH	$11,980	Actual FOH	$103,540
Applied VOH (46,000 × $0.25)	(11,500)	Applied FOH (23,000 × $3.90)	(89,700)
Underapplied VOH	$ 480	Underapplied FOH	$ 13,840

Note that the large underapplication of FOH was caused mainly by a difference between the number of machine hours used to set the rate (27,000) and the number of machine hours that were actually used (23,000): 4,000 × $3.90 = $15,600. The underapplication of FOH was constrained by the fact that the company incurred only $103,540 of FOH rather than the $105,300 the company expected to incur. The total underapplication is the combination of the negative machine hour effect and the positive total expenditure effect: $15,600 − ($105,300 − $103,540) = $13,840.

b.

	2008	2009
Net sales	$ 300,000	$ 330,000
Variable cost of goods sold	(60,000)	(66,000)
Product contribution margin	$ 240,000	$ 264,000
Variable operating expenses	(50,000)	(55,000)
Total contribution margin	$ 190,000	$ 209,000
Fixed costs		
Manufacturing	$ 100,000	$ 100,000
Operating	32,500	33,500
Total fixed costs	$(132,500)	$(133,500)
Income before tax	$ 57,500	$ 75,500

c. Reconciliation 2008

Absorption costing income before tax	$77,500
− Fixed manufacturing overhead in ending inventory ($4.00 × 5,000)	(20,000)
Variable costing income before tax	$57,500

Reconciliation 2009

Absorption costing income before tax	$67,500
+ Fixed manufacturing overhead released from beginning inventory ($4.00 × 2,000)	8,000
Variable costing income before tax	$75,500

Key Terms

absorption costing, **p. 73**	normal capacity, **p. 65**
applied overhead, **p. 62**	outlier, **p. 67**
contribution margin, **p. 74**	overapplied overhead, **p. 63**
dependent variable, **p. 69**	phantom profit, **p. 78**
direct costing, **p. 73**	practical capacity, **p. 65**
expected capacity, **p. 66**	product contribution margin, **p. 74**
flexible budget, **p. 71**	regression line, **p. 69**
full costing, **p. 73**	simple regression, **p. 69**
functional classification, **p. 73**	theoretical capacity, **p. 65**
high–low method, **p. 67**	underapplied overhead, **p. 63**
independent variable, **p. 69**	variable costing, **p. 73**
least squares regression analysis, **p. 69**	volume variance, **p. 77**
multiple regression, **p. 69**	

Questions

1. What is the difference between a variable and a mixed cost, considering that each changes in total with changes in activity levels?
2. The high–low method of analyzing mixed costs uses only two observation points: the high and the low points of activity. Are these always the best points for prediction purposes? Why or why not?
3. Discuss the reasons a company would use a predetermined overhead rate rather than apply actual overhead to products or services.
4. Why are departmental predetermined OH rates more useful for managerial decision making than plantwide OH rates? Why do firms use separate variable and fixed rates rather than total rates?
5. Why would regression analysis provide a more accurate cost formula than the high–low method for a mixed cost?
6. How does absorption costing differ from variable costing in cost accumulation and income statement presentation?
7. What is meant by classifying costs (a) functionally and (b) behaviorally? Why would a company be concerned about functional and behavioral classifications?
8. Is variable or absorption costing generally required for external reporting? Why is this method required compared to the alternative?
9. Why does variable costing provide more useful information than absorption costing for making internal decisions?
10. What are the income relationships between absorption and variable costing when production differs from sales? What causes these relationships to occur?

Exercises

11. **LO.1 (OH application)** Use the information in Exercise 14 and assume that Waterloo Mfg. has decided to use units to apply overhead to production. In April 2008, the company produced 900 units and incurred $7,000 and $27,000, of variable and fixed overhead, respectively.
    a. What amount of variable manufacturing overhead should be applied to production in April 2008?
    b. What amount of fixed manufacturing overhead should be applied to production in April 2008?
    c. Calculate the under- or overapplied variable and fixed overhead for April 2008.
12. **LO.1 (Predetermined OH rate)** For 2008, Southwest Industrial has a monthly overhead cost formula of $42,900 + $6 per direct labor hour. The firm's 2008 expected annual capacity is 156,000 direct labor hours, to be incurred evenly each month. Making one unit of the company's product requires three direct labor hours.
    a. Determine the total overhead to be applied per unit of product in 2008.

b. Prepare journal entries to record the application of overhead to Work in Process Inventory and the incurrence of $128,550 of actual overhead in January 2008, when 12,780 direct labor hours were worked.

c. Given the actual direct labor hours in part (b), how many units would you have expected to be produced in January?

13. **LO.1 (Predetermined OH rate)** Cairo Products applies overhead using a combined rate for fixed and variable overhead. The rate is 125 percent of direct labor cost. During the first three months of the current year, actual costs were incurred as follows:

	Direct Labor Cost	Actual Overhead
January	$360,000	$440,000
February	330,000	420,400
March	340,000	421,000

a. What amount of overhead was applied to production in each of the three months?

b. What was the underapplied or overapplied overhead for each of the three months and for the first quarter?

14. **LO.1 (Predetermined OH rates)** Waterloo Mfg. prepared the following 2008 abbreviated flexible budget for different levels of machine hours:

	20,000	22,000	24,000	26,000
Variable manufacturing overhead	$ 80,000	$ 88,000	$ 96,000	$104,000
Fixed manufacturing overhead	325,000	325,000	325,000	325,000

Each product requires two hours of machine time, and the company expects to produce 10,000 units in 2008. Production is expected to be evenly distributed throughout the year.

a. Calculate separate predetermined variable and fixed OH rates using as the basis of application (1) units of product and (2) machine hours.

b. Calculate the combined predetermined OH rate using (1) units of product and (2) machine hours.

c. Assume that all actual overhead costs are equal to expected overhead costs in 2008, but that Waterloo Mfg. produced 11,000 units of product. If the separate rates based on units of product calculated in part (a) were used to apply overhead, what amounts of underapplied or overapplied variable and fixed overhead exist at year-end 2008?

15. **LO.2 (Predetermined OH rates and underapplied/overapplied OH)** Empire Glassworks had the following information in its Work in Process Inventory account for June 2008:

Work in Process Inventory

Beginning balance	5,000	Transferred out	167,500
Materials added	75,000		
Labor (5,000 DLHs)	45,000		
Applied overhead	60,000		
Ending balance	17,500		

All workers are paid the same rate per hour. Factory overhead is applied to Work in Process Inventory on the basis of direct labor hours. The only work left in process at the end of the month had a total of 1,430 direct labor hours accumulated to date.

a. What is the total predetermined OH rate per direct labor hour?

b. If actual total overhead for June is $60,750, what is the amount of underapplied or overapplied overhead?

c. Given your answer to part (b), how would you recommend the over- or underapplied overhead be closed?

16. **LO.1 (Plantwide vs. departmental OH rates)** Houston Corp. has gathered the following information to develop predetermined OH rates for 2008. The company produces a wide variety of products that are processed through two departments, Assembly (automated) and Finishing (labor intensive).

Budgeted total overhead: $300,200 in Assembly and $99,800 in Finishing
Budgeted total direct labor hours: 5,000 in Assembly and 20,000 in Finishing
Budgeted total machine hours: 38,000 in Assembly and 2,000 in Finishing

a. Compute a plantwide predetermined OH rate using direct labor hours.

b. Compute a plantwide predetermined OH rate using machine hours.

c. Compute departmental predetermined OH rates using machine hours for Assembly and direct labor hours for Finishing.

d. Determine the amount of overhead that would be assigned to a product that required five machine hours in Assembly and one direct labor hour in Finishing using the answers developed in parts (a), (b), and (c).

17. LO.2 (Underapplied or overapplied overhead) At the end of 2008, Westmeier Corporation's accounts showed a $33,000 credit balance in Manufacturing Overhead Control. In addition, the company had the following account balances:

Work in Process Inventory	$192,000
Finished Goods Inventory	48,000
Cost of Goods Sold	360,000

a. Prepare the necessary journal entry to close the overhead account if the balance is considered immaterial.
b. Prepare the necessary journal entry to close the overhead account if the balance is considered material.
c. Which method do you believe is more appropriate for the company and why?

18. LO.4 (High–low method) Information about SnoCo's utility cost for the last six months of 2008 follows. The high–low method will be used to develop a cost formula to predict 2009 utility charges, and the number of machine hours has been found to be an appropriate cost driver. Data for the first half of 2008 are not being considered because the utility company imposed a significant rate change as of July 1, 2008.

Month	Machine Hours	Utility Cost
July	33,750	$6,500
August	34,000	6,100
September	33,150	5,070
October	32,000	5,980
November	31,250	5,750
December	31,000	5,860

a. What is the cost formula for utility expense?
b. What is the budgeted utility cost for September 2009 if 33,175 machine hours are projected?

19. LO.3 (Predetermined OH rates; capacity measures) Quality Ware makes toasters and uses a normal cost system that applies overhead based on machine hours. The following 2008 budgeted data are available:

Variable factory overhead at 100,000 machine hours	$625,000
Variable factory overhead at 150,000 machine hours	937,500
Fixed factory overhead at all levels between 10,000 and 180,000 machine hours	720,000

Practical capacity is 180,000 machine hours; expected capacity is two-thirds of practical.
a. What is Quality Ware's predetermined variable OH rate?
b. What is the predetermined fixed OH rate using practical capacity?
c. What is the predetermined fixed OH rate using expected capacity?
d. During 2008, the firm incurs 110,000 machine hours and $1,360,000 of overhead costs. How much variable overhead is applied? How much fixed overhead is applied using the rate found in part (b)? How much fixed overhead is applied using the rate found in part (c)? Calculate the total under- or overapplied overhead for 2007 using both fixed OH rates.

20. LO.3 (Capacity measures) For 2008, Rydex Manufacturing has estimated its production capacities as follows:

Theoretical capacity	200,000 units
Practical capacity	150,000 units
Normal capacity	130,000 units
Expected capacity	100,000 units

Rydex is trying to choose which capacity measure it should use to develop its predetermined OH rates for 2008.
a. Why does the choice of capacity measure affect the amount of under- or overapplied overhead the firm will have at the end of 2008?
b. Which capacity measure choice would likely result in the least amount of under- or overapplied overhead?
c. Which of the alternative capacity measures makes allowances for possible cycles in the industry?

21. LO.2 (Underapplied or overapplied overhead) At year-end 2008, Power Co. has a $40,000 debit balance in its Manufacturing Overhead Control account. Overhead is applied to products based on direct labor cost. Relevant account balance information at year-end follows:

	Work in Process Inventory	Finished Goods Inventory	Cost of Goods Sold
Direct material	$ 40,000	$ 80,000	$120,000
Direct labor	20,000	40,000	50,000
Factory overhead	40,000	80,000	100,000
	$100,000	$200,000	$270,000

a. What predetermined OH rate was used during the year?
b. Provide arguments to be used for deciding whether to prorate the balance in the overhead account at year-end.
c. Prorate the overhead account balance based on the relative balances of the appropriate accounts.
d. Identify some possible reasons that the company had a debit balance in the overhead account at year-end.

22. **LO.4 (High–low method)** Architectural Models Inc. builds replicas of residences of famous and infamous people. The company is highly automated, and the new accountant-owner has decided to use machine hours as the basis for predicting maintenance costs. The following data are available from the company's most recent eight months of operations:

Machine Hours	Maintenance Costs
8,000	$1,470
14,000	1,200
7,000	1,680
12,000	1,100
6,000	1,960
18,000	880
16,000	1,020
11,000	1,200

a. Using the high–low method, determine the cost formula for maintenance costs with machine hours as the basis for estimation.
b. What aspect of the estimated equation is bothersome? Provide an explanation for this situation.
c. Within the relevant range, can the formula be reliably used to predict maintenance costs? Can the a and b values in the cost formula be interpreted as fixed and variable costs? Why or why not?

23. **LO.4 (High–low method)** Midwest Supply has gathered the following data on the number of shipments received and the cost of receiving reports for the first seven weeks of 2008.

Number of Shipments Received	Weekly Cost of Receiving Reports
100	$175
87	162
80	154
70	142
105	185
115	200
120	202

a. Using the high–low method, develop the equation for predicting weekly receiving report costs based on the number of shipments received.
b. What is the predicted amount of receiving report costs for a week in which 340 shipments are received?
c. What are the concerns you have regarding your prediction from part (b)?

24. **LO.4 (Least squares)** Alberta Mfg. has compiled the following data to analyze utility costs:

Month	Machine Hours	Utility Cost
January	200	$150
February	325	220
March	400	240
April	410	245
May	525	310
June	680	395
July	820	420
August	900	450

Use the least squares method to develop a formula for budgeting utility cost.

25. **LO.5 (Least squares)** Refer to the information in Exercise 23 for Midwest Supply.

a. Using the least squares method, develop the equation for predicting weekly receiving report costs based on the number of shipments received.
b. What is the predicted amount of receiving report costs for a month (assume a month is exactly four weeks) in which 340 shipments are received?

26. LO.5 (Flexible budget; variances; cost control) The South Dakota plant of Blackhills Corp. prepared the following flexible overhead budget for three levels of activity within the plant's relevant range.

	12,000 units	16,000 units	20,000 units
Variable overhead	$24,000	$32,000	$40,000
Fixed overhead	16,000	16,000	16,000
Total overhead	$40,000	$48,000	$58,000

After discussion with the home office, the plant expected to produce 16,000 units of its single product during 2008. However, demand for the product was exceptionally strong, and actual production for 2008 was 17,600 units. Actual variable and fixed overhead costs incurred in producing the 17,600 units were $34,500 and $16,400, respectively.

The production manager was upset because the company planned to incur $48,000 of costs and actual costs were $50,900. Prepare a memo to the production manager regarding the following questions.

a. Should the $50,900 actual total cost be compared to the $48,000 expected total cost for control purposes? Explain the rationale for your answer.

b. Analyze the costs and explain where the company did well or poorly in controlling its costs.

27. LO.4 & LO.5 (High–low method; flexible budget) Santa Fe Tile has gathered the following information on its utility costs for the past six months.

Machine Hours	Utility Cost
1,300	$ 940
1,700	1,075
1,250	900
1,800	1,132
1,900	1,160
1,500	990

a. Using the high–low method, determine the cost formula for utility costs.

b. Prepare a flexible budget with separate variable and fixed categories for utility costs at 1,000, 1,500, and 2,000 machine hours.

28. LO.6 & LO.7 (Absorption vs. variable costing) Uzzo's Umbrellas manufactures umbrellas for the upscale market. In May 2008, the company manufactured 18,000 and sold 16,560 umbrellas. The cost per unit for the 18,000 umbrellas produced was as follows:

Direct material	$ 8.00
Direct labor	4.00
Variable overhead	2.00
Fixed overhead	3.00
Total	$17.00

There was no beginning inventory for May.

a. What is the value of ending inventory using absorption costing?

b. What is the value of ending inventory using variable costing?

c. Which accounting method, variable or absorption, would have produced the higher net income for May?

29. LO.5 (Flexible budget) Tom's Shoe Repair provides a variety of shoe and repair services. Analysis of monthly costs revealed the following cost formulas when direct labor hours are used as the basis of cost determination:

Supplies: $y = \$0 + \$4.00X$
Production supervision and direct labor: $y = \$500 + \$7.00X$
Utilities: $y = \$350 + \$5.40X$
Rent: $y = \$450 + \$0.00X$
Advertising: $y = \$75 + \$0.00X$

a. Prepare a flexible budget at 250, 300, 350, and 400 direct labor hours.

b. Calculate a total cost per direct labor hour at each level of activity.

c. Tom usually incurs 350 direct labor hours per month. The average shoe repair requires 1.25 labor hours to complete. Tom wants to earn a 40 percent margin on his cost. What should be the average charge per customer, rounded to the nearest dollar to achieve Tom's profit objective?

30. LO.6 & LO.7 (Production cost; absorption vs. variable costing) Arizona Olive Oil began business in 2008, during which it produced 104,000 quarts of olive oil. In 2008, the company sold 100,000 quarts of olive oil. Costs incurred during the year were as follows:

Ingredients used	$224,000
Direct labor	104,000
Variable overhead	192,000
Fixed overhead	93,600
Variable selling expenses	40,000
Fixed selling and administrative expenses	112,000
Total actual costs	$765,600

a. What was the actual production cost per quart under variable costing? Under absorption costing?
b. What was variable cost of goods sold for 2008 under variable costing?
c. What was cost of goods sold for 2008 under absorption costing?
d. What was the value of ending inventory under variable costing? Under absorption costing?
e. How much fixed overhead was charged to expense in 2008 under variable costing? Under absorption costing?

31. LO.6 & LO.7 (Absorption vs. variable costing) Eastern Chemical Company uses variable costing to manage its internal operations. The following data relate to the company's first year of operation, when 50,000 units were produced and 46,000 units were sold.

Variable costs per unit	
Direct material	$50
Direct labor	30
Variable overhead	14
Variable selling costs	12
Fixed costs	
Selling and administrative	$750,000
Manufacturing	500,000

How much higher (or lower) would the company's first-year net income have been if absorption costing had been used rather than variable costing? Show computations.

32. LO.6 & LO.7 (Convert variable to absorption) The April 2008 income statement for Kickin' Sportswear has just been received by Bobby Cox, vice president of marketing. The firm uses a variable costing system for internal reporting purposes.

KICKIN' SPORTSWEAR
Income Statement
For the Month Ended April 30, 2008

Sales		$7,200,000
Variable standard cost of goods sold		(3,600,000)
Product contribution margin		$3,600,000
Fixed expenses		
Manufacturing (budget and actual)	$2,250,000	
Selling and administrative	1,200,000	(3,450,000)
Income before tax		$ 150,000

The following notes were attached to the statements:
- Unit sales price for April averaged $72.
- Unit manufacturing costs for the month were:

Variable cost	$36
Fixed cost	15
Total cost	$51

- The predetermined OH rate for fixed manufacturing costs was based on normal monthly production of 150,000 units.
- April production was 7,500 units in excess of sales.
- April ending inventory consisted of 12,000 units.

a. The marketing vice president is not familiar with variable costing.
  1. Recast the April income statement on an absorption costing basis.
  2. Reconcile and explain the difference between the variable costing and the absorption costing income figures.
b. Explain the features of variable costing that should appeal to the marketing vice president.

(CMA adapted)

33. LO.6 & LO.7 (Net income; absorption vs. variable costing) Eastland Company produces lampposts. In 2008, fixed overhead was applied to products at the rate of $16 per unit. Variable cost per unit remained

constant throughout the year. In July 2008, income under variable costing was $188,000. July's beginning and ending inventories were 20,000 and 10,400 units, respectively.
a. Calculate income under absorption costing assuming no variances.
b. Assume instead that the company's July beginning and ending inventories were 10,000 and 12,000 units, respectively. Calculate income under absorption costing.

34. LO.6 & LO.7 (Essay) Because your professor is scheduled to address a national professional meeting at the time your class ordinarily meets, the class has been divided into teams to discuss selected issues. Your team's assignment is to prepare a report arguing whether fixed manufacturing overhead should be included as a component of product cost. You are also expected to draw your own conclusion about this issue and provide the rationale for your conclusion in your report.

35. LO.6 & LO.7 (Variable and absorption costing) The John Hancock Co. manufactures novel ballpoint pens. Data pertaining to the company's 2008 operations follow:

Production for the year	90,000 units
Sales for the year (sales price per unit, $8)	97,500 units
Beginning 2008 inventory	17,500 units

Costs to produce 1 unit (2007 & 2008):	
Direct material	$3.60
Direct labor	1.00
Variable overhead	0.60
Fixed overhead	0.40

Selling and administrative costs:	
Variable (per unit sold)	$0.40
Fixed (per year)	$150,000

Fixed manufacturing overhead is assigned to units of production based on a predetermined OH rate using an expected production capacity of 100,000 units per year.
a. What is budgeted annual fixed manufacturing overhead?
b. If budgeted fixed overhead equals actual fixed overhead, what is underapplied or overapplied fixed overhead in 2008 under absorption costing? Under variable costing?
c. What is the product cost per unit under absorption costing? Under variable costing?
d. How much total expense is charged against revenues in 2008 under absorption costing? Under variable costing?
e. Is income higher under absorption or variable costing? By what amount?

Problems

36. LO.1–LO.3 (Overhead Application) Ludwig Enterprises makes only one product. The company has a theoretical capacity of 50,000 units annually. Practical capacity is 80 percent of theoretical capacity, and normal capacity is 80 percent of practical capacity. The firm is expecting to produce 30,000 units next year. The company president, Mandy Moss, has budgeted the following factory overhead costs for the coming year:

Indirect materials: $2.00 per unit
Indirect labor: $144,000 plus $2.50 per unit
Utilities for the plant: $6,000 plus $0.04 per unit
Repairs and maintenance for the plant: $20,000 plus $0.34 per unit
Material handling costs: $16,000 plus $0.12 per unit
Depreciation on plant assets: $210,000 per year
Rent on plant building: $50,000 per year
Insurance on plant building: $12,000 per year

a. Determine the cost formula for total factory overhead in the format of $y = a + bX$.
b. Determine the total predetermined OH rate for each possible overhead application base.
c. Assume that Ludwig produces 35,000 units during the year and that actual costs are exactly as budgeted. Calculate the overapplied or underapplied overhead for each possible overhead allocation base.

37. LO.1 (Overhead application) Last June, Jordan Johnson had just been appointed CFO of McGiver Mfg. Company when he received some interesting reports about the profitability of the company's three most important product lines. One of the products, K1, was produced in a very labor intensive production process, another product, K7, was produced in a very machine-intensive production process, and the third product, K4, was produced in a manner that was equally labor and machine intensive. Johnson observed that all three products were produced in high volume and were priced in the marketplace similarly to competitive products of other manufacturers. Prior to receiving the profit report, Johnson had expected the three products to be roughly equally profitable. However, according to the profit report, K1 was actually losing a significant amount of money and K7 was generating an impressively high profit. In the middle, K4 was producing an average profit. After viewing the profit data, Johnson developed a theory that the "real" profitability of each product was substantially different from the reported profits. To test his theory, Johnson gathered cost data from the firm's accounting records. Johnson was quickly satisfied that the direct material and direct labor costs were charged to products properly; however, he surmised that the manufacturing overhead allocation was distorting product costs. To further investigate, he gathered the following information.

	K1	K4	K7
Monthly direct labor hours	2,000	400	100
Monthly machine hours	800	2,400	12,800
Monthly allocated overhead cost	$80,000	$16,000	$4,000

Johnson noted that the current cost accounting system assigned all overhead to products based on direct labor hours using a predetermined overhead rate.
a. Using the data gathered by Johnson, calculate the predetermined OH rate based on direct labor hours.
b. Find the predetermined OH rate per machine hour that would allocate the current total amount of overhead ($100,000) to the three product lines.
c. Johnson believes the current overhead allocation is distorting the profitability of the product lines; determine the amount of overhead that would be allocated to each product line if machine hours were the basis of overhead allocation.
d. Why are the overhead allocations using direct labor hours and machine hours so different? Which is the better allocation?

38. **LO.1 & LO.3 (Plant vs. departmental OH rates)** Warton Industrial has two departments: Fabrication and Finishing. Three workers oversee the 25 machines in Fabrication. Finishing uses 35 crafters to hand polish output, which is then run through buffing machines. Warton's Product CG9832-09 uses the following amounts of direct labor and machine time in each department:

	Fabrication	Finishing
Machine hours	8.00	0.15
Direct labor hours	0.02	2.00

Following are the budgeted overhead costs and volumes for each department for the upcoming year:

	Fabrication	Finishing
Budgeted overhead	$317,670	$162,000
Budgeted machine hours	72,000	9,300
Budgeted direct labor hours	4,800	48,000

a. What is the plantwide OH rate based on machine hours for the upcoming year? How much overhead will be assigned to each unit of Product CG9832-09 using this rate?
b. Warton's auditors inform management that departmental predetermined OH rates using machine hours in Fabrication and direct labor hours in Finishing would be more appropriate than a plantwide rate. What would the OH rates be for each department? How much overhead would have been assigned to each unit of Product CG9832-09 using departmental rates?
c. Discuss why departmental rates are more appropriate than plantwide rates for Warton Industries.

39. **LO.1–LO.3 (Predetermined OH rates; flexible budget; capacity)** Kreaton Company budgeted the following factory overhead costs for the upcoming year to help calculate variable and fixed predetermined overhead rates.

Indirect material: $1.25 per unit produced
Indirect labor: $1.00 per unit produced
Factory utilities: $3,000 plus $0.02 per unit produced
Factory machine maintenance: $10,000 plus $0.17 per unit produced
Material handling charges: $8,000 plus $0.06 per unit produced
Machine depreciation: $0.03 per unit produced
Building rent: $25,000
Supervisors' salaries: $72,000
Factory insurance: $6,000

The company produces only one type of product that has a theoretical capacity of 100,000 units of production during the year. Practical capacity is 80 percent of theoretical, and normal capacity is 95 percent of practical. The company's expected production for the upcoming year is 72,000 units.

a. Prepare a flexible budget for Kreaton Company using each level of capacity.

b. Calculate the predetermined variable and fixed overhead rates for each capacity measure (round to the nearest cent when necessary).

c. Kreaton Company decides to apply overhead to products using expected capacity as the budgeted level of activity. The firm actually produces 70,000 units during the year. All actual costs are as budgeted.

   1. Prepare journal entries to record the incurrence of actual overhead costs and to apply overhead to production. Assume cash is paid for costs when appropriate.

   2. What is the amount of underapplied or overapplied fixed overhead at year-end?

d. Which measure of capacity would be of most benefit to management and why?

40. LO.2 (Under/Overapplied OH; OH disposition) Hastings Co. budgeted the following variable and fixed overhead costs for 2008:

Variable indirect labor	$100,000
Variable indirect materials	20,000
Variable utilities	80,000
Variable portion of other mixed costs	120,000
Fixed machinery depreciation	62,000
Fixed machinery lease payments	13,000
Fixed machinery insurance	16,000
Fixed salaries	75,000
Fixed utilities	12,000

The company allocates overhead to production using machine hours. For 2008, machine hours have been budgeted at 20,000.

a. Determine the predetermined variable and fixed OH rates for Hastings Co. The company uses separate variable and fixed manufacturing overhead control accounts.

b. During 2008, Hastings Co. used 21,000 machine hours during production and incurred a total of $273,600 of variable overhead costs and $185,680 of fixed overhead costs. Prepare journal entries to record the incurrence of the actual overhead costs and the application of overhead to production.

c. What amounts of underapplied or overapplied overhead exist at year-end 2008 for Hastings?

d. Hastings' management believes that the fixed overhead amount calculated in part (a) should be considered immaterial. Prepare the entry to close the Fixed Overhead Control account at the end of the year.

e. Hastings' management believes that the variable overhead amount calculated in part (a) should be considered material and should be prorated to the appropriate accounts. At year-end, Hastings had the following balances in its inventory and Cost of Goods Sold accounts:

Raw Material Inventory	$ 25,000
Work in Process Inventory	234,000
Finished Goods Inventory	390,000
Cost of Goods Sold	936,000

Prepare the entry to close the Variable Overhead Control account at the end of the year.

41. LO.1 & LO.3 (Plant vs. departmental OH rates) Green River Manufacturing makes a wide variety of products, all of which must be processed in the Cutting and Assembly departments. For the year 2008, Green River budgeted total overhead of $969,020, of which $383,400 will be incurred in Cutting and the remainder will be incurred in Assembly. Budgeted direct labor and machine hours are as follows:

	Cutting	Assembly
Budgeted direct labor hours	27,000	3,000
Budgeted machine hours	2,100	65,800

Two products made by Green River are the RW22SKI and the SD45ROW. The following cost and production time information on these items has been gathered:

	RW22SKI	SD45ROW
Direct material	$34.85	$19.57
Direct labor rate in Cutting	$14.00	$14.00
Direct labor rate in Assembly	$6.50	$6.50
Direct labor hours in Cutting	6.00	4.80
Direct labor hours in Assembly	0.03	0.05
Machine hours in Cutting	0.06	0.15
Machine hours in Assembly	5.90	9.30

a. What is the plantwide predetermined OH rate based on (1) direct labor hours and (2) machine hours for the upcoming year? Round all computations to the nearest cent.

b. What are the departmental predetermined OH rates in Cutting and Assembly using the most appropriate base in each department? Round all computations to the nearest cent.

c. What are the costs of products RW22SKI and SD45ROW using (1) a plantwide rate based on direct labor hours, (2) a plantwide rate based on machine hours, and (3) departmental rates calculated in part (b)?

d. A competitor manufactures a product that is extremely similar to RW22SKI and sells each unit of it for $270. Discuss how Green River's management might be influenced by the impact of the different product costs calculated in part (c).

42. **LO.4 (High–low; least squares regression)** Green Shade manufactures insulated windows. The firm's repair and maintenance (R&M) cost is mixed and varies most directly with machine hours worked. The following data have been gathered from recent operations:

EXCEL

Month	MHs	R&M Cost
May	1,400	$ 9,000
June	1,900	10,719
July	2,000	10,900
August	2,500	13,000
September	2,200	11,578
October	2,700	13,160
November	1,700	9,525
December	2,300	11,670

a. Use the high–low method to estimate a cost formula for repairs and maintenance.

b. Use least squares regression to estimate a cost formula for repairs and maintenance.

c. Does the answer to part (a) or to part (b) provide the better estimate of the relationship between repairs and maintenance costs and machine hours? Why?

43. **LO.4 (Analyzing mixed costs)** Queen Dairy determined that the total predetermined OH rate for costing purposes is $26.80 per cow per day (referred to as an *animal day*). Of this, $25.20 is the variable portion. Overhead cost information for two levels of activity within the relevant range follow:

	4,000 Animal Days	6,000 Animal Days
Indirect materials	$25,600	$38,400
Indirect labor	56,000	80,000
Maintenance	10,400	13,600
Utilities	8,000	12,000
All other	15,200	21,600

a. Determine the fixed and variable values for each of the preceding overhead items, and determine the total overhead cost formula.

b. Assume that the total predetermined OH rate is based on expected annual capacity. What is this level of activity for the company?

c. Determine expected overhead costs at the expected annual capacity.

d. If the company raises its expected capacity by 3,000 animal days above the present level, calculate a new total overhead rate for product costing.

44. **LO.5 (Flexible budgets)** Doggie Doos, a dog grooming business, has determined that the following formulas describe its costs:

Grooming supplies (variable) $y = \$0 + \$4.00X$
Direct labor (variable) $y = \$0 + \$12X$
Overhead (mixed) $y = \$8,000 + \$1.00X$

Top Dogg is the owner of Doggie Doos and has determined that direct labor is the best cost driver for all three cost categories.

a. Prepare a flexible budget for each of the following activity levels: 550, 600, 650, and 700 direct labor hours.

b. Determine the total cost per direct labor hour at each of the levels of activity.

c. Groomers at Doggie Doos normally work 650 direct labor hours during a month. Each grooming job typically takes 1.25 hours of groomer time. Dogg wants to earn a profit equal to 40% of the costs incurred. What should he charge each pet owner for grooming?

EXCEL

45. LO.4 (Least squares) Caribbean Holiday provides charter cruises in the Virgin Islands. Lois Martin, the owner, wants to understand how her labor costs change per month. She recognizes that the cost is neither strictly fixed nor strictly variable. She has gathered the following information and has identified two potential predictive bases: number of charters and gross receipts:

Month	Labor Costs	Number of Charters	Gross Receipts ($000)
January	$ 8,000	10	$ 12
February	9,200	14	18
March	12,000	22	26
April	14,200	28	36
May	18,500	40	60
June	28,000	62	82
July	34,000	100	120
August	30,000	90	100
September	24,000	80	96

Using the least squares method, develop a labor cost formula using
a. number of charters
b. gross receipts

46. LO.5 (Flexible budgets) John Ralston is a staff accountant for BigBiz Corp. Ralston was recently given the task of developing a monthly flexible budget formula for several manufacturing costs. He was told that his equations would be used as an aid in developing future budgets for these manufacturing costs and he was told to put his results into an equation in the form $y = a + bX$ for each cost. Ralston gathered data and used high–low analysis to obtain the flexible budget formulas. Rather than using a single activity measure, Ralston decided to use two. Thus, for each manufacturing cost analyzed, he developed two equations. However, after analyzing several equations, Ralston became perplexed over his results because the results from the two equations were very different in some cases. Ralston has asked you, his colleague, how he should decide which of the two estimated equations for each manufacturing cost he should submit to his boss. To illustrate his dilemma, Ralston provided you with his two equations for repairs and maintenance expense, which follow.

Using machine hours:	$y = \$10,000 + \$14X$
Using direct labor hours:	$y = \$250,000 + \$27X$

What advice will you give Ralston?

47. LO.1 & LO.5 (Flexible budgets; predetermined OH rates) Cool Pool makes large fiberglass swimming pools and uses machine hours and direct labor hours to apply overhead in the Production and Installation departments, respectively. The monthly overhead cost formula in Production is $y = \$7,950 + \$4.05$ MH; in Installation, the overhead cost formula is $y = \$6,150 + \$14.25$ DLH. These formulas are valid for a relevant range of activity up to 6,000 machine hours in Production and 9,000 direct labor hours in Installation.

Each pool is estimated to require 25 machine hours in Production and 60 hours of direct labor in Installation. Expected capacity for the year is 120 pools.
a. Prepare a flexible budget for Production at possible annual capacities of 2,500, 3,000, and 3,500 machine hours. Prepare a flexible budget for Installation at possible annual capacities of 6,000, 7,000, and 8,000 machine hours.
b. Prepare a budget for next month's variable, fixed, and total overhead costs for each department assuming that expected production is eight pools.
c. Calculate the total overhead cost to be applied to each pool scheduled for production in the coming month if expected capacity is used to calculate the predetermined OH rates.

48. LO.6 & LO.7 (Absorption and variable costing) Gotcha manufactures radar detectors. For each unit, the following costs apply: $40 for direct material, $120 for direct labor, and $40 for variable overhead. The company's annual fixed cost is $750,000; it uses expected capacity of 12,500 units produced as the basis for applying fixed overhead to products. A commission of 10 percent of the selling price is paid on each unit sold. Annual fixed selling and administrative expenses are $180,000. The following additional information is available:

	2008	2009
Selling price per unit	$400	$400
Number of units sold	10,000	12,000
Number of units produced	12,500	11,000
Beginning inventory (units)	7,500	10,000
Ending inventory (units)	10,000	?

Prepare pre-tax income statements under absorption and variable costing for the years ended 2008 and 2009, with any volume variance being charged to Cost of Goods Sold. Reconcile the differences in income for the two methods.

49. **LO.6 & LO.7 (Convert variable to absorption; ethics)** Georgia Shacks produces small outdoor buildings. The company began operations in 2008, producing 2,000 buildings and selling 1,500. A variable costing income statement for 2008 follows. During the year, variable production costs per unit were $800 for direct material, $300 for direct labor, and $200 for overhead.

GEORGIA SHACKS
Income Statement (Variable Costing)
For the Year Ended December 31, 2008

Sales		$3,750,000
Variable cost of goods sold		
Beginning inventory	$ 0	
Cost of goods manufactured	2,600,000	
Cost of goods available for sale	$2,600,000	
Less ending inventory	(650,000)	(1,950,000)
Product contribution margin		$1,800,000
Less variable selling and administrative expenses		(270,000)
Total contribution margin		$1,530,000
Less fixed expenses		
Fixed factory overhead	$1,500,000	
Fixed selling and administrative expenses	190,000	(1,690,000)
Income before taxes		$ (160,000)

The company president is upset about the net loss because he wanted to borrow funds to expand capacity.

a. Prepare a pre-tax absorption costing income statement.
b. Explain the source of the difference between the pre-tax income and loss figures under the two costing systems.
c. Would it be appropriate to present an absorption costing income statement to the local banker, considering the company president's knowledge of the net loss determined under variable costing? Explain.
d. Assume that during the second year of operations, Georgia Shacks produced 2,000 buildings, sold 2,200, and experienced the same total fixed costs as in 2008. For the second year:
   1. Prepare a variable costing pre-tax income statement.
   2. Prepare an absorption costing pre-tax income statement.
   3. Explain the difference between the incomes for the second year under the two systems. ▲

50. **LO.1, LO.6, & LO.7 (Overhead application; absorption costing; ethics)** Prior to the start of fiscal 2008, managers of MultiTech hosted a Web conference for their shareholders, financial analysts, and members of the financial press. During the conference, the CEO and CFO released the following financial projections for 2008 to the attendees (amounts in millions):

Sales	$40,000
Cost of Goods Sold	32,000
Gross Margin	$ 8,000
Operating expenses	4,000
Operating income	$ 4,000

As had been their custom, the CEO and CFO projected confidence that the firm would achieve these goals, even though their projections had been significantly more positive than the actual results for 2007. Not surprisingly, the day following the Web conference, MultiTech's stock rose 15%.

In early October 2008, the CEO and CFO of MultiTech met and developed revised projections for fiscal 2008, based on actual results for the first three quarters of the year and projections for the final quarter. Their revised projections for 2008 follow:

Sales	$38,000
Cost of Goods Sold	30,500
Gross Margin	$ 7,500
Operating expenses	4,000
Operating income	$ 3,500

Upon reviewing these numbers, the CEO turned to the CFO and stated, "I think the market will be forgiving if we come in 5% light on the top line (sales), but if we miss operating income by 12.5% ($500 ÷ $4,000) our stock is going to get hammered when we announce fourth quarter and annual results."

The CFO mulled the situation over for a couple of days and started to develop a strategy to increase reported income by increasing production above planned levels. She believed this strategy could successfully move $500 million from Cost of Goods Sold to Finished Goods Inventory. If so, the firm could meet its early profit projections.

a. How does increasing production, relative to the planned level of production, decrease Cost of Goods Sold?

b. What other accounts are likely affected by a strategy of increasing production to increase income?

c. Is the CFO's plan ethical? Explain.

d. If you were a stockholder of MultiTech and carefully examined the 2008 financial statements, how might you detect the results of the CFO's strategy? ▲

51. LO.6 & LO.7 (Absorption costing vs. variable costing) Since opening in 2007, Precision Motors has built light aircraft engines and has gained a reputation for reliable and quality products. Factory overhead is applied to production using direct labor hours and any underapplied or overapplied overhead is closed at year-end to Cost of Goods Sold. The company's inventory balances for the past three years and income statements for the past two years follow.

Inventory Balances	12/31/07	12/31/08	12/31/09
Direct Material	$22,000	$30,000	$10,000
Work in Process			
Costs	$40,000	$48,000	$64,000
Direct labor hours	1,335	1,600	2,100
Finished Goods			
Costs	$25,000	$18,000	$14,000
Direct labor hours	1,450	1,050	820

	COMPARATIVE INCOME STATEMENTS			
	2008		2009	
Sales		$840,000		$1,015,000
Cost of goods sold				
Finished goods, 1/1	$ 25,000		$ 18,000	
Cost of goods manufactured	548,000		657,600	
Total available	$573,000		$675,600	
Finished goods, 12/31	(18,000)		(14,000)	
CGS before overhead adjustment	$555,000		$661,600	
Underapplied factory overhead	36,000		14,400	
Cost of goods sold		(591,000)		(676,000)
Gross margin		$249,000		$ 339,000
Selling expenses	$ 82,000		$ 95,000	
Administrative expenses	70,000		75,000	
Total operating expenses		(152,000)		(170,000)
Operating income		$ 97,000		$ 169,000

The same predetermined OH rate was used to apply overhead to production orders in 2008 and 2009. The rate was based on the following estimates:

Fixed factory overhead	$ 25,000
Variable factory overhead	$155,000
Direct labor cost	$150,000
Direct labor hours	25,000

In 2008 and 2009, actual direct labor hours expended were 20,000 and 23,000, respectively. Raw material costing $292,000 was issued to production in 2008 and $370,000 in 2009. Actual fixed overhead was $37,400 for 2008 and $42,300 for 2009, and the planned direct labor rate per hour was equal to the actual direct labor rate.

For both years, all of the reported administrative costs were fixed. The variable portion of the reported selling expenses results from a commission of 5 percent of sales revenue.

a. For the year ended December 31, 2009, prepare a revised income statement using the variable costing method.

b. Prepare a numerical reconciliation of the difference in operating income between the 2009 absorption and variable costing statements.

c. Describe both the advantages and disadvantages of using variable costing.

(CMA adapted)

52. LO.6 & LO.7 (Absorption vs. variable costing) Jersey Jerseys is a New York–based company that produces and sells cotton jerseys. The firm uses variable costing for internal purposes and absorption costing for external purposes. At year-end, financial information must be converted from variable costing to absorption costing to satisfy external requirements.

At the end of 2007, management anticipated that 2008 sales would be 20 percent above 2007 levels. Thus, production for 2008 was increased by 20 percent to meet the expected demand. However, economic conditions in 2008 kept sales at the 2007 unit level of 40,000. The following data pertain to 2007 and 2008:

	2007	2008
Selling price per unit	$20	$20
Sales (units)	40,000	40,000
Beginning inventory (units)	4,000	4,000
Production (units)	40,000	48,000
Ending inventory (units)	4,000	?

Per-unit production costs (budgeted and actual) for 2007 and 2008 were:

Material	$2.25
Labor	3.75
Overhead	1.50
Total	$7.50

Annual fixed costs for 2007 and 2008 (budgeted and actual) were:

Production	$117,000
Selling and administrative	125,000
Total	$242,000

The predetermined OH rate under absorption costing is based on an annual capacity of 60,000 units. Any volume variance is assigned to Cost of Goods Sold. Taxes are to be ignored.

a. Present the income statement based on variable costing for 2008.
b. Present the income statement based on absorption costing for 2008.
c. Explain the difference, if any, in the income figures. Assuming that there is no Work in Process Inventory, provide the entry necessary to adjust the book income amount to the financial statement income amount if an adjustment is necessary.
d. The company finds it worthwhile to develop its internal financial data on a variable costing basis. What advantages and disadvantages are attributed to variable costing for internal purposes?
e. Many accountants believe that variable costing is appropriate for external reporting; many others oppose its use for external reporting. List the arguments for and against the use of variable costing in external reporting.

(CMA adapted)

4

Activity-Based Management and Activity-Based Costing

Objectives

After completing this chapter, you should be able to answer these questions:

LO.1 What are value-added and non-value-added activities?

LO.2 How do value-added and non-value-added activities affect manufacturing cycle efficiency?

LO.3 Why must cost drivers be designated in an activity-based costing system?

LO.4 How are costs computed using an activity-based costing system?

LO.5 How can the information generated from an activity-based management or activity-based costing system be used by management?

LO.6 Under what conditions is activity-based costing useful in an organization?

Introduction

To succeed in today's global marketplace, companies must generate high-quality products or services and have competitive cost structures. Actions taken to create cost efficiencies require an understanding of the drivers, or underlying causes, of costs and not merely recognition of cost predictors. Chapter 3 discusses computation of predetermined overhead (OH) rates using what are typically considered traditional activity bases: direct labor costs, direct labor hours, and machine hours. However, many alternative activity bases are available that can improve management information and enhance the competitive advantage of an organization.

This chapter discusses activity-based management and activity-based costing. Activity-based management (ABM) focuses on controlling production or performance activities to improve customer value and enhance profitability. Activity-based costing (ABC) is a cost accounting system that focuses on an organization's activities and collects costs on the basis of the underlying nature and extent of those activities. Multiple predetermined OH rates are then calculated using the various cost drivers of organizational activities.

Activity-Based Management

Although specifically designated as an accounting function, determination of product cost is of major concern for all managers. The profitability of a particular product or market, product pricing policies, and investments to support production are issues that extend beyond accounting to the areas of corporate strategy, marketing, and finance. In theory, the cost to produce a product or to perform a service would not matter if enough customers were willing to buy that product or service at a price high enough to cover its cost and provide a reasonable profit margin. In reality, customers purchase a product or service only if they perceive an acceptable value for the price.

Management, then, should be concerned about an equitable relationship between selling price and value. Activity-based management includes a variety of topics, as is shown in Exhibit 4–1. These concepts help companies to produce more efficiently, determine costs more accurately, and control and evaluate performance more effectively. A primary component of activity-based management is activity analysis, which is the process of studying activities both to classify them and to devise ways of minimizing or eliminating non-value-added activities.

Value-Added versus Non-Value-Added Activities

LO.1
What are value-added and non-value-added activities?

In a business context, an activity is defined as a repetitive action performed in fulfillment of business functions. If one takes a black-or-white perspective, activities are either value-added (VA) or non-value-added (NVA). A value-added activity increases the worth of a product or service to a customer and is one for which the customer is willing to pay. Alternatively, a non-value-added activity increases the time spent on a product or service but does not increase its worth. Non-value-added activities are unnecessary from the customer's perspective. Therefore, NVA activities can be reduced, redesigned, or eliminated without affecting the product's or service's market value or quality. Often an easy way to determine the value provided by an activity is to ask "why" five times: if the answers represent valid business reasons, the activity generally adds value; otherwise, it adds no value. For example, one necessary step in making a pizza crust is to mix flour and water, but storing flour until it is needed would be considered unnecessary as indicated by the following manager–employee "conversation."

- Why are we storing flour? Because it was acquired before it was actually needed.
- Why was it acquired prior to use? Because the flour was acquired in a bulk shipment.
- Why was the flour bought in bulk? Because flour is cheaper that way.
- Why is it cheaper if buying in bulk creates costs for storing and moving the flour as well as possible costs of spilling or spoilage of the flour? Hmmm; that thought never occurred to me; maybe there's a better way. (In this case, the "why" questions never made it past four times!)

EXHIBIT 4–1

Components of Activity-Based Management

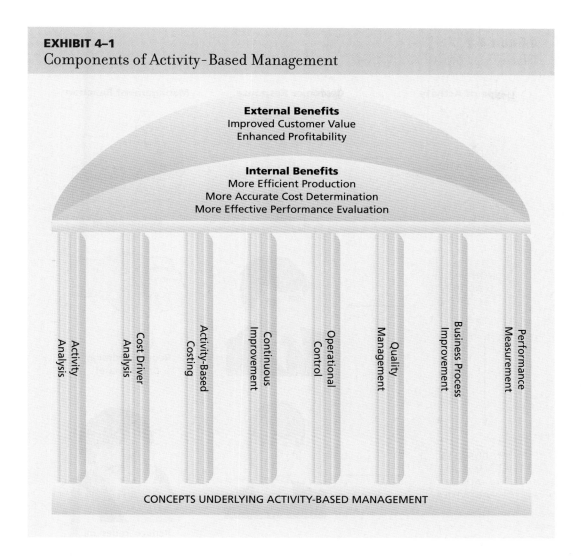

External Benefits
Improved Customer Value
Enhanced Profitability

Internal Benefits
More Efficient Production
More Accurate Cost Determination
More Effective Performance Evaluation

- Activity Analysis
- Cost Driver Analysis
- Activity-Based Costing
- Continuous Improvement
- Operational Control
- Quality Management
- Business Process Improvement
- Performance Measurement

CONCEPTS UNDERLYING ACTIVITY-BASED MANAGEMENT

Businesses can also engage in some activities that are essential (or appear to be essential) to business operations but for which customers would not willingly choose to pay (refer to Exhibit 4–2). These activities are known as **business-value-added activities**. For instance, companies must prepare invoices for documenting sales and collections. Customers realize this activity must occur, that it creates costs, and that product selling prices must be set to cover the costs of this activity. However, because invoice preparation adds no direct value to products and services, customers would prefer not to pay for this activity through a higher selling price.

From a management perspective, the cost of making products or performing services must be determined so that the company can charge a satisfactory price for the items and produce profits. Activities drive the consumption of resources, and, in turn, resource consumption drives costs. Because most prices are set by the marketplace rather than by individual companies based on their costs, companies that reduce or eliminate NVA activities can obtain a larger profit margin when selling at market price than those companies with higher costs. Additionally, if a company can reduce the "going" market price because costs have declined, it might be able to increase its market share.

To begin activity analysis, managers should first identify organizational processes. A **process** is a series of activities that, when performed together, satisfy a specific objective. Companies engage in processes for production, distribution, selling, administration, and other company functions. Processes should be defined before a company tries to determine relationships among activities. Most processes occur horizontally across organizational functions and, thus, overlap multiple functional

EXHIBIT 4–2
Classifications of Activities

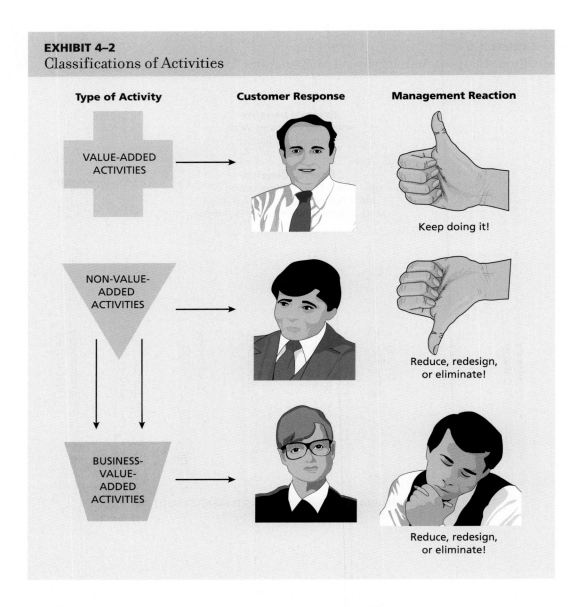

Type of Activity	Customer Response	Management Reaction

VALUE-ADDED ACTIVITIES → (smiling man) → (thumbs up) Keep doing it!

NON-VALUE-ADDED ACTIVITIES → (frowning man) → (thumbs down) Reduce, redesign, or eliminate!

BUSINESS-VALUE-ADDED ACTIVITIES → (person with glasses) → (thinking man) Reduce, redesign, or eliminate!

areas. For example, a production process also affects engineering, purchasing, receiving, warehousing, accounting, human resources, and marketing. Exhibit 4–3, which does not include the sales process for the product, provides a depiction of why a process should be defined in a more limited manner than "production."

For each distinct process, a **process map** (or detailed flowchart) should be prepared to indicate *every* step in *every* area that goes into making or doing something. Some of the steps included on the process map are necessary and, therefore, *must* be performed for the process to be completed. Other steps are those activities for which a valid business answer to the question of "why" cannot be found and, as such, are unnecessary.

After a process map has been developed, a **value chart** can be constructed to identify the stages and time spent in those stages from the beginning to the end of a process. Time is usually classified in four ways. The actual time that it takes to perform all *necessary* functions to manufacture the product or to perform the service is called the **processing (service) time**; this time adds value. Performing quality control other than what is internal to the process results in **inspection time**; moving products or components from one place to another constitutes **transfer time**. Storage time and time spent waiting at a production operation for processing are considered **idle time**. Inspection time, transfer time, and idle time add no value. Thus, the **cycle (lead) time** from the receipt to completion of an

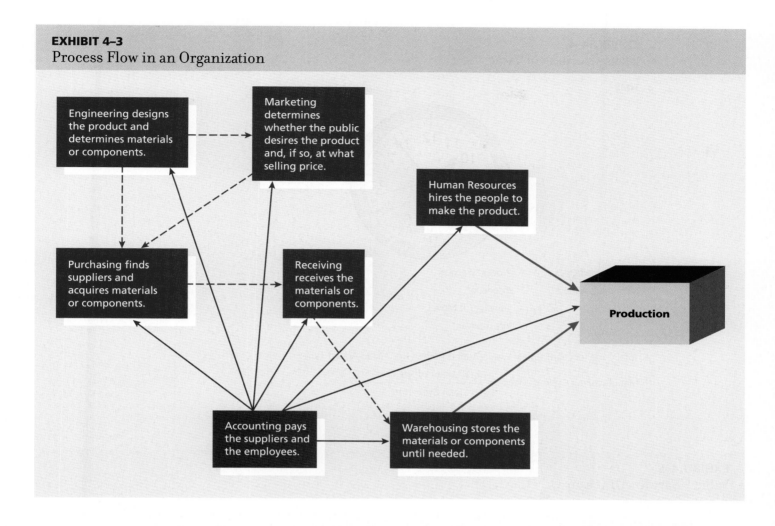

EXHIBIT 4–3
Process Flow in an Organization

order for a product or service is equal to value-added processing time plus non-value-added time. Time concepts are illustrated in Exhibit 4–4.

Although viewing inspection time and transfer time as non-value-added activities is theoretically correct, few companies can completely eliminate all quality control functions and all transfer time. Understanding the NVA nature of these functions, however, should help managers strive to minimize such activities to the extent possible. Thus, companies should view VA and NVA activities as occurring on a continuum and strive to eliminate or minimize those activities that add the most time and cost *and* the least value.

Exhibit 4–5 provides a value chart for a chemical produced by Dinosaur Oil. Note the excessive time consumed by storing and moving materials. Value is added to products only when production actually occurs; thus, Dinosaur Oil's entire production sequence has only 11 days of VA time.

Packaging may be a VA activity for some companies and a NVA activity for others. Some products, such as liquids, require packaging; other products need little or no packaging. Because packaging takes up about a third of the U.S. landfills and creates a substantial amount of cost, companies and consumers are beginning to focus their attention on reducing or eliminating packaging. For instance, in 2006, Wal-Mart announced that in 2008 it planned to begin using a "packaging scorecard" to measure its suppliers on their ability to develop more environmentally friendly packaging and reduce overall packaging by 5 percent.[1]

---

[1] This initiative is expected to prevent millions of pounds of trash from reaching landfills and 667,000 metric tons of CO_2 from entering the atmosphere—the equivalent of taking 213,000 trucks off the road annually and saving 323,800 tons of coal and 66.7 million gallons of diesel fuel from being burned. (Source: http://www.walmartstores.com/GlobalWMStoresWeb/navigate.do?catg=667; last accessed 6/3/07.)

EXHIBIT 4–4
Classifications of Time

TIME

Value-Added:	Process (Service)
Non-Value-Added:	Inspection
	Transfer (or Move)
	Idle (or Wait)

Total Cycle (or Lead) Time = Value-Added Time + Non-Value-Added Time

$$\text{Manufacturing Cycle Efficiency} = \frac{\text{Total Value-Added Time}}{\text{Total Cycle Time}}$$

EXHIBIT 4–5
Value Chart for Dinosaur Oil

Assembling

Operations	Receiving	Quality control	Storage	Move to production	Waiting for use	Setup of machinery	Assembly	Move to inspection	Move to finishing
Average time (days)	4	2	20–30	1	6	1	6	1	1

Finishing

Operations	Receiving	Move to production	Waiting for use	Setup of machinery	Finishing	Inspection	Packaging	Move to dockside	Storage	Ship to customer
Average time (days)	1	1	10–24	1	4	1	1	1	3	2–8

Total time in Assembling:	42 – 52 days	Assembling value-added time:	6 days	
Total time in Finishing:	25 – 45 days	Finishing value-added time:	5 days	
Total processing time:	67 – 97 days	**Total value-added time:**	**11 days**	
Total value-added time:	11 – 11 days			
Total non-value-added time:	**56 – 86 days**			

Non-value-added activities ▮

Value-added activities ▮

Manufacturing Cycle Efficiency

Dividing total value-added processing time by total cycle time results in a measurement referred to as manufacturing cycle efficiency (MCE). (A service company would compute service cycle efficiency by dividing total actual service time by total cycle time.) Using the information from Exhibit 4–5, Dinosaur Oil's MCE is 16 percent ($11 \div 67$) if the company operates with the least amount of NVA time or 11 percent ($11 \div 97$) if it operates with the greatest amount of NVA time.

Although 100 percent efficiency can never be achieved, most production processes add value to products only approximately 10 percent of the time from the receipt of the raw material until shipment to the customer. In other words, about 90 percent of manufacturing cycle time is wasted time. But products act like magnets in regard to costs: the longer the cycle time, the more time the product has to "pull" costs to it.

A just-in-time (JIT) manufacturing process (discussed in detail in Chapter 18) seeks to achieve substantially higher efficiency by producing components and goods at the precise time they are needed by either the next production station or the consumer. Thus, the use of JIT eliminates a significant amount of idle time (especially in storage) and increases manufacturing cycle efficiency. JIT also often relies on the use of automated technologies, such as flexible manufacturing systems, which reduce processing time and increase MCE.

In a retail environment, cycle time relates to the length of time from ordering to selling an item. NVA activities in retail include shipping time from the supplier, delays occurring in the Receiving Department in order to count the merchandise, and any storage time between receipt and sale. In a service company, cycle time refers to the time between service order and service completion. All time spent on activities that are not actual service performance or are "non-activities" (such as delays in beginning a job) are considered NVA activities for that job.

Non-value-added activities can be attributed to systemic, physical, and human factors. For example, a systemic cause is the need to manufacture products in large batches to minimize setup cost or the need to respond to service jobs in order of urgency. Physical factors often contribute to NVA activities because the plant and machine layout do not provide the most efficient transfer of products. This factor is especially apparent in multistory buildings in which receiving and shipping are on the ground floor but storage and production are on upper floors. NVA activities are also caused by people who have improper skills, received inadequate training, or have the need to socialize during work.

Attempts to reduce NVA activities should be directed at all of these causes, but it is imperative that the "Willie Sutton" rule be applied. This rule is named for the bank robber who, when asked why he robbed banks, reportedly replied, "Because that's where the money is." The NVA activities that create the highest costs should be the ones on which management concentrates its efforts to reduce or eliminate. Systemic factors must be modified to reflect a new management philosophy regarding performance measures and determination of product cost. Physical layout must be changed to improve product flow and alleviate machine bottlenecks, and managers must convince employees to accept responsibility for their work and strive for total quality control. Focusing attention on eliminating NVA activities should cause product/service quality to increase and cycle time and cost to decrease.

Constructing a value chart for every product or service would be extremely time consuming, but a few such charts can quickly indicate where a company is losing time and money through NVA activities. The cost of such activities can be approximated by using estimates for storage facility depreciation, property taxes and insurance charges, wages for employees who handle warehousing, and the cost of capital on working capital funds tied up in stored inventory. Multiplying these cost estimates by times shown in the value chart will indicate the amount by which costs could be reduced by eliminating NVA activities.

Cost-Driver Analysis

Companies engage in many activities that consume resources and cause costs to be incurred. All activities have cost drivers, defined in Chapter 2 as the factors that have direct cause-and-effect relationships to a cost. Many cost drivers can be identified for an individual business unit. For

LO.2
How do value-added and non-value-added activities affect manufacturing cycle efficiency?

example, cost drivers for factory insurance are number of employees; value of property, plant, and equipment; and number of accidents or claims during a specified time period. Cost drivers affecting the entire plant include inventory size, physical layout, and number of different products produced. Cost drivers are classified as either volume-related (such as machine hours) or non-volume-related (such as setups, work orders, or distance traveled), which generally reflect the incurrence of specific transactions.

More cost drivers can generally be identified for a given activity than should be used for cost accumulation or activity elimination. Management should limit the cost drivers selected to a reasonable number and make certain that the cost of measuring a driver does not exceed the benefit of using it. A cost driver should be easy to understand, directly related to the activity being performed, and appropriate for performance measurement. For example, Exhibit 4–6 shows six possible cost drivers for shipping cost, but the one that is the easiest to track and measure is the distance of the trip.

Costs have traditionally been accumulated into one or two groups of costs (generally known as pools), such as total factory overhead or variable factory overhead and fixed factory overhead. These pooled costs have then been assigned to products or services using one or two drivers, such as direct labor hours and/or machine hours. Such a procedure causes few, if any, problems for financial statement preparation. However, the use of a minimal number of cost pools or drivers can produce illogical product or service costs for internal managerial use in complex production (or service) environments.

EXHIBIT 4–6
Potential Cost Drivers for Shipping Cost

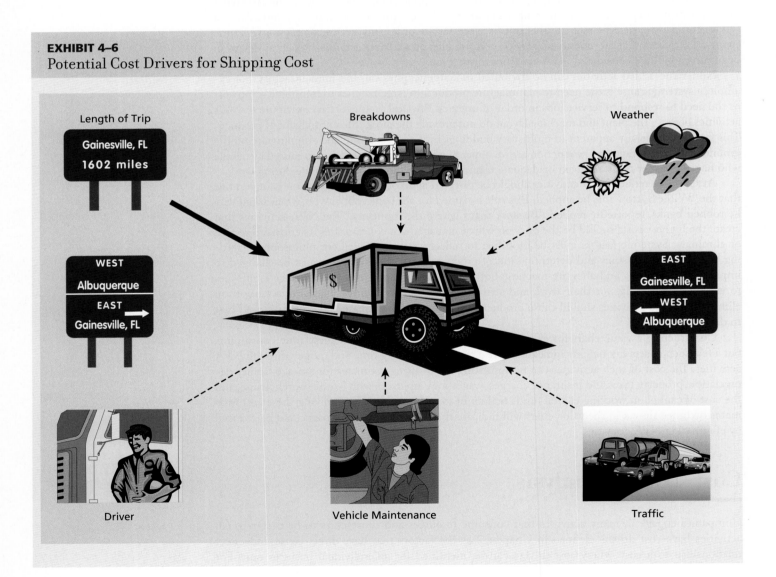

Exhibit 4–7 indicates how cost driver analysis is combined with activity analysis to create a tool for managing costs. Cost driver analysis identifies the activities causing costs to be incurred; activity analysis highlights the activities that do not add value and, as such, can be targeted for elimination to reduce costs and increase profitability. This combined information provides the basis for management's decisions for improving the process and increasing profitability.

To reflect more complex environments, the accounting system must first recognize that costs are created and incurred because their drivers occur at different levels.[2] This realization necessitates using cost driver analysis, which investigates, quantifies, and explains the relationships of drivers to their related costs. Traditionally, cost drivers were viewed as existing only at the unit level; for example, labor hours or machine time expended to produce a product or render a service. These unit-level costs are caused by the production or acquisition of a single unit of product or the delivery of a single unit of service. Other drivers and their costs are incurred for broader-based categories or levels of activity. These broader-based activity levels have successively wider scopes of influence on products and product types. The levels are batch, product or process, and organizational or facility. Exhibit 4–8 provides examples of the types of costs that occur at the various levels.

Costs that are caused by a group of things being made, handled, or processed at a single time are referred to as batch-level costs. An example of a batch-level cost is the cost of machine setup. Assume that to prepare a machine to cast product parts costs $900. Two different part types are to be manufactured during the day; therefore, two setups will be needed at a total cost of $1,800. After the first setup, production will generate 3,000 Type A parts; the machine will then be reset to generate 600 Type B parts. These specific numbers of parts are needed for production because the company is on a just-in-time production system. As the following calculations show, the cost per unit depends on whether setup costs are considered unit-level or batch-level costs.

LO.3
Why must cost drivers be designated in an activity-based costing system?

2 setups × $900 per setup = $1,800 total setup cost

	Unit-level Cost Assignment $1,800 ÷ 3,600 = $0.50			Batch-level Cost Assignment			
	# of Parts	Cost per Part	Cost Assignment	Cost per Batch	# of Parts in Batch	Cost per Part	Cost Assignment
Type A Parts	3,000	$0.50	$1,500	$ 900	3,000	$0.30	$ 900
Type B Parts	600	$0.50	300	900	600	1.50	900
Total	3,600		$1,800	$1,800			$1,800

EXHIBIT 4–7
Activity-Based Data and Cost Management

Benchmark: How do we do against competitors?

Activity analysis: How can we get better?

Pricing analysis: How much will the customer or end consumer pay?

Accumulated costs

Cost drivers

Source: Adapted from Michael Gering, "Activity-Based Costing and Performance Improvement," *Management Accounting* (London) (March 1999), p. 25. Reprinted with permission.

[2]This hierarchy of costs was introduced by Robin Cooper in "Cost Classification in Unit-Based and Activity-Based Manufacturing Cost Systems," *Journal of Cost Management* (Fall 1990), p. 6.

EXHIBIT 4–8
Levels of Costs

Classification Levels	Types of Costs	Necessity of Cost
Unit-Level Costs	■ Direct material ■ Direct labor ■ Some machine costs, if traceable	Incur once for each unit produced
Batch-Level Costs	■ Purchase orders ■ Setup ■ Inspection ■ Movement ■ Scrap, if related to the batch	Incur once for each batch produced
Product/Process-Level Costs	■ Engineering change orders ■ Equipment maintenance ■ Product development ■ Scrap, if related to product design	Support a product type or a process
Organizational/Facility-Level Costs	■ Building depreciation ■ Plant or division manager's salary ■ Organizational advertising	Support the overall production or service process

The unit-level method assigns the majority of setup cost to Type A parts. However, because setup cost is actually created by a batch-level driver, the batch-level cost assignments are more appropriate. The batch-level perspective shows the commonality of the cost to the parts within the batch and is more indicative of the relationship between the activity (setup) and the driver (different production runs).

A cost caused by the development, production, or acquisition of different items is called a *product-level (process-level) cost*. To illustrate this cost, assume that the engineering department of Dinosaur Oil issued five engineering change orders (ECOs) during May. Of these ECOs, four relate to Product R, one relates to Product S, and none relates to Product T. Each ECO costs $6,000 to issue. During May, the company produced a total of 7,500 units of product: 1,000 units of Product R, 1,500 units of Product S, and 5,000 units of Product T. If ECO costs are treated as unit-level costs, the following allocations would occur:

5 ECOs × $6,000 per ECO = $30,000 total ECO cost

	Unit-level Cost Assignment			Product-level Cost Assignment		
		$30,000 ÷ 7,500 = $4.00				
	# of Units	Cost per Unit	Cost Assignment	# of ECOs	Cost per ECO	Cost Assignment
Product R	1,000	$4.00	$ 4,000	4	$6,000	$24,000
Product S	1,500	$4.00	6,000	1	$6,000	6,000
Product T	5,000	$4.00	20,000	0		0
Total	7,500		$30,000	5		$30,000

Note that the unit-level method inappropriately assigns $20,000 of ECO cost to Product T, which had no ECOs issued for it! Using a product- or process-level driver (number of ECOs) for ECO costs would assign $24,000 of costs to Product R and $6,000 to Product S, but these costs do not attach solely to the current month's production. The product-level ECO cost should be allocated to all the Product R and Product S units that are manufactured while these ECOs are in effect because all similar products manufactured using the changed design benefit from the ECOs. Thus, because future production of Products R and S is unknown at the end of May, no per-unit cost is shown in the product-level cost assignment table. If management believes it is necessary to assign such costs, estimates can be made about future production levels. Using estimates is common in accounting, and, if the estimates are reasonable, no significant product cost distortions should arise for either internal or external reporting.

Certain costs, called organizational-level costs, are incurred for the sole purpose of supporting facility operations. Such costs are common to many different activities and products or services and can be prorated to products only on an arbitrary basis. Although organizational-level costs should theoretically not be assigned to products at all, some companies attach them to goods produced or services rendered because the amounts are insignificant relative to all other costs.

Accountants have traditionally (and incorrectly) assumed that when costs did not vary with changes in production at the unit level, those costs were fixed rather than variable. In reality, batch, product/process, and organizational level costs are all variable, but they vary for reasons other than changes in production volume. Therefore, to determine a valid estimate of product or service cost, costs should be accumulated by cost level. Because unit, batch, and product/process level costs are all associated with units of products or services (merely at different levels), these costs can be summed at the product/service level to match with the revenues generated by product sales. Organizational-level costs are not product-related, so they should be subtracted only in total from net product revenues.

Exhibit 4–9 illustrates how costs collected at the unit, batch, and product/process levels can be aggregated to estimate a total product cost. Each product cost is multiplied by the number of units sold, and that amount of cost of goods sold is subtracted from total product revenues to obtain a product line profit or loss amount. These computations would be performed for each product line and summed to determine net product income or loss from which the unassigned organizational-level costs would be subtracted to find company profit or loss for internal management use. In this model, the traditional distinction between product and period costs (discussed in Chapter 2) can be and is ignored. The emphasis is on modifying product profitability analysis for a focus on internal management purposes rather than on external reporting. Because the approach in Exhibit 4–9 ignores the product/period cost distinction required by generally accepted accounting principles (GAAP), it is not currently acceptable for external reporting.

Data for Wainwright Manufacturing are presented in Exhibit 4–10 to illustrate the difference in information that would result from recognizing multiple cost levels. Prior to recognizing that some costs were incurred at the batch, product, and organizational levels, Wainwright Manufacturing accumulated and allocated its factory overhead costs among its three products (C, D, and E) on a machine-hour basis. Each product requires one machine hour, but Product D is a low-volume, special-order line. In the first section of Exhibit 4–10, cost information indicates that all three products are profitable for Wainwright Manufacturing to produce and sell. After analyzing company activities, Wainwright's cost accountant began capturing costs at the different levels and assigning them to products based on appropriate cost drivers. The individual details for this overhead assignment are not shown, but the final assignments and resulting product profitability figures are presented in the second section of Exhibit 4–10. This more refined approach to assigning costs shows that Product D is actually unprofitable for the company to produce.

Costs are incurred because firms engage in activities that consume resources. Accountants have traditionally accumulated costs as transactions occurred and thus focused on the cost's amount rather than its source. However, this lack of consideration for underlying causes of costs has often resulted in both a lack of ability to control costs and flawed product cost data. Traditional cost allocations tend to subsidize low-volume specialty products by misallocating overhead to high-volume, standard products. This problem occurs because costs of the extra activities needed to make specialty products are assigned using the one or very few drivers of traditional costing—and usually these drivers are volume based. Interestingly, in 1954, Professor William J. Vatter noted that when cost accounting

EXHIBIT 4–9
Determining Product Profitability and Company Profit

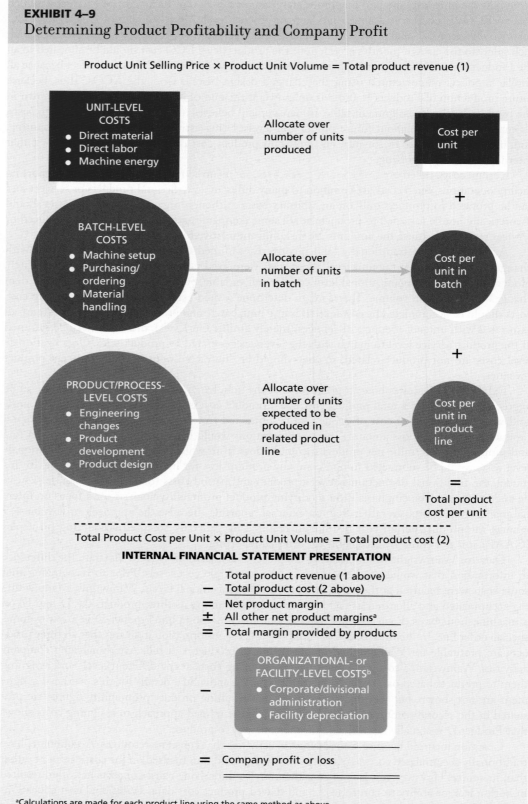

Product Unit Selling Price × Product Unit Volume = Total product revenue (1)

UNIT-LEVEL COSTS
- Direct material
- Direct labor
- Machine energy

Allocate over number of units produced

Cost per unit

+

BATCH-LEVEL COSTS
- Machine setup
- Purchasing/ordering
- Material handling

Allocate over number of units in batch

Cost per unit in batch

+

PRODUCT/PROCESS-LEVEL COSTS
- Engineering changes
- Product development
- Product design

Allocate over number of units expected to be produced in related product line

Cost per unit in product line

=

Total product cost per unit

Total Product Cost per Unit × Product Unit Volume = Total product cost (2)

INTERNAL FINANCIAL STATEMENT PRESENTATION

Total product revenue (1 above)
− Total product cost (2 above)
= Net product margin
± All other net product margins[a]
= Total margin provided by products

− **ORGANIZATIONAL- or FACILITY-LEVEL COSTS[b]**
- Corporate/divisional administration
- Facility depreciation

= Company profit or loss

[a]Calculations are made for each product line using the same method as above.
[b]Some of these costs could be assignable to specific products or services and would be included in determining product cost per unit.

EXHIBIT 4–10

Wainwright Manufacturing Product Profitability Analysis

Total overhead cost = $1,505,250

Total machine hours = 111,500

Overhead rate per machine hour = $13.50

	Product C (5,000 Units)		Product D (1,500 Units)		Product E (105,000 Units)		
	Unit	**Total**	**Unit**	**Total**	**Unit**	**Total**	**Total**
Product revenue	$50.00	$250,000	$45.00	$67,500	$40.00	$4,200,000	$4,517,500
Product costs							
Direct	$20.00	$100,000	$20.00	$30,000	$ 9.00	$ 945,000	
Overhead	13.50	67,500	13.50	20,250	13.50	1,417,500	
Total	$33.50	$167,500	$33.50	$50,250	$22.50	$2,362,500	(2,580,250)
Net income		$ 82,500		$17,250		$1,837,500	$1,937,250

	Product C (5,000 Units)		Product D (1,500 Units)		Product E (105,000 Units)		
	Unit	**Total**	**Unit**	**Total**	**Unit**	**Total**	**Total**
Product revenue	$50	$250,000	$45	$ 67,500	$40	$4,200,000	$4,517,500
Product costs							
Direct	$20	$100,000	$20	$ 30,000	$ 9	$ 945,000	
Overhead							
Unit level	8	40,000	12	18,000	6	630,000	
Batch level	9	45,000	19	28,500	3	315,000	
Product level	3	15,000	15	22,500	2	210,000	
Total	$40	$200,000	$66	$ 99,000	$20	$2,100,000	(2,399,000)
Product line income or (loss)		$ 50,000		$(31,500)		$2,100,000	$2,118,500
Organizational-level costs							(181,250)
Net income							$1,937,250

could no longer fulfill the management information needs it was developed to meet, either it would have to change or it would be replaced with something else.[3] The time may have come for cost accounting to change by adopting new bases on which to collect and assign costs. Those bases are the activities that drive or create the costs.

Activity-Based Costing

LO.4
How are costs computed using an activity-based costing system?

Recognizing that costs are incurred at different organizational levels, accumulating costs into related cost pools, and using multiple cost drivers to assign costs to products and services are the three fundamental components of activity-based costing. ABC focuses on attaching costs to products and services based on the activities conducted to produce, perform, distribute, and support those products and services.

[3]William J. Vatter, "Tailor-Making Cost Data for Specific Uses," in L. S. Rosen, ed., *Topics in Managerial Accounting* (Toronto: McGraw-Hill Ryerson Ltd., 1954), p. 194.

Managers in many manufacturing companies are concerned about the product costing information being provided by traditional cost accounting systems. Although such product costs are reasonable for use in preparing financial statements, they often have limited value for management decision making and cost control—the latter being the "top concern" of almost 72 percent of managers participating in a 2005 survey by *Industry Week* magazine.[4] On the other hand, companies that have the following characteristics might want to reevaluate their cost systems and implement activity-based costing:

- production or performance of a wide variety of products or services;
- high overhead costs that are not proportional to the unit volume of individual products;
- significant automation that has made it increasingly difficult to assign overhead to products using the traditional direct labor or machine-hour bases;
- profit margins that are difficult to explain; and/or
- difficult-to-make products that show big profits and easy-to-make products that show losses.[5]

Two-Step Allocation

After being recorded in the general ledger and subledger accounts, costs in an ABC system are accumulated in activity center cost pools. An activity center is any segment of the production or service process for which management wants a separate reporting of costs. In defining these centers, management should consider the following issues: geographical proximity of equipment, defined centers of managerial responsibility, magnitude of product costs, and the need to keep the number of activity centers manageable. Costs having the same driver are accumulated in pools reflecting the appropriate level of cost incurrence (unit, batch, or product/process). The fact that a relationship exists between a cost pool and a cost driver indicates that if the cost driver can be reduced or eliminated, the related cost should also be reduced or eliminated.

Gathering costs in pools having the same cost drivers allows managers to view an organization's activities cross-functionally. Some companies not using an ABC system accumulate overhead in departmental, rather than plantwide, cost pools, reflecting a vertical-function approach to cost accumulation, but production and service activities are horizontal by nature. A product or service flows through an organization, affecting numerous departments as it goes. Using a cost driver approach to develop cost pools allows managers to more clearly focus on the various cost impacts created in making a product or performing a service than was traditionally possible.

After accumulation, costs are allocated out of the activity center cost pools and assigned to products and services by use of a second type of driver. An activity driver measures the demands placed on activities and, thus, the resources consumed by products and services. An activity driver often indicates an activity's output. The process of cost assignment is the same as the overhead application process illustrated in Chapter 3. Exhibit 4–11 illustrates this two-step allocation process of tracing costs to products and services in an ABC system.

As illustrated in Exhibit 4–11, the cost drivers for the collection stage can differ from the activity drivers used for the allocation stage because some activity center costs are not traceable to lower levels of activity. Costs at the lowest (unit) level of activity should be allocated to products by use of volume- or unit-based drivers. Costs incurred at higher (batch and product/process) levels can also be allocated to products by use of volume-related drivers, but the volume measure should include only those units associated with the batch or the product/process—not with total production or service volume. Exhibit 4–12 provides some common drivers for various activity centers.

Three significant cost drivers that have traditionally been disregarded are related to variety and complexity. Product variety refers to the number of different types of products made; product complexity refers to the number of components included in a product; process complexity refers to the number of processes through which a product flows. These characteristics create additional overhead costs for activities such as warehousing, purchasing, setups, and inspections—all of which can be seen as long-term variable costs because they will increase as the number and types of products increase. Therefore, accountants should consider using items such as number of product types, number of components, and number of necessary processes as the cost drivers for applying ABC.

---

[4]Tonya Vinas, Jill Jusko, and Bruce Vernyi, "A Map of the World," *Industry Week* (September 2005), pp. 27ff.
[5]Robin Cooper, "You Need a New Cost System When...," *Harvard Business Review* (January–February 1989), pp. 77–82.

EXHIBIT 4–11
Tracing Costs in an Activity-Based Costing System

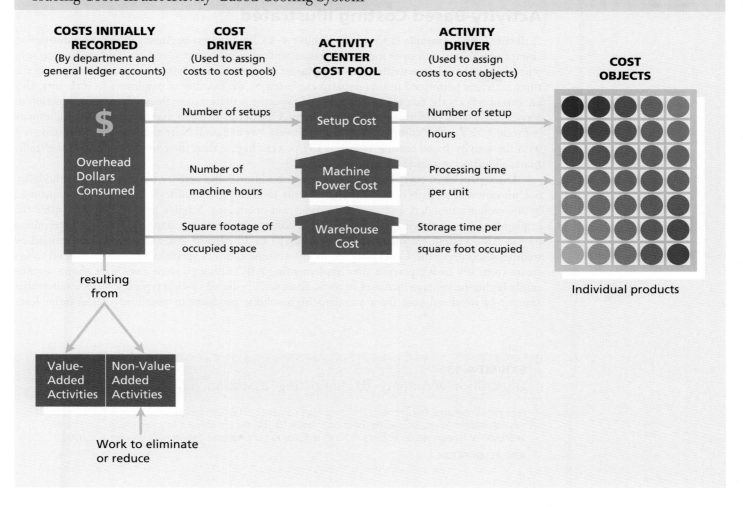

| COSTS INITIALLY RECORDED (By department and general ledger accounts) | COST DRIVER (Used to assign costs to cost pools) | ACTIVITY CENTER COST POOL | ACTIVITY DRIVER (Used to assign costs to cost objects) | COST OBJECTS |

$
Overhead Dollars Consumed

Number of setups → Setup Cost → Number of setup hours

Number of machine hours → Machine Power Cost → Processing time per unit

Square footage of occupied space → Warehouse Cost → Storage time per square foot occupied

Individual products

resulting from

Value-Added Activities | Non-Value-Added Activities

Work to eliminate or reduce

EXHIBIT 4–12
Activity Drivers

Activity Center	Activity Drivers
Accounting	Reports requested; dollars expended
Human resources	Job change actions; hiring actions; training hours; counseling hours
Data processing	Reports requested; transactions processed; programming hours; program change requests
Production engineering	Hours spent in each shop; job specification changes requested; product change notices processed
Quality control	Hours spent in each shop; defects discovered; samples analyzed
Plant services	Preventive maintenance cycles; hours spent in each shop; repair and maintenance actions
Material services	Dollar value of requisitions; number of transactions processed; number of personnel in direct support
Utilities	Direct usage (metered to shop); space occupied
Production shops	Fixed per-job charge; setups made; direct labor; machine hours; number of moves; material applied

Source: Michael D. Woods, "Completing the Picture: Economic Choices with ABC," *Management Accounting* (December 1992), p. 54. Reprinted from *Management Accounting*. Copyright by Institute of Management Accountants, Montvale, N.J.

Activity-Based Costing Illustrated

A detailed ABC example is shown in Exhibit 4–13. The process begins by gathering information about the activities and costs for a factory maintenance department. Costs are then assigned to specific products based on activities. This department allocates its total human resources cost among the three activities performed in that department based on the number of employees in each area. This allocation reflects the fact that occurrences of a specific activity, rather than volume of production or service, drive work performed in the department. One of the products manufactured by the company is Product Z, a rather complex unit with relatively low demand. Note that the cost allocated to it with the activity-based costing system is 132 percent higher than the cost allocated with the traditional allocation system ($1.564 vs. $0.675)!

Discrepancies in cost assignments between traditional and activity-based costing methods are not uncommon. Activity-based costing systems indicate that significant resources are consumed by low-volume products and complex production operations. Studies have shown that, after the implementation of activity-based costing, the costs of high-volume standard products determined by the ABC system are often anywhere from 10 to 30 percent lower than costs determined by traditional cost systems. Costs assigned to low-volume complex specialty product costs tend to increase from 100 to 500 percent after implementing ABC, although some cases have shown significantly higher percentage increases in costs. Thus, activity-based costing typically shifts a substantial amount of overhead cost from standard high-volume products to premium special-order low-

EXHIBIT 4–13
Illustration of Activity-Based Costing Allocation

Factory Maintenance Department: The company's conventional system assigns the human resources costs of this department to products using direct labor hours (DLHs); the department has 9 employees and incurred $450,000 of human resources costs in 2008 or $50,000 per employee. Expected DLHs were 200,000.

ABC ALLOCATION

Stage 1
Trace costs from general ledger and subsidiary ledger accounts to activity center pools according to number of employees:

- Regular maintenance—uses 5 employees; $250,000 is allocated to this activity; second-stage allocation to be based on machine hours (MHs)
- Preventive maintenance—uses 2 employees; $100,000 is allocated to this activity; second-stage allocation to be based on number of setups
- Repairs—uses 2 employees; $100,000 is allocated to this activity; second-stage allocation is based on number of machine starts

Stage 2
Allocate activity center cost pools to products using cost drivers chosen for each cost pool.
2008 activity of second-stage drivers: 500,000 MHs; 5,000 setups; 100,000 machine starts

Step 1:   Allocate costs per unit of activity of second-stage cost drivers.

- Regular maintenance—$250,000 ÷ 500,000 MHs = $0.50 per MH
- Preventive maintenance—$100,000 ÷ 5,000 setups = $20 per setup
- Repairs—$100,000 ÷ 100,000 machine starts = $1 per machine start

Step 2:   Allocate costs to products using quantity of second-stage cost drivers consumed in making these products. The following quantities of activity are relevant to Product Z: 30,000 MHs; 30 setups; 40 machine starts; and 3,000 DLHs out of a total of 200,000 DLHs in 2008. Ten thousand units of Product Z were manufactured during 2008.

ABC Allocation to Product Z = (30,000 × $0.50) + (30 × $20) + (40 × $1) = $15,640 for 10,000 units, or $1.564 per unit

Traditional Allocation to Product Z = $450,000 ÷ 200,000 DLHs = $2.25 per DLH; (3,000 × $2.25) = $6,750 for 10,000 units, or $0.675 per unit volume products, as shown in Exhibit 4–14. The ABC costs of moderately complex products and services (those that are neither extremely simple nor complex nor produced in extremely low or high volumes) tend to remain approximately the same as the costs calculated using traditional costing methods.

Although the preceding discussion addresses costs normally considered product costs, activity-based costing is just as applicable to selling and administrative department costs. Many companies use an activity-based costing system to allocate corporate overhead costs to their revenue-producing units based on the number of reports, documents, customers, or other reasonable measures of activity.

Determining Whether ABC Is Useful

LO.5
How can the information generated from an activity-based management or activity-based costing system be used by management?

Although not every accounting system using direct labor or machine hours to assign overhead costs produces inaccurate cost information, a great deal of information can be lost in the accounting systems of companies that ignore activity and cost relationships. Some general indicators can alert managers to the need to review the relevance of the cost information their system is providing. Several of these indicators are more relevant to manufacturing entities, whereas others are equally appropriate to both manufacturing and service businesses. Factors to consider include the:

- number and diversity of products or services produced,
- diversity and differential degree of support services used for different products,
- extent to which common processes are used,

EXHIBIT 4–14
Traditional versus ABC Overhead Allocations

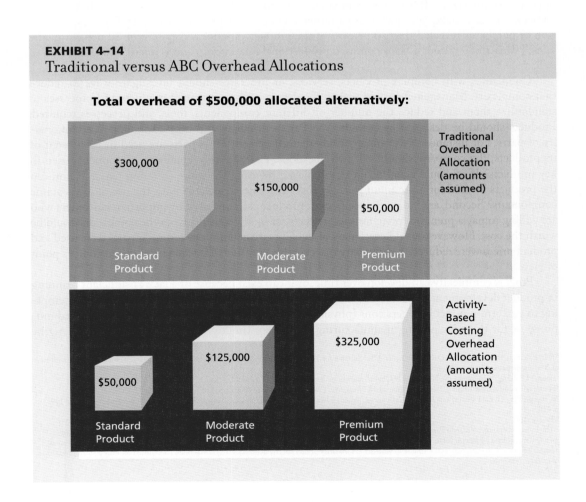

■ effectiveness of current cost allocation methods, and

■ rate of growth of period costs.[6]

Additionally, if ABC is implemented, the new information will change management decisions only if management is free to set product/service prices, there are no strategic constraints in the company, and the company has developed a culture of cost reduction. The following circumstances could indicate the need to consider using ABC.

LO.6
Under what conditions
is activity-based costing
useful in an organization?

Large Product Variety and High Product Complexity

Product variety is commonly associated with the need to consider activity-based costing. Whether products are variations of the same product line (such as Hallmark's different types of greeting cards) or whether products are in numerous product families (such as Procter & Gamble's detergents, diapers, fabric softeners, and shampoos), adding products causes numerous overhead costs to increase. Consider, for example, that one food-products manufacturer experienced an increase in the number of stock-keeping units (SKUs) in a single product line from 40 to more than 800.[7]

In the quest for product variety, many companies are striving for mass customization of products through the use of flexible manufacturing systems. Such personalized production can often be conducted at a relatively low cost. For example, Selve, a European manufacturer of women's shoes, lets customers create their own shoes from various materials and designs and "offers a true custom fit based on a 3-D scan of customers' feet. All shoes are made-to-order in Italy, delivered in about three weeks, and cost $180 to $285."[8] Although such customization can please some customers, it has some drawbacks. First, there could be too many choices. For instance, at one time, Nissan reportedly had 87 different varieties of steering wheels, but customers did not want many of them and disliked having to choose from so many options.[9] Second, mass customization creates a tremendous opportunity for errors. Third, most companies have found that customers, given a wide variety of choices, typically make selections from a rather small percentage of the total. At Toyota, investigation of purchases revealed that 20 percent of the product varieties accounted for 80 percent of the sales.[10] This 20:80 ratio is a fairly common proportional relationship and is referred to as the Pareto principle.[11]

Companies with complex products, services, or processes should investigate ways to reduce that complexity. Management could review the design of the company's products and processes to standardize them and reduce the number of different components, tools, and processes required. Products should be designed to consider the Pareto principle and take advantage of commonality of parts. For instance, if a company finds that 20 percent of its parts are used in 80 percent of its products, the company should ask two questions. First, are the remaining components used in key products? If so, could equal quality be achieved by using the more common parts? If not, can the products be sold for a premium price to cover the costs associated with the use of low-volume components? Second, are the parts specified for product use purchased by important customers who are willing to pay a premium price for the products? If so, the benefits from the complexity could be worth the cost. However, would customers be equally satisfied if more common parts were used and product prices were reduced? Complexity is acceptable *only* if it adds value from the customer's point of view.

Process complexity can develop over time, or it can exist because of a lack of sufficient planning in product development. Processes are complex when they create difficulties for the people attempting to perform production operations (physical straining, awkwardness of motions, and wasted motions) or for the people using manufacturing machinery (multiple and/or detailed setups, lengthy

[6]T. L. Estrin, Jeffrey Kantor, and David Albers, "Is ABC Suitable for Your Company?" *Management Accounting* (April 1994), p. 40. Copyright Institute of Management Accountants, Montvale, N.J.

[7]Leonard Sahling, "Scourge of the Lean Supply Chain," *Journal of Commerce* (October 9, 2006), p. 1.

[8]Frank Pillar and Ashok Kumar, "For Each, Their Own," *Industrial Engineer* (September 2006), pp. 40ff.

[9]B. Joseph Pine II, Bart Victor, and Andrew C. Boynton, "Making Mass Customization Work," *Harvard Business Review* (September–October 1993), p. 110.

[10]Ibid, p. 108.

[11]The Italian economist Vilfredo Pareto found that about 85 percent of Milan's wealth was held by about 15 percent of the people. The term *Pareto principle* was coined by Joseph Juran in relationship to quality problems. Juran found that a high proportion of such problems were caused by a small number of process characteristics (the vital few) whereas the majority of process characteristics (the trivial many) accounted for only a small proportion of quality problems.

transfer time between machine processes, recalibration of instruments, and so on). Process complexity reflects numerous non-value-added activities, causing time delays and cost increases.

Many traditional cost systems are not designed to account for information such as the number of different parts that are used in a product, so management cannot identify products made with low-volume or unique components. ABC systems are flexible and can gather such details so that persons involved in reengineering efforts have information about relationships among activities and cost drivers. With these data, reengineering efforts can be focused both on the primary causes of process complexity and on the causes that create the highest levels of waste.

Lack of Commonality in Overhead Costs

Certain products and services create substantially more overhead costs than others do. Although some of these additional overhead costs are caused by product variety or product/process complexity, others are related to support services. For instance, some products require high levels of advertising; some use expensive distribution channels; and some require the use of high-technology machinery. If only one or two overhead pools are used, overhead related to specific products will be spread over all products. The result will be increased costs for products that are not responsible for the increased overhead.

Problems in Current Cost Allocations

If a company has undergone one or more significant changes in its products or processes (such as increasing product variety or business process reengineering), managers and accountants need to investigate whether the existing cost system still provides a reasonable estimate of product or service cost. After automating their production processes, many companies have experienced large reductions in labor cost with equal or greater increases in overhead cost. In such companies, using direct labor as an overhead allocation base produces extraordinarily high application rates. Consider the fact that some companies are using predetermined OH rates that range from 500 to 2,000 percent of the direct labor cost. Products made using automated equipment tend to be charged an insufficient amount of overhead whereas products made using high proportions of direct labor tend to be overcharged.

Traditional overhead cost allocations also generally emphasize the assignment of product costs to products at the same time the majority of period costs are expensed as incurred. ABC recognizes that some period costs (such as R&D and distribution) are distinctly and reasonably associated with specific products and, therefore, should be traced and allocated to those products. This recognition changes the traditional view of product versus period cost.

Changes in Business Environment

A change in a company's competitive environment could also require better cost information. Increased competition can occur because (1) other companies have recognized the profit potential of a particular product or service, (2) other companies now find the product or service has become cost feasible to make or perform, or (3) an industry or market has been deregulated. If many new companies are competing for old business, the best estimate of product or service cost must be available to management so that reasonable profit margins can be maintained or obtained.

Changes in management strategy can also signal the need for a new cost system. For example, if management wants to start a new production operation, the cost system must be capable of providing information on how costs will change. Showing costs as conforming only to the traditional unit-level variable and fixed classifications might not allow usable information to be developed. Viewing costs as batch-level, product/process-level, or organizational-level focuses on cost drivers and on the changes the planned operations will have on activities and costs.

Continuous improvement recognizes the concepts of eliminating NVA activities to reduce cycle time, making products (or performing services) with zero defects, reducing product costs on an ongoing basis, and simplifying products and processes. ABC, by promoting an understanding of cost drivers, allows the NVA activities to be identified and their causes eliminated or reduced.

Criticisms of Activity-Based Costing

Realistically assessing new models and accounting approaches to determine what they can help managers accomplish is always important. However, no accounting technique or system provides management exact cost information for every product or the information needed to make consistently perfect decisions. Activity-based costing, though typically providing better information for certain types of companies than that generated under a traditional overhead allocation process, is not a cure-all for all managerial concerns. Following are some shortcomings of ABC.

First, ABC requires a significant amount of time and, thus, cost to implement. If implementation is to be successful, substantial support is needed throughout the firm. Management must create an environment for change that overcomes a variety of individual, organizational, and environmental barriers. Individual barriers are typically related to (1) fear of the unknown or shift in status quo, (2) potential loss of status, or (3) a necessity to learn new skills. Organizational barriers are often related to "territorial," hierarchical, or corporate culture issues. Environmental barriers are often built by employee groups (including unions), regulatory agencies, or other stakeholders of interest.

To overcome these barriers, a firm must recognize that these barriers exist, investigate their causes, and communicate information about the "what," "why," and "how" of ABC to all concerned parties. Top management must be involved with, and support, the implementation process; a shortfall in this area will make any progress toward the new system slow and difficult. Additionally, everyone in the company must be educated in new terminology, concepts, and performance measurements. Even if both of these conditions (support and education) are met, substantial time is needed to properly analyze the activities taking place in the activity centers, trace costs to those activities, and determine the cost drivers.

Another problem with ABC is that it does not conform specifically to GAAP. ABC suggests that some nonproduct costs (such as those for R&D) *should* be allocated to products, whereas certain other traditionally designated product costs (such as factory building depreciation) *should not* be allocated to products. Therefore, most companies have used ABC for internal reporting but continue to prepare their external financial statements with a more traditional system—requiring even more costs to be incurred. As ABC systems become more accepted, more companies could choose to refine how ABC and GAAP determine product cost to make those definitions more compatible and, thereby, eliminate the need for two costing systems.

Activity-based costing encourages allocating research & development costs to any products that R&D generates.

Companies attempting to implement ABC as a cure-all for product failures, sales volume declines, or financial losses will quickly find that the system is ineffective for these purposes. However, companies can implement ABC and its related management techniques in support of and in conjunction with total quality management (TQM), JIT, or any of the other world-class methodologies. Companies doing so will provide the customer with the best variety, price, quality, service, and lead time of which they are capable. Not coincidentally, they might even find their businesses booming. ABC and ABM are effective in supporting continuous improvement, short lead times, and flexible manufacturing by helping managers to

■ identify and monitor significant technology costs;

■ trace many technology costs directly to products;

■ increase market share;

■ identify the cost drivers that create or influence cost;

■ identify activities that do not contribute to perceived customer value (i.e., non-value-added activities or waste);

■ understand the impact of new technologies on all elements of performance;

■ translate company goals into activity goals;

■ analyze the performance of activities across business functions;

■ analyze performance problems; and

■ promote standards of excellence.

In summary, ABC is a cost accounting tool that allocates overhead to products and services in a manner different from that of a traditional system. ABC does not, by its implementation, cause the amount of overhead incurred by a company to be reduced; that outcome results from the implementation of activity-based management through its focus on identifying and reducing or eliminating non-value-added activities. Together, ABM and ABC help managers operate in the top right quadrant of the graph in Exhibit 4–15, so that they can produce products and perform services most efficiently and effectively and, thus, be highly competitive in the global business environment.

EXHIBIT 4–15
Efficiency and Effectiveness of Operations

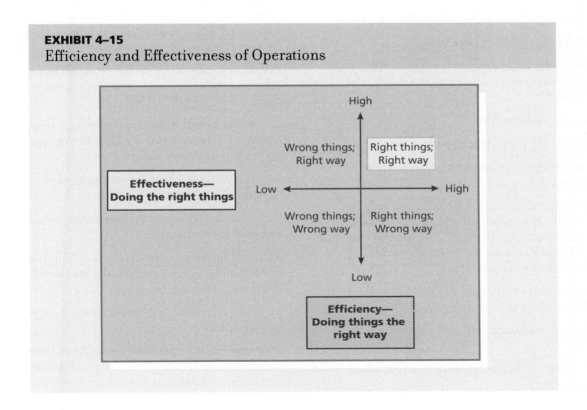

Comprehensive Review Module

Chapter Summary

1. Activity-based management

   - analyzes activities and identifies their cost drivers.

   - classifies activities as value-added or non-value-added (which includes business-value-added) and strives to eliminate or minimize the non-value-added costs.

   - helps to assure that customers perceive an equitable relationship between product selling price and value.

   - improves processes and operational controls.

   - analyzes performance problems.

   - translates company goals into organizational activities.

2. A value-added activity

   - increases the worth of a product or service.

   - is one for which the customer is willing to pay.

   - is an actual production or service task.

   - increases manufacturing cycle efficiency (calculated as total value-added time divided by total cycle time).

3. A non-value-added activity

   - lengthens the production or performance time.

   - is one for which the customer would not be willing to pay.

   - is an inspection (except in industries such as food and pharmaceutical) task, a transfer task, or manufacturing inactivity; packaging may be NVA (unless essential to the convenient or proper delivery of a product).

   - increases the cost of product or services without adding product or service value.

   - decreases manufacturing (service) cycle efficiency.

4. A cost driver is designated in an activity-based costing system to

   - identify what causes a cost to be incurred so that it can be controlled.

   - indicate at what level (unit, batch, product/process, or organizational) a cost occurs.

   - allow costs with similar drivers to be pooled together and a single, appropriate activity basis be used to allocate those costs to products or services.

   - manage costs more effectively and efficiently.

   - identify the costs related to product variety and product/process complexity.

5. Activity-based costing differs from a traditional cost accounting system in that ABC

   - identifies several levels of costs rather than the traditional concepts of variable (at the unit level) or fixed.

   - collects costs in cost pools based on the underlying nature and extent of activities.

   - assigns costs within the multiple cost pools to products or services using multiple drivers (both volume and non-volume related) that best reflect the factor causing the costs to occur.

   - does not consider some product costs for internal purposes when those costs are considered product costs for external reporting.

   - may, under certain conditions, provide a more realistic picture of actual production cost than has traditionally been available.

6. Installation of an activity-based management/costing system will allow management to

   - recognize the cost impact of cross-functional activities in an organization.

   - recognize that fixed costs are, in fact, long-run variable costs that change based on an identifiable driver.

   - recognize the value of preparing process maps and value charts.

   - recognize that the traditional bases (direct labor and machine hours) might not produce the most logical costs for products or services.

- recognize that standard products/services often financially support premium products/services.

- set prices that are more reflective of the activities needed to produce special or premium products or to decide whether such products are actually profitable for the company.

- calculate manufacturing cycle efficiency and use it to measure organizational performance.

- recognize that the most effective way to control costs is to minimize or eliminate non-value-added activities.

- recognize that all customers should not necessarily be retained.

7. Activity-based costing is appropriate in an organization that

- produces and sells a wide variety of products or services.

- customizes products to customer specifications.

- uses a wide diversity of techniques to manufacture its products or to provide its services.

- has a lack of commonality in overhead costs related to products or services.

- has experienced problems with its current overhead allocation system.

- has experienced significant changes in its business environment, including widespread adoption of new technologies.

Potential Ethical Issues

1. Ignoring non-value-added activities and times in the development of a value chart to improve cycle efficiency as a performance measurement

2. Using an unsubstantiated designation of "non-value-added" for specific activities merely to justify the elimination of the jobs of the individuals performing those activities

3. Misclassifying batch- or product/process-level activities as unit-level to spread the costs of those activities to higher-volume products/services and, thereby, reduce the cost of lower-volume products to justify a reduced selling price on the lower-volume products/services

4. Selecting an inappropriate cost driver to allocate costs to products or services in a way that intentionally distorts realistic cost calculations

5. Using activity-based costing to unethically justify no longer purchasing from a particular vendor or selling to a particular customer

6. Using activity-based costing to justify not allocating corporate funds to social or environmental causes

7. Using distorted activity-based costing allocations to transfer costs from fixed-price contracts to cost-plus contracts ▲

Solution Strategies

Manufacturing Cycle Efficiency

Total Cycle Time
= Value-Added Processing Time + Inspection Time + Transfer Time + Idle Time
MCE = Value-Added Processing Time ÷ Total Cycle Time

Note: Depending on the organization, packaging time may be part of value-added processing time or an additional type of non-value-added time. In either case, packaging time will add to total cycle time.

Activity-Based Costing

1. Determine the organization's activity centers.

2. Determine departmental activities and efforts, that is, the cost drivers needed to conduct those activities.

3. Determine departmental resources consumed in conducting activities, and allocate costs of these resources to activity centers based on the cost drivers.

4. Determine activities needed to manufacture products or provide revenue-producing services, that is, the activity drivers.

5. Allocate costs to products and services based on activities and cost drivers involved.

Demonstration Problem

Potter Inc. manufactures wizard figurines. All figurines are approximately the same size, but some are plain ceramic while others are "fancy," with purple leather capes and a prism-headed wand. Management is considering producing only the fancy figurines because the rate of return on sales is so much higher than it is on the ceramic figurines. The company's total production overhead is $5,017,500. Some additional data follow:

	Ceramic	Fancy
Revenues	$15,000,000	$16,800,000
Direct costs	$8,250,000	$8,750,000
Production (units)	1,500,000	350,000
Machine hours	200,000	50,000
Direct labor hours	34,500	153,625
Number of inspections	1,000	6,500

Required:

a. Potter Inc. has consistently used machine hours to allocate overhead. Determine the profitability of each line of figurines, and decide whether the company should stop producing the ceramic figurines.

b. The cost accountant has determined that production overhead costs can be assigned to separate cost pools. Pool #1 contains $1,260,000 of overhead costs for which the most appropriate cost driver is machine hours; Pool #2 contains $2,257,500 of overhead costs for which the most appropriate cost driver is direct labor hours; and Pool #3 contains $1,500,000 of overhead costs for which the most appropriate cost driver is number of inspections. Compute the overhead cost that should be allocated to each type of figurine using this methodology.

c. Discuss whether the company should continue to manufacture both types of figurines.

Solution to Demonstration Problem

a. Overhead rate per MH = $5,017,500 ÷ 250,000 = $20.07 per MH

		Ceramic		Fancy
Revenue		$15,000,000		$16,800,000
Direct costs	$8,250,000		$8,750,000	
Overhead	4,014,000		1,003,500	
Total costs		(12,264,000)		(9,753,500)
Gross margin		$ 2,736,000		$ 7,046,500
Rate of return on sales (rounded)		18%		42%

b.

	Ceramic	Fancy	Total
Machine hours	200,000	150,000	350,000
Rate per MH ($1,260,000 ÷ 350,000)	× $3.60	× $3.60	× $3.60
Pool #1 OH cost allocations	$720,000	$540,000	$1,260,000
Direct labor hours	34,500	153,625	188,125
Rate per DLH ($2,257,500 ÷ 188,125)	× $12	× $12	× $12
Pool #2 OH cost allocations	$414,000	$1,843,500	$2,257,500
Number of inspections	1,000	6,500	7,500
Rate per inspection ($1,500,000 ÷ 7,500)	× $200	× $200	× $200
Pool #3 OH cost allocations	$200,000	$1,300,000	$1,500,000
Total allocated overhead costs	$1,334,000	$3,683,500	$5,017,500

		Ceramic		Fancy
Revenue		$15,000,000		$16,800,000
Direct costs	$8,250,000		$8,750,000	
Overhead	1,334,000		3,683,500	
Total costs		(9,584,000)		(12,433,500)
Gross margin		$ 5,416,000		$ 4,366,500
Rate of return on sales		36%		26%

c. Given the new allocations, management should continue to produce both types of figurines because both appear to be profitable. However, the cost accountant could consider developing additional overhead pools because of the large number of costs charged to Pool #2.

Key Terms

activity, *p. 100*

activity analysis, *p. 100*

activity-based costing (ABC), *p. 100*

activity-based management (ABM), *p. 100*

activity center, *p. 112*

activity driver, *p. 112*

batch-level cost, *p. 107*

business-value-added activity, *p. 101*

continuous improvement, *p. 117*

cost driver analysis, *p. 107*

cycle (lead) time, *p. 102*

idle time, *p. 102*

inspection time, *p. 102*

manufacturing cycle efficiency (MCE), *p. 105*

mass customization, *p. 116*

non-value-added activity, *p. 100*

organizational-level cost, *p. 109*

Pareto principle, *p. 116*

process, *p. 101*

process complexity, *p. 112*

process map, *p. 102*

processing (service) time, *p. 102*

product complexity, *p. 112*

product-level (process-level) cost, *p. 108*

product variety, *p. 112*

service cycle efficiency, *p. 105*

transfer time, *p. 102*

unit-level cost, *p. 107*

value-added activity, *p. 100*

value chart, *p. 102*

Questions

1. What is activity-based management (ABM), and what specific management tools are used in ABM?
2. What is activity analysis, and how is it used in concert with cost driver analysis to manage costs?
3. Why are value-added activities defined from a customer viewpoint?
4. In a televised football game, what activities are value-added? What activities are non-value-added? Would everyone agree with your choices? Why or why not?
5. If five people from the same organization calculated manufacturing cycle efficiency for one specific process, would each compute the same MCE? Why or why not?
6. Do cost drivers exist in a traditional accounting system? Are they designated as such? How, if at all, does the use of cost drivers in a traditional accounting system differ from those in an activity-based costing system?
7. Why do the more traditional methods of overhead assignment "overload" standard high-volume products with overhead costs, and how does ABC improve overhead assignments?
8. Are all companies likely to benefit to an equal extent from adopting ABC? Discuss.
9. Significant hurdles, including a large time commitment, are often encountered in adopting ABC. What specific activities associated with ABC adoption require large investments of time?

Exercises

10. **LO.1 (Activity analysis)** Go to a local department or grocery store.
    a. List five packaged items for which it is readily apparent that packaging is essential and, therefore, would be considered value-added.
    b. List five packaged items for which it is readily apparent that packaging is nonessential and therefore adds no value.

c. For each item listed in part (b), indicate why you think the item was packaged rather than left unpackaged.

11. **LO.1 (Activity analysis)** Recently, the manager at the Sioux Falls plant of Gillespie Mfg. has noticed the plant has had numerous schedule changes on its production line. She has asked you to assess the problem's financial implications. You have gathered the following information on the activities, estimated times, and average costs required for a single schedule change.

Activity	Est. Time	Average Cost
Review impact of orders	30 min.–2 hrs.	$ 300
Reschedule orders	15 min.–24 hrs.	800
Reschedule production orders	15 min.–1 hr.	75
Stop production and change over	10 min.–3 hrs.	150
Return and locate material (excess inventory)	20 min.–6 hrs.	1,500
Generate new production paperwork	15 min.–4 hrs.	500
Change purchasing schedule	10 min.–8 hrs.	2,100
Collect paperwork from the floor	15 min.	75
Review new line schedule	15 min.–30 min.	100
Overtime premiums	3 hrs.–10 hrs.	1,000
Total		$6,600

a. Which of these, if any, are value-added activities?
b. What is the cost driver in this situation?
c. How can the cost driver be controlled and the NVA activities eliminated?

12. **LO.1 (Activity analysis)** Your boss wants to know whether quality inspections at your company add value. Use the "why" methodology to help your boss make this determination if you work at (a) a clothing manufacturer that sells to a discount chain and (b) a pharmaceutical manufacturer.

13. **LO.1 (Activity analysis)** Choose an activity related to this class, such as attending lectures or doing homework. Write down the answers to the question "why" five times to determine whether your activity is value-added or non-value-added.

14. **LO.1 & LO.2 (Activity analysis; MCE)** Log Cabins Unlimited constructs vacation houses in the North Carolina mountains. The company has developed the following value chart:

Operations	Average Number of Days
Receiving materials	1
Storing materials	5
Measuring and cutting materials	3
Handling materials	7
Setting up and moving scaffolding	6
Assembling materials	7
Building fireplace	9
Pegging logs	4
Cutting and framing doors and windows	2
Sealing joints	4
Inspecting property (county inspectors)	3

a. What are the value-added activities and their total time?
b. What are the non-value-added activities and their total time?
c. Calculate the manufacturing cycle efficiency of the process.
d. Explain the difference between value-added and non-value-added activities.

15. **LO.1 & LO.2 (Activity analysis; MCE)** Spice-a-licious produces creole seasoning using the following process for each batch.

Function	Time (Minutes)
Receiving ingredients	120
Moving ingredients to stockroom	80
Storing ingredients in stockroom	7,160
Moving ingredients from stockroom	80
Mixing ingredients	360
Packaging ingredients	150
Moving packaged seasoning to warehouse	100
Storing packaged seasoning in warehouse	20,000
Moving packaged seasoning from warehouse to trucks	120

   a. Calculate the total cycle time of this manufacturing process.
   b. Which of the functions add value?
   c. Calculate the manufacturing cycle efficiency of this process.
   d. What could Spice-a-licious do to improve its MCE?

16. **LO.1 & LO.2 (Activity analysis; MCE)** Declerque Company makes flavored water and performs the following tasks in the beverage manufacturing process:

	Hours
Receiving and transferring ingredients to storage	6
Storing ingredients	180
Transferring the ingredients from storage	3
Mixing and cooking the ingredients	3
Bottling the water	2
Transferring the bottles to await customer shipment	6

   a. Calculate the total cycle time of this manufacturing process.
   b. Calculate the manufacturing cycle efficiency of this process.

17. **LO.1 & LO.2 (Activity analysis)** Mark Dickenson plans to build a concrete walkway for his home during his vacation. The following schedule shows how project time will be allocated:

	Hours
Purchase materials	5
Obtain rental equipment	3
Remove sod and level site	10
Build forms for concrete	12
Mix and pour concrete into forms	5
Level concrete and smooth	2
Let dry	22
Remove forms from concrete	1
Return rental tools	1
Clean up	2

   a. Identify the value-added activities. How much of the total is value-added time?
   b. Identify the non-value-added activities. How much total time is spent performing non-value-added activities?
   c. Calculate the manufacturing cycle efficiency.

18. **LO.3 (Cost drivers)** For each of the following costs commonly incurred in a manufacturing company, identify a cost driver and explain why it is an appropriate choice.
   a. Equipment maintenance
   b. Machine setup cost
   c. Engineering changes
   d. Computer operations
   e. Material handling
   f. Freight costs for materials
   g. Quality control
   h. Advertising expense
   i. Material storage
   j. Building utilities
   k. Factory depreciation

19. **LO.2 (Value chart)** Malvaney Corporation manufactures special-order office cubicle systems. Production time is two days, but the average cycle time for any order is three weeks. The company president has asked you, as the new controller, to discuss missed delivery dates. Prepare an oral presentation for the executive officers in which you address the following:
   a. Possible causes of the problem.
   b. How a value chart could be used to address the problem.

20. **LO.3 (Cost drivers)** Cruise-IN fast-food restaurant relies on computer-controlled equipment to prepare food for customers. Classify each of the following costs as unit-level (U), batch-level (B), product/process-level (P), or organizational-level (O).
   a. Store manager's salary
   b. Cardboard boxes for food order

    c. Oil for the deep-fat fryer (changed every four hours)
    d. Maintenance of the restaurant building
    e. Wages of employees who clear and clean tables
    f. Refrigeration of raw materials
    g. Property taxes
    h. Electricity expense for the pizza oven
    i. French fries
    j. Depreciation on equipment

21. LO.3 (Cost drivers) Sheldon Lansing developed the following list of cost pools for Lansing's Temporary Services. For each pool, identify a cost driver and explain why it is appropriate.
    a. Advertising cost
    b. Utilities
    c. Information technology
    d. Accounts receivable department
    e. Property taxes and insurance on office building
    f. Payroll department

22. LO.4 (Levels of costs) Newell & Smith, CPAs, has four partners and ten staff accountants. The partners each work 2,000 hours per year and earn $200,000 annually. The staff accountants each work 2,500 hours per year and earn $60,000 annually. The firm's total annual budget for professional support available to partners and staff accountants is $250,000. The firm also spends $80,000 for administrative support that is used only by the partners.
    a. Assume that total support cost is considered a unit-level cost based on number of work hours. What is the support rate per labor hour?
    b. If an audit engagement requires 50 partner hours and 200 staff accountant hours, how much professional support cost would be charged to the engagement using the rate determined in part (a)?
    c. Assume that support costs are considered batch-level costs based on number of work hours. What are the support rates per labor hour?
    d. If an audit engagement requires 50 partner hours and 200 staff accountant hours, how much support cost would be charged to the engagement using the rates determined in part (c)?

23. LO.4 (OH allocation using cost drivers) LeBlanc Industries has decided to implement an activity-based costing system for its in-house legal department. The legal department's primary expense is professional salaries, which are estimated for associated activities as follows:

Reviewing supplier or customer contracts (Contracts)	$180,000
Reviewing regulatory compliance issues (Regulation)	250,000
Court actions (Court)	575,500

    Management has determined that the appropriate cost allocation base for Contracts is the number of pages in the contract reviewed, for Regulation is the number of reviews, and for Court is professional hours. For 2008, the legal department reviewed 300,000 pages of contracts, responded to 500 regulatory review requests, and logged 2,500 professional hours in court.
    a. Determine the allocation rate for each activity in the legal department.
    b. What amount would be charged to a producing department that had 14,000 pages of contracts reviewed, made 18 regulatory review requests, and consumed 210 professional hours in court services during the year?
    c. How can the developed rates be used for evaluating output relative to cost incurred in the legal department? What alternative does the firm have to maintaining an internal legal department and how might this choice affect costs?

24. LO.4 (ABC) Ezella Enterprises is in the process of instituting an activity-based costing project in its 10-person purchasing department. Annual departmental overhead costs are $585,000. Because finding the best supplier takes the majority of effort in the department, most of the costs are allocated to this activity area. Many purchase orders are received in a single shipment.

Activity	Allocation Measure	Quantity	Total Cost
Find best suppliers	Number of telephone calls	300,000	$300,000
Issue purchase orders	Number of purchase orders	37,500	150,000
Review receiving reports	Number of receiving reports	22,500	135,000

One special order product manufactured by the company required the following purchasing department activities: 150 telephone calls, 40 purchase orders, and 20 receipts.

a. What amount of purchasing department cost should be assigned to this product?

b. If 80 units of the product are manufactured during the year, what is the purchasing department cost per unit?

c. If purchasing department costs had been allocated using telephone calls as the allocation base, how much cost would have been assigned to this product?

25. LO.4 (Levels of costs) Cargill Inc. has a casting machine that is used for three of the company's products. Setup cost for the machine is $4,500. During June, the casting machine was set up for six different production runs. The following information shows the units of output from each of the setups.

Setup #	Product #453	Product #529	Product #663
1	420		
2		11,400	
3			6,000
4		13,800	
5	30		
6		8,550	

a. If total machine setup cost is allocated to all units of product, what is the setup cost per unit and total setup cost for Products #453, 529, and 663 during June?

b. If machine setup cost is allocated to each type of product made, what is the setup cost per unit of Products #453, 529, and 663 and the total cost of those products during June?

c. If Cargill Inc. had manufactured all similar products in a single production run, how would unit and total costs have changed during June?

26. LO.5 (Product profitability) Reeves Inc. manufactures lawn mowers and garden tractors. Lawn mowers are relatively simple to produce and are made in large quantities. Garden tractors are customized to individual wholesale customer specifications. The company sells 200,000 lawn mowers and 20,000 garden tractors annually. Revenues and costs incurred for each product are as follows:

	Lawn Mowers	Garden Tractors
Revenue	$13,000,000	$11,900,000
Direct material	2,000,000	1,800,000
Direct labor ($20 per hour)	1,200,000	4,000,000
Overhead	?	?

Manufacturing overhead totals $2,640,000, and administrative expenses equal $3,600,000.

a. Calculate the profit (loss) in total and per unit for each product if overhead is assigned to product using a per-unit basis.

b. Calculate the profit (loss) in total and per unit for each product if overhead is assigned to products using a direct labor hour basis.

c. Assume that manufacturing overhead can be divided into two cost pools as follows: $1,490,000, which has a cost driver of direct labor hours (totaling 260,000), and $1,150,000, which has a cost driver of machine hours (totaling 100,000). Lawn mower production uses 60,000 direct labor hours and 30,000 machine hours; garden tractor production uses 200,000 direct labor hours and 70,000 machine hours. Calculate the profit (loss) in total and per unit for each product if overhead is assigned to products using these two overhead bases.

d. Does your answer in part (a), (b), or (c) provide the best representation of the profit contributed by each product? Explain.

27. LO.4 (ABC) Eloquence Publishing is concerned about the profitability of its regular dictionaries. Company managers are considering producing only the top-quality, hand-sewn dictionaries with gold-edged pages. Eloquence is currently assigning the $1,000,000 of overhead costs to both types of dictionaries based on machine hours. Of the overhead, $400,000 is utilities-related and the remainder is primarily related to quality control inspectors' salaries. The following information about the products is also available:

	Regular	Hand-Sewn
Number produced	1,000,000	700,000
Machine hours	85,000	15,000
Inspection hours	5,000	25,000
Revenues	$3,200,000	$2,800,000
Direct costs	$2,500,000	$2,200,000

  a. Determine the total overhead cost that is being assigned to each type of dictionary using the current allocation system.
  b. Determine the total overhead cost that would be assigned to each type of dictionary if more appropriate cost drivers were used.
  c. Should the company stop producing the regular dictionaries? Explain.

28. **LO.5 (Benefits of ABC)** The cost systems at many companies selling multiple products have become less than adequate in today's global competition. Managers often make important product decisions based on distorted cost information because the cost systems have been primarily designed to focus on inventory measurement. Current literature suggests that many manufacturing companies should have at least three cost systems, one each for inventory measurement, operational control, and activity-based costing.
  a. Identify the purpose and characteristics of each of the following cost systems:
     1. Inventory measurement
     2. Activity-based costing
  b. Discuss why a cost system developed for inventory valuation could distort product cost information.
  c. Describe the benefits that management can obtain from using activity-based costing.
  d. List the steps that a company using a traditional cost system would take to implement activity-based costing.

(CMA adapted)

29. **LO.5 (Controlling OH)** Starshine Company is in the process of analyzing and updating its cost information and pricing practices. Since the company's product line changed from general paints to specialized marine coatings, there has been tremendous overhead growth, including costs in customer service, production scheduling, inventory control, and laboratory work. Factory overhead has doubled following the shift in product mix. Although some large orders are still received, most current business is generated from products designed and produced in small lot sizes to meet specifically detailed environmental and technical requirements. Management believes that large orders are being penalized and small orders are receiving favorable cost (and, thus, selling price) treatment.
  a. Indicate why the shift in product lines would have caused such major increases in overhead.
  b. Is it possible that management is correct in its belief about the costs of large and small orders? If so, why?
  c. Write a memo to management suggesting how it might change the cost accounting system to reflect the changes in the business.

30. **LO.5 (Decision making; ethics)** Many manufacturers are deciding to service only customers that buy $10,000 or more of products from the manufacturers annually. Manufacturers defend such policies by stating that they can provide better service to customers that handle more volume and more diverse product lines.
  a. Relate the concepts in the chapter to the decision of manufacturers to drop small customers.
  b. Are there any ethical implications of eliminating groups of customers that could be less profitable than others?
  c. Does activity-based costing adequately account for all costs that are related to a decision to eliminate a particular customer base? (*Hint:* Consider opportunity costs such as those related to reputation.)▲

Problems

31. **LO.3–LO.5 (Cost drivers; ABC; analysis)** Rocky Mount Community Hospital has been under increasing pressure to be accountable for its patient charges. The hospital's current pricing system is ad hoc, based on pricing norms for the geographical area; only direct costs for surgery, medication, and other treatments are explicitly considered. The hospital's controller has suggested that the hospital improve pricing policies by seeking a tighter relationship between costs and pricing. This approach would make prices for services less arbitrary. As a first step, the controller has determined that most costs can be assigned to one of three cost pools. The three cost pools follow along with the estimated amounts and activity drivers.

Activity Center	Amount	Activity Driver	Quantity
Professional salaries	$10,500,000	Professional hours	60,000 hours
Building costs	4,950,000	Square feet used	45,000 sq. ft.
Risk management	680,000	Patients served	2,000 patients

The hospital provides service in three broad categories. The services follow with their volume measures for the activity centers.

Service	Professional Hours	Square Feet	Number of Patients
Surgery	3,000	10,000	400
Housing patients	56,000	22,000	1,000
Outpatient care	1,000	13,000	600

a. What bases might be used as cost drivers to allocate the service center costs among the patients served by the hospital? Defend your selections.

b. The hospital currently charges an "add-on" rate calculated using professional hours to patients' direct charges. What rate is Rocky Mount Community Hospital charging per hour?

c. Determine the allocation rates for each activity center cost pool.

d. Allocate the activity center costs to the three services provided by the hospital.

e. Rocky Mount has decided to estimate costs by activity center using professional hours. What is the cost per professional hour of each activity center? What would cause the cost per hour difference for three services?

32. **LO.3 (Activity analysis)** Elsinore Manufacturing is concerned about its ability to control factory labor-related costs. The company has recently finished an analysis of these costs for 2008. Following is a summary of the major categories of labor costs identified by the company's accounting department:

EXCEL

Category	Amount
Base wages	$42,000,000
Health care benefits	7,000,000
Payroll taxes	3,360,000
Overtime	5,798,400
Training	1,250,000
Retirement benefits	4,599,000
Workers' compensation	799,960

Following are some of the potential cost drivers identified by the company for labor-related costs, along with their 2008 volume levels.

Potential Activity Driver	2008 Volume Level
Average number of factory employees	1,400
Number of new hires	200
Number of regular labor hours worked	2,100,000
Number of overtime hours worked	192,000
Total factory wages paid	$47,798,400
Volume of production in units	8,000,000
Number of production process changes	400
Number of production schedule changes	250

a. For each cost pool, determine the cost per unit of the activity driver using the activity driver that you believe has the closest relationship to the cost pool.

b. Based on your judgments and calculations in part (a), which activity driver should receive the most attention from company managers in their efforts to control labor-related costs? How much of the total labor-related cost is attributable to this activity driver?

c. In the contemporary environment, many firms ask their employees to work record levels of overtime. What activity driver does this practice suggest is a major contributor to labor-related costs? Explain.

33. **LO.4 (ABC)** Huxstable Inc. has a total of $1,551,000 in production overhead costs. The company's products and related statistics follow:

	Product A	Product B
Direct material in pounds	93,000	127,000
Direct labor hours	20,000	25,000
Machine hours	35,000	15,000
Number of setups	200	500
Number of units produced	10,000	5,000

Additional data: The 220,000 pounds of material were purchased for $363,000. One direct labor hour costs $12.

a. Assume that Huxstable Inc. uses direct labor hours to apply overhead to products. Determine the total cost for each product and the cost per unit.

b. Assume that Huxstable Inc. uses machine hours to apply overhead to products. Determine the total cost for each product and the cost per unit.

c. Assume that Huxstable Inc. uses the following activity centers, cost drivers, and costs to apply overhead to products.

Cost Pool	Cost Driver	Cost	Volume
Utilities	# of machine hours	$500,000	50,000
Setup	# of setups	105,000	700
Material handling	pounds of material	946,000	220,000

Determine the total cost for each product and the cost per unit.

34. LO.3 & LO.5 (ABC; pricing) Dozier Desks makes gray metal five-drawer desks and, occasionally, takes custom orders. The company's overhead costs for a month in which no custom desks are produced are as follows:

Purchasing Department for raw material and supplies (10 purchase orders per month)	$ 5,000
Setting up machines for production runs (4 times per month after maintenance checks)	1,240
Utilities (based on 3,200 machine hours)	160
Supervisor salaries	8,000
Machine and building depreciation (fixed)	5,500
Quality control and inspections performed on random selection of desks each day; one quality control worker	2,500
Total overhead costs	$22,400

Factory operations are highly automated, and overhead is allocated to products based on machine hours. This allocation process has resulted in a factory overhead rate of $7 per machine hour ($22,400 ÷ 3,200 MHs).

In July 2008, six orders were filled for custom desks. Selling prices were based on charges for actual direct material, actual direct labor and the $7 per machine hour charge for 200 hours of machine time. During July, the following costs were incurred for 3,200 hours of machine time:

Purchasing Department for raw material and supplies (22 purchase orders per month)	$ 6,200
Setting up machines for production runs (18 times)	1,640
Utilities (based on 3,200 machine hours)	160
Supervisor salaries	8,000
Machine and building depreciation (fixed)	5,500
Quality control and inspections performed on random selection of desks each day; one quality control worker	2,980
Engineering design and specification costs	3,000
Total overhead costs	$27,480

a. How much of the purchasing department cost is variable and how much is fixed? What types of purchasing costs would fit into each of these categories?

b. Why might the number of machine setups have increased from 4 to 18 when only six custom orders were received?

c. Why might the cost of quality control and inspections have increased?

d. Why were engineering design and specification costs included during July?

e. If Dozier Desks were to adopt activity-based costing, what would you suggest as the cost drivers for each of the overhead cost items?

f. Do you think the custom orders should have been priced using the predetermined rate of $7 per machine hour? Explain the reasoning for your answer.

35. LO.4 (ABC) Jankowski Corp. manufactures two products. Following is a production and cost analysis for each product for the year 2008.

Cost Component	Product A	Product B	Both Products	Cost
Units produced	10,000	10,000	20,000	
Raw material used (units)				
X	50,000	50,000	100,000	$ 800,000
Y		100,000	100,000	$ 200,000
Labor hours used				
Department 1				$ 682,000
Direct labor	20,000	5,000	25,000	$ 375,000
Indirect labor				
Inspection	2,500	2,400	4,900	

Machine operations	5,000	10,000	15,000	
Setups	252	248	500	
Department 2				$ 462,000
Direct labor	5,000	5,000	10,000	$ 200,000
Indirect labor				
Inspection	2,680	5,000	7,680	
Machine operations	1,000	3,860	4,860	
Setups	250	310	560	
Machine hours used				
Department 1	5,000	10,000	15,000	$ 400,000
Department 2	5,000	20,000	25,000	$ 800,000
Power used (kW hours)				$ 400,000
Department 1			1,500,000	
Department 2			8,500,000	
Other activity data				
Building occupancy				$1,000,000
Purchasing				$ 100,000
Number of purchase orders				
Material X			200	
Material Y			300	
Square feet occupied				
Purchasing			10,000	
Power			40,000	
Department 1			200,000	
Department 2			250,000	

Sabrina Teasdale, the firm's cost accountant, has just returned from a seminar on activity-based costing. To apply the concepts she has learned, she decides to analyze the costs incurred for Products A and B from an activity basis. In doing so, she specifies the following first and second allocation processes:

FIRST STAGE: ALLOCATIONS TO DEPARTMENTS

Cost Pool	Cost Object	Activity Allocation Base
Power	Departments	Kilowatt hours
Purchasing	Material	Number of purchase orders
Building occupancy	Departments	Square feet occupied

SECOND STAGE: ALLOCATIONS TO PRODUCTS

Cost Pool	Cost Object	Activity Allocation Base
Departments		
Indirect labor	Products	Hours worked
Power	Products	Machine hours
Machinery-related	Products	Machine hours
Building occupancy	Products	Machine hours
Material purchasing	Products	Materials used

Source: Adapted from Harold P. Roth and A. Faye Borthick, "Getting Closer to Real Product Costs," *Management Accounting* (May 1989), pp. 28–33. Reprinted from *Management Accounting*. Copyright by Institute of Management Accountants, Montvale, N.J.

a. Determine the total overhead for Jankowski Corp.
b. Determine the plantwide overhead rate for the company, assuming the use of direct labor hours.
c. Determine the cost per unit of Product A and Product B, using the overhead rate found in part (b).
d. Determine the cost allocations to departments (first-stage allocations). Allocate costs from the departments in the following order: building occupancy, purchasing, and power. Finish the cost allocations for one department to get an "adjusted" cost to allocate to the next department.
e. Using the allocations found in part (d), determine the cost allocations to products (second-stage allocations).
f. Determine the cost per unit of Product A and Product B using the overhead allocations found in part (e).

36. **LO.4 (ABC)** Tejas Time-Out makes umbrellas, gazebos, and chaise lounges. The company uses a traditional overhead allocation scheme and assigns overhead to products at the rate of $20 per direct labor hour. In 2008, the company produced 200,000 umbrellas, 20,000 gazebos, and 60,000 chaise lounges and incurred $8,000,000 of manufacturing overhead costs. The cost per unit for each product group in 2008 was as follows:

EXCEL

	Umbrellas	Gazebos	Chaise Lounges
Direct material	$ 8	$ 80	$ 8
Direct labor	12	90	30
Overhead	16	120	40
Total	$36	$290	$78

Because profitability has been lagging and competition has been getting more intense, Tejas Time-Out is considering implementing an activity-based costing system for 2009. In analyzing the 2008 data, management determined that all $8,000,000 of factory overhead could be assigned to four basic activities: quality control, setups, material handling, and equipment operation. Data from 2008 on the costs associated with each of the four activities follow:

Quality Control	Setups	Material Handling	Equipment Operation	Total Costs
$400,000	$400,000	$1,200,000	$6,000,000	$8,000,000

Management determined that the following allocation bases and total 2008 volumes for each allocation base could have been used for ABC:

Activity	Base	Volume
Quality control	Number of units produced	280,000
Setups	Number of setups	2,000
Material handling	Pounds of material used	4,000,000
Equipment operation	Number of machine hours	2,000,000

Volume measures for 2008 for each product and each allocation base were as follows:

	Umbrellas	Gazebos	Chaise Lounges
Number of units	200,000	20,000	60,000
Number of setups	400	800	800
Pounds of material	800,000	2,000,000	1,200,000
Number of machine hours	400,000	800,000	800,000

a. How much direct labor time is need to produce an umbrella, a gazebo, and a chaise lounge?
b. For 2008, determine the total overhead allocated to each product group using the traditional allocation based on direct labor hours.
c. For 2008, determine the total overhead that would have been allocated to each product group if activity-based costing were used. Compute the cost per unit for each product group.
d. Tejas Time-Out has a policy of setting sales prices based on product costs. How would the sales prices using activity-based costing differ from those obtained using the traditional overhead allocation?

37. LO.4 & LO.5 (ABC; pricing) Walla Walla Doors has consistently charged manufacturing overhead costs to products using machine hours. However, the company president has decided that the use of ABC would provide more realistic cost estimates and, in turn, give the company an edge in pricing over its competitors. Walla Walla's accountant and production manager have provided the following budgeted information for 2008, given a budgeted capacity of 1,000,000 machine hours:

Type of Manufacturing Cost	Cost Amount
Electric power	$ 500,000
Work cells	3,000,000
Material handling	1,000,000
Quality control inspections	1,000,000
Machine setups	350,000
Total budgeted overhead costs	$5,850,000

Type of Manufacturing Cost	Activity Drivers
Electric power	200,000 kilowatt hours
Work cells	300,000 square feet
Material handling	200,000 material moves
Quality control inspections	50,000 inspections
Machine setups	25,000 setups

A national construction company approached Sandy Withers, the VP of marketing, about a bid for 2,500 doors. Withers asked the cost accountant to prepare a cost estimate for producing the 2,500 doors; she received the following data:

Direct material cost	$50,000
Direct labor cost	$150,000
Machine hours	5,000
Direct labor hours	2,500
Electric power—kilowatt hours	500
Work cells—square feet	1,000
Number of material handling moves	20
Number of quality control inspections	15
Number of setups	6

Source: Adapted from Nabil Hassa, Herbert E. Brown, and Paul M. Saunders, "Management Accounting Case Study: Beaver Window Inc.," *Management Accounting Campus Report* (Fall 1990). Copyright Institute of Management Accountants, Montvale, N.J.

a. What is the predetermined overhead rate if the traditional measure of machine hours is used?
b. What is the manufacturing cost per door as presently accounted for?
c. What is the manufacturing cost per door under the proposed ABC method?
d. If the two cost systems will result in different cost estimates, which cost accounting system is preferable as a pricing base and why?
e. If activity-based management were implemented prior to an ABC system, which of the manufacturing overhead costs might be reduced or eliminated? Why?

38. **LO.4 & LO.5 (ABC; pricing)** Rushmore Corp. has identified activity centers to which overhead costs are assigned. The cost pool amounts for these centers and their selected activity drivers for 2008 follow:

EXCEL

Activity Centers	Costs	Activity Drivers
Utilities	$1,200,000	60,000 machine hours
Scheduling and setup	1,092,000	780 setups
Material handling	2,560,000	1,600,000 pounds of material

The company's products and other operating statistics follow:

	PRODUCTS		
	A	B	C
Direct costs	$80,000	$80,000	$90,000
Machine hours	30,000	10,000	20,000
Number of setups	130	380	270
Pounds of material	500,000	300,000	800,000
Number of units produced	40,000	20,000	60,000
Direct labor hours	32,000	18,000	50,000

a. Determine unit product cost using the appropriate cost drivers for each product.
b. Before it installed an ABC system, the company used a traditional costing system that allocated factory overhead to products using direct labor hours. The firm operates in a competitive market and sets product prices at cost plus a 20 percent markup.
   1. Calculate unit costs based on traditional costing.
   2. Determine selling prices based on unit costs for traditional costing and for ABC.
c. Discuss the problems related to setting prices based on traditional costing and explain how ABC improves the information.

39. **LO.4 & LO.5 (ABC; product profitability)** Colorado Consulting provides a wide range of engineering and architectural consulting services through its three branch offices in Aspen, Durango, and Golden. The company allocates resources and bonuses to the three branches based on the net income reported for the period. The following presents the performance results of 2008.

	Aspen	Durango	Golden	Total
Sales	$1,500,000	$1,419,000	$1,067,000	$ 3,986,000
Less: Direct material	(281,000)	(421,000)	(185,000)	(887,000)
Direct labor	(382,000)	(317,000)	(325,000)	(1,024,000)
Overhead	(725,800)	(602,300)	(617,500)	(1,945,600)
Net income	$ 111,200	$ 78,700	$ (60,500)	$ 129,400

Overhead items are accumulated in one overhead pool and allocated to the branches based on direct labor dollars. For 2008, this predetermined overhead rate was $1.90 for every direct labor dollar incurred by an office.

The overhead pool includes rent, depreciation, taxes, etc., regardless of which office incurred the expense. This method of accumulating costs forces the offices to absorb a portion of the overhead incurred by other offices.

Management is concerned with the results of the 2008 performance reports. During a review of overhead costs, it became apparent that many items of overhead are not correlated with direct labor dollars as previously assumed. Management decided that applying overhead based on activity-based costing and direct tracing, when possible, should provide a more accurate picture of the profitability of each branch. An analysis of the overhead revealed that the following dollars for rent, utilities, depreciation, and taxes could be traced directly to the office that incurred the overhead.

	Aspen	Durango	Golden	Total
Office overhead	$195,000	$286,100	$203,500	$684,600

Activity pools and activity drivers were determined from the accounting records and staff surveys as follows:

Activity Pools		Activity Driver	NUMBER OF ACTIVITIES BY LOCATION		
			Aspen	Durango	Golden
General administration	$ 409,000	Direct labor	$386,346	$305,010	$325,344
Project costing	48,000	# of timesheet entries	6,300	4,060	3,640
Accounts payable/receiving	139,000	# of vendor invoices	1,035	874	391
Accounts receivable	47,000	# of client invoices	572	429	99
Payroll/Mail sort & delivery	30,000	# of employees	34	39	27
Personnel recruiting	38,000	# of new hires	8	4	8
Employee insur. processing	14,000	# of insur. claims filed	238	273	189
Proposals	139,000	# of proposals	195	245	60
Sales meetings, sales aids	202,000	Contracted sales	$1,821,600	$1,404,150	$569,250
Shipping	24,000	# of projects	100	125	25
Ordering	48,000	# of purchase orders	126	102	72
Duplicating costs	46,000	# of copies duplicated	160,734	145,782	67,284
Blueprinting	77,000	# of blueprints	38,790	31,032	16,378
	$1,261,000				

a. How much overhead cost should be assigned to each office based on activity-based costing concepts?
b. What is the contribution of each office before subtracting the results obtained in part (a)?
c. What is the profitability of each office using activity-based costing?
d. Evaluate the concerns of management regarding the traditional costing technique currently used.

(IMA adapted)

40. **LO.4 & LO.5 (ABC; decision making)** MindMatters manufactures multiple types of products; however, most of the company's sales are from Product #347 and Product #658. Product #347 has been a standard in the industry for several years; the market for this product is competitive and price sensitive. MindMatters plans to sell 65,000 of Product #347 in 2008 at a price of $150 per unit. Product #658 is a recent addition to Mind-Matters' product line. This product incorporates the latest technology and can be sold at a premium price; the company expects to sell 40,000 units of this product in 2008 for $300 per unit.

MindMatters' management group is meeting to discuss 2008 strategies, and the current topic of conversation is how to spend the sales and promotion budget. The sales manager believes that the market share for Product #347 could be expanded by concentrating MindMatters' promotional efforts in this area. However, the production manager wants to target a larger market share for Product #658. She says, "The cost sheets I get show that the contribution from Product #658 is more than twice that from Product #347. I know we get a premium price for this product; selling it should help overall profitability." MindMatters has the following costs for the two products:

	Product #347	Product #658
Direct material	$80	$140
Direct labor	1.5 hours	4.0 hours
Machine time	0.5 hours	1.5 hours

Variable manufacturing overhead is currently applied on the basis of direct labor hours. For 2008, variable manufacturing overhead is budgeted at $1,120,000 for a total of 280,000 direct labor hours. The hourly rates for machine time and direct labor are $10 and $14, respectively. MindMatters applies a material handling charge at 10 percent of material cost; this material handling charge is not included in variable manufacturing overhead. Total 2008 expenditures for materials are budgeted at $10,800,000.

Dina Lucchia, MindMatters' controller, believes that before management decides to allocate marketing funds to individual products, it might be worthwhile to look at these products on the basis of the activities involved in their production. Lucchia has prepared the following schedule to help the management group understand this concept.

	Budgeted Cost	Cost Driver	Annual Activity for Cost Driver
Material overhead			
Procurement	$ 400,000	Number of parts	4,000,000 parts
Production scheduling	220,000	Number of boards	110,000 boards
Packaging and shipping	440,000	Number of boards	110,000 boards
	$1,060,000		
Variable overhead			
Machine setup	$ 446,000	Number of setups	278,750 setups
Hazardous waste disposal	48,000	Pounds of waste	16,000 pounds
Quality control	560,000	Number of inspections	160,000 inspections
General supplies	66,000	Number of boards	110,000 boards
	$1,120,000		
Manufacturing			
Machine insertion	$1,200,000	Number of parts	3,000,000 parts
Manual insertion	4,000,000	Number of parts	1,000,000 parts
Wave soldering	132,000	Number of boards	110,000 boards
	$5,332,000		

	REQUIRED PER UNIT	
	Product #347	Product #658
Parts	25	55
Machine insertions of parts	24	35
Manual insertions of parts	1	20
Machine setups	2	3
Hazardous waste	0.02 lb	0.35 lb
Inspections	1	2

Lucchia wants to calculate a new cost, using appropriate cost drivers, for each product. The new cost drivers would replace the direct labor, machine time, and overhead costs in the current costing system.
a. Identify at least four general advantages associated with activity-based costing.
b. On the basis of current costs, calculate the total contribution expected in 2008 for
   1. Product #347.
   2. Product #658.
c. On the basis of activity-based costs, calculate the total contribution expected in 2008 for
   1. Product #347.
   2. Product #658.
d. Explain how the comparison of the results of the two costing methods could impact the decisions made by MindMatters' management group.

(CMA adapted)

41. **LO.5 & LO.6 (Product complexity)** Superior Electronics is a world leader in the production of electronic test and measurement instruments. The company experienced almost uninterrupted growth through the 1990s, but in the 2000s, the low-priced end of the Portables Division's product line was challenged by the aggressive low-price strategy of several Japanese competitors. These Japanese companies set prices 25 percent below Superior's prevailing prices. To compete, the division needed to reduce costs and increase customer value by increasing operational efficiency.

The division took steps to implement just-in-time delivery and scheduling techniques as well as a total quality control program and to involve people techniques that moved responsibility for problem solving down to the operating level of the division. The results of these changes were impressive: substantial reductions in cycle time, direct labor hours per unit, and inventory levels as well as increases in output dollars per person per day and in operating income. The cost accounting system was providing information, however, that did not seem to support the changes.

Total overhead cost for the division was $10,000,000; of this, 55 percent seemed to be related to materials and 45 percent to conversion. Material-related costs pertain to procurement, receiving, inspection, stockroom personnel, and so on. Conversion-related costs pertain to direct labor, supervision, and process-related engineering. All overhead was applied on the basis of direct labor.

The division decided to concentrate efforts on revamping the application system for material-related overhead. Managers believed the majority of material overhead (MOH) costs were related to the maintenance and handling of each different part number. Other types of MOH costs were driven by the value of parts, absolute number of parts, and each use of a different part number.

At this time, the division used 8,000 different parts, each in extremely different quantities. For example, annual usage of one part was 35,000 units; usage of another part was only 200 units. The division decided that MOH costs would decrease if a smaller number of different parts were used in the products.

Source: Adapted from Michael A. Robinson, ed., *Cases from Management Accounting Practice*, No. 5 (Montvale, N.J.: National Association of Accountants, 1989), pp. 13–17. Copyright by Institute of Management Accountants (formerly National Association of Accountants), Montvale, N.J.

a. Why would MOH have decreased because parts were standardized?
b. Using the numbers given, develop a cost allocation method for MOH to quantify and communicate the strategy of parts standardization.
c. Explain how the use of the method developed in part (b) would support the strategy of parts standardization.
d. Is any method that applies the entire MOH cost pool on the basis of one cost driver sufficiently accurate for complex products? Explain.
e. Are MOH product costing rates developed for management reporting appropriate for inventory valuation for external reporting? Why or why not?

42. **LO.4 & LO.5 (ABC; pricing)** Burtie Gonzales owns and manages a commercial cold-storage warehouse that has 100,000 cubic feet of storage capacity. Historically, she has charged customers a flat rate of $0.08 per pound per month for goods stored.

In the past two years, Gonzales has become dissatisfied with the profitability of the warehouse operation. Despite the fact that the warehouse remains relatively full, revenues have not kept pace with operating costs. Recently, Gonzales asked her accountant, Seth Parker, to improve her understanding of how activity-based costing could help her revise the pricing formula. Parker has determined that most costs can be associated with one of four activities. Those activities and their related costs, volume measures, and volume levels for 2008 follow:

Activity	Cost	Monthly Volume Measure	
Send/receive goods	$25,000	Weight in pounds	500,000
Store goods	8,000	Volume in cubic feet	80,000
Move goods	10,000	Volume in square feet	5,000
Identify goods	4,000	Number of packages	500

Source: Adapted from Harold P. Roth and Linda T. Sims, "Costing for Warehousing and Distribution," *Management Accounting* (August 1991), pp. 42–45. Reprinted from *Management Accounting*. Copyright by Institute of Management Accountants, Montvale, N.J.

a. Based on the activity cost and volume data, determine the amount of cost assigned to the following customers, whose goods were all received on the first day of last month.

Customer	Weight of Order in Pounds	Cubic Feet	Square Feet	Number of Packages
Butler	40,000	3,000	300	5
Rutledge	40,000	2,000	200	20
Morris	40,000	1,000	1,000	80

b. Determine the price to be charged to each customer under the existing pricing plan.
c. Determine the price to be charged using ABC, assuming Gonzales would base the price on the cost determined in part (a) plus a markup of 30 percent.
d. How well does Gonzales' existing pricing plan capture the costs incurred of providing the warehouse services? Explain.

43. **LO.5 & LO.6 (Decision making; ethics)** As the chief executive officer of a large corporation, you have decided after discussion with production and accounting personnel to implement activity-based management concepts. Your goal is to reduce cycle time and, in turn, costs. A primary way to accomplish this goal is to install highly automated equipment in your plant, which would then displace approximately 60 percent of your workforce. Your company is the major employer in the area of the country where it is located.

a. Discuss the pros and cons of installing the equipment from the perspective of your (1) stockholders, (2) employees, and (3) customers.

b. How would you explain to a worker that his or her job is a non-value-added activity?

c. What alternatives might you have that could accomplish the goal of reducing cycle time but not create economic havoc for the local area? ▲

44. **LO.5 & LO.6 (Decision making)** Companies that want to be more globally competitive can consider the implementation of activity-based management (ABM). Such companies often have used other initiatives that involve higher efficiency, effectiveness, or output quality. These same initiatives are typically consistent with and supportive of ABM.

a. In what other types of "initiatives" might such global companies engage?

b. How might ABM and activity-based costing (ABC) help a company in its quest to achieve world-class status?

c. For any significant initiative, senior management commitment is generally required. Would it be equally important to have top management support if a company was instituting ABC rather than ABM? Justify your answer.

d. Assume that you are a member of top management in a large organization. Do you think implementation of ABM or ABC would be more valuable? Explain the rationale for your answer.

5 | Job Order Costing

Objectives

After completing this chapter, you should be able to answer the following questions:

LO.1 How do job order and process costing systems, as well as their related valuation methods, differ?

LO.2 What are the primary documents supporting a job order costing system and what purposes are served by each of them?

LO.3 What journal entries are used to accumulate costs in a job order costing system?

LO.4 How do costs flow in a job order costing system?

LO.5 How are standard costs used in a job order costing system?

LO.6 How does information from a job order costing system support management decision making?

LO.7 How are losses treated in a job order costing system?

Introduction

The primary use of a product costing system is to assign production costs to products or services for purposes of internal and external financial reporting. Product costing systems range from very simple to very complex. The more complex systems are more expensive to operate and maintain because they require substantially more input data. When specifying the details of a product costing system, the cost of generating such information must be less than the benefits of that information to management. For companies that produce homogeneous output in batch or continuous production processes, only an "average" product cost is required to support most reporting needs. Thus, an elaborate system is not necessary and a costing system is satisfactory if it accurately tracks costs by production process or by batch. Such costing systems are called process costing systems.

However, for firms that produce heterogeneous and custom outputs, product costs must be tracked to the product or customer level. Such a job order costing system is more expensive and elaborate than a process costing system because it requires the input of more cost and operating data. This chapter discusses job order costing systems and is the first in a sequence of product costing chapters. The chapter begins by distinguishing between job order and process costing and by addressing the three methods of valuation that can be used within these systems (actual, normal, and standard).

LO.1
How do job order and process costing systems, as well as their related valuation methods, differ?

Methods of Product Costing

Before product cost can be computed, a determination must be made about the (1) cost accumulation system and (2) valuation method to be used. The cost accumulation system defines the cost object and method of assigning costs to production; the valuation method specifies how product costs are measured. Companies must have both a cost system and a valuation method; six possible combinations exist as shown in Exhibit 5–1.[1]

Cost Accumulation Systems

Job order and process costing are the two primary cost accumulation systems. A job order costing system is used by companies that make relatively small quantities of distinct products or services that conform to specifications designated by the purchaser. Thus, job order costing is appropriate for a cobbler making custom shoes and boots, a publishing company producing educational textbooks, an accountant preparing tax returns, an architectural firm designing commercial buildings, and a research firm performing product development studies. In these various settings, the word job is synonymous with client, engagement, project, or contract.

In contrast, process costing systems (covered in Chapter 6) are used by companies that make large quantities of homogeneous goods such as breakfast cereal, candy bars, detergent, gasoline, and bricks. Given the mass manufacturing process, one unit of output cannot be readily identified with specific input costs within a given period—making the use of a cost averaging approach necessary.

Valuation Methods

As indicated in Exhibit 5–1, job order or process costing systems may be based on three alternative valuation methods: actual, normal, or standard. Actual cost systems use the actual costs of direct material, direct labor, and overhead to determine Work in Process (WIP) Inventory cost. Service businesses that have few customers and/or low volume may use an actual cost system. However, because of the reasons discussed in Chapter 3, many companies prefer to use a normal cost system that combines actual direct material and direct labor costs with predetermined overhead (OH) rates. If

---

[1]A third and fourth dimension (cost accumulation and cost presentation) are also necessary in this model. These dimensions relate to the use of absorption or variable costing and are covered in Chapter 3.

EXHIBIT 5–1
Costing Systems and Inventory Valuation

	METHOD OF VALUATION		
COST ACCUMULATION SYSTEM	**Actual**	**Normal**	**Standard**
JOB ORDER	Actual Direct Material Actual Direct Labor Actual Overhead (assigned to job at end of period)	Actual Direct Material Actual Direct Labor Overhead applied using predetermined rate(s) at completion of job or end of period (predetermined rate times actual input)	Standard Direct Material Standard Direct Labor Overhead applied using predetermined rate(s) when goods are completed or at end of period (predetermined rate times standard input)
PROCESS	Actual Direct Material Actual Direct Labor Actual Overhead (assigned to job at end of period using FIFO or weighted average cost flow)	Actual Direct Material Actual Direct Labor Overhead applied using predetermined rate(s) (using FIFO or weighted average cost flow)	Standard Direct Material Standard Direct Labor Standard Overhead using predetermined rate(s) (will always be FIFO cost flow)

the predetermined OH rate is substantially equivalent to what the actual OH rate would have been for an annual period, predetermined rates provide acceptable and useful costs.

Companies using either job order or process costing may employ standards (or predetermined benchmarks) for costs to be incurred and/or quantities to be used. In a **standard cost system**, unit norms or standards are developed for direct material and direct labor quantities and/or costs. Overhead is applied to production using a predetermined rate that is considered the standard. These standards can then be used to plan for future activities and cost incurrence and to value inventories. Both actual and standard costs are recorded in the accounting records to provide an essential element of cost control—norms against which actual operating costs can be compared. A standard cost system allows companies to quickly recognize deviations or variances from expected production costs and to correct problems resulting from excess usage and/or costs. Actual costing systems do not provide this benefit, and normal costing systems cannot provide it in relation to material and labor. Although standards are most useful in environments characterized by repetitive manufacturing, standard costing can be used in some circumstances in a job order costing environment.

Because the use of predetermined OH rates is more common than the use of actual overhead costs, this chapter addresses a job order, normal cost system and describes several job order, standard cost combinations.[2]

Job Order Costing System

Product costing is concerned with (1) cost identification, (2) cost measurement, and (3) product cost assignment. In a job order costing system, costs are accumulated by job. A job is a single unit

---

[2]Although actual overhead may be assigned to jobs, such an approach would be less customary because total overhead would not be known until the period was over, causing an unwarranted delay in overhead assignment. Activity-based costing can increase the validity of tracing overhead costs to specific products or jobs.

or group of units that is identifiable as being produced to distinct customer specifications.[3] Each job is treated as a unique cost entity or cost object. Costs of different jobs are maintained in separate subsidiary ledger accounts and are not added together in the ledger.

The job order costing system provides information important to managing profitability and setting prices for output. Custom manufacturers typically price their goods using two methods. A cost-plus contract may be used, which allows producers to cover all direct costs and some indirect costs and to generate an acceptable profit margin. In other cases, producers may use a competitive bidding technique. In such instances, the company must accurately estimate the costs of making the unique products associated with each contract; otherwise, the company can incur significant losses when actual costs exceed those that were estimated during the bidding process.

Use of cost-plus contracts or competitive bidding is complicated by the nature of custom manufacturing, in which each job may be uniquely different from the next. In such circumstances, pricing and cost control cannot be based on an accounting system that aggregates costs across contracts. Thus, job order costing is used to accumulate the costs of each job (contract) separately from all other jobs.

The logic of separating costs for individual jobs is illustrated by an example for Dean's Custom Fabricating, a firm that specializes in custom ornamental metal products. During February, the company completed three small contracts; each job required a different quantity and type of material, number of labor hours, and conversion operations. Exhibit 5–2 provides Dean's Custom Fabricating WIP Inventory control and subsidiary ledger accounts at the end of February. Because each job is distinctive, costs of the products cannot logically be averaged—a unique cost must be determined for each job.

Actual direct material and actual direct labor costs are combined with an applied overhead cost that is computed as a predetermined OH rate multiplied by some actual cost driver (such as cost or quantity of materials used or number of direct labor hours required). Normal cost valuation is used because, although actual direct material and direct labor costs are fairly easy to identify and associate with a particular job, overhead costs are usually not traceable to specific jobs and must be allocated to production. For example, at Dean's Custom Fabricating, utility costs are related to all jobs worked on during that month. Accurately determining which jobs created the need for a given amount of water, heat, or electricity would be impossible.

A job can consist of a single unit or multiple similar or dissimilar units. If multiple outputs are produced, a per-unit cost can be computed only if the units are similar or if costs are accumulated for each separate unit (such as through an identification number). For example, Master Halco produces many different styles of ornamental fencing. The company could determine the average cost per foot of "Universal," "Picket," or "Spear" fencing by accumulating the total costs per batch of homogeneous products in different production runs and treating each production run as a separate job. In such cases, an average production cost can be determined for each foot of fencing within each batch because the units within the batch are indistinguishable. If, however, the output consists of dissimilar units for which individual cost information is not gathered, no cost per unit can be determined although it is still possible to know the total job cost.

Job Order Costing: Details and Documents

A job can be categorized by the stage of its production cycle. There are three stages of production: (1) contracted for but not yet started, (2) in process, and (3) completed.[4]

Because a company using job order costing makes products to user specifications, jobs occasionally require unique raw material. Thus, some raw material may not be acquired until a job is under contract and it is known that production will occur. The raw material acquired, although often separately distinguishable and related to specific jobs, is accounted for in a single general ledger control account (Raw Material Inventory) with subsidiary ledger backup. The material may, however,

[3]To eliminate the need for repetition, the term *units* should be read to mean either products or services because job order costing is applicable to both manufacturing and service companies. For the same reason, the term *produced* can mean manufactured or performed.
[4]In concept, there could be four categories. The third and fourth categories would distinguish between products completed but not sold and products completed and sold. However, the usual case is that firms using a job order costing system produce only products for which there is current demand. Consequently, there is no need for an inventory of finished products that await sale.

Separate Subsidiary Ledger Accounts for Jobs

JOB #412 Ornamental Fence	**JOB #414** Interior Railing	**JOB #417** Window Guards

GENERAL LEDGER

Work in Process Inventory Control

Direct material (actual)	XXX	Transferred to finished goods	
Direct labor (actual)	XXX	or next department	XXX
Overhead (predetermined rate × actual activity)	XX		
Ending balance	25,400		

SUBSIDIARY LEDGER

Job #412, Ornamental Fence

Direct material (actual)	XXX
Direct labor (actual)	XXX
Overhead (predetermined rate × actual activity)	XX
Ending balance	10,250

Job #414, Interior Railing

Direct material (actual)	XXX
Direct labor (actual)	XXX
Overhead (predetermined rate × actual activity)	XX
Ending balance	9,170

Job #417, Window Guards

Direct material (actual)	XX
Direct labor (actual)	XX
Overhead (predetermined rate × actual activity)	X
Ending balance	5,980

be designated in the storeroom and possibly in the subsidiary records as being "held for use in Job #407." Such designations should keep the material from being used on a job other than the one for which it was acquired.

Material Requisitions

LO.2
What are the primary documents supporting a job order costing system and what purposes are served by each of them?

To begin a job, a material requisition form (shown in Exhibit 5–3) is prepared so material can be released from the warehouse and sent to the production area. This source document indicates the types and quantities of material to be issued to production or used to perform a service job. Such documents are usually prenumbered and come in multiple-copy sets so that completed copies can be maintained in the warehouse, in the production department, and with each job. Completed material requisition forms verify material flow from the warehouse to the requisitioning department and allow responsibility for material cost to be traced to users. Although hard-copy material requisition forms may still be used, it is increasingly common for this document to exist only electronically.

LO.3
What journal entries are used to accumulate costs in a job order costing system?

The Raw Material Inventory account may contain the costs of both direct and indirect materials. When material is issued, its cost is released from Raw Material Inventory. If the material is considered direct to a job, the cost is assigned to WIP Inventory; if the material is indirect, the cost is assigned to Manufacturing Overhead Control. Thus, the journal entry is as follows:

Work in Process Inventory (for direct material)	XXX	
Manufacturing Overhead Control (for indirect material)	XXX	
Raw Material Inventory		XXX
To issue direct and indirect material to production		

When the first direct material associated with a job is issued to production, that job moves to the second stage of its production cycle—work in process. When a job enters this stage, cost accumulation must begin using the primary accounting document in a job order system—the job order cost sheet (or job cost record).

Job Order Cost Sheet

The source document that provides virtually all financial information about a particular job is the job order cost sheet. The set of job order cost sheets for all incomplete jobs composes the WIP Inventory subsidiary ledger. Total costs contained on the job order cost sheets for all incomplete jobs

EXHIBIT 5–3
Material Requisition Form

Date _____				No. 341			
Job Number _____			Department _____				
Authorized by _____			Issued by _____				
Received by _____			Inspected by _____				
Item No.	Part No.	Description	Unit of Measure	Quantity Required	Quantity Issued	Unit Cost	Total Cost

should reconcile to the WIP Inventory control account balance in the general ledger (as shown in Exhibit 5–2).

A job order cost sheet includes a job number, a description of the job, customer identification, various scheduling information, delivery instructions, and contract price as well as details regarding actual costs for material, labor, and applied overhead. The form also might include budgeted cost information, especially if such information is used to estimate the job's selling price or to support a bid price. In bid pricing, budgeted and actual costs should be compared at the end of a job to determine any deviations from estimates. Like material requisition forms, job cost sheets currently exist only electronically in many companies.

Exhibit 5–4 illustrates a job order cost sheet for Dean's Custom Fabricating. This job is for the construction and installation of a decorative fence; the customer is the Willowdale Homeowners'

EXHIBIT 5–4
Dean's Custom Fabricating Job Order Cost Sheet

Job Number   PF108

Customer Name and Address:

Willowdale Homeowners' Assoc.
200 Willow Avenue
Willow, Texas

Description of Job:

2,000 feet of 6' steel fence per
    contract dated 8/13/2008

Contract Agreement Date:	8/13/08
Scheduled Starting Date:	9/01/08
Agreed Completion Date:	11/15/08
Actual Completion Date:	

Contract Price $35,250

Delivery Instructions: Full installation per contract

FABRICATION

DIRECT MATERIAL			**DIRECT LABOR**			**OVERHEAD BASED ON**					
						# OF LABOR HOURS			**# OF MACHINE HOURS**		
(EST. $5,000)			(EST. $7,200)			(EST. $3,000)			(EST. $2,000)		
Date	**Source**	**Amount**	**Date**	**Source**	**Amount**	**Date**	**Source**	**Amount**	**Date**	**Source**	**Amount**

INSTALLATION
(SAME FORMAT AS ABOVE BUT WITH DIFFERENT OH RATES)

FINISHING
(SAME FORMAT AS ABOVE BUT WITH DIFFERENT OH RATES)

SUMMARY

	FABRICATION		INSTALLATION		FINISHING	
	Actual	**Budget**	**Actual**	**Budget**	**Actual**	**Budget**
Direct material		$ 5,000		$ 0		$1,500
Direct labor		7,200		1,800		3,000
Overhead (labor)		3,000		1,500		1,200
Overhead (machine)		2,000		2,000		
Totals		$17,200		$5,300		$5,700

		Actual	**Budget**
Final Costs:	Fabrication		$17,200
	Installation		5,300
	Finishing		5,700
	Totals		$28,200

Association. All of Dean's Custom Fabricating job order cost sheets include a section for budgeted data so that budget-to-actual comparisons can be made for planning and control purposes. Direct material and direct labor costs are assigned and posted to jobs as work on the job is performed. Direct material information is gathered from the material requisition forms, and direct labor information is found on employee time sheets or employee labor tickets. (Employee time sheets are discussed in the next section.)

Overhead is applied to production at Dean's Custom Fabricating based on departmental predetermined OH rates. The company is organized into three departments: Fabrication, Installation, and Finishing. Each department may have more than one rate. For example, in the Fabrication Department, the overhead rates for 2008–2009 are as follows:

Labor-related costs: $12 per direct labor hour
Machine-related costs: $30 per machine hour

Employee Time Sheets

An employee time sheet indicates the jobs on which each employee worked and the direct labor time consumed. Exhibit 5–5 provides an illustration of a time sheet that would be completed manually by employees; such time sheets are most reliable if the employees keep them current as the day progresses. Work arriving at an employee station is accompanied by a tag or bar code specifying its job order number. The times that work is started and stopped are noted on the time sheet.[5] These time sheets should be collected and reviewed by supervisors to ensure that the information is accurate.

Large businesses often use electronic time-keeping software rather than manual time sheets. Employees simply swipe their employee ID cards and job cards through an electronic scanner when they switch from one job to another. This software allows labor costs to be accumulated by both job and department. In highly automated factories, employee time sheets may not be used because of the low proportion of direct labor cost to total cost. However, machine time can be tracked through

EXHIBIT 5–5
Employee Time Sheet

| For Week Ending _____ |
| Department _____ |
| Employee Name _____ |
| Employee ID No. _____ |

Type of Work		Job Number	Start Time	Stop Time	Day (circle)	Total Hours
Code	Description					
					M T W Th F S	
					M T W Th F S	
					M T W Th F S	
					M T W Th F S	
					M T W Th F S	
					M T W Th F S	

Employee Signature   Supervisor's Signature (for overtime)

[5]Alternatives to daily time sheets are job time tickets that supervisors give to employees as they are assigned new jobs and supervisors' records of which employees worked on what jobs for what period of time. The latter alternative is extremely difficult if a supervisor is overseeing a large number of employees or if employees are dispersed through a large section of the plant.

the use of machine clocks or counters in the same way as human labor is tracked. As jobs are transferred from one machine to another, the clock or counter can be reset to mark the start and stop times. Machine times can then be equated to employee-operator time. Another convenient way to track employee time is through bar codes that can be scanned as products pass through individual workstations. There are also numerous time-and-attendance software tools.

Transferring employee time sheet (or alternative source document) information to the job order cost sheet requires knowledge of employee labor rates. Wage rates are found in employee personnel files. Time spent on the job is multiplied by the employee's wage rate, and the amounts are summed to find total direct labor cost for the period. The summation is recorded on the job order cost sheet. Time sheet information is also used for payroll preparation; the journal entry to record the labor cost is

Work in Process Inventory (for direct labor)	XXX	
Manufacturing Overhead Control (for indirect labor)	XXX	
Salaries and Wages Payable		XXX
To record direct and indirect labor wages		

After these uses, time sheets are filed and retained so they can be referenced if necessary for any future information needs. If total actual labor costs for the job differ significantly from the original estimate, the manager responsible for labor cost control may be asked to explain the discrepancy. In addition, if a job is billed on a cost-plus basis, the number of hours worked may be audited by the buyer. This situation is quite common and especially important when dealing with government contracts. Hours not worked directly on the contracted job cannot be arbitrarily or incorrectly charged to the cost-plus job without the potential for detection. Last, time sheets provide information on overtime hours. Under the Fair Labor Standards Act, overtime must generally be paid at a time-and-a-half rate to all nonmanagement employees when they work more than 40 hours in a week.

Overhead

Overhead costs can be substantial in manufacturing and service organizations. Actual overhead incurred during production is debited to the Manufacturing Overhead control account. If actual overhead is applied to jobs, the cost accountant waits until the end of the period and divides the actual overhead incurred in each designated cost pool by a related measure of activity or cost driver to obtain an application rate. Actual overhead is applied to jobs by multiplying the actual overhead application rate by the actual measure of activity associated with each job.

More commonly, normal costing is used, and overhead is applied to jobs with one or more annualized predetermined OH rates. Overhead is assigned to jobs by multiplying the predetermined rate by the actual measure of the activity base that was incurred for each job during the period. If a job is completed within a period, overhead is applied at completion of production so that a full product cost can be transferred to Finished Goods Inventory. If, however, a job is not complete at the end of a period, overhead must be applied at that time so that WIP Inventory on the period-end balance sheet contains costs for all three product elements (direct material, direct labor, and overhead). The journal entry for applying overhead to WIP Inventory follows:

Work in Process Inventory	XXX	
Manufacturing Overhead Control		XXX
To apply overhead to WIP Inventory		

Completion of Production

When a job is completed, its total cost is added (debited) to Finished Goods Inventory and removed from (credited to) Work in Process Inventory. Job order cost sheets for completed jobs are removed from the WIP Inventory subsidiary ledger and become the subsidiary ledger for the Finished Goods Inventory control account. When a job is sold, its cost is transferred from Finished Goods Inventory to Cost of Goods Sold. The job cost sheet then becomes a subsidiary record for Cost of Goods Sold.

Finished Goods (FG) Inventory	XXX	
Work in Process Inventory		XXX
To transfer completed goods to FG Inventory		

Cost of Goods Sold (CGS)	XXX	
Finished Goods Inventory		XXX
To transfer goods sold from FG Inventory to CGS		

This cost transfer presumes the use of a perpetual inventory system, which is common in a job order costing environment because goods are generally easily identified and tracked.

Job order cost sheets for completed jobs are kept in a company's permanent files. A completed job order cost sheet provides management with a historical summary about total costs and, if appropriate, the cost per finished unit for a given job. The cost per unit may be helpful for planning and control purposes as well as for bidding on future contracts. If a job was exceptionally profitable, management might decide to pursue additional similar jobs. If a job was unprofitable, the job order cost sheet may indicate areas in which cost control was lax. Such areas are more readily identifiable if the job order cost sheet presents the original, budgeted cost information.

Most businesses that use job order costing have no Finished Goods Inventory because production occurs only when a specific customer contracts for a particular good or service. Upon completion, the product or service cost may flow immediately to Cost of Goods Sold.

Job Order Costing and Technology

The trend in job order costing is to automate data collection and data entry functions supporting the accounting system. Automating recordkeeping functions relieves production employees of that task, and electronically stored data can be accessed to serve many purposes. For example, data from a completed job can be used as input to project the costs of a future job on which a bid is to be made, to understand a client's purchasing habits, or to estimate profit for next year. However, regardless of whether the data entry process is automated, virtually all product costing software, even very inexpensive off-the-shelf programs, contains a job costing module.

Many companies have created intranets to manage information, especially that pertaining to jobs produced. An **intranet** is a restricted network for sharing information and delivering data from corporate databases to local-area network (LAN) desktops. Exhibit 5–6 indicates some types of information that can be accessed on an intranet. As shown in the exhibit, much information relevant to managing a particular job's production is available online to managers. Data related to contract information and technical specifications, budgeted costs, actual costs, and stage of production measurements are instantly available to managers. Because input functions are automated, the intranet data become more closely correlated with real time.

In any job order costing system, the individual job is the cost object. The next section presents a comprehensive job order costing situation using information from Dean's Custom Fabricating, the company introduced earlier.

LO.4
How do costs flow in a job order costing system?

Job Order Costing Illustration

Dean's Custom Fabricating establishes prices based on costs incurred. Over the long term, the company's goal is to realize a gross profit equal to 20 percent of sales revenue. This level of gross profit is sufficient to generate a reasonable profit after covering selling and administrative costs. In more competitive circumstances, such as when a company has too much unused capacity, prices and gross margin may be reduced to increase the likelihood of gaining job contracts. Dean's Custom Fabricating has little unused capacity, so the company sets prices somewhat high to reduce the possibility of successfully obtaining too many contracts.

To help in establishing the price for the Willowdale Homeowners' Association, Dean's cost accountant provided the sales manager with the budgeted cost information shown earlier in Exhibit 5–4. The sales manager believed that a normal selling price was appropriate and, thus, set the sales price to yield a gross margin of roughly 20 percent [($35,250 − $28,200) ÷ $35,250]. The customer agreed to this sales price in a contract dated August 13, 2008. Dean's production manager scheduled the job to begin on September 1, 2008, and to be completed by November 15, 2008. The job is assigned the number PF108 for identification purposes.

EXHIBIT 5–6
Project Management Site Content

Project Management Library
- Instructions on how to use the project intranet site
- Project manager manuals
- Policy and procedure manuals
- Templates and forms
- Project management training exercises

General Project Information
- Project descriptions
- Photos of project progress
- Contract information
- Phone and e-mail directories
- Project team rosters
- Document control logs
- Scope documents
- Closure documents
- Links to project control tools
- Links to electronic document retrieval systems

Technical Information
- Drawing logs
- Detailed budgets and physical estimates
- Specifications
- Bill of materials by department
- Punch lists
- Links to drawing databases

Management Information
- Meeting minutes
- Daily logs
- Project schedules
- Task and resource checklists
- Shutdown and look-ahead reports
- Work-hour estimates
- Change notices
- Labor hours worked
- Earned value

Financial Information
- Project cost sheet
- Funding requests for each cost account
- Cash flow projections and budgets
- Original cost budgets and adjustments
- Contract status reports
- Departmental budget reports
- Links to mainframe sessions for requisitions and purchase order tracking
- Companywide financial statements

Source: Lawrence Barkowski, "Intranets for Project and Cost Management in Manufacturing," *Cost Engineering* (June 1999), p. 36. Reprinted with permission of AACE International, 209 Prairie Ave., Suite 100, Morgantown, WV 25601 USA. Internet: http://www.aacei.org. E-mail: info@aacei.org

---

The following journal entries illustrate the flow of costs for the Fabrication Department during September 2008. Work on several jobs, including Job #PF108, was performed in Fabrication during that month. In entries 1, 2, and 4 in the list that follows, separate WIP Inventory accounts are shown for costs related either to Job #PF108 or to other jobs. In practice, the Work in Process Inventory account for a given department would be debited only once for all costs assigned to it. The details for posting to the individual job cost records would be presented in the journal entry explanations.

1. During September 2008, material requisition forms #L40–L55 indicated that raw materials costing $5,420 were issued from the warehouse to the Fabrication Department. This amount included $4,875 of direct material used on Job #PF108 and $520 of direct material used on other jobs. The remaining $25 of raw materials issued during September were indirect.

Work in Process Inventory—Fabrication (Job #PF108)	4,875	
Work in Process Inventory—Fabrication (other jobs)	520	
Manufacturing Overhead Control—Fabrication (indirect material)	25	
Raw Material Inventory		5,420
To record direct and indirect materials issued per September requisitions		

2. The September time sheets and payroll summaries for the Fabrication Department workers were used to trace direct and indirect labor to that department. Total labor cost for the Fabrication Department for September was $9,599. Job #PF108 required $6,902 of direct labor cost combining the two biweekly pay periods in September. The remaining jobs in process required $1,447 of direct labor cost, and indirect labor cost for the month totaled $1,250.

Work in Process Inventory—Fabrication (Job #PF108)	6,902	
Work in Process Inventory—Fabrication (other jobs)	1,447	
Manufacturing Overhead Control—Fabrication (indirect labor)	1,250	
Wages Payable		9,599
To record September wages		

3. The Fabrication Department incurred overhead costs in addition to indirect material and indirect labor during September. Factory building and equipment depreciation of $2,500 was recorded. Insurance on the factory building ($200) for the month had been prepaid and had expired. The $1,900 bill for factory utility costs was received and would be paid in October. Repairs and maintenance costs of $500 were paid in cash. Additional miscellaneous overhead costs of $800 were incurred; these costs are credited to "Various accounts" for illustrative purposes. The following entry summarizes the accumulation of these other actual overhead costs for September.

Manufacturing Overhead Control—Fabrication	5,900	
Accumulated Depreciation		2,500
Prepaid Insurance		200
Utilities Payable		1,900
Cash		500
Various accounts		800
To record actual September overhead costs exclusive of indirect material and indirect, nonsalaried labor		

4. Dean's prepares financial statements monthly. To do so, Work in Process Inventory must include all production costs: direct material, direct labor, and overhead. The company allocates overhead to the Fabrication Department WIP Inventory based on two predetermined OH rates: $12 per direct labor hour and $30 per machine hour. In September, the employees committed 260 hours of direct labor time to Job #PF108, and 65 machine hours were consumed on that job. The other jobs advanced during the month received total applied overhead of $900 [25 direct labor hours (assumed) × $12] + [20 machine hours (assumed) × $30].

Work in Process Inventory—Fabrication (Job #PF108)	5,070	
Work in Process Inventory—Fabrication (other jobs)	900	
Manufacturing Overhead Control—Fabrication		5,970
To apply overhead for September using predetermined rates		

Notice that the $5,900 actual amount of September overhead in the Fabrication Department is not equal to the $5,970 of overhead applied to that department's Work in Process Inventory. This $70 difference is the overapplied overhead for the month. Because the predetermined OH rates were based on annual estimates, differences in actual and applied overhead accumulate during the year. Underapplied or overapplied overhead will be closed (as shown in Chapter 3) at year-end to Cost of Goods Sold (if the amount is immaterial) or allocated among Work in Process Inventory, Finished Goods Inventory, and Cost of Goods Sold accounts (if the amount is material).

The preceding entries for the Fabrication Department would be similar to the entries made in each of the other departments of Dean's Custom Fabricating. Direct material and direct labor data are posted to each job order cost sheet frequently (usually daily or weekly); entries are posted to the general ledger control accounts for longer intervals (usually monthly).

Job #PF108 will pass consecutively through the three departments of Dean's Custom Fabricating. In other types of job shops, different departments may work on the same job concurrently. Similar entries for Job #PF108 are made throughout the production process, and Exhibit 5–7 shows the cost sheet at the job's completion. Note that direct material requisitions, direct labor cost, and applied overhead shown previously in entries 1, 2, and 4 are posted on the job cost sheet. The actual costs of Installation and Finishing are given in the job order cost sheet in Exhibit 5–7, but the details are omitted in this discussion.

When the job is completed, its costs are transferred to Finished Goods Inventory. The journal entries related to transfers among departments as well as the completion and sale of the goods are as follows:

Work in Process Inventory—Installation	16,847	
Work in Process Inventory—Fabrication		16,847
To transfer Job #PF108 from Fabrication to Installation		

| Work in Process Inventory—Finishing | 22,376 | |
| Work in Process Inventory—Installation | | 22,376 |

To transfer Job #PF108 from Installation to Finishing

| Finished Goods Inventory—Job #PF108 | 28,091 | |
| Work in Process Inventory—Finishing | | 28,091 |

To transfer completed Job #PF108 to FG Inventory

| Accounts Receivable—Willowdale Homeowners' Association | 35,250 | |
| Sales | | 35,250 |

To record the sale of goods on account

| Cost of Goods Sold—Job #PF108 | 28,091 | |
| Finished Goods Inventory—Job #PF108 | | 28,091 |

To record the CGS for the above sale

Managers in all departments can use the completed job order cost sheet to determine how well costs were controlled. Overall, costs were slightly below the budgeted level, which is indicative of effective cost control, particularly in the Fabrication Department.

EXHIBIT 5–7

Dean's Custom Fabricating Completed Job Order Cost Sheet

Job Number PF108

Customer Name and Address:

Willowdale Homeowners' Assoc.
200 Willow Avenue
Willow, Texas

Contract Agreement Date: 8/13/08
Scheduled Starting Date: 9/01/08
Agreed Completion Date: 11/15/08
Actual Completion Date:

Delivery Instructions: Full installation per contract

Description of Job:

2,000 feet of 6' steel fence per contract dated 8/13/2008

Contract Price $35,250

FABRICATION

	DIRECT MATERIAL (EST. $5,000)			DIRECT LABOR (EST. $7,200)			OVERHEAD BASED ON # OF LABOR HOURS (EST. $3,000)			# OF MACHINE HOURS (EST. $2,000)		
Date	Source	Amount	Date	Source	Amount	Date	Source	Amount	Date	Source	Amount
9/30	MR L40-L55	$4,875	9/30	payroll	$6,902	7/31	payroll	$3,120	9/30	Machine hour meters	$1,950
---	---	---	---	---	---	---	---	---	---	---	---

INSTALLATION
(SAME FORMAT AS ABOVE BUT WITH DIFFERENT OH RATES)

FINISHING
(SAME FORMAT AS ABOVE BUT WITH DIFFERENT OH RATES)

SUMMARY

	FABRICATION Actual	Budget	INSTALLATION Actual	Budget	FINISHING Actual	Budget
Direct material	$ 4,875	$ 5,000	$ 0	$ 0	$1,605	$1,500
Direct labor	6,902	7,200	1,805	1,800	2,970	3,000
Overhead (labor)	3,120	3,000	1,610	1,500	1,140	1,200
Overhead (machine)	1,950	2,000	2,114	2,000	0	0
Totals	$16,847	$17,200	$5,529	$5,300	$5,715	$5,700

		Actual	Budget
Final Costs:	Fabrication	$16,847	$17,200
	Installation	5,529	5,300
	Finishing	5,715	5,700
	Totals	$28,091	$28,200

In the remainder of this chapter, the use of job order costing data to support management decision making and improve cost control is discussed. The next section discusses how standard, rather than actual, costs can be used to improve cost management.

LO.5
How are standard costs used in a job order costing system?

Job Order Costing Using Standard Costs

The Dean's Custom Fabricating example illustrates the use of actual historical cost data for direct material and direct labor in a job order costing system. However, using actual direct material and direct labor costs may cause the costs of similar units to fluctuate from period to period or from job to job because of changes in component costs. Use of standard costs for direct material and direct labor can minimize the effects of such cost fluctuations in the same way that predetermined rates do for overhead costs.

A standard cost system determines product cost by using predetermined norms in the inventory accounts for prices and/or quantities of cost components. After production is complete, standard production cost is compared to actual production cost to determine production efficiency. A difference between the actual quantity, price, or rate and its related standard is called a variance. Standard costing is covered in detail in Chapter 7.

Standards can be used in a job order system only if a company typically engages in jobs that produce fairly similar products. One type of standard job order costing system uses standards only for input prices of material or only for labor rates. Such a process is reasonable if all output relies on similar kinds of material or labor. If standards are used for price or rate amounts only, the debits to WIP Inventory become a hybrid of actual and standard information: actual quantities at standard prices or rates.

A Coat of Many Colors, a house-painting company located in Denver, illustrates the use of price and rate standards. Management has decided that, because of the climate, one specific brand of paint (costing $30 per gallon) is the best to use. Painters employed by the company are paid $12 per hour. These two amounts can be used as price and rate standards for A Coat of Many Colors. No standards can be set for the quantity of paint that will be used on a job or the amount of time that will be spent on the job. These items will vary based on the quantity and texture of wood of the structure as well as on the size of the structure being painted.

Assume that A Coat of Many Colors paints a house requiring 50 gallons of paint and 80 hours of labor time. The standard paint and labor costs, respectively, are $1,500 (50 × $30) and $960 (80 × $12). The paint was purchased on sale for $1,350, or $27 per gallon. A comparison of this price to the standard results in a $150 favorable (50 gallons × $3 per gallon) material price variance. If the actual labor rate paid to painters was $11 per hour, there would be an $80 favorable (80 hours × $1 per hour) labor rate variance.

Other job order companies produce output that is homogeneous enough to allow standards to be developed for both quantities and prices of material and labor. Such compa-

The output of painting companies is heterogeneous, so no set standard quantity of paint can be established across all jobs.

nies usually use distinct production runs for numerous similar products. In such circumstances, the output is homogeneous for each run, unlike the heterogeneous output of A Coat of Many Colors.

Green Manufacturing Inc. is a job order manufacturer that uses both price and quantity material and labor standards. Green produces wooden flower boxes from recycled wood that are retailed through several chains of garden supply stores. Retailers contract for the boxes on a job order basis because of the changes in style, color, and size with each spring gardening season. Green produces the boxes in distinct production runs each month for each retail chain. Price and quantity standards for direct material and direct labor have been established and are used to compare the estimated and actual costs of monthly production runs for each type of box produced.

Material and labor standards set for the boxes sold to Mountain Gardens are as follows: 8 linear feet of 1" × 10" redwood plank at $0.60 per linear foot and 1.4 direct labor hours at $9.00 per direct labor hour (DLH). In June, 2,000 boxes were produced for Mountain Gardens. Actual wood used was 16,300 linear feet, which was purchased at $0.58 per linear foot. Direct labor employees worked 2,700 hours at an average labor rate of $9.10.

Given this information, Green used 300 linear feet of redwood above the standard quantity for the job [16,300 − (8 × 2,000)]. This excess usage caused a $180 unfavorable material quantity variance at the $0.60 standard price ($0.60 × 300 linear feet). The actual redwood used was purchased at $0.02 below the standard price per linear foot, which resulted in a $326 favorable ($0.02 × 16,300) material price variance.

The actual DLHs used were 100 less than standard [2,700 − (1.4 hours × 2,000)], which resulted in a $900 favorable ($9 standard rate × 100 hours) labor quantity variance. The work crew earned $0.10 per hour above standard, which created a $270 unfavorable ($0.10 × 2,700) labor rate variance. A summary of variances follows:

Direct material quantity variance	$ 180 unfavorable
Direct material price variance	(326) favorable
Direct labor quantity variance	(900) favorable
Direct labor rate variance	270 unfavorable
Net variance (cost less than expected)	$(776) favorable

From a financial perspective, Green controlled its total material and labor costs well on the Mountain Gardens job.

Variances can be computed for actual-to-standard differences regardless of whether standards have been established for both quantities and prices or for prices or rates only. Standard costs for material and labor provide the same types of benefits as predetermined OH rates: more timely information and comparisons against actual amounts. In fact, a predetermined OH rate is simply a type of standard. It establishes a constant amount of overhead assignable as a component of product cost and eliminates any immediate need for actual overhead information in the calculation of product cost.

Standard cost job order systems are reasonable substitutes for actual or normal costing systems as long as the standards provide managers with useful information. Any type of product costing system is acceptable in practice if it is effective and efficient in serving the company's unique production needs, provides information desired by management, meets external reporting demands, and can be maintained at a cost that is reasonable when compared to the benefits received. These criteria apply equally well to both manufacturers and service companies.

Job Order Costing to Assist Managers

LO.6
How does information from a job order costing system support management decision making?

Managers are interested in controlling costs in each department as well as for each job. Actual direct material, direct labor, and factory overhead costs are accumulated in departmental accounts and are periodically compared to budgets so that managers can respond to significant deviations. Transactions must be recorded in a consistent, complete, and accurate manner to have information on actual costs available for periodic comparisons.

Managers in different types of job order organizations may stress different types of cost control. Companies such as Aston Martin are extremely concerned about labor hours and their related costs: unlike most cars that are built on a moving assembly line, each Aston Martin DB9 takes about

200 labor-hours to handmake in a series of workstations at the Gaydon, England, plant.[6] Other companies, such as jewelers, implement significant cost and physical controls for direct materials that include platinum, gold, diamonds, and Australian black opals. Hospitals must be careful to control overhead costs created by long waiting periods or delays in recording and communicating patient information.

One primary difference between job order costing for manufacturing and service organizations is that most service organizations use a fairly insignificant amount of materials relative to the value of labor for each job. In such cases, only direct labor may be traced to each job and all materials may be treated (for the sake of convenience) as part of overhead. Overhead then needs to be allocated to the various jobs, most commonly using a predetermined rate per direct labor hour or direct labor dollar. Other cost drivers that can effectively assign overhead to jobs may also be identified.

Knowing the costs of individual jobs allows managers to better estimate future job costs and to establish realistic bids and selling prices. Using budgets and standards in a job order costing system also provides information against which actual costs can be compared at regular time intervals for control purposes. These comparisons can also furnish some performance evaluation information. The following two examples demonstrate the usefulness of job order costing to managers.

Concrete Café

Concrete Café specializes in concrete structures. The firm has a diverse set of clients and job types. Its president, Josh Bradley, wants to know which of the firm's clients are the most profitable and which are the least profitable. To determine this information, he requested a breakdown of profits per job measured on both a percentage and an absolute dollar basis.

Bradley found that no records of costs for each client's job were kept. Costs had been accumulated only by type—travel, entertainment, and so forth. Stan Tobias, the sales manager, was certain that the largest profits came from Concrete Café's largest accounts. Careful job cost analysis found that the largest accounts contributed most of the firm's revenue but the smallest percentage and absolute dollars of incremental profits. Until Bradley requested this information, no one had totaled the costs of recruiting each client or the travel, entertainment, and other costs associated with maintaining each client.

A company that has a large number of jobs that vary in size, time, or effort may not know which jobs are responsible for disproportionately large costs. Job order costing can assist in both determining which jobs are truly profitable and helping managers to better monitor costs. As a result of the cost analysis, Bradley changed the company's marketing strategy. The firm began concentrating its efforts on smaller clients who were located closer to the primary office, causing a substantial increase in profits because significantly fewer costs were incurred for travel and entertainment. A job order costing system was implemented to track each client's costs. Unprofitable accounts were dropped, and account managers felt more responsibility to monitor and control costs related to their particular accounts.

Paula's Pirogues

Paula Boudreaux is a unique individual: a female boat builder. She and her employees custom manufacture small wooden boats to customer specifications. Before completing her MBA and learning about job order costing, Boudreaux had merely "guess-timated" the costs associated with each boat's production. She would estimate selling prices by using vague information from past jobs and specifications for the new design and adding what she considered a reasonable profit margin. Often customers who indicated they thought the selling price was too high could convince Boudreaux to make price reductions.

After implementing a job order costing system, Boudreaux had better cost control over the jobs that were in process, maintained better inventory valuations for financial statements, and had available better information with which to prevent part stockouts (not having parts in inventory) and production stoppages. The use of material requisitions helped make certain that materials acquired for a particular custom boat actually were used for that job. The job order cost sheets also gave her more up-to-date information that enhanced her ability to judge whether to accept additional work

[6]http://www.astonmartin.com/companynews; last accessed 7/20/07.

and when current work would be completed. Most important, the job order costing system gave Boudreaux an informed means by which to understand how costs were incurred on jobs, to estimate costs that would be incurred on future jobs, and to justify price quotes on future jobs.

Whether an entity is a manufacturer or a service organization that tailors its output to customer specifications, company management will find that job order costing techniques help in performing managerial functions. This type of cost system is useful for determining the cost of goods produced or services rendered in companies that are able to attach costs to specific jobs. As product variety increases, the size of production lots for many items shrinks, and job order costing becomes more applicable. Custom-made goods may become the norm rather than the exception in an environment that relies on flexible manufacturing systems and computer-integrated manufacturing.

Product and Material Losses in Job Order Costing

LO.7
How are losses treated in a job order costing system?

Production processes may result in losses of direct material or partially completed products. Some losses, such as evaporation, leakage, or oxidation, are inherent in the manufacturing process; such reductions are called shrinkage. Modifying the production process to reduce or eliminate shrinkage may be difficult, impossible, or simply not cost-beneficial. At other times, production process errors (either by humans or by machines) cause a loss of units through rejection at inspection for failure to meet appropriate quality standards or designated product specifications. Such units are considered either defects, if they can be economically reworked and sold, or spoilage, if this cannot be done.

If units do not meet quality specifications, they may be reworked to meet product specifications or sold as irregulars. Rework cost is a product or period cost depending on whether the rework relates to defective production that is considered to be normal or abnormal. A normal loss of units falls within a tolerance level that is expected during production. For example, if a company sets its quality goal as 99 percent of goods produced, the company expects a normal loss of 1 percent. Any loss in excess of the set expectation level is considered an abnormal loss. Thus, the difference between normal and abnormal loss is merely one of degree and is determined by management.

In a job order situation, the accounting treatment for lost units depends on two issues: (1) Is a loss generally incurred for most jobs, or is it specifically identified with a particular job? (2) Is the loss considered normal or abnormal?

Generally Anticipated on All Jobs

If a normal loss is anticipated on all jobs, the predetermined OH rate should include an amount for the net cost of the loss, which is equal to the cost of defective or spoiled work less the estimated disposal value, if any, of that work. This approach assumes that losses are naturally inherent and unavoidable in the production of good units, and the estimated loss should be allocated to the good units produced.

Assume that Kyndo Corp. produces special order cleaning compounds for use by manufacturers. Regardless of the job, however, some spoilage always occurs in the mixing process. In computing the predetermined OH rate related to the custom compounds, the following estimates are made:

Overhead costs other than spoilage		$121,500
Estimated spoilage cost	$10,300	
Sales of improperly mixed compounds to foreign distributors	(4,300)	6,000
Total estimated overhead		$127,500
Estimated gallons of production during the year		÷150,000
Predetermined OH rate per gallon		$ 0.85

During the year, Kyndo Corp. accepted a job (#38) from Husserl Co. to manufacture 500 gallons of cleaning compound. Direct material cost for this job was $4,660, direct labor cost totaled $640, and applied overhead was $425 ($0.85 × 500 gallons), for a total job cost of $5,725. Kyndo Corp. put 500 gallons of compounds into production. Five gallons (or 1 percent) of the compounds became defective during the production process when a worker accidentally added a thickening agent meant for another job into a container of Job #38's cleaning compound. Actual cost of the defective mixture was $57.25 (0.01 × $5,725), and it can be sold for $22. The following entry is made to account for the actual defect cost:

Disposal Value of Defective Work	22.00	
Manufacturing Overhead Control	35.25	
Work in Process Inventory—Job #38		57.25
To record disposal value of defective work incurred on Job #38 for Husserl Co.		

The estimated cost of spoilage was originally included when calculating the predetermined OH rate. Therefore, as defects or spoilage occur, the disposal value of nonstandard work is included in an inventory account (if salable), and the net cost of the normal, nonstandard work is charged to the Manufacturing Overhead Control account as is any other actual overhead cost.

Specifically Identified with a Particular Job

If defects or spoilage are not generally anticipated but are occasionally experienced on specific jobs because of job-related characteristics, the estimated cost should not be included in setting the predetermined OH rate. Because the defect/spoilage cost attaches to the job, disposal value of such goods reduces the cost of the job that created those goods. If no disposal value exists for the defective/spoiled goods, the cost of those lost units remains with the job that caused the defect or spoilage.

Assume that Kyndo Corp. did not typically experience spoilage in its production process. The company's predetermined OH rate would have been calculated as $0.81 per gallon ($121,500 ÷ 150,000). Thus, the total cost for the Husserl Co. job would have been $5,705 [$4,660 + $640 + ($0.81 × 500)]. A greater than normal quantity of ammonia was added to 5 gallons of the batch at Husserl Co.'s request. After inspecting those 5 gallons, Husserl Co. was unsatisfied and asked Kyndo Corp. to keep the original formula for the remaining gallons. The 5 gallons could be sold to another company for $22; this amount would reduce the cost of the Husserl Co. job as shown in the following entry:

Disposal Value of Defective Work	22	
Work in Process Inventory—Job #38		22
To record disposal value of defective work incurred on Job #38 for Husserl Co.		

Abnormal Spoilage

The cost of all abnormal losses (net of any disposal value) should be written off as a period cost. This treatment is justified because asset cost should include only those costs that are necessary to acquire or produce inventory; unnecessary costs should be written off in the period in which they are incurred. Abnormal losses are not necessary to the production of good units and the cost is avoidable in the future. This cost should be separately identified and the cause investigated to determine how to prevent future similar occurrences.

The following entry assumes that Kyndo Corp. normally anticipates some loss of partially completed products on its custom orders and that the estimated cost of those products was included in the development of a predetermined OH rate. Assume that on Job #135, the cost of defective units was $198 but $45 of disposal value was associated with those units. Of the remaining $153 of cost, $120 was related to normal defects and $33 was related to abnormal defects. The following journal entry records these facts.

Disposal Value of Defective Work	45	
Manufacturing Overhead Control	120	
Loss from Abnormal Spoilage	33	
Work in Process Inventory—Job #135		198
To record reassignment of cost of defective and spoiled work on Job #135		

The first debit represents the defective inventory's disposal value; the debit to Manufacturing Overhead Control is for the net cost of normal spoilage. The debit to Loss from Abnormal Spoilage is for the portion of the net cost of spoilage that was unnecessary and unanticipated in setting the predetermined application rate.

Comprehensive Review Module

Chapter Summary

1. Job order and process costing systems differ in that job order costing

   - is used in companies that make limited quantities of customer-specified products or perform customer-specific services; process costing is used in companies that make mass quantities of homogeneous output on a continuous flow or batch basis.

   - requires the use of a job order cost sheet to track the direct material, direct labor, and actual or applied overhead to each customer-specific job; process costing simply accounts for direct material, direct labor, and actual or applied overhead by batch of goods per department.

   - does not allow for the computation of a cost per unit unless all units within the job are similar; process costing can and does create a cost per unit for each cost element.

   - may use an actual cost system (combining actual direct material, direct labor, and overhead), a normal cost system (combining actual direct material and direct labor as well as applied overhead using a predetermined OH rate), or a standard cost system (combining budgeted norms for direct material, direct labor, and overhead); process costing may use the same type of cost valuation systems but standard cost systems are significantly more prevalent in process costing than job order costing.

2. From an accounting standpoint, a "job"

   - is the cost object for which costs are accumulated.

   - can consist of one or more units of output.

   - has its costs accumulated on a job order cost sheet.

3. The primary documents used in a job order costing system are the

   - material requisition forms, which trace the issuance of raw material to the specific jobs in WIP Inventory so that direct material can be included on the job order cost sheets.

   - job order cost sheets, which, for incomplete jobs, serve as the Work in Process Inventory subsidiary ledger; cost sheets for completed jobs not yet delivered to customers constitute the Finished Goods Inventory subsidiary ledger; and cost sheets for completed and sold jobs comprise the Cost of Goods Sold subsidiary ledger.

   - employee time sheets, which record the hours worked and jobs associated with work by employees so that direct labor cost can be included on the job order cost sheets.

4. The typical journal entries used to accumulate costs in a job order costing system record the

   - purchase, for cash or on credit, of raw material for use in production.

   - issuance of direct material to WIP Inventory.

   - incurrence of direct labor hours and cost.

   - incurrence of actual overhead costs.

   - application of predetermined overhead to jobs in process.

   - transfer of jobs and their related costs between departments.

   - completion of jobs and transfer of those jobs to Finished Goods Inventory.

   - sale of the products for cash or credit.

   - removal of products from Finished Goods Inventory upon sale and the expensing of the total production cost to Cost of Goods Sold.

5. Technological changes have impacted the gathering and use of information in job order costing systems by

   - including a job order costing module in even basic accounting software.

   - aiding the product management of jobs through software programs that allow operational and financial data about jobs to be shared throughout the firm, often disseminated on company intranets.

   - tracking job costs because more accurate and timely data are gathered and employees are relieved of the recurring burden of logging data.

- allowing electronic tracking, through scanners and bar codes, of employee work information and flow of parts and components.

6. Standard costs may be used in a job order costing system by

   - establishing standards for quantities and/or costs of production inputs.

   - providing a basis for managers to evaluate the efficiency of operations through comparisons of actual and standard costs. Differences between actual costs and standard costs are captured in variance accounts, and, by analyzing the variances, managers gain an understanding of the factors that cause costs to differ from the expected amounts.

7. Job order costing information helps support management decision making by

   - assisting managers in their planning, controlling, decision-making, and performance evaluating functions.

   - allowing managers to trace costs associated with

specific current jobs to better estimate costs for future jobs.

   - providing a way by which managers can better control the costs associated with current production, especially if comparisons with budgets or standards are used.

   - attaching costs correctly to jobs that are contracted on a cost-plus basis.

   - highlighting those jobs or types of jobs that are most profitable to the organization.

8. Both normal and abnormal losses may occur in a job order system, and they are accounted for in the following manner:

   - normal losses that are generally anticipated on all jobs are estimated and included in the development of the predetermined OH rate.

   - normal losses that are associated with a particular job are charged to that job (net of any disposal value of the spoiled items).

   - abnormal losses are always charged to a loss account in the period in which they are incurred.

Potential Ethical Issues

1. Inflating costs of cost-plus contracts so that the price of the contract increases as does the profit for the contract

2. Assigning costs from a fixed-fee contract to a cost-plus contract so that both contracts become more profitable

3. Substituting materials of a lower quality than specified in the contract to reduce costs and increase profits

4. Shifting costs from completed jobs (in Cost of Goods Sold) to incomplete jobs (in Work in Process Inventory) to both increase profits reported for financial accounting purposes and inflate assets on the balance sheet

5. Using manufacturing methods or materials that violate the intellectual property rights of other firms (e.g., patent rights of competitors)

6. Recording the disposal value from the sale of defective work in a cost-plus contract job as "Other Revenue" rather than reducing the inventory cost of the related job ▲

Solution Strategies

BASIC JOURNAL ENTRIES IN A JOB ORDER COSTING SYSTEM		
Raw Material Inventory	XXX	
Accounts Payable		XXX
To record the purchase of raw material		
Work in Process Inventory—Dept. (Job #)	XXX	
Manufacturing Overhead Control	XXX	
Raw Material Inventory		XXX
To record the issuance of direct and indirect material		
requisitioned for a specific job.		
Work in Process Inventory—Dept. (Job #)	XXX	
Manufacturing Overhead Control	XXX	
Wages Payable		XXX
To record direct and indirect labor payroll for		
production employees		

Manufacturing Overhead Control	XXX	
Various accounts		XXX
To record the incurrence of actual overhead costs.		
(Account titles to be credited must be specified in		
an actual journal entry.)		
Work in Process Inventory—Dept. (Job #)	XXX	
Manufacturing Overhead Control		XXX
To apply overhead to a specific job (This may		
be actual OH or OH applied using a predetermined		
rate. Predetermined OH is applied at job completion		
or end of period, whichever is earlier.)		
Finished Goods Inventory (Job #)	XXX	
Work in Process Inventory		XXX
To transfer completed goods to FG Inventory		
Accounts Receivable	XXX	
Sales		XXX
To record the sale of goods on account		
Cost of Goods Sold	XXX	
Finished Goods Inventory		XXX
To record CGS		

Demonstration Problem

Modern Building Solutions builds portable buildings to clients' specifications. The firm has two departments: Parts Fabrication and Assembly. The Parts Fabrication Department designs and cuts the major components of the building and is highly automated. The Assembly Department assembles and installs the components and this department is highly labor intensive. The Assembly Department begins work on the buildings as soon as the floor components are available from the Parts Fabrication Department.

In its first month of operations (March 2008), Modern Building Solutions obtained contracts for three buildings:

Job 1: A 20- by 40-foot storage building
Job 2: A 35- by 35-foot commercial utility building
Job 3: A 30- by 40-foot portable classroom

Modern Building Solutions bills its customers on a cost-plus basis, with profit equal to 25 percent of costs. The firm uses a job order costing system based on normal costs. Overhead is applied in Parts Fabrication at a predetermined rate of $100 per machine hour (MH). In the Assembly Department, overhead is applied at a predetermined rate of $10 per direct labor hour (DLH). The following significant transactions occurred in March 2008.

1. Direct material was purchased on account: $80,000.

2. Direct material was issued to the Parts Fabrication Department for use in the three jobs: Job #1, $8,000; Job #2, $14,000; and Job #3, $45,000. Direct material was issued to the Assembly Department: Job #1, $500; Job #2, $1,200; and Job #3, $6,600.

3. Time sheets and payroll summaries indicated that the following direct labor costs were incurred:

	Parts Fabrication Department	Assembly Department
Job #1	$1,000	$2,400
Job #2	3,000	3,500
Job #3	5,000	9,500

4. The following indirect costs were incurred in each department:

	Parts Fabrication Department	Assembly Department
Labor	$ 4,200	$4,500
Utilities/Fuel	5,900	2,300
Depreciation	10,300	3,600

The labor and utilities/fuel costs were accrued at the time of the journal entry.

5. Overhead was applied based on the predetermined rates in effect in each department. The Parts Fabrication Department had 200 MHs (20 MHs on Job #1, 35 MHs on Job #2, and 145 MHs on Job #3), and the Assembly Department worked 950 DLHs (40 DLHs on Job #1, 110 DLHs on Job #2, and 800 DLHs on Job #3) for the month.

6. Job #1 was completed and sold for cash in the amount of the cost-plus contract. At month-end, Jobs #2 and #3 were only partially complete.

7. Any underapplied or overapplied overhead at month-end is considered immaterial and is assigned to Cost of Goods Sold.

Required:

a. Record the journal entries for transactions 1 through 7.

b. As of the end of March 2008, determine the total cost assigned to Jobs #2 and #3.

Solution to Demonstration Problem

a.	1.	Raw Material Inventory	80,000	
		Accounts Payable		80,000
		To record purchase of direct material		
	2.	WIP Inventory—Parts Fabrication (Job #1)	8,000	
		WIP Inventory—Parts Fabrication (Job #2)	14,000	
		WIP Inventory—Parts Fabrication (Job #3)	45,000	
		Raw Material Inventory		67,000
		To record requisition and issuance of direct material		
		to Parts Fabrication Department		
		WIP Inventory—Assembly (Job #1)	500	
		WIP Inventory—Assembly (Job #2)	1,200	
		WIP Inventory—Assembly (Job #3)	6,600	
		Raw Material Inventory		8,300
		To record requisition and issuance of direct material		
		to Assembly Department		
	3.	WIP Inventory—Parts Fabrication (Job #1)	1,000	
		WIP Inventory—Parts Fabrication (Job #2)	3,000	
		WIP Inventory—Parts Fabrication (Job #3)	5,000	
		Wages Payable		9,000
		To record direct labor cost for Parts Fabrication Department		
		WIP Inventory—Assembly (Job #1)	2,400	
		WIP Inventory—Assembly (Job #2)	3,500	
		WIP Inventory—Assembly (Job #3)	9,500	
		Wages Payable		15,400
		To record direct labor cost for Assembly Department		
	4.	Manufacturing Overhead Control—Parts Fabrication	20,400	
		Manufacturing Overhead Control—Assembly	10,400	
		Wages Payable		8,700
		Utilities/Fuel Payable		8,200
		Accumulated Depreciation		13,900
		To record various overhead costs		
	5.	WIP Inventory—Parts Fabrication (Job #1)	2,000	
		WIP Inventory—Parts Fabrication (Job #2)	3,500	
		WIP Inventory—Parts Fabrication (Job #3)	14,500	
		Manufacturing Overhead Control—Parts Fabrication		20,000
		To apply overhead in Parts Fabrication Department		
		WIP Inventory—Assembly (Job #1)	400	
		WIP Inventory—Assembly (Job #2)	1,100	
		WIP Inventory—Assembly (Job #3)	8,000	
		Manufacturing Overhead Control—Assembly		9,500
		To apply overhead in Assembly Department		
	6.	Finished Goods Inventory[a]	14,300	
		WIP Inventory—Parts Fabrication		11,000
		WIP Inventory—Assembly		3,300
		To record completion of Job #1		

Cash	17,875	
Sales Revenue [b]		17,875
To record sale of Job #1		
Cost of Goods Sold	14,300	
Finished Goods Inventory		14,300
To record CGS for Job #1		

7.

Cost of Goods Sold	1,300	
Manufacturing Overhead Control—Parts Fabrication		400
Manufacturing Overhead Control—Assembly		900
To assign underapplied overhead to CGS		

[a]Job #1 costs = $8,000 + $500 + $1,000 + $2,400 + $2,000 + $400 = $14,300
[b]Revenue, Job #1 = $14,300 × 1.25 = $17,875

b.

	Job #2	Job #3
Direct material—Parts Fabrication	$14,000	$45,000
Direct labor—Parts Fabrication	3,000	5,000
Overhead—Parts Fabrication	3,500	14,500
Direct material—Assembly	1,200	6,600
Direct labor—Assembly	3,500	9,500
Overhead—Assembly	1,100	8,000
Totals	$26,300	$88,600

Key Terms

abnormal loss, ***p. 155***

cost-plus contract, ***p. 142***

defect, ***p. 155***

employee time sheet, ***p. 146***

intranet, ***p. 148***

job, ***p. 140***

job order cost sheet, ***p. 144***

job order costing system, ***p. 140***

material requisition form, ***p. 144***

normal loss, ***p. 155***

process costing system, ***p. 140***

shrinkage, ***p. 155***

spoilage, ***p. 155***

standard cost system, ***p. 141***

variance, ***p. 152***

Questions

1. In choosing a product costing system, what are the two choices available for a cost accumulation system? How do these systems differ?

2. In choosing a product costing system, what are the three valuation method alternatives? Explain how these methods differ.

3. In a job order costing system, what key documents support the cost accumulation process and what is the purpose of each?

4. In a standard costing system, discuss how information about variances can be used to improve cost control.

5. If normal spoilage is generally anticipated to occur on all jobs, how should the cost of that spoilage be treated?

6. How can information produced by a job order costing system assist managers in operating their firms more efficiently?

7. Why are normal and abnormal spoilage accounted for differently? Typically, how does one determine which spoilage is normal and which is abnormal?

Exercises

8. **LO.2 (Job costing documents; ethics)** You work for a public accounting firm in a litigation support role. One of your clients, OakTex Industries, contracted for a specialized production machine from a tool company on a cost-plus basis. Specifically, the contract specified a price equal to "production cost plus 15% of production cost." Prior to executing the contract with the tool company, OakTex was told by a sales executive at the tool company that the approximate price of the machine would be $862,500 based on the following estimates:

Direct material cost	$250,000
Direct labor cost	200,000
Manufacturing overhead (applied based on machine time)	300,000
Markup	112,500
Estimated price to OakTex	$862,500

The tool company delivered the completed machinery, configured and manufactured per the contract. However, the invoice that accompanied the machinery caught executives at OakTex by surprise. The invoice provided the following:

Direct material cost	$ 450,000
Direct labor cost	200,000
Manufacturing overhead (applied based on machine time)	300,000
Markup	142,500
Estimated price to OakTex	$1,092,500

Upon receiving the invoice, OakTex executives requested an audit of the direct material charges because they were nearly twice the estimated amount. The tool company granted the request and OakTex hired your firm to conduct the audit.

a. Describe your strategy for validating the $450,000 charge for direct material and discuss specific documents you will request from the tool company as part of the audit.

b. Even if the $450,000 charge is validated, do you perceive the tool company's behavior in this case as ethical? Explain. ▲

9. **LO.2 (Job order costing documents; accounts)** Following are specific types of information that can be located in a particular account (such as WIP Inventory) or on a particular document (such as an employee time card). For each item listed, identify the account or document that would provide the relevant information.

a. Total product cost assigned to a particular job
b. Total cost of material issued to production for a period
c. Total hours worked on a particular job by a particular employee
d. Total cost of goods completed during a period
e. Total cost of goods sold during a period
f. Total cost of material purchased during a period
g. Total manufacturing overhead cost incurred for a period
h. Total overhead cost assigned to a particular job
i. Total direct labor cost incurred during a period
j. Total indirect labor cost incurred during a period

10. **LO.1 (Costing system choice)** For each of the following firms, determine whether it is more likely to use job order or process costing. This firm

a. is a health care clinic.
b. makes custom jewelry.
c. manufactures hair spray and hand lotion.
d. provides public accounting services.
e. manufactures paint.
f. cans vegetables and fruits.
g. is an automobile repair shop.
h. provides landscaping services for corporations.
i. manufactures baby food.
j. provides property management services for a variety of real estate developments.
k. designs custom software.
l. produces candles.

11. LO.1 (Costing system/valuation method) Jackson Brown, after spending 20 years working for a large engineering firm, has decided to start his own business. Working in his garage during weekends, Brown developed a consumer product that removes jar lids with little physical effort. Brown believes the potential market for this product is nearly one million units annually. Brown has protected his design with appropriate patents, has acquired production space and required machinery, and is now training his newly hired employees to manufacture the product.

Brown has been a friend of your family for your entire life and he has asked your advice about what type of product cost accounting system he should use. He has researched the topic on the Internet and understands that there are job order costing and process costing systems as well as several valuation methods that can be coupled with those costing systems. Based on the limited information given here, what recommendation would you make to Brown? Why?

12. LO.3 & LO.4 (Journal entries; cost flows) The following costs were incurred in February 2008 by Container Corp., which produces customized steel storage bins.

Direct material purchased on account		$ 38,000
Direct material used for jobs:		
Job #217	$22,400	
Job #218	3,600	
Other jobs	26,800	52,800
Direct labor costs for month:		
Job #217	$ 5,200	
Job #218	7,000	
Other jobs	9,800	22,000
Actual overhead costs for February		110,000

The balance in Work in Process Inventory on February 1 was $8,400, which consisted of $5,600 for Job #217 and $2,800 for Job #218. The February beginning balance in Direct Material Inventory was $22,300. Actual overhead is applied to jobs on the basis of direct labor cost. Job #217 was completed and transferred to Finished Goods Inventory during February. Job #217 was then sold for cash at 135 percent of cost.

a. Prepare journal entries to record the preceding information.

b. Determine the February ending balance in WIP Inventory. How much of this balance relates to Job #218?

13. LO.3 & LO.4 (Journal entries) Midwest Ceramics produces custom-made floor tiles. During April 2008, the following information was obtained relating to operations and production:

1. Direct material purchased on account, $92,000.
2. Direct material issued to jobs, $81,900.
3. Direct labor hours incurred, 1,700. All direct factory employees were paid $15 per hour.
4. Actual factory overhead costs incurred for the month totaled $34,350. This overhead consisted of $9,000 of supervisory salaries, $10,750 of depreciation charges, $3,600 of insurance, $6,250 of indirect material, and $4,750 of utilities. Salaries, insurance, and utilities were paid in cash, and indirect material was taken from supplies inventory.
5. Overhead is applied to production at the rate of $20 per direct labor hour.

Beginning balances of Raw Material Inventory and Work in Process Inventory were, respectively, $2,150 and $11,200. Ending Work in Process Inventory was $2,350.

a. Prepare journal entries for transactions 1–5.

b. Determine the balance in Raw Material Inventory at the end of the month.

c. Determine the cost of the goods completed during April. If 5,000 similar units were completed, what was the cost per unit?

d. What is the amount of underapplied or overapplied overhead at the end of April?

14. LO.4 (Cost flows) For 2008, Edgar Mfg. decided to apply overhead to units based on direct labor hours. The company's WIP Inventory account on January 31 appeared as follows:

Work in Process Inventory			
Beginning balance	68,000	Cost of completed jobs	??
Direct material	130,700		
Direct labor	87,500		
Applied overhead	62,300		

The direct labor cost contained in the $68,000 beginning balance of WIP Inventory was for a total of 5,000 direct labor hours. During January, 7,000 direct labor hours were recorded. Only one job was still in process on January 31. That job had $20,250 in direct material and 1,850 direct labor hours assigned to it.

   a. What was the predetermined OH rate for 2008?
   b. What was the average direct labor rate per hour?
   c. What was the balance in WIP Inventory at the end of January?
   d. What was the total cost of jobs completed in January?

15. LO.4 (Cost flows) LeBlanc Designs began operations on May 1, 2008. Its Work in Process Inventory account on May 31 appeared as follows:

Work in Process Inventory

Direct material	277,200	Cost of completed jobs	??
Direct labor	192,000		
Applied overhead	211,200		

The company applies overhead on the basis of direct labor cost. Only one job was still in process on May 31. That job had $66,300 in direct material and $46,800 in direct labor cost assigned to it.
   a. What was the predetermined overhead application rate?
   b. What was the balance in WIP Inventory at the end of May?
   c. What was the total cost of jobs completed in May?

16. LO.4 (Cost flows) On March 18, 2008, a fire destroyed Riverside Mfg.'s WIP Inventory, which consisted of two custom jobs (B325 and Q428). The following information had, however, been contained in some off-site records:

   ■ Riverside Mfg. applies overhead at the rate of 85 percent of direct labor cost.
   ■ The cost of goods sold for the company averages 75 percent of selling price. Sales from January 1 to the date of the fire totaled $637,000.
   ■ The company's wage rate for production employees is $8.90 per hour.
   ■ As of March 18, $21,000 of direct material and 28 hours of direct labor had been recorded for Job B325. Also at that time, $14,700 of direct material and 40 hours of direct labor had been recorded for Job Q428.
   ■ January 1, 2008, inventories were as follows: $19,500 of Direct Material and $68,900 of Finished Goods. The amount of Work in Process Inventory is unknown. Jobs B325 and Q428 were not in process on January 1.
   ■ One job, R91, was completed and in the warehouse awaiting shipment on March 18. The total cost of this job was $53,600.

Determine the following amounts:
   a. Cost of goods sold for the year
   b. Cost of goods manufactured during the year
   c. Amount of applied overhead contained in each job in WIP Inventory
   d. Cost of WIP Inventory destroyed by the fire

EXCEL

17. LO.4 (Cost flows) Indiana Industries applies overhead to jobs at a rate of 120 percent of direct labor cost. On December 31, 2008, a flood destroyed many of the firm's cost records, leaving only the following information:

Direct Material Inventory

Beg. balance	12,300		?
Purchases	?		
	4,100		

Work in Process Inventory

Beg. balance	28,000		?
Direct material	?		
Direct labor	90,000		
Overhead	?		
	24,000		

Finished Goods Inventory

Beg. balance	45,000	685,000	
Goods completed	?		
	42,000		

Cost of Goods Sold

?		

As the cost accountant of Indiana Industries, you must find the following for 2008:
   a. Cost of goods sold
   b. Cost of goods manufactured
   c. Amount of overhead applied to production

d. Cost of direct material used

e. Cost of direct material purchased

18. LO.4 (Cost flows in two departments) Red River Products uses a normal cost, job order costing system. In the Mixing Department, overhead is applied using machine hours; in Paving, overhead is applied using direct labor hours. In December 2007, the company estimated the following data for its two departments for 2008:

	Mixing Department	Paving Department
Direct labor hours	6,000	14,000
Machine hours	30,000	6,000
Budgeted overhead cost	$240,000	$392,000

a. Compute the predetermined OH rate for each department of Red River.

b. Job #220 was started and completed during March 2008. The job cost sheet shows the following information:

	Mixing Department	Paving Department
Direct material	$22,600	$3,400
Direct labor cost	$ 1,250	$4,050
Direct labor hours	24	120
Machine hours	160	44

Compute the overhead applied to Job #220 for each department and in total.

c. If the company had computed a companywide predetermined OH rate rather than departmental rates, would such a rate have indicated the actual overhead cost of each job? Explain.

19. LO.4 (Cost allocation to jobs) Bitter & Butter, LLP, is a law firm that currently has four cases in process. Following is information related to those cases as of the end of March 2008:

	Case #1	Case #2	Case #3	Case #4
Direct material	$220	$4,400	$1,850	$410
Direct labor hours ($190 per hour)	20	45	36	8
Estimated court hours	6	45	150	20

Bitter & Butter allocates overhead to cases based on a predetermined rate of $100 per estimated court hour. Determine the total cost assigned to each case as of March 31, 2008.

20. LO.4 (Cost flows; assigning costs to jobs) Dawn's Designs, an interior decorating firm, uses a job order costing system and applies overhead to jobs using a predetermined rate of 60 percent of direct labor cost. On June 1, 2008, Job #918 was the only job in process. Its costs included direct material of $8,250, direct labor of $1,200, and applied overhead of $720. During June, the company began work on Jobs #919, #920, and #921. Direct material used for June totaled $17,350. June's direct labor cost totaled $6,300. Job #920 had not been completed at the end of June, and its direct material and direct labor charges were $3,350 and $650, respectively. All other jobs were completed in June.

a. What was the total cost of Job #920 as of the end of June 2008?

b. What was the cost of goods manufactured for June 2008?

c. If actual overhead for June was $4,350, was the overhead underapplied or overapplied for the month? By how much?

21. LO.4 (Cost flows; assigning costs to jobs) Custom Cabinetry uses a job order costing system and applies overhead to jobs at a predetermined rate of $2.20 per direct labor dollar. During April 2008, the company spent $14,800 on direct material and $23,900 on direct labor for Job #344. Budgeted factory overhead for the company for the year was $660,000.

a. How did Custom Cabinetry compute the predetermined OH rate for 2008?

b. Journalize the application of overhead to all jobs, assuming that April's total direct labor cost was $30,700.

c. How much overhead was assigned to Job #344 during April?

d. If Job #344 had a balance of $18,350 on April 1, what was the balance on April 30?

22. LO.5 (Standard costing) Fine Print Inc. incurred the following direct material costs in November 2008 for high-volume routine print jobs:

Actual unit purchase price	$0.016 per sheet
Standard unit price	$0.018 per sheet
Quantity purchased and used in November	490,000 sheets
Standard quantity allowed for good production	492,000 sheets

Calculate the material price variance and the material quantity variance.

23. **LO.5 (Standard costing)** United Services provides a number of routine maintenance services to oil and gas firms in their production facilities. Although the services provided to each client are relatively unique, some services provided are repetitive. The firm negotiates prices for its services with each individual client. The CFO of United Services has recently completed examination of the profitability of a sample of the firm's service contracts. She was surprised that the amount of profit generated for each contract varied significantly. Further, the CFO discovered that the production inputs (e.g., material and labor) for contracts often varied substantially from amounts budgeted at the time the service contracts were negotiated. As you are an accounting intern at United Services, the CFO has asked you to write a memo to her describing how the adoption of standard costing could improve cost control and profit management for the firm's service contracts.

24. **LO.6 (Job costing and decision making)** Kelly Shiro owns a small firm that manufactures computers from commodity components. Her clientele is diverse and the computer configurations her clients demand are equally diverse. Shiro has historically tracked only the cost of components to the computers her firm builds. She has based the selling prices, or bids, of the computers on the cost of components plus a markup sufficient to cover the other costs of operating her firm. In recent years, Shiro has encountered increasing price pressure from her customers and as a result she often has priced her computers below the full-markup price. The result of the price discounting has been lower profits for the firm.

   As you have provided other financial services to Shiro's firm in the past, she has turned to you for guidance regarding approaches she could take to better manage her firm's profits and prices. You decide that a job order costing system could be helpful to Shiro.

   a. Explain how a job order costing system could help Shiro better control the costs and profits of her firm.
   b. Explain why Shiro should not base her computer prices only on component costs plus a markup.

25. **LO.5 (Standard costing)** Delaware Inc. uses a standard cost system. The company experienced the following results related to direct labor in December 2008:

Actual hours worked	49,500
Standard hours for production	46,200
Actual direct labor rate	$9.25
Standard direct labor rate	$9.75

   a. Calculate the total actual payroll.
   b. Determine the labor rate variance.
   c. Determine the labor quantity variance.
   d. What concerns do you have about the variances in parts (b) and (c)?

26. **LO.6 (Cost control)** Tom Tom makes steel storage canisters for various chemical products. The company uses a job order costing system and obtains jobs based on competitive bidding. For each project, a budget is developed.

   One of the firm's products is a 55-gallon drum. In the past year, the company made this drum on four separate occasions for four different customers. Financial details for the four orders follow:

Date	Job No.	Quantity	Bid Price	Budgeted Cost	Actual Cost
Jan. 17	2118	30,000	$150,000	$120,000	$145,000
Mar. 13	2789	25,000	125,000	100,000	122,000
Oct. 20	4300	40,000	200,000	160,000	193,000
Dec. 3	4990	35,000	175,000	140,000	174,000

   Assume that you are the company's controller. Write a memo to management describing any problems that you perceive in the data presented and the steps that should be taken to eliminate recurrence of these problems.

27. **LO.6 (Job cost and pricing)** Ace Crawford is an attorney who uses a job order costing system to collect costs relative to client engagements. Crawford is currently working on a case for Peter Paul. During the first three months of 2008, Crawford logged 75 hours on the Paul case.

   In addition to direct hours spent by Crawford, his office assistant has worked 25 hours typing and copying 1,450 pages of documents related to the Paul case. Crawford's assistant works 160 hours per month and is paid a salary of $4,800 per month. The average cost per copy is $0.05 for paper, toner, and machine rental. Telephone charges for long-distance calls on the case totaled $310.25. Last, Crawford has estimated that total office overhead for rent, utilities, parking, and so on, amount to $9,600 per month and that, during a normal month, he is at the office 120 hours.

a. Crawford desires to earn, at a minimum, $90 per hour, and he wishes to cover all direct and allocated indirect costs related to a case. What minimum charge per hour (rounded to the nearest $10) should Crawford charge Paul? (Hint: Be sure to include office overhead.)

b. All the hours that Crawford spends at the office are not necessarily billable hours. In addition, Crawford did not consider certain other expenses such as license fees, country club dues, automobile costs, and other miscellaneous expenses when he determined the amount of overhead per month. Therefore, to cover nonbillable time as well as other costs, Crawford desires to bill each client for direct costs plus allocated indirect costs plus 50 percent margin on his time and overhead. What will Crawford charge Paul in total for the time spent on his case?

28. **LO.7 (Accounting for losses)** Describe how the following occurrences should be accounted for based on the fact pattern presented.

a. A certain amount of spoilage and waste are normal in the production system and affect all jobs.

b. A certain amount of spoilage occurs that is unique to a particular job. There is no disposal value for the spoiled units.

c. Because of a nonroutine malfunction in a production machine, a number of products in Work in Process Inventory were ruined. The quantity of work lost is assumed to be abnormal. There is some salvage value for the spoiled units.

29. **LO.6 (Cost Control; ethics)** Companies use time sheets for two primary reasons: to know how many hours an employee works and, in a job order production situation, to trace work hours to products. An article ("Altering of Worker Time Cards Spurs Growing Number of Suits" by Steven Greenhouse) in the *New York Times* on April 4, 2004, described a recent corporate practice of deleting worker hours to increase organizational profitability. Use your library database to obtain this article and discuss the following:

a. What companies were mentioned as having been found to engage in this practice?

b. Why is it easier now than in the past to engage in this practice?

c. As a member of upper management, how would you respond to finding out that this practice was being used in some of your stores? Provide an answer that addresses both the short run and the long run. ▲

30. **LO.7 (Job order costing; rework)** Rex's Rigging manufactures pulley systems to customer specifications and uses a job order system. Fort Bend Mechanical recently ordered 10,000 pulleys, and the job was assigned #BA468. Information for Job #BA468 revealed the following:

Direct material	$20,400
Direct labor	24,600
Overhead	18,400

Final inspection of the pulleys revealed that 230 were defective. In correcting the defects, an additional $850 of cost was incurred ($150 for direct material and $700 for direct labor). After the defects were corrected, the pulleys were included with the other good units and shipped to the customer.

a. Journalize the entry to record incurrence of the rework costs if rework is normal but specific to this job.

b. Journalize the entry to record incurrence of the rework costs if Rex's Rigging's predetermined overhead rate includes normal rework costs.

c. Journalize the entry to record incurrence of the rework costs, assuming that all rework is abnormal.

Problems

31. **LO.3 (Journal entries)** Main Spars uses an actual cost, job order system. The following transactions are for August 2008. At the beginning of the month, Direct Material Inventory was $4,000, Work in Process Inventory was $12,500, and Finished Goods Inventory was $10,500.

- Direct material purchases on account totaled $45,000.
- Direct labor cost for the period totaled $37,800 for 4,000 direct labor hours; these costs were paid in cash.
- Actual overhead costs were $41,000 and are applied to production based on direct labor hours.
- The ending inventory of Direct Material Inventory was $1,500.
- The ending inventory of Work in Process Inventory was $5,750.
- Goods costing $121,850 were sold for $173,025 cash.

a. What was the actual OH rate per direct labor hour?

b. Journalize the preceding transactions.

c. Determine the ending balance in Finished Goods Inventory.

32. LO.3 (Journal entries) Summer Shade installs awnings on residential and commercial structures. The company had the following transactions for February 2008:
- Purchased $395,000 of building (raw) material on account.
- Issued $285,000 of building (direct) material to jobs.
- Issued $60,000 of building (indirect) material for use on jobs.
- Accrued wages payable of $437,000, of which $397,000 could be traced directly to particular jobs.
- Applied overhead to jobs on the basis of 55 percent of direct labor cost.
- Completed jobs costing $523,000. For these jobs, revenues of $671,000 were collected.

Journalize the above transactions.

33. LO.3 & LO.4 (Journal entries; cost flows) Minneapolis Machinery began 2008 with three jobs in process:

	TYPE OF COST			
Job No.	Direct Material	Direct Labor	Overhead	Total
247	$ 38,600	$ 45,700	$17,366	$101,666
251	88,300	104,900	39,862	233,062
253	72,700	84,800	32,224	189,724
Totals	$199,600	$235,400	$89,452	$524,452

During 2008, the following transactions occurred:
1. The firm purchased and paid for $271,000 of raw material.
2. Factory payroll records revealed the following:
   - Indirect labor incurred was $27,000.
   - Direct labor incurred was $301,400 and was associated with the jobs as follows:

Job No.	Direct Labor Cost
247	$ 8,700
251	4,400
253	10,500
254	68,300
255	72,500
256	47,300
257	89,700

3. Material requisition forms issued during the year revealed the following:
   - Indirect material issued totaled $38,000.
   - Direct material issued totaled $233,200 and was associated with jobs as follows:

Job No.	Direct Material Cost
247	$ 6,200
251	3,100
253	8,400
254	52,600
255	59,900
256	36,400
257	66,600

4. Overhead is applied to jobs on the basis of direct labor cost. Management budgeted overhead of $120,000 and total direct labor cost of $300,000 for 2008. Actual total factory overhead costs (including indirect labor and indirect material) for the year totaled $122,200.
5. Jobs #247 through #255 were completed and delivered to customers, who paid for the goods in cash. The revenue on these jobs was $1,132,387.
   a. Journalize all preceding events.
   b. Determine the ending balances for the jobs still in process.
   c. Determine the cost of jobs completed, adjusted for underapplied or overapplied overhead.

34. LO.3 & LO.4 (Journal entries; assigning costs to jobs; cost flows) Vital Ventures uses a job order costing system. On September 1, 2008, the company had the following account balances:

Raw Material Inventory	$ 166,200
Work in Process Inventory	756,300
Cost of Goods Sold	2,432,000

On September 1, the three jobs in Work in Process Inventory had the following balances:

Job #75	$293,200
Job #78	116,800
Job #82	346,300

The following transactions occurred during September:

Sept. 1   Purchased $970,000 of raw material on account.

4   Issued $950,000 of raw material as follows: Job #75, $144,800; Job #78, $126,300; Job #82, $496,100; Job #86, $156,200; and indirect material, $26,600.

15   Prepared and paid the $378,500 factory payroll for Sept. 1–15. Analysis of this payroll showed the following information:

Job #75	4,830 hours	$ 42,300
Job #78	13,160 hours	133,600
Job #82	10,150 hours	101,500
Job #86	5,140 hours	55,400
Indirect wages		45,700

15   On each payroll date, Vital Ventures applies manufacturing overhead to jobs at a rate of $8.50 per direct labor hour.

15   Job #75 was completed, accepted by the customer, and billed at a selling price of cost plus 25 percent. Selling prices are rounded to the nearest whole dollar.

20   Paid the following monthly factory bills: utilities, $19,800; rent, $35,300; and accounts payable (accrued in August), $98,400.

24   Purchased raw material on account, $312,000.

25   Issued $386,100 of raw material as follows: Job #78, $77,400; Job #82, $106,300; Job #86, $174,500; and indirect material, $27,900.

30   Recorded additional factory overhead costs as follows: depreciation, $104,500; expired prepaid insurance, $32,700; and accrued taxes and licenses, $16,200.

30   Recorded and paid the factory payroll for Sept. 16–30 of $357,200. Analysis of the payroll follows:

Job #78	8,940 hours	$ 88,700
Job #82	13,650 hours	114,200
Job #86	9,980 hours	121,800
Indirect wages		32,500

30   Applied overhead for the second half of the month to jobs.

a. Journalize the September transactions.

b. Use T-accounts to post the information from the journal entries in part (a) to the job cost subsidiary accounts and to general ledger accounts.

c. Reconcile the September 30 balances in the subsidiary ledger with the Work in Process Inventory account in the general ledger.

d. Determine the amount of underapplied or overapplied overhead for September.

35. **LO.3 & LO.4 (Job cost sheet analysis)** As a candidate for a cost accounting position with Casper Building Components, you have been asked to take a quiz to demonstrate your knowledge of job order costing. Casper's job order costing system is based on normal costs, and overhead is applied based on direct labor cost. The following records pertaining to May have been provided to you:

Job No.	Direct Material	Direct Labor	Applied Overhead	Total Cost
67	$ 17,703	$ 6,920	$7,960	$32,583
69	54,936	7,240	8,328	70,504
70	1,218	2,000	2,300	5,518
71	154,215	28,500	?	?
72	28,845	2,200	2,532	33,577

To explain the missing job number, you are informed that Job #68 had been completed in April. You are also told that Job #67 was the only job in process at the beginning of May. At that time, the job had been assigned $12,900 for direct material and $3,600 for direct labor. At the end of May, Job #71 had not been completed; all others had. You are to provide answers to the following questions:

a. What predetermined overhead rate does Casper Building Components use?

b. What was the total cost of beginning Work in Process Inventory?

c. What were total direct manufacturing costs incurred for May?

d. What was cost of goods manufactured for May?

36. LO.3 & LO.4 (Simple inventory calculation) Production data for the first week in November 2008 for Florida Fabricators were as follows:

WORK IN PROCESS INVENTORY

Date	Job No.	Material	Labor	Machine Time (Overhead)
Nov. 1	411	$950	18 hours	25 hours
1	412	620	5 hours	15 hours
7	417	310	4 hours	8 hours

Finished Goods Inventory, Nov. 1: $11,900
Finished Goods Inventory, Nov. 7: $ 0

MATERIAL RECORDS

Type	Inv. 11/1	Purchases	Issuances	Inv. 11/7
Aluminum	$4,150	$49,150	$29,350	$?
Steel	6,400	13,250	17,100	$?
Other	2,900	11,775	12,950	$?

Direct labor hours worked: 340. Labor cost is $15 per direct labor hour. Machine hours worked: 600. Overhead for first week in November:

Depreciation	$ 4,500
Supervisor salaries	7,200
Indirect labor	4,175
Insurance	1,400
Utilities	1,125
Total	$18,400

Overhead is applied to production at a rate of $30 per machine hour. Underapplied or overapplied overhead is treated as an adjustment to Cost of Goods Sold at year-end. (All company jobs are consecutively numbered, and all work not in ending Finished Goods Inventory has been completed and sold.)

What is the value on November 7 of (1) the three raw material accounts, (2) Work in Process Inventory, and (3) Cost of Goods Sold?

37. LO.3 & LO.4 (Comprehensive) Jackson Construction Company uses a job order costing system. In May 2008, Jackson made a $1,650,000 bid to build a pedestrian overpass over the beach highway in Gulfport, Mississippi. Jackson Construction won the bid and assigned #515 to the project. Its completion date was set at December 15, 2008. The following costs were estimated for completion of the overpass: $620,000 for direct material, $335,000 for direct labor, and $201,000 for overhead.

During July, direct material cost assigned to Job #515 was $60,900, and direct labor cost associated with it was $87,520. The firm uses a predetermined OH rate of 60 percent of direct labor cost. Jackson Construction also worked on several other jobs during July and incurred the following costs:

Direct material (including Job #515)	$289,650
Direct labor (including Job #515)	292,000
Indirect labor	27,900
Administrative salaries and wages	19,800
Depreciation on construction equipment	13,200
Depreciation on office equipment	3,900
Client entertainment (on accounts payable)	5,550
Advertising for firm (paid in cash)	3,300
Indirect material (from supplies inventory)	9,300
Miscellaneous expenses (design related; to be paid in the following month)	5,100
Accrued utilities (for office, $900; for construction, $2,700)	3,600

During July, Jackson Construction completed several jobs that had been in process before the beginning of the month. These completed jobs generated $612,000 of revenues for the company. The related job cost sheets showed costs associated with those jobs of $414,500. At the beginning of July, Jackson Construction had Work in Process Inventory of $435,900.

a. Prepare a job order cost sheet for Job #515, including all job details, and post the appropriate cost information for July.

b. Prepare journal entries for the preceding information.

c. Prepare a Cost of Goods Manufactured Schedule for July for Jackson Construction Company.

d. Assuming that the company pays income tax at a 40 percent rate, prepare an income statement for Jackson Construction Company.

38. **LO.3 & LO.4 (Departmental rates)** Connie's Cubicles has two departments: Fabrication and Assembly. All jobs go through each department, and the company uses a job order costing system. Overhead is applied to jobs based on machine hours in Fabrication and on labor hours in Assembly. In December 2007, corporate management estimated the following production data for 2008 in setting its predetermined OH rates:

	Fabrication	Assembly
Machine hours	52,000	22,000
Direct labor hours	25,200	160,000
Departmental overhead	$780,000	$880,000

Two jobs completed during 2008 were #2296 and #2297. The job order cost sheets showed the following information about these jobs:

	Job #2296	Job #2297
Direct material cost	$59,250	$73,600
Direct labor hours—Fabrication	450	230
Machine hours—Fabrication	900	450
Direct labor hours—Assembly	425	200
Machine hours—Assembly	54	23

Direct labor workers are paid $12 per hour in the Fabrication Department and $10 per hour in Assembly.

a. Compute the predetermined OH rates used in Fabrication and Assembly for 2008.

b. Compute the direct labor cost associated with each job for both departments.

c. Compute the amount of overhead assigned to each job in each department.

d. Determine the total cost of Jobs #2296 and #2297.

e. Actual data for 2008 for each department follow.

	Fabricating	Assembly
Machine hours	51,600	21,600
Direct labor hours	23,900	162,000
Departmental overhead	$764,000	$895,000

What is the amount of underapplied or overapplied overhead for each department for the year ended December 31, 2008?

39. **LO.4 (Cost flows; assigning costs to jobs)** Charles Weber is an advertising consultant; he tracks costs for his jobs using a job order costing system. During September, Weber and his staff worked on and completed jobs for the following companies:

	Douglas Company	Palacios Manufacturing	El Campo Inc.
Direct material cost	$3,900	$7,100	$ 9,900
Direct labor cost	$2,790	$9,000	$14,175
Number of promotions designed	3	10	8

Direct material can be traced to each job because these costs are typically associated with specific advertising campaigns. Based on historical data, Weber has calculated an overhead charge of $58 per direct labor hour. The normal labor cost per hour is $45.

a. Determine the total cost for each of the advertising accounts for the month.

b. Determine the cost per promotion developed for each client.

c. Weber charges $4,300 per promotion. What was his net income for the month, assuming actual overhead for the month was $25,000?

d. You suggest to Weber that he bill ads on a cost-plus basis and suggest a markup of 30 percent on cost. How would his income have compared to his income computed in part (c) if he had used this method? How would his clients feel about such a method?

40. **LO.3 & LO.4 (Comprehensive)** Fast Fence designs and manufactures perimeter fencing for large retail and commercial buildings. Each job goes through three stages: design, production, and installation. Three jobs were started and completed during the first week of May 2008. No jobs were in process at the end of April 2008. Information for the three departments for the first week in May follows:

	DEPARTMENT		
Job #2019	**Design**	**Production**	**Installation**
Direct labor hours	400	NA	380
Machine hours	NA	360	NA
Direct labor cost	$40,800	$17,000	$5,040
Direct material	$ 4,800	$58,200	$5,200
Job #2020	**Design**	**Production**	**Installation**
Direct labor hours	340	NA	320
Machine hours	NA	1,200	NA
Direct labor cost	$34,680	$ 29,800	$ 5,760
Direct material	$ 4,100	$134,400	$18,400
Job #2021	**Design**	**Production**	**Installation**
Direct labor hours	360	NA	1,640
Machine hours	NA	480	NA
Direct labor cost	$36,720	$ 10,800	$7,600
Direct material	$ 8,800	$116,000	$5,200

Overhead is applied using departmental rates. Design and Installation use direct labor cost as the base, with rates of 30 and 90 percent, respectively. Production uses machine hours as the base, with a rate of $15 per hour. Actual overhead for the month was $52,800 in Design, $30,000 in Production, and $15,600 in Installation.

a. Determine the overhead to be applied to each job. By how much is the overhead underapplied or overapplied in each department? For the company?

b. Assume that no journal entries have been made to Work in Process Inventory. Journalize all necessary entries to both the subsidiary ledger and general ledger accounts.

c. Calculate the total cost for each job.

41. **LO.1 & LO.4 (Comprehensive)** Pip Squeaks Inc. is a manufacturer of furnishings for infants and children. The company uses a job order cost system. Pip Squeaks' Work in Process Inventory on April 30, 2008, consisted of the following jobs:

Job No.	Items	Units	Accumulated Cost
CBS102	Cribs	20,000	$ 900,000
PLP086	Playpens	15,000	420,000
DRS114	Dressers	25,000	1,570,000

The company's Finished Goods Inventory, carried on a FIFO (first-in, first-out) basis, consists of five items:

Item	Quantity and Unit Cost	Total Cost
Cribs	7,500 units × $64	$ 480,000
Strollers	13,000 units × $23	299,000
Carriages	11,200 units × $102	1,142,400
Dressers	21,000 units × $55	1,155,000
Playpens	19,400 units × $35	679,000
Total		$3,755,400

Pip Squeaks applies factory overhead on the basis of direct labor hours. The company's factory overhead budget for the fiscal year ending May 31, 2008, totaled $4,500,000, and the company planned to work 600,000 direct labor hours during this year. Through the first 11 months of the year, a total of 555,000 direct labor hours were worked, and total factory overhead amounted to $4,273,500.

At the end of April, the balance in Pip Squeaks' Raw Material Inventory account, which includes both raw material and purchased parts, was $668,000. Additions to and requisitions from the material inventory during May included the following:

	Raw Material	Parts Purchased
Additions	$242,000	$396,000
Requisitions:		
Job #CBS102	51,000	104,000
Job #PLP086	3,000	10,800
Job #DRS114	124,000	87,000
Job #STR077 (10,000 strollers)	62,000	81,000
Job #CRG098 (5,000 carriages	65,000	187,000

During May, Pip Squeaks' factory payroll consisted of the following:

Job No.	Hours	Cost
CBS102	12,000	$122,400
PLP086	4,400	43,200
DRS114	19,500	200,500
STR077	3,500	30,000
CRG098	14,000	138,000
Indirect	3,000	29,400
Supervision		57,600
Total		$621,100

The jobs that were completed in May and the unit sales for May follow:

Job No.	Items	Quantity Completed
CBS102	Cribs	20,000
PLP086	Playpens	15,000
STR077	Strollers	10,000
CRG098	Carriages	5,000

Items	Quantity Shipped
Cribs	17,500
Playpens	21,000
Strollers	14,000
Dressers	18,000
Carriages	6,000

a. Describe when it is appropriate for a company to use a job order costing system.
b. Calculate the dollar balance in Pip Squeaks' Work in Process Inventory account as of May 31, 2008.
c. Calculate the dollar amount related to the playpens in Pip Squeaks' Finished Goods Inventory as of May 31, 2008.
d. Explain the treatment of underapplied or overapplied overhead when using a job order costing system.

(CMA adapted)

42. **LO.3 & LO.4 (Comprehensive; job cost sheet)** Lincoln Construction Company builds bridges. In October and November 2008, the firm worked exclusively on a bridge spanning the Calamus River in northern Nebraska. Lincoln Construction's Precast Department builds structural elements of the bridges in temporary plants located near the construction sites. The Construction Department operates at the bridge site and assembles the precast structural elements. Estimated costs for the Calamus River Bridge for the Precast Department were $1,550,000 for direct material, $220,000 for direct labor, and $275,000 for overhead. For the Construction Department, estimated costs for the Calamus River Bridge were $350,000 for direct material, $130,000 for direct labor, and $214,500 for overhead. Overhead is applied on the last day of each month. Overhead application rates for the Precast and Construction Departments are $25 per machine hour and 165 percent of direct labor cost, respectively.

TRANSACTIONS FOR OCTOBER

1 Purchased $1,150,000 of material (on account) for the Precast Department to begin building structural elements. All of the material was issued to production; of the issuances, $650,000 was considered direct.
5 Installed utilities at the bridge site at a total cost of $25,000. This amount will be paid at a later date.
8 Paid rent for the temporary construction site housing the Precast Department, $5,000.
15 Completed bridge support pillars by the Precast Department and transferred to the construction site.
20 Paid machine rental expense of $60,000 incurred by the Construction Department for clearing the bridge site and digging foundations for bridge supports.
24 Purchased additional material costing $1,485,000 on account.
31 Paid the following bills for the Precast Department: utilities, $7,000; direct labor, $45,000; insurance, $6,220; and supervision and other indirect labor costs, $7,900. Departmental depreciation was recorded, $15,200. The company also paid bills for the Construction Department: utilities, $2,300; direct labor, $16,300; indirect labor, $5,700; and insurance, $1,900. Departmental depreciation was recorded on equipment, $8,750.
31 Issued a check to pay for the material purchased on October 1 and October 24.
31 Applied overhead to production in each department; 6,000 machine hours were worked in the Precast Department in October.

TRANSACTIONS FOR NOVEMBER

1	Transferred additional structural elements from the Precast Department to the construction site. The Construction Department incurred a cash cost of $5,000 to rent a crane.
4	Issued $1,000,000 of material to the Precast Department. Of this amount, $825,000 was considered direct.
8	Paid rent of $5,000 in cash for the temporary site occupied by the Precast Department.
15	Issued $425,000 of material to the Construction Department. Of this amount, $200,000 was considered direct.
18	Transferred additional structural elements from the Precast Department to the construction site.
24	Transferred the final batch of structural elements from the Precast Department to the construction site.
29	Completed the bridge.
30	Paid final bills for the month in the Precast Department: utilities, $15,000; direct labor, $115,000; insurance, $9,350; and supervision and other indirect labor costs, $14,500. Depreciation was recorded, $15,200. The company also paid bills for the Construction Department: utilities, $4,900; direct labor, $134,300; indirect labor, $15,200; and insurance, $5,400. Depreciation was recorded on equipment, $18,350.
30	Applied overhead in each department. The Precast Department recorded 3,950 machine hours in November.
30	Billed the state of Nebraska for the completed bridge at the contract price of $3,450,000.

a. Journalize the entries for the preceding transactions. For purposes of this problem, it is not necessary to transfer direct material and direct labor from one department into the other.

b. Post all entries to T-accounts.

c. Prepare a job order cost sheet, which includes estimated costs, for the construction of the bridge.

d. Discuss Lincoln Construction Company's estimates relative to its actual costs.

43. LO.5 (Standard costing) C3PO specializes in making robotic conveyor systems to move materials within a factory. Model #89 accounts for approximately 60 percent of the company's annual sales. Because the company has produced and expects to continue to produce a significant quantity of this model, C3PO uses the following standard costs to account for Model #89 production costs.

Direct material (14,000 pounds)	$28,000
Direct labor (860 hours at $20 per hour)	17,200
Overhead	38,000
Total standard cost	$83,200

For the 200 units of Model #89 produced in 2008, the actual costs were

Direct material (3,000,000 pounds)	$ 5,800,000
Direct labor (178,400 hours)	3,478,800
Overhead	7,400,000
Total actual cost	$16,678,800

a. Compute a separate variance between actual and standard cost for direct material, direct labor, and manufacturing overhead for the Model #89 units produced in 2008.

b. Is the direct material variance found in part (a) driven primarily by the price per pound difference between standard and actual or the quantity difference between standard and actual? Explain.

44. LO.4 (Missing amounts) Riveredge Manufacturing Company realized too late that it had made a mistake locating its controller's office and its electronic data processing system in the basement. Because of the spring thaw, the Mississippi River overflowed its banks on May 2 and flooded the company's basement. Electronic data storage was destroyed, and the company had not provided off-site storage of data. Some of the paper printouts were located but were badly faded and only partially legible. On May 3, when the flooding subsided, company accountants were able to assemble the following factory-related data from the debris and from discussions with various knowledgeable personnel. Data about the following accounts were found:

- Raw Material (includes indirect material) Inventory: Balance April 1 was $4,800.
- Work in Process Inventory: Balance April 1 was $7,700.
- Finished Goods Inventory: Balance April 30 was $6,600.
- Total company payroll cost for April was $29,200.
- Accounts payable balance April 30 was $18,000.
- Indirect material used in April cost $5,800.
- Other nonmaterial and nonlabor overhead items for April totaled $2,500.

Payroll records, kept at an across-town service center that processes the company's payroll, showed that April's direct labor amounted to $18,200 and represented 4,400 labor hours. Indirect factory labor amounted to $5,400 in April.

The president's office had a file copy of the production budget for the current year. It revealed that the predetermined overhead application rate is based on planned annual direct labor hours of 50,400 and expected factory overhead of $151,200.

Discussion with the factory superintendent indicated that only two jobs remained unfinished on April 30. Fortunately, the superintendent also had copies of the job cost sheets that showed a combined total of $2,400 of direct material and $4,500 of direct labor. The direct labor hours on these jobs totaled 1,072. Both of these jobs had been started during April.

A badly faded copy of April's Cost of Goods Manufactured and Sold Schedule showed cost of goods manufactured was $48,000, and the April 1 Finished Goods Inventory was $8,400.

The treasurer's office files copies of paid invoices chronologically. All invoices are for raw material purchased on account. Examination of these files revealed that unpaid invoices on April 1 amounted to $6,100; $28,000 of purchases had been made during April; and $18,000 of unpaid invoices existed on April 30.

a. Calculate the cost of direct material used in April.
b. Calculate the cost of raw material issued in April.
c. Calculate the April 30 balance of Raw Material Inventory.
d. Determine the amount of underapplied or overapplied overhead for April.
e. What is the Cost of Goods Sold for April?

45. **LO.6 (Ethics)** Two types of contracts are commonly used when private firms contract to provide services to governmental agencies: cost-plus and fixed-price contracts. The cost-plus contract allows the contracting firm to recover the costs associated with providing the product or service plus a reasonable profit. The fixed-price contract provides for a fixed payment to the contractor. When a fixed-price contract is used, the contractor's profits are based on its ability to control costs relative to the price received.

In recent years, a number of contractors have either been accused or found guilty of improper accounting or fraud in accounting for contracts with the government. One deceptive accounting technique that is sometimes the subject of audit investigations involves cases in which a contractor is suspected of shifting costs from fixed-priced contracts to cost-plus contracts. In shifting costs from the fixed-priced contract, the contractor not only influences costs assigned to that contract but also receives a reimbursement plus an additional amount on the costs shifted to the cost-plus contract.

a. Why would a company that conducts work under both cost-plus and fixed-price contracts have an incentive to shift costs from the fixed-price to the cost-plus contracts?
b. From an ethical perspective, do you believe such cost shifting is ever justified? Explain. ▲

46. **LO.5 (Standard costing)** During July 2008, Hip Hop Hitch worked on two production runs (Jobs #918 and #2002) of the same product, a trailer hitch component. Job #918 consisted of 1,200 units of the product, and Job #2002 contained 2,000 units. The hitch components are made from 1/2" sheet metal. Because this component is routinely produced for one of Hip Hop Hitch's long-term customers, standard costs have been developed for its production. The standard cost of material for each unit is $4.50; each unit contains 6 pounds of material. The standard direct labor time per unit is 6 minutes for workers earning a rate of $20 per hour. The actual costs recorded for each job were as follows:

	Direct Material	Direct Labor
Job #918	(7,500 pounds) $5,250	(130 hours) $2,470
Job #2002	(11,800 pounds) 9,440	(230 hours) 4,255

a. What is the standard direct cost of each trailer hitch component?
b. What was the total standard direct cost assigned to each of the jobs?
c. Compute the variances for direct material and for direct labor for each job.
d. Why should variances be computed separately for each job rather than for the aggregate annual trailer hitch component production?

47. **LO.6 (Ethics)** One of the main points of using a job order costing system is to achieve profitability by charging a price for each job that is proportionate to the related costs. The fundamental underlying concept is that the buyer of the product should be charged a price that exceeds all costs related to the job contract; thus, the price reflects the cost.

However, there are settings in which the price charged to the consumer does not reflect the costs incurred by the vendor to serve that customer. This is the situation in a recent case heard by the U.S. Supreme Court. The case involves the University of Wisconsin, which charges all students a user fee and then redistributes these fees to student organizations.

The purpose of collecting the fee is to ensure that money is available to support diversity of thought and speech in student organizations. The user fee supports even unpopular causes so that the students hear a variety of voices. In total, the fee subsidized about 125 student groups. However, a group of students filed suit, claiming that students should not be required to fund causes that are inconsistent with their personal beliefs.

a. In your opinion, how would diversity of thought be affected if a student were allowed to select the organizations that would receive the student's user fee (e.g., as with dues)?

b. Is the University of Wisconsin treating its students ethically by charging them to support student organizations for causes that conflict with their personal beliefs? ▲

48. LO.6 (Research; quality) Timbuk2 is a San Francisco company that makes a variety of messenger, cyclist, and laptop bags. The company's Web site (Timbuk2.com) allows customers to design their own size, color, and fabric bags with specific features and accessories; then the company sews the bags to the customers' specifications.

a. Visit the company's Web site and custom design a bag. Compare the quoted price with a bag of similar quality and features at a local store. Explain whether you think the Timbuk2 bag is a good value.

b. Why would Timbuk2 be able to produce custom-made messenger bags for almost the same cost as mass-produced ones?

c. Would you expect the quality of the custom-produced messenger bags to be higher or lower than the mass-produced ones? Discuss the rationale for your answer.

d. Why would the custom-made messenger bags show a high profit margin?

49. LO.7 (Defective units and rework) PlastiCo produces plastic pipe to customer specifications. Losses of less than 5 percent are considered normal because they are inherent in the production process. The company applies overhead to products using machine hours. PlastiCo used the following information in setting its predetermined OH rate for 2008:

Expected overhead other than rework	$425,000
Expected rework costs	37,500
Total expected overhead	$462,500
Expected machine hours for 2008	50,000

During 2008, the following production and cost data were accumulated:

Total good production completed	2,000,000 feet of pipe
Total defects	40,000 feet of pipe
Ending inventory	75,000 feet of pipe
Total cost of direct material for Job #B316	$343,550
Total cost of conversion for Job #B316	$ 78,875
Total machine hours for Job #B316	1,540
Cost of reworking defects during 2008	$ 37,750
Total actual overhead cost for 2008	$431,000

a. Determine the overhead application rate for 2008.

b. Determine the cost for Job #B316 in 2008.

c. Assume that the rework is normal and those units can be sold for the regular selling price. How will PlastiCo account for the $37,750 of rework cost?

d. Assume that PlastiCo does not include rework costs in developing the overhead application rate because rework is related to specific jobs. Determine the cost of Job #B316.

e. Using the information from part (d), assume that 20 percent of the rework cost was specifically related to 200 feet of pipe produced for Job #B316. The reworked pipe can be sold for $1.50 per foot. What is the total cost of Job #B316?

50. LO.7 (Defective units and rework) Detroit Chemicals produces a variety of chemicals that are used by auto manufacturers in their painting processes. With each batch of chemicals produced, some spoilage naturally occurs. Detroit Chemicals includes normal spoilage cost in its predetermined OH rate. For 2008, Detroit Chemicals estimated the following:

Overhead costs, other than spoilage	$300,000
Estimated spoilage cost	25,000
Estimated sales value of spoiled materials	10,000
Estimated direct labor hours	20,000

a. Detroit Chemicals applies overhead based on direct labor cost. Calculate the predetermined OH rate for 2008.

b. For a batch of chemicals mixed in May 2008, the firm experienced normal spoilage on Job #788. The cost of the spoiled material amounted to $612 and the company estimated the salvage value of those materials to be $265. Journalize the entry for the spoilage.

6 Process Costing

Objectives

After completing this chapter, you should be able to answer the following questions:

LO.1 How does process costing differ from job order costing?

LO.2 Why are equivalent units of production used in process costing?

LO.3 How are equivalent units of production, unit costs, and inventory values determined using the weighted average method of process costing?

LO.4 How are equivalent units of production, unit costs, and inventory values determined using the FIFO method of process costing?

LO.5 How are equivalent units of production, unit costs, and inventory values determined using the standard costing method of process costing?

LO.6 Why would a company use a hybrid costing system?

LO.7 (*Appendix 1*) What alternative methods can be used to calculate equivalent units of production?

LO.8 (*Appendix 2*) How are normal and abnormal spoilage losses treated in an EUP schedule?

Introduction

Companies choose product costing systems based, in part, on the nature of the products they produce and the customers they serve. When a company manufactures products or performs services to customer specifications and in limited quantities, it will use job order costing. In contrast, other companies manufacture products in a continuous flow process or in batches of output, in which each unit is basically identical to all others. For example, Kellogg's produces Rice Krispies in batches and all "rice puffs" in each batch are the same. However, with Pop-Tarts, the external pastry is the same for all batches, but the flavoring inside may differ or some Pop-Tarts may be frosted whereas others are not. Kellogg's would use process costing rather than job order costing to accumulate and assign costs to units of production. Manufacturers of food products, bricks, gasoline, candles, and paper, among many other types of firms, commonly use this costing method.

LO.1
How does process costing differ from job order costing?

Both job order and process costing systems accumulate costs by cost component in each production department. However, the two systems assign costs to departmental output differently. In a job order system, costs are assigned to specific jobs and then, if possible, to units contained within the job. Process costing uses an averaging technique to assign costs directly to units produced during the period. In both systems, unit costs are transferred as goods are moved from one department to the next so that a total production cost can be accumulated.

This chapter first illustrates the weighted average (WA) and first-in, first-out (FIFO) methods of calculating unit cost in a process costing system. These two methods differ only in the treatment of beginning Work in Process (WIP) Inventory units and costs. After unit cost has been determined, total costs are assigned to the units transferred out of a department and to that department's ending WIP Inventory. The chapter also describes a standard-cost process costing system, which is an often-used simplification of the FIFO process costing system. Appendix 2 to this chapter provides a brief introduction to the issue of spoilage in a process costing production system.

Introduction to Process Costing

Assigning costs to units of production requires the use of an averaging process. In the easiest situation, a product's actual unit cost is found by dividing a period's departmental production costs by that period's departmental production quantity as expressed by the following formula:

$$\text{Unit Cost} = \text{Production Costs} \div \text{Production Quantity}$$

Production Costs: The Numerator

The formula numerator is obtained by accumulating departmental costs incurred in a single period. Because most companies make more than one type of product, costs must be accumulated by product within each department. The accumulation can occur by using either separate WIP Inventory accounts for each product or a single WIP Inventory control account that is supported by detailed subsidiary ledgers containing specific product information.

Cost accumulation in a process costing system differs from that in a job order costing system in two ways: (1) the quantity of production for which costs are accumulated, and (2) the cost object to which the costs are assigned. Assume that Colorful Candles typically makes 6", 9", and 12" taper candles but occasionally contracts to make custom candles for a client's promotions. For its specialty production, Colorful Candles uses job order costing. Direct material and direct labor costs associated with each distinctive order would be accumulated and assigned directly to the individual buyer's job. After each job is completed, the total material, labor, and allocated overhead costs are known and job cost can be determined.

In contrast, for its basic product lines, Colorful Candles would use a process costing system to accumulate periodic costs for each department and each product. Because the company manufactures several types of candles each period, the costs assignable to each product type must be individually designated and attached to the specific production runs. Production run costs are then assigned to the units processed during the period.

Exhibit 6–1 presents the source documents used to make initial cost assignments to production departments during a period. Costs are reassigned at the end of the period (usually each month) from the departments to the units produced. As goods are transferred from one department to the next, related departmental production costs are also transferred. When products are complete, their costs are transferred from WIP Inventory to Finished Goods (FG) Inventory.

As in job order costing, direct material and direct labor costs present relatively few problems for cost accumulation and assignment. Direct material cost can be measured from material requisition slips; direct labor cost can be determined from employee time sheets and wage rates for the period.

Overhead, however, must be allocated to output. If total overhead costs are relatively constant from period to period and production volume is relatively steady over time, actual overhead costs may be used for product costing. Otherwise, using actual overhead for product costing would result in fluctuating unit costs and, therefore, predetermined application rates are more appropriate. As managers find new ways to structure production activities and develop new management methods, the bases on which overhead is assigned to production may change. For example, as a production plant becomes less labor intensive and more automated, management should change from a labor-based to a machine-based overhead allocation.

EXHIBIT 6–1
Cost Flows and Cost Assignment

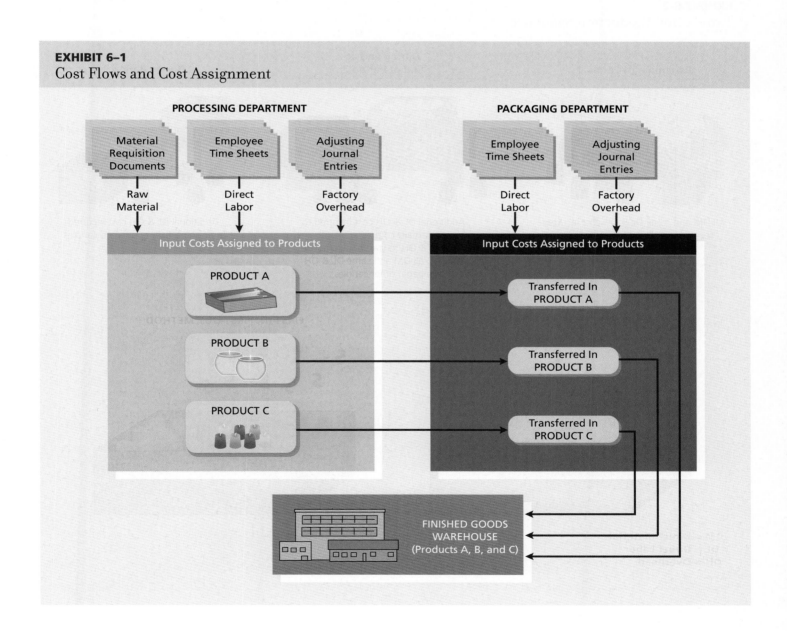

LO.2
Why are equivalent units
of production used in
process costing?

Production Quantity: The Denominator

The denominator in the unit cost formula represents total departmental production for the period. If all units were 100 percent complete at the end of each accounting period, units could simply be counted to obtain the denominator. In most production processes, however, partially completed units comprise WIP Inventory at the end of one period and become the partially completed beginning WIP Inventory of the next period. Process costing assigns costs to both fully and partially completed units by mathematically converting partially completed units to equivalent whole units.

Units in beginning WIP Inventory were started last period but will be completed during the current period. This two-period production sequence means that some costs for these units were incurred last period and additional costs will be incurred in the current period. Additionally, the partially completed units in ending WIP Inventory were started in the current period but will not be completed until next period. Therefore, current period production efforts caused units in ending WIP Inventory to absorb some costs in this period, and more costs will be absorbed next period. This production sequence is illustrated in Exhibit 6–2.

EXHIBIT 6–2
Two-Period Production Sequence

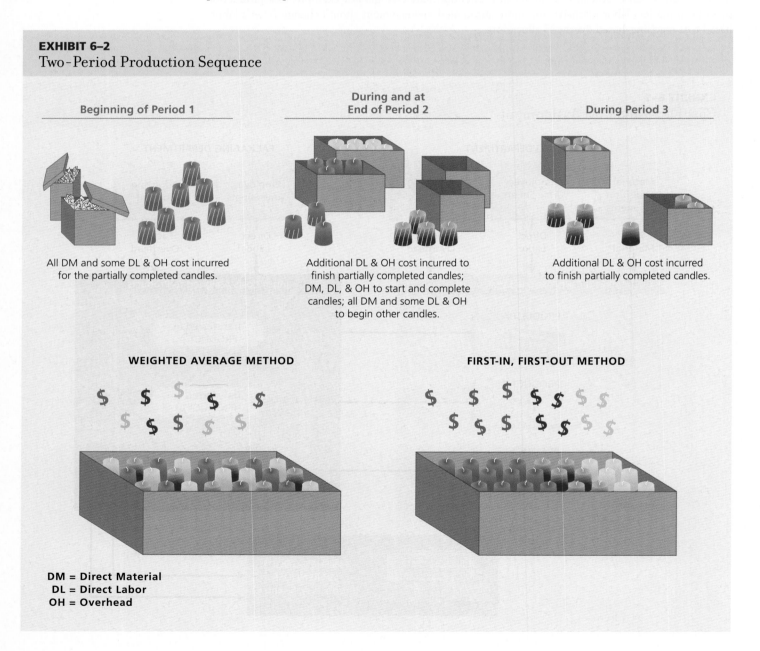

Beginning of Period 1	During and at End of Period 2	During Period 3
All DM and some DL & OH cost incurred for the partially completed candles.	Additional DL & OH cost incurred to finish partially completed candles; DM, DL, & OH to start and complete candles; all DM and some DL & OH to begin other candles.	Additional DL & OH cost incurred to finish partially completed candles.

WEIGHTED AVERAGE METHOD   **FIRST-IN, FIRST-OUT METHOD**

DM = Direct Material
DL = Direct Labor
OH = Overhead

Physical inspection of ending WIP Inventory units is needed to determine the proportion of direct material, direct labor, and overhead work that was incurred during the current period. One hundred percent minus this proportion represents the proportion of work to be completed in a future period. Inspection at the end of last period provided information on the proportion of work that needed to be completed this period on beginning WIP Inventory.

Equivalent Units of Production

Units typically flow through a production department in first-in, first-out order. Goods that were incomplete at the end of the previous period are completed first in the current period; then units are started and completed during the current period; and, finally, some units are started but not completed during the current period. Because manufacturing efforts benefit a variety of different units, production cannot be measured by counting whole units. Accountants use a concept known as equivalent units of production to measure the quantity of production achieved during a period.

Equivalent units of production (EUP) are approximations of the number of whole units of output that could have been produced during a period from the actual effort expended during that period. The following simple example indicates how EUP are calculated. Assume Colorful Candles had no WIP Inventory on November 1. During November, the company processed 220,000 units: 200,000 units were fully completed and 20,000 units were 40 percent complete at the end of the period. The EUP for the period are [(200,000 × 100%) + (20,000 × 40%)] or 208,000.

Some quantity of direct material must be introduced at the start of production to begin the conversion process. For example, to make its various products, Colorful Candles' production process begins with candle wax. Any material added at the start of production is 100 percent complete throughout the process, regardless of the percentage of completion of labor and overhead.

Most production processes require multiple direct materials. Additional materials may be added at any point or even continuously during processing. A material, such as a box or a glass container, may even be added at the end of processing. Until the end of the production process, the product would be 0 percent complete as to the box but may be totally complete with regard to other materials. The production flow for candles in Exhibit 6–3 visually illustrates the need for separate EUP computations for each cost component. Wicks and wax are 100 percent complete at any point in the process after the start of production; no additional quantities of these materials are added later in production. When enough labor and overhead have been added to reach the 20 percent completion point, additional materials (color and scent) are added. Prior to 20 percent completion, these materials were 0 percent complete; after the 20 percent point, these materials are 100 percent complete. Once the candles are completed, they are boxed and the product is 100 percent complete. Thus, boxes are 0 percent complete until the candles are completely finished; when the candles are boxed, the product is complete and transferred to the finished goods warehouse or directly to customers.

Assume that enough wicks and wax are started to make 8,000 candles. At the end of the period, the process is 75 percent complete as to labor and overhead. The candles would be 100 percent complete as to wicks, wax, color, and scent, but 0 percent complete as to boxes. The materials EUP calculations would indicate that there are 8,000 EUP for wicks, wax, color, and scent and zero EUP for boxes. The labor and overhead (conversion) cost components would have an equivalency of 6,000 candles because the product is 75 percent complete and labor and overhead are added continuously during the process.[1]

When overhead is applied on a direct labor basis, or when direct labor and overhead are added to the product at the same rate, a single percentage of completion estimate can be used for both conversion cost components. However, because cost drivers other than direct labor are increasingly being used to apply overhead costs, single computations for "conversion EUP" are being made less often. For example, whereas the cost driver for the utilities portion of overhead cost may be machine hours, that of the materials handling portion of overhead cost may be pounds of material. The increased use of multiple cost pools and/or activity-based costing concepts makes it less likely that the degrees of completion for the direct labor and overhead components of processing will be equal.

---

[1] Although the same number of equivalent units results for wicks, wax, color, and scent and for labor and overhead, separate calculations of unit cost may be desirable for each component. These separate calculations would give managers more information for planning and control purposes. Managers must weigh the costs of making separate calculations against the benefits from having the additional information. For illustrative purposes, however, single computations will be made when cost components are at equal percentages of completion.

EXHIBIT 6–3
Candle Manufacturing Process—Production Department

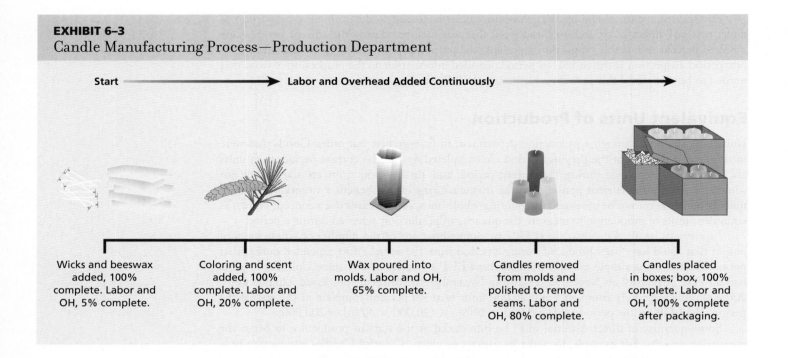

Start ⟶ **Labor and Overhead Added Continuously** ⟶

| Wicks and beeswax added, 100% complete. Labor and OH, 5% complete. | Coloring and scent added, 100% complete. Labor and OH, 20% complete. | Wax poured into molds. Labor and OH, 65% complete. | Candles removed from molds and polished to remove seams. Labor and OH, 80% complete. | Candles placed in boxes; box, 100% complete. Labor and OH, 100% complete after packaging. |

Weighted Average and First-In, First-Out Process Costing Methods

The two methods of accounting for cost flows in process costing are (1) weighted average and (2) first-in, first-out. The methods reflect the way in which cost flows are assumed to occur in the production process. In a very general way, these process costing approaches can be related to the cost flow methods used in financial accounting.

Retail businesses use the weighted average method to determine an average cost per unit of inventory. This cost is computed by dividing the total cost of goods available for sale by the total units available for sale. Total cost and total units are found by adding purchases to beginning inventory. Costs and units of the current period are not distinguished in any way from those on hand at the end of the prior period. In contrast, the first-in, first-out method of accounting for merchandise inventory separates goods according to when they were purchased and at what cost. The costs of beginning inventory are the first costs sent to Cost of Goods Sold, with other costs following in the order in which they were incurred; units remaining in the ending inventory are assigned costs based on the most recent purchases.

Use of these methods for costing the production of a manufacturing firm is similar to their use by a retailer. The weighted average method computes a single average cost per unit of the combined beginning WIP Inventory and current period production. The first-in, first-out method separates beginning WIP Inventory and current period production as well as their costs so that a current period cost per unit can be calculated. The denominator in the EUP cost formula differs, depending on which of the two methods is used.[2]

One purpose of any costing system is to determine a product cost for use on financial statements. When goods are transferred from Work in Process Inventory to Finished Goods Inventory (or another department), a cost must be assigned to those goods. In addition, at the end of any period, a value must be assigned to goods that are only partially complete and still remain in Work in

[2]Note that the term *denominator* is used here rather than equivalent units of production. Based on its definition, equivalent units of production are related to current period productive activity. Thus, for any given set of production facts, there is only one true measure of equivalent units produced—regardless of the cost flow assumption used—and that measure is FIFO EUP. However, this fact has been obscured over time due to continued references to the "EUP" computation for weighted average. Thus, the term *EUP* has taken on a generic use to mean "the denominator used to compute the unit cost of production for a period in a process costing system." The term is used in this generic manner throughout the process costing discussion.

Process Inventory. The determination of both cost of goods manufactured and cost of ending WIP Inventory require the specification of a process cost flow method (WA or FIFO).

Exhibit 6–4 outlines the steps necessary in a process costing system for determining the costs assignable to the units completed and to those still in ending inventory at the end of a period. Each of these steps is discussed, and then a complete example is provided for both weighted average and FIFO costing.

EXHIBIT 6–4
Steps in Process Costing

				COMMENTS
(1)	Calculate the physical units to account for	+	Units in beginning WIP Inventory / Units started	Determine the units in the process.
(2)	Calculate the physical units accounted for	+	Units transferred out / Units in ending WIP Inventory	Identify groups of units to be costed (beginning WIP Inventory, started and completed, and ending WIP Inventory).
	Verify that the units in Steps (1) and (2) are equal			If not, recalculate Steps (1) and (2).
(3)	Calculate the equivalent units of production	or	Weighted average method / FIFO method	Identify the related work effort incurred for each unit group by cost component (i.e., material, labor, and overhead).
(4)	Calculate the total cost to account for	+	Cost in beginning WIP Inventory / Cost of current period	Determine the costs that have been incurred in total (and by cost component).
(5)	Calculate the cost per equivalent unit of production	or	Weighted average method / FIFO method	Determine the EUP cost to be assigned per cost component.
(6)	Assign the costs to inventory accounts	or	Transferred out (to FG Inventory or to the next department) / Ending WIP Inventory	Determine the total cost to be assigned to each group of units worked on during the period.
	Verify that the costs in Steps (4) and (6) are equal	+	Cost transferred out / Cost in ending WIP Inventory = Total cost to account for	If not, recalculate Steps (4), (5), and (6).

The first step is to calculate the total physical units for which the department is responsible. This amount is equal to the sum of fully and partially completed units processed in the department during the current period: it is equal to the actual beginning WIP Inventory units plus the actual units started.

Second, calculate the total physical units accounted for by determining what happened to the units during the period. At the end of the period, the total physical units will be either (1) completed and transferred out or (2) partially completed and remaining in ending WIP Inventory.[3] At this point, verify that the total physical units to account for are equal to the total physical units accounted for. If these amounts are not equal, any additional computations will be incorrect.

Third, use either the WA or FIFO method to determine the EUP for each cost component. If all direct material is added at the same degree of completion, a single computation for direct material can be made. If multiple materials are used and are placed into production at different points in the production process, multiple EUP calculations for direct materials are necessary. If overhead is based on direct labor or if these two factors are always at the same degree of completion, a single EUP can be computed for conversion. If neither condition exists, separate EUP schedules must be prepared for labor and overhead.[4]

Fourth, calculate the **total cost to account for**. This amount is the sum of the balance in WIP Inventory at the beginning of the period plus all current costs for direct material, direct labor, and overhead.

Fifth, calculate the cost per equivalent unit for each cost component using either the WA or the FIFO EUP calculated in step 3.

Sixth, use the costs computed in step 5 to assign production costs to units completed and transferred out of WIP Inventory and to units remaining in WIP Inventory.

The Colorful Candles example is used to demonstrate the steps involved in the computation of EUP and cost assignment for both methods of process costing. Colorful Candles makes a variety of candles, including a 7-inch unscented pillar candle, popular with restaurants and hotels because of allergy concerns of customers. The company views the manufacturing process of this product as a single department with a single direct material: wax. Costs of wicks and coloring are insignificant and are considered indirect materials and part of overhead. Candles are shipped in reusable containers to a central warehouse. From there, candles are distributed to wholesalers and retailers. Because wax is added at the start of processing, inventory is 100 percent complete as to this material as soon as processing begins. Labor and overhead are assumed to be at the same degree of completion throughout the production process. Actual overhead is assigned to production at the end of each period. Exhibit 6–5 presents April 2008 information regarding Colorful Candles' inventories and costs.

Although quantities are given for candles transferred out and for those in the ending WIP Inventory, both quantities are not essential. The number of candles remaining in the ending WIP Inventory can be calculated as total candles to account for minus the candles that were completed and transferred to FG Inventory during April. Alternatively, the number of candles transferred to FG Inventory can be calculated as the total candles to account for minus the candles in ending WIP Inventory. Next, Colorful Candles information is used to illustrate each step listed in Exhibit 6–4.

LO.3
How are equivalent units of production, unit costs, and inventory values determined using the weighted average method of process costing?

Weighted Average Method

Step 1: Calculate the Total Physical Units to Account For

Candles in beginning WIP Inventory	10,000
Candles started during current period	401,400
Candles to account for	411,400

Step 2: Calculate the Physical Units Accounted For

Candles completed and transferred to FG Inventory	406,000
Candles in ending WIP Inventory	5,400
Candles accounted for	411,400

[3]A third category (spoilage/breakage) does exist. These occurrences are considered later in the chapter. Appendix 2 in this chapter describes the accounting for spoilage in process costing situations.
[4]As discussed in Chapter 4, overhead can be applied to products using a variety of traditional (direct labor hours or machine hours) or nontraditional (such as number of machine setups, pounds of material moved, and/or number of material requisitions) bases. The number of equivalent unit computations necessary results from the number of different cost pools and overhead allocation bases established in a company. Some highly automated manufacturers may not have a direct labor category. The quantity of direct labor may be so nominal that it is included in a conversion category and not accounted for separately.

EXHIBIT 6–5

Production and Cost Information for Colorful Candles for April 2008

Candles in beginning WIP Inventory (40% complete as to labor and overhead or conversion)		10,000
Candles started during current period		401,400
Candles completed and transferred to FG Inventory		406,000
Candles in ending WIP Inventory (80% complete as to labor and overhead or conversion)		5,400
Costs of beginning WIP Inventory		
Direct material	$ 11,886	
Direct labor	3,600	
Overhead	29,916	$ 45,402
Current period costs		
Direct material	$642,240	
Direct labor	345,372	
Overhead	975,168	1,962,780
Total cost to account for		$2,008,182

The items detailed in this step indicate the categories to which costs will be assigned in the final step. The number of candles accounted for in step 2 equals the number of candles to account for in step 1.

Step 3: Calculate the Equivalent Units of Production

The WA EUP computation uses the number of candles in the beginning WIP Inventory and the number of candles started and completed during the period. Units started and completed during a period equal units completed during the period minus units in the beginning inventory. Units started and completed can also be computed as units started during the period minus the units in the ending inventory. For Colorful Candles, the candles started and completed in April are 198,000 (203,000 − 5,000) or (200,700 − 2,700). Exhibit 6–6 illustrates the concepts of total units to account for, total units accounted for, and units started and completed.

The ending WIP Inventory is 100 percent complete as to material because wax is added at the start of production. The ending WIP Inventory is 80 percent complete as to labor and overhead (conversion); one EUP computation can be made because these cost elements are assumed to be added at the same rate throughout the production process. The WA computation for equivalent units of production is as follows:[5]

	DM	Conversion (Labor & Overhead)
Beginning WIP Inventory (whole units)	10,000	10,000
Candles started and completed	396,000	396,000
Ending WIP Inventory (candles × % complete)	5,400	4,320
Equivalent units of production	411,400	410,320

Step 4: Calculate the Total Cost to Account For

Total cost to account for equals beginning WIP Inventory cost plus current period costs. Note that the information provided in Exhibit 6–5 gives the cost for each component of production—direct material, direct labor, and overhead. Production costs can be determined from transfers of direct material from the warehouse, incurrence of direct labor, and either actual or applied overhead amounts.

[5]Different approaches exist to compute equivalent units of production and unit costs under WA and FIFO. In addition to the computations shown in the chapter, two other valid and commonly used approaches for computing and reconciling WA and FIFO equivalent units of production and unit costs are presented in appendix 1 in this chapter.

EXHIBIT 6–6
Unit Concepts

Total Units to Account For	Total Units Accounted For	Units Started and Completed
Beginning WIP Inventory Units	Units Completed	Units Completed
+ Units Started	+ Ending WIP Inventory Units	− Beginning WIP Inventory Units
		OR
		Units Started
		− Ending WIP Inventory Units

The sum of direct labor and overhead costs is the conversion cost. For Colorful Candles, the total cost to account for is $2,008,182 ($45,402 + $1,962,780).

	DM	DL	OH	Total
Beginning WIP Inventory costs	$ 11,886	$ 3,600	$ 29,916	$ 45,402
Current period costs	642,240	345,372	975,168	1,962,780
Total cost to account for	$654,126	$348,972	$1,005,084	$2,008,182

The total cost to account for must be assigned to the goods transferred to FG Inventory (or, if appropriate, to the next department) and to the ending WIP Inventory. Assignments are made in relation to the whole or equivalent whole units contained in each type of inventory.

Step 5: Calculate the Cost per Equivalent Unit of Production

A cost per EUP must be computed for each cost component for which a separate calculation of EUP is made. Under the WA method, the costs of the beginning WIP Inventory and those of the current period are summed for each cost component and divided by that component's weighted average EUP to obtain the per-unit cost. This calculation for each cost component at the end of the period follows:

$$\text{Unit Cost} = \frac{\text{Total Cost Incurred}}{\text{Total Equivalent Units of Effort}}$$

$$= \frac{(\text{Beginning WIP Inventory Cost} + \text{Current Period Cost})}{\text{WA EUP}}$$

This computation divides total cost by total units, which is the common WA approach that produces an average component cost per unit. Because labor and overhead are at the same degree of completion, their costs can be combined and shown as a single conversion cost per equivalent unit. Colorful Candles' WA cost per EUP calculations for material and conversion follow:

	Direct Material	+	Conversion	=	Total
Beginning WIP Inventory costs	$ 11,886		$ 33,516		$ 45,402
Current period costs	642,240		1,320,540		1,962,780
Total cost per component	$654,126		$1,354,056		$2,008,182
Divided by EUP (step 3)	÷ 411,400		÷ 410,320		
Cost per EUP	$1.59		$3.30		$4.89

The amounts for the product cost components (material and conversion) are summed to find the total production cost of $4.89 for equivalent whole candles completed during April by Colorful Candles.

Step 6: Assign Costs to Inventories

This step assigns total production costs to units of product by determining the cost of (1) goods completed and transferred out during the period and (2) units in the ending WIP Inventory.

Using the WA method, the cost of goods transferred out is found by multiplying the total number of units transferred by the total cost per EUP. Because this method is based on an averaging technique that combines both prior and current period work, it does not matter in which period the transferred units were started. All units and all costs are commingled. The total cost transferred for Colorful Candles for April is $1,985,340 (406,000 × $4.89).

Ending WIP Inventory cost is calculated by multiplying the EUP for each cost component by the component cost per EUP computed in step 5. Cost of the ending WIP Inventory using the WA method is as follows:

Ending WIP Inventory
Direct material (5,400 × $1.59) $ 8,586
Conversion (4,320 × $3.30)   14,256
Total cost of ending WIP Inventory $22,842

The total cost assigned to units transferred out and to units in the ending WIP Inventory must equal the total cost to account for. For Colorful Candles, total cost to account for (step 4) was determined as $2,008,182, which equals transferred-out cost ($1,985,340) plus the cost of the ending WIP Inventory ($22,842).

The steps just discussed can be combined into a **cost of production report**, which details all manufacturing quantities and costs, shows the computation of cost per EUP, and indicates the cost assigned to goods produced during the period. Exhibit 6–7 shows Colorful Candles' cost of production report using the WA method.

Information contained on the cost of production report indicates the actual flow of goods and dollar amounts through the general ledger accounting system. The following T-accounts show how the information in Exhibit 6–7 "moves" through the WIP and FG Inventory accounts. The total cost to account for must either be transferred out of WIP Inventory or remain as the ending balance of that account.

FIFO Method

LO.4
How are equivalent units of production, unit costs, and inventory values determined using the FIFO method of process costing?

Steps 1 and 2 are the same for the FIFO method as for the WA method because these two steps involve the use of physical units.

Step 3: Calculate the Equivalent Units of Production

Using the FIFO method, the work performed last period is *not* commingled with work of the current period. Only the work performed on the beginning WIP Inventory during the current period is shown in the EUP schedule; this work equals the whole units in the beginning WIP Inventory times (1− percentage of work done in the prior period). No additional material is needed in April to complete the 10,000 candles in the beginning WIP Inventory. Because the beginning WIP Inventory was 40 percent complete as to labor and overhead, the company will do 60 percent of the conversion work on those goods in the current period or the equivalent of 6,000 candles (10,000 × 60%).

The EUP schedule for the FIFO method is:

	DM	Conversion
Candles in beginning WIP Inventory completed in the current period	0	6,000
Candles started and completed	396,000	396,000
Ending WIP Inventory (candles × % complete)	5,400	4,320
Equivalent units of production	401,400	406,320

Except for the different treatment of units in the beginning WIP Inventory, the remaining amounts in the FIFO EUP schedule are the same as those for the WA method. Thus, the

EXHIBIT 6–7

Colorful Candles' Cost of Production Report for the Month Ended April 30, 2008 (Weighted Average Method)

Production Data	Whole Units	Direct Material	Conversion
		EQUIVALENT UNITS OF PRODUCTION	
Beginning WIP Inventory[a]	10,000		
Candles started	401,400		
Candles to account for	411,400		
Beginning WIP Inventory (completed)	10,000	10,000	10,000
Started and completed	396,000	396,000	396,000
Candles completed	406,000		
Ending WIP Inventory	5,400	5,400	4,320
Candles accounted for[b]	411,400	411,400	410,320

Cost Data	Total	Direct Material	Conversion
Costs in beginning WIP Inventory	$ 45,402	$ 11,886	$ 33,516
Current period costs	1,962,780	642,240	1,320,540
Total cost to account for	$2,008,182	$654,126	$1,354,056
Divided by EUP		÷ 411,400	÷ 410,320
Cost per EUP	$4.89	$1.59	$3.30

Cost Assignment			
Transferred out (406,000 × $4.89)		$1,985,340	
Ending WIP Inventory			
Direct material (5,400 × $1.59)	$ 8,586		
Conversion (5,400 × 80% × $3.30)	14,256	22,842	
Total cost accounted for		$2,008,182	

[a]Fully complete as to material; 40% complete as to conversion
[b]Fully complete as to material; 80% complete as to conversion

only difference between the EUPs of the two methods is equal to the number of candles in the beginning WIP Inventory times the percentage of work performed in the prior period, as shown here:

	DM	Conversion
FIFO EUP	401,400	406,320
+ Beginning WIP Inventory (5,000 units × % work done in prior period: 100% material, 40% conversion)	10,000	4,000
= WA EUP	411,400	410,320

Step 4: Calculate the Total Cost to Account For

This step is the same as it was for the WA method; the total cost to account for is $2,008,182.

Step 5: Calculate the Cost per Equivalent Unit of Production

The FIFO EUP calculation ignores the work performed in the prior period on beginning WIP Inventory; thus, the FIFO cost per EUP computation also ignores prior period costs. Because the EUP computations and the costs used to compute cost per EUP both differ between the FIFO and weighted average methods, different cost per EUP results will be obtained for the WA and FIFO methods. The FIFO cost per EUP calculation is:

	Direct Material	+	Conversion	=	Total
Current period costs	$642,240		$1,320,540		$1,962,780
Divided by EUP (step 3)	÷ 401,400		÷ 406,320		
Cost per EUP	$1.60		$3.25		$4.85

It is useful to understand the underlying difference between the WA and FIFO total cost computations. The WA total cost of $4.89 is the average cost of each candle completed during April, regardless of when production began. The FIFO total cost of $4.85 is the average cost of each candle started and completed solely during the current period. The $0.04 difference is caused by the difference in treatment of beginning WIP Inventory costs.

Step 6: Assign Costs to Inventories

The FIFO method assumes that the units in beginning WIP Inventory are the first units completed during the current period and, thus, are the first units transferred out. The remaining units transferred out during the period were both started and completed in the current period. As shown in the cost of production report in Exhibit 6–8, the two-step computation needed to determine the cost of goods transferred out distinctly presents this FIFO logic.

The first part of the cost assignment for units transferred out relates to beginning WIP Inventory units. On April 1, these units had all material cost and some labor and overhead cost in WIP Inventory. These costs were *not* included in the EUP cost calculations in step 5. The costs to finish these units were incurred during the current period, and, thus, completion is shown using current period costs. Total cost of producing the units contained in the beginning WIP Inventory is equal to the beginning WIP Inventory costs plus the current period completion costs. Next, the cost of units started and completed in the current period is computed using current period costs. This cost assignment process for Colorful Candles is as follows:

```
Transferred out
 (1)  Beginning inventory (prior period costs)              $   45,402
        Completion of beginning inventory
           Direct material (0 × $1.60)                              0
           Conversion (10,000 × 60% × $3.25)                   19,500
             Total cost of beginning inventory transferred  $   64,902
 (2)  Candles started and completed (396,000 × $4.85)        1,920,600
      Total cost transferred                                $1,985,502
```

The total cost for all units completed and transferred to FG Inventory for April is $1,985,502.[6]

The process of calculating the FIFO cost of the ending WIP Inventory is the same as under the WA method. Ending WIP cost using FIFO is as follows:

```
Ending WIP Inventory
   Direct material (5,400 × $1.60)                     $ 8,640
   Conversion (4,320 × $3.25)                           14,040
   Total cost of ending WIP Inventory                  $22,680
```

The total cost of the candles transferred out ($1,985,502) plus the cost of the candles in the ending WIP Inventory ($22,680) equals the total cost to be accounted for ($2,008,182).

Summary journal entries and T-accounts for Colorful Candles for April are given in Exhibit 6–9. It is assumed that the company began April with no FG Inventory, 400,000 candles

---

[6]Because of FIFO's two-step process to determine cost of units transferred, a question exists as to how to calculate a per-unit cost for the units that were in the beginning WIP Inventory and those that were started and completed in the current period. The resolution of this question is found in the use of either the strict or the modified FIFO method.

If strict FIFO is used, beginning inventory units are transferred out at their total completed cost; the units started and completed during the current period are transferred at a separate and distinct current period cost. For Colorful Candles, use of strict FIFO means that the 5,000 candles in the beginning inventory are transferred at an approximate cost per unit of $6.49 ($32,451 ÷ 5,000). The candles started and completed in April are transferred at the current period cost of $4.85 (computed in step 5). If strict FIFO is used, the costs of these two groups should be reported separately, not added together, to get a total transferred cost.

However, unless the difference between the unit costs of beginning inventory and of units started and completed is significant, there is no need to maintain the distinction. The costs of the two groups can be combined and averaged over all of the units transferred in a process known as the modified FIFO method. For Colorful Candles, modified FIFO assigns an approximate average cost of $4.89 per candle ($1,985,502 ÷ 406,000) to all candles transferred from the department. Modified FIFO allows the next department or Finished Goods Inventory to account for all units received during the period at the same cost per unit. This method is useful when products are processed through several departments so that the number of separate unit costs to be accounted for does not become excessive.

EXHIBIT 6–8

Colorful Candles' Cost of Production Report for the Month Ended
April 30, 2008 (FIFO Method)

Production Data	Whole Units	EQUIVALENT UNITS OF PRODUCTION	
		Direct Material	Conversion
Beginning WIP Inventory[a]	10,000		
Candles started	401,400		
Candles to account for	411,400		
Beginning WIP Inventory completed[b]	10,000	0	6,000
Started and completed	396,000	396,000	396,000
Candles completed	406,000		
Ending WIP Inventory[c]	5,400	5,400	4,320
Candles accounted for	411,400	401,400	406,320

Cost Data	Total	Direct Material	Conversion
Costs in beginning WIP Inventory	$ 45,402		
Current period costs	1,962,780	$642,240	$1,320,540
Total cost to account for	$2,008,182		
Divided by EUP		÷ 401,400	÷ 406,320
Cost per EUP	$4.85	$1.60	$3.25

Cost Assignment			
Transferred out			
Beginning WIP Inventory costs	$45,402		
Cost to complete			
Conversion (6,000 × $3.25)	19,500	$ 64,902	
Started and completed (396,000 × $4.85)		1,920,600	
Total cost transferred		$1,985,502	
Ending WIP Inventory			
Direct material (5,400 × $1.60)	$ 8,640		
Conversion (5,400 × 80% × $3.25)	14,040	22,680	
Total cost accounted for		$2,008,182	

[a]Fully complete as to material; 40% complete as to conversion
[b]0% additional material added; 60% additional conversion required
[c]Fully complete as to material; 80% complete as to conversion

were sold on account for $9 each, and a perpetual FIFO inventory system is in use. Weighted average amounts are shown where they would differ from FIFO.

Process Costing in a Multidepartment Setting

Most companies have multiple, rather than single, department processing facilities. In a multide-partment production environment, goods are transferred from a predecessor (upstream) department to a successor (downstream) department. For example, if the candles at Colorful Candles were boxed

EXHIBIT 6–9

Colorful Candles' Process Costing Journal Entries and T-Accounts for April 2008

1.	Work in Process Inventory	642,240	
	Raw Material Inventory		642,240
	To record issuance of material to production (Exhibit 6–5)		
2.	Work in Process Inventory	345,372	
	Wages Payable		345,372
	To accrue wages for direct labor (Exhibit 6–5)		
3.	Manufacturing Overhead	975,168	
	Various accounts		975,168
	To record actual overhead costs (Exhibit 6–5)		
4.	Work in Process Inventory	975,168	
	Manufacturing Overhead		975,168
	To apply actual overhead to production		
5.	Finished Goods Inventory	1,985,502	
	Work in Process Inventory		1,985,502
	To transfer cost of completed candles to finished goods (Exhibit 6–8) (Entry would be for $1,985,340 if weighted average was used—Exhibit 6–7.)		
6.	Accounts Receivable	3,600,000	
	Sales		3,600,000
	To record sales on account (400,000 candles × $9.00)		
	Cost of Goods Sold	1,956,402	
	Finished Goods Inventory		1,956,402
	To transfer cost of goods sold, using strict FIFO:		

First 10,000 units	*$ 64,902*	
Remaining 390,000 units at $4.85	*1,891,500*	
	$1,956,402	

(Entry would be for $1,956,000 if weighted average was used: 400,000 × $4.89.)

Work in Process Inventory

Beginning balance	45,402	Cost of goods	
Direct material	642,240	manufactured	1,985,502
Direct labor	345,372		
Applied overhead	975,168		
Ending balance	22,680		

Finished Goods Inventory

Beginning balance	0	Cost of goods sold	1,956,402
Cost of goods			
manufactured	1,985,502		
Ending balance			
(6,000 × $4.85)	29,100		

Cost of Goods Sold

April CGS	1,956,402	

in house, the company's manufacturing activities could be viewed as occurring in two departments: Processing and Packaging.

Manufacturing costs *always* follow the physical flow of goods; thus, when goods are transferred from one department to another, costs are also transferred. Thus, costs of the completed units of predecessor departments are treated as input costs in successor departments. Such a sequential treatment requires the use of an additional cost component called *transferred-in cost* or *prior department cost*. This cost component is always 100 percent complete because the goods would not have been transferred out of the predecessor department if processing there were not complete. The transferred-in cost component is treated the same as any other cost component in the calculations of EUP and cost per EUP.

A successor department might add additional raw material to the units transferred in or might simply provide additional labor with a corresponding incurrence of overhead. Anything added in the successor department requires its own cost component column for calculating EUP and cost per EUP (unless the additional components have the same degree of completion, in which case they can be combined).

Occasionally, successor departments change the unit of measure used in predecessor departments. For example, at Colorful Candles, the measure in the Processing Department might be number of candles but the measure in the Packaging Department might be number of 24-unit boxes of candles.

The demonstration problem at the end of the chapter provides a complete example of predecessor and successor department activities.

LO.5
How are equivalent units of production, unit costs, and inventory values determined using the standard costing method of process costing?

Process Costing with Standard Costs

Companies may prefer to use standard rather than actual costs for inventory valuation purposes. Actual costing requires that a new production cost be computed each period. Once a production process is established, however, the "new" costs are often not materially different from the "old" costs, so standards for each cost component can be developed and used as predetermined benchmarks to simplify the costing process and eliminate periodic cost recomputations. Standards should be reviewed, and possibly revised, at a minimum of once per year to keep quantities and amounts current.

EUP calculations for standard process costing are identical to those of FIFO process costing. Unlike the WA method, the emphasis of both standard costing and FIFO are on the measurement and control of current production activities and current period costs. The WA method commingles prior and current period units and costs, which reduces the emphasis on current effort that standard costing is intended to represent and measure.

Use of standard quantities and costs allows material, labor, and overhead variances to be computed during the period. To illustrate the differences between using actual and standard process costing, the Colorful Candles example is continued. The company's April production and standard cost information is given in Exhibit 6–10. Beginning inventory cost data have been restated from the original to reflect standard costs and to demonstrate the effect of consistent use of standard costs over successive periods. Beginning WIP Inventory consisted of 10,000 units that were fully complete as to material and 40 percent complete as to conversion. Therefore, the standard cost of the beginning inventory is as follows:

Material (10,000 × 100% × $1.59)	$15,900
Labor (10,000 × 40% × $0.85)	3,400
Overhead (10,000 × 40% × $2.35)	9,400
Total	$28,700

Exhibit 6–11 presents the cost of production report using Colorful Candles' standard cost information.[7]

---

[7]Total material, labor, and overhead variances are shown for Colorful Candles in Exhibit 6–11. Additionally, variances from actual costs must be closed at the end of a period. If the variances are immaterial, they can be closed to Cost of Goods Sold; otherwise, they should be allocated among the appropriate inventory accounts and Cost of Goods Sold.

EXHIBIT 6–10
Colorful Candles' Production and Standard Cost Data for April 2008

Production data

Beginning WIP Inventory (BI) (100%, 40%)	10,000
Candles started	401,400
Ending WIP Inventory (EI) (100%, 80%)	5,400

Standard cost of production

Direct material	$1.59
Direct labor	0.85
Overhead	2.35
Total	$4.79

Equivalent units of production (repeated from Exhibit 6–8):

	DM	Conversion
BI (candles × percentage not complete at start of period)	0	6,000
Candles started and completed	396,000	396,000
EI (candles × percentage complete at end of period)	5,400	4,320
Equivalent units of production	401,400	406,320

When a standard cost system is used, inventories are stated at standard rather than actual costs. Summary journal entries for Colorful Candles' April production, assuming a standard cost FIFO process costing system and amounts from Exhibit 6–11, are as follows:

1. WIP Inventory is debited for $638,226: the standard cost ($629,640) of material used to complete 396,000 units started in April plus the standard cost ($8,586) for the material used to produce the units in ending WIP Inventory. Raw Material Inventory is credited for the actual cost of the material withdrawn during April ($642,240).

Work in Process Inventory	638,226	
Direct Material Variance	4,014	
Raw Material Inventory		642,240

To record issuance of material at standard and variance from standard

2. WIP Inventory is debited for the standard cost of labor allowed based on the equivalent units produced in April. The EUP for the month reflect the production necessary to complete the beginning WIP Inventory candles (6,000), the candles started and completed (396,000), and the work performed on the ending inventory candles (4,320), or a total of 406,320 EUP. Multiplying this equivalent production by the standard labor cost per candle of $0.85 gives a total of $345,372.

Work in Process Inventory	345,372	
Wages Payable		345,372

To accrue direct labor cost and assign labor cost to WIP Inventory at standard; there was no direct labor variance

3. Actual factory overhead incurred in April is $975,168.

Manufacturing Overhead	975,168	
Various accounts		975,168

To record actual overhead cost for April

4. WIP Inventory is debited for the standard cost of overhead based on the EUP produced in April. Because labor and overhead are at the same percentage of completion, equivalent production is the same as in entry 2 or 406,320 EUP. Multiplying the EUP by the standard overhead application rate of $2.35 per candle gives $954,852.

EXHIBIT 6–11

Colorful Candles' Cost of Production Report for the Month Ended April 30, 2008 (Standard Costing)

Costs to Be Accounted for	Direct Material	Direct Labor	Overhead	Total
Total costs				
Beginning WIP Inventory (at standard)	$ 15,900	$ 3,400	$ 9,400	$ 28,700
Current period (actual)	642,240	345,372	975,168	1,962,780
(1) Total	$658,140	$348,772	$984,568	$1,991,480
Cost Assignment (at standard)				
Transferred out				
Beginning WIP Inventory cost*	$ 15,900	$ 3,400	$ 9,400	$ 28,700
Cost to complete				
DL (6,000 × $0.85)		5,100		
OH (6,000 × $2.35)			14,100	
Total cost to complete				19,200
Started and completed				
DM (396,000 × $1.59)	629,640			
DL (396,000 × $0.85)		336,600		
OH (396,000 × $2.35)			930,600	
Total started and completed				1,896,840
Ending WIP Inventory				
DM (5,400 × $1.59)	8,586			
DL (4,320 × $0.85)		3,672		
OH (4,320 × $2.35)			10,152	
Total ending WIP Inventory				22,410
(2) Total standard cost assigned	$654,126	$348,772	$964,252	$1,967,150
Variances from actual (1 − 2)*	4,014	0	20,316	24,330
Total costs accounted for	$658,140	$348,772	$984,568	$1,991,480

NOTE: Favorable variances would have been shown in parentheses.
*Beginning WIP inventory is carried at standard costs rather than actual. Therefore, no portion of the variance is attributable to beginning WIP inventory. Any variance that might have been associated with beginning WIP inventory was measured and identified with the prior period.

```
Work in Process Inventory                        954,852
Manufacturing Overhead Variance                   20,316
      Manufacturing Overhead                                       975,168
      To apply overhead to WIP Inventory and record the overhead variance
```

5. Finished Goods Inventory is debited for the total standard cost ($1,944,740) of the 406,000 candles completed during the month (406,000 × $4.79).

```
Finished Goods Inventory                        1,944,740
      Work in Process Inventory                                  1,944,740
      To transfer standard cost of completed candles to FG Inventory
```

A standard costing system eliminates the need to be concerned about differentiating between the per-unit cost of the beginning WIP Inventory units that were completed and the per-unit cost of the units started and completed in the current period. All units transferred out of a department are costed at the standard or "normal" production cost for each cost component. Thus, recordkeeping is simplified, and variations from the norm are highlighted in the period of incurrence. Standard cost systems are discussed in depth in Chapter 7.

Standard costing not only simplifies the cost flows in a process costing system but also provides a useful tool to control costs. By developing standards, managers have a benchmark against which actual costs can be compared. Managers may also use these standards as targets for balanced score-card performance measurements. For example, meeting standard costs 98 percent of the time may be set as a goal for the internal business process perspective. Variances serve to identify differences between the benchmark (standard) cost and the actual cost. By striving to control variances, managers control costs. Managers should also benchmark, to the extent possible, their firm's costs against costs incurred by other firms. Such information may help indicate the organization's cost strengths and weaknesses.

Hybrid Costing Systems

LO.6
Why would a company use a hybrid costing system?

Many companies now customize what were previously mass-produced items. In such circumstances, neither job order nor process costing techniques are perfectly suited to attach costs to output. Thus, companies may choose to use a hybrid costing system that is appropriate for their particular processing situation. A hybrid costing system combines characteristics of both job order and process costing systems. A hybrid system would be used, for example, in a manufacturing environment in which various product lines have different direct materials but similar processing techniques.

To illustrate the need for hybrid systems, assume that you order an automobile with the following options: heated leather seats, a Bose stereo system, an iPod plug-in, and pearlized paint. Costs of these options must be traced specifically to your car, but the assembly processes for all cars produced by the plant are similar. A hybrid system allows the job order costing feature of tracing direct material to specific jobs to be combined with the process costing feature of averaging labor and overhead costs over all homogeneous production to derive the total cost of your automobile. It would not be feasible to use a job order costing system to trace labor or overhead cost to your car individually, and it would be improper to average the costs of your options over all the cars produced during the period.

A hybrid costing system might be used by a table manufacturer if it uses a variety of raw materials, such as teak, oak, pine, and mahogany, in the production process.

A hybrid costing system may be appropriate for companies producing items such as furniture, clothing, or jam. In each instance, numerous kinds of raw materials could be used to create similar output. A table may be made from oak, teak, or mahogany; a blouse may be made from silk, cotton, or polyester; and jam may be made from peaches, strawberries, or apricots. The material cost for a batch run would be traced separately, but the production process of the batch is repetitive.

Hybrid costing systems provide a more accurate accounting picture of the actual type of manufacturing activities in certain companies. Job order costing and process costing are two ends of a continuum and, as is typically the case for any continuum, neither end is necessarily the norm. As the use of flexible manufacturing processes increases, so will the use of hybrid costing systems.

LO.7
What alternative methods can be used to calculate equivalent units of production?

Appendix 1

Alternative Calculations of Weighted Average and FIFO Methods

Various methods can be used to compute equivalent units of production under the WA and FIFO methods. One common variation of the weighted average EUP calculation presented in the chapter is the following:

> Units transferred out (whole units)
> + Ending WIP Inventory (equivalent units)
> = WA EUP

Once the WA EUP figure is available, the FIFO EUP can be quickly derived by subtracting the equivalent units in the beginning WIP Inventory that had been produced in the previous period:

> WA EUP
> − Beginning WIP Inventory (equivalent units)
> = FIFO EUP

This computation is appropriate because the WA method concentrates on both units completed and units started but not completed during the period. Unlike the FIFO method, the WA method does not exclude the equivalent units in the beginning WIP Inventory. Thus, converting from WA to FIFO requires removal of the equivalent units produced in the previous period from beginning WIP Inventory.

The April production data for Colorful Candles are repeated here to illustrate these alternative calculations for the weighted average and FIFO methods.

Candles in beginning WIP Inventory (100% complete as to material; 40% complete as to conversion costs)	10,000
Candles started during the month	401,400
Candles completed during the month	406,000
Candles in ending WIP Inventory (100% complete as to material; 80% complete as to conversion costs)	5,400

Using these data, the EUP are computed as follows:

	DM	Conversion
Candles transferred out	406,000	406,000
+ Ending WIP Inventory EUP		
(5,400 × 100%; 5,400 × 80% complete)	5,400	4,320
= **WA EUP**	411,400	410,320
− Beginning WIP Inventory EUP		
manufactured in previous period (10,000 × 100%;		
10,000 × 40% complete)	(10,000)	(4,000)
= **FIFO EUP**	401,400	406,320

The distinct relationship between the WA and FIFO methods can also be used in another manner to generate EUP. This method begins with the total number of units to account for in the period. From this amount, the EUP to be completed next period are subtracted to give the WA EUP. Next, as in the method just shown, the equivalent units completed in the prior period (the beginning

Work in Process Inventory) are deducted to give the FIFO EUP. Using Colorful Candles' data, these computations are as follows:

	DM	Conversion
Total units to account for	411,400	411,400
− EUP to be completed next period (ending WIP Inventory × % not completed: 5.400 × 0%; 5.400 × 20%)	0	(1,080)
= WA EUP	411,400	410,320
− EUP completed in prior period (beginning WIP Inventory × % completed last period: 10,000 × 100%; 10,000 × 40%)	(10,000)	(4,000)
= FIFO EUP	401,400	406,320

These alternative calculations can be used either as a confirmation of answers found by using beginning WIP Inventory units, units started and completed, and ending WIP Inventory units or as a shortcut to initially compute EUP.

Appendix 2

Spoilage

LO.8
How are normal and abnormal spoilage losses treated in an EUP schedule?

The chapter examples assumed that all units to be accounted for have either been transferred out or are in the ending WIP Inventory. However, almost every process produces some units that do not meet production specifications. In other situations, addition or expansion of materials after the start of the process may cause the number of units accounted for to be higher than those to be accounted for originally or in a previous department. This appendix addresses two simple examples of spoilage in a process costing system.

Losses in a production process may occur continuously or at a specific point. For example, the weight loss in roasting coffee beans would be considered a continuous loss because it occurs fairly uniformly through the process. In contrast, a discrete loss is assumed to occur at a specific point and is detectable only when a quality check is performed. Control points can be either mechanically included into the production process or performed by inspectors.

Several methods can be used to account for units lost during production. Selection of the most appropriate method depends on whether the loss is considered normal or abnormal and whether the loss occurred continuously in the process or at a discrete point.[8] Exhibit 6–12 summarizes the accounting for the cost of lost units.

The costs of normal shrinkage and normal continuous losses in a process costing environment are handled through the method of neglect, which simply excludes the spoiled units in the equivalent units of production schedule. Ignoring the spoilage results in a smaller number of EUP, and dividing production costs by a smaller EUP raises the cost per equivalent unit. Thus, the cost of lost units is spread proportionately over the good units transferred out and those remaining in WIP Inventory.

Alternatively, the cost of normal discrete losses should be assigned only to units that have passed the inspection point. Such units should be good units (relative to the inspected characteristic), whereas the units prior to this point may be good or they may be defective or spoiled. Assigning loss costs to units that may be found to be defective or spoiled in the next period would not be reasonable.

The cost of all abnormal losses should be accumulated and treated as a loss in the period in which those losses occurred. Abnormal loss cost is always accounted for on an equivalent unit basis.

Hanks Inc. will be used to illustrate the method of neglect for a normal loss and an abnormal loss. Hanks produces glass jars in a single department; the jars are then sold to candle manufacturers. All materials are added at the start of the process, and conversion costs are applied uniformly throughout the production process. Breakage commonly occurs after the jars are formed when a machine pushes air into them to form their openings. The company expects a maximum of 5 percent of the material started into production to be "lost" during processing. For convenience,

---

[8]Normal and abnormal losses are defined in Chapter 5.

EXHIBIT 6–12
Continuous versus Discrete Losses

Type	Assumed to Occur	May Be	Cost Handled How?	Cost Assigned To?
Continuous	Uniformly throughout process	Normal or Abnormal	Absorbed by all units in ending inventory and transferred out on an EUP basis	Product
			Written off as a loss on an EUP basis	Period
Discrete	At inspection point or at end of process	Normal or Abnormal	Absorbed by all units past inspection point in ending inventory and transferred out on an EUP basis	Product
			Written off as a loss on an EUP basis	Period

EXHIBIT 6–13
Production and Cost Data for Hanks Inc. for June 2008

Jars

Beginning WIP Inventory (60% complete)	12,000
Started during month	90,000
Jars completed and transferred	79,200
Ending WIP Inventory (75% complete)	15,000
Spoiled jars	7,800

Costs

Beginning WIP Inventory		
Material	$ 16,230	
Conversion	3,459	$ 19,689
Current period		
Material	$101,745	
Conversion	19,041	120,786
Total cost to be accounted for		$140,475

quantities will be discussed in terms of jars rather than raw material inputs. Recyclable shipping containers are provided by buyers and, therefore, are not a cost to Hanks Inc. The company uses the WA method of calculating equivalent units. Exhibit 6–13 provides the basic information for June 2008.

The company is accountable for 102,000 jars: 12,000 in the beginning WIP Inventory plus 90,000 started into processing during June. Only 94,200 jars (79,200 completed and 15,000 in ending WIP Inventory) are accounted for prior to considering the processing loss. The 7,800 "spoiled" jars are included to balance the total 102,000 jars. Hanks Inc. considers 4,500 (90,000 × 0.05) of the spoiled jars as normal spoilage; the remaining 3,300 (7,800 − 4,500) are considered abnormal spoilage. Under the method of neglect, the normal spoilage is not extended into the computation of EUP. This method simply allows the normal spoilage to "disappear" in the EUP schedule. Therefore, the cost per equivalent "good" jar made during the period is higher for each cost component.[9]

Exhibit 6–14 presents the cost of production report for Hanks Inc. for June 2008. Had FIFO process costing been used, there would have been a difference in the number of equivalent units of production, the cost per equivalent unit, and the cost assignment schedule.[10]

EXHIBIT 6–14

Hanks Inc.'s Cost of Production Report for the Month Ended June 30, 2008 (Normal and Abnormal Loss)

		EQUIVALENT UNITS OF PRODUCTION	
Production Data	**Whole Units**	**Direct Material**	**Conversion**
Beginning WIP Inventory (100%; 60%)	12,000		
Jars started	90,000		
Jars to account for	102,000		
Beginning WIP Inventory (completed)	12,000	12,000	12,000
Jars started and completed	67,200	67,200	67,200
Total jars completed	79,200		
Ending inventory (100%; 75%)	15,000	15,000	11,250
Normal spoilage (not extended)	4,500		
Abnormal spoilage (100%; 100%)	3,300	3,300	3,300
Jars accounted for	102,000	97,500	93,750

Cost Data	**Total**	**Direct Material**	**Conversion**
Beginning WIP Inventory cost	$ 19,689	$ 16,230	$ 3,459
Current costs	120,786	101,745	19,041
Total cost to account for	$140,475	$117,975	$22,500
Divided by EUP		÷ 97,500	÷ 93,750
Cost per WA EUP	$1.45	$1.21	$0.24

Cost Assignment			
Transferred out (79,200 × $1.45)		$114,840	
Ending WIP Inventory			
Direct material (15,000 × $1.21)	$18,150		
Conversion (11,250 × $0.24)	2,700	20,850	
Abnormal loss (3,300 × $1.45)		4,785	
Total cost accounted for		$140,475	

[9]There is a theoretical problem with the use of the method of neglect when a company uses weighted average process costing. Units in the ending Work in Process Inventory have spoiled unit cost assigned to them in the current period and will have lost unit cost assigned again in the next period. But even with this flaw, this method provides a reasonable measure of unit cost if the rate of spoilage is consistent from period to period.

[10]For FIFO costing, the EUP would be 85,500 and 86,550, respectively, for DM and Conversion. Cost per EUP would be $1.19 and $0.22, respectively, for DM and Conversion. Total cost transferred out would be $115,497; total cost of the ending Work in Process Inventory would be $20,325; and cost of abnormal loss would be $4,653.

Comprehensive Review Module

Chapter Summary

1. Process costing

   - is an alternative to job order costing for assigning costs to output in manufacturing companies.

   - differs from job order costing in that process costing is used in companies making large quantities of homogeneous products; job order costing is used in companies making smaller quantities of distinctive, custom-ordered products.

   - differs from job order costing in that process costing uses either the weighted average (WA) or first-in, first-out (FIFO) method to compute equivalent units of production (EUP); job order costing does not use either type of cost flow assumption and does not compute EUP.

2. EUP are used in process costing to

   - approximate the number of whole units of output that could have been produced during a period from the actual effort expended during that period.

   - assign production costs for direct material, direct labor, and overhead to completed and incomplete output of the period; a separate EUP calculation is required for each cost component that is at a different percentage of completion in the production process.

3. The WA method of process costing

   - combines the beginning WIP Inventory and current period production activity.

   - determines

     ➤ EUP (by cost component) by adding the physical units in the beginning WIP Inventory, the physical units started and completed during the period, and the equivalent units in the ending WIP Inventory.

     ➤ unit cost (by cost component) by dividing total cost (equal to the beginning-of-the-period costs plus current period costs) by EUP.

     ➤ transferred-out value by multiplying total units transferred out by the total cost per EUP.

     ➤ ending WIP Inventory value by multiplying the EUP for each cost component by the related cost per EUP.

4. The FIFO method of process costing

   - does not commingle the beginning WIP Inventory and current period production activity or costs.

   - determines

     ➤ EUP (by cost component) by the equivalent units in the beginning WIP Inventory that were completed in the current period, the physical units started and completed during the period, and the equivalent units in the ending WIP Inventory.

     ➤ unit cost (per cost component) by dividing current period cost by EUP.

     ➤ transferred-out value by adding the cost of the beginning WIP Inventory, the current period cost needed to complete the beginning WIP Inventory, and the cost of the units started and completed in the current period.

     ➤ ending WIP Inventory value by multiplying the EUP for each cost component by the related cost per EUP.

5. Standard costs can be used in a process costing system in combination with the FIFO method to

   - assign a "normal" production cost to EUP each period.

   - allow managers to quickly recognize and investigate significant deviations from expected production costs.

6. A hybrid costing system allows companies to

   - combine the characteristics of both job order and process costing systems.

   - trace direct material and/or direct labor that is related to a particular batch of goods to those specific goods using job order costing.

   - use process costing techniques to account for cost components that are common to numerous batches of output.

Potential Ethical Issues

1. Estimating too high (or too low) a completion percentage for ending WIP Inventory to decrease (or increase) the cost per EUP and, thereby, distorting ending WIP and ending FG inventories on the balance sheet and Cost of Goods Sold on the income statement

2. Not updating standard costs to reflect new quantities or costs and, thereby, distorting ending WIP and ending FG inventories on the balance sheet and Cost of Goods Sold on the income statement and creating potentially significant variances that could be written off without management review

3. Ignoring the necessity to trace significant, direct costs to specific jobs in hybrid manufacturing situations and, thereby, understating the cost of products containing high-cost components or materials and overstating the cost of products containing low-cost components or materials

4. Treating abnormal spoilage as normal spoilage and, thereby, inflating the cost of "good" units and not reporting the abnormal spoilage as a current period loss on the income statement ▲

Solution Strategies

Steps in Process Costing Computations

1. Calculate the physical units to account for:

    $$\text{Beginning WIP Inventory in physical units}$$
    $$+ \text{ Units started (or transferred in) during period}$$

2. Calculate the physical units accounted for. This step involves identifying the groups to which costs are to be assigned (transferred out or remaining in ending WIP Inventory).

    $$\text{Units completed and transferred}$$
    $$+ \text{ Units in ending WIP Inventory}$$

3. Calculate the equivalent units of production per cost component. The cost components include transferred-in (if multidepartment), direct material, direct labor, and overhead. In cases of multiple materials having different degrees of completion, each material is considered a separate cost component. If overhead is applied on a direct labor basis or is incurred at the same rate as direct labor, labor and overhead can be combined as one cost component and referred to as conversion.

    a. WA

    $$\text{Beginning WIP Inventory in physical units}$$
    $$+ \text{ Units started and completed*}$$
    $$+ \text{ (Ending WIP Inventory} \times \text{ \% complete)}$$

    b. FIFO

    $$\text{(Beginning WIP Inventory} \times \text{ \% not complete at start of period)}$$
    $$+ \text{ Units started and completed*}$$
    $$+ \text{ (Ending WIP Inventory} \times \text{ \% complete)}$$

    *Units started and completed = (Units transferred out − Units in beginning WIP Inventory)

4. Calculate total cost to account for:

    $$\text{Cost in beginning WIP Inventory}$$
    $$+ \text{ Costs of the current period}$$

5. Calculate cost per equivalent unit for each cost component:

    a. WA

    $$\text{Cost of component in beginning WIP Inventory}$$
    $$+ \underline{\text{Cost of component for current period}}$$
    $$= \text{ Total cost of component}$$
    $$\div \text{ EUP for component}$$

b. FIFO

$$\text{Cost of component for current period} \div \text{EUP for component}$$

6. Assign the costs to inventory accounts using the WA or FIFO method. The total cost assigned to units transferred out plus the units in the ending WIP Inventory must equal the total cost to account for.

a. WA
    1. Transferred out:

$$\text{Units Transferred Out} \times \text{Total Cost per EUP for all components}$$

    2. Ending WIP Inventory:

$$\text{The sum of (EUP for each component)} \times \text{(Cost per EUP for each component)}$$

b. FIFO
    1. Transferred out:

Beginning WIP Inventory cost
+ (Beginning WIP Inventory × % not complete at beginning of period for each component × Cost per EUP for each component)

    2. Ending WIP Inventory:

$$\text{The sum of (EUP for each component} \times \text{Cost per EUP for each component)}$$

Demonstration Problem

Plaid-Clad manufactures golf bags in a two-department process: Assembly and Finishing. The Assembly Department uses weighted average costing; the percentage of completion of overhead in this department is unrelated to direct labor. The Finishing Department adds hardware to the assembled bags and uses FIFO costing; overhead is applied in this department on a direct labor basis. For June, the following production data and costs were gathered:

Assembly Department: Units

Beginning WIP Inventory (100% complete for DM; 40% complete for DM; 30% complete for OH)	250
Units started	8,800
Ending WIP Inventory (100% complete for material; 70% complete for labor; 90% complete for overhead)	400

Assembly Department: Costs

	DM	DL	OH	Total
Beginning WIP Inventory	$ 3,755	$ 690	$ 250	$ 4,695
Current	100,320	63,606	27,681	191,607
Total costs	$104,075	$64,296	$27,931	$196,302

Finishing Department: Units

Beginning WIP Inventory (100% complete for transferred in; 15% complete for DL; 40% complete for conversion)	100
Units transferred in	8,650
Ending WIP Inventory (100% complete for transferred in; 30% complete for DL; 65% complete for conversion)	200

Finishing Department: Costs

	Transferred In	DM	Conversion	Total
Beginning inventory	$ 2,176	$ 30	$ 95	$ 2,301
Current	188,570	15,471	21,600	225,641
Totals	$190,746	$15,501	$21,695	$227,942

Required:

a. Prepare a cost of production report for the Assembly Department.

b. Prepare a cost of production report for the Finishing Department.

c. Prepare T-accounts to show the flow of costs through the Assembly and Finishing Departments.

d. Prepare the journal entries for the Finishing Department for June.

Solution to Demonstration Problem

a.

EQUIVALENT UNITS OF PRODUCTION

	Whole Units	DM	DL	OH
Beginning WIP Inventory	250			
Units started	8,800			
Units to account for	9,050			
Beginning WIP Inventory (completed)	250	250	250	250
Started and completed	8,400	8,400	8,400	8,400
Units completed	8,650			
Ending WIP Inventory	400	400	280	360
Units accounted for	9,050	9,050	8,930	9,010

Cost Data	Total	DM	DL	OH
Beginning WIP Inventory	$ 4,695	$ 3,755	$ 690	$ 250
Current period	191,607	100,320	63,606	27,681
Total cost to account for	$196,302	$104,075	$64,296	$27,931
Divided by EUP		÷ 9,050	÷ 8,930	÷ 9,010
Cost per EUP	$21.80	$11.50	$7.20	$3.10

Cost Assignment

Transferred out (8,650 × $21.80)		$188,570
Ending WIP Inventory		
Direct material (400 × $11.50)	$4,600	
Direct labor (280 × $7.20)	2,016	
Overhead (360 × $3.10)	1,116	7,732
Total cost accounted for		$196,302

b.

EQUIVALENT UNITS OF PRODUCTION

	Whole Units	Transferred In	DM	Conversion
Beginning WIP Inventory	100			
Units started	8,650			
Units to account for	8,750			
Beginning WIP Inventory (completed)	100	0	85	60
Started and completed	8,450	8,450	8,450	8,450
Units completed	8,550			
Ending WIP Inventory	200	200	60	130
Units accounted for	8,750	8,650	8,595	8,640

Cost Data	Total	Transferred In	DM	Conversion
Beginning WIP Inventory	$ 2,301			
Current period	225,641	$188,570	$15,471	$21,600
Total cost to account for	$227,942			
Divided by EUP		÷ 8,650	÷ 8,595	÷ 8,640
Cost per EUP	$26.10	$21.80	$1.80	$2.50

Cost Assignment

Transferred out		
Beginning inventory cost	$2,301	
Cost to complete		
Transferred in (0 × $21.80)	0	
Direct material (85 × $1.80)	153	
Conversion (60 × $2.50)	150	$ 2,604
Started and completed (8,450 × $26.10)		220,545
Ending inventory		
Transferred in (200 × $21.80)	$4,360	
Direct material (60 × $1.80)	108	
Conversion (130 × $2.50)	325	4,793
Total cost accounted for		$227,942

c.

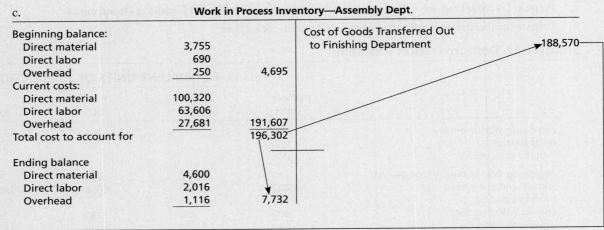

Work in Process Inventory—Assembly Dept.

Beginning balance:			Cost of Goods Transferred Out
Direct material	3,755		to Finishing Department
Direct labor	690		188,570
Overhead	250	4,695	
Current costs:			
Direct material	100,320		
Direct labor	63,606		
Overhead	27,681	191,607	
Total cost to account for		196,302	
Ending balance			
Direct material	4,600		
Direct labor	2,016		
Overhead	1,116	7,732	

Work in Process Inventory—Finishing Dept.

Beginning balance:			Cost of Goods Manufactured
Transferred in	2,176		(Transferred out to Finished Goods):
Direct material	30		Goods in BI completed 2,604
Conversion	95	2,301	Goods Started & Completed 220,545 223,149
Current costs:			
Transferred in	188,570		
Direct material	15,471		
Conversion	21,600	225,641	
Total cost to account for		227,942	
Ending balance			
Transferred in	4,360		
Direct material	108		
Conversion	325	4,793	

Finished Goods Inventory

Beginning balance	XXX	Cost of Goods Sold	$$$
Cost of goods manufactured	223,149		
Ending balance	YYY		

d. **Assembly Dept.**

Work in Process Inventory—Assembly	100,320	
Raw Material Inventory		100,320
To transfer in direct material		

Work in Process Inventory—Assembly	63,606	
Wages Payable		63,606
To record direct labor costs		

Work in Process Inventory—Assembly	27,681	
Factory Overhead Control—Assembly		27,681
To apply overhead costs to WIP		

Work in Process Inventory—Finishing	188,570	
Work in Process Inventory—Assembly		188,570
To transfer completed goods to next department		

Finishing Dept.

Work in Process Inventory—Finishing	15,471	
Raw Material Inventory		15,471
To transfer in direct material		

Work in Process Inventory—Finishing	21,600	
Conversion Cost Control—Finishing		21,600
To apply direct labor and overhead costs to WIP		
Finished Goods Inventory	223,149	
Work in Process Inventory—Finishing		223,149
To transfer completed goods to FG		

Key Terms

continuous loss, **p. 197**

cost of production report, **p. 187**

discrete loss, **p. 197**

equivalent units of production (EUP), **p. 181**

first-in, first-out (FIFO) method (of process costing), **p. 182**

hybrid costing system, **p. 195**

method of neglect, **p. 197**

total cost to account for, **p. 184**

total units to account for, **p. 185**

units started and completed, **p. 185**

weighted average (WA) method (of process costing), **p. 182**

Questions

1. What are the characteristics of a company that would be more likely to use process costing than job order costing?

2. How do the WA and FIFO methods of process costing differ in the manner in which the beginning Work in Process Inventory units are treated?

3. What is an "equivalent unit of production," and why is it a necessary concept to employ in a process costing system?

4. Is one equivalent unit computation sufficient for all cost components? Explain your answer.

5. Describe the six steps of process costing. What is the objective to be achieved by applying the six steps?

6. Which cost component can be found in a downstream department that will not be present in the most upstream department? Discuss.

7. What is meant by the term *transferred-out cost*? Why does the transferred-out cost under the WA method include only one computation but the FIFO method includes multiple computations?

8. A company has two sequential processing departments. On the cost of production reports for the departments, will the cost per unit transferred out of the first department always be equal to the cost per unit transferred in to the second department? Explain.

9. Why does standard costing make process costing more clerically and computationally efficient?

10. What is a hybrid costing system? In what circumstances are hybrid costing systems typically employed?

11. (Appendix 2) What is meant by the "method of neglect"? How does the use of this method affect cost of good production?

12. (Appendix 2) In a process costing system, how are normal and abnormal spoilage typically treated? Why are normal and abnormal spoilage treated differently?

Exercises

13. **LO.3 (WA EUP)** In manufacturing its products, LaJolla Corp. adds all direct material at the beginning of the production process. The company's direct labor and overhead are considered to be continuously at the same degree of completion. September production information follows:

Beginning WIP Inventory	32,000 pounds
Started during September	800,000 pounds
Completed during September	808,000 pounds

As of September 1, the beginning WIP Inventory was 60 percent complete as to labor and overhead. On September 30, the ending WIP Inventory was 35 percent complete as to conversion.

a. Determine the total number of pounds to account for.

b. Determine the equivalent units of production for direct material.

c. Determine the equivalent units of production for direct labor and overhead.

14. **LO.2 (Research)** In a team of three or four people, choose a company whose mass production process you would like to study. Use the library, the Internet, and (if possible) personal resources to gather information. Prepare a visual representation (similar to Exhibit 6–3) of that production process. In this illustration, indicate the approximate percentage of completion points at which various materials are added and where/how labor and overhead flow into and through the process.

  Assume that 1,000 units of product are flowing through your production process and are now at the 60 percent completion point as to labor. Prepare a written explanation about the quantity of direct material equivalent units that are included in the 1,000 units. Also explain how much overhead activity and cost have occurred and why the overhead percentage is the same as or different from the percentage of completion for labor.

15. **LO.3 (WA EUP)** For each of the following situations, use the weighted average method to determine the equivalent units of production for labor and overhead, assuming that they are continuously at the same percentage of completion.

a.	Beginning WIP Inventory (60% complete)	40,000
	Units started in production	280,000
	Units transferred out	200,000
	Ending WIP Inventory (75% complete)	120,000
b.	Beginning WIP Inventory (25% complete)	40,000
	Units started in production	240,000
	Units transferred out	?
	Ending WIP Inventory (60% complete)	60,000
c.	Beginning WIP Inventory (30% complete)	15,000
	Units started in production	135,000
	Units transferred out	130,000
	Ending WIP Inventory (90% complete)	?
d.	Beginning WIP Inventory (20% complete)	10,000
	Units started in production	?
	Units transferred out	180,000
	Ending WIP Inventory (70% complete)	20,000

16. **LO.3 (WA EUP)** Delbert Inc. uses a weighted average process costing system. All material is added at the start of the production process. Direct labor and overhead are added at the same rate throughout the process. Delbert's records indicate the following production for October 2008:

Beginning WIP Inventory (25% complete as to conversion)	540,000 units
Started during October	765,000 units
Ending WIP Inventory (60% complete as to conversion)	135,000 units

a. What are the equivalent units of production for direct material?

b. What are the equivalent units of production for conversion?

17. **LO.4 (FIFO EUP)** Assume that Delbert Inc. in Exercise 16 uses the FIFO method of process costing.

a. What are the equivalent units of production for direct material?

b. What are the equivalent units of production for conversion?

18. **LO.4 (FIFO EUP)** Assume that LaJolla Corp. in Exercise 13 uses the FIFO method of process costing.

a. What are the equivalent units of production for direct material?

b. What are the equivalent units of production for conversion?

19. **LO.3, LO.4, & LO.7 (WA & FIFO EUP)** Glasgow Inc. makes small metal toys in a one-department production process. All metal is added at the beginning of the process. Paint for the toys and plastic bags for packaging are considered indirect materials and part of overhead. The following information is available relative to September 2008 production activities:

Beginning WIP Inventory: 50,000 toys (70% complete as to labor; 75% complete as to overhead)
Started into production: metal for 560,000 toys, which were cast during the month
Ending WIP Inventory: 60,000 toys (40% complete as to labor; 60% complete as to overhead)

a. Compute the EUP for direct material, direct labor, and overhead using weighted average process costing.

b. Compute the EUP for direct material, direct labor, and overhead using FIFO process costing.

c. Reconcile the calculations in parts (a) and (b).

20. **LO.4 (FIFO EUP)** Assume that the company in Exercise 15 uses the FIFO method of process costing. Determine the equivalent units of production for labor and overhead, assuming that they are continuously at the same percentage of completion for each situation.

21. **LO.3 & LO.4 (WA & FIFO EUP)** Clarisse Corp. produces steel and uses a process costing system to assign production costs. During March 2008, the firm had a beginning Work in Process Inventory of 180,000 tons of steel that were 100 percent complete as to material and 40 percent complete as to conversion. During the month, the raw material needed to produce 2,400,000 tons of steel was started in process. At month-end, 105,000 tons remained in WIP Inventory; these units were 100 percent complete as to material and 45 percent complete as to conversion.
    a. Compute the total units to account for.
    b. Determine how many units were started and completed.
    c. Determine the equivalent units of production using the weighted average method.
    d. Determine the equivalent units of production using the FIFO method.
    e. Reconcile your answers to parts (c) and (d).

22. **LO.3, LO.4, & LO.7 (WA & FIFO EUP)** CleanSweep produces outdoor brooms. On April 30, 2008, the firm had 7,200 units in process that were 60 percent complete as to material, 40 percent complete as to direct labor, and 20 percent complete as to overhead. During May, 374,000 brooms were started. Records indicate that 368,400 units were transferred to Finished Goods Inventory in May. Ending units in process were 70 percent complete as to material, 25 percent complete as to direct labor, and 10 percent complete as to overhead.
    a. Calculate the physical units to account for in May.
    b. How many units were started and completed during May?
    c. Determine May's EUP for each category using the weighted average method.
    d. Determine May's EUP for each category using the FIFO method.
    e. Reconcile your answers to parts (c) and (d).

23. **LO.4 (Cost per FIFO EUP)** Assume that Joyner Inc. in Exercise 24 had 3,600 EUP for direct material in October's beginning WIP Inventory, 4,000 EUP for direct labor, and 3,960 EUP for overhead. What was the October FIFO cost per EUP for direct material, direct labor, and overhead?

24. **LO.3 (Cost per WA EUP)** Joyner Inc. manufactures pillar candles. In October 2008, company production was 26,800 equivalent units for direct material, 24,400 equivalent units for labor, and 21,000 equivalent units for overhead. During October, direct material, conversion, and overhead costs incurred were as follows:

Direct material	$ 78,880
Conversion	138,480
Overhead	42,600

Beginning WIP Inventory costs for October were $14,920 for direct material, $20,020 for labor, and $9,900 for overhead. What was the October weighted average cost per equivalent unit for direct material, direct labor, and overhead?

25. **LO.3 (WA EUP; cost per WA EUP)** Ouch! manufactures canisters of insect repellent. On August 1, 2008, the company had 9,800 units in the beginning WIP Inventory that were 100 percent complete as to canisters, 60 percent complete as to other materials, 40 percent complete as to direct labor, and 20 percent complete as to overhead. During August, Ouch! started 81,500 units in the manufacturing process. Ending WIP Inventory included 4,600 units that were 100 percent complete as to canisters, 40 percent complete as to other materials, 20 percent complete as to direct labor, and 10 percent complete as to overhead.

    Cost information for the month follows:

Beginning WIP Inventory	
Canisters	$ 7,382
Other direct materials	6,671
Direct labor	3,963
Overhead	3,432
August costs	
Canisters	65,658
Other direct materials	86,296
Direct labor	79,276
Overhead	157,814

Prepare a schedule showing the Ouch! August 2008 computation of weighted average equivalent units of production and cost per equivalent unit.

26. LO.3 & LO.4 (Cost per WA & FIFO EUP) Alonzo Mfg. produces concrete garden border sections. May 2008 production and cost information were as follows:

WA EUP	
Direct material	80,000 sections
Direct labor	76,000 sections
Overhead	75,000 sections
FIFO EUP	
Direct material	60,000 sections
Direct labor	62,000 sections
Overhead	66,000 sections
Beginning WIP Inventory costs	
Direct material	$ 9,800
Direct labor	3,160
Overhead	5,010
Current period costs	
Direct material	$27,000
Direct labor	17,360
Overhead	42,240

All material is added at the beginning of processing.
a. What is the total cost to account for?
b. Using weighted average process costing, what is the cost per equivalent unit for each cost component?
c. Using FIFO process costing, what is the cost per equivalent unit for each cost component?
d. How many units were in beginning inventory and at what percentage of completion was each cost component?

27. LO.3 (WA cost assignment) The following production and cost per EUP data are available for Manet Corp. for February 2008:

Units completed during February	780,000
Units in ending inventory (100% complete as to direct material;	
30% complete as to direct labor; 25% complete as to overhead)	111,000
Direct material cost per EUP	$3.75
Direct labor cost per EUP	$4.50
Overhead cost per EUP	$5.10

a. What is the cost of the goods completed during February?
b. What is the cost of the goods in the ending inventory at February 29, 2008?
c. What is the total cost to account for during February?

28. LO.4 (FIFO EUP; cost per FIFO EUP) K-Bam makes skateboards and uses a FIFO process costing system. On May 1, 2008, the company had 1,000 boards in process that were 70 percent complete as to material and 85 percent complete as to conversion. During the month, 3,800 additional boards were started. On May 31, 800 boards were still in process (40 percent complete as to material and 60 percent complete as to conversion). Cost information for May 2008 is as follows:

Beginning WIP Inventory costs	
Direct material	$12,481
Conversion	11,732
Current period costs	
Direct material	66,970
Conversion	44,649

a. Calculate EUP for each cost component using the FIFO method.
b. Calculate cost per EUP for each cost component.

29. LO.3 & LO.4 (EUP; cost per EUP; cost assignment; FIFO & WA) HowLoud? Company mass-produces miniature speakers for personal sound systems. The following T-account presents the firm's cost information for June 2008:

Work in Process Inventory	
6/1 Direct material cost in BI	3.853
6/1 Conversion cost in BI	3,146
June DM issued	62.928
June DL incurred	13.070
June OH applied to production	7,990

The company had 1,000 units in process on June 1. These units were 60 percent complete as to material and 30 percent complete as to conversion. During June, the firm started 8,400 units and ended the month with 300 units still in process. The units in the ending WIP Inventory were 80 percent complete as to material and 70 percent complete as to conversion.

a. Compute the unit costs for June under the FIFO method for direct material and for conversion.
b. Determine the total costs transferred to Finished Goods Inventory during June using the FIFO method.
c. Prepare the entries for the direct material, direct labor, and overhead applied to production during June as well as the transfer of the goods completed during June.
d. Compute the unit costs for June under the weighted average method for direct material and for conversion.
e. Determine the cost of inventory on June 30, using the weighted average method.

30. LO.4 (FIFO cost assignment) In November 2008, Paloma PLC computed its equivalent unit costs under FIFO process costing as follows:

Direct material	$14.75
Packaging	1.50
Direct labor	5.42
Overhead	3.84

Direct material and packaging are added at the start and end of processing, respectively.

Beginning inventory cost was $513,405 and consisted of
- $394,520 direct material cost for 27,000 EUP.
- $45,931 direct labor cost for 8,100 EUP.
- $72,954 overhead cost for 9,450 EUP.

Paloma transferred a total of 185,000 units to finished goods during November and had 6,000 units in ending WIP Inventory. The ending inventory units were 30 percent complete as to direct labor and 55 percent complete as to overhead.

a. What percentage complete were the beginning inventory units as to direct material? Packaging? Direct labor? Overhead?
b. What was the total cost of the completed beginning inventory units?
c. What was the cost of the units started and completed in November?
d. What was the cost of November's ending inventory?

31. LO.4 (FIFO EUP; second department) Use the information in Exercise 32 and assume that DuCharm Inc. uses the FIFO method of process costing. For the Assembly Department, compute the following:

a. equivalent units of production for each cost component.
b. cost per EUP for each cost component.
c. cost transferred to Finished Goods Inventory.
d. cost of ending WIP Inventory.

32. LO.3 (WA EUP; second department) DuCharm Inc. produces calendars in a two-process, two-department operation. In the Printing Department, calendars are printed and cut. In the Assembly Department, the material received from Printing is assembled into individual calendars and bound. Each department maintains its own Work in Process Inventory, and costs are assigned using weighted average process costing. In Assembly, conversion costs are incurred evenly throughout the process; direct material is added at the end of the process. For November 2008, the following production and cost information is available for the Assembly Department:

Beginning WIP Inventory: 20,000 calendars (30% complete as to conversion);
  transferred in cost, $25,000; conversion cost, $2,900
Transferred in during November: 80,000 calendars
Current period costs: transferred in, $80,000; direct material, $10,500; conversion, $14,960
Ending WIP Inventory: 30,000 calendars (80% complete as to conversion)

For the Assembly Department, compute the following:
a. equivalent units of production for each cost component.
b. cost per EUP for each cost component.
c. cost transferred to Finished Goods Inventory.
d. cost of ending WIP Inventory.

33. LO.5 (Standard process costing; variances) Squiggles manufactures plastic float toys and uses a standard process costing system. All plastic is added at the start of production, and labor and overhead are incurred at equal rates throughout the process. The standard cost of one float toy is as follows:

Direct material	$0.10
Direct labor	0.02
Overhead	0.07
Total cost	$0.19

The following production and cost data are applicable to April 2008:

Beginning WIP Inventory (45% complete)	180,000 units
Units started in April	1,300,000 units
Ending WIP Inventory (65% complete)	144,000 units
Current cost of direct material	$184,000
Current cost of direct labor	26,980
Current cost of overhead	93,000

a. What amount is carried as the April beginning balance of WIP Inventory?
b. What amount is carried as the April ending balance of WIP Inventory?
c. What amount is transferred to Finished Goods Inventory for April?
d. Using the FIFO method, what are the total direct material, direct labor, and overhead variances for April?
e. Record the journal entries to recognize the direct material, direct labor, and overhead variances.

34. LO.3 & LO.4 (WA & FIFO EUP; two departments) Dali Metals has two processing departments: Fabrication and Assembly. Metal is placed into production in the Fabrication Department, where it is cut and formed into various components. These components are transferred to Assembly, where they are welded, polished, and coated with sealant. Production data follow for these two departments for March 2008:

Fabrication

Beginning WIP Inventory (100% complete as to material; 25% complete as to conversion)	5,000
Units started during month	40,000
Ending WIP Inventory (100% complete as to material; 60% complete as to conversion)	6,800

Assembly

Beginning WIP Inventory (0% complete as to sealant; 35% complete as to conversion)	2,000
Units started during month	?
Ending WIP Inventory (0% complete as to sealant; 15% complete as to conversion)	6,100

a. Determine the equivalent units of production for each cost component for each department under the WA method.
b. Determine the equivalent units of production for each cost component for each department under the FIFO method.

35. LO.6 (Hybrid costing) Windy City Co. makes one-size-fits-most capes. Each cape goes through the same conversion process, but three types of fabric (Dacron, denim, and cotton) are available. The company uses a standard costing system, and standard costs for each type of cape follow:

	Dacron	Denim	Cotton
Material (2 yards)	$10	$ 8	$12
Direct labor (1 hour)	12	12	12
Overhead (based on 1.5 machine hours)	9	9	9
Total	$31	$29	$33

Material is added at the start of production. In March 2008, there was no beginning WIP Inventory and 2,500 capes were started into production. Of these, 300 were Dacron, 500 were denim, and 1,700 were cotton. At the end of March, 100 capes (20 Dacron, 30 denim, and 50 cotton) were not yet complete. The stage of completion for each cost component for the 100 unfinished capes is as follows:

Material	100% complete
Direct labor	25% complete
Overhead	35% complete

a. Determine the total cost of the capes completed and transferred to Finished Goods Inventory.
b. Determine the total cost of the capes in the ending WIP Inventory.

36. LO.5 (Standard process costing) Sivitanides Company uses a standard costing system to account for its pita bread manufacturing process. The pita bread is sold in packages of one dozen pieces. The company has set the following standards for production of each package:

Direct material—ingredients	$0.25
Direct material—packaging	0.05
Direct labor	0.07
Overhead	0.31
Total cost	$0.68

On June 1, the company had 12,000 pitas in process; these were 100 percent complete as to ingredients, 0 percent complete as to packaging, and 70 percent complete as to labor and overhead. During June, 310,000 pitas were started and 314,000 were finished. Ending inventory was 100 percent complete as to ingredients, 0 percent complete as to the packaging, and 60 percent complete as to labor and overhead.

a. What were the equivalent units of production for June for each cost component?

b. What was the cost of the packages transferred to Finished Goods Inventory during June?

c. What was the cost of the ending WIP Inventory for June?

37. **LO.8 (Appendix 2; FIFO EUP computations; normal loss)** Reeves Inc. produces paint in a process in which spoilage occurs continually. Spoilage of 2 percent or fewer of the gallons of raw material placed into production is considered normal. The following operating statistics are available for June 2008:

Beginning WIP Inventory (60% complete as to material;	
70% complete as to conversion)	8,000 gallons
Started during June	180,000 gallons
Ending WIP Inventory (40% complete as to material;	
20% complete as to conversion)	4,000 gallons
Spoiled	1,400 gallons

a. How many gallons were transferred out?

b. What are the FIFO equivalent units of production for material? For conversion?

38. **LO.6 (Hybrid costing)** After reading about hybrid costing, Linda Schneider finally realized that all of the beaded necklaces she made did not cost her the same amount of money, even though they took the same amount of time and effort to manufacture. She makes three primary types of necklaces: those made from glass beads, metal beads, and natural beads. After doing some online research, Schneider developed the following standard costs for each type of necklace:

	Glass	Metal	Natural
Beads	$19	$11	$ 7
Direct labor (1/2 hour)	8	8	8
Overhead (based on 1/2 hour)	5	5	5
Total	$32	$24	$20

Schneider began 2008 with no beginning WIP Inventory after she experienced an extreme holiday rush. During January, Schneider started 200 necklaces: 60 were glass, 30 were metal, and 110 were natural. At the end of January, 30 necklaces were not yet complete: 5 glass, 18 metal, and 7 natural. The stage of completion for each cost component for the 30 unfinished necklaces was as follows:

Material	100% complete
Direct labor	50% complete
Overhead	60% complete

a. Calculate the cost of necklaces completed during January.

b. Calculate the cost of necklaces in ending WIP Inventory.

39. **LO.8 (Appendix 2; WA; normal vs. abnormal spoilage)** Lang Industries uses a weighted average process costing system, and company management has specified that the normal loss from shrinkage cannot exceed 5 percent of the units started in a period. All raw material is added at the start of the production process. March processing information follows:

Beginning WIP Inventory (30% complete as to conversion)	10,000 units
Started during March	60,000 units
Completed during March	58,200 units
Ending WIP Inventory (20% complete as to conversion)	8,000 units

a. How many total units are there to account for?

b. How many units were spoiled during processing? Of the spoiled units, how many should be treated as a normal loss? As an abnormal loss?

c. What are the equivalent units of production for direct material? For conversion?
d. How are costs associated with the normal spoilage handled?
e. How are costs associated with the abnormal spoilage handled?

40. **LO.8 (Appendix 2; FIFO; normal loss)** Rodin Inc. produces dog food. During the production process, some shrinkage occurs. Management believes that shrinkage of less than 8 percent is normal. All direct material is entered at the beginning of the process. October 2008 data follow:

Beginning WIP Inventory (45% complete as to conversion)	18,000 pounds
Started during the month	60,000 pounds
Transferred to FG Inventory	63,000 pounds
Ending WIP Inventory (15% complete as to conversion)	10,800 pounds
Loss	? pounds

The following costs are associated with October production:

Beginning WIP Inventory:		
Material	$ 7,000	
Conversion	5,400	$12,400
Current period:		
Material	$19,530	
Conversion	16,956	36,486
Total cost to account for		$48,886

Prepare an October 2008 cost of production report for Rodin Inc. using FIFO process costing.

41. **LO.8 (Appendix 2; FIFO; normal and abnormal loss)** Waykita Foods manufactures corn meal in a continuous, mass production process. Corn is added at the beginning of the process. Normal losses are minimal and abnormal losses infrequently occur when foreign materials are found in the corn meal. Routine inspection occurs at the 95 percent completion point as to conversion.

During May, a machine malfunctioned and dumped salt into 8,000 pounds of corn meal. This abnormal loss occurred when conversion was 70 percent complete on those pounds of product. The error was immediately noticed, and those pounds of corn meal were pulled from the production process. An additional 2,000 pounds of meal were detected as unsuitable at the routine inspection point. The 2,000 lost pounds were considered within reasonable limits. May production data follow:

Beginning WIP Inventory (85% complete)	40,000 pounds
Started during the month	425,000 pounds
Ending WIP Inventory (25% complete)	10,000 pounds

a. Determine the number of EUP for direct material and for conversion, assuming a FIFO cost flow.
b. If the costs per EUP are $2.40 and $4.70 for direct material and conversion, respectively, what is the cost of the ending WIP Inventory?
c. What is the cost of abnormal loss? How is this cost treated in May?

Problems

42. **LO.3 (WA EUP; cost assignment)** Seattle Products manufactures computer cases. All material is added at the start of production and overhead is applied to each product at the rate of 70 percent of direct labor cost. At the beginning of July, there were no units in the Finished Goods Inventory. The firm's inventory cost records provide the following information:

	Units	DM Cost	DL Cost
Work in Process Inventory 7/1			
(70% complete as to labor and overhead)	100,000	$ 750,000	$215,000
Units started in production	1,500,000		
Costs for July	5,650,000	4,105,000	
Work in Process Inventory 7/31			
(60% complete as to labor and overhead)	400,000		

At the end of July, the cost of the Finished Goods Inventory was determined to be $124,000.
a. Compute the following:
   1. Equivalent units of production using the weighted average method.

2. Unit production costs for material, labor, and overhead.

3. Cost of goods sold.

b. Prepare the journal entries to record the July transfer of completed goods and the July cost of goods sold.

(CPA adapted)

43. **LO.3 (WA EUP & cost assignment)** Pardner Inc. manufactures belt buckles in a single-step production process. To determine the proper valuations for inventory balances and Cost of Goods Sold, you have obtained the following information for August 2008:

	Whole Units	Cost of Material	Cost of Labor
Beginning work in process	400,000	$ 400,000	$ 576,000
Units started during period	2,000,000	2,600,000	3,204,000
Units transferred to finished goods	1,800,000		

Beginning inventory units were 100 percent complete as to material and 80 percent complete as to labor. The ending inventory units were 100 percent complete as to material and 50 percent complete as to labor. Overhead is applied to production at the rate of 60 percent of direct labor cost.

a. Prepare a schedule to compute equivalent units of production by cost component assuming the weighted average method.

b. Determine the unit production costs for material and conversion.

c. Calculate the costs assigned to completed units and ending inventory for August 2008.

44. **LO.4 (FIFO cost per EUP)** Zack's Corp. makes a variety of snack mixes. The following information for August 2008 relates to a dried fruit trail mix. Materials are added at the beginning of processing; overhead is applied on a direct labor basis. The mix is transferred to a second department for packaging. Zack's uses a FIFO process costing system.

Beginning WIP Inventory (40% complete as to direct labor)	10,000 pounds
Mix started in August	160,800 pounds
Ending WIP Inventory (80% complete as to labor)	8,000 pounds
Material cost incurred in August	$776,664
Conversion cost incurred in August	$214,760

Beginning inventory cost totaled $53,580. For August 2008, compute the following:

a. Equivalent units of production by cost component.

b. Cost per equivalent unit by cost component.

c. Cost of mix transferred to the packaging department in August.

d. Cost of August's ending inventory.

45. **LO.3 (WA cost of production report; journal entries)** Bangor Products manufactures electronic language translators. Analysis of beginning Work in Process Inventory for July 2008 revealed the following:

800 Units	Percent Complete	Costs Incurred
Direct material	45	$ 6,748
Direct labor	65	8,680
Overhead	40	5,710
Total beginning inventory		$21,138

Direct labor costs were extremely high during June, because the company had a labor strike and paid a high premium to get production workers that month.

During July, Bangor Products started production of another 11,400 translators and incurred $259,012 for material, $58,200 for direct labor, and $188,210 for overhead. At the end of July, the company had 400 units in process (70 percent complete as to material, 90 percent complete as to direct labor, and 80 percent complete as to overhead).

a. Prepare a cost of production report for July using the weighted average method.

b. Journalize the July transactions.

c. Prepare T-accounts to represent the flow of costs for Bangor Products for July. Use XXX where amounts are unknown and identify what each unknown amount represents.

46. **LO.4 (FIFO cost of production report)** Use the information from Problem 45 for Bangor Products.

a. Prepare a cost of production report for July using the FIFO method.

b. In general, what differences exist between the WA and FIFO methods of process costing and why do these differences exist?

47. LO.4 (FIFO cost assignment) Fresh Seasons Processors is a contract manufacturer for Delectable Dressing Company. Fresh Seasons uses a FIFO process costing system to account for its salad dressing production. All ingredients are added at the start of the process. Delectable provides reusable vats to Fresh Seasons for the completed product to be shipped to Delectable for bottling, so Fresh Seasons incurs no packaging costs. April 2008 production and cost information for Fresh Seasons Processors is as follows:

Gallons of dressing in beginning WIP Inventory	36,000
Gallons completed during April	242,000
Gallons of dressing in ending WIP Inventory	23,500
Costs of beginning WIP Inventory	
Direct material	$ 178,000
Direct labor	39,100
Overhead	81,740
Costs incurred in April	
Direct material	$1,136,025
Direct labor	451,450
Overhead	723,195

The beginning and ending WIP Inventories had the following percentages of completion for labor and overhead:

	Beginning Inventory	Ending Inventory
Direct labor	55%	15%
Overhead	70%	10%

a. How many gallons of dressing ingredients were started in April?
b. What is the total cost of the completed beginning inventory?
c. What is the total cost of goods completed during April?
d. What is the average cost per gallon of all goods completed during April?
e. What is the cost of April's ending WIP Inventory?

48. LO.3 & LO.4 (WA and FIFO; cost of production report) Springtime Paints makes quality paint in one production department. Production begins with the blending of various chemicals, which are added at the beginning of the process, and ends with the canning of the paint. Canning occurs when the mixture reaches the 90 percent stage of completion. The gallon cans are then transferred to the Shipping Department for crating and shipment. Labor and overhead are added continuously throughout the process. Factory overhead is applied at the rate of $3 per direct labor hour.

Prior to May, when a change in the process was implemented, work in process inventories were insignificant. The change in process enables more production but results in large amounts of work in process. The company has always used the weighted average method to determine equivalent production and unit costs. Now production management is considering changing from the weighted average method to the first-in, first-out method. The following data relate to actual production during May:

WIP Inventory, May 1	
Direct material—chemicals	$ 45,100
Direct labor ($10 per hour)	5,250
Factory overhead	1,550
Costs for May	
Direct material—chemicals	$228,900
Direct material—cans	7,000
Direct labor ($10 per hour)	35,000
Factory overhead	11,000
Units for May (Gallons)	
WIP Inventory, May 1 (25% complete)	4,000
Sent to Shipping Department	20,000
Started in May	21,000
WIP Inventory, May 31 (80% complete)	5,000

a. Prepare a cost of production report for May using the WA method.
b. Prepare a cost of production report for May using the FIFO method.
c. Discuss the advantages and disadvantages of using the WA method versus the FIFO method, and explain under what circumstances each method should be used.

(CMA adapted)

49. LO.3 & LO.4 (WA & FIFO; cost of production report) In a single-process production system, Phunky Phingers produces wool gloves. For November 2008, the company's accounting records reflected the following:

Beginning WIP Inventory
  (100% complete as to material; 30% complete as to direct labor;
  60% complete as to overhead)   12,000 units
Units started during the month   90,000 units
Ending WIP Inventory (100% complete as to material;
  40% complete as to direct labor; 80% complete as to overhead)   20,000 units

Cost Component	November 1	During November
Direct material	$13,020	$90,000
Direct labor	1,908	45,792
Overhead	4,636	70,824

a. For November, prepare a cost of production report, assuming that the company uses the weighted average method.

b. For November, prepare a cost of production report, assuming that the company uses the FIFO method.

50. **LO.3 (Two departments; WA)** Almost Real makes artificial Christmas trees in two departments: Cutting and Boxing. In the Cutting Department, wire wrapped with green "needles" is placed into production at the beginning of the process and is cut to various lengths, depending on the size of the trees being made at that time. The "branches" are then transferred to the Boxing Department where the lengths are separated into the necessary groups to make a tree. These are then placed in boxes and immediately sent to Finished Goods. The following data are available related to the October 2008 production in each of the two departments:

EXCEL

		PERCENT OF COMPLETION		
	Units	Transferred In	Material	Conversion
Cutting Department				
Beginning WIP Inventory	8,000	N/A	100	30
Started in process	36,000			
Ending inventory	3,600	N/A	100	70
Boxing Department				
Beginning WIP Inventory	2,500	100	0	55
Transferred in	?			
Ending inventory	1,200	100	0	60

	COSTS		
	Transferred In	Material	Conversion
Cutting Department			
Beginning WIP Inventory	N/A	$ 293,000	$ 80,000
Current period	N/A	1,379,000	1,293,440
Boxing Department			
Beginning WIP Inventory	$166,420	$ 0	$ 8,400
Current period	?	383,640	246,120

a. Prepare a cost of production report for the Cutting Department assuming a weighted average method.

b. Using the data developed from part (a), prepare a cost of production report for the Boxing Department, also using the weighted average method.

51. **LO.4 (FIFO; second department; advanced)** Xena Corp. makes porcelain sinks in a process requiring operations in three separate departments: Molding, Curing, and Finishing. Materials are introduced in Molding; additional material is added in Curing. The following information is available for the Curing Department for May 2008:

Beginning WIP Inventory (degree of completion: transferred in, 100%;
  direct material, 80%; direct labor, 40%; overhead, 30%)   8,000 units
Transferred in from Molding   40,000 units
Ending WIP Inventory (degree of completion: transferred in, 100%;
  direct material, 70%; direct labor, 50%; overhead, 40%)   4,000 units
Transferred to Finishing   ? units

Cost Component	Beginning Inventory	Current Period
Transferred in	$154,000	$760,000
Direct material	24,960	161,600
Direct labor	20,080	256,800
Overhead	6,970	129,600

Prepare, in good form, a FIFO cost of production report for the Curing Department for May 2008.

52. LO.4 (Comprehensive; FIFO; two departments) Safe-N-Sound, which uses FIFO process costing, makes a backyard fencing system for pet owners in a two-stage production system. In the Cutting Dept., wood is cut and assembled into 6-foot fence sections. In the Coating Dept., the sections are pressure treated to resist the effects of weather and then coated with a preservative. The following production and cost data are available for March 2008 (units are 6-foot fence sections):

Units	Cutting Dept.	Coating Dept.
Beginning WIP Inventory (March 1)	1,300	900
Complete as to material	80%	0%
Complete as to conversion	75%	60%
Units started in March	4,800	?
Units completed in March	:	4,500
Ending WIP Inventory (March 31)	1,100	?
Complete as to material	40%	0%
Complete as to conversion	20%	40%

Costs		
Beginning WIP Inventory		
Transferred in		$11,840
Material	$ 8,345	0
Conversion	⁊,⁊20	1,674
Current		
Transferred in	?	?
Material	35,200	4,950
Conversion	21,225	11,300

a. Prepare EUP schedules for both the Cutting and Coating Departments.
b. Determine the cost per EUP for the Cutting Department.
c. Assign costs to goods transferred out of and in ending WIP Inventory in the Cutting Department.
d. Determine the cost per EUP in the Coating Department. Use the modified FIFO basis. (See footnote 6, page 189.)
e. Assign costs to goods transferred out of and in ending WIP Inventory in the Coating Department.
f. Assuming there was no beginning or ending Finished Goods Inventory for March, what was Cost of Goods Sold for March?

53. LO.3 (Cost flows: multiple departments) Kennedy Corporation produces accent stripes for automobiles in 50-inch rolls. Each roll passes through three departments (Striping, Adhesion, and Packaging) before it is ready for shipment to automobile dealers and detailing shops. Product costs are tracked by department and assigned using a process costing system. Overhead is applied to production in each department at a rate of 80 percent of the department's direct labor cost.

The following T-account information pertains to departmental operations for June 2008:

Work in Process—Striping				Work in Process—Adhesion			
Beginning	20,000			Beginning	70,000		
DM	90,000			Transferred in	?		
DL	80,000	?	?	DM	22,600	?	480,000
Overhead	?			DL	?		
				Overhead	?		
Ending	17,000						
				Ending	20,600		

Work in Process—Packaging				Finished Goods			
Beginning	150,000			Beginning	185,000		
Transferred in	?			TI	880,000	?	720,000
DM	?	CGM	?				
DL	?						
Overhead	90,000			Ending	?		
Ending	40,000						

a. What was the cost of goods transferred from the Striping Department to the Adhesion Department for the month?
b. How much direct labor cost was incurred in the Adhesion Department? How much overhead was assigned to production in the Adhesion Department for the month?

c. How much direct material cost was charged to products in the Packaging Department?
d. Prepare the journal entries for all interdepartmental transfers of products and the cost of the units sold during June 2008.

54. **LO.6 (Multiproduct; hybrid costing)** Be-at-Ease Industries manufactures a series of three models of molded plastic chairs: standard (without arms), deluxe (with arms), and executive (with arms and padding). All are variations of the same design. The company uses batch manufacturing and has a hybrid costing system.

Be-at-Ease has an extrusion operation and subsequent operations to form, trim, and finish the chairs. Plastic sheets are produced by the extrusion operation, some of which are sold directly to other manufacturers. During the forming operation, the remaining plastic sheets are molded into chair seats and the legs are added; the standard model is sold after this operation. During the trim operation, the arms are added to the deluxe and executive models, and the chair edges are smoothed. Only the executive model enters the finish operation where the padding is added. All units produced complete the same steps within each operation.

The July production run had a total manufacturing cost of $898,000. The units of production and direct material costs incurred were as follows:

	Units Produced	Extrusion Materials	Form Materials	Trim Materials	Finish Materials
Plastic sheets	5,000	$ 60,000			
Standard model	6,000	72,000	$24,000		
Deluxe model	3,000	36,000	12,000	$ 9,000	
Executive model	2,000	24,000	8,000	6,000	$12,000
Totals	16,000	$192,000	$44,000	$15,000	$12,000

Manufacturing costs applied during July were as follows:

	Extrusion Operation	Form Operation	Trim Operation	Finish Operation
Direct labor	$152,000	$60,000	$30,000	$18,000
Factory overhead	240,000	72,000	39,000	24,000

a. For each product produced by Be-at-Ease during July, determine the
1. Unit cost.
2. Total cost.
Account for all costs incurred during the month, and support your answer with appropriate calculations.
b. Without prejudice to your answer in part (a), assume that only 1,000 units of the deluxe model remained in the Work in Process Inventory at the end of the month. These units were 100 percent complete as to material and 60 percent complete as to conversion in the trim operation. Determine the value of the 1,000 units of the deluxe model in Be-at-Ease's Work in Process Inventory at the end of July.

(CMA adapted)

55. **LO.5 (Standard process costing)** Dark Out manufactures sunglass and ski goggle lenses. The company uses a standard process costing system and carries inventories at standard. For May 2008, the following data are available:

Standard Cost of 1 Unit

Direct material	$ 5.50
Conversion	12.50
Total manufacturing cost	$18.00
Beginning WIP Inventory	10,000 units (100% DM; 70% conversion)
Started in May	180,000 units
Completed in May	160,000 units
Ending WIP Inventory	? units (100% DM; 60% conversion)
Actual costs for May	
Direct material	$ 981,000
Conversion	2,145,000
Total actual cost	$3,126,000

a. Prepare an equivalent units of production schedule.
b. Prepare a cost of production report and assign costs to goods transferred and to inventory.
c. Calculate and label the variances and close them to Cost of Goods Sold.

56. **LO.3 & LO.8 (Appendix 2; WA; normal and abnormal spoilage)** Wood Tools manufactures one of its products in a two-department process. A separate Work in Process Inventory account is maintained for each department, and the company uses a weighted average process costing system. The first department is Molding;

the second is Grinding. At the end of production in Grinding, a quality inspection is made and then packaging is added. Overhead is applied in the Grinding Department on a machine-hour basis. Production and cost data for the Grinding Department for August 2008 follow:

Production Data

Beginning WIP Inventory (% complete: material, 0%;	
labor, 30%; overhead, 40%)	1,000 units
Transferred in from Molding	50,800 units
Normal spoilage (found at the end of processing during quality control)	650 units
Abnormal spoilage (found at end of processing during quality control)	350 units
Ending WIP Inventory (% complete: material, 0%;	
labor, 40%; overhead, 65%)	1,800 units
Transferred to finished goods	? units

Cost Data

Beginning WIP Inventory		
Transferred in	$ 6,050	
Material (label and package)	0	
Direct labor	325	
Overhead	980	$ 7,355
Current period		
Transferred in	$149,350	
Material (label and package)	12,250	
Direct labor	23,767	
Overhead	50,190	235,557
Total cost to account for		$242,912

a. Prepare a cost of production report for the Grinding Department for August.

b. Prepare the journal entry to dispose of the cost of abnormal spoilage.

57. LO.3 & LO.8 (Appendix 2; WA; normal and abnormal loss) Umm-Umm Good produces frozen hamburgers. In the Forming Department, ground beef is formed into patties and cooked; an acceptable shrinkage loss for this department is 3 percent of the pounds started. The patties are then transferred to the Finishing Department where they are placed on buns, boxed, and frozen.

Umm-Umm Good uses a weighted average process costing system and has the following production and cost data for the Forming Department for May 2008:

Beginning WIP Inventory (80% complete as to conversion)	2,000 pounds
Started	250,000 pounds
Transferred to Finishing (357,300 patties)	238,200 pounds
Ending inventory (30% complete as to conversion)	6,000 pounds
Beginning inventory cost of ground beef	$1,906
May cost of ground beef	$227,924
Beginning inventory conversion cost	$150
May conversion cost	$23,880

a. What is the total shrinkage (in pounds)?

b. How much of the shrinkage is classified as normal? How is it treated for accounting purposes?

c. How much of the shrinkage is classified as abnormal? How is it treated for accounting purposes?

d. What are the May 2008 equivalent units of production in the Forming Department for direct materials and conversion?

e. What is the total cost of the patties transferred to the Finishing Department? Cost of ending inventory? Cost of abnormal spoilage?

f. How might Umm-Umm Good reduce its shrinkage loss? How, if at all, would your solution(s) affect costs and selling prices?

58. LO.3 & LO.8 (Appendix 2; WA; normal and abnormal spoilage) Blanchard Company produces door pulls that are inspected at the end of production. Spoilage may occur because the door pull is improperly stamped or molded. Any spoilage in excess of 3 percent of the completed good units is considered abnormal. Direct material is added at the start of production. Labor and overhead are incurred evenly throughout production.

The company's May 2008 production and cost data follow:

Beginning WIP Inventory (50% complete)	5,600
Units started	74,400
Good units completed	70,000
Ending WIP Inventory (1/3 complete)	7,500

	DM	Conversion	Total
Beginning inventory	$ 6,400	$ 1,232	$ 7,632
Current period	74,400	31,768	106,168
Total	$80,800	$33,000	$113,800

Calculate the equivalent units schedule, prepare a weighted average cost of production report, and assign all costs.

59. **LO.3 & LO.8 (Appendix 2; WA; normal and abnormal spoilage)** Grand Monde Company manufactures various lines of bicycles. Because of the high volume of each type of product, the company employs a process cost system using the weighted average method to determine unit costs. Bicycle parts are manufactured in the Molding Department and transferred to the Assembly Department where they are partially assembled. After assembly, the bicycle is sent to the Packing Department.

Cost-per-unit data for the 20-inch dirt bike has been completed through the Molding Department. Annual cost and production figures for the Assembly Department follow:

PRODUCTION DATA

Beginning WIP Inventory (100% complete as to transferred in; 100% complete as to material; 80% complete as to conversion)	3,000 units
Transferred in during the year (100% complete as to transferred in)	45,000 units
Transferred to Packing	40,000 units
Ending WIP Inventory (100% complete as to transferred in; 50% complete as to material; 20% complete as to conversion)	4,000 units

COST DATA

	Transferred In	Direct Material	Conversion
Beginning WIP Inventory	$ 82,200	$ 6,660	$ 13,930
Current period	1,237,800	96,840	241,430
Totals	$1,320,000	$103,500	$255,360

Damaged bicycles are identified on inspection when the assembly process is complete. The normal rejection rate for damaged bicycles is 5 percent of those reaching the inspection point. Any damaged bicycles above the 5 percent quota are considered to be abnormal. Damaged bikes are removed from the production process, and, when possible, parts are reused on other bikes. However, such salvage is ignored for the purposes of this problem.

Grand Monde does not want to assign normal spoilage cost either to the units in ending inventory (because they have not yet been inspected) or to the bikes that are considered "abnormal spoilage." Thus, the company includes both normal and abnormal spoilage in the equivalent units schedule (at the appropriate percentage of completion). The cost of the normal spoilage is then added to the bikes transferred to the Packing Department. Abnormal spoilage is treated as a period loss.

a. Compute the number of damaged bikes that are considered to be
   1. Normal spoilage.
   2. Abnormal spoilage.
b. Compute the weighted average equivalent units of production for the year for
   1. Bicycles transferred in from the Molding Department.
   2. Bicycles produced with regard to Assembly material.
   3. Bicycles produced with regard to Assembly conversion.
c. Compute the cost per equivalent unit for the fully assembled dirt bike.
d. Compute the amount of total production cost that will be associated with the following items:
   1. Normal damaged units.
   2. Abnormal damaged units.
   3. Good units completed in the Assembly Department.
   4. Ending Work in Process Inventory in the Assembly Department.
e. What amount will be transferred to the Packing Department?
f. Discuss some potential reasons for spoilage to occur in this company. Which of these reasons would you consider important enough to correct and why? How might you attempt to correct these problems?

(CMA adapted)

60. **LO.4 & LO.8 (Appendix 2; FIFO; normal and abnormal spoilage)** Use the Blanchard Company data given in Problem 58. Prepare a May 2008 cost of production report using the FIFO method.

7 | Standard Costing and Variance Analysis

Objectives

After completing this chapter, you should be able to answer the following questions:

LO.1 How are standards for material, labor, and overhead set?

LO.2 What documents are associated with standard cost systems, and what information do those documents provide?

LO.3 How are material, labor, and overhead variances calculated and recorded?

LO.4 Why are standard cost systems used?

LO.5 What changes have occurred in the setting and use of standards?

LO.6 How will standard costing be affected if a single conversion element is used rather than the traditional labor and overhead elements?

LO.7 (*Appendix*) How do multiple material and labor categories affect variances?

Introduction

As discussed in Chapter 5, a standard is a performance benchmark. Organizations develop and use standards for almost all tasks. For example, businesses set standards for employee sales expenses, hotels set standards for performing housekeeping tasks and delivering room service, and casinos set standards for revenue to be generated per square foot of playing space. McDonald's standards state that 1 pound of beef will provide 10 hamburger patties, a bun will be toasted for 17 seconds, and one packet of sanitizer will be used for every 2.5 gallons of water when cleaning the shake machine.[1] Instructions for the proper preparation of doughnuts indicate that, after being fried in 375°F grease, a doughnut should be cooled to 160°F before being glazed—a process that takes a standard time of approximately 1 to 2 minutes.[2]

Because of the variety of organizational activities and information objectives, no single standard costing system is appropriate for all situations. Some systems use standards for prices but not for quantities; other systems (especially in service businesses) use standards for labor but not material. Accountants help explain the financial consequences of either exceeding the target performance levels or failing to achieve them. Without a predetermined performance measure, managers have no way of knowing what level of performance is expected. And, without comparing the actual result to the predetermined measure, managers have no way either of knowing whether the company met expectations or of exercising control.

This chapter discusses a traditional standard cost system that provides price and quantity standards for each cost component: direct material, direct labor, and manufacturing overhead. The chapter discusses how standards are developed, how variances are calculated, and what information can be gained from detailed variance analysis. It also presents journal entries used in a standard cost system. The chapter appendix covers mix and yield variances that can arise from using multiple materials or groups of labor.

Development of a Standard Cost System

Although manufacturing companies originally initiated the use of standard cost systems, service and not-for-profit organizations also use standards. A standard cost system tracks both standard and actual costs in the accounting records. This dual recording provides an essential element of cost control: having norms against which actual operations can be compared. Standard cost systems use standards, which specify the expected costs and quantities needed to manufacture a single unit of product or perform a single service. Developing a standard cost involves judgment and practicality in identifying the material and labor types, quantities, and prices as well as understanding the types of organizational overhead and how they behave.

A primary objective in manufacturing a product is to minimize unit cost while achieving certain quality specifications. Almost all products can be manufactured from a variety of alternative inputs that would generate similar output and output quality. The input choices that are made affect the standards that are set.

Some possible input resource combinations are not necessarily practical or efficient. For instance, a work team might consist only of craftspersons or skilled workers, but such a team might not be cost beneficial if the wage rates of skilled and unskilled workers differ significantly. Also, providing high-technology equipment to unskilled labor is possible, but to do so would not be an efficient use of resources.

After the desired output quality and the input resources needed to achieve that quality at a reasonable cost have been determined, price and quantity standards can be developed. Experts from cost accounting, industrial engineering, personnel, data processing, purchasing, and management contribute information and expertise toward developing standards. To ensure credibility of the stan-

---

[1]Daniel Kruger, "You Want Data with That?" *Forbes* (March 29, 2004), pp. 58–59.
[2]SweetHaven Publishing Services, "Fundamentals of Cafeteria/Banquet Food Preparation: Section IV: Yeast-Raised Doughs," http://www.free-ed.net/sweethaven/Culinary/FoodPrep01/lessonmain.asp?iNum=module0204.htm (last accessed 5/20/07).

dards and to motivate people to achieve the standards, standard-setting involvement of managers and workers whose performance will be compared to the standards is vital. The discussion of the standard-setting process begins with material.

Material Standards

The first step in developing material standards is to identify and list the specific direct material(s) used to manufacture the product. This list is often available on product specification documents prepared by the engineering department prior to initial production. Without such documentation, material specifications can be determined by observing the production area, questioning production personnel, inspecting material requisitions, and reviewing the product-related cost accounts. Four things must be known about material inputs: type, quantity, quality, and price. For example, the direct material used in producing a baseball glove is cured and tanned cowhide; indirect materials include nylon thread and small plastic reinforcements at the base of the thumb and small finger. Each cowhide provides enough leather for three or four gloves. Higher quality and a shorter breaking-in period can be achieved by using kangaroo leather. Attempts have been made to use a variety of synthetic materials for manufacturing baseball gloves, but these have not achieved the resilience, stretchability, or "feel" of real leather.

In making quality decisions, managers should remember that as the material grade rises, so generally does price; decisions about material inputs usually seek to balance the relationships of price, quality, and projected selling prices with company objectives. The resulting trade-offs affect material mix, material yield, finished product quality and quantity, overall product cost, and product salability. Thus, quantity and cost estimates become direct functions of quality decisions. Tanning is important in the manufacturing process of baseball gloves because that process is what provides the gloves with their flexibility and durability; if hides are not properly tanned, the gloves quickly crack and flake. Because of the quality selected for each component, estimates of the physical quantity of weight, size, volume, or some other measure can be made. These estimates are based on the results of engineering tests, opinions of managers and workers using the material, past material requisitions, and review of the cost accounts.

Unlike baseball gloves, most products require multiple direct material inputs. The specifications for materials, including quality and quantity, are compiled on a **bill of materials**; Exhibit 7–1 shows the bill of materials for one type of mountain bike manufactured by Harris Corporation. Even companies without formal standard cost systems develop bills of materials for products as guides for production activity.

When converting quantities from the bill of materials into costs, companies often make allowances for normal waste of components.[3] After standard quantities have been developed, component prices that reflect quantity discounts allowed and freight/receiving costs must be determined. Purchasing agents can often influence prices by being aware of the company's purchasing habits and of alternative suppliers that can provide the most appropriate material in the most reasonable time at the most reasonable price. Incorporating such information into price standards should make it easier for the purchasing agent to later determine the causes of any significant differences between actual and standard prices.

When all quantity and price information is available, component quantities are multiplied by unit prices to obtain the total cost of each component. (Remember that cost equals price times quantity.) These totals are summed to determine the total standard material cost of one unit of product.

Labor Standards

Developing labor standards requires the same basic procedures as those used for material. Each production operation performed by workers (such as bending, reaching, lifting, moving material, and packing) or by machinery (such as drilling, cooking, and assembling) should be identified. In specifying operations and movements, activities such as cleanup, setup, and rework are considered. All

LO.1
How are standards for material, labor, and overhead set?

LO.2
What documents are associated with standard cost systems, and what information do those documents provide?

---

[3]Although such allowances are often made, they do not result in the most effective use of a standard cost system. Problems arising from their inclusion are discussed later in this chapter.

EXHIBIT 7–1

Harris Corporation's Bill of Materials

Product Name: <u>Mountain Bike (unassembled)</u>
Product # <u>15</u>
Date Established: <u>January 10, 2008</u>

COMPONENT ID#	QUANTITY REQUIRED	DESCRIPTION	COMMENTS
WF-05	1	Front wheel, tire & tube	Stumpjumper
WR-05	1	Rear wheel, tire & tube	Stumpjumper
B-05	2	Front & rear brakes	Includes derailleur, levers, and calipers
HB-05	1	Handlebar and stem	Stainless steel
B-21	16	2.5" x 5/16" bolts	Includes nuts and flat washers
S-18	12	3" clamps	Stainless steel
SPS-05	1	Seat post and seat	Nylon and black
P-05	2	Pedals	Black rubber
F-05	1	Frame	Fiberglass

unnecessary movements of workers and of material should be disregarded when time standards are set. Exhibit 7–2 indicates that a manufacturing worker's day is not spent entirely in productive work.

To develop effective standards, a company must obtain quantitative information for each production operation. Such information can be gathered from industrial engineering methods, in-house time-and-motion studies, or historical data. Methods-time measurement (MTM) is an industrial engineering process that analyzes work tasks to determine the time a trained worker requires to perform a given operation at a rate that can be sustained for an eight-hour workday. In-house studies may result in employees engaging in "slowdown" tactics when they are being monitored to establish a longer time as the standard, which makes employees appear more efficient when actual results are measured. Slowdowns may also occur because employees, knowing they are being observed, want to make certain that they are performing the task correctly. Rather than monitoring task performance, the average time needed to manufacture a product during the prior year can be calculated from employee time sheets and used to set a current time standard. A problem with this method is that historical data can include inefficiencies. To compensate for biases in internal estimations, management and supervisory personnel normally adjust standards for slowdowns or past inefficiencies by making subjective adjustments to any internal information gathered.

After all labor tasks have been analyzed, a company prepares an operations flow document that lists all tasks necessary to make one unit of product or perform a specific service. When products are manufactured individually, the operations flow document shows the time necessary to produce one unit. In a process that produces goods in batches, individual times cannot be specified accurately and time is specified for the batch. Exhibit 7–3 presents the operations flow document for a mountain bike produced by Harris Corporation.

EXHIBIT 7–2

Where Did the Day Go?

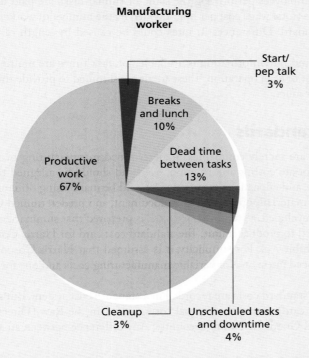

Source: John R. Hayes, "Memo Busters," *Forbes* (April 24, 1995), p. 174. Reprinted by permission of Forbes magazine. © 2004 Forbes Inc.

EXHIBIT 7–3

Harris Corporation's Operations Flow Document

Product: <u>Mountain Bike</u>
Product # <u>15</u>
Date Established: <u>January 10, 2008</u>

Operation ID#	Department	Standard Time	Description of Task
009	Painting	3 hours	Spray primer, clear coat, and paint on frame
012	Assembly	5 hours	Assemble bike
015	Oiling	1 hour	Oil all gear parts
018	Testing	0.50 hour	Inspect and test bike
210	Packaging	0.25 hour	Place bike in corrugated packaging

Labor rate standards should reflect employee wages and the related employer costs for fringe benefits, FICA (Social Security), and unemployment taxes. In the simplest situation, all departmental personnel are paid the same wage rate as, for example, when wages are task-specific or tied to a labor contract. If employees performing the same or similar tasks are paid different wage rates, a weighted average rate (total wage cost per hour divided by the number of workers) must be computed and used as the standard. Differences in rates could be caused by length of employment or skill level.

When all time and rate information is available, job task times are multiplied by wage rates to generate the total cost of each operation. These totals are summed to provide the total standard labor cost of one unit of product.

Overhead Standards

Overhead standards are merely companies' predetermined manufacturing overhead rates. To provide the most appropriate costing information, overhead should be assigned to separate cost pools based on cost drivers, and allocations to products should be made using different activity drivers.

After the bill of materials, operations flow document, and predetermined OH rates per activity measure have been developed, a standard cost card is prepared that summarizes the standard quantities and costs needed to produce a unit. The standard cost card for Harris Corporation's mountain bike is shown in Exhibit 7–4. For simplicity, it is assumed that Harris Corporation uses only two predetermined overhead rates: one for variable manufacturing costs and one for fixed manufacturing costs.

Both actual and standard costs are recorded in a standard cost system. But standard costs (based on the standard cost card), rather than actual costs, appear in the Raw (Direct) Material, Work in Process, and Finished Goods Inventory accounts.[4] Any difference between an actual and a standard cost is a variance.

LO.3
How are material, labor, and overhead variances calculated and recorded?

General Variance Analysis Model

A total variance is the difference between the total actual cost for the production inputs and the total standard cost applied to the production output. This variance can be diagrammed as follows:

Total variances do not provide useful information for determining why standard and actual costs differed. For instance, the preceding variance computation does not indicate whether the variance was caused by price factors, quantity factors, or both. To provide additional information, total variances are subdivided into price and usage components. The total variance diagram can be expanded to provide the following general model indicating the two subvariances:

The price component of the total variance shows the difference between what was actually paid for inputs and the amount expected to be paid for inputs. The price/rate variance is calculated as the

---

[4]The standard cost of each cost element (direct material, direct labor, variable overhead, and fixed overhead) is said to be applied or allocated to the goods produced. This terminology is the same as that used when overhead is assigned to inventory based on a predetermined rate.

EXHIBIT 7–4

Harris Corporation's Standard Cost Card for Mountain Bikes

Product: Mountain Bike
Product # 15
Date Established: January 10, 2008

DIRECT MATERIAL

Component ID#	Quantity Required	Unit Cost	Total Cost
WF-05	1	$ 20.00	$ 20
WR-05	1	25.00	25
B-05	2	20.00	40
HB-05	1	23.00	23
B-21	16	0.75	12
S-18	12	1.25	15
SPS-05	1	17.00	17
P-05	2	14.00	28
F-05	1	200.00	200
Total cost			$380

DIRECT LABOR

ID#	Wage Rate/Hr	Total Hrs	Painting	Assembling	Oiling	Testing	Packaging	Total Cost
009	$12	3.00	$36					$ 36
012	15	5.00		$75				75
015	8	1.00			$8			8
Testing	20	0.50				$10		10
Packaging	8	0.25					$2	2
Totals		9.75	$36	$75	$8	$10	$2	$131

MANUFACTURING OVERHEAD

Variable overhead ($14 per labor hour) (9.75 direct labor hours)	$136.50
Fixed overhead ($120,000 expected annual FOH ÷ 5,000 budgeted capacity of bikes)	24.00
Total overhead	$160.50

difference between the actual price (AP) and the standard price (SP) per unit of input multiplied by the actual input quantity (AQ):

$$\text{Price/Rate Variance} = (AP - SP)(AQ)$$

The diagram of the general model moves from actual cost of actual input quantity in the left column to standard cost of actual output in the right column. The middle column of the measure of input is a hybrid of actual quantity and standard price. The change from input to output reflects the fact that the actual ratio of inputs to outputs will not necessarily equal the standard ratio of inputs to outputs.

The usage component of the total variance shows the efficiency of results or the relationship of input to output. The far right column in the model shows a total standard cost, which reflects a measure of output known as the **standard quantity**. This quantity, depicted in Exhibit 7–5, translates

EXHIBIT 7–5
Depiction of Standard Quantity

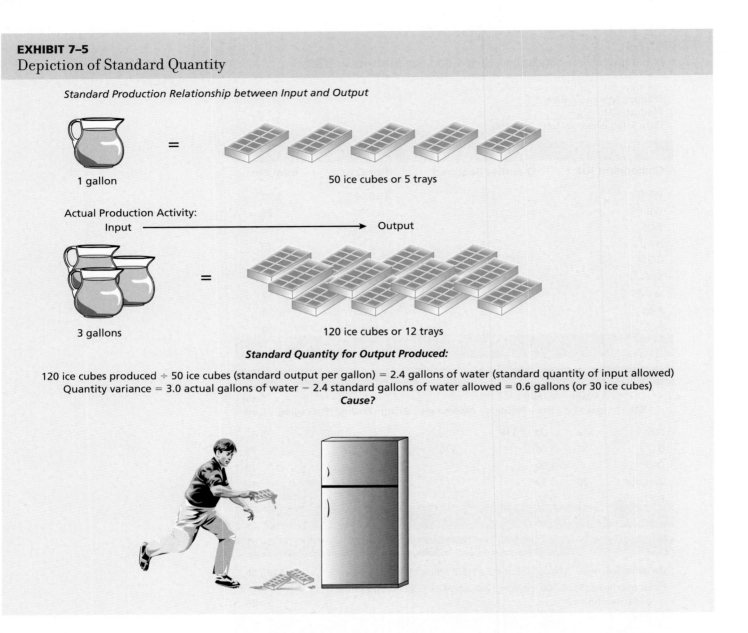

Standard Production Relationship between Input and Output

1 gallon

=

50 ice cubes or 5 trays

Actual Production Activity:
Input ⟶ Output

3 gallons

=

120 ice cubes or 12 trays

Standard Quantity for Output Produced:

120 ice cubes produced ÷ 50 ice cubes (standard output per gallon) = 2.4 gallons of water (standard quantity of input allowed)
Quantity variance = 3.0 actual gallons of water − 2.4 standard gallons of water allowed = 0.6 gallons (or 30 ice cubes)
Cause?

actual production output into the standard input quantity that should have been used to achieve that output. The monetary amount shown in the right-hand column of the general variance analysis model is computed as the standard quantity multiplied by the standard input price. This computation provides a monetary measure that can be recorded in the accounting records. The quantity/efficiency variance is calculated as the difference between the AQ and standard quantity of input allowed (SQ) multiplied by the standard price per unit of input:

$$\text{Quantity/Efficiency Variance} = (\text{AQ} - \text{SQ})(\text{SP})$$

The following sections illustrate variance computations for each cost element.

Material and Labor Variance Computations

The standard costs of production for 400 mountain bikes (the actual quantity made by Harris Corporation in January 2008) are shown in the top half of Exhibit 7–6. The lower half of the exhibit

EXHIBIT 7-6

Standard and Actual Cost Data for Harris Corporation's January 2008 Production of 400 Mountain Bikes

STANDARD COST FOR 400 MOUNTAIN BIKES

Direct Material Component ID#	Quantity	Unit Cost	Total Cost
WF-05	400	$ 20.00	$ 8,000
WR-05	400	25.00	10,000
B-05	800	20.00	16,000
HB-05	400	23.00	9,200
B-21	6,400	0.75	4,800
S-18	4,800	1.25	6,000
SPS-05	400	17.00	6,800
P-05	800	14.00	11,200
F-05	400	200.00	80,000
Total standard direct material cost			$152,000

Direct Labor Department	Total Hours	Rate	Total Cost
Painting	1,200	$12.00	$14,400
Assembling	2,000	15.00	30,000
Oiling	400	8.00	3,200
Testing	200	20.00	4,000
Packaging	100	8.00	800
Total standard direct labor hours and cost	3,900		$52,400

Variable overhead		$54,600
Fixed overhead		10,000
Total standard overhead cost		$64,600

ACTUAL JANUARY COST FOR 400 MOUNTAIN BIKES

Direct Material Component ID#	Quantity	Unit Cost	Total Cost
WF-05	413	$ 19.00	$ 7,847
WR-05	400	24.00	9,600
B-05	810	20.00	16,200
HB-05	400	24.00	9,600
B-21	6,700	0.74	4,958
S-18	4,850	1.20	5,820
SPS-05	400	18.00	7,200
P-05	800	15.00	12,000
F-05	400	197.00	78,800
Total actual direct material cost			$152,025

Direct Labor Department	Total Hours	Rate	Total Cost
Painting	1,100	$12.00	$13,200
Assembling	1,900	16.00	30,400
Oiling	390	7.90	3,081
Testing	200	19.50	3,900
Packaging	90	8.00	720
Total actual direct labor hours and cost	3,680		$51,301

Variable overhead		$50,784
Fixed overhead		8,480
Total actual overhead cost		$59,264

shows actual January 2008 material, labor, and overhead quantities and cost data. This information is used to compute the January 2008 variances.

Material Variances

The general variance analysis model is used to compute price and quantity variances for each type of direct material. To illustrate the calculations, direct material item WF-05 is used.

If the actual price or quantity amounts are higher than the standard price or quantity amounts, the variance is unfavorable (U); if the actual amounts are lower than the standard amounts, the variance is favorable (F). However, *unfavorable* is not necessarily equated with bad nor is *favorable* equated with good. An unfavorable variance (higher actual cost or usage than standard) has a negative effect on income, and a favorable variance (lower actual cost or usage than standard) has a positive effect on income. However, determination of "bad" or "good" must be made after identifying the cause of the variance and the implications of that variance for other cost elements.

The material price variance (MPV) indicates whether the amount paid for material was less than or more than standard price. For item WF-05, the price paid was $19 rather than the standard price of $20 per unit. The $413 F MPV can also be calculated as: $(\$19 - \$20)(413) = (-\$1)(413) = -\$413$ F; this variance is favorable because the actual price is less than the standard. A favorable variance *reduces* the cost of production and, thus, a negative sign indicates a favorable variance. The purchasing manager should be able to explain why the price paid for item WF-05 was less than standard.

The material quantity variance (MQV) indicates whether the actual quantity used was less than or more than the standard quantity for the actual output. This difference is multiplied by the standard price per unit of material because quantities cannot be entered into the accounting records—only dollar amounts. Production used 13 more units of WF-05 than the standard allowed, resulting in a $260 unfavorable material quantity variance: $(\$20)(413 - 400) = (\$20)(13) = \$260$ U. The production manager should be able to explain why the additional WF-05 components were used in January.

The total material variance ($153 F) can be calculated by subtracting the total standard cost ($8,000) for component WF-05 from the total actual cost ($7,847) of WF-05. The total material variance also represents the summation of the individual variances: $-\$413$ F $+$ \$260 U $=$ $-\$153$ F.

To find the total direct material variances, price and quantity variance computations would be made for each of the remaining direct material components. These component variances then would be summed to obtain the total price and quantity variances. Such a summation, however, would not provide useful information for cost control.

Point-of-Purchase Material Variance Model

A total variance for a cost component generally equals the sum of the price and usage variances. An exception to this rule occurs when the quantity of material purchased is not the same as the quantity of material placed into production. Because the material price variance relates to the purchasing (rather than the production) function, the point-of-purchase model calculates the material price variance using the quantity of materials purchased (Q_p) rather than the quantity of materials used (Q_u). The general variance analysis model is altered slightly to isolate the variance as early as possible to provide more rapid information for management control purposes.

Assume that Harris Corporation purchased 450 WF-05s at $19 per unit during January, but only used 413 for the 400 bikes produced that month. Using the point-of-purchase variance model, the computation for the material price variance is adjusted, but the computation for the material quantity variance remains the same as previously shown. The point-of-purchase material variance model is a "staggered" one as follows:

The material quantity variance is still computed on the actual quantity used and, thus, remains at $260 U. Because the price and quantity variances have been computed using different bases, they should not be summed, and no total material variance can be meaningfully determined.

Labor Variances

The labor variances for mountain bicycle production in January 2008 would be computed on a departmental basis and then summed across departments. To illustrate the computations, the Painting Department data are used. Each mountain bike requires 3 hours in the Painting Department; thus, the standard labor time allowed for 400 bikes is (400 × 3) or 1,200 hours. The actual labor time used in the Painting Department is shown on Exhibit 7–6 as 1,100 hours. Calculations of the labor variances are as follows:

The **labor rate variance** (LRV) is the difference between the actual wages paid to labor for the period and the standard cost of actual hours worked. The LRV can also be computed as: $(\$12 - \$12)(1,100) = (\$0)(1,100) = \$0$. The **labor efficiency variance** (LEV) indicates whether the amount of time worked was less than or more than the standard quantity for the actual output. This difference is multiplied by the standard rate per hour of labor time. The Painting Department worked 100 hours less than hours allowed to produce 400 mountain bikes, and the LEV is $(1,100 - 1,200)(\$12) = (-100)(\$12) = -\$1,200$ F.

The total labor variance ($1,200 F) for the Painting Department can be calculated by subtracting the total standard labor cost ($14,400) from the total actual labor cost ($13,200). The total labor variance also represents the summation of the individual variances: $\$0 + -\$1,200$ F $= -\$1,200$ F.

Overhead Variances

Because total variable overhead changes in direct relationship with changes in activity and fixed overhead per unit changes inversely with changes in activity, a specific capacity level must be selected to compute budgeted overhead costs and to develop a predetermined overhead (OH) rate. To compute the predetermined OH rates, managers at Harris Corporation used a capacity level of 5,000 mountain bikes or 48,750 direct labor hours (5,000 bikes × 9.75 hours each). Budgeted variable overhead costs at that level of direct labor hours (DLHs) were $682,500 and budgeted annual fixed overhead costs were $120,000. Harris Corporation managers computed the predetermined variable

OH rate using DLHs and the predetermined fixed OH rate using number of mountain bikes. Thus, the predetermined variable and fixed OH rates are, respectively, $14 per DLH ($682,500 ÷ 48,750) and $24 per bike ($120,000 ÷ 5,000).

Because Harris Corporation uses separate variable and fixed overhead application rates, separate price and usage components are calculated for each type of overhead. This four-variance approach provides managers the greatest detail and, thus, the greatest flexibility for control and performance evaluation.

Variable Overhead

The computations for variable overhead (VOH) variances are as follows:

Actual VOH cost is debited to the Variable Manufacturing Overhead Control account with appropriate credits to various accounts. Applied VOH is debited to Work in Process Inventory and credited to Variable Manufacturing Overhead Control. The applied VOH reflects the standard predetermined OH rate multiplied by the standard quantity of activity for the period's actual output. The total VOH variance is the balance in Variable Manufacturing Overhead Control at the end of the period and is equal to the amount of underapplied or overapplied VOH.

Using the actual January 2008 VOH cost information in Exhibit 7–6, the VOH variances for mountain bike production are calculated as follows:

The difference between actual VOH and budgeted VOH based on actual hours is the **variable overhead spending variance**. VOH spending variances are caused by both price and volume differences. For example, an unfavorable variable overhead spending variance could be caused by either paying a higher price or using more indirect material than standards allow. Variable overhead spending variances associated with price differences can occur because, over time, changes in VOH prices have not been included in the standard rate. For example, average indirect labor wage rates or utility rates could have changed since the predetermined VOH rate was computed. Managers usually have little control over prices charged by external parties and should not be held accountable for variances arising because of such price changes. In these instances, the standard rates should be adjusted.

Variable overhead spending variances associated with quantity differences can be caused by waste or shrinkage of production inputs (such as indirect material). For example, deterioration of material during storage or from lack of proper handling can be recognized only after the material is placed into production. Such occurrences usually have little relationship to the input activity basis used, but they do affect the VOH spending variance. If waste or spoilage is the cause of the VOH spending variance, managers should be held accountable and encouraged to implement more effective controls.

The difference between budgeted VOH for actual hours and applied VOH is the **variable overhead efficiency variance**. This variance quantifies the effect of using more or less of the activity or resource which is the base for variable overhead application. For example, Harris Corporation applies variable overhead to mountain bikes using direct labor hours. If Harris uses direct labor time inefficiently, one effect of the inefficiency is higher variable overhead costs. When actual input exceeds standard input allowed, production operations are considered to be inefficient. Excess input also indicates that an increased VOH budget is needed to support the additional activity base being used.

Fixed Overhead

The total fixed overhead (FOH) variance is divided into its price and production volume components by inserting budgeted FOH as a middle column into the general variance analysis model as follows:

The left column is the total actual fixed overhead incurred. Actual FOH cost is debited to Fixed Manufacturing Overhead Control and credited to various accounts. The budgeted FOH is a constant amount throughout the relevant range of activity and was the amount used to develop the predetermined FOH rate; thus, the middle column is a constant figure regardless of the actual quantity of input or the standard quantity of input allowed.

Applied FOH is debited to Work in Process Inventory and credited to Fixed Manufacturing Overhead Control. The applied FOH reflects the standard predetermined OH rate multiplied by the standard quantity of activity for the period's actual output. The total FOH variance is the balance in Fixed Manufacturing Overhead Control at the end of the period and is equal to the amount of underapplied or overapplied FOH.

Total budgeted FOH for the year is $120,000. Assuming that FOH is incurred steadily throughout the year, the monthly budgeted FOH is $10,000. Using the actual January 2008 FOH cost information in Exhibit 7–6, the FOH variances for mountain bike production are calculated as follows:

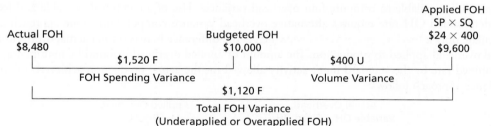

The difference between actual and budgeted FOH is the fixed overhead spending variance. This amount normally represents the differences between budgeted and actual costs for the numerous FOH components, although it can also reflect resource mismanagement. Individual FOH components would be shown in the company's flexible overhead budget, and individual spending variances should be calculated for each component.

As with variable overhead, applied FOH is related to the standard application rate and the standard quantity for the actual production level achieved. Relative to FOH, the standard input allowed for the achieved production level measures capacity utilization for the period. The fixed overhead volume variance is the difference between budgeted and applied fixed overhead. This variance is caused solely by producing at a level that differs from that used to compute the predetermined OH rate. In the case of Harris Corporation, the predetermined FOH rate is $24 per unit. This rate resulted from dividing expected FOH cost of $120,000 by a capacity level of 5,000 bikes. Had any other capacity level been chosen, the predetermined FOH rate would have differed, even though the total amount of budgeted monthly fixed overhead ($10,000) would have remained the same. If actual capacity usage differs from that used in determining the application rate used to apply FOH, a volume variance will occur. For example, if the company had chosen 4,800 bikes as the capacity level used to set the predetermined FOH rate, there would be no volume variance for January 2008: expected volume for the month (4,800 ÷ 12, or 400 units) would equal actual production volume. A volume variance occurs because, by using an application rate per unit of activity, FOH is treated as if it were a variable cost even though it is not.

Although capacity utilization is controllable to some degree, the volume variance is the one over which managers have the least influence and control, especially in the short run. Thus, a volume variance is also called a noncontrollable variance. Although they cannot control the capacity level chosen to compute the predetermined FOH rate, managers do have the ability to control capacity utilization. The level of capacity utilization should always be viewed in relation to inventory level and sales demand. Managers must understand that underutilization of capacity is not always undesirable; it is more appropriate to properly regulate production than to produce goods that will end up in inventory stockpiles. Producing unneeded inventory generates substantial costs for material, labor, and overhead (including storage and handling costs). The positive impact that such unneeded production will have on the volume variance is insignificant because this variance is of little or no value for managerial control purposes.

Management is usually aware, as production occurs, of capacity utilization even if a volume variance is not reported. The volume variance merely translates under- or overutilization into a dollar amount. An unfavorable volume variance indicates less-than-expected utilization of capacity. If available capacity is commonly being used at a level higher (or lower) than that which was anticipated or is available, managers should recognize that condition, investigate the reasons for it, and (if possible and desirable) initiate appropriate action. Sometimes managers can influence capacity utilization by modifying work schedules, taking measures to relieve any obstructions to or congestion of production activities, and carefully monitoring the movement of resources through the production process. Preferably, such actions should be taken before production rather than after it. Efforts made after production is completed might improve next period's operations but will have no impact on past production.

Alternative Overhead Variance Approaches

If the accounting system does not distinguish between variable and fixed overhead costs, insufficient data will be available to compute four overhead variances. Use of a combined (variable and fixed) predetermined OH rate requires alternative overhead variance computations. One approach is to calculate only a total overhead variance, which is the difference between total actual overhead and total overhead applied to production. The amount of applied overhead is found by multiplying the combined rate by the standard input activity allowed for the actual production achieved. The one-variance approach follows:

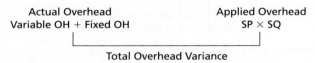

Like other total variances, the total overhead variance provides limited information to managers.

A two-variance analysis is performed by inserting a middle column in the one-variance model:

The middle column is the expected total overhead cost for the period's actual output. This amount represents total budgeted VOH at the standard quantity measure allowed plus the budgeted FOH, which is constant at all activity levels in the relevant range.

The budget variance equals total actual overhead minus budgeted overhead for the period's actual output. This variance is also referred to as the controllable variance because managers are able to exert influence on this amount during the short run. The difference between total applied overhead and budgeted overhead for the period's actual output is the volume variance; this variance is the same as would be computed under the four-variance approach.

Inserting another column between the left and middle columns of the two-variance model provides a three-variance analysis by separating the budget variance into spending and efficiency variances. The new column represents the flexible budget based on the actual input measure(s).[5] The three-variance model is as follows:

Actual Overhead VOH + FOH	Budgeted Overhead (for actual input used)	Budgeted Overhead (for actual output)	Applied Overhead SP × SQ
	OH Spending Variance	OH Efficiency Variance	Volume Variance
		Total Overhead Variance	

The total overhead spending variance is computed as total actual overhead minus total budgeted overhead at the actual input activity level; this amount equals the sum of the VOH and FOH spending variances of the four-variance approach. The overhead efficiency variance is related solely to variable overhead and is the difference between total budgeted overhead at the actual input activity level and total budgeted overhead at the standard activity level. This variance measures, at standard cost, the approximate amount of VOH caused by using more or fewer inputs than were standard for the actual production. The sum of the overhead spending and overhead efficiency variances of the three-variance analysis equals the budget variance of the two-variance analysis. The volume variance is the same amount as that calculated using the two-variance or the four-variance approach.

If VOH and FOH are applied using a combined rate, the one-, two-, and three-variance approaches will have the interrelationships shown in Exhibit 7–7. The amounts in the exhibit represent the data provided earlier for Harris Corporation. Managers should select the method that provides the most useful information and that conforms to the company's accounting system. As more companies begin to recognize the existence of multiple cost drivers for overhead and to use multiple bases for applying overhead to production, computation of the one-, two-, and three-variance approaches will diminish.

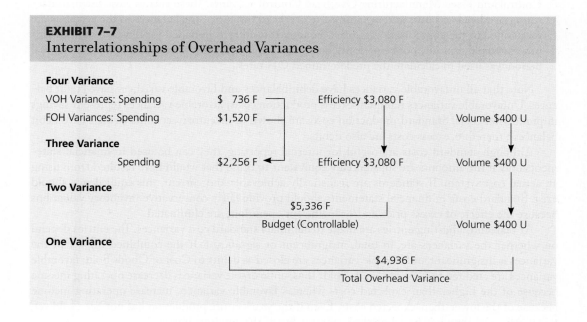

EXHIBIT 7–7
Interrelationships of Overhead Variances

Four Variance

VOH Variances: Spending	$ 736 F	Efficiency $3,080 F		
FOH Variances: Spending	$1,520 F		Volume $400 U	

Three Variance

Spending	$2,256 F	Efficiency $3,080 F	Volume $400 U

Two Variance

$5,336 F	
Budget (Controllable)	Volume $400 U

One Variance

$4,936 F
Total Overhead Variance

---

[5]Flexible budgets are discussed in Chapter 3.

Standard Cost System Journal Entries

See Exhibit 7–8 for selected journal entries using Harris Corporation's mountain bike production data for January 2008. The following explanations apply to the numbered journal entries.

1. The debit to Raw Material Inventory is for the standard price of the actual quantity of component WF-05 purchased in January. The credit to Accounts Payable is for the actual price of the actual quantity of component WF-05 purchased. The variance credit reflects the favorable material price variance for that component. Similar entries would be made for purchases of all other components.

2. The debit to Work in Process Inventory is for the standard price of the standard quantity of the WF-05 component used in January; the Raw Material Inventory credit is for the standard price of the actual quantity of WF-05 components used in production. The debit to the Material Quantity Variance account reflects the overuse (by 13 units) of WF-05s, valued at the standard price. Similar entries would be made for issuances of all other components to production.

3. The debit to Work in Process Inventory is for the standard hours in the Painting Department to produce 400 mountain bikes multiplied by the standard wage rate. The Wages Payable credit is for the actual amount of direct cost for painters during the period. The Labor Efficiency Variance credit reflects the difference between actual and standard hours multiplied by the standard wage rate. Similar entries would be made for wages incurred and standard direct labor wages allowed for all other departments.

4. During January, actual costs incurred for variable and fixed overhead are debited to the Manufacturing Overhead Control accounts. These costs are caused by a variety of transactions including indirect material and labor usage, depreciation, and utility costs. This entry reflects the incurrence of all company overhead for the month.

5. Overhead is applied to production using the predetermined rates multiplied by the standard input allowed. Overhead application is recorded at completion of production or at the end of the period, whichever occurs first. The difference between actual debits and applied credits in each overhead account represents the total variable and fixed overhead variances and is also the underapplied or overapplied overhead for the period. For January, variable overhead and fixed overhead are applied at the respective $14 per direct labor hour and $24 per unit predetermined rates.

6. & 7. These entries assume an end-of-month closing of the Variable Manufacturing Overhead Control and Fixed Manufacturing Overhead Control accounts. These entries close the manufacturing overhead accounts and recognize the overhead variances. The balances in the accounts are reclassified to the appropriate variance accounts. This entry is provided for illustration only. This process would typically not be performed at month-end but rather at year-end because an annual period was used to calculate the predetermined OH rates.

Note that all unfavorable variances have debit balances and favorable variances have credit balances. Unfavorable variances represent excess production costs; favorable variances represent savings in production costs. Standard production costs are shown in inventory accounts (which have debit balances); therefore, excess costs are also debits.

Although standard costs are useful for internal reporting, they can be used in financial statements only if the amounts are substantially equivalent to those that would have resulted from using an actual cost system. If standards are realistically achievable and current, this equivalency should exist. Standard costs in financial statements should provide fairly conservative inventory valuations because the effects of excess price and/or inefficient operations are eliminated.

At year-end, adjusting entries are made to eliminate standard cost variances. The entries depend on whether the variances are, in total, insignificant or significant. If the combined impact of the variances is insignificant, unfavorable variances are closed as debits to Cost of Goods Sold; favorable variances are credited to Cost of Goods Sold. Thus, unfavorable variances decrease operating income because of the higher-than-expected costs whereas favorable variances increase operating income because of the lower-than-expected costs. Even if the year's entire production has not been sold yet, this variance treatment is based on the immateriality of the amounts involved.

In contrast, large variances are prorated at year-end among ending inventories and Cost of Goods Sold so that the balances in those accounts approximate actual costs. Proration is based on

EXHIBIT 7–8
Selected Journal Entries for Harris Corporation's Mountain Bike Production, January 2008

(1)	Raw Material Inventory ($20 × 450)	9,000	
	Material Purchase Price Variance [($20 − $19) × 450]		450
	Accounts Payable		8,550
	To record the acquisition of 450 WF-05s		
(2)	Work in Process Inventory ($20 × 400 × 1)	8,000	
	Material Quantity Variance {$20 × [(400 × 1) − 413]}	260	
	Raw Material Inventory ($20 × 413)		8,260
	To record issuance of WF-05s to production		
(3)	Work in Process Inventory [$12 × (400 × 3)]	14,400	
	Labor Rate Variance [($12 − $12) × 1,100]	0	
	Labor Efficiency Variance {$12 × [(400 × 3) − 1,100]}		1,200
	Wages Payable ($12 × 1,100)		13,200
	To record incurrence of direct labor costs by the Painting Department (Note: In an actual organization, no journal entry debit would have been made for the labor rate variance because the amount was $0.)		
(4)	Variable Manufacturing Overhead Control	50,784	
	Fixed Manufacturing Overhead Control	8,480	
	Various accounts		59,264
	To record actual overhead costs		
(5)	Work in Process Inventory	64,200	
	Variable Manufacturing Overhead Control ($14 × 400 × $9.75)		54,600
	Fixed Manufacturing Overhead Control ($24 × 400 × 1)		9,600
	To apply predetermined overhead to the month's production		
(6)	Variable Manufacturing Overhead Control ($54,600 − $50,784)	3,816	
	Variable Overhead Spending Variance		736
	Variable Overhead Efficiency Variance		3,080
	To close variable OH and recognize the variable OH variances		
(7)	Fixed Manufacturing Overhead Control	1,120	
	Volume Variance [($24 × 400 × 1) − ($120,000 ÷ 12)]	400	
	Fixed Overhead Spending Variance [$8,480 − ($120,000 ÷ 12)]		1,520
	To close fixed OH and recognize the fixed OH variances		

the relative size of the account balances. Disposition of significant variances is similar to the disposition of large amounts of underapplied or overapplied overhead as shown in Chapter 3.

To illustrate the disposition of significant variances, assume that Nailz Company has a $20,000 unfavorable (debit) year-end Material Purchase Price Variance. The company considers this amount significant. Nailz makes one type of product, which requires a single raw material input. Other relevant year-end account balances for Nailz Company are as follows:

Raw Material Inventory	$ 49,126
Work in Process Inventory	28,072
Finished Goods Inventory	70,180
Cost of Goods Sold	554,422
Total of affected accounts	$701,800

The theoretically correct allocation of the material price variance would use actual material cost in each account at year-end. However, as was mentioned in Chapter 3 with regard to overhead, after the conversion process has begun, cost elements within account balances are commingled and tend to lose their identity. Thus, unless a significant misstatement would result, disposition of the variance can be based on the proportions of each account balance to the total, as follows:

Raw Material Inventory	7%	($49,126 ÷ $701,800)
Work in Process Inventory	4	($28,072 ÷ $701,800)
Finished Goods Inventory	10	($70,180 ÷ $701,800)
Cost of Goods Sold	79	($554,422 ÷ $701,800)
Total	100%	

Applying these percentages to the $20,000 material price variance gives the amounts in the following journal entry to assign to the affected accounts:

Raw Material Inventory ($20,000 × 0.07)	1,400	
Work in Process Inventory ($20,000 × 0.04)	800	
Finished Goods Inventory ($20,000 × 0.10)	2,000	
Cost of Goods Sold ($20,000 × 0.79)	15,800	
Material Purchase Price Variance		20,000
To dispose of the material purchase price variance at year-end		

All variances other than the material price variance occur as part of the conversion process. Because conversion includes raw material put into production (rather than raw material purchased), all remaining variances are prorated only to Work in Process Inventory, Finished Goods Inventory, and Cost of Goods Sold. The preceding discussion about standard setting, variance computations, and year-end adjustments indicates that a substantial commitment of time and effort is required to implement and use a standard cost system. Companies are willing to make such a commitment for a variety of reasons.

LO.4
Why are standard cost systems used?

Why Standard Cost Systems Are Used

Standard cost systems are designed to provide information for management to use in performing its functions. The first reason for the use of a standard cost system is that it allows management to plan for costs to be incurred in performing production or service activities. Second, the system collects information on the actual costs incurred. Third, the system allows management to control operations by comparing expected costs with actual costs and to evaluate performance based on the size and explanations for the period's variances. These basic functions result in the following six distinct benefits of standard cost systems.

Clerical Efficiency

Less clerical time and effort are required in a standard cost system than in an actual cost system. A standard cost system assigns costs to inventory and Cost of Goods Sold accounts at predetermined amounts per unit regardless of actual conditions. With an actual cost system, actual unit costs change continuously with changes in prices and usage of inputs. A standard cost system holds unit costs constant for some period.

Motivating

Standards help communicate management's expectations to workers. When standards are achievable and rewards for attaining them are available, workers are likely to be motivated to strive to meet them. The attainment of standards, however, must require a reasonable amount of effort on the workers' part.

Planning

Financial and operational planning requires estimates about future prices and usage of inputs. Managers can use current standards to estimate future quantity needs and costs. These estimates help determine purchasing needs for material, staffing needs for labor, and capacity needs related to overhead and planning for company cash flows. In addition, use of a standard simplifies budget preparation because a standard is, in fact, a budget for one unit of product or service. Standards are also used to provide the cost basis needed to analyze relationships among the organization's costs, sales volume, and profits.

Controlling

The control process begins with the establishment of standards as a basis against which actual costs can be measured and variances calculated. Variance analysis is the process of categorizing the nature (favorable or unfavorable) of the differences between actual and standard costs and seeking explanations for those differences. A well-designed variance analysis system computes variances as early as possible subject to cost–benefit assessments. The system should help managers determine who or what is responsible for each variance and who is best able to explain it. An early measurement and reporting system allows managers to monitor operations, take corrective action if necessary, evaluate performance, and motivate workers to achieve performance standards.

In analyzing variances, managers must recognize that they have a specific scarce resource: their time. They must distinguish between situations that can be ignored and those that need attention. To do this, managers establish upper and lower tolerance limits of acceptable deviations from the standard. If variances are small and within an acceptable range, no managerial action is required. If a variance is significantly different from standard, the manager responsible for the cost is expected to identify the variance cause(s) and then take actions to eliminate future unfavorable variances, or, perhaps, perpetuate favorable variances.

Setting upper and lower tolerance limits for deviations (as illustrated in Exhibit 7–9) allows managers to implement the management-by-exception concept. In the exhibit, the only significant deviation from standard occurred on Day 5, when the actual cost exceeded the upper limit of acceptable performance. An exception report should be generated on this date so that the manager can investigate the underlying variance causes.

Variances large enough to fall outside the acceptability ranges often indicate problems. However, a variance does not reveal the problem's cause nor the person or group responsible for it. To determine variance causality, managers must investigate significant variances through observation, inspection, and inquiry. The investigation involves people at the operating level as well as accounting personnel. Operations personnel should spot variances as they occur and record the reasons for the variances to the extent that those reasons are discernable. For example, operating personnel could readily detect and report causes such as machine downtime or material spoilage.

EXHIBIT 7–9
Illustration of Management by Exception Concept

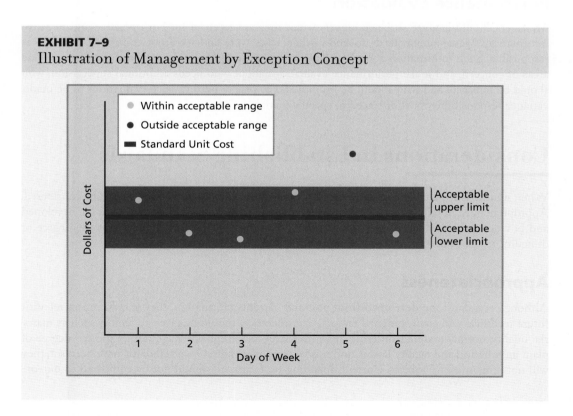

One important point about variances must be made: An extremely favorable variance is not necessarily a good variance. Although people often want to equate the "favorable" designation with "good," an extremely favorable variance could mean that an error was made when the standard was set or that a related, offsetting unfavorable variance exists. For example, if low-grade material is purchased, a favorable price variance may result, but additional material might have to be used to overcome defective production. Also, an unfavorable labor efficiency variance might result because more time was required to complete a job as a result of using the inferior material. Another common situation begins with labor rather than material. Using lower-paid workers will result in a favorable rate variance but can cause excessive use of raw material and labor time because the workers are not as skilled at their production jobs. Managers must be aware that such relationships exist and that variances cannot be analyzed in isolation.

The time frame for which variance computations are made is being shortened. Monthly variance reporting is still common, but there is movement toward shorter reporting periods. As more companies integrate total quality management and just-in-time production into their operations, variance reporting and analysis will become more frequent.[6] Additionally, standards should definitely be updated as an organization implements changes in production technology.

Decision Making

Standard cost information facilitates decision making. For example, managers can compare a standard cost with a quoted price to determine whether an item should be manufactured in-house or purchased. Using actual cost information in such a decision could be inappropriate because the actual cost could fluctuate each period. Also, in deciding whether to offer a special price to customers, managers can use standard product cost to determine the lowest price limit. Similarly, a company bidding on contracts must have some idea of estimated product costs. Bidding too low and winning the contract could cause substantial operating income (and, possibly, cash flow) problems; bidding too high could be noncompetitive and cause the contract to be awarded to another company.

Performance Evaluation

Managers should analyze variance reports when they are received for both positive and negative information. Management needs to know when costs were and were not controlled and who is responsible. Such information allows management to provide feedback to subordinates, investigate areas of concern, and make performance evaluations about who needs additional supervision, who should be replaced, and who should be promoted. For proper performance evaluations to be made, variance responsibility must be traced to specific managers.[7]

Considerations in Establishing Standards

When standards are established, the issues of appropriateness and attainability should be considered. Appropriateness, in relation to a standard, refers to the basis on which the standards are developed and how long they will be viable. Attainability refers to management's belief about the degree of difficulty or rigor that should be incurred in achieving the standard.

Appropriateness

Although standards are developed from past and current information, they should reflect relevant future technical and environmental factors. Consideration should be given to factors such as material quality, normal material-ordering quantities, expected employee wage rates, expected degree of plant automation and facility layout, and mix of employee skills. Once standards have been set, they will not remain useful forever. Current operating performance should not be compared to out-of-

---

[6]Total quality management is discussed in Chapter 17, and just-in-time production is discussed in Chapter 18.
[7]Cost control relative to variances is discussed in greater depth in Chapter 16. Performance evaluation is discussed in greater depth in Chapter 14.

date standards. Standards must evolve to reflect an organization's changing methods and processes. Out-of-date standards produce variances that do not provide logical bases for planning, controlling, decision making, or performance evaluation.

Attainability

Standards provide a target level of performance and can be set at various levels of rigor. This level affects motivation; one reason for using standards is to motivate employees. Similar to the capacity levels discussed in Chapter 3, standards can be classified as expected, practical, and ideal. Depending on the type of standard in effect, the acceptable ranges used to apply the management-by-exception principle will differ. This difference is especially notable on the unfavorable side.

Expected standards reflect what is actually expected to occur. Such standards anticipate future waste and inefficiencies and allow for them. As such, expected standards are not of significant value for motivation, control, or performance evaluation. A company using expected standards should set a very small range of acceptable variation because actual costs should conform closely to standards. In addition, expected standards tend to generate favorable variances.

Standards that can be reached or slightly exceeded approximately 60 to 70 percent of the time with reasonable effort are called practical standards. These standards allow for normal, unavoidable delays such as those caused by machine downtime and worker breaks. Practical standards represent an attainable challenge and traditionally have been thought to be the most effective in motivating workers and determining their performance levels. Both favorable and unfavorable variances result from the use of such moderately rigorous standards.

Standards that provide for no inefficiency of any type are called ideal standards (or theoretical standards); they encompass the highest level of rigor and do not allow for normal operating delays or human limitations such as fatigue, boredom, or misunderstanding. Unless a plant is entirely automated (and then the possibility of human error or power failure still exists), ideal standards are impossible to attain. Applying such standards traditionally resulted in discouraged and resentful workers who ultimately ignored the standards. Variances from ideal standards will always be unfavorable and were commonly not considered useful for constructive cost control or performance evaluation. Such a perspective has begun to change, however.

Changes in Standards Usage

Many accountants and managers believe that variances are not currently being used correctly for control and performance evaluation purposes. For example, material standards generally include a factor for waste, and labor standards are commonly set at the expected level of attainment even though this level includes downtime and human error. Use of standards that are not aimed at the highest possible (ideal) level of attainment are now being questioned in business environments concerned with world-class operations.

Use of Ideal Standards and Theoretical Capacity

The Japanese influence on Western management philosophy and production techniques has been significant. Both total quality management (TQM) and just-in-time (JIT) production systems evolved as a result of an upsurge in Japanese productivity. These two concepts are inherently based on ideal standards. Rather than including waste and inefficiency in the standards and then accepting additional waste and spoilage deviations under a management-by-exception principle, both TQM and JIT begin with the premises of zero defects, zero inefficiency, and zero downtime. Under TQM and JIT, ideal standards become expected standards and there is no (or only a minimal allowable) level of acceptable deviation from standards.

When a standard is set at a less-than-ideal level, managers are allowing and encouraging inefficient resource utilization. Ideal standards result in the most useful information for managerial purposes as well as the highest quality products and services at the lowest possible cost. If no inefficiencies are built into or tolerated in the system, deviations from standard should be minimized

LO.5
What changes have occurred in the setting and use of standards?

and overall organizational performance improved. Workers may, at first, resent the introduction of standards set at a "perfection" level, but it is in their own and management's best long-run interest to have such standards. Higher standards for efficiency automatically mean lower costs because of the elimination of non-value-added activities such as waste, idle time, and rework.

Implementing ideal standards requires that employees in the organizations communicate and work together to improve performance. The implementation process begins with identifying current problems and causes of those problems. For example, where and why are variances occurring? Second, use the answers to the previous questions to determine what needs to change. For example, if variances are caused by the equipment, facility, or workers, management must be ready to invest in plant and equipment, workplace reorganization, or worker training so that the standards are amenable to the operations. Training is essential if workers are to perform at the high levels of efficiency demanded by ideal standards. If variances are related to external sources (such as poor-quality material), management must be willing to change suppliers and/or pay higher prices for higher grade input. Third, setting standards at the ideal level in part assigns the responsibility for quality to workers; thus, management must also give those workers the authority to react to problems. Fourth, requiring people to work at their maximum potential demands recognition, which means that management must provide rewards for achievement.

In addition to setting standards at an ideal level, world-class companies can also use theoretical capacity to set fixed OH rates. If a company were totally automated or if people consistently worked at their full potential, such a capacity measure would provide the lowest and most appropriate predetermined OH rate. Any underapplied OH resulting from a difference between theoretical and actual capacity would indicate capacity that should be either used or eliminated; the underapplied OH could also indicate human capabilities that have not been fully developed. Also, any end-of-period underapplied OH would be viewed as a period cost and closed to a loss account (such as Loss from Inefficient Operations) on the income statement. Showing the underapplied OH in this manner should attract managerial attention to the inefficient and ineffective use of resources.

Whether setting standards at the ideal level and using theoretical capacity to set predetermined fixed OH rates will become norms of non-Japanese companies cannot be determined at this time. However, standards will slowly move from the expected or practical to closer to the ideal, if only because of competition. A competitor that produces goods based on the highest possible standards and the highest level of capacity is more likely to have lower costs and higher quality—which, in turn, will often result in lower prices.

Adjusting Standards

Standards are generally set after comprehensive investigation of prices and quantities for the various cost elements. Traditionally, these standards were retained for at least one year and, sometimes, for multiple years. Currently, the business environment (which includes suppliers, technology, competition, product design, and manufacturing methods) changes so rapidly that a standard may no longer be useful for management control purposes for an entire year.

Company management must consider whether to modify standards during a year when significant cost or quantity changes occur. Ignoring the changes is a simplistic approach that allows the same type of cost to be recorded at the same amount all year. Thus, for example, any material purchased during the year would be recorded at the same standard cost regardless of when it was purchased. Although making recordkeeping easy, this approach eliminates any opportunity to adequately control costs or evaluate performance. Additionally, such an approach could create large differentials between standard and actual costs, making standard costs unacceptable for external reporting.

Adjusting the standards to reflect price or quantity changes would make some aspects of management control and performance evaluation more effective and others more difficult. For instance, budgets prepared using the original standards would need to be adjusted before appropriate actual comparisons could be made against them. Changing standards also creates a problem for recordkeeping and inventory valuation. Should products be valued at the standard cost that was in effect when they were produced or the standard cost in effect when the financial statements were prepared? Although production-point standards would be more closely related to actual costs, the use of such standards might undermine many of the benefits discussed earlier in the chapter.

If possible, management should consider combining these two choices in the accounting system. The original standards can be considered "frozen" for budget purposes and a revised budget can be prepared using the new current standards. Differences between these two budgets would reflect variances related to business environment cost changes. These variances could be designated as uncontrollable (such as those related to changes in the market price of raw material) or internally initiated (such as changes in standard labor time resulting from employee training or equipment rearrangement). Comparing the budget based on current standards with actual costs would provide variances that more adequately reflect internally controllable causes, such as excess material and/or labor time usage caused by inferior material purchases.

Material Price Variance Based on Purchases Rather Than on Usage

The material price variance computation has traditionally been based on purchases rather than on usage to calculate the variance as quickly as possible relative to the cost incurrence. Although calculating the material price variance at the purchase point allows managers to see the impact of buying decisions more rapidly, such information might not be most relevant in a just-in-time environment. Buying material that is not needed for current production requires that the material be stored and moved, both of which are non-value-added activities. The trade-off in price savings should be measured against the additional costs to determine the cost–benefit relationship of such a purchase.

Additionally, computing a material price variance on purchases rather than on usage can reduce the probability of recognizing a relationship between a favorable material price variance and an unfavorable material quantity variance. If a favorable price variance resulted from buying low-grade material, effects of that purchase will not be known until the material is actually used.

Decline in Direct Labor

As the proportion of product cost related to direct labor declines, the necessity for direct labor variance computations is minimized. The increase in automation often relegates labor to an indirect category because workers become machine overseers rather than product producers. Accordingly, direct labor can be combined with overhead to become viewed as the "conversion cost" of a product.

Conversion Cost as an Element in Standard Costing

LO.6
How will standard costing be affected if a single conversion element is used rather than the traditional labor and overhead elements?

As discussed in Chapter 2, conversion cost consists of direct labor and manufacturing overhead. The traditional view of separating product cost into three categories (direct material, direct labor, and overhead) is appropriate in a labor-intensive production setting. However, in more highly automated factories, direct labor cost generally represents only a small part of total product cost. In such circumstances, one worker might oversee a large number of machines and deal more with troubleshooting machine malfunctions than with converting raw material into finished products. These new conditions mean that workers are probably considered indirect rather than direct labor and, therefore, their wages should be considered overhead.

Many highly automated companies have adapted their standard cost systems to provide for only two elements of product cost: direct material and conversion. In these situations, conversion cost is likely to be separated into variable and fixed components. Conversion cost can also be separated into direct and indirect categories based on the ability to trace such costs to a machine rather than to a product. Overhead can be applied under an activity-based costing methodology (see Chapter 4) using a variety of cost drivers such as number of machine hours, material cost, number of production runs, number of machine setups, or throughput time.

Variance analysis for conversion cost in automated plants normally focuses on the following: (1) spending variances for overhead costs, (2) efficiency variances for machinery and production costs rather than labor costs, and (3) a volume variance for production. These types of analyses are

Advanced automation in factories translates into lower direct labor cost as a percentage of total product cost.

similar to the traditional three-variance overhead approach. In an automated system, managers are better able to control not only the spending and efficiency variances but also the volume variance. The idea of planned output is essential in a JIT system. Variance analysis under a conversion cost approach is illustrated in Exhibit 7–10. Regardless of how variances are computed, managers must analyze those variances and use them for cost control purposes to the extent that such control can be exercised.

Assume that Harris Corporation makes a bike frame in a new facility that is fully automated; all labor required for this product is considered indirect. For simplicity, it is assumed that all overhead is applied on the basis of budgeted machine hours. Necessary 2008 production and cost information for bike frames follows:

Expected production	12,000 units
Actual production	13,000 units
Actual machine time	25,000 MHs
Standard machine time allowed per unit	2 MHs
Budgeted variable conversion cost	$ 96,000
Budgeted fixed conversion cost	$192,000
Actual variable conversion cost	$ 97,500
Actual fixed conversion cost	$201,000

Variable conversion rate: $96,000 ÷ 24,000 = $4 per MH
Fixed conversion rate: $192,000 ÷ 24,000 = $8 per MH
Standard machine hours allowed: 13,000 units × 2 hours per unit = 26,000 MHs

The variance computations for conversion costs follow.

Actual Conversion Cost ($97,500 + $201,000) $298,500	Flexible Budget at Actual Hours [($4 × 25,000) + $192,000] $292,000	Flexible Budget at Standard Hours [($4 × 26,000) + $192,000] $296,000	Standard Cost ($12 × 26,000) $312,000
	$6,500 U	$4,000 F	$16,000 F
	Spending Variance	Efficiency Variance	Volume Variance

$13,500 F

Total Conversion Cost Variance

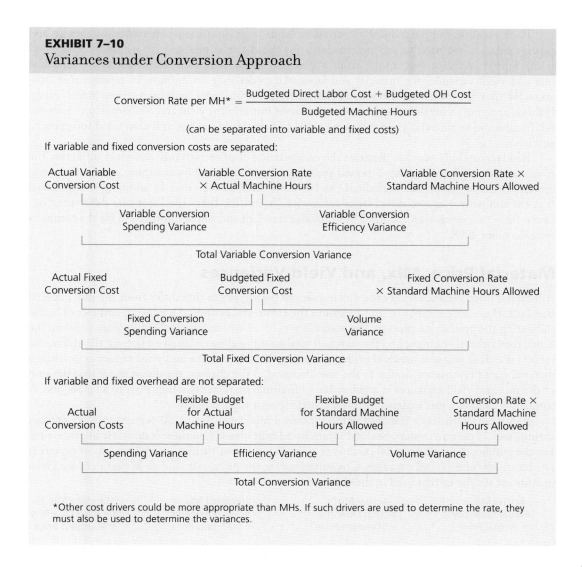

EXHIBIT 7–10
Variances under Conversion Approach

$$\text{Conversion Rate per MH* } = \frac{\text{Budgeted Direct Labor Cost} + \text{Budgeted OH Cost}}{\text{Budgeted Machine Hours}}$$

(can be separated into variable and fixed costs)

If variable and fixed conversion costs are separated:

Actual Variable Conversion Cost	Variable Conversion Rate × Actual Machine Hours	Variable Conversion Rate × Standard Machine Hours Allowed

Variable Conversion Spending Variance | Variable Conversion Efficiency Variance

Total Variable Conversion Variance

Actual Fixed Conversion Cost	Budgeted Fixed Conversion Cost	Fixed Conversion Rate × Standard Machine Hours Allowed

Fixed Conversion Spending Variance | Volume Variance

Total Fixed Conversion Variance

If variable and fixed overhead are not separated:

Actual Conversion Costs	Flexible Budget for Actual Machine Hours	Flexible Budget for Standard Machine Hours Allowed	Conversion Rate × Standard Machine Hours Allowed

Spending Variance | Efficiency Variance | Volume Variance

Total Conversion Variance

*Other cost drivers could be more appropriate than MHs. If such drivers are used to determine the rate, they must also be used to determine the variances.

Appendix

Mix and Yield Variances

Most companies combine many materials and various classes of direct labor to produce goods. In such settings, the material and labor variance computations presented in this chapter are insufficient.

When a product is made from more than one material, a goal is to combine the materials in a way that produces the desired quality in the most cost beneficial manner. Sometimes materials can be substituted for one another without affecting product quality. In other instances, only one specific material or type of material can be used. For example, a furniture manufacturer might use either oak or maple to build a couch frame and still have the same basic quality. However, a perfume manufacturer might have to use a very specific fragrance oil to achieve a desired scent.

Labor, like materials, can be combined in many different ways to make the same product. Some combinations are less expensive or more efficient than others. As with materials, some amount of interchangeability among labor categories is assumed. However, all potential combinations could not be viable; for example, unskilled workers could not be substituted for skilled craftspeople to cut Baccarat or Waterford crystal. The goal is to find the most effective and efficient selection of workers to perform specific tasks.

LO.7
How do multiple material and labor categories affect variances?

Each possible combination of materials or labor is called a mix. Experience, judgment, and experimentation are used to set the standards for the material mix and labor mix. Process yield is the output quantity that results from a specified input. Mix standards are used to calculate mix and yield variances for material and labor. An underlying assumption in product mix situations is that the potential for substitution among the material and labor components exists. If this assumption is invalid, changing the mix cannot improve the yield and could even prove wasteful. In addition to mix and yield variances, price and rate variances are still computed for material and labor.

Randazzo's Deli is used to illustrate the computation of price/rate, mix, and yield variances. The company recently began selling 1-pound packages of seafood gumbo containing crab, shrimp, and oysters. To some extent, one ingredient can be substituted for the other. In addition, it is assumed that the company uses two direct labor categories (A and B). There is a labor rate differential between these two categories. Exhibit 7–11 provides standard and actual information for the company for December 2008.

Material Price, Mix, and Yield Variances

A material price variance shows the dollar effect of paying prices that differ from the raw material standard. The material mix variance measures the effect of substituting a nonstandard mix of material during the production process. The material yield variance measures the difference between the actual total quantity of input and the standard total quantity allowed based on output; this difference reflects standard mix and standard prices. Summing the material mix and yield variances provides a material quantity variance similar to the one discussed in the chapter; the difference is that the sum of the mix and yield variances is attributable to multiple ingredients rather than to a single one. A company can have a mix variance without experiencing a yield variance.

Randazzo's Deli has a standard gumbo material mix consisting of 30 percent crab, 45 percent shrimp, and 25 percent oysters. Seafood is purchased fully cleaned, so there is no waste in processing. For the gumbo, the yield from 60 pounds of crab, 90 pounds of shrimp, and 50 pounds of oysters is one lot of 200 one-pound packages. Computations for the price, mix, and yield variances are given in a format similar to that used in the chapter:

Actual Mix × Actual Quantity × Actual Price	Actual Mix × Actual Quantity × Standard Price	Standard Mix × Actual Quantity × Standard Price	Standard Mix × Standard Quantity × Standard Price
	Material Price Variance	Material Mix Variance	Material Yield Variance

Given the information in Exhibit 7–11, Randazzo's Deli used 8,020 total pounds of ingredients to make 40 lots of frozen gumbo. The standard quantity necessary to produce this quantity is 8,000 total pounds of ingredients. The actual mix of crab, shrimp, and oysters was 28.5, 45.5, and 26.0 percent, respectively:

Crab	(2,285.7 pounds of 8,020) = 28.5%
Shrimp	(3,649.1 pounds of 8,020) = 45.5%
Oysters	(2,085.2 pounds of 8,020) = 26.0%

Computations necessary for the material variances are shown in Exhibit 7–12.

Actual M, Q, & P* $43,520.53	Actual M & Q; Standard P $43,303.99	Standard M; Actual Q; Standard P $43,588.70	Standard M, Q, & P $43,480.00
	$216.54 U	$284.71 F	$108.70 U
	Material Price Variance	Material Mix Variance	Material Yield Variance

$40.53 U

Total Material Variance

*Note: M = mix, Q = quantity, and P = price.

EXHIBIT 7–11

Standard and Actual Information for December 2008

Material standards for one lot (200 1-pound packages):

Crab	60 pounds at $7.20 per pound	$ 432
Shrimp	90 pounds at $4.50 per pound	405
Oysters	50 pounds at $5.00 per pound	250
Total	200 pounds	$ 1,087

Labor standards for one lot (200 1-pound packages):

Category A workers	20 hours at $10.50 per hour	$210
Category B workers	10 hours at $14.30 per hour	143
Total	30 hours	$353

Actual production and cost data for December:

Production   40 lots

Material:

Crab	Purchased and used	2,285.7 pounds at $7.50 per pound
Shrimp	Purchased and used	3,649.1 pounds at $4.40 per pound
Oysters	Purchased and used	2,085.2 pounds at $4.95 per pound
Total		8,020.0 pounds

Labor:

Category A workers	903 hours at $10.50 per hour =	$ 9,481.50
Category B workers	387 hours at $14.35 per hour =	5,553.45
Total	1,290 hours	$15,034.95

EXHIBIT 7–12

Computations for Material Mix and Yield Variances

(1) Total actual data (mix, quantity, and prices):

Crab—2,285.7 pounds at $7.50	$17,142.75	
Shrimp—3,649.1 pounds at $4.40	16,056.04	
Oysters—2,085.2 pounds at $4.95	10,321.74	$43,520.53

(2) Actual mix and quantity; standard prices:

Crab—2,285.7 pounds at $7.20	$16,457.04	
Shrimp—3,649.1 pounds at $4.50	16,420.95	
Oysters—2,085.2 pounds at $5.00	10,426.00	$43,303.99

(3) Standard mix; actual quantity; standard prices:

Crab—30% × 8,020 pounds × $7.20	$17,323.20	
Shrimp—45% × 8,020 pounds × $4.50	16,240.50	
Oysters—25% × 8,020 pounds × $5.00	10,025.00	$43,588.70

(4) Total standard data (mix, quantity, and prices):

Crab—30% × 8,000 pounds × $7.20	$17,280.00	
Shrimp—45% × 8,000 pounds × $4.50	16,200.00	
Oysters—25% × 8,000 pounds × $5.00	10,000.00	$43,480.00

These computations show a single price variance being calculated for all of the materials. To be more useful to management, separate price variances should be calculated for each material used. For example, the material price variance for crab is $685.71 U ($17,142.75 − $16,457.04), for shrimp is $364.91 F ($16,056.04 − $16,420.95), and for oysters is $104.26 F ($10,321.74 − $10,426.00). The savings on shrimp and oysters did not offset the higher price for crab, so the total price variance was unfavorable. Also, less than the standard proportion of the most expensive ingredient (crab) was used, so it is reasonable that there would be a favorable mix variance. Randazzo's Deli also experienced an unfavorable yield because total pounds of material allowed for output (8,000) was less than actual total pounds of material used (8,020).

Labor Rate, Mix, and Yield Variances

The two labor categories used by Randazzo's Deli are helpers (A) and cooks (B). When labor standards are prepared, the labor categories needed to perform various tasks and the amount of time each task is expected to take are established. During production, variances will occur if workers are not paid the standard rate, do not work in the standard mix on tasks, or do not perform those tasks in the standard time.

The labor rate variance is a measure of the cost of paying workers at other than standard rates. The labor mix variance is the financial effect associated with changing the proportionate amount of higher or lower paid workers in production. The labor yield variance reflects the monetary impact of using a higher or lower number of hours than the standard allowed. The sum of the labor mix and yield variances equals the labor efficiency variance. The diagram for computing labor rate, mix, and yield variances is as follows:

Standard rates are used to make both the mix and yield computations. To make the gumbo, the standard mix of A and B labor shown in Exhibit 7–11 is two-thirds and one-third (20 and 10 hours), respectively. The actual mix is 70 percent (903 of 1,290 total hours) A and 30 percent (387 of 1,290) B. See Exhibit 7–13 for the labor computations for the gumbo production. Because 30 hours is the standard for producing one lot of gumbo, the standard number of hours allowed for production of 40 lots is 1,200 (800 hours of A and 400 hours of B).

Using the amounts from Exhibit 7–13, the labor variances for Randazzo's Deli's gumbo production in December are calculated as follows:

*Note: M = mix, H = hours, and R = rate.

As with material price variances, separate rate variances should be calculated for each class of labor. Because category A does not have a labor rate variance, the total rate variance for December relates solely to category B.

Randazzo's Deli saved $163.40 by using the actual mix of labor rather than the standard. A higher proportion of the less expensive, unskilled class of labor (category A) than specified in the standard mix was used. One result of substituting a higher proportion of lower-paid workers seems to be that an unfavorable yield occurred because total actual hours (1,290) were higher than standard (1,200).

Because there are trade-offs in mix and yield when component qualities and quantities are changed, management should observe the integrated nature of price, mix, and yield. The effects of changes of one element on the other two need to be considered for managing cost efficiency and output quality. If mix and yield can be increased by substituting less expensive resources while maintaining quality, managers and product engineers should change the standards and the proportions of components. If costs are reduced but quality is maintained, selling prices could be reduced to gain a larger market share.

EXHIBIT 7–13
Computations for Labor Mix and Yield Variances

(1) Total actual data (mix, hours, and rates):
    Category A—903 hours at $10.50 $9,481.50
    Category B—387 hours at $14.35   5,553.45 $15,034.95

(2) Actual mix and hours; standard rates:
    Category A—903 hours at $10.50 $9,481.50
    Category B—387 hours at $14.30   5,534.10 $15,015.60

(3) Standard mix; actual hours; standard rates:
    Category A—2/3 × 1,290 × $10.50 $9,030.00
    Category B—1/3 × 1,290 × $14.30   6,149.00 $15,179.00

(4) Total standard data (mix, hours, and rates):
    Category A—2/3 × 1,200 × $10.50 $8,400.00
    Category B—1/3 × 1,200 × $14.30   5,720.00 $14,120.00

Comprehensive Review Module

Chapter Summary

1. Setting standards for
   - material requires that management identify the
     ➢ types of material inputs needed to make the product or perform the service.
     ➢ quality of material inputs needed to make the product or perform the service.
     ➢ quantity of material inputs needed to make the product or perform the service.
     ➢ prices of the material inputs, given normal purchase quantities.
   - labor requires that management identify the
     ➢ types of labor tasks needed to make the product or perform the service.
     ➢ amount of labor time needed to make the product or perform the service.
     ➢ skill levels of personnel needed to make the product or perform the service.

   ➢ wage rates or salary levels for the classes of labor skills needed.
   - overhead requires that management identify the
     ➢ variable and fixed overhead costs incurred in the organization.
     ➢ estimated level of activity to be used in computing the predetermined overhead rate(s).
     ➢ estimated variable and fixed overhead costs at the estimated level of activity.
     ➢ predetermined overhead rate(s) used to apply overhead to production or service performance.

2. The documents used in a standard cost system include the
   - bill of materials, which contains all quantity and quality raw material specifications to make one unit (or batch) of output.
   - operations flow document, which contains all labor operations necessary to make one unit

(or batch) of output or perform a particular service.

- standard cost card, which summarizes the standard quantities and costs needed to complete one unit of product or perform a particular service.

3. A variance is the difference between an actual and a standard cost. Standard costs are recorded in the Work in Process Inventory account, and variances are recorded as either debit (unfavorable) or credit (favorable) differences between the standard cost and the actual cost incurred. In general, variances are calculated as follows for

- direct material:
  - ➤ Material Price Variance = (Actual Price × Actual Quantity) − (Standard Price × Actual Quantity)
  - ➤ Material Quantity Variance = (Standard Price × Actual Quantity) − (Standard Price × Standard Quantity)
  - ➤ Total Material Variance = Material Price Variance + Material Quantity Variance

- direct labor
  - ➤ Labor Rate Variance = (Actual Price × Actual Quantity) − (Standard Price × Actual Quantity)
  - ➤ Labor Efficiency Variance = (Standard Price × Actual Quantity) − (Standard Price × Standard Quantity)
  - ➤ Total Labor Variance = Labor Rate Variance + Labor Efficiency Variance

- variable overhead
  - ➤ VOH Spending Variance = Actual VOH − (Standard Price × Actual Quantity)
  - ➤ VOH Efficiency Variance = (Standard Price × Actual Quantity) − Applied VOH

  - ❖ Applied VOH = (Standard Price × Standard Quantity)
  - ➤ Total VOH Variance = VOH Spending Variance + VOH Efficiency Variance

- fixed overhead
  - ➤ FOH Spending Variance = Actual FOH − Budgeted FOH
    - ❖ Budgeted FOH = Constant FOH amount per period
  - ➤ Volume Variance = Budgeted FOH − Applied FOH
    - ❖ Applied FOH = (Standard Price × Standard Quantity)
  - ➤ Total FOH Variance = FOH Spending Variance + Volume Variance

4. A standard cost system is used to

- provide clerical efficiency.
- assist management in its planning, controlling, decision making, and performance evaluation functions.
- motivate employees when the standards are
  - ➤ set at a level to encourage high-quality production and promote cost control.
  - ➤ seen as expected performance goals.
  - ➤ updated periodically so that they reflect actual economic conditions.

5. In highly automated companies, the standard cost system can use

- only two elements of production cost: direct material and conversion.
- ideal standards rather than expected or practical standards.
- predetermined fixed overhead rates based on theoretical capacity rather than expected, normal, or practical capacity.

Potential Ethical Issues

1. Setting labor time standards extremely high so that variances on which performance is evaluated are consistently favorable

2. Evaluating each manager on the variances generated in his or her production area without regard for potential implications on other production areas

3. Estimating production at levels significantly higher than is necessary to meet current and anticipated sales, thereby lowering the predetermined fixed OH rate per unit and inventory cost, while increasing reported operating income

4. Producing unnecessary inventory to generate a high, favorable volume variance

5. Not adjusting standards for changed production conditions so that favorable variances will result

6. Using inappropriate material or labor mixes that create favorable price or rate variances but result in a lower quality product ▲

Solution Strategies

Actual Costs (AC)

1. Direct material:

$$\text{Actual Price (AP)} \times \text{Actual Quantity Purchased or Used (AQ)}$$
$$\text{DM: AP} \times \text{AQ} = \text{AC}$$

2. Direct labor:

$$\text{Actual Price (Rate)} \times \text{Actual Quantity of Hours Worked}$$
$$\text{DL: AP} \times \text{AQ} = \text{AC}$$

Standard Costs (SC)

1. Direct material:

$$\text{Standard Price} \times \text{Standard Quantity}$$
$$\text{DM: SP} \times \text{SQ} = \text{SC}$$

2. Direct labor:

$$\text{Standard Price (Rate)} \times \text{Standard Quantity of Hours}$$
$$\text{DL: SP} \times \text{SQ} = \text{SC}$$

General Variance Format

AP × AQ	SP × AQ	SP × SQ
Material Price Variance	Material Quantity Variance	
Labor Rate Variance	Labor Efficiency Variance	
VOH Spending Variance	VOH Efficiency Variance	

Variances in Formula Format

The following abbreviations are used:

AFOH = actual fixed overhead
AM = actual mix
AP = actual price or rate
AQ = actual quantity or hours
AVOH = actual variable overhead
BFOH = budgeted fixed overhead (remains at constant amount regardless of activity level as long as within the relevant range)
SM = standard mix
SP = standard price
SQ = standard quantity
TAOH = total actual overhead

$$\text{Material price variance} = (AP \times AQ) - (SP \times AQ)$$
$$\text{Material quantity variance} = (SP \times AQ) - (SP \times SQ)$$
$$\text{Labor rate variance} = (AP \times AQ) - (SP \times AQ)$$
$$\text{Labor efficiency variance} = (SP \times AQ) - (SP \times SQ)$$

Four-Variance Approach:

Variable OH spending variance = AVOH − (VOH rate × AQ)
Variable OH efficiency variance = (VOH rate × AQ) − (VOH rate × SQ)
Fixed OH spending variance = AFOH − BFOH
Volume variance = BFOH − (FOH rate × SQ)

Three-Variance Approach:

Spending variance = TAOH − [(VOH rate × AQ) + BFOH]
Efficiency variance = [(VOH rate × AQ) + BFOH] − [(VOH rate × SQ) + BFOH]
Volume variance = [(VOH rate × SQ) + BFOH] − [(VOH rate × SQ) + (FOH rate × SQ)] (This is equal to the volume variance of the four-variance approach.)

Two-Variance Approach:

Budget variance = TAOH − [(VOH rate × SQ) + BFOH]
Volume variance = [(VOH rate × SQ) + BFOH] − [(VOH rate × SQ) + (FOH rate × SQ)] (This is equal to the volume variance of the four-variance approach.)

One-Variance Approach:

Total OH variance = TAOH − (Combined OH rate × SQ)

Mix and Yield Variances

Multiple Materials

Material price variance = (AM × AQ × AP) − (AM × AQ × SP)
Material mix variance = (AM × AQ × SP) − (SM × AQ × SP)
Material yield variance = (SM × AQ × SP) − (SM × SQ × SP)

Multiple Labor Categories

Labor rate variance = (AM × AQ × AP) − (AM × AQ × SP)
Labor mix variance = (AM × AQ × SP) − (SM × AQ × SP)
Labor yield variance = (SM × AQ × SP) − (SM × SQ × SP)

Variances in Diagram Format

Direct Material

Point of Purchase

Actual Price ×   Standard Price ×
Actual Quantity Purchased   Actual Quantity Purchased

Material Price Variance

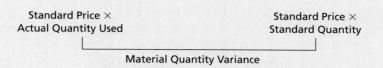

Standard Price × Actual Quantity Used	Standard Price × Standard Quantity

Material Quantity Variance

Point of Usage

Actual Price × Actual Quantity Used	Standard Price × Actual Quantity Used	Standard Price × Standard Quantity

Material Price Variance   Material Quantity Variance

Total Material Variance

Direct Labor

Actual Price × Actual Quantity of Hours Worked	Standard Price × Actual Quantity of Hours Worked	Standard Price × Standard Quantity of Hours

Labor Rate Variance   Labor Efficiency Variance

Total Labor Variance

Overhead Four-Variance Approach:

Variable Overhead

Actual VOH	VOH Rate × Actual Quantity	Applied VOH VOH Rate × Standard Quantity
	(a)	(b)

VOH Spending Variance   VOH Efficiency Variance

Total Variable OH Variance

Fixed Overhead

Actual FOH	Budgeted FOH	Applied FOH FOH Rate × Standard Quantity
	(c)	(d)

FOH Spending Variance   Volume Variance

Total Fixed OH Variance

Overhead One-, Two-, and Three-Variance Approaches:

Actual Actual VOH + Actual FOH	**Budget Based on Input Hours** VOH Rate × AQ + Budgeted FOH	**Budget Based on Output Hours** VOH Rate × SQ + Budgeted FOH	**Applied** VOH Rate × SQ + FOH Rate × SQ
(a) + (c)	(b)	(d)	

Spending Variance   Efficiency Variance   Volume Variance

(a) + (b) + (c)   (d)

Budget Variance   Volume Variance

(a) + (b) + (c) + (d)

Total Overhead Variance
(Total Under/Overapplied Overhead)

Mix and Yield Variances

Multiple Materials

Actual Mix ×	Actual Mix ×	Standard Mix ×	Standard Mix ×
Actual Quantity	Actual Quantity	Actual Quantity	Standard Quantity
× Actual Price	× Standard Price	× Standard Price	× Standard Price

Material Price Variance   Material Mix Variance   Material Yield Variance

Multiple Labor Categories

Actual Mix ×	Actual Mix ×	Standard Mix ×	Standard Mix ×
Actual Hours ×	Actual Hours ×	Actual Hours ×	Standard Hours ×
Actual Rate	Standard Rate	Standard Rate	Standard Rate

Labor Rate Variance   Labor Mix Variance   Labor Yield Variance

Demonstration Problem

Hopkins Containers makes 300-gallon plastic water tanks for a variety of commercial uses. The standard per unit material, labor, and overhead costs are as follows:

Direct material: 80 pounds × $2	$160
Direct labor: 1.25 hours × $16 per hour	20
Variable overhead: 30 minutes of machine time × $50 per hour	25
Fixed overhead: 30 minutes of machine time × $40 per hour	20

The predetermined OH rates were developed using a practical capacity of 6,000 units per year. Production is assumed to occur evenly throughout the year.

During May 2008, the company produced 525 tanks. Actual data for May 2008 are as follows:

Direct material purchased: 46,000 pounds × $1.92 per pound
Direct material used: 43,050 pounds (all from May's purchases)
Total labor cost: $10,988.25 for 682.5 hours
Variable overhead incurred: $13,770 for 270 hours of machine time
Fixed overhead incurred: $10,600 for 270 hours of machine time

Required:

a. Calculate the following:

1. Material price variance based on purchases
2. Material quantity variance
3. Labor rate variance
4. Labor efficiency variance
5. Variable overhead spending and efficiency variances
6. Fixed overhead spending and volume variances
7. Overhead variances using a three-variance approach
8. Overhead variances using a two-variance approach
9. Overhead variance using a one-variance approach

b. Record the entries to recognize the variances

Solution to Demonstration Problem

a. 1.

$$AP \times AQ_p \qquad\qquad SP \times AQ_p$$
$$\$1.92 \times 46,000 \qquad \$2.00 \times 46,000$$
$$\$88,320 \qquad\qquad \$92,000$$
$$\$3,680\ F$$
$$MPV$$

2. SQ = 525 × 80 pounds = 42,000 pounds

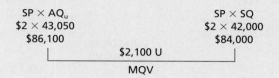

$$SP \times AQ_u \qquad\qquad SP \times SQ$$
$$\$2 \times 43,050 \qquad\qquad \$2 \times 42,000$$
$$\$86,100 \qquad\qquad \$84,000$$
$$\$2,100\ U$$
$$MQV$$

3. & 4. AR = \$10,988.25 ÷ 682.5 hours = \$16.10 per hour
SQ = 525 × 1.25 hours = 656.25 hours

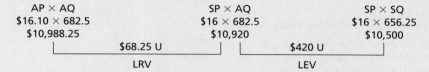

$$AP \times AQ \qquad\qquad SP \times AQ \qquad\qquad SP \times SQ$$
$$\$16.10 \times 682.5 \qquad \$16 \times 682.5 \qquad \$16 \times 656.25$$
$$\$10,988.25 \qquad\qquad \$10,920 \qquad\qquad \$10,500$$
$$\$68.25\ U \qquad\qquad \$420\ U$$
$$LRV \qquad\qquad LEV$$

5. SQ = 525 × 0.5 = 262.5 hours

$$\qquad\qquad SP \times AQ \qquad\qquad SP \times SQ$$
$$Actual\ VOH \qquad \$50.00 \times 270 \qquad \$50.00 \times 262.5$$
$$\$13,770 \qquad\qquad \$13,500 \qquad\qquad \$13,125$$
$$\$270\ U \qquad\qquad \$375\ U$$
$$VOH\ Spending\ Variance \qquad VOH\ Efficiency\ Variance$$

6. BFOH, annually = 6,000 × \$20 = \$120,000
BFOH, monthly = \$120,000 ÷ 12 months = \$10,000

SQ = 262.5 hours [from part (5)].

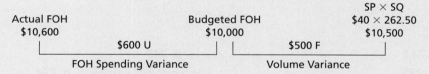

$$\qquad\qquad\qquad\qquad\qquad\qquad SP \times SQ$$
$$\qquad\qquad\qquad\qquad\qquad\qquad \$40 \times 262.50$$
$$Actual\ FOH \qquad\qquad Budgeted\ FOH \qquad \$10,500$$
$$\$10,600 \qquad\qquad \$10,000$$
$$\$600\ U \qquad\qquad \$500\ F$$
$$FOH\ Spending\ Variance \qquad Volume\ Variance$$

7.–9. Combined overhead application rate = \$50 + \$40 = \$90 per MH;
SQ = 262.5 hours [from part (5)].

Actual VOH + Actual FOH	VOH Rate × AQ + Budgeted FOH	VOH Rate × SQ + Budgeted FOH	Applied OH (SP × SQ)
\$13,770	\$50 × 270 = \$13,500	\$50 × 262.5 = \$13,125	\$50 × 262.5 = \$13,125
+ 10,600	+ 10,000	+ 10,000	+ 40 × 262.5 = 10,500
\$24,370	\$23,500	\$23,125	\$90 × 262.5 = \$23,625

$$\$870\ U \qquad\qquad \$375\ U \qquad\qquad \$500\ F$$
$$Spending\ Variance \qquad Efficiency\ Variance \qquad Volume\ Variance$$

$$\qquad\qquad VOH\ Rate \times SQ$$
$$\qquad\qquad + Budgeted\ FOH$$
$$\qquad\qquad \$50 \times 262.50 = \$13,125$$
$$Actual\ OH \qquad\qquad + 10,000 \qquad\qquad Applied\ OH$$
$$\$24,370 \qquad\qquad \$23,125 \qquad\qquad (SP \times SQ)$$
$$\qquad\qquad\qquad\qquad\qquad \$90 \times 262.50 = \$23,625$$
$$\$1,245\ U \qquad\qquad \$500\ F$$
$$Budget\ Variance \qquad\qquad Volume\ Variance$$

Actual OH		Applied OH
$24,370		SP × SQ
		$90 × 262.50 = $23,625

$745 U

Total Overhead Variance
(Total Under/Overapplied Overhead)

b.   **All amounts are taken from the computations shown in part (a).**

Raw Material Inventory	92,000.00	
Material Purchase Price Variance		3,680.00
Accounts Payable		88,320.00
To record acquisition of material		
Work in Process Inventory	84,000.00	
Material Quantity Variance	2,100.00	
Raw Material Inventory		86,100.00
To record issuance of material to production		
Work in Process Inventory	10,500.00	
Labor Rate Variance	68.25	
Labor Efficiency Variance	420.00	
Wages Payable		10,988.25
To record direct labor costs in all departments		
Variable Overhead Efficiency Variance	375.00	
Variable Overhead Spending Variance	270.00	
Variable Manufacturing Overhead Control		645.00
To close variable OH		
Fixed Overhead Spending Variance	600.00	
Fixed Manufacturing Overhead Control		100.00
Volume Variance		500.00
To close fixed OH		

Key Terms

bill of materials, **p. 223**

budget variance, **p. 235**

controllable variance, **p. 235**

expected standard, **p. 241**

fixed overhead spending variance, **p. 233**

ideal standard, **p. 241**

labor efficiency variance, **p. 231**

labor mix variance, **p. 248**

labor rate variance, **p. 231**

labor yield variance, **p. 248**

management by exception, **p. 239**

material mix variance, **p. 246**

material price variance, **p. 230**

material quantity variance, **p. 230**

material yield variance, **p. 246**

methods-time measurement (MTM), **p. 224**

mix, **p. 246**

noncontrollable variance, **p. 234**

operations flow document, **p. 224**

overhead efficiency variance, **p. 235**

overhead spending variance, **p. 235**

practical standard, **p. 241**

standard, **p. 222**

standard cost card, **p. 226**

standard quantity, **p. 227**

total overhead variance, **p. 234**

total variance, **p. 226**

variable overhead efficiency variance, **p. 232**

variable overhead spending variance, **p. 232**

variance analysis, **p. 239**

volume variance, **p. 233**

yield, **p. 246**

Questions

1. What is a standard cost card? What information does it contain? How does it relate to a bill of materials and an operations flow document?
2. How is the material standard developed? Why are the quantities shown in the bill of materials not always the same quantities shown in the standard cost card?
3. A total variance can be calculated for each cost component of a product. Into what variances can this total be separated and to what does each relate? (Discuss separately for material and labor.)
4. What is meant by the term *standard hours*? Does the term refer to inputs or outputs?
5. Why are the overhead spending and overhead efficiency variances said to be controllable? Is the volume variance controllable? Why or why not?
6. How are actual and standard costs recorded in a standard cost system?
7. How are insignificant variances closed at the end of an accounting period? How are significant variances closed at the end of an accounting period? Why is there a difference in treatment?
8. What are the three primary uses of a standard cost system? In a business that routinely manufactures the same products or performs the same services, why are standards helpful?
9. What is management by exception? How do managers use a standard cost system in their efforts to control costs?
10. Why do managers care about the utilization of capacity? Are they controlling costs when they control utilization?
11. (Appendix) What variances can be computed for direct material and direct labor when some materials or labor inputs are substitutes for others? What information does each of these variances provide?

Exercises

12. **LO.1 (Standard setting; team project)** As a three-person team, choose an activity that is commonly performed every day, such as taking a shower/bath, preparing a meal, or doing homework. Have each team member time him- or herself performing that activity for two days and then develop a standard time for the team. Now have the team members time themselves performing the same activity for the next five days.
    a. Using an assumed hourly wage rate of $12, calculate the labor efficiency variance for your team.
    b. Prepare a list of reasons for the variance.
    c. How could some of the variance have been avoided?

13. **LO.1 & LO.2 (Developing standard cost card and discussion)** Yum-Yum Company produces frozen desserts. Company products have typically had strong regional sales, but other companies have recently begun marketing similar products in the area. Price competition has become increasingly important. Betty Donovan, the company's controller, is in the process of implementing a standard cost system because of its usefulness in cost control and in making better pricing decisions.

    The company's most popular product is raspberry sherbet, which is manufactured in 10-gallon batches. Each batch requires 6 quarts of raspberries. The raspberries are sorted by hand before entering the production process. Because of imperfections in the raspberries, 1 quart of berries is discarded for every 4 quarts of acceptable berries. The standard direct labor sorting time to obtain 1 quart of acceptable raspberries is 3 minutes. The acceptable raspberries are then blended with other ingredients; blending requires 12 minutes of direct labor time per batch. During blending, some material is lost. After blending, the sherbet is packaged in quart containers. Donovan has gathered the following cost information:

    - Raspberries are purchased for $0.80 per quart.
    - All other ingredients cost a total of $0.45 per gallon.
    - Direct labor is paid $9.00 per hour.
    - The total cost of material and labor required to package the sherbet is $0.38 per quart.
    a. Develop the standard cost for the direct cost components of a 10-gallon batch of raspberry sherbet. The standard cost should identify standard quantity, standard price/rate, and standard cost per batch for each direct cost component.
    b. As part of implementing the company's standard cost system, Donovan plans to train those responsible for maintaining the standards on how to use variance analysis. She is particularly concerned with the causes of unfavorable variances.

1. Discuss the possible causes of unfavorable material price variances, and identify the individual(s) who should be held responsible for these variances.
2. Discuss the possible causes of unfavorable labor efficiency variances, and identify the individual(s) who should be held responsible for these variances.

(CMA adapted)

14. **LO.3 (DM variances)** Humphrey Patio makes wrought iron table and chair sets. During April, the purchasing agent bought 12,800 pounds of scrap iron at $0.97 per pound. During the month, 10,700 pounds of scrap iron were used to produce 300 table and chair sets. Each set requires a standard quantity of 35 pounds at a standard cost of $0.95 per pound.
    a. For April, compute the direct material price variance (based on the quantity purchased) and the direct material quantity variance (based on quantity used).
    b. Identify the titles of individuals in the firm who would be responsible for each of the variances.
    c. Provide some possible explanations for the variances computed in part (a).

15. **LO.3 (DM variances)** In November 2008, DayTime Publishing Company's costs and quantities of paper consumed in manufacturing its 2009 Executive Planner and Calendar were as follow:

Actual unit purchase price	$0.065 per page
Standard unit price	$0.070 per page
Standard quantity for good production	195,800 pages
Actual quantity purchased during November	230,000 pages
Actual quantity used in November	200,000 pages

   a. Calculate the total cost of purchases for November.
   b. Compute the material price variance (based on quantity purchased).
   c. Calculate the material quantity variance.

16. **LO.3 (DL variances)** Hammersteen & Rogers, CPAs, set the following standard for its inventory audit of La Bamba Co.: 350 hours at an average hourly billing rate of $195. The firm actually worked 330 hours during the inventory audit process. The total labor variance for the audit was $2,500 unfavorable.
    a. Compute the total actual payroll. Record the entry to accrue payroll costs.
    b. Compute the labor efficiency variance.
    c. Compute the labor rate variance.
    d. Write a memo to the appropriate personnel regarding feedback about the labor efficiency variance. The memo should also offer a brief explanation that is consistent with the labor rate and efficiency variances.

17. **LO.3 (DL variances)** Mendlow Construction builds standard prefabricated wooden frames for walls. Each frame requires 10 direct labor hours and employees are paid a standard hourly rate of $16. During May, the company produced 630 frames and worked 6,200 direct labor hours. Payroll records indicate that workers earned $102,300.
    a. What were the standard hours for May construction?
    b. Calculate the direct labor variances.
    c. What was the actual hourly wage rate?

18. **LO.3 (DM & DL variances)** In December, Donna Levinson, president of Levinson Inc., received the following information from Danny Sweeten, the new controller, in regard to November production of travel bags:

November production	2,400 bags
Actual cost of material purchased and used	$20,375
Standard material allowed	0.5 square yard per bag
Material quantity variance	$800 U
Actual hours worked	5,000 hours
Standard labor time per bag	2 hours
Labor rate variance	$650 F
Standard labor rate per hour	$17
Standard price per yard of material	$6

Levinson asked Sweeten to provide the following information:
   a. Standard quantity of material allowed for November production
   b. Standard direct labor hours allowed for November production
   c. Material price variance
   d. Labor efficiency variance
   e. Standard prime (direct material and direct labor) cost to produce one travel bag
   f. Actual cost to produce one travel bag in November

EXCEL

g. An explanation for the difference between standard and actual cost; be sure that the explanation is consistent with the pattern of the variances.

19. LO.3 (DM & DL variances) NatureWay produces 100 percent cotton T-shirts, with the following standard direct material and labor quantities and costs:

Direct material	2.0 yards × $3.00
Direct labor	0.7 hour × $2.50

Actual September production and costs for the company to produce 10,000 T-shirts were as follows:

	Quantity	Cost
Direct material		
Purchased	30,000 yards	$89,700
Requisitioned into production	23,000 yards	69,900
Direct labor	9,500 hours	24,000

a. Compute the direct material and direct labor variances.
b. How might the sales and production managers explain the direct material variances?
c. How might the production and human resources managers explain the direct labor variances?
d. Record the year-end adjusting entry to close the material and labor variances.

20. LO.3 (Missing information for DM & DL) For each independent case, fill in the missing figures.

	Case A	Case B	Case C	Case D
Units produced	800	?	240	1,500
Standard hours per unit	3	0.8	?	?
Standard hours	?	600	480	?
Standard rate per hour	$7	?	$9.50	$6
Actual hours worked	2,330	675	?	4,875
Actual labor cost	?	?	$4,560	$26,812.50
Labor rate variance	$466 F	$1,080 F	$228 U	?
Labor efficiency variance	?	$780 U	?	$2,250 U

21. LO.3 (OH variances) Joy Ride Corp. has a fully automated production facility in which almost 97 percent of overhead costs are driven by machine hours. As the company's cost accountant, you have computed the following overhead variances for May:

Variable overhead spending variance	$17,000 F
Variable overhead efficiency variance	20,600 F
Fixed overhead spending variance	14,000 U
Fixed overhead volume variance	10,000 U

The company's president is concerned about the variance amounts and has asked you to show her how the variances were computed and to answer several questions. Budgeted fixed overhead for the month is $500,000; the predetermined variable and fixed overhead rates are, respectively, $10 and $20 per machine hour. Budgeted capacity is 10,000 units.

a. Using the four-variance approach, prepare an overhead analysis in as much detail as possible.
b. What is the standard number of machine hours allowed for each unit of output?
c. How many actual hours were worked in May?
d. What is the total spending variance?
e. What additional information about the manufacturing overhead variances is gained by inserting detailed computations into the variable and fixed manufacturing overhead variance analysis?
f. How would the overhead variances be closed if the three-variance approach were used?

22. LO.3 (OH variances) The manager of Texas Department of Transportation has determined that it typically takes 30 minutes for the department's employees to register a new car. In Travis County, the predetermined fixed overhead rate was computed on an estimated 9,000 direct labor hours per month and is $8 per direct labor hour, whereas the predetermined variable overhead rate is $3 per direct labor hour.

During July, 17,600 cars were registered in Travis County and 8,950 direct labor hours were worked in registering those vehicles. For the month, variable overhead was $25,900 and fixed overhead was $72,600.

a. Compute overhead variances using a four-variance approach.
b. Compute overhead variances using a three-variance approach.
c. Compute overhead variances using a two-variance approach.

23. **LO.3 (Four OH variances; journal entries)** Kemp Manufacturing set 60,000 direct labor hours as the 2008 capacity measure for computing its predetermined variable overhead rate. At that level, budgeted variable overhead costs are $270,000. Kemp will apply budgeted fixed overhead of $118,800 on the basis of 3,300 budgeted machine hours for the year. Both machine hours and fixed overhead costs are expected to be incurred evenly each month.

    During March 2008, Kemp incurred 4,900 direct labor hours and 250 machine hours. Actual variable and fixed overhead were $22,275 and $9,600, respectively. The standard times allowed for March production were 4,980 direct labor hours and 240 machine hours.
    a. Using the four-variance approach, determine the overhead variances for March 2008.
    b. Prepare all journal entries related to overhead for Kemp Manufacturing for March 2008.

24. **LO.3 (Missing data; three OH variances)** Fletcher Corporation's flexible budget formula for total overhead is $720,000 plus $16 per direct labor hour. The combined overhead rate is $40 per direct labor hour. The following data have been recorded for 2008:

Actual total overhead	$1,160,000
Total overhead spending variance	32,000 U
Volume variance	48,000 U

    Use a three-variance approach to determine the following:
    a. Standard hours for actual production
    b. Actual direct labor hours worked

25. **LO.3 (OH variances)** Longhorn Inc.'s total predetermined overhead rate is $40 per hour based on a monthly capacity of 48,000 machine hours. Overhead is 30 percent variable and 70 percent fixed.

    During September 2008, Longhorn Inc. produced 4,600 units of product and incurred 53,000 machine hours. September's actual overhead cost was $1,985,760. Each unit of product requires 12 machine hours.
    a. What were standard hours for September?
    b. What is total monthly budgeted fixed overhead cost?
    c. What is the controllable overhead variance?
    d. What is the noncontrollable overhead variance?

26. **LO.3 (Variance journal entries)** At year-end 2008, the trial balance of Prestonwood Corp. showed the following accounts and amounts:

	Debit	Credit
Direct Material Inventory	$ 36,600	
Work in Process Inventory	43,920	
Finished Goods Inventory	65,880	
Cost of Goods Sold	585,600	
Material Price Variance	7,250	
Material Quantity Variance		$10,965
Labor Rate Variance		1,100
Labor Efficiency Variance	4,390	
VOH Spending Variance		3,600
VOH Efficiency Variance	300	
FOH Spending Variance	650	
Volume Variance	1,475	

    Assume that, taken together, the variances are believed to be significant. Prepare the journal entries to close the variances at year-end.

27. **LO.4 (Behavioral implications of standard costing)** Contact a local company that uses a standard cost system. Make an appointment with a manager at that company to interview her or him on the following issues:
    - the characteristics that should be present in a standard cost system to encourage positive employee motivation
    - how a standard cost system should be implemented to positively motivate employees
    - the meaning of management by exception and how variance analysis often results in the use of this concept
    - how employee behavior could be adversely affected when "actual to standard" comparisons are used as the basis for performance evaluation

    Prepare a short report and an oral presentation based on your interview.

28. **LO.4 (Cost control evaluation)** The Joe Haslett Concrete Company makes precast concrete steps for use with manufactured housing. The company had the following 2008 budget based on expected production of 3,200 units:

	Standard Cost	Amount Budgeted
Direct material	$22.00	$ 70,400
Direct labor	12.00	38,400
Variable overhead		
Indirect material	4.20	13,440
Indirect labor	1.75	5,600
Utilities	1.00	3,200
Fixed overhead		
Supervisory salaries		40,000
Depreciation		15,000
Insurance		9,640
Total		$195,680

Cost per unit = $195,680 ÷ 3,200 = $61.15

Actual production for 2008 was 3,500 units, and actual costs for the year were as follows:

Direct material used	$ 80,500
Direct labor	42,300
Variable overhead	
Indirect material	14,000
Indirect labor	6,650
Utilities	3,850
Fixed overhead	
Supervisory salaries	41,000
Depreciation	15,000
Insurance	8,800
Total	$212,100

Cost per unit = $212,100 ÷ 3,500 = $60.60

The plant manager, Taesha Farrell, whose annual bonus includes (among other factors) 20 percent of the net favorable cost variances, states that she saved the company $1,925 [($61.15 − $60.60) × 3,500]. She has instructed the plant cost accountant to prepare a detailed report to be sent to corporate headquarters comparing each component's actual per-unit cost with the per-unit amounts in the preceding annual budget to prove the $1,925 cost savings.

a. Is the actual-to-budget comparison proposed by Farrell appropriate? If her comparison is not appropriate, prepare a more appropriate comparison.

b. How would you, as the plant cost accountant, react if Farrell insisted on her comparison? Suggest what alternatives are available to you. ▲

29. **LO.4 (Ethics)** Hotel rooms have become more extravagant over the past decade and the time needed to clean a room has increased. According to a study entitled "Creating Luxury, Enduring Pain" by Unite Here (the primary union representing hotel workers in the United States), housekeepers have the most dangerous jobs at hotels and have an injury rate of more than one in ten workers—almost twice that of other hotel employees. Since 9/11, the standard number of rooms for a housekeeper to clean has risen from 12 per day to 18 per day. At one pricey hotel chain, it is estimated that a housekeeper who cleans 15 rooms strips approximately 500 pounds of soiled linens and replaces those with 500 pounds of clean linens ... resulting in back and shoulder injuries, carpel tunnel syndrome, and bursitis.

Two articles relating to this situation are Komp, "Hotel Housekeepers Report Staggering Job Injury Rate," *The New Standard* (May 3, 2006) (http://newstandardnews.net/content/index.cfm/items/3122; last accessed 8/11/07) and Labor Research Association, "Bargaining Hotel Workers Defending Benefits in Contract Talks with Las Vegas Casinos," LRA Online (May 8, 2002) (http://www.laborresearch.org/print.php?id=196; last accessed 8/11/07).

a. Why is it necessary for hotels to establish a standard for number of rooms to be cleaned by housekeepers?

b. One of the articles states that the average hourly wage of housekeepers is $8.32, although this may be higher (approximately $12 per hour) at the larger hotel chains. The large hotel chains are, however, attempting to eliminate health care benefits with the wage increases. Given the rate of job injuries, do you believe that the housekeepers are better off with the lower wage and health care benefits or a higher wage and no health care benefits? Explain.

c. In an 8-hour day (480 minutes), cleaning 15 rooms amounts to approximately 32 minutes per room. What makes it difficult for a housekeeper to strip and remake a bed, vacuum, lightly dust, and clean a bathroom in that period of time? ▲

30. LO.4 (DL & OH; use of standard cost systems; ethics) Many companies face the prospect of paying workers overtime wages; some of these payments are at time-and-a-half wages.

a. How does overtime pay affect direct labor cost? Variable overhead?

b. Obviously, paying overtime to already employed workers makes better financial business sense than does hiring additional workers. If workers would prefer not to work overtime but do so to maintain their jobs, how does overtime affect the ethical contract between employers and employees?

c. What effects might overtime have on job efficiency? On job effectiveness (such as quality of production)?

d. Would you be in favor of limiting allowable hours of overtime to have more individuals employed? Discuss this question from the standpoint of (1) the government, (2) the employer, (3) a currently employed worker, and (4) an unemployed individual. ▲

31. LO.4 (Ethics) An HMO medical program began reimbursing hospitals according to diagnostic-related groups (DRGs). Each DRG has a specified standard "length of stay." If a patient leaves the hospital early, the hospital is financially impacted favorably, but a patient staying longer than the specified time costs the hospital money.

a. From the hospital administrator's point of view, would you want favorable length-of-stay variances? How might you try to obtain such variances?

b. From a patient's point of view, would you want favorable length-of-stay variances? Answer this question from the point of view of (1) a patient who has had minor surgery and (2) a patient who has had major surgery.

c. Would favorable length-of-stay variances necessarily equate to high-quality care? ▲

32. LO.6 (Variances and conversion cost category) Brake-Easy manufactures brake rotors and has always applied overhead to production using direct labor hours. Recently, company facilities were automated, and the accounting system was revised to show only two cost categories: direct material and conversion. Estimated variable and fixed conversion costs for the current month were $340,000 and $152,000, respectively. Expected output for the current month was 10,000 rotors and the estimated number of machine hours was 20,000. During July 2008, the firm actually used 18,000 machine hours to make 9,600 rotors while incurring $456,000 of conversion costs. Of this amount, $300,000 was variable cost.

a. Using the four-variance approach, compute the variances for conversion costs.

b. Evaluate the effectiveness of the firm in controlling the current month's costs.

33. LO.7 (Appendix) Herminey Company produces 12-ounce cans of mixed pecans and cashews. Standard and actual information follows.

Standard Quantities and Costs (12-oz. can)

Pecans: 6 ounces at $3.00 per pound	$1.125
Cashews: 6 ounces at $4.00 per pound	1.500

Actual Quantities and Costs for Production of 18,000 Cans

Pecans: 7,473 pounds at $2.90 per pound
Cashews: 6,617 pounds at $4.25 per pound

Determine the material price, mix, and yield variances.

34. LO.7 (Appendix) Casey Shannen Ltd. employs engineers and draftspeople. The average hourly rates are $80 for engineers and $40 for draftspeople. For one project, the standard was set at 375 hours of engineer time and 625 hours of draftsperson time. Actual hours worked on this project were:

Engineers—500 hours at $85 per hour
Draftspeople—500 hours at $42.00 per hour

Determine the labor rate, mix, and yield variances for this project.

35. LO.7 (Appendix) Wisnowski Services has three labor classes: administrative assistants, paralegals, and attorneys. Standard wage rates are as follows: administrative assistants, $25 per hour; paralegals, $40 per hour; and attorneys, $85 per hour. The firm has established a standard of 0.5 hours of administrative assistant time and 2.0 hours of paralegal time for each hour of attorney time in probate cases. For October, the numbers of actual direct labor hours worked and of standard hours for probate cases were as follows:

	Actual DLHs	Number of Standard Hours Allowed
Administrative assistant	500	500
Paralegal	1,800	2,000
Attorney	1,100	1,000

a. Calculate October's direct labor efficiency variance and decompose the total into the following components:
   1. Direct labor mix variance
   2. Direct labor yield variance
b. Prepare a memo addressing whether management used an efficient mix of labor.

(CMA adapted)

Problems

36. **LO.3 (DM & DL variances)** Aquatica uses a standard cost system for materials and labor in producing small fishing boats. Production requires three materials: fiberglass, paint, and a prepurchased trim package. The standard costs and quantities for materials and labor are as follows:

Standards for One Fishing Boat

2,500 pounds of fiberglass × $0.80 per pound	$2,000
6 quarts gel coat paint × $60.00 per gallon	90
1 trim package	400
40 hours of labor × $25.00 per hour	1,000
Standard cost for DM and DL	$3,490

The following actual data related to the production of 600 boats was recorded for July:

Material Purchased

Fiberglass—1,640,000 pounds × $0.83 per pound
Paint—1,000 gallons × $55.50 per gallon
Trim packages—640 × $405 per package

Material Used

Fiberglass—1,580,000 pounds
Paint—924 gallons
Trim packages—608

Direct Labor Used

24,200 hours × $23.50 per hour

Calculate the material and labor variances for Aquatica for July. The material price variance should be computed for each type of material and on the quantity of material purchased.

37. **LO.3 (DM & DL variances; journal entries)** Lilliputian Corp. makes small plastic dog toys with the following material and labor standards:

	Standard Quantity	Standard Cost
Material	0.5 pound	$4.00 per pound ($2.00 per unit of output)
Labor	12 minutes	16.00 per hour ($3.20 per unit of output)

During October, 58,000 pounds of material were acquired at $4.15 per pound; only 50,600 pounds of that were used in production during the month to make 100,000 toys. Factory payroll for October showed 20,600 direct labor hours at a total cost of $331,660.

a. Compute material and labor variances, basing the material price variance on the quantity of material purchased.
b. Assuming a perpetual inventory system is used, prepare the relevant general journal entries for October.

38. **LO.3 (Incomplete data; variances)** Forensic Supply produces latex surgical gloves. Machines perform the majority of the processing for 400 pairs of gloves per hour. Each pair of gloves requires 0.85 square foot of latex, which has a standard price of $0.80 per square foot. Machine operators are considered direct labor and are paid $25 per hour.

During one week in May, Forensic Supply produced 30,000 pairs of gloves and experienced a $1,496 unfavorable material quantity variance. The company had purchased 1,500 more square feet of material than had been used in production that week. The unfavorable material price variance for the week was $577.40. A $104 favorable total labor variance was generated based on 77 total actual labor hours to produce the gloves. Determine the following amounts:

a. Standard quantity of material for production achieved
b. Actual quantity of material used
c. Actual quantity of material purchased
d. Actual price of material purchased
e. Standard hours for actual production
f. Labor efficiency variance
g. Labor rate variance
h. Actual labor rate

39. **LO.3 (Incomplete data; variances)** Smart Products makes wooden lap desks. A small fire on October 1 partially destroyed the records relating to September's production. The charred remains of the standard cost card appear here.

	Standard Quantity	Standard Price
Direct material	5.0 board feet	
Direct labor		$12.50 per hour

From other fragments of records and several discussions with employees, you learn the following:

- The standard quantity of material allowed for September's production was 4,000 board feet.
- The September payroll for direct labor was $19,220 based on 1,550 actual hours worked.
- The production supervisor distinctly remembered being held accountable for 50 more hours of direct labor than should have been worked. She was upset because top management failed to consider that she saved several hundred board feet of material by creative efforts that required extra time.
- The purchasing agent's files showed that 4,300 board feet had been purchased in September at $2.05 per board foot. He was proud of the fact that this price was $0.05 below standard cost per foot. All purchased material had been used during the month.

a. How many units were produced during September?
b. Calculate all variances for direct material and direct labor for September.
c. What is the standard number of hours allowed for the production of each unit?
d. Prepare general journal entries reflecting direct material and direct labor activity and variances for September, assuming a standard cost, perpetual inventory system.

40. **LO.5 (Adjusting standards)** ALOHA Corp., started in January 2001, manufactures Hawaiian muumuus. At that time, the following material and labor standards were developed:

Material	3.0 yards at $6 per yard
Labor	1.5 hours at $10 per hour

In January 2008, ALOHA Corp. hired a new cost accountant, Anulu Haoki. At the end of the month, Haoki was reviewing the production variances and was amazed to find that the company's material and labor standards had never been revised. Actual material and labor data for January when 17,200 muumuus were produced follow:

Material	Purchased, 50,000 yards at $7.00
	Used 50,000 yards
Labor	17,800 hours at $13.50 per hour

Material prices have risen 4 percent each year beginning in 2002, but the company can now buy at 94 percent of regular price due to increased purchase volume. Also, direct material waste has been reduced from 1/4 yard to 1/8 yard per muumuu; waste has always been included in the standard material quantity. Beginning in 2002, each annual labor contract has specified a 5 percent cost-of-living adjustment. Revision of the plant layout and acquisition of more efficient machinery has decreased the labor time per muumuu by one-third since the company began.

a. Determine the material and labor variances based on the company's original standards.
b. Determine the new standards against which Haoki should measure the January 2008 results. (Round adjustments annually to the nearest cent.)
c. Compute the variances for material and labor using the revised standards.

41. LO.4 (OH variances) Braunfels Corp. has an expected monthly capacity of 9,000 units but only 5,700 units were produced and 6,000 direct labor hours were used during August 2008 due to a flood in the manufacturing facility. Actual variable overhead for August was $48,120 and actual fixed overhead was $132,000. Standard cost data follow:

	Standard Cost per Unit (One Unit Takes One Labor Hour)
Direct material	$ 9.00
Direct labor	15.00
Variable overhead	8.00
Fixed overhead	16.00
Total	$48.00

a. Compute and compare the actual overhead cost per unit with the expected overhead cost per unit.
b. Calculate overhead variances using the four-variance method.

42. LO.4 (OH variances; journal entries) All Natural Products makes wooden picnic tables, swings, and benches. Standard hours for each product are as follows:

Picnic table	10 standard direct labor hours
Swing	3 standard direct labor hours
Bench	12 standard direct labor hours

The standard variable overhead rate is $4 per direct labor hour. The standard fixed overhead rate, computed using an expected annual capacity of 36,000 direct labor hours, is $2 per direct labor hour. The company estimates stable fixed overhead costs and direct labor hours each month of the annual period. March production was 100 picnic tables, 400 swings, and 60 benches; production required 3,020 actual direct labor hours. Actual variable and fixed overhead for March were $12,800 and $5,900, respectively.

a. Prepare a variance analysis using the four-variance approach. (Hint: Convert the production of each type of product into standard hours for all work accomplished for the month.)
b. Prepare journal entries to record actual overhead costs, application of overhead to production, and closing of the overhead variance accounts (assuming those variances are immaterial).
c. Evaluate the effectiveness of the managers in controlling costs.

43. LO.4 (OH variances with unknowns) During December 2008, Gharigh Corp. manufactured products requiring 8,000 standard labor hours. The following variance and actual information is available:

Labor rate variance	$ 4,500 U
Labor efficiency variance	12,000 U
Actual variable overhead	154,000
Actual fixed overhead	79,000

Gharigh Corp.'s standard costs for labor and overhead were set at the beginning of 2008 and have remained constant through the year as follows:

Direct labor (4 hours × $12 per hour)	$ 48
Factory overhead (10,000 DLH expected capacity)	
Variable (4 hours × $16 per direct labor hour)	64
Fixed (4 hours × $8 per direct labor hour)	32
Total unit conversion cost	$144

Calculate the following unknown amounts:
a. Number of units manufactured
b. Total applied factory overhead
c. Volume variance
d. Variable overhead spending variance
e. Variable overhead efficiency variance
f. Total actual overhead

44. LO.4 (OH variances) Melbourne Mfg. produces comforter sets with the following standard cost information:
- Each comforter set requires 1/2 hour of machine time to produce.
- Variable overhead is applied at the rate of $9 per machine hour.
- Fixed overhead is applied at the rate of $6 per machine hour, based on an expected annual capacity of 30,000 machine hours.

Production Statistics for 2008

Number of comforter sets produced	62,000 units
Actual number of machine hours	66,600 hours
Variable overhead cost incurred	$265,400
Fixed overhead cost incurred	$177,250

a. Using a combined overhead rate, calculate variances using the two-variance approach.
b. Using a combined overhead rate, calculate variances using the three-variance approach.

45. LO.4 (Comprehensive) Dole Manufacturing produces metal products with the following standard quantity and cost information:

Direct Material

Aluminum	4 sheets at $2	$ 8
Copper	3 sheets at $4	12
Direct labor	7 hours at $8	56
Variable overhead	5 machine hours at $3	15
Fixed overhead	5 machine hours at $2	10

Overhead rates were based on normal monthly capacity of 6,000 machine hours.

During November, the company produced only 850 units because of a labor strike that occurred during union contract negotiations. After the dispute was settled, the company scheduled overtime to try to meet regular production levels. The following costs were incurred in November:

Material

Aluminum	4,000 sheets purchased at $2; used 3,500 sheets
Copper	3,000 sheets purchased at $4.20; used 2,600 sheets

Direct Labor

Regular time	5,200 hours at $8.00 (pre-contract settlement)
Regular time	900 hours at $8.50 (post-contract settlement)

Variable Overhead

$11,650 (based on 4,175 machine hours)

Fixed Overhead

$9,425 (based on 4,175 machine hours)

Determine the following:
a. Total material price variance
b. Total material usage (quantity) variance
c. Labor rate variance
d. Labor efficiency variance
e. Variable overhead spending variance
f. Variable overhead efficiency variance
g. Fixed overhead spending variance
h. Volume variance
i. Budget variance

46. LO.4 (Comprehensive; all variances; all methods) Hellier Contractors paints interiors of residences and commercial structures. The firm's management has established cost standards per 100 square feet of area to be painted.

Direct material ($18 per gallon of paint)	$1.50
Direct labor	2.00
Variable overhead	0.60
Fixed overhead (based on 600,000 square feet per month)	1.25

Management has determined that 400 square feet can be painted by the average worker each hour. During May, the company painted 600,000 square feet of space and incurred the following costs:

Direct material (450 gallons purchased and used)	$ 8,300.00
Direct labor (1,475 hours)	12,242.50
Variable overhead	3,480.00
Fixed overhead	7,720.00

a. Compute the direct material variances.
b. Compute the direct labor variances.
c. Use a four-variance approach to compute overhead variances.
d. Use a three-variance approach to compute overhead variances.
e. Use a two-variance approach to compute overhead variances.
f. Reconcile your answers for parts (c) through (e).
g. Discuss other cost drivers that could be used as a basis for measuring activity and computing variances for this company.

47. **LO.4 (Variance disposition)** The following variances existed at year-end 2008 for Mendalena Production Company:

Material price variance	$46,800 U
Material quantity variance	49,800 F
Labor rate variance	10,500 F
Labor efficiency variance	73,800 U
Variance overhead spending variance	6,000 U
Variance overhead efficiency variance	3,600 F
Fixed overhead spending variance	13,200 F
Volume variance	33,600 U

In addition, the following inventory and Cost of Goods Sold account balances existed at year-end 2008:

Raw Material Inventory	$ 338,793
Work in Process Inventory	914,277
Finished Goods Inventory	663,663
Cost of Goods Sold	2,724,267

a. Prepare the journal entry at December 31 to dispose of the variances, assuming that all are insignificant.
b. After posting your entry in part (a), what is the balance in Cost of Goods Sold?
c. Prepare the journal entries at December 31 to dispose of the variances, assuming that all are significant.
d. After posting your entries in part (c), what are the balances in each inventory account and in Cost of Goods Sold?

48. **LO.4 (Variances and variance responsibility)** Weizel Industries manufactures children's footballs with the following standard costs per unit:

Material: one square foot of leather at $2.00	$ 2.00
Direct labor: 1.6 hours at $9.00	14.40
Variable overhead cost	3.00
Fixed overhead cost	3.00
Total cost per unit	$22.40

Per-unit overhead cost was calculated from the following annual overhead budget for 180,000 footballs.

Variable Overhead Cost

Indirect labor—90,000 hours at $7.00	$630,000	
Supplies (oil)—180,000 gallons at $0.50	90,000	
Allocated variable service department costs	90,000	
Total variable overhead cost		$810,000

Fixed Overhead Cost

Supervision	$ 1,000	
Depreciation	135,000	
Other fixed costs	45,000	
Total fixed overhead cost		261,000
Total budgeted overhead cost at 180,000 units		$1,071,000

Following are the charges to the manufacturing department for November when 15,000 units were produced:

Material (15,900 square feet at $2.00)	$ 31,800
Direct labor (24,600 hours at $9.10)	223,860
Indirect labor (7,200 hours at $7.10)	51,120
Supplies (oil) (18,000 gallons at $0.55)	9,900
Allocated service department variable OH costs	9,600

Supervision	7,425
Depreciation	11,250
Other fixed costs	3,750
Total	$348,705

Purchasing normally buys about the same quantity as is used in production during a month. In November, it purchased 15,600 square feet of material at a price of $2.10 per foot.

a. Calculate the following variances from standard costs for the data given:
   1. Material purchase price
   2. Material quantity
   3. Direct labor rate
   4. Direct labor efficiency
   5. Overhead budget

b. The company has divided its responsibilities so that the Purchasing Department is responsible for the purchase price of materials and the Manufacturing Department is responsible for the quantity of materials used. Does this division of responsibilities solve the conflict between price and quantity variances? Explain your answer.

c. Prepare a report detailing the overhead budget variance. The report, which will be given to the Manufacturing Department manager, should show only that part of the variance that is her responsibility and should highlight the information in ways that would be useful to her in evaluating departmental performance and when considering corrective action.

d. Assume that the departmental manager performs the timekeeping function for this manufacturing department. From time to time, analyses of overhead and direct labor variances have shown that the manager has deliberately misclassified labor hours (that is, listed direct labor hours as indirect labor hours and vice versa) so that only one of the two labor variances is unfavorable. It is not feasible economically to hire a separate timekeeper. What should the company do, if anything, to resolve this problem?

(CMA adapted)

49. **LO.5 (Standards revision)** Ripper Corp. uses a standard cost system for its aircraft component manufacturing operations. Recently, the company's direct material supplier went out of business, but Ripper's purchasing agent found a new source that produces a similar material. The price per pound from the original supplier was $7.00; the new source's price is $7.77. The new source's material reduces scrap and, thus, each unit requires only 1.00 pound rather than the previous standard of 1.25 pounds per unit. In addition, use of the new source's material reduces direct labor time from 24 to 22 minutes per unit because there is less machine setup time. At the same time, the recently signed labor contract increased the average direct labor wage rate from $12.60 to $14.40 per hour.

The company began using the new direct material on April 1, the same day that the new labor agreement went into effect. However, Ripper Corp. is still using the following standards that were set at the beginning of the calendar year:

Direct material	1.2 pounds at $6.80 per pound	$ 8.16
Direct labor	20 minutes at $12.30 per DLH	4.10
Standard DM and DL cost per unit		$12.26

Steve Wenskel, cost accounting supervisor, had been examining the following April 30 variance report.

PERFORMANCE REPORT
STANDARD COST VARIANCE ANALYSIS FOR APRIL 2008

Standard	Price Variance	Quantity Variance	Actual
DM $ 8.16	($0.97 × 1.0) $0.97 U	($6.80 × 0.2) $1.36 F	$ 7.77
DL 4.10	[$2.10 × (22/60)] 0.77 U	[$12.30 × (2/60)] 0.41 U	5.28
$12.26			$13.05

COMPARISON OF 2008 ACTUAL COSTS

	Average 1st Quarter Costs	April Costs	Percent Increase (Decrease)
DM	$ 8.75	$ 7.77	(11.2)
DL	5.04	5.28	4.8
	$13.79	$13.05	(5.4)

When Cynthia Dirope, assistant controller, came into Wenskel's office, he said, "Cynthia, look at this performance report! Direct material price increased 11 percent, and the labor rate increased over 14 percent during April. I expected greater variances, yet prime costs decreased over 5 percent from the $13.79 we experienced during the first quarter of this year. The proper message just isn't coming through."

Dirope said, "This has been an unusual period. With all the unforeseen changes, perhaps we should revise our standards based on current conditions and start over."

Wenskel replied, "I think we can retain the current standards but expand the variance analysis. We could calculate variances for the specific changes that have occurred to direct material and direct labor before we calculate the normal price and quantity variances. What I really think would be useful to management right now is to determine the impact the changes in direct material and direct labor had in reducing our prime costs per unit from $13.79 in the first quarter to $13.05 in April—a reduction of $0.74."

a. Discuss the advantages of (1) immediately revising the standards and (2) retaining the current standards and expanding the analysis of variances.

b. Prepare an analysis that reflects the impact of the new direct material and new labor contract on reducing Ripper Corp.'s standard costs per unit from $13.79 to $13.05. The analysis should show the changes in direct material and direct labor costs per unit that are caused by (1) the use of the new direct material and (2) the labor rates of the new contract. This analysis should be in sufficient detail to identify the changes due to direct material price, direct labor rate, the effect of direct material quality on direct material usage, and the effect of direct material quality on direct labor usage.

(CMA adapted)

50. **LO.6 (Conversion cost variances)** The May budget for the Brinker Company shows $1,080,000 of variable conversion costs, $360,000 of fixed conversion costs, and 72,000 machine hours for the production of 24,000 units of product. During May, 76,000 machine hours were worked and 24,000 units were produced. Variance and fixed conversion costs for the month were $1,128,800 and $374,500, respectively.

a. Calculate the four conversion cost variances assuming that variable and fixed costs are separated.

b. Calculate the three conversion cost variances assuming that fixed and variable costs are combined.

51. **LO.6 (Conversion cost variances)** Kieve Company makes men's suit alterations for a major clothing store chain. No direct materials are used in the alterations process and overhead costs are primarily variable and relate very closely to direct labor charges. The company owner has decided to compute variances on a conversion cost basis. Standards for 2008 are as follows:

Expected direct labor hours (DLHs; to be incurred evenly throughout the year)	60,000
Number of suits altered in October	1,800
Standard DLHs per suit	3
Actual DLHs worked in October 2008	5,490
Budgeted variable conversion cost per DLH	$18
Budgeted annual fixed conversion cost	$72,000
Actual variable conversion cost for October 2008	$103,100
Actual fixed conversion cost for October 2008	$5,750

a. How many suits does Kieve Company expect to alter during 2008?

b. What is the predetermined fixed OH rate for Kieve Company?

c. How many standard direct labor hours were allowed for October 2008?

d. Calculate the four conversion cost variances assuming that variable and fixed costs are separated.

e. Calculate the three conversion cost variances assuming that fixed and variable costs are combined.

52. **LO.7 (Appendix)** It'Z Italiano produces three-topping, 18-inch frozen pizzas and uses a standard cost system. The three pizza toppings (in addition to cheese) are onions, olives, and mushrooms. To some extent, discretion may be used to determine the actual mix of these toppings. The company has two classes of labor, and discretion also may be used to determine the mix of the labor inputs. The standard cost card for a pizza follows:

Onions	3 ounces at $0.10 per ounce
Olives	3 ounces at $0.35 per ounce
Mushrooms	3 ounces at $0.50 per ounce
Labor category 1	5 minutes at $12 per hour
Labor category 2	6 minutes at $8 per hour

During May 2008, the company produced 48,000 pizzas and used the following inputs:

Onions	8,000 pounds
Olives	12,000 pounds
Mushrooms	8,000 pounds
Labor category 1	5,200 hours
Labor category 2	4,000 hours

During the month there were no deviations from standards on material prices or labor rates.
a. Determine the material quantity, mix, and yield variances.
b. Determine the labor efficiency, mix, and yield variances.
c. Prepare the journal entries to record the above mix and yield variances.

53. **LO.7 (Appendix)** Levy Products makes HealthPlus, a nutritional aid. For a 50-pound batch, standard material and labor costs are as follows:

	Quantity	Unit Price	Total
Wheat	25.0 pounds	$ 0.20 per pound	$5.00
Barley	25.0 pounds	0.10 per pound	2.50
Corn	10.0 pounds	0.05 per pound	0.50
Skilled labor	0.8 hour	12.00 per hour	9.60
Unskilled labor	0.2 hour	8.00 per hour	1.60

During June, the following materials and labor were used in producing 600 batches of HealthPlus:

Wheat	18,000 pounds at $0.22 per pound
Barley	14,000 pounds at $0.11 per pound
Corn	10,000 pounds at $0.04 per pound
Skilled labor	400 hours at $12.25 per hour
Unskilled labor	260 hours at $8.00 per hour

a. Calculate the material quantity, mix, and yield variances.
b. Calculate the labor efficiency, mix, and yield variances.

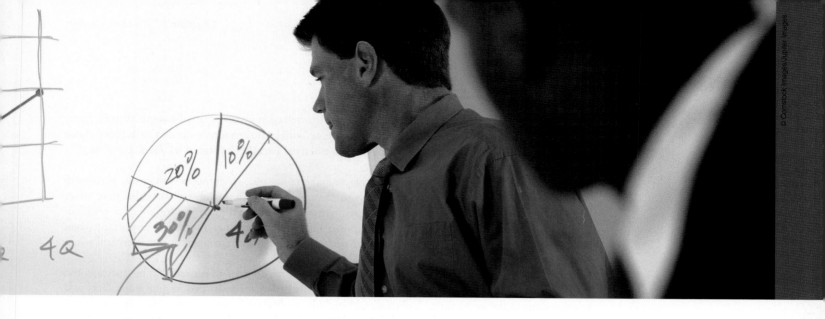

8 | The Master Budget

Objectives

After completing this chapter, you should be able to answer the following questions:

LO.1 How is strategic planning related to budgeting?

LO.2 What is the starting point of a master budget and why?

LO.3 What are the various components of a master budget, and how are they prepared?

LO.4 Why is the cash budget so important in the master budgeting process?

LO.5 How and why are budgeted financial statements prepared at the end of the budgeting process?

LO.6 What benefits are provided by a budget?

LO.7 (*Appendix*) How does a budget manual facilitate the budgeting process?

Introduction

In virtually any endeavor, organizing and coordinating behavior involves visualizing the future, specifying the desired outcomes, and determining the activities and resources needed to achieve those results. The last part of the behavioral process is essential because, as stated in *The Little Prince*, "a goal without a plan is just a wish."

Planning is the cornerstone of effective management, and, in complex situations, successful planning requires that managers predict, with reasonable precision, the key variables that affect company performance. These predictions provide management the foundation for effective problem solving, control, and resource allocation. Planning (especially in financial terms) is important when future conditions are expected to be approximately the same as current ones, and it is critical when conditions are expected to change.

As plans become more involved, the means of obtaining desired results should be documented because of the human tendency to forget and the difficulty of mentally processing many facts and relationships at the same time. A plan should include qualitative narratives of goals, objectives, and means of accomplishment. However, if plans consisted only of qualitative narratives, comparisons between actual results and expectations would be vague generalizations, and there would be no way to measure how well the organization met its specified objectives. The process of formalizing plans and translating qualitative narratives into a documented, quantitative format is called budgeting. The end result of this process is a budget, which quantitatively expresses an organization's commitment to planned activities and to resource acquisition and use.

This chapter covers the budgeting process and preparation of the master budget. Budgeting is important for organizations of all sizes, especially those with large quantities of monetary, human, and physical resources.

The Budgeting Process

Budgeting is an important part of an organization's planning process, in part because it determines a direction or path chosen from many alternatives. Inclusion of quantifiable amounts provides specific criteria against which future performance (also recorded in accounting terms) can be compared. Thus, a budget is a type of standard that allows variances to be computed and feedback about those variances to be given to appropriate individuals.

Strategic Planning

LO.1
How is strategic planning related to budgeting?

Although budgets are typically expressed in financial terms, the budgeting process must begin with consideration of nonquantitative factors and all organizational resources—raw material, inventory, supplies, personnel, and facilities—and can be viewed from a long-term or a short-term perspective.

Managers who plan on a long-range basis (5 to 10 years) are engaged in strategic planning. Top-level management conducts this process, often with the assistance of key staff members. The result is a statement of long-range organizational goals and the strategies and policies that will help achieve those goals. Strategic planning is not concerned with day-to-day operations, although the strategic plan is the foundation on which short-term planning is based. Managers engaging in strategic planning should identify key variables that are believed to be the direct causes of the achievement or nonachievement of organizational goals and objectives. Key variables can be internal (under the control of management) or external (normally noncontrollable by management). Effective strategic planning requires that managers build plans and budgets that integrate the following external considerations and influences with the firm's internal factors, such as core competencies, product development, and product life cycles.

- Competitor actions
- Local and global market conditions

- Political/regulatory climates in which the company operates
- Current and emerging production technology
- Outsourcing opportunities
- Consumer trends and attitudes
- Demographics of the areas in which the company operates

During the strategic planning process, managers agree both on organizational goals and objectives and on how to achieve them. Typically, goals are stated as desired abstract achievements (such as "to become a market leader for a particular product"), and objectives are stated as desired quantifiable results for a specified time (such as "to manufacture 200,000 units of Product X with fewer than 1 percent defects next year"). Achieving goals and objectives requires organizing complex activities, managing diverse resources, and formalizing plans.

Tactical Planning

After identifying key variables, management should gather information useful for managing or reacting to changes in these variables. Often this information is historical and qualitative and provides a useful starting point for tactical planning activities. Tactical planning determines how the strategic plans will be achieved. Some tactical plans, such as corporate policy statements, exist for the long term and address repetitive situations. Most tactical plans, however, are short term (1 to 18 months); they are considered "single-use" plans and are developed to address a given set of circumstances or to cover a specific period of time.

The annual budget is an example of a single-use tactical plan. Although this budget is typically prepared for a one-year period, shorter horizon (quarterly and monthly) plans should also be included if the budget is to contain the details necessary for the plan to work effectively. The budget is the quantified end product that results from the predictions and assumptions that were made about achieving both financial and nonfinancial goals and objectives. Financial goals could include targets for net income, earnings per share, or sales revenue. Nonfinancial performance goals and objectives could include a designated customer satisfaction level, defect reduction rates, and percentage of on-time deliveries. By quantifying potential difficulties in achieving organizational goals and objectives and by making those difficulties visible, budgets can help stimulate managers to think of ways to overcome problems before they are realized.

Budgets are also an effective means of communicating objectives, constraints, and expectations to all organizational personnel. Such communication promotes understanding of what is to be accomplished, how those accomplishments are to be achieved, and the manner in which resources are to be allocated. Resource allocations are made, in part, from a process of obtaining information, justifying requests, and negotiating compromises.

Employee participation is needed to effectively integrate necessary information from various sources as well as to obtain individual managerial commitment to the resulting budget. Participation helps to produce a spirit of cooperation, motivate employees, and instill teamwork. At the same time, the greater the degree of participation of all personnel affected in the budgeting process, the greater the time and cost involved. Traditionally, to say that a company uses a highly participative budgeting process has implied that budgets have been built from the bottom of the organization upward.

A well-prepared budget serves as a guide for company activities. Exhibit 8–1 illustrates the relationships among strategic planning, tactical planning, and budgeting. Both strategic planning and tactical planning require that the latest information regarding the economy, environment, governmental regulations, technology, and available resources be incorporated into setting goals and objectives. This information is used to adjust the previously gathered historical information for any changes in the key variables for the planning period. The planning process also demands that, as activity unfolds and plans are implemented, a monitoring system provide feedback so that the control function can be put into operation.

Managers review the budget prior to approving and implementing it to determine whether the forecasted results are acceptable. The budget could indicate that results expected from the planned activities do not achieve the desired objectives. In this case, planned activities are reconsidered and revised so that they more effectively achieve the desired outcomes expressed in the tactical planning stage.

After a budget has been accepted, it is implemented and becomes a performance benchmark. The budget sets the resource constraints under which managers must operate for the upcoming budget period. The control phase includes making actual-to-budget comparisons, determining variances, investigating variance causes, taking necessary corrective action, and providing feedback to operating managers. Feedback, both positive and negative, is essential to the control process and must be provided in a timely manner. This cyclical process is illustrated in Exhibit 8–2.

EXHIBIT 8–1
Relationships among Planning Processes

Who?	What?	How?	Why?
Top management	Strategic planning	State organizational mission, goals, and strategies; long range (5–10 years)	Establish a long-range vision of the organization and provide a sense of unity of and commitment to specified purposes
Top management and mid-management	Tactical planning	State organizational plans; short range (1–18 months)	Provide direction for achievement of strategic plans; state strategic plans in terms on which managers can act; furnish a basis against which results can be measured
Top management, mid-management, and operational management	Budgeting	Prepare quantitative and monetary statements that coordinate company activities for a year or less	Allocate resources effectively and efficiently; indicate a commitment to objectives; provide a monetary control device

EXHIBIT 8–2
Cyclical Nature of Budgeting Process

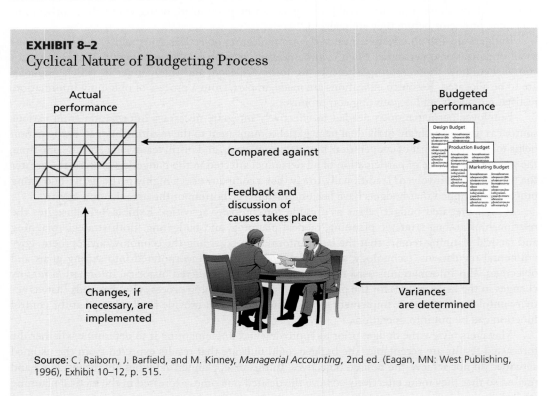

Source: C. Raiborn, J. Barfield, and M. Kinney, *Managerial Accounting*, 2nd ed. (Eagan, MN: West Publishing, 1996), Exhibit 10–12, p. 515.

The preceding discussion describes a budgeting process, but, as with many other business practices, budgeting can be unique to individual countries. For example, the lengthy and highly specific budgeting process used by many U.S. companies differs dramatically from that used by many Japanese companies. Japanese companies tend to view the budget more as a device to help focus personnel and resources on achieving group and firm-level targets than as a control device by which to gauge individual performance.

Regardless of the manner in which it is carried out, the budgeting process results in a **master budget**. This "budget" is actually a comprehensive set of budgets, budgetary schedules, and budgeted (pro forma) organizational financial statements.

The Master Budget

As shown in Exhibit 8–3, operating and financial budgets compose the master budget. An **operating budget** is a budget that is expressed in both units and dollars. When an operating budget relates to revenues, the units are those expected to be sold, and the dollars reflect selling prices. In contrast, when an operating budget relates to costs, the input units are those expected to be either transformed into output units or consumed, and the dollars reflect costs.

Monetary details from the various operating budgets are combined to prepare **financial budgets**, which indicate the funds to be generated or consumed during the budget period. Financial budgets include cash and capital budgets as well as the budgeted financial statements that are the ultimate focal points for top management.

The master budget is prepared for a specific period and is static in the sense that it is based on a single level of output demand.[1] Developing the budget using a single demand level is necessary to identify the specific input quantities to be acquired. Arrangements must be made to assure that an adequate number of personnel are hired, that needed production and/or storage space is available, and that suppliers, prices, delivery schedules, and quality of resources are confirmed.

EXHIBIT 8–3
Components of a Master Budget

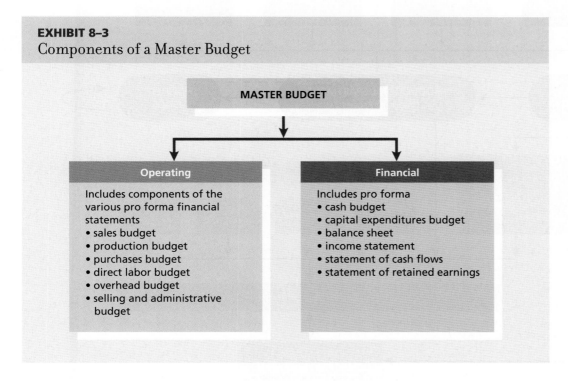

[1]Companies can engage in contingency planning, providing for multiple budgeting paths. For example, a company could construct three budgets, such as for a high level of activity, an expected level of activity, and a low level of activity. If actual activity turns out to be either higher or lower than expected, management has a budget ready.

The sales demand level selected for use in the master budget affects all other budget components. Because of the many budgetary relationships, all departmental budgets must interact in a coordinated manner. A budget developed by one department is often an essential ingredient in developing another department's budget.

The budgetary process shown in Exhibit 8–4 illustrates how the various functional areas of a manufacturing organization interact and are involved with master budget preparation. The process begins with the Sales Department's estimates of the types, quantities, and timing of sales for the company's products. The budget is typically prepared for a year and then subdivided into quarterly and monthly periods.

A production manager combines sales estimates with information from Purchasing, Human Resources, Operations, and Capital Facilities to specify the types, quantities, and timing of products to be manufactured. Sales estimates, in conjunction with estimated cash collection patterns, are used to determine the amounts and timing of cash receipts.

For the treasurer to properly manage the organization's funds, cash receipts and disbursements information must be matched from all areas so that cash is available when, and in the amount, needed.

Departments involved in the budgeting process both generate and consume information. For example, the Sales Department must receive finished goods information to know whether goods are in stock (or can be produced) before selling products. In addition, the treasurer must receive continual cash information as well as provide information to various organizational units on funds availability so that proper funds management can be maintained.

EXHIBIT 8–4

The Budgetary Process in a Manufacturing Organization

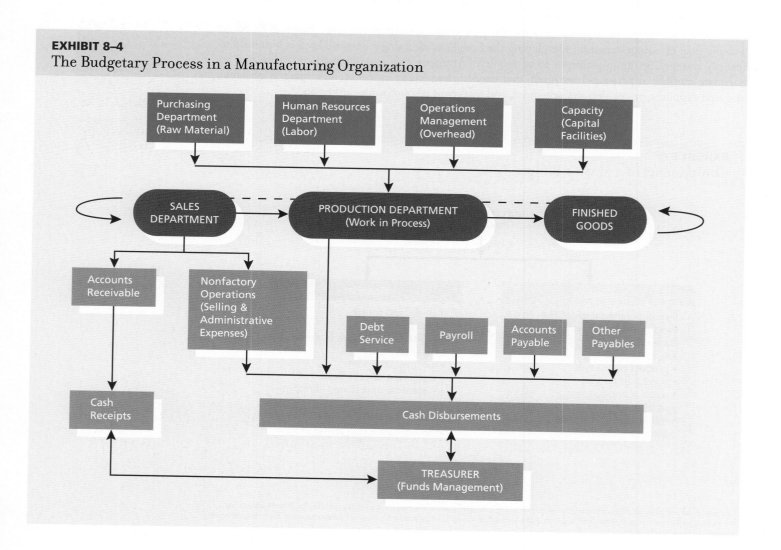

If top management encourages participation of lower-level managers in the budgeting process, each department either prepares its own budget or provides information for inclusion in a budget. Exhibit 8–5 presents an overview of the budget preparation sequence, indicates departmental budget preparation responsibility, and illustrates how the budgets interface.

The master budget begins with the sales budget. Next, production and other resource requirements are budgeted based on the sales budget. Cash flows from the sales and resource consumption budgets are then integrated into budgeted financial statements. Exhibit 8–5 depicts information flow but not the necessary details; thus, the chapter next discusses the specifics of preparing a master budget.

LO.2
What is the starting point of a master budget and why?

EXHIBIT 8–5
The Master Budget: An Overview

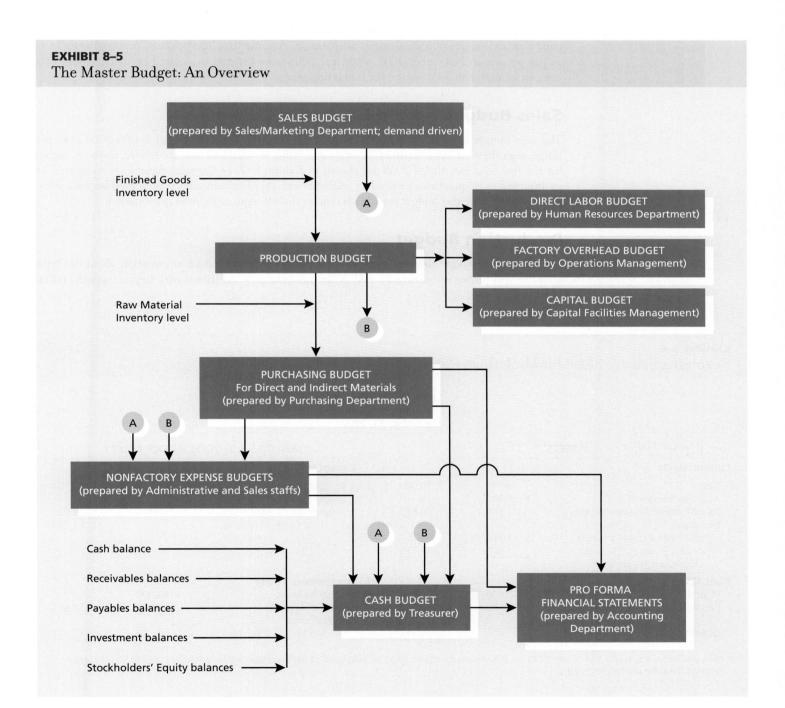

LO.3
What are the various components of a master budget, and how are they prepared?

The Master Budget Illustrated

This illustration uses information from Midlothian Corp., an illustrative company that has been in business for several years. The company, which produces a single type of 6-foot, made-to-stock steel hinge, is preparing its 2008 budget and has estimated total annual sales at 350,000 hinges. Although annual sales would be detailed on a monthly basis, the Midlothian Corp. illustration focuses on the budgets for only the first quarter of 2008. The process of developing the master budget is the same regardless of whether the time frame is one year or one quarter.

The December 31, 2007, balance sheet presented in Exhibit 8–6 provides account balances needed to begin preparation of the master budget. The December 31, 2007, balances are estimates rather than actual figures because the budget process for 2008 must begin significantly before December 31, 2007. The company's budgetary time schedule depends on many factors, including company size and degree of forecasting sophistication. Assume that Midlothian Corp. begins its budgeting process in November 2007, when the 2008 sales forecast is received by management or a committee designated to oversee the budgeting process.

Sales Budget

The sales budget is prepared in both units and sales dollars. The selling price set for 2008 is $5 per hinge, regardless of sales territory or customer. Monthly demand and its related revenue impact for the first four months of 2008 are shown in Exhibit 8–7. Dollar sales figures are computed by multiplying sales quantities by product selling prices. April information is presented because some elements of the master budget for March require the subsequent month's information.

Production Budget

The production budget follows from the sales budget and is based on information about the type, quantity, and timing of units to be sold. Sales information is combined with beginning and ending

---

EXHIBIT 8–6
Beginning Balance Sheet for Midlothian Corp.

Midlothian Corp.
Balance Sheet
December 31, 2007

ASSETS			LIABILITIES & STOCKHOLDERS' EQUITY		
Current Assets			**Current Liabilities**		
Cash		$ 10,000	Accounts Payable		$ 42,504
Accounts Receivable	$ 69,840		Dividends Payable (payment		
Less Allowance for Uncollectibles	(1,248)	68,592	scheduled for March 31)		45,000
Inventories			Total Current Liabilities		$ 87,504
Raw Material (3,443 pounds)	$ 7,919*				
Finished Goods (1,500 units)	4,800	12,719			
Total Current Assets		$ 91,311			
Plant Assets			**Stockholders' Equity**		
Property, Plant, and Equipment	$370,000		Common Stock	$180,000	
Less Accumulated Depreciation	(90,000)	280,000	Retained Earnings	103,807	283,807
			Total Liabilities and		
Total Assets		$371,311	Stockholders' Equity		$371,311

*This amount is actually $7,918.90, or 3,443 pounds of steel multiplied by $2.30 per pound. It has been rounded for simplicity in this exhibit. Retained Earnings has been similarly rounded.

EXHIBIT 8–7

Sales Budget for the Three Months and Quarter Ending March 31, 2008

	January	February	March	Total for Quarter	April*
Sales in units	30,000	28,000	33,000	91,000	32,000
Sales in dollars	$150,000	$140,000	$165,000	$455,000	$160,000

*Information for April is needed for subsequent computations.

Finished Goods (FG) Inventory information so that managers can schedule necessary production. The following formula provides the computation for units to be produced:

Number of units to be sold (from sales budget)	XXX
+ Number of units desired in ending FG Inventory	XXX
= Total units needed during period	XXX
− Number of units in beginning FG Inventory	(XXX)
= Units to be produced	XXX

Company management determines ending inventory policy. Desired ending FG Inventory balance is generally a function of the quantity and timing of demand in the upcoming period as related to the firm's capacity and speed to produce particular units. Frequently, management stipulates that ending FG Inventory be equal to a given percentage of the next period's projected sales. Other alternatives include a constant amount of inventory, a buildup of inventory for future high-demand periods, or near-zero inventory under a just-in-time system (discussed in depth in Chapter 18). The decision about ending inventory levels results from the consideration of whether a firm wants to have constant production with varying inventory levels or variable production with constant inventory levels.

Managers should consider the high costs of stockpiling inventory before making a decision about how much inventory to keep on hand. Demand for Midlothian Corp.'s products is relatively constant year-round. Because most sales are to recurring customers, Midlothian's policy is that ending FG Inventory should be 5 percent of the next month's unit sales. Considering this policy and using the sales information from Exhibit 8–7, the production budget shown in Exhibit 8–8 is prepared.

January's beginning FG Inventory is the 1,500 units on hand at December 31, 2007, or 5 percent of January's estimated sales of 30,000 units. Desired March ending inventory is 5 percent of the April sales of 32,000 hinges (given in Exhibit 8–7). Midlothian does not have any Work in Process Inventory because all units placed into production are assumed to be fully completed during each period.[2]

Note that a retail or service company would not have a production budget included in its master budget.

Purchases Budget

Direct material must be purchased each period in sufficient quantities to meet production needs. In addition, the quantities of direct material purchased must conform with the company's desired ending inventory policies. Midlothian Corp.'s management ties its policy for ending Direct Material Inventory to its production needs for the following month. Because of occasional difficulty in obtaining the high quality of steel needed, Midlothian's ending inventory for direct material is set at 10 percent of the quantity needed for the following month's production.

Companies may have different policies for the direct material associated with different products or for different seasons of the year. For example, a company may maintain only a minimal ending

---

[2]Most manufacturing entities do not produce only whole units during the period. Normally, partially completed beginning and ending Work in Process inventories will exist. These inventories create the need to use equivalent units of production when computing the production budget.

EXHIBIT 8–8
Production Budget for the Three Months and Quarter Ending March 31, 2008

	January	February	March	Total
Sales in units (from Exhibit 8–7)	30,000	28,000	33,000	91,000
+ Desired ending inventory	1,400	1,650	1,600	1,600
= Total needed	31,400	29,650	34,600	92,600
− Beginning inventory	(1,500)	(1,400)	(1,650)	(1,500)
= Units to be produced	29,900	28,250	32,950	91,100

inventory of a direct material that is consistently available in the quantity and quality desired. Alternatively, if a material is difficult to obtain at certain times of the year, a company may stockpile that material for use in future periods.

The purchases budget is first stated in whole units of finished products and then converted to direct material component requirements and dollar amounts. Production of a Midlothian hinge requires only one direct material: steel. Steel cost has been estimated by the purchasing agent at $2.30 per pound, and it takes 1.1 pounds of steel to produce one 6-foot hinge. Exhibit 8–9 shows Midlothian's purchases cost for each month of the first quarter of 2008. Note that beginning and ending inventory quantities are expressed first in terms of hinges and then are converted to the appropriate quantity measure (pounds of steel). Total budgeted cost of direct material purchases for the first quarter of 2008 is $231,292.60.

Personnel Budget

Given expected production, the Engineering and Human Resources Departments can work together to determine the necessary labor requirements for the factory, sales force, and office staff. Labor requirements are stated in terms of total number of people, specific number of worker types (skilled laborers, setup helpers, salespeople, clerical personnel, etc.), and production hours needed for factory employees. Labor costs are computed from items such as union labor contracts, minimum wage laws, fringe benefit costs, payroll taxes, and bonus arrangements. The various personnel amounts are shown, as appropriate, in the direct labor budget, manufacturing overhead budget, or selling and administrative budget.

Direct Labor Budget

Midlothian Corp.'s management has reviewed the staffing requirements and has developed the direct labor cost estimates shown in Exhibit 8–10 for the first quarter of 2008. Factory direct labor costs are based on standard hours of labor needed to produce the units in the production budget. The average wage rate includes the direct labor payroll rate, payroll taxes, and fringe benefits; these items usually add between 25 and 30 percent to the base labor cost. All compensation is paid in the month in which it is incurred.

Overhead Budget

Overhead costs are the third production cost that must be budgeted by month and for the quarter. Midlothian Corp. has determined that machine hours are the best predictor of overhead costs and has prepared the overhead budget shown in Exhibit 8–11. Ten units can be produced per machine hour.

In estimating overhead, all fixed and variable costs must be specified, and mixed costs must be separated into their fixed (a) and variable (b) components. Each overhead amount shown is calcu-

EXHIBIT 8–9

Purchases Budget for the Three Months and Quarter Ending March 31, 2008

	January	February	March	Quarter
Units to be produced (from Exhibit 8–8)	29,900	28,250	32,950	91,100
+ Ending inventory (10% of next month's production)	2,825	3,295	3,450[a]	3,450
= Total whole units needed	32,725	31,545	36,400	94,450
− Beginning inventory	(3,130)[b]	(2,825)	(3,295)	(3,130)
= Finished units for which purchases are required	29,595	28,720	33,105	91,420
STEEL PURCHASES				
Finished units	29,595	28,720	33,105	91,420
× Pounds needed per unit	× 1.1	× 1.1	× 1.1	× 1.1
= Total pounds to be purchased	32,554.5	31,592	36,415.5	100,562
× Price per pound	× $2.30	×$2.30	× $2.30	× $2.30
= Total cost of steel purchases	$74,875.35	$72,661.60	$83,755.65	$231,292.60

[a]April production is assumed to be 34,500 units.
[b]Beginning inventory of raw material (RM) was 3,443 pounds; each unit requires 1.1 pounds, so there was enough RM for 3,130 units, or 10% of the following month's production.

EXHIBIT 8–10

Direct Labor Budget for the Three Months and Quarter Ending March 31, 2008

	January	February	March	Total
Units to be produced	29,900	28,250	32,950	91,100
× Standard hours allowed	× 0.025	× 0.025	× 0.025	× 0.025
= Total hours allowed	747.50	706.25	823.75	2,277.50
× Average wage rate (including fringe benefits)	× $9.00	× $9.00	× $9.00	× $9.00
= Direct labor cost	$ 6,728	$ 6,356	$ 7,414	$ 20,498

Note: The costs for January and March have been rounded up to the next whole dollar, whereas the cost for February has been rounded down to the next whole dollar; these adjustments allow the quarter total to balance at a rounded up whole dollar.

lated using the $y = a + bX$ formula discussed in Chapter 3. For example, March maintenance cost is $575 fixed cost plus $988.50 ($0.30 × 3,295 estimated machine hours) variable cost for a total of $1,563 (rounded). Both total cost and cost net of depreciation are shown in the budget. The net of depreciation cost is expected to be paid in cash during the month and will affect the cash budget.

Selling and Administrative Budget

Selling and administrative (S&A) expenses can be predicted in the same manner as overhead costs. Exhibit 8–12 presents Midlothian Corp.'s first-quarter 2008 S&A budget. Sales figures, rather than production levels, are the activity measure used to prepare this budget. The company has two sales-

282

EXHIBIT 8–11
Overhead Budget for the Three Months and Quarter Ending March 31, 2008

			January	February	March	Total
Estimated machine hours (X) (Units of production ÷ 10)			2,990	2,825	3,295	9,110

	Value of					
	(fixed) *a*	**(variable)** *b*				
Overhead item						
Depreciation	$1,700	$0.00	$ 1,700	$ 1,700	$ 1,700	$ 5,100
Indirect material	0	0.20	598	565	659	1,822
Indirect labor	6,000	1.50	10,485	10,238	10,942	31,665
Utilities	500	0.10	799	783	829	2,411
Property tax	500	0.00	500	500	500	1,500
Insurance	450	0.00	450	450	450	1,350
Maintenance	575	0.30	1,472	1,423	1,563	4,458
Total cost (y)	$9,725	$2.10	$16,004	$15,659	$16,643	$48,306
Total cost net of depreciation			$14,304	$13,959	$14,943	$43,206

Note: The costs for February have been rounded up to the next whole dollar, and the costs for March have been rounded down to balance to the appropriate quarter total.

EXHIBIT 8–12
Selling and Administrative Budget for the Three Months and Quarter Ending March 31, 2008

			January	February	March	Total
Predicted sales (from Exhibit 8–7)			$150,000	$140,000	$165,000	$455,000

	Value of					
	(fixed) *a*	**(variable)** *b*				
S&A item						
Supplies	$ 0	$0.02	$ 3,000	$ 2,800	$ 3,300	$ 9,100
Depreciation	500	0.00	500	500	500	1,500
Miscellaneous	100	0.01	1,600	1,500	1,750	4,850
Compensation						
Salespeople	2,000	0.02	5,000	4,800	5,300	15,100
Administrative	9,000	0.00	9,000	9,000	9,000	27,000
Total cost (y)	$11,600	$0.05	$ 19,100	$ 18,600	$ 19,850	$ 57,550
Total cost net of depreciation			$ 18,600	$ 18,100	$ 19,350	$ 56,050

people who are paid $1,000 per month plus a 2 percent commission on sales. Administrative salaries total $9,000 per month.

Capital Budget

The master budget focuses on the short-term or upcoming fiscal period. Managers, however, must also assess long-term needs such as plant and equipment purchases and budget for those expenditures. This assessment is referred to as capital budgeting and is discussed in Chapter 15. The capital budget is prepared separately from the master budget, but, because current expenditures are involved, capital budgeting does affect the master budgeting process.

As shown in Exhibit 8–13, Midlothian Corp.'s managers have decided to purchase a new $28,000 machine in January and to pay for it in February. The machine will be placed into service in April after installation, testing, and employee training. Depreciation on the new machine will not be included in the overhead calculation until installation is complete.

Cash Budget

After the preceding budgets have been developed, a cash budget can be constructed. The cash budget could be the most important schedule prepared during the budgeting process because, without cash, a company cannot survive.

The following model can be used to summarize cash receipts and disbursements in a way that assists managers in devising appropriate financing measures to meet company needs.

LO.4
Why is the cash budget so important in the master budgeting process?

Cash Budget Model

Beginning cash balance		XXX
+ Cash receipts (collections)		XXX
= Cash available for disbursements exclusive of financing		XXX
− Cash needed for disbursements (purchases, direct labor, overhead, S&A, taxes, bonuses, etc.)		(XXX)
= Cash excess or deficiency (a)		XXX
− Minimum desired cash balance		(XXX)
= Cash needed or available for investment or loan repayment		XXX
Financing methods		
± Borrowing (repayments)	XXX	
± Issue (reacquire) capital stock	XXX	
± Sell (acquire) investments	XXX	
± Sell (acquire) plant assets	XXX	
± Receive (pay) interest or dividends	XXX	
Total impact (+ or −) of planned financing (b)		XXX
= Ending cash balance (c), where [(c) = (a) ± (b)]		XXX

Cash Receipts and Accounts Receivable

Because not all sales are made on a cash basis, managers must translate sales information into cash receipts through the use of an expected collection pattern. This process considers the collection patterns experienced in the recent past and management's judgment about changes that could disturb current collection patterns. For example, changes that could weaken current collection patterns include recessionary conditions, increases in interest rates, less strict credit-granting policies, and ineffective collection practices.

EXHIBIT 8–13

Capital Budget for the Three Months and Quarter Ending March 31, 2008

	January	February	March	Total
Acquisition—machinery	$28,000	$ 0	$0	$28,000
Cash payment for machinery	0	28,000	0	28,000

In specifying collection patterns, managers should recognize that different types of customers pay in different ways. Any sizable, unique category of clientele should be segregated. Midlothian Corp. has two types of customers: (1) cash customers who never receive a discount and (2) credit customers. Of the credit customers, manufacturers and wholesalers are allowed a 2 percent cash discount; retailers are not allowed the discount.

Midlothian Corp. has determined from historical data that the collection pattern diagrammed in Exhibit 8–14 is applicable to its customers. Of each month's sales, 20 percent will be for cash, and 80 percent will be on credit. The 40 percent of the credit customers who are allowed the discount pay in the month of the sale. Collections from the remaining credit customers are as follows: 20 percent in the month of sale, 50 percent in the month following the sale, and 29 percent in the second month following the sale. Uncollectible accounts amount to 1 percent of the credit sales that do not take a discount.

Using the sales budget, information on November and December 2007 sales, and the collection pattern, management can estimate cash receipts from sales during the first three months of 2008. Management must have November and December sales information because collections for credit sales extend over three months, meaning that collection of some of the previous year's sales occur in the current year. Midlothian Corp.'s November and December sales were $125,000 and $135,000, respectively. Using Midlothian's expected collection pattern, projected monthly collections in the first quarter of 2008 are shown in Exhibit 8–15.

The amounts for November and December collections can be reconciled to the 12/31/07, balance sheet (Exhibit 8–6), which indicated a balance of $69,840 in Accounts Receivable. This amount appears in the collection schedule as follows:

December 31, 2007, Balance in Accounts Receivable

January collections of November sales	$17,400
Estimated November bad debts	600
January collections of December sales	32,400
February collections of December sales	18,792
Estimated December bad debts	648
December 31, 2007, Accounts Receivable balance	$69,840

EXHIBIT 8–14
Collection Pattern for Sales

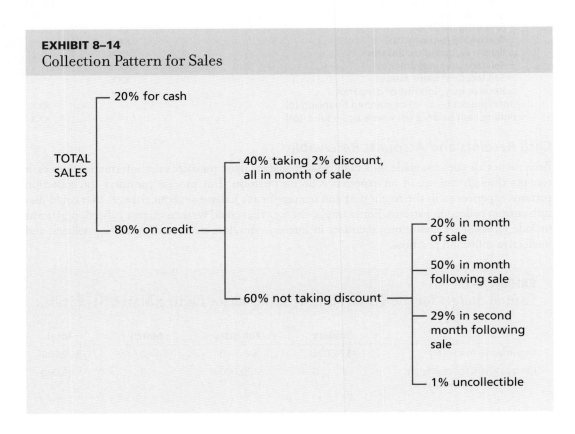

EXHIBIT 8–15

Cash Collections for the Three Months and Quarter Ending March 31, 2008

	January	February	March	Total	Discount	Uncollectible
From						
November 2007 sales						
$125,000(0.8)(0.6)(0.29)	$ 17,400			$ 17,400		
$125,000(0.8)(0.6)(0.01)						$ 600
December 2007 sales						
$135,000(0.8)(0.6)(0.5)	32,400			32,400		
$135,000(0.8)(0.6)(0.29)		$ 18,792		18,792		
$135,000(0.8)(0.6)(0.01)						648
January 2008 sales						
$150,000(0.2)	30,000			30,000		
$150,000(0.8)(0.4)(0.98)	47,040N*			47,040	$ 960	
$150,000(0.8)(0.6)(0.2)	14,400			14,400		
$150,000(0.8)(0.6)(0.5)		36,000		36,000		
$150,000(0.8)(0.6)(0.29)			$ 20,880	20,880		
$150,000(0.8)(0.6)(0.01)						720
February 2008 sales						
$140,000(0.2)		28,000		28,000		
$140,000(0.8)(0.4)(0.98)		43,904N		43,904	896	
$140,000(0.8)(0.6)(0.2)		13,440		13,440		
$140,000(0.8)(0.6)(0.5)			33,600	33,600		
March 2008 sales						
$165,000(0.2)			33,000	33,000		
$165,000(0.8)(0.4)(0.98)			51,744N	51,744	1,056	
$165,000(0.8)(0.6)(0.2)			15,840	15,840		
Totals	$141,240	$140,136	$155,064	$436,440	$2,912	$1,968

*N stands for "net of discount." To determine the gross amount, divide the net amount by 0.98 (i.e., 100% − 2%).

January 2008 sales of $150,000 are used to illustrate the collection calculations in Exhibit 8–15. The first line for January represents cash sales of 20 percent of total sales, or $30,000. The next line represents the 80 percent of the customers who buy on credit and who take the discount:

Sales to credit customers (80% of $150,000)	$120,000
Sales to customers allowed discount (40% × $120,000)	$ 48,000
− Discount taken by customers (0.02 × $48,000)	(960)
= Net collections from customers allowed discount	$ 47,040

The third line reflects the 60 percent of credit customers who paid in the month of sale but were not allowed the discount. The remaining amounts in Exhibit 8–15 are computed similarly.

After the cash collections schedule has been prepared, balances for Accounts Receivable, Allowance for Uncollectibles, and Sales Discounts can be projected. These T-accounts for Midlothian Corp. follow. Balances will be used to prepare budgeted, quarter-end 2008 financial statements. For illustrative purposes only, all sales are initially recorded as Accounts Receivable. Immediate cash collections are then deducted from the Accounts Receivable balance.

Accounts Receivable (A/R)

12/31/07 Balance (Exhibit 8–6)	69,840	Collections in January from beginning A/R ($17,400 + $32,400)	49,800
January 2008 sales (Exhibit 8–7)	150,000	Cash sales in January (Exhibit 8–15)	30,000
		Credit collections subject to discount (cash received, $47,040)	48,000
		Credit collections not subject to discount	14,400
February 2008 sales (Exhibit 8–7)	140,000	Collections in February from beginning A/R	18,792
		Cash sales in February (Exhibit 8–15)	28,000
		Collections in February from Jan. sales	36,000
		Credit collections subject to discount (cash received, $43,904)	44,800
		Credit collections not subject to discount	13,440
March 2008 sales (Exhibit 8–7)	165,000	Cash sales in March (Exhibit 8–15)	33,000
		Collections in March from January sales	20,880
		Collections in March from February sales	33,600
		Credit collections subject to discount (cash received, $51,744)	52,800
		Credit collections not subject to discount	15,840
3/31/08 Balance	85,488		

Allowance for Uncollectible Accounts

		12/31/07 Balance (Exhibit 8–6)	1,248
		January estimate (Exhibit 8–15)	720
		February estimate [$140,000(80%)(60%)(1%)]	672
		March estimate [$165,000(80%)(60%)(1%)]	792
		3/31/08 Balance	3,432

Sales Discounts

January discounts	960	
February discounts	896	
March discounts	1,056	
3/31/08 Balance	2,912	

Note that the estimated uncollectible accounts from November 2007 through March 2008 have not been written off as of the end of the first quarter of 2008. Companies continue to make collection efforts for a substantial period before accounts are acknowledged as truly worthless. Thus, these receivables may remain on the books for six months or more from the original sales date. When accounts are written off, Accounts Receivable and the Allowance for Uncollectibles will both decrease; however, there will be no income statement impact relative to the write-off.

Cash Disbursements and Accounts Payable

Using the purchases information from Exhibit 8–9, management can prepare a cash disbursements schedule for Accounts Payable. Midlothian Corp. buys all raw material on account. It pays for 40 percent of each month's purchases in the month of purchase and is allowed a 2 percent discount for prompt payment. The remaining 60 percent is paid in the month following purchase, and no discounts are taken.

Exhibit 8–16 presents the first-quarter 2008 cash disbursements information for purchases. The December 31, 2007, Accounts Payable balance of $42,504 (Exhibit 8–6) represents 60 percent of December purchases of $70,840. All amounts have been rounded to whole dollars.

Accounts payable activity is summarized in the following T-account. The March 31 balance represents 60 percent of March purchases that will be paid during April.

EXHIBIT 8–16

Cash Disbursements for Accounts Payable for the Three Months and Quarter Ending March 31, 2008

Payment for Purchases of	January	February	March	Total	Discount
December 2007	$42,504			$ 42,504	
January 2008 (from Exhibit 8–9)					
$74,875.35(0.40)(0.98)	29,351N*			29,351	$ 599
$74,875.35(0.60)		$44,925		44,925	
February 2008 (from Exhibit 8–9)					
$72,661.60(0.40)(0.98)		28,483N		28,483	581
$72,661.60(0.60)			$43,597	43,597	
March 2008 (from Exhibit 8–9)					
$83,755.65(0.40)(0.98)			32,832N	32,832	670
Total disbursements for A/P	$71,855	$73,408	$76,429	$221,692	$1,850

*N stands for "net of discount." The total amount of gross purchases paid for in the month of purchase is the sum of the net of discount payment plus the amount shown on the same line in the Discount column.

Accounts Payable

		12/31/07 Balance (Exhibit 8–6)	42,504
January payments for December purchases (Exhibit 8–16)	42,504	January 2008 purchases (Exhibit 8–9)	74,875
January payments for January purchases subject to discount (cash paid, $29,351)	29,950	February 2008 purchases (Exhibit 8–9)	72,661
February payments for January purchases (Exhibit 8–16)	44,925	March 2008 purchases (Exhibit 8–9)	83,756
February payments for February purchases subject to discount (cash paid, $28,483)	29,064		
March payments for February purchases (Exhibit 8–16)	43,597		
March payments for March purchases subject to discount (cash paid, $32,832)	33,502		
		3/31/08 Balance	50,254

Purchases Discounts

	January discounts	599
	February discounts	581
	March discounts	670
	3/31/08 Balance	1,850

Given the cash receipts and disbursements information for Midlothian Corp., the cash budget model is used to formulate the cash budget shown in Exhibit 8–17. The company has established $10,000 as its desired minimum cash balance. There are two primary reasons for having a desired minimum cash balance: one is internal; the other is external. The first reason reflects the uncertainty associated with the budgeting process. Because managers cannot budget with absolute precision, they maintain a "cushion" to protect the company from potential errors in forecasting collections and payments. The second reason is that the company's banks may require a minimum cash balance in relation to an open line of credit.

EXHIBIT 8–17
Cash Budget for the Three Months and Quarter Ending March 31, 2008

	January	February	March	Total
Beginning cash balance	$ 10,000	$ 10,753	$ 10,211	$ 10,000
Cash collections (Exhibit 8–15)	141,240	140,136	155,064	436,440
Cash available exclusive of financing	$151,240	$150,889	$165,275	$446,440
Disbursements				
Accounts payable (for purchases, Exhibit 8–16)	$ 71,855	$ 73,408	$ 76,429	$221,692
Direct labor (Exhibit 8–10)	6,728	6,356	7,414	20,498
Overhead (Exhibit 8–11)*	14,304	13,959	14,943	43,206
S&A expenses (Exhibit 8–12)*	18,600	18,100	19,350	56,050
Total disbursements	$111,487	$111,823	$118,136	$341,446
Cash excess (inadequacy)	$ 39,753	$ 39,066	$ 47,139	$104,994
Minimum balance desired	(10,000)	(10,000)	(10,000)	(10,000)
Cash available (needed)	$ 29,753	$ 29,066	$ 37,139	$ 94,994
Financing				
Borrowings (repayments)	$ 0	$ 0	$ 0	$ 0
Issue (reacquire) stock	0	0	0	0
Sell (acquire) investments	(29,000)	(1,000)	8,000	(22,000)†
Sell (acquire) plant assets	0	(28,000)	0	(28,000)
Receive (pay) interest‡	0	145	150	295
Receive (pay) dividends	0	0	(45,000)	(45,000)
Total impact of planned financing	$ (29,000)	$ (29,855)	$ (36,850)	$ (94,705)
Ending cash balance	$ 10,753	$ 10,211	$ 10,289	$ 10,289

*These amounts are net of depreciation.
†This is the net result of investments and disposals of investments.
‡Interest is calculated assuming a 6 percent annual rate (0.005 percent per month) and investments and disposals of investments are made at the end of the month in $1,000 increments.

For simplicity, it is assumed that any investments or sales of investments are made in end-of-month $1,000 increments. Interest on company investments at 6 percent per annum or .005 percent per month is added to the company's bank account at month's end.

Exhibit 8–17 indicates that Midlothian Corp. expects a $39,753 excess of cash available over disbursements in January. Such an excess, however, does not consider the need for the $10,000 minimum balance. Thus, the company has $29,753 available. It will use $29,000 of that amount to purchase temporary investments at the end of January.

In February, Midlothian Corp. again will meet its desired minimum cash balance, pay for the machine, and make an additional $1,000 temporary investment. In March, Midlothian will have enough excess cash available, coupled with the liquidation of $8,000 of investments, to pay the $45,000 dividend declared in 2007.

Cash flow provides the short-run source of power in a business to negotiate and act. In addition to preparing and executing a sound cash budget, a business can take other measures. Exhibit 8–18 offers some suggestions in this regard for small businesses, although the same prescriptions are applicable to businesses of all sizes.

EXHIBIT 8–18
Ten Ways to Improve Small Business Cash Flow

Cash flow is the lifeblood of any small business. A healthy stream is essential if a business is to succeed. In general, the key is to accelerate the flow of money coming in and delay what goes out. Having written credit and collection policies can also help. Here are 10 tips a business can use to improve cash flow.

1. **Establish sound credit practices.** Before dealing with a new customer, always get at least three trade references and one bank reference. Credit reports, available from Dun and Bradstreet and others, report on a company's general financial health as well as how quickly—or slowly—it pays its bills. Never give credit until you are comfortable with a customer's ability to pay.

2. **Expedite fulfillment and shipping.** Fill orders accurately and efficiently, and then use the quickest means available to deliver products and services to customers. Unnecessary delays can add days or weeks to customer payments.

3. **Bill promptly and accurately.** The faster you mail an invoice, the faster you will be paid. When possible, send an invoice with the order. If deliveries do not automatically trigger an invoice, establish a set billing schedule, preferably weekly. Check invoices for accuracy before mailing them. All invoices should include a payment due date. An invoice without payment terms may fall to the bottom of a customer's pile of bills.

4. **Offer discounts for prompt payment.** Given an incentive, some customers will pay sooner rather than later. Trade discounts typically give 1– 2 percent off the total amount due if customers pay in 10 days.

5. **Aggressively follow up on past due accounts.** As soon as a bill becomes overdue, call the customer and ask when you can expect payment. Keep a record of the conversation and the customer's response. Set a follow-up date in the event the promised payment is not received. Ask delinquent customers with genuine financial problems to try to pay at least a small amount every week. When necessary, don't hesitate to seek professional help from an attorney or collection agency.

6. **Deposit payments promptly.** Don't let checks sit in a drawer waiting to be deposited. The sooner you make a deposit, the sooner you can put the money to work for your business. If you are really serious about speeding up your cash flow, a post office box or bank lockbox can accelerate receipt of checks.

7. **Seek better payment terms from suppliers and banks.** Better payment terms from suppliers are the simplest way to slow down a company's cash outflow. Whereas most suppliers provide 30-day terms, 60 or 90 days are sometimes available, though it might mean changing suppliers. Better credit terms translate into borrowing money interest free. Some banks also could be willing to restructure business loans to make them easier to repay.

8. **Keep a tight control on inventory.** Less cash tied up in inventory generally means better cash flow. Although some suppliers offer deeper discounts on volume purchases, if inventory sits on the shelf too long, it ties up money that could be put to better use elsewhere.

9. **Review and reduce expenses.** Take a critical look at all expenses. If you're not sure an expense is necessary, hold back until you are confident it will have a favorable impact on the bottom line. Consider ways to decrease operating costs, such as switching from a weekly to a biweekly payroll to reduce payroll processing costs. Be careful not to cut costs that could hurt profits. For instance, rather than cutting the marketing budget, redirect the money to areas where it will have a more positive impact.

10. **Pay bills on time, but never before they are due.** The basic rule is to take as long as you are allowed to pay bills—without incurring late fees or interest charges. Make an exception to this rule only when you are offered a trade discount for early payment.

Source: "10 Ways to Improve Small Business Cash Flow," *Journal of Accountancy* (March 1, 2000), http://www.aicpa.org/pubs/jofa/mar2000/checklist .htm (last accessed 8/6/07). Copyright 2000 by American Institute of Certified Public Accountants. Reproduced with permission of American Institute of Certified Public Accountants in the format Textbook via Copyright Clearance Center.

Budgeted Financial Statements

The final step in the budgeting process is the development of budgeted financial statements for the period. These financial statements reflect the results that will be achieved if the estimates and assumptions used for all previous budgets actually occur. Such statements allow management to determine whether the predicted results are acceptable. If results are not acceptable, management has the opportunity to make adjustments before the beginning of the period for which the budget is being prepared.

When expected net income is unacceptably low, management can investigate the possibility of raising selling prices or finding ways to decrease costs. Any changes considered by management might have related effects that must be included in the revised projections. For example, raising selling prices could decrease volume. Alternatively, cost reductions from using lower-grade material could increase spoilage during production or cause a decline in demand. With the availability of computer software, changes in budget assumptions and their resultant effects can be simulated quickly and easily.

Cost of Goods Manufactured Schedule

In a manufacturing environment, management must prepare a schedule of cost of goods manufactured before it can prepare an income statement. This schedule is necessary to determine cost of

LO.5
How and why are budgeted financial statements prepared at the end of the budgeting process?

goods sold. Using information from previous budgets, Midlothian Corp.'s budgeted cost of goods manufactured schedule is shown in Exhibit 8–19. Because it was assumed that no beginning or ending Work in Process Inventories exist, cost of goods manufactured equals the manufacturing costs of the period. Had a partially completed Work in Process Inventory existed, the computations would be more complex and would have involved the use of equivalent units of production (discussed in Chapter 6).

Income Statement

Midlothian Corp.'s budgeted income statement for the first quarter of 2008 is presented in Exhibit 8–20. This statement uses much of the information previously developed in determining the revenues and expenses for the period.

Balance Sheet

On completion of the income statement, a March 31, 2008, balance sheet (Exhibit 8–21) can be prepared.

Statement of Cash Flows

Information found on the income statement, balance sheet, and cash budget is also used to prepare a statement of cash flows (SCF). This statement can assist managers in judging the company's ability to handle fixed cash outflow commitments, adapt to adverse changes in business conditions, and undertake new commitments. Furthermore, because the SCF identifies the relationship between net income and net cash flow from operations, it assists managers in judging the quality of the company's earnings.

EXHIBIT 8–19
Budgeted Cost of Goods Manufactured Schedule

Midlothian Corp.
Budgeted Cost of Goods Manufactured Schedule
For Quarter Ending March 31, 2008

Beginning Work in Process Inventory		$ 0
Cost of raw material used		
Beginning balance (Exhibit 8–6)	$ 7,919	
Net purchases (from Accounts Payable		
and Purchases Discounts, p. 287)	229,442	
Total raw material available	$237,361	
Ending balance of raw material (Note A; rounded)	(8,729)	
Cost of raw material used	$228,632	
Direct labor (Exhibit 8–10)	20,498	
Factory overhead (Exhibit 8–11)	48,306	
Total costs to be accounted for		297,436
Ending Work in Process Inventory		(0)
Cost of goods manufactured		$297,436
Note A: Steel		
Ending balance (Exhibit 8–9) required for finished goods	3,450	
Pounds per unit	× 1.1	
Total pounds of raw material required	3,795	
Price per pound	× $2.30	
Ending balance of raw material	$8,728.50	

EXHIBIT 8–20
Budgeted Income Statement

Midlothian Corp.
Budgeted Income Statement
For Quarter Ending March 31, 2008

Sales (Exhibit 8–7)			$455,000
Less sales discounts (p. 286)			(2,912)
Net sales			$452,088
Cost of goods sold			
Finished goods—12/31/07 (Exhibit 8–6)		$ 4,800	
Cost of goods manufactured (Exhibit 8–19)		297,436	
Cost of goods available for sale		$302,236	
Finished goods—3/31/08 (Note A)		(5,120)	(297,116)
Gross margin			$ 154,972
Expenses			
Uncollectible accounts expense (Note B)		$ 2,184	
S&A expenses (Exhibit 8–12)		57,550	(59,734)
Income from operations			$ 95,238
Other revenue—interest earned (Exhibit 8–17)			295
Income before income taxes			$ 95,533
Income taxes (assumed rate of 40%)			(38,213)
Net income			$ 57,320

Note A

Beginning finished goods units		1,500
Production (Exhibit 8–8)		91,100
Units available for sale		92,600
Sales (Exhibit 8–7)		(91,000)
Ending finished goods units		1,600
Cost per unit:		
Material	$2.53	
Conversion (assumed)	0.67	× $3.20
Cost of ending inventory		$ 5,120

Note B

Total sales	$455,000
× % credit sales	× 0.80
= Credit sales	$364,000
× % not taking discount	× 0.60
= Potential bad debts	$218,400
× % estimated uncollectible	× 0.01
= Estimated bad debts	$ 2,184

Whereas the cash budget is essential to current cash management, the budgeted SCF gives managers a more comprehensive view of cash flows by rearranging them into three distinct major activities (operating, investing, and financing). Such a rearrangement permits management to judge whether the specific anticipated flows are consistent with the company's strategic plans. In addition, the SCF would incorporate a schedule or narrative about significant noncash transactions if any have occurred, such as an exchange of stock for land.

EXHIBIT 8–21
Budgeted Balance Sheet

Midlothian Corp.
Budgeted Balance Sheet
March 31, 2008

ASSETS			LIABILITIES AND STOCKHOLDERS' EQUITY		
Current Assets			**Current Liabilities**		
Cash (Exhibit 8–17)		$ 10,289	Accounts Payable (p. 287)		$ 50,254
Accounts Receivable (p. 286)	$ 85,488		Income Tax Payable		
Less Allowance for Uncollectibles			(Exhibit 8–20)		38,213
(p. 286)	(3,432)	82,056	Total Current Liabilities		$ 88,467
Inventories					
Raw Material (3,795 pounds)					
(Exhibit 8–19, Note A, rounded)	$ 8,729				
Finished Goods (1,600 units)					
(Exhibit 8–20, Note A)	5,120	13,849			
Investment		22,000			
Total Current Assets		$128,194			
Plant Assets			**Stockholders' Equity**		
Property, Plant, and Equipment					
(Note A)	$398,000		Common Stock	$180,000	
Less Accumulated Depreciation			Retained Earnings	161,127	341,127
(Note B)	(96,600)	301,400	Total Liabilities and Stockholders' Equity		$429,594
Total Assets		$429,594			
Note A					
Beginning balance (Exhibit 8–6)	$370,000				
Purchased new machine	28,000				
Ending balance	$398,000				
Note B					
Beginning balance (Exhibit 8–6)	$ 90,000				
Factory depreciation (Exhibit 8–11)	5,100				
S&A depreciation (Exhibit 8–12)	1,500				
Ending balance	$ 96,600				
Note C					
Beginning balance (Exhibit 8–6)	$103,807				
Net income (Exhibit 8–20)	57,320				
Ending balance	$161,127				

The operating section (prepared on either a direct or an indirect basis) of the SCF is acceptable for external reporting. The direct basis uses pure cash flow information (cash receipts and cash disbursements) for operating activities. The operating section of a SCF prepared on an indirect basis begins with net income and makes reconciling adjustments to arrive at cash flow from operations. Exhibit 8–22 provides a statement of cash flows for Midlothian Corp. using the information from the cash budget in Exhibit 8–17. The bottom of Exhibit 8–22 shows the indirect method of presenting operating cash flows and uses the information from the budgeted income statement in Exhibit 8–20 and the balance sheets in Exhibits 8–6 and 8–21.

EXHIBIT 8–22
Budgeted Statement of Cash Flows

Midlothian Corp.
Budgeted Statement of Cash Flows
For Quarter Ending March 31, 2008

Operating activities			
Cash collections from sales		$436,440	
Interest earned		295	
Total		$436,735	
Cash payments			
For inventory:			
Raw material	$221,692		
Direct labor	20,498		
Overhead	43,206	(285,396)	
For S&A costs		(56,050)	
Net cash inflow from operating activities			$ 95,289
Investing activities			
Purchase of plant asset		$ (28,000)	
Short-term investment		(22,000)	
Net cash outflow from investing activities			(50,000)
Financing activities			
Dividends paid		$ (45,000)	
Net cash outflow from financing activities			(45,000)
Net increase in cash			$ 289
Beginning balance of cash (1/1/06)			10,000
Ending balance of cash (12/31/06)			$ 10,289
Alternative (indirect) basis for operating activities			
Net income		$ 57,320	
+ Depreciation (Exhibit 8–11 and Exhibit 8–12)	$ 6,600		
− Increase in net Accounts Receivable ($68,592 − $82,056)	(13,464)		
− Increase in total inventory ($12,719 − $13,849)	(1,130)		
+ Increase in Taxes Payable ($0 − $38,213)	38,213		
+ Increase in Accounts Payable ($42,504 − $50,254)	7,750	37,969	
= Net cash inflow from operating activities		$ 95,289	

Midlothian Corp.'s cash flow from operations ($95,289) is low compared to net sales revenue of $455,000; however, its net income per net sales dollar (20.9 percent) is fairly high. Midlothian Corp. may want to review its hinge sales price and its production costs. Another issue that might be discussed is whether such a high proportion of retained earnings should be paid out as dividends.

Concluding Comments

LO.6
What benefits are provided by a budget?

A well-prepared master budget can act as:

1. a guide to help managers align activities and resource allocations with organizational goals;
2. a vehicle to promote employee participation, cooperation, and departmental coordination;

3. a tool to enhance conduct of the managerial functions of planning, controlling, problem solving, and performance evaluating;
4. a basis on which to sharpen management's responsiveness to changes in both internal and external factors; and
5. a model that provides a rigorous view of future performance of a business in time to consider alternative measures.

Because of its fundamental nature in the budgeting process, sales demand must be predicted as accurately and with as many details as possible. Sales forecasts should indicate type and quantity of products to be sold, geographic locations of the sales, types of buyers, and timing of sales. Such detail is necessary because different products require different production and distribution facilities, different customers have different credit terms and payment schedules, and different seasons or months can necessitate different shipping schedules or methods.

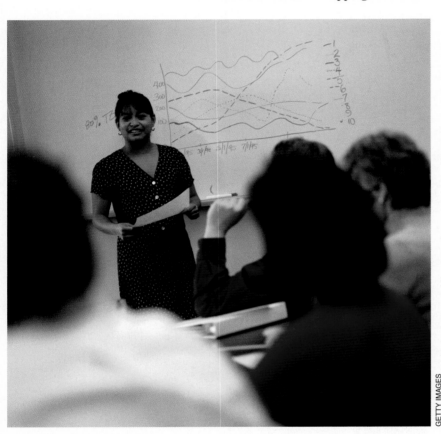

Estimated sales demand has a pervasive impact on the master budget. To arrive at a valid prediction, managers use as much information as is available and can combine several estimation approaches. Combining prediction methods provides managers a way to confirm estimates and reduce uncertainty. Some ways of estimating future demand are (1) canvassing sales personnel for a subjective consensus, (2) making simple extrapolations of past trends, (3) using market research, and (4) employing statistical and other mathematical models.

Care should be taken to use realistic, rather than optimistic or pessimistic, forecasts of revenues and costs. Firms can develop computer models that allow repetitive simulations to be run after changes are made to one or more factors. These simulations permit managers to review results that would be obtained under various circumstances.

The master budget is normally prepared for a year and is detailed by quarters and months within those quarters. Some companies use a **continuous budget** (or **rolling budget**), which means that an ongoing 12-month budget is presented by successively adding a new budget month (12 months into the future) as each current month expires. Such a process allows management to work, at any time, within the present 1-month component of a full 12-month annual budget. Continuous budgets make the planning process less sporadic. Rather than having managers "go into the bud-

Sales forecasts should specify type and quantity of product to be sold, geographic locations of sales, buyer types, and when sales are to be made.

geting period" at a specific time, they are continuously involved in planning and budgeting. Benefits of a continuous budget include:

■ eliminating a fiscal year mind-set by recognizing that business is an ongoing operation and should be managed accordingly;

■ allowing management to take corrective steps as forecasted business conditions change;

■ eliminating the unrealistic "gap" that occurs with the first iteration of each annual budget;

■ reducing or eliminating the budget planning process that occurs at the end of each fiscal year.[3]

Another recent survey jointly conducted by the American Productivity Quality Center and IBM Global Business Services found that companies focusing on "planning, budgeting and forecast-

[3]Stephen Hunt and Paula Klein, "Budgets Roll with the Times," *Optimize* (August 2003), p. 85.

ing as a business strategy are higher performers in all areas than those that focus on cost accounting, control and cost management."[4] The study also showed that high-performing organizations tend to complete their budgeting cycle in 30 days compared to 90 days in low-performing organizations—and most of the high-performers used rolling budgets.

If actual results differ from plans, managers should find the causes of the differences and then consider budget revisions. Arrangements usually cannot be made rapidly enough to revise the current month's budget. However, under certain circumstances and if desired, managers could revise future months' budgets. If actual performance deviates substantially from what was expected, management could adjust the budget, depending on the variance causes.

If the causes are beyond the organization's control and are cost related, management can decide to revise budget cost estimates upward or downward to be more realistic. If the causes are internal (such as the sales staff not selling the product), management can leave the budget in its original form so that the effects of operational control are visible in the comparisons. Regardless of whether the budget is revised, managers should commend those individuals responsible for positive performance and communicate the effects of such performance to other related departments. For example, if the sales force has sold significantly higher quantities of product than expected in the original budget, production and purchasing must be notified to increase the number of units manufactured and amount of raw material purchased.

Budget revisions, however, may not occur because the system in use is too complex or detailed. In a 2005 survey of senior finance executives in the United States, the United Kingdom, France, and Germany, almost two-thirds of the respondents said they update their financial plans only twice a year or less. The survey also showed that respondents' current forecasting systems were highly inaccurate: 84 percent said their financial forecasts were off by 5 percent or more; 54 percent said the error differential was 10 percent or more. Exhibit 8–23 provides other information obtained from the same survey respondents relative to the primary objectives of their planning processes.

EXHIBIT 8–23
Primary Objectives of the Planning Process

Objective	ALL COMPANIES Rank	ALL COMPANIES % of Respondents	LARGE COMPANIES Rank	LARGE COMPANIES % of Respondents	MID-SIZE COMPANIES Rank	MID-SIZE COMPANIES % of Respondents	SMALL COMPANIES Rank	SMALL COMPANIES % of Respondents
Driving operational plans from strategic plans	1	76	1	77	2	80	1	69
Cost control	2	57	5	59	1	81	2	60
Prioritizing investments; allocating resources	3	62	4	60	3	68	3	60
Maximizing revenue or gross margin	4	60	3	60	4	60	4	57
Optimizing return on capital	5	54	2	62	5	54	5	47
Increasing accountability of line managers	6	43	6	46	6	44	7	40
Accuracy	7	42	7	43	7	41	6	43
Determining incentive targets	8	30	8	21	8	38	8	34
Other objectives	9	5	9	6	9	9	9	4

Source: Fay Hansen, Laurie Brannen, and John Cummings, "Global Planning Perspectives," *Business Finance* (March 2006), p. 12. Copyright © 2006 Penton Media.

[4]Anonymous, "Focus on Control, Cost Management Falls Short," *Business Finance* (March 2007), p. 11.

When budgets are used for performance evaluations, management often encounters the problem of budget slack, which is the intentional underestimation of revenues and/or overestimation of expenses. Slack can be incorporated into the budget during the development process in a participatory budget. A participatory budget is developed through joint decision making by top management and operating personnel. However, slack is not often found in imposed budgets, which top management prepares with little or no input from operating personnel. After the budget has been developed, operating personnel are informed of the budget goals and constraints. The budgeting process can be represented by a continuum with participatory budgets on one end and imposed budgets on the other. Only rarely is a budget either purely participatory or purely imposed. The budget process in a company is usually defined by the degree to which the process is either participatory or imposed.

Having budget slack allows subordinate managers to achieve their objectives with less effort than would be necessary without the slack. Slack also creates problems because of the significant interaction of the budget factors. For example, if sales volumes are understated or overstated, problems in the production, purchasing, and personnel areas can arise.

Top management can try to reduce slack by tying actual performance to the budget through a bonus system. Operating managers are rewarded with large bonuses for budgeting relatively high performance levels and achieving those levels. If performance expectations are low, achievement of that performance is either not rewarded or only minimally rewarded. Top management must be aware that budget slack has a tremendous negative impact on organizational effectiveness and efficiency.

Managers could consider expanding their budgeting process to recognize the concepts of activities and cost drivers in a manner consistent with activity-based management. An activity budget can be created by mapping the line items in the conventional budget to a list of activities. This type of budget can increase managerial awareness of non-value-added (NVA) activities and make managers question why such costs are being incurred. Based on this enhanced awareness, managers can plan to reduce or eliminate some of these NVA activities.

Appendix

LO.7
How does a budget manual facilitate the budgeting process?

Budget Manual

To be useful, a budget requires a substantial amount of time and effort from the persons who prepare it. This process can be improved by the availability of an organizational budget manual, which is a detailed set of information and guidelines about the budgetary process. These materials are frequently maintained on a company's intranet so they are available continuously and can be economically updated. The manual should include:

1. statements of the budgetary purpose;
2. a listing of specific budgetary activities to be performed;
3. a calendar of scheduled budgetary activities;
4. sample budgetary forms; and
5. original, revised, and approved budgets.

The statements of budgetary purpose and desired results communicate the reasons behind the process. These statements should flow from general to specific details. An example of a general statement of budgetary purpose follows: "The cash budget provides a basis for planning, reviewing, and controlling cash flows from and for various activities; this budget is essential to the preparation of a pro forma statement of cash flows." Specific statements could include references to minimum desired cash balances and periods of intense cash needs.

Budgetary activities should be listed by position rather than person because the responsibility for actions should be assigned to the individual holding the designated position at the time the budget is being prepared. The manual's activities section should indicate who has the final authority for revising and approving the budget. Budget approval can be delegated to a budget committee or reserved by one or several members of top management.

The budget calendar helps coordinate the budgetary process; it should indicate a timetable for all budget activities and be keyed directly to the activities list. The timetable for the budget process is unique to each organization. The larger the organization, the more time will be needed to gather and coordinate information, identify weak points in the process or the budget itself, and take corrective action. The calendar should also indicate control points for the upcoming periods at which budget-to-actual comparisons are to be made and feedback provided to managers who are responsible for operations.

Sample forms and templates are extremely useful because they provide for consistent presentations of budget information from all individuals, making summarization of information easier and quicker. The templates should be easy to understand and may include standardized worksheets or programmed spreadsheets that allow managers to update historical information to arrive at budgetary figures. This section of the budget manual may also provide standard cost tables for items on which the organization has specific guidelines or policies. For example, in estimating employee fringe benefit costs, the company rule of thumb could be 25 percent of base salary. Or, if company policy states that each salesperson's per diem meal allowance is $50, meal expenses would be budgeted as estimated travel days multiplied by $50.

The final section of the budget manual contains the budgets generated during the budgeting process. Numerous budgets may be proposed and rejected prior to actual budget acceptance and implementation. Understanding this revision process and why changes were made is helpful for future planning. The final approved master budget is included in the budget manual as a control document.[5]

[5]In the event of changes in economic conditions or strategic plans, the "final" budget can be revised during the budget period.

Comprehensive Review Module

Chapter Summary

1. Budgeting is important so that managers

    - can visualize the future and move in a focused direction.

    - plan effectively.

    - agree on and communicate organizational goals and objectives.

    - develop quantitative translations of strategic goals and objectives.

    - commit resources to desired activities.

    - establish financial performance indicators of success.

    - engage people to participate in the planning process.

    - produce a spirit of cooperation among employees and organizational departments or divisions.

    - control operations and resource usage.

2. Strategic planning and budgeting are related because they

    - tie the long-term and short-term (tactical) plans together.

    - use the same underlying key variables to identify success.

    - harmonize external considerations and internal factors.

    - require current information regarding the economy, business environment, technological developments, and available resources.

3. The starting point of a master budget

    - reflects a single level of output demand (sales).

- is static to facilitate the numerous arrangements (employees, suppliers, prices, resource quality, capacity availability, etc.) that must be in place before operations begin.

4. Master budget components

- include the

  ➢ sales budget, which reflects units and dollars.

  ➢ production budget, which adds unit sales to desired units in ending Finished Goods Inventory and subtracts units in beginning Finished Goods Inventory. There is no production budget for retail or service companies.

  ➢ purchases budget, which adds production requirements to desired ending raw material or component inventories and subtracts beginning raw material or component inventories; purchases quantities are then multiplied by raw material or component costs.

  ➢ personnel budget, which indicates the number and types of employees needed as well as salary amounts and wage rates.

  ➢ direct labor budget, which multiplies production by standard hours allowed and then by average wage rate.

  ➢ overhead budget, which is the sum of (variable manufacturing OH costs multiplied by the quantity of the cost driver) and fixed manufacturing OH costs.

  ➢ selling and administrative budget, which is the sum of (variable nonmanufacturing costs multiplied by the quantity of the cost driver) and fixed nonmanufacturing costs.

  ➢ capital budget, which contains fixed asset purchases and payment points for those assets.

  ➢ cash budget, which reflects all cash received from and spent on items included in the other budgets.

- are combined to prepare budgeted financial statements for management review and assessment.

5. The cash budget is critical to the master budgeting process because it

- is essential for an organization to have cash to survive.

- translates accrual-based information (such as sales revenues and purchases) into actual cash flows.

- can help indicate whether credit practices are effective (i.e., whether customers are paying for purchases within the designated credit period).

- allows the organization to forecast when cash borrowings could be necessary or when cash investments could be made (and for how long).

- can be used to help prepare the budgeted statement of cash flows.

6. Budgets benefit organizations by

- guiding management to align organizational goals with activities and resource commitments.

- promoting employee participation and departmental coordination.

- enhancing the managerial functions of planning, controlling, and problem solving.

- allowing management to forecast future performance to determine acceptability and, if necessary, provide an opportunity for change.

- providing a benchmark against which to judge how effectively and efficiently organizational goals were met.

7. (Appendix) A budget manual should include

- statements of the budgetary purposes;

- a listing of specific budgetary activities to be performed;

- a calendar of scheduled budgetary activities;

- sample budgetary forms; and

- original, revised, and approved budgets.

Potential Ethical Issues

1. Using a single budgeting system globally that may conflict with national cultures

2. Knowingly introducing, or allowing employees to introduce, budget slack into the process that will misallocate resources or generate inequitable performance rewards

3. Treating short-term conditions as long-term conditions (or vice versa) to intentionally distort the effects of those conditions on the budgeting process

4. Pressuring employees to meet or exceed budget goals through the use of fraudulent accounting techniques

5. Encouraging employee participation in the budgeting process merely to disregard that input

6. Engaging in "backwards budgeting" that justifies management decisions that have been previously determined—especially relative to employee layoffs and plant closures

7. Disregarding contingencies during budget preparation because those conditions cannot be quantified with extreme accuracy

8. Ignoring external performance measures and benchmarks (such as comparisons with competitors or customer satisfaction levels) and concentrating only on meeting internally selected financial targets

9. Allowing lower-level managers to participate in the budgeting process but not communicating necessary "big picture" assumptions—causing participatory budgets to be unrealistic and managers to fail to achieve targets

10. Promoting a "spend-it-or-lose-it" attitude, whereby organizational units that engage in cost savings are punished, and units that spend unnecessarily are rewarded, in future periods

11. Mandating a uniform "across-the-board" organizational budget cut without giving employees the opportunity to justify current expenditures or to suggest alternative methods of achieving the desired cost reduction ▲

Solution Strategies

Sales Budget
Units of sales
× Selling price per unit
= Dollars of sales

Production Budget
Units of sales
+ Units desired in ending inventory
− Units in beginning inventory
= Units to be produced

Purchases Budget
Units to be produced
+ Units desired in ending inventory
− Units in beginning inventory
= Units to be purchased

Direct Labor Budget
Units to be produced*
× Standard time allowed per unit
= Standard labor time allowed
× Per hour direct labor cost
= Total direct labor cost

*Converted to direct material component requirements, if necessary

Overhead Budget
Predicted activity base
× Variable overhead rate per unit of activity
= Total variable overhead cost
+ Fixed overhead cost
= Total overhead cost

Selling and Administrative Budget
Predicted sales dollars (or other variable measure)
× Variable S&A rate per dollar (or other variable measure)
= Total variable S&A cost
+ Fixed S&A cost
= Total S&A cost

Schedule of Cash Receipts (Collections) from Sales
Dollars of credit sales for month
× Percent collection for month of sale

= Credit to accounts receivable for month's sales
− Allowed and taken sales discounts
= Receipts for current month's credit sales
+ Receipts from cash sales
+ Current month's cash receipts for prior months' credit sales
= Cash receipts for current month

Schedule of Cash Payments for Purchases
  Units to be purchased
× Cost per unit
= Total cost of purchases
× Percent payment for current purchases
= Debit to accounts payable for month's purchases
− Purchase discounts taken
= Cash payments for current month's purchases
+ Cash purchases
+ Current month's payments for prior months' purchases
= Cash payments for accounts payable for current month

Cash Budget
  Beginning cash balance
+ Cash receipts (collections)
= Cash available for disbursements
− Cash needed for disbursements:
    Cash payments for accounts payable for month
    Cost of compensation
    Total cost of overhead minus depreciation
    Total S&A cost minus depreciation
= Cash excess or deficiency
− Minimum desired cash balance
= Cash needed or available for investment or financing
± Various financing measures
= Ending cash balance

Demonstration Problem

The July 31, 2008, balance sheet for Zachary Cabinets Inc. includes the following information:

Cash	$30,000 debit
Accounts Receivable	92,000 debit
Allowance for Uncollectible Accounts	1,000 credit
Merchandise Inventory	6,000 debit

The firm's management has designated $15,000 as the firm's monthly minimum cash balance. Other information about Zachary Cabinets follows:
- Revenues of $200,000, $240,000, and $275,000 are expected for August, September, and October, respectively. All goods are sold on account.
- The collection pattern for accounts receivable is 55 percent in the month of sale, 44 percent in the month following the sale, and 1 percent uncollectible.
- Cost of goods sold (CGS) approximates 60 percent of sales revenues.
- Management wants to end each month with units costing the equivalent of 5 percent of the following month's cost of goods sold. Unit costs are assumed to be stable.
- All accounts payable for inventory are paid in the month of purchase.
- Other monthly expenses are $26,000, which includes $4,000 of depreciation but does not include uncollectible accounts expense.
- Investments of excess cash are made in $5,000 increments.

Required:
a. Forecast the August cash collections.
b. Forecast the August and September cost of purchases.
c. Prepare the cash budget for August including the effects of financing (borrowing or investing).

Solution to Demonstration Problem

a. August Collections

From July ($92,000 − $1,000)	$ 91,000
From August ($200,000 × 0.55)	110,000
Total	$201,000

b.

August CGS = $200,000 × 0.60 = $120,000
September CGS = $240,000 × 0.60 = $144,000; desired August EI = $144,000 × 0.05 = $7,200
October CGS = $275,000 × 0.6 = $165,000; desired September EI = $165,000 × 0.05 = $8,250

	August	September
Sales	$200,000	$240,000
Cost of goods sold (60%)	$120,000	$144,000
Add desired ending balance	7,200	8,250
Total needed	$127,200	$152,250
Less beginning balance	(6,000)	(7,200)
Cost of purchases	$121,200	$145,050

c. August Cash Budget

Beginning cash balance		$ 30,000
August collections		201,000
Total cash available for disbursements		$ 231,000
Disbursements		
Purchase of merchandise	$121,200	
Other monthly expenses ($26,000 − $4,000)	22,000	(143,200)
Cash excess or deficiency (a)		$ 87,800
Less minimum cash balance desired		(15,000)
Cash available		$ 72,800
Financing:		
Acquire investment (b)		(70,000)
Ending cash balance (c); (c = a − b)		$ 17,800

Key Terms

budget, *p. 272*

budgeting, *p. 272*

budget manual, *p. 296*

budget slack, *p. 296*

continuous budget, *p. 294*

financial budget, *p. 275*

imposed budget, *p. 296*

master budget, *p. 275*

operating budget, *p. 275*

participatory budget, *p. 296*

rolling budget, *p. 294*

strategic planning, *p. 272*

tactical planning, *p. 272*

Questions

1. How does budgeting provide important information to managers and operating personnel?

2. How does the strategic plan influence preparation of the master budget?

3. Distinguish between a tactical plan and a strategic plan. How are these plans related?

4. After a master budget has been prepared, what is its role in managerial control?

5. Differentiate between the operating and financial budgets that are contained in a master budget. Why are both types needed?

6. Discuss the sequence in which the major components of the master budget are prepared. Why is it necessary to prepare the components in such a sequence?
7. Why is a firm's production budget influenced by the finished goods inventory policy?
8. Assume that in preparing the cash budget, the accountant discovers that a cash shortage will likely occur in a specific month. What actions might the accountant recommend to management to deal with the cash shortage?
9. The cash budget and the budgeted statement of cash flows both provide information about cash. What information about cash is common to these two sources, and what information is unique to the two sources?
10. Why is continuous (rolling) budgeting becoming more popular?
11. If the majority of companies find that their forecasts are inaccurate, why should managers engage in budgeting at all?
12. What is budgetary slack, and what might top managers do to rid their firms' budgets of slack?
13. (Appendix) Why is it helpful for a company to prepare a budget manual?

Exercises

14. **LO.1 (Strategic planning)** Before a budget can be prepared, company management considers "what if" changes that might occur during the forecast period. Prepare a list of five possible questions about changes that you might want to consider if you were a manager in a
    a. global manufacturing company.
    b. local retailer.
15. **LO.1 (Strategic planning; research)** When engaging in strategic planning, company management often prepares a SWOT analysis.
    a. What is a SWOT analysis and why is it useful in the planning process?
    b. Choose an organization with which you are familiar and develop a SWOT analysis for that organization.
16. **LO.1 (Tactical planning)** People, as well as businesses, need to budget. Assume that you and your spouse are having difficulties living within your combined incomes. Prepare a list of at least ten recommendations on how to "do things differently" to help manage your finances.
17. **LO.2 (Revenue budget)** In 2008, University Credit Union (UCU) had $2,000,000 in business loans at an average interest rate of 5.5 percent as well as $1,600,000 in consumer loans with an average rate of 10 percent. UCU also has $500,000 invested in government securities that pay interest at an average rate of 2 percent.
    For 2009, UCU estimates that the volume of business loans will increase to $3,000,000, and the interest rate will rise to 6.5 percent. It projects that consumer loans will be $2,000,000 and have an average interest rate of 13 percent. The credit union's government security investment will be $800,000 and will bear an average interest rate of 3.5 percent. What is UCU's projected revenue for 2009?
18. **LO.2 (Sales budget)** The sales manager of Guding Co. estimates that the company will sell 1,000,000 units of product RI#698 during 2009. The selling price of RI#698 is expected to decline due to technology changes during the year and estimates of the sales price are as follows:

1st Quarter	2nd Quarter	3rd Quarter	4th Quarter
$15	$14	$12	$10

In talking with customers, the sales department discovered that sales quantities per quarter could vary substantially and, as such, the sales manager has prepared the following three sets of quarterly sales projections:

	1st Quarter	2nd Quarter	3rd Quarter	4th Quarter	Total
Scenario A	300,000	150,000	320,000	230,000	1,000,000
Scenario B	200,000	350,000	125,000	325,000	1,000,000
Scenario C	265,000	240,000	400,000	95,000	1,000,000

If the sales department for Guding Co. is able to influence customers, which of the potential sales scenarios would be most financially beneficial to Guding Co.? Would that scenario possibly cause the company any difficulties?
19. **LO.3 (Production budget)** Alonzo Inc. has the following projected unit sales for the first four months of 2009:

January	51,200
February	48,000
March	64,000
April	76,800

Company policy is to have an ending monthly inventory equal to 10% of next month's estimated sales; however, this criterion was not in effect at the end of 2008. Ending inventory at that time was 7,000 units. Determine the company's production requirements for each month of the first quarter of 2009.

20. **LO.3 (Production budget)** Katherine Company's sales budget has the following unit sales projections for each quarter of calendar year 2009:

January–March	540,000
April–June	680,000
July–September	490,000
October–December	550,000
Total	2,260,000

Sales for the first quarter of 2010 are expected to be 600,000 units. Ending inventory of finished goods for each quarter is scheduled to equal 5 percent of the next quarter's budgeted sales. The company is expected to be in compliance with this policy as of December 31, 2008. Develop a quarterly production budget for 2009 and for the year in total.

21. **LO.3 (Material purchases budget)** Santa Fe Boots has projected sales of 42,960 pairs of cowboy boots in October. Each pair of boots requires 2.5 linear feet of leather. The beginning inventory of leather and boots, respectively, are 2,000 yards and 2,152 pairs. Santa Fe Boots wants to have 3,000 yards of leather and 5,800 pairs of boots on hand at the end of October due to high sales projections for the holiday season. To convert linear feet of leather to yards, simply divide by three because the leather comes in a standard width. If Santa Fe Boots has no beginning or ending Work in Process Inventory, how many yards of leather must the company purchase in October?

22. **LO.3 (Material purchases budget)** Ida OK Company has budgeted sales of 380,000 feet of its concrete culvert products for June 2009. Each foot of product requires 8 pounds of concrete ($0.11 per pound) and 15 pounds of gravel ($0.05 per pound). Actual beginning inventories and projected ending inventories follow:

	June 1	June 30
Finished Goods Inventory (in feet)	24,500	20,000
Concrete (in pounds)	82,000	68,600
Gravel (in pounds)	65,300	92,500

a. How many pounds of concrete does Ida OK Company plan to purchase in June? What will be the cost of those purchases?

b. How many pounds of gravel does Ida OK Company plan to purchase in June? What will be the cost of those purchases?

23. **LO.3 (Production and related schedules)** Clark Corp. manufactures and sells plastic boxes and trays. Sales are projected to be evenly spread over the annual period. Estimated product sales and material needs for each unit of product follow:

	Boxes	Trays
Annual sales	84,000	60,000
Material A	2.0 pounds	1.0 pound
Material B	3.0 pounds	4.0 pounds
Direct labor	2.0 hours	0.5 hour

Overhead is applied at a rate of $1.60 per direct labor hour.

	Expected Beginning Inventories	Desired Ending Inventories
Material A	2,000 pounds	2,500 pounds
Material B	5,000 pounds	3,400 pounds
Material A	2,000 pounds	2,500 pounds
Material B	5,000 pounds	3,400 pounds
Boxes	1,000 units	1,200 units
Boxes	1,000 units	1,200 units
Trays	300 units	450 units

Material A costs $0.05 per pound, and Material B costs $0.08 per pound. Prepare the following information:

a. Production schedule by product and in total.

b. Purchases budget in units by product and in total as well as in dollars.

c. Direct labor budget in hours by product and in total.

d. Overhead to be charged to production by product and in total.

24. LO.4 (Cash collections) Anthony Inc. is preparing its first-quarter monthly cash budget for 2009. The following information is available about actual 2008 sales and expected 2009 sales:

November	December	January	February	March
$41,500	$38,000	$39,500	$44,000	$29,500

Tracing collections from prior year monthly sales and discussions with the credit manager helped develop a profile of collection behavior patterns.

Of a given month's sales, 40 percent is typically collected in the month of sale. Because the company terms are 1 percent (end of month) net 30, all collections within the month of sale are net of the 1 percent discount. Of a given month's sales, 30 percent is collected in the month following the sale. The remaining 30 percent is collected in the second month following the month of the sale. Bad debts are negligible and should be ignored.

a. Prepare a schedule of cash collections for Anthony Inc. for January, February, and March 2009.

b. Calculate the Accounts Receivable balance at March 31, 2009.

25. LO.4 (Cash collections) Myra Catlett is president of Catlett Corp. The interior design firm is doing quite well, and Ms. Catlett has decided to finally take a month's vacation with her family to Australia, New Zealand, and Antarctica. Ms. Catlett has researched the trip and determined that the total cost of the trip for her family will be approximately $100,000—she wants to go first-class on everything! Her travel agent says that a 10% discount can be obtained if Ms. Catlett can write a check for the cost of the trip by the end of November. Ms. Catlett says she sees no problem in doing that given that the company's expected billings for October, November, and December, respectively, are $200,000, $130,000, and $30,000 (when Ms. Catlett will be on vacation).

As of October 31, 2009, Catlett Corp.'s accountant has estimated cash collections from billings to be 15% in the month of sale, 55% in the month following sale, and 30% in the second month following the sale. Accounts Receivable at September 30, 2009, are $22,000; all of that amount is expected to be collected in October. Average monthly business costs sum to $45,000.

a. What are Catlett Corp.'s expected cash collections for October, November, and December?

b. Can Ms. Catlett pay for her trip in November and obtain the 10% discount? Explain.

c. What would you suggest that Ms. Catlett do?

26. LO.4 (Cash collections, accounts receivable) Nino's Catering is developing a forecast for June 2009 cash receipts from sales. Total sales for June 2009 are expected to be $850,000. Of each month's sales, 75 percent is expected to be on credit. The Accounts Receivable balance at May 31 is $173,250, of which $135,000 represents the remainder of May credit sales. There are no receivables from months prior to April 2009. The collection pattern of Nino's Catering credit sales is 60 percent in the month of sale, 25 percent in the month following the sale, and 15 percent in the second month following the sale. Nino's Catering has no uncollectible accounts.

a. What were total sales for April 2009?

b. What were credit sales for May 2009?

c. What are projected cash collections for June 2009?

d. What is the expected balance of Accounts Receivable at June 30, 2009?

27. LO.4 (Cash budget) The October 1, 2009, Accounts Receivable balance for Langely Landscaping is $607,500. Of that balance, $450,000 represents remaining accounts receivable from September billings. The normal collection pattern for the firm is 20 percent of billings in the month of service, 55 percent in the month after service, and 22 percent in the second month following service. The remaining billings are uncollectible. October billings are expected to be $900,000.

a. What were August billings for Langely Landscaping?

b. What amount of September billings is expected to be uncollectible?

c. What are the firm's projected cash collections in October?

28. **LO.4 (Cash balance)** The following budgeted May 2009 cash information is available for Cameron Corp.:

Net after-tax income	$147,000
Accrued income tax expense	41,000
Decrease in Accounts Receivable for month	4,000
Decrease in Accounts Payable for month	3,500
Depreciation expense	28,100
Estimated bad debts expense	2,050
Dividends declared in May	15,000
Dividends declared in January and paid in May	20,000

If Cameron's May 1, 2009, cash balance is $13,500, what is the company's budgeted May 31, 2009, cash balance?

29. **LO.4 (Cash disbursements)** The following budgeted information about Enid Co. is available for September 2009:

Sales for September	$2,400,000
Gross profit on sales	35%
Wages expense for September	$312,500
Increase in Wages Payable for September	$37,000
Other cash expenses for September	$235,250
Decrease in Accounts Payable during September	$40,000
Decrease in Merchandise Inventory during September	$33,750

Enid Co. only uses its Accounts Payable for inventory purchases.
a. How much does Enid Co. expect to pay for inventory in September 2009?
b. What are total budgeted cash disbursements for September 2009?

30. **LO.4 (Cash budget)** The following cash budget is for the second quarter of next year. Complete the missing numbers on the cash budget, assuming that the accountant has requested a minimum cash balance of $3,500 at the start of each month. All borrowings, repayments, and investments are made in even $500 amounts. No borrowings or investments exist at the beginning of April.

	April	May	June	Total
Beginning cash balance	$ 3,700	$?	$?	$?
Cash receipts	8,200	10,100	?	?
Total cash available	$?	$?	$20,500	$38,900
Cash disbursements				
Payments on account	$?	$ 3,900	$ 5,700	$?
Wages expense	5,000	?	6,200	17,300
Overhead costs	4,000	4,600	?	13,000
Total disbursements	$10,300	$?	$16,300	$?
Cash excess (deficiency)	$?	$?	$?	$?
Minimum cash balance	(3,500)	(3,500)	?	?
Cash available (needed)	$?	$(4,400)	$?	$ (5,800)
Financing				
Borrowings (repayments)	$ 2,000	$?	$ (500)	$?
Acquire (sell) investments	0	0	?	?
Receive (pay) interest	0	0	?	(10)
Ending cash balance	$ 3,600	$?	$?	$ 3,690

31. **LO.3 & LO.4 (Various budgets)** Compute the required answer for each of the following independent situations.
a. For next year, Harrington Suits projects $20,000,000 of sales and total fixed manufacturing costs of $5,000,000. Variable manufacturing costs are estimated at 40 percent of sales. Assuming no change in inventory, what is the company's projected cost of goods sold?
b. Bea Company has projected the following information for October:

Sales	$900,000
Gross profit (based on sales)	35%
Increase in Merchandise Inventory in October	$40,000
Decrease in Accounts Payable for October	$34,000

What are expected cash disbursements for inventory purchases for October?
c. Buda Corp. is attempting to budget its overhead costs for March 2009. Overhead is a mixed cost with the following flexible budget formula: $y = \$320,000 + \$14.25X$, where X represents machine hours. Fixed overhead includes $125,000 of depreciation. If Buda Corp. expects to utilize 12,000 machine hours in March, what is

the company's budgeted March overhead cost? How much cash will the company pay for budgeted overhead in March?

d. O'Neill Enterprises expects to begin 2009 with a cash balance of $10,000. Cash collections from sales and on account during the year are expected to be $468,600. The firm wants to maintain a minimum cash balance of $5,000. Budgeted cash disbursements for the year are as follows:

Payoff of note payable	$ 45,000
Interest on note payable	4,200
Purchase of computer system	14,800
Payments for operating costs and inventory purchases	190,000
Direct labor payments	100,000
Cash overhead payments	127,000
Cash selling and administrative payments	93,000

The company can, if necessary, borrow in $1,000 amounts. Prepare a cash budget for 2009.

32. LO.5 (Budgeted income statement) Last year's income statement for Cosper Company follows:

Sales (50,000 × $10)		$ 500,000
Cost of goods sold		
Direct material	$200,000	
Direct labor	100,000	
Overhead	50,000	(350,000)
Gross profit		$ 150,000
Expenses		
Selling	$ 52,000	
Administrative	60,000	(112,000)
Income before taxes		$ 38,000

This year, unit sales are expected to increase by 25 percent; material and labor costs are expected to increase by 10 percent per unit. Overhead is applied to production based on a percentage of direct labor costs. Fixed selling expenses total $12,000; the remainder varies with sales dollars. All administrative costs are fixed.

Management desires to earn 10 percent on sales this year and will adjust the unit selling price if necessary. Develop a budgeted income statement for the year for Cosper Company that incorporates the indicated changes.

33. LO.3–LO.5 (Budgeted accounts receivable; cash; and income statement) In preparing its budget for July, Rosario Inc. has the following information available:

Accounts Receivable at June 30	$750,000
Estimated credit sales for July	900,000
Estimated collections in July for credit sales in July and prior months	660,000
Estimated write-offs in July for uncollectible credit sales	27,000
Estimated provision for uncollectible accounts for credit sales in July	20,000

a. What is the projected balance of Accounts Receivable at July 31?
b. Which of these amounts (if any) will affect the cash budget?
c. Which of these amounts (if any) will affect the budgeted income statement for July?

(CPA adapted)

34. LO.5 (Budgeted income statement) The following budget information is available for Lohman Corp. for May 2009.

- Sales are expected to be $400,000. All sales are on account, and a provision for bad debts is made monthly at 3 percent of sales.
- Inventory was $35,000 on April 30 and an increase of $10,000 is planned for May.
- All inventory is marked to sell at cost plus 60 percent.
- Estimated cash disbursements for selling and administrative expenses for the month are $55,000.
- Depreciation for May is projected at $8,000.

Prepare a budgeted income statement for Lohman Corp. for May 2009.

(CPA adapted)

35. LO.5 (Budgeted income statement) Alyssa Co. is planning to purchase a new piece of production equipment. The equipment will increase fixed overhead by $350,000 per year in depreciation but reduce variable expenses per unit by 20 percent. Budgeted 2009 sales of the company's products are 120,000 units at an average selling price of $25. Variable expenses are currently 65 percent of sales, and fixed costs total $700,000 per year.

a. Prepare an income statement assuming that the new equipment is not purchased.
b. What is the current variable cost per unit? What will be the new variable cost per unit if the equipment is purchased?

c. Prepare an income statement assuming that the new equipment is purchased.

d. Should the equipment be acquired?

36. **LO.6 (Budgeting attitudes)** Many managers believe that if all amounts in their spending budgets are not spent during a period, they will lose allocations in future periods and that they will receive little or no recognition for the cost savings.

Prepare an essay that discusses the behavioral and ethical issues involved in a spend-it-or-lose-it attitude. Include in your discussion the issue of negotiating budget allocation requests prior to the beginning of the period.▲

37. **LO.6 (Continuous budgeting)** You own a small boat manufacturing company. At a recent manufacturers' association meeting, you overheard one of the other company owners say that he liked using a continuous budgeting process. Discuss in a report to your top management group what you believe are the advantages and disadvantages of continuous budgeting for your company.

38. **LO.6 (Research)** Find the Web page for a charitable organization that operates internationally as well as domestically.

a. Prepare a list of activities in which this organization is currently involved.

b. What would be the greatest challenges in budgeting for such an organization?

c. Do you think not-for-profits should be as concerned as for-profit organizations with budgeting? Explain the rationale for your answer.

39. **LO.6 (Planning)** High-level executives have often indicated that competitors' actions are the top external factor affecting their businesses and their business plans.

a. Why are competitors' actions so important to business planning?

b. How would competitors' actions affect a business's internal planning?

c. What other internal and external factors are key elements in a business's budgeting process?

Problems

40. **LO.3 (Production and purchases budgets)** Birmingham Inc. has prepared the following unit sales forecast for 2009:

	January–June	July–December	Total
Sales	580,000	720,000	1,300,000

Estimated ending Finished Goods Inventories are 25,000 units at December 31, 2008; 36,000 units at June 30, 2009; and 60,000 units at December 31, 2009.

In manufacturing a unit of this product, Birmingham Inc. uses 3 pounds of Material A and 0.75 gallons of Material B. Materials A and B cost, respectively, $2.50 per pound and $1.80 per gallon.

The company carries no Work in Process Inventory. Ending inventories of direct material are projected as follows:

	December 31, 2008	June 30, 2009	December 31, 2009
Material A (in pounds)	120,000	135,000	142,000
Material B (in gallons)	45,000	35,000	38,000

Prepare a production and purchases budget for each semiannual period of 2009.

41. **LO.3 (Production and purchases budgets)** George Gorges Manufacturing has budgeted monthly unit sales for the first quarter of 2009 as follows:

	January	February	March	Total
Sales in units	36,000	32,000	30,000	98,000

April sales are expected to be 28,000.

The following are estimates of finished units and pounds of direct material at month's end for December 2008 and the first quarter of 2009:

	December	January	February	March
Finished units	9,000	8,000	7,500	7,000
Direct material M	6,750	6,000	5,625	5,250
Direct material N	4,500	4,000	3,750	3,500
Direct material O	9,000	8,000	7,500	7,000

The production process requires 3 pounds of Material M, 2 pounds of Material N, and 4 pounds of Material O.

a. Prepare a monthly production and purchases budget for the first quarter of 2009.

b. The production supervisor wants to purchase new production equipment for 2009. Such equipment would largely replace the current labor-intensive production system. Write a memo to corporate management explaining why new production equipment could affect the production and purchases budget.

c. Who should be consulted to determine the new material requirements per unit if the new production equipment is installed?

42. **LO.3 & LO.4 (Production; purchases; cash disbursements)** Yi Fan's Tea Company has budgeted sales of 300,000 cans of iced tea mix during June 2009 and 375,000 cans during July. Production of the mix requires 14 ounces of tea and 2 ounces of sugar. June 1 inventories of tea and sugar are as follows:

Iced tea mix	12,300 cans of finished product
Tea	750 pounds
Sugar	200 pounds

The company generally carries an inventory equal to 5 percent of the following month's needs for finished goods; the ending inventory for raw material should equal 5 percent of Finished Goods Inventory. Assuming that the ending inventory policy is met, answer the following questions.

a. How many cans of iced tea mix will be produced in June?

b. How many pounds of tea will be purchased in June?

c. How many pounds of sugar will be purchased in June?

d. If tea and sugar cost $2.50 and $0.18 per pound, respectively, what dollar amount of purchases is budgeted for June?

e. If the company normally pays for 30 percent of its budgeted purchases during the month of purchase and takes a 2 percent discount, what are budgeted cash disbursements in June for June purchases?

43. **LO.3 (Production; purchases; direct labor & OH budgets)** Earhart Reliable Tools makes two products that use similar raw materials: #587Q and #253X. Estimated production needs for a unit of each product follow:

	#587Q	#253X
Steel (in pounds)	2	4
Wood (in board feet)	.5	.2
Direct labor (in hours)	3	6
Machine hours	.5	3

Estimated sales in units by product for 2009 are 40,000 of #587Q and 15,000 of #253X. Additionally, estimated beginning and desired ending inventory quantities for 2009 follow:

	Beginning	Ending
Steel (in pounds)	1,000	700
Wood (in board feet)	400	300
#587Q (units)	400	320
#253X (units)	600	450

Overhead is applied to production at the rate of $16 per machine hour and the direct labor wage rate is $12.50 per hour. Prepare the production, purchases, direct labor, and overhead budgets for 2009.

44. **LO.3 & LO.4 (Production; purchases; cash budgets)** Iberville Furniture Co. makes bookstands and expects sales and collections for the first three months of 2009 to be as follows:

	January	February	March	Total
Sales quantity (units)	6,400	5,200	7,400	19,000
Revenue	$128,000	$104,000	$148,000	$380,000
Collections	$116,200	$ 81,300	$101,500	$299,000

The December 31, 2008, balance sheet revealed the following selected account balances: Cash, $18,320; Direct Material Inventory, $8,230; Finished Goods Inventory, $23,200; and Accounts Payable, $5,800. The Direct Material Inventory balance represents 1,580 pounds of scrap iron and 1,200 bookstand bases. The Finished Goods Inventory consists of 1,220 bookstands.

Each bookstand requires 2 pounds of scrap iron, which costs $3 per pound. Bookstand bases are purchased from a local lumber mill at a cost of $2.50 per unit. Company management decided that, beginning in 2009, the ending balance of Direct Material Inventory should be 25 percent of the following month's production requirements and that the ending balance of Finished Goods Inventory should be 20 percent of the next month's sales. Sales for April and May are expected to be 8,000 bookstands per month.

The company normally pays for 75 percent of a month's purchases of direct material in the month of purchase (on which it takes a 1 percent cash discount). The remaining 25 percent is paid in full in the month following the month of purchase.

Direct labor is budgeted at $0.70 per bookstand produced and is paid in the month of production. Total cash manufacturing overhead is budgeted at $14,000 per month plus $1.30 per bookstand. Total cash selling and administrative costs equal $13,600 per month plus 10 percent of sales revenue. These costs are all paid in the month of incurrence. In addition, the company plans to pay executive bonuses of $25,000 in January 2009 and make an estimated quarterly tax payment of $4,800 in March 2009.

Management requires a minimum cash balance of $15,000 at the end of each month. If the company borrows funds, it will do so only in $1,000 multiples at the beginning of a month at a 12 percent annual interest rate. Loans are to be repaid at the end of a month in multiples of $1,000. Interest is paid only when a repayment is made. Investments are made in $1,000 multiples at the end of a month, and the return on investment is 8 percent per year.

a. Prepare a production budget by month and in total for the first quarter of 2009.
b. Prepare a direct material purchases budget by month and in total for the first quarter of 2009.
c. Prepare a schedule of cash payments for purchases by month and in total for the first quarter of 2009.
d. Prepare a combined payments schedule for manufacturing overhead and selling and administrative cash costs for each month and in total for the first quarter of 2009.
e. Prepare a cash budget for each month and in total for the first quarter of 2009.

45. **LO.1, LO.3, & LO.4 (Budgeted sales and S&A; other computations)** Cairo Caftans has projected cost of goods sold (CGS) for June 2009 of $1,200,000. Of this amount, $75,000 represents fixed overhead costs. Total variable costs for the company each month average 70 percent of sales. The company's cost to retail (CGS to sales) percentage is 60 percent, and the company normally generates net income equal to 15 percent of sales. All purchases and expenses (except depreciation) are paid in cash: 65 percent in the month incurred and 35 percent in the following month. Depreciation is $37,500 per month.

a. What are Cairo Caftans' expected sales for June?
b. What are Cairo Caftans' expected variable selling and administrative costs for June?
c. What are Cairo Caftans' total fixed costs? How much of this is fixed selling and administrative cost?
d. Cairo Caftans normally collects 55 percent of its sales in the month of sale and the rest in the next month. What are expected cash receipts and disbursements related only to June's transactions?

46. **LO.4 (Cash budget)** The March 31, 2009, balance sheet of Lazee Fair follows:

Assets		Liabilities and Stockholders' Equity		
Cash	$ 12,000	Accounts Payable		$ 70,200
Accounts Receivable (net of Allowance for Uncollectibles of $1,440)	34,560			
Merchandise Inventory	52,400	Common Stock	$25,000	
Plant Assets (net of Accumulated Depreciation of $60,000)	36,000	Retained Earnings	39,760	64,760
		Total Liabilities and Stockholders' Equity		
Total Assets	$134,960			$134,960

Additional information about the company follows:
- Expected sales for April and May are $120,000 and $130,000, respectively. All sales are made on account.
- The monthly collection pattern from the month of sale forward is 50 percent, 48 percent, and 2 percent uncollectible.
- Cost of goods sold is 65 percent of sales.
- Purchases each month are 60 percent of the current month's sales and 30 percent of the next month's projected sales. All purchases are paid for in full in the month following purchase.
- Dividends of $10,000 will be declared and paid in April 2009.
- Selling and administrative expenses each month are $21,500, of which $4,000 is depreciation.
- Investments and borrowings must be made in $1,000 amounts.

a. What will be budgeted cash collections for April 2009?
b. What will be the Merchandise Inventory balance at April 30, 2009?

   c. What will be the projected balance in the Retained Earnings account at April 30, 2009?

   d. If the company wishes to maintain a minimum cash balance of $8,000, how much will be available for investment or need to be borrowed at the end of April 2009?

47. LO.4 (Cash budget) Kalamazoo-Rama typically makes 80 percent of its sales on credit. The company bills sales twice monthly, on the 10th of the month for the last half of the prior month's sales and on the 20th of the month for the first half of the current month's sales. All sales are made with terms of 2/10, n/30. Based on past experience, accounts receivable are collected as follows:

Within the discount period	80%
On the 30th day	18%
Uncollectible	2%

Sales for May 2009 were $600,000, and projected sales for the next four months are

June	$800,000
July	700,000
August	800,000
September	600,000

Kalamazoo-Rama's average profit margin on its products is 30 percent of selling price.

   Kalamazoo-Rama purchases merchandise to meet the current month's sales demand and to maintain a desired monthly ending inventory of 25 percent of the next month's sales. All purchases are on account with terms of n/30. The company pays for one-half of a month's purchases in the month of purchase and the other half in the month following the purchase. All sales and purchases occur evenly throughout the month.

   a. How much cash can Kalamazoo-Rama plan to collect from credit sales during July 2009?

   b. How much cash can Kalamazoo-Rama plan to collect in September 2009 from sales made in August?

   c. What will be the budgeted dollar value of Kalamazoo-Rama's inventory on August 31, 2009?

   d. How much merchandise should Kalamazoo-Rama plan to purchase during June 2009?

   e. What are Kalamazoo-Rama's budgeted cash payments for merchandise during August 2009?

(CPA adapted)

48. LO.4 (Cash budget) Livingston Inc. has incurred substantial losses for several years and has decided to declare bankruptcy. The company petitioned the court for protection from creditors on March 31, 2008, and submitted the following balance sheet:

LIVINGSTON INC.
Balance Sheet
March 31, 2008

	Book Value	Liquidation Value
Assets		
Accounts Receivable	$100,000	$ 50,000
Inventories	90,000	40,000
Plant Assets (net)	150,000	160,000
Totals	$340,000	$250,000

Livingston's liabilities and stockholders' equity at this date follow:

Accounts Payable—General Creditors	$600,000
Common Stock	60,000
Retained Earnings Deficit	(320,000)
Total	$340,000

Livingston's management informed the court that the company has developed a new product and that a prospective customer is willing to sign a contract for the purchase of 10,000 units of this product during the year ending March 31, 2009, 12,000 units during the year ending March 31, 2010, and 15,000 units during the year ending March 31, 2011, at a price of $90 per unit. This product can be manufactured using Livingston's present facilities. Monthly production with immediate delivery is expected to be uniform within each year. Receivables are expected to be collected during the calendar month following sales. Unit production costs of the new product are estimated as follows:

Direct material	$20
Direct labor	30
Variable overhead	10

Fixed costs of $130,000 (excluding depreciation) are incurred per year. Purchases of direct material will be paid during the calendar month following purchase. Fixed costs, direct labor, and variable overhead will be paid as incurred. Inventory of direct material will equal 60 days' usage. After the first month of operations, 30 days' usage will be ordered each month.

The general creditors have agreed to reduce their total claims to 60 percent of their March 31, 2008, balances under the following conditions:

- Existing accounts receivable and inventories are to be liquidated immediately, with the proceeds turned over to the general creditors.
- The reduced balance of accounts payable is to be paid as cash is generated from future operations but no later than March 31, 2010. No interest will be paid on these obligations.

Under this proposed plan, the general creditors would receive $110,000 more than the current liquidation value of Livingston's assets. The court has engaged you to determine the feasibility of this plan.

Ignoring any need to borrow and repay short-term funds for working capital purposes, prepare a cash budget for the years ending March 31, 2009 and 2010, showing the cash expected to be available for paying the claims of the general creditors, the amount of payments to general creditors, and the cash remaining after payment of claims.

(CPA adapted)

49. **LO.4 (Cash budget)** Collegiate Management Education (CME) Inc. is a nonprofit organization that sponsors a wide variety of management seminars throughout the Southwest. In addition, it is heavily involved in research into improved methods of teaching and motivating college administrators. Its seminar activity is largely supported by fees, and the research program is supported by membership dues.

CME operates on a calendar-year basis and is finalizing the budget for 2009. The following information has been taken from approved plans, which are still tentative at this time:

Seminar Program

Revenue:

The scheduled number of programs should produce $12,000,000 of revenue for the year. Each program is budgeted to produce the same amount of revenue. The revenue is collected during the month the program is offered. The programs are scheduled during the basic academic year and are not held during June, July, August, or December. Of the revenue, 12 percent is generated in each of the first five months of the year and the remainder is distributed evenly during September, October, and November.

Direct expenses:

The seminar expenses are made up of three types:

- Instructors' fees are paid at the rate of 70 percent of seminar revenue in the month following the seminar. The instructors are considered independent contractors and are not eligible for CME employee benefits.
- Facilities fees total $5,600,000 for the year. They are the same for each program and are paid in the month the program is given.
- Annual promotional costs of $1,000,000 are spent equally in all months except June and July when there is no promotional effort.

Research Program

Research grants:

The research program has a large number of projects nearing completion. The main research activity this year includes feasibility studies for new projects to be started in 2010. As a result, the total grant expense of $3,000,000 for 2009 is expected to be incurred at the rate of $500,000 per month during the first six months of the year.

Salaries and Other CME Expenses

- Office lease—annual amount of $240,000 paid monthly at the beginning of each month.
- General administrative expenses—$1,500,000 annually, or $125,000 per month, paid in cash as incurred.
- Depreciation expense—$240,000 per year.
- General CME promotion—annual cost of $600,000, paid monthly.
- Salaries and benefits are as follows:

Number of Employees	Annual Cash Salary	Total Annual Salaries
1	$50,000	$ 50,000
3	40,000	120,000
4	30,000	120,000
15	25,000	375,000

5	15,000	75,000
22	10,000	220,000
50		$960,000

Employee benefits are $240,000, or 25 percent of annual salaries. Except for the pension contribution, the benefits are paid as salaries are paid. The annual pension payment of $24,000, based on 2.5 percent of total annual salaries, is due on April 15, 2009.

Other Information

- Membership income—CME has 100,000 members, each of whom pays a $100 annual fee. The fee for the calendar year is invoiced in late June.
- Collection schedule—July, 60 percent; August, 30 percent; September, 5 percent; and October, 5 percent.
- Capital expenditures—this program calls for a total of $510,000 in cash payments to be spread evenly over the first five months of 2009.
- Cash and temporary investments at January 1, 2009, are estimated at $750,000.
- a. Prepare a budget of the annual cash receipts and disbursements for 2009.
- b. Prepare a cash budget for CME for January 2009.
- c. Using the information developed in parts (a) and (b), identify two important operating problems of CME.

(CPA adapted)

50. LO.4 (Cash budget) CrossMan Corp., a rapidly-expanding crossbow distributor, is in the process of formulating plans for 2009. Joan Caldwell, director of marketing, has completed her 2009 forecast and is confident that sales estimates will be met or exceeded. The following forecasted sales figures show the growth expected and will provide the planning basis for other corporate departments.

	SALES			SALES
January	$1,800,000		July	$3,000,000
February	2,000,000		August	3,000,000
March	1,800,000		September	3,200,000
April	2,200,000		October	3,200,000
May	2,500,000		November	3,000,000
June	2,800,000		December	3,400,000

George Brownell, assistant controller, has been given the responsibility for formulating the cash flow projection, a critical element during a period of rapid expansion. The following information will be used in preparing the cash analysis:

- CrossMan has experienced an excellent record in accounts receivable collections and expects this trend to continue. The company collects 60 percent of its billings in the month after the sale and 40 percent in the second month after the sale. Uncollectible accounts are insignificant and should not be considered in the analysis.
- The purchase of crossbows is CrossMan's largest expenditure; the cost of these items equals 50 percent of sales. The company receives 60 percent of the crossbows one month prior to sale and 40 percent during the month of sale.
- Prior experience shows that 80 percent of accounts payable is paid by CrossMan one month after receipt of the purchased crossbows, and the remaining 20 percent is paid the second month after receipt.
- Hourly wages, including fringe benefits, are a function of sales volume and are equal to 20 percent of the current month's sales. These wages are paid in the month incurred.
- Administrative expenses are projected to be $2,640,000 for 2009. All of these expenses are incurred uniformly throughout the year except the property taxes. Property taxes are paid in four equal installments in the last month of each quarter. The composition of the expenses is:

Salaries	$ 480,000
Promotion	660,000
Property taxes	240,000
Insurance	360,000
Utilities	300,000
Depreciation	600,000
Total	$2,640,000

- Income tax payments are made by CrossMan in the first month of each quarter based on income for the prior quarter. CrossMan's income tax rate is 40 percent. CrossMan's net income for the first quarter of 2009 is projected to be $612,000.

- CrossMan has a corporate policy of maintaining an end-of-month cash balance of $100,000. Cash is invested or borrowed monthly, as necessary, to maintain this balance.
- CrossMan uses a calendar year reporting period.

a. Prepare a budgeted schedule of cash receipts and disbursements for CrossMan Corp., by month, for the second quarter of 2009. Ignore interest expense and/or interest income associated with the borrowing/investing activities.

b. Discuss why cash budgeting is particularly important for a rapidly expanding company such as CrossMan Corp.

c. Do monthly cash budgets ignore the pattern of cash flows within the month? Explain.

(CPA adapted)

51. **LO.4 & LO.5 (Cash budget; budgeted income statement)** Frank's Fresh Fruit Stand purchases, wholesales, and retails fresh fruits and vegetables. Company estimates reveal the following for the first three months of the company's 2009 fiscal year:

	PURCHASES	SALES
June	$66,000	$102,000
July	58,000	92,000
August	80,000	116,000

The company usually pays 60 percent of any month's purchases in the month of purchase and is granted a 2 percent discount on those payments. The remaining amount is paid in the following month, with no discount given. Other monthly payments for expenses are $24,000 plus 12 percent of sales revenue. Depreciation is $4,000 per month. The company maintains a minimum cash balance of $28,000. Borrowings and repayments must be made in $500 amounts.

All retail sales are for cash and all wholesale transactions are on credit. Experience indicates the following expected collection pattern for credit sales: 25 percent in the month of sale, 60 percent in the month following the sale, and 15 percent in the second month following the sale. The company has no debt other than what is currently owed for purchases on account.

a. Calculate the July 31 balances for Accounts Receivable and Accounts Payable.

b. Calculate the expected total cash collections in August.

c. Calculate the expected total cash disbursements in August.

d. Prepare a cash budget for August, assuming that the beginning balance of cash was $28,470.

e. Prepare a budgeted income statement for August. Assume an average gross profit rate of 40 percent and ignore income taxes.

f. Explain how and why inventory management must be different for perishable commodities than for nonperishable commodities.

52. **LO5 (Budgeted results)** Shiffer Corp. manufactures decorative, high-quality nutcrackers. All nutcrackers, regardless of design, sell for the same price, which the company has set at full production cost plus 30 percent (rounded to the nearest $5 increment). Variable production cost is $50 per unit, and total fixed costs are $2,000,000. Fixed manufacturing costs are 80 percent of total fixed costs and are allocated to the product based on the number of units produced. There are no variable selling or administrative costs. Variable and fixed costs are expected to increase by 15 and 8.75 percent, respectively, next year. Estimated production and sales are 300,000 units.

a. What is the expected full production cost per unit of Shiffer Corp.'s nutcrackers for next year?

b. What is the product's expected selling price?

c. What is budgeted income before tax using the selling price computed in part (b)?

d. What is the required selling price (rounded to the nearest dollar) for the company to earn income before tax equal to 25 percent of sales?

53. **LO.5 (Budgeted income statement and balance sheet)** The projected October 31, 2009, balance sheet for Laredo Co. follows:

ASSETS

Cash	$ 16,000,000
Accounts Receivable (net of Allowance for Uncollectibles of $4,000,000)	76,000,000
Inventory	32,000,000
Property, Plant, and Equipment (net of Accumulated Depreciation of $25,000,000)	70,000,000
Total Assets	$194,000,000

LIABILITIES AND STOCKHOLDERS' EQUITY

Accounts Payable	$165,000,000
Common Stock	100,000,000
Retained Earnings (deficit)	(71,000,000)
Total Liabilities and Stockholders' Equity	$194,000,000

Additional information is as follows:

- Sales for November and December are budgeted at $220,000,000 and $240,000,000, respectively.
- Collections are expected to be 60 percent in the month of sale, 38 percent in the following month, and 2 percent uncollectible.
- The company's gross profit is projected at 25 percent of sales.
- Purchases each month are 75 percent of the following month's projected sales. Purchases are paid in full in the month following the purchase.
- Other monthly cash expenses are $31,000,000. Monthly depreciation is $10,000,000.

    a. Prepare a budgeted income statement for November 2009.

    b. Prepare a budgeted balance sheet for November 2009.

    c. Describe any special problems this company may encounter because of its weak balance sheet. Recommend actions the firm might take to improve the balance sheet.

54. LO.2–LO.5 (Comprehensive) KneadIt produces and sells upscale mixers and breadmakers. In October 2008, KneadIt's budget department gathered the following data to meet budget requirements for 2009.

2009 PROJECTED SALES

Product	Units	Price
Mixers	60,000	$ 90
Breadmakers	40,000	140

2009 INVENTORIES (UNITS)

Product	Expected 1/1/09	Desired 12/31/09
Mixers	15,000	20,000
Breadmakers	4,000	5,000

To produce one unit of each product, the following major internal components are used (in addition to the plastic housing for products, which is subcontracted in a subsequent operation):

Component	Mixer	Breadmaker
Motor	1	1
Beater	2	4
Fuse	2	3

Projected data for 2009 with respect to components are as follows:

Component	Anticipated Purchase Price	Expected Inventory 1/1/09	Desired Inventory 12/31/09
Motor	$18.00	2,000	3,600 units
Beater	1.75	21,000	24,000 units
Fuse	2.40	6,000	7,500 units

Projected direct labor requirements for 2009 and rates are as follows:

Product	Hours per Unit	Rate per Hour
Mixers	2	$ 8
Breadmakers	3	10

Overhead is applied at a rate of $5 per direct labor hour.

    Based on these projections and budget requirements for 2009 for mixers and breadmakers, prepare the following budgets for 2009:

    a. Sales budget (in dollars).

    b. Production budget (in units).

    c. Internal components purchases budget (in units and dollars).

    d. Direct labor budget (in dollars).

    e. What is the total production cost, excluding subsequent departments, per mixer and per breadmaker?

(CPA adapted)

55. **LO.2–LO.5 (Master budget preparation)** Caputto Colors manufactures industrial dye. The company is preparing its 2009 master budget and has presented you with the following information.
   a. The December 31, 2008, balance sheet for the company follows:

CAPUTTO COLORS
Balance Sheet
December 31, 2008

Assets			Liabilities and Stockholders' Equity		
Cash		$ 5,080	Notes Payable		$ 25,000
Accounts Receivable		26,500	Accounts Payable		2,148
Raw Material Inventory		800	Dividends Payable		10,000
Finished Goods Inventory		2,104	Total Liabilities		$ 37,148
Prepaid Insurance		1,200	Common Stock	$100,000	
Building	$300,000		Paid-in Capital	50,000	
Accum. Depreciation	(20,000)	280,000	Retained Earnings	128,536	278,536
			Total Liabilities and		
Total Assets		$315,684	Stockholders' Equity		$315,684

   b. The Accounts Receivable balance at 12/31/08 represents the remaining balances of November and December credit sales. Sales were $70,000 and $65,000, respectively, in those two months.
   c. Estimated sales in gallons of dye for January through May 2009 follow:

January	8,000
February	10,000
March	15,000
April	12,000
May	11,000

   Each gallon of dye sells for $12.
   d. The collection pattern for accounts receivable is as follows: 70 percent in the month of sale, 20 percent in the first month after the sale, and 10 percent in the second month after the sale. Caputto Colors expects no bad debts and gives no cash discounts.
   e. Each gallon of dye has the following standard quantities and costs for direct material and direct labor:

1.2 gallons of direct material (some evaporation occurs during	
processing) × $0.80 per gallon	$0.96
0.5 hour of direct labor × $6 per hour	3.00

   f. Variable overhead (VOH) is applied to the product on a machine-hour basis. Processing 1 gallon of dye takes 5 hours of machine time. The variable overhead rate is $0.06 per machine hour; VOH consists entirely of utility costs. Total annual fixed overhead is $120,000; it is applied at $1 per gallon based on an expected annual capacity of 120,000 gallons. Fixed overhead per year is composed of the following costs:

Salaries	$78,000
Utilities	12,000
Insurance—factory	2,400
Depreciation—factory	27,600

   Fixed overhead is incurred evenly throughout the year.
   g. There is no beginning Work in Process Inventory. All work in process is completed in the period in which it is started. Raw Material Inventory at the beginning of the year consists of 1,000 gallons of direct material at a standard cost of $0.80 per gallon. There are 400 gallons of dye in Finished Goods Inventory at the beginning of the year carried at a standard cost of $5.26 per gallon: direct material, $0.96; direct labor, $3.00; variable overhead, $0.30; and fixed overhead, $1.00.
   h. Accounts Payable relates solely to raw material and is paid 60 percent in the month of purchase and 40 percent in the month after purchase. No discounts are received for prompt payment.
   i. The dividend will be paid in January 2009.
   j. A new piece of equipment costing $9,000 will be purchased on March 1, 2009. Payment of 80 percent will be made in March and 20 percent in April. The equipment has a useful life of three years and will have no salvage value.
   k. The note payable has a 12 percent interest rate; interest is paid at the end of each month. The principal of the note is repaid as cash is available to do so.

l. Caputto Colors' management has set a minimum cash balance at $5,000. Investments and borrowings are made in even $100 amounts. Interest on any borrowings is expected to be 12 percent per year and investments will earn 4 percent per year.

m. The ending Finished Goods Inventory should include 5 percent of the next month's needs. This is not true at the beginning of 2009 due to a miscalculation in sales for December. The ending inventory of raw materials also should be 5 percent of the next month's needs.

n. Selling and administrative costs per month are as follows: salaries, $18,000; rent, $7,000; and utilities, $800. These costs are paid in cash as they are incurred.

o. The company's tax rate is 35 percent. (Round to the nearest dollar.)

Prepare a master budget for each month of the first quarter of 2009 and pro forma financial statements as of the end of the first quarter of 2009.

56. **LO.3, LO.5, & LO.6 (Preparing and analyzing a budget)** Daniels & Co., LLP, a local accounting firm, has a formal budgeting system. The firm has five partners, two managers, four seniors, two secretaries, and two bookkeepers. The budgeting process has a bottom-line focus; that is, the budget and planning process continues to iterate and evolve until an acceptable budgeted net income is obtained. The determination of an acceptable level of net income is based on two factors: (1) the amount of salary the partners could generate if they were employed elsewhere and (2) a reasonable return on the partners' investment in the firm's net assets.

For 2009, after careful consideration of alternative employment opportunities, the partners agreed that the best alternative employment would generate the following salaries:

Partner 1	$150,000
Partner 2	225,000
Partner 3	110,000
Partner 4	90,000
Partner 5	125,000
Total	$700,000

The second input to determining the desired net income level is more complex. This part of the desired net income is based on the value of the net assets owned by the accounting firm. The partners have identified two major categories of assets: tangible and intangible. The partners have agreed that the net tangible assets are worth $230,000. The intangible assets, consisting mostly of the accounting practice itself, are worth 1.1 times gross fees billed in 2009, which totaled $1,615,000. The partners have also agreed that a reasonable rate of return on the net assets of the accounting firm is 12 percent. Thus, the partners' desired net income from return on investment is as follows:

Tangible assets	$ 230,000
Intangible assets ($1,615,000 × 110%)	1,776,500
Total investment	$2,006,500
Rate of return	× 0.12
Required dollar return	$ 240,780

The experience of the accounting firm indicates that other operating costs are incurred as follows:

Fixed expenses (per year)
Salaries (other than partners)	$300,000
Overhead	125,000

Variable expenses
Overhead	15% of gross billings
Client service	5% of gross billings

Source: Adapted from Jerry S. Huss, "Better Budgeting for CPA Firms," *Journal of Accountancy* (November 1977), pp. 65–72. Reprinted with permission from the *Journal of Accountancy*. Copyright © 2000 by American Institute of CPAs. Opinions of the authors are their own and do not necessarily reflect policies of the AICPA.

a. Determine the minimum level of gross billings that would allow the partners to realize their net income objective. Prepare a budget of costs and revenues at that level.

b. If the partners believe that the level of billings you have projected in part (a) is not feasible given the time constraints at the partner, manager, and senior levels, what changes can they make to the budget to preserve the desired level of net income?

57. **LO.3, LO.5, & LO.6 (Revising and analyzing an operating budget)** Kosciusko Ltd., a division of Jackson Industries (JI), offers consulting services to clients for a fee. JI's corporate management is pleased with the performance of Kosciusko Ltd. for the first nine months of the current year and has recommended that

Kosciusko's division manager, Jason Newport, submit a revised forecast for the remaining quarter because the division has exceeded the annual year-to-date plan by 20 percent of operating income. An unexpected increase in billed hour volume over the original plan is the main reason for this gain in income. The original operating budget for the first three quarters for Kosciusko Ltd. follows:

2008 OPERATING BUDGET

	1st Quarter	2nd Quarter	3rd Quarter	Total 9 Months
Consulting fees				
Management consulting	$ 315,000	$ 315,000	$ 315,000	$ 945,000
EDP consulting	421,875	421,875	421,875	1,265,625
Total	$ 736,875	$ 736,875	$ 736,875	$ 2,210,625
Other revenue	10,000	10,000	10,000	30,000
Total	$ 746,875	$ 746,875	$ 746,875	$ 2,240,625
Expenses				
Consultant salaries	$(386,750)	$(386,750)	$(386,750)	$(1,160,250)
Travel and entertainment	(45,625)	(45,625)	(45,625)	(136,875)
Administrative	(100,000)	(100,000)	(100,000)	(300,000)
Depreciation	(40,000)	(40,000)	(40,000)	(120,000)
Corporate allocation	(50,000)	(50,000)	(50,000)	(150,000)
Total	$(622,375)	$(622,375)	$(622,375)	$(1,867,125)
Operating income	$ 124,500	$ 124,500	$ 124,500	$ 373,500

When comparing the actuals for the first three quarters to the original plan, Newport analyzed the variances and will reflect the following information in his revised forecast for the fourth quarter.

The division currently has 25 consultants on staff, 10 for management consulting and 15 for EDP consulting, and has hired 3 additional management consultants to start work at the beginning of the fourth quarter to meet the increased client demand.

The hourly billing rates for consulting revenues will remain at $90 for each management consultant and $75 for each EDP consultant. However, due to the favorable increase in billing hour volume when compared to the plan, the hours for each consultant will be increased by 50 hours per quarter. New employees are equally as capable as current employees and their time will be billed at the same rates.

The annual budgeted salaries and actual salaries, paid monthly, are $50,000 for a management consultant and 8 percent less for an EDP consultant. Corporate management has approved a merit increase of 10 percent at the beginning of the fourth quarter for all 25 existing consultants, but the new consultants will be compensated at the planned rate.

The planned salary expense includes a provision for employee fringe benefits amounting to 30 percent of the annual salaries; however, the improvement of some corporate-wide employee programs will increase the fringe benefit allocation to 40 percent.

The original plan assumes a fixed hourly rate for travel and other related expenses for each billing hour of consulting. These expenses are not reimbursed by the client, and the previously determined hourly rate has proven to be adequate to cover these costs.

Other revenues are derived from temporary rentals and interest income and remain unchanged for the fourth quarter.

Administrative expenses are 7 percent below the plan; this 7 percent savings on fourth-quarter expenses will be reflected in the revised plan.

Depreciation for office equipment and computers will stay constant at the projected straight-line rate.

Due to the favorable experience for the first three quarters and the division's increased ability to absorb costs, JI corporate management has increased the corporate expense allocation by 50 percent.

a. Prepare a revised operating budget for the fourth quarter for Kosciusko Ltd. that Jason Newport will present to Jackson Industries. Be sure to furnish supporting calculations for all revised revenue and expense amounts.
b. Discuss the reasons that an organization would prepare a revised forecast.
c. Discuss your feelings about the 50 percent increase in corporate expense allocations.

(CPA adapted)

58. **LO.6 (Budgeting internationally)** Preparing budgets for a multinational organization is significantly more complex than doing so for a solely domestic organization. What costs might managers find in budgets for international companies that might not commonly be included (or included at similar amounts) in budgets for domestic companies?

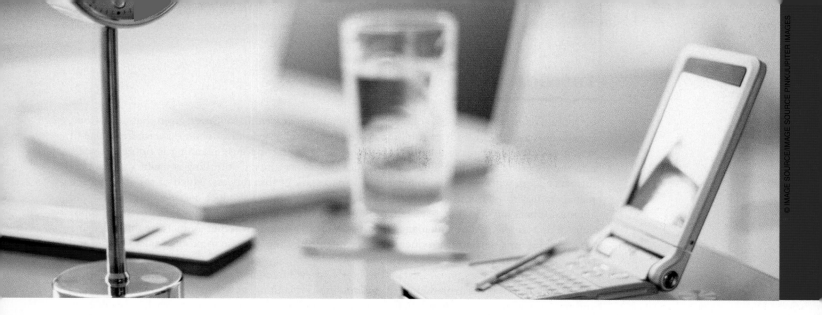

9

Break-Even Point and Cost-Volume-Profit Analysis

Objectives

After completing this chapter, you should be able to answer the following questions:

LO.1 Why is variable costing more useful than absorption costing in determining the break-even point (BEP) and performing cost-volume-profit (CVP) analysis?

LO.2 How is the BEP determined using the formula approach, graphing approach, and income statement approach?

LO.3 How do companies use CVP analysis information in decision making?

LO.4 How do break-even and CVP analysis differ for single-product and multi-product firms?

LO.5 How are margin of safety and operating leverage concepts used in business?

LO.6 What are the underlying assumptions of CVP analysis?

Introduction

Corporate managers have a goal of maximizing shareholder wealth. However, given that no obvious, single course of action leads to fulfillment of that goal, managers must choose a specific course of action and develop plans and controls to pursue that course. Because planning is future-oriented, uncertainty exists and information helps reduce that uncertainty. Controlling is making actual performance align with plans, and information is necessary in that process. Much of the information managers use to plan and control reflects relationships among product costs, selling prices, and volumes. Changing one of these essential components in the mix will cause changes in other components. For example, a company manager would want to estimate whether an increase in advertising expenditures for a particular product would be justified by the increase in product sales volume and contribution margin that would be generated.

This chapter focuses on understanding how costs, volumes, and profits interact. Understanding these relationships helps in predicting future conditions (planning) as well as in explaining, evaluating, and acting on results (controlling). Before generating profits, a company must first reach its break-even point, which means that it must generate sufficient sales revenue to cover all costs. Then, by linking cost behavior and sales volume, managers can use the cost-volume-profit model to plan and control.

The chapter also presents the concepts of margin of safety and degree of operating leverage. Information provided by these models helps managers focus on the implications that volume changes would have on organizational profitability.

LO.1

Why is variable costing more useful than absorption costing in determining the break-even point (BEP) and performing cost-volume-profit (CVP) analysis?

Break-Even Point

As discussed in Chapter 3, absorption costing is the traditional approach to product costing and is primarily used for external reporting. Alternatively, variable costing is more commonly used for internal purposes because it makes cost behavior more transparent. The variable costing presentation of separating variable from fixed costs facilitates the use of this chapter's models: break-even point, cost-volume-profit, margin of safety, and degree of operating leverage.

A variable costing budgeted income statement for Baldwin Corporation is presented in Exhibit 9–1. Baldwin Corporation manufactures a high-quality line of desk clocks. Product specifications have been established for several years and will continue at least until model year 2010. In addition to the traditional income statement information, per-unit amounts are shown for sales revenue, variable costs, and contribution margin. The company has a total variable production cost of 62.5 percent, a variable selling expense of 10 percent, and a contribution margin ratio of 27.5 percent. These Baldwin Corporation data are used throughout this chapter to illustrate break-even and cost-volume-profit computations.

A company's break-even point (BEP) is that level of activity, in units or dollars, at which total revenues equal total costs. Thus, at BEP, the company incurs neither a profit nor a loss on operating activities. Companies, however, do not wish merely to "break even" on operations. The BEP is calculated to establish a point of reference. Knowing BEP, managers are better able to set sales goals that should result in profits from operations rather than losses.

Finding the BEP first requires understanding company revenues and costs. A short summary of revenue and cost assumptions is presented at this point to provide a foundation for BEP calculation and cost-volume-profit (CVP) analysis. These assumptions, and some challenges to them, are discussed in more detail at the end of the chapter.

- *Relevant range*: The company is assumed to be operating within the relevant range of activity specified in determining the revenue and cost information used in each of the following assumptions.[1]

- *Revenue*: Revenue per unit is assumed to remain constant; fluctuations in per-unit revenue for factors such as quantity discounts are ignored. Thus, total revenue fluctuates in direct proportion to level of activity or volume.

---

[1]As discussed in Chapter 2, the relevant range is the range of activity over which a variable cost will remain constant per unit and a fixed cost will remain constant in total.

EXHIBIT 9–1
Baldwin Corporation Budgeted Income Statement for 2009

	Total		Per Unit	Percentage
Sales (600,000 units)		$ 24,000,000	$40.00	100.0
Variable costs				
Production	$15,000,000		$25.00	62.5
Selling	2,400,000		4.00	10.0
Total variable costs		(17,400,000)	(29.00)	(72.5)
Contribution margin		$ 6,600,000	$11.00	27.5
Fixed costs				
Production	$ 3,200,000			
Selling and administrative	1,400,000			
Total fixed costs		(4,400,000)		
Income before income tax		$ 2,200,000		

- *Variable costs*: On a per-unit basis, variable costs are assumed to remain constant. Therefore, total variable costs fluctuate in direct proportion to level of activity or volume. Variable production costs include direct material, direct labor, and variable overhead; variable selling costs include charges for items such as commissions and shipping. Variable administrative costs can exist in areas such as purchasing; however, in the illustrations that follow, administrative costs are assumed to be fixed.

- *Fixed costs*: Total fixed costs are assumed to remain constant, and, as such, per-unit fixed cost decreases as volume increases. (Per-unit fixed cost increases as volume decreases.) Fixed costs include both fixed manufacturing overhead and fixed selling and administrative expenses.

- *Mixed costs*: Mixed costs are separated into their variable and fixed elements before they are used in BEP or CVP analysis. Any method (such as regression analysis or the high–low method) that validly separates these costs in relation to one or more predictors can be used.

An important measure in break-even analysis is contribution margin (CM), which can be defined on either a per-unit or a total basis. CM per unit equals selling price per unit minus total variable cost per unit, which includes production, selling, and administrative costs. Unit contribution margin is constant because revenue and variable cost have been defined as being constant per unit. Total CM is the difference between total revenues and total variable costs for all units sold. This amount fluctuates in direct proportion to sales volume. On either a per-unit or a total basis, contribution margin indicates the amount of revenue remaining after all variable costs have been covered.[2] This amount contributes to the coverage of fixed costs and the generation of profits.

Break-even calculations can be demonstrated using the formula, graph, and income statement approaches. Data needed to compute the break-even point and perform CVP analysis are given in the income statement shown in Exhibit 9–1 for Baldwin Corporation.

Formula Approach to Breakeven

LO.2
How is the BEP determined using the formula approach, graphing approach, and income statement approach?

The formula approach to break-even analysis uses an algebraic equation to calculate the BEP. In this analysis, sales volume, rather than production activity, is the focus of the relevant range. The equation represents the variable costing income statement and shows the relationships among revenue, fixed cost, variable cost, volume, and profit as follows:

$$R(X) - VC(X) - FC = P$$

[2]Contribution margin refers to the total contribution margin. Product contribution margin is the difference between revenues and total variable product costs included in cost of goods sold.

where   R = revenue (selling price) per unit
                 X = volume (number of units)
              R(X) = total revenue
                VC = variable cost per unit
             VC(X) = total variable cost
                FC = total fixed cost
                 P = total profit

Because this equation is simply a formulaic representation of an income statement, P can be set equal to zero to solve for the break-even point. At the point where P = $0, total revenues are equal to total costs, and break-even point (BEP) in units can be found by solving the equation for X.

$$R(X) - VC(X) - FC = \$0$$
$$R(X) - VC(X) = FC$$
$$(R - VC)(X) = FC$$
$$X = FC \div (R - VC)$$
$$X = FC \div CM$$

Break-even volume equals total fixed cost divided by contribution margin per unit (revenue per unit minus the variable cost per unit). Using the information in Exhibit 9–1 for Baldwin Corporation ($40 selling price per clock, $29 variable cost per clock, and $4,400,000 of total fixed costs), the BEP for the company is calculated as

$$\$40(X) - \$29(X) - \$4,400,000 = \$0$$
$$\$40(X) - \$29(X) = \$4,400,000$$
$$\$11(X) = \$4,400,000$$
$$X = \$4,400,000 \div \$11$$
$$X = 400,000 \text{ clocks}$$

BEP can be expressed in either units or dollars of revenue. One way to convert a unit BEP to dollars is to multiply the number of units by the selling price per unit. For Baldwin, the BEP in sales dollars is $16,000,000 (400,000 clocks × $40 per clock).

Another method of computing BEP in sales dollars requires the computation of a **contribution margin ratio (CM%)**, which is calculated as contribution margin divided by revenue. This ratio indicates what proportion of revenue remains after variable costs have been deducted from sales or that portion of the revenue dollar that can be used to cover fixed costs and provide profit. The CM% can be calculated using either per-unit, or total, revenue and variable cost information. Dividing total fixed cost by the CM% gives the BEP in sales dollars. The CM% allows the BEP to be determined even if unit selling price and unit variable cost are not known. Subtracting the contribution margin ratio from 100 percent gives the **variable cost ratio (VC%)**, which represents variable cost as a proportion of revenue.[3]

The CM% for Baldwin Corporation is given in Exhibit 9–1 as 27.5 percent ($11 ÷ $40). Thus, break-even sales dollars are ($4,400,000 ÷ 0.275), or $16,000,000. BEP in units can be determined by dividing the BEP in sales dollars by the unit selling price, or $16,000,000 ÷ $40 = 400,000 clocks.

The BEP provides a starting point for planning future operations. Managers want to earn operating profit rather than simply cover costs. Substituting an amount other than zero for the profit (P) term in the break-even formula converts break-even analysis to cost-volume-profit analysis.

---

[3]Derivation of the contribution margin ratio formula follows:

$$\text{Sales} - [(VC\%)(\text{Sales})] = FC$$
$$(1 - VC\%)\text{Sales} = FC$$
$$\text{Sales} = FC \div (1 - VC\%)$$
$$\text{because } (1 - VC\%) = CM\%$$
$$\text{then Sales} = FC \div CM\%$$

where VC% = variable cost ratio or variable costs as a percentage of sales
    CM% = contribution margin ratio or contribution margin as a percentage of sales

Thus, the VC% plus the CM% is equal to 100 percent.

CVP Analysis

Because profit cannot be achieved until the BEP is reached, the starting point of CVP analysis is the break-even point. Examining shifts in costs and volume and the resulting effects on profits is called cost-volume-profit (CVP) analysis. CVP analysis can be used to calculate the sales volume necessary to achieve a target profit, stated as either a fixed or variable amount on a before- or after-tax basis.

Managers use CVP analysis to effectively plan and control by concentrating on the relationships among revenues, costs, volume changes, taxes, and profits. The CVP model can be expressed mathematically or graphically. The CVP model considers all costs, regardless of whether they are product, period, variable, or fixed. The analysis is usually performed on a companywide basis. The same basic CVP model and calculations can be applied to a single- or multiproduct business.

Using CVP Analysis

CVP analysis requires substitution of known amounts in the formula to solve for an unknown amount. The formula mirrors the income statement when known amounts are used for selling price per unit, variable cost per unit, volume of units, and fixed costs to find the amount of profit generated under given conditions. Because CVP analysis is concerned with relationships among the elements affecting continuing operations, in contrast with nonrecurring activities and events, profits—as used in this chapter—refer to operating profits before extraordinary and other nonoperating, nonrecurring items. The following quote indicates the pervasive utility of the CVP model:

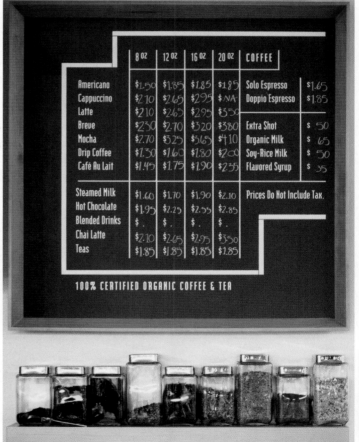

A product's selling price is often market related and is not a management decision variable.

> *Cost Volume Profit analysis (CVP) is one of the most hallowed, and yet one of the simplest, analytical tools in management accounting. [CVP] allows managers to examine the possible impacts of a wide range of strategic decisions [in] such crucial areas as pricing policies, product mixes, market expansions or contractions, outsourcing contracts, idle plant usage, discretionary expense planning, and a variety of other important considerations in the planning process. Given the broad range of contexts in which CVP can be used, the basic simplicity of CVP is quite remarkable. Armed with just three inputs of data—sales price, variable cost per unit, and fixed costs—a managerial analyst can evaluate the effects of decisions that potentially alter the basic nature of a firm.*[4]

An important application of CVP analysis allows managers to set a desired target profit and focus on the relationships between it and other known income statement amounts to find an unknown. One common unknown in such applications is the sales volume that is needed to generate a particular profit amount.

Selling price is generally not as commonly unknown as volume because selling price is often market determined and is not a management decision variable. Additionally, because selling price and volume are often directly related and because certain costs are considered fixed, managers can use CVP to determine how high variable cost can be while allowing the company to produce a desired amount of profit. Variable cost can be affected

[4]Flora Guidry, James O. Horrigan, and Cathy Craycraft, "CVP Analysis: A New Look," *Journal of Managerial Issues* (Spring 1998), p. 74ff.

by modifying product specifications or material quality as well as by being more efficient or effective in the production, service, and/or distribution processes.

The following examples continue using the Baldwin Corporation data with different amounts of target profit.

Fixed Amount of Profit

Because contribution margin represents the sales dollars remaining after variable costs are covered, each dollar of CM generated by product sales goes first to cover fixed costs and then to produce profits. After the BEP is reached, each dollar of contribution margin is a dollar of before-tax profit.

Before Tax

Profit can be treated in the break-even formula as an additional cost to be covered. Inclusion of a target profit changes the break-even formula to a CVP equation.

$$R(X) - VC(X) - FC = PBT$$
$$R(X) - VC(X) = FC + PBT$$
$$X = (FC + PBT) \div (R - VC)$$

or

$$X = (FC + PBT) \div CM$$

where PBT = fixed amount of profit before tax

Assume that Baldwin's management desires a $3,300,000 before-tax profit. The calculations in Exhibit 9–2 show that, to achieve this profit before tax, the company must sell 700,000 clocks and generate $28,000,000 of revenue.

After Tax

In choosing a target profit amount, managers must recognize that income tax represents a significant influence on business decision making. A company wanting a particular amount of profit after tax must first determine, given the applicable tax rate, the amount of profit that must be earned on a before-tax basis. The CVP formulas that designate a fixed after-tax profit amount follow:

EXHIBIT 9–2
Baldwin CVP Analysis—Fixed Amount of Profit before Tax

In units:

Profit before tax (PBT) desired = $3,300,000

$$R(X) - VC(X) = FC + PBT$$
$$CM(X) = FC + PBT$$
$$(\$40 - \$29)X = \$4,400,000 + \$3,300,000$$
$$\$11X = \$7,700,000$$
$$X = \$7,700,000 \div \$11 = \underline{700,000} \text{ clocks}$$

In sales dollars:

$$Sales = (FC + PBT) \div CM\%$$
$$Sales = \$7,700,000 \div 0.275*$$
$$Sales = \underline{\$28,000,000}$$

*From Exhibit 9–1

$$\text{PBT} - [(\text{TR})(\text{PBT})] = \text{PAT}$$

and

$$\text{R}(X) - \text{VC}(X) - \text{FC} - [(\text{TR})(\text{PBT})] = \text{PAT}$$

where PBT = fixed amount of profit before tax
      PAT = fixed amount of profit after tax
       TR = tax rate

PAT is further defined so that it can be integrated into the original CVP formula:

$$\text{PBT} (1 - \text{TR}) = \text{PAT}$$

or

$$\text{PBT} = \text{PAT} \div (1 - \text{TR})$$

Substituting into the formula,

$$\text{R}(X) - \text{VC}(X) - \text{FC} = \text{PBT}$$
$$\text{R}(X) - \text{VC}(X) = \text{FC} + \text{PBT}$$
$$(\text{R} - \text{VC})(X) = \text{FC} + [\text{PAT} \div (1 - \text{TR})]$$
$$\text{CM}(X) = \text{FC} + [\text{PAT} \div (1 - \text{TR})]$$

Assume the managers at Baldwin Corporation want to earn $3,300,000 of profit after tax and the company's average tax rate is 25 percent. The number of clocks (800,000) and dollars of sales ($32,000,000) needed are calculated in Exhibit 9–3.

Set Amount of Profit per Unit

Managers may want to conduct an analysis of profit on a per-unit basis. As in the prior examples, profit can be stated on either a before-tax or an after-tax basis. For these alternatives, the CVP formula must be adjusted to recognize that profit is related to volume of activity.

EXHIBIT 9–3
Baldwin CVP Analysis—Fixed Amount of Profit after Tax

In units:

$$\text{PAT desired} = \$3,300,000; \text{ tax rate} = 25\%$$
$$\text{PBT} = \text{PAT} \div (1 - \text{TR})$$
$$\text{PBT} = \$3,300,000 \div (1 - 0.25)$$
$$\text{PBT} = \$3,300,000 \div 0.75$$
$$\text{PBT} = \$4,400,000$$

$$\text{CM}(X) = \text{FC} + \text{PBT}$$
$$\$11X = \$4,400,000 + \$4,400,000$$
$$\$11X = \$8,800,000$$
$$X = \$8,800,000 \div \$11$$
$$X = \underline{800,000} \text{ clocks}$$

In sales dollars:

$$\text{Sales} = (\text{FC} - \text{PBT}) \div \text{CM ratio}$$
$$\text{Sales} = (\$4,400,000 + \$4,400,000) \div 0.275$$
$$\text{Sales} = \$8,800,000 \div 0.275$$
$$\text{Sales} = \underline{\$32,000,000}$$

Before Tax

In this situation, the adjusted CVP formula for computing the necessary unit sales volume to earn a specified amount of profit before tax per unit is

$$R(X) - VC(X) - FC = P_uBT(X)$$

where P_uBT = amount of profit per unit before tax

Solving for X (volume) gives the following:

$$R(X) - VC(X) - P_uBT(X) = FC$$
$$CM(X) - P_uBT(X) = FC$$
$$X = FC \div (CM - P_uBT)$$

The per-unit profit is treated in the CVP formula as if it were an additional variable cost to be covered. This treatment effectively "adjusts" the original contribution margin and contribution margin ratio. When setting the desired profit as a percentage of selling price, the profit percentage cannot exceed the contribution margin ratio. If it does, an infeasible problem is created because the "adjusted" contribution margin is negative. In such a case, the variable cost ratio plus the desired profit percentage would exceed 100 percent of the selling price, and such a condition cannot exist.

Assume that Baldwin's president wants to know what level of sales (in clocks and dollars) would be required to earn a 15 percent before-tax profit on sales. This rate of return translates into a set amount of profit per unit of $6. The calculations shown in Exhibit 9–4 provide the answers to these questions.

After Tax

Adjusting the CVP formula to determine unit profit on an after-tax basis involves stating profit in relation to both the volume and the tax rate. Algebraically, the formula is:

EXHIBIT 9–4
Baldwin CVP Analysis—Set Amount of Profit per Unit before Tax

In units:

$$P_uBT \text{ desired} = 15\% \text{ of sales revenue}$$
$$P_uBT = 0.15(\$40)$$
$$P_uBT = \$6$$

$$CM(X) - P_uBT(X) = FC$$
$$\$11X - \$6X = \$4,400,000$$
$$\$5X = \$4,400,000$$
$$X = \$8,800,000$$
$$X = \underline{880,000} \text{ clocks}$$

In sales dollars, the following relationships exist:

	Per Clock	Percentage
Selling price	$ 40	100.0
Variable costs	(29)	(72.5)
Set amount of profit before tax	(6)	(15.0)
"Adjusted" contribution margin ratio	$ 5	12.5

$$\text{Sales} = FC \div \text{"Adjusted" CM\%*}$$
$$\text{Sales} = \$4,400,000 \div .125$$
$$\text{Sales} = \underline{\$35,200,000}$$

*It is not necessary to have per-unit data; all computations can be made with percentage information only.

$$R(X) - VC(X) - FC - \{(TR)[P_uBT(X)]\} = P_uAT(X)$$

where P_uAT = amount of profit per unit after tax

P_uAT is further defined so that it can be integrated into the original CVP formula:

$$P_uAT(X) = P_uBT(X) - \{(TR)[P_uBT(X)]\}$$
$$P_uAT(X) = P_uBT(X)[(1 - TR)]$$
$$P_uBT(X) = [P_uAT \div (1 - TR)](X)$$

Thus, the following relationship exists:

$$R(X) - VC(X) = FC + [P_uAT \div (1 - TR)](X)$$
$$CM(X) = FC + P_uBT(X)$$
$$CM(X) - P_uBT(X) = FC$$
$$X = FC \div (CM - P_uBT)$$

Baldwin managers want to earn an after-tax profit of 10 percent of revenue and the company has a 25 percent tax rate. The necessary sales in units and dollars are given in Exhibit 9–5.

Each of the preceding CVP illustrations used a variation of the formula approach. The graphing approach is an alternative method of presenting CVP solutions.

Graphing Approach to Breakeven

Although solutions to BEP and CVP problems can be determined using equations, sometimes the information is more effectively conveyed to managers in a visual format. Exhibit 9–6 graphically

---

EXHIBIT 9–5
Baldwin CVP Analysis—Set Amount of Profit per Unit after Tax

In units:

$$P_uAT \text{ desired} = 10\% \text{ of revenue; tax rate} = 25\%$$
$$P_uAT = 0.10(\$40)$$
$$P_uAT = \$4$$

$$P_uBT = \$4 \div (1.00 - 0.25)$$
$$P_uBT = \$4 \div 0.75$$
$$P_uBT = \$5.33 \text{ (rounded)}$$

$$CM(X) - P_uBT(X) = FC$$
$$\$11.00X - \$5.33X = \$4,400,000$$
$$\$5.67X = \$4,400,000$$
$$X = \$4,400,000 \div \$5.67$$
$$X = \underline{776,014} \text{ clocks (rounded)}$$

	Per Clock	Percentage
Selling price	$40.00	100.00
Variable costs	(29.00)	(72.50)
Set amount of profit before tax	(5.33)	(13.33) (rounded)
"Adjusted" contribution margin	$ 5.67	14.17

$$\text{Sales} = FC \div \text{"Adjusted" CM ratio}$$
$$\text{Sales} = \$4,400,000 \div 0.1417$$
$$\text{Sales} = \underline{\$31,051,517} \text{ (rounded)}$$

presents each income statement item for Baldwin Corporation's original budgeted data (see Exhibit 9–1) providing visual representations of revenue, costs, and contribution margin behaviors.

Although illustrating individual behaviors, the graphs presented in Exhibit 9–6 are not very useful for determining the relationships among the income statement amounts. A break-even chart can be prepared to graph the relationships among revenue, volume, and costs. The BEP on a break-even chart is located at the point where the total cost and total revenue lines intersect. Two approaches to graphing can be used in preparing break-even charts: the traditional (or CVP) approach and the profit-volume graph approach.

Traditional Approach

The traditional approach break-even graph shows the relationships among revenues, costs, and profits (or losses). This graph does not show contribution margin. A traditional break-even graph for Baldwin Corporation is prepared as discussed on the next page.

EXHIBIT 9–6
Baldwin Graphing Presentation of Income Statement Items

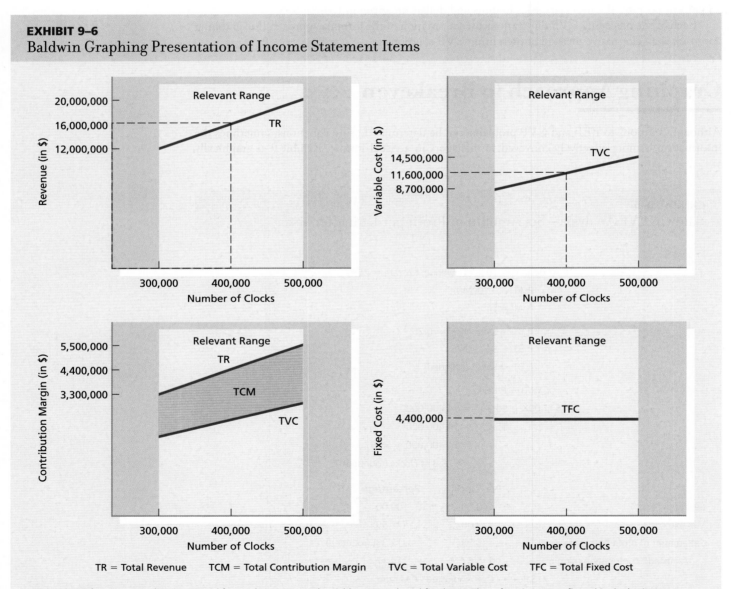

TR = Total Revenue   TCM = Total Contribution Margin   TVC = Total Variable Cost   TFC = Total Fixed Cost

Note: Linear functions are always assumed for total revenue, total variable cost, and total fixed cost. These functions are reflected in the basic assumptions given on pp. 337–338.

EXHIBIT 9–7
Baldwin Graph of Total and Variable Costs

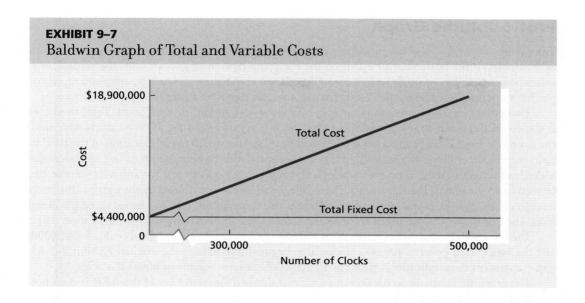

Step 1: As shown in Exhibit 9–7 above, label each axis and graph the total cost and fixed cost lines. The fixed cost line is drawn parallel to the x-axis (volume). The variable cost line begins where the fixed cost line intersects the y-axis. The slope of the variable cost line is the per-unit variable cost ($29). The resulting line represents total cost. The distance between the fixed cost and the total cost lines represents total variable cost at each activity level.

Step 2: Chart the revenue line, beginning at $0. The BEP is located at the intersection of the revenue line and the total cost line. The vertical distance to the right of the BEP and between the revenue and total cost lines represents profit; the distance between the revenue and total cost lines to the left of the BEP represents loss. If exact readings could be taken on the graph in Exhibit 9–8, the break-even point for Baldwin Corporation would be $16,000,000 of sales, or 400,000 clocks.

EXHIBIT 9–8
Baldwin Traditional Approach of Graphing Breakeven

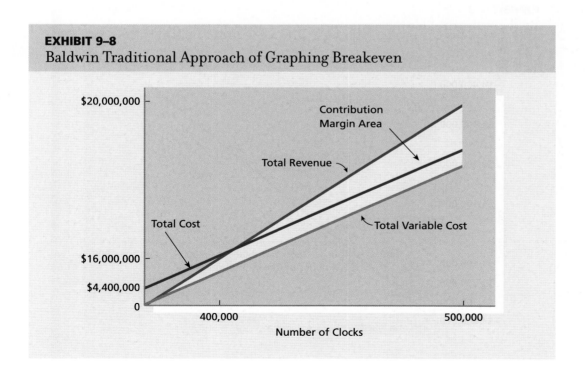

Profit-Volume Graph

The profit-volume (PV) graph provides a depiction of the amount of profit or loss associated with each sales level. The horizontal, or *x*, axis on the PV graph represents sales volume; the vertical, or *y*, axis represents dollars of profit or loss. Amounts shown above the *x*-axis are positive and represent profits; amounts shown below the *x*-axis are negative and represent losses.

Two points can be located on the graph: total fixed cost and break-even point. Total fixed cost is shown on the *y*-axis below the sales volume line as a negative amount. If no products were sold, the fixed cost would still be incurred and a loss of that amount would result. Location of the BEP in units may be determined algebraically and is shown at the point where the profit line intersects the *x*-axis; at that point, there is no profit or loss. The amount of profit or loss for any sales volume can be read from the *y*-axis. The slope of the profit (diagonal) line is determined by the unit contribution margin ($11), and the points on the line represent the contribution margin earned at each volume level. The line shows that no profit is earned until total contribution margin covers total fixed cost.

The PV graph for Baldwin Corporation is shown in Exhibit 9–9. Total fixed cost is $4,400,000, and the break-even point is 400,000 clocks. The diagonal line reflects the original Exhibit 9–1 income statement data indicating a profit of $2,200,000 at a sales volume of 600,000 clocks.

The graphing approach to breakeven provides a detailed visual display of the BEP. It does not, however, provide a precise solution because exact points cannot be determined on a graph. A definitive computation of the BEP can be found algebraically using the formula approach or a computer software application. A third approach to illustrating breakeven is the income statement approach.

Income Statement Approach

The income statement approach to CVP analysis allows accountants to prepare budgeted statements using available revenue and cost information. Income statements can also be used to prove the accuracy of computations made using the CVP formula, or the statements can be prepared merely to determine the impact of various sales levels on profit after tax (net income). The income statement

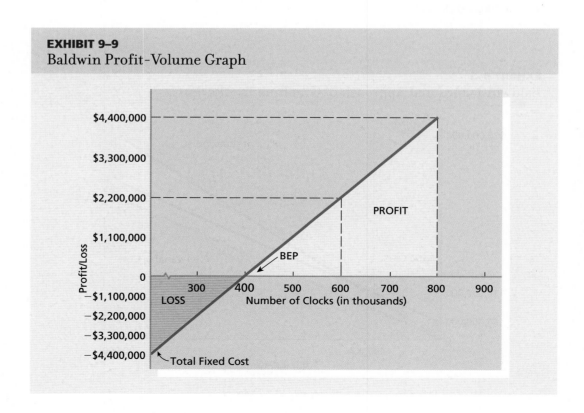

EXHIBIT 9–9
Baldwin Profit-Volume Graph

approach can be readily adapted to computerized spreadsheets, which can be used to quickly obtain the results of many different combinations of the CVP factors.

Because the formula, graphing, and income statement approaches are based on the same relationships, each should align with the other. Exhibit 9–10 proves each of the computations made in Exhibits 9–2 through 9–5 for Baldwin Corporation. The answers provided by break-even or CVP analysis are valid only in relation to specific selling prices and cost relationships. Changes that occur in the company's selling price or cost structure will cause a change in the BEP or in the sales needed to obtain a desired profit. However, the effects of revenue and cost changes on a company's BEP or sales volume can be determined through incremental analysis.

Incremental Analysis for Short-Run Changes

LO.3
How do companies use CVP analysis information in decision making?

The break-even point can increase or decrease, depending on revenue and cost changes. Other things being equal, the BEP will increase if there is an increase in the total fixed cost or a decrease in the unit (or percentage) contribution margin. A decrease in contribution margin could arise because of a reduction in selling price, an increase in variable cost per unit, or a combination of the two. The BEP will decrease if total fixed cost decreases or unit (or percentage) contribution margin increases. A change in the BEP will also cause a shift in total profit or loss at any level of activity.

Incremental analysis is a process that focuses only on factors that change from one course of action or decision to another. In CVP situations, incremental analysis is focused on changes occurring in revenues, costs, and/or volume. Following are some examples of changes that could occur in a company and the incremental computations that can be used to determine the effects of those

EXHIBIT 9–10
Baldwin's Income Statement Approach to CVP—Proof of Computations

Previous computations:

Break-even point: 400,000 clocks

Fixed profit ($255,000) before tax: 700,000 clocks

Fixed profit ($3,300,000) after tax: 800,000 clocks

Set amount of profit (15% on revenues) before tax: 880,000 clocks

Set amount of profit (10% on revenues) after tax: 776,014 clocks

R = $40 per clock; VC = $29 per clock; FC = $4,400,000;

Tax rate = 25% for Exhibits 9–3 and 9–5

Clocks sold	Basic Data 400,000	Exh. 9–2 700,000	Exh. 9–3 800,000	Exh. 9–4 880,000	Exh. 9–5 776,014
Sales	$16,000,000	$28,000,000	$32,000,000	$35,200,000	$31,040,560
Total variable cost	(11,600,000)	(20,300,000)	(23,200,000)	(25,520,000)	(22,504,406)
Contribution margin	$ 4,400,000	$ 7,700,000	$ 8,800,000	$ 9,680,000	$ 8,536,154
Total fixed cost	(4,400,000)	(4,400,000)	(4,400,000)	(4,400,000)	(4,400,000)
Profit before tax	$ 0	$ 3,300,000	$ 4,400,000	$ 5,280,000[a]	$ 4,136,154
Tax (25%)			(1,100,000)		(1,034,039)
Profit after tax (NI)			$ 3,300,000		$ 3,102,115[b]

[a]Desired profit before tax = 15% on revenue; 0.15 × $35,200,000 = $5,280,000
[b]Desired profit after tax = 10% on revenue; 0.10 × $31,040,560 = $3,104,050 (differs from $3,102,115 only because of rounding error)

changes on the BEP or on profit. In most situations, incremental analysis is sufficient to determine the feasibility of contemplated changes, and a complete income statement need not be prepared. The basic facts presented for Baldwin Corporation in Exhibit 9–1 are continued. All of the following examples use before-tax information to simplify the computations. After-tax analysis would require the application of the (1 − tax rate) adjustment to all profit figures.

Case 1

Baldwin Corporation wants to earn a before-tax profit of $2,750,000. How many clocks must the company sell to achieve that profit? The incremental analysis relative to this question addresses the number of clocks above the BEP that must be sold. Because each dollar of contribution margin after BEP is a dollar of profit, the incremental analysis focuses only on the profit desired:

$$\$2,750,000 \div \$11 = 250,000 \text{ clocks above BEP}$$

Because the BEP has already been computed as 400,000 clocks, the company must sell a total of 650,000 clocks.

Case 2

Baldwin Corporation estimates that spending an additional $425,000 on advertising will result in an additional 50,000 clocks being sold. Should the company incur this extra fixed cost? The contribution margin from the additional clocks must first cover the additional fixed cost before additional profits can be generated.

Increase in contribution margin (50,000 clocks × $11 CM per clock)	$550,000
− Increase in fixed cost	(425,000)
= Net incremental benefit	$125,000

Because there is a net incremental profit of $125,000, the company should undertake the advertising campaign.

An alternative computation is to divide the additional fixed cost of $425,000 by the $11 contribution margin. The result indicates that 38,636 clocks (rounded) would be required to cover the additional cost. Because the company expects to sell 50,000 clocks, the remaining 11,364 clocks would produce $11 of profit per clock, or $125,004.

Case 3

Baldwin Corporation estimates that reducing a clock's selling price to $37.50 will result in an additional 90,000 clocks per year being sold. Should the company reduce the clock's selling price? Budgeted sales volume, given in Exhibit 9–1, is 600,000 clocks. If the selling price is reduced, the contribution margin per unit will decrease to $8.50 per clock ($37.50 SP − $29.00 VC). Sales volume will increase to 690,000 clocks (600,000 + 90,000).

Total new contribution margin (690,000 clocks × $8.50 CM per clock)	$5,865,000
− Total fixed cost (unchanged)	(4,400,000)
= New profit before tax	$1,465,000
− Current budgeted profit before tax (from Exhibit 9–1)	(2,200,000)
= Net incremental loss	$ (735,000)

Because the reduction in sales price will cause profit to decrease by $735,000, Baldwin should not reduce the clock's selling price. The company, however, might want to investigate the possibility that a reduction in price could, in the long run, increase demand to more than the additional 90,000 clocks per year and, thus, make the price reduction a profitable action.

Case 4

Baldwin Corporation has an opportunity to sell 100,000 clocks to a nonrecurring customer for $27 per clock. The clocks will be packaged and sold using the customer's own logo. Packaging costs will increase by $1 per clock, but the company will not incur any of the current variable selling costs. If

Baldwin accepts the job, it will pay a $30,000 commission to the salesperson calling on this customer. This sale will not interfere with budgeted sales and is within the company's relevant range of activity. Should Baldwin make this sale?

The new variable cost per clock is $26 ($25 total budgeted variable production costs + $1 additional variable packaging cost + $0 variable selling costs). The $27 selling price minus the $26 new total variable cost provides a contribution margin of $1 per clock sold to the contractor.

Total additional contribution margin (100,000 clocks × $1 CM per clock)	$100,000
− Additional fixed cost (commission) related to this sale	(30,000)
= Net incremental benefit	$ 70,000

The total CM generated by the sale more than covers the additional fixed cost. Thus, the sale produces a net incremental profit and, therefore, should be made.

However, as with all proposals, this one should be evaluated on the basis of its long-range potential. Is the commission a one-time payment? Will sales to the customer continue for several years? Will such sales affect regular business in the future? Is the sales price to the new customer a legal one?[5] If all of these questions can be answered "yes," Baldwin should seriously consider this opportunity. In addition, referral business by the new customer could also increase sales.

The incremental approach is often used to evaluate alternative pricing strategies in economic downturns. In such stressful times, companies must confront the reality that they might be unable to sell a normal volume of goods at normal prices. With this understanding, companies can choose to maintain normal prices and sell a lower volume of goods or reduce prices and attempt to maintain market share and normal volume.

CVP Analysis in a Multiproduct Environment

LO.4
How do break-even and CVP analysis differ for single-product and multiproduct firms?

Companies typically produce and sell a variety of products, some of which may be related (such as bats and baseballs or sheets, towels, and bedspreads). To perform CVP analysis in a multiproduct company, one must assume either that the product sales mix stays constant as total sales volume changes or that the average contribution margin ratio stays constant as total sales volume changes. The constant mix assumption can be referred to as the "bag" (or "basket") assumption. The analogy is that the sales mix represents a bag of products that are sold together. For example, when some product A is sold, set amounts of products B and C are also sold. Use of an assumed constant sales mix allows a weighted average contribution margin ratio to be computed for the bag of products being sold. Without the assumption of a constant sales mix, BEP cannot be calculated, nor can CVP analysis be used effectively.[6]

In a multiproduct company, the CM% is weighted by the quantities of each product included in the "bag." This weighting process means that the CM% of the product composing the largest proportion of the bag has the greatest impact on the average contribution margin of the product mix.

Suppose that, because of the success of its desk clocks, Baldwin management is considering the production of clock wall-mounting kits. The vice president of marketing estimates that, for every three clocks sold, the company will sell one clock wall-mounting kit. Therefore, the "bag" of products has a 3:1 product ratio. Baldwin will incur an additional $514,000 in fixed plant asset costs (depreciation, insurance, and so forth) to support a higher relevant range of production. Exhibit 9–11 provides relevant company information and shows the break-even computations. Break-even occurs at sales of 126,000 "bags" of product, which contain 378,000 clocks and 126,000 wall-mounting kits.

Any shift in the product sales mix will change the weighted average CM% and BEP. If the sales mix shifts toward a product with a lower dollar contribution margin, the BEP will increase and profits will decrease unless there is a corresponding increase in total revenues. A shift toward higher dollar contribution margin products without a corresponding decrease in revenues will cause

---

[5]The Robinson-Patman Act addresses the legal ways in which companies can price their goods for sale to different purchasers.
[6]After the constant percentage contribution margin in a multiproduct firm has been determined, all situations regarding profit points can be treated in the same manner as they were earlier in the chapter. One must remember, however, that the answers reflect the "bag" assumption.

EXHIBIT 9–11
Baldwin CVP Analysis—Multiple Products

	Clocks		Clock Wall-Mounting Kits	
Product Cost Information				
Selling price	$40	100.0%	$10	100%
Total variable cost	(29)	(72.5)%	(4)	(40)%
Contribution margin	$11	27.5%	$ 6	60%

Total fixed costs (FC) = $4,400,000 previous + $514,000 additional = $4,914,000

	Clocks		Clock Wall-Mounting Kits		Total	Percentage
Number of products per bag		3		1		
Revenue per product	$40		$10			
Total revenue per "bag"		$120		$10	$130	100
Variable cost per product	(29)		(4)			
Total variable cost per "bag"		(87)		(4)	(91)	(70)
Contribution margin—product	$11		$ 6			
Contribution margin—"bag"		$ 33		$ 6	$ 39	30

BEP in units (where B = number of "bags" of products)

$$CM(B) = FC$$
$$\$39B = \$4,914,000$$
$$B = 126,000 \text{ bags}$$

Note: Each "bag" consists of 3 clocks and 1 clock wall-mounting kit; therefore, it will take 378,000 clocks and 126,000 clock wall-mounting kits to break even, assuming the constant 3:1 mix.

BEP in sales dollars (where S$ = sales dollars; CM% = weighted average CM per "bag"):

$$S\$ = FC \div CM\%$$
$$S\$ = \$4,914,000 \div 0.30$$
$$S\$ = \$16,380,000$$

Note: The break-even sales dollars also represent the assumed constant sales mix of $120 of sales of clocks to $10 of sales of clock wall-mounting kits to represent a 92.3% (rounded) to 7.7% (rounded) ratio. Thus, the company must have $15,120,000 ($16,380,000 × 92.3%) in sales of clocks and $1,260,000 in sales of clock wall-mounting kits to break even.

Proof of these computations using the income statement approach:

	Clocks	Clock Wall-Mounting Kits	Total
Sales	$15,120,000	$1,260,000	$16,380,000
Variable costs	(10,962,000)	(504,000)	(11,466,000)
Contribution margin	$ 4,158,000	$ 756,000	$ 4,914,000
Fixed costs			(4,914,000)
Income before tax			$ 0

a lower BEP and increase profits. The financial results shown in Exhibit 9–12 indicate that a shift toward the product with the lower dollar contribution margin (clock wall-mounting kits) causes a higher BEP and lower profits. This exhibit assumes that Baldwin sells 126,000 "bags" of product (the break-even level in Exhibit 9–11), but the mix was not in the exact proportions assumed in Exhibit 9–11. Instead of a 3:1 ratio, the sales mix was 2.5 clocks to 1.5 clock wall-mounting kits. A

EXHIBIT 9–12

Baldwin's Effects of Product Mix Shift

	Clocks	Clock Wall-Mounting Kits		Total	Percentage
Number of products per bag	2.5	1.5			
Revenue per product	$40	$10			
Total revenue per "bag"		$100.00	$15	$115.00	100.0
Variable cost per product	(29)	(4)			
Total variable cost per "bag"		(72.50)	(6)	(78.50)	(68.3)
Contribution margin—product	$11	$ 6			
Contribution margin—"bag"		$ 27.50	$ 9	$ 36.50	31.7

BEP in units (where B = number of "bags" of products)

$$CM(B) = FC$$
$$\$36.50B = \$4,914,000$$
$$B = 134,631 \text{ bags (rounded up)}$$

Actual results: 126,000 "bags" with a sales mix ratio of 2.5 clocks to 1.5 clock wall-mounting kits; thus, the company sold 315,000 clocks and 189,000 clock wall-mounting kits.

	315,000 Clocks	189,000 Clock Wall-Mounting Kits	Total
Sales	$12,600,000	$1,890,000	$14,490,000
Variable costs	(9,135,000)	(756,000)	(9,891,000)
Contribution margin	$ 3,465,000	$1,134,000	$ 4,599,000
Fixed cost			(4,914,000)
Net loss			$ (315,000)

loss of $315,000 resulted because Baldwin sold a higher proportion of the clock wall-mounting kits, which have a lower dollar contribution margin than the clocks.

Margin of Safety

LO.5

How are margin of safety and operating leverage concepts used in business?

When making decisions about business opportunities and changes in sales mix, managers often consider the **margin of safety (MS)**, which is the excess of budgeted or actual sales over break-even sales. The MS is the amount that sales can drop before reaching the BEP and, thus, provides a measure of the amount of "cushion" against losses.

The MS can be expressed in units, in dollars, or as a percentage (MS%). The following formulas are applicable:

Margin of safety in units = Actual sales in units − Break-even sales in units

Margin of safety in $ = Actual sales in $ − Break-even sales in $

Margin of safety % = Margin of safety in units ÷ Actual unit sales

or

MS % = Margin of safety in $ ÷ Actual sales $

The BEP for Baldwin (using the original, single-product data) is 400,000 units or $16,000,000 of sales. The company's budgeted income statement presented in Exhibit 9–1 shows sales for 2009 of $24,000,000 for 600,000 clocks. Baldwin's MS is quite high because the company is operating far above its BEP (see Exhibit 9–13).

MS calculations allow management to determine how close to a "danger level" the company is operating and, as such, provides an indication of risk. The lower the MS, the more carefully management must watch sales and control costs so that it will not generate a net loss. At low margins of safety, managers are less likely to take advantage of opportunities that, if incorrectly analyzed or forecasted, could send the company into a loss position.

Operating Leverage

Another measure that is closely related to the MS and provides useful management information is the company's degree of operating leverage. The relationship between a company's variable and fixed costs is reflected in its operating leverage. Typically, highly labor-intensive organizations have high variable costs and low fixed costs; these organizations have low operating leverage. (An exception to this rule is a sports team, which is highly labor intensive, but its labor costs are fixed rather than variable.)

Conversely, organizations that are highly capital intensive or automated have cost structures that include low variable and high fixed costs, providing high operating leverage. Because variable costs are low relative to selling prices, the contribution margin is high. However, high fixed costs mean that BEP also tends to be high. If the market predominantly sets selling prices, volume has the primary impact on profitability. As companies become more automated, they face this type of cost structure and become more dependent on volume increases to raise profits. Thus, a company's cost structure strongly influences the degree to which its profits respond to changes in volume.

Companies with high operating leverage have high contribution margin ratios. Although such companies must establish fairly high sales volumes to initially cover fixed costs, once those costs are covered, each unit sold after breakeven produces large profits. Thus, a small increase in sales can have a major impact on a company's profits.

The degree of operating leverage (DOL) measures how a percentage change in sales from the current level will affect company profits. In other words, DOL indicates how sensitive the company's profit is to sales volume increases and decreases. The computation for DOL follows.

$$\text{DOL} = \text{CM} \div \text{Profit before tax}$$

This calculation assumes that fixed costs do not increase when sales increase.

Assume that Baldwin Corporation is currently selling 600,000 clocks. The income statement in Exhibit 9–14 reflects this sales level and shows that the company has a DOL of 3.00. If Baldwin increases sales by 20 percent, the 60 percent change in profits equals the DOL multiplied by the percentage change in sales or (3.00 × 20%). If sales decrease by the same 20 percent, the impact on profits is a negative 60 percent. These amounts are confirmed in Exhibit 9–14.

EXHIBIT 9–13
Baldwin's Margin of Safety

In units: 600,000 actual − 400,000 BEP = 200,000 clocks

In sales $: $24,000,000 actual sales − $16,000,000 BEP sales = $8,000,000

As a percentage: 200,000 ÷ 600,000 = 33.33%

or

$8,000,000 ÷ $24,000,000 = 33.33%

EXHIBIT 9–14
Baldwin's Degree of Operating Leverage

	Current (600,000 clocks)	20% Increase (720,000 clocks)	20% Decrease (480,000 clocks)
Sales	$24,000,000	$28,800,000	$ 19,200,000
Variable costs ($29.00 per clock)	(17,400,000)	(20,880,000)	(13,920,000)
Contribution margin	$ 6,600,000	$ 7,920,000	$ 5,280,000
Fixed costs	(4,400,000)	(4,400,000)	(4,400,000)
Profit before tax	$ 2,200,000	$ 3,520,000[a]	$ 880,000[b]

Degree of operating leverage = Contribution margin ÷ Profit before tax

($6,600,000 ÷ $2,200,000)	3.00		
($7,920,000 ÷ $3,520,000)		2.25	
($5,280,000 ÷ 880,000)			6.00

[a]Profit increase = $3,520,000 − 2,200,000 = $1,320,000 (or 60.00% of the original profit)
[b]Profit decrease = $880,000 − $2,200,000 = ($1,320,000) (or −60% of the original profit)

The DOL decreases as sales move upward from the BEP. Thus, when the margin of safety is small, the degree of operating leverage is large. In fact, at the BEP, the DOL is infinite because any increase from zero is an infinite percentage change. If a company is operating close to BEP, each percentage increase in sales can make a dramatic impact on net income. As sales increase from break-even sales, margin of safety increases but the degree of operating leverage declines. The relationship between the MS percentage (MS%) and DOL follows:

$$MS \% = 1 \div DOL$$
$$DOL = 1 \div MS \%$$

This relationship is proved in Exhibit 9–15 using the 600,000-clock sales level information for Baldwin. Therefore, if one of the two measures is known, the other can be easily calculated.

Underlying Assumptions of CVP Analysis

LO.6
What are the underlying assumptions of CVP analysis?

CVP analysis is a short-run model that focuses on relationships among selling price, variable costs, fixed costs, volume, and profits. This model is a useful planning tool that can provide information about the impact on profits when changes are made in the cost structure or in the sales level. Although limiting the accuracy of the results, several important but necessary assumptions are made in the CVP model. These assumptions follow:

1. All revenue and variable cost behavior patterns are constant per unit and linear within the relevant range.
2. Total contribution margin (total revenue − total variable cost) is linear within the relevant range and increases proportionally with output. This assumption follows directly from assumption 1.
3. Total fixed cost is constant within the relevant range. This assumption, in part, indicates that no capacity additions will be made during the period under consideration.
4. Mixed costs can be accurately separated into their fixed and variable elements. Although accuracy of separation can be questioned, reliable estimates can be developed from the use of regression analysis or the high–low method (as discussed in Chapter 3).

> **EXHIBIT 9–15**
> **Baldwin's Margin of Safety and Degree of Operating Leverage Relationship**
>
> Break-even sales = 400,000 units; Current sales = 600,000 units
>
> Margin of Safety % = Margin of Safety in Units ÷ Actual Sales in Units
>
> $$= [(600,000 - 400,000) \div 600,000]$$
>
> $$= 0.33, \text{ or } 33\% \text{ (rounded)}$$
>
> Degree of Operating Leverage = Contribution Margin ÷ Profit before Tax
>
> $$= \$6,600,000 \div \$2,200,000$$
>
> $$= 3$$
>
> Margin of Safety = (1 ÷ DOL) = (1 ÷ 3) = 0.33, or 33% (rounded)
>
> Degree of Operating Leverage = (1 ÷ MS %) = (1 ÷ 0.33) = 3 (rounded)

5. Sales and production are equal; thus, there is no material fluctuation in inventory levels. This assumption is necessary because fixed cost can be allocated to inventory at a different rate each year. Thus, variable costing information must be available. Because CVP and variable costing both focus on cost behavior, they are distinctly compatible with one another.
6. In a multiproduct firm, the sales mix remains constant. This assumption is necessary so that a weighted average contribution margin and CM% can be computed.
7. Labor productivity, production technology, and market conditions will not change. If any of these changes were to occur, costs would change correspondingly, and selling prices might change. Such changes would invalidate assumptions 1 through 3.

These assumptions limit the activity volume for which the calculations can be made as well as the time frame for the usefulness of the calculations. If changes occur in selling prices or costs, new computations must be made for break-even and CVP analyses.

The preceding seven assumptions are the traditional ones associated with CVP analysis. An additional assumption must be noted with regard to the distinction between variable and fixed costs. Accountants have generally assumed that cost behavior, once classified, remains constant as long as operations remain within the relevant range. Thus, for example, once a cost was determined to be "fixed," it would be fixed next year, the year after, and 10 years from now.

It is more appropriate, however, to regard fixed costs as long-term variable costs. Over the long run, through managerial decisions, companies can change fixed costs; thus, fixed costs are not fixed forever. Generating cost information in a manner that yields a longer-run perspective is presented in Chapter 4 on activity-based costing/management. Part of the traditional "misclassification" of fixed costs has been caused by improperly specifying drivers of costs. As production and sales volumes are less often viewed as cost drivers, companies will begin to recognize that a "fixed cost" exists only in a short-term perspective.

Such a reclassification of costs simply means that cost drivers for long-term variable costs must be specified in break-even and CVP analyses. The formula will need to be expanded to include these additional drivers, and more information and a longer time frame will be needed to make the calculations. No longer will sales volume necessarily be the overriding nonmonetary force in the computations.

These adjustments to the CVP formula will force managers to take a long-run, rather than a short-run, view of product opportunities. Such a perspective could produce better organizational decisions. As the time frame is extended, both the time value of money and life cycle costing become necessary considerations. Additionally, the traditional income statement becomes less useful for developing projects that will take several years to mature. A long-run perspective is important in a variety of circumstances, such as when variable or fixed costs arise only in the first year that a product or service is provided to customers.

Comprehensive Review Module

Chapter Summary

1. Variable costing, rather than absorption costing, is used to conduct cost-volume-profit (CVP) analysis because variable costing

   - organizes costs by behavior rather than by functional classification as in absorption costing.

   - shows fixed costs in lump-sum amounts rather than being allocated to products on a per-unit basis as in absorption costing.

   - does not allow for the deferral or release of fixed costs to or from inventory when production and sales volumes differ as happens in absorption costing.

2. Break-even point (BEP) can be determined using the

   - formula approach by solving the following formulas for X:

     ➤ X = Fixed Cost ÷ Contribution Margin per unit, where X = BEP in units

     ➤ X = Fixed Cost ÷ Contribution Margin Ratio, where X = BEP in sales dollars

   - graphing approach

     ➤ by reading the y-axis at the point where the total revenue and total cost lines intersect using the traditional CVP graph.

     ➤ by reading where the profit line intersects the x-axis using the profit-volume graph.

   - income statement approach which

     ➤ requires developing complete income statements showing total revenue minus total costs as being equal to a profit figure.

     ➤ is often used to prove the solutions found with other approaches.

3. CVP analysis can be used by a company to

   - determine BEP by assigning a zero value to the profit figure.

   - study the interrelationships of

     ➤ prices,

     ➤ volumes,

     ➤ fixed and variable costs, and

     ➤ contribution margins.

   - calculate the level of sales volume necessary to achieve specific before- or after-tax target profit objectives.

   - enhance a manager's ability to positively influence current operations and to predict future operations, thereby reducing the risk of uncertainty.

4. In a multiproduct environment, break-even and CVP analysis

   - require that a constant product sales mix or "bag" assumption be used for the various products.

   - require that a weighted average contribution margin or CM ratio be calculated for each "bag" of product sold.

   - state solutions in terms of "bags" of product, which means the solutions must be converted (using the original product sales mix) to actual units (or sales dollars) of individual products.

5. Companies use the margin of safety (MS) and degree of operating leverage (DOL) concepts as follows:

   - the MS indicates how far (in units, in sales dollars, or as a percentage) a company is operating from its BEP; the MS% is equal to (1 − DOL).

   - the DOL shows the percentage change that would occur in profit given a specified percentage change in sales from the current level; the DOL is equal to (1 − MS%).

6. The break-even and CVP models are based on several assumptions that limit their ability to reflect reality. Underlying assumptions are that

   - revenue and variable cost per unit are constant and linear within the relevant range.

   - contribution margin is linear within the relevant range.

- total fixed cost is constant within the relevant range.

- mixed costs can be accurately separated into their variable and fixed components.

- sales and production levels are equal.

- sales mix is constant in a multiproduct setting.

- labor productivity, production technology, and market conditions will not change during the period under consideration.

Potential Ethical Issues

1. Ignoring the relevant range when setting assumptions about cost behavior to disregard the implications of cost changes on the calculation of BEP or CVP analysis

2. Treating some or all fixed costs as per-unit costs (i.e., using absorption costing) in calculating BEP or performing CVP analysis

3. Using untested or inaccurate assumptions about the relationship between variables such as advertising and sales volume or sales price and sales volume to assure a particular decision outcome

4. Assuming a constant sales mix ratio while ignoring expected changes in demand for individual products when conducting CVP analysis for multiproduct firms

5. Using CVP analyses to support long-term cost management strategies

6. Visually distorting BEP graphs to project improper conclusions

7. Including irrelevant information in incremental analysis to manipulate calculation results▲

Solution Strategies

Cost-Volume-Profit (CVP)

The basic equation for break-even and CVP problems is

$$\text{Total Revenue} - \text{Total Costs} = \text{Profit}$$

CVP problems can also be solved by using a numerator/denominator approach. All numerators and denominators and the types of problems that each relates to follow. The formulas relate to both single- and multiproduct firms, but results for multiproduct firms are per bag and should be converted to units of individual products.

Problem Situation	Numerator	Denominator
Simple BEP in units	FC	CM
Simple BEP in dollars	FC	CM%
CVP with fixed profit in units	FC + P	CM
CVP with fixed profit in dollars	FC + P	CM%
CVP with specified profit in units	FC	$CM - P_U$
CVP with profit specified as a % of sales	FC	$CM\% - P_U\%$

where FC = fixed cost
CM = contribution margin per unit
$CM\%$ = contribution margin percentage
P = total profit (on a before-tax basis)
P_U = profit per unit (on a before-tax basis)
$P_U\%$ = profit percentage per unit (on a before-tax basis)

To convert after-tax profit to before-tax profit, divide after-tax profit by $(1 - \text{tax rate})$.

Margin of Safety (MS)

Margin of Safety in Units = Actual Sales in Units − Break-Even Sales in Units
Margin of Safety in Dollars = Actual Sales \$ − Break-Even Sales \$
Margin of Safety % = (Margin of Safety in Units or \$) ÷ (Actual Sales in Units or \$)

Degree of Operating Leverage (DOL)

Degree of Operating Leverage = Contribution Margin ÷ Profit Before Tax

Predicted Profit = [1 + (DOL × Percent Change in Sales)] × Current Profit

Demonstration Problem

Top Gardner makes small plant stands that sell for $25 each. The company's annual level of production and sales is 120,000 units. In addition to $430,500 of fixed manufacturing overhead and $159,050 of fixed administrative expenses, the following per-unit costs have been determined for each plant stand:

Direct material	$ 6.00
Direct labor	3.00
Variable manufacturing overhead	0.80
Variable selling expense	2.20
Total variable cost	$12.00

Required:

a. Prepare a variable costing income statement at the current level of production and sales.

b. Calculate the unit contribution margin in dollars and the contribution margin ratio for a plant stand.

c. Determine the break-even point in number of plant stands.

d. Calculate the dollar break-even point using the contribution margin ratio.

e. Determine Top Gardner's margin of safety in units, in sales dollars, and as a percentage.

f. Compute the company's degree of operating leverage. If sales increase by 25 percent, by what percentage will before-tax income increase?

g. How many plant stands must the company sell to earn $996,450 in before-tax income?

h. If the company wants to earn $657,800 after tax and is subject to a 20 percent tax rate, how many units must be sold?

i. How many plant stands must be sold to break even if Top Gardner's fixed manufacturing costs increased by $7,865? (Use the original data.)

j. The company has received an offer from a Brazilian company to buy 4,000 plant stands at $20 per unit. The per-unit variable selling cost of the additional units will be $2.80 (rather than $2.20), and $18,000 of additional fixed administrative cost will be incurred. This sale would not affect domestic sales or their costs. Based on quantitative factors alone, should Top Gardner accept this offer?

Solution to Demonstration Problem

a.

Top Gardner
Variable Costing Income Statement

Sales (120,000 × $25.00)		$3,000,000
Variable production costs		
Direct material (120,000 × $6.00)	$720,000	
Direct labor (120,000 × $3.00)	360,000	
Overhead (120,000 × $0.80)	96,000	
Variable selling expenses (120,000 × $2.20)	264,000	(1,440,000)
Contribution margin		$1,560,000
Fixed costs		
Manufacturing overhead	$430,500	
Administrative	159,050	(589,550)
Income before income tax		$ 970,450

b. CM = SP − VC = $25 − $12 = $13 per unit

   CM% = CM ÷ SP = $13 ÷ $25 = 52%

c. BEP = FC ÷ CM = $589,550 ÷ $13 = 45,350 plant stands

d. BEP = FC ÷ CM% = $589,550 ÷ 0.52 = $1,133,750 in sales

e. MS_u = Current unit sales − BEP unit sales = 120,000 − 45,350 = 74,650 plant stands

MS$ = Current sales in dollars − BEP sales in dollars = $3,000,000 − $1,133,750 = $1,866,250

MS% = MS in units ÷ Current unit sales = 74,650 ÷ 120,000 = 62% (rounded)

f.   DOL = Current CM ÷ Current Pre-Tax Income = $1,560,000 ÷ $970,450 = 1.61 (rounded)

Increase in Income = DOL × % Increase in Sales = 1.61 × 0.25 = 40.25%

Proof:

New Sales = 120,000 × 1.25 = 150,000
New CM = 150,000 × $13.00 = $1,950,000
New Pre-Tax Profit = New CM − FC = $1,950,000 − $589,550 = $1,360,450
Increase = New Pre-Tax Profit − Old Pre-Tax Profit = $1,360,450 − $970,450 = $390,000
Increase in % terms = $390,000 ÷ $970,450 = 40.19% (rounded)

g. $13X = $589,550 + $996,450

X = $1,586,000 ÷ $13

X = 122,000 plant stands

h.   PBT = PAT ÷ (1 − tax rate) = $657,800 ÷ (1 − 0.20) = $657,800 ÷ 0.80 = $822,250

$13X = $589,550 + $822,250

X = $1,411,800 ÷ $13

X = 108,600 plant stands

i.   X = Increase in FC ÷ CM

X = $7,865 ÷ $13

X = 605 units over BEP

New BEP = 45,350 + 605 = 45,955 plant stands

j.   New CM for each additional unit = $20.00 − $12.60 = $7.40

Total New CM = $7.40 × 4,000 = $29,600

Increase in Pre-Tax Profit = Increase in CM − Increase in FC = $29,600 − $18,000 = $11,600

Yes, the company should accept the offer.

Key Terms

break-even chart, **p. 328**

break-even point (BEP), **p. 320**

contribution margin ratio (CM%), **p. 322**

cost-volume-profit (CVP) analysis, **p. 323**

degree of operating leverage (DOL), **p. 336**

incremental analysis, **p. 331**

margin of safety (MS), **p. 335**

operating leverage, **p. 336**

profit-volume (PV) graph, **p. 330**

variable cost ratio (VC%), **p. 322**

Questions

1. What information provided by a variable costing income statement is used in computing the break-even point? Is this information on an absorption costing income statement? Explain your answer.

2. How is "break-even point" defined? What are the differences among the formula, graph, and income statement approaches for computing breakeven?

3. What is the contribution margin ratio? How is it used to calculate the break-even point?

4. Why is CVP analysis generally used as a short-run tool? Would CVP ever be appropriate as a long-run model?

5. How is the "bag" assumption used in CVP analysis for a multiproduct firm? What additional assumption must be made in multiproduct CVP analysis that doesn't pertain to a single-product CVP situation?

6. A multiproduct company has a sales mix of nine widgees to three squigees. Widgees have a contribution margin ratio of 45 percent, and squigees have a contribution margin ratio of 80 percent. If the sales mix changes to six widgees to six squigees, will the company have a higher or lower weighted average contribution margin ratio and a higher or lower break-even point (in sales dollars)? Explain the rationale for your answer.

7. Define and explain the relationship between margin of safety and degree of operating leverage.

Exercises

8. **LO.1 (Variable costing income statement)** SuperCaf Beverages began business in 2008 selling bottles of a thirst-quenching drink. Production for the first year was 104,000 bottles of SuperCaf, and sales were 98,000 bottles. The selling price per bottle was $1.55. Costs incurred during the year were as follows:

Ingredients used	$28,000
Direct labor	13,000
Variable overhead	24,000
Fixed overhead	2,600
Variable selling expenses	5,000
Fixed selling and administrative expenses	14,000
Total actual costs	$86,600

For 2008:
a. What was the production cost per bottle under variable costing?
b. What was variable cost of goods sold?
c. What was the contribution margin per bottle?
d. What was the contribution margin ratio?

9. **LO.1 (Variable costing income statement)** Top Hat Sports Gear manufactures baseball caps. The following information is available for 2008, the company's first year in business when it produced 150,000 caps. Revenue of $240,000 was generated by the sale of 90,000 caps.

EXCEL

	Variable Costs	Fixed Costs
Production		
Direct material	$75,000	
Direct labor	50,000	
Overhead	37,500	$56,250
Selling and administrative	45,000	50,000

a. What is the variable production cost per unit?
b. What is the total contribution margin per unit?
c. Prepare a variable costing income statement.

10. **LO.2 (Cost and revenue behavior)** The following financial data have been determined from analyzing the records of Leroy's Axles (a one-product firm):

Contribution margin per unit	$ 25
Variable costs per unit	21
Annual fixed cost	90,000

How does each of the following measures change when product volume goes up by one unit at Leroy's Axles?
a. Total revenue
b. Total cost
c. Income before tax

11. **LO.2 (Break-even point)** California Coastal has the following revenue and cost functions:

$$\text{Revenue} = \$30 \text{ per unit}$$
$$\text{Costs} = \$60,000 + \$15 \text{ per unit}$$

a. What is the break-even point in units?
b. What is the break-even point in dollars?

12. **LO.2 (Break-even point)** Jason's Jewelry makes and sells class rings for local schools. Operating information follows:

Selling price per ring	$500
Variable costs per ring	
Rings and stones	$180
Sales commissions	36
Overhead	16
Annual fixed costs	
Selling expenses	$ 84,000
Administrative expenses	112,000
Manufacturing	60,000

a. What is Jason's break-even point in rings?
b. What is Jason's break-even point in sales dollars?
c. What would Jason's break-even point be if sales commissions increased to $44?
d. What would Jason's break-even point be if selling expenses decreased by $10,000?

13. **LO.2 (Formula; graph; income statement)** Karsten Chemical had the following income statement for 2008:

Sales (30,000 gallons × $4)		$120,000
Variable costs		
Production (40,000 gallons × $1.50)	$60,000	
Selling (40,000 gallons × $0.25)	10,000	(70,000)
Contribution margin		$ 50,000
Fixed costs		
Production	$23,000	
Selling and administrative	3,100	(26,100)
Income before tax		$ 23,900
Income tax (40%)		(9,560)
Net income		$ 14,340

a. Compute the break-even point using the equation approach.
b. Prepare a CVP graph to reflect the relationships among costs, revenues, profit, and volume.
c. Prepare a profit-volume graph.
d. Prepare a short explanation for company management about each of the graphs.
e. Prepare an income statement at break-even point using variable costing.

14. **LO.3 (Sales price computation)** Leisure Sport has designed a new athletic suit. The company plans to produce and sell 60,000 units of the new product in the coming year. Annual fixed costs are $600,000, and variable costs are 70 percent of selling price. If the company wants a pre-tax profit of $300,000, at what minimum price must it sell its product?

15. **LO.3 (CVP)** Indiana Industries makes portable garden sheds that sell for $1,500 each. Costs are as follows:

	Per Unit	Total
Direct material	$700	
Direct labor	75	
Variable production overhead	40	
Variable selling and administrative cost	35	
Fixed production overhead		$100,000
Fixed selling and administrative		30,000

a. How many garden sheds must Indiana Industries sell to break even?
b. If Indiana Industries' management wants to earn a pre-tax profit of $195,000, how many garden sheds must it sell?
c. If Indiana Industries' management wants to earn a pre-tax profit of $260,000, how many garden sheds must it sell?

16. **LO.3 (CVP)** Reno Corp. sells a product for $180 per unit. The company's variable costs per unit are $30 for direct material, $25 per unit for direct labor, and $17 per unit for overhead. Annual fixed production overhead is $37,400, and fixed selling and administrative overhead is $25,240.
a. What is the contribution margin per unit?
b. What is the contribution margin ratio?
c. What is the break-even point in units?

d. Using the contribution margin ratio, what is the break-even point in sales dollars?

e. If Reno Corp. wants to earn a pre-tax profit of $25,920, how many units must the company sell?

17. **LO.3 (CVP; taxes)** Use the information for Indiana Industries in Exercise 15 and assume a tax rate for the company of 40 percent.

    a. If Indiana Industries' management wants to earn an after-tax profit of $134,400, how many garden sheds must it sell?

    b. How much revenue is needed to yield an after-tax profit of 10 percent of revenue? How many garden sheds does this revenue amount represent?

18. **LO.3 (CVP; taxes)** Use the information for Reno Corp. in Exercise 16 and assume a tax rate for the company of 30 percent.

    a. If Reno Corp. wants to earn an after-tax profit of $67,900, how many units must the company sell?

    b. If Reno Corp. wants to earn an after-tax profit of $2.80 on each unit sold, how many units must the company sell?

19. **LO.3 (Incremental sales)** Omaha Office Systems has annual sales of $4,500,000 with variable expenses of 60 percent of sales and fixed expenses per month of $50,000. By how much must annual sales increase for Omaha Office Systems to have pre-tax income equal to 30 percent of sales?

20. **LO.3 (CVP; taxes)** Easy Rider makes gasoline-powered golf carts. The selling price is $4,000 each, and costs are as follows:

Costs	Per Unit	Total
Direct material	$1,600	
Direct labor	500	
Variable overhead	250	
Variable selling	25	
Annual fixed production overhead		$200,000
Annual fixed selling and administrative		80,420

Easy Rider's income is taxed at a 35 percent rate.

    a. How many golf carts must Easy Rider sell to earn $500,000 after tax?

    b. What level of revenue is needed to yield an after-tax income equal to 20 percent of sales?

21. **LO.3 (Essay; Internet)** A significant trend in business today is the increasing use of outsourcing. Go to the Internet and search Web sites with the objective of gaining an understanding for the vast array of outsourcing services that are available. Prepare a presentation in which you discuss the extensive use of outsourcing today and how it could be used as a tool to manage a firm's cost structure and in CVP planning.

22. **LO.3 (Volume and pricing)** Dim Witt is the county commissioner of Clueless County. He decided to institute tolls for local ferry boat passengers. After the tolls had been in effect for four months, Astra Astute, county accountant, noticed that collecting $1,450 in tolls incurred a daily cost of $1,800. The toll is $0.50 per passenger.

    a. How many people are using the ferry boats each day?

    b. If the $1,800 cost is entirely fixed, how much must each passenger be charged for the toll process to break even? How much must each passenger be charged for the toll process to make a profit of $250 per day?

    c. Assume that only 80 percent of the $1,800 is fixed and the remainder varies by passenger. If the toll is raised to $0.60 per person, passenger volume is expected to fall by 10 percent. If the toll is raised and volume falls, will the county be better or worse off than it is currently and by what amount?

    d. Assume that only 80 percent of the $1,800 is fixed and the remainder varies by passenger. If passenger volume will decline by 5 percent for every $0.20 increase from the current $0.50 rate, at what level of use and toll amount would the county first make a profit?

    e. Discuss the saying "We may be showing a loss, but we can make it up in volume."

23. **LO.3 (CVP analysis)** Following are abbreviated income statements for two companies, A and B.

	A	B
Sales	$1,000,000	$1,000,000
Variable costs	(700,000)	0
Contribution margin	$ 300,000	$1,000,000
Fixed costs	0	(700,000)
Operating income	$ 300,000	$ 300,000

A and B produce identical products and sell them at an identical price, $20. Both companies are searching for ways to increase operating income. Managers of both companies are considering three identical strategies. Consider each of the following strategies, and discuss which company is best situated to adopt that strategy.

   a. Decrease sales price 30% to increase sales volume 50%.
   b. Increase sales price per unit 20% which will cause sales volume to decline by 10%.
   c. Increase advertising by $100,000 to increase sales volume by 7,500 units.

24. **LO.4 (CVP; multiproduct)** Anne's Accessories sells men's wallets and money clips. Historically, the firm's sales have averaged three wallets for every money clip. Each wallet has an $8 contribution margin, and each money clip has a $6 contribution margin. Anne's Accessories incurs fixed costs in the amount of $180,000. The selling prices of wallets and money clips, respectively, are $30 and $15. The corporatewide tax rate is 40 percent.

   a. How much revenue is needed to break even? How many wallets and money clips does this represent?
   b. How much revenue is needed to earn a pre-tax profit of $150,000?
   c. How much revenue is needed to earn an after-tax profit of $150,000?
   d. If Anne's Accessories earns the revenue determined in part (b) but does so by selling five wallets for every two money clips, what would be the pre-tax profit (or loss)? Why is this amount not $150,000?

25. **LO.4 (Multiproduct)** Green Machine makes three types of electric scooters. The company's total fixed costs are $1,080,000,000. Selling prices, variable costs, and sales percentages for each type of scooter follow:

	Selling Price	Variable Cost	Percent of Total Unit Sales
Mod	$2,200	$1,900	30%
Rad	3,700	3,000	50
X-treme	6,000	5,000	20

   a. What is Green Machine's break-even point in units and sales dollars?
   b. If the company has an after-tax income goal of $1 billion and the tax rate is 50 percent, how many units of each type of scooter must be sold for the goal to be reached at the current sales mix?
   c. Assume the sales mix shifts to 50 percent Mod, 40 percent Rad, and 10 percent X-treme. How does this change affect your answer to part (a)?
   d. If Green Machine sold more X-treme scooters and fewer Mod scooters, how would your answers to parts (a) and (b) change? No calculations are needed.

26. **LO.5 (CVP; margin of safety)** Norman Myers wants to cash in on the increased demand for ethanol. Accordingly he purchased a corn farm in Iowa. Myers believes his corn crop can be sold to an ethanol plant for $3.80 per bushel. Variable cost associated with growing and selling a bushel of corn is $2.80. Myers's annual fixed costs are $132,000.

   a. What is the break-even point in sales dollars and bushels of corn? If Myers's farm is 1,200 acres, how many bushels must he produce per acre to break even?
   b. If Myers actually produces 174,000 bushels, what is the margin of safety in bushels, in dollars, and as a percentage?

27. **LO.5 (CVP; operating leverage)** Wisconsin Rubber Co. manufactures tires for all-terrain vehicles. The tires sell for $50 and variable cost per tire is $20; monthly fixed costs are $450,000.

   a. What is the break-even point in units and sales dollars?
   b. If Jim Wallace, the company's CEO, wants the business to earn a pre-tax profit of 25 percent of revenues, how many tires must be sold each month?
   c. If the company is currently selling 20,000 tires monthly, what is the degree of operating leverage?
   d. If the company can increase sales by 15 percent above the current level, what will be the increase in net income? What will be the new net income? Prove your calculations with an income statement.

28. **LO.5 (Operating leverage; margin of safety)** Atomic Energy Co. makes a high-energy protein drink. The selling price per gallon is $7.20, and variable cost of production is $4.32. Total fixed costs per year are $316,600. The company is currently selling 125,000 gallons per year.

   a. What is the margin of safety in gallons?
   b. What is the degree of operating leverage?
   c. If the company can increase sales in gallons by 30 percent, what percentage increase will it experience in income? Prove your answer using the income statement approach.
   d. If the company increases advertising by $41,200, sales in gallons will increase by 15 percent. What will be the new break-even point? The new degree of operating leverage?

29. **LO.5 (Leverage factors; essay)** A group of prospective investors has asked for your help in understanding the comparative advantages and disadvantages of starting a company that is either labor intensive or, in

contrast, one that uses significant cutting-edge technology and is therefore capital intensive. Prepare a report addressing the issues. Include discussions regarding cost structure, BEP, CVP, MS, DOL, risk, customer satisfaction, and the relationships among these concepts.

30. **LO.6 (Product cost; essay)** A friend of yours, attending another university, states that she learned CVP is a short-run-oriented model and is, therefore, of limited usefulness. Your professor, however, has often discussed CVP in presentations about long-run planning to your cost accounting class. You decide to investigate your friend's allegation by preparing a report addressing your friend's contention. Your professor is also asking you to prepare a separate report for internal management's use that addresses how the CVP model could be adapted to become more useful for making long-run decisions. Prepare these two reports, one for your friend's understanding and one for your professor.

31. **LO.2–LO.4 (Comprehensive)** Compute the answers to each of the following independent situations.
   a. Orlando Ray sells liquid and spray mouthwash in a sales mix of 1:2, respectively. The liquid mouthwash has a contribution margin of $10 per unit; the spray's CM is $5 per unit. Annual fixed costs for the company are $100,000. How many units of spray mouthwash would Orlando Ray sell at the break-even point?
   b. Piniella Company has a break-even point of 4,000 units. At BEP, variable costs are $6,400 and fixed costs are $1,600. If one unit over breakeven is sold, what will be the company's pre-tax income?
   c. Montreal Company's product sells for $10 per bottle. Annual fixed costs are $216,000 and variable cost is 40 percent of selling price. How many units would Montreal Company need to sell to earn a 25 percent pre-tax profit on sales?
   d. York Mets Company has a BEP of 2,800 units. The company currently sells 3,200 units at $65 each. What is the company's margin of safety in units, in sales dollars, and as a percentage?

32. **LO.6 (Ethics; essay)** Frisco Chemical Company's new president has learned that, for the past four years, the company has been dumping its industrial waste into the local river and falsifying reports to authorities about the levels of suspected cancer-causing materials in that waste. The plant manager says that there is no proof that the waste causes cancer and that only a few fishing villages are within 100 miles downriver. If the company must treat the substance to neutralize its potentially injurious effects and then transport it to a legal dump site, the company's variable and fixed costs would rise to a level that might make the firm uncompetitive. If the company loses its competitive advantage, 10,000 local employees could become unemployed and the town's economy could collapse.

   a. What specific variable and fixed costs can you identify that would increase (or decrease) if the waste were treated rather than dumped? How would these costs affect product contribution margin?
   b. What ethical conflicts does the president face?
   c. What rationalizations can you detect that plant employees have devised?
   d. What options and suggestions can you offer the president?▲

33. **LO.6 (CVP assumptions)** Identify which of the CVP assumptions is violated in the circumstances described below.
   a. Price per unit declines as the volume of sales and production increase.
   b. Labor productivity increases as the volume of production declines.
   c. The sales mix in a multiproduct firm varies as the volume of total sales changes.
   d. Mixed costs cannot be separated into variable and fixed components.
   e. Costs behave according to a curvilinear function.
   f. Sales and production volume differ.
   g. Fixed costs and capacity can be adjusted within the period.

34. **LO.6 (CVP assumptions)** A local businesswoman, Ms. Hogarth, has hired you and a colleague, Steve, from your cost accounting class to advise her regarding her small manufacturing business that makes leather valises. The business was organized just two years ago and has failed to become profitable ... which is why the business owner has hired you and Steve. After analyzing the client's books, Steve prepared the following simple income statement for the current year.

Sales	$100,000
Variable costs	(60,000)
Contribution margin	$ 40,000
Fixed costs	(70,000)
Operating loss	$ (30,000)

After studying the income statement, Steve worked out the break-even point for the firm and advised the client, "Ms. Hogarth you will need to achieve sales of $175,000 before this business is producing enough revenues to cover all costs."

Ms. Hogarth replied, "That's a 75% increase over existing sales; I don't see any way this business will reach that level of sales."

"Then," said Steve, "You should shut the business down today to cut your losses."

After considering Steve's income statement and the conversation between Steve and Ms. Hogarth, discuss whether you agree with Steve's recommendation.

Problems

35. LO.1 & LO.2 (Absorption vs. variable costing; ethics) In its first year of operations, Belleville Utility Trailers incurred the following costs:

Variable production costs	$1,400 per unit
Variable selling and administrative costs	100 per unit
Fixed production costs	$100,000
Fixed selling and administrative costs	40,000

For this year, the company reported the following results:

Sales ($2,500 per unit)	$250,000
Cost of Goods Sold	(200,000)
Gross Margin	$ 50,000
Selling and Administrative Costs	(50,000)
Operating Income	$ 0

a. Using the contribution margin ratio approach, compute the break-even point for this company.
b. How many units did the firm produce in its first year of operations?
c. Provide an explanation that reconciles your result in (a) to the income statement provided above.
d. Prepare a variable costing income statement for sales of 100 units.
e. Assume that Belleville Utility Trailers is in need of a bank loan. Would it be unethical to use the income statement above, rather than the income statement compiled in part (d) to present to the loan officer? Explain. ▲

36. LO.1–LO.3 (CVP) Beloit Baskets manufactures a three-wheeled shopping cart that sells for $120. Variable manufacturing and variable selling costs are, respectively, $70 and $20 per unit. Annual fixed costs are $1,950,000.

a. What is the contribution margin per unit and the contribution margin ratio?
b. What is the break-even point in units?
c. How many units must the company sell to earn a pre-tax income of $1,800,000?
d. If the company's tax rate is 40 percent, how many units must be sold to earn an after-tax profit of $1,500,000?
e. If labor costs are 60 percent of the variable manufacturing costs and 40 percent of the fixed costs, how would a 10 percent decrease in both variable and fixed labor costs affect the break-even point?
f. Assume that the total market for three-wheeled shopping carts is 600,000 units per year and that Beloit currently has 18 percent of the market. Beloit wants to obtain a 25 percent market share and also wants to earn a pre-tax profit of $2,700,000. By how much must variable costs be reduced? Provide some suggestions for variable cost reductions.

37. LO.1–LO.3 & LO.5 (CVP single product; comprehensive) Sacramento Spheres makes baseballs that sell for $6.50 per two-pack. Current annual production and sales are 840,000 baseballs. Costs for each baseball are as follows:

Direct material	$1.00
Direct labor	0.50
Variable overhead	0.40
Variable selling expenses	0.10
Total variable cost	$2.00
Total fixed overhead	$700,000

a. Calculate the unit contribution margin in dollars and the contribution margin ratio for the company.
b. Determine the break-even point in number of baseballs.
c. Calculate the dollar break-even point using the contribution margin ratio.
d. Determine the company's margin of safety in number of baseballs, in sales dollars, and as a percentage.

e. Compute the company's degree of operating leverage. If sales increase by 25 percent, by what percentage would before-tax income increase?

f. How many baseballs must the company sell if it desires to earn $996,450 in before-tax profit?

g. If the company wants to earn $657,800 after tax and is subject to a 20 percent tax rate, how many baseballs must be sold?

h. How many baseballs would the company need to sell to break even if its fixed costs increased by $25,000? (Use original data.)

i. Sacramento Spheres has received an offer to provide a one-time sale of 8,000 baseballs at $5 per two-pack to a network of sports superstores. This sale would not affect other sales, nor would the cost of those sales change. However, the variable cost of the additional units would increase by $0.20 for shipping, and fixed costs would increase by $4,000. Based solely on financial information, should the company accept this offer? Show your calculations. What other factors might the company wish to consider in accepting or rejecting this offer?

38. LO.1–LO.3 (CVP) Swim Fit, in business since 2005, makes swimwear for professional athletes. Analysis of the firm's financial records for the current year reveals the following:

Average swimsuit selling price	$140
Variable swimsuit expenses	
Direct material	56
Direct labor	24
Variable overhead	16
Annual fixed costs	
Selling	$20,000
Administrative	48,000

The company's tax rate is 40 percent. Louise Abraham, company president, has asked you to help her answer the following questions.

a. What is the break-even point in number of swimsuits and in dollars?

b. How much revenue must be generated to produce $80,000 of pre-tax earnings? How many swimsuits would this level of revenue represent?

c. How much revenue must be generated to produce $80,000 of after-tax earnings? How many swimsuits would this represent?

d. What amount of revenue would be necessary to yield an after-tax profit equal to 20 percent of revenue?

e. Swim Fit is considering purchasing a faster sewing machine that will save $12 per swimsuit in cost but will raise annual fixed costs by $8,000. If the equipment is purchased, the company expects to make and sell an additional 5,000 swimsuits. Should the company make this investment?

f. A marketing consultant told Swim Fit managers that they could increase the number of swimsuits sold by 30 percent if the selling price was reduced by 10 percent and the company spent $20,000 on advertising. The company has been selling 3,000 swimsuits. Should the company make the changes advised by the consultant?

39. LO.1, LO.3 & LO.4 (CVP decision alternatives) Flash Riprock owns a sports brokerage agency and sells tickets to major league baseball, football, and basketball games. He also sells sports travel packages that include game tickets, airline tickets, and hotel accommodations. Revenues are commissions based as follows:

Game ticket sales	8% commission
Airline ticket sales	10% commission
Hotel bookings sales	20% commission

Monthly fixed costs include advertising ($2,200), rent ($1,800), utilities ($500), and other costs ($4,400). There are no variable costs. A typical month generates the following sales amounts that are subject to the stated commission structure:

Game tickets	$60,000
Airline tickets	9,000
Hotel bookings	14,000
Total	$83,000

a. What is Riprock's normal monthly profit or loss?

b. Riprock estimates that airline bookings can be increased by 40 percent if he increases advertising by $1,200. Should he increase advertising?

c. Riprock's friend Rusty has asked him for a job in the travel agency. Rusty has proposed that he be paid 50 percent of whatever additional commissions he can bring to the agency plus a salary of $400 per month. Riprock has estimated that Rusty can generate the following additional bookings per month:

Game tickets	$ 8,000
Airline tickets	1,500
Hotel bookings	6,000
Total	$15,500

Hiring Rusty would also increase fixed costs by $600 per month inclusive of salary. Should Riprock hire Rusty?

d. Riprock hired Rusty and in the first month Rusty generated an additional $13,000 of bookings for the agency. The bookings, however, were all airline tickets. Was the decision to hire Rusty a good one? Why or why not?

40. LO.2 (Graph) The Club House is a social organization that performs charitable work in its local community. The club has the following monthly cost and fee information: monthly membership fee per member, $60; monthly variable cost of service per member, $25; and monthly fixed service cost, $3,500. Costs are extremely low because volunteers provide almost all services and supplies. Excess of fees over service costs are used to support charitable activities.

a. Prepare a break-even chart for The Club House.

b. Prepare a profit-volume graph for The Club House.

c. At this time, The Club House has only 120 members. Which of the preceding items (break-even chart or profit-volume graph) would you use in a speech to the membership about the benefits of recruiting additional members? Why?

41. LO.3 & LO.4 (Multiproduct firm) Green Machine manufactures commercial and residential riding lawn-mowers. The company sells one commercial mower per three residential mowers sold. Selling prices for the commercial and residential mowers are, respectively, $5,600 and $1,800, and variable selling and production costs are, respectively, $3,800 and $1,000. The company's annual fixed costs are $8,400,000. Compute the sales volume of each engine type needed to:

a. Break even.

b. Earn $1,260,000 of income before tax.

c. Earn $1,008,000 of income after tax, assuming a 40 percent tax rate.

d. Earn 12 percent on sales revenue in before-tax income.

e. Earn 8 percent on sales revenue in after-tax income, assuming a 40 percent tax rate.

42. LO.3 & LO.4 (Multiproduct firm) Lucky Duck makes small pressed resin ducks and ducklings. For every duck sold, the company sells five ducklings. The following information is available about the company's selling prices and costs:

	Ducks	Ducklings
Selling price	$12	$6
Variable cost	6	4
Annual fixed costs	$144,000	

a. What is the average contribution margin ratio?

b. Calculate the monthly break-even point if fixed costs are incurred evenly throughout the year. At the BEP, indicate how many units of each product will be sold monthly.

c. If the company wants to earn $48,000 pre-tax profit monthly, how many units of each product must it sell?

d. Company management has specified $15,840 as monthly net income, and the company is in a 40 percent tax bracket. However, marketing information has indicated that the sales mix has changed to one duck to nine ducklings. How much total revenue and what number of products must be sold to achieve the company's profit objective?

e. Refer to the original information. If the company can reduce variable cost per duckling to $2 by raising monthly fixed costs by $4,250, how will the break-even point change? Should the company make these changes?

43. LO.3–LO.5 (Multiproduct firm) Happy Holidays Inc. manufactures plastic lawn ornaments. Currently the firm manufactures three items: reindeer, snowmen, and Santas. For each reindeer, two snowmen and four Santas are sold.

	Reindeer	Snowmen	Santas
Variable product costs	$12.00	$15.00	$25.00
Variable selling expenses	6.00	4.50	8.00
Variable administrative expenses	3.00	5.50	6.00
Selling price	40.00	35.00	60.00
Annual fixed factory overhead	$420,000		
Annual fixed selling expenses	150,000		
Annual fixed administrative expenses	80,178		

The firm is in a 40 percent tax bracket.

a. What is the annual break-even point in revenues?
b. How many reindeer, snowmen, and Santas are expected to be sold at the break-even point?
c. If the firm desires pre-tax income of $250,428, how much total revenue is required, and how many units of each product must be sold?
d. If the firm desires after-tax income of $155,718, how much total revenue is required, and how many units of each product must be sold?
e. If the firm achieves the revenue determined in part (d), what is its margin of safety in dollars and as a percentage?

44. LO.2–LO.5 (Comprehensive; multiproduct) Authentic Wood Flooring makes three types of wood flooring: Oak, Parquet, and Cherry. The company's tax rate is 40 percent. The following costs are expected for 2009:

	Oak	Parquet	Cherry
Variable costs (on a per-square-yard basis)			
Direct material	$10.40	$6.50	$17.60
Direct labor	3.60	0.80	12.80
Production overhead	2.00	0.30	3.50
Selling expense	1.00	0.50	4.00
Administrative expense	0.40	0.20	0.60
Fixed overhead	$760,000		
Fixed selling expense	240,000		
Fixed administrative expense	200,000		

Per-yard expected selling prices are as follows: Oak, $32.80; Parquet, $16.00; and Cherry, $50.00. The expected sales mix is as follows:

	Oak	Parquet	Cherry
Square yards	9,000	72,000	6,000

a. Calculate the break-even point for 2009.
b. How many square yards of each product are expected to be sold at the break-even point?
c. If the company wants to earn pre-tax profits of $800,000, how many square yards of each type of flooring would it need to sell? How much total revenue would be required?
d. If the company wants to earn an after-tax profit of $680,000, determine the revenue needed using the contribution margin percentage approach.
e. If the company achieves the revenue determined in part (d), what is the margin of safety (1) in dollars and (2) as a percentage?

45. LO2–LO.4 (CVP analysis; multiproduct) Buck Taylor owns Slam Dunk Hotel, a luxury hotel with 60 two-bedroom suites for coaches and their players. Capacity is 10 coaches and 50 players. Each suite is equipped with extra long king-sized beds, super-tall and extended shower heads, extra-tall bathroom vanities, a laptop, and a printer. Each suite has a Pacific Ocean view. Hotel services include airport limousine pickup and drop-off, a daily fruit basket, champagne on the day of arrival, and a Hummer for transportation. Coaches and players are interviewed about their dietary restrictions and room service requirements before arrival. The hotel's original cost was $1,920,000, and depreciation is $160,000 per year. Other hotel operating costs include:

Labor	$320,000 per year plus $5 per suite per day
Utilities	$158,000 per year plus $1 per suite per day
Miscellaneous	$100,000 per year plus $6 per suite per day

In addition to these costs, costs are incurred for food and beverage for each guest. These costs are strictly variable and (on average) are $40 per day for coaches and $15 per day for players.

a. Assuming that the hotel is able to maintain an average annual occupancy of 80 percent in both coach and player suites (based on a 360-day year), determine the minimum daily charge that must be assessed per suite per day to generate $240,000 of income before tax.

b. Assume that the per-day price Taylor charges is $240 for coaches and $200 for players. If the sales mix is 12 to 48 (12 coach days of occupancy for every 48 player days of occupancy), compute the following:

    1. The break-even point in total occupancy days.

    2. Total occupancy days required to generate $400,000 of income before tax.

    3. Total occupancy days to generate $400,000 of after-tax income. Taylor's personal tax rate is 35 percent.

c. Taylor is considering adding a massage service for guests to complement current hotel services. He has estimated that the costs of providing such a service would largely be fixed because all necessary facilities already exist. He would, however, need to hire five certified masseurs at a cost of $500,000 per year. If Taylor decides to add this service, how much would he need to increase his daily charges (assume equal dollar increases to coach and player room fees) to maintain the break-even point computed in part (b)?

46. LO.3 (CVP analysis; advanced) Rudolph Railways is a luxury passenger carrier in Alaska. All seats are first class, and the following data are available:

Number of seats per passenger train car	120
Average load factor (percentage of seats filled)	75%
Average full passenger fare	$70
Average variable cost per passenger	$30
Fixed operating costs per month	$1,200,000

a. What is the break-even point in passengers and revenues?

b. What is the break-even point in number of passenger train cars?

c. If Rudolph raises its average passenger fare to $85, it is estimated that the load factor will decrease to 60 percent. What will be the break-even point in number of passenger cars?

d. (Refer to original data.) Fuel cost is a significant variable cost to any railway. If fuel charges increase by $8 per barrel, it is estimated that variable cost per passenger will rise to $40. What would be the new break-even point in passengers and in number of passenger train cars?

e. Rudolph has experienced an increase in variable cost per passenger to $35 and an increase in total fixed costs to $1,500,000. The company has decided to raise the average fare to $80. If the tax rate is 40 percent, how many passengers are needed to generate an after-tax profit of $400,000?

f. (Use original data.) Rudolph is considering offering a discounted fare of $50, which the company believes would increase the load factor to 80 percent. Only the additional seats would be sold at the discounted fare. Additional monthly advertising costs would be $80,000. How much pre-tax income would the discounted fare provide Rudolph if the company has 40 passenger train cars per day, 30 days per month?

g. Rudolph has an opportunity to obtain a new route that would be traveled 15 times per month. The company believes it can sell seats at $75 on the route, but the load factor would be only 60 percent. Fixed costs would increase by $100,000 per month for additional crew, additional passenger train cars, maintenance, and so on. Variable cost per passenger would remain at $30.

    1. Should the company obtain the route?

    2. How many passenger train cars must Rudolph operate to earn pre-tax income of $50,500 per month on this route?

    3. If the load factor could be increased to 75 percent, how many passenger train cars must be operated to earn pre-tax income of $50,500 per month on this route?

    4. What qualitative factors should be considered by Rudolph in making its decision about acquiring this route?

47. LO.2, LO.3 & LO.5 (Incremental analysis) Sunny Day Co. makes canvas window awnings. You have been asked to predict the potential effects of some proposed company changes. The following information is available:

Variable costs per unit	
Direct material	$9.20
Direct labor	6.50
Production overhead	4.30
Selling expenses	2.30
Administrative expenses	1.50
Annual fixed costs	
Production overhead	$600,000
Selling	480,000
Administrative	240,000

The selling price is $47.00 per unit, and expected sales volume for the current year is 150,000 units. Following are some changes proposed by various members of the company.

1. Engineers suggest that adding color accents to each unit at a cost of $7.20 would increase product sales by 20 percent.
2. The sales manager suggests that a $260,000 increase in advertising will increase sales by 15 percent.
3. The sales force believes that lowering the price by 5 percent will increase demand in units by 10 percent.
a. Compute the current break-even point in units and dollars.
b. Compute the current margin of safety in dollars, in units, and as a percentage.
c. Compute the independent effects on profit and dollar break-even point of each of the suggestions. For each proposal, advise company management about acceptability.

48. **LO.1–LO.3 & LO.5 (MS; DOL; PV graph)** You are considering buying one of two local firms (Olson Corp. and Miami Inc.). Olson Corp. uses a substantial amount of direct labor in its manufacturing operations and its salespeople work on commission. Miami Inc. uses the latest automated technology in manufacturing; its salespeople are salaried. The following financial information is available for the two companies:

	OLSON CORP.		MIAMI INC.	
	2008	**2009**	**2008**	**2009**
Sales	$600,000	$960,000	$600,000	$840,000
Expenses including taxes	(528,000)	(823,200)	(528,000)	(667,200)
Net income	$ 72,000	$136,800	$ 72,000	$172,800

After examining cost data, you find that the fixed costs for Olson Corp. are $60,000; the fixed costs for Miami Inc. are $300,000. The tax rate for both companies is 40 percent.
a. Recast the income statements into a variable costing format.
b. What are the break-even sales for each firm for each year?
c. Assume that you could acquire either firm for $1,200,000, and you want an after-tax return of 12 percent on your investment. Determine what sales level for each firm would allow you to reach your goal.
d. What is the margin of safety for each firm for each year? What is the degree of operating leverage?
e. Assume that product demand for 2010 is expected to rise by 15 percent from the 2009 level. What will be the expected net income for each firm?
f. Assume that product demand for 2010 is expected to fall by 20 percent from the 2009 level. What will be the expected net income for each firm?
g. Prepare a profit-volume graph for each firm.

49. **LO.5 (CVP; DOL; MS—two quarters; comprehensive)** Following is information pertaining to Langley Co.'s operations of the first and second quarter of 2008:

	QUARTER	
	First	**Second**
Units		
Production	70,000	60,000
Sales	60,000	70,000
Expected activity level	65,000	65,000
Unit selling price	$75.00	$75.00
Unit variable costs		
Direct material	$34.50	$34.50
Direct labor	16.50	16.50
Factory overhead	7.80	7.80
Selling and administrative	5.70	5.70
Fixed costs		
Factory overhead	$195,000	$195,000
Selling and administrative	42,800	42,800

Additional Information
- There were no finished goods at January 1, 2008.
- Langley Co. writes off any quarterly underapplied or overapplied overhead as an adjustment to Cost of Goods Sold.
- Langley Co.'s income tax rate is 35 percent.
a. Prepare a variable costing income statement for each quarter.
b. Calculate each of the following for 2008 if 260,000 units were produced and sold:

1. Unit contribution margin.
2. Contribution margin ratio.
3. Total contribution margin.
4. Net income.
5. Degree of operating leverage.
6. Annual break-even unit sales volume.
7. Annual break-even dollar sales volume.
8. Annual margin of safety as a percentage.
9. Annual margin of safety in units.

50. **LO.6 (CVP assumptions)** You were talking to your roommate one day about CVP analysis and the approaches that are used to calculate the break-even point. You also described the assumptions that underlie this type of analysis.

    Your roommate proclaimed, "Wow, you people in accounting are pretty simple. Do you realize how unrealistic it is to assume that, no matter how many units you sell, you will realize the same price per unit? And, I've never heard any serious person suggest that costs are linear. How can you possibly state that assumption with a straight face? In your world, profit maximization is simple . . . just produce the maximum amount possible."

    Provide a written justification of the assumptions accountants make in conducting CVP analysis that will satisfy your critical economist roommate.

10 | Relevant Information for Decision Making

Objectives

After completing this chapter, you should be able to answer the following questions:

LO.1 What factors determine the relevance of information to decision making?

LO.2 What are sunk costs, and why are they not relevant in making decisions?

LO.3 What information is relevant in an outsourcing decision?

LO.4 How can management achieve the highest return from use of a scarce resource?

LO.5 What variables do managers use to manipulate sales mix?

LO.6 How are special prices set, and when are they used?

LO.7 How do managers determine whether a product line should be retained or discontinued?

LO.8 (*Appendix*) How is linear programming used to optimally manage multiple resource constraints?

Introduction

This chapter introduces the topic of relevant costing, which focuses managerial attention on a decision's relevant (or pertinent) information. Relevant costing techniques are applied in virtually all business decisions in both short-term and long-term contexts. The chapter examines the application of relevant costing techniques to recurring business decisions, such as replacing an asset, outsourcing a product or part, allocating scarce resources, manipulating sales mix, and evaluating specially priced orders. Discussion of analysis tools that are applied to longer-term decisions is deferred to Chapter 15. Long-term decisions generally require consideration of costs and benefits that are mismatched in time; that is, the cost is incurred currently but the benefit is derived in future periods.

LO.1
What factors determine the relevance of information to decision making?

The Concept of Relevance

In decision making, managers should consider all relevant costs and revenues associated with each decision alternative. In this process, there is a relationship between time and relevance. As the decision time horizon is reduced, fewer costs and revenues are relevant because the majority of such amounts cannot be changed by short-term management actions. In the longer term, management action can influence virtually all costs. Regardless of whether the decision is a short- or long-term one, all decision making requires analysis of relevant information.

For information to be relevant, it must possess three characteristics: (1) be associated with the decision under consideration, (2) be important to the decision maker, and (3) have a connection to, or bearing on, some future endeavor.

Association with Decision

Cost accountants can assist managers in determining which costs and revenues are decision relevant. Costs or revenues are relevant when they are logically related to a decision and vary from one decision alternative to another by being either incremental or differential. Incremental revenue (or differential revenue) is the amount of revenue that differs across decision choices; incremental cost (or differential cost) is the amount of cost that varies across decision choices. For example, if the annual operating cost of an existing machine is $30,000 and that of a potential replacement machine is $22,000, the incremental annual cost to operate the existing machine is $8,000 ($30,000 − $22,000).

The process of relevant costing requires comparing the incremental revenues and incremental costs of alternative choices. Although incremental costs can be variable or fixed, a general guideline is that most variable costs are relevant but most fixed costs are not. The logic of this guideline is that, as an activity measure (such as sales or production volume) changes within the relevant range, total variable cost changes, but total fixed cost remains constant. However, as is often the case, there are exceptions to this general rule.

The difference between the incremental revenue and the incremental cost of a particular alternative is the incremental profit (incremental loss) of that course of action. Management can compare incremental effects of alternatives in deciding on the most profitable (or least costly) alternative. Although such a comparison sounds simple, for two reasons it often is not. First, the concept of relevance is an inherently individualistic determination; second, technological changes have increased the amount of available information to consider in making a decision. One challenge is to get as much information as possible that reflects relevant costs and benefits.

Some relevant factors, such as sales commissions or direct production costs, are easily identified and quantified because they are captured by the accounting system. Other factors are relevant and quantifiable but are not captured by the accounting system. Such factors cannot be ignored simply because they are difficult to obtain or require the use of estimates. For instance, opportunity costs represent the benefits forgone because one course of action is chosen over another. These costs are extremely important in decision making but are not included in the accounting records.

To illustrate the concept of opportunity cost, assume that on August 1, Tonya bought a ticket for $70 to attend a play in December. In October, Tonya's friend offers to buy the ticket for $120. The $120 price offered by Tonya's friend is an opportunity cost, a benefit that Tonya will sacrifice if she chooses to attend the play rather than sell the ticket.

Importance to Decision Maker

The need for specific information depends on how important that information is relative to the achievement of managerial objectives. Additionally, managers give more weight in the decision process to information that is more, rather than less, precise. However, if information is extremely important but less precise, a manager must weigh importance against precision.

Bearing on the Future

Information may pertain to past or present events but is relevant only if it pertains to a future decision choice. All managerial decisions are made to affect future events, so the information on which decisions are based should reflect future effects. The future can be the short run (two hours from now, or next month) or the long run (three years from now).

Only future costs and revenues can be influenced by current decisions, and, as the time horizon lengthens, the greater is the set of future costs that are controllable, avoidable, and relevant. The challenge in relevant costing is to filter out of consideration those costs that are not relevant. Costs incurred in the past to acquire an asset or a resource are called sunk costs. One common misconception or error in decision making is treating a sunk cost, such as a previously purchased asset's acquisition cost or book value, as though it were relevant.

Sunk Costs

LO.2
What are sunk costs, and why are they not relevant in making decisions?

Sunk costs cannot be changed no matter what future course of action is taken because historical transactions cannot be reversed currently. For example, after acquiring an asset or a resource, managers could find that it is no longer adequate for its intended purpose, does not perform to expectations, is technologically obsolete, or is no longer marketable. Managers must then decide whether to keep the asset. This decision uses the current or future selling price that can be obtained for the old asset, but that price is the result of current or future conditions and does not "recoup" the historical or sunk cost. The historical cost is irrelevant to the decision.

Although asset acquisition decisions are covered in depth in Chapter 15, they provide an excellent introduction to the concept of relevant information. The following illustration includes simplistic assumptions regarding asset acquisitions but demonstrates why sunk costs are not relevant costs.

Assume that Ace Home Appliances purchases a robotic warehouse management system for $12,000,000 on December 9, 2008. This "original" system is expected to have a useful life of five years and no salvage value. Five days later, on December 14, Cory Coppel, vice president of production, notices an advertisement for a similar system for $10,800,000. This "new" system also has an estimated life of five years and no salvage value, but it has features that enable it to perform better than, and save $355,000 per year in labor costs over, the original system. On investigation, Coppel discovered that the original system can be sold for only $8,900,000. Exhibit 10–1 provides data on the original and new robotic warehouse management systems.

Ace Home Appliances has two options: (1) use the original system or (2) sell it and buy the new system. Exhibit 10–2 indicates the relevant costs Coppel should consider in making his decision. As the computations show, the original system's $12,000,000 purchase price does not affect the decision outcome. This amount was "gone forever" when the company bought the system. However, by selling the original system, the company would have net cash outlay for the new system of only $1,900,000 because $8,900,000 will be received from selling the old system. Using either system, Ace will incur operating costs over the next five years, but it will spend $355,000 less each year using the new system for lifetime operating savings of $1,775,000.

EXHIBIT 10–1

Ace Home Appliances: Robotic Warehouse Management System Replacement Decision Data

	Original System (Purchased December 9)	New System (Available December 14)
Cost	$12,000,000	$10,800,000
Life in years	5	5
Salvage value	$0	$0
Current resale value	$8,900,000	Not applicable
Annual operating cost	$855,000	$500,000

EXHIBIT 10–2

Relevant Costs Related to Ace Home Appliances' Alternatives

Alternative (1): Use original system		
Operating cost over life of original system ($855,000 × 5 years)		$ 4,275,000
Alternative (2): Sell original system and buy new		
Cost of new system	$10,800,000	
Resale value of original system	(8,900,000)	
Effective net outlay for new system	$ 1,900,000	
Operating cost over life of new system ($500,000 × 5 years)	2,500,000	
Total cost of new system		(4,400,000)
Benefit of keeping the old system		$ (125,000)
The alternative incremental calculation follows:		
Savings from operating the new system for 5 years		$ 1,775,000
Less effective incremental outlay for new system		(1,900,000)
Incremental advantage of keeping the old system		$ (125,000)

A common analytical tendency is to include the $12,000,000 cost of the old system in the analysis. However, this cost does not differ between the decision alternatives. If Ace keeps the original system, the company will deduct the $12,000,000 as depreciation expense over the system's life. Alternatively, if Ace sells the system, it will charge the $12,000,000 against the revenue realized from the system's sale. Thus, the $12,000,000 depreciation charge or its equivalent loss is the same in magnitude whether the company retains the original system or disposes of it and buys the new one. Because the amount is the same under both alternatives, it is not relevant to the decision process.

Coppel must consider only the following relevant factors in deciding whether to purchase the new system:

1. cost of the new system ($10,800,000).
2. current resale value of the original system ($8,900,000).

3. annual savings of the new system ($355,000) and the number of years (5) such savings would be enjoyed.[1]

This example demonstrates the difference between relevant and irrelevant costs, including sunk costs. The next section discusses how the concepts of relevant costing, incremental revenues, and incremental costs are applied in making some routine, recurring managerial decisions.

Relevant Costs for Specific Decisions

In evaluating courses of action, managers should select the alternative that provides the highest incremental benefit to the company. In doing so, they must compare the net benefits of all courses of action against a baseline alternative. One course of action that is often used as the baseline alternative is the "change nothing" or "do nothing" option.

Although certain incremental revenues and incremental costs are associated with other alternatives, the "change nothing" alternative has a zero incremental benefit because it reflects the status quo. Some situations involve specific government regulations or mandates in which a "change nothing" alternative does not exist. For example, if a licensed governmental agency issues an injunction against a company for polluting river water, the company would be forced to correct the pollution problem (assuming that it wishes to continue in business). It could delay the installation of pollution control devices at the risk of fines or closure. Management should consider such fines as incremental costs; closure would create an opportunity cost amounting to the income that would have been generated had sales continued.

Rational decision-making behavior includes a comprehensive evaluation of the monetary effects of all alternative courses of action. The chosen course should be one that will make the business better off than it is currently. In making decisions, managers must also find a way to include any inherently nonquantifiable considerations. Inclusion can be made by attempting to quantify those items or by simply making instinctive value judgments about nonmonetary benefits and costs.

Outsourcing Decisions

Deciding how to source required inputs is an important decision for every business. Traditionally, many companies ensured the availability as well as the desired level of quality of parts and services by controlling all functions internally. However, there is a growing trend to purchase more of the required materials, components, and services through an outsourcing process. Outsourcing refers to having work performed for one company by an off-site, nonaffiliated supplier; it allows a company to buy a product (or service) from an outside supplier rather than to make the product or perform the service in-house.

The outsourcing trend is global in scope and has become a hotly debated topic in the United States. Central to the debate is the effect on U.S. employment that outsourcing has when it involves offshoring, which sends work formerly performed in the home country to other countries. However, a careful analysis of outsourcing suggests that more work is outsourced to U.S. firms from other countries than is exported from the United States to foreign firms.[2] Information technology work is the most common work taken offshore followed by manufacturing and back-office processing work (e.g., customer service).[3]

The outsourcing decision (or make-or-buy decision) is made only after performing an analysis that compares internal production and opportunity costs to external purchase cost and then assesses the best use of facilities. Having an insourcing (make) option implies that the company has the capacity available for that purpose or has considered the cost of obtaining the necessary capacity.

LO.3
What information is relevant in an outsourcing decision?

---

[1]In addition, two factors that were not discussed are important: the potential tax effects of the transactions and the time value of money. The authors have chosen to defer consideration of these items to Chapter 15, which covers capital budgeting. Because of the time value of money, both systems were assumed to have zero salvage values at the end of their lives—a fairly unrealistic assumption.
[2]See Michael M. Phillips, "More Work Is Outsourced to U.S. Than Away From It, Data Show," *Wall Street Journal* (April 3, 2004), p. A1.
[3]See Kate O'Sullivan and Don Durfee, "Offshoring by the Numbers," *CFO* (June 2004), pp. 51 ff.

Relevant information for this type of decision includes both quantitative and qualitative factors. Exhibit 10–3 summarizes the primary motivations for companies to pursue outsourcing.

As shown in the graphic on the next page, most outsourcing is not related to an organization's strategic core but to the management of operating costs.[4] Thus, routine activities such as information processing are more often outsourced than activities that constitute core competencies or new strategies.

EXHIBIT 10–3
Reasons to Outsource

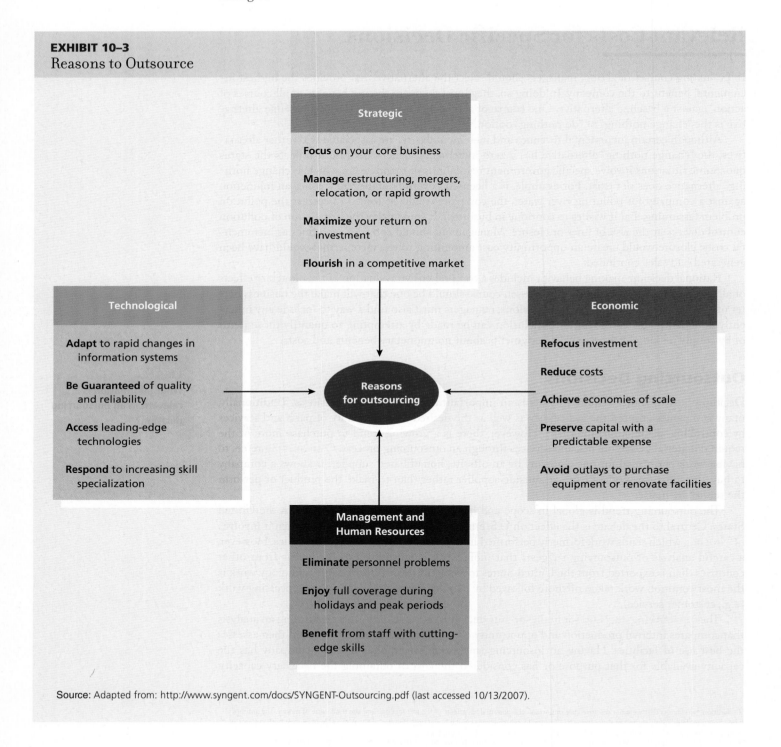

Strategic

Focus on your core business

Manage restructuring, mergers, relocation, or rapid growth

Maximize your return on investment

Flourish in a competitive market

Technological

Adapt to rapid changes in information systems

Be Guaranteed of quality and reliability

Access leading-edge technologies

Respond to increasing skill specialization

Reasons for outsourcing

Economic

Refocus investment

Reduce costs

Achieve economies of scale

Preserve capital with a predictable expense

Avoid outlays to purchase equipment or renovate facilities

Management and Human Resources

Eliminate personnel problems

Enjoy full coverage during holidays and peak periods

Benefit from staff with cutting-edge skills

Source: Adapted from: http://www.syngent.com/docs/SYNGENT-Outsourcing.pdf (last accessed 10/13/2007).

[4]See Jerry Bowles, "Outsourcing for Competitive Advantage," *Forbes* (June 7, 2004), p. 101.

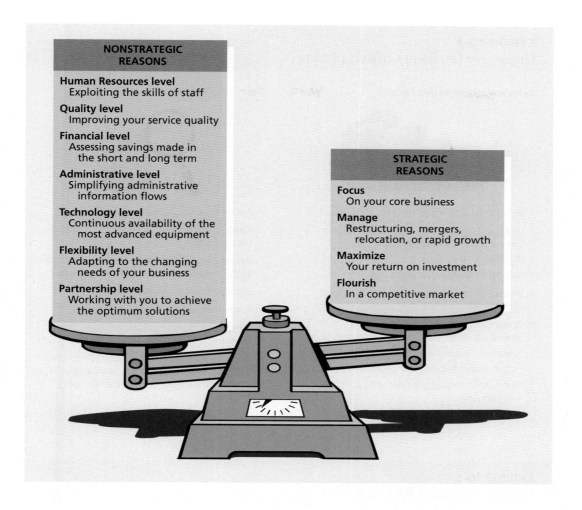

Numerous factors, such as those included in Exhibit 10–4, should be considered in the outsourcing decision. Several quantitative factors, such as incremental direct material and direct labor costs per unit, are known with a high degree of certainty. Other factors, such as the variable overhead per unit and the opportunity cost associated with production facilities, must be estimated. The qualitative factors should be evaluated by more than one individual so personal biases do not distort business judgment.

Although companies can gain the best knowledge, experience, and methodology available in a process through outsourcing, they also lose some control. Thus, company management should carefully evaluate the activities to be outsourced. The pyramid in Exhibit 10–5 is one model for assessing outsourcing risk. Factors to consider include whether (1) a function is considered critical to the organization's long-term viability (such as product research and development), (2) the organization is pursuing a core competency relative to this function, and (3) issues such as product/service quality, time of delivery, flexibility of use, or reliability of supply can be resolved to the company's satisfaction.

Exhibit 10–6 (p. 363) provides information about the casing for a microwave oven manufactured by Ace Home Appliances. The total cost to manufacture one microwave oven case is $7.90, or cases can be purchased externally for $7.00 each. Ace's cost accountant is preparing an analysis to determine whether the company should continue making the cases or buy them from the outside supplier.

Production of each case costs $6.20 per unit for material, labor, and variable overhead. In addition, $0.50 of the fixed overhead is considered a direct product cost because that amount can specifically be traced to the manufacture of cases. This $0.50 is an incremental cost because it could be avoided if Ace does not produce the microwave cases. The remaining fixed overhead ($1.20) is

EXHIBIT 10–4
Outsource Decision Considerations

Relevant Quantitative Factors

- Incremental production costs for each unit
- Unit cost of purchasing from outside supplier (price less any discounts available plus shipping, etc.)
- Number of available suppliers
- Production capacity available to manufacture components
- Opportunity costs of using facilities for production rather than for other purposes
  * Amount of space available for storage
  * Costs associated with carrying inventory
  * Increase in throughput generated by buying components

Relevant Qualitative Factors

- Reliability of supply sources
- Ability to control quality of inputs purchased from outside
- Nature of the work to be subcontracted (such as the importance of the part to the whole)
- Impact on customers and markets
- Future bargaining position with supplier(s)
- Perceptions regarding possible future price changes
- Perceptions about current product prices (are the prices appropriate or, in some cases with international suppliers, is product dumping involved?)

EXHIBIT 10–5
Outsourcing Risk Pyramid

Outsourcing Risk Pyramid

Never Outsource
- Strategic Direction of Firm
- Unique Core Competencies

Outsource under Tight Control
- Tax, Audit, Legal Services
- Information Technology Sharing

Outsource under Service Levels
- Help Desk, Call Centers, Data Centers, Logistics

Low-Risk Outsourcing
- Facility Management, Network Management, Temporary Staffing, Supply-Chain Management
- Payroll, Security Services, Food Service

Source: The Yankee Group, "Innovators in Outsourcing," *Forbes* (October 23, 1995), p. 266. Reprinted with permission from The Yankee Group.

EXHIBIT 10–6
Ace Home Appliances—Outsource Decision Cost Information

	Present Manufacturing Cost per Microwave Case	Relevant Cost of Manufacturing Microwave Case
Direct material	$2.40	$2.40
Direct labor	3.00	3.00
Variable factory overhead	0.80	0.80
Fixed factory overhead*	1.70	0.50
Total unit cost	$7.90	$6.70
Quoted price from supplier		$7.00

*Of the $1.70 fixed factory overhead, only $0.50 is actually caused by microwave case production and could be avoided if the firm chooses not to produce cases. The remaining $1.20 of fixed factory overhead is allocated to indirect (common) costs that would continue even if case production ceases.

not relevant to the outsourcing decision. This amount is a common cost incurred by general production activity that is unassociated with the cost object (cases). Therefore, because the $1.20 of fixed overhead cost would continue under either alternative, it is not relevant.

The relevant cost for the insource alternative is $6.70—the cost that would be avoided if the company purchases the case externally. This amount should be compared to the $7.00 cost quoted by the supplier under the outsource alternative. The $6.70 and $7.00 are the incremental costs of making and buying, respectively. All else being equal, management should choose to make the cases rather than purchase them because the company will save $0.30 on each case. Relevant costs, regardless of whether they are variable or fixed, are avoidable because one decision alternative was chosen over another. In an outsourcing decision, variable production costs are relevant. Fixed production costs are relevant only if they can be avoided by discontinuing production.

The opportunity cost of the facilities being used by production is also relevant in this decision. Choosing to outsource a product component rather than to make it allows the company to use its facilities for an alternative purpose. If a more profitable alternative is available, management should consider diverting the capacity to this use. Assume that Ace Home Appliances can lease out the physical space now used to produce microwave cases for $360,000 per year. If the company produces 600,000 cases annually, it has an opportunity cost of $0.60 per unit ($360,000 ÷ 600,000 cases) for using rather than renting the production space. The lease opportunity makes the outsource alternative more attractive to Ace because it would forgo this amount if it chooses to make the cases; thus, the lease opportunity cost is essentially an "additional" production cost. Sacrificing potential revenue is as much a relevant cost as is the incurrence of expenses. See Exhibit 10–7 for calculations relating to this decision on both a per unit and a total cost basis. Under either format, the comparison indicates that there is a $0.30 per unit advantage to outsourcing over insourcing.

Another opportunity cost that can be associated with insourcing is an increase in plant production activity (or throughput) that is lost because a component is being made. Assume that case production at Ace Home Appliances uses a resource that has been determined to be a bottleneck in the manufacturing plant. Management calculates that plant throughput can be increased by 1 percent per year on all products if the company buys rather than makes the cases. This increase in throughput would provide an estimated additional annual contribution margin of $210,000 with no incremental fixed costs. Dividing this amount by the 600,000 cases currently being produced results in a $0.35 per-unit opportunity cost related to manufacturing. When added to the previously calculated relevant cost of $7.30, the relevant cost of manufacturing cases becomes $7.65. Based on the information in Exhibit 10–7 (even without the inclusion of the throughput opportunity cost), Ace Home Appliances' cost accountant should inform company management that it is more economical

EXHIBIT 10–7
Ace Home Appliances' Opportunity Cost and Outsource Decision

	Insource	Outsource	Difference in Favor of Outsourcing
Per unit			
Direct production costs	$ 6.70		
Opportunity cost (revenue)	0.60		
Purchase cost		$ 7.00	
Cost per case	$ 7.30	$ 7.00	
In total			
Revenue from renting capacity	$ 0	$ 360,000	$ 360,000
Cost for 600,000 cases	(4,020,000)	(4,200,000)	(180,000)
Net cost	$(4,020,000)	$(3,840,000)	$ 180,000*

*The $180,000 represents the net purchase benefit of $0.30 per unit multiplied by the 600,000 units to be purchased during the year.

to purchase cases for $7.00 than to manufacture them. This type of analysis—determining which alternative is preferred based on the quantitative considerations—is the typical starting point of the decision process. Managers then use judgment to assess the decision's qualitative aspects.

Suppose Ace Home Appliances' purchasing agent read a newspaper article that the case supplier being considered is in poor financial condition and might file for bankruptcy. In this instance, management would decide to insource rather than to outsource the cases from this supplier. Although quantitative analysis supports the purchase of the units, qualitative considerations suggest outsourcing would not be a wise action because the supplying source's stability as a going concern is questionable.

This additional consideration also shows that a theoretically short-run decision can have many potentially long-run effects. If Ace had stopped case production and rented out its facilities and the supplier had then gone bankrupt, Ace would face high start-up costs to reestablish its case production process. At one point Stonyfield Farm, a New Hampshire–based yogurt company, faced such a situation: the firm subcontracted its yogurt production and one day found its supplier bankrupt, making Stonyfield unable to fill customer orders. It took Stonyfield two years to acquire the necessary production capacity and regain market strength.

This viewpoint suggests that the term *fixed cost* may actually be a misnomer because, although such costs do not vary with volume in the short run, they will vary in the long run. Thus, fixed costs are relevant for long-run decision making.

To illustrate this reasoning, assume that a company manufactures (rather than outsources) a particular part and expects demand for that part to increase in the future. If the company expands capacity in the future, it will incur additional "fixed" capacity costs. In turn, product costs would likely increase as a result of additional overhead allocated to production. To suggest that products made before capacity is increased would cost less than those made afterward is a short-run view. The long-run viewpoint should consider both the current and long-run variable costs over the product life cycle: capacity costs were "fixed" only until the relevant range of capacity changed. However, many firms actively engage in cooperative efforts with their suppliers to control costs and reduce prices. Strong supplier relationships are required for companies using the just-in-time (JIT) technologies discussed in Chapter 18.

Outsourcing decisions are not confined solely to manufacturing entities. Many service organizations also make such decisions. For example, accounting and law firms must decide whether to

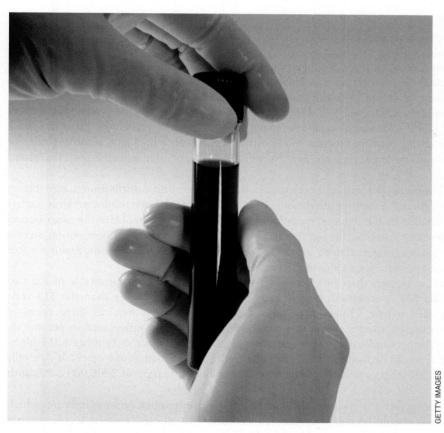

Many doctors' offices, especially if space is an issue, opt to outsource blood testing to independent labs.

prepare and present in-house continuing education programs or to outsource them. Some of the larger accounting firms have established a presence in India and other countries, where they prepare routine client tax reports for the IRS. Many schools use independent contractors to bus their students. Doctors investigate the differences in cost, quality of results, and convenience to patients from having blood samples drawn and tested in the office or at an independent lab. Outsourcing can include product and process design activities, accounting and legal services, utilities, engineering services, and employee health services.

As discussed earlier, outsourcing decisions include the opportunity costs of facilities. If capacity is occupied in one way, it cannot be used at the same time for another purpose. Limited capacity is only one type of scarce resource that managers need to consider when making decisions.

Scarce Resource Decisions

Managers frequently confront the short-run problem of making the best use of **scarce resources** that are essential to production activity or service provision but have limited availability. Scarce resources include machine hours, skilled labor hours, raw materials, production capacity, and other inputs. In the long run, company management could obtain a higher quantity of a scarce resource, such as by purchasing additional machines to increase the number of machine hours available. However, in the short run, management must make the most efficient use of the currently available scarce resources.

Determining the best use of a scarce resource requires management to designate company objectives. If an objective is to maximize company profits, a scarce resource is best used to produce and sell the product generating the highest contribution margin *per unit of the scarce resource*. This strategy assumes that the company must ration only one scarce resource.

LO.4
How can management achieve the highest return from use of a scarce resource?

Exhibit 10–8 gives information on two products that Ace Home Appliances manufactures: toasters and microwave ovens. Each toaster requires 1 electronic switch, and each microwave oven requires 3 electronic switches. Currently, Ace has access to only 62,000 switches per month to make toasters, microwave ovens, or some combination of both. Because Ace's demand for switches is more than the 62,000 per month that are available, the purchased switch is a scarce resource for the company. As shown in Exhibit 10–8, the per-unit contribution margins of a toaster and a microwave oven are, respectively, $13 and $27. Fixed annual overhead related to these two product lines totals $9,220,000 and is allocated to products for purposes of inventory valuation. Fixed overhead, however, does not change with production levels within the relevant range and, accordingly, is not relevant in a short-run scarce resource decision. No variable selling or administrative costs are related to either product.

Because fixed overhead per unit is not relevant in the short run, unit contribution margin rather than unit gross margin is the appropriate measure of profitability of the two products.[5] Unit contribution margin is divided by the required quantity of the scarce resource to obtain the contribution margin per unit of scarce resource. The last line in Exhibit 10–8 shows the $13 contribution margin per switch for the toaster compared to $9 for the microwave oven. Thus, it is more profitable for Ace Home Appliances to produce toasters than microwave ovens.

At first glance, it appears that the microwave oven would be the more profitable of the two products because its $27 contribution margin per unit is significantly higher than the $13 contribution margin of a toaster. However, because the microwave oven requires three times as many switches as a toaster, toaster production generates a higher contribution margin per switch. If Ace Home Appliances makes only these two types of products and wants to achieve the highest possible profit, it would dedicate all available switches to the production of toasters. If Ace sells all units produced, this strategy would provide a total contribution margin of $806,000 per month (62,000 × $13).

When one limiting factor is involved, the outcome of a scarce resource decision indicates which single type of product should be manufactured and sold. Most situations, however, involve several factors that limit attainment of business objectives. Linear programming, discussed in the appendix to this chapter, is one method used to solve problems with several limiting factors.

In addition to considering the monetary effects related to scarce resource decisions, managers must remember that all factors cannot be readily quantified and that a situation's qualitative aspects must be evaluated in addition to the quantitative ones. For example, before choosing to produce only toasters, Ace Home Appliances' managers should assess the potential damage to the firm's reputation

EXHIBIT 10–8
Ace Home Appliances—Toaster and Microwave Oven Information

	Toaster	Microwave Oven
Selling price per unit (a)	$80.00	$120.00
Variable production cost per unit:		
Direct material	$45.00	$ 60.00
Direct labor	12.50	15.00
Variable overhead	9.50	18.00
Total variable cost (b)	$67.00	$ 93.00
Unit contribution margin [c = a − b]	$13.00	$ 27.00
Number of switches required per unit (d)	÷ 1	÷ 3
Contribution margin per switch [c ÷ d]	$13.00	$ 9.00

[5]Gross margin (or gross profit) is unit selling price minus total production cost per unit. Total production cost includes allocated fixed overhead.

and customer markets if the company were to limit its product line to a single item. Such a choice severely restricts a company's customer base and is especially important if the currently manufactured products are competitively related. For example, if Ace Home Appliances stopped manufacturing microwave ovens, some customers who wanted a combination conventional/microwave oven would purchase their products from another company.

Concentrating on a single product can also create market saturation or company stagnation. Customers infrequently purchase some products, such as refrigerators and Rolex watches, or purchase items in single units. Making only products such as these limits the company's opportunity for repeat business. If a company concentrates on the wrong single product (such as VCRs or laser video disks), that exclusionary choice can be the beginning of the company's end.

In some cases, the revenues and expenses of a group of products must be considered as a set of decisions in allocating scarce resources. Multiple products could be complementary or part of a package in which one product cannot be used effectively without another product or is the key to revenue generation in future periods. To illustrate these possibilities, consider the following products: Cross's ballpoint pen and mechanical pencil sets, Gillette's Atra razor and razor blades, and Mattel's Barbie "family" of products. Would it be reasonable for Cross to make only pens, Gillette to make only razors, or Mattel to make only Barbie dolls? In the case of Gillette, the company is known for giving away its razors to 18-year-old males—only because Gillette realizes the future benefit of razor blade purchases. Mattel's management would probably choose to manufacture and sell Barbie dolls at zero contribution margin because of the profits that Barbie accessories earn.

Thus, company management could decide that production and sale of some number of less profitable products is necessary to maintain either customer satisfaction or sales of other products. The revenue side of production mix is sales mix, which is discussed in the following section.

Sales Mix Decisions

LO.5
What variables do managers use to manipulate sales mix?

Managers continuously strive to achieve a variety of company objectives such as maximization of profit, maintenance of or increase in market share, and generation of customer goodwill and loyalty. Managers must be effective in selling products or performing services to accomplish these objectives. Regardless of whether the company is a retailer, manufacturer, or service organization, sales mix refers to the relative product quantities composing a company's total sales. Some important factors affecting a company's sales mix are product selling prices, sales force compensation, and advertising expenditures. Because a change in one or all of these factors could cause sales mix to shift, managing it is fundamental to managing profit.

Assume that Ace Home Appliances has a meat slicer line in addition to toasters and microwave ovens. Exhibit 10–9 provides information on that line; the information is used to illustrate the effects of the three factors—selling prices, sales compensation, and advertising—on sales mix. The product line includes standard, home deluxe, and professional slicers, each with different features and targeted at a different market segment. All slicers compete on the basis of high quality and are priced at the high end of their market niches.

Sales Price Changes and Relative Profitability of Products

A company must continually monitor the sales prices of its products, with respect to both each other and competitors. Such monitoring can provide information that causes management to change one or more sales prices. Factors that might influence price changes include fluctuations in demand or production/distribution cost, economic conditions, and competition. Any shift in the selling price of one product in a multiproduct firm normally causes a change in sales mix of that firm because of the economic law of demand elasticity with respect to price.[6]

For Ace Home Appliances, profit maximization is the primary corporate objective. This strategy does not necessarily translate into maximizing unit sales of the product with the highest selling prices and minimizing unit sales of the product with the lowest selling price; this is because the highest selling price per unit does not necessarily yield the highest contribution margin per unit or

[6]The law of demand elasticity indicates how closely price and demand are related. Product demand is highly elastic if a small price reduction generates a large demand increase. If demand is less elastic, large price reductions are needed to bring about moderate sales volume increases. In contrast, if demand is highly elastic, a small price increase results in a large drop in demand.

EXHIBIT 10–9
Ace Home Appliances—Meat Slicer

PRODUCT INFORMATION	Standard	Home Deluxe	Professional
Unit selling price (SP)	$80	$450	$900
Variable costs			
Direct material	$33	$185	$425
Direct labor	12	75	245
Variable factory overhead	15	45	90
Total variable production cost	$60	$305	$760
Product contribution margin	$20	$145	$140
Variable selling expense (10% of SP)	(8)	(45)	(90)
Contribution margin per unit	$12	$100	$ 50
Total fixed costs:			
Production	$4,200,000		
Selling & administrative	1,100,000		
Total	$5,300,000		

per dollar of sales. In Ace Home Appliances' case, the slicer with the highest sales price (the professional model) yields the second highest unit contribution margin of the three products but the lowest contribution margin as a percent of sales. The company generates more profit by selling a dollar's worth of the home deluxe slicer than a dollar's worth of either the standard or the professional model. A dollar of sales of the home deluxe slicer yields $0.22 (rounded) of contribution margin compared to $0.12 for the standard and $0.056 (rounded) for the professional.

If profit maximization is their goal, managers should consider each product's sales volume and unit contribution margin. Total company contribution margin is the sum of the contribution margins provided by the sale of all products. Exhibit 10–10 shows product sales volumes and the respective total contribution margins from the three slicer types. To maximize profits from the slicers, Ace's management must maximize total contribution margin rather than per-unit contribution margin.

A product's sales volume typically is related to its selling price. Generally, when the price of a product or service increases and demand is elastic with respect to price, demand for that product decreases.[7] Thus, in an attempt to increase profits, if Ace Home Appliances' management decides to raise the standard slicer price to $100, the company should experience some decline in demand. The marketing research personnel have indicated that such a price increase would cause demand for that product to drop from 52,000 to 30,000 slicers per period. The effect of this pricing decision on Ace Home Appliances' slicer product line income is shown in Exhibit 10–11.

Because contribution margin per unit of the standard slicer increased, the total dollar contribution margin generated by sales of that product increased despite the decrease in unit sales. This example assumed that customers did not switch their purchases from the standard slicer to other Ace Home Appliances products when the price of the standard slicer went up. When some product prices in a product line remain stable and others increase, customers might substitute one product for another. This instance ignored switching within the company, but some customers would likely purchase one of the more expensive slicers after the price of the standard slicer increased. For example, customers might believe that the difference in functionality between the standard and the home deluxe slicers is worth the price difference and make such a purchasing switch.

---

[7]Such a decline in demand would generally not occur when the product in question has no close substitutes or is not a major expenditure in consumers' budgets.

EXHIBIT 10–10
Ace Home Appliances—Relationship between Contribution Margin, Sales Volume, and Profit

	Unit Contribution Margin (from Exhibit 10–9)	Current Sales Volume in Units	Income Statement Information
Standard slicers	$ 12	52,000	$ 624,000
Home deluxe slicers	100	39,000	3,900,000
Professional slicers	50	15,000	750,000
Total contribution margin of product sales mix			$ 5,274,000
Fixed expenses (from Exhibit 10–9)			(5,300,000)
Product line income at present volume and sales mix			$ (26,000)

EXHIBIT 10–11
Ace Home Appliances—Relationship between Sales Price Change, Sales Volume, and Profit

	Unit Contribution Margin (from Exhibit 10–9)	New Sales Volume in Units	Income Statement Information
Standard slicers	$ 30*	30,000	$ 900,000
Home deluxe slicers	100	39,000	3,900,000
Professional slicers	50	15,000	50,000
Total contribution margin of product sales mix			$ 5,550,000
Fixed expenses (from Exhibit 10–9)			(5,300,000)
Product line income at new volume and sales mix			$ 250,000

*New price of $100 minus [total variable production costs of $60 + variable selling expense of $10 (10% of new selling price)].

In making decisions to raise or lower prices, relevant quantitative factors include (1) new contribution margin per unit of product, (2) short-term and long-term changes in product demand and production volume because of the price change, and (3) best use of the company's scarce resources. Some relevant qualitative factors involved in pricing decisions are (1) impact of changes on customer goodwill toward the company, (2) customer loyalty toward company products, and (3) competitors' responses to the firm's new pricing structure.[8] Also, changes in the competitive environment create opportunities for producing new products; exploiting such opportunities leads to sales mix changes.

When determining prices for proposed new products, management should take a long-run view of the product's life cycle. This view should include assumptions about consumer behavior, competitor behavior, pace of technology changes, government posture, environmental concerns, size of the potential market, and demographic changes. These considerations would affect product price estimates at the various stages in the product's life cycle.

[8]With regard to the actions of competitors, consider what occurs when one airline lowers its fares on a particular route. It typically does not take very long for all other airlines flying that route to adjust their fares accordingly. Thus, any competitive advantage is only for a short time span.

Sales Compensation Changes

Many companies compensate salespeople by paying a fixed rate of commission on gross sales dollars. This approach motivates salespeople to sell the highest priced product rather than the product providing the highest contribution margin to the company. If the company has a profit maximization objective, such a compensation policy will be ineffective in achieving that objective.

Assume that Ace Home Appliances has set a price structure for its slicers as follows: standard, $100; home deluxe, $450; and professional, $900. The company's current policy is to pay sales commissions equal to 10 percent of selling price. This commission structure encourages sales of professional slicers rather than home deluxe or standard slicers. Ace is considering a new sales force compensation structure that would provide base salaries for all salespeople totaling $925,000 per period.[9] In addition, Ace would pay salespeople a commission equal to 15 percent of product contribution margin (selling price minus total variable production cost). The per-unit product contribution margins of the slicers are $40, $145, and $140 for standard, home deluxe, and professional slicers, respectively. The new compensation policy should motivate sales personnel to sell more of the slicers that produce the highest commission, which would correspondingly be the company's most profitable products.[10]

Refer to Exhibit 10–12 for a comparison of Ace Home Appliances' total contribution margin using the current sales mix and commission structure with that of the new compensation structure focused on total contribution margin. The new structure would increase profits by shifting sales from the slicers with a lower contribution margin ratio to those with the higher contribution margin ratio. Salespeople also benefit from the new pay structure through higher total compensation. Reflected in the sales mix change is the fact that standard slicers can be sold with substantially less salesperson effort per unit than that required for the other models.

Fixed expenses would not be considered in setting compensation structures unless those expenses were incremental relative to the new policy or to changes in sales volumes. The new base salaries were an incremental cost of Ace Home Appliances' proposed compensation plan.

EXHIBIT 10–12

Ace Home Appliances—Impact of Change in Commission Structure

	Product Contribution Margin	−	Commission	=	Contribution Margin after Commission	×	Volume	=	Total Contribution Margin
Old Policy—Commissions Equal 10% of Selling Price									
Standard	$ 40		(0.1 × $100) = $10		$ 30.00		30,000		$ 900,000
Home deluxe	145		(0.1 × $450) = $45		100.00		39,000		3,900,000
Professional	140		(0.1 × $900) = $90		50.00		15,000		750,000
Total contribution margin for product sales							84,000		$5,550,000
New Policy—Commissions Equal 15% of Product Contribution Margin per Unit and Incremental Base Salaries of $925,000									
Standard	$ 40		(0.15 × $40) = $6.00		$ 34.00		40,000		$1,360,000
Home deluxe	145		(0.15 × $145) = $21.75		123.25		49,000		6,039,250
Professional	140		(0.15 × $140) = $21.00		119.00		10,000		1,190,000
Total contribution margin for product sales							99,000		$8,589,250
Less sales force base salaries									(925,000)
Contribution margin adjusted for sales force base salaries									$7,664,250

[9]The revised compensation structure should allow the sales personnel to achieve the same or higher income as before the change given a similar level of effort.

[10]This statement relies on the assumption that the salespersons' efforts are more highly correlated with unit sales than dollar sales. If this assumption is accurate, the commission structure should encourage sales of products with higher contribution margin ratios.

Advertising Budget Changes

Adjusting the advertising budgets of specific products or increasing the company's total advertising budget could lead to shifts in the sales mix. This section uses the data for Ace Home Appliances from Exhibit 10–11 and examines a proposed increase in the company's total advertising budget.

Ace Home Appliances' advertising manager, Joe Malanga, has proposed increasing the advertising budget from $500,000 to $650,000 per year. He believes the increased advertising will result in the following additional slicer sales during the coming year: standard, 2,500; home deluxe, 1,500; and professional, 750. Company management wants to know whether spending the additional $150,000 for advertising to generate the additional 4,750 units of sales will produce higher profits than the slicer line is currently generating.

The original fixed costs, as well as the contribution margin generated by the current sales levels, are irrelevant to the decision. The relevant items are the increased sales revenue, increased variable costs, and increased fixed cost—the incremental effects of the advertising change. The difference between incremental revenues and incremental variable costs is the incremental contribution margin from which the incremental fixed cost is subtracted to obtain the incremental benefit (or loss) of the decision.[11]

See Exhibit 10–13 for calculations of the expected increase in contribution margin if the company makes the increased advertising expenditure. The $262,500 of additional contribution margin more than covers the $150,000 incremental cost for advertising, indicating that company management should increase its advertising by $150,000.

Increased advertising can cause changes in the sales mix or in the number of units sold by targeting advertising efforts at specific products. Sales can also be influenced by opportunities that allow companies to obtain business at a sales price that differs from the normal price.

Special Order Decisions

In a special order decision, management computes sales prices for production or service jobs that are not part of the company's normal operations. Special order situations include jobs that require a bid, are accepted during slack periods, or are made to a particular buyer's specifications. Typically, the sales price quoted on a special order job should be high enough to cover the job's variable and incremental fixed costs and generate a profit.

Sometimes companies depart from their price-setting routine and bid "low-ball" selling prices. A low-ball bid could cover only costs and produce no profit or even be below cost. The rationale of low-ball bids is to obtain the job and have the opportunity to introduce company products or services to a particular market segment. Special pricing of this nature could provide work for a period of time, but it cannot be continued over the long run. To remain in business, a company must set selling prices to cover total costs and provide a reasonable profit margin.[12]

LO.6
How are special prices set, and when are they used?

EXHIBIT 10–13
Ace Home Appliances—Analysis of Increased Advertising Cost

	Standard	Home Deluxe	Professional	Total
Increase in volume	2,500	1,500	750	4,750
Contribution margin per unit	× $30	× $100	× $50	
Incremental contribution margin	$75,000	$150,000	$37,500	$ 262,500
Incremental fixed cost of advertising				(150,000)
Incremental benefit from increased advertising expenditure				$ 112,500

---

[11]This same type of incremental analysis is shown in Chapter 9 in relation to cost-volume-profit computations.
[12]An exception to this general rule can occur when a company produces related or complementary products. For instance, an electronics company can sell a video game at or below cost and allow the ancillary software program sales to be the primary source of profit.

Special pricing also arises for private-label orders in which the buyer's (rather than the producer's) name is attached to the product. Companies may accept these jobs during slack periods to more effectively use available capacity. Fixed costs are typically not allocated to special order, private-label products. Some variable costs (such as sales commissions) can be reduced or eliminated by the very nature of the private-label process. Prices on this type of special order are typically set high enough to generate a positive contribution margin.

Special prices can also be justified when orders are of an unusual nature (because of the quantity, method of delivery, or packaging) or when products are tailor-made to customer instructions. Last, special pricing is used when goods are produced for a one-time job, such as an overseas order that will not affect domestic sales.

Assume that Ace Home Appliances has the opportunity to bid on a special order for 60,000 private-label slicers for a major kitchen products retailer. Company management wants to obtain the order if the additional business will provide a satisfactory contribution to profit. Ace has unused production capacity available, and can obtain the necessary components and raw material from suppliers. Also, Ace has no immediate opportunity to apply its currently unused capacity in another way, so there is no opportunity cost.

Management has gathered the information shown in Exhibit 10–14 to determine a price to bid on the private-label slicers. Direct material and components, direct labor, and variable factory overhead costs are relevant to setting the bid price because these costs will be incurred for each slicer produced. Although all variable costs are normally relevant to a special pricing decision, variable selling expense is irrelevant in this instance because no sales commission will be paid on this sale. Fixed manufacturing overhead and fixed selling and administrative expenses are not expected to increase because of this sale, so these expenses are not relevant in the pricing decision.

Using the available cost information, the relevant cost for determining the bid price for each slicer is $150 (direct material and components, direct labor, and variable overhead). This cost is the minimum price at which the company should sell one slicer. Any price higher than $150 will provide some profit.

Assume that Ace Home Appliances' slicer line is currently experiencing a $3,100,000 net loss and company managers want to set a bid price that would cover the net loss and create $200,000 of before-tax profit. In this case, Ace would spread the total $3,300,000 desired contribution margin over the 60,000-unit special order at $55 per slicer. This approach would indicate a bid price of $205 per slicer ($150 variable cost + $55). However, any price above the $150 variable cost will contribute toward reducing the $3,100,000 product line loss.

In setting the bid price, management may specify a "reasonable" profit on the special order. Ace's management believes that a normal profit margin of $25 per slicer, or 11.4 percent (rounded) of the $220 full cost is reasonable. Setting the special order bid price at $167.10 would cover the

EXHIBIT 10–14
Ace Home Appliances—Private-Label Slicer Product Information

	Normal Costs	Relevant Costs
Per-unit cost for slicers:		
Direct material and components	$ 90	$ 90
Direct labor	25	25
Variable overhead	35	35
Variable selling expense (commission)	20	0
Total variable cost	$170	$150
Fixed factory overhead (allocated)	30	
Fixed selling & administrative expense	20	
Total cost per slicer	$220	

$150 variable production costs and provide the 11.4 percent profit margin ($17.10) on incremental unit cost. This computation illustrates a simplistic cost-plus approach to pricing but ignores both product demand and market competition. Ace's bid price should also reflect these considerations. In addition, company management should consider any effects that the additional job will have on normal company activities and whether this job will create additional, unforeseen costs. As discussed in Chapter 4, activities create costs, so management must be aware of the company's cost drivers.

When setting a special order price, management must consider qualitative as well as quantitative issues. For instance, management should answer questions such as the following: Will setting a low bid price set a precedent for future prices? Will the contribution margin on a bid, set low enough to acquire the job, be sufficient to justify the additional burdens placed on management and employees by this activity? Will the additional production activity require the use of bottleneck resources and reduce company throughput? How will special order sales affect the company's normal sales? If production of the special order is scheduled during a period of low business activity (off-season or recession), is management willing to take the business at a lower contribution or profit margin simply to keep a trained workforce employed?

A final consideration in making special pricing decisions in the United States is the Robinson-Patman Act, which prohibits companies from pricing the same product at different levels when those amounts do not reflect related cost differences. Cost differences must result from actual variations in the cost to manufacture, sell, or distribute a product because of different methods of production or quantities sold.

Companies may, however, give ad hoc discounts, which are price concessions that relate to real (or imagined) competitive pressures rather than to location of the merchandising chain or volume purchased. Such discounts are not usually subject to detailed justification because they are based on a competitive market environment. Although ad hoc discounts do not require intensive justification under the law, other types of discounts do because they could reflect some type of price discrimination. Prudent managers must understand the legalities of special pricing and the factors that allow for its implementation. For normally stocked merchandise, the only support for pricing differences is a difference in distribution costs.

In making pricing decisions, managers typically first analyze the market environment, including the degree of industry competition and competitors' prices. Then managers consider full production cost in setting normal sales prices. Full production cost includes an allocated portion of the fixed costs of the production process, which in a multiproduct environment could include common costs of production relating to more than one type of product. Allocations of common costs can distort the results of operations shown for individual products.

Product Line and Segment Decisions

LO.7
How do managers determine whether a product line should be retained or discontinued?

Operating results of multiproduct environments are often presented in a disaggregated format showing disaggregated results by product lines. In reviewing these disaggregated statements, managers must distinguish relevant from irrelevant information regarding individual product lines. If all costs (variable and fixed) are allocated to product lines, a product line or segment could be perceived as operating at a loss when actually it is not. The commingling of relevant and irrelevant information on the statements could cause such perceptions.

Exhibit 10–15 provides basic earnings information for the Oven Division of Ace Home Appliances, which manufactures three oven lines: Economy, Standard, and Deluxe. The data in the exhibit make it appear that the Deluxe line is operating at a net loss of $165,000. Managers reviewing such results might reason that the Division would be $165,000 more profitable if the Deluxe oven line were dropped. Such a conclusion could be premature because of the mixture of relevant and irrelevant information in the income statement presented.

All fixed expenses have been allocated to the individual product lines in Exhibit 10–15. Such allocations are traditionally based on one or more measures of "presumed" equity for each product line, such as the following: square footage occupied in the manufacturing plant, number of machine hours incurred for production, and number of direct labor employees. In all cases, however, allocations could force fixed expenses into specific product line operating results even though some of those expenses were not actually incurred for the benefit of the specific product line.

EXHIBIT 10–15

Oven Division of Ace Home Appliances Product Line Income Statements (in $ooos)

	Economy	Standard	Deluxe	Total
Sales	$ 8,000	$ 9,800	$ 3,000	$ 20,800
Total direct variable expenses	(5,400)	(5,700)	(2,200)	(13,300)
Total contribution margin	$ 2,600	$ 4,100	$ 800	$ 7,500
Total fixed expenses	(2,100)	(3,700)	(965)	(6,765)
Net income (loss)	$ 500	$ 400	$ (165)	$ 735
Details of fixed expenses				
(1) Avoidable fixed expenses	$ 1,200	$ 3,000	$ 450	$ 4,650
(2) Unavoidable fixed expenses	600	420	300	1,320
(3) Allocated common expenses	300	280	215	795
Total	$ 2,100	$ 3,700	$ 965	$ 6,765

Exhibit 10–16 segregates the Oven Division's fixed expenses into three subcategories: (1) avoidable if the particular product line is eliminated (these expenses can also be referred to as *attributable expenses*), (2) directly associated with a particular product line but not avoidable, and (3) incurred for the benefit of the company as a whole (common expenses) and that are allocated to the individual product lines. The latter two subcategories are irrelevant in deciding whether to eliminate a product line. An unavoidable expense merely shifts to another product line if the one with which it is associated is eliminated. Common expenses will be incurred regardless of which product lines are eliminated. An example of a common cost is the insurance premium on a manufacturing facility that houses all product lines.

If the Oven Division eliminates the Deluxe line, total divisional profit will decline by the $350,000 segment margin of that line. **Segment margin** represents the excess of revenues over direct variable expenses and avoidable fixed expenses. It is the amount remaining to cover unavoidable direct fixed expenses and common expenses and to provide profits.[13] The appropriate figure on which to base the continuation or elimination decision is segment margin because it measures the segment's contribution to the coverage of indirect and unavoidable expenses. The new net income of $385,000 that would result from having only two product lines (Economy and Standard) is in the following alternative computations.

	(In $000)
Current net income	$ 735
Decrease in income due to elimination of Deluxe (segment margin)	(350)
New net income	$ 385
Proof:	
Total contribution margin of Economy and Standard lines	$ 6,700
Less avoidable fixed expenses of the Economy and Standard lines	(4,200)
Segment margin of Economy and Standard lines	$ 2,500
Less all remaining unavoidable and allocated expenses	
in Exhibit 10–16 ($1,320 + $795)	(2,115)
Remaining income with two product lines	$ 385

Based on the information in Exhibit 10–16, the Oven Division should not eliminate the Deluxe product line because it is generating a positive segment margin and covering its relevant expenses.

In classifying product line costs, managers should be aware that some costs can appear to be avoidable but are actually not. For example, the salary of a supervisor working directly with a product

[13]All common expenses are assumed to be fixed; this is not always the case. Some common costs could be variable, such as expenses of processing purchase orders or computer time-sharing expenses for payroll or other corporate functions.

EXHIBIT 10–16

Oven Division of Ace Home Appliances Segment Margin Income
Statements (in $ooos)

	Economy	Standard	Deluxe	Total
Sales	$ 8,000	$ 9,800	$ 3,000	$ 20,800
Total direct variable expenses	(5,400)	(5,700)	(2,200)	(13,300)
Total contribution margin	$ 2,600	$ 4,100	$ 800	$ 7,500
(1) Avoidable fixed expenses	(1,200)	(3,000)	(450)	(4,650)
Segment margin	$ 1,400	$ 1,100	$ 350	$ 2,850
(2) Unavoidable fixed expenses	(600)	(420)	(300)	(1,320)
Product line result	$ 800	$ 680	$ 50	$ 1,530
(3) Allocated common expenses	(300)	(280)	(215)	(795)
Net income (loss)	$ 500	$ 400	$ (165)	$ 735

line appears to be an avoidable fixed cost if the product line is eliminated. However, if the company generally retains such supervisors and transfers them to another area when product lines are cut, the supervisor's salary will continue and must be treated as unavoidable. These types of determinations must be made before costs can be appropriately classified in product line elimination decisions.

Depreciation on factory equipment used to manufacture a specific product is an irrelevant cost in product line decisions. But if the equipment can be sold, the selling price is relevant to the decision because the sale increases the benefit of discontinuing the product line. Even if the equipment will be kept in service and used to make other products, the depreciation expense is unavoidable and irrelevant to the decision.

Before deciding to discontinue a product line, management should carefully consider what resources would be required to turn the product line around and consider the long-term ramifications of product line elimination. For example, elimination of a product line shrinks market assortment, which could cause some customers to seek other suppliers that maintain a broader market assortment. And, as in other relevant costing situations, this decision has qualitative as well as quantitative factors that must be analyzed. Individual customers also should be assessed (in the same manner as product lines) for profitability. When necessary, ways to improve the cost–benefit relationship should be determined.

Management's task is to effectively and efficiently allocate its finite stock of resources to accomplish its objectives. A cost accountant must learn what uses management will make of requested information to ensure that it is relevant and provided in the appropriate form. Managers must have a reliable quantitative basis on which to analyze problems, compare viable solutions, and choose the best course of action. Because management is a social rather than a natural science, it has no fundamental "truths," and few related problems are susceptible to black-or-white solutions. Relevant costing is a process of making human approximations of the costs of alternative decision results.

Appendix

Linear Programming

Some factors restrict the immediate attainment of almost any objective. For example, assume that the Brazos County Humane Society's objective is to care for more neglected pets during the coming year. Factors restricting the attainment of that objective include the physical constraints

LO.8
How is linear programming used to optimally manage multiple resource constraints?

related to the size of its facility, size of its staff, hours per week the staff is allowed to work, and amount of funding available. Each factor reflects a limited or scarce resource; to achieve its objective, Brazos County Humane Society must find a way to allocate its limited resources efficiently and effectively.

Managers must allocate scarce resources among competing uses. If a company has only one scarce resource, managers will schedule production or other activity in a way that maximizes the scarce resource's use. Most situations, however, involve several limiting factors that compete with one another during the process of striving to attain business objectives. Solving problems having several limiting factors requires the use of mathematical programming, which refers to a variety of techniques used to allocate limited resources among activities to achieve a specific goal or purpose. This appendix introduces linear programming, which is one form of mathematical programming.[14]

Basics of Linear Programming

Linear programming (LP) is a method used to find the optimal allocation of scarce resources in a situation involving one objective and multiple limiting factors.[15] The objective and restrictions on achieving that objective must be expressible as linear equations.[16] The equation that specifies the objective is called the objective function, which typically is either to maximize or to minimize some measure of performance, such as maximizing contribution margin or minimizing product cost.

A constraint hampers management's pursuit of the objective. Resource constraints involve limited availability of labor time, machine time, raw material, space, or production capacity. Demand or marketing constraints restrict the quantity of product that can be sold during a time period. Constraints can also be in the form of technical product requirements. For example, requirements as to calories or vitamin content could constrain the mix and quantity of foods used in production of frozen meals.

A final constraint in all LP problems is a non-negativity constraint, which states that negative values for physical quantities cannot exist in a valid solution. Constraints represent the limits imposed on optimizing the objective function and, like the objective function, are specified in mathematical equations.

Almost every allocation problem has multiple feasible solutions that satisfy all constraints. Different solutions generally give different values for the objective function, although some problems have several solutions that provide the same value for the objective function. Solutions in fractional values can be generated. If solutions must be restricted to whole numbers, integer programming techniques must be used to constrain solutions accordingly. The optimal solution to a maximization or a minimization goal provides the best answer to the allocation problem.

Formulating an LP Problem

Linear programming techniques are commonly applied to production scheduling and combination of ingredients. Management's goal in determining production mix in a multiproduct environment is to find the product mix that, when sold, maximizes the company's contribution margin. The goal in determining the mix of ingredients for a specific product is to find the mix providing the specified level of quality at the minimum variable cost.

Each LP problem contains one dependent variable, two or more independent (or decision) variables, and one or more constraints. A decision variable is the unknown element, such as number of units, for which the problem is being solved. The first and most important step in solving linear programming problems is to set up the information in mathematical equation form. The objective function and each constraint must be identified. The objective function is frequently stated in such a

---

[14]This appendix discusses basic linear programming concepts; it is not an all-inclusive presentation. Any standard management science text should be consulted for an in-depth presentation of the subject.

[15]Finding the best allocation of resources when multiple goals exist is called goal programming. This text does not address this topic.

[16]If the objective and/or restrictions cannot be expressed in linear equations, the technique of nonlinear programming must be used. No general method has been developed that can solve all types of nonlinear programming problems.

way that the solution either maximizes contribution margin or minimizes variable costs. Basic objective function formats for maximization and minimization problems follow:

Maximization problem

$$\text{Objective function: MAX CM} = CM_1X_1 + CM_2X_2$$

Minimization problem

$$\text{Objective function: MIN VC} = VC_1X_1 + VC_2X_2$$

where
- CM = contribution margin
- CM_1 = contribution margin per unit of the first product
- CM_2 = contribution margin per unit of the second product
- X_1 = number of units of the first product
- X_2 = number of units of the second product
- VC = variable cost
- VC_1 = variable cost per unit of the first product
- VC_2 = variable cost per unit of the second product

Resource constraints are usually expressed as inequalities.[17] The following is the general formula for a less-than-or-equal-to resource constraint:

$$\text{Resource constraint(1): } A_1X_1 + A_2X_2 \leq \text{Resource 1}$$

where
- X_1 = number of units of the first product
- X_2 = number of units of the second product

The coefficients (A_1 and A_2) are input–output coefficients that indicate the rate at which each decision variable uses or depletes the scarce resource.

Machine time is an example of a resource constraint. Assume that Ace Home Appliances has only 10,000 machine hours available to produce blenders and mixers. Producing one blender unit requires 0.50 machine hour, and producing one mixer requires 0.25 machine hour. The resource constraint is shown as:

$$0.5X_1 + 0.25X_2 \leq 10,000$$

where
- X_1 = number of blenders
- X_2 = number of mixers

If Ace Home Appliances were to manufacture only one of the two types of products, it could produce 20,000 (10,000 ÷ 0.5) blenders or 40,000 mixers (10,000 ÷ 0.25). In manufacturing both products, the company must recognize that manufacturing one blender precludes manufacturing two mixers. The contribution margin of each product and the other constraints under which the company operates determine the mix of units to be produced.

All general concepts of formatting a linear programming problem are illustrated in the following maximization problem using data for Office Storage Corporation (OSC), which sells two office storage products: file cabinets and storage shelves. Exhibit 10–17 provides information on these products and the constraints that must be considered. OSC managers want to know the mix of products that will generate the maximum contribution margin. The company produces the items for future sale and must store them for the near term in its warehouse. The problem is composed of the following factors: (1) the objective is to maximize contribution margin (CM), (2) the decision variables are the file cabinet (X_1) and storage shelves (X_2), and (3) the constraints are labor time, machine time, and warehouse storage space.

Equations used to express objective functions should indicate the purpose of the problem and how that purpose is to be realized. OSC's purpose (objective) is to maximize its contribution margin by producing and selling the combination of file cabinets and storage shelves that provide contribution margins of $25 and $9, respectively. The objective function is stated as

---

[17]It is also possible to have strict equality constraints. For example, in producing a 10-pound bag of dog food, ingredients could be combined in a variety of ways, but total weight is required to be 10 pounds.

EXHIBIT 10–17
Office Storage Corporation Product Information and Constraints

File cabinet	
Contribution margin per unit	$25
Labor hours to manufacture 1 unit	3
Machine hours to assemble 1 unit	2
Cubic feet of warehouse space per unit	8
Storage shelves	
Contribution margin per unit	$ 9
Labor hours to manufacture 1 unit	2
Machine hours to assemble 1 unit	1
Cubic feet of warehouse space per unit	3
Constraints	
Total labor time available each month	2,100 hours
Total machine time available each month	850 hours
Warehouse space available	4,000 cubic feet

$$\text{MAX CM} = 25X_1 + 9X_2$$

The constraint inequalities represent the demands made by each decision variable on scarce resource availability. Total labor time for producing the two products must be less than or equal to 2,100 hours per month. Each file cabinet and storage shelf produced takes 3 and 2 labor hours, respectively. The labor constraint is expressed as

$$3X_1 + 2X_2 \leq 2,100$$

Expressing the machine time constraint equation is similar to that of the labor time constraint: 2 hours of machine time are required for each file cabinet and 1 hour is needed for each storage shelf. Total machine time available per month is 850 hours. This resource constraint is

$$2X_1 + 1X_2 \leq 850$$

The file cabinets and storage shelves produced cannot exceed available warehouse storage space. Each file cabinet consumes substantially more space than each storage shelf. The production constraint is expressed as

$$8X_1 + 3X_2 \leq 4,000$$

Although not shown in Exhibit 10–17, non-negativity constraints exist for this problem. They state that production of either product cannot be less than zero units and are shown as

$$X_1 \geq 0$$

$$X_2 \geq 0$$

See Exhibit 10–18 for the mathematical formulas needed to solve the Office Storage Corporation LP production problem. Next, methods for solving the problem are discussed.

Solving an LP Problem

Linear programming problems can be solved by a graphical approach or by the simplex method. Graphs are simple to use and provide a visual representation to aid in solving linear programming

---

EXHIBIT 10–18
Office Storage Corporation LP Problem Statement

Objective Function: MAX CM = $25X_1 + 9X_2$

Constraints (subject to):

$3X_1 + 2X_2 \leq 2,100$	(labor time in hours)
$2X_1 + 1X_2 \leq 850$	(machine time in hours)
$8X_1 + 3X_2 \leq 4,000$	(warehouse storage space)
$X_1 \geq 0$	(non-negativity of file cabinets)
$X_2 \geq 0$	(non-negativity of storage shelves)

---

problems. Graphical methods are useful, however, only when the problem has two decision variables and few constraints or two constraints and few decision variables.

The graphical method of solving a linear programming problem consists of five steps:

1. State the problem in terms of a linear objective function and linear constraints.
2. Graph the constraints and determine the feasible region, which is the graphical space contained within and on all of the constraint lines.
3. Determine the coordinates of each corner (or vertex) of the feasible region.
4. Calculate the value of the objective function at each vertex.
5. Select the optimal solution. The optimal solution for a maximization problem is the one with the highest objective function value and for a minimization problem is the one with the lowest objective function value.

Labeled constraint lines and the corner values are identified in Exhibit 10–19.

The feasible region whose corners are A–B–C is shaded. Only the machine hours constraint is binding; the other two constraint lines fall outside the machine hour constraint and, therefore, do not impact the solution. The total contribution margin at each corner is calculated as follows:

	VALUES		
Corner	X_1	X_2	
A	0	0	CM = $25(0) + $9(0) = $0
B	425	0	CM = $25(425) + $9(0) = $10,625
C	0	850	CM = $25(0) + $9(850) = $7,650

Inspection reveals that the contribution margin is at its highest ($10,625) at point B. The corners that are not part of the feasible region are not evaluated because they do not satisfy all of the constraints of the problem.

The simplex method is a more efficient way to handle complex linear programming problems. It is an iterative (sequential) algorithm that solves multivariable, multiconstraint linear programming problems. An algorithm is a logical step-by-step problem-solving technique (generally utilizing a computer) that continuously searches for an improved solution relative to the one previously computed. The simplex method does not check every feasible solution but only those occurring at the corners of the feasible region. Because corners always represent the extremities of the feasible region, the maximum or minimum value of the objective function is always located at a corner.

The simplex method begins with a mathematical statement of the objective function and constraints. The inequalities in the constraints must be expressed as equalities to solve the problems algebraically. Expressing inequalities as equalities is accomplished by introducing slack or surplus variables (S) into constraint equations. A slack variable represents the unused amount of a resource

EXHIBIT 10–19
Office Storage Corporation Production Constraints

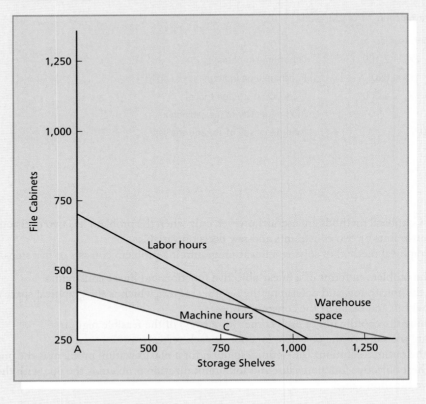

at any level of operation. The amount of the slack variable can range from zero to the total amount of the constrained resource. Slack variables are associated with "less than or equal to" ($\leq$) constraints and are added to the left side of the constraint equation. A surplus variable represents overachievement of a minimum requirement and is associated with "greater than or equal to" ($\geq$) constraints. Surplus variables are subtracted from the left side of a constraint equation. The formulas for Office Storage Corporation in Exhibit 10–18 are repeated here with the inclusion of slack variables (S1, S2, and S3) for each constrained resource. There are no surplus variables for Office Storage Corporation because all constraints were "less than or equal to" constraints.

$$\text{Objective Function: MAX CM} = 25X_1 + 9X_2$$

Constraints (subject to):

$$3X_1 + 2X_2 + S1 = 2{,}100 \text{ (labor time in hours)}$$
$$2X_1 + 1X_2 + S2 = 850 \text{ (machine time in hours)}$$
$$8X_1 + 3X_2 + S3 = 4{,}000 \text{ (warehouse storage in cubic feet)}$$

Solving a linear programming problem using the simplex method requires either the use of matrix algebra or a computer.

Comprehensive Review Module

Chapter Summary

1. Because of their association with the decision, importance to the decision maker, and bearing on the future, the following items are relevant in decision making:

   • costs that vary between decision choices (incremental or differential costs).

   • benefits sacrificed by pursuing one decision choice rather than another (opportunity costs).

2. Sunk costs

   • are costs incurred in the past to acquire assets or resources.

   • are not relevant to decision making because they cannot be changed regardless of which decision choice is selected.

   • are not recoverable regardless of current circumstances.

3. Relevant considerations in outsourcing (or offshoring) decisions include

   • quantitative factors such as

     ➢ incremental/differential production costs,

     ➢ opportunity costs,

     ➢ external purchase costs, and

     ➢ cash flow.

   • qualitative factors such as

     ➢ capacity availability,

     ➢ quality control,

     ➢ technology availability,

     ➢ organizational core competencies,

     ➢ employee skill levels in-house and externally,

     ➢ business risk, and

     ➢ supplier availability and reliability.

4. A scarce resource

   • is essential to production but is available only in limited quantity.

   • includes machine hours, skilled labor hours, raw materials or components, and production capacity.

   • requires management to base decisions on the contribution margin per unit of scarce resource available from alternative uses of the scarce resources; organizational profitability will be maximized by producing and selling the product or service that has the highest contribution margin per unit of scarce resource.

5. Sales mix is a key determinant of organizational profitability; it can be managed by manipulating

   • sales prices,

   • sales compensation methods, or

   • advertising budgets.

6. Special prices for products or services

   • are generally set based on relevant variable production and selling costs and, if any, incremental fixed costs.

   • may or may not include a profit amount.

   • are used when companies bid on special order jobs, such as those that

     ➢ require a bid,

     ➢ are accepted during slack periods,

     ➢ are made to a particular buyer's specifications, or

     ➢ are of an unusual nature because of the order quantity, method of delivery, or packaging.

7. Segment margin

   • is the excess of revenues over direct variable expenses and avoidable fixed expenses for a specific product/service line.

   • measures the segment's contribution to the coverage of indirect and unavoidable expenses and profit.

- is used to decide whether a product line should be retained or eliminated; a positive segment margin indicates retention and a negative segment margin indicates elimination.

8. (Appendix) Linear programming

 - is used to find the optimal allocation of scarce resources.

 - uses equations to express the problem's objective function and constraints.

- generates multiple feasible solutions, but the optimal solution will always be at a corner (vertex) of the feasible region.

- can be handled through the use of the graphical approach or the simplex method; the simplex method uses slack and surplus variables to translate inequalities in constraints to equalities.

Potential Ethical Issues

1. Ignoring important qualitative factors in making relevant decisions, such as the impact on domestic employees in offshoring decisions

2. Choosing to move production offshore to a developing country to exploit lax environmental and labor regulations

3. Making decisions based on how they will impact reported financial earnings rather than by using relevant information

4. Using bait-and-switch advertising techniques to manage sales mix

5. Pricing products or services at amounts that violate the Robinson-Patman Act or other jurisdictional pricing regulations, especially if the prices are meant to be discriminatory against any type of protected group

6. Handling a scarce material circumstance by substituting materials that pose high risks to human health or the environment for the scarce material ▲

Solution Strategies

General rule of decision making: Choose the alternative that yields the greatest incremental benefit.

$$
\begin{array}{l}
\text{Incremental (additional) revenues} \\
-\ \underline{\text{Incremental (additional) costs}} \\
\text{Incremental benefit (positive or negative)}
\end{array}
$$

Relevant Costs

- Direct material
- Direct labor
- Variable production overhead
- Variable selling expenses related to each alternative (can be greater or less than the "change nothing" alternative)
- Avoidable fixed production overhead
- Avoidable fixed selling/administrative costs (if any)
- Opportunity cost of choosing some other alternative (either increases the cost of one alternative or reduces the cost of another alternative)

Relevant Cost Analysis of Specific Decisions

Single Scarce Resource

1. Identify the scarce resource.

2. Determine the per-unit consumption of the scarce resource for each product.

3. Determine the contribution margin per unit of the scarce resource for each product.

4. Produce and sell the product with the highest contribution margin per unit of scarce resource to maximize profits.

Product Line Analysis

Sales
- Direct variable expenses
= Product line contribution margin
- Avoidable fixed expenses
= Segment (product line) margin*
- Unavoidable fixed expenses
= Product line operating results

*Make decision to retain or eliminate based on this line item.

Demonstration Problem

Thompson Theatre produces various equipment for home theatre and sound systems. One key component in all of its products is a speaker module that requires two specific speakers and is configured from a custom combination of the two speakers. The firm currently incurs the following costs to make each speaker module:

Direct material	$24
Direct labor	16
Variable overhead	10
Fixed overhead	20

Of the per-unit fixed overhead, the firm could avoid $8 if the modules were purchased from a company that has offered to sell an equivalent module for $56. Thompson Theatre produces 20,000 modules annually.

Required:

(Consider each requirement to be independent of the others.)

a. Should Thompson Theatre outsource the production of the module? Show calculations.

b. Thompson Theatre's vice president, Fred Flick, estimates that the company can rent out the facilities used to make the modules for $120,000 annually. What should the company do? Show calculations.

c. What are some qualitative factors that Thompson Theatre should consider in making this speaker module outsourcing decision?

Solution to Demonstration Problem

a. Relevant cost of making:

Direct material	$24
Direct labor	16
Variable overhead	10
Avoidable fixed overhead	8
Total	$58
Cost to outsource	$56

The cost to outsource is below the relevant cost to manufacture. Therefore, Thompson Theatre should outsource the speaker module.

b. **$120,000 rental income ÷ 20,000 modules = $6 opportunity cost per module**

Relevant cost to insource [part (a)]	$58
Opportunity cost	6
Total	$64

The cost to insource is now even more inferior to outsourcing. Therefore, Thompson Theatre should outsource the item.

c. Some qualitative factors include the following:

- Thompson Theatre's future control of quality, supply, cost, and price of the speaker module
- Supplier's long-run going concern prospects
- Existence and number of other suppliers
- Impact on customers and markets
- Impact on employees
- Reaction of financial and business press

Key Terms

ad hoc discount, **p. 373**

algorithm, **p. 379**

constraint, **p. 376**

decision variable, **p. 376**

differential cost, **p. 356**

differential revenue, **p. 356**

feasible region, **p. 379**

feasible solution, **p. 376**

incremental cost, **p. 356**

incremental revenue, **p. 356**

input–output coefficients, **p. 377**

integer programming, **p. 376**

linear programming (LP), **p. 376**

make-or-buy decision, **p. 359**

mathematical programming, **p. 376**

non-negativity constraint, **p. 376**

objective function, **p. 376**

offshoring, **p. 359**

opportunity cost, **p. 356**

optimal solution, **p. 376**

outsourcing, **p. 359**

outsourcing decision, **p. 359**

relevant costing, **p. 356**

Robinson-Patman Act, **p. 373**

sales mix, **p. 367**

scarce resource, **p. 365**

segment margin, **p. 374**

simplex method, **p. 379**

slack variable, **p. 379**

special order decision, **p. 371**

sunk cost, **p. 357**

surplus variable, **p. 380**

vertex, **p. 379**

Questions

1. What does the term relevance mean in the context of making management decisions?
2. How does the passage of time affect the set of costs that is relevant to a decision?
3. What are opportunity costs and why are they often the most difficult costs to analyze in decision making?
4. Describe sunk costs. Are there circumstances in which sunk costs are relevant to decisions? Discuss.
5. What is outsourcing? Why is the practice heatedly debated in the United States?
6. What is a scarce resource? Why is an organization's most scarce resource likely to change from time to time?
7. What is the objective of managing the sales mix of products? What are the major factors that influence sales mix?
8. What is a special order decision? Under what circumstances would a company refuse to accept a special order?
9. What is segment margin? How is segment margin used in the quantitative analysis of a decision to drop or keep a product line?
10. (Appendix) Under what circumstances is linear programming needed to analyze a scarce resource decision?
11. (Appendix) What is the objective function in a linear programming model? What are the two common types of objective functions?

Exercises

12. **LO.1–LO.3 (Relevant costs; sunk costs)** Prior to the 2007 Super Bowl, a Chicago-area retailer ordered 50,000 T-shirts that read: Chicago Bears—2007 Super Bowl Champs. The company paid $10.25 for each of the custom T-shirts. Following the loss of Chicago to the Indianapolis Colts, the retailer found itself with 15,000 unsold T-shirts after the Super Bowl. Before the Super Bowl, the retailer was able to sell 35,000 of the T-shirts at an average per-unit price of $35. The company is currently deciding how to dispose of the 15,000 remaining T-shirts. The retailer has learned from one of its suppliers that each shirt could be reworked at an average cost of $4.50 per shirt (which involves removing the Super Bowl reference from the shirts). Management of the retailer believes the reworked shirts could be sold at an average price of $9.25 during the coming football season. Alternatively, the company could sell the shirts at an average price of $3.00 as scrap material.

a. Identify at least three alternative courses of action management could take with regard to the leftover T-shirts.

b. Which costs are sunk in this decision?

c. Identify the relevant costs of each alternative you listed in part (a).

d. Based on your answer to part (c), what is the best alternative and what is the relative financial advantage of the best alternative over the second best alternative?

13. **LO.1 & LO.2 (Relevant costs)** Because of a monumental error committed by its purchasing department, Olson's Grocery ordered 5,000 heads of lettuce rather than the 1,000 that should have been ordered. The company paid $0.75 per head for the lettuce. Although management is confident that it can sell 2,000 units through regular sales, the market is not large enough to absorb the other 3,000 heads. Management has identified two ways to dispose of the excess heads of lettuce. First, a wholesaler has offered to purchase them for $0.35 each. Second, a restaurant chain has offered to purchase the lettuce if Olson's will agree to convert it into packaged lettuce for salads. This option would require Olson's to incur $4,500 for conversion and the heads of lettuce could then be sold for the equivalent of $0.53 each.

a. Which costs are sunk in this decision?

b. Actually, Olson's can consider three alternatives in this decision. Describe the alternative that is not mentioned in the problem.

c. What are the relevant costs of each decision alternative, and what should the company do?

14. **LO.1 & LO.2 (Relevant costs)** Robco manufactures and sells UHF radios. Information on last year's operations (sales and production of the 2008 model) follows:

Sales price per unit	$30
Costs per unit	
Direct material	$7
Direct labor	4
Overhead (50% variable)	6
Selling costs (40% variable)	10
Production in units	10,000
Sales in units	9,500

At this time (April 2009), the 2009 model is in production and it renders the 2008 model obsolete. If the remaining 500 units of the 2008 model radios are to be sold through regular channels, what is the minimum price the company would accept for the radios?

15. **LO.1 & LO.2 (Relevant costs)** Assume that you are about to graduate from your university and are deciding whether to apply for graduate school or enter the job market. To help make the decision, you have gathered the following data:

Costs incurred for the bachelor's degree	$163,000
Out-of-pocket costs for a master's degree	$ 72,000
Estimated starting salary with B.A.	$ 48,400
Estimated starting salary with M.A.	$ 56,800
Estimated time to complete master's degree	2 years
Estimated time from the present to retirement	40 years

a. Which of these factors are relevant to your decision?

b. What is the opportunity cost associated with earning the master's degree?

c. What is the out-of-pocket cost to obtain the master's degree?

d. What other factors should you consider before making a decision?

16. **LO.1 & LO.2 (Relevant vs. sunk costs)** Your roommate, Jackson Robards, purchased a new portable DVD player just before this school term for $90. Shortly after the semester began, Jackson's DVD player was crushed by an errant "flying plant" during a party at his apartment. Returning the equipment to the retailer, Jackson was informed that the estimated cost of repairs was $65 because the damage was not covered by the manufacturer's warranty.

Pondering the figures, Jackson was ready to decide to make repairs; after all, he had recently paid $90 for the equipment. However, before making a decision, he asked for your advice.

a. Using concepts from this chapter, prepare a brief presentation outlining factors that Jackson should consider in making his decision.

b. Continue the presentation in part (a) by discussing the options Jackson should consider in making his decision. Start by defining a base case against which alternatives can be compared.

17. **LO.1 & LO.2 (Asset replacement)** Certain production equipment used by Eastern Industrial has become obsolete relative to current technology. The company is considering whether it should keep or replace its existing equipment. To aid in this decision, the company's controller gathered the following data:

	Old Equipment	New Equipment
Original cost	$150,000	$198,000
Remaining life	5 years	5 years
Accumulated depreciation	$79,000	$0
Annual cash operating costs	$34,000	$8,000
Current salvage value	$44,000	NA
Salvage value in 5 years	$0	$0

   a. Identify any sunk costs in the data.
   b. Identify any irrelevant (nondifferential) future costs.
   c. Identify all relevant costs to the equipment replacement decision.
   d. What are the opportunity costs associated with the alternative of keeping the old equipment?
   e. What is the incremental cost to purchase the new equipment?
   f. What qualitative considerations should be considered before making any decision?

18. **LO.1 & LO.2 (Asset replacement)** On April 1, 2008, Hutchinson Hydraulics purchased new computer-based production scheduling software for $240,000. On May 15, 2008, a representative of a computerized manufacturing technology company demonstrated new software that was clearly superior to that purchased by the firm in April. The price of this software is $420,000. Corporate managers estimate that the new software would save the company $32,000 annually in schedule-related costs compared to the recently installed software. Both software packages should last 10 years (the expected life of the computer hardware) and have no salvage value at that time. The company can sell its existing software for $178,000 if the new software is purchased. Should the company keep and use the software purchased earlier or buy the new software? Show computations to support your answer.

19. **LO.3 (Outsourcing)** Glass Technologies manufactures fiberglass housings for portable generators. One part of a housing is a metal latch. Currently, the company produces the 120,000 metal latch units required annually. Company management is considering purchasing the latch from an external vendor. The following data are available for making the decision:

Cost per Unit to Manufacture

Direct material	$0.80
Direct labor	0.68
Variable overhead	0.36
Fixed overhead—applied	0.56
Total cost	$2.40

Cost per Unit to Purchase

Purchase price	$1.96
Freight charges	0.04
Total cost	$2.00

   a. Assuming that all of Glass Technologies' internal production costs are avoidable if the company purchases rather than makes the latch, what would be the net annual cost advantage to purchasing the latches?
   b. Assume that some of Glass Technologies' fixed overhead costs could not be avoided if it purchases rather than makes the latches. How much of the fixed overhead must be avoidable for the company to be indifferent as to making or buying the latches?

20. **LO.3 (Outsourcing)** Witchita Metal Co. produces pickup truck bumpers that it sells on a wholesale basis to new car retailers. The average bumper sales price is $160. Normal annual sales volume is 150,000 units, which is the company's maximum production capacity. At this capacity, the company's per-unit costs are as follows:

Direct material	$ 53 (including mounting hardware @ $15 per unit)
Direct labor	17
Overhead (2/3 is fixed)	45
Total	$115

A key component in producing bumpers is the mounting hardware used to attach the bumpers to the vehicles. Birmingham Mechanical has offered to sell Witchita Metal as many mounting units as the company needs for $20 per unit. If Witchita Metal accepts the offer, the released facilities currently used to produce mounting hardware could be used to produce an additional 4,800 bumpers. What alternative is more desirable and by what amount? (Assume that the company is currently operating at its capacity of 150,000 units.)

21. LO.3 (Outsourcing) Pneu Shoe Company manufactures various types of athletic shoes. Several types require a built-in air pump. Presently, the company makes all air pumps it requires. However, management is evaluating an offer from Ram Air Co. to provide air pumps at a cost of $1.80 each. Pneu Shoe's management has estimated that the variable production costs of the air pump total $1.35 per unit and that the company could avoid $13,500 per year in fixed costs if it purchased rather than produced the air pumps.

   a. If 25,000 pumps per year are required, should Pneu Shoe make them or buy them from Ram Air Co.?
   b. If 60,000 pumps per year are required, should Pneu Shoe make them or buy them?
   c. Assuming that all other factors are equal, at what level of production would the company be indifferent between making and buying the pumps?

22. LO.4 (Allocation of scarce resources) Because the employees of one of the company's plants are on strike, the Dallas Digital plant is operating at peak capacity. It makes two electronic products: MP3 players and PDAs. Presently, the company can sell as many of each product as can be made, but making a PDA takes twice as long in production labor time as an MP3 player. The company's production capacity is 100,000 labor hours per month. Data on each product follow:

	MP3 players	PDAs
Sales	$ 72	$128
Variable costs	(60)	(108)
Contribution margin	$ 12	$ 20
Labor hours required	1	2

Fixed costs are $240,000 per month.

   a. How many of each product should Dallas Digital make? Explain your answer.
   b. What qualitative factors would you consider in making this product mix decision?

23. LO.4 (Allocation of scarce resources) Takisha White received her accounting degree in 1986. Since graduating, she has obtained significant experience in a variety of job settings. Her skills include auditing, income and estate taxation, and business consulting. White currently has her own practice, and her skills are in such demand that she limits her practice to taxation issues. Most of her engagements are one of three types: individual income taxation, estate taxation, or corporate taxation. Following are data pertaining to the revenues and costs of each tax area (per tax return):

EXCEL

	Individual	Estate	Corporate
Revenue	$350	$1,200	$750
Variable costs	$ 50	$ 200	$150
Hours per return of White's time	2	8	5

Fixed costs of operating the office are $50,000 per year. White has such significant demand for her work that she must ration her time. She desires to work no more than 2,500 hours in the coming year. She can allocate her time so that she works only on one type of tax return or on any combination of the three types.

   a. How should White allocate her time in the coming year to maximize her income?
   b. Based on the optimal allocation, what is White's projected pre-tax income for the coming year?
   c. What other factors should White consider in allocating her time?
   d. What could White do to overcome the scarce resource constraint?

24. LO.5 (Sales mix) Doggie 'Doos provides two types of services to dog owners: grooming and training. All company personnel can perform each service equally well. To expand sales and market share, Doggie 'Doos' manager, Sally Switzer, relies heavily on radio and billboard advertising, but the 2008 advertising budget is expected to be very limited. Information on projected operations for 2008 follows:

	Grooming	Training
Revenue per billable hour	$ 40	$ 60
Variable cost of labor	$ 10	$ 21
Material cost per billable hour	$ 6	$ 7
Allocated fixed cost per year	$270,000	$230,000
Projected billable hours for 2008	30,000	20,000

   a. What is Doggie 'Doos' projected pre-tax profit or (loss) for 2008?

b. If $1 spent on advertising could increase grooming revenue by $20 or training revenue by $20, on which service should the advertising dollar be spent?

c. If $1 spent on advertising could increase either grooming billable time or training billable time by 1 hour, on which service should the advertising dollar be spent?

25. LO.5 (Sales mix) One product produced and sold by Oregon Outfitters is an ATV gun rack for which 2008 projections follow:

Projected volume in units	120,000
Sales price per unit	$30
Variable production cost per unit	$12
Variable selling cost per unit	$6
Fixed production cost	$825,000
Fixed selling and administration costs	$425,000

a. Compute the projected pre-tax profit to be earned on the ATV gun rack during 2008.

b. Corporate management estimates that unit volume could be increased by 20 percent if sales price were decreased by 10 percent. How would such a change affect the profit level projected in part (a)?

c. Rather than cutting the sales price, management is considering holding the sales price at the projected level and increasing advertising by $220,000. Such a change would increase volume by 25 percent. How would the level of profit under this alternative compare to the profit projected in part (a)?

26. LO.5 (Sales mix) Matrix Communications manufactures cell phones and two cell phone accessories: ear buds and a 12-volt (automotive) battery charger. (Each ear bud package contains a set of ear buds.) The ear buds and charger are compatible only with the Matrix cell phone. Sales prices and variable costs for each product follow:

	Cell phones	Set of ear buds	Charger
Sales	$ 75	$ 20	$ 20
Variable production costs	(60)	(4)	(5)
Variable selling costs	(4)	(1)	(2)
Contribution margin	$ 11	$ 15	$ 13
Unit sales (next year's budget)	2,000,000	400,000	200,000

The historical data of Matrix Communications suggest that, for each ten cell phones sold, two ear bud sets and one battery charger are sold. The company is currently exploring two options to increase overall corporate income for the upcoming year. The alternatives that follow would maintain the historical sales mix ratios.

1. Increase corporate advertising by $3,000,000. The company estimates doing so would increase cell phone sales to 2,200,000 units.

2. Decrease the price of cell phones to $70. The company estimates doing so would increase cell phone sales to 2,150,000 units.

a. Determine the effect of each proposal on budgeted profits for the coming year. Which alternative is preferred and what is the relative financial benefit of that alternative?

b. How could the firm's management increase the ratio of ear buds and chargers to cell phone unit sales?

27. LO.6 (Special order) Great Plain's Wire Co. produces 12.5-gauge barbed wire that is retailed through farm supply companies. Presently, the company has the capacity to produce 100,000 tons of wire per year. It is operating at 80 percent of annual capacity and, at this level of operations, the cost per ton of wire is as follows:

Direct material	$540
Direct labor	50
Variable overhead	60
Fixed overhead	150
Total	$800

The average sales price for the output produced by the firm is $900 per ton. The State of Texas has approached the firm to supply 200 tons of wire for the state's prisons for $620 per ton. No production modifications would be necessary to fulfill the order from the State of Texas.

a. What costs are relevant to the decision to accept this special order?

b. What would be the dollar effect on pre-tax income if this order were accepted?

28. LO.6 (Special order) For The Ages Inc. produces solid-oak umbrella stands. Each stand is handmade and hand finished using the finest materials available. The firm has been operating at capacity (2,000 stands per year) for the past three years. Based on this capacity of operations, the firm's costs per stand are as follows:

Material	$ 50
Direct labor	40
Variable overhead	10
Fixed overhead	30
Total cost	$130

All selling and administrative expenses incurred by the firm are fixed. The average selling price of stands is $225. Recently, a large retailer approached Bill Wood, the president of For The Ages, about supplying three special stands to give as gifts to CEOs of key suppliers. Wood estimates that the following per-unit costs would be incurred to make the three stands:

Material	$250
Direct labor	350
Variable overhead	90
Total direct costs	$690

To accept the special order, the firm would have to sacrifice production of 20 regular units.

a. Identify all relevant costs that Wood should consider in deciding whether to accept the special order.

b. Assume the retailer offers to pay For The Ages a total of $3,600 for the three stands. How would accepting this offer affect For The Ages' pre-tax income?

29. **LO.7 (Product line)** Operations of Del Rio Oil Drilling Services are separated into two geographical divisions: United States and Mexico. The operating results of each division for 2008 follow:

	United States	Mexico	Total
Sales	$ 7,200,000	$ 3,600,000	$10,800,000
Variable costs	(4,740,000)	(2,088,000)	(6,828,000)
Contribution margin	$ 2,460,000	$ 1,512,000	$ 3,972,000
Direct fixed costs	(900,000)	(480,000)	(1,380,000)
Segment margin	$ 1,560,000	$ 1,032,000	$ 2,592,000
Corporate fixed costs	(1,800,000)	(900,000)	(2,700,000)
Operating income (loss)	$ (240,000)	$ 132,000	$ (108,000)

Corporate fixed costs are allocated to the divisions based on relative sales. Assume that all of a division's direct fixed costs could be avoided by eliminating that division. Because the U.S. division is operating at a loss, Del Rio's president is considering eliminating it.

a. If the U.S. division had been eliminated at the beginning of the year, what would have been Del Rio's pre-tax income?

b. Recast the income statements into a more meaningful format than the one given. Why would total corporate operating results change from the $108,000 loss to the results determined in part (a)?

30. **LO.7 (Product line)** Akron Associates provides outsourcing services for three areas: payroll, general ledger (GL), and tax compliance. The company is currently contemplating the elimination of the GL area because it is showing a pre-tax loss. An annual income statement follows:

AKRON ASSOCIATES
Income Statement by Service Line
For the Year Ended July 31, 2008
(in thousands)

	Payroll	GL	Tax	Total
Sales	$ 4,400	$ 3,200	$ 3,600	$11,200
Cost of sales	(2,800)	(2,000)	(2,160)	(6,960)
Gross margin	$ 1,600	$ 1,200	$ 1,440	$ 4,240
Avoidable fixed and variable costs	$ 1,260	$ 1,450	$ 1,040	$ 3,750
Allocated fixed costs	180	160	210	550
Total fixed costs	$ 1,440	$ 1,610	$ 1,250	$ 4,300
Operating profit	$ 160	$ (410)	$ 190	$ (60)

a. Should corporate management drop the GL area? Support your answer with appropriate schedules.

b. If the GL area were dropped, how would the company's pre-tax profit be affected?

31. **LO.8 (Appendix)** The contribution margins for three different products are $18.00, $10.00, and $3.50. State the objective function in equation form to maximize the contribution margin.

32. **LO.8 (Appendix)** The variable costs for four different products are $4.65, $3.93, $4.39, and $9.72. State the objective function in equation form to minimize the variable costs.

33. **LO.8 (Appendix)** Florida Fashions makes three clothing items: pants, shorts, and shirts. Contribution margins for the products are $3.25, $2.05, and $2.60 per unit, respectively. The company's manager must decide what mix of clothes to make. Florida Fashions has 800 labor hours and 4,000 yards of material available. Additional information for labor and material requirements follows:

	Sewing Time	Fabric Needed
Pants	2.5 hours	2.5 yards
Shorts	1.0 hour	2.0 yards
Shirts	2.5 hours	1.0 yard

Write the objective function and constraints for the clothes manufacturer.

34. **LO.8 (Appendix)** Josie Galvez is a college student with a food budget of $120 per month. She wants to get a certain level of nutritional benefits from the food she buys. The following table lists the foods she can buy with the nutritional information per serving.

	Carbohydrates	Protein	Potassium	Calories	Cost
Pizza	38 g	10 g	0	500	$3.99
Tuna	1 g	13 g	0	60	1.29
Cereal	35 g	7 g	120 mg	190	0.93
Macaroni & cheese	23 g	3 g	110 mg	110	2.12
Spaghetti	42 g	8 g	100 mg	210	3.42
Recommended daily allowance	50 g	10 g	100 mg	2,000	

Write the objective function and constraints to minimize the cost yet meet the recommended daily nutritional allowances.

Problems

35. **LO.1 & LO.2 (Relevant costs)** John McGuire is the manager of AllFlex Sporting Goods, a division of All-Flex Global. McGuire's division sells a variety of sporting goods and supplies to wholesalers and retail chains throughout the Pacific northwest and Canada. AllFlex has a single manufacturing facility located in Salem, Oregon. As the manager of AllFlex, McGuire is paid a salary and a bonus based on the profit he generates for the company. Recently, McGuire has been contemplating selling a warehouse owned by the division in Salem. He has gathered the following information regarding the warehouse.

Acquisition date	10/10/1992
Acquisition price	$15,500,000
Accumulated depreciation	$5,300,000
Current market value	$7,000,000

Because the company has adopted JIT-based inventory management, the warehouse is no longer needed to store finished goods inventory. Furthermore, if the warehouse were sold, the $7,000,000 of current market value would be realized on the sale. McGuire has consulted you, the CFO of the division, about the effect of the warehouse sale on divisional profits. You provided McGuire the following calculation:

Sales price	$ 7,000,000
Less net book value ($15,500,000 − $5,300,000)	(10,200,000)
Projected profit (loss) on sale	$ (3,200,000)

a. Discuss whether the loss that would be recognized on the sale is relevant to the decision to sell the warehouse.
b. What would you recommend that McGuire do with respect to the warehouse?

36. **LO.1 & LO.2 (Asset replacement)** Tucson Tools recently created a new product, a computer-controlled, laser-precise lathe, and Ohio Ornamental Metals is considering purchasing one. Ohio's CFO received the following information from the accounting department regarding the company's existing lathe and the new Tucson lathe. The savings in operating costs offered by the new lathe would mostly derive from reduced waste, reduced labor, and energy cost savings:

Old Machine

Original cost	$775,000
Present book value	$150,000
Annual cash operating costs	$450,000
Market value now	$200,000
Market value in 5 years	$0
Remaining useful life	5 years

New Machine

Cost	$1,400,000
Annual cash operating costs	$185,000
Market value in 5 years	$0
Useful life	5 years

a. Based on financial considerations alone, should Ohio Ornamental Metals purchase the new lathe? Show computations to support your answer.

b. What qualitative factors should Ohio Ornamental Metals consider before making a decision about purchasing the new lathe?

37. LO.1 & LO.2 (Asset replacement) Niobrara Energy Company provides electrical services to several rural counties in Nebraska and South Dakota. Its efficiency has been greatly affected by changes in technology. The company is currently considering the replacement of its main steam turbine, which was put in place in the 1980s but is now obsolete. The turbine's operation is very reliable, but it is much less efficient than newer, computer-controlled turbines. The controller presented the following financial information to corporate management:

	Old Turbine	New Turbine
Original cost	$2,000,000	$4,000,000
Market value now	$400,000	$4,000,000
Remaining life	8 years	8 years
Quarterly operating costs	$160,000	$45,000
Salvage value in 8 years	$0	$0
Accumulated depreciation	$400,000	N/A

a. Identify the costs that are relevant to the company's equipment replacement decision.

b. Determine whether it is more financially sound to keep the old turbine or replace it. Provide your own computations based on relevant costs only.

c. For this part only, assume that the acquisition cost of the new technology is unknown. What is the maximum amount that Niobrara could pay for the new technology and be in the same financial condition as it is in currently?

d. What other considerations would come into play if, rather than a new turbine, the company were considering solar-powered technology to replace the old turbine system?

38. LO.3 (Outsourcing; ethics; essay) Tate Electronics manufactures computers and all required components. Its purchasing agent informed the company owner, Mervin Tate, that another company had offered to supply keyboards for Tate computers at prices below the variable costs at which Tate can make them. Incredulous, Tate hired an industrial consultant to explain how the supplier could offer the keyboards at less than Tate's variable costs.

The consultant suspects the supplier is using many undocumented laborers to work in its plant. These people are poverty stricken and will take work at substandard wages. Tate's purchasing agent and the plant manager recommend to Mr. Tate that Tate Electronics should outsource the keyboards because "no one can blame us for the supplier's hiring practices and if those practices come to light, no one will be able to show that we knew of those practices."

a. What are the ethical issues involved in this case?

b. What are the advantages and disadvantages of buying from this supplier?

c. What do you think Mr. Tate should do and why? ▲

39. LO.3 (Outsourcing) Sure Grip Inc. manufactures handles for suitcases and other luggage. Attaching each handle to the luggage requires, depending on the size of the luggage piece, between two and six standard fasteners, which the company has historically produced. The costs to produce one fastener (based on capacity operation of 4,000,000 units per year) are:

Direct material	$0.08
Direct labor	0.06
Variable factory overhead	0.04
Fixed factory overhead	0.14
Total	$0.32

Fixed factory overhead includes $200,000 of depreciation on equipment for which there is no alternative use and no market value. The balance of the fixed factory overhead pertains to the salary of the production supervisor, Jeff Wittier. Wittier has a lifetime employment contract and the skills that could be used to replace Brenda Gibbons, supervisor of floor maintenance. She draws a salary of $50,000 per year but is due to retire from the company.

Saratoga Suitcase Co. recently approached Sure Grip with an offer to supply all required fasteners for $0.26 per unit. Anticipated sales demand for the coming year will require 4,000,000 fasteners.

a. Identify the costs that are relevant in this outsourcing decision.

b. What is the total annual advantage or disadvantage (in dollars) of outsourcing the fasteners rather than making them?

c. What qualitative factors should be taken into account in making this decision?

40. **LO.3 (Outsourcing)** Modern Building Systems manufactures steel buildings for agricultural and home applications. Currently, managers are trying to decide between two alternatives regarding a major overhead door assembly for the company's buildings. The alternatives are as follows:

- Purchase new equipment with a five-year life and no salvage value at a cost of $5,000,000. Modern Building Systems uses straight-line depreciation and allocates that amount on a per unit of production basis.
- Purchase the assemblies from an outside vendor who will sell them for $240 each under a five-year contract.

Following is Modern Building System's present cost to produce one door assembly based on current and normal activity of 50,000 units per year.

Direct material	$139
Direct labor	66
Variable overhead	43
Fixed overhead*	36
Total	$284

*The fixed overhead includes $7 supervision cost, $9 depreciation, and $20 general company overhead.

The new equipment would be more efficient than the old equipment and would reduce direct labor costs and variable overhead costs by 25 percent. Supervisory costs of $350,000 would be unaffected. The new equipment would have a capacity of 75,000 assemblies per year. Modern Building Systems could lease the space occupied by current assembly production to another firm for $114,000 per year if the company decides to buy from the outside vendor.

a. Show an analysis, including relevant unit and total costs, for each alternative of producing or buying the assemblies. Assume 50,000 assemblies are needed each year.

b. How would your answer differ if 60,000 assemblies were needed?

c. How would your answer differ if 75,000 assemblies were needed?

d. In addition to quantitative factors, what qualitative factors should be considered?

41. **LO.1, LO.2, & LO.5 (Relevant costs; sales mix)** In November 2005, Microsoft introduced its highly anticipated new video game player, the Xbox 360. In early July 2007, Microsoft announced it was extending the warranty on its Xbox 360 to three years for a certain type of malfunction indicated by three flashing red lights on the game console. The warranty extension would apply to previously sold units; however, the warranty for any other type of failure would not be extended beyond the original one-year warranty term. In making this announcement, Microsoft indicated it would take a charge of $1.05 to $1.15 billion in the quarter ending June 30, 2007, for the costs of the warranty extension. [Source: Nick Wingfield, "Microsoft's Videogame Efforts Take a Costly Hit," *Wall Street Journal* (July 6, 2007), p. A3.]

a. What relevant costs were likely considered by Microsoft management in reaching the decision to extend the warranty on the Xbox 360 and, in so doing, incur in excess of $1 billion of additional costs?

b. Conduct research to determine how Microsoft's stock price was affected by the announcement of the warranty extension and its associated costs on July 6, 2007. Explain why the stock price reacted as it did.

c. Assume that one of the rationalizations for Microsoft to extend the warranty on the Xbox 360 was to manage sales mix. How could the extension of the Xbox warranty affect the sales mix of Microsoft's entertainment and devices division?

d. Comment on whether Microsoft was ethically obligated to extend the warranty on the Xbox 360 to three years. ▲

42. LO.5 (Sales mix) Anchorage Accessories produces leather belts and key fobs that sell for $40 and $10, respectively. The company currently sells 100,000 units of each type with the following operating results:

Belts

Sales (100,000 × $40)		$ 4,000,000
Variable costs		
Production (100,000 × $22)	$2,200,000	
Selling (100,000 × $6)	600,000	(2,800,000)
Contribution margin		$ 1,200,000
Fixed costs		
Production	$ 400,000	
Selling and administrative	180,000	(580,000)
Income		$ 620,000

Key Fobs

Sales (100,000 × $10)		$ 1,000,000
Variable costs		
Production (100,000 × $5)	$ 500,000	
Selling (100,000 × $1)	100,000	(600,000)
Contribution margin		$ 400,000
Fixed costs		
Production	$ 100,000	
Selling and administrative	80,000	(180,000)
Income		$ 220,000

Corporate management has expressed its disappointment with the income being generated from the sales of these two products. Managers have asked for your help in analyzing three alternative plans to improve operating results.

1. Change the sales commission to 12 percent of sales price less variable production costs for each product from the current 5 percent of selling price. The marketing manager believes that the sales of the belts will decline by 5,000 units but those of key fobs will increase by 15,000 units.
2. Increase the advertising budget for belts by $75,000. The marketing manager believes this will increase the sales of belts by 19,000 units but will decrease the sales of key fobs by 9,000 units.
3. Raise the per-unit price of belts by $5 and of key fobs by $3. The marketing manager believes this will cause a decrease in the sales of belts by 6,000 units and of key fobs by 10,000 units.
a. Determine the effects on the income of each product line and the company in total if each alternative plan is put into effect.
b. What is your recommendation to the management of Anchorage Accessories?

43. LO.4 & LO.5 (Sales mix with scarce resources) Bangor Bikes manually manufactures three unique bicycle models: racing, touring, and basic. All of the skilled craftspeople employed at Bangor Bikes can make each of the three models. Because it takes about a year to train each craftsperson, labor is a fixed production constraint over the short term. For 2008, the company expects to have available 34,000 labor hours. The average hourly labor rate is $25. Data regarding the current product line follow:

	Racing	Touring	Basic
Selling price	$1,800	$1,360	$480
Variable costs			
Direct material	$ 440	$ 320	$120
Direct labor	600	550	150
Variable factory overhead	360	240	82
Variable selling	40	30	20
Fixed costs			
Factory	$300,000		
Selling and administrative	150,000		

The company pays taxes at the rate of 50 percent of operating income.
a. If the company can sell an unlimited amount of any of the products, how many of each product should it make? What pre-tax income will the company earn given your answer?

b. How many of each product must the company make if it has the policy to devote no more than 50 percent of its available skilled labor capacity to any one product but at least 20 percent to every product? What pre-tax income will the company earn given your answer?

c. Given the nature of the three products, is it reasonable to believe that there are market constraints on the mix of products that can be sold? Explain.

d. How does the company's tax rate enter into the calculation of the optimal labor allocation?

44. LO.6 (Special order) Victoria Valves manufactures a variety of industrial valves and pipe fittings sold primarily to customers in the United States. Currently, the company is operating at 70 percent of capacity and is earning a satisfactory return on investment.

Prince Industries Ltd. of Scotland has approached Victoria's management with an offer to buy 120,000 pressure valves. Prince manufactures an almost identical pressure valve, but a fire in Prince's valve plant has closed its manufacturing operations. Prince needs the 120,000 valves over the next four months to meet commitments to its regular customers; the company is prepared to pay $19 each for the valves.

Victoria Valves' product cost for the pressure valve based on current attainable standards is

Direct material	$ 5
Direct labor	6
Manufacturing overhead	9
Total cost	$20

Manufacturing overhead is applied to production at the rate of $18 per standard direct labor hour. This overhead rate is made up of the following components:

Variable factory overhead	$ 6
Fixed factory overhead—direct	8
Fixed factory overhead—allocated	4
Applied manufacturing overhead rate	$18

Additional costs incurred in connection with sales of the pressure valve include 5 percent sales commissions and $1 freight expense per unit. However, the company does not pay sales commissions on special orders that come directly to management.

In determining selling prices, Victoria adds a 40 percent markup to product cost, which provides a $28 suggested selling price for the pressure valve. The marketing department, however, has set the current selling price at $27 to maintain market share.

Production management believes that it can handle Prince Industries' order without disrupting its scheduled production. The order would, however, require additional fixed factory overhead of $12,000 per month in the form of supervision and clerical costs.

If management accepts the order, Victoria will manufacture 30,000 pressure valves and ship them to Prince Industries each month for the next four months.

a. Determine how many additional direct labor hours would be required each month to fill the Prince Industries order.

b. Prepare an incremental analysis showing the impact of accepting the Prince Industries order.

c. Calculate the minimum unit price that Victoria Valves' management could accept for the Prince Industries order without reducing net income.

d. Identify the factors, other than price, that Victoria Valves should consider before accepting the Prince Industries order.

(CMA adapted)

45. LO.7 (Product line) Franzen Food Service sells high-quality ice cream and steaks via overnight delivery. Income statements showing revenues and costs of fiscal year 2008 for each product line follow:

	Ice Cream	Steaks
Sales	$ 4,000,000	$ 1,800,000
Less: Cost of merchandise sold	(2,400,000)	(1,300,000)
Commissions to salespeople	(400,000)	(150,000)
Delivery costs	(600,000)	(120,000)
Depreciation on equipment	(200,000)	(100,000)
Salaries of division managers	(80,000)	(75,000)
Allocated corporate costs	(100,000)	(100,000)
Net income (loss)	$ 220,000	$ (45,000)

Management is concerned about profitability of steaks and is considering dropping the line and estimates that the equipment currently used to process steaks could be rented to a competitor for $8,500 annually. If the steaks line is dropped, allocated corporate costs would decrease from a total of $200,000 to $170,000, and all employees, including the manager of the product line, would be dismissed. The depreciation would be unaffected by the decision, but $105,000 of the delivery costs charged to the steaks line could be eliminated if it is dropped.

a. Recast the preceding income statements in a format that provides more information in making this decision regarding the steaks product line.

b. What is the net advantage or disadvantage (change in total company pre-tax profits) of continuing sales of steaks?

c. Should the company be concerned about losing sales of ice cream products if it drops the steaks line? Explain.

d. How would layoffs that would occur as a consequence of dropping the steaks line adversely affect the whole company?

46. LO.7 (Product line) You have been hired to assist the management of Carson Chair Company in resolving certain issues. Carson Chair has its home office in Montana and leases facilities in Montana, Idaho, and North Dakota, where it produces a high-quality bean bag chair designed for residential use. Carson management has provided you a projection of operations for fiscal 2009, the forthcoming year, as follows:

	Total	Montana	Idaho	North Dakota
Sales	$ 8,800,000	$ 4,400,000	$ 2,800,000	$ 1,600,000
Fixed costs				
Factory	$ 2,200,000	$ 1,120,000	$ 560,000	$ 520,000
Administration	700,000	420,000	220,000	60,000
Variable costs	2,900,000	1,330,000	850,000	720,000
Allocated home office costs	1,000,000	450,000	350,000	200,000
Total costs	$(6,800,000)	$(3,320,000)	$(1,980,000)	$(1,500,000)
Pre-tax profit from operations	$ 2,000,000	$ 1,080,000	$ 820,000	$ 100,000

The sales price per unit is $50.

Due to the marginal results of operations in North Dakota, Carson Chair has decided to cease its operations there and sell that factory's machinery and equipment by the end of 2009. Managers expect proceeds from the sale of these assets to exceed their book value by enough to cover termination costs.

However, Carson Chair would like to continue serving its customers in that area if it is economically feasible. It is considering the following three alternatives:

1. Expand the operations of the Idaho factory by using space that is currently idle. This move would result in the following changes in that factory's operations:

	Increase over Factory's Current Operations
Sales	50%
Fixed costs	
Factory	20%
Administration	10%

Under this proposal, variable costs would be $16 per unit sold.

2. Enter into a long-term contract with a competitor who will serve that area's customers and will pay Carson a royalty of $8 per unit based on an estimate of 30,000 units being sold.

3. Close the North Dakota factory and not expand the operations of the Idaho factory.
   Note: Total home office costs of $1,000,000 will remain the same under each situation.

To assist the company's management in determining which alternative is most economically feasible, prepare a schedule computing its estimated pre-tax profit from total operations that would result from each of the following methods:

a. Expansion of the Idaho factory.

b. Negotiation of a long-term contract on a royalty basis.

c. Close the North Dakota operations with no expansion at other locations.

(AICPA adapted)

47. LO.1, LO.2, & LO.7 (Comprehensive) Pittsburg Products has processing plants in Kentucky and Pennsylvania. Both plants use recycled glass to produce jars that a variety of food processors use in food canning. The jars sell for $10 per hundred units. Budgeted revenues and costs for the year ending December 31, 2009, in thousands of dollars, are:

EXCEL

	Kentucky	Pennsylvania	Total
Sales	$1,100	$2,000	$3,100
Variable production costs			
Direct material	$ 275	$ 500	$ 775
Direct labor	330	500	830
Factory overhead	220	350	570
Fixed factory overhead	350	450	800
Fixed regional promotion costs	50	50	100
Allocated home office costs	55	100	155
Total costs	$1,280	$1,950	$3,230
Operating income (loss)	$ (180)	$ 50	$ (130)

Home office costs are fixed and are allocated to manufacturing plants on the basis of relative sales levels. Fixed regional promotional costs are discretionary advertising costs needed to obtain budgeted sales levels.

Because of the budgeted operating loss, Pittsburg Products is considering ceasing operations at its Kentucky plant. If it does so, proceeds from the sale of plant assets will exceed asset book values and exactly cover all termination costs; fixed factory overhead costs of $25,000 would not be eliminated. Pittsburg Products is considering the following three alternative plans:

PLAN A: Expand Kentucky's operations from its budgeted 11,000,000 units to a budgeted 17,000,000 units. It is believed that this can be accomplished by increasing Kentucky's fixed regional promotional expenditures by $120,000.

PLAN B: Close the Kentucky plant and expand the Pennsylvania operations from the current budgeted 20,000,000 units to 31,000,000 units to fill Kentucky's budgeted production of 11,000,000 units. The Kentucky region would continue to incur promotional costs to sell the 11,000,000 units. All sales and costs would be budgeted by the Pennsylvania plant.

PLAN C: Close the Kentucky plant and enter into a long-term contract with a competitor to serve the Kentucky region's customers. This competitor would pay a royalty of $1.25 per 100 units sold to Pittsburg, which would continue to incur fixed regional promotional costs to maintain sales of 11,000,000 units in the Kentucky region.

a. Without considering the effects of implementing Plans A, B, and C, compute the number of units that the Kentucky plant must produce and sell to cover its fixed factory overhead costs and fixed regional promotional costs.

b. Prepare a schedule by plant and in total of Pittsburg's budgeted contribution margin and operating income resulting from the implementation of each of the following:
  1. Plan A.
  2. Plan B.
  3. Plan C.

(AICPA adapted)

48. **LO.1, LO.2, & LO.7 (Sales and profit improvement)** Forward Fashions is a retail organization in the Northeast that sells upscale clothing. Each year, store managers in consultation with their supervisors establish financial goals, and then a monthly reporting system captures actual performance.

One of the firm's sales districts, District A, has three stores but has historically been a very poor performer. Consequently, the district supervisor has been searching for ways to improve the performance of her three stores. For May, she set performance goals with the managers of Stores 1 and 2. The managers will receive bonuses if the stores exceed certain performance measures. The manager of Store 3 decided not to participate in the bonus scheme. Because the district supervisor is unsure what type of bonus will encourage better performance, she offered the manager of Store 1 a bonus based on sales in excess of budgeted sales of $570,000; she offered the manager of Store 2 a bonus based on net income in excess of budgeted net income. The company's net income goal for each store is 12 percent of sales. The budgeted sales for Store 2 are $530,000.

Other pertinent data for May follow:
- At Store 1, sales were 40 percent of total District A sales; sales at Store 2 were 35 percent of total District A sales. The cost of goods sold at both stores was 42 percent of sales.
- Variable selling expenses (sales commissions) were 6 percent of sales for all stores and districts.
- Variable administrative expenses were 2.5 percent of sales for all stores and districts.
- Maintenance cost including janitorial and repair services is a direct cost for each store. The store manager has complete control over this outlay; however, it should not be below 1 percent of sales.

- Advertising is considered a direct cost for each store and is completely under the store manager's control. Store 1 spent two-thirds of District A's total outlay for advertising, which was 10 times more than Store 2 spent on advertising.
- The rental expense at Store 1 is 40 percent of District A's total and at Store 2 is 30 percent of District A's total.
- District A expenses are allocated to the stores based on sales.

a. Will Store 1 or Store 2 generate more profit under the new bonus scheme?
b. Will Store 1 or Store 2 generate more revenue under the new bonus scheme?
c. Why would Store 1 have an incentive to spend so much more on advertising than Store 2?
d. Which store manager has the most incentive to spend money on regular maintenance? Explain.
e. Which bonus scheme appears to offer the most incentive to improve the profit performance of the district in the short term? Long term?

(CMA adapted)

49. **LO.1, LO.2, & LO.7 (Comprehensive; product line)** Clean-N-Brite is a multiproduct company with several manufacturing plants. The Cincinnati plant manufactures and distributes two household cleaning and polishing compounds, regular and heavy duty, under the HouseSafe label. The forecasted operating results for the first six months of 2009, when 100,000 cases of each compound are expected to be manufactured and sold, are presented in the following statement:

HOUSESAFE COMPOUNDS—CINCINNATI PLANT
Forecasted Results of Operations
For the Six-Month Period Ending June 30, 2009

	(IN $000)		
	Regular	Heavy-Duty	Total
Sales	$ 2,000	$ 3,000	$ 5,000
Cost of sales	(1,600)	(1,900)	(3,500)
Gross profit	$ 400	$ 1,100	$ 1,500
Selling and administrative expenses			
Variable	$ 400	$ 700	$ 1,100
Fixed*	240	360	600
Total selling and administrative expenses	$ (640)	$(1,060)	$(1,700)
Income (loss) before taxes	$ (240)	$ 40	$ (200)

*The fixed selling and administrative expenses are allocated between the two products on the basis of dollar sales volume on the internal reports.

The sales price per case for the regular compound will be $20 and for the heavy duty will be $30 during the first six months of 2009. The manufacturing costs by case of product follow.

	COST PER CASE	
	Regular	Heavy-Duty
Raw material	$ 7.00	$ 8.00
Direct labor	4.00	4.00
Variable manufacturing overhead	1.00	2.00
Fixed manufacturing overhead*	4.00	5.00
Total manufacturing cost	$16.00	$19.00
Variable selling and administrative costs	$ 4.00	$ 7.00

*Depreciation charges are 50 percent of the fixed manufacturing overhead of each line.

Each product is manufactured on a separate production line. Annual normal manufacturing capacity is 200,000 cases of each product. However, the plant is capable of producing 250,000 cases of regular compound and 350,000 cases of heavy-duty compound annually.

The following schedule reflects top management consensus regarding the price/volume alternatives for the HouseSafe products for the last six months of 2009, which are essentially the same as those during its first six months.

REGULAR COMPOUND		HEAVY-DUTY COMPOUND	
Alternative Prices (per case)	Sales Volume (in cases)	Alternative Prices (per case)	Sales Volume (in cases)
$18	120,000	$25	175,000
20	100,000	27	140,000
21	90,000	30	100,000
22	80,000	32	55,000
23	50,000	35	35,000

Top management believes the expected loss for the first six months reflects a tight profit margin caused by intense competition and that many competitors will be forced out of this market by next year, so the company's profits should improve.

a. What unit selling price should Clean-N-Brite select for each HouseSafe compound for the remaining six months of 2009? Support your answer with appropriate calculations.

b. Without prejudice to your answer for requirement (a), assume that the optimum price/volume alternatives for the last six months will be a selling price of $23 and volume level of 50,000 cases for the regular compound and a selling price of $35 and volume of 35,000 cases for the heavy-duty compound.

    1. Should Clean-N-Brite consider closing its Cincinnati operations until 2010 to minimize its losses? Support your answer with appropriate calculations.

    2. Identify and discuss the qualitative factors that should be considered in deciding whether the Cincinnati plant should be closed during the last six months of 2009.

(CMA adapted)

50. **LO.8 (Linear Programming)** Buffalo Mfg. makes three outdoor leisure products: chairs, tables, and umbrellas. The company has significant demand for all three products but must manage certain constraints in its operations. Following are sales price, demand and cost information for each product.

	Chairs	Tables	Umbrellas
Sales price	$25	$90	$75
Variable production cost	15	60	50
Variable selling cost	5	10	10

The company faces machine time and labor time constraints in producing the three products. In total, the company has 15,000 machine hours and 30,000 labor hours available for production in the coming year. Following are the per unit production requirements for the three products.

	Chairs	Tables	Umbrellas
Machine hours	.5	1.5	1
Labor hours	1.0	1.5	1

a. In managing its constrained resources, what is the objective function of Buffalo Mfg.?

b. What are the production constraint equations for Buffalo Mfg.?

c. What are non-negativity constraint equations for Buffalo Mfg.?

11

Allocation of Joint Costs and Accounting for By-Product/Scrap

Objectives

After completing this chapter, you should be able to answer the following questions:

LO.1 How are the outputs of a joint process classified?

LO.2 What management decisions must be made before beginning a joint process?

LO.3 How is the joint cost of production allocated to joint products?

LO.4 How are by-product and scrap accounted for?

LO.5 How should not-for-profit organizations account for the cost of a joint activity?

Introduction

Almost every company produces and sells multiple products. Some companies engage in multiple production processes to manufacture a variety of products; other companies have a single process that simultaneously generates different outputs. For example, a chicken processing plant generates whole chickens, chicken parts, ground chicken, and fertilizer from a single input. Similarly, crude oil refining can produce gasoline, motor oil, heating oil, and kerosene; mining can produce copper, silver, and gold.

A process during which one product cannot be manufactured without producing others is known as a **joint process**. Such processes are common in the food, extractive, agricultural, and chemical industries. Additionally, the process of producing first-quality merchandise and factory seconds in a single operation can be viewed as a joint process. For example, if a manufacturing process is unstable in that it cannot "maintain output at a uniform quality level, [then] . . . the products that emerge from the [process] vary across one or more quality dimensions."[1]

This chapter discusses joint manufacturing processes, their related product outputs, and the accounting treatment of the costs of those processes. Costs incurred for material, labor, and overhead during a joint process are referred to as the **joint cost** of the production process. Joint cost is allocated only to the primary products of a joint process using either a physical or a monetary measure. Although joint cost allocations are necessary to determine financial statement valuations, such allocations should not be used in making internal decisions.[2] For example, in evaluating the profitability of a specific joint product, the decision maker must understand that the product's profitability is determined largely by the method used to allocate the joint cost and that allocation process is always arbitrary to some extent. Following incurrence of the joint cost, additional **separate costs** that are assignable to specific products may be incurred in later stages of production.

In addition, advertising and marketing expenditures can be joint costs. For example, a not-for-profit (NFP) organization could produce a brochure that serves the concurrent purposes of providing public service information and requesting donations. Joint costs for NFPs are covered in the last section of the chapter.

LO.1
How are the outputs of a joint process classified?

Outputs of a Joint Process

A joint process inexorably produces more than one product line. A product that has a sales value resulting from a joint process is classified as (1) a joint product, (2) a by-product, or (3) scrap. **Joint products** are the primary outputs of a joint process; each joint product has substantial revenue-generating ability. Joint products provide the financial motive for entering into the production process. These products are also called *primary products*, *main products*, or *co-products*.

Joint products are not necessarily products that differ intentionally. The definition of joint products includes similar products of differing quality that result from the same process. For example, a poultry processor generates different grades of turkeys, and, depending on certain characteristics defined by the U.S. Department of Agriculture, ready-to-cook poultry is graded as A, B, or C quality.

In contrast, **by-product** and **scrap** are incidental outputs of a joint process. Both are salable, but their sales values alone would not be sufficient for management to justify undertaking the joint process. For example, Perdue Farms would never undertake poultry processing simply to generate the by-product that is made into fertilizer or livestock feed. Krispy Kreme would never undertake doughnut manufacturing to generate the doughnut holes sold to customers. Weyerhaeuser would never undertake lumber production merely to generate the bark that is sold for burning to produce power and steam.[3] By-product is distinguished from scrap by having a higher sales value.

---

[1]James F. Gatti and D. Jacque Grinnell, "Joint Cost Allocations: Measuring and Promoting Productivity and Quality Improvements," *Cost Management* (July–August 2000), pp. 13–21.
[2]Sometimes correctly pricing a product depends on knowledge of the full cost of making the product, particularly when contractual agreements require cost-plus pricing. Joint cost allocation is also necessary to the costing of products for financial reporting.
[3]Weyerhaeuser's Web site has a virtual tour of a lumber production process; go to http://www.weyerhaeuser.com/ourbusinesses/pulppaperpckging/newsprint/virtualtour and click on virtual tour (last accessed 8/4/07).

A final output from a joint process is waste, which is a residual output that has no sales value. The expense incurred in the disposal of waste can exceed its production costs in some industries. However, many companies have learned either to minimize their production waste by changing their processing techniques or to reclassify waste as by-product or scrap by finding a use that generates some minimal amount of revenue.

Over time, a company can change a product classification because of changes in technology, consumer demand, or ecological factors. Some products originally classified as by-products can be reclassified as joint products, and some joint products can be reduced to the by-product category. Even products originally viewed as scrap or waste can be upgraded to joint product status. For example, years ago, poultry processors considered chicken litter, bones, beaks, and feet to be waste. These items are now recycled and processed further to produce valuable organic fertilizer. Therefore, depending on the company, these items can be classified as either by-product or scrap. Furthermore, the litter produced by chickens that was once considered waste can, when gasified, be used to produce electricity.

Classification of joint process output is based on management's judgment about the relative sales values of the outputs.

Finding an alternative use for what previously had been classified as waste (such as converting chicken litter and bones into organic fertilizer) allows a company to reclassify that item as a by-product or scrap.

Classifications are unique to each company. For example, assume that Companies A and B are both poultry processors. Company A might classify whole chickens and breast meat as the only joint products and all other chicken parts as by-product, whereas Company B might classify whole chickens, thighs, legs, and wings as joint products and all other chicken parts as by-product. These classifications could be based on the fact that Company A's processing facilities are large enough only to clean the chickens and remove the breast section; any additional processing would require a capital investment that would not be cost beneficial. Poultry Company B could have significantly larger facilities that allow further processing at costs substantially less than the sales value of the multiple products.

The Joint Process

Joint products are typically manufactured in companies using mass production processes and a process costing accounting method.[4] As shown in Exhibit 11–1, the outputs of steer processing would include a wide variety of meat cuts for retail sales (joint products); fat, entrails, bones, horns, and hooves that are classified as by-product or scrap; and some nonusable waste that is discarded.

The point at which joint process outputs are first identifiable as individual products is called the split-off point. A joint process can have one or more split-off points, depending on the number and types of output produced. Output may be sold at the split-off point if a market exists for products at that degree of completion. Alternatively, some or all of the products can be processed beyond the split-off point.

Joint cost includes all direct material, direct labor, and overhead costs incurred up to the split-off point. For financial reporting purposes, the cost principle requires that all necessary and reasonable costs of production be attached to products. Thus, at split-off, the joint cost is allocated to the joint products because their creation was the financial incentive for management to undertake the joint production process. Allocation of joint cost to the "extra" by-product, scrap, or waste would be both

---

[4]For simplicity, Chapter 6, on process costing, included examples in which calculating equivalent units was relatively straightforward.

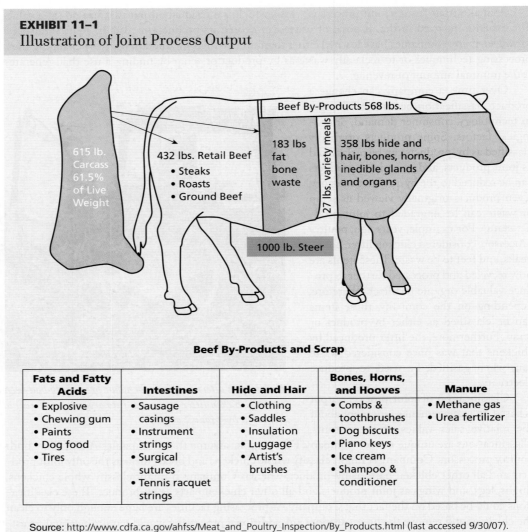

EXHIBIT 11–1
Illustration of Joint Process Output

Beef By-Products 568 lbs.

615 lb. Carcass 61.5% of Live Weight

432 lbs. Retail Beef
• Steaks
• Roasts
• Ground Beef

183 lbs fat bone waste

27 lbs. variety meals

358 lbs hide and hair, bones, horns, inedible glands and organs

1000 lb. Steer

Beef By-Products and Scrap

Fats and Fatty Acids	Intestines	Hide and Hair	Bones, Horns, and Hooves	Manure
• Explosive • Chewing gum • Paints • Dog food • Tires	• Sausage casings • Instrument strings • Surgical sutures • Tennis racquet strings	• Clothing • Saddles • Insulation • Luggage • Artist's brushes	• Combs & toothbrushes • Dog biscuits • Piano keys • Ice cream • Shampoo & conditioner	• Methane gas • Urea fertilizer

Source: http://www.cdfa.ca.gov/ahfss/Meat_and_Poultry_Inspection/By_Products.html (last accessed 9/30/07).

improper and not cost beneficial. Although joint cost allocation is necessary for financial statement valuations, such an allocation is not relevant to internal decision making. When the split-off point is reached, the joint cost has already been incurred and is a sunk cost (discussed in Chapter 10).

If any of the joint outputs are processed further, additional costs will be incurred. Any costs incurred after split-off are assigned to the separate products for which those costs were incurred. Exhibit 11–2 describes a joint process with multiple split-off points and the allocation of costs to products. For simplicity, none of the output of this joint process is considered a by-product; some amounts of scrap and waste are produced from Joint Process 1 but no joint cost is assigned to such output. Note that two of the joint products of Joint Process 1 (products B and C) become direct material for Joint Process 2. For accounting purposes, the joint cost allocations will follow products B and C into Joint Process 2, but these allocated costs should not be used in making decisions about further processing in Departments 2, 3, or 4. Such decisions should be made only after considering whether the expected additional revenues from further processing are higher than the expected additional costs.

The Joint Process Decision

LO.2
What management decisions must be made before beginning a joint process?

Exhibit 11–3 shows the four management decision points in a joint production process. Before committing resources to a joint production process, management must first decide whether the total

EXHIBIT 11–2
Model of a Joint Process

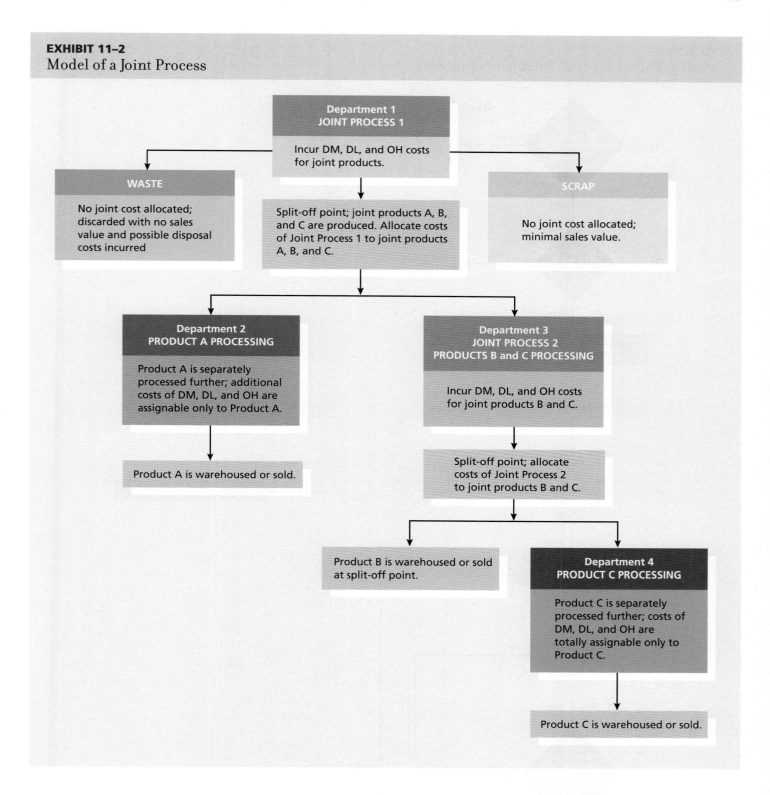

expected revenues from the sale of the joint output are likely to exceed the total expected processing costs. Joint cost, separate processing costs after split-off, and selling or disposal costs should be included in this calculation. Because the joint process results in a "basket" of products, some additional processing costs might be incurred to make products salable, or some disposal costs might be necessary for waste materials. Once the joint process costs are incurred, they are sunk costs regardless of whether the output is salable at the end of the joint process or at what amount.

EXHIBIT 11–3
Decision Points in a Joint Production Process

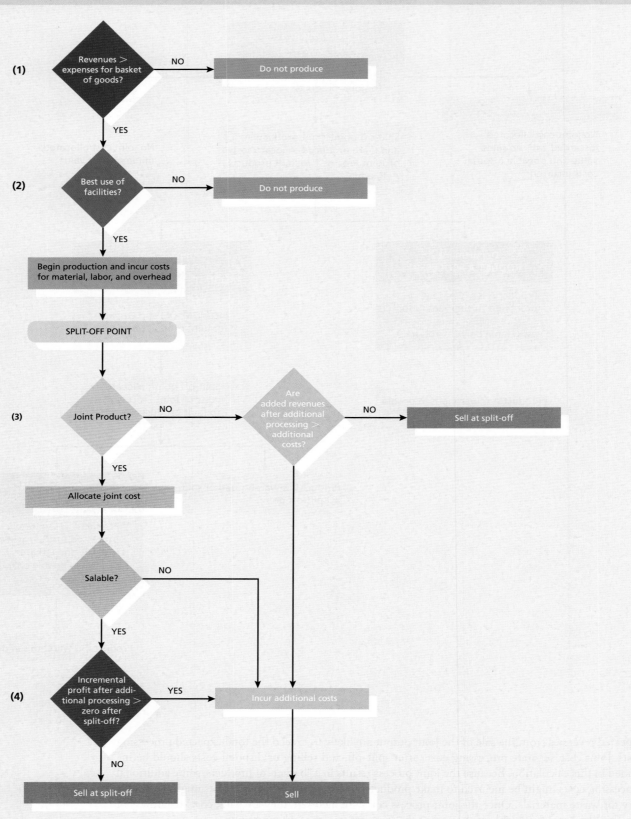

If total anticipated revenues from the basket of products exceed the anticipated joint and separate costs, managers should compare the income from this use of resources to that provided by the best alternative use of company resources. If joint process income exceeds that from other uses, management would decide that this joint production process is the best use of capacity and would begin production.

The next two decisions are made at split-off. The third decision is to determine how to classify joint process outputs. Some output will be primary; others will be by-product, scrap, or waste. This classification decision is necessitated by the fact that joint cost is assigned only to joint products. Before allocating the joint cost, however, it is possible that the total cost incurred to this point may be reduced by the sales value of the by-product and scrap. Treatment of by-product and scrap value is discussed later in the chapter.

The fourth decision is the most complex. Management must decide whether to sell (any or all of) the joint output at split-off or to process it further. If primary products are salable at split-off, further processing should be undertaken only if the value added to the product, as reflected by the incremental revenue, exceeds the incremental cost. If a primary product is not salable at split-off, additional costs must be incurred to make that product salable. For nonprimary output, management must also estimate whether the incremental revenue from additional processing will exceed the additional processing cost. If additional processing provides no net benefit, the nonsalable output should be sold without further processing after the split-off point.

To illustrate a further processing decision, assume that a whole chicken has a selling price of $0.96 per pound at split-off and that the minimum selling price for edible chicken parts after further processing is $1.06 per pound. If the additional processing cost is less than $0.10 per pound, the $0.10 incremental revenue ($1.06 − $0.96) exceeds the incremental cost and additional processing should occur. Note that no part of the joint cost is used in this decision process because that cost is "sunk" and cannot be recouped, and, thus, the only relevant items in the decision to process further are the incremental revenue and incremental cost.[5]

In making decisions at any potential sales point, managers must have a reasonable estimate of the selling price for each type of joint output. Expected selling prices should be based on both cost and market factors. In the long-run, the selling prices and volumes of products must be sufficient to cover their total costs. However, immediate economic influences on setting selling prices, such as competitors' prices and consumers' sensitivity to price changes, must be considered when estimating selling prices and forecasting revenues.

Allocation of Joint Cost

LO.3
How is the joint cost of production allocated to joint products?

Gobble Gobble Inc. is used to demonstrate alternative methods of allocating joint processing cost. The company manufactures three primary products from a joint process: turkey breasts, ground turkey, and whole turkeys. (All remaining parts are considered by-products of the joint process.) All joint products either can be sold at split-off or can be processed further at an additional separate cost. Breasts can be processed further to produce deli meats; ground turkey can be processed further and included in turkey sausage; whole turkeys can be processed further to make precooked or marinated roasters. Certain marketing and disposal costs for advertising, commissions, and transportation are incurred regardless of when the products are sold. Exhibit 11–4 provides assumed information on Gobble Gobble's processing operations and joint products for October 2008. The company started processing 10,000 tons of turkey during that month; approximately 10 percent of the tonnage started will become a by-product used in fertilizer pellets. Thus, an input of 10,000 tons results in 9,000 tons of joint product output and 1,000 tons of by-product.

Physical Measure Allocation

An easy, objective way to prorate joint cost at the split-off point is to use a physical measure. Physical measure allocation uses a common physical characteristic of the joint products as the

[5]See Chapter 10 for a detailed discussion of incremental and relevant costs.

EXHIBIT 11–4

Joint Cost Information for Gobble Gobble

Joint processing cost for period: $5,400,000

(1) Joint Product	(2) Tons Produced	(3) Sales Price per Ton at Split-Off	(4) Marketing Cost per Ton Regardless of When Sold	(5) Separate Cost per Ton if Processed Further	(6) Final Sales Price per Ton
Breast	3,800	$2,800	$200	$100	$3,200
Ground	2,400	1,800	100	100	2,100
Whole	2,800	1,200	50	60	1,500

Diagram of problem assuming products are sold at split-off

proration base. All joint products must be measurable by the same characteristic, such as one of these:

- tons of meat, bone, and hide in the meat packing or turkey processing industry
- tons of ore in the mining industry
- linear board feet in the lumber milling industry
- barrels of oil in the petroleum refining industry
- number of computer chips in the semiconductor industry

Using the physical measure allocation, Gobble Gobble's $5,400,000 of joint cost is assigned as shown in Exhibit 11–5. This allocation process treats each weight unit of output as equally desirable and assigns each the same per-unit cost. For Gobble Gobble, physical measure allocation assigns a cost of approximately $600 ($5,400,000 ÷ 9,000 tons) per ton of turkey, regardless of type.

The journal entries for recognizing the joint processing cost, allocating it to the joint products, and recognizing the separate processing cost (assuming that all joint products are processed further) follow:

EXHIBIT 11–5

Gobble Gobble's Joint Cost Allocation Based on Physical Measure

Cost per Physical Measure = Total Joint Cost ÷ Total Units of Physical Measurement

= $5,400,000 ÷ 9,000 tons = $600 per ton

Joint Product	Tons Produced	Cost per Ton	Total Allocated Cost	Revenue at Split-Off	Cost at Split-Off	Gross Profit at Split-Off
Breast	3,800	$600	$2,280,000	$2,800	$600	$2,200
Ground	2,400	600	1,440,000	1,800	600	1,200
Whole	2,800	600	1,680,000	1,200	600	600
Total	9,000		$5,400,000			

Work in Process Inventory—Turkey Processing	5,400,000	
Various accounts		5,400,000
To record joint processing cost		
Work in Process Inventory—Breast	2,280,000	
Work in Process Inventory—Ground	1,440,000	
Work in Process Inventory—Whole	1,680,000	
Work in Process Inventory—Turkey Processing		5,400,000
To allocate joint processing cost		
Work in Process Inventory—Breast (3,800 tons × $100)	380,000	
Work in Process Inventory—Ground (2,400 tons × $100)	240,000	
Work in Process Inventory—Whole (2,800 tons × $60)	168,000	
Various accounts		788,000
To record separate processing costs		

Marketing costs are recorded at the point of sale of the products.

Unlike monetary measures, physical measures provide an unchanging yardstick of output. Assuming that it is agreed that use of the word *ton* means "short ton" or 2,000 pounds (rather than a "long ton" or a "metric ton"), a ton of output produced from a process 10 years ago is the same measurement as a ton produced from that process today. Physical measures are useful in allocating joint cost to products that have extremely unstable selling prices. These measures are also necessary in rate-regulated industries that use cost to determine selling prices. For example, assume that a rate-regulated company has the right to set the selling price of its product at 20 percent above cost. It would be circular logic to allocate joint cost using selling prices that were set based on the cost to produce the output.

Allocating joint cost based on a physical measure, however, ignores the revenue-generating ability of individual joint products. Products that weigh the most or that are produced in the largest quantity will receive the highest proportion of joint cost allocation—regardless of their ability to bear that cost when they are sold. In the case of Gobble Gobble, each ton of whole turkey has been assigned a cost of $600. However, the computations in Exhibit 11–5 show that, by allocating the same amount of joint cost to each ton of joint product, whole turkeys generate the lowest gross profit per ton of the three joint products.

Monetary Measure Allocation

All commonly used allocation methods employ a process of proration. Because the physical measure allocation process is so simple, a detailed proration scheme is unnecessary. However, the following steps can be used to prorate joint cost to joint products in more complex monetary measure allocations:

1. Choose a monetary allocation base.
2. List the values that compose the base for each joint product.
3. Sum the values in step 2 to obtain a total value for the list.

4. Divide each individual value in step 2 by the total in step 3 to obtain a numerical proportion for each value. The sum of these proportions should be 1.00, or 100 percent.
5. Multiply the joint cost by each proportion to obtain the amount allocated to each product.
6. Divide the prorated joint cost for each product by the number of equivalent units of production (EUP) for each product to obtain a cost per EUP for valuation purposes.

The primary benefit of monetary over physical measure allocations is that the former recognizes the relative ability of each product to generate a profit at sale.[6] A problem with monetary measure allocations is that the basis used is dynamic. Because of fluctuations in general and specific price levels, a dollar's worth of output today is different from a dollar's worth of output from the same process five years ago. However, accountants customarily ignore price level fluctuations when recording or processing data, so this particular flaw of monetary measures is manageable.

Although there are many monetary measures that can be used to allocate joint cost to primary output, only three are presented in this text: sales value at split-off; net realizable value at split-off, and approximated net realizable value at split-off.

Sales Value at Split-Off

The sales value at split-off allocation method assigns joint cost to joint products based on the relative sales values of the products at the split-off point. To use this method, all joint products must be salable at split-off. Exhibit 11–6 presents Gobble Gobble's assignment of joint cost to production using the sales value at split-off allocation method. The low selling price per ton of whole turkeys relative to the other joint products results in a lower allocated cost per ton than the allocated cost using the physical measure allocation technique. This allocation method uses a weighting technique based on both quantity produced and selling price of production. The account titles for the entries to incur joint cost, allocate it to the joint products, and recognize separate processing cost are the same as those used earlier; however, the amounts allocated will be those shown in Exhibit 11–6.

Net Realizable Value at Split-Off

The net realizable value at split-off allocation method assigns joint cost based on the relative magnitudes of net realizable values of the joint products at the split-off point. Net realizable value (NRV) is equal to product sales revenue at split-off minus any costs necessary to prepare and dispose of the product. This method requires that all joint products be salable at the split-off point and considers the additional costs that must be incurred at split-off to realize the estimated sales revenue.

EXHIBIT 11–6
Gobble Gobble's Joint Cost Allocation Based on Sales Value at Split-Off

Joint Product	Tons Produced	Selling Price	Total Revenue	Proportion	Joint Cost	Amount Allocated	Cost per Ton
Breast	3,800	$2,800	$10,640,000	0.58[a]	$5,400,000	$3,132,000	$824.21
Ground	2,400	1,800	4,320,000	0.24[b]	5,400,000	1,296,000	540.00
Whole	2,800	1,200	3,360,000	0.18[c]	5,400,000	972,000	347.14
Total	9,000		$18,320,000	1.00		$5,400,000	

Proportions = Total Revenue of Respective Joint Product ÷ Total Revenue

[a]$10,640,000 ÷ $18,320,000 = 0.58 (rounded)
[b]$4,320,000 ÷ $18,320,000 = 0.24 (rounded)
[c]$3,360,000 ÷ $18,320,000 = 0.18 (rounded)

[6]Monetary measures are more reflective of the primary reason a joint process is undertaken: profit. Physical measure allocations are sometimes of dubious value because they are based on the flawed assumption that all physical units are equally desirable.

The marketing costs (shown in the fourth column of Exhibit 11–4) for Gobble Gobble's products are incurred whether the product is sold at split-off or after further processing. Exhibit 11–7 provides the joint cost allocations based on each product's relative proportion of total NRV. Results in Exhibits 11–6 and 11–7 are very similar because marketing costs incurred for each primary product are relatively low. When disposal costs are relatively high, cost allocations based on sales value at split-off and net realizable value can differ substantially.

Approximated Net Realizable Value at Split-Off

Often, some or all of the joint products are not salable at the split-off point. To be sold, these products must be processed additionally after split-off, which causes additional costs to be incurred. This lack of marketability at split-off means that neither the sales value at split-off nor the net realizable value at split-off approach can be used. Approximated net realizable value at split-off allocation requires that a simulated NRV at the split-off point be calculated to distribute the joint cost proportionately.[7] For each product, this value is computed as final sales price minus incremental separate costs. Incremental separate cost refers to all processing, marketing, and disposal costs that are incurred between the split-off point and the point of sale. An underlying assumption of this method is that the incremental revenue from further processing is equal to or greater than the incremental costs of further processing and selling. Using the information in Exhibit 11–4, approximated NRVs at split-off are determined for each of Gobble Gobble's joint products.

Joint Product	Final Sales Price per Ton	Separate Cost per Ton after Split-Off*	Approximated NRV at Split-Off
Breast	$3,200	$300[a]	$2,900
Ground	2,100	200[b]	1,900
Whole	1,500	110[c]	1,390

*Separate Cost after Split-Off = Separate Processing Cost + Marketing Cost at Point of Sale:
[a]$200 + $100 = $300
[b]$100 + $100 = $200
[c]$60 + $50 = $110

Further processing should be undertaken only if the incremental revenues will exceed the incremental costs based on the following computations.

EXHIBIT 11–7
Gobble Gobble's Joint Cost Allocation Based on Net Realizable Value at Split-Off

Joint Product	Tons Produced	Unit NRV per Ton	Total NRV	Proportion	Joint Cost	Amount Allocated	Cost per Ton
Breast	3,800	$2,600[a]	$ 9,880,000	0.57[d]	$5,400,000	$3,078,000	$810.00
Ground	2,400	1,700[b]	4,080,000	0.24[e]	5,400,000	1,296,000	540.00
Whole	2,800	1,150[c]	3,220,000	0.19[f]	5,400,000	1,026,000	366.43
Total	9,000		$17,180,000	1.00		$5,400,000	

Unit NRV per Ton = Sales Value at Split-Off − Marketing Costs at Point of Sale

[a]Unit NRV per ton = $2,800 − $200 = $2,600
[b]Unit NRV per ton = $1,800 − $100 = $1,700
[c]Unit NRV per ton = $1,200 − $50 = $1,150

Proportions = Total Revenue of Respective Joint Product ÷ Total Revenue

[d]$9,880,000 ÷ $17,180,000 = 0.57 (rounded)
[e]$4,080,000 ÷ $17,180,000 = 0.24 (rounded)
[f]$3,220,000 ÷ $17,180,000 = 0.19 (rounded)

[7]Another name for this method is *artificial net realizable value at split-off allocation*.

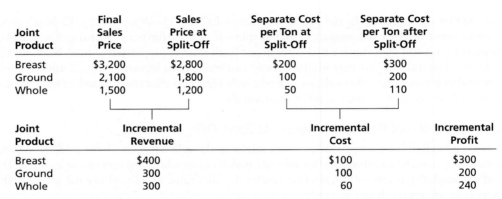

Joint Product	Final Sales Price	Sales Price at Split-Off	Separate Cost per Ton at Split-Off	Separate Cost per Ton after Split-Off
Breast	$3,200	$2,800	$200	$300
Ground	2,100	1,800	100	200
Whole	1,500	1,200	50	110

Joint Product	Incremental Revenue	Incremental Cost	Incremental Profit
Breast	$400	$100	$300
Ground	300	100	200
Whole	300	60	240

For all products, the incremental revenues from further processing beyond the split-off point exceed the incremental costs. Thus, Gobble Gobble Inc. will be better off if all joint products are processed further than if they are sold at split-off. The same conclusion can be reached by comparing the NRVs at split-off with the approximated NRVs at split-off:

Joint Product	Net Realizable Value at Split-Off	Approximated Net Realizable Value at Split-Off	Difference
Breast	$2,600	$2,900	$300
Ground	1,700	1,900	200
Whole	1,150	1,390	240

The decisions made about further processing affect the values used to allocate joint cost in the approximated NRV method. If it is uneconomical to further process one or more products, the value base used for allocation of joint cost will be a mixture of actual and approximated NRVs at split-off. Products that will not be processed further will be valued at their actual NRVs at split-off; whereas products that will be processed further are valued at approximated NRVs at split-off. However, using a mixed base is unnecessary in this case because all products will be processed further. Using the approximated NRV at split-off method, the $5,400,000 joint cost is allocated among the products as shown in Exhibit 11–8.

Gobble Gobble can process some or all of the breast meat, ground turkey, and whole turkeys further to create additional types of output (Exhibit 11–9). This further processing does not change the allocation of joint cost previously made to the joint products. Assume that Gobble Gobble used the allocations from Exhibit 11–8 and decided to further process 1,000 tons of breast meat into deli meat, 900 tons of ground turkey into turkey sausage, and 1,200 tons of whole turkey into marinated turkeys. The further processing would require assigning to the new products some of the original joint cost as well as the processing cost incurred to specifically manufacture these alternative products, as shown in the following journal entries. For simplicity, the separate costs of processing the "new" output are assumed to be the same as those for processing their related joint product counterpart.

EXHIBIT 11–8

Gobble Gobble's Joint Cost Allocation Based on Approximated Net Realizable Value at Split-Off

Joint Product	Tons Produced	NRV per Ton	Approximated Total NRV	Proportion	Joint Cost	Amount Allocated	Cost per Ton
Breast	3,800	$2,900	$11,020,000	0.57	$5,400,000	$3,078,000	$810.00
Ground	2,400	1,900	4,560,000	0.23	5,400,000	1,242,000	517.50
Whole	2,800	1,390	3,892,000	0.20	5,400,000	1,080,000	385.71
Total	9,000		$19,472,000	1.00		$5,400,000	

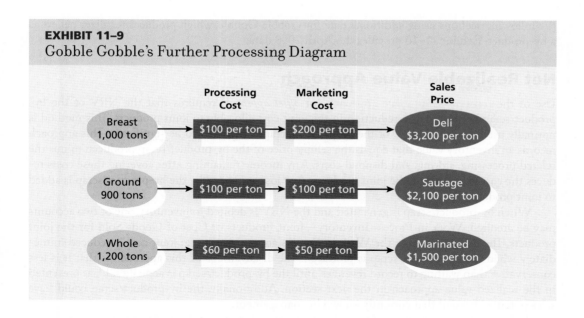

EXHIBIT 11–9

Gobble Gobble's Further Processing Diagram

	Work in Process		
Work in Process Inventory—Deli (1,000 tons × $810.00)	810,000	
Work in Process Inventory—Sausage (900 tons × $517.50)	465,750	
Work in Process Inventory—Marinated (1,200 tons × $385.71)	462,852	
Work in Process Inventory—Breast		810,000
Work in Process Inventory—Ground		465,750
Work in Process Inventory—Whole		462,852
To transfer allocated costs to new product inventories		
Work in Process Inventory—Deli (1,000 tons × $100)	100,000	
Work in Process Inventory—Sausage (900 tons × $100)	90,000	
Work in Process Inventory—Marinated (1,200 tons × $60)	72,000	
Various accounts		262,000
To record separate processing costs		

The marketing costs per ton have not been recorded because the products have not yet been sold.

Each method discussed allocates a different amount of joint cost to the joint products and results in a different per-unit cost for each product. Each method has advantages and disadvantages. For most companies, approximated NRV at split-off provides the most logical joint cost assignment. The most rational joint cost allocation matches the costs of joint processing with its benefits. Approximated NRV is considered the "best" method of joint cost allocation because, for each joint product, approximated NRV captures the intended level of separate processing, the costs of separate processing, the expected selling costs of each joint product, and the expected selling price of each joint product. Thus, approximated NRV is the best measure of the expected contribution of each product line to the coverage of joint costs. It is, however, more complex than the other methods because estimations must be made about additional processing costs and potential future sales values.

Accounting for By-Product and Scrap

LO.4
How are by-product and scrap accounted for?

Because the distinction between by-product and scrap is one of degree, these categories are discussed together by presenting several of the treatments found in practice. The appropriate choice of method depends on the magnitude of the net realizable value of the by-product/scrap and the need for additional processing after split-off. As the sales value of the by-product/scrap increases, so does the need for inventory recognition. Sales value of the by-product/scrap is generally recorded under either (1) the NRV approach or (2) the realized value approach. These approaches are discussed in the following sections using additional data for Gobble Gobble, which produces fertilizer pellets as a by-product. Exhibit 11–10 provides the April 2008 data.

Net Realizable Value Approach

Use of the net realizable value approach (or *offset approach*) requires that the NRV of the by-product/scrap be treated as a reduction in the joint cost allocable to joint products. This method is normally used when the NRV of the by-product/scrap is expected to be significant. This approach records an inventory value that equals the selling price of the by-product/scrap produced minus the related processing, storing, and disposal costs. Any income remaining after covering these costs reduces the cost of producing the joint products. Any loss generated by the by-product/scrap is added to joint product cost.

When by-product/scrap is generated and the NRV is debited to inventory, one of two accounts may be credited: Work in Process Inventory—Joint Products or Cost of Goods Sold for the joint products. The benefit of using the Work in Process account is timing: joint cost is reduced immediately when the by-product/scrap is produced. The disadvantage of this approach is that it is less conservative than waiting to record revenues until the by-product/scrap is actually sold, as presented in the realized value approach in the next section. Additionally, the by-product/scrap could have sales potential beyond that currently known by management.

The journal entries to record by-product/scrap production and the additional processing, completion, and sale of the by-product/scrap follow. Note that in the first journal entry, an alternative credit could have been made to the Cost of Goods Sold of the joint products.

Work in Process Inventory—Fertilizer Pellets (2,000,000 × $0.20)	400,000	
Work in Process Inventory—Joint Products		400,000
To record production of by-product		
Work in Process Inventory—Fertilizer Pellets (2,000,000 × $0.10)	200,000	
Various accounts		200,000
To record additional processing costs		
Finished Goods Inventory—Fertilizer Pellets (2,000,000 × $0.30)	600,000	
Work in Process Inventory—Fertilizer Pellets		600,000
To transfer completed by-product to finished goods		
Cash (or Accounts Receivable) (2,000,000 × $0.30)	600,000	
Finished Goods Inventory—Fertilizer Pellets		600,000
To record sale of by-product		

Although reducing joint cost by the NRV of the by-product/scrap is the traditional method used to account for such goods, it is not necessarily the best method for internal decision making or the management of by-product/scrap. By-product/scrap can be treated either as having no assignable cost or as having costs equal to the net sales value. However, when management considers by-product/scrap to be a moderate source of income, the accounting and reporting methods used should help managers monitor production and further processing of the by-product/scrap and make effective decisions regarding this resource.[8] The NRV method does not indicate the revenues,

EXHIBIT 11–10
April 2008 Data for By-Products of Gobble Gobble

Total processing for month: 10,000 tons of turkey, resulting in 9,000 tons of joint products

By-products from joint product production: 1,000 tons (or 2,000,000 pounds) of fertilizer pellet ingredients

Selling price of fertilizer pellets: $0.30 per pound

Processing costs per pound of fertilizer pellets: $0.08 for labor and $0.02 for overhead

Net realizable value per pound of fertilizer pellets: $0.20

[8]Advances in technology and science have turned many previous "by-product" or "scrap" items into main products. Management should not ignore the significance of such products and should seek new uses or markets for them.

expenses, or profits from the by-product/scrap and, thus, does not provide sufficient information to induce management to maximize the inflows from by-product/scrap disposal.

Realized Value Approach

Under the realized value approach (or *other income approach*), no value is recognized for the by-product/scrap until it is sold. This method is the simplest approach to accounting for by-product/scrap. Several reporting techniques can be used with the realized value approach.

One presentation shows total sales of by-product/scrap on the income statement under the Other Revenue caption. Costs of additional processing or disposal of the by-product/scrap are included in the cost of producing the joint products. This presentation provides little useful information to management because it does not match the costs of producing the by-product/scrap with its revenues. Gobble Gobble Inc. entries for the incurrence of labor and overhead costs and sale of by-product using the Other Revenue method follow:

Work in Process Inventory—Joint Products (2,000,000 × $0.08)	160,000	
Manufacturing Overhead Control (2,000,000 × $0.02)	40,000	
Various accounts		200,000
To record the labor and overhead costs of by-product processing		
(Note: All costs are included in the cost of joint products.)		
Cash (or Accounts Receivable) (2,000,000 × $0.30)	600,000	
Other Revenue		600,000
To record sale of by-product		

A second presentation for the realized value approach shows by-product/scrap revenue on the income statement net of additional costs of processing and disposal. This method presents the net by-product/scrap revenue as an enhancement of net income in the period of sale under the Other Income caption. This presentation allows management to recognize the monetary benefit realized by the company from managing the costs and revenues related to by-product/scrap. The entries using the Other Income method for the incurrence of labor and overhead costs and sale of by-product for Gobble Gobble Inc. are as follows:

Work in Process Inventory—Fertilizer Pellets (2,000,000 × $0.10)	200,000	
Various accounts		200,000
To record the labor and overhead costs of by-product processing		
(Note: All costs are included in the cost of by-product.)		
Cash (or Accounts Receivable)	600,000	
Work in Process Inventory—Fertilizer Pellets		200,000
Other Income		400,000
To record sale of by-product net of processing/disposal costs		

Because the Other Income method matches by-product/scrap revenue with related storage, further processing, transportation, and disposal costs, this method provides detailed information on financial responsibility and accountability for disposition of these secondary outputs, provides better control, and could improve performance. Managers are more apt to look for new or expanded sales potential because the net benefits of doing so are provided on the income statement.

Other alternative presentations include showing the realized value from the sale of by-product/scrap as (1) an addition to gross margin, (2) a reduction of the cost of goods manufactured, or (3) a reduction of the cost of goods sold. The major advantage of these simplistic approaches is clerical efficiency.

Regardless of whether a company uses the NRV or the realized value approach, the specific method used to account for by-product/scrap should be established before the joint cost is allocated to the joint products. Exhibit 11–11 shows four comparative income statements using different methods of accounting for by-product/scrap income for Gobble Gobble. Some assumed amounts have been included to provide complete income statements.

By-product, scrap, and waste are created in all types of businesses, not just manufacturers. Managers might not see the need to determine the cost of these secondary types of products. However, with the trend toward more emphasis on cost and quality control, many companies are becoming aware of the potential value of by-product, scrap, and waste as substantial sources of revenue and are devoting time and attention to developing those innovative revenue sources.

EXHIBIT 11–11
Gobble Gobble Comparative Income Statements—By-Product Presentations

(a) Net Realizable Value Approach: Reduce Cost of Goods Sold (CGS)

Sales		$ 6,200,000
Cost of goods sold		
Beginning finished goods (FG)	$ 400,000	
Cost of goods manufactured (CGM)	3,600,000	
Cost of goods available (CGA)	$4,000,000	
Ending FG	(380,000)	
Unadjusted CGS	$3,620,000	
NRV of by-product	(400,000)	(3,220,000)
Gross margin		$ 2,980,000
Operating expenses		(2,600,000)
Income from principal operations		$ 380,000
Other income		
Royalties		80,000
Income before income taxes		$ 460,000

(b) Net Realizable Value Approach: Reduce Cost of Goods Manufactured (CGM)

Sales		$6,200,000
Cost of goods sold		
Beginning FG	$ 400,000	
CGM ($3,600,000 − $400,000)	3,200,000	
CGA	$3,600,000	
Ending FG [assumed to be smaller than under (a)]	(342,000)	(3,258,000)
Gross margin		$2,942,000
Operating expenses		(2,600,000)
Income from principal operations		$ 342,000
Other income		
Royalties		80,000
Income before income taxes		$ 422,000

(c) Net Realized Value Approach: Increase Revenue

Sales		$6,200,000
Other revenue		
By-product sales		600,000
Total revenue		$6,800,000
Cost of goods sold		
Beginning FG	$ 400,000	
CGS (main products)	3,600,000	
CGS (processing by-product)	200,000	
CGA	$4,200,000	
Ending FG	(380,000)	(3,820,000)
Gross margin		$2,980,000
Operating expenses		(2,600,000)
Income from principal operations		$ 380,000
Other income		
Royalties		80,000
Income before income taxes		$ 460,000

(d) Net Realized Value Approach: Present as Other Income

Sales		$6,200,000
Cost of goods sold		
Beginning FG	$ 400,000	
CGM	3,600,000	
CGA	$4,000,000	
Ending FG	(380,000)	(3,620,000)
Gross margin		$2,580,000
Operating expenses		(2,600,000)
Loss from principal operations		$ (20,000)
Other income		
Royalties	$ 80,000	
By-product sales (NRV)	400,000	480,000
Income before income taxes		$ 460,000

By-Product and Scrap in Job Order Costing

Although joint products are not normally associated with job order costing systems, accounting for by-product or scrap is common in these systems. Either the NRV or the realized value approach can be used to recognize the value of by-product/scrap.

In a job order system, the value of by-product/scrap is appropriately credited to either manufacturing overhead or the specific jobs in process. The former account is credited if by-product/scrap is typically created by most jobs undertaken. The effect of crediting manufacturing overhead is to reduce the amount of overhead that is applied to all products for the period. In contrast, if only a few or specific jobs generate substantial amounts of by-product/scrap, the individual jobs causing the by-product/scrap should be credited with this value. The effect of crediting specific jobs with the value of by-product/scrap is to reduce the total costs assigned to those jobs.[9]

To illustrate, assume that Gobble Gobble Inc. occasionally prepares special turkey products for large institutional clients. Every special order generates scrap meat that is sold to Canine Catering Corporation. In October 2008, Gobble Gobble received an order for 20,000 turkey casseroles from the Bexar County Public School District. The casseroles are prepared using a combination of breast, thigh, and wing meat. After production of the casseroles, Gobble Gobble sold $250 of scrap meat. Using the realized value approach, the entry to record the sale of the scrap is:

Cash	250	
Manufacturing Overhead		250
To record the sale of scrap		

In contrast, assume that Gobble Gobble seldom has salable scrap on its special order jobs. However, during October 2008, the company contracted with Green Cove Convalescent Centers to prepare 25,000 frozen chicken croquettes. Because Gobble Gobble normally does not process chicken, it must acquire specific raw material for the job and will charge the cost of all raw material directly to Green Cove. Preparation of the chicken croquettes generates some scrap that can be sold for $375 to Tortilla Soup Cannery. Because the raw material cost is directly related to the Green Cove job, the sale of scrap from that raw material also relates to that job. Under these circumstances, the production and sale of the scrap are recorded (using the NRV approach) as follows:

Scrap Inventory—Chicken	375	
Work in Process Inventory—Green Cove Convalescent Centers		375
To record the NRV of scrap produced by Green Cove job		
Cash	375	
Scrap Inventory—Chicken		375
To record sale of the scrap		

In this case, the NRV approach is preferred because of the recognition timing. To affect the specific job cost that caused an unusual incidence and quantity of scrap, it could be necessary to recognize the by-product/scrap upon production; otherwise, the job could be completed before the by-product/scrap can be sold.

Allocation of joint costs is not unique to manufacturing organizations; some costs incurred in service businesses and in not-for-profit organizations may be allocated among product lines, organizational locations, or types of activities performed by the organizations.

Joint Costs in Service Businesses and Not-For-Profit Organizations

LO.5
How should not-for-profit organizations account for the cost of a joint activity?

Joint costs in service businesses and NFP organizations often relate to marketing and promotion rather than to production processes. Service businesses and NFPs incur joint costs for advertising multiple products, printing multipurpose documents, or holding multipurpose events. NFPs often develop and distribute brochures providing information about the organization, its purposes, and its programs as well as making an appeal for funds.

---

[9]Conceptually, the treatment of the profitability of by-product/scrap in a job order system is similar to the treatment of the costs of spoilage in a job order system, as discussed in Chapter 5.

A service business can choose either a physical or a monetary allocation base to allocate joint costs. For example, a local bicycle and lawn mower repair company could advertise a sale and list all store locations in a single newspaper ad. The ad cost could be allocated equally to all locations or be allocated on sales volume for each location during the period of the sale. As another example, a grocery delivery service could deliver several customers' orders on the same trip. The cost of the trip could be allocated based on the number of bags or pounds of food delivered for each customer.

Although service businesses may decide that allocating joint cost is not necessary, financial accounting requires that NFPs (and state and local government entities) allocate the costs of "joint activities" among fundraising, organizational program (program activities), and administrative functions (management and general activities).[10] No specific allocation method is prescribed; the SOP only states that the method must be rational and systematic, result in reasonable allocations, and be applied in the same manner under similar situations. A major purpose of this allocation process is to ensure that external users of financial statements are able to clearly determine amounts spent by the organization for various activities—especially fundraising. High fundraising costs may harm an NFP's credibility with philanthropists who measure the effectiveness of an organization by the percentage of funds that actually goes toward programs that further the entity's mission rather than the percentage that goes to raise more funds. High fundraising percentages may also jeopardize an NFP's standing with charity regulators.▲

There are three tests that must be met for allocation; if all the tests are not met, all the costs associated with the "joint activity" (such as advertising) must be charged to fundraising.[11] The tests relate to (in order) purpose, audience, and content. The purpose criterion demonstrates that the activity's purpose includes accomplishing some program or management/general function. The audience criterion demonstrates that the NFP chose the audience because it is suitable for accomplishing the activity's program or management/general functions. The content criterion demonstrates that the activity's content supports program or management/general functions. The commonality among the criteria is that each creates some type of "call for action"—thus, a brochure that simply informs the audience about the NFP's purpose or a particular disease is not considered a call for action.

A critical element under the purpose criterion is the compensation test. If a majority of compensation or fees for anyone performing a part of the activity is tied to contributions raised, the activity automatically fails the purpose criterion and all costs of the activity must be charged to fundraising. Thus, if professional fundraisers are used and paid a percentage of the amount raised, all costs of the activity must be charged to fundraising.

---

[10]American Institute of Certified Public Accountants, *Statement of Position 98-2: Accounting for Costs of Activities of Not-for-Profit Organizations and State and Local Governmental Entities That Include Fund Raising* (August 1998).

[11]An exception to the rule is that costs for goods and services provided in exchange transactions (such as a meal provided at a function that failed to meet the three required criteria) that are part of joint activities should not be reported as fundraising costs; such costs should be reported as cost of sales for the activity.

Comprehensive Review Module

Chapter Summary

1. The possible outputs of a joint process include

   - joint products—output with a relative high sales value.

   - by-product—output with a higher sales value than scrap but less than joint products.

   - scrap—output with a low sales value.

   - waste—residual output with no sales value.

2. Joint products

   - provide the primary incentive for undertaking production.

   - are identified at the split-off point.

- are assigned the joint cost of the production process.
- could have the related joint cost reduced by the net realizable value or realized value of by-product and scrap.

3. Questions that must be answered in a joint production process include

- two that are made before the joint process is started:
  - ➢ Do total revenues exceed total (joint and separate) costs?
  - ➢ Is this process the best use of available facilities?
- two that are made at the split-off point:
  - ➢ Which products will be classified as joint products, by-product, scrap, and waste?
  - ➢ Which products will be sold at split-off, and which will be processed further?

4. Joint cost is commonly allocated to joint products using one of two common methods:

- physical measures that provide an unchanging yardstick of output over time and treat each unit of product as equally desirable.
- monetary measures that consider different valuations of the individual joint products; these valuations can be based on
  - ➢ sales value at split-off,
  - ➢ net realizable value at split-off, or
  - ➢ approximated net realizable value at split-off.

5. By-product and scrap can be accounted for by using the

- net realizable value (offset) approach in which the NRV of the by-product/scrap reduces either the
  - ➢ Work in Process Inventory of the joint products when the by-product/scrap is produced or the
  - ➢ Cost of Goods Sold of the joint products when the by-product/scrap is produced.
- realized value (other income) approach in which the NRV of the by-product/scrap is shown on the income statement as either
  - ➢ other revenue when the by-product/scrap is sold or
  - ➢ other income when the by-product/scrap is sold.

6. Not-for-profit organizations must either

- allocate the cost incurred for a "joint activity" among the categories of
  - ➢ fundraising,
  - ➢ program, and/or
  - ➢ management/general activities
- or charge the entire cost of the joint activity to fundraising if all of the following three criteria are not met:
  - ➢ purpose,
  - ➢ audience, and
  - ➢ content.

Potential Ethical Issues

1. Making product decisions based on the sum of allocated joint cost and separate processing costs

2. Classifying a joint product as a by-product or scrap so that no joint cost will be allocated to that product and, thereby, increase that product's appearance of profitability

3. Classifying a salable product as "waste" and then selling that product "off the books" for the personal benefit of a manager

4. Manipulating the assignment of joint costs such that joint products in inventory at the end of a period are assigned a disproportionately higher cost than joint products sold during the period so that higher income and higher values for inventory are reported at period-end

5. Using the sales value of by-product or scrap generated by specific jobs to offset total manufacturing overhead and, thus, the overhead allocation rate on all production rather than using that sales value to reduce the cost of the job specifically generating the by-product/scrap

6. Reducing or not incurring expenses by disposing of hazardous waste in a manner that causes harm to the environment or threatens humans and wildlife

7. Misallocating the cost of an activity to program and management/general activities solely to reduce the fundraising cost of a not-for-profit organization▲

Solution Strategies

Allocation of Joint Cost

Joint cost is allocated only to joint products; however, joint cost can be reduced by the value of by-product/scrap before the allocation process begins.

For physical measure allocation: Divide joint cost by the products' total physical measurements to obtain a cost per unit of physical measure.

For monetary measure allocation:

1. Choose an allocation base.

2. List the values that compose the allocation base for each joint process.

3. Sum the values in step 2.

4. Calculate the percentage of the total base value associated with each joint product.

5. Multiply the joint cost by each percentage calculated in step 4 to obtain the amount to be allocated to each joint product.

6. Divide the prorated joint cost for each product by the number of equivalent units of production (EUP) for each product to obtain a cost per EUP for valuation purposes.

Allocation bases, measured at the split-off point, by which joint cost is prorated to the joint products include the following:

Type of Measure	Allocation Base
Physical output	Physical measure of units of output (e.g., tons, feet, barrels, liters)
Monetary	Currency units of value
Sales value	Revenues of the several products
Net realizable value	Sales value minus incremental processing and disposal costs
	Final sales price minus incremental separate costs
	Approximated net realizable value

Demonstration Problem

Circle City Inc. produces two joint products—JP#89-43-A and JP#89-43-B—from a single input. Further processing of product JP#89-43-A results in a by-product designated BP#89-43-X. A summary of production and sales for 2008 follows:

- Circle City Inc. input 600,000 tons of raw material into the Processing Department. Total joint processing cost was $520,000,000. During the joint processing, 90,000 tons of material were lost.
- After joint processing, 60 percent of the joint process output was transferred to Division 1 to produce JP#89-43-A, and 40 percent of the joint process output was transferred to Division 2 to produce JP#89-43-B.
- Further processing in Division 1 resulted in 70 percent of the input tons becoming JP#89-43-A and 30 percent of the input tons becoming BP#89-43-X. The separate processing cost for JP#89-43-A in Division 1 was $648,884,000.
- Total packaging costs for JP#89-43-A were $321,300,000. After Division 1 processing and packaging, product JP#89-43-A is salable at $6,000 per ton.
- Each ton of BP#89-43-X can be sold for $120 after total selling cost of $5,000,000. The company accounts for the by-product using the net realizable value method and showing the NRV as a reduction in the cost of goods sold of the joint products.
- In Division 2, product JP#89-43-B was further processed at a separate cost of $408,000,000. A completed ton of JP#89-43-B sells for $3,700.
- Selling cost for both products JP#89-43-A and JP#89-43-B is $200 per ton.

Required:

a. Prepare a process diagram similar to the one shown in Exhibit 11–4 or 11–9.

b. Record the journal entry to

1. recognize incurrence of joint cost.

2. allocate joint costs to the joint products using tonnage as a physical measure and transfer the products into Divisions 1 and 2.

3. record incurrence of separate processing costs for products JP#89-43-A and JP#89-43-B in Divisions 1 and 2.

4. record incurrence of packaging cost for product JP#89-43-A.

5. transfer completed products JP#89-43-A and JP#89-43-B to finished goods.

c. Allocate the joint cost to products JP#89-43-A and JP#89-43-B using approximated net realizable values at split-off.

d. Circle City Inc. had no Work in Process or Finished Goods Inventory at the beginning of 2008. Prepare an income statement through gross margin for Circle City Inc. assuming that:

- 80 percent of product JP#89-43-A and 90 percent of product JP#89-43-B produced were sold.

- all the by-product BP#89-43-X that was produced during the year was sold.

- joint cost was allocated using the physical measurement method in part (b).

Solution to Demonstration Problem

a.

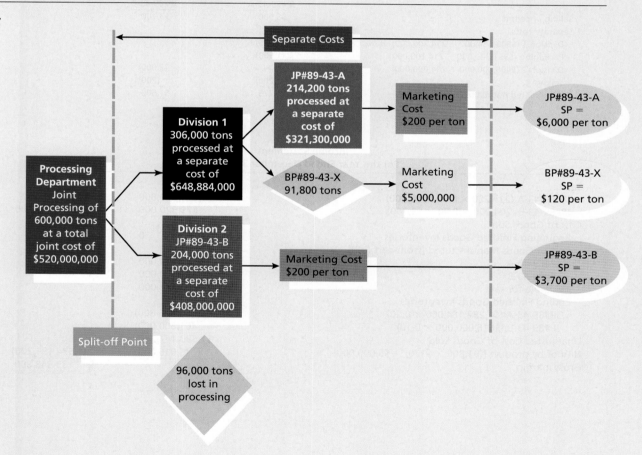

b.

1.	Work in Process Inventory—Processing	520,000,000	
	Various accounts		520,000,000
	To record 2008 joint processing costs		
2.	Work in Process Inventory—Division 1	312,000,000	
	Work in Process Inventory—Division 2	208,000,000	
	Work in Process Inventory—Processing		520,000,000
	To allocate joint cost to joint products		

3. Work in Process—Division 1 648,884,000
   Work in Process—Division 2 408,000,000
       Various accounts 1,056,884,000
   To record separate processing costs

4. Work in Process Inventory—Division 1 321,300,000
       Various accounts 321,300,000
   To record packaging costs for JP#89-43-A

5. Finished Goods Inventory—JP#89-43-A 1,282,184,000
   Finished Goods Inventory—JP#89-43-B 616,000,000
       Work in Process Inventory—Division 1 1,282,184,000
       Work in Process Inventory—Division 2 616,000,000
   To transfer completed production to finished goods

c. **Approximated NRV Method**

Product	Tons Produced	NRV per Ton at Split-off*	Total NRV	Proportion	Joint Cost	Allocated Joint Cost
JP#89-43-A	214,200	$1,275	$273,105,000	0.47	$520,000,000	$244,400,000
JP#89-43-B	204,000	1,500	306,000,000	0.53	520,000,000	275,600,000
			$579,105,000	1.00		$520,000,000

	JP#89-43-A	JP#89-43-B
Selling price/ton	$6,000	$3,700
Separate costs		
Division 1 ($648,884,000 ÷ 214,200,000)	(3,025)	
Packaging ($321,300,000 ÷ 214,200,000)	(1,500)	
Division 2 ($408,000,000 ÷ 204,000,000)		(2,000)
Selling	(200)	(200)
Approximated net realizable value	$1,275	$1,500

d.

Circle City Inc.
Income Statement
For the Year Ended December 31, 2008

Sales		
JP#89-43-A (214,200 × 0.80 × $6,000)	$1,028,160,000	
JP#89-43-B (204,000 × 0.90 × $3,700)	679,320,000	$ 1,707,480,000
Cost of Goods Sold		
Beginning Finished Goods Inventories	$ 0	
Cost of Goods Manufactured [from part (b5)]		
JP#89-43-A	1,282,184,000	
JP#89-43-B	616,000,000	
Available for sale	$1,898,184,000	
Ending Finished Goods Inventories		
JP#89-43-A ($1,282,184,000 × 0.20)	(256,436,800)	
JP#89-43-B ($616,000,000 × 0.10)	(61,600,000)	
Unadjusted Cost of Goods Sold	$1,580,147,200	
NRV of by-product [(91,800 × $120) − $5,000,000]	(6,016,000)	(1,574,131,200)
Gross margin		$ 133,348,800

Key Terms

approximated net realizable value at split-off
     allocation, **p. 409**

by-product, **p. 400**

joint cost, **p. 400**

joint process, **p. 400**

joint product, **p. 400**

net realizable value (NRV), **p. 408**

net realizable value approach, **p. 412**

net realizable value at split-off allocation, **p. 408**

physical measure allocation, **p. 405**

realized value approach, **p. 413**

sales value at split-off allocation, **p. 408**

scrap, **p. 400**

separate cost, **p. 400**

split-off point, **p. 401**

waste, **p. 401**

Questions

1. How does management determine how to classify each type of output from a joint process? Is this decided before or after production?
2. In a company that engages in a joint production process, will all processing stop at the split-off point? Discuss the rationale for your answer.
3. By what criteria would management determine whether to proceed with processing at each decision point in a joint production process?
4. Why is cost allocation necessary in accounting? Why is it necessary in a joint process?
5. Compare the advantages and disadvantages of the two primary methods used to allocate joint cost to joint products.
6. Why are approximated, rather than actual, net realizable values at split-off sometimes used to allocate joint cost?
7. Which of the two common approaches used to account for by-product provides better information to management? Discuss the rationale for your answer.
8. When is by-product/scrap cost considered in setting the predetermined overhead rate in a job order costing system? When is it not considered?
9. Why must not-for-profit organizations allocate any cost for a joint activity among fundraising, program, and administrative activities?

Exercises

10. **LO.1 (Essay; Internet)** Use the Internet to find five examples of businesses that have joint processes. For each business, describe:
    a. The various outputs from the processes; using logic, determine whether each output would be classified as a joint product, a by-product, scrap, or waste.
    b. Your recommendation of the most appropriate methods of allocating joint cost to the outputs you described in part (a); express, in nontechnical terms, your justification for each of your recommendations.
    c. For one of the businesses, diagram the flow of costs.
11. **LO.2 (Joint process decision making)** Tom Schaefer's uncle has asked him to take over the family poultry processing plant. Provide Schaefer, who graduated in engineering, answers to the following issues.
    a. What are the important questions to be answered about joint processes in a poultry processing plant? Also indicate the points in a joint process at which these questions should be answered.
    b. How should joint costs be used in managerial decision making? When and why might a joint cost be used inappropriately in decision making?
    c. How are joint process outputs similar and dissimilar?
12. **LO.3 (Physical measure allocation)** Elgin Timber uses a joint process to manufacture two grades of wood: A and B. During October 2008, the company incurred $24,000,000 of joint production cost in producing 36,000,000 board feet of grade A and 12,000,000 board feet of grade B wood. The company allocates joint cost on the basis of board feet of wood produced. The company can sell grade A wood at the split-off point for $0.50 per board foot. Alternatively, grade A wood can be further processed at a cost of $0.75 per

board foot and then sold for $1.60 per board foot. No opportunity exists for processing grade B wood after split-off.

a. How much joint cost should be allocated to grade A and to grade B wood?

b. If grade A wood is processed further and then sold, what is the incremental effect on Elgin's net income? Should the additional processing be performed?

13. **LO.3 (Sales value and physical value allocation)** Deby's Dairy produces milk and sour cream from a joint process. During June, the company produced 240,000 quarts of milk and 320,000 pints of sour cream (there are two pints in a quart). Sales value at split-off point was $100,000 for the milk and $220,000 for the sour cream. The milk was assigned $43,200 of the joint cost.

a. Using the sales value at split-off approach, determine the total joint cost for June.

b. Assume, instead, that the joint cost was allocated based on the number of quarts produced. What was the total joint cost incurred in June?

14. **LO.3 (Physical and sales value allocations)** FINS produces three products from its fish farm: fish, fish oil, and fish meal. During July 2008, FINS produced the following average quantities of each product from each pound (16 ounces) of fish processed:

Product	Obtained from Each Pound of Fish
Fish	8 ounces
Fish oil	4
Fish meal	2
Total	14 ounces

Of each pound of fish processed, 2 ounces are waste. In July, FINS processed 50 tons of fish (1 ton equals 2,000 pounds). Joint cost amounted to $190,400. On average, each pound of product has the following selling prices: fish, $6; fish oil, $9; and fish meal, $3.

a. Allocate the joint cost using weight as the basis. (Round to nearest whole percentage.)

b. Allocate the joint cost using sales value as the basis. (Round to nearest whole percentage.)

c. Discuss the advantages and disadvantages of the answers to parts (a) and (b).

15. **LO.3 (Net realizable value allocation)** B. Wood Communications has three operating groups: Games, News, and Documentaries. In May, the company incurred $12,000,000 of joint cost for facilities and administration. May revenues and separate production costs of each group follow:

	Games	News	Documentaries
Revenue	$17,920,000	$15,360,000	$94,720,000
Separate costs	16,480,000	8,160,000	55,360,000

a. What amount of joint cost is allocated to each operating group using the net realizable value approach? Compute the profit for each operating area after the allocation.

b. What amount of joint cost is allocated to each operating group if the allocation is based on revenues? Compute the profit for each operating group after the allocation.

c. Assume you are head of the Games Group. Would the difference in allocation bases create significant problems for you when you report to the top management of the company? Develop a short presentation for top management if the allocation base in part (b) is used to determine each operating group's relative profitability. Be certain to discuss important differences in revenues and cost figures for the Games and Documentaries groups.

16. **LO.3 (Approximated net realizable value method)** BellaBella Perfume Company makes three products that can either be sold at split-off or processed further and then sold. The joint cost for April 2008 is $720,000.

Product	Bottles of Output	Sales Price at Split-Off	Separate Cost after Split-Off	Final Sales Price
Perfume	15,000	$6.00	$2.00	$15.50
Eau de toilette	20,000	4.00	1.00	12.00
Body splash	25,000	4.00	1.50	11.00

The number of ounces in a bottle of each product is: perfume, 1; eau de toilette, 2; and body splash, 3. Assume that all products are processed further after split-off.

a. Allocate the joint cost based on the number of bottles, weight, and approximated net realizable values at split-off. (Round to the nearest whole percentage.)

b. Assume that all products are processed further and completed. At the end of the period, the inventories are as follows: perfume, 450 bottles; eau de toilette, 1,000 bottles; and body splash, 1,500 bottles. Determine the values of the inventories based on answers obtained in part (a).

c. Do you see any problems with the allocation based on approximated net realizable value?

17. **LO.3 (Allocating joint cost)** In one joint process, Hardahl Chemical produces three joint products and one by-product. The following information is available for September 2008:

Product	Gallons	Sales Value at Split-Off per Gallon	Cost after Split-Off	Final Selling Price
JP-4539	4,000	$12	$3	$21
JP-4587	16,000	8	5	14
JP-4591	12,000	15	2	19

Allocate the joint cost of $465,000 to the production based on the
a. number of gallons;
b. sales value at split-off; and
c. approximated net realizable values at split-off.
(Round all percentages to the nearest whole percentage.)

18. **LO.3 (Processing beyond split-off and cost allocations)** Hive Corp. makes three products from a joint production process using honey. Joint cost for the process in 2008 is $60,800.

Product	Units of Output	Per Unit Selling Price at Split-Off	Incremental Processing Cost	Final Sales Price
Honey butter	5,000	$2.00	$1.50	$3.00
Honey jam	10,000	3.20	2.00	7.00
Honey syrup	500	1.50	0.20	1.80

Each container of honey butter, jam, and syrup, respectively, contains 16 ounces, 8 ounces, and 3 ounces of product.
a. Determine which products should be processed beyond the split-off point.
b. Assume honey syrup should be treated as a by-product. Allocate the joint cost based on units produced, weight, and sales value at split-off. Use the net realizable value method in accounting for the by-product. (Round to nearest whole percentage.)

19. **LO.3 (Sell or process further)** Winnovia Mills processes cotton in a joint process that yields two joint products: fabric and yarn. May's joint cost is $80,000, and the sales values at split-off are $240,000 for fabric and $200,000 for yarn. If the products are processed beyond split-off, the final sales value will be $360,000 for fabric and $280,000 for yarn. Additional costs of processing are expected to be $80,000 for fabric and $68,000 for yarn.
a. Should the products be processed further? Show computations.
b. Were any revenues and/or costs irrelevant to the decision? If so, what were they and why were they irrelevant?

20. **LO.3 (Processing beyond split-off)** Washington Cannery makes three products from a single joint process. For 2008, the cannery processed all three products beyond split-off. The following data were generated for the year:

Joint Product	Incremental Separate Cost	Total Revenue
Candied apples	$26,000	$620,000
Apple jelly	38,000	740,000
Apple jam	15,000	270,000

Analysis of 2008 market data reveals that candied apples, apple jelly, and apple jam could have been sold at split-off for $642,000, $706,000, and $253,000, respectively.
a. Based on hindsight, evaluate management's production decisions in 2008.
b. How much additional profit could the company have generated in 2008 if it had made optimal decisions at split off?

21. **LO.3 (Sell or process further)** In a joint process, Venobe Clothing produces precut fabrics for three products: dresses, jackets, and blouses. Joint cost is allocated on the basis of relative sales value at split-off. The company can choose to process each of the products further rather than sell the fabric at split-off. Information related to these products follows:

	Dresses	Jackets	Blouses	Total
Number of units produced	5,000	8,000	3,000	16,000
Joint cost allocated	$87,000	?	?	$180,000
Sales values at split-off point	?	?	$40,000	$300,000
Additional costs of processing further	$13,000	$10,000	$39,000	$62,000
Sales values after all processing	$150,000	$134,000	$105,000	$389,000

a. What amount of joint cost should be allocated to jackets and blouses?
b. What are the sales values at split-off for dresses and jackets?
c. Should any of the products be processed beyond the split-off point? Show computations.
d. If 4,000 jackets are processed further and sold for $67,000, what is the gross profit on the sale?

22. **LO.3 (Retail organization joint cost)** Wilke Realty separates its activities into two operating divisions: Rental and Sales. In March 2008, the firm spent $15,000 for general company promotions (as opposed to advertisements for specific properties). Wilke's corporate controller must allocate the promotion costs to the two operating divisions and she is debating between two alternatives: expected increase in divisional revenue from the promotions and expected increase in divisional profit from the promotions (before allocated promotion costs). The promotions are expected to have the following effects on the two divisions:

	Rental	Sales
Increase in divisional revenue	$400,000	$800,000
Increase in profit (before allocated promotion costs)	91,000	39,000

a. Allocate the total promotion cost to the two divisions using change in revenue.
b. Allocate the total promotion cost to the two divisions using change in profit before joint cost allocation.
c. Which of the two approaches is more appropriate? Explain.

23. **LO.3 (Service organization joint cost)** Smithfield Soccer Camp holds two types of league training: one for high schools and one for adults. During 2008, the camp had the following operating data:

	High School Leagues	Adult Leagues
Training hours taught	2,000	1,000
Hourly tuition	$35	$65

Direct instructional costs for 2008 were $60,000; overhead costs for the two programs were $27,750. Camp owners want to know the cost of each program.
a. Determine each program's cost using a physical measure base.
b. Determine each program's cost using the sales value at split-off method.
c. Make a case for each allocation method in parts (a) and (b).

24. **LO.4 (By-product/scrap; net realizable value vs. realized value)** Indicate whether each item that follows is associated with (1) the realized value approach or (2) the net realizable value approach.
a. ignores value of by-product/scrap until it is sold
b. has the advantage of better timing
c. should be used when the by-product's net realizable value is large
d. is easier
e. is used to reduce the cost of main products when the by-product is produced
f. presents proceeds from sale of the by-product as other revenue or other income
g. is appropriate if the by-product's net realizable value is small
h. credits either cost of goods sold of main products or the joint cost when the by-product inventory is recorded
i. is less conservative
j. is the most clerically efficient

25. **LO.4 (By-product and cost allocation)** Wabash Farms raises tomatoes that, at harvest, are separated into three grades: premium, good, and fair. Joint cost is allocated to products based on bushels of output. The $225,000 joint cost for one harvest yielded the following output quantities.

Product	Output in Bushels
Premium	9,680
Good	25,960
Fair	8,360

The joint process also created by-product that had a total net realizable value of $30,000. The company records the by-product inventory at the time of production. Allocate the joint cost to the joint products using bushels of output.

26. LO.4 (By-product; net realizable value method) Peitro Processing produces fillet, smoked, and canned salmon in a single process. The same amount of disposal cost is incurred whether a product is sold at split-off or after further processing. In October 2008, the joint cost of the production process is $71,000.

Product	Pounds Produced	Separate Cost	Final Selling Price
Fillet	9,000	$1.50	$8.00
Smoked	10,000	2.60	6.50
Remnants	1,000	0.15	0.75

a. The remnants are considered a by-product of the process and are sold to cat food processors. Allocate the joint cost based on approximated net realizable value at split-off. Use the net realizable value method to account for the by-product.

b. Determine the value of ending Finished Goods Inventory, assuming that 8,000 pounds of salmon fillets, 9,400 pounds of smoked salmon, and 950 pounds of salmon remnants were sold. (Round cost per pound to the nearest penny.)

27. LO.4 (By-product accounting method selection) Your employer engages in numerous joint processes that produce significant quantities and types of by-product. You have been asked to give a report to management on the best way to account for by-product. Develop a set of criteria for making such a choice and provide reasons for each criterion selected. On the basis of your criteria, along with any additional assumptions you wish to provide about the nature of the company you work for, recommend a particular method of accounting for by-product and explain why you consider it to be better than the alternatives.

28. LO.4 (By-product and cost allocation) Forensic Productions shot hundreds of hours of footage that cost $16,000,000. From this footage, the company produced two movies: *Greedy CEOs* and *Greedy CEOs: The Sequel*. The sequel used better sound effects than the original and was significantly more expensive to produce. However, audiences seemed to be more interested in the careers of Kendra Leigh and Dan Gosouthski, discussed in the sequel, than the CEOs portrayed in the original movie and the sequel was much better received at the box office.

Forensic Productions also generated revenue from admissions paid by numerous forensic accountants who wanted to tour the movie production set. The company accounted for this revenue as a by-product and used it to reduce joint cost before making allocations to the two feature-length movies.

The following information pertains to the two movies:

Products	Total Receipts	Separate Costs
Greedy CEOs	$ 8,000,000	$ 4,800,000
Greedy CEOs: The Sequel	54,000,000	37,200,000
Studio tours	700,000	380,000

a. If joint cost is allocated based on net realizable value, how much of the joint cost is allocated to each movie?

b. Based on your allocations in part (a), how much profit was generated by each movie?

29. LO.4 (Accounting for by-product) Imposito Lumber manufactures various wood products that yield sawdust as a by-product. Selling costs associated with the sawdust are $150 per ton sold. The company accounts for sawdust sales by deducting the sawdust's net realizable value from the major products' cost of goods sold. Sawdust sales in 2008 were 24,000 tons at $210 each. If Imposito Lumber changes its method of accounting for sawdust sales to show the net realizable value as Other Revenue (presented at the bottom of the income statement), how would its gross margin be affected?

30. LO.4 (Accounting for by-product) In making potato chips and frozen hash browns, Wendall's Snacks generates potato skins as a by-product. The potato skins are sold to restaurants for use in appetizers. Processing and disposal costs associated with by-product sales are $0.06 per pound of potato skins. During May 2008, Wendall's Snacks produced and sold 90,000 pounds of potato skins for $13,500. In addition, the joint cost for producing potato chips and hash browns was $82,000; separate costs of production were $48,000. In May, 80 percent of all joint production was sold for $290,000. Nonfactory operating expenses for May were $13,800.

a. Prepare an income statement for Wendall's Snacks assuming that by-product sales are shown as Other Revenue and the processing and disposal costs for the by-product are shown as additional cost of goods sold of the joint products.

b. Prepare an income statement for Wendall's Snacks assuming that the net realizable value of the by-product is shown as other income.

c. Prepare an income statement for Wendall's Snacks assuming that the net realizable value of the by-product is subtracted from the joint cost of the main products.

d. Would the presentation in (a), (b), or (c) be most helpful to managers? Why?

31. **LO.4 (Accounting for scrap)** Hammatt Inc. provides a variety of services for commercial clients. Hammatt destroys any paper client records after seven years and the shredded paper is sold to a recycling company. The net realizable value of the recycled paper is treated as a reduction to operating overhead. The following data pertain to 2008 operations:

Budgeted operating overhead	$205,200
Actual operating overhead	$210,500
Budgeted net realizable value of recycled paper	$9,200
Actual net realizable value of recycled paper	$9,700
Budgeted billable hours	70,000
Actual billable hours	70,900

a. Assuming that billable hours is the allocation base, what was the company's predetermined overhead rate?

b. Record the journal entry for the sale of the recycled paper.

c. What was the company's underapplied or overapplied overhead for 2008?

32. **LO.4 (Accounting for scrap)** Renaissance Creations restores antique stained glass windows. All jobs generate some breakage or improper cuts. This scrap can be sold to stained glass hobbyists. Renaissance Creations expects to incur approximately 30,000 direct labor hours during 2008. The following estimates are made in setting the predetermined overhead rate for 2008:

Overhead costs other than breakage		$185,600
Estimated cost of scrap	$16,800	
Estimated sales value of scrap	(7,400)	9,400
Total estimated overhead		$195,000

One job that Renaissance Creations completed during 2008 was a stained glass window of the McCrory family crest that took 80 hours. Total direct material cost $590; direct labor is invoiced at $25 per hour. Scrap that was generated from this job was sold for $68.

a. What predetermined overhead rate was set for 2008?

b. What was the cost of the McCrory stained glass window?

c. Prepare the journal entry to record the sales value of the scrap from the McCrory stained glass window.

d. Assume instead that only certain jobs generate scrap. What was the cost of the McCrory stained glass window?

33. **LO.4 (Accounting for scrap)** Ruthie Architects offers a variety of architectural services for commercial construction clients. For each major job, architectural models of the completed structures are built for client presentations. The company uses a job order cost system. At the completion of a job, models not wanted by clients are sold to an arts and crafts retailer. Ruthie Architects uses the realized value method of accounting for sale of the models. The sales value of each model is credited to the cost of the specific job for which the model was built. During 2008, the model for the Frost Center building was sold for $2,500.

a. Using the realized value approach, give the entry to record the sale.

b. Independent of your answer to part (a), assume that the sales value of the models is not credited to specific jobs. Give the entry to account for the sale of the Frost Center model.

34. **LO.5 (NFP program and support cost allocation)** Memphis Jazz Company is preparing a pamphlet that will provide information on the types of jazz, jazz terminology, and biographies of some of the more well-known jazz musicians. In addition, the pamphlet will include a request for funding to support the jazz company. The company has tax-exempt status and operates on a not-for-profit basis.

The 10-page pamphlet cost $180,000 to design and print. Only 200,000 copies of the pamphlet were printed because the director of the company will be leaving and the pamphlet will soon be redesigned. One page of the pamphlet is devoted to fund solicitation; however, 98 percent of the design time was spent on developing and writing the jazz information.

a. If space is used as the allocation measure, how much of the pamphlet's cost should be assigned to program activities? To fund-raising activities?

b. If design time is used as the allocation measure, how much of the pamphlet's cost should be assigned to program activities? To fund-raising activities?

35. LO.5 (NFP; research) Choose a not-for-profit organization with which you are familiar. Go to that organization's Web site and find a recent annual report or IRS filing.

a. How much did the organization spend on joint costs during the period?
b. To what activities were the joint costs allocated?
c. What bases might the organization have used to allocate the joint costs?

Problems

36. LO.2 (Joint product decision; ethics) Production of ethanol, made from corn, is on the rise. Some states
are even requiring that ethanol be blended in small amounts with gasoline to reduce pollution. The problem
is that there is not enough corn being produced: either the consumption of corn as a food product (in all of
its many forms) or as a fuel product will have to suffer. Research the issues regarding ethanol production from
corn, and discuss what must be considered by farmers when determining whether corn output should be sold
for consumption or for fuel.▲

37. LO.3 (Joint costs; journal entries) Natural Beauty Corp. uses a joint process to make two main products:
Forever perfume and Fantasy lotion. Production is organized in two sequential departments: Combining and
Heating. The products do not become separate until they have been through the heating process. After heating,
the perfume is removed from the vats and bottled without further processing. The residue remaining in the vats
is then blended with aloe and lanolin to become the lotion.

   The following costs were incurred in the Combining Department during October 2008: direct material,
$28,000; direct labor, $7,560; and applied manufacturing overhead, $4,250. Prior to separation of the joint
products, October costs in the Heating Department were direct material, $6,100; direct labor, $2,150; and applied manufacturing overhead, $3,240. After split-off, the Heating Department incurred separate costs for each
product line as follows: bottles in which to package the Forever perfume, $2,120; and direct material, direct
labor, and applied manufacturing overhead of $1,960, $3,120, and $4,130, respectively, for Fantasy lotion.

   Neither department had beginning Work in Process Inventory balances, and all work that started in
October was completed in that month. Joint costs are allocated to perfume and lotion using approximated net
realizable values at split-off. For October, the approximated net realizable values at split-off were $158,910 for
perfume and $52,970 for lotion.
a. Determine the joint cost allocated to and the total cost of Forever perfume and Fantasy lotion.
b. Prepare journal entries for the Combining and Heating Departments for October 2008.
c. Post the entries to the accounts.

38. LO.3 (Physical measure joint cost allocation) North Dakota Soybeans operates a processing plant in
which soybeans are crushed to create soybean oil and soybean meal. The company purchases soybeans by the
bushel (60 pounds). From each bushel, the normal yield is 11 pounds of soybean oil, 44 pounds of soybean
meal, and 5 pounds of waste. For March, Midwest purchased and processed 5,000,000 bushels of soybeans.
The yield in March on the soybeans was equal to the normal yield. The following costs were incurred for the
month:

Soybeans	$47,500,000
Conversion costs	2,300,000

At the end of March there was no in-process or raw material in inventory. Also, there was no beginning Finished
Goods Inventory. For the month, 60 percent of the soybean oil and 75 percent of the soybean meal was sold.
a. Allocate the joint cost to the joint products on the basis of pounds of product produced.
b. Calculate the cost of goods sold for March.
c. Calculate the cost of Finished Goods Inventory at the end of March.

39. LO.3 (Physical measure joint cost allocation) Ladysmith Dairy began operations at the start of
May 2008. Ladysmith operates a fleet of trucks to gather whole milk from local farmers. The whole milk is
then separated into two joint products: skim milk and cream. Both products are sold at the split-off point to
dairy wholesalers. For May, the firm incurred the following joint costs:

Whole milk purchase cost	$200,000
Direct labor costs	90,000
Overhead costs	146,000
Total product cost	$436,000

During May, the firm processed 1,000,000 gallons of whole milk, producing 777,750 gallons of skim milk and 137,250 gallons of cream. The remaining gallons of the whole milk were lost during processing. There were no Raw Material or Work in Process Inventories at the end of May.

After the joint process, the skim milk and cream were separately processed at costs, respectively, of $33,830 and $41,655. Of the products produced, Ladysmith Dairy sold 775,000 gallons of skim milk for $736,250 and 137,000 gallons of cream for $141,110 to wholesalers.

a. Ladysmith uses a physical measure (gallon) to allocate joint costs. Allocate the joint cost to production.

b. Calculate ending Finished Goods Inventory cost, Cost of Goods Sold, and gross margin for May.

c. A manager at Ladysmith Dairy noted that the milk fat content of whole milk can vary greatly from farmer to farmer. Because milk fat content determines the relative yields of skim milk and cream from whole milk, the ratio of joint products can be partly determined based on the milk fat content of purchased whole milk. How could Ladysmith Dairy use information about milk fat content in the whole milk it purchases to optimize the profit realized on its joint products?

40. LO.3 (Monetary measure joint cost allocation) Refer to the information in Problem 38.

a. Assume the net realizable values of the joint products are as follows:

Soybean oil $0.35 per pound
Soybean meal $0.18 per pound

Allocate the joint cost incurred in March on the basis of net realizable value.

b. Calculate the cost of goods sold for March using the answer to part (a).

c. Calculate the cost of Finished Goods Inventory at the end of March based on the answer to part (a).

d. Compare the answers to parts (b) and (c) of Problem 38 to the answers to parts (b) and (c) of this problem. Explain why the answers differ.

41. LO.3 (Monetary measure joint cost allocation) Refer to the information in Problem 39.

a. Calculate the sales price per gallon for skim milk and cream.

b. Using relative sales value, allocate the joint cost to the joint production.

c. Calculate ending Finished Goods Inventory cost, Cost of Goods Sold, and the gross margin for the month.

42. LO.3 & LO.4 (Joint cost allocation; by-product; income determination) Bitterroot Bank & Trust has two main service lines: commercial checking and credit cards. The bank also generates some revenue from selling identity fraud insurance as a by-product of its two main services. The monthly joint cost for conducting the two main services is $400,000 and includes expenses for facilities, legal support, equipment, record keeping, and administration. The joint cost is allocated on the basis of total revenues generated from each main service.

The following table presents the results of operations and revenues for June:

Service	Number of Accounts	Total Revenues
Commercial checking	6,000	$957,000
Credit cards	14,000	693,000
Identity theft insurance	5,000	40,000

To account for the identity theft insurance, management views it as a reduction of Cost of Services Rendered for main services. The commissions are accounted for on a realized value basis as the policies are received.

For June, separate costs for commercial checking accounts and credit cards were $425,000 and $190,000, respectively.

a. Allocate the joint cost.

b. Determine the income for each main service and the company's overall gross margin for June.

43. LO.3 & LO.4 (Joint products; by-product) Georgia Peach is a fruit-packing business. The firm buys peaches by the truckload in season and separates them into three categories: premium, good, and fair. Premium peaches can be sold as is to supermarket chains and to specialty gift stores. Good peaches are sliced and canned in light syrup and sold to supermarkets. Fair peaches are considered a by-product and are sold to Yum-Yum Company, which processes the peaches into jelly.

Georgia Peach has two processing departments: (1) Cleaning and Sorting (joint cost) and (2) Cutting and Canning (separate costs). During the month, the company paid $15,000 for one truckload of fruit and $700 for labor to sort the fruit into categories. Georgia Peach uses a predetermined overhead rate of 40 percent of direct labor cost. The following yield, costs, and final sales value resulted from the month's truckload of fruit.

	Premium	Good	Fair
Yield in pecks	1,500	2,000	500
Cutting and canning costs	0	$2,000	0
Total packaging and delivery costs	$1,500	$2,200	$500
Total final sales value	$30,000	$15,000	$4,500

a. Determine the joint cost.

b. Diagram Georgia Peach's process in a manner similar to Exhibits 11–4 and 11–9.

c. Allocate joint cost using the approximated net realizable value at split-off method, assuming that the by-product is recorded when realized and is shown as Other Income on the income statement.

d. Using the allocations from part (c), prepare the necessary entries assuming that the by-product is sold for $4,500 and that all costs were as shown.

e. Allocate joint cost using the approximated net realizable value at split-off method, assuming that the by-product is recorded using the net realizable value approach and that the joint cost is reduced by the net realizable value of the by-product.

f. Using the allocations from part (d), prepare the necessary entries, assuming that the estimated realizable value of the by-product is $4,000.

44. **LO.3 & LO.4 (Process costing; joint cost allocation; by-product)** True Challenge provides personal training services for, and sells apparel products to, its clients. True Challenge also generates a limited amount of revenue from the sale of protein drinks. The net realizable value from drink sales is accounted for as a reduction in the joint cost assigned to the Personal Training Services and Apparel Products. Protein drinks sell for $2.50 per bottle. The costs associated with making and packaging the drinks are $1.00 per bottle.

The following information is available for 2008 on apparel products, which are purchased by True Challenge:

Beginning inventory	$ 35,000
Ending inventory	21,500
Purchases	181,350

Joint cost is to be allocated to Personal Training Services and Apparel Products based on approximated net realizable values. For 2008, total revenues were $753,000 from Personal Training Services and $289,000 from Apparel. The following joint costs were incurred:

Rent	$36,000
Insurance	43,750
Utilities	3,000

Separate costs were as follows:

	Personal Training	Apparel
Labor	$231,000	$36,000
Supplies	151,300	700
Equipment depreciation	165,000	1,200
Administration	103,000	3,700

For the year, 2,500 bottles of protein drinks were sold.

a. What is the total net realizable value of protein drinks used to reduce the joint cost assigned to Personal Training and Apparel?

b. What is the joint cost to be allocated to Personal Training and Apparel?

c. What is the approximated pre-tax realizable value of each main product or service for 2008?

d. How much joint cost is allocated to each main product or service?

e. Determine the net income produced by each main product or service.

45. **LO.3 & LO.4 (Joint cost allocation; by-product)** Taste of San Bernardino produces orange juice and orange marmalade from a joint process. Second-stage processing of the marmalade creates an orange pulp by-product that can be sold for $0.05 per gallon. Expenses to distribute pulp total $90.

In May 2008, 140,000 pounds of oranges costing $44,200 were processed in Department 1, with labor and overhead costs of $33,800 incurred. Department 1 processing resulted in 56,000 gallons of output, of which 40 percent was transferred to Department 2 to become orange juice and 60 percent was transferred to Department 3. Of the input going to Department 3, 20 percent resulted in pulp and 80 percent resulted in marmalade. Joint cost is allocated to orange juice and marmalade on the basis of approximated net realizable values at split-off.

The orange juice in Department 2 was processed at a total cost of $9,620; the marmalade in Department 3 was processed at a total cost of $6,450. The net realizable value of pulp is accounted for as a reduction in the separate processing costs in Department 3. Selling prices per gallon are $5.25 and $3.45 for orange juice and marmalade, respectively.

a. Diagram Taste of San Bernardino's process in a manner similar to Exhibits 11–4 and 11–9.
b. How many gallons leaving Department 1 were sent to Department 2 for further processing? To Department 3?
c. How many gallons left Department 3 as pulp? As marmalade?
d. What is the net realizable value of pulp?
e. What is the total approximated net realizable value of the orange juice? The marmalade?
f. What amount of joint cost is assigned to each main product?
g. If 85 percent of the final output of each main product was sold during May and Taste of San Bernardino had no beginning inventory of either product, what is the value of the ending inventory of orange juice and marmalade?

46. **LO.3 & LO.4 (By-product/joint product journal entries)** Natasha Inc. is a 5,000-acre farm that produces two products: Zilla and Corma. Zilla sells for $3.50 per bushel (assume that a bushel weighs 60 pounds). Without further processing, Corma sells for $30 per ton (a ton equals 2,000 pounds). If the Corma is processed further, it can be sold for $45 per ton. In 2008, total joint cost up to the split-off point was $875,000. In 2008, Natasha Inc. produced 70 bushels of Zilla and 1 ton of Corma per acre. If all the Corma were processed further, separate costs would be $50,000.

Prepare the 2008 journal entries for Corma if it is:

a. transferred to storage at sales value as a by-product without further processing with a corresponding reduction of Zilla's production costs.
b. further processed as a by-product and transferred to storage at net realizable value with a corresponding reduction of the manufacturing costs of Zilla.
c. further processed and transferred to finished goods with joint cost being allocated between Zilla and Corma based on relative sales value at the split-off point.

47. **LO.3 & LO.4 (Joint cost allocation; ending inventory valuation; by-product)** During March 2008, the first month of operations, Oink Oink's Pork Co. had the operating statistics shown in the following table.

Products	Weight in Pounds	Sales Value at Split-Off	Pounds Produced	Pounds Sold
Tenderloin	8,600	$132,000	6,440	5,440
Roast	13,400	86,000	16,740	14,140
Ham	10,800	22,400	8,640	7,640
Hooves	4,600	4,600	9,200	8,000

Costs of the joint process were direct material, $40,000; direct labor, $23,400; and overhead, $10,000. The company's main products are pork tenderloin, roast pork, and ham; pork hooves are a by-product of the process. The company recognizes the net realizable value of by-product inventory at split-off by reducing total joint cost. Neither the main products nor the by-product requires any additional processing or disposal costs, although management could consider additional processing.

a. Calculate the ending inventory values of each joint product based on (1) relative sales value and (2) pounds. (Round to nearest whole percentage.)
b. Discuss the advantages and disadvantages of each allocation base for (1) financial statement purposes and (2) decisions about the desirability of processing the joint products beyond the split-off point.

48. **LO.3 & LO.4 (Joint cost allocation; scrap)** Linda's Linens produces terrycloth products for hotels. The company buys fabric in 60-inch-wide bolts. In the first process, the fabric is set up, cut, and separated into pieces. Setup can be for either robes and beach towels or bath towels, hand towels, and washcloths.

During July, the company set up and cut 6,000 robes and 12,000 beach towels. Because of the irregular pattern of the robes, the process produces scrap that is sold to various prisons and hospitals for rags at $0.45 per pound. July production and cost data for Linda's Linens are as follows:

Fabric used, 25,000 feet at $1.50 per foot	$37,500
Labor, joint process	$12,000
Overhead, joint process	$11,000
Pounds of scrap produced	3,600

Linda's Linens assigns the joint processing cost to the robes and beach towels based on approximated net realizable value at split-off. Other data gathered include these:

	Per Robe	Per Beach Towel
Final selling prices	$20.00	$7.00
Costs after split-off are	6.80	1.60

The selling price of the scrap is treated as a reduction of joint cost.

a. Determine the joint cost to be allocated to the joint products for July.

b. How much joint cost is allocated to the robes in July? To the beach towels? Prepare the journal entry necessary at the split-off point.

c. What amount of cost for robes is transferred to Finished Goods Inventory for July? What amount of cost for beach towels is transferred to Finished Goods Inventory for July?

49. **LO.4 (Scrap; essay; ethics)** Some waste, scrap, or by-product material have little value. In fact, for many meat and poultry producers, animal waste represents a significant liability because it is considered hazardous and requires significant disposal costs. Some companies, such as Smithfield Foods Inc. (the largest hog processor in the United States), gather the animal waste in "lagoons" and allow it to be used as "liquid fertilizer."

a. Review Smithfield Foods: A Corporate Profile at http://www.citizen.org/documents/Smithfield.pdf as well as the environmental policies at the company's Web site (http://www.smithfieldfoods.com/Enviro/Policies; last accessed 8/6/07). Discuss the ethical and legal implications of disposing of industrial waste in this manner.

b. What actions can people take to reduce this type of disposal?

c. Ethically, what obligation does the vendor/manufacturer of potentially toxic pollutants have to the consumer of the company's products?▲

50. **LO.4 (By-product; research)** Choose a fairly common product that you believe would generate multiple by-products.

a. Without doing any research, prepare a list of some items that you believe would be by-products from that product.

b. After you have completed your list, use the Web to find what by-products are actually associated with the product you have chosen.

51. **LO.5 (NFP joint cost)** Andrea's Alzheimer's Foundation was started by a family whose mother had died after suffering for several years with Alzheimer's. A lecture that cost the Foundation $180,000 was held in November, which is national Alzheimer's awareness month. Advertisements were placed in all local newspapers and were broadcast on local media channels. During the lecture, information was provided about the causes, symptoms, and treatment of Alzheimer's, about help available for caregivers, and about the Foundation and its mission. In addition to requesting contributions, members of the Foundation asked attendees to take a quiz about Alzheimer's, volunteer to distribute pamphlets about the disease to local businesses, write letters to their insurance companies about additional coverage availability, and participate in the Medicare Advocacy Program to gather information and identify problems encountered by beneficiaries and providers.

a. Would the lecture meet the audience criterion? Why or why not?

b. Did the lecture include a call for action? Explain.

c. Assume that 65% of the lecture time was related to the disease, 25% of the lecture was related to the Foundation, and 10% was related to fundraising. Allocate the joint cost to the three activities.

d. Assume that the topics discussed at the lecture were not in specific order and, often, discussion was in response to questions that were asked by the attendees. How else might the joint cost be allocated among program, management, and fundraising activities?

e. Andrea's Alzheimer's Foundation hired a consultant to help with the lecture. The consultant was paid $20,000 but has been informed that, if the lecture raises between $200,001 and $250,000, the fee would increase to $25,000; if the lecture raises over $250,000, the consultant would be paid $35,000. The consultant's fee was not included in the $180,000 joint cost. The Foundation was excited to find that the lecture raised $270,000. The time allocation given in part (c) was representative of the time spent on topics during the lecture. How much of the $215,000 ($180,000 + $35,000) should be allocated to the three activities?

52. **LO.5 (NFP joint cost; research; ethics)** Read Joseph McCafferty's article entitled "Misgivings" in *CFO.com* (January 2007); http://www.cfo.com/article.cfm/8477078/c_8483311?f=singlepage&x=1 (last accessed 8/6/07).

a. Discuss your thoughts about not-for-profits claiming to raise funds without incurring any costs.

b. What would you consider a "reasonable" cost of fundraising ratio and why?

c. Why would some types of not-for-profits (such as educational institutions) have different types of fundraising ratios than others (such as museums or health-related organizations)?▲

53. **LO.1–3 & LO.5 (NFP joint cost; joint revenues; decision making)** Throughout your college career, you have been employed on a part-time basis by the Executive Development Center of your business college. The Development Center provides executive training for a fee to individuals and organizations located throughout the state. For 2008, the condensed income statement that follows summarizes the operating results of the center.

Fees	$5,250,000
Faculty and staff salaries	(2,100,000)
Facilities cost	(1,100,000)
Training materials	(750,000)
Marketing and promotions	(800,000)
Other costs of operations	(1,000,000)
Net operating loss	$ (500,000)

Given that the center operated at a loss in 2008, the dean of the business college has asked the director to provide a justification for not closing the center. As the dean stated, "We're charged with a fundamental obligation of being good stewards of the state's resources. We cannot justify spending net resources to subsidize educational programs to corporations and other profit-oriented organizations."

The center director has made the dean's comments known to all employees and faculty of the center and all are concerned about losing their employment should the center be closed.

Having just completed a chapter in your accounting course addressing joint products, you become curious as to whether the preceding income statement fairly reflects the value of all outputs of the center. Particularly, you believe that the center plays a crucial role in the generation of contributions made to the college by alumni and friends of the business college and university.

a. Discuss how the existence of joint products of the Executive Development Center would potentially modify the preceding income statement.

b. Discuss how you could use the concepts of joint products and joint cost allocation to demonstrate to the dean that the Executive Development Center is not consuming "net resources" of the state or college and that the center should continue its operations.

12 | Introduction to Cost Management Systems

Objectives

After completing this chapter, you should be able to answer the following questions:

LO.1 Why do organizations have management control systems?

LO.2 What is a cost management system, and what are its primary goals?

LO.3 What factors influence the design of a cost management system?

LO.4 What are the three groups of elements that comprise a cost management system, and what are the purposes of these elements?

LO.5 What is gap analysis, and how is it used in the evolution of a cost management system?

Introduction

A fundamental concern of managers in executing their duties is how their actions affect organizational costs and benefits. This concern arises from the managerial focus on revenue growth and profit generation. Managers use models and information systems to improve their comprehension of costs and benefits and to identify drivers of costs and revenues. Many models used by managers are comparative analyses of costs and benefits. Financial experts, especially accountants, bear the primary responsibility for providing managers information about measurements of those costs and benefits.

Chapter 1 discussed the differences and similarities among the disciplines of financial, management, and cost accounting. Cost accounting is described as playing a role in both internal and external reporting. As such, this field of accounting is cast into separate, often competing, roles that the financial reporting role often dominates. Thus, even though directly linked to the managerial functions of planning, controlling, decision making, and performance evaluation, cost accounting information is frequently found to be of limited value to managers because that information is shaped by financial reporting demands.

The problem is that the dictates of financial reporting are very different from those of cost management. For financial reporting purposes, cost information can be highly aggregated and historical and must be consistent with GAAP. In contrast, cost information required for management purposes may be segmented, current, and relevant only for a particular purpose. Consequently, information provided by the financial reporting system is often of little value for cost management purposes.[1] In designing cost accounting systems, the general internal use of information and the specific application of information to manage costs are receiving increased attention. The first section of this chapter introduces management information and control systems, which offer a foundation and context for understanding the roles of the cost management system (CMS), first introduced in Chapter 2. This chapter then discusses concepts and approaches to designing information systems that support the internal use of accounting and other information to manage costs. A CMS is presumed to be an integral part of an organization's overall management information and control systems. The discussion emphasizes the main factors that determine the structure and success of a CMS, the factors that influence the design of such a system, and the elements that compose the system.

Introduction to Management Information and Control Systems

A CMS is part of an overall management information and control system. Exhibit 12–1 illustrates the types of information needed in an organization to meet the requirements of individuals in performing their managerial functions as well as requirements of external parties in performing their investment and credit-granting functions. A management information system (MIS) is a structure of interrelated elements used to collect, organize, and communicate data to managers so they can plan, control, make decisions, and evaluate performance. An MIS emphasizes satisfying internal, rather than external, demands for information. Most organizations have computerized the MIS for ease of access to information, reliability of input and processing, and ability to simulate outcomes of alternative situations.

The accounting function is charged with the task of providing information to interested external parties such as creditors and suppliers relative to payments and purchases as well as to the government for mandatory reporting such as to the Internal Revenue Service, Securities and Exchange Commission, and other regulatory bodies. In addition, external intelligence is also gathered from these parties as well as from competitors and contained within the information system. Managers use internally and externally generated information to govern their organizations.

---

[1]Robin Cooper and Regine Slagmulder, "Strategic Cost Management: Introduction to Enterprisewide Cost Management," *Management Accounting* (August 1998), p. 17.

EXHIBIT 12–1
Information Flows and Types of Information

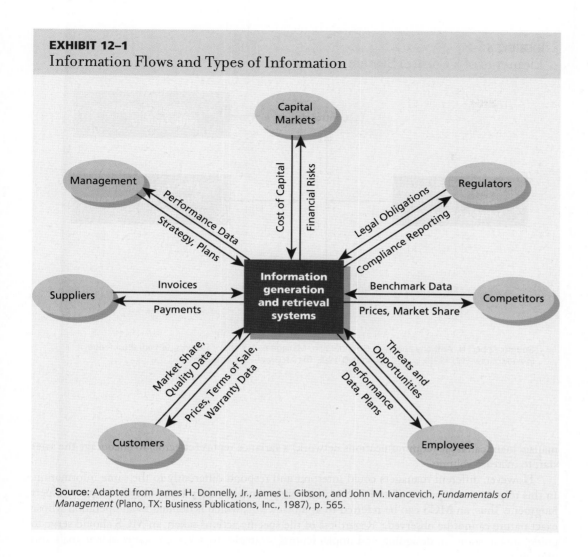

Source: Adapted from James H. Donnelly, Jr., James L. Gibson, and John M. Ivancevich, *Fundamentals of Management* (Plano, TX: Business Publications, Inc., 1987), p. 565.

Because one of the managerial functions requiring information is control, the MIS is part of the **management control system (MCS)**. As illustrated in Exhibit 12–2, a control system has the following four primary components:

1. A detector or sensor, which is a measuring device that identifies what is actually happening in the process being controlled.
2. An assessor, which is a device for determining the significance of what is happening. Usually, significance is assessed by comparing the information on what is actually happening with some standard or expectation of what should be happening.
3. An effector, which is a device that alters behavior if the assessor indicates the need for doing so. This device is often called feedback.
4. A communications network, which transmits information between the detector and the assessor and between the assessor and the effector.[2] The arrows in Exhibit 12–2 depict the communication network.

Through these system components, information about actual organizational occurrences is gathered, comparisons are made against plans, changes are made when necessary, and communications take place among appropriate parties. For example, source documents (detectors) gather information about sales that is compared to the budget (assessor). If sales revenues are below budget,

LO.1
Why do organizations have management control systems?

[2]Robert N. Anthony and Vijay Govindarajan, *Management Control Systems*, 9th ed. (Burr Ridge, IL: Irwin/McGraw-Hill, 1998), pp. 1–2.

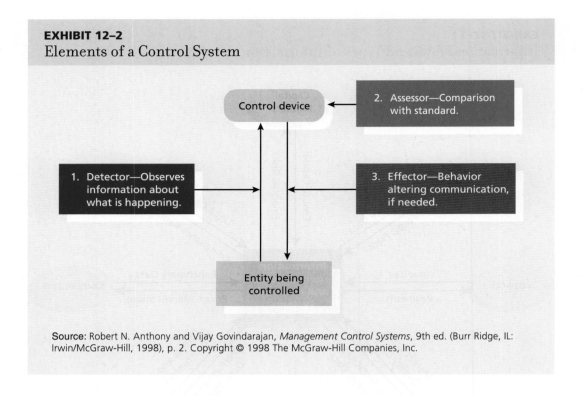

EXHIBIT 12–2
Elements of a Control System

Source: Robert N. Anthony and Vijay Govindarajan, *Management Control Systems*, 9th ed. (Burr Ridge, IL: Irwin/McGraw-Hill, 1998), p. 2. Copyright © 1998 The McGraw-Hill Companies, Inc.

management can issue (communications network) a variance report (effector) to encourage the sales staff to increase volume.

However, different managers could interpret and respond differently to the same information. In this respect, development of an MCS is not merely a mechanical process but also requires expert judgment. Thus, an MCS can be referred to as a **black box**, which is defined as an operation whose exact nature cannot be observed.[3] Regardless of the specific actions taken, an MCS should serve to guide organizations in designing and implementing strategies to achieve organizational goals and objectives.

Most businesses have a variety of control systems in place. For example, a control system could reflect a set of procedures for screening potential suppliers or employees, a set of criteria to evaluate potential and existing investments, or a statistical control process to monitor and evaluate quality.

Defining a Cost Management System

A cost management system consists of a set of formal methods developed for planning and controlling an organization's cost-generating activities relative to its short-term objectives and long-term strategies. Business entities face two major challenges: achieving profitability in the short run and maintaining a competitive position in the long run. An effective CMS provides managers the information needed to meet both of these challenges.

Exhibit 12–3 illustrates the organizational role of a cost management system. The CMS helps provide information useful to managing an organization's core competencies so the organization can exploit perceived opportunities in the marketplace and develop tactics and strategies to fend off threats. Similarly, the CMS links plans and strategies to actual organizational performance.

Refer to Exhibit 12–4 for a summary of the differences in the information requirements for organizational success in both the short run and the long run. In the short run, revenues must

[3]Ibid., p. 5.

EXHIBIT 12–3
Organizational Role of a Cost Management System

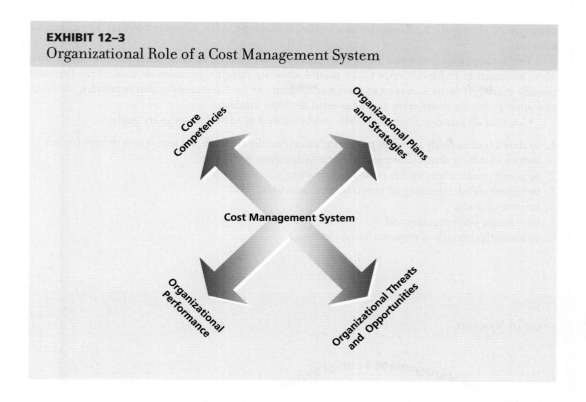

EXHIBIT 12–4
Dual Focus of a Cost Management System

	Short Run	**Long Run**
Objective	Organizational efficiency	Survival
Focus	Specific costs: • manufacturing • service • marketing • administration	Cost categories: • customers • suppliers • products • distribution channels
Important characteristics of information	Timely Accurate Highly specific Short term	Periodic Reasonably accurate Broad focus Long term

Source: Adapted from Robin Cooper and Regine Slagmulder, "Operational Improvement and Strategic Costing," *Management Accounting* (September 1998), pp. 12–13. Copyright 1998 by Institute of Management Accountants. Reproduced with permission of Institute of Management Accountants in the format Textbook via Copyright Clearance Center.

exceed costs and the organization must make efficient use of its resources relative to the revenues that are generated. Specific cost information is needed and must be delivered in a timely fashion to an individual who is in a position to influence the cost. Short-run information requirements are often described as relating to organizational efficiency.

Meeting the long-run objective of survival depends on acquiring the right inputs from the right suppliers, selling the right mix of products to the right customers, and using the most appropriate channels of distribution. These decisions require only periodic information that is reasonably accurate.

The information generated from the CMS should benefit all functional areas of the entity. Thus, as shown in Exhibit 12–5, a CMS should integrate information from all areas of the firm and provide managers faster access to an increased quantity of cost information that is relevant, detailed, and appropriate for short-term and long-term decision making.

Crossing all functional areas, a CMS can be viewed as having six primary goals:

LO.2
What is a cost management system, and what are its primary goals?

1. to develop reasonably accurate product costs, especially through the use of cost drivers (or activities that have direct cause-and-effect relationships with costs);
2. to assess product/service life cycle performance;
3. to improve understanding of processes and activities;
4. to control costs;
5. to measure performance; and
6. to allow the pursuit of organizational strategies.

EXHIBIT 12–5
An Integrated Cost Management System

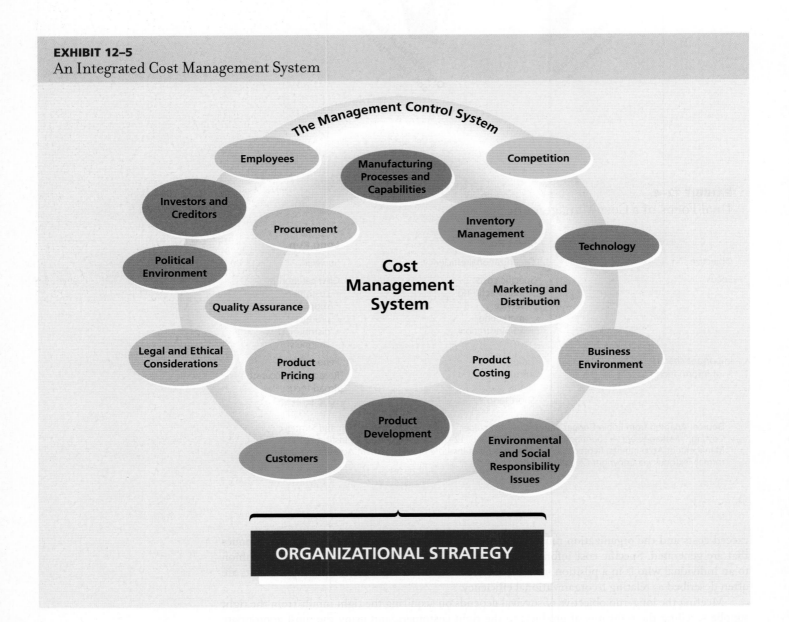

Primarily, a CMS should provide the means of developing accurate product or service costs; thus, the system must be designed to use cost driver information to trace costs to products and services. The system is not required to be the most accurate, but it should match the benefits of additional accuracy with expenses of achieving such accuracy. Traceability has been made easier by improved information technology, including bar coding and radio frequency identification (RFID), which uses exceptionally small "flakes" of silicon to transmit a code for the item to which it is attached. Although patented in 1952, bar coding was not used commercially until 1966 when a system was installed in a Kroger store and did not become popular until Wal-Mart required all of its suppliers to begin using them in 1984.[4] Nationwide, Wal-Mart is currently the largest proponent of RFID technology and is pushing the RFID technology down to its suppliers.[5] Today, this technology is also used to identify pets and commercial livestock.

The product/service costs generated by the CMS are the inputs to managerial processes. These costs are used to plan, prepare financial statements, assess individual product/service profitability and period profitability, establish prices for cost-plus contracts, and create a basis for performance measurements. If the input costs generated by the CMS are not reasonably accurate, the output of the preceding processes will be inappropriate for control and decision-making purposes.

Although product/service profitability may be calculated periodically (possibly as a requirement for external reporting), the financial accounting system does not provide information about the profitability of a product over its entire life; rather the financial accounting system provides only a

Traceability has been made easier by information technology such as bar coding, popularized by Wal-Mart in the early '80s.

period-by-period look at product profitability. The CMS should provide information about the life cycle performance of a product or service. Without life cycle information, managers will not have a basis to relate costs incurred in one part of the life cycle to costs and profitability of other parts. For example, managers might not recognize that strong investment in the early life of a product could provide significant rewards later by minimizing costs of engineering changes and potential quality-related costs. Further, if development/design cost is not traced to the related product or service, managers could be unable to recognize organizational investment "disasters."

A CMS should also help managers understand business processes and organizational activities. Only by understanding how an activity is accomplished and the reasons for cost incurrence can managers make cost beneficial improvements in the production and processing systems. Managers of a company desiring to implement new technology or production systems must recognize what costs and benefits will flow from such actions. Such assessments can be made only if the managers understand how the processes and activities will differ after the change.

[4]Anonymous, "Bar Code History Page," http://www.adams1.com/pub/russadam/history.html (last accessed 8/2/07).
[5]Anonymous, "Wal-Mart RFID Plans Change," *RFid Gazette,* http://www.rfidgazette.org/walmart/ (last accessed 8/2/07).

A cost accounting system's original purpose was to control costs, and, given the current global competitive environment, this is still an important function of a CMS. As discussed in Chapter 4, a cost can be controlled only when the related activity is monitored, the cost driver is known, and the information is available. For example, if units are spoiled in a process, the CMS should provide information on spoilage quantity and cost rather than "burying" that information in other cost categories. Additionally, the cost management system should allow managers to understand the process so that the underlying causes of the spoilage can be determined. Having this information available allows managers to compare the costs of fixing the process with the benefits to be gained.

Information generated from a CMS should help managers measure and evaluate performance. The measurements can be used to evaluate human or equipment performance as well as future investment opportunities.

Finally, to maintain a competitive position in an industry, a firm must generate the information necessary to define and implement its organizational strategies. Strategy is the link between an organization's goals, objectives, and operational activities. In the current global market, firms must be certain that such a linkage exists. Information provided by a CMS enables managers to perform strategic analyses on issues such as determining core competencies and organizational constraints from a cost–benefit perspective and assessing the positive and negative financial and nonfinancial factors of strategic and operational plans. Thus, the CMS is essential to the generation of information for effective strategic resource management.

Because the world of business competition is dynamic and creative managers are constantly devising new business practices and innovative approaches to competition, a CMS must be flexible. The following section discusses the issues affecting the design and ongoing development of cost management systems in a continually evolving organization.

LO.3

What factors influence the design of a cost management system?

Designing a Cost Management System

In designing or revising a CMS, managers and accountants must be attuned to the unique characteristics of their firms. A generic cost management system cannot be taken "off the shelf" and applied to any organization because the CMS should be tailored to the specific situation of each firm. However, some overriding factors important in designing a CMS are shown in Exhibit 12–6 and are described in this section.

Organizational Form, Structure, and Culture

An entity's legal nature reflects its organizational form. Selecting the organizational form is one of the most important decisions business owners make. This choice affects the costs of raising capital, operating the business (including taxation issues), and, possibly, litigating.

The most popular organizational form for large, publicly traded businesses is the corporation. Smaller businesses or cooperative ventures between large businesses use general partnerships, limited partnerships, limited liability partnerships (LLPs), and limited liability companies (LLCs). Both the LLP and LLC provide more protection than a general partnership for an investor's personal assets in the event of litigation that leads to the firm's liquidation. Accordingly, LLPs and LLCs can offer better control for legal costs than general partnerships can.

Organizational form also helps determine who has the statutory authority to make decisions for the firm. In a general partnership, all partners are allowed to make business decisions as a mere incidence of ownership unless specified to the contrary. Alternatively, in a corporation, individual shareholders act through a board of directors who, in turn, typically rely on professional managers. This ability to "centralize" authority is regarded as one of the primary advantages of the corporate organizational form and, to some extent, is available in limited partnerships, LLPs, and LLCs.

After the organizational form has been selected, top managers are responsible for creating a structure that is best suited to achieving the firm's goals and objectives. Organizational structure, introduced in Chapter 1, refers to how authority and responsibility for decision making are

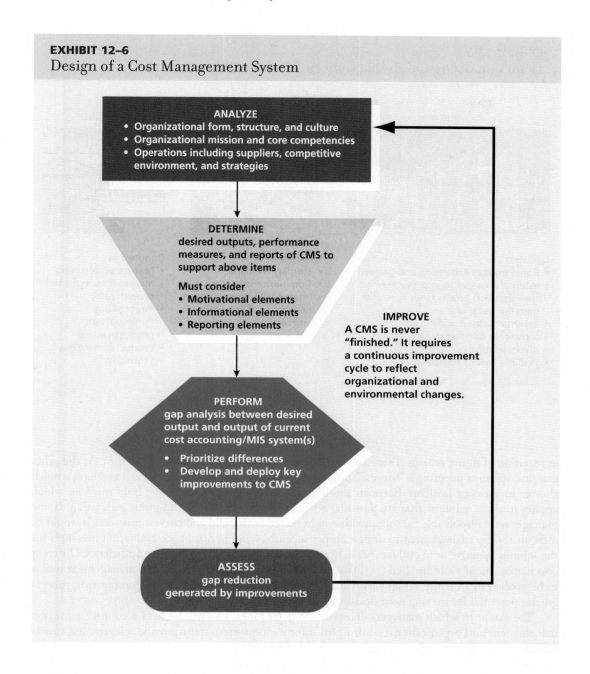

EXHIBIT 12–6
Design of a Cost Management System

ANALYZE
- Organizational form, structure, and culture
- Organizational mission and core competencies
- Operations including suppliers, competitive environment, and strategies

DETERMINE
desired outputs, performance measures, and reports of CMS to support above items

Must consider
- Motivational elements
- Informational elements
- Reporting elements

IMPROVE
A CMS is never "finished." It requires a continuous improvement cycle to reflect organizational and environmental changes.

PERFORM
gap analysis between desired output and output of current cost accounting/MIS system(s)

- Prioritize differences
- Develop and deploy key improvements to CMS

ASSESS
gap reduction generated by improvements

distributed in the entity. Top managers make judgments about how to organize subunits and the extent to which authority will be distributed among managers and employees. Although the current competitive environment is conducive to a high degree of delegation, top managers usually retain authority over operations that can be performed more economically centrally because of scale economies. For instance, financing, human resources, research and development, and certain accounting functions typically are maintained "at headquarters" rather than being delegated to organizational subunits.

In designing the organizational structure, top managers normally try to group subunits either geographically or by similar missions or natural product clusters. These aggregation processes provide effective cost management because of proximity or similarity of the subunits under a single manager's control.

To illustrate, relative to similarity of mission, business subunits could pursue one of three generic missions (build, harvest, or hold); these missions are described in Exhibit 12–7. Subunits pursuing a "build" mission use more cash than they generate. Such subunits invest cash today with an

EXHIBIT 12–7
Depiction of Organizational Generic Missions

BUILD	HOLD	HARVEST

Denoted by:
- Rapid market expansion and growth
- Internal changes to improve (or find new uses for) products/services and gain market share
- External related acquisitions (upstream or downstream) or diversification
- Possible lack of competitors

Denoted by:
- Stability of market
- Dominance in market
- Internal changes to create new demand for product and retain market share

Denoted by:
- Mature or declining market (low expected growth rate)
- Strategically "unimportant" product/service
- Product/service is a "cash cow"

expectation of future returns. These are the high-growth-oriented subunits of the firm. At the other extreme, subunits pursuing a "harvest" mission are expected to generate excess cash and have a much shorter investment horizon. Between the build and harvest missions is the hold mission, which applies to those subunits that are pursuing a balance between growth and profit generation. If one manager were responsible for subunits that represented both build and harvest missions, it would be difficult for top management to design proper incentives and performance evaluation measures for the subunit manager or to evaluate his or her cost management effectiveness and efficiency. Different cost management tools are used for different subunit missions. If a specific cost management tool is to be applied to an entire subunit with a mix of missions across that subunit's components, there is greater potential for making poor decisions.

The extent to which managers delegate also determines who will be held accountable for cost management and organizational control. An information system must provide relevant and timely information to persons who are making decisions that have cost control implications, and a control system must be in place to evaluate the quality of those decisions.

An entity's culture also plays an important role in setting up a CMS. Organizational culture refers to the underlying set of assumptions about the entity and the goals, processes, practices, and values that its members share. To illustrate the effect of organizational culture on the CMS, consider AT&T in the early 1980s prior to its divestiture. It was an organization characterized by "bureaucracy, centralized control, nepotism, a welfare mentality in which workers were 'taken care of,' strong socialization processes, [and] little concern for efficiency. . . ."[6] Such a culture would have limited the requirements of a CMS because few individuals needed information, decisions were made at the top of the organization, and cost control was not a consideration because costs were passed on to customers through the rate structure. After divestiture, the company's culture changed to embrace decision making at multiple organizational levels, cost efficiency, and individual responsibility and accountability. Supporting such a changed culture requires different types, quantities, and distributions of cost management information.

[6]Thomas S. Bateman and Scott A. Snell, *Management Building Competitive Advantage* (Burr Ridge, IL: Irwin, 1996), p. 268.

The values-based aspects of organizational culture are also extremely important in assessing the CMS. For example, two parts of SETECH Ltd.'s mission statement are to "provide ongoing cost savings through technical leadership, and to develop and maintain the most efficient logistics systems in the industry through continuous improvement."[7] Without a well-designed CMS, SETECH could not evaluate its progress toward accomplishing that mission. Thus, a CMS is instrumental in providing a foundation for companies with an organizational culture that emphasizes cost savings and continuous improvement.

Organizational Mission and Core Competencies

Knowledge of the organization's mission and core competencies is a key consideration in the design of a cost management system. The mission provides a long-term goal toward which the organization wishes to move. If the entity's mission is unknown, it does not matter what information is generated by the CMS—or any other information system!

In pursuing the business mission, companies can either avoid or confront competition. For example, companies could try to avoid competition by attempting to be more adept in some way than other entities. The generic paths a company could take to avoid competition include product differentiation and cost leadership as defined in Chapter 1.

In the current global environment, it is often difficult to maintain a competitive advantage under either a differentiation or a cost leadership strategy. Competitors are becoming skilled at duplicating the specific competencies that gave rise to the original competitive advantage. For many companies, the key to future success could be to confront competition by identifying and exploiting temporary opportunities for advantage. In a confrontation strategy, companies "still try to differentiate their products by introducing new features, or try to develop a price leadership position by dropping prices, . . . [but, the companies] assume that their competitors will rapidly bring out products that are equivalent and match any price changes."[8] Although it could be necessary, a confrontation strategy is, by its very nature, less profitable for companies than differentiation or cost leadership.

See Exhibit 12–8 for an illustration of how the strategy of the firm, together with the life cycle stages of products, determines what a firm must do well to be successful at any point in time. This exhibit illustrates how the information requirements of managers change over time as the life cycle evolves and, thus, depend on the strategy being pursued.

The globalization of markets has created, in many industries, competition among equals. Today, many firms are capable of delivering products and services that are qualitatively and functionally equivalent. Without being able to distinguish one competitor's products from those of another based on quality or functionality, the consumer's focus switches to price. In turn, price-based competition changes the internal focus to costs.

An organization can clarify its mission by identifying core competencies or the operational dimensions that are key to survival. Most organizations would consider timeliness, quality, customer service, efficiency and cost control, and responsiveness to change as five critical competencies. Once managers have gained consensus on an entity's core competencies, the CMS can be designed (1) to gather information related to measurement of those items and (2) to generate output about those competencies in forms that are useful to interested parties.

Operations and Competitive Environment and Strategies

Once the organizational "big picture" has been established, managers can assess internal specifics related to the design of a CMS. A primary consideration is the firm's cost structure. Traditionally, cost structure has been defined in terms of relative proportions of fixed and variable costs and, thus, how costs change relative to changes in production or sales volume.[9]

[7]SETECH Inc., "About Us: Mission Statement," http://www.setechusa.com/AboutUs/MissionStatement.htm (last accessed 8/2/07).
[8]Robin Cooper, *When Lean Enterprises Collide* (Boston: Harvard Business School Press, 1995), p. 11.
[9]An organization's cost structure reflects its operating leverage as discussed in Chapter 9.

EXHIBIT 12–8
Critical Organizational Activities by Strategy and Life Cycle Stage

Life Cycle Stage	Product Strategy		
	Cost Leadership	Product Differentiation	Confrontation
Build	Research and development Parts standardization Develop efficient distribution channels	Research and development Advertising Product customization Customer relationship management	Time-to-market Activity-based management Process flexibility Business intelligence
Hold	Process standardization Engineering change elimination Kaizen costing	Advertising Distribution channels Customer relationship management	Process dependability Service emphasis Advertising Engineering changes
Harvest	Cost control Product changeover speed Capacity control Outsource Distribution cost management	Product replacement Continue marketing efforts Exit strategy Enhance service	Distribution channel development Service differentiation Focus on distribution network

Manufacturing and service firms have aggressively adopted advanced technology, and, as they become increasingly dependent on automated technology, firms find it more difficult to control costs. Many technology costs are associated with the plant, equipment, and infrastructure investments that provide the capacity to produce goods and services. These costs are higher in industries that depend on technology for competing on the bases of quality and price.

The cost management implications of this shift in cost structure are significant. Most important, because most technology costs are not susceptible to short-run control, cost management efforts are increasingly directed toward the longer term. Also, managing costs is increasingly a matter of capacity management: high capacity utilization (if accompanied by high sales volume) allows a firm to reduce its per-unit costs in pursuing a cost leadership strategy. A second implication of the changing cost structure is the firm's flexibility to respond to changing short-term conditions. As the proportion of costs relating to technology investment increases, a firm has less flexibility to take short-term actions to reduce costs with no long-term adverse consequences.

In pursuing either a differentiation or a cost leadership strategy, the management of high technology costs requires beating competitors to the market with new products. Being first to market can enable a company to set a price that leads to a larger market share that, in turn, can lead to an industry position of cost leader. Alternatively, the leading-edge company can set a product price that provides a substantial per-unit profit for all sales generated before competitors are able to offer alternative products. For example, in mid-2007 there was no direct competitor for Apple's iPhone. Rapid time to market requires fast development of new products and services. Time to market is critical in the high-tech industry because profitability depends on selling an adequate number of units at an acceptable price. Because the price per unit has been falling steadily for years, getting a new product to the market late can be disastrous. Richard O'Brien, an economist for Hewlett-Packard, describes the risk: "Product life cycles keep shrinking. If you can't get to market on time, you will have missed your chance because the price point will have moved."[10]

Reducing time to market is one way a company can cut costs; other techniques are indicated in Exhibit 12–9. Most actions to reduce product cost are associated with the early product life cycle stages. Thus, as has been previously mentioned, product profitability is largely determined by an effective design and development process.

Getting products to market quickly and profitably requires a compromise between product innovation and superior product design. Rapid time to market could mean that a firm incurs costs associated with design flaws (such as the costs of engineering changes) that could have been avoided if more time had been allowed for the product's development. This strategy was evident in Microsoft's release of its Xbox 360 in 2006. Although the product was very innovative and widely anticipated by the marketplace, the product was discovered to have a higher-than-expected failure rate, which caused the company to accrue extraordinary warranty costs in 2007. When a flawed product is marketed, costs will likely be incurred for returns, warranty work, or customer "bad will" regarding the firm's reputation for product quality. Time to market is important because of the competitive advantages it offers and because of compressed product life cycles. The faster a product gets to market, the fewer competitive products will exist; consequently, a greater market share can be captured (see Exhibit 12–10).

Supplier relationships constitute another aspect of an organization's operating environment. Many companies that have formed strategic alliances with suppliers have found such relationships

---

EXHIBIT 12–9

Actions to Substantially Reduce Product Costs

- Reduce non-value-added activities
- Standardize product parts and processes
- Reduce variability of processes
- Increase product and process quality
- Manufacture products to order
- Design products to limit engineering change orders
- Implement new technologies
- Increase capacity utilization
- Minimize investment in inventories
- Outsource non-core competencies
- Find and eliminate process bottlenecks
- Redesign factory layout
- Reduce setup time
- Train employees to obtain learning curve effects
- Engage in benchmarking to find better methodologies
- Develop long-term and sole-source supplier relationships
- Stress the importance of a quality culture
- Encourage employee suggestions
- Engage in life-cycle and target costing

---

[10]Darren McDermott, "Cost Consciousness Beats 'Pricing Power,'" *Wall Street Journal* (May 3, 1999), p. A1.

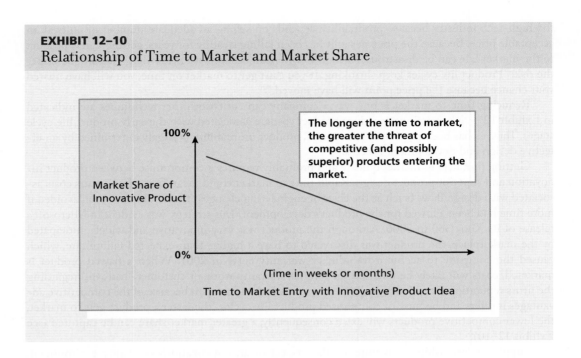

EXHIBIT 12–10
Relationship of Time to Market and Market Share

to be effective cost control mechanisms. For example, by involving suppliers early in the design and development stage of new products, a company should achieve a better design for manufacturability and improve the likelihood of meeting cost targets. Additionally, if the information systems of customers and suppliers are linked electronically, the capabilities and functions of these systems must be considered in designing the CMS.

An internal operating environment consideration in the design of a CMS is the need to integrate the organization's current information systems. The "feeder" systems (such as payroll, inventory valuation, budgeting, and costing) that are in place should be evaluated to answer the following questions:

- What input data are being gathered and in what form?
- What outputs are being generated and in what form?
- How do the current systems interact with one another, and how effective are those interactions?
- Is the current chart of accounts appropriate for the cost management information desired?
- What significant information issues (such as yield, spoilage, and cycle time) are not currently being addressed by the information system, and could those issues be integrated into the current feeder systems?

With knowledge of the preceding information, management must analyze the cost–benefit trade-offs that relate to the design of the CMS. As the costs of gathering, processing, and communicating information decrease, or as the quantity and intensity of competition increase, more sophisticated cost management systems are required. Additionally, as companies focus on customer satisfaction and expand their product or service offerings, more sophisticated CMSs are needed. In these conditions, the generation of "better" cost information is essential to long-run organizational survival and short-run profitability.

Even with appropriate information systems in place, there is no guarantee that managers' decisions will be consistent with organizational strategies. Proper incentives and reporting systems must be incorporated into the CMS for managers to make appropriate decisions, as discussed in the following section.

Determine Desired Components of CMS

A CMS is composed of three primary elements: motivational, informational, and reporting. These elements are detailed in Exhibit 12–11. The elements as a whole must be internally consistent, and the individually selected elements must be consistent with the strategies and missions of the subunits. Different aspects of these elements can be used for different purposes. For example, numerous measures of performance can be specified, but only certain measures will be appropriate for specific purposes.

Motivational Elements

Performance measurements are chosen to be consistent with organizational goals and objectives and to motivate or "drive" managers toward designated achievements. These measurements can be quantitative or nonquantitative, financial or nonfinancial, and short term or long term. For example, if a subunit is expected to generate a specified amount of profit for the year, the performance measure has been set to be quantitative, financial, and short term. A longer-term performance measure might be an average increase in profit or change in stock price over a 5- to 10-year period.

The motivational elements create a linkage between the internal information systems (information elements of the CMS) and the performance of the firm as perceived by the stockholders. Exhibit 12–12 indicates how this linkage typically is operationalized. Top managers' compensation contracts with the stockholders are based on earnings as measured by the financial accounting system and on stock price performance. In turn, top managers drive the performance of lower-level managers by contracting with them based on performance versus the budget. Thus, the motivational elements link the performance of all managers to the welfare of stockholders through compensation contracting that cascades down through the organizational hierarchy. These motivational

EXHIBIT 12–11
Cost Management System Elements

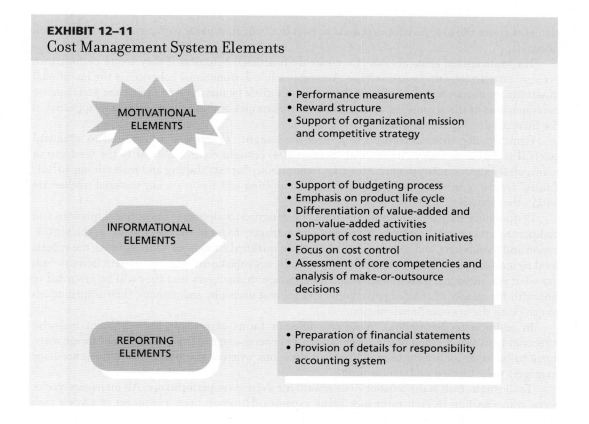

MOTIVATIONAL ELEMENTS
- Performance measurements
- Reward structure
- Support of organizational mission and competitive strategy

INFORMATIONAL ELEMENTS
- Support of budgeting process
- Emphasis on product life cycle
- Differentiation of value-added and non-value-added activities
- Support of cost reduction initiatives
- Focus on cost control
- Assessment of core competencies and analysis of make-or-outsource decisions

REPORTING ELEMENTS
- Preparation of financial statements
- Provision of details for responsibility accounting system

EXHIBIT 12–12
Managerial Contracting Process

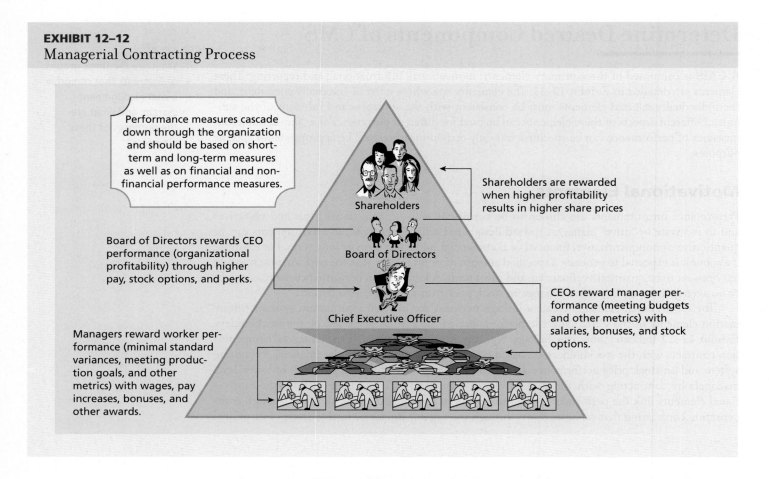

Performance measures cascade down through the organization and should be based on short-term and long-term measures as well as on financial and non-financial performance measures.

Shareholders are rewarded when higher profitability results in higher share prices

Shareholders

Board of Directors rewards CEO performance (organizational profitability) through higher pay, stock options, and perks.

Board of Directors

CEOs reward manager performance (meeting budgets and other metrics) with salaries, bonuses, and stock options.

Chief Executive Officer

Managers reward worker performance (minimal standard variances, meeting production goals, and other metrics) with wages, pay increases, bonuses, and other awards.

elements create the incentive for managers to beat the budget, increase earnings, and increase stock price.

The motivational elements can also create dysfunctional behaviors if they create performance pressure on managers that is too intense. Among possible dysfunctional behaviors is the intentional misstatement of transactions and accruals or deferrals made by managers to distort the performance measurements of the accounting system. Numerous examples of these occurrences have appeared in the financial press in recent years.

Firms develop internal controls to protect the integrity of financial reports and to safeguard assets. The Sarbanes-Oxley Act of 2002 (Section 404) brought control systems to the forefront of managerial focus: companies must now take responsibility for establishing and maintaining an "adequate" system of internal controls over financial reporting and report on any material weaknesses within that system.

Performance measures and rewards should be designed to support organizational missions and competitive strategies, to motivate employees and managers to act in the best interest of the organization and its subunits, and to help recruit and retain qualified employees. Once defined, the criteria used to measure performance should be linked to the organizational incentive system because "you get what you measure." This linkage sends the message to managers that they will be rewarded in line with the quality of their organizational and subunit decisions and, thereby, their contributions to achieving the organizational mission.

In addition to performance measures, different forms of rewards have different incentive effects and can reflect different time orientations. In general, longer-term incentives encourage managers to be more long-term oriented in their decisions whereas short-term incentives encourage managers to be focused on the near future.

To illustrate, cash is the most obvious reward for short-term performance. All managers receive some compensation in cash to finance living expenses. However, once a manager receives a cash reward, its value does not depend on the firm's future performance. In contrast, a stock option that is not exercisable until a future time provides a manager an incentive to be more concerned about long-term performance. The ultimate value of the stock option is determined in the future when the option is exercised rather than on the date it is received. Thus, the option's value is related more to long-term than to short-term organizational performance.

Performance rewards for top management can consist of both short-term and long-term incentives. Normally, a major incentive is performance-based pay that is tied to the firm's stock price. The rewards for subunit managers should be based on the specific subunit's mission. For example, managers of subunits charged with a "build" mission should receive long-term incentives. These managers need to be concerned about long-term success and be willing to make short-term sacrifices for long-term gains. In contrast, managers of subunits charged with a "harvest" mission must be more oriented to the short term. These subunits are expected to squeeze out as much cash and profit as possible from their operations. Accordingly, incentives should be in place to encourage these managers to have a short-term focus in decision making.

Today's companies experiment with a variety of incentives as "carrots" to induce employees and managers to act in the best interest of customers and shareholders. **Profit sharing** refers to compensation that is contingent on the level of organizational profit generated. This type of pay is a powerful incentive and is now used in virtually every U.S. industry.

Selection of performance measurements and the reward structure is important because managers evaluate decision alternatives based on how the outcomes could impact the selected performance (measurement and reward) criteria.[11] Because higher performance equals a larger reward, the cost management system must have specified performance "yardsticks" and provide measurement information to the appropriate individuals for evaluation purposes. Performance measurement is meaningful only in a comparative or relative sense. Typically, current performance is assessed relative to past or expected performance or relative to customer expectations.

Informational Elements

An organization's accounting function is expected to support managers' abilities to plan, control, make decisions, and evaluate performance. These functions converge in a system designed for cost management. Relative to the planning role, the CMS should provide a sound foundation for the financial budgeting process.

Budgets provide both a specification of expected achievement and a benchmark against which to compare actual performance. A CMS should both supply the financial information needed for budget preparation and disclose the cost drivers of activities so that more useful simulations of alternative scenarios can be made. The system should be able to highlight any activities that have a poor cost–benefit relationship so that they can be reduced or eliminated and, in turn, reduce organizational costs and improve profits.

As firms find it more difficult to maintain a competitive advantage, they must place greater emphasis on managing the product life cycle. As discussed earlier in this chapter, most actions available to managers to control costs are concentrated in the earliest stages of the product life cycle. Accordingly, information relevant to managing costs must be focused on decisions made during those stages. That information will be provided by a well-designed and integrated CMS.

Product life cycles are getting shorter as firms become more and more adept at duplicating their competitors' offerings. In the future, managers will confront the fact that products will spend less time in the maturity stage of the product life cycle. Firms will be forced to find ways to continue to "squeeze" cash from their mature products to support new product development. Additionally, the future will place greater emphasis on a firm's ability to adapt to changing competitive conditions. Flexibility will be an important organizational attribute and will cause managers to change the emphasis of control systems (see Exhibit 12–13).

To provide information relevant to product design and development, the CMS must be able to relate resource consumption and cost to alternative product and process designs. Computer simulation models are useful in relating products to activities. In addition to focusing information on the front end of the product life cycle, capital spending is becoming an increasingly important tool in cost management, especially relative to new technology acquisition decisions. Decisions about capi-

---

[11]Performance measurements and rewards are discussed in greater depth in Chapter 14.

tal investments affect a firm's future cost structure and, hence, the extent to which short-term actions can effect a change in the level of total costs.

Finally, the system should produce cost information with minimal distortions from improper or inaccurate allocations or from improper exclusions. Improper exclusions usually relate to the influence of financial accounting, such as the mandate to expense product development and distribution costs. If the system minimizes these cost distortions, cost assignments are more relevant for control purposes and for internal decision making.

The information required to support decisions depends on the unique situational factors of the firm and its subunits. The information system must enable the decision maker to evaluate how alternative decision choices would impact the items that are used to measure and evaluate the decision maker's performance. Techniques discussed in other chapters, such as relevant costing, quality cost management, job order and process costing, and cost-volume-profit analysis, relate to the role of cost information in decision making. Many decisions involve comparing the benefit received from some action (such as serving a given customer) to the costs of that action. Only if the cost data contain minimal distortion can managers make valid cost–benefit assessments.

Reporting Elements

The reporting elements of a cost management system refer to methods of providing information to persons in evaluative roles. First and foremost, the CMS must be effective in generating fundamental financial statement information such as inventory valuations and cost of sales. Regardless of

EXHIBIT 12–13
Shift in Control Emphasis in Future Competitive Environments

Activity	From		To
Product design	Releasing early to gain market share	⟶	Designing for manufacturability and reliability
Product offerings	Developing a limited number of product styles	⟶	Engaging in mass customization to entice a wide variety of customers
Budgeting	Developing annual budgets	⟶	Developing rolling budgets
Cost standards	Using expected standards	⟶	Using ideal standards
Overhead allocation	Using expected capacity	⟶	Using theoretical capacity
Quality	Inspecting for quality problems	⟶	Building quality into the production system
Outsourcing	Turning product and process control over to the outsource provider	⟶	Working in partnership with the outsource provider
Strategy	Focusing on the short-term as the primary indicator of success	⟶	Focusing on the short-term as a means for long-term success
Employee involvement and procedures	Emphasizing the need to comply with policies	⟶	Encouraging participation in change and understanding of organizational functions
Performance measurement	Concentrating on financial results	⟶	Concentrating on multiple types of critical success measurements
Product marketing	Selling what the firm makes	⟶	Focusing on sales mix that maximizes customer value

whether such information is used for internal planning, control, decision making, or performance evaluation, there should be little difficulty generating an "external" product or service cost if the feeder systems to the CMS have been appropriately integrated and the system itself is designed to minimize distortions.

In addition to financial statement valuations, the reporting elements of the CMS must address internal needs of a responsibility accounting system that provides information to top management about the performance of organizational subunits and their managers.[12] Such a system should separately track costs and, if appropriate, revenues for each organizational subunit.

Performance reports are useful only to the extent that the actual performance of a given manager or subunit can be compared to a meaningful baseline, such as a measure of expected performance. Expected performance can be denoted in financial terms, such as budgetary amounts, or in nonfinancial terms, such as throughput, customer satisfaction measures, lead time, capacity utilization, and research and development activities. As illustrated by balanced scorecards, performance reports can be multidimensional. By comparing actual to expected performance, top managers are able to determine which managers and subunits performed according to expectations and which exceeded or failed to meet expectations. Using this information that has been processed and formulated by the CMS, top managers link decisions about managerial rewards to performance.

The movement toward delegation of authority has increased the importance of an effective reporting system because top managers must depend on the reporting system to keep all organizational subunits aligned with their subunit missions as well as with organizational goals and objectives. A CMS is not designed to "cut" costs. It exists to ensure that a satisfactory yield (revenue) is realized from the incurrence of costs. Accordingly, cost management begins with an understanding that different costs are incurred for different purposes. Some costs are incurred to yield immediate benefits; others are expected to yield benefits in the near or distant future.

Only by linking costs to activities and activities to strategies can the yield on costs be understood. Thus, to achieve effective cost management, it is useful to start by sorting organizational activities according to their strategic roles. This logic suggests that organizational management is made easier by breaking down operations into subunits. By so doing, top managers can assign responsibility and accountability for distinct subunit missions to a particular manager. In turn, by creating the proper incentives for each subunit manager, top management will have set the stage for each subunit manager to act in the best interest of the overall organization. This linkage is the start of a process that focuses a specific subunit manager's attention on a set of costs and activities that uniquely relates to the subunit's organizational mission.

Costs can be effectively managed by subunit managers only when they are provided with relevant information. Because the nature and time horizon of decisions made by managers vary across subunits, each manager requires unique information. Accountants face the task of providing information that is tailored to each subunit manager's context. In addition to information about decision alternatives, managers need to know how the alternatives are likely to impact their expected rewards.

The role of a reporting system is to compare actual performance to benchmark performance for each manager. On the basis of this comparison, the relative rewards of subunit managers are determined. Accordingly, this comparison is a key source of motivation for subunit managers to act in the best interest of the organization. Optimal organizational performance is realized only if there is consistency for each subunit across the motivational, informational, and reporting elements. Managers of subunits with a "build" mission need information tailored to their competitive strategies and focused on the early stages of the product life cycle. Their incentives to manage costs must be relatively long term, and their reward structures should emphasize success in the areas of product development and design and market share growth. Alternatively, subunit managers of mature businesses need information that pertains more to short-term competition. Their reward and reporting structures should emphasize near-term profit and cash flow.

One of the evolving challenges in today's business environment is the management of activities across an entire supply chain. Competition is prevalent among supply or "value" chains as well as individual businesses. Thus, future financial specialists will develop cost management systems that include activities not occurring within single firms but occurring within a supply chain and involving several firms.

---

[12]Responsibility accounting concepts are discussed in detail in Chapter 13.

Because most businesses have some type of CMS in place, design and implementation issues primarily relate to modifications of the current system. The analysis of existing systems is discussed next.

LO.5
What is gap analysis, and how is it used in the evolution of a cost management system?

Perform Gap Analysis and Assess Improvements

After the organization and its subunits have been structured and the CMS elements have been determined, the current information system(s) should be evaluated. Gap analysis is the study of the differences between two information systems, often a current system and a proposed system. To assess deficiencies in the existing system, gap analysis compares the information that is currently available with the information that is needed. Any differences represent spaces or "gaps" to be overcome. In many situations, it is impossible to eliminate all system gaps in the short term potentially because of software or hardware capability or availability. Methods of reducing or eliminating the gaps, including all related technical requirements and changes to existing feeder systems, should be specified in detail. These details should be expressed, qualitatively and quantitatively, in terms of costs and benefits.

In the common circumstance of limited resources, top management can prioritize which gap issues should be addressed and in what order. As system implementation proceeds, management should assess the effectiveness of the improvements and determine the need for others. Once the CMS has been established, previously identified gaps can become irrelevant or can rise in rank of priority. Only through continuous improvement efforts can the CMS provide an ongoing, viable network of information to users.

Technological impact on cost management system design and implementation is significant. With advancements in technology, it is becoming possible to link a company's feeder systems into a truly integrated CMS. Enterprise resource planning (ERP) systems are packaged business software systems that allow companies to do the following:[13]

- standardize information systems and replace different "legacy" systems;
- integrate information systems and automate the transfer of data among systems;
- improve the quality of information, including purchase preferences of customers; and
- improve the timeliness of information by providing real-time, online reporting.

ERP software often involves a large number of separate modules that collect data from individual processes in the firm (sales, shipping, distribution, and so forth) and assemble that data in a form accessible by all managers. ERP is discussed in detail in Chapter 19.

Appendix

Cost Management System Conceptual Design Principles

"In 1986, Computer Aided Manufacturing-International Inc. (CAM-I) formed a consortium of progressive industrial organizations, professional accounting firms, and government agencies to define the role of cost management in the new advanced manufacturing environment."[14] One outcome of this consortium was a conceptual framework of principles (listed in Exhibit 12–14) for designing a cost management system. If a CMS provides the suggested information relating to costs, performance measurements, and investment management, that system will be relevant to management's decision-making needs. Although compatible with existing cost accounting systems, the set of principles as a whole suggests a radical departure from traditional practices. The practices focus management attention on organizational activities, product life cycles, integrating cost management and performance measurement, and integrating investment management and strategic management.

---

[13]Emily Brodeur and Paul Sharman, "ERP Cost and Performance Systems: Risks and Opportunities," *Journal of Cost Management* (March/April 2002), p. 21.
[14]Callie Berliner and James A. Brimson, eds., *Cost Management for Today's Advanced Manufacturing* (Boston: Harvard Business School Press, 1988), p. vii.

EXHIBIT 12–14
CMS Conceptual Design Principles

Cost Principles

- Identify costs of non-value-added activities to improve use of resources.
- Recognize holding costs as a non-value-added activity traceable directly to a product.
- Significant costs should be directly traceable to management reporting objectives.
- Separate cost centers should be established for each homogeneous group of activities consistent with organizational responsibility.
- Activity-based cost accumulation and reporting will improve cost traceability.
- Separate bases for allocations should be developed to reflect causal relations between activity costs and management reporting objectives.
- Costs should be consistent with the requirement to support life cycle management.
- Technology costs should be assigned directly to products.
- Actual product cost should be measured against target cost to support elimination of waste.
- Cost-effective approaches for internal control should be developed as a company automates.

Performance Measurement Principles

- Performance measures should establish congruence with a company's objectives.
- Performance measures should be established for significant activities.
- Performance measures should be established to improve visibility of cost drivers.
- Financial and nonfinancial activities should be included in the performance measurement system.

Investment Management Principles

- Investment management should be viewed as more than the capital budgeting process.
- Investment management decisions should be consistent with company goals.
- Multiple criteria should be used to evaluate investment decisions.
- Investments and attendant risks should be considered interrelated elements of an investment strategy.
- Activity data should be traceable to the specific investment opportunity.
- Investment management decisions should support the reduction or elimination of non-value-added activities.
- Investment management decisions should support achieving target cost.

Source: Callie Berliner and James A. Brimson, eds., *Cost Management for Today's Advanced Manufacturing* (Boston: Harvard Business School Press, 1988), pp. 13–18. Reprinted by permission of Harvard Business School Press. Copyright 1988 by CAM-1. All rights reserved.

Comprehensive Review Module

Chapter Summary

1. Organizations have management control systems to

   - implement strategic and operating plans.

   - provide a means for comparison of actual to planned results for management control purposes.

2. A cost management system (CMS)

   - is a set of formal methods developed for planning and controlling an organization's cost-generating activities relative to its short-term objectives and long-term strategies.

   - has a short-term goal of making efficient use of organizational resources.

   - has a long-term goal of ensuring the organization's survival.

Chapter 12 Introduction to Cost Management Systems

3. The design of a CMS is influenced by the
   - organizational form through, for example, laws that determine who within the organization is entitled to be a decision maker.
   - organizational structure because it
     - ➤ determines how authority and responsibility are distributed in an organization.
     - ➤ indicates who is accountable, what they are accountable for, and the nature of information needed by each decision maker.
   - organizational culture because it determines
     - ➤ how people interact with each other in the organization.
     - ➤ the extent to which individuals take authority and assume responsibility for organizational outcomes.
   - organizational mission.
   - organizational core competencies.
   - external environment because it determines the
     - ➤ nature and extent of competitive pressures bearing on the organization.
     - ➤ industry's competitive dimensions and the bases on which organizations compete.
   - organizational strategies that influence the
     - ➤ organizational cost structure.
     - ➤ managerial preferences in responding to competitive pressures.

4. Elements that affect the design of a CMS are
   - motivational, which are used to influence managers and employees to exert high effort and to act in the organization's interests.
   - informational, which are selected to provide the appropriate information to managers who are responsible for making decisions and for making the organization effective and efficient in its operations.
   - reporting, which are selected to provide feedback to, and to provide consequences for, managers and employees.

5. Gap analysis
   - is a tool that can help identify and prioritize necessary changes in a CMS.
   - assesses differences between an organization's ideal CMS and the organization's existing CMS.

Key Terms

black box, **p. 436**

cost management system (CMS), **p. 434**

cost structure, **p. 443**

enterprise resource planning (ERP) system, **p. 452**

gap analysis, **p. 452**

management control system (MCS), **p. 435**

management information system (MIS), **p. 434**

organizational culture, **p. 442**

organizational form, **p. 440**

profit sharing, **p. 449**

radio frequency identification (RFID), **p. 439**

Questions

1. How can a company evaluate whether it is effectively managing its costs?
2. What is a control system? What purpose does a control system serve in an organization?
3. Why does a cost management system necessarily have both a short-term and long-term focus?
4. Why is it not possible simply to take a cost management system "off the shelf"?
5. How does the choice of organizational form influence the design of a firm's cost management system?
6. What information could be generated by a cost management system that would help an organization manage its core competencies?
7. How could an organization's culture be used as a control mechanism?

8. How does a product's life cycle stage influence the nature of information required to successfully manage costs of that product?

9. In the present highly competitive environment, why has cost management risen to such a high level of concern whereas price management has declined in importance?

10. (Appendix) What was CAM-I, and why was it organized?

Exercises

11. **LO.1 (Management control systems)** A few years after graduation, Oram and four of his friends from college organized an engineering consulting business called 5Q. All five individuals had earned degrees in engineering fields and were anxious to pool their expertise and work together in a successful business venture. Even though the business was very successful in attracting clients, the business failed within two years of its founding because the entrepreneurs were unable to control their costs. Discuss how the adoption of management controls could have improved the odds that the business would have been successful.

12. **LO.1 (Management control systems)** Following are activities that are components of a management control system in a production department. For each item listed, discuss whether it is a detector, assessor, effector, or communications network.
    a. comparing actual costs to budgeted costs.
    b. reporting results of comparing actual to budgeted costs.
    c. implementing changes in production systems to correct the largest negative variances.
    d. measurement of actual costs.

13. **LO.2 (Cost management and strategy)** As a financial analyst, you have just been handed the 2008 financial report of Firm Z, a large, global pharmaceutical company. Firm Z competes in both traditional pharmaceutical products and in evolving biotechnology products. The following data (in billions) on Firm Z and the pharmaceutical industry are available:

	Firm Z	Industry Average
Sales	$2.00	$0.960
Net income	0.54	0.096
Advertising	0.04	0.160
Research and development	0.16	0.240
New investment in facilities	0.20	0.240

Given these data, evaluate the cost management performance of Firm Z.

14. **LO.2 (Cost management and strategy)** Following are descriptions of three businesses. For each, assume that you are the CEO. Identify the most critical information you would need to manage the strategic decisions of that business.
    a. Private hospital that competes on the basis of delivering high-quality services to an upscale clientele.
    b. Small, high-technology firm that has just developed its first product and will begin sales in the coming quarter; five other products are under development.
    c. American Sugar Company, which is a large firm that competes in the commodity sugar industry.

15. **LO.3 (Organizational form)** Write a paper that compares and contrasts the corporate, general partnership, limited partnership, LLP, and LLC forms of business. At a minimum, discuss issues related to formation, capital generation, managerial authority and responsibility, taxation, ownership liability, and implications for success in mission and objectives.

16. **LO.3 (Cost management and organizational culture)** Use Internet resources to gather information on any two firms in the same industry. The following examples are possible pairs to compare.
    - Delta Air Lines and Southwest Airlines
    - ChevronTexaco and BP
    - Nordstrom's and Wal-Mart
    - Oracle and Microsoft
    - Gateway and Dell Computer

    In your discussion, address the following questions:
    a. Compare and contrast the organizational cultures of the firms.
    b. Compare and contrast the operating performance of the firms.

c. Which of the pair is the better operating performer? Discuss the criteria used to make this determination.

d. Do you believe that organizational culture has any relationship to the differences in operations? Why?

17. **LO.3 (Cost management and technology)** Many firms now engage in some form of B2B (business-to-business) Internet-based commerce. A specific type is B2B buy-side, which is Internet technology that allows firms to solicit bids on inputs that firms require to support production, sales, and administration. Interested and qualified vendors can view the bid specifications and then electronically submit offers to sell the firms the needed inputs. Search the Internet to learn about B2B buy-side systems, and then discuss how a small firm could use a B2B buy-side system to reduce its supply chain costs.

18. **LO.3 (Organizational strategy)** Use Internet resources to find a company (regardless of where it is domiciled) whose managers have chosen to (a) avoid competition through differentiation, (b) avoid competition through cost leadership, and (c) confront competitors head on. Analyze each of these strategies and discuss your perception of how well each strategy has worked.

19. **LO.3 (Cost management and organizational objectives)** Prepare an oral presentation discussing how accounting information can (a) help and (b) hinder an organization's progress toward its mission and objectives. Be sure to differentiate between the effects of what you perceive as "traditional" versus "nontraditional" accounting information.

20. **LO.3 (Organizational culture)** Write a paper describing the organizational culture at a job you have held or at the college or university you attend. Be sure to include a discussion of the value system and how it was communicated to new employees or new students.

21. **LO.4 (Elements of management control system)** In recent years, many firms have been forced to restate their earnings which were previously reported in their public financial reports. A number of these restatements have been linked to attempts by top management to manipulate the reported accounting information for the purpose of achieving higher compensation. For example, some firms accelerated the recognition of revenue (in a manner not consistent with GAAP) so that the profit on those sales could be reported in the current period rather than in the following period. These reporting anomalies often require manual intervention with the normal reporting policies of the firms.

a. Discuss which elements in the management control system might cause the manipulative behavior described.

b. Is the described behavior ethical? Discuss.▲

22. **LO.4 (Elements of management control system)** The use of stock options to compensate executives has become much more common in recent years. The increased use of options to compensate executives is based on efforts of boards of directors to align the interests of managers and stockholders. Prior to the implementation of FAS 123R, firms would often report the stock options expense only in a footnote—the expense did not flow through the income statement.

a. Discuss why firms would desire to report the expense of stock options in the footnotes of the financial statements rather than in the body of the income statement.

b. Discuss whether the practice of reporting stock option expense in the footnotes was unethical or misleading.

c. Research the topic "backdating stock options." Discuss the motivation for backdating options and whether this is an ethical practice.▲

23. **LO.5 (Gap analysis)** Carlos Sanchez is the CFO of Car Plastics, a small company that makes specialized lighting equipment for the car industry. Because of intensified competition from foreign companies, Car Plastics has experienced extreme price pressure for its products. In response to this pressure, top management has decided to focus more intently on the role of product quality to improve the competitive position of the company.

With this change in competitive focus, Sanchez recognizes that the company must revise its CMS to better manage product quality. As an intern working for Sanchez, write him a memo describing how gap analysis could be used to revise the CMS.

24. **LO.5 (Gap analysis)** Performance Solutions manufactures after-market parts for lawn mowers and recreational all-terrain vehicles (ATVs). Because of the growth in the ATV market, sales of Performance Solutions' products have grown at double-digit rates over the past five years and the firm's information systems no longer adequately provide the information managers need to run the business. For example, the accounting system cannot provide information needed to control the high rate of growth in costs, or even to relate the growth in costs to the growth in sales. As a consultant hired by Performance Solutions, discuss how you could use gap analysis to identify the deficiencies in the firm's CMS and to prioritize the firm's efforts to close the gaps.

Problems

25. **LO.1 (Management control systems)** In many organizations the operating budget is the primary control tool. The use of a budget to control activities is more appropriate in some circumstances than in others, and always a key criterion in evaluating the efficacy of a control is whether the control is helping to implement the firm's strategy. Consider the following activities and circumstances, and discuss whether use of a budget as a primary control is appropriate:
    a. research and development department of a mature manufacturing firm
    b. marketing expense of a start-up technology company
    c. travel expense for the sales force of an insurance company
    d. energy costs for a public utility company
    e. costs of environmental remediation for a chemical manufacturer
    f. production costs in a car manufacturing company
    g. operational costs of classroom buildings in a public university

26. **LO.1 (Information and cost management)** The price of a product or service is a function of the total costs of producing that product or service. In turn, the total cost of producing a product or service is a function of the aggregate of costs incurred throughout the supply chain.

    Higher education is one industry that has been characterized by rapidly rising costs and rapidly rising prices. Study the supply chain of your college or university and prepare a table identifying specific ways in which an improved system of communications with suppliers and customers could result in specific cost savings for the institution, its suppliers, or its customers (students). Organize your table in three columns as follows:

Specific Information to Be Obtained	Information Source	Specific Cost to Be Reduced

27. **LO.2 (Cost management and strategy)** You are the product manager at a silicone chip manufacturer. One of your products is a commodity chip that the electronics industry widely uses in cell phones, printers, digital cameras, and so forth. As product manager, you have full profit responsibility for the commodity chip.

    The commodity chip is a "cash cow" for your company and enjoys an enviable market share in the industry. Because your company's chip is approximately the same as chips available from competitors, market competition for this product is primarily based on price.

    Because of your success in managing the commodity chip, you were recently promoted to product manager of ZX chip, the most innovative chip your company has ever developed because of its data processing speed, miniature size, and incredible functionality. The ZX chip has just completed final testing and will be ready to be presented to the market in two weeks.

    You were successful in managing the commodity chip because you kept unit production cost low by achieving high volume and efficient production. Identify and discuss the key variables you will try to manage to make the ZX chip as successful as the commodity chip. Discuss how your efforts to manage costs will be similar to and different from your efforts to manage costs of the commodity chip.

28. **LO.2 (Alternative cost management strategies)** In 1993, Procter & Gamble (P&G) management tried to control costs by eliminating many of its brands' coupons while increasing print advertising. Only a miniscule portion of the hundreds of billions of coupons distributed annually by P&G were ever redeemed by customers. Eliminating coupons allowed P&G to reduce its prices on most brands. After testing a market in the northeastern United States, P&G found that it lost 16 percent of its market share because competitors did not follow P&G in this move. Instead, competitors countered P&G's decrease in price promotions by increasing their price promotions. Although price promotions had been unprofitable, discontinuing them while competitors did not was even more unprofitable for the company. P&G probably anticipated losing some market share in exchange for more profitability and equity for its brands but not to the degree that occurred. Advertising was expected to reverse the damage to penetration.

    Source: Raju Narisetti, "P&G Ad Chief Plots Demise of the Coupon," *Wall Street Journal* (April 17, 1996), pp. B1, B5A; and Tim Amber, "P&G Learnt the Hard Way from Dropping Its Price Promotions," *Marketing* (June 7, 2001), pp. 22–23.

    a. What costs and benefits did P&G likely consider in its discontinuance of coupons?
    b. What was P&G's apparent strategy in deciding to lower prices? Explain.

29. **LO.2 (Cost management and customer service)** Companies sometimes experience difficult financial times . . . sometimes so drastic that they declare bankruptcy. If a firm does not invest sufficient resources in its growth, then at some point it will experience diminishing revenues as its product revenues decline.

Alternatively, if a firm invests too heavily in growth, costs can spiral out of control. Commonly companies striving to maintain profitability switch back and forth between a focus on cost management or cost reduction and revenue growth. Often cost reduction is achieved by tactics such as across-the-board cost cutting. Seldom do companies maintain a balance of focus on cost management and revenue generation; however, one company, Alcoa, has taken a more strategic approach to both revenue growth and cost management. Even while in the middle of an effort to reduce costs by $1 billion per year, the company was focused on generating significant revenue growth. To achieve growth, the company breaks down its current revenue streams into five categories, including sales from existing customers and sales won from the competitors' customers. By segmenting its revenue streams, the company can better evaluate the profitability of obtaining additional sales from different streams and focus on cost management and revenue growth simultaneously. The underlying idea is that growth in costs should occur only where there is a significant opportunity to increase profitability. Further, the company believes that cost management and revenue generation must be managed jointly so that managers understand how cost cutting affects customer value and revenue growth.

Source: Joseph McCafferty, "Testing the Top Line: Analyzing a Company's Sources of Revenues Can Bring Insights into Growth," *CFO Magazine* (October 19, 2004), http://www.cfo.com/article.cfm/3219980/2/c_2984272?f=archives (last accessed 8/16/07).

a. When are across-the-board spending cuts a rational approach to cost management?
b. How can a cost management system help avoid adverse effects from cost cutting?
c. Why is it necessary for managers to focus attention on both generating new revenue and managing costs to be successful?

30. **LO.3 (Cost management: short term vs. long term)** Component Metals produces steel products for a variety of customers. One division of the company is the Garage Door Division, created in the late 1940s. Since that time, this division's principal products have been galvanized steel components used in garage door installations. The division has been continuously profitable since 1950, and, in 2008, it generated $10 million of profits on $300 million of sales.

However, over the past 10 years, divisional growth has been slow; profitability has become stagnant, and few new products have been developed, although the garage door components market has matured. Company president John Stamp has asked his senior staff to evaluate operations of the Garage Door Division and to recommend changes that would improve its operations. The staff uncovered the following facts:

■ Tonya Calley, age 53, has been division president for the past 15 years. Her compensation package includes an annual salary of $175,000 plus a cash bonus based on achievement of the budgeted level of annual profit.
■ Growth in sales in the residential metal products industry has averaged 12 percent annually over the past decade. Most of the growth has occurred in ornamental products used in residential privacy fencing.
■ Nationally, the division's market share in the overall residential metal products industry has dropped from 12 percent to 7 percent during the past 10 years and has dropped from 40 percent to 25 percent for garage door components.
■ The division maintains its own information systems, which are essentially the same systems that were in place 15 years ago; however, some of the manual systems have been computerized (e.g., payroll, accounts payable, accounting).
■ The division has no customer service department. A small sales staff solicits and takes orders by phone from national distribution chains.
■ The major intradivision communication tool is the annual operating budget. No formal statements have been prepared in the division regarding strategies, mission, values, goals and objectives, or identifying core competencies.

Given this information, identify the major problems in the Garage Door Division and develop recommendations to address the problems you have identified.

31. **LO.3 (Cost management and profitability)** After graduating last year from an Ivy League university, Sonya Tyson was hired as a stock analyst. Wanting to make her mark on the industry, Tyson issued a scathing report on a major discount department store retailer, Smart-Mart. The basis of her attack was a comparative analysis between Smart-Mart and Tracy's Department Store, an upscale, full-service department store. Some of the information cited in Tyson's report follows:

Items as Percent of Sales	Smart-Mart	Tracy's
Cost of goods sold	65%	55%
Gross margin	35	45
Selling and administrative	27	33
Profit	8	12

Based on the comparative analysis, Tyson issued to her clients a "sell" recommendation for Smart-Mart and a "buy" recommendation for Tracy's. The gist of Tyson's rationale for the recommendations was that Tracy's Department Store was outperforming Smart-Mart in the crucial area of cost management as evidenced by both a higher profit as a percent of sales and a higher gross margin as a percent of sales.

a. Evaluate Tyson's recommendations given the limited evidence available.

b. Because the two firms contrasted by Tyson have different strategies, what performance criteria would you use to evaluate their competitiveness in the industry?

32. **LO.3 (Cost management; product life cycle)** In August 2007, Heelys, a Texas-based maker of wheeled shoes, reported quarterly profits that beat the street estimates by three cents per share. Upon receiving the news, the market price of Heelys dropped 48 percent. Why? Although the profit reported for the current quarter was better than the market expected, the company simultaneously informed the market that sales for the balance of the year were being revised downward because the company's shoes were piling up in retail stores.

Source: Rob Curran, "Anthracite, DGSE Rise; Heelys Slip," *The Wall Street Journal* (August 9, 2007), p. C2.

a. Using Internet resources, identify the economic reasons cited by Heelys' management for the profit warning issued in August 2007.

b. Applying your understanding of product life cycle, explain why Heelys' stock price dropped so significantly following the profit warning.

c. Following the profit warning in August 2007, what specific actions did managers take to improve profitability? Do any of these actions suggest that Heelys had revised its strategy in August 2007?

33. **LO.3 (Stakeholders; cost management)** Laura Thompson, newly appointed controller of Allied Networking Services Inc. (ANSI), a rapidly growing company, has just been asked to serve as lead facilitator of a team charged with designing a cost management system (CMS) at ANSI. Also serving on the team are Tom Weiss, company president; Susan Turner, vice president of finance; and George Wipple, vice president of marketing.

At the team's organizational meeting, Weiss suggested that the performance measurements to be built into the CMS should have a primary focus based on ANSI's ultimate goal. Thompson advised the team that it would therefore be necessary for the team to gain consensus on the issue of an appropriate goal on which to focus the emphasis for the CMS's primary measurements.

When the team members pressed Weiss for what he thought ANSI's goal should be, he indicated that he believed that maximization of company profits was the most reasonable choice. At this, Wipple chimed in that because sales are the lifeblood of the company, the team should think about making customer satisfaction ANSI's ultimate goal.

Turner, who had been silently listening to the discussion, was prompted by Thompson to give her opinion on the issue. Turner said that much of the professional literature advocates maximization of shareholder wealth as the ultimate goal of business. She did not see why it should not be the same at ANSI. After all, the stockholders provide the financial capital, take the ultimate risk, and are responsible for organizing the company. Therefore, she asserted, the primary emphasis of measurements in the CMS should focus on whether or not stockholder wealth is being maximized.

A heated debate ensued. Wipple said, "Look, without customers, the company has no reason for being in existence—how profitable is a company without customers, and how well off would its managers and stockholders be without revenues?" To this, Turner replied, "Without stockholder funds, you have no company!" Weiss responded, "Unless we manage ANSI profitably, there'll be no company to provide customers with products and services or to provide a basis for stockholder wealth!" The team decided to reconvene after everyone had a chance to assess what had been said.

a. Should the CMS design team be deciding the company's ultimate goal? If not, who should make such a decision?

b. What do you believe should be the ultimate goal for a business? Defend your answer.

c. Can one group of stakeholders effectively be served at the expense of the other stakeholders? Discuss.

34. **LO.1 & LO.4 (CMS; MIS; ethics in reporting)** The value of an oil and gas company is tied to two fundamental circumstances. The first is the amount of oil and gas the company is presently producing. This amount, along with unit prices, determines the revenue and cash inflow that the company generates. The second circumstance is the level of oil and gas reserves controlled by the company. Over the long run, the reserve level is a constraint on the amount and cost of current oil and gas production. Accordingly, the capital markets evaluate the performance of oil and gas companies as much on management of reserves as on management of current production. Because investors use information about reserves to value oil and gas companies, the SEC has developed rules for classifying and reporting reserves.

In a series of several announcements in early 2004, Shell Oil (Royal Dutch/Shell Group of Cos.) downgraded its proven oil and gas reserves by more than 20 percent, or about 4.5 billion barrels. Most of the misstatements of reserves, which were revealed to the public in 2004, had been booked in the years 1997 to 2000. Following the 2004 disclosures, regulatory bodies, including the SEC and the U.S. Justice Department, opened inquiries into the misreporting of reserves to determine if there had been violations of reporting rules or other laws.

    a. Assume that the misreporting of reserves by Shell resulted from the MIS's generation of unintentional but inaccurate information. From a cost management perspective, how might the CMS, built on inaccurate data, have caused managers to take actions that were not in the company's best long-run interests? What actions could managers have taken to ensure the reliability of the data?

    b. Assume that Shell intentionally misreported reserves. Discuss how the CMS, if not properly designed, could have contributed to the misreporting.

    c. Discuss the ethics of manipulating financial and fundamental data for the purpose of managing (misleading) perceptions of investors and other interested users of company information. ▲

35. LO.4 (Cost management; social responsibility) Through its three sets of elements (motivational, informational, and reporting), a CMS focuses the attention of a given decision maker on the data and information that are crucial to that decision maker's responsibilities in the organization. However, the nature and scope of information generated by the CMS for that decision maker are often limited by traditions of financial reporting and the imaginations of CMS designers. A common omission from a CMS is information useful in meeting a firm's social responsibility.

    Consider the possibility that a CMS could be developed that would be informative relative to organizational performance from the following perspectives: minorities, local community, customers, employees, and the environment. Discuss how this information could be used to manage the following specific expenses:

    a. product liability costs

    b. local property taxes

    c. pollution remediation

    d. costs associated with employee turnover

    e. warranty expense ▲

36. LO.3–LO.5 (CMS design) Boston Bottling was founded in the late 1800s and was owned by the same family until 1960 when the firm went public. Throughout its life as a public firm, the company has been continuously profitable and recorded slow, but steady, growth. Historically, the company has maintained a steady focus on cost control as the key to profit generation. However, since about 2000 the company has struggled to significantly increase profits. In 1980, the firm bottled merely five brands of product and sold its output through four large wholesalers. Today, the firm bottles 40 brands of product, and product life averages only four years. Consequently, the firm is constantly adding and deleting brands in its product line. Further, to market the 40 brands of product, the company sells to dozens of wholesalers, brokers, and large retail chains. The company uses multiple pricing models to accommodate the various outlets.

    a. Discuss how the changes in the operating environment of Boston Bottling could negatively affect its ability to generate profit.

    b. The firm's cost management system has not evolved with the changing complexity of the business environment. Discuss how gap analysis could be used to update the cost management system.

13

Responsibility Accounting, Support Department Cost Allocations, and Transfer Pricing

▶

Objectives

After completing this chapter, you should be able to answer the following questions:

LO.1 Which factors determine whether a firm should be decentralized or centralized?

LO.2 How are decentralization and responsibility accounting related?

LO.3 What are the four primary types of responsibility centers, and what distinguishes them from each other?

LO.4 How are revenue variances computed?

LO.5 Why and how are support department costs allocated to operating departments?

LO.6 What types of transfer prices are used in organizations, and why are such prices used?

LO.7 What difficulties can be encountered by multinational companies using transfer prices?

Introduction

As an organization grows, its customer-base size and locations, product or service offerings, level of technology, distribution channels, and number of employees change. To cope with such changes, managers must recognize when and how the company's authority structure should be altered to support decision making, communication, and employee motivation. Global operations demand that managers in all regions effectively use corporate human and physical resources; product customization demands that managers be in close touch with customers; and coordination of larger and more diverse workforces demands that managers be more adept at employee training and development. Decisions often need to be made rapidly at a "grass-roots" level rather than at "the top" of the organizational hierarchy. Thus, one of the most common progressions made by high-growth companies is from highly centralized organizational structures to highly decentralized structures. When an organization adopts centralization of decision making, top management retains the major portion of decision-making authority. When top management delegates decision-making authority to subunit managers, decentralization exists. This chapter describes the accounting methods—responsibility accounting, support department cost allocations, and transfer pricing—that are appropriate in decentralized organizations.

Decentralization

The degree of centralization can be viewed as a continuum. In a completely centralized firm, a single individual (usually the company owner or president) makes all major decisions and retains full authority and responsibility for that organization's activities. Alternatively, a purely decentralized organization would have virtually no central authority, and each subunit would act as a totally independent entity. Decentralization is a transfer of authority, responsibility, and decision-making rights from the top to the bottom of the organization structure. Decentralization has both advantages and disadvantages, which are summarized in Exhibit 13–1.

EXHIBIT 13–1
Advantages and Disadvantages of Decentralization

Advantages

- Helps top management recognize and develop managerial talent.
- Allows managerial performance to be comparatively evaluated.
- Can often lead to greater job satisfaction and provides job enrichment.
- Makes the accomplishment of organizational goals and objectives easier.
- Reduces decision-making time.
- Allows the use of management by exception.

Disadvantages

- Can result in a lack of goal congruence or suboptimization by subunit managers.
- Requires more effective communication abilities because decision making is removed from the home office.
- Can create personnel difficulties upon introduction, especially if managers are unwilling or unable to delegate effectively.
- Can be extremely expensive, including costs of training and of making poor decisions.

Either extreme of the centralization–decentralization continuum represents a clearly undesirable arrangement. In the totally centralized company, a single individual would have neither the expertise nor sufficient and timely information to make effective decisions in all functional areas. In the totally decentralized firm, subunits could act in ways that are inconsistent with the organization's goals. Organizations tend to structure themselves according to the pure centralization versus pure decentralization factors in Exhibit 13–2. Most businesses are somewhere along the continuum. The combination of the managers' personal characteristics, the nature of decisions required for organizational growth, and the types of organizational activities lead a company to find the appropriate degree of decentralization.

Decentralization does not necessarily mean that a unit manager has the authority to make all decisions concerning that unit. Top management selectively determines the types of authority to delegate to and withhold from lower-level managers. Decentralized companies often have certain organizational functions, such as cash management and purchasing, made at a central location. A 2006 survey found that one-third of financial executives listed centralization of the treasury function as a top priority of their companies: centralization provides "better control of cash positions and operational risk," "a layer of oversight for reviewing information and transactions," and reduces costs and redundant operations.[1]

Even when functions and the decision-making authority for those functions are delegated, top management retains ultimate responsibility for decision outcomes. Thus, a sophisticated accounting and reporting system must be implemented to provide top management information about overall subunit accountability as well as the ability to measure it.

LO.1
Which factors determine whether a firm should be decentralized or centralized?

EXHIBIT 13–2
Degree of Decentralization in an Organizational Structure

FACTOR	CONTINUUM		
	Pure Centralization	⟶	**Pure Decentralization**
Age of firm	Young	⟶	Mature
Size of firm	Small	⟶	Large
Stage of product development	Stable	⟶	Growth
Growth rate of firm	Slow	⟶	Rapid
Expected impact on profits of incorrect decisions	High	⟶	Low
Top management's confidence in subordinates	Low	⟶	High
Historical degree of control in firm	Tight	⟶	Moderate or loose
Geographical diversity of operations	Local	⟶	Widespread
Cost of communications	Low	⟶	High
Ability to resolve conflicts	Easy	⟶	Difficult
Level of employee motivation	Low	⟶	Moderate to high
Level of organizational flexibility	Low	⟶	High
Time of response to changes	Slow	⟶	Rapid

---

[1] Karen M. Kroll, "Centralization Nation," *Business Finance* (March 2007), pp. 27ff.

LO.2
**How are decentralization
and responsibility
accounting related?**

Responsibility Accounting Systems

A responsibility accounting system facilitates decentralization by providing information about the performance, efficiency, and effectiveness of organizational subunits and their managers. Responsibility accounting is the key management control tool in a decentralized organization.

A responsibility accounting system produces responsibility reports that assist each successively higher level of management in evaluating the performances of subordinate managers and their respective organizational units. The reports should be tailored to fit the planning, controlling, and decision-making needs of subordinate managers and should include both monetary and nonmonetary information. Exhibit 13–3 provides examples of information that can be shown in responsibility reports. Depending on the type of responsibility unit for which the report is being generated, all types of information shown are not necessarily available.

A manager's responsibility report should reflect the degree of influence that he or she has and should include only the revenues and/or costs under that manager's control. Normally, some of an organizational unit's revenues or costs are not controllable (or are only partially or indirectly controllable) by the unit manager. In such instances, the responsibility accounting report should separately classify all reported monetary information as controllable or noncontrollable by the manager. Alternatively, separate reports should be prepared for the organizational unit (showing all monetary amounts) and for the unit manager (showing only those monetary amounts under his or her control).

EXHIBIT 13–3
Information for Responsibility Reports

Monetary

- Budgeted and actual revenues
- Budgeted and actual costs (computed on a comparable basis)
- Variance computations for revenues and costs
- Asset investment base

Nonmonetary

- Capacity measures (theoretical and that used to compute predetermined overhead rates)
- Target rate of earnings on investment base
- Desired and actual market share
- Departmental/divisional throughput
- Number of defects (by product, product line, supplier)
- Number of orders backlogged (by date, cost, and selling price)
- Number of customer complaints (by type and product); method of complaint resolution
- Percentage of orders delivered on time
- Manufacturing (or service) cycle efficiency
- Percentage of reduction of non-value-added time from previous reporting period (broken down by idle time, storage time, move time, and quality control time)
- Number and percentage of employee suggestions considered significant and practical
- Number and percentage of employee suggestions implemented
- Number of unplanned production interruptions
- Number of schedule changes
- Number of engineering change orders; percentage change from previous period
- Number of safety violations; percentage change from previous period
- Number of days of employee absences; percentage change from previous period

A responsibility accounting system helps organizational unit managers to conduct the five basic control functions:

1. Prepare a plan (for example, using budgets and standards) and use it to communicate output expectations and delegate authority.
2. Gather actual data classified in accordance with the activities and categories specified in the plan. The responsibility accounting system can be used to record and summarize data for each organizational unit.
3. Monitor the differences between planned and actual data at scheduled intervals. Responsibility reports for subordinate managers and their immediate supervisors normally include comparisons of actual results with flexible budget figures. In contrast, responsibility reports can provide comparisons of actual performance to the master budget.
4. Exert managerial influence in response to significant differences. Because of day-to-day contact with operations, unit managers should be aware of any significant variances before they are reported, identify the variance causes, and attempt to correct them. Top management, on the other hand, could not know about operational variances until it receives responsibility reports. By the time top management receives the reports, the problems causing the variances should have been corrected, or subordinate managers should have explanations as to why the problems were not or could not be resolved.
5. Continue comparing data and responding, then at the appropriate time, begin the process again.

Responsibility reports reflect the upward flow of information from operational units to company top management and illustrate the broadening scope of responsibility. Managers receive detailed information on the performance of their immediate areas of control and summary information on all organizational units for which they are responsible. Summarizing results causes a pyramiding of information. Reports at the lowest level of units are highly detailed, whereas more general information is reported to the top of the organization. Upper-level managers desiring more detail than is provided in summary reports can obtain it by reviewing the responsibility reports prepared by their subordinates.

Exhibit 13–4 illustrates the June 2008 responsibility report for Frazier Manufacturing Company. Each area's budget is presented for comparative purposes. Production department data are aggregated with data of the other departments under the production vice president's control. (These combined data are shown in the middle section of Exhibit 13–4.) Similarly, the total costs of the production vice president's area of responsibility are combined with other costs for which the company president is responsible (in the top section of Exhibit 13–4).

Variances are itemized in performance reports at the lower levels so that the appropriate manager has the necessary details to take any required corrective action related to significant variances.[2] Under the management-by-exception principle, major deviations from expectations are highlighted under the subordinate manager's reporting section to assist upper-level managers in determining whether they need to become involved in subordinates' operations. In addition, such detailed variance analyses alert operating managers to items that require explanations for superiors. For example, the unfavorable direct material and favorable direct labor amounts in the production department manager's section of Exhibit 13–4 would probably be considered significant and require explanations to the production vice president.

The process of responsibility accounting creates some issues for management. For example, the idea of "rolling up" (or aggregating) information to each successively higher level allows potentially important details to be buried. If different units within the responsibility accounting system are competing with each other for resources, managers could try to "promote their own agendas" by blaming other organizational units for problems; alternatively, the competition could lead to a lack of goal congruence between or among organizational units. (**Goal congruence** exists when the personal and organizational goals of decision makers throughout the firm are consistent and mutually supportive.) Additionally, by partitioning each responsibility unit as a separate part of the report, interdependencies among units might be obscured. As mentioned in Chapter 4, organizational processes are typically horizontal and, thereby, the activities in one unit may affect activities in other responsibility accounting units.

---

[2]In practice, the variances presented in Exhibit 13–4 would be further separated into the portions representing price and quantity effects as shown in Chapter 7 on standard costing.

EXHIBIT 13–4

Frazier Manufacturing Company Responsibility Report (June 2008)

President's Performance Report

	Budget	Actual	Variance Fav. (Unfav.)
Administrative office—president	$1,192,000	$1,196,800	$ (4,800)
Financial vice president	944,000	936,400	7,600
Production vice president	2,951,984	2,977,600	(25,616) ◄
Sales vice president	1,100,000	1,105,600	(5,600)
Totals	$6,187,984	$6,216,400	$(28,416)

Production Vice President's Performance Report

	Budget	Actual	Variance Fav. (Unfav.)
Administrative office—vice president	$ 720,000	$ 728,800	$ (8,800)
Distribution and storage	498,800	504,000	(5,200) ◄
Production department	1,733,184	1,744,800	(11,616) ◄
Totals	$2,951,984	$2,977,600	$(25,616)

Distribution and Storage Manager's Performance Report

	Budget	Actual	Variance Fav. (Unfav.)
Direct material	$ 144,000	$ 141,600	$ 2,400
Direct labor	218,000	221,200	(3,200)
Supplies	18,800	21,200	(2,400)
Indirect labor	94,400	95,200	(800)
Repairs and maintenance	14,000	14,800	(800)
Other	9,600	10,000	(400)
Totals	$ 498,800	$ 504,000	$ (5,200)

Production Department Manager's Performance Report

	Budget	Actual	Variance Fav. (Unfav.)
Direct material	$ 477,200	$ 490,000	$(12,800)
Direct labor	763,520	752,108	11,412
Supplies	70,624	74,000	(3,376)
Indirect labor	185,152	188,080	(2,928)
Depreciation	154,612	154,612	0
Repairs and maintenance	49,628	51,600	(1,972)
Other	32,448	34,400	(1,952)
Totals	$1,733,184	$1,744,800	$(11,616)

Responsibility accounting's focus is on the manager who has control over a particular cost object. In a decentralized company, the cost object is an organizational unit or responsibility center, such as a division, department, or geographical region.

LO.3

What are the four primary types of responsibility centers, and what distinguishes them from each other?

Types of Responsibility Centers

Responsibility accounting systems identify, measure, and report on the performance of responsibility centers and their managers. Responsibility centers are generally classified according to their manager's scope of authority and type of financial responsibility: costs, revenues, profits, and/or asset base. The four primary types of responsibility centers are illustrated in Exhibit 13–5 and discussed in the following sections.

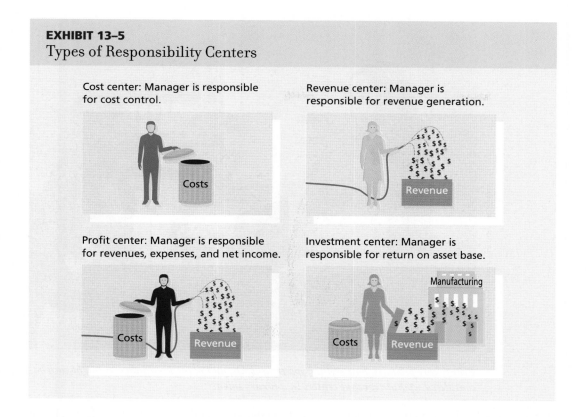

EXHIBIT 13–5
Types of Responsibility Centers

Cost center: Manager is responsible for cost control.

Revenue center: Manager is responsible for revenue generation.

Profit center: Manager is responsible for revenues, expenses, and net income.

Investment center: Manager is responsible for return on asset base.

Cost Center

A cost center is an organizational unit whose manager has the authority only to incur costs and is specifically evaluated on the basis of how well costs are controlled. Cost centers commonly include service and administrative (or support) departments. For example, a company's human resources and accounting departments could be considered cost centers because these units do not generate revenues or charge for services, but they do incur costs. Controlling costs in these types of areas is discussed in Chapter 16.

In the traditional manufacturing environment, the production department is the largest cost center and the highest priority in that cost center is normally to minimize standard cost variances (as discussed in Chapter 7). Top management often concentrates only on the unfavorable variances reported in a cost center and ignores the efficient performance indicated by favorable variances. However, significant favorable variances should not be disregarded if the management-by-exception principle is applied appropriately. Using this principle, top management should investigate all variances (both favorable and unfavorable) that fall outside the range of acceptable deviations.

In some instances, a cost center can generate revenues, but the revenues are either not under the manager's control or not effectively measurable. The first situation exists in a community library that is provided a specific proration of property tax dollars but has no authority to levy or collect the related taxes. The second situation exists in discretionary cost centers, such as a research and development center, in which the outputs (revenues or benefits generated from the cost inputs) are not easily measured.[3] In these situations, the revenues should *not* be included in the manager's responsibility accounting report.

Revenue Center

A revenue center is strictly defined as an organizational unit that is responsible for the generation of revenues and has no control over setting selling prices or budgeting costs. For instance, in many retail

[3]Discretionary costs are discussed in Chapter 16.

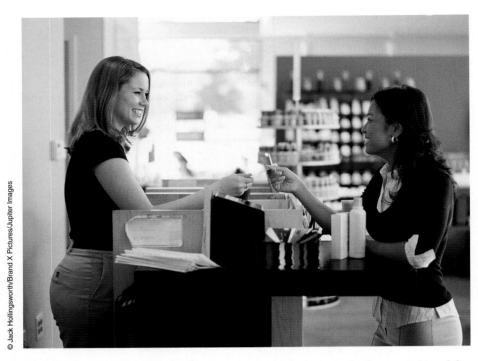

Beauty care products, hair styling, spa treatments, and manicures/pedicures might each be considered separate revenue centers in a luxury salon.

stores, each sales department is considered an independent unit and managers are evaluated based on the total revenues their departments generate. Departmental managers, however, may have no authority to adjust selling prices to affect volume, and often they do not participate in the budgeting process. Additionally, the departmental managers may have no ability to affect costs.

LO.4
How are revenue variances computed?

In a revenue center, performance evaluations are limited because the manager has control over only one item: revenues. Actual performance in revenue centers (as well as in any other area that has control over revenue) should be compared against budgeted performance to determine variances from expectations. Budgeted and actual revenues may differ because of either volume of units sold or price of units sold. To compare budgeted and actual revenues, the price and volume components of revenue must be distinguished from one another.[4] The sales price variance is calculated by multiplying the actual number of units sold by the difference between actual and budgeted sales prices. This variance indicates the portion of the total revenue variance that is related to a change in selling price. The sales volume variance is calculated by multiplying the budgeted sales price by the difference between the actual and budgeted sales volumes. The model for computing revenue variances follows:

where

ASP = actual sales price
ASV = actual sales volume
BSP = budgeted sales price
BSV = budgeted sales volume

In most instances, pure revenue centers do not exist because managers are also responsible for managing some costs in their centers. A more appropriate term for such organizational units is a *revenue and limited cost center.*

---

[4]Separating the price and volume elements of a revenue variance is similar to the separation of the price and usage elements of cost variances discussed in Chapter 7.

Profit Center

A profit center is an organizational unit whose manager is responsible for generating revenues and managing expenses related to current activity. Thus, profit centers should be independent organizational units whose managers have the ability to obtain resources at the most economical prices and to sell products at prices that will maximize revenue. A profit center manager's goal is to maximize the center's profit. Costs not under a profit center manager's control are those related to long-term investments in plant assets; as such, separate evaluations should be made for the subunit and its manager.

Investment Center

An investment center is an organizational unit whose manager is responsible for managing revenues and current expenses. In addition, the center's manager has the authority to acquire, use, and dispose of plant assets to earn the highest feasible rate of return on the center's asset base. Many investment centers are independent, freestanding divisions or corporate subsidiaries. This independence gives investment center managers the opportunity to make decisions about all matters affecting their organizational units and to be judged on the outcomes of those decisions. Because of their closeness to daily divisional activities, investment center managers should have more current and detailed knowledge than top management has about sales prices, costs, and other market information.

After top management has delegated authority to lower-level responsibility center managers, the possibility exists that those managers will not act harmoniously to accomplish the organization's goals. Rather, each responsibility center manager may act to optimize only his or her own isolated performance and that of his or her responsibility center. Losing sight of the organizational goals while working to achieve an independent responsibility center's conflicting goal results in suboptimization, or a situation in which individual managers pursue goals and objectives that are in their own and/or their segments' particular interests rather than in the company's best interests.

A unique challenge for the design of responsibility centers arises from the instance in which one responsibility center supplies its outputs largely to other internal responsibility centers. In determining the responsibility classification of such an organizational unit, top management often makes judgments about the nature and extent of the costs and revenues to include in those responsibility centers. Frequently, rather than attempting to make performance assessments about cost centers, management assigns the costs incurred in cost centers to operating areas through a process of support department cost allocation. Alternatively, management can attempt to "create" revenues for the cost center by using an internal transfer pricing system for the center's tangible or intangible output that is used by other company units.

Support Department Cost Allocation

LO.5
Why and how are support department costs allocated to operating departments?

Organizations incur two types of overhead costs: manufacturing and support (or nonmanufacturing). Typically, as the number of product lines or service types increases, so does the need for additional support activities. An organization's support activities occur in service and administrative departments. A service department is an organizational unit (such as central purchasing, maintenance, engineering, security, or warehousing) that provides specific functional tasks for other internal units. Administrative departments perform management activities that benefit the entire organization and include the human resources, accounting, legal, and insurance departments as well as organizational headquarters. Service and administrative departments can be referred to collectively as support departments.

All support department costs are incurred to benefit production or service-rendering activities. Thus, support department costs must be covered in the long run by sales of products and services. These costs may be allocated to production departments to meet the objectives of full cost computation, managerial motivation, and managerial decision making. Exhibit 13–6 identifies reasons for and against allocating support department costs in relationship to each allocation objective.

EXHIBIT 13–6
Allocating Service Department Costs: Pros and Cons

OBJECTIVE: TO COMPUTE FULL COST

Reasons *for*:

1. Provides for cost recovery.
2. Instills a consideration of support costs in production managers.
3. Reflects production's "fair share" of support costs.
4. Meets regulations in some pricing instances.

Reasons *against*:

1. Provides costs that are beyond production manager's control.
2. Provides arbitrary costs that are not useful in decision making.
3. Confuses the issues of pricing and costing. Prices should be set high enough for each product to provide a profit margin that should cover all nonproduction costs.

OBJECTIVE: TO MOTIVATE MANAGERS

Reasons *for*:

1. Instills a consideration of support costs in production managers.
2. Relates individual production unit's profits to total company profits.
3. Reflects usage of services on a fair and equitable basis.
4. Encourages production managers to help support departments control costs.
5. Encourages the usage of certain services.

Reasons *against*:

1. Distorts production division's profit figures because allocations are subjective.
2. Includes costs that are beyond production manager's control.
3. Will not materially affect production division's profits.
4. Creates interdivisional ill will when there is lack of agreement about allocation base or method.
5. Is not cost beneficial.

OBJECTIVE: TO COMPARE ALTERNATIVE COURSES OF ACTION

Reasons *for*:

1. Provides relevant information in determining corporatewide profits generated by alternative actions.
2. Provides best available estimate of expected changes in costs due to alternative actions.

Reasons *against*:

1. Is unnecessary if alternative actions will not cause costs to change.
2. Presents distorted cash flows or profits from alternative actions because allocations are arbitrary.

Source: Adapted from *Statements on Management Accounting Number 4B: Allocation of Service and Administrative Costs* (June 13, 1985), pp. 9–10. Copyright by Institute of Management Accountants.

Allocation Bases

If support department costs are to be assigned to operating areas, a rational and systematic means by which to make the assignment must be developed. An improper cost allocation base will yield distorted cost allocations. A valid allocation base should

- ■ Measure the benefit the operating department receives from the support department;
- ■ Capture the causal relationship existing between factors in the operating department and costs incurred in the support department;
- ■ Reflect the fairness or equity of the allocations between operating departments; and
- ■ Measure the ability of operating departments to bear the allocated costs.

The first two criteria are used most often to select allocation bases because these criteria are reasonably objective and will produce rational allocations. Fairness is a valid theoretical basis for allocation, but its use can cause dissension because everyone does not agree on what is fair or equitable. The ability-to-bear criterion often results in unrealistic or profit-detrimental actions: managers might manipulate operating data related to the allocation base to minimize support department allocations. Exhibit 13–7 indicates some appropriate bases for assigning various types of support department costs.

Methods of Allocating Support Department Costs

The idea underlying support department cost allocations is that the responsibility centers that benefit from the services provided by support units should bear the costs of such support units. Thus, the alternative methods all intend to accomplish the same result: assign the cost of support departments to their customers. All methods addressed in the following discussion accomplish the objective of assigning support costs to operating departments. The methods differ in their complexity and reliability of results. The direct method is the simplest support department cost allocation method.

The direct method assigns support department costs only to operating areas. For example, the human resources department costs can be assigned to production departments based on number of employees, and purchasing department costs can be assigned to production departments based on number of purchase orders generated. The direct method is the simplest allocation method, but it may result in distorted cost allocations if there is significant exchange of services among support departments as well as operating departments.

The step method allows a partial recognition of the effects of interactions among support departments in assigning costs. This method ranks the quantity of services provided by each support department to other support areas. A benefits-provided ranking begins with the support department providing the most service to all other support areas and ends with the support department providing the least service to all other support areas. Then, support department costs are sequentially allocated down the ranking until all costs have been assigned to the operating areas. For example, the human resources department might be the first department listed in the ranking because it provides assistance to all company areas; all other areas, including support areas, would receive an allocation of the human resources department's costs based on the proportion of human resources services used. Although many approaches are used to implement the benefits-provided ranking, the two most common are the dollar volume of services and the percentage of total assistance to other support areas.

EXHIBIT 13–7
Appropriate Service/Administrative Cost Allocation Bases

Type of Cost	Acceptable Allocation Bases
Research and development	Estimated time or usage, sales, assets employed, new products developed
Personnel functions	Number of employees, payroll, number of new hires
Accounting functions	Estimated time or usage, sales, assets employed, employment data
Public relations and corporate promotion	Sales
Purchasing function	Dollar value of purchase orders, number of purchase orders, estimated time of usage, percentage of material purchases
Corporate executives' salaries	Sales, assets employed, pretax operating income
Treasurer's functions	Sales, estimated time or usage, assets or liabilities employed
Legal and governmental affairs	Estimated time or usage, sales, assets employed
Tax department	Estimated time or usage, sales, assets employed
Income taxes	Pretax operating income
Property taxes	Square feet, real estate valuation

Source: Adapted from *Statements on Management Accounting Number 4B: Allocation of Service and Administration Costs* (June 13, 1985), p. 8. Copyright by Institute of Management Accountants.

The algebraic method of allocating support department costs considers all departmental inter-relationships and reflects these relationships in simultaneous equations. These equations provide for reciprocal allocation of total support costs among the support departments as well as to the operating departments. No benefits-provided ranking is needed. The algebraic method is the most complex of all the allocation techniques, but it is also the most theoretically correct and, if relationships are properly formulated, provides the most accurate and reliable allocations.

Service Department Cost Allocation Illustration

Data for Wisconsin Wellness Corp. (WWC) illustrate the three methods of allocating budgeted support department costs. WWC has two operating divisions: nutritionals and vision care. WWC's support departments are corporate administration, human resources, and maintenance. Budgeted costs of each support department are first allocated to each operating division using one of the three methods of support area cost allocation and are then added to the budgeted overhead costs of those divisions to determine an appropriate divisional overhead application rate. Exhibit 13–8 provides an abbreviated 2008 budget of the direct and indirect costs for each support department and operating division of WWC.

Exhibit 13–9 presents the bases selected for allocating WWC's support department costs. These bases are proxies for the quantity of services consumed by each service area and operating division. Assume that support departments are listed in a benefits-provided ranking. Management determined that administration provides the most assistance to all other support areas, human resources is second in the rank ordering, and maintenance supports only the operating areas (equipment used in other areas is under a lease maintenance arrangement and is not serviced by the company's maintenance department). All product research and development is conducted in a separate subsidiary company.

Direct Method Allocation

In the direct method of allocation, support department costs are assigned using the specified bases only to the operating areas. The direct method cost allocation for Wisconsin Wellness Corp. is shown in Exhibit 13–10.

Use of the direct method of support department allocation produces the total budgeted costs for nutritionals and vision care (Exhibit 13–11). If budgeted revenues and costs equal actual revenues and costs, nutritionals would show a 2008 profit of $1,730,563, or 22.3 percent on revenues, and vision care would show a profit of $1,210,287, or 26.9 percent.

EXHIBIT 13–8
Wisconsin Wellness Corp. 2008 Budgeted Departmental and Divisional Costs

	Administration	Human Resources	Maintenance	Nutritionals	Vision Care	Total
Direct departmental costs:						
Material	$ 0	$ 0	$ 0	$1,275,600	$ 669,600	$1,945,200
Labor	1,350,000	150,000	360,000	736,200	864,000	3,460,200
Total	$1,350,000	$150,000	$360,000	$2,011,800	$1,533,600	$5,405,400
Departmental overhead*	1,651,200	69,750	238,200	1,677,000	267,600	3,903,750
Total initial departmental costs	$3,001,200	$219,750	$598,200	$3,688,800	$1,801,200	$9,309,150

*Would be specified by type and cost behavior in actual budgeting process.

EXHIBIT 13–9
Service Department Allocation Bases

Administration costs—allocated based on dollars of assets employed

Human resources costs—allocated based on number of employees

Maintenance costs—allocated based on machine hours used

	Dollars of Assets Employed	Number of Employees	Number of Machine Hours Used
Administration	$12,000,000	24	0
Human resources	3,600,000	6	0
Maintenance	6,000,000	18	0
Nutritionals	30,000,000	75	258,000
Vision care	24,000,000	21	64,500

EXHIBIT 13–10
Direct Allocation of Service Department Costs

	Base	Proportion of Total Base	Amount to Allocate	Amount Allocated
Administration costs				
(dollars of assets employed)				
Nutritionals	$30,000,000	30,000,000 ÷ 54,000,000 = 56%*	$3,001,200	$1,680,672
Vision care	24,000,000	24,000,000 ÷ 54,000,000 = 44*	3,001,200	1,320,528
Total	$54,000,000	100%		$3,001,200
Human resouces costs				
(number of employees)				
Nutritionals	75	75 ÷ 96 = 78%*	$219,750	$ 171,405
Vision care	21	21 ÷ 96 = 22*	219,750	48,345
Total	96	100%		$ 219,750
Maintenance costs				
(number of machine hours used)				
Nutritionals	258,000	258,000 ÷ 322,500 = 80%	$598,200	$ 478,560
Vision care	64,500	64,500 ÷ 322,500 = 20	598,200	119,640
Total	322,500	100%		$ 598,200

*Rounded

Step Method Allocation

To apply the step method allocation, a benefits-provided ranking must be specified. This ranking for Wisconsin Wellness Corp. was given in Exhibit 13–9. Costs are assigned using an appropriate, specified allocation base to the departments receiving support. After costs have been assigned from a department, no costs are charged back to that department. Step method allocation of WWC support costs is shown in Exhibit 13–12.

   In this case, the amount of support department costs assigned to each operating area differs only slightly between the step and direct methods. However, in many situations, the difference can be

EXHIBIT 13–11
Direct Method Allocation to Revenue-Producing Areas

	Nutritionals	Vision Care	Total
Total (assumed) budgeted revenues (a)	$7,750,000	$4,500,000	$12,250,000
Allocated overhead			
From administration	$1,680,672	$1,320,528	$ 3,001,200
From human resources	171,405	48,345	219,750
From maintenance	478,560	119,640	598,200
Subtotal	$2,330,637	$1,488,513	$ 3,819,150
Departmental overhead	1,677,000	267,600	1,944,600
Total overhead (for OH application rate determination)	$4,007,637	$1,756,113	$ 5,763,750
Direct costs	2,011,800	1,533,600	3,545,400
Total budgeted costs (b)	$6,019,437	$3,289,713	$ 9,309,150
Total budgeted pretax profits (a − b)	$1,730,563	$1,210,287	$ 2,940,850

VERIFICATION OF ALLOCATION TO

	Administration	Human Resources	Maintenance	Nutritionals	Vision Care	Total
Initial costs	$3,001,200	$219,750	$598,200			$3,819,150
Costs from						
Administration	(3,001,200)			$1,680,672	$1,320,528	
Human resources		(219,750)		171,405	48,345	
Maintenance			(598,200)	478,560	119,640	
Totals	$ 0	$ 0	$ 0	$2,330,637	$1,488,513	$3,819,150

substantial. If budgeted revenues and costs equal actual revenues and costs, the step method allocation process will cause nutritionals and vision care to show the following profits:

	Nutritionals	Vision Care
Revenues	$7,750,000	$4,500,000
Direct costs	(2,011,800)	(1,533,600)
Indirect departmental costs	(1,677,000)	(267,600)
Allocated support department costs	(2,420,270)	(1,398,880)
Profit	$1,640,930	$1,299,920

These profit figures reflect rates of return on revenues of 21.2 percent and 28.9 percent, respectively.

The step method is a hybrid between the direct and the algebraic methods. This allocation approach is more realistic than the direct method in that the step method partially recognizes relationships among support departments, although it does not recognize the mutual exchange of services among support departments. Under the step method allocation process, a support department is "eliminated" once its costs have been assigned. If a support department further down the ranking sequence provides assistance to support areas higher in the benefits-provided ranking, then this assistance is not recognized.

Algebraic Method Allocation

The algebraic method of allocation eliminates the two disadvantages of the step method because it recognizes all interrelationships among departments and no decision must be made about a rank ordering of support departments. The algebraic method involves formulating a set of equations that

EXHIBIT 13–12

Step Method Allocation to Revenue-Producing Areas

	Base	Proportion of Total Base	Amount to Allocate	Amount Allocated
Administration costs				
(dollars of assets employed)				
Human resources	$ 3,600,000	3,600,000 ÷ 63,600,000 = 6%[a]	$3,001,200	$ 180,072
Maintenance	6,000,000	6,000,000 ÷ 63,600,000 = 9[a]	3,001,200	270,108
Nutritionals	30,000,000	30,000,000 ÷ 63,600,000 = 47[a]	3,001,200	1,410,564
Vision care	24,000,000	24,000,000 ÷ 63,600,000 = 38[a]	3,001,200	1,140,456
Total	$63,600,000	100%		$3,001,200
Human resources costs				
(number of employees)				
Maintenance	18	18 ÷ 114 = 16%[a]	$399,822[b]	$ 3,972
Nutritionals	75	75 ÷ 114 = 66[a]	399,822	263,882
Vision care	21	21 ÷ 114 = 18[a]	399,822	71,968
Total	114	100%		$ 399,822
Maintenance costs				
(number of machine hours used)				
Nutritionals	258,000	258,000 ÷ 322,500 = 80%	$932,280[c]	$ 745,824
Vision care	64,500	64,500 ÷ 322,500 = 20	932,280	186,456
Total	322,500	100%		$ 932,280

[a]Rounded
[b]Personnel costs = Original cost + Allocated from administration = $219,750 + $180,072 = $399,822
[c]Maintenance costs = Original cost + Allocated from administration + Allocated from human resources = $598,200 + $270,108 + $63,972 = $932,280

VERIFICATION OF ALLOCATION TO

	Administration	Human Resources	Maintenance	Nutritionals	Vision Care	Total
Initial costs	$ 3,001,200	$ 219,750	$ 598,200			$3,819,150
Costs from						
Administration	(3,001,200)	180,072	270,108	$1,410,564	$1,140,456	
Human resources		(399,822)	63,972	263,882	71,968	
Maintenance			(932,280)	745,824	186,456	
Totals	$ 0	$ 0	$ 0	$2,420,270	$1,398,880	$3,819,150

reflect reciprocal service among departments. Solving these equations simultaneously recognizes the fact that support departments both give and receive services.

The starting point of the algebraic method is choosing which base to use for measuring the consumption of services by each department (shown in Exhibit 13–9). A schedule is created to show the proportionate usage by each department of the other departments' services. These proportions are then used to develop equations that, when solved simultaneously, give cost allocations that fully recognize the reciprocal services provided.

The allocation proportions for all departments of WWC are shown in Exhibit 13–13. The human resources department allocation is discussed to illustrate the derivation of these proportions.

EXHIBIT 13–13
Interdepartmental Proportional Relationships

	ADMINISTRATION (DOLLARS OF ASSETS EMPLOYED)		HUMAN RESOURCES (NUMBER OF EMPLOYEES)		MAINTENANCE (NUMBER OF MACHINE HOURS USED)	
	Base	**Percent***	**Base**	**Percent***	**Base**	**Percent***
Administration	n/a	n/a	24	18%	0	0%
Human resources	$ 3,600,000	6%	n/a	n/a	0	0
Maintenance	6,000,000	9	18	13	n/a	n/a
Nutritionals	30,000,000	47	75	54	258,000	80
Vision care	24,000,000	38	21	15	64,500	20
Total	$63,600,000	100%	138	100%	322,500	100%

*Rounded

The allocation basis for human resources cost is number of employees. WWC has 138 employees, excluding those in the human resources department. Human resources employees are ignored because costs are being removed from that department and assigned to other areas. Because maintenance has 18 employees, the proportionate amount of human resources services used by maintenance is 18 ÷ 138, or 13 percent (rounded).

By using the calculated percentages, algebraic equations representing the interdepartmental usage of services can be formulated. The departments are labeled A, H, and M in the equations for administration, human resources, and maintenance, respectively. The initial costs of each support department are shown first in the formulas:

$$A = \$3,001,200 + 0.18H + 0.00M$$
$$H = \$ \ 219,750 + 0.06A + 0.00M$$
$$M = \$ \ 598,200 + 0.09A + 0.13H$$

These equations are solved simultaneously by substituting one equation into the others, gathering like terms, and reducing the unknowns until only one unknown exists. The value for this unknown is then computed and substituted into the remaining equations. This process is continued until all unknowns have been eliminated.

1. Substituting the equation for A into the equation for H gives the following:

$$H = \$219,750 + 0.06(\$3,001,200 + 0.18H)$$

Multiplying and combining terms produces the following results:

$$H = \$219,750 + \$180,072 + 0.01H$$
$$H = \$399,822 + 0.01H$$
$$H - 0.01H = \$399,822$$
$$0.99H = \$399,822$$
$$H = \$403,861$$

2. The value for H is now substituted in the formula for administration:

$$A = \$3,001,200 + 0.18(\$403,861)$$
$$A = \$3,001,200 + \$72,695$$
$$A = \$3,073,895$$

3. Substituting the values for A and H into the equation for M gives the following:

$$M = \$598,200 + 0.09(\$3,073,895) + 0.13(\$403,861)$$
$$M = \$598,200 + \$276,651 + \$52,502$$
$$M = \$927,353$$

The amounts provided by these equations are then allocated among all the departments; costs are allocated both to and from the support areas. The resulting allocations are shown in Exhibit 13–14. Note that the net amount assigned to all support areas is $0.

The $3,073,895 of administration costs is used to illustrate the computation of the amounts in Exhibit 13–14. Administration costs are assigned to the other areas based on dollars of assets employed. Exhibit 13–14 indicates that human resources has 6 percent of WWC's total asset dollars; thus, $184,434 (0.06 × $3,073,895) is assigned to that area. A similar proration process is used for the other departments. Allocations from Exhibit 13–14 are used in Exhibit 13–15 to determine the reallocated costs and finalize the total budgeted overhead of nutritionals and vision care.

When a company has few support department interrelationships, the algebraic method can be solved by hand. If a large number of support area interactions exist, this method must be performed by a computer. Results obtained from the algebraic method provide the most rational and appropriate means of allocating support department costs, although it does take a substantial amount of time to accurately determine the proportional relationships.

EXHIBIT 13–14
Algebraic Solution of Service Department Costs

Costs are allocated based on percentages computed in Exhibit 13–13.

	ADMINISTRATION		HUMAN RESOURCES		MAINTENANCE	
	Percent	Amount	Percent	Amount	Percent	Amount
Administration	n/a	n/a	18%	$ 72,695	0%	$ 0
Human resources	6%	$ 184,434	n/a	n/a	0	0
Maintenance	9	276,650	13	52,502	n/a	n/a
Nutritionals	47	1,444,731	54	218,085	80	741,882
Vision care	38	1,168,080	15	60,579	20	185,471
Total*	100%	$3,073,895	100%	$403,861	100%	$927,353

*Total costs are the solution results of the set of algebraic equations.

EXHIBIT 13–15
Algebraic Method Allocation to Revenue-Producing Areas

	Total Service Department Cost (from equations)	Administration	Human Resources	Maintenance	Nutritionals	Vision Care
Administration	$3,073,895	$ 0	$184,434	$276,650	$1,444,731	$1,168,080
Human resources	403,861	72,695	0	52,502	218,085	60,579
Maintenance	927,353	0	0	0	741,882	185,471
Total costs	$4,405,109	$72,695	$184,434	$329,152	$2,404,698	$1,414,130
Less reallocated costs	(586,281)	(72,695)	(184,434)	(329,152)		
Budgeted costs	$3,818,828	$ 0	$ 0	$ 0		
Departmental OH costs of operating areas					1,677,000	267,600
Total budgeted cost for OH application rate determination					$4,081,698	$1,681,730

Regardless of the method used to allocate support department costs, the final step is to determine the overhead application rates for the operating areas. After support department costs have been assigned to production, they are included as part of production overhead and allocated to products or jobs through normal overhead assignment procedures.

As shown in Exhibit 13–15, the total allocated overhead costs of $4,081,698 and $1,681,730 for nutritionals and vision care, respectively, will be divided by an appropriate overhead allocation base to assign both manufacturing and nonmanufacturing overhead to products. For example, assume that WWC has chosen total ounces of eye products as the overhead allocation base for vision care. If the division expects to produce 2,250,000 ounces of eye products in 2008, the overhead cost assigned to each ounce of product would be $0.75, or ($1,681,730 ÷ 2,250,000).

For simplicity, cost behavior in all departments has been ignored. A more appropriate allocation process would specify different bases in each department for the variable and fixed costs. Such differentiation would not change the allocation process but would change the results of the three methods (direct, step, or algebraic). Separation of variable and fixed costs would provide more accurate allocation; use of the computer makes this process more practical than otherwise.

Before making any allocations, management should be certain that the allocation bases are reasonable. Allocations are often based on the easiest available measure, such as number of people employed or number of documents processed. Use of such measures can distort the allocation process.

Allocating support department costs to operating divisions makes managers more aware of, and responsible for, controlling support service usage. However, if such allocations are made, evaluation of the operating division managers' performance should exclude these allocations. The operating division managers can control their usage of support services but not the actual incurrence of support department costs. The financial performance of an operating department manager should be evaluated using an incremental, rather than a full allocation, approach. For example, the vision care manager's performance should be evaluated using a predetermined overhead rate of approximately $0.12 per unit ($267,600 ÷ 2,250,000 ounces of product) rather than the $0.75 rate discussed earlier.

An alternative to using cost allocation to assign support costs to operating units is to use a transfer pricing system. A transfer price for goods or services may be set internally so that the "selling" segment can measure its revenue and the "buying" segment can measure its costs.

Transfer Pricing

For an organization to be profitable, revenues must cover all costs, including those incurred by support departments. These costs can be allocated internally to user departments based on the methods shown earlier in this chapter, or support services can be "sold" to user departments using transfer prices. In either case, support department costs are included in the costs of operating departments. Top management must determine which method (allocation or transfer pricing) produces the most useful information.

Because they are internally set, transfer prices are always eliminated for external reporting purposes, leaving only the actual cost of the items on balance sheets or income statements.[5] The practice of using transfer prices for products is well established; using transfer prices for services is becoming more prevalent. A pseudo-profit center is created when one responsibility center uses a transfer price to artificially "sell" goods or services to another responsibility center: the selling center has artificial revenues and profits, and the buying center has an artificially inflated product or service cost.[6]

Various motivations exist for adopting transfer pricing systems. Transfer prices can be established to promote goal congruence, make performance evaluation among segments more comparable, and/or "transform" a cost center into a profit center. A typical reason includes the desire to motivate managers and make them more entrepreneurial. If used, transfer prices should ensure

[5]Elimination of transfer prices within a company is similar to the elimination of any markup on the sale of inventory between a company and its subsidiaries (or among the subsidiaries of a single company) in preparing consolidated financial statements.
[6]Pseudo-profit centers have been discussed for many years. One article by Ralph L. Benke Jr. and James Don Edwards, "Should You Use Transfer Pricing to Create Pseudo-Profit Centers?" appeared in *Management Accounting* (now *Strategic Finance*) in February 1981. Such centers (termed *microprofit centers*) were also discussed at great length by Robin Cooper in *When Lean Enterprises Collide* (Boston: Harvard Business School Press, 1995).

optimal resource allocation and promote operating efficiency. Often transfer pricing systems are used when the selling unit offers services both inside and outside of the organization. Using transfer prices for services between organizational units has several advantages, as described in Exhibit 13–16.

Transfer prices for goods or services can be calculated in a number of ways, but the following general rules are appropriate.

- The maximum price should be no higher than the lowest market price at which the buying segment can acquire the goods or services externally.

- The minimum price should be no less than the sum of the selling segment's incremental costs associated with the goods or services plus the opportunity cost of the facilities used.[7]

To illustrate these rules, assume that a product is available from external suppliers at a price below the minimum price of the internal supplier. The immediate short-run decision could be for the internal selling division to stop production and for the purchasing division to buy the product from the external suppliers. This decision might be reasonable because, compared with the external suppliers, the selling division does not appear to be cost-efficient in its production activities. Stopping production would release the facilities for other, more profitable, purposes. A longer-run solution could be to have the selling division improve its efficiency and reduce the cost of making the product internally. This solution could be implemented without stopping internal production, but some external purchases might be made until costs have been reduced.

The difference between the upper and lower transfer price limits is the corporate "profit" (or savings) generated by producing internally rather than buying externally. Transfer prices act to "divide the corporate profit" between the buying and selling segments. For external statements, such "divided profits" are irrelevant because they are eliminated. For internal reporting, these "profits" can be extremely important. If managerial performance is evaluated on a competitive basis, both buying and selling segment managers want to maximize their financial results in the responsibility accounting reports. The supplier-segment manager tries to obtain the highest transfer (selling) price, whereas the buying-segment manager tries to acquire the goods or services at the lowest transfer (purchase) price. Thus, transfer prices should be agreed on by the company's selling and buying segments.

EXHIBIT 13–16
Advantages of Transfer Prices for Services

	Revenue Departments	Service Departments
User Involvement	Encourage ways to improve services to benefit users	Promote development of services more beneficial to users
Cost Consciousness	Relate to services used; restrict usage to those that are necessary and cost beneficial	Relate to cost of services provided; must justify transfer price established
Performance Evaluations	Include costs for making performance evaluations if control exists over amount of services used	Promote making a service department a profit center rather than a cost center and thus provide more performance evaluation measures

[7]Typically, the cost-based amount used by the buying division reflects only the variable costs of the selling division.

LO.6
What types of transfer prices are used in organizations, and why are such prices used?

Types of Transfer Prices

There are three traditional types of transfer prices: cost-based, market-based, and negotiated. Exhibit 13–17 lists some questions that should be addressed for each type of transfer price. A discussion of each method and its advantages and disadvantages follows. Numerical examples of transfer price calculations are given in the Demonstration Problem at the end of the chapter.

Cost-Based Transfer Prices

A cost-based transfer price would seem simple to implement until one realizes there are many definitions of the term *cost*, ranging from variable production cost to absorption cost plus additional amounts for selling and administrative costs (and, possibly, opportunity cost) of the selling unit. If only variable costs are used to set a transfer price, the selling division has little incentive to sell to another internal division because no contribution margin is generated on the transfer to help cover fixed costs. Transfer prices based on absorption cost at least provide a contribution toward covering the selling division's fixed production overhead.

Modifications can be made to reduce the problems of cost-based transfer prices. When variable cost is used as a base, an additional amount can be added to cover some fixed costs and provide a measure of profit to the selling division. This adjustment is an example of a cost-plus arrangement. Some managers think cost-plus arrangements are acceptable substitutes for market-based transfer

---

EXHIBIT 13–17
Types of Transfer Prices and Related Questions of Use

Cost Based

1. What should be included in cost?
   Variable production costs
   Total variable cost
   Absorption production costs
   "Adjusted" absorption production costs

2. Should cost be actual or standard?

3. Should a profit margin for the selling division be included?

Market Based

1. What if there is no exact counterpart in the market?

2. What if internal sales create a cost savings (such as not having bad debts) that would not exist in external sales?

3. What if the market price is currently depressed?

4. Which market price should be used?

Negotiated

1. Do both parties have the ability to bargain with autonomy?

2. How will disputes be handled?

3. Are comparable product substitutes available externally?

prices, especially when market prices for comparable substitute products are unavailable. Absorption cost can be modified by adding an amount equal to an average of the nonproduction costs associated with the product and/or an amount for profit to the selling division. In contrast, a transfer price could be set at less than absorption cost if there is no other use for the idle capacity or if there are estimated savings (such as reduced packaging) in production costs on internally transferred goods.

Another consideration in a cost-based transfer price is whether actual or standard cost is used. Actual costs can vary according to the season, production volume, and other factors, whereas standard costs can be specified in advance and are stable measures of efficient production costs. Thus, standard costs provide a superior basis for transfer pricing. Any variances from standard are borne by the selling segment; otherwise, the selling division's efficiencies or inefficiencies are passed on to the buying division. Relative to services, cost-based transfer prices are generally used for low-cost and low-volume services such as temporary maintenance and temporary office staff assistance.

Market-Based Transfer Prices

To eliminate the problems of defining "cost," some companies simply use a market price approach to setting transfer prices. Market price is believed to be an objective, arm's-length measure of value that simulates the selling price that would be offered and paid if the subunits were independent, autonomous companies. If operating efficiently relative to the competition, a selling division should be able to show a profit when transferring products or services at market prices. Similarly, an efficiently operating buying division should not be troubled by a market-based transfer price because that is what would have to be paid for the goods or services if the alternative of buying internally did not exist. Relative to the transfer of services, market-based transfer prices are effective for common high-cost and high-volume standardized services such as storage and transportation.

Several problems can exist, however, with the use of market prices for intracompany transfers. First, transfers can involve products having no exact counterpart in the external market, which means there will be no established market price. Second, market price is not entirely appropriate for some transfers because internal sales can provide cost savings by reducing bad debts and/or packaging, advertising, or delivery expenditures. Third, if the external market is experiencing a temporary reduction in demand for the product, there is a question of whether the current "depressed" price or the expected long-run market price should be used as the transfer price. Fourth, different prices, discounts, and credit terms are allowed to different buyers, so there is a question of which is the "right" market price to use.

Negotiated Transfer Prices

Because of the problems associated with both cost- and market-based prices, negotiated transfer prices are often set through a process of bargaining between the selling and purchasing unit managers. Such prices are typically below the normal market price paid by the buying unit but above the selling unit's combined incremental and opportunity costs. If internal sales would eliminate any variable selling costs, such costs are not considered. If external sales do not exist or a division cannot downsize its facilities, no opportunity cost is involved.

Ability to negotiate a transfer price implies that segment managers have the autonomy to sell or buy products externally if internal negotiations fail. Because such extensive autonomy could lead to dysfunctional behavior and suboptimization, top management can provide a means of arbitrating a price in the event that the units cannot agree.

Negotiated transfer prices are often used for services because their value—as shown through expertise, reliability, convenience, or responsiveness—is often qualitative and can be assessed only judgmentally from the perspective of the parties involved. The transfer price should depend on the cost and volume level of the service as well as whether comparable substitutes are available. Negotiated transfer prices are commonly used for customized high-cost and high-volume services such as risk management and specialized executive training.

To encourage cooperation between the transferring divisions, top management can consider joint divisional profits as one performance measurement for both the selling and the buying unit managers. Another way of reducing the difficulties in establishing a transfer price is simply to use a dual pricing approach.

Dual Pricing

A **dual pricing arrangement** provides different transfer prices for the selling and buying segments by allowing the seller to record the transfer of goods or services at a market or negotiated market price and the purchaser to record the transfer at a cost-based amount.[8] This arrangement provides a profit margin on the goods transferred from the selling division but a minimal cost to the buying division. Dual pricing eliminates the problem of having to artificially divide the profits between the selling and buying segments and allows managers to have the most relevant information for decision making and performance evaluation. However, an internal reconciliation (similar to that used in preparing consolidated statements when intercompany sales are made between the consolidated entities at an amount other than cost) is needed to adjust revenues and costs when company external financial statements are prepared.

Selecting a Transfer Pricing System

Setting a reasonable transfer price is not an easy task. Everyone involved in the process must be aware of both positive and negative aspects of each type of transfer price and be responsive to suggestions for change. Determination of which type of transfer pricing system to use should reflect the organizational units' characteristics as well as corporate goals. No single method of setting a transfer price is best in all instances. Also, transfer prices are not intended to be permanent; they are frequently revised in relation to changes in costs, supply, demand, competitive forces, and other factors. Flexibility by the selling segment to increase a transfer price when reduced productive capacity is present or to decrease a transfer price when excess productive capacity exists is a strong management lever. Regardless of what method is used, a good transfer price provides

- an appropriate basis for the calculation and evaluation of segment performance,
- the rational acquisition or use of goods and services between corporate divisions,
- the flexibility to respond to changes in demand or market conditions, and
- a means of motivation to encourage and reward goal congruence by managers in decentralized operations.

  In contrast, transfer prices can also create the following potential problems:

- Disagreement between organizational unit managers as to how the transfer price should be set.
- Additional organizational costs and employee time.
- The inability to work equally well for all departments or divisions. For example, support departments that do not provide measurable benefits or cannot show a distinct cause-and-effect relationship between cost behavior and service use by other departments should not attempt to use transfer prices.
- Dysfunctional behavior among organizational units or underutilization or overutilization of services.
- Complicated tax planning in multinational companies.

A company should weigh the advantages and disadvantages of transfer prices before instituting such a system.

LO.7
What difficulties can be encountered by multinational companies using transfer prices?

Transfer Prices in Multinational Settings

Because of the differences in tax systems, customs duties, freight and insurance costs, import/export regulations, and foreign-exchange controls, setting transfer prices for products and services becomes extremely difficult when the company is engaged in multinational operations. In addition, as shown in Exhibit 13–18, the internal and external objectives of transfer pricing policies differ in multinational entities.

[8]Opportunity cost is discussed in Chapter 10.

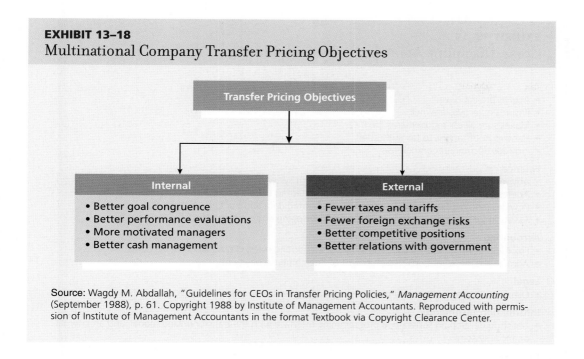

EXHIBIT 13–18
Multinational Company Transfer Pricing Objectives

Source: Wagdy M. Abdallah, "Guidelines for CEOs in Transfer Pricing Policies," *Management Accounting* (September 1988), p. 61. Copyright 1988 by Institute of Management Accountants. Reproduced with permission of Institute of Management Accountants in the format Textbook via Copyright Clearance Center.

Whereas multinational companies can use one transfer price when they send a product to or receive it from one country, they can use a totally different transfer price for the same product when it is sent to or received from another country. However, the company should set guidelines on transfer pricing policies that are followed on a consistent basis. For example, a company should not price certain parent company services to foreign subsidiaries in a manner that would send the majority of those costs to the subsidiary in the country with the highest tax rate unless that method of pricing is reasonable and equitable to all subsidiaries. The general test of reasonableness is that a transfer price should reflect an arm's-length transaction. In establishing a transfer pricing system, a company should utilize a group of individuals who represent numerous discipline areas. Exhibit 13-19 indicates which areas should be involved and what the functions of those areas should be.

Tax authorities in both the home and host countries carefully scrutinize multinational transfer prices because such prices determine which country taxes the income from the transfer. The U.S. Congress is concerned about both U.S. multinationals operating in low-tax-rate countries and foreign companies operating in the United States. In either situation, Congress believes that companies could avoid paying U.S. corporate income taxes because of misleading or inaccurate transfer pricing. Thus, the Internal Revenue Service (IRS) can be quick to investigate U.S. subsidiaries that operate in low-tax areas and suddenly have unusually high profits. The IRS will grant advance pricing agreements (APAs), which are binding contracts with a company that provide details of how a transfer price is to be set and establishes that no adjustments or penalties will be made if the agreed-upon methodology is used. These agreements usually run for three to five years and may be renewed if no major changes occur. APAs also help eliminate the possibility of double taxation on the exchange of goods or services. Information from the U.S. IRS Web site indicates that the majority of transfer pricing methods used in APAs for tangible and intangible property as well as services are based on cost plus a profit margin.[9] One disadvantage of seeking an APA is that several years typically pass before IRS approval is granted, but an important advantage is that APAs may fulfill documentation requirements under the Sarbanes-Oxley Act of 2002 (SOX) to substantiate "proper allocation of revenues and expenses" making the "development of effective, SOX-compliant internal controls more attainable and acceptable."[10]

[9]Internal Revenue Service, "Announcement and Report Concerning Advance Pricing Agreements" (March 30, 2004); http://www.irs.gov/pub/irs-utl/apa03.pdf (last accessed 8/13/07).
[10]Mitch McGhee, "SOX and APAs: A Look at Their Compatibility," *Strategic Finance* (May 2007), p. 15ff.

EXHIBIT 13–19
Cross-Discipline Approach to Transfer Pricing

Tax
- Acts as project driver
- Ensures objectives are met
- Makes sure all tax requirements are met
- Handles notifications to tax authorities
- Provides documentation/defense

Finance
- Advises on and develops solutions for management systems
- Addresses the ability of the financial reporting system to handle implications of transfer pricing
- Provides required financial data, including segmented data and budgets
- Assists in (or takes primary responsibility for) developing and running transfer pricing models

Accounting
- Provides information on accounting systems, accounting rules, consolidation of accounts
- Administers invoicing/booking/settlement of intercompany payments

Legal
- Oversees development of intercompany legal agreements and legal pricing requirements

Information Technology
- Assists in developing software, a programming interface with the transfer pricing model, and an internal financial system

Customs
- Assesses valuation, duty impacts, and representation and notification requirements

Operations: Members with Global Business Experience
- Assist in determining foreign implications of transfer pricing policy
- Act as intermediaries between U.S. and foreign businesspeople
- May be structured similarly to U.S. core team

Outside Advisers
- Bring industry best practices to the internal team
- Provide access to resources around the world experienced in international tax, transfer pricing, valuation, VAT, and customs
- Offer insight into expectations of auditors with respect to tax provision, including FAS 109, FIN 48, and Sarbanes-Oxley requirements

Source: KPMG LLP (U.S.), *Improving Transfer Pricing Risk Management in High-Technology Companies* (2007), p. 12 (http://www.kpmg.com/NR/rdonlyres/49B2DD91-314E-41F6-AB81-5E150AAC8B76/0/ImprovingTransferPricingRiskManagementinHighTechnologyCompanies.pdf).

According to the *Ernst & Young 2005–2006 Global Transfer Pricing Surveys*, transfer pricing is often the most important international tax issue for governments and multinational enterprises (MNEs); additionally, audits by tax authorities are becoming the rule rather than the exception, with almost 70 percent of the survey respondents having undergone a transfer pricing audit in the three years prior to the survey.[11] Exhibit 13-20 indicates the types of circumstances that often trigger transfer pricing audits.

More countries are adopting transfer pricing legislation and, as MNEs begin doing business in a new country, they must comply with that country's tax requirements relative to transfer pricing. The Organization for Economic Cooperation and Development has been actively involved in helping to establish internationally accepted procedures for APAs. In February 2007, the European Commission adopted EU-wide guidelines on APAs so as "to avoid costly and time-consuming tax examinations into the transactions included in the APA, relieve the large administrative burden on taxpayers, and eliminate double taxation" within the EU.[12]

[11]Ernst & Young, *2005–2006 Global Transfer Pricing Surveys: Global Transfer Pricing Trends, Practices, and Analysis* (November 2005); http://www.ey.com/global/download.nsf/International/Transfer_Pricing_Global_Surveys_Q4_2005/$file/GlobalTPSurvey_Q4_2005.pdf (last accessed 8/13/07).
[12]PricewaterhouseCoopers, "New EU Guidelines to Avoid Transfer Pricing Disputes," *International Tax Review* (April 2007), p. 1.

EXHIBIT 13–20
Circumstances Most Likely to Trigger Transfer Pricing Audits (in Parent Companies)

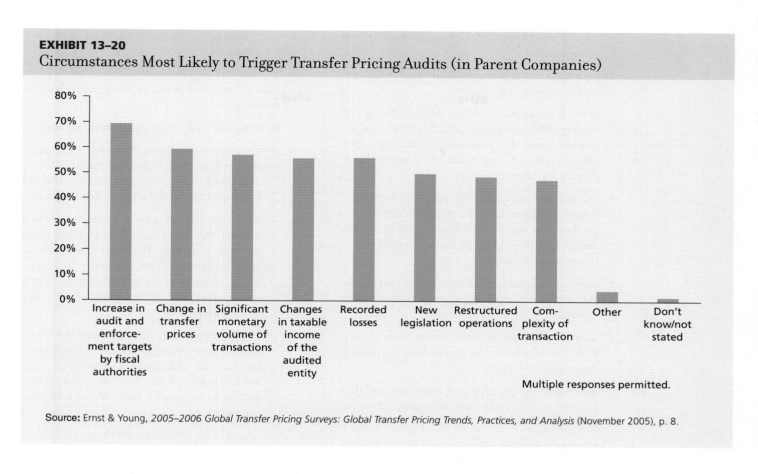

Multiple responses permitted.

Source: Ernst & Young, *2005–2006 Global Transfer Pricing Surveys: Global Transfer Pricing Trends, Practices, and Analysis* (November 2005), p. 8.

Similar to those in international settings, multistate firms can employ transfer pricing strategies to move profits from state to state. Firms can take advantage not only of different income tax rates across states using transfer pricing arrangements but also of the fact that a few states impose no income tax at all.

Comprehensive Review Module

Chapter Summary

1. Decentralization is generally appropriate for companies that

    -   are mature.

    -   are large.

    -   are in a growth stage of product development.

    -   are growing rapidly.

    -   can financially withstand incorrect decisions.

    -   have high confidence in the employees' decision-making ability.

    -   have widespread operations.

    -   want to challenge, motivate, and mentor employees.

- require rapid response to changing conditions or opportunities.

2. Decentralization and responsibility accounting are related in that decentralization

   - is made to work effectively through the use of responsibility accounting, which provides information about the performance, efficiency, and effectiveness of organizational responsibility centers and their managers.

   - implies the acceptance of authority by subordinate managers, and the responsibility reports produced by the responsibility account system indicate the "rolling up" of that authority back to upper management.

   - requires each responsibility center to report on the activities under its manager's immediate control.

   - uses the principle of management by exception, which is reflected in the successively aggregated responsibility reports.

   - seeks goal congruence and uses responsibility reports to highlight any suboptimization of resources.

3. The four primary types of responsibility centers and the characteristics of each are

   - cost centers, in which managers are primarily responsible for controlling costs.

   - revenue centers, in which managers are primarily responsible for generating revenues; in some instances, managers have control over revenues and some costs. Revenue centers can calculate variances as follows:

   where
   ASP = actual sales price
   ASV = actual sales volume
   BSP = budgeted sales price
   BSV = budgeted sales volume

   - profit centers, in which managers are responsible for generating revenue, controlling costs, and maximizing their units' incomes.

   - investment centers, in which managers are responsible for generating revenue, controlling costs, and producing a satisfactory return on the asset base under their control.

4. Support department costs are allocated to producing departments

   - to meet the objectives of full cost computation, managerial motivation, or managerial decision making.

   - by using the direct, step, or algebraic method.

     ➤ The direct method assigns support department costs only to operating departments but does not consider assistance that can be provided from one support department to another.

     ➤ The step method uses a benefits-provided ranking that lists support departments from the one providing the most assistance to other departments to the one providing assistance primarily to the operating areas. Costs are assigned from each department in order of the ranking.

     ➤ The algebraic method recognizes the interrelationships among all departments through the use of simultaneous equations. This method provides the best allocation information and is readily adaptable to computer computations.

5. Transfer prices are intracompany charges for goods or services bought and sold between segments of a decentralized company. Such prices are

   - typically cost-based, market-based, or negotiated; a dual pricing system can also be used to assign different transfer prices to the selling and buying units.

   - set between an upper price bound, which is the lowest market price at which the product/service can be acquired externally, and the lowest price bound, which is the incremental cost of production or performance plus the opportunity cost of the facilities used.

   - used in organizations to

     ➤ enhance goal congruence.

     ➤ make performance evaluations among segments more comparable.

     ➤ change a cost center into a pseudo–profit center.

     ➤ ensure optimal resource allocations.

     ➤ promote responsibility center autonomy.

     ➤ encourage motivation and communication among responsibility center managers.

6. Multinational companies using transfer prices encounter difficulties, including

- differences in tax systems, customs duties, freight and insurance costs, import/export regulations, and foreign-exchange controls.

- the ability to determine what transfer price would be considered "reasonable," as though generated in an arm's-length transaction.

- the increase in transfer pricing audits by tax authorities.

- the length of time required to have an advanced pricing agreement approved by appropriate tax authorities.

Potential Ethical Issues

1. Having managers engage in suboptimization techniques that benefit themselves to the detriment of the overall firm

2. Creating responsibility reports that "bury" important details needed to accurately evaluate managerial performance in summary data

3. Allocating support department costs using an "ability-to-bear" criterion that results in profit-detrimental actions

4. Improperly estimating the benefits provided between departments to shift support department costs inappropriately

5. Establishing a transfer pricing system that does not allow managers who will be judged on profitability performance to buy or sell externally

6. Engaging in transfer pricing techniques that improperly shift costs to low- or no-tax locations ▲

Solution Strategies

Transfer Prices (Cost-Based, Market-Based, Negotiated, Dual)

Upper limit: Lowest price available from external suppliers

Feasible region for setting a transfer price

Lower limit: Incremental costs of producing and selling the transferred goods or services plus the opportunity cost of the facilities used

Service Department Cost Allocation

Direct Method

1. Determine rational and systematic allocation bases for each support department.

2. Assign costs from each support department directly to operating areas using specified allocation bases. No costs are assigned to support areas.

Step Method

1. Determine rational and systematic allocation bases for each support department.

2. List support departments in a benefits-provided ranking from the one that provides the most assistance to all other areas (both operating and support) to the one that provides assistance only to operating areas.

3. Beginning with the first support department listed, allocate the costs from that department to all remaining departments; repeat the process until only operating departments remain.

Algebraic Method

1. Determine rational and systematic allocation bases for each department.

2. Develop equations that express the costs of, and service relationships among, each support area.

3. Solve the simultaneous equations for the support departments through an iterative process or by computer until all values are known.

4. Allocate costs using allocation bases developed in step 2. Eliminate "reallocated" costs from consideration.

Demonstration Problem

RaceFest Inc. has two operating divisions. The Ski Division (SD) makes water and snow skis, and the Binding Division (BD) makes rubber boots for water skis. The Binding Division estimates that 800,000 pairs of boots will be produced in 2008; of those, 600,000 pairs will be sold internally and 200,000 pairs will be sold externally. Managers of the two divisions are in the process of determining a transfer price for a pair of boots. The following information for the Binding Division is available:

Direct material	$27	
Direct labor	12	
Variable overhead	7	
Variable S&A (both for external and internal sales)	4	
Total variable cost		$50
Fixed overhead (rate based on estimated annual production)	$10	
Fixed selling and administrative (rate based on estimated annual sales)	5	
Total fixed cost		15
Total cost per pair of boots		$65
Markup on total variable cost (40%)		20
List price to external customers		$85

Required:

a. Determine a transfer price based on variable production cost.

b. Determine a transfer price based on total variable production cost plus normal markup.

c. Determine a transfer price based on full production cost.

d. Determine a transfer price based on total cost per pair of boots.

e. Prepare the journal entries for the Binding (selling) and Ski (buying) segments if the transfer is made at the external selling price for the selling division and the full production cost for the buying division.

f. Assume that the Binding Division has no alternative use for the facilities that make the rubber boots for internal transfer. Also assume that the Ski Division can buy equivalent boots externally for $80. Calculate the upper and lower limits for which the transfer price should be set.

g. Compute a transfer price that divides the "profit" between the two divisions equally.

h. In contrast to the assumption in part (f), assume that a large portion of the facilities in which boots are produced can be rented for $600,000 if the Binding Division makes boots only for external sale. Determine the lower limit of the transfer price.

Solution to Demonstration Problem

a.	Direct material	$27
	Direct labor	12
	Variable overhead	7
	Transfer price	$46

b.

Total variable cost	$50
Markup (40%)	20
Transfer price	$70

c.

Variable production cost	$46
Fixed production cost	10
Transfer price	$56

d.

Total variable cost	$50
Total fixed cost	15
Transfer price	$65

e. Binding Division:

Accounts Receivable—Ski Division (600,000 × $56)	33,600,000	
Intracompany Profits* (600,000 × $29)	17,400,000	
Intracompany Sales* (600,000 × $85)		51,000,000
Intracompany Cost of Goods Sold (CGS)* (600,000 × $56)	33,600,000	
Finished Goods (600,000 × $56)		33,600,000

Note: When company income statements are prepared, these amounts would be eliminated as follows:

Intracompany Sales	51,000,000	
Intracompany CGS		33,600,000
Intracompany Profits		17,400,000

In addition, any remaining amounts of intracompany Accounts Receivable and Accounts Payable shown by the two divisions would be eliminated.

Ski Division:

Inventory (600,000 × $56)	33,600,000	
Accounts Payable—Binding Division		33,600,000

f. Upper limit: Ski Division's external purchase price = $80
Lower limit: Total variable cost of Binding Division = $50

g. (Lower limit + Upper limit) ÷ 2 = ($50 + $80) ÷ 2 = $130 ÷ 2 = $65

h. $600,000 ÷ 600,000 pairs of boots = $1 opportunity cost per pair
Lower limit: Incremental variable cost of Binding Division + Opportunity cost = $50 + $1 = $51

Key Terms

administrative department, **p. 469**

advance pricing agreement (APA), **p. 483**

algebraic method, **p. 472**

benefits-provided ranking, **p. 471**

centralization, **p. 462**

cost center, **p. 467**

decentralization, **p. 462**

direct method, **p. 471**

dual pricing arrangement, **p. 482**

goal congruence, **p. 465**

investment center, **p. 469**

negotiated transfer price, **p. 481**

profit center, **p. 469**

pseudo-profit center, **p. 478**

responsibility accounting system, **p. 464**

responsibility center, **p. 466**

responsibility report, **p. 464**

revenue center, **p. 467**

sales price variance, **p. 468**

sales volume variance, **p. 468**

service department, **p. 469**

step method, **p. 471**

suboptimization, **p. 469**

support department, **p. 469**

transfer price, **p. 478**

Questions

1. Billi Barnes is the president and chief operating officer of Barnes Electronics. She founded the company and has led it to its prominent place in the electronics field. She has manufacturing plants and outlets in 40 states. Barnes is finding, however, that she cannot "keep track" of things the way she did in the past. Discuss the advantages and disadvantages of decentralizing the firm's decision-making activities among the various local and regional managers. Also discuss what functions Barnes might want to be performed centrally and why she would choose these functions.

2. Why are responsibility reports prepared? Is it appropriate for a single responsibility report to be prepared for a division of a major company? Why or why not?

3. What is suboptimization, and what factors contribute to it in a decentralized firm?

4. Why are support department costs often allocated to operating departments? Is such an allocation process always useful from a decision-making standpoint? How might support department cost allocation create a feeling of cost responsibility among managers of operating departments?

5. "The four criteria for selecting an allocation base for support department costs should be applied equally." Discuss the merits of this statement.

6. Compare and contrast the direct, step, and algebraic methods of allocating support department costs. What are the advantages and disadvantages of each method?

7. When the algebraic method of allocating support department costs is used, total costs for each support department increase from what they were prior to the allocation. Why does this occur, and how are the additional costs treated?

8. What are transfer prices, and why do companies use them? How could the use of transfer prices improve or impair goal congruence?

9. Would transfer prices be used in each of the following responsibility centers: cost, revenue, profit, and investment? If so, how would they be used?

10. What problems might be encountered when attempting to implement a cost-based transfer pricing system? A market-based transfer pricing system?

11. What is dual pricing? What is the intended effect of dual pricing on the performance of each division affected by the dual price?

12. How can support departments use transfer prices, and what advantages do transfer prices have over cost allocation methods?

13. Explain why the determination of transfer prices is more complex in a multinational, rather than in a domestic, setting.

Exercises

14. **LO.1 (Centralization vs. decentralization)** Indicate whether a firm exhibiting each of the following characteristics would more likely be centralized (C) or decentralized (D).
    a. Two years old
    b. Widely dispersed operating units
    c. Growth stage of product development
    d. Tight management control
    e. High level of organizational flexibility
    f. Wary of financial impacts of incorrect subordinate management decisions
    g. Stable market environment
    h. Subordinates highly trained and mentored in decision-making skills
    i. Few employees
    j. Slow growth rate
    k. Large number of employees who telecommute

15. **LO.1 (Decentralization advantages and disadvantages)** Indicate whether each of the following is a potential advantage (A) or disadvantage (D) of decentralization. If an item is neither an advantage nor a disadvantage, use N.
    a. Speed of decisions
    b. Provision of increased job satisfaction

    c. Development of leadership qualities
    d. Placement of decision maker closer to time and place of problem
    e. Support of training in decision making
    f. Promotion of goal congruence
    g. Delegation of ultimate responsibility
    h. Use of management-by-exception principle by top management
    i. Cost of developing the planning and reporting system
    j. Complication of communication process

16. **LO.1 (Centralization vs. decentralization)** Many companies are trying to determine the best organizational structure for information technology (IT) operations. In the 1980s, the reduced cost of computing technology and human resources caused many companies to decentralize the IT operations; this trend began to shift back to centralization during the past 10 years. Gather research to compare and contrast the advantages and disadvantages of centralized and decentralized IT operations. What other important information would you need to make a decision on such an organizational structure?

17. **LO.1 & LO.6 (Decentralization; transfer prices; research)** Search the Internet to identify three highly decentralized companies. Based on the information you find on each, either determine directly or infer the types of responsibility centers used by these companies. Also, determine or speculate about whether the companies use transfer prices or allocation of costs for intracompany transfers of services. Prepare a report on your findings and inferences. In cases for which you had to infer, explain what information or reasoning led you to that inference. Why is decentralization appropriate for some companies but not for others?

18. **LO.3 (Responsibility centers)** For each of the following organizational units, indicate whether the unit would most likely be classified as a cost center (C), a revenue center (R), a profit center (P), or an investment center (I).
    a. Housekeeping department of a hotel
    b. City ticket office of an airline
    c. Laundry of a for-profit hospital
    d. Corporate-owned local outlet of a fast-food restaurant
    e. Fine jewelry counter in a local department store
    f. Long-term parking lot at a regional airport
    g. London office of an international public accounting firm
    h. Gift shop in a national state park
    i. Grounds department of a private university
    j. Bloodmobile of a local hospital
    k. Local public television station's fund-raising telethon staffed by volunteers
    l. Sales representative for a college textbook publisher

19. **LO.3 (Responsibility centers; research)** Go to your university's Web site and review the various organizational units within the university. Assuming no transfer pricing exists, make a list of the units that you believe would be classified as cost centers and profit centers.

20. **LO.3 (Profit centers and allocations; research)** Multiple-doctor medical practices are often structured with each doctor acting as a profit center.
    a. Discuss why such an organizational structure would be useful.
    b. Go to the Web and find some software packages that could be used to account for such an organizational structure.
    c. List some costs of a medical practice that would be directly traceable to each physician.
    d. List some costs of a medical practice that might not be directly traceable to each physician. Provide possible allocation bases for such costs.

21. **LO.4 (Revenue variances)** For 2008, Bach Company planned to sell 200,000 units at a $40 selling price. In early 2009, the company president asked the manager of the Marketing Division why budgeted revenue had not been achieved. Investigation revealed the following information:

Actual sales volume	206,000 units
Actual selling price	$38 per unit

Analyze the information given and prepare an explanation for Bach's president.

22. **LO.4 (Revenue variances)** As sales manager of a dairy, you have been asked by the company owner why sales of milk are below budget. Review of the budget indicates that revenue was expected to be $210,000, based on expected sales of 420,000 gallons at $0.50. The sales records indicate that 430,000 gallons of milk were actually sold at $0.48 per gallon. Analyze revenues and explain what occurred.

23. **LO.4 (Revenue variances)** James Cook delivers two-day statistical process control seminars for manufacturing workers. For each program, a $4,000 fee is normally paid. In 2007, Cook presented 30 seminars, and he budgeted a 20 percent increase in seminars for 2008. At the end of 2008, Cook is disappointed that his actual revenue is only $136,500. He presented 39 seminars during the year.
   a. What was Cook's expected revenue for 2008?
   b. What were Cook's sales price and sales volume variances?
   c. Discuss why Cook did not achieve his budgeted 2008 revenue.

24. **LO.5 (Direct method)** Griffin Corporation uses the direct method to allocate support department costs to production departments (fabricating and finishing). Information for June 2008 follows:

	Human Resources	Administration
Service department costs	$420,000	$300,000
Services provided to other departments		
Human resources		10%
Administration	15%	
Fabricating	40%	55%
Finishing	45%	35%

   a. What amounts of human resources and administration costs should be assigned to fabricating for June?
   b. What amounts of human resources and administration costs should be assigned to finishing for June?

25. **LO.5 (Direct method)** Cressida Bank has three support areas (administration, human resources, and accounting) and three revenue-generating areas (checking accounts, savings accounts, and loans). Monthly direct costs and the interdepartmental support structure are shown in the following benefits-provided ranking.

		PERCENTAGE OF SERVICE USED BY					
Department	Direct Costs	Admin.	Human Resources	Accounting	Checking	Savings	Loans
Administration	$360,000		10%	10%	30%	40%	10%
Human Resources	240,000	10%		10	30	20	30
Accounting	200,000	10	10		40	20	20
Checking	280,000						
Savings	150,000						
Loans	300,000						

   Compute the total cost for each revenue-generating area of the bank using the direct method.

26. **LO.5 (Step method)** Use the information in Exercise 25 to compute total cost for each revenue-generating area if Cressida Bank uses the step method of cost allocation. (The support department columns will not sum to zero because of rounding.)

27. **LO.5 (Step method)** Leander Mfg. has three support departments (human resources, administration, and maintenance) and two revenue-generating departments (assembly and finishing). The company uses the step method to allocate support department costs to operating departments. In October 2008, human resources incurred $240,000 of costs, administration incurred $370,000, and maintenance incurred $110,000. Proportions of services provided to other departments for October 2008 follow:

	Human Resources	Administration	Maintenance
Human resources		10%	5%
Administration	15%		10
Maintenance	10	15	
Assembly	45	50	50
Finishing	30	25	35

   a. Assuming that the departments are listed in a benefits-provided ranking, what amount of cost should be assigned from human resources to each of the other departments? From administration? From maintenance?
   b. What total support department cost was assigned to assembly in October? To finishing?
   c. Explain why the cost allocation is affected by the order in which costs are assigned.

28. **LO.5 (Algebraic method)** Use the information for Cressida Bank in Exercise 25 to compute the total cost for each revenue-generating area using the algebraic method.

29. **LO.5 (Algebraic method)** The following chart indicates the percentage of support department services used by other departments. Service departments are designated S1, S2, and S3; operating departments are designated RP1 and RP2.

Department	SERVICES USED				
	S1	S2	S3	RP1	RP2
S1	n/a	10%	20%	30%	40%
S2	40%	n/a	30	20	10
S3	20	30	n/a	40	10

Costs of the period were $112,000, $240,000, and $360,000 for S1, S2, and S3, respectively. Allocate the support department costs to the operating departments using the algebraic method.

30. **LO.6 (Transfer pricing in support departments)** Indicate whether each of the following statements constitutes a potential advantage (A), disadvantage (D), or neither (N) of using transfer prices for support department costs.

a. Can increase resource waste

b. Can make a support department into a profit center

c. Can cause certain services to be under- or overutilized

d. Can put all support departments on an equal footing

e. Can require additional organizational data and employee time

f. Can reduce goal congruence

g. Can increase communication about what additional services are needed and which can be reduced or eliminated

h. Can make users and providers more cost conscious

i. Can improve ability to evaluate performance

j. Can increase disagreements among departments

31. **LO.6 (Transfer pricing)** Irmela Division, a subsidiary of Siberia Ltd., manufactures computer chips with the following costs:

Direct material	$10.00
Direct labor	17.50
Variable overhead	8.50
Fixed overhead	12.00
Total	$48.00

Some of the chips are sold externally for $108.75; others are transferred internally to the Gerhardt Division. Irmela Division's plant manager wants to establish a reasonable transfer price for chips transferred to Gerhardt. The purchasing manager of Gerhardt Division has informed the plant manager that comparable chips can be purchased externally in a price range from $75 to $115.

a. Determine the upper and lower limits for the transfer price between Irmela Division and Gerhardt Division.

b. If Irmela Division is presently selling all the chips it can produce to external buyers, what minimum price should be set for transfers to Gerhardt Division?

32. **LO.6 (Transfer pricing)** Electronics and Appliances are two investment centers of Alonzo Company. Electronics produces a microprocessor used by Appliances to manufacture several of its products; the microprocessor is also sold externally for $62. The following information is available about the microprocessor:

Total production annually (75% sold internally; 25% sold externally)	800,000 units
Variable production costs	$37
Variable selling costs (includes $4 per unit in advertising cost)	$13
Fixed overhead (allocated on the basis of units of production)	$1,200,000
Fixed selling costs	$1,600,000

Determine the transfer price under each of the following methods:

a. total variable cost

b. full production cost

c. total variable production cost plus necessary selling costs

d. market price

33. **LO.6 (Transfer pricing)** Claremont Co., a profit center of California Enterprises, manufactures brake pads to sell internally to other company divisions as well as externally. A set of Claremont brake pads normally sells for $36. Production and selling costs for a set of brake pads follow:

Direct material	$4.50
Direct labor	5.70
Variable overhead	2.40
Fixed overhead (based on production of 700,000 sets)	8.25
Variable selling expense	1.50

Angeles Co., another division of California Enterprises, wants to purchase 50,000 sets of brake pads from Claremont Co. during the next year. No selling costs are incurred on internal sales.

a. If Claremont's manager can sell all the brake pads it produces externally, what should the minimum transfer price be? Explain.

b. Assume that Claremont Co. is experiencing a slight slowdown in external demand and will be able to sell only 600,000 sets of brake pads externally next year at the $36 selling price. What should be the minimum selling price to Angeles Co. under these conditions? Explain.

c. Assume that Joe Massoud, the manager of Angeles Co., offers to pay Claremont Co.'s production cost plus 25 percent for each set of brake pads. Massoud receives an invoice for $1,303,125 but was planning on only $787,500. How were these amounts determined? What created the confusion? Explain.

34. **LO.6 (Transfer pricing; management motivation)** Yummy's Food Stores operates 20 large supermarkets in the Midwest. Each store is evaluated as a profit center, and store managers have complete control over their purchases and inventory policy. Company policy is that transfers between stores will be made at cost if a store runs short of an item and another store has a sufficient supply.

During a recent period of rapid increases in food prices, company managers noticed that interstore transfers had decreased sharply. Store managers indicated that it was almost impossible to find another store with sufficient inventory to make a transfer when one store ran short of inventory. However, more in-depth checking revealed that many of the other stores did actually have the inventory items on hand.

a. Why would the store managers be reluctant to make the interstore transfers?

b. How could the transfer pricing policy be changed to avoid this type of situation?

35. **LO.6 (Transfer pricing)** Walsdorf Company's information technology department is developing a support department transfer price based on minutes of computer time. For 2008, its expected capacity was 350,000 minutes, and theoretical capacity was 500,000 minutes. Costs of the IT department for 2008 were expected to total $332,500.

a. What is the IT transfer price based on expected capacity?

b. What is the IT transfer price based on full capacity?

c. Actual operating costs in the IT department for 2008 were $350,000, and actual capacity usage was 365,000 minutes. What were the total variances from budget if the IT department used a transfer price based on expected capacity? On full capacity? What are some possible causes of that variance?

36. **LO.7 (International transfer pricing; research)** Use the Internet to identify a multinational company encountering tax problems related to transfer pricing between its organizational units in different countries. Prepare a brief discussion of the issues and the actual or potential consequences.

Problems

37. **LO.1 (Decentralization; ethics)** A large U.S. corporation participates in a highly competitive industry. Company management has decided that decentralization will best allow the company to meet the competition and achieve profit goals. Each responsibility center manager is evaluated on the basis of profit contribution, market penetration, and return on investment. Failure to meet the objectives established by corporate management for these measures is not acceptable and usually results in demotion or dismissal of a center manager.

An anonymous survey of company managers showed that they felt extreme pressure to compromise their personal ethical standards to achieve corporate objectives. For example, managers at certain plants felt it necessary, for cost control purposes, to reduce quality control to such a level that it was uncertain whether all unsafe products were being rejected. Also, sales and human resources were encouraged to use questionable tactics to obtain orders, including offering gifts and other incentives to purchasing agents.

The chief executive officer is disturbed by the survey findings. In her opinion, the company cannot condone such behavior. She concludes that the company should do something about this problem.

a. Discuss what might be the causes for the ethical problems described.

b. Outline a program that could be instituted by the company to help reduce the pressures on managers to compromise personal ethical standards in their work.▲

(CMA adapted)

38. **LO.1 (Decentralization; ethics)** Although centralization and decentralization are commonly discussed in the context of business organizations and distinct, often "far-flung" subunits, the concepts are also applicable within a single building! Consider that, in the 1970s, most hospitals began shifting from centralized nursing stations to decentralized stations that were close to patients' rooms. This trend was thought to make it easier for nurses to attend to patients and to maintain their charts.

a. Why did the shift from centralized stations to decentralized stations take place?

b. What problems could be created by the decentralized nurse stations that did not exist when centralized stations were more common?▲

39. **LO.2 (Responsibility accounting reports)** Rushmore Industries manufactures industrial tools and has annual sales of approximately $3.5 million with no evidence of cyclical demand. R&D is very important to Rushmore because its market share expands only in response to product innovation.

The company controller has designed and implemented a new annual budget system divided into 12 equal segments for use for monthly performance evaluations. The vice president of operations was upset upon receiving the following responsibility report for the machining department for October 2008:

MACHINING DEPARTMENT
Responsibility Report
For the Month Ended October 31, 2008
(in $000s)

	Budget	Actual	Variance
Volume in units	3,000	3,185	185 F
Variable manufacturing costs			
Direct material	$24,000	$ 24,843	$ 843 U
Direct labor	27,750	29,302	1,552 U
Variable factory overhead	33,300	35,035	1,735 U
Total	$85,050	$ 89,180	$4,130 U
Fixed manufacturing costs			
Indirect labor	$ 3,300	$ 3,334	$ 34 U
Depreciation	1,500	1,500	0
Property tax	300	300	0
Insurance	240	240	0
Other	930	1,027	97 U
Total	$ 6,270	$ 6,401	$ 131 U
Corporate costs			
Research and development	$ 2,400	$ 3,728	$1,328 U
Selling and administration	3,600	4,075	475 U
Total	$ 6,000	$ 7,803	$1,803 U
Total costs	$97,320	$103,384	$6,064 U

a. Identify the weaknesses in the responsibility report for the machining department.

b. Prepare a revised responsibility report for the machining department that reduces or eliminates the weaknesses indicated in part (a).

c. Deviations in excess of 5 percent of budget are considered material and worthy of investigation. Should any of the machining department's variances be investigated? Regardless of materiality, is there any area that the vice president of operations might wish to discuss with the manager of the machining department?

(CMA adapted)

40. **LO.2 (Responsibility reports)** To respond to increased competition and a reduction in profitability, a nationwide law firm, Branson Longview & Tonala, recently instituted a responsibility accounting system. One of the several responsibility centers established was the Civil Litigation Division. This division is treated as a cost center for control purposes. In the first year (2008) after the new system was established, the responsibility report for the Civil Litigation Division contained the following comparisons:

	Budget	Actual	Variance
Variable costs			
Professional labor	$1,000,000	$ 940,000	$60,000 F
Travel	50,000	40,000	10,000 F
Supplies	100,000	90,000	10,000 F
Fixed costs			
Professional labor	400,000	405,000	5,000 U
Facilities	250,000	265,000	15,000 U
Insurance	80,000	78,000	2,000 F
Total	$1,880,000	$1,818,000	$62,000 F

For 2008, the division projected it would handle 1,000 cases, but its actual case load was 990.

a. What are the major weaknesses in the preceding responsibility report?

b. Recast the responsibility report in a more meaningful format for cost control evaluation.

c. If Branson Longview & Tonala uses a management-by-exception philosophy, which costs are likely to receive additional investigation? Explain.

41. LO.2 (Responsibility report; performance evaluation) On January 1, 2008, Michelle Sarwally was promoted to production manager of The Fish Factory. The firm buys raw fish, cooks and processes it, and then cans it in single-portion containers. The canned fish is sold to several wholesalers that specialize in providing food to school lunch programs in the northwest United States and western Canada. All processing is conducted in the firm's highly automated plant in Seattle, Washington. The production manager's performance is evaluated on the basis of a comparison of actual costs to standard costs. Only variable costs that the manager controls are included in the comparison. Fish cost is noncontrollable. Standard costs per pound of fish for 2008 follow:

Direct labor	$0.25
Repairs	0.05
Maintenance	0.30
Indirect labor	0.05
Power	0.10

For 2008, the company purchased 5 million pounds of fish and canned 3 million pounds. There were no beginning or ending inventories of raw, in-process, or canned fish for the year. Actual 2008 costs were:

Direct labor	$600,000
Repairs	160,000
Maintenance	650,000
Indirect labor	155,000
Power	315,000

a. Prepare a responsibility report for Michelle Sarwally for 2008.

b. As her supervisor, evaluate Sarwally's performance based on the report in part (a).

c. Sarwally believes her 2008 performance is so good that she should be considered for immediate promotion to vice president of operations. Do you agree? Discuss the rationale for your answer.

d. Do you believe that all of the costs shown on Sarwally's responsibility report are truly under her control? Discuss the rationale for your answer.

42. LO.3 (Profit center performance) Celine Laythram, head of the accounting department at Springfield College, has felt increasing pressure to raise external funds to compensate for dwindling state financial support. She decided to offer a three-day accounting workshop on income taxation for local CPAs in late February 2008. Joe Bennett, a tenured tax professor, offered to supervise the seminar's planning process. In mid-January, Bennett presented the following budget to Laythram:

Revenues ($900 per participant)		$ 90,000
Expenses		
Speakers ($2,500 each)	$15,000	
Rent on facilities	3,600	
Advertising	4,000	
Meals and lodging	33,390	
Departmental overhead allocation	23,560	(79,550)
Profit		$ 10,450

The $3,600 facilities rent is a fixed rental, which is to be paid to a local hotel for the use of a meeting room. Advertising is also a fixed cost. Meal expense is budgeted at $10 per person per meal (a total of nine meals to be provided for each participant and each speaker); lodging is budgeted at the rate of $75 per participant and speaker per night. Departmental overhead includes a $10 charge per participant and speaker for supplies as well as a general allocation of 25 percent of revenues for use of departmental secretarial and production resources. After reviewing the budget, Laythram gave Bennett approval to proceed with the seminar.

a. Recast the budget in a segment margin income statement format.

b. The seminar's actual financial results were as follows:

Revenues (120 participants)		$96,000
Expenses		
Speakers ($3,050 each)	$18,300	
Rent on facilities	4,200	
Advertising	4,500	
Meals and lodging	39,690	
Departmental overhead allocation	25,260	(91,950)
Profit		$ 4,050

Because signups were below expectations, the seminar fee was reduced from $900 to $800 and advertising expense was increased. In budgeting for the speakers, Bennett neglected to include airfare, which averaged $550 per speaker. With the increased attendance, a larger meeting room had to be rented from the local hotel. Recast the actual results in a segment margin income format.

c. Identify and discuss the factors that are primarily responsible for the difference between the budgeted and the actual profit on the tax seminar.

43. **LO.3 (Responsibility centers; research)** Organizational spending on outsourced contact centers (previously referred to as call centers) continues to increase. Contact centers are critical to organizational success because these units often have primary responsibility for interactions with customers. In some companies, the contact centers are established primarily for customer support; in other companies (especially in the financial services sector), these centers not only provide customer support but also sell additional services to customers who call. Use library, Web, or interview research to gather information on contact centers.

a. Contact centers often have a large responsibility for customer relationship management (CRM). What is CRM, and why is it so important to companies?

b. List five well-known companies that use such centers and indicate the primary purpose of those contact centers.

c. For each company identified in part (b), do you think that its contact center would primarily be considered a cost or a profit center? Discuss the rationale for your answers.

d. For each company in part (b), list three possible methods of allocating the costs of contact centers to operating departments. Discuss the rationale for your answers.

e. Although outsourced contact centers (especially those that are offshore) may create cost reductions, what other measurements might be useful in gauging contact center performance and customer satisfaction?

44. **LO.3 (Cost and profit centers; ethics; research)** Many companies provide on-site child care facilities for employees' children. In some situations, this service is provided free of charge; in other situations, employees are charged, usually on a sliding scale basis relative to pay, for such services.

a. If a company provides, but does not charge for, employee child care, the cost of such facilities would be considered a cost center. What potential ethical issues might arise when child care facilities are viewed as a cost center?

b. If a company charges for employee child care, do you think the company should establish a designated percentage of profitability that it wishes to earn on the facilities? Discuss the reason for your answer.

c. Find information on two companies that have child care facilities for their employees and determine whether employees are charged for such facilities. What benefits are gained from the companies' perspectives from having such on-site facilities?▲

45. **LO.4 (Revenue variances)** McMillan Sporting Goods sells footballs and shoulder pads. For 2008, company management budgeted the following:

	Footballs	Shoulder Pads
Sales revenue	$800,000	$1,200,000
Unit sales price	$40	$30

At the end of 2008, management was told that actual sales of footballs were 21,000 units and the sales price variance was $63,000 unfavorable. Sales of shoulder pads generated $1,120,000 of revenue, with an unfavorable sales volume variance of $240,000.

a. Compute the budgeted sales volume for each product.
b. Compute the sales volume variance for footballs.
c. Compute the sales price variance for shoulder pads.
d. What conditions might have contributed to the revenue variances?

46. LO.4 (Revenue variances) Juan Navarez manages the marketing department at Electronic Village. Company management has been concerned about the sales of three products and has informed Navarez that, regardless of other sales, his performance in 2008 will be evaluated on whether he has met the sales budget for the following items:

	Sales Price per Unit	Budgeted Unit Sales
HD radio tuners	$240	1,600
Satellite radios	$135	4,200
MP3 car decks	$120	2,100

Actual sales for these three products, generated in 2008, were as follows:

	Sales Price per Unit	Sales Revenue
HD radio tuners	$230	$391,000
Satellite radios	$140	282,800
MP3 car decks	$110	456,500

a. For 2008, compute the sales price variances by product.
b. For 2008, compute the sales volume variances by product.
c. Assuming that the variances computed in parts (a) and (b) are controllable by Navarez, discuss what actions he may have taken to cause actual results to deviate from budgeted results.
d. What problems might be caused by the manner in which Navarez was evaluated during 2008?

47. LO.5 (Direct method) Management of Mount Holly Community Hospital has decided to allocate the budgeted costs of its three support departments (administration, public relations, and maintenance) to its three operating programs (surgery, in-patient care, and out-patient services). Budgeted information for 2008 follows:

Budgeted costs	
Administration	$2,700,000
Public relations	550,000
Maintenance & janitorial	850,000
Allocation bases:	
Administration	Dollars of assets employed
Public relations	Number of employees
Maintenance & janitorial	Hours of equipment operation

	EXPECTED UTILIZATIONS		
	Dollars of Assets Employed	Number of Employees	Hours of Equipment Operation
Administration	$ 740,090	4	1,020
Public relations	450,100	7	470
Maintenance & janitorial	825,680	5	1,530
Surgery	1,974,250	10	12,425
In-Patient care	1,229,250	18	14,200
Out-Patient services	521,500	22	8,875

Using the direct method, allocate the expected support department costs to the operating areas.

48. LO.5 (Step method) Winfield Realty classifies its operations into three departments: commercial sales, residential sales, and property management. The owner, Leo Winfield, wants to know the full cost of operating each department. Direct departmental costs and several allocation bases associated with each follow:

		AVAILABLE ALLOCATION BASES		
	Direct Costs	Number of Employees/ Salespersons	Dollars of Assets Employed	Dollars of Revenue
Administration	$ 750,000	10	$1,240,000	n/a
Accounting	495,000	5	682,000	n/a
Promotion	360,000	6	360,000	n/a
Commercial sales	5,245,000	21	500,000	$4,500,000
Residential sales	4,589,510	101	725,000	9,500,000
Property management	199,200	13	175,000	500,000

The support departments are shown in a benefits-provided ranking. Winfield has selected the following allocation bases for each department: number of employees/salespersons for administration, dollars of assets employed
for accounting, and dollars of revenue for promotion.

a. Use the step method to allocate the support department costs to the revenue-generating departments.
b. Which department is apparently the most profitable?

49. LO.5 (Algebraic method) Prieto Press has two support departments (administration and editorial) and two
operating divisions (college texts and professional publications). Following are the direct costs and allocation
bases for each of these areas:

		ALLOCATION BASES	
Department	**Direct Costs**	**Dollars of Assets Employed**	**Number of Employees**
Administration	$ 450,000	$ 620,000	10
Editorial	350,000	144,000	5
College texts	2,250,000	1,200,000	55
Professional publications	950,000	1,056,000	35

Company management has decided to allocate administration and editorial costs using dollars of assets employed and number of employees, respectively. Use the algebraic method to allocate the support department costs
and determine the total operating costs of college textbooks and professional publications.

50. LO.5 (Comprehensive support department allocations) Management at Thomason Media has decided
to allocate the costs of the paper's two support departments (administration and human resources) to the two
revenue-generating departments (advertising and circulation). Administration costs are to be allocated on the
basis of dollars of assets employed; human resources costs are to be allocated on the basis of number of employees. The following costs and allocation bases are available:

Department	**Direct Costs**	**Number of Employees**	**Dollars of Assets Employed**
Administration	$ 781,500	10	$ 387,100
Human resources	492,700	7	291,700
Advertising	957,800	12	762,400
Circulation	1,352,600	25	1,870,300
Totals	$3,584,600	54	$3,311,500

a. Using the direct method, allocate the support department costs to the revenue-generating departments.
b. Using your answer to part (a), what are the total costs of the revenue-generating departments after the
allocations?
c. Assuming that the benefits-provided ranking is the order shown in the table, use the step method to allocate
the support department costs to the revenue-generating departments.
d. Using your answer to part (b), what are the total costs of the revenue-generating departments after the
allocations?
e. Using the algebraic method, allocate the support department costs to the revenue-generating departments.

51. LO.5 (Comprehensive support department allocations) Wakowski Company's annual budget for its
three support departments (administration, legal/accounting, and maintenance/engineering) and its two production departments (processing and finishing) follows:

		ANNUAL BUDGET ($000 omitted)				
	Administration	**Legal/ Accounting**	**Maintenance/ Engineering**	**Processing**	**Finishing**	**Total**
Direct labor	$ 700	$500	$ 900	$2,800	$2,000	$ 6,900
Direct material	70	200	90	400	1,200	1,960
Insurance	175	50	75	300	220	820
Depreciation	90	70	80	200	150	590
Miscellaneous	30	20	40	60	30	180
Total	$1,065	$840	$1,185	$3,760	$3,600	$10,450

		ANNUAL BUDGET ($000 omitted)				
	Administration	Legal/ Accounting	Maintenance/ Engineering	Processing	Finishing	Total
Number of employees	40	20	30	200	150	440
Sq. ft. of floor space	400	300	200	800	1,000	2,700
Maint./Eng. hours	15	20	15	68	102	220

a. Prepare a cost distribution that allocates support department costs using the step method. Assume the benefits-provided ranking is the order in which the departments are listed. The allocation bases for the support department are (1) administration: number of employees, (2) legal/accounting: floor space, and (3) maintenance/engineering: number of hours. Calculate the factory overhead (OH) rates using 400,000 direct labor hours in processing and 300,000 direct labor hours in finishing. Round OH rates to the nearest $0.10.

b. Calculate the factory overhead rates per direct labor hour using the direct method. Round OH rates to the nearest $0.10.

c. Calculate the factory overhead rates per direct labor hour using the algebraic method. Round percentages to three decimal points. Round OH rates to the nearest $0.10.

52. **LO.5 (Effect of support department allocations on reporting and evaluation)** Kendra Corporation is a diversified manufacturing company with corporate headquarters in Eagan, Minnesota. The three operating divisions are Kennedy Division, Plastic Products Division, and Outerspace Products Division. Much of Kennedy Division's manufacturing activity is related to work performed for the government space program under negotiated contracts.

Kendra Corporation headquarters provides general administrative support and computer services to each of the three operating divisions. The computer services are provided through a computer time-sharing arrangement. The central processing unit (CPU) is located in St. Paul, and the divisions have remote terminals connected to the CPU by telephone lines. One standard from the Cost Accounting Standards Board provides that the cost of general administration may be allocated to negotiated defense contracts. Furthermore, the standards provide that, in situations in which computer services are provided by corporate headquarters, the actual costs (fixed and variable) of operating the computer department may be allocated to the Kennedy Division based on a reasonable measure of computer usage.

The general manager of each of the three divisions is evaluated based on the division's before-tax performance. The November 2008 performance evaluation reports (in millions of dollars) for each division follow:

	Kennedy Division	Plastics Products Division	Outerspace Products Division
Sales	$ 23	$ 15	$ 55
Cost of goods sold	(13)	(7)	(38)
Gross profit	$ 10	$ 8	$ 17
Selling and administrative			
Division selling and administration costs	$ 5	$ 5	$ 8
Corporate general administration costs	1	0	0
Corporate computing	1	0	0
Total	$ 7	$ 5	$ 8
Profit before taxes	$ 3	$ 3	$ 9

Without a charge for computing services, the operating divisions might not make the most cost-effective use of the computer systems resources. Outline and discuss a method for charging the operating divisions for use of computer services that would promote cost consciousness by the operating divisions and operating efficiency by the computer systems services.

(CMA adapted)

53. **LO.6 (Transfer prices)** In each of the following cases, the Speaker Division can sell all of its production of audio speakers externally or some internally to the Sound System Division and the remainder to outside customers. The Speaker Division's production capacity is 400,000 units annually. The data related to each independent case are as follows:

Speaker Division	Case 1	Case 2
Selling price to outside customers	$75	$60
Production costs per unit		
Direct material	30	20
Direct labor	10	8
Variable overhead	3	2
Fixed overhead (based on capacity)	1	1
Other variable selling and delivery costs per unit*	6	3
Sound System Division		
Number of speakers needed annually	80,000	80,000
Current unit price being paid to outside supplier	$65	$52

*In either case, $1 of the selling expenses will *not* be incurred on intracompany transfers.

a. For each case, determine the upper and lower limits for a transfer price for speakers.

b. For each case, determine a transfer price for the Speaker Division that will provide a $10 contribution margin per unit.

c. Using the information developed for part (b), determine a dual transfer price for Case 1 assuming that Sound System will acquire the speakers from the Speaker Division at $10 below Sound System's purchase price from outside suppliers.

54. **LO.6 (Transfer price)** O'Doulan Company has two divisions: Engine and Mobile Systems. The Engine Division produces engines used by both the Mobile Systems Division and a variety of external industrial customers. External sales orders are generally produced in 50-unit lots. Using this typical lot size, the cost per engine is as follows:

Variable production cost	$2,100
Fixed manufacturing overhead	900
Variable selling expense	300
Fixed selling expense	420
Fixed administrative expense	640
Total unit cost	$4,360

An engine's external selling price is $5,232, providing the Engine Division with a normal profit margin of 20 percent. Because a significant number of sales are being made internally, Engine Division managers have decided that the external selling price should be used to transfer all engines to Mobile Systems.

When the Mobile Systems Division manager learned of the new transfer price, she became very upset because it would have a major negative impact on her division's profit. Mobile Systems has asked for a lower transfer price from the Engine Division so that it earns a profit margin of only 15 percent. Mobile Systems' manager has asked corporate management whether the division can buy engines externally. Tom Hawkins, O'Doulan's president, has gathered the following information on transfer prices to help the two divisional managers negotiate an equitable transfer price:

Current external sales price	$5,232
Total variable production cost plus a 20 percent profit margin ($2,100 × 1.2)	2,520
Total production cost plus a 20 percent profit margin ($3,000 × 1.2)	3,600
Bid price from external supplier (if motors are purchased in 50-unit lots)	4,640

a. Discuss advantages and disadvantages of each of these transfer prices to both the selling and buying divisions and to O'Doulan Company.

b. If the Engine Division could sell all of its production externally at $5,232, what is the appropriate transfer price and why?

55. **LO.6 (Transfer pricing journal entries)** Travel Inc.'s Roll-Em-On Division makes computer bags. The bags are sold to another internal division, SkyWheels, for inclusion in a luggage set and to external buyers. During the month just ended, SkyWheels acquired 4,000 bags from the Roll-Em-On Division, whose standard unit costs follow:

Direct material	$20
Direct labor	6
Variable factory overhead	8
Fixed factory overhead	12
Variable selling expense	4
Fixed selling and administrative expense	6

SkyWheels can acquire comparable bags externally for $80 each. Give the entries for each division and for Roll-Em-On (assuming that no bags acquired by SkyWheels have been sold) for the past month if the transfer is to be recorded

a. at SkyWheels' external purchase price and no selling expenses were incurred on, or allocated to, internal transfers.

b. at a negotiated price of total variable cost plus 15 percent of full production cost.

c. by Roll-Em-On Division at SkyWheels' external price, and by SkyWheels at Roll-Em-On's variable production cost.

d. at Roll-Em-On's absorption cost.

56. **LO.6 (Internal vs. external sale)** The president of Bangor Inc. has given the managers of the company's three decentralized divisions (Oxford, Aroostook, and Somerset) the authority to decide whether to sell externally or internally at a transfer price the division managers determine. Market conditions are such that internal or external sales will not affect market or transfer prices. Intermediate markets will always be available for the divisions to purchase their manufacturing needs or sell their product. Division managers attempt to maximize their contribution margin at the current level of operating assets for their divisions.

The Aroostook Division manager is considering the following two alternative orders.

■ Somerset Division needs 3,000 units of a motor that Aroostook Division can supply. To manufacture these motors, Aroostook would purchase components from Oxford Division at a transfer price of $600 per unit; Oxford's variable cost for these components is $300 per unit. Aroostook Division would further process these components at a variable cost of $500 per unit.

If Somerset cannot obtain the motors from Aroostook, it will purchase the motors from Melbourne Company for $1,500 per unit. Melbourne Company would also purchase 3,000 components from Oxford at a price of $400 for each motor; Oxford's variable cost for these components is $200 per unit.

■ Langton Company wants to buy 3,500 similar motors from the Aroostook Division for $1,250 per unit. Aroostook would again purchase components from Oxford Division, in this case at a transfer price of $500 per unit; Oxford's variable cost for these components is $250 per unit. Aroostook Division would further process these components at a variable cost of $400 per unit.

Aroostook Division's plant capacity is limited, and therefore the company can accept either the Langton contract or the Somerset order but not both. The president of Bangor Inc. and the manager of Aroostook Division agree that it would not be beneficial in the short or long run to increase capacity.

a. If the Aroostook Division manager wants to maximize the short-run contribution margin, determine whether Aroostook Division should (1) sell motors to Somerset Division at the prevailing market price or (2) accept Langton Company's contract. Support your answer with appropriate calculations.

b. Without prejudice to your answer to part (a), assume that Aroostook Division decides to accept the Langton contract. Determine whether this decision is in the best interest of Bangor Inc. Support your answer with appropriate calculations.

(CMA adapted)

57. **LO.5 & LO.6 (Direct method; transfer price)** Massengale & Phinney LLC has three revenue departments: litigation (Lit.), family practice (FP), and legal consulting (LC). In addition, the company has two support departments, administration and EDP. Administration costs are allocated to the three revenue departments on the basis of number of employees. EDP's fixed costs are allocated to revenue departments on the basis of peak hours of monthly service expected to be used by each revenue department. EDP's variable costs are assigned to the revenue departments at a transfer price of $40 per hour of actual service. Following are the direct costs and the allocation bases associated with each of the departments:

	Direct Costs (before transfer costs)	ALLOCATION BASES: NUMBER OF		
		Employees	Peak Hours	EDP Hours Used
Administration	$450,000	4	30	290
EDP—Fixed	300,000	2	n/a	n/a
EDP—Variable	90,640	2	n/a	n/a
Lit.	200,000	10	80	1,220
FP	255,000	5	240	650
LC	340,000	3	25	190

a. Was the variable EDP transfer price of $40 adequate? Explain.

b. Allocate all support department costs to the operating departments using the direct method.

c. What are the total costs of the operating departments after the allocation in part (b)?

58. LO.6 (Interdivisional transfers; deciding on alternatives) Amy Keeler, a management accountant, has recently been employed as controller in the Fashions Division of Deluxe Products Inc. The company is organized on a divisional basis with considerable vertical integration.

Fashions Division makes several leather products, including a portfolio. Product sales have been steady, and the marketing department expects continued strong demand. Keeler is looking for ways the Fashions Division can contain its costs and thus boost its earnings from future sales. She discovered that Fashions Division has always purchased its supply of leather from LeatherWorks, another part of Deluxe Products. LeatherWorks has been providing the 3 square feet of tanned leather needed for each portfolio for $9 per square foot.

Keeler wondered whether it might be possible to purchase Fashions' leather needs at comparable quality from an external supplier at a lower price. Top management at Deluxe Products reluctantly agreed to allow the Fashions Division to consider purchasing outside the company.

Fashions Division management has issued an RFP (request for proposal) for the leather needed for 100,000 portfolios during the coming year. The two best supplier bids are $8 and $7 per square foot from Koenig and Thompson, respectively. Keeler has been informed that another subsidiary of Deluxe Products, Barrows Chemical, supplies Thompson the chemicals that are an essential ingredient of Thompson's tanning process. Barrows Chemical charges Thompson $2 for enough chemicals to prepare 3 square feet of leather. Barrows' profit margin is 30 percent.

LeatherWorks Division wants to continue supplying Fashions' leather needs at the same price per square foot as in the past. Tom Reed, LeatherWorks' controller, has made it clear that he believes Fashions Division should continue to purchase all its needs from LeatherWorks to preserve that division's healthy profit margin of 40 percent of sales.

As Deluxe Products' vice president of finance, you have called a meeting of the controllers of Fashions and LeatherWorks. Keeler is eager to accept Thompson's bid of $7. She points out that Fashions' earnings will show a significant increase if the division can buy from Thompson.

Reed, however, wants Deluxe Products to keep the business within the company and suggests that you require Fashions to purchase its needs from LeatherWorks. He emphasizes that LeatherWorks' profit margin should not be lost from the company.

From whom should the Fashions Division buy the leather? Consider both Fashions' desire to minimize its costs and Deluxe Products' corporate goal of maximizing profit on a companywide basis.

(IMA adapted)

59. LO.6 (Transfer prices; discussion) Bison Inc. is a decentralized company, and each investment center has its own sales force and production facilities. Top management uses return on investment (income divided by assets) for performance evaluation. Laramie Division has just been awarded a contract for a product that uses a component manufactured by Rawlins Division and by outside suppliers. Laramie used a cost figure of $7.60 for the component when the bid was prepared for the new product. Rawlins supplied this cost figure in response to Laramie's request for the average variable cost of the component.

Rawlins has an active sales force that is continually soliciting new customers, and sales of the component are expected to increase. Rawlins' regular selling price is $13 for the component that Laramie needs for the new product. Rawlins has the following costs associated with the component:

Standard variable manufacturing cost	$ 6.40
Standard variable selling and distribution cost	1.20
Standard fixed manufacturing cost	2.40
Total	$10.00

The two divisions have been unable to agree on a transfer price for the component. Corporate management has never established a transfer price because interdivisional transactions have never occurred. The following suggestions have been made for the transfer price:
- regular selling price,
- regular selling price less variable selling and distribution expenses,
- standard manufacturing cost plus 15 percent, or
- standard variable manufacturing cost plus 20 percent.

a. Compute each suggested transfer price.
b. Discuss the effect that each of the transfer prices might have on the attitude of Rawlins Division management toward intracompany business.

c. Is the negotiation of a price between the Laramie and Rawlins Divisions a satisfactory method for solving the transfer price problem? Explain your answer.

d. Should the corporate management of Bison Inc. become involved in this transfer controversy? Explain your answer.

(CMA adapted)

60. **LO.6 (Transfer prices)** Big Sky Industries consists of eight divisions that are evaluated as profit centers. All transfers between divisions are made at market price. Precision Regulators, a division of Big Sky, sells approximately 20 percent of its output externally. The remaining 80 percent of Precision Regulators' output is transferred to other divisions within Big Sky. No other Big Sky Industries division transfers internally more than 10 percent of its output.

With respect to any profit-based measure of performance, Precision Regulators is the leading division within Big Sky Industries. Other divisional managers always find that their performance is compared to that of Precision Regulators. These managers argue that the transfer pricing situation gives Precision Regulators a competitive advantage.

a. What factors could contribute to any advantage that the Precision Regulators Division might have over the other divisions?

b. What alternative transfer price or performance measure might be more appropriate in this situation?

61. **LO.7 (International transfer prices; research)** Go to the Ernst & Young Web site to find information on the 2006 *Transfer Pricing Global Reference Guide*. Choose five countries (other than the United States) and compare and contrast the transfer pricing survey results for those countries, including APAs.

62. **LO.7 (International transfer prices; research)** Go to the Deloitte Web site to find information on the 2007 *Strategy Matrix for Global Transfer Pricing*. Choose eight characteristics of the transfer pricing regimes and compare the requirements for those characteristics of four countries with the same characteristics/requirements for the United States. Which of the five countries (including the United States) seem to have the most stringent requirements for each characteristic?

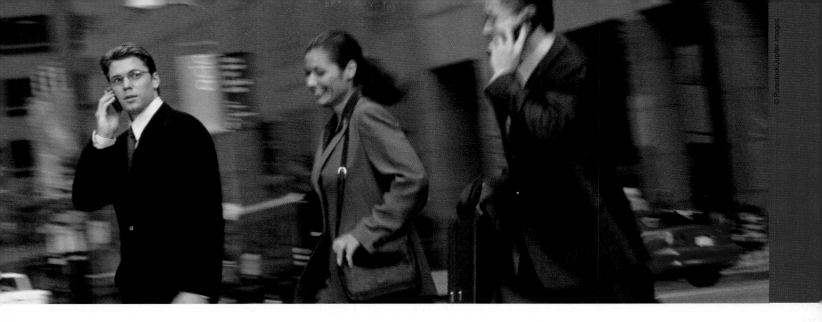

14 Performance Measurement, Balanced Scorecards, and Performance Rewards

Objectives

After completing this chapter, you should be able to answer the following questions:

LO.1 Why is a mission statement important to an organization?

LO.2 What roles do performance measures serve in organizations?

LO.3 What guidelines or criteria apply to the design of performance measures?

LO.4 What are the common short-term financial performance measures, and how are they calculated and used?

LO.5 Why should company management focus on long-run performance?

LO.6 What factors should managers consider when selecting nonfinancial performance measures?

LO.7 Why is it necessary to use multiple measures of performance?

LO.8 How can a balanced scorecard be used to measure performance?

LO.9 What is compensation strategy, and what factors must be considered in designing the compensation plan?

LO.10 What difficulties are encountered in trying to measure performance and design compensation plans for multinational firms?

505

Introduction

Managers recognize that, to achieve profitability in the face of global competition, the single most important variables are to attract and satisfy customers. Historically, managers focused almost exclusively on short-run financial performance measures and ignored the long-run and critical nonfinancial activities. Such tunnel vision was partially created by two circumstances: (1) managers were commonly judged on a short-term basis and (2) long-run and nonfinancial performance data were often unavailable from the accounting system. Because many of the recent accounting scandals resulted from intense pressure on managers to achieve short-term performance targets, more managers are recognizing the need for a longer horizon on which to gauge performance. Additionally, with the ability of new technology to implement strategic cost management systems, world-class companies have begun implementing multiple types of performance measures and reward systems.

An organization's performance evaluation and reward systems are key tools for aligning the goals of workers, managers, and owners.[1] The primary function of managers is to maximize stockholder value or stockholder wealth. When employees help control costs and profits increase, stockholders benefit through increased dividends and/or stock market prices. One of the most important ways of motivating employees to maximize stockholder wealth is through the design and implementation of effective employee performance measurement and reward systems.

LO.1
Why is a mission statement important to an organization?

Organization Mission Statements

Every organization has a reason or mission for which it exists. The mission statement expresses an organization's purpose and should identify how the organization will meet targeted customers' needs through its products or services. For example, at Intel, the mission statement is "Delight our customers, employees, and shareholders by relentlessly delivering the platform and technology advancements that become essential to the way we work and live."[2] Mission statements must be communicated not only externally to customers but also to employees throughout the organization; internal communication can be made in numerous ways, including by conference room posters and printed cards that employees can add to their identification badges.

In addition to a mission statement, many companies have developed a **values statement** that reflects the organization's culture by identifying fundamental beliefs about what is important to the organization. These values may be objective (such as profitability and increased market share) or subjective (such as ethical behavior and respect for individuals). Intel's values statement contains six primary items: (1) risk taking, (2) quality, (3) great place to work, (4) discipline, (5) results orientation, and (6) customer orientation. All new Intel employees are required to take a class on company values.

Mission and values statements are two of the underlying bases for setting organizational goals (abstract targets to be achieved) and objectives (quantified targets with expected completion dates). Goals and objectives can be short term or long term, but they are inexorably linked. Without achieving at least some short-run success, there will never be long-run success. Without engaging in long-run planning, short-run success will rapidly fade.

LO.2
What roles do performance measures serve in organizations?

Organizational Roles of Performance Measures

In fulfilling organizational missions, managers design and implement strategies that apply organizational resources to activities. The organizational structure reflects the manner in which a firm assigns and coordinates its people in deploying strategies. Subunits can be created and charged with making specific contributions to the business strategy. The extent to which each subunit succeeds in

---

[1]The authors use the term *employees* to refer to all personnel of an organization. The terms *workers* and *managers* are used to identify mutually exclusive groups of employees.
[2]http://www.intel.com/intel/company/corp1.htm#anchor1 (last accessed 8/12/07).

its mission can be assessed using carefully designed performance measures that capture the subunit's important performance dimensions.

Management talent and time are dedicated to planning, controlling, decision making, and evaluating performance with respect to activities. For an organization to be successful, managers must devise appropriate information systems to track and gauge the effective and efficient use of organizational resources. Two conditions must exist in order to make such determinations: (1) the terms *effective* and *efficient* must be defined, and (2) measures consistent with those definitions must be formulated. Definitions of *effective* and *efficient* could relate to historical organizational performance, competitive benchmarks, or stakeholder expectations. Once defined, effectiveness and efficiency can be assessed by comparing measures of actual performance with defined and targeted performance goals.

As indicated in Exhibit 14–1, performance measures should exist for all elements that are critical to an organization's success in a competitive market. Management must recognize that progress toward a goal can be achieved only if the goal is specified and communicated to the organization's members. Thus, not setting performance measures for any of an organization's critical elements is tantamount to stating that the ignored element is unimportant. All elements are linked because high performance in one element should lead to high performance in the others.

EXHIBIT 14–1

Critical Elements for Performance Measurement and Examples of Measurements

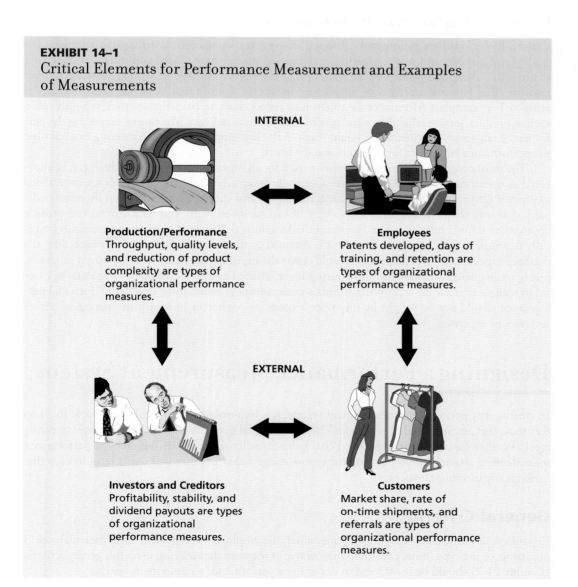

INTERNAL

Production/Performance
Throughput, quality levels, and reduction of product complexity are types of organizational performance measures.

Employees
Patents developed, days of training, and retention are types of organizational performance measures.

EXTERNAL

Investors and Creditors
Profitability, stability, and dividend payouts are types of organizational performance measures.

Customers
Market share, rate of on-time shipments, and referrals are types of organizational performance measures.

Internal Performance Measures

Internal measures that provide a focus on the efficiency and effectiveness of production processes must be developed by management. Inadequate processes make it more difficult for a company to manufacture a product or perform a service that will engender both employee pride and customer satisfaction. Internal process measures must reflect concern for streamlined production, high quality, and minimization of product complexity. Products and services compete with others on the dimensions of price, quality, and product features. Superior performance in any of these three areas can provide the competitive advantage needed for success. Developing performance measures for each competitive dimension can help to identify alternative ways to leverage a firm's competencies.

Employee performance is also a critical element of organizational success. Each successive level of management establishes target measures for subordinates. These measures communicate organizational mission, goals, and strategies and motivate subordinates to accomplish the stated targets. Measures are also used for implementing organizational control over activities, such as using responsibility accounting reports to compare actual to budgeted results. Performance comparisons of employees are used in decisions about promotions and retention. A firm searching for new ways to provide customers with more value at less cost must develop an organizational culture that promotes employee learning, job satisfaction, and production efficiency.

External Performance Measures

Externally, performance measures must signal an organization's ability to satisfy its customers. The quality and quantity of firms competing in the global market have placed consumers at the center of attention. Although profit may be the ultimate measure of success in serving customers, other measures that indicate relative accomplishment in specific areas of market performance can be developed. For example, performance measures must reflect characteristics that customers highly value, such as product/service reliability, value, quality, and on-time delivery. Meeting or exceeding the performance targets set for customers should result in the increased likelihood of meeting or exceeding the performance targets set for investors and creditors.

The most common performance measure used for all organizations is profit, which can be measured as operating income or net income. Generally accepted accounting principles are formulated to provide information that is comparable across firms. This comparability facilitates investor/creditor judgments about which firms are worthy of capital investments and which firms can provide appropriate returns relative to the investment risks assumed. Financial performance measures typically determine whether top management is retained or dismissed. And, meeting or exceeding the market's expectations of performance should create the capital inflows that fund improved processes, hiring more qualified employees, and creating more satisfied customers. Management must be careful to realize, after recent accounting scandals in the business community, that "good" financial performance should not be sought by improper accounting—whether in regard to "managing" either revenues or expenses.

LO.3
What guidelines or criteria apply to the design of performance measures?

Designing a Performance Measurement System

In creating any performance measurement system, it is important to remember that people focus on the items that are measured by superiors. Thus, an essential question to address when implementing a performance measurement system is, What behavior will this metric encourage? The performance measurement system should be designed to encourage behaviors that will result in outcomes that generate organizational success.

General Criteria

Regardless of the results that are being measured, the employee level at which the measurement is occurring, or the type (monetary or nonmonetary) of measure that is being used, five general criteria (Exhibit 14–2) should be considered in designing a performance measurement system:

EXHIBIT 14–2
Criteria for Designing a Performance Measurement System

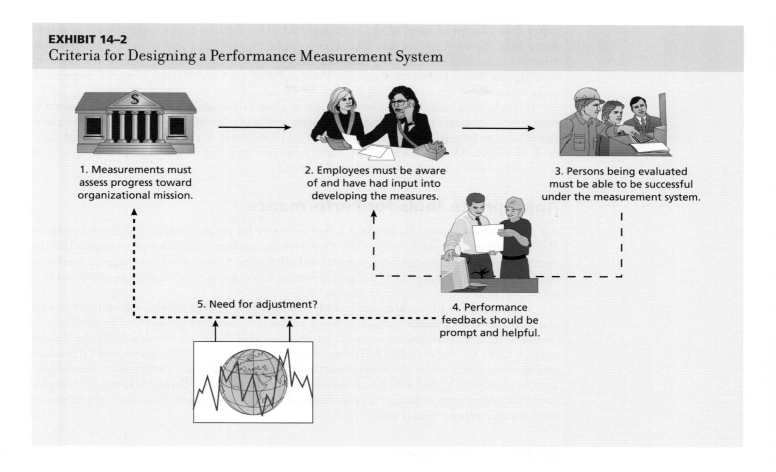

1. The measures should be established to assess progress toward the organizational mission and its related goals and objectives.
2. The persons being evaluated should be aware of the measurements being used and have had some input in developing them.
3. The persons being evaluated should have the appropriate skills, equipment, information, and authority to be successful under the measurement system.
4. Feedback of accomplishment should be provided in a timely and useful manner.
5. The system should be flexible enough to adapt to new conditions in the organization's environment.

Assess Progress toward Mission

Organizations have a variety of objectives, including the need to be financially viable. Therefore, financial performance measures must be relevant for the type of organization or subunit being evaluated and must reflect an understanding of accounting information and its potential for manipulation. In addition to financial success, many companies are now establishing operational targets of total customer satisfaction, zero defects, minimal lead time to market, and environmental and social responsibility. These goals generally cannot be defined directly using traditional, short-term financial methods. Alternative measures are needed to capture the nonfinancial dimensions of performance. Nonfinancial performance measures that indicate progress—or lack thereof—toward the achievement of a world-class company's critical success factors can be developed.

Awareness of and Participation in Performance Measures

Regardless of the number or types of measures chosen, top management must set high performance standards and communicate them to others. The measures should promote harmonious operations rather than suboptimization among organizational units. Because people normally act in accordance with the way they are measured, they must be aware of and understand the performance measures being used. Withholding measurement information does not allow people to perform at their highest level, which is frustrating for them and does not foster feelings of mutual respect and cooperation.

If standards or budget comparisons are used to assess performance, people should be involved in setting those standards or the budget. Participation results in a "social contract" between participants and evaluators by generating an understanding and acceptance of the reasonableness of the standards or budget. Also, people who have participated in setting targets generally attempt to achieve the results to affirm that the plans were well founded.

Appropriate Tools for Performance

For performance measures to be fair, it is first necessary for people to either possess or be able to obtain the appropriate skills for their jobs. Given job competence, people must then be provided the necessary tools (equipment, information, and authority) to perform their jobs in a manner consistent with the measurement process. If the appropriate tools are unavailable, it cannot be presumed that people will be able to accomplish their tasks.

In decentralized firms, there may be little opportunity to directly observe subordinates' actions and managers have to make evaluations based on the outcomes that are captured by performance measures. Thus, the performance measures selected should (1) be highly correlated with the subunit mission, (2) be fair and complete reflections of the subunit manager's performance, and (3) measure performance that is under the subunit manager's control. To evaluate performance, benchmarks must be established against which accomplishments can be measured. Benchmarks can be monetary (such as standard costs or budget appropriation amounts) or nonmonetary (such as zero defects or another organization's market share).

Need for Feedback

Performance should be monitored, and feedback (both positive and negative) should be provided on a continuing basis to the appropriate individuals. Waiting to give feedback on performance until a known evaluation point is reached allows employees no opportunity for early adjustment. Thus, if employee performance reviews and evaluations are to be performed annually at a certain date, feedback on performance should be provided periodically during the year so that employees are aware of how they are doing, have ample opportunities to maximize positive results and correct negative results, and are not negatively "blindsided" during their performance reviews.

The ultimate feedback is that organizational stakeholders exhibit belief in the firm's viability. The primary determinant of this belief is typically provided by short-run financial performance measures.

LO.4
What are the common short-term financial performance measures, and how are they calculated and used?

Short-Term Financial Performance Measures for Management

As discussed in Chapter 13 relative to responsibility centers and responsibility accounting, each manager in a firm is expected to make an organizational contribution. Measurements selected to gauge managerial performance must be appropriate for the types of responsibility assigned and behavior desired. Traditionally, managerial performance was primarily judged on monetary measures such as profits, achievement of and variations from budget objectives, and cash flow.

The ability to use monetary measures is, however, affected by the type of responsibility center being evaluated because managers should be evaluated only with metrics that reflect authority and responsibility. In a cost center, the primary financial performance measurements are the variances from budgeted or standard costs. Performance in a pure revenue center can be primarily judged by comparing budgeted revenues with actual revenues. Profit and investment center managers are responsible for revenues, expenses, and return on investment; thus, a variety of measures are appropriate.

Divisional Profits

The segment margin of a profit or investment center is a frequently used measure of divisional performance.[3] This amount is compared with the center's budgeted income, and variances are computed to determine where targets were exceeded or not achieved. Thus, segment margin does not include allocated common costs.

One problem with using segment margin to measure performance is that its individual components (like many other accounting measures) are subject to manipulations, such as the following:

- If a cost flow method other than first-in, first-out is used, inventory purchases can be accelerated or deferred at the end of the period to manage the period's Cost of Goods Sold for retailing and wholesaling firms.
- Replacement of workers who have resigned or been dismissed can be deferred to minimize salary expense for the period.
- Routine maintenance can be delayed or eliminated to reduce perceived expenses in the short run.
- If fixed overhead is being allocated to inventory, production can be increased so that cost per unit declines.
- Sales recognition can be delayed or accelerated.
- Advertising expenses or other discretionary costs can be delayed or accelerated.
- Depreciation methods can be changed to affect depreciation expense.

These tactics can be used to "cause" reported segment margin to conform to budget expectations, but such manipulations are normally not in the center's long-run best interest and could even be improper accounting.

Cash Flow

For an entity or an investment center to succeed, it must meet two requirements: (1) long-run profitability and (2) continuous liquidity. The statement of cash flows (SCF) provides information about the sources and uses of cash from operating, investing, and financing activities. Such information is useful when managing cash outflow commitments, adapting to adverse changes in business conditions, and assessing new cash commitments. Furthermore, because this statement identifies the relationships between segment margin (or net income) and net cash flow from operations, the SCF assists managers in judging reliability of the entity's earnings. Analysis of the SCF in conjunction with budgets and other financial reports provides information on cost reductions, collection policies, dividend payout, impact of capital projects on total cash flows, and liquidity position. Many useful financial ratios (such as the current ratio, quick ratio, and number of days' collections in accounts receivable) involve cash flow and are useful to managers, aiding them in effectively conducting their responsibilities.

Return on Investment

Return on investment (ROI) is a ratio relating income generated by an investment center to the resources (or asset base) used to produce that income. The return on investment formula is

$$ROI = Income \div Assets\ Invested$$

To use ROI, both terms in the formula must be specifically defined; alternative definitions and preferred definitions are provided in Exhibit 14–3. Once definitions have been assigned to the terms, ROI can be used to evaluate individual investment centers or organizations and to make intracompany, intercompany, and multinational comparisons. However, managers making these comparisons must consider differences in the entities' characteristics and accounting methods.

---

[3]The term *segment margin* is defined in Chapter 10 as segment sales minus (direct variable expenses and avoidable fixed expenses).

EXHIBIT 14–3
ROI Definitional Questions and Answers

Question	Preferable Answer
Is income defined as segment or operating income?	Segment income Because the manager does not have short-run control over unavoidable fixed expenses and allocated corporate costs.
Is income on a before-tax or after-tax basis?	Before-tax Because investment centers might pay higher or lower tax rates if they were separated from the organization.
Should assets be defined as • total assets utilized; • total assets available for use; or • net assets (equity)?	Total assets available for use Because if duplicate or unused assets were eliminated from the formula, there would be no encouragement for managers to dispose of those assets and gain additional cash flow that could be used for more profitable projects. Alternatively, if the objective is to measure how well the segment is performing, given the funds provided for that segment, then net assets should be used to measure return on equity.
Should plant assets be included at • original cost; • depreciated book value; or • current value?	Current value Because as assets age and net book value declines, an investment center earning the same income each year would show a continuously increasing ROI. Although more difficult to obtain and possibly subjective, current values measure the opportunity cost of using the assets.
Should beginning, ending, or average assets be used?	Average assets Because the numerator income amount is for a period of time, the denominator base should be calculated for the same time frame.

Data for Midwest Controls (Exhibit 14–4) are used to illustrate return on investment computations. The company has investment centers in Omaha, Las Vegas, and Pittsburgh. All three divisions operate in the same industry, offer the same types of services to customers, and are charged with similar missions. Similarity in business lines and missions allows for comparisons among the three centers.

Exhibit 14–5 provides the return on investment rates (using a variety of bases) for Midwest Controls's investment centers. The rates vary because different definitions are used in each case for the numerator and denominator. These variations demonstrate why the income and assets involved must be defined before making computations or comparisons.

The ROI formula can be restated to provide useful information about two individual factors that compose the rate of return: profit margin and asset turnover. This restatement, called the Du Pont model, is

$$\text{ROI} = \text{Profit Margin} \times \text{Asset Turnover}$$
$$= (\text{Income} \div \text{Sales}) \times (\text{Sales} \div \text{Assets})$$

EXHIBIT 14–4
Data for Midwest Controls

	IN THOUSANDS			
	Omaha	Las Vegas	Pittsburgh	Total
Revenues	$ 3,200,000	$ 675,000	$430,000	$4,305,000
Direct costs				
Variable	(1,120,000)	(310,000)	(172,000)	(1,602,000)
Fixed (avoidable)	(550,000)	(118,000)	(60,000)	(728,000)
Segment margin	$ 1,530,000	$ 247,000	$198,000	$1,975,000
Unavoidable fixed				
and allocated costs	(372,000)	(78,000)	(50,000)	(500,000)
Operating income	$ 1,158,000	$ 169,000	$148,000	$1,475,000
Taxes (34%)	(393,720)	(57,460)	(50,320)	(501,500)
Net income	$ 764,280	$ 111,540	$ 97,680	$ 973,500
Current assets	$ 48,500	$ 33,120	$ 20,000	
Fixed assets	6,179,000	4,610,000	900,000	
Total asset cost	$ 6,227,500	$4,643,120	$920,000	
Accumulated				
Depreciation (b)	(1,232,500)	(1,270,000)	(62,500)	
Total asset book value	$ 4,995,000	$3,373,120	$857,500	
Liabilities	(2,130,000)	(600,000)	(162,500)	
Net assets	$ 2,865,000	$2,773,120	$695,000	
Proportion of total				
assets utilized	100%	93%	85%	
Current value of				
fixed assets	$ 5,500,000	$2,400,000	$780,000	
Market value of				
invested capital (for EVA)	$18,250,000	$2,400,000	$500,000	

Note: A summarized corporate balance sheet would not balance with the investment center balance sheets because of the existence of general corporate assets and liabilities.

Profit margin is the ratio of income to sales. It indicates what proportion of each sales dollar is *not* used for expenses and, thus, becomes profit. Profit margin can be used to judge management's efficiency with regard to the relationship between sales and expenses. **Asset turnover** measures asset productivity and shows the number of sales dollars generated by each dollar of assets. This metric can be used to judge management's effective utilization of assets relative to revenue production.

Exhibit 14–6 shows the calculations of the ROI components for each of Midwest Controls's investment centers using segment margin and total historical cost as the income and asset base definitions. Thus, ROI is the same as that given in the third calculation of Exhibit 14–5.

The Omaha investment center has both the highest profit margin and highest turnover. This center may be benefiting from scale economies relative to the other divisions, which could partially account for its superior performance. Additionally, Omaha is better at leveraging its assets; as shown in Exhibit 14–4, the center's assets are 100 percent utilized.

The Las Vegas center is performing very poorly compared to the other two investment centers. Based on the relationship between the accumulated depreciation and fixed asset cost amounts, the Las Vegas center appears to be the oldest, which could be a factor driving its poor performance.

EXHIBIT 14–5
ROI Computations

	Omaha	Las Vegas	Pittsburgh
Operating Income	$1,158,000	$169,000	$148,000
Assets Utilized	$4,995,000	$3,137,002	$728,875
ROI	23.2%	5.4%	20.3%
Operating Income	$1,158,000	$169,000	$148,000
Asset Current Value	$5,500,000	$2,400,000	$780,000
ROI	21.1%	7.0%	19.0%
Segment Margin	$1,530,000	$247,000	$198,000
Total Asset Cost	$6,227,500	$4,643,120	$920,000
ROI	24.6%	5.3%	21.5%
Segment Margin	$1,530,000	$247,000	$198,000
Asset Book Value	$4,995,000	$3,373,120	$857,500
ROI	30.6%	7.3%	23.1%
Segment Margin	$1,530,000	$247,000	$198,000
Asset Current Value	$5,500,000	$2,400,000	$780,000
ROI	27.8%	10.3%	25.4%
Segment Margin	$1,530,000	$247,000	$198,000
Net Assets	$2,865,000	$2,773,120	$695,000
ROI	53.4%	8.9%	28.5%

EXHIBIT 14–6
ROI Components–Du Pont Formula

Omaha Investment Center

ROI = (Income ÷ Sales) × (Sales ÷ Assets)

= ($1,530,000 ÷ $3,200,000) × ($3,200,000 ÷ $6,227,500)

= 0.478 × 0.514

= 24.6%

Las Vegas Investment Center

ROI = (Income ÷ Sales) × (Sales ÷ Assets)

= ($247,000 ÷ $675,000) × ($675,000 ÷ $4,643,120)

= 0.366 × 0.145

= 5.3%

Pittsburgh Investment Center

ROI = (Income ÷ Sales) × (Sales ÷ Assets)

= ($198,000 ÷ $430,000) × ($430,000 ÷ $920,000)

= 0.460 × 0.467

= 21.5%

Las Vegas's manager should consider purchasing more modern facilities to generate more sales and greater profits. Such an investment could, however, cause ROI to decline because the asset base would increase. Rate of return computations can encourage managers to retain and use old plant assets (especially when accumulated depreciation is deducted from the asset base) to keep ROIs high as long as those assets can keep revenues up and expenses down.

The Pittsburgh investment center is the newest of the three based on the low proportion of accumulated depreciation to fixed asset cost. With increased asset utilization, the Pittsburgh investment center should generate a higher asset turnover and raise its ROI.

Sales prices, volume and mix of products sold, expenses, and capital asset acquisitions and dispositions affect ROI. Return on investment can be increased through various management actions including (1) raising sales prices if demand will not be impaired, (2) decreasing expenses, and (3) decreasing dollars invested in assets, especially nonproductive ones. Actions should be taken only after considering relationships among the factors that determine ROI. For instance, a sales price increase could reduce sales volume if demand is elastic with respect to price.

Profit margin, asset turnover, and ROI can be assessed as favorable or unfavorable only if each component is compared with a valid benchmark. Comparison bases include expected results, prior results, or results of other similar entities.

Residual Income

An investment center's residual income (RI) is the profit earned that exceeds an amount "charged" for funds committed to the center. The "charged" amount is equal to a specified target rate of return multiplied by the asset base and is comparable to an imputed rate of interest on the divisional assets used.[4] The rate can be changed to compensate for market rate fluctuations or for risk. The residual income computation is as follows:

$$\text{Residual Income} = \text{Income} - (\text{Target Rate} \times \text{Asset Base})$$

Residual income yields a dollar figure rather than a percentage. Expansion (or additional investments in assets) should occur in an investment center if positive residual income (dollars of return) is expected on the dollars of additional investment. Continuing the Midwest Controls example, Exhibit 14–7 illustrates the calculation of each investment center's RI. Midwest Controls has established a 15 percent target return on total assets and has defined income as segment margin and asset base as total historical cost of assets. Omaha and Pittsburgh show positive residual incomes, but Las Vegas's negative RI indicates that income is significantly low relative to asset investment.

EXHIBIT 14–7
Residual Income Calculations

Omaha

RI = $1,530,000 − (0.15 × $6,227,500) = $1,530,000 − $934,125 = $595,875

Las Vegas

RI = $247,000 − (0.15 × $4,643,120) = $247,000 − $696,468 = $(449,468)

Pittsburgh

RI = $198,000 − (0.15 × $920,000) = $198,000 − $138,000 = $60,000

[4]This target rate is similar to the discount rate used in capital budgeting (discussed in Chapter 15). For management to invest in a capital project, that project must earn at least a minimum specified rate of return. In the same manner, the ROI of an investment center must be equal to or higher than the target rate used to compute residual income.

Economic Value Added

A measure that has been developed to more directly align the interests of managers with interests of common shareholders is economic value added (EVA®).[5] Conceptually similar to RI, EVA is a measure of the profit produced above the cost of capital. However, EVA applies the target rate of return to the market value of the capital invested in the investment center or organization rather than the book value of assets that is used to calculate RI. Furthermore, EVA is calculated on net income, or the after-tax profits available to stockholders. The EVA calculation is as follows:

$$\text{EVA} = \text{After-Tax Profits} - (\text{Cost of Capital \%} \times \text{Market Value of Invested Capital})$$

Using information on net income and market values given in Exhibit 14–4, calculations of EVA for each Midwest Controls investment center are given in Exhibit 14–8. The after-tax cost of capital is assumed to be 13 percent.

As the difference between the market value of invested capital (total equity and interest-bearing debt) and the book value of assets increases, so do the relative benefits of using EVA rather than RI as a performance measure. The results given in Exhibit 14–8 show a different portrayal of performance than those given by ROI and RI. EVA shows the Pittsburgh center to be the stellar performer. By failing to capture the large difference between the market and book values of the Omaha investment center, ROI and RI significantly overstate Omaha's performance. Las Vegas still appears to be performing poorly, although better than Omaha.

Despite its popularity, EVA cannot measure all dimensions of performance and is short-term focused. Accordingly, the EVA measure can discourage investment in long-term projects because whereas such investments cause an immediate increase in the amount of invested capital, only at some future time do they increase after-tax profits. For greatest benefit, EVA should be supplemented with longer-term financial and nonfinancial performance measures.

Limitations of Return on Investment, Residual Income, and Economic Value Added

Each financial measure of performance discussed has certain limitations. For example, the limitations of divisional profit and cash flow are their potential for income and cash flow manipulation.

ROI, RI, and EVA have three primary limitations. The first limitation reflects the use of accounting income. Income can be manipulated or managed in the short run, depending on the accounting methods selected to account for items such as inventory or depreciation. For valid comparisons to be made, all investment centers must use the same accounting methods. Because neither cash flows nor the time value of money are considered, income may not always provide the best basis for evaluating performance.

EXHIBIT 14–8
Economic Value Added Calculations

Omaha

EVA = $764,280 − (0.13 × $18,250,000) = $764,280 − $2,372,500 = $(1,608,220)

Las Vegas

EVA = $111,540 − (0.13 × $2,400,000) = $111,540 − $312,000 = $(200,460)

Pittsburgh

EVA = $97,680 − (0.13 × $500,000) = $97,680 − $65,000 = $32,680

---

[5]EVA is a registered trademark of Stern Stewart & Co. It was first discussed by Alfred Marshall, an English economist, in about 1890. More information about EVA can be found at http://www.sternstewart.com/evaabout/whatis.php (last accessed 8/12/07).

The second limitation of ROI, RI, and EVA relates to the asset investment base used. Asset investment can be difficult to properly measure and assign to center managers. Some investments (such as research and development costs) have value beyond the accounting period but are not capitalized and, thus, create an understated asset base. Previous managers could have acquired assets, and, if those managers are no longer heading the center, current managers can potentially be judged on investment decisions over which they had no control. If fixed assets and inventory are not restated for price-level increases, net income could be overstated (or understated, in the event of price-level decreases) and the investment base could be understated (or overstated). Managers who keep and use older assets can report much higher ROIs than managers using new assets. For EVA, this situation exists for the income measure but not for the asset measure because EVA focuses on the market value of capital employed.

The third limitation of these measures is a single, potentially critical problem: they direct attention to how well an investment center performed in isolation rather than relative to companywide objectives. Such focus can result in suboptimization of resources so that the firm is not maximizing its operational effectiveness and efficiency. Assume that the Pittsburgh investment center of Midwest Controls (shown in Exhibit 14–6 to have an ROI of 21.5 percent) has an opportunity to increase income by $40,000 by installing a new $200,000 robot on the production line. This specific investment has an ROI of 20 percent ($40,000 ÷ $200,000), and, as shown in the following calculation, installing the robot would cause Pittsburgh's ROI to decline:

$$\text{New Pittsburgh ROI} = (\$198,000 + \$40,000) \div (\$920,000 + \$200,000)$$
$$= \$238,000 \div \$1,120,000$$
$$= 21.25\%$$

If Midwest Controls evaluates investment center managers based only on ROI, the Pittsburgh center manager will not accept this investment opportunity. If, however, Midwest Controls has a 15 percent target rate of return on investment, the Pittsburgh manager's decision to reject the new opportunity suboptimizes companywide returns. This venture should be accepted because it provides a return higher than the firm's target rate. Top management should be informed of such opportunities, made aware of the effects that acceptance might have on divisional performance measurements, and be willing to reward such acceptance based on the impact on company performance.

Differences in Perspectives

Concentrating solely on financial results is similar to a basketball coach focusing solely on the game score. Both the financial measures and the score are lagging indicators, or reflections of past decisions. Succeeding in business or sports requires that considerable attention be placed on actionable steps for effectively competing, whether in the global marketplace or on the court. Measurements for improving performance should involve tracking leading indicators or statistical data about the actionable steps that will create the results desired. Thus, as illustrated in Exhibit 14–9, leading indicators reflect causes and lagging indicators reflect effects or outcomes.

Managing for the long run has commonly been viewed as managing a series of short runs. Theoretically, if a firm performs well in each successive short run, its future is secure. Although appealing, this approach fails when the firm does not keep pace with long-range technical and competitive trends. Thinking only of short-run performance and ignoring the time required to make long-term improvements can doom a firm in the globally competitive environment.

Short-run objectives focus on the effective and efficient management of current operating, investing, and financing activities. A firm's long-term objectives involve resource investments and proactive efforts, such as customer satisfaction, quality, delivery, price, and service, to enhance competitive position. Because competitive position results from the interaction of a variety of factors, a firm must identify the most important drivers (not just predictors) of the achievement of a particular long-run objective. For example, predictors of increased market share might include increased spending on employee training, research and development, or capital improvements. The true drivers of increased market share for a firm, however, are likely to be product and service quality, speed of delivery, and reputation relative to the competitors. Measurements of success in these areas would be leading indicators of increased market share and profitability.

LO.5
Why should company management focus on long-run performance?

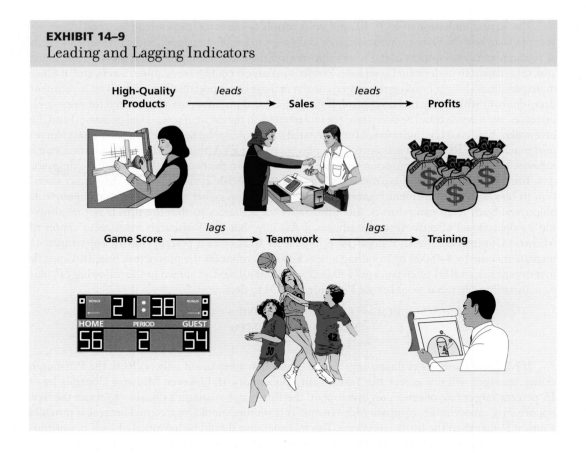

EXHIBIT 14–9
Leading and Lagging Indicators

LO.6
What factors should managers consider when selecting nonfinancial performance measures?

Nonfinancial Performance Measures

Performance can be evaluated qualitatively and quantitatively. Qualitative measures are often subjective; for example, a manager could be evaluated using low-to-high rankings on job skills such as knowledge, quality of work, and need for supervision. Rankings can be given for an individual on a stand-alone basis, in relationship to other managers, or on a group or team basis. Although such measures provide useful information, at some point and in some way, performance should also be compared to a quantitative—but not necessarily financial—standard. People are generally more comfortable with, and respond better to, quantitative rather than qualitative measures of performance because quantitative measures provide a defined target at which to aim. Quantitative performance measures are of two types: financial and nonfinancial.

Selection of Nonfinancial Measures

Nonfinancial performance measures (NFPMs) use information contained in the cost management, rather than the financial accounting, system. Thus, NFPMs are based on nonmonetary details, such as time (e.g., manufacturing cycle time or setup time), quantities (e.g., number of patents generated or pounds of material moved), and ratios (e.g., percentage of good units to total units produced or percentage of sales generated from repeat customers). Appropriate nonfinancial metrics are those that

- can be clearly articulated and defined,
- are relevant to the objective,
- can trace responsibility,

■ rely on valid data,

■ have target objectives, and

■ have established internal and/or external benchmarks.

As indicated in Exhibit 14–10, NFPMs have many distinct advantages over financial performance measures.

Using a very large number of NFPMs is counterproductive and wasteful. Additionally, there may be considerable interdependence among some of the measures. For example, increased product quality should increase customer satisfaction, and additional worker training should decrease poor service performance. An organization must determine which factors are essential to long-term success and develop short-run and long-run metrics for these factors to steer the company toward success. A short-run success measure for quality is the number of customer complaints in the current period; a long-range success measure for quality is the number of patents obtained for quality improvements of company products. Choosing appropriate performance measures can also help a company focus on the activities that cause costs to be incurred and, thus, control costs and improve processes. As discussed in Chapter 4 on activity-based management (ABM), if the activity is controlled, the cost resulting from that activity is controlled.

The following discussion addresses three important nonfinancial performance measures.

Throughput

One significant NFPM is **throughput**, or the number of good units or quantity of services that are produced and sold or provided by an organization within a specified time. Because its primary goal is to earn income, a for-profit organization must sell (not simply produce) inventory for throughput to be achieved.

Throughput can be analyzed as a set of component elements (in a manner similar to the way the Du Pont model includes components of ROI). Components of throughput include manufacturing

---

EXHIBIT 14–10
Advantages of Nonfinancial over Financial Performance Measures

Compared to financial measures, nonfinancial performance measures are more

• **relevant** to nonmanagement employees who are generally more familiar with nonfinancial items (such as times and quantities) than financial items (such as costs or profits).

• **timely** than historical financial data and, thus, more apt to identify problems or where benefits can be obtained.

• **reflective** of the leading indicators of activities that create shareholder wealth, such as manufacturing and delivering quality goods and services and providing service for the customer.

• **causal** of goal-congruent behavior (rather than suboptimization) because they promote long-term success rather than the short-term success promoted by financial measures.

• **integrated** with organizational effectiveness because they can be designed to focus on processes rather than simply outputs.

• **indicative** of productive activity and the direction of future cash flows.

• **appropriate** for gauging teamwork because they can focus on outputs that result from organizational effort (such as quality) rather than inputs (such as costs).

• **cross functional** than financial measures, which are generally related to one function.

• **comparable** for benchmarking externally than financial measures (which can be dramatically affected by differences in accounting methods).

• **aligned** with the reward system because they are more likely to be under the control of lower-level employees than are financial measures.

cycle efficiency, process productivity, and process quality yield.[6] Throughput can be calculated as follows:

$$\frac{\text{Manufacturing}}{\text{Cycle Efficiency}} \times \frac{\text{Process}}{\text{Productivity}} \times \frac{\text{Process}}{\text{Quality Yield}} = \text{Throughput}$$

$$\frac{\text{Value-Added}}{\frac{\text{Processing Time}}{\text{Total Time}}} \times \frac{\text{Total Units}}{\frac{\text{Value-Added}}{\text{Processing Time}}} \times \frac{\text{Good Units}}{\text{Total Units}} = \text{Throughput}$$

Manufacturing cycle efficiency (defined in Chapter 4) is the proportion of value-added (VA) processing time to total processing time. VA processing time reflects activities that increase the product's worth to the customer. Total units produced during the period divided by the VA processing time determines **process productivity**. Production activities can produce both good and defective units. The proportion of good units resulting from activities is the **process quality yield**. An example of these calculations is given in Exhibit 14–11.

Management should strive to increase throughput by decreasing non-value-added (NVA) activities, increasing total unit production and sales, decreasing the per-unit processing time, increasing process quality yield, or a combination of these. Some companies have increased throughput significantly by the use of flexible manufacturing systems and, in some cases, by reorganizing production operations. Computer technologies such as bar coding, computer-integrated manufacturing, electronic data interchange and sophisticated production scheduling technology have also enhanced throughput at many firms. Improved throughput means a greater ability to respond to customer needs and demands, to reduce production costs, and to reduce inventory levels and, therefore, the NVA costs of moving and storing goods.

EXHIBIT 14–11
Throughput Calculation Example

Total processing time	80,000 hours
Total value-added processing time	20,000 hours
Total quantity of product HD#240 manufactured	100,000 tons
Total quantity of good production manufactured and sold	88,000 tons

Manufacturing Cycle Efficiency = VA Processing Time ÷ Total Processing Time
         = 20,000 ÷ 80,000 = 25%
         (means that 75% of processing time is non-value-added)

Process Productivity = Total Units ÷ VA Processing Time
         = 100,000 ÷ 20,000 = 5
         (means that 5 tons can be produced per hour)

Process Quality Yield = Good Units ÷ Total Units
         = 88,000 ÷ 100,000 = 88%
         (means that 88% of the tons were good, or 12% were defective)

Throughput = MCE × PP × PQY
         = 0.25 × 5 × 0.88 = 1.1
         (means that 1.1 good tons are produced per hour of total processing time, compared with the 5 tons actually produced per value-added hour)

    or

Throughput = Good Units ÷ Total Time
         = 88,000 ÷ 80,000 = 1.1

---

[6]These terms and formulas are based on the following article: Carole Cheatham, "Measuring and Improving Throughput," *Journal of Accountancy* (March 1990), pp. 89–91. One assumption that must be made with regard to this model is that the quantity labeled "throughput" is sold. Another assumption is that the units started are always completed before the end of the measurement period.

Cost of Quality

Companies operating in the global environment are also generally concerned with high product and service quality and the need to develop quality measurements such as those presented in Exhibit 14–12. For example, if a performance measurement is the cost of defective units produced during a period, the expectation is that defects will occur and management will accept some amount of defect cost. If, instead, the performance measurement is zero defects, the expectation is that no defects will occur and such a standard would create an atmosphere more conducive to eliminating defects than would the first. As quality improves, management's threshold of "acceptable" performance becomes more demanding and performance is evaluated against progressively more rigorous benchmarks.

Lead Time

An NFPM of customer service is lead time, or how quickly customers receive their goods after placing their orders. Measuring lead time should result in products becoming more rapidly available for customers. In addition, using fewer parts, interchangeable parts, and parts that require few or no engineering changes after the start of production shortens lead time. Lead time incentives could also drive changes in facility layout to speed work flow, to increase workforce productivity, and to reduce defects and rework. Last, lead time incentives should cause managers to observe and correct any NVA activities or constraints that are creating production, performance, or processing delays. Some companies are implementing ABM techniques to remove any implied acceptance of NVA activities. ABM can provide information on the overhead impact created by reengineered processes meant to streamline activities and minimize nonquality work.

EXHIBIT 14–12
Nonfinancial Quality Measurements

Element	Measure
Prevention	Design review (number of hours) Preventive maintenance (number of hours) Employee training (number of hours) Quality circles (number of hours) Quality engineering (number of hours)
Appraisal	Material inspection (number of inspections) Work in Process inspection (number of inspections) Finished Goods inspection (number of inspections) Sample preparation (number of samples) Product simulation (number of simulations)
Internal failure	Scrap (number of units) Rework (number of units) Spoilage (number of units) Quality related downtime (number of hours) Reinspection of rework (number of units)
External failure	Warranty claims (number of claims) Complaint processing (number of complaints) Loss of goodwill (percentage of nonreturning customers*) Liability suits (number of suits) Product recalls (number of recalls)

*Not as originally listed in article.

Source: Ronald C. Kettering, "Accounting for Quality with Nonfinancial Measures: A Simple No-Cost Program for the Small Company," *Management Accounting Quarterly* (Spring 2001), p. 17. Copyright 2001 by Institute of Management Accountants. Reproduced with permission of Institute of Management Accountants in the format Textbook via Copyright Clearance Center.

Establishment of Comparison Bases

Once the NFPMs are selected, benchmark performance levels should be established as bases of comparison against which actual data can be compared. These levels can be developed internally (such as from another world-class division) or determined from external sources (such as competitors or companies in other industries). In addition, a system of monitoring and reporting comparative performance levels should be established at appropriate intervals. Typically, lower-level results are monitored more frequently (continuously, daily, or weekly) than upper-level results (monthly, quarterly, and annually). Measures used by middle management are intermediate links between the lower- and upper-level performance measures and require monitoring at intermediate points (weekly, monthly, and annually). Annual measurements can be plotted to reveal long-run trends and progress toward long-run objectives.

A general model for measuring the relative success of an activity compares a numerator representing number of successes with a logical and valid denominator representing total outcome volume. For example, delivery success could be measured for a period based on success or failure information. Assume that Midwest Controls made 1,000 deliveries during a period; of those, 922 were on time and 78 were late. The company's measurement of delivery success is 92.2 percent (922 ÷ 1,000), or its delivery failure rate is 7.8 percent (78 ÷ 1,000). Determination of how well or poorly the company performed for the period would require comparison with previous periods, a target rate of success (such as 100 percent on-time deliveries), or a benchmark with a world-class competitor. Analysis of the types and causes of the 78 late deliveries should allow management to determine what actions would eliminate these causes in the process of continuous long-term improvement.

Use of Multiple Measures

LO.7
Why is it necessary to use multiple measures of performance?

A performance measurement system should encompass a variety of measures, especially those that track factors considered necessary for mission achievement and long-run success. Although internal measures of performance are useful, only a company's customers can truly assess organizational performance. Good performance is typically defined as providing a product or service that equals or exceeds a customer's quality, price, and delivery expectations. This definition is totally unrelated to internal measurements such as standard cost variances or capacity utilization. Companies that cannot meet quality, price, and delivery expectations will find themselves at some point without customers and without any need for financial performance measures.

Knowing that performance is to be judged using external criteria should cause companies to implement concepts such as just-in-time inventory, total quality management, and continuous improvement. Two common themes of these concepts are to make the organization, its products, and its processes (production as well as customer responsiveness) more effective and efficient and to generate higher value through lower costs.

Exhibit 14–13 provides ideas for judging managerial performance in four areas. Some of these measures should be monitored for both short-run and long-run implications. For example, a short-run measure of market improvement is the growth rate of sales. A long-run measure is change in market share. Brainstorming about both short-run and long-run measures can be an effective approach to identifying measurements. Because measures should reflect the organization's mission and culture in addition to management's expectations and philosophies, changes in any of these factors should also create changes in performance measures.

LO.8
How can a balanced scorecard be used to measure performance?

Using a Balanced Scorecard for Measuring Performance

In recognition of the multiple facets of performance, some companies and not-for-profit organizations have begun to use a balanced scorecard (BSC) approach to performance measurement. The BSC provides a set of measurements that "complements financial measures of past performance

EXHIBIT 14–13

Examples of Performance Measurements

		QUANTITATIVE	
	Qualitative	**Nonfinancial**	**Financial**
HUMAN RESOURCES	Acceptance of additional responsibility Increased job skills Need for supervision Interaction with upper- and lower-level employees	Proportion of direct to indirect labor (low or high depending on degree of automation) Diversity of ethnic background in hiring and promotion Scores on standardized examinations	Comparability of personnel pay levels with those of competitors Savings from using part-time personnel
MARKET	Addition of new product features Increased product durability Improved efficiency (and/ or effectiveness) of product	Number of sales transactions Percentage repeat customers Number of new ideas generated Number of customer complaints Delivery time	Increase in revenue from previous period Percent of total market revenue Revenue generated per advertising dollar (by product or product line)
COSTS	Better traceability of costs Increased cost consciousness Better employee suggestions for cost reductions Increased usage of automated equipment for routine tasks	Time to design new products Number of engineering change orders issued Length of process time Proportion of products with defects Number of different product parts Number of days of inventory Proportion of material generated as scrap/waste Reduction in setup time since prior period	Reduction in production cost (DM, DL, & OH and in total) since prior period Reduction in distribution and scrap/waste cost since prior period Variances from standard Cost of engineering changes
RETURNS (PROFITABILITY)	Customer satisfaction Product brand loyalty	Proportion of on-time deliveries Degree of accuracy in sales forecasts of demand	Change in market price per share Return on investment Change in net income

with measures of the drivers of future performance."[7] The scorecard should reflect an organization's mission and strategy and typically includes performance measures from four perspectives: financial, internal business, customer, and learning and growth. Managers choosing to apply the BSC demonstrate a belief that traditional financial performance measures alone are insufficient to assess how the firm is doing and how it is likely to do in the future. Exhibit 14–14 shows how Crown Castle International uses the balanced scorecard to drive its strategy. Crown Castle owns and manages wireless infrastructures including towers for the communications industry.

Companies adapt the balanced scorecard to fit their own structures and environments. Financial measures of the BSC should reflect stakeholder-relevant issues of profitability, organizational growth, and market price of stock. Such measures are lag indicators of the other perspectives and can include subunit operating income, bottom-line net income, cash flow, change in market share, and return on assets. Customer measures lead financial perspective measures and should indicate how the organization is faring relative to customer issues of speed (lead time), quality, service, and price (both at purchase and after purchase). Internal process measures should focus on things the organization needs to do to meet customer needs and expectations. Measures in this area are usually quantitative and could include process quality yields, manufacturing or service cycle efficiency, time to market on new products, on-time delivery, and cost variances. Learning and growth measures lead customer perspective measures and should focus on using the organization's intellectual capital to adapt to

[7]Robert S. Kaplan and David P. Norton, *The Balanced Scorecard* (Boston: Harvard Business School Press, 1996), p. 8.

EXHIBIT 14–14
Using the Balanced Scorecard to Drive Strategy

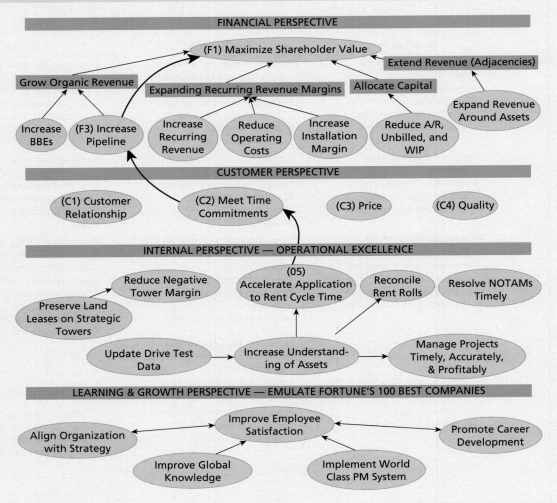

Source: Robert E. Paladino, "Balanced Forecasts Drive Value," *Strategic Finance* (January 2005) p. 36. Copyright 2005 by Institute of Management Accountants. Reproduced with permission of Institute of Management Accountants in the format Textbook via Copyright Clearance Center.

changing customer needs or influence new customer needs and expectations through product or service innovations. Learning and growth measures tend to be quantitative, long-term targets. These measures might include number of patents or copyrights applied for, percentage of research and development projects resulting in patentable products, average time of R&D project from conception to commercialization, and percentage of capital investments on "high-tech" projects. Learning and growth measures can help an organization ascertain its ability to learn, grow, improve, and survive.

BSCs may be used in organizations at multiple levels: top management, subunit, and even individual employees. When a BSC is implemented at lower levels of the organization, care should be taken to make certain that the measurements used can "roll up" into higher level measurements that will ultimately provide the organizational results desired. Regardless of the managerial level at which the scorecard is used or the type of organization using the scorecard, this technique allows measurement data to be compiled in a way that reflects the organizational mission. "Taken together, the measures provide a holistic view of what is happening both inside and outside the organization

Differences in exchange rates and property values might make it more expensive for a U.S. company to start a Japanese subsidiary than an Indonesian one.

or level, thus allowing all constituents of the organization to see how their activities contribute to attainment of the organization's overall mission."[8]

No single BSC, measurement system, or set of performance measurements is appropriate for all organizations or, possibly, even all responsibility centers within the same company. Although some performance measurements, such as financial viability, zero defects, and customer service, are important regardless of the type of organization or its location, foreign operations may require some additional considerations in performance measurement and evaluation compared to domestic operations.

Performance Evaluation in Multinational Settings

Many large companies have overseas operations whose performance must be measured and evaluated. Use of only one measurement criterion such as income is even less appropriate for multinational segments than it is for domestic responsibility centers.

The investment cost necessary to create the same type of organizational unit in different countries can differ substantially. For example, because of exchange rates and legal costs, it is significantly more expensive for a U.S. company to open a Japanese subsidiary than an Indonesian one. If performance were measured using residual income calculated with the same target rate of return, the Japanese unit would be placed at a distinct disadvantage because of its larger investment base. However, the company could believe that the possibility of future Japanese joint ventures or market inroads

[8]Chee W. Chow, Denise Ganulin, Kamal Haddad, and Jim Williamson, "The Balanced Scorecard: A Potent Tool for Energizing and Focusing Healthcare Organization Management," *Journal of Healthcare Management* (May–June 1998), pp. 263–280.

justifies the larger investment. One method of handling such a discrepancy in investment bases is to assign a lower target rate when computing residual income for the Japanese subsidiary than for the Indonesian one. This type of differential might also be appropriate because of the lower political, financial, and economic risks.

Income comparisons between multinational units could be invalid because of differences in trade tariffs, income tax rates, currency fluctuations, political risks, and the possibility of restrictions on the transfer of goods or currency from a country. Income earned by a multinational unit can also be affected by conditions totally outside its control, such as protectionism of local companies, government aid, or varying wage rates caused by differing standards of living, levels of industrial development, and/or the amount of social services. If the multinational subunit adopts the local country's accounting practices, differences in international standards can make income comparisons among units difficult and inconvenient even after the statements are translated to a single currency basis.

Firms with multinational profit or investment centers (or subsidiaries) need to establish flexible systems of measuring performance. Such systems should recognize that differences in sales volumes, accounting standards, economic conditions, and risk might be outside the control of an international subunit's manager. Qualitative performance measures such as market share increases, quality improvements (defect reductions), improvement of inventory management with the related reduction in working capital, and new product development could become significantly more useful.

Regardless of location, the measurement of performance is the measurement of people. Because people are unique and have multiple facets, the performance measurement system must reflect those characteristics. By linking performance measures to an organization's mission and reward structure, employees are motivated to improve performance that will result in long-run organizational viability.

Compensation Strategy

LO.9
What is compensation strategy, and what factors must be considered in designing the compensation plan?

The many organizational changes (technological advances, globalization, and a focus on customers and product/service quality) that have occurred in the recent past have created opportunities and challenges in establishing responsibility and rewarding individuals for their performance. Each organization should determine a compensation strategy that addresses the role that compensation should play in the firm. The foundation for the actual compensation plan should tie organizational goals, mission, and strategies to performance measurements and employee rewards. The relationships among the activities underlying an integrated planning, performance, and reward structure are shown in Exhibit 14–15.

The traditional U.S. compensation strategy differentiates among three employee groups: top management, middle management, and workers. Top managers usually receive compensation including a salary element and significant incentives that are provided for meeting or exceeding targeted objectives such as companywide net income or earnings per share. Middle managers are typically given salaries with the opportunity for future raises (and possibly bonuses) based on some performance measure such as segment income or divisional return on investment. Workers are paid wages (usually specified by union contract, established by skill level or seniority, or tied to the minimum wage law) for the number of hours worked or production level achieved; current or year-end bonuses can arise when performance exceeds some specified quantitative measure.

The most basic reward plan consists of hourly, weekly, monthly, or other periodic compensation, which is related to time spent at work rather than on tasks accomplished. However, this type of compensation provides no immediate link between performance and reward. The only motivational aspects of periodic compensation are the prospects for advancement to a higher periodic pay rate/amount, demotion to a lower pay rate/amount, or dismissal.

Pay-for-Performance Plans

Compensation plans should encourage higher levels of employee performance and loyalty, while lowering overall costs and raising profits. The plans must encourage behavior essential to achieving organizational goals and maximizing stockholder value.

EXHIBIT 14–15
Plan–Performance–Reward Model

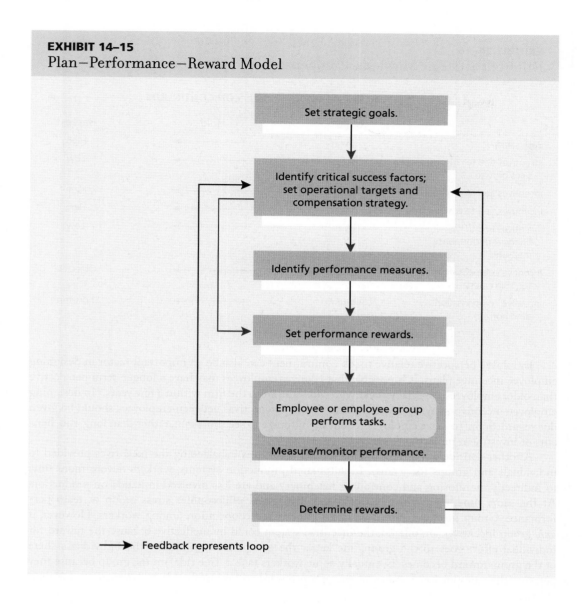

In a pay-for-performance plan, the defined performance measures must be highly correlated with the organization's operational targets. Otherwise, suboptimization can occur, and workers can earn incentive pay even though the organization's broader objectives are not achieved. More than any other goal or objective, maximization of shareholder wealth (a long-term goal) drives the design of reward systems.

A second important consideration when designing a performance-based reward system is that the measures should not focus solely on the short run. Short-run measures are not necessarily viable proxies for the long-run wealth maximization that is the primary objective of U.S. businesses. Pay-for-performance criteria should encourage workers to adopt a long-run perspective. Many financial incentives now involve shares of corporate common stock or stock options. Employees (regardless of level) who become stockholders in their employing company tend to develop, to some degree, the same perspective as other stockholders: long-run wealth maximization.

Because each organizational subunit has a unique mission and possesses unique competencies, the performance measurement system and reward structure should be crafted with the subunit's mission in mind. What is measured and rewarded affects the focus of employees, and that focus should be directed toward factors that determine the success of the whole organization as well as its subunits. Exhibit 14–16 indicates how the form of reward is influenced by the subunit mission.

EXHIBIT 14–16
Different Strategic Missions: Compensation Implications

	Build	Hold	Harvest
		MISSION CONTINUUM	
Base salary	Low	⟶	High
Incentives tied to sales growth	High	⟶	Low
Incentives tied to profitability	Low	⟶	High
Incentives tied to cost control	Low	⟶	High
Incentives tied to non-financial performance measures	High	⟶	Low
Incentive compensation formula criteria	Subjective	⟶	Objective
Incentive compensation time horizon	Long-term	⟶	Short-term

Employee perspective relative to job commitment can also be an important factor in designing employee incentive plans. It is possible that younger employees may have a longer-term perspective than older employees, especially those who will retire from the firm within a few years.[9] In designing employee incentives, any difference in time frame perspectives between employees should be given due regard. Soon-to-leave employees could suboptimize to see short-run, rather than long-run, benefits of investment projects.

Another consideration in designing worker incentives is balancing the incentives provided to individuals and groups (or teams). In automated production systems, workers devote more time to indirectly monitoring and controlling machinery and are less involved in hands-on production. At the same time, many organizational and managerial philosophies stress group or team performance. Group incentives are necessary to encourage cooperation among workers. However, if *only* group incentives are offered, the incentive system could be ineffective because the reward for individual effort goes to the group. The larger the group size, the smaller the individual's share of the group reward becomes. Eventually, some workers take a "free ride" on the group because they perceive their proportional shares of the group reward to be insufficient to compensate for their efforts.

Links between Performance Measures and Rewards

When the compensation strategy and target objectives are known, performance measures for individual employees or employee groups can be determined based on their required contributions to the operational plan. Performance measures should, directly or indirectly, link individual actions with basic business strategies. Rewards in a performance-based compensation plan should use both monetary and nonmonetary, short-term and long-term measures. If an organization makes numerous measurements but only rewards financial outcomes, employees will quickly realize what is truly important in the work environment and what is being measured simply for the sake of measurement.

[9]Although younger workers in the past were always presumed to have a longer time-frame perspective, such a presumption is no longer necessarily true. Today's younger workers (from the Gen X and "millennium student" populations) tend not to have the same level of organizational commitment that workers of the past had; these younger workers often see their current job as merely a short-run "stepping stone" to their next position—meaning that their perspective is little different from the soon-to-retire employees. "Young workers don't care if they have 10 or 12 jobs in the course of a career [and] new recruits leave in as little as six months," was a comment made by one chief operating officer. [Source: Pamela Ganer, "Older Companies Look to Woo, and Keep, Younger Workers," PostGazette.com (June 26, 2005); http://www.postgazette.com/pg/05177/528317.stm (last accessed 8/12/07).]

Degree of Control over Performance Output

Actual performance is a function of employee effort, employee skill, and random effects. Random effects include performance measurement error, problems or inefficiencies created by co-workers or adjacent workstations, illness, and weather-related production problems. After the actual performance is measured, determining the contributions of the controllable and noncontrollable factors to the achieved performance is impossible in many instances. Using performance-based pay systems causes employees to bear more risk than does the use of less comprehensive input–output measurements to determine compensation. Efforts should be made to identify performance measures that minimize the risk borne by employees.

At the worker level, performance measures should be specific and typically have a short-run focus—usually on cost and/or quality control. Each higher level in the organizational hierarchy should include increasingly more elements related to the critical success factors under an individual's control and responsibility. As the level of responsibility increases, performance measures should, by necessity, become less specific, focus on a longer time horizon, and be more concerned with organizational longevity than with short-run cost control or income. When the compensation strategy, operational targets, and performance measurements have been determined, appropriate target rewards can be specified. Rewards should motivate employees to contribute in a manner congruent with the operational objectives, and employees must be able to relate their performance to the reward structure.

Incentives Relative to Organizational Level

Individuals at different organizational levels typically view monetary rewards differently because of the relationship of pay to standard of living. Relative pay scales are essential to recognizing the value of monetary rewards to different employees. At lower employee levels, most incentives should be monetary and short term (to enhance current lifestyles), but some nonmonetary and long-term incentives should also be included so these individuals will take a long-run organizational ownership view. At higher levels, most incentives should be nonmonetary and long term (such as stock and stock options) so that top management will be more concerned about the organization's continuing well-being rather than their own short-term personal gains.[10]

Performance Plans and Feedback

As employees perform their required tasks, their performance related to the measurement standards is monitored. The two feedback loops in the model shown in Exhibit 14–15 exist so that problems identified in one period can be corrected in future periods. The first feedback loop relates to monitoring and measuring performance, which must be considered in setting targets for the following periods. The second feedback loop relates to the rewards given and the compensation strategy's effectiveness. Both loops are essential in the managerial planning process.

Worker Pay and Performance Links

The competitive environment in many industries has evolved to use more automation and less labor-intensive technology. Also, management philosophies now emphasize the need for workers to perform in teams and groups. An interesting paradox has been created by these changes. Workers are more detached from the production function and more involved with higher technology tasks. Thus, the trend is to rely more on performance-based evaluation and less on direct supervision to control worker behavior. This trend is consistent with the movement to empower workers and decrease levels of supervision and layers of management.

Promoting Overall Success

Many performance-based plans have the expressed goal of getting common stock into the hands of employees. One popular arrangement is profit sharing, which provides incentive payments to

[10]Two Web sites useful for benchmarking salary information are www.salary.com and www.salaryexpert.com (last accessed 8/9/07).

employees. These current and/or deferred incentive payments are contingent on organizational performance and can be in the form of cash or stock. Allocation of the total profit-sharing payment among individual employees is made on the basis of personal performance, seniority, team performance, managerial judgment, and/or specified formulas. One popular profit-sharing compensation program is the employee stock ownership plan (ESOP), in which investments are made in the employer's securities. An ESOP conforming to Internal Revenue Code rules offers both tax and incentive advantages. Under an ESOP, the employer makes tax-deductible payments of cash or stock to a trust fund. If cash is contributed, it is used by the trust to purchase shares of the employing company's stock. Trust beneficiaries are the employees, and their wealth grows with both the employer contributions and advances in the stock price. Of course, as was so dramatically illustrated at Enron, employees are at risk of losing some or all of these benefits if the employing company goes bankrupt.

Nonfinancial Incentives

Besides various forms of monetary compensation, workers can also be motivated by nonfinancial factors. Although all employees value and require money to satisfy basic human needs, other human needs cannot necessarily be fulfilled with monetary wealth. Employees are typically more productive in environments in which they think their efforts are appreciated. Supervisors can formally recognize contributions of subordinates through simple gestures such as compliments and small awards. For example, Intel has spontaneous recognition of employee contributions as well as quarterly department events. Allowing employees to participate in decisions affecting their own and the firm's welfare also contributes to making employment socially fulfilling and lets employees know that superiors are attentive to, and appreciative of, their contributions.

Tax Implications of Compensation Elements

Differences in tax treatments of employee compensation are important because they affect the after-tax income received by employees and the after-tax employer cost of the pay plan. There are three different tax treatments for employee compensation: full and immediate taxation, deferral of taxation, and exemption from taxation. Tax deferral indicates that taxation occurs in the future rather than currently. Tax exemption is the most desirable form of tax treatment because the amount is never subject to income taxation.

When analyzing the compensation plan, employers and employees must consider the entire package—not simply one element of the package. For employers, compensation beyond wages and salaries creates additional costs; for employees, such compensation creates additional benefits. Fringe benefits can include employee health insurance, child care, physical fitness facilities, and pension plans. However, different types of fringe benefits have different tax consequences. Certain employee fringe benefits are tax exempt to the employee but are fully deductible by the employer.

Global Compensation

LO.10
What difficulties are encountered in trying to measure performance and design compensation plans for multinational firms?

As more companies engage in multinational operations, compensation systems must be developed that reward all employees and managers on a fair and equitable basis. A very important issue related to global compensation is the manner in which expatriates are compensated. Expatriates (expats) are parent-company and third-country nationals assigned to a foreign subsidiary or foreign nationals assigned to the parent company. Relocating individuals to foreign countries requires consideration of compensation. A fair and reasonable compensation package in one locale might not be fair and reasonable in another.

The compensation package paid to expats must reflect labor market factors, cost-of-living considerations, and currency fluctuations as well as recognize tax consequences. Typically, an expat's base salary and fringe benefits should reflect what he or she would have been paid domestically—adjusted for reasonable cost-of-living factors. These factors could be quite apparent (such as obtaining housing, education, and security needs similar to those that would have been obtained in the home country or compensating for a spouse's loss of employment), or they could be less obvious (such as a need to hire someone in the home country to care for an elderly relative or to handle real estate investments).

Expats can be paid in the currency of the country in which they reside, in their home currency, or in a combination of both. Frequently, price-level adjustment clauses are built into the compensation system to counteract any local currency inflation or deflation. Regardless of the national currency that comprises the pay package, fringe benefits related to retirement must be related to the home country and should be paid in that currency.

Tying compensation to performance is essential because all workers recognize that what gets measured and rewarded is what gets accomplished. Organizations must focus their reward structures to motivate employees to succeed at all activities that will create shareholder, stakeholder, and personal value. In this highly competitive age, the new paradigm of success in for-profit businesses is to provide quality products and services at a reasonable price while generating a reasonable profit margin. Top management compensation has traditionally been tied to financial measures of performance; more and more organizations are beginning to tie the compensation of all levels of workers to one or more nonfinancial performance measures.

Ethical Considerations of Compensation

A major issue of discussion and contention involves perceptions of disparity between the pay of ordinary workers and top managers. Plato argued that no one should earn more than five times the income earned by the lowest-paid worker. In the early 1900s, however, J. P. Morgan stated that the differential should be no more than 20 times. Today, there are numerous examples of CEOs earning many times the pay of the average worker.[11]

The greatest ethical compensation dilemmas involve circumstances that pit the welfare of employees against that of stockholders or the welfare of managers against the welfare of workers. Only if there is a perception of equity across the contributions and entitlements of labor, management, and capital will the organization be capable of achieving the efficiency to compete in global markets.▲

[11]In April of each year, *The Wall Street Journal* provides a special report on executive pay.

Comprehensive Review Module

Chapter Summary

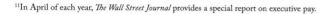

1. A mission statement is important to an organization because it

   - expresses the organization's purpose.

   - identifies how the organization intends to meet its customers' needs through its products/services.

   - communicates organizational purpose and intentions to employees.

   - acts as a foundation for setting organizational strategy.

2. Performance measures in organizations serve to

   - assess organizational performance.

   - relate organizational goals and missions to managerial performance.

- foster growth of subordinate managers.
- motivate managers.
- enhance organizational communication.
- evaluate comparative managerial performance.
- implement organizational control.

3. The design of performance measures should be guided by

- assessing progress toward organizational mission, goals, and objectives.
- allowing the people being evaluated to participate in the development of the measures.
- hiring people who have the appropriate skills and talents (or training people to have such) and providing those people with the necessary equipment, information, and authority to be successful.
- providing feedback to people in a timely and useful manner.
- establishing a set of multiple measures that will provide a variety of information about performance.

4. Common short-term financial performance measures include

- divisional profits or segment margin, which is
  - ➢ calculated as segment sales minus (direct variable expenses and avoidable fixed expenses).
  - ➢ used to assess whether segmental profitability goals were achieved.
- cash flow (by segment or responsibility unit), which is
  - ➢ calculated as cash provided (used) from operating activities, investing activities, and (if appropriate) financing activities.
  - ➢ used to assess the profitability of the responsibility unit, liquidity to pay debts as they arise, adaptability to adverse conditions, and ability to undertake new commitments.
- return on investment, which is
  - ➢ calculated as profit margin multiplied by asset turnover.
  - ➢ used to assess the generation of income relative to the resources used to produce that income.

- residual income, which is
  - ➢ calculated as income earned above a target rate on the unit's asset base.
  - ➢ used to assess the generation of income relative to the resources used to produce that income.
- economic value added, which is
  - ➢ calculated as after-tax profits less the product of the market value of invested capital multiplied by the cost of capital percentage.
  - ➢ used to assess the generation of income relative to the market value of the resources used to produce that income.

5. Company management should focus on long-run performance because such a perspective reflects

- leading indicators of future performance.
- technical and competitive trends.
- a more intensive investigation of resource allocations.
- proactive efforts to enhance competitive position.

6. When selecting nonfinancial performance measures, managers should consider that

- people are more comfortable with quantitative rather than qualitative measures.
- the measures need to be clearly defined and communicated to those who will be evaluated by the measures.
- the measures must be relevant to the objective, trace responsibility, and benchmark internally and/or externally.
- the measures use valid data that can be obtained in a cost-beneficial manner.
- too many measures are counterproductive.

7. Multiple measures of performance should be used because an organization's success depends on a variety of factors, each of which should be reviewed for contribution toward the organization's mission, goals, and objectives.

8. A balanced scorecard can be used to measure performance by providing a set of measurements that reflect the organization's mission and strategy from a(n)

- financial perspective.
- customer perspective.

- internal process perspective.

- learning and growth perspective.

9. Measuring performance for multinational firms often creates difficulties because of differing

   - labor and tax laws.

   - employee work ethics.

   - market and political stability.

   - inflation, exchange, and labor rates.

   - consumer wealth and purchasing power.

   - financing costs.

   - accounting practices.

10. Compensation strategy

- addresses the role compensation should play in an organization.

- forms the underlying structure for the compensation plan, including consideration of

   ➢ employees' control over performance output.

   ➢ employees' positions in the organization.

   ➢ employees' opportunities to gain feedback and adapt performance.

   ➢ the alignment of organizational mission, goals, and objectives with the performance measurements and employee rewards.

   ➢ tax and ethical implications of compensation.

Potential Ethical Issues

1. Creating an unbalanced performance measurement system that places excessive emphasis on short-term performance

2. Putting excessive emphasis on accounting earnings such that managers experience extreme pressure to manipulate financial reports

3. Reporting fraudulent or manipulated accounting numbers in order to be paid a higher bonus or to avoid the adverse effects of the actual performance on compensation

4. Evaluating mid- and lower-level managers using performance criteria that are beyond the influence of such managers

5. Backdating managerial stock options so that the options are immediately "in the money"

6. Not informing or explaining fully all performance criteria by which employees and managers will be evaluated

7. Not providing timely feedback to employees and managers during the period so that corrective action can be taken on a timely basis

8. Rewarding only financial performance and ignoring other important performance criteria such as innovation and organizational learning

9. Engaging in suboptimization practices that are personally beneficial to the detriment of the entire organization

10. Compensating expats or employees in foreign operations in a manner that would be considered "inappropriate" from an external perspective because of the wage rate/salary being paid, work hours being demanded, or work conditions being provided▲

Solution Strategies

Performance Measures for Responsibility Centers

- **Cost Center**

  Budgeted costs
  − Actual costs
  Variances (consider materiality)

- **Revenue Center**

  Budgeted revenues
  − Actual revenues
  Variances (consider materiality)

- **Profit Center**

  Budgeted profits
  − Actual profits
  Variances (consider materiality)

  Cash inflows
  − Cash outflows
  Net cash flow (adequate for operations?)

- **Investment Center**

  Budgeted profits
  − Actual profits
  Variances (consider materiality)

  Cash inflows
  − Cash outflows
  Net cash flow (adequate for operations?)

Return on Investment = Income ÷ Assets (high enough rate?)

Du Pont Model ROI = Profit Margin × Asset Turnover
= (Income ÷ Sales) × (Sales ÷ Assets) (high enough rate?)

Residual Income = Income − (Target Rate × Asset Base) (positive or negative? amount?)

Economic Value Added = Income − (Cost of Capital % × Market Value of Capital Invested)
(positive or negative? amount?)

Throughput

$$\frac{\text{Manufacturing}}{\text{Cycle Efficiency}} \times \frac{\text{Process}}{\text{Productivity}} \times \frac{\text{Process}}{\text{Quality Yield}} = \text{Throughput}$$

$$\frac{\text{Value-Added Processing Time}}{\text{Total Time}} \times \frac{\text{Total Units}}{\text{Value-Added Processing Time}} \times \frac{\text{Good Units}}{\text{Total Units}} = \text{Throughput}$$

Reward System

The design of an effective reward structure depends heavily on each organization's unique characteristics. It is impossible to design a generic incentive model that would be effective in all firms. However, affirmative answers to the following questions provide guidance as to the applicability of a proposed incentive and reward plan for a particular organization.

1. Are the organizational objectives more likely to be achieved if the proposed compensation structure is implemented?
2. Is the proposed structure consistent with organizational design and culture as well as management philosophy?
3. Are there reasonable and objective performance measures that are good surrogates for the organizational objectives and subunit missions?
4. Are factors beyond employee/group control minimized under the performance measures of the proposed compensation structure?
5. Is there limited ability of employees to manipulate the performance measurements tied to the proposed compensation structure?
6. In light of the interests of managers, workers, and stockholders, is the proposed reward structure fair and does it encourage and promote ethical behavior?
7. Is the proposed reward structure arranged to take advantage of potential employee/employer tax benefits?
8. Does the proposed reward structure promote harmony among employee groups?
9. Is there an adequate balance between group and individual incentives?
10. Can the system be adapted to accommodate international constraints and considerations?

Demonstration Problem 1

Cougar Technologies is a division of Global Enterprises. The division had the following performance targets for 2008:

Asset turnover	3.1
Profit margin	6%
Target rate of return on investments for RI	15%
Cost of capital	9%
Income tax rate	35%

At the end of 2008, the following actual information concerning the company's performance is available:

Total assets at beginning of year	$12,400,000
Total assets at end of year	14,800,000
Average fair market value of invested capital	18,000,000
Sales	34,000,000
Variable operating costs	17,400,000
Direct fixed costs	13,720,000
Allocated fixed costs	1,350,000

Required:

a. Compute the 2008 segment margin and average assets for Cougar Technologies.

b. Based on segment margin and average assets, compute the profit margin, asset turnover, and ROI.

c. Evaluate the ROI performance of Cougar Technologies.

d. Using your answers from part (b), compute the residual income for Cougar Technologies.

e. Compute the EVA for Cougar Technologies using segment margin as pre-tax income. What causes EVA and RI to differ?

f. Based on the data given in the problem, discuss why ROI, EVA, and RI could be inappropriate measures of performance for Cougar Technologies.

Solution to Demonstration Problem 1

a.
Sales	$34,000,000
Variable operating costs	(17,400,000)
Direct fixed costs	(13,720,000)
Segment margin	$ 2,880,000

Average assets = ($12,400,000 + $14,800,000) ÷ 2 = $13,600,000

b. Profit margin = $2,880,000 ÷ $34,000,000 = 8.5%
Asset turnover = $34,000,000 ÷ $13,600,000 = 2.50
ROI = 8.5% × 2.5 = 21.25%

c. The target ROI for the division was 18.6% (6% × 3.1). The division generated an ROI of 21.25%. The division exceeded its target profit margin but fell short of its target asset turnover. Because the profit margin effect dominated the asset turnover effect, the achieved ROI was above the target ROI by more than 2.5%.

d. RI = $2,880,000 − (0.15 × $13,600,000)
= $2,880,000 − $2,040,000
= $840,000

e. After-Tax Profits = Pre-tax Segment Income − Taxes
= $2,880,000 − ($2,880,000 × 0.35)
= $2,880,000 − $1,008,000
= $1,872,000

EVA = $1,800,000 − ($18,000,000 × 0.09)
= $1,800,000 − $1,620,000
= $180,000

EVA and RI differ for three reasons. First, RI is based on pre-tax, rather than after-tax, income; RI is based on the book value of investment whereas EVA is based on the market value of investment; and the target rates of return differ between the methods.

f. ROI, RI, and EVA are all measures of short-term performance. These measures may be particularly inappropriate for divisions that have long-term missions (such as high growth). In this case, the relatively large growth (19.35%) in assets of Cougar Technologies from the beginning to the end of the period could indicate that this division is oriented toward growth. If so, the ROI, RI, and EVA measures will provide an incentive contrary to the growth mission.

Demonstration Problem 2

Patagonia Plastics makes keyboard casings. During November 2008, managers compiled the following data:

Total casings manufactured	925,000
Good casings produced and sold	865,500
Total processing time (minutes)	10,560
Value-added processing time (minutes)	3,460

Required:

a. Calculate the manufacturing cycle efficiency (MCE).

b. Calculate the process productivity (PP).

c. Calculate the process quality yield (PQY).

d. Calculate throughput using one ratio.

e. Confirm your answer to part (d) using the results of parts (a), (b), and (c).

Solution to Demonstration Problem 2

a. MCE = Value-Added Processing Time $\div$ Total Processing Time
$= 3,460 \div 10,560 = 32.76\%$

b. PP = Total Casings Manufactured $\div$ Value-Added Processing Time
$= 925,000 \div 3,460 = 267.34$ casings per minute of VA time

c. PQY = Good Casings Manufactured $\div$ Total Casings Manufactured
$= 865,500 \div 925,000 = 93.57\%$

d. Throughput = Good Casings Manufactured $\div$ Total Processing Time
$= 865,500 \div 10,560 = 81.96$ casings per minute

e. Throughput = MCE $\times$ PP $\times$ PQY
$= .3276 \times 267.34 \times .9357 = 81.95$ casings per minute (rounded)

Note that the answers in parts (d) and (e) differ only because of rounding error.

Key Terms

asset turnover, **p. 513**

compensation strategy, **p. 526**

Du Pont model, **p. 512**

economic value added (EVA®), **p. 516**

employee stock ownership plan (ESOP), **p. 530**

expatriate, **p. 530**

lagging indicator, **p. 517**

leading indicator, **p. 517**

process productivity, **p. 520**

process quality yield, **p. 520**

profit margin, **p. 513**

residual income (RI), **p. 515**

return on investment (ROI), **p. 511**

tax deferral, **p. 530**

tax exemption, **p. 530**

throughput, **p. 519**

values statement, **p. 506**

Questions

1. What are the benefits of organizational mission and values statements? How are organizational missions and strategies related to performance measures?

2. Why is performance measurement important to the success of businesses? Should performance measures be qualitative, quantitative, or both? Justify your answer. For performance measurements to be meaningful, why is it necessary to establish benchmarks?

3. What benefits can be gained by allowing a manager to participate in developing the performance measures that will be used to assess that manager's performance?

4. On what basis should the performance of a responsibility center be measured? What are the traditional financial performance measures for each type of responsibility center? Why can the same quantitative measures of performance *not* be used for all types of responsibility centers?

5. How can cash flow be used as a performance measure? In what ways is cash flow a relatively stronger or weaker performance measure than accrual measures such as segment income?

6. The president of Toys for Boys evaluates the performance of Annie and Andy, the divisional managers, on the basis of a variety of net income measures. Drew, the controller, informs the president that such measures could be misleading. What are the major concerns in defining the "income" measures? Are internal or external measures more susceptible to manipulation? Explain.

7. What is residual income, and how is it used to measure divisional performance? How is it similar to, and different from, the return on investment measure? How is residual income similar to, and different from, economic value added? How is economic value added superior to residual income as a performance measure?

8. In designing a performance measurement system, why should managerial rewards be linked to performance measures? Why would an effective compensation strategy treat top managers, middle managers, and other workers differently?

9. What is the balanced scorecard? What perspectives are considered in selecting performance measures for the balanced scorecard, and why is each of these perspectives important?

10. Why is the trend in U.S. business away from automatic pay increases and toward increased use of incentive compensation plans?

11. If worker performance measures used in a pay-for-performance plan are not highly correlated with corporate goals, what is the likely result for the organization? For the workers?

12. How does the time perspective of a performance-based plan affect the selection of performance measures?

13. Why should different missions for two subunits result in different performance reward structures for the managers of those subunits? How does the mission of an organizational subunit affect the mix of financial and nonfinancial, and short-term and long-term, rewards?

14. How can feedback, both positive and negative, be used to improve managerial performance? How is feedback used in a performance-based reward system?

15. Many pay structures involve compensation that is both cash and stock based. Why do firms want employees to be holders of the firm's common stock? Why are additional performance measurement and reward issues created when managers are not shareholders in the firms they manage?

16. What are some of the important equity issues in designing reward structures? Why is the achievement of equity in the reward structure important?

Exercises

17. **LO.1–LO.3 (Selecting performance measures)** Jorja Property Management provides management services for commercial real estate development projects. The firm recently started a new division to market video game services to existing clients. The new division will purchase and maintain the video equipment placed in client buildings. Clients will be paid 20 percent of gross video equipment revenues.

    Jorja Property Management has hired you to report on recommended performance measures to be used in monitoring and evaluating the success of the new division and its manager. Begin your report with a discussion of your perception of the new division's strategic mission.

18. **LO.1–LO.3 & LO.6 (Selecting performance measures)** Choose a company that has either gone out of business or is currently in poor financial condition. Use the Web to research that company's history. Prepare a report on your findings, concentrating on indicators that might have provided a perspective of failure. Describe these indicators as short term or long term and as leading or lagging.

19. **LO.1–LO.3 (Performance measurement)** Recall the various ways in which your academic performance has been measured and rewarded. Have the ways that your class grades have been determined always provided the best indications of performance? Provide at least two positive and two negative examples. What would you have done to change the measurement system in the negative examples?

20. **LO.1–LO.3 (Performance measurement)** Research suggests that as people work over a certain number of hours, productivity goes down, stress goes up, and work is not as good. You have taken this observation to heart and want to establish some performance measures in your accounting firm to help indicate that there is a reasonable balance between work and leisure for employees. Use all resources available to research this topic and prepare your list of performance measures. How will you benchmark these measures? How will you react to employees who are "workaholics"?

21. **LO.1–LO.3 & LO.5 (Measuring long-run performance)** The company president has asked you, as the new controller, to comment on any deficiencies of the firm. After saying you believe that the firm needs long-run performance measurements, the president says that the long run is really just a series of short runs. He says that if you do a good job of evaluating these short-run performances, the long run will take care of itself. He sees that you are unconvinced and agrees to keep an open mind if you can make a good case for measuring and evaluating long-run performance. He suggests that you prepare a report stating your case. Do so.

22. **LO.4 (ROI)** Data for the three autonomous divisions of Hazzard Inc. for fiscal year 2008 follow:

	Division 1	Division 2	Division 3
Segment income	$ 250,000	$ 350,000	$ 4,000,000
Asset investment	2,500,000	2,000,000	30,000,000

Compute the return on investment for each division.

23. **LO.4 (ROI)** For the most recent fiscal year, the Canadian Division of Hudson Corporation generated an asset turnover ratio of 3 and a profit margin (as measured by the segment margin) ratio of 5 percent on sales of $3,600,000.
   a. Compute the average assets employed.
   b. Compute the segment margin.
   c. Compute the ROI.

24. **LO.4 (ROI; RI)** The following 2008 information is available for Westfall Industries: average assets invested, $14,400,000; revenues, $52,800,000; and expenses, $49,200,000.
   a. Calculate return on investment.
   b. Calculate profit margin.
   c. Calculate asset turnover.
   d. Using parts (b) and (c), prove your answer to part (a).
   e. Assuming Westfall's cost of capital is 12%, compute the 2008 residual income.

25. **LO.4 (RI)** Kilrud Corp. has established a 10 percent target ROI for 2008 for its Jamestown Division. The following data have been gathered for the division's operations for 2008: average total assets, $11,200,000; revenues, $30,000,000; and expenses, $28,000,000. What is the division's residual income? Did the division successfully meet the target ROI?

26. **LO.4 (RI)** London Ltd. operates its two divisions as investment centers. Information about these divisions follows:

	Division 1	Division 2
Sales	$2,100,000	$1,200,000
Total variable costs	1,260,000	300,000
Total fixed costs	250,000	700,000
Average assets invested	3,050,000	1,100,000

   a. What is the residual income of each division if the "charge" on invested assets is 12 percent? Which division is doing a better job?
   b. If the only change expected for next year is a sales increase of 22 percent, what will be the residual income of each division? Which division will be doing a better job financially?
   c. Why did the answers to the second questions in parts (a) and (b) differ?

27. **LO.4 (ROI; RI)** Schulz GmbH, a German company, set a 16 percent target rate of return for its U.S. Division for 2008. For 2008, the U.S. Division generated $78,000,000 of revenue on average assets of $50,000,000. The division's variable costs were 45 percent of sales, and fixed costs were $13,500,000. Compute the following items for the U.S. Division for 2008:
    a. ROI
    b. Residual income
    c. Profit margin
    d. Asset turnover

28. **LO.4 (EVA)** Mountain Mist Inc.'s cost of capital is 11 percent. In 2008, one of the firm's divisions generated an EVA of $1,130,000. The fair market value of the capital investment in that division was $26,500,000. How much after-tax income was generated by the division in 2008?

29. **LO.4 (EVA)** EVA is used by top management at Denver Technologies to measure and evaluate the performance of segment managers. The company's cost of capital is 13 percent. In 2008, its Schnepel subsidiary generated after-tax income of $13,260,000, with $8,900,000 fair market value of invested capital.
    a. Compute the subsidiary's EVA.
    b. As the controller of Denver Technologies, how would you determine the fair value of capital investment for a particular division?

30. **LO.4 (Performance measurement changes)** Following is a list of transactions that affected one division within a multiple-division company. Indicate, for the current fiscal year, whether each transaction would increase (I), decrease (D), have no effect (N), or have an indeterminate (?) effect on asset turnover, profit margin, ROI, and RI. Each transaction is independent.
    a. In September, the division fired its R&D manager; the position will not be filled during the current fiscal year.
    b. At mid-year, the division manager increased scheduled annual production by 5,000 units. This decision has no effect on scheduled sales.
    c. Equipment with an original cost of $680,000 was sold for $139,000. At the time of sale, the book value of the equipment was $170,000. The equipment sale had no effect on production or sales activities.
    d. The division wrote down obsolete finished goods by debiting Cost of Goods Sold and crediting Finished Goods Inventory for $96,000.
    e. The division manager automated a previously labor-intensive operation. The action had no effect on sales, but total annual operating expenses declined by 17 percent.
    f. Because of significant changes in its cost of capital, the company lowered the division's target rate of return from 12 to 10 percent.
    g. A special overseas order was accepted at a selling price significantly less than that for domestic business. The selling price, however, was sufficient to cover all traceable costs of the order.
    h. During the year, the division manager spent an additional $165,800 on advertising, which sparked an immediate increase in sales.

31. **LO.4 (Throughput)** Just Nuts, a macadamia nut cannery, is analyzing its throughput for September. The following statistics are obtained for the month:

Cans packed and sold	350,000
Total cans packed	371,020
Value-added processing time	650 hours
Total processing time	2,450 hours

    a. Calculate the manufacturing cycle efficiency.
    b. Calculate the process productivity.
    c. Calculate the process quality yield.
    d. Calculate the throughput using only good units and total time.
    e. Verify your answer to part (d) by using your answers to parts (a), (b), and (c).

32. **LO.4 (Throughput)** Kishiyama Corp. wants to compute its throughput for August 2008. The following production data are available:

Good units produced and sold	2,923,200
Total units produced	3,360,000
Total processing time	288,000 hours
Value-added time	100,800 hours

a. Determine the manufacturing cycle efficiency.
b. Determine the process productivity.
c. Determine the process quality yield.
d. Determine the throughput.
e. What can company management do to raise hourly throughput?

33. **LO.4 (Throughput)** Management at MidSouth Corp. has decided to begin using throughput as a divisional performance measure. The Charlotte Division is a job shop that carefully crafts furniture to customer specifications. The following first quarter information is available for the division:

Good units started, completed, and sold	49,200
Total units completed	52,224
Total value-added hours of processing time	15,360
Total hours of divisional time	24,000

a. What is the division's manufacturing cycle efficiency?
b. What is the division's process productivity?
c. What is the division's process quality yield?
d. What is the total hourly throughput?
e. Discuss whether throughput is as useful a performance measurement in a job shop as in an automated plant. Why would you expect process quality yield to be high in a job shop? Why might a job shop such as Charlotte Division have a low manufacturing cycle efficiency?

34. **LO.9 (Pay plan and suboptimization)** Pierre Wilke is a division manager of English Manufacturing Inc. He is in the process of evaluating a $2,000,000 investment. The following net annual increases, before depreciation, in divisional income are expected during the investment's five-year life:

Year 1	$ 200,000
Year 2	300,000
Year 3	380,000
Year 4	1,600,000
Year 5	1,600,000

All company assets are depreciated using the straight-line method. Wilke receives an annual salary of $300,000 plus a bonus of 2 percent of divisional pre-tax profits. Before consideration of the potential investment project, he anticipates that his division will generate $4,000,000 annually in pre-tax profit.

a. Compute the effect of the new investment on the level of divisional pre-tax profits for years 1 through 5.
b. Determine the effect of the new project on Wilke's compensation for each of the five years.
c. Based on your computations in part (b), will Wilke want to invest in the new project? Explain.
d. Would upper management likely view the new investment favorably? Explain.

35. **LO.9 (Variable pay and incentives)** In recent years, salaries for chief financial officers (CFOs) of large U.S. corporations averaged only about 20 percent of the total CFO compensation package; the other 80 percent is performance-based, variable compensation that includes mostly stock options and short-term and long-term incentive bonuses. Among major corporate officers, typically, only CEOs have a higher percentage of pay that is variable.

a. What does the high portion of variable CFO pay indicate about the importance of CFOs to their organizations?
b. Discuss any concerns investors should have about such a high percentage of CFO pay being variable.

Problems

36. **LO.4 (Divisional profit)** The Executive Consulting Division (ECD) of Global Financial Services is evaluated by corporate management based on a comparison of budgeted and actual pre-tax income. For 2008, ECD's budgeted income statement was as follows:

Sales	$ 18,000,000
Variable costs	(12,600,000)
Contribution margin	$ 5,400,000
Fixed costs	(3,600,000)
Pre-tax income	$ 1,800,000

At the end of 2008, ECD's actual results were as follows:

Sales	$ 19,500,000
Variable costs	(14,625,000)
Contribution margin	$ 4,875,000
Fixed costs	(3,615,000)
Pre-tax income	$ 1,260,000

a. Based on the preceding information, evaluate ECD's performance. What was the principal reason for the poor profit performance?

b. Why do complete income statements provide a more comprehensive basis for evaluating the profit performance of a manager than mere comparisons of the bottom lines of the budgeted and actual income statements?

37. LO.4 (Statement of cash flows) Delta G's controller prepared the following cash flow statements (in thousands of dollars) for the past two years, the current year, and the upcoming year (2009):

	2006	2007	2008	Budget 2009
Net cash flows from operating activities				
Net income	$ 1,700	$ 39,200	$ 43,700	$ 45,100
Add net reconciling items	2,200	4,300	3,000	4,000
Total	$ 43,900	$ 43,500	$ 46,700	$ 49,100
Net cash flows from investing activities				
Purchase of plant and equipment	$(18,700)		$(12,200)	$ (4,600)
Sale (purchase) of investments	8,700	$ (3,600)	(12,600)	(15,800)
Other investing inflows	1,200	800	600	2,400
Total	$ (8,800)	$ (2,800)	$(24,200)	$(18,000)
Net cash flows from financing activities				
Payment of notes payable	$(12,000)	$(24,000)	$(15,000)	$ (7,000)
Payment of dividends	(20,000)	(7,000)	(13,300)	(20,000)
Total	$(32,000)	$(31,000)	$(28,300)	$(27,000)
Net change in cash	$ 3,100	$ 9,700	$ (5,800)	$ 4,100

After preparation of the budgeted cash flow statement for 2009, Lana Kaslowski, the company president, asked you to recompile it based on a separate set of facts. She is evaluating a proposal to purchase a local-area network (LAN) computer system for the company at a total cost of $50,000. The proposal has been deemed to provide a satisfactory rate of return. However, she does not want to issue additional stock and would prefer not to borrow any more money to finance the project.

Projecting the market value of the accumulated investments for the previous two years ($3,600 and $12,600) reveals an estimate that these investments could be liquidated for $18,400. Kaslowski said the investments scheduled for 2009 could be delayed indefinitely and that dividends could be reduced to 40 percent of the budgeted amount. These are the only changes that can be made to the original forecast.

a. Evaluate the cash trends for the company during the 2006–2009 period.

b. Giving effect to the preceding changes, prepare a revised 2009 budgeted statement of cash flows and present the original and the revised version in a comparative format.

c. Based on the revised budgeted SCF, can the LAN computer system be purchased if Kaslowski desires an increase in cash of at least $1,000?

d. Comment on the usefulness of the report prepared in part (b) to Kaslowski.

38. LO.3, LO.4, LO.6 & LO.7 (Cash flow; ethics) Michael O'Day, the controller of Irish Potato Co., is disillusioned with the company's system of evaluating the performance of divisional profit centers and their managers. The present system focuses on a comparison of budgeted to actual income from operations. O'Day's major concern with the current system is the ease with which profit center managers can manipulate the measure "Income from operations." Most corporate sales are made on credit and most purchases are made on account. The profit centers are organized according to product line. Following is the second quarter 2008 income statement for one of the company's profit centers:

Sales	$ 63,000,000
Cost of goods sold	(51,000,000)
Gross profit	$ 12,000,000
Selling and administrative expenses	(9,000,000)
Income from operations	$ 3,000,000

O'Day has suggested that company management replace the accrual-based income from operations evaluation measure with a cash flow from operations measure. He believes this measure will be less susceptible to manipulation by profit center managers. To defend his position, he compiles a cash flow income statement for the same profit center:

Cash receipts from customers	$ 52,800,000
Cash payments for production labor, materials, and overhead	(43,200,000)
Cash payments for selling and administrative activities	(8,400,000)
Cash flow from operations	$ 1,200,000

a. If O'Day is correct that profit center managers are manipulating the income measure, where are manipulations likely taking place?
b. Explain whether the proposed cash flow measure would be less subject to manipulation than the income measure.
c. Explain whether manipulation would be reduced if both the cash flow and income measures were utilized.
d. Do the cash and income measures reveal different information about profit center performance? Explain.
e. How could the existing income statement be used more effectively in evaluating performance?▲

39. **LO.4 (ROI)** Spruce Enterprises operates a chain of lumber stores. In 2008, corporate management examined industry-level data and determined the following performance targets for lumber retail stores:

Asset turnover	1.7
Profit margin	8.0%

The actual 2008 results for the company's lumber retail stores follow:

Total assets at beginning of year	$10,200,000
Total assets at end of year	12,300,000
Sales	28,250,000
Operating expenses	25,885,000

a. For 2008, how did the lumber retail stores perform relative to their industry norms?
b. Where, as indicated by the performance measures, are the most likely areas to improve performance in the retail lumber stores?
c. What are the advantages and disadvantages of setting a performance target at the start of the year compared with one that is determined at the end of the year based on actual industry performance?

40. **LO.4 (ROI; RI)** Salvador Ceramics sells pottery to specialty retail and department stores. For 2008, the company's New Mexico Division had the following performance targets:

Asset turnover	2.7
Profit margin	6.0%

Actual information concerning the performance of the New Mexico Division in 2008 follows:

Total assets at beginning of year	$ 7,400,000
Total assets at end of year	9,900,000
Sales	24,000,000
Operating expenses	23,160,000

a. For 2008, did the New Mexico Division achieve its target objectives for ROI, asset turnover, and profit margin?
b. Where, as indicated by the performance measures, are the most likely areas to improve performance?
c. If the company has an overall target return of 12 percent, what was the New Mexico Division's residual income for 2008?

41. **LO.4 (Adjusting income for ROI purposes; ethics)** Imelda Sanchez, manager of the Arias Division of Poncé Chemical, is evaluated based on the division's return on investment and residual income. Near the end of November 2008, she was reviewing the division's financial information as well as some activities projected for the remainder of the year. The information she was reviewing follows.
1. Annual sales were projected at 100,000 units, each with a selling price of $30. Sanchez has received a purchase order from a new customer for 5,000 units. The purchase order states that the units should be shipped on January 3, 2009, for arrival on January 5.
2. The division's 2008 beginning inventory was 500 units, each with a cost of $11. Purchases of 99,500 units have been made steadily throughout the year, and the per-unit cost has been constant at $10. Sanchez intends to make a purchase of 5,200 units before year-end, providing a 200-unit balance in inventory after

making the shipment to the new customer. Carrying costs for the units are quite high, but ordering costs are extremely low. The division uses a last-in, first-out (LIFO) cost flow assumption for inventory.

3. Shipping expenses are $0.50 per unit sold.

4. Sanchez has just received a notice from her primary supplier that he is going out of business and is selling his remaining stock of 15,000 units for $9 each. She makes a note to herself to place her final order for the year from this supplier.

5. Division advertising is $5,000 per month for newspaper inserts and television spots. No advertising has yet been purchased for December, but Sanchez intends to have her sales manager call the paper and TV station early next week.

6. Salaries through the end of the year are projected at $700,000. This amount assumes that the position to be vacated by the division's personnel manager will be filled on December 1. The personnel manager's job pays $66,000 per year. Sanchez has an interview on Monday with an individual who appears to be a good candidate for the position.

7. Other general and administrative costs for the full year are estimated to total $590,000.

8. As Sanchez was reviewing the divisional information, she received a phone call from the division's maintenance supervisor. He informed her that $10,000 of electrical repairs to the office heating system is necessary. When asked if the repairs were essential, the supervisor replied, "No, the office won't burn down if you don't make them, but they are advisable for energy efficiency and long-term operation of the system." Sanchez tells the supervisor to see her on Monday at 8:00 A.M.

Using her information, Sanchez prepared a budgeted income statement and was fairly pleased with the division's results. Although providing the 13 percent rate of return on investment desired by corporate management, the results did not reach the 16 percent rate needed for Sanchez to receive a bonus for the year.

a. Prepare a 2008 budgeted income statement for the Arias Division. Determine the division's residual income, assuming that the division has an asset investment base of $4,500,000.

b. Sanchez's less-than-scrupulous friend, John Greer, walked into the house at this time. When he heard that she was not going to receive a bonus, Greer said, "Here, let me take care of this for you." He proceeded to recompute the budgeted income statement and showed Sanchez that, based on his computation of $723,000 in income, she would receive her bonus. Prepare Greer's budgeted income statement.

c. What future difficulties might arise if Sanchez acts in a manner that will make Greer's pro forma income statement figures a reality?▲

42. **LO.4 (ROI; RI)** Northwest Industries produces stamping machinery for manufacturers. In 2005, the company expanded vertically by acquiring a supplier, Corvalis Company. To manage the two separate businesses, Corvalis is now operated as a divisional investment center.

Northwest monitors its divisions on the basis of both unit contribution and return on investment (ROI), with investment defined as average operating assets employed. Management bonuses are determined based on ROI. All investments in operating assets are expected to earn a minimum return of 11 percent before income taxes.

Corvalis's cost of goods sold is entirely variable, whereas the division's administrative expenses are totally fixed. Selling expenses are a mixed cost with 40 percent attributed to sales volume. Corvalis's ROI has ranged from 11.8 percent to 14.7 percent since 2005. During the fiscal year ended November 30, 2008, Corvalis contemplated a capital acquisition with an estimated ROI of 11.5 percent; however, division management decided that the investment would decrease Corvalis's overall ROI.

The division's operating assets employed were $15,750,000 at November 30, 2008, a 5 percent increase over the 2007 year-end balance. The division's 2008 income statement follows:

CORVALIS DIVISION
Income Statement
For the Year Ended November 30, 2008
($000 omitted)

Sales revenue		$ 25,000
Less expenses		
Cost of goods sold	$16,500	
Administrative expenses	3,955	
Selling expenses	2,700	(23,155)
Income from operations before income taxes		$ 1,845

a. Calculate the segment margin for the Corvalis Division, assuming that 1,484,000 units were produced and sold during the year ended November 30, 2008.

b. Calculate the following performance measures for 2008 for the Corvalis Division:
   1. pre-tax ROI, and
   2. residual income calculated on the basis of average operating assets employed.
c. Explain why the management of the Corvalis Division would have been more likely to accept the contemplated capital acquisition if residual income rather than ROI were used as a performance measure.
d. Identify several items that Corvalis should control if it is to be evaluated fairly by either the ROI or residual income performance measures.

(CMA adapted)

43. LO.4 (Decisions based on ROI and RI) Destin Marine uses ROI to evaluate the performance of both its Powerboat and its Sailboat Division managers. The following estimates of relevant measures have been made for the upcoming year:

	Powerboats	Sailboats	Total Company
Sales	$36,000,000	$96,000,000	$132,000,000
Expenses	32,400,000	84,000,000	116,400,000
Divisional assets	30,000,000	60,000,000	90,000,000

Both division managers have the autonomy to make decisions regarding new investments. The Powerboat manager is considering investing in a new asset that would generate a 14 percent ROI; the Sailboat manager is considering an investment that would generate an 18 percent ROI.
a. Compute the projected ROI for each division, disregarding the contemplated new investments.
b. Based on your answer in part (a), which of the managers is likely to actually invest in the additional assets under consideration?
c. Are the outcomes of the investment decisions in part (b) likely to be consistent with overall corporate goals? Explain.
d. If the company evaluated the division managers' performances using a residual income measure with a target return of 17 percent, would the outcomes of the investment decisions be different from those described in part (b)? Explain.

44. LO.4 (EVA) As one of the division managers for Lawson Inc. your performance is evaluated primarily on a single measure: after-tax divisional segment income less the cost of capital invested in divisional assets. The fair value of invested capital in your division is $37,500,000, the required return on capital is 10 percent, and the tax rate is 35 percent. Income projections for 2008 follow:

Sales	$ 60,000,000
Expenses	(52,500,000)
Segment income	$ 7,500,000
Taxes	(2,625,000)
After-tax segment income	$ 4,875,000

You are considering an investment in a new product line that would, according to projections, increase 2008 pre-tax segment income by $600,000. The investment cost is not yet determinable because negotiations about several factors are still under way.
a. Ignoring the new investment, what is your projected EVA for 2008?
b. In light of your answer in part (a), what is the maximum amount that you would be willing to invest in the new product line?
c. Assuming that the new product line would require an investment of $2,100,000, what would be the revised projected EVA for your division in 2008 if the investment were made?

45. LO.4 (Throughput) Miguel Prieto manages the Springfield Division of Wilson Corporation. Prieto is concerned about the amount of the division's production. The following production data are available for April 2008:

Total units completed	423,360
Total good units completed and sold	359,856
Total value-added hours of processing time	15,680
Total hours of processing time	56,000

Determine each of the following for this division for April.
a. What is the manufacturing cycle efficiency?
b. What is the process productivity?
c. What is the process quality yield?

d. What is the total throughput per hour?

e. If only 280,000 of the units produced in April had been sold, would your answers to any of the preceding questions differ? If so, how? If not, why not?

f. If Prieto can eliminate 20 percent of the NVA time, how would throughput per hour for these data differ?

g. If Prieto can increase quality output to a yield of 90 percent and eliminate 20 percent of the NVA time, how would throughput per hour for these data differ?

h. How would Prieto determine how the NVA time was being spent in the division? What suggestions do you have for decreasing NVA time and increasing yield?

46. **LO.3 & LO.5 (ROI; new investment evaluation)** Cincinnati Industrial produces tool and die machinery for manufacturers. The company expanded vertically in 2005 by acquiring one of its suppliers of alloy steel plates, Louisville Metal Division. To manage the two separate businesses, the operations of Louisville Metal are reported separately as an investment center.

Cincinnati Industrial monitors its divisions on the basis of both unit contribution and return on investment (ROI), with investment defined as average operating assets employed. Management bonuses are determined based on ROI. All investments in operating assets are expected to earn a minimum return of 11 percent before income taxes.

Louisville Metal's cost of goods sold is considered to be entirely variable, and the division's administrative expenses are not dependent on volume. Selling expenses are a mixed cost with 40 percent attributed to sales volume. Louisville Metal's ROI has ranged from 11.8 percent to 14.7 percent since 2005. During the fiscal year ended November 30, 2008, Louisville Metal contemplated a capital acquisition with an estimated ROI of 11.5 percent; however, division management decided that the investment would decrease Louisville Metal's overall ROI.

The 2008 operating income statement for Louisville Metal follows. The division's operating assets employed were $15,750,000 at November 30, 2008, a 5 percent increase over the 2007 year-end balance.

Louisville Metal Division
Operating Income Statement
For the Year Ended November 30, 2008
($000 omitted)

Sales revenue		$25,000
Less expenses		
Cost of goods sold	$16,500	
Administrative expenses	3,955	
Selling expenses	2,700	(23,155)
Operating income before taxes		$ 1,845

a. Calculate the unit contribution for Louisville Metal Division if 1,484,000 units were produced and sold during the year ended November 30, 2008.

b. Calculate the following performance measures for 2008 for the Louisville Metal Division:
   1. Pre-tax return on investment (ROI) on average operating assets employed
   2. Residual income calculated on the basis of average operating assets employed

c. Explain why the management of the Louisville Metal Division would have been more likely to accept the contemplated capital acquisition if residual income rather than ROI was used as a performance measure.

d. The Louisville Metal Division is a separate investment center within Cincinnati Industrial. Identify several items that Louisville Metal should control if it is to be evaluated fairly by either the ROI or the residual income performance measure.

(CMA)

47. **LO.2, LO.3 & LO.6 (Providing feedback on performance)** Terry Travers is the manufacturing supervisor of the Aurora Manufacturing Company, which produces a variety of plastic products. Some of these products are standard items that are listed in the company's catalog, whereas others are made to customer specifications. Each month, Travers receives a performance report displaying the budget for the month, the actual activity for the period, and the variance between budget and actual. Part of Travers' annual performance evaluation is based on his department's performance against budget. Aurora's purchasing manager, Bob Christensen, also receives monthly performance reports and is evaluated in part on the basis of these reports.

The most recent monthly reports were just distributed when Travers met Christensen in the hallway outside their offices. Scowling, Travers began the conversation, "I see we have another set of monthly performance reports hand delivered by that not very nice junior employee in the budget office. He seemed pleased to tell me that I was in trouble with my performance again."

Christensen: "I got the same treatment. All I ever hear about are the things I haven't done right. Now, I'll have to spend a lot of time reviewing the report and preparing explanations. The worst part is that the information is almost a month old, and we spend all this time on history."

Travers: "My biggest gripe is that our production activity varies a lot from month to month, but we're given an annual budget that's written in stone. Last month, we were shut down for three days when a strike delayed delivery of the basic ingredient used in our plastic formulation, and we had already exhausted our inventory. You know that, of course, since we had asked you to call all over the country to find an alternate source of supply. When we got what we needed on a rush basis, we had to pay more than we normally do."

Christensen: "I expect problems like that to pop up from time to time—that's part of my job—but now we'll both have to take a careful look at the report to see where charges are reflected for that rush order. Every month, I spend more time making sure I should be charged for each item reported than I do making plans for my department's daily work. It's really frustrating to see charges for things I have no control over."

Travers: "The way we get information doesn't help, either. I don't get copies of the reports you get, yet a lot of what I do is affected by your department, and by most of the other departments we have. Why do the budget and accounting people assume that I should be told only about my operations even though the president regularly gives us pep talks about how we all need to work together as a team?"

Christensen: "I seem to get more reports than I need, and I am never getting asked to comment until top management calls me on the carpet about my department's shortcomings. Do you ever hear comments when your department shines?"

Travers: "I guess they don't have time to review the good news. One of my problems is that all the reports are in dollars and cents. I work with people, machines, and materials. I need information to help me solve this month's problems—not another report of the dollars expended last month or the month before."

a. Based on the conversation between Travers and Christensen, describe the likely motivation and behavior of these two employees resulting from Aurora Manufacturing Company's performance reporting system.

b. 1. When performance reporting systems have been properly implemented, both employees and companies should benefit from them. Describe the benefits that can be realized from using a performance reporting system.

   2. Based on the situation presented here, recommend ways for Aurora Manufacturing Company to improve its performance system to increase employee motivation.

(CMA adapted)

48. **LO.6–LO.8 (Performance measurement; BSC)** For each of the following items, indicate two performance measurements that could be obtained from a cost management system. Classify each item into one of the four balanced scorecard perspectives.

   a. Quality
   b. Cost
   c. Production line flexibility
   d. People productivity and development
   e. Inventory management
   f. Lead time
   g. Responsive after-sale service
   h. Customer satisfaction and retention
   i. Product and process design
   j. Manufacturing planning process
   k. Procurement process
   l. Manufacturing process
   m. Management accomplishments
   n. Marketing/sales and customer service
   o. Delivery performance
   p. Financial accounting services

49. **LO.8 (Balanced scorecard)** You have been elected president of your university's newly chartered accounting honor society. The society is a chapter of a national organization that has the following mission: "To promote the profession of accountancy as a career and to imbue members with high ethical standards."

   a. Determine the balanced scorecard categories that you believe would be appropriate for the honor society.
   b. Under each category, determine between four and six important performance measures.
   c. How would you choose benchmarks against which to compare your chapters to others of the national organization?

50. LO8 (Balanced scorecard) One of the fundamental performance measurements in an organization's balanced scorecard learning and growth perspective is number of patents obtained. The following information from the U.S. Patent & Trademark Office [and cited in Cecily Fluke and Lesley Kump, "Innovation," *Forbes* (July 5, 2004), p. 44] indicates the total U.S. patents issued for five years prior to July 2004:

Company	Total Patents
IBM	15,756
Canon	9,447
NEC	8,818
Micron Technology	7,420
Samsung Electronics	7,007
Matsushita	6,947
Sony	6,903
Hitachi	6,809
Fujitsu	6,018
Toshiba	5,895

In a team of three or four people, research these companies on the Web and prepare a written report on their financial performance, customers' perceptions of their service and product quality, and manufacturing operations (such as level of automation in plants).

51. LO.2–LO.8 (Balanced scorecard; EVA) Colson Manufacturing makes a variety of glass products having both commercial and household applications. One of its newest divisions, ColOptics, manufactures fiber optic cable and other high-tech products. Recent annual operating results (in millions) for ColOptics and two older divisions follow:

	ColOptics	Industrial Glass	Kitchenware
Sales	$250	$900	$750
Segment income	25	92	85

Colson Manufacturing uses economic value added (EVA) as its only segment performance measure. Claudia Levy, CEO of Colson, posed some serious questions in a memo to the controller, Andy Jacobs, after studying the operating results.

Dear Andy:

    I'm concerned about ColOptics. Its key competitor's sales and market share are growing at about twice the pace of ColOptics. I'm not comforted by the fact that ColOptics is generating substantially more profits than the competitor. The mission we have established for ColOptics is high growth. Do you think we should use EVA to measure the division's performance and as a basis to compensate ColOptics's divisional management? Do we need to change our performance criteria?
Claudia

After pondering the memo and studying the operating results, Jacobs passed the memo and operating results to you, his newest employee in the controller's office, and asked you to respond to the following questions.
a. Why would the use of EVA discourage a high-growth strategy?
b. Could the concept of the balanced scorecard be used to encourage a higher rate of growth in ColOptics? Explain.

52. LO.8 (Balanced scorecard) As the cost of health care continues to increase, hospital and clinic managers need to be able to evaluate the performance of their organizations. Numerous articles have been written on performance measurements for health care organizations. Obtain some of these articles and prepare a report on what you believe to be the best set of balanced scorecard measures for such an organization.

53. LO.2, LO.3 & LO.9 (Performance evaluation; ethics) In September 2008, Electronic Mind Corporation (EMC) decided to launch an expansion plan for some product lines. To finance this expansion, the firm has decided to issue $200,000,000 of new common stock in November 2008.

Historically, the firm's personal digital assistant (PDA) was a significant contributor to corporate profits. However, a competitor has recently introduced a PDA that has rendered EMC's PDA obsolete. The controller has informed EMC's president that the inventory value of the PDAs needs to be reduced to its net realizable value. Because EMC has a large inventory of the PDAs in stock, the write-down will have a very detrimental effect on both the balance sheet and income statement.

The president, whose compensation is determined in part by corporate profits and in part by stock price, has suggested that the write-downs be deferred until January 2009. He argues that, by deferring the write-down, existing shareholders will realize more value from the shares to be sold in November because the stock market will not be informed of the pending write-downs.

a. What effects are the performance evaluation measures of the president likely to have on his decision to defer the write-down of the obsolete inventory?

b. Is the president's decision to defer the write-down of the inventory an ethical treatment of existing shareholders? Of potential new shareholders?

c. If you were the controller of Electronic Mind Corporation, how would you respond to the president's decision to defer the write-down until after issuance of the new stock?▲

54. **LO.9 (Compensation)** Relative to worker compensation, no topic is more hotly debated than the minimum wage law. Using concepts from this chapter, prepare a report in which you explain why increases in the minimum wage are not desirable and how alternative mechanisms could be used to increase the compensation of low-paid workers.

55. **LO.7 & LO.9 (Pay plans and goal congruence)** In 2008, the lead story in your college newspaper reports the details of the hiring of the current football coach. The previous football coach was fired for failing to win games and attract fans. In his last season, his record was 1 win and 11 losses. The news story states that the new coach's contract provides for a base salary of $200,000 per year plus an annual bonus computed as follows:

Win less than 5 games	$ 0
Win 5 to 7 games	25,000
Win 8 games or more	75,000
Win 8 games and conference championship	95,000
Win 8 games, win conference, and get a bowl bid	150,000

The coach's contract has essentially no other features or clauses.

The first year after the new coach is hired, the football team wins three games and loses eight. In the second year, the team wins six games and loses five. In the third year, the team wins nine games, wins the conference championship, and is invited to a prestigious bowl. Shortly after the bowl game, articles appear on the front page of several national sports publications announcing that your college's football program has been cited by the National Collegiate Athletic Association (NCAA) for nine major rule violations including cash payoffs to players, playing academically ineligible players, illegal recruiting tactics, illegal involvement of alumni in recruiting, and so on. The national news publications agree that the NCAA will disband your college's football program. One article also mentioned that during the past three years, only 13 percent of senior football players managed to graduate on time. Additional speculation suggests that the responsible parties, including the coaching staff, athletic director, and college president, will be dismissed by the board of trustees.

a. Compute the amount of compensation paid to the new coach in each of his first three years.

b. Did the performance measures in the coach's contract foster goal congruence? Explain.

c. Would the coach's actions have been different if other performance measures had been added to the compensation contract? Explain.

d. What performance measures should be considered for the next coach's contract, assuming the football program is allowed to continue?

56. **LO.5 & LO.9 (Compensation; ethics; research)** Beginning in the 1990s, American firms increasingly adopted the practice of using stock options to compensate mid- to high-level managers. Companies were motivated to use stock options as a large portion of the compensation mix for two reasons. First, accounting rules allowed the expense of the stock options to be charged directly against Retained Earnings rather than against income of the period. Accordingly, reported income would be higher than if the compensation were paid in another form such as cash. Second, boards of directors viewed stock options as aligning manager and stockholder interests better than most other forms of compensation. Conduct research on the use of stock options during the past 20 years and write a report that answers the following questions.

a. The Financial Accounting Standards Board recently issued FAS 123R, which can be found at www.fasb.org under Pronouncements & EITF Abstracts. Discuss the motivation for revising this financial reporting standard.

b. Discuss whether it is misleading to stockholders to report the cost of stock options in the footnotes to the financial statements rather than reporting the cost as an expense on the income statement.

c. Research the linkage between reported accounting abuses (e.g., manipulating reported earnings) and the increased use of stock options for managerial compensation. Discuss your findings.▲

57. LO.5, LO.7 & LO.9 (Performance evaluation; compensation; ethics) A recent survey of U.S. chief financial officers provides compelling evidence that managers are willing to take extraordinary measures to achieve financial earnings targets. For example, the survey found 26 percent were willing to sacrifice some long-term value of the firm to achieve short-term earnings goals. Further 55 percent were willing to delay the start of new projects to achieve higher earnings and 80 percent indicated they would reduce spending on research and development to achieve short-term earnings targets.

Source: J.R. Graham, C.R. Harvey and S. Rajgopal, "The Economic Implications of Corporate Financial Reporting," *Journal of Accounting and Economics* 40, 2005, pp. 3–73.

a. Discuss the ethics of managers forfeiting long-term value of their firms to achieve short-term earnings goals and earn higher short-term compensation.

b. How can boards of directors create incentives and performance measures that will discourage top managers from optimizing reported short-run performance at the expense of long-term performance?▲

58. LO.4 & LO.9 (Performance evaluation; compensation; ethics) Chalmette Manufacturing has just initiated a formula bonus plan that rewards plant managers for various achievements. One of the current criteria for bonuses is the improvement of asset turnover. The plant manager of the Violet Plant asked Sam Jensen, his assistant, to meet him Saturday when the plant is closed. Without explanation, the plant manager specified that certain raw materials were to be loaded on one of the plant's dump trucks. When the truck was loaded, the plant manager and Jensen drove to a secluded mountain road where, to Jensen's astonishment, the plant manager flipped a switch and the truck dumped the raw materials down a steep ravine. The plant manager grinned and said that these raw materials were obsolete and the company would run more smoothly without them. For the next several weekends, Jensen observed the plant manager do the same thing. The following month, the plant manager was officially congratulated for improving asset turnover.

a. How did the dumping improve asset turnover?

b. What are the ethical problems in this case?

c. What are Jensen's options? Which should he choose and why?▲

59. LO.3, LO.5 & LO.9 (Performance and compensation) Performance Offroad Co. (POC), a subsidiary of Suchihara Automotive, manufactures go-carts and other recreational vehicles. Family recreational centers that feature go-cart tracks, miniature golf, batting cages, and arcade games have increased in popularity. As a result, POC has been receiving some pressure from Suchihara Automotive top management to diversify into some of these other recreational areas. Kid Games Inc. (KGI), one of the largest firms that leases arcade games to family recreation centers, is looking for a friendly buyer. Suchihara Automotive management believes that KGI's assets could be acquired for an investment of $3.2 million and has strongly urged Bill Grieco, division manager of POC, to consider acquiring KGI.

Grieco has reviewed KGI's financial statements with his controller, Marie Donnelly, and they believe that the acquisition may not be in POC's best interests. "If we decide not to do this, the Suchihara Automotive people are not going to be happy," said Grieco. "If we could convince them to base our bonuses on something other than return on investment, maybe this acquisition would look more attractive. How would we do if the bonuses were based on residual income using the company's 15 percent cost of capital?"

Suchihara Automotive has traditionally evaluated all of its divisions on the basis of return on investment, which is defined as the ratio of operating income to total assets; the desired rate of return for each division is 20 percent. The management team of any division reporting an annual increase in the return on investment is automatically eligible for a bonus. The management of divisions reporting a decline in the return on investment must provide convincing explanations for the decline to be eligible for a bonus, and this bonus is limited to 50 percent of the bonus paid to divisions reporting an increase. Presented below are condensed financial statements for both POC and KGI for the fiscal year ended May 31, 2008.

	POC	KGI
Sales revenue	$10,500,000	
Leasing revenue		$2,800,000
Variable expenses	(7,000,000)	(1,000,000)
Fixed expenses	(1,500,000)	(1,200,000)
Operating income	$ 2,000,000	$ 600,000

Current assets	$ 2,300,000	$1,900,000
Long-term assets	5,700,000	1,100,000
Total assets	$ 8,000,000	$3,000,000

	POC	KGI
Current liabilities	$ 1,400,000	$ 850,000
Long-term liabilities	3,800,000	1,200,000
Shareholders' equity	2,800,000	950,000
Total liabilities and shareholders' equity	$ 8,000,000	$3,000,000

a. Under the present bonus system how would the acquisition of KGI affect Grieco's bonus expectations?

b. If Grieco's suggestion to use residual income as the evaluation criterion is accepted, how would acquisition of KGI affect Grieco's bonus expectations?

c. Given the present bonus arrangement, is it fair for Suchihara Automotive management to expect Grieco to acquire KGI?

d. Is the present bonus system consistent with Suchihara Automotive's goal of expansion of POC into new recreational products?

(CMA)

60. LO.10 (Expatriate compensation) Assume you are the newly appointed CFO of an international engineering services firm. As one of your first assignments you need to appoint a new controller for the branch of your firm located in Buenos Aires. You have identified an assistant controller in your New York office who has the requisite skills and knowledge to perform effectively in this assignment. You are aware of the candidate's current salary and that she owns an apartment in Manhattan, is married, and has three children. Discuss how you would assemble a compensation package for this candidate that would entice her to (1) accept the Buenos Aires assignment, and (2) be motivated to perform at a high level in that assignment.

61. LO.10 (Global performance evaluation and compensation; ethics; research) Many domestic companies have chosen to offshore their production operations to countries with lower wage rates. Some of the countries being used have been accused of allowing sweatshops, child labor, and polluting conditions that would not be allowed domestically. Research the benefits of, and problems with, offshoring and answer the following items.

a. How should offshoring affect the establishment of performance measurements?

b. If you were an expat manager for a division in a lesser-developed country, how would you defend the fact that the wages being paid to your employees are so much less than the minimum wage required domestically? ▲

15 | Capital Budgeting

Objectives

After completing this chapter, you should be able to answer the following questions:

LO.1 Why do most capital budgeting methods focus on cash flows?

LO.2 How is payback period computed, and what does it measure?

LO.3 How are the net present value and profitability index of a project computed, and what do they measure?

LO.4 How is the internal rate of return on a project computed, and what does it measure?

LO.5 How do taxation and depreciation affect cash flows?

LO.6 What are the underlying assumptions and limitations of each capital project evaluation method?

LO.7 How do managers rank investment projects?

LO.8 How is risk considered in capital budgeting analyses?

LO.9 How and why should management conduct a postinvestment audit of a capital project?

LO.10 (*Appendix 1*) How are present values calculated?

LO.11 (*Appendix 2*) What are the advantages and disadvantages of the accounting rate of return method?

Introduction

Choosing the assets in which an organization will invest is one of the most important business decisions for managers. In most organizations, investments must be made in some short-term working capital assets, such as merchandise inventory, supplies, and raw material. Organizations must also invest in capital assets, which are long-term assets used to generate future revenues or cost savings or to provide distribution, service, or production capacity. A capital asset can be a tangible fixed asset (such as a piece of machinery or a building) or an intangible asset (such as a capital lease or drug patent).

Providing information about the estimated financial returns of potential capital projects is an important task of cost accountants. This chapter discusses techniques used in evaluating the potential financial costs and benefits of proposed capital projects. Several of these techniques are based on an analysis of the amounts and timing of investment cash flows.

Capital Asset Acquisition

Financial managers, assisted by cost accountants, are responsible for analyzing alternative investment opportunities through a process of capital budgeting. Capital budgeting involves the evaluation and ranking of alternative future investments to effectively and efficiently allocate limited capital resources. The process includes planning for and preparing the capital budget as well as reviewing past investments to assess the success of past decision processes and to enhance decision processes in the future. Planned annual expenditures for capital projects for the near term (less than 5 years) and summary information for the long term (6 to 10 years) are shown in the capital budget, which is a key instrument in implementing organizational strategies.

Capital budgeting involves comparing and evaluating alternative projects within a budgetary framework. Managers and accountants apply quantitative and qualitative criteria to evaluate the feasibility of alternative projects. Although financial criteria are used to judge virtually all projects, firms now also use nonfinancial criteria to critically assess activities that have benefits that are difficult to monetarily quantify. For example, high-technology and R&D investments are often difficult to evaluate using only financial criteria.

Exhibit 15–1 provides quantitative and qualitative criteria used by the forest products industry to evaluate capital projects. These criteria were obtained from a survey of practices in the forest products industry and are not presented in rank order in the exhibit. Most firms evaluate projects using multiple criteria and include quantitative and qualitative considerations in their analyses. By evaluating potential capital projects using a portfolio of criteria, managers can be confident that they have considered all possible costs and contributions of projects. Additionally, using multiple criteria allows for a balanced evaluation of short- and long-term benefits as well as the effects of capital spending on all significant stakeholders in the organization.

LO.1
Why do most capital budgeting methods focus on cash flows?

Use of Cash Flows in Capital Budgeting

Any investment made by an organization is expected to earn some type of return. For example, investments in bonds are expected to earn interest and investments in other companies are expected to earn dividends. In general, such interest and dividends are cash amounts. Similarly, investments in capital assets are evaluated from a financial perspective based on their cash costs and cash benefits. Accordingly, accounting accruals are typically not considered in capital budget analysis. Accrual accounting recognizes revenues when they are earned rather than when cash is received and recognizes expenses when they are incurred rather than when cash is paid. Converting operating income to cash flow information puts all investment returns on an equivalent basis.

Capital budgeting investment decisions can be made using a variety of techniques (see Exhibit 15–1) such as payback period, net present value, profitability index, internal rate of return, and accounting rate of return. All of these methods, except the accounting rate of return, focus on

EXHIBIT 15–1
Project Evaluation Criteria

Quantitative Criteria

1. Accounting rate of return
2. Payback period
3. Discounted payback period
4. Net present value
5. Internal rate of return
6. Profitability index

Qualitative Criteria

1. Employee morale
2. Employee safety
3. Employee responsibility
4. Corporate image
5. Social responsibility
6. Market share
7. Growth
8. Strategic planning
9. Ensure wood supply

Source: Liliya S. Hogaboam and Steven R. Shook, "Capital Budgeting Practices in the U.S. Forest Products Industry: A Reappraisal," *Forest Products Journal* (December 2004), p. 149.

the amounts and timing of cash flows (receipts or disbursements of cash). Cash receipts include revenues from a capital project that have been earned and collected, savings in cash operating costs, and any cash inflow from selling the asset at the end of its useful life. Cash disbursements include asset acquisition expenditures, additional cash invested in working capital, and cash costs of project-related direct material, direct labor, and overhead.

In evaluating capital projects, a distinction is made between operating cash flows and financing cash flows. Interest expense is a cash outflow associated with debt financing and is *not* part of the project selection process. Project funding is a financing, not an investment, decision. A financing decision is a judgment regarding the method of raising capital to fund an investment. Financing is based on an entity's ability to issue and service debt and equity securities. On the other hand, an investment decision is a judgment about which assets to acquire to accomplish an entity's mission. Cash flows generated by the two types of decisions should not be combined. Company management must justify an asset's acquisition and use prior to justifying the method of financing that asset.

Including financing receipts and disbursements with other project cash flows confuses the evaluation of a project's profitability because financing costs relate to all projects of an entity rather than to a specific project. The assignment of financing costs to a specific project is often arbitrary, which causes problems in comparing projects that are acquired with different financing sources. In addition, including the financing effects in an investment decision creates a problem in assigning responsibility. Divisional managers, or top managers with input from divisional managers, make investment decisions. An organization's treasurer in conjunction with top management typically makes financing decisions.

Cash flows from a capital project are received and paid at different points in time over the project's life. Some cash flows occur at the beginning of a period, some during the period, and others at the end. To simplify capital budgeting analysis, most analysts assume that all cash flows occur at a specific, single point in time—typically, either at the beginning or end of the time period in which they actually occur. The following example illustrates how cash flows are treated in capital budgeting situations.

Cash Flows Illustrated

Assume that various capital projects are being considered by Parker Stores, a retail chain selling consumer goods in 55 locations throughout the Midwest. One investment being considered by the firm is the acquisition of photovoltaic solar power technology to light all parking lots owned by the chain. In addition to long-term cost savings, this investment would reduce the company's carbon footprint.

The expected cost to purchase and install the technology as well as the operating cost savings appear in Exhibit 15–2. This detailed information can be simplified to a net cash flow for each year. For Parker Stores, the project generates a net negative flow in the first year and net positive cash flows thereafter. This cash flow information can be illustrated through the use of a time line.

Time Lines

A time line visually illustrates the points in time when projected cash flows are received or paid, making it a helpful tool for analyzing cash flows of a capital investment proposal. Cash inflows are shown as positive amounts on a time line, and cash outflows are shown as negative amounts.

The following time line represents the cash flows (in millions) associated with Parker Stores' potential solar technology investment.

End of period	0	1	2	3	4	5	6	7
Inflows	$ 0	$2,700	$2,900	$3,200	$3,900	$4,200	$2,100	$1,000
Outflows	(13,500)	(500)	(300)	(0)	(0)	(0)	(0)	(0)
Net cash flow	$(13,500)	$2,200	$2,600	$3,200	$3,900	$4,200	$2,100	$1,000

On a time line, the date of initial investment represents time point 0, which marks the start of the cash flows pertaining to a project. Each year after the initial investment is represented as a full time period; periods serve only to separate the timing of cash flows. Nothing is presumed to happen during a period. Thus, for example, cash inflows each year from product sales are shown as occurring at the end of, rather than during, the time period. A less conservative assumption would show the cash flows occurring at the beginning of the period.

EXHIBIT 15–2
Parker Stores' Photovoltaic Technology Decision Information

Cash Outflows

Year 0	$13,500,000
Year 1	500,000
Year 2	300,000

Cash Inflows

Electricity cost savings:

Year 1	$2,700,000
Year 2	2,900,000
Year 3	3,200,000
Year 4	3,900,000
Year 5	4,200,000
Year 6	2,100,000
Year 7	1,000,000

Note: After year 7, the technology will be obsolete and subject to replacement.

Payback Period

LO.2
How is payback period computed, and what does it measure?

Information on the timing of net cash flows is an input to a simple and often used capital budgeting technique called payback period. This method measures the time required for a project's cash inflows to equal the original investment. The payback for a project is complete when the organization has recouped its investment.

In one sense, payback period measures a dimension of project risk by focusing on the timing of cash flows. The assumption is that the longer it takes to recover the initial investment, the greater the project's risk, because cash flows in the more distant future are more uncertain than relatively near-term cash flows. Another reason for concern about long payback periods relates to capital reinvestment. The faster that capital is returned from an investment, the more rapidly it can be invested in other projects.

Payback period for a project having unequal cash inflows is determined by accumulating cash flows until the original investment is recovered. Thus, using the information shown in Exhibit 15–2 and the time line presented earlier, the solar technology investment payback period is calculated using a yearly cumulative total of inflows (in millions) as follows:

Year	Annual Cash Flow	Cumulative Total
0	$(13,500)	$(13,500)
1	2,200	(11,300)
2	2,600	(8,700)
3	3,200	(5,500)
4	3,900	(1,600)
5	4,200	2,600
6	2,100	4,700
7	1,000	5,700

At the end of the fourth year, all but $1,600 of the initial investment of $13,500 has been recovered. The $4,200 inflow in the fifth year is assumed to occur evenly throughout the year. Therefore, it should take approximately 38 percent ($1,600 ÷ $4,200) of the fifth year to cover the rest of the original investment, giving a payback period for this project of 4.38 years (or 4 years and 4.6 months).

When the cash flows from a project are equal each period (an annuity), the payback period is determined as follows:

$$\text{Payback Period} = \text{Investment} \div \text{Annuity}$$

Assume that another investment being considered by Parker Stores requires an initial investment of $50,000 and is expected to generate equal annual cash flows of $8,000 in each of the next 10 years. In this case, the payback period would equal the $50,000 net investment cost divided by $8,000, or 6.25 years (6 years and 3 months).

Company management typically sets a maximum acceptable payback period as one of the financial evaluation criteria for capital projects. If Parker Stores has set five years as the longest acceptable payback period, the solar technology investment would be considered acceptable, but the second investment project would be considered unacceptable.

Most companies use payback period in conjunction with other quantitative criteria. After being found acceptable in terms of payback period, a project is then evaluated using other financial capital budgeting techniques. A second evaluation is usually necessary because the payback period method ignores three things: cash inflows occurring after the payback period has been reached, the company's desired rate of return, and the time value of money. These issues are considered in the decision process using discounted cash flow techniques.

Discounting Future Cash Flows

A time value is associated with money because interest is paid or received on money.[1] For example, $1 received today has more value than $1 received one year from today because money received

---

[1] The time value of money and present value computations are covered in appendix 1 of this chapter. These concepts are essential to understanding the rest of this chapter; be certain they are clear before continuing.

today can be invested to generate a return that will cause it to accumulate to more than $1 over time; this effect is referred to as the time value of money. Discounted cash flow techniques are used in most capital budgeting situations to account for the effect of the time value of money.

Discounting means reducing future cash flows to their time 0 amounts (present values) by removing the portion of the future values representing interest. This "imputed" amount of interest is based on two considerations: the length of time until the cash flow is received or paid and the rate of interest assumed. After discounting, all future values associated with a project are stated in a common base of current dollars, also known as their present values (PVs). Cash receipts and disbursements occurring at the beginning of a project (time 0) are already stated in their present values and are not discounted.

Capital project information involves the use of estimates. It is extremely important, therefore, to have the best possible estimates of all potential cash inflows and outflows. To appropriately discount cash flows, managers must estimate the rate of return on capital required by the company in addition to the project's cost and cash flow estimates. This rate of return, called the discount rate, is used to determine the imputed interest portion of future cash receipts and expenditures. The discount rate should equal or exceed the company's cost of capital (COC), which is the weighted average cost of the various sources of funds (debt and equity) that compose a firm's financial structure.[2] For example, if a company has a COC of 10 percent, it annually costs an average of 10 percent of each capital dollar to finance investment projects. To determine whether a capital project is a worthwhile investment, this company should generally use a minimum rate of 10 percent to discount its projects' future cash flows.

A distinction must be made between cash flows representing a return *of* capital and those representing a return *on* capital. A return of capital is the recovery of the original investment (or the return of principal), whereas a return on capital is income and equals the discount rate multiplied by the investment amount. For example, $1.00 invested in a project that yields a 10 percent rate of return will grow to a sum of $1.10 in one year. Of the $1.10, $1.00 represents the return of capital and $0.10 represents the return on capital. The return on capital is computed for each period of the investment life. For a company to benefit from making an investment, a project must produce cash inflows that exceed the investment made and the cost of capital. To determine whether a project meets a company's desired rate of return, one of several discounted cash flow methods can be used.

Discounted Cash Flow Methods

Three discounted cash flow techniques are the net present value method, the profitability index, and the internal rate of return. Each of these methods is defined and illustrated in the following subsections.

Net Present Value Method

LO.3
How are the net present value and profitability index of a project computed, and what do they measure?

The net present value method determines whether a project's rate of return is equal to, higher than, or lower than the desired rate of return. All cash flows from a project are discounted to their present values using the company's desired rate of return. Subtracting the total present value of all cash outflows of an investment project from the total present value of all cash inflows yields the project's net present value (NPV). A 7 percent discount rate is used in Exhibit 15–3 to illustrate the net present value calculations for the cash flow data shown in Exhibit 15–2.

The factors used to compute the net present value are obtained from the present value tables provided in Appendix A at the end of the text. Each period's cash flow is multiplied by a factor obtained from Table 1 (PV of $1) for 7 percent and the appropriate time period designated for the cash flow.

The net present value represents the net cash benefit (or, if negative, the net cash cost) of acquiring and using the proposed asset. If the NPV is zero, the project's actual rate of return is equal to the required rate of return. If the NPV is positive, the actual rate is more than the required rate of return. If the NPV is negative, the actual rate is less than the required rate of return. Note that the

---

[2]All examples in this chapter use an assumed discount rate or cost of capital. The computations required to find a company's cost of capital rate are discussed in any basic finance text.

EXHIBIT 15–3
Net Present Value Calculation for Solar Technology Investment

		DISCOUNT RATE = 7%		
		a ×	b =	c
Cash Flow	Time	Amount	Discount Factor	Present Value
Initial investment	t_0	$(13,500,000)	1.0000	$(13,500,000)
Year 1 net cash flow	t_1	2,200,000	0.9346	2,056,120
Year 2 net cash flow	t_2	2,600,000	0.8734	2,271,840
Year 3 net cash flow	t_3	3,200,000	0.8163	2,612,160
Year 4 net cash flow	t_4	3,900,000	0.7629	2,975,310
Year 5 net cash flow	t_5	4,200,000	0.7130	2,995,600
Year 6 net cash flow	t_6	2,100,000	0.6663	1,399,230
Year 7 net cash flow	t_7	1,000,000	0.6228	622,800
Net present value				$ 1,433,060

exact rate of return is not indicated under the NPV method, but its relationship to the desired rate can be determined. If all estimates about the investment are correct, the solar technology investment being considered by Parker Stores has an NPV of $1,433,060 and will provide a rate of return of more than 7 percent.

If Parker Stores chose any rate other than 7 percent and used that rate in conjunction with the same facts, a different net present value would have resulted. For example, if Parker Stores set 9 percent as the discount rate, an NPV of $469,310 would have resulted for the project (see Exhibit 15–4, which gives net present values at other selected discount rates). The computations for these values are made in a manner similar to those at 7 and 9 percent. (To confirm your understanding of the NPV method, you may want to prove these computations.)

The information in Exhibit 15–4 indicates that the NPV is not a single, unique amount, but is a function of several factors. First, changing the discount rate while holding the amounts and timing of cash flows constant affects the NPV. Increasing the discount rate causes NPV to decrease; decreasing the discount rate causes NPV to increase. Second, changes in estimated amounts and/or timing of cash inflows and outflows affect a project's net present value. Effects of cash flow changes on NPV depend on the changes themselves. For example, decreasing the estimate of cash outflows causes NPV to increase; reducing the stream of cash inflows causes NPV to decrease. When amounts and timing of cash flows change in conjunction with one another, the effects of the changes can be determined only by calculation.

The NPV method, although not providing a project's actual rate of return, provides information on how that rate compares with the desired rate. This information allows managers to eliminate any project producing a negative NPV from consideration because such a project would have an unacceptable rate of return. This method can also be used to select the best project when choosing among investments that can perform the same task or achieve the same objective. However, this method should *not* be used to compare independent projects requiring different levels of initial investment. Such a comparison favors projects having higher net present values over those with lower net present values without regard to the capital invested in the project.

To illustrate, assume that Parker Stores could spend $400,000 on investment A or $80,000 on investment B. The net present values of investments A and B are $8,000 and $4,000, respectively. If only NPVs were compared, the company would conclude that Investment A was a "better" investment because it has a higher NPV. However, investment A provides an NPV of only 2 percent ($8,000 ÷ $400,000), whereas investment B provides a 5 percent ($4,000 ÷ $80,000) NPV. Logically, organizations should invest in projects that produce the highest return per investment dollar. Comparisons of projects requiring different levels of investment are made using a variation of the NPV method known as the profitability index.

EXHIBIT 15–4
Net Present Value Calculation for Solar Technology Investment

		DISCOUNT RATE = 9%		
		a	× b =	c
Cash Flow	Time	Amount	Discount Factor	Present Value
Initial investment	t_0	$(13,500,000)	1.0000	$(13,500,000)
Year 1 net cash flow	t_1	2,200,000	0.9174	2,018,280
Year 2 net cash flow	t_2	2,600,000	0.8417	2,188,420
Year 3 net cash flow	t_3	3,200,000	0.7722	2,471,040
Year 4 net cash flow	t_4	3,900,000	0.7084	2,762,760
Year 5 net cash flow	t_5	4,200,000	0.6499	2,729,580
Year 6 net cash flow	t_6	2,100,000	0.5963	1,252,230
Year 7 net cash flow	t_7	1,000,000	0.5470	547,000
Net present value				$ 469,310

Net present value with a 5% discount rate: $2,494,590
Net present value with an 8% discount rate: $938,060
Net present value with a 10% discount rate: $23,210
Net present value with an 11% discount rate: $(402,030)

Profitability Index

The profitability index (PI) is a ratio of a project's net cash inflows to the project's net investment. The PI is calculated as

$$PI = \text{Present Value of Net Cash Flows} \div \text{Net Investment}$$

The present value (PV) of net cash flows equals the PV of future cash inflows minus the PV of future cash outflows. The PV of net cash inflows represents an output measure of the project's worth, whereas the net investment represents an input measure of the project's cost. By relating these two measures, the profitability index gauges the efficiency of the firm's use of capital. The higher the index, the more efficient the capital investment.

The following information illustrates the calculation and use of the profitability index. Parker Stores is considering two investments: a distribution warehouse costing $3,440,000 and distribution equipment costing $1,700,000 for an existing storage facility. Corporate managers have computed the present values of the investments by discounting all future expected cash flows at a rate of 12 percent. Present values of the expected net cash inflows are $4,200,000 for the distribution warehouse and $2,360,000 for the distribution equipment. Dividing the PV of the net cash inflows by initial cost gives the PI for each investment. Subtracting asset cost from the present value of the net cash inflows provides the NPV. Results of these computations follow:

	PV of Inflows	Cost	PI	NPV
Warehouse	$4,200,000	$3,440,000	1.22	$760,000
Distribution equipment	2,360,000	1,700,000	1.39	660,000

Although the net present value of the warehouse is higher, the profitability index indicates that the distribution equipment is a more efficient use of corporate capital.[3] The higher PI reflects a higher rate of return on the distribution equipment than on the warehouse. The higher a project's PI, the more profitable that project is per investment dollar.

[3]Two conditions must exist for the PI to provide better information than the NPV method. First, the decision to accept one project must require that the other project be rejected. Second, the availability of funds for capital acquisitions must be limited.

If a capital investment is to provide a return on capital, the PI should be equal to or greater than 1.00. This criterion is the equivalent of an NPV equal to or greater than zero. Like the NPV method, the PI does not indicate the project's expected rate of return. However, another discounted cash flow method, the internal rate of return, provides the expected rate of return to be earned on an investment.

Internal Rate of Return

LO.4
How is the internal rate of return on a project computed, and what does it measure?

A project's **internal rate of return (IRR)** is the discount rate that causes the present value of the net cash inflows to equal the present value of the net cash outflows. The IRR is the project's expected rate of return. If the IRR is used as the discount rate to determine a project's NPV, the NPV will be zero. Data in Exhibit 15–4 indicate that Parker Stores' solar technology investment would generate an IRR slightly over 10 percent because a discount rate of 10 percent produced an NPV of $23,210 and a discount rate of 11 percent produced an NPV of $(402,030).

The following formula can be used to determine NPV:

$$\text{NPV} = -\text{Investment} + \text{PV of Cash Inflows} - \text{PV of Cash Outflows}$$
$$\text{Other than Investment}$$
$$= -\text{Investment} + \text{Cash Inflows (PV Factor)} - \text{Cash Outflows}$$
$$(\text{PV Factor})$$

Capital project information should include amounts for the investment, cash inflows, and cash outflows. Thus, the only missing data in the preceding formula are the PV factors. By inserting the known amounts into the formulas, the missing PV factors can be calculated and then can be found in the PV tables. The interest rate with which the factors are associated is the internal rate of return.

The IRR is most easily computed for projects having equal annual net cash flows. When an annuity exists, the NPV formula can be restated as follows:

$$\text{NPV} = -\text{Net Investment} + \text{PV of Annuity Amount}$$
$$= -\text{Net Investment} + (\text{Cash Flow Annuity Amount} \times \text{PV Factor})$$

The investment and annual cash flow amounts are known from the expected data, and the NPV is known to be zero at the IRR. The IRR and its present value factor are unknown. To determine the internal rate of return, substitute known amounts into the formula, rearrange terms, and solve for the unknown (the PV factor):

$$\text{NPV} = -\text{Net Investment} + (\text{Annuity} \times \text{PV Factor})$$
$$0 = -\text{Net Investment} + (\text{Annuity} \times \text{PV Factor})$$
$$\text{Net Investment} = (\text{Annuity} \times \text{PV Factor})$$
$$\text{Net Investment} \div \text{Annuity} = \text{PV Factor}$$

The solution yields a present value factor for the number of annuity periods corresponding to the project's life at an interest rate equal to the internal rate of return. Finding this factor in the PV of an annuity table and reading the interest rate at the top of the column in which the factor is found provides the internal rate of return.

To illustrate an IRR computation for a project with a simple annuity, assume that Parker Stores is considering the purchase of a warehouse distribution management system. The system would cost $1,500,000, be installed immediately, and generate cost savings of $300,000 per year over its seven-year life. The system has no expected salvage value.

The NPV equation is solved for the present value factor.

$$\text{NPV} = -\text{Net Investment} + (\text{Annuity} \times \text{PV Factor})$$
$$\$0 = -\$1,500,000 + (\$300,000 \times \text{PV Factor})$$
$$\$1,500,000 = (\$300,000 \times \text{PV Factor})$$
$$\$1,500,000 \div \$300,000 = \text{PV Factor}$$
$$5.0000 = \text{PV Factor}$$

The PV of an ordinary annuity table (Appendix A, Table 2) is examined to find the IRR. In the table, find the row representing the project's life (in this case, seven periods) and find the PV factor resulting from the equation solution. In row 7, a factor of 5.0330 appears under the column headed

9 percent. Thus, the internal rate of return for this investment is very near 9 percent. By using interpolation, a computer program, or a programmable calculator, the exact IRR can be found.[4] A computer program indicates that the IRR of the warehouse distribution management system is 9.2 percent.

Refer to Exhibit 15–5 for a plot of the NPVs that result from discounting the warehouse distribution management system cash flows at various rates of return. For example, the NPV at 7 percent is $109,146 and at 11 percent is ($77,785). (These computations are not provided here but can be performed by discounting the $300,000 annual cash flows and subtracting $1,500,000 of investment cost.)

The internal rate of return is located on the graph's horizontal axis at the point where the NPV equals zero [9.2 percent (rounded)]. Note that the graph reflects an inverse relationship between rates of return and NPVs. Higher rates yield lower present values because, at the higher rates, fewer dollars are invested to obtain the same future value.

Manually finding the IRR of a project that has unequal annual cash flows is more complex and requires an iterative trial-and-error process. An initial estimate is made of a rate believed to be close to the IRR and the NPV is computed. If the resulting NPV is negative, a lower rate is estimated (because of the inverse relationship mentioned earlier), and the NPV is computed again. If the NPV is positive, a higher rate is selected and the NPV is calculated. This process is continued until the NPV equals zero, at which time the IRR has been found.

The project's IRR is then compared with management's preestablished **hurdle rate**, which is the rate of return specified as the lowest acceptable return on investment. Like the discount rate mentioned earlier, this rate should generally be at least equal to the cost of capital. In fact, the hurdle rate is commonly the discount rate used in computing NPV amounts. If a project's IRR is equal to or greater than the hurdle rate, the project is considered viable from a financial perspective.

The higher the IRR, the more financially attractive the investment proposal. In choosing among alternative investments, however, managers cannot look solely at the internal rates of return on projects, because the rates do not reflect the dollars involved. An investor would normally rather have a 20 percent return on $1,000 than a 100 percent return on $10!

Using the IRR has three drawbacks. First, when uneven cash flows exist, the iterative process is inconvenient. Second, unless PV tables that provide factors for fractional interest rates are available, finding the precise IRR on a project is difficult. These two problems can be eliminated with the use

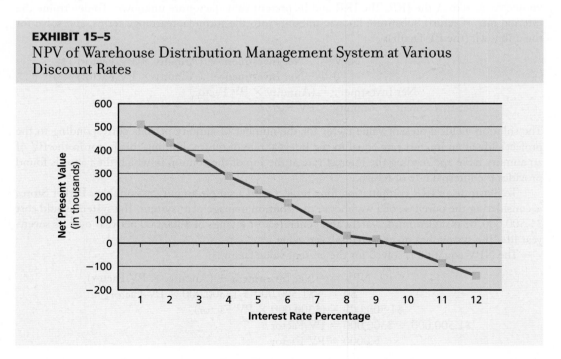

EXHIBIT 15–5
NPV of Warehouse Distribution Management System at Various Discount Rates

---

[4]*Interpolation* is the process of finding a term between two other terms in a series.

of a computer or a programmable calculator. The last problem is that sometimes it is possible to find several rates of return that will make the NPV of the cash flows equal zero. This phenomenon usually occurs when there are net cash inflows in some years and net cash outflows in other years of the investment project's life (other than at time 0).

In performing discounted cash flow analyses, accrual-based accounting information generally must be converted to cash flow data. One accrual that deserves special attention is depreciation. Although depreciation is not a cash flow item, it has cash flow implications because of its effect on income tax payments—which *are* cash flows.

Effect of Depreciation on After-Tax Cash Flows

LO.5
How do taxation and depreciation affect cash flows?

Income taxes represent a significant cash expense for businesses and, therefore, are the subject of managerial planning and decision-making processes. Tax considerations have a large impact on overall business profitability and managers typically make decisions only after examining how those decisions will affect company taxes. In evaluating capital projects, managers should use after-tax cash flows to determine project acceptability.

Depreciation expense is *not* a cash flow item: no funds are paid or received for it. However, depreciation on capital assets, similar to interest on debt, affects cash flows by reducing a company's income tax expense. Thus, depreciation provides a **tax shield** against the payment of taxes. The tax shield produces a **tax benefit** equal to the amount of taxes saved (the depreciation amount multiplied by the tax rate). The concepts of tax shield and tax benefit are shown on the following income statements. The tax rate is assumed to be 40 percent.

No Depreciation Deduction Income Statement		Depreciation Deduction Income Statement	
Sales	$ 500,000	Sales	$ 500,000
Cost of goods sold	(350,000)	Cost of goods sold	(350,000)
Gross margin	$ 150,000	Gross margin	$ 150,000
Expenses other than		Expenses other than	
depreciation	(75,000)	depreciation	(75,000)
Depreciation expense	0	Depreciation expense	(75,000)
Income before taxes	$ 75,000	Income before taxes	$ 0
Tax expense (40%)	(30,000)	Tax expense (40%)	0
Net income	$ 45,000	Net income	$ 0

In this example, the tax shield is the $75,000 depreciation expense amount and the tax benefit is $30,000 (the difference between $30,000 of tax expense on the first income statement and $0 of tax expense on the second income statement). The tax benefit also equals the depreciation tax shield of $75,000 multiplied by the 40 percent tax rate. Because taxes are reduced by $30,000 when depreciation is taken, the pattern of cash flows is improved.

It is the depreciation taken for income tax purposes rather than the depreciation taken for financial accounting purposes that is relevant in discounted cash flow analysis. Income tax laws regarding depreciation deductions are subject to frequent revision. For example, in recent years, Congress has allowed very rapid depreciation of certain assets to stimulate economic growth in the United States. In making analyses of capital investments, managers should use the most current tax regulations for depreciation. Different depreciation methods can have significant impacts on after-tax cash flows. For a continuously profitable business, an accelerated method of depreciation, such as the modified accelerated cost recovery system (MACRS) allowed for U.S. tax computations, will produce higher tax benefits in the early years of an asset's life than will the straight-line method. These higher tax benefits will translate into a higher NPV for the investment's cash flows.

Depreciation methods and asset depreciable lives that are available for tax purposes could dramatically affect projected after-tax cash flows, net present value, profitability index, and internal rate of return expected from a capital investment. Because capital projects are analyzed and evaluated before investments are made, managers should be aware of the inherent risk of tax law changes. Original assumptions made about the depreciation method or asset life could be invalid by the time an investment is actually made and an asset is placed into service. However, an asset can generally be depreciated using the method and tax life allowed when the asset was purchased and placed into service regardless of the tax law changes occurring after that time.

Relatively unpredictable changes may also occur in the tax rate structure. For example, the Tax Reform Act of 1986 lowered the maximum federal corporate tax rate from 46 percent to 34 percent; the present top U.S. tax rate is 35 percent.[5] With state income taxes added to the federal income tax, the combined rate for large U.S. corporations is approximately 40 percent.[6] A tax rate reduction lowers the tax benefit provided by depreciation because such a reduction lessens the impact on cash flow. Tax law changes (such as asset tax-life changes) can cause the expected outcomes of the capital investment analysis to vary from the project's actual outcomes.[7]

To illustrate such variations, assume that Parker Stores is considering a $6 million investment in new point-of-sale equipment for its stores that will have a 10-year economic life and produce expected net annual cash operating savings of $850,000. The company's after-tax cost of capital is 5 percent. Further, corporate assets are depreciated on a straight-line basis for tax purposes.[8] Recent tax law changes have dramatically accelerated the rate of cost recovery for many types of assets. Under current law, the cost of some assets can be deducted entirely in the year of acquisition.

In late 2008, prior to making the point-of-sale equipment investment, Parker Stores' cost accountant, Sarah Brown, calculated the project's NPV. At the time of Brown's analysis, Parker Stores' tax rate was 30 percent, and the tax laws allowed a 10-year depreciable life on this property. See Situation A in Exhibit 15–6 for the results of her calculations. Note that depreciation is added to income after tax to obtain the amount of after-tax cash flow. Even though depreciation is deductible for tax purposes, it is a noncash expense. The PV amounts are obtained by multiplying the after-tax cash flows by the appropriate PV of an annuity factor from Table 2 in Appendix A at the end of the text. The NPV evaluation technique indicates the acceptability of the capital investment.

Because Brown was concerned about proposed changes in the U.S. tax rate, she also analyzed the project assuming that tax rates changed. See Exhibit 15–6 for the different after-tax cash flows and NPVs that result if the same project is subjected to either a 25 percent (Situation B) or 40 percent (Situation C) tax rate. Based on the net present value criterion, a decrease in the tax rate makes the point-of-sale equipment a more acceptable investment; an increase has the opposite effect.

Understanding how depreciation and taxes affect the various capital budgeting techniques allows managers to make the most informed decisions about capital investments. If the substantial resource commitment required can be justified, managers are more likely to have confidence in capital investments made by the company. Justification is partially achieved by determining whether a capital project fits into an organization's strategic plans. To be confident of their conclusions, managers must also comprehend the assumptions and limitations of each capital budgeting method.

LO.6
What are the underlying assumptions and limitations of each capital project evaluation method?

Assumptions and Limitations of Methods

As summarized in Exhibit 15–7 (page 564), each capital budget evaluation method has underlying assumptions and limitations. To maximize benefits of the capital budgeting process, managers should understand the similarities and differences of the various methods and use multiple methods to evaluate projects.

All methods in Exhibit 15–7 have two similar limitations. First, except to the extent that payback indicates promptness of investment recovery, none of the methods provides a mechanism to

---

[5]Surtaxes that apply to corporations can drive the top marginal rate above 35 percent for certain income brackets.
[6]http://www.us.kpmg.com/microsite/Global_Tax/Ctr_Survey/2004CTRS.pdf (last accessed 9/12/07).
[7]Additionally, managers should be careful to consider effects of applicable foreign and state tax laws.
[8]To simplify the presentation, the authors have elected to ignore a tax rule requirement called the *half-year* (or *mid-quarter*) *convention* that applies to personal assets and a mid-month convention that applies to most real estate improvements. Under tax law, only a partial year's depreciation may be taken in the year an asset is placed into service. The slight difference that such a tax limitation would make on the amounts presented is immaterial for purposes of illustrating these capital budgeting concepts.

EXHIBIT 15–6
Point-of-Sale Equipment Investment Analyses

Assumed Facts

Initial investment	$6,000,000
Expected annual before-tax cash flows	850,000
Straight-line depreciation (10 years)	600,000
Expected economic life	10 years

Situation A: Tax rate of 30% (actual rate in effect)
Situation B: Tax rate of 25%
Situation C: Tax rate of 40%

	SITUATION		
Years 1–10	**A**	**B**	**C**
Before-tax cash flow	$850,000	$850,000	$850,000
Depreciation	(600,000)	(600,000)	(600,000)
Income before tax	$250,000	$250,000	$250,000
Tax	(75,000)	(62,500)	(100,000)
Net income	$175,000	$187,500	$150,000
Depreciation	600,000	600,000	600,000
Cash flow after tax	$775,000	$787,500	$750,000

SITUATION A—NPV CALCULATIONS ASSUMING A 5% DISCOUNT RATE

Cash Flow	Time	Amount	Discount Factor	Present Value
Investment	t_0	$(6,000,000)	1.0000	$(6,000,000)
Annual inflows	t_1–t_{10}	775,000	7.7217	5,984,318
Net present value				$ (15,682)

SITUATION B—NPV CALCULATIONS ASSUMING A 5% DISCOUNT RATE

Cash Flow	Time	Amount	Discount Factor	Present Value
Investment	t_0	$(6,000,000)	1.0000	$(6,000,000)
Annual inflows	t_1–t_{10}	787,500	7.7217	6,080,839
Net present value				$ 80,839

SITUATION C—NPV CALCULATIONS ASSUMING A 5% DISCOUNT RATE

Cash Flow	Time	Amount	Discount Factor	Present Value
Investment	t_0	$(6,000,000)	1.0000	$(6,000,000)
Annual inflows	t_1–t_{10}	750,000	7.7217	5,791,275
Net present value				$ (208,725)

include management preferences with regard to the timing of cash flows. This limitation can be partially overcome by discounting cash flows occurring further in the future at higher rates than those in earlier years, assuming that earlier cash flows are preferred. Second, all methods use single, deterministic measures of cash flows rather than probabilities. This limitation can be minimized through the use of probability estimates of cash flows. Such estimates can be input into a computer program to determine a distribution of answers for each method under various conditions of uncertainty.

EXHIBIT 15–7
Assumptions and Limitations of Capital Budgeting Methods

ASSUMPTIONS	LIMITATIONS
Payback Method	
• Speed of investment recovery is the key consideration. • Timing and size of cash flows are accurately predicted. • Risk (uncertainty) is lower for a shorter payback project.	• Cash flows after payback are ignored. • Cash flows and project life are treated as deterministic without explicit consideration of probabilities. • Time value of money is ignored. • Cash flow pattern preferences are not explicitly recognized.
Net Present Value	
• Discount rate used is valid. • Timing and size of cash flows are accurately predicted. • Life of project is accurately predicted. • If the shorter-lived of two projects is selected, the proceeds of that project will continue to earn the discount rate of return through the theoretical completion of the longer-lived project.	• Cash flows and project life are treated as deterministic without explicit consideration of probabilities. • Alternative project rates of return are not known. • Cash flow pattern preferences are not explicitly recognized. • IRR on project is not reflected.
Profitability Index	
• Assumptions are the same as NPV. • Size of PV of net inflows relative to size of present value of investment measures efficient use of capital.	• Assumptions are the same as NPV. • A relative answer is given but dollars of NPV are not reflected.
Internal Rate of Return	
• Hurdle rate used is valid. • Timing and size of cash flows are accurately predicted. • Life of project is accurately predicted. • If the shorter lived of two projects is selected, the proceeds of that project will continue to earn the IRR through the theoretical completion of the longer-lived project.	• The IRR, rather than dollar size, is used to rank projects for funding. • Dollars of NPV are not reflected. • Cash flows and project life are treated as deterministic without explicit consideration of probabilities. • Cash flow pattern preferences are not explicitly recognized. • Multiple rates of return can be calculated on the same project.
Accounting Rate of Return **(presented in appendix 2 of this chapter)**	
• Effect on accounting earnings relative to average investment is key consideration. • Timing and size of increase in earnings, investment cost, project life, and salvage value can be accurately predicted.	• Cash flows are not considered. • Time value of money is not considered. • Earnings, investment, and project life are treated as deterministic without explicit consideration of probabilities.

Investment Decision

Management must identify the best asset(s) to acquire for fulfilling the company's goals and objectives; to do so requires answers to the questions appearing in the following four subsections.

Is the Activity Worthy of an Investment?

A company acquires assets when they have value in relation to specific activities in which the company is engaged. For example, Amazon.com invests heavily in product and service development because that activity is the primary path to new revenues. Before making asset acquisition decisions, company management must be certain that the activity for which the assets are needed justifies an investment.

An activity's worth is measured by cost–benefit analysis. For most capital budgeting decisions, costs and benefits are measured in monetary terms. If the dollars of benefits exceed the dollars of costs, the activity is potentially worthwhile. In some cases, though, the benefits provided by capital projects are difficult to quantify. Difficulty in quantification is no reason to exclude such benefits from capital budgeting analyses. Often surrogate quantifiable measures can be obtained for qualitative benefits. For example, benefits from investments in day care centers for employees' children could be estimated through the reduction in employee time off and turnover. At a minimum, managers should attempt to subjectively include qualitative benefits in the analytical process.

In other circumstances, management could know in advance that the monetary benefits of the capital project will not exceed the costs but that the project is essential for other reasons. For instance, a company could consider renovating the employee workplace with new carpet, furniture, paint, and artwork. The renovation would not make the employees' work any easier, faster, or safer but would make the workplace more comfortable. Such a project could be deemed "worthy" regardless of the results of a cost–benefit analysis. Companies could also invest in unprofitable products to maintain market share of a product group and, therefore, protect the market position of profitable products. Further, a company may invest in technology that reduces energy consumption and pollution even though the investment is not wholly justified on financial grounds alone.

Which Assets Can Be Used for the Activity?

Determination of available and suitable assets to use when conducting the intended activity is closely related to an evaluation of the activity's worth. Management must determine how much the needed assets will cost to decide whether the activity should be pursued. Management should gather the following specific monetary and nonmonetary information for each asset to make this determination: initial cost, estimated life and salvage value, raw material and labor requirements, operating costs (both fixed and variable), output capacity, serviceability and service costs, maintenance expectations, and revenues to be generated (if any) (see Exhibit 15–8). As mentioned in the previous section, information used in a capital project analysis may include surrogate, indirect measures. Management must have both quantitative and qualitative information on each asset and recognize that some projects are simply more crucial to the firm's future than others.

Of the Available Assets for Each Activity, Which Is the Best Investment?

Using all available information, management should select the best asset from the candidates and end consideration of all others. In most instances, companies have committees that discuss, evaluate, and approve capital projects. In judging capital project acceptability, a committee should recognize that two types of capital budgeting decisions must be made: screening decisions and preference decisions. A *screening decision* determines whether a capital project is desirable based on some previously established minimum criterion or criteria. A project that does not meet the minimum standard(s) is excluded from further consideration. The second decision is a *preference decision* in which projects are ranked according to their impact on the achievement of company objectives.

Deciding which asset is the best investment requires the use of one or more of the evaluation techniques discussed previously. Some techniques are used to screen the acceptability of projects; other techniques are used to rank the projects in order of preference. Although different companies use different techniques for screening and ranking purposes, payback period is commonly used only for screening decisions because payback focuses only on the short run and does not consider the time value of money. The remaining techniques can be used to screen or rank capital projects.

Of the "Best Investments" for All Worthwhile Activities, in Which Ones Should the Company Invest?

Although many worthwhile investment activities exist, each company has limited resources available and must allocate them in the most profitable manner. Therefore, after choosing the best asset for

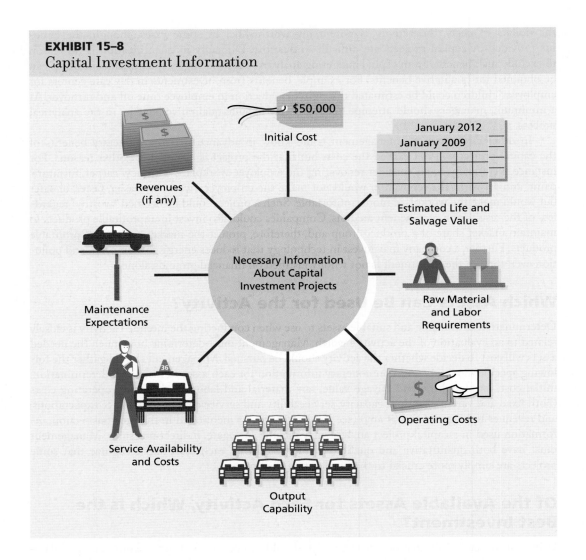

EXHIBIT 15–8
Capital Investment Information

$50,000
Initial Cost

Revenues
(if any)

January 2012
January 2009
Estimated Life and
Salvage Value

Maintenance
Expectations

Necessary Information
About Capital
Investment Projects

Raw Material
and Labor
Requirements

Service Availability
and Costs

Operating Costs

Output
Capability

each activity, management must decide which activities and assets to fund. Investment projects are classified as mutually exclusive, independent, or mutually inclusive.

Mutually exclusive projects fulfill the same function. One project will be chosen from such a group, excluding all others from further consideration. A proposal under consideration could be to replace a current asset with one that provides the same functionality. If the company keeps the old asset, it will not buy the new one; if it purchases the new one, it will sell the old asset. Thus, the two assets are mutually exclusive. For example, if a small bakery decides to buy a new delivery truck, it would no longer need the existing truck and would sell it to help finance the new one.

Other investments could be independent projects because they have no specific bearing on one another. For example, the acquisition of an office computer system is not related to the purchase of a factory machine. These project decisions are analyzed and accepted or rejected independently of one another. Although limited resources can preclude the acquisition of all acceptable projects, the projects themselves are not mutually exclusive.

Management may consider acquiring a mutually inclusive project in which multiple investments are all related to a primary project. In such a situation, if the primary project is chosen, all related projects are also selected. Alternatively, rejection of the primary project dictates rejection of the others. For example, when a firm chooses to invest in new technology, investing in an employee training program for the new technology would also be necessary.

Exhibit 15–9 illustrates a typical investment decision process in which a company is determining the best way to provide transportation for its sales force. Answers to the four questions asked in the subheadings to this section are provided for the transportation decision.

For a small business, if the purchase of a new delivery truck would result in the sale of the existing truck, the decision to purchase or keep is a mutually exclusive one.

EXHIBIT 15–9
Typical Investment Decision Process

Activity—Provide transportation for a sales force of 10 people.

1. Is the activity worthy of an investment?
    Yes; this decision is based on an analysis of the cost of providing transportation in relationship to the dollars of gross margin to be generated by the sales force.

2. Which assets can be used for the activity?
    Available: Bus passes, bicycles, motorcycles, automobiles (purchased), automobiles (leased), automobiles (currently owned), small airplanes.
    Infeasible: Bus passes, bicycles, and motorcycles are rejected as infeasible because of inconvenience and inability to carry a reasonable quantity of merchandise; airplanes are rejected as infeasible because of inconvenience and lack of proximity of landing sites to customers.
    Feasible: Various types of automobiles to be purchased (assume asset options A through G); various types of leasing arrangements (assume availability of leases 1 through 5); current fleet.
    Gather all relevant quantitative and qualitative information on all feasible assets (assets A–G; leases 1–5; current fleet).

3. Of the available assets of each activity, which is the best investment?
    Compare all relevant information and choose the best asset candidate from the purchase group (assume asset D) and the lease group (assume lease 2).

4. Of the "best investments" for all worthwhile activities, in which ones should the company invest?
    Comparing the best asset candidate from the purchase group (asset D) and the lease group (lease 2) represents a mutually exclusive, multiple-candidate project decision. The best candidate is found to be type D assets. Comparing the type D assets to the current fleet is a mutually exclusive, replacement project. The best investment is the purchase of a new fleet of 10 type D automobiles concurrently with the sale of the old fleet.

To ensure that capital funds are invested in the best projects available, managers must carefully evaluate all projects and decide which of them represents the most effective and efficient use of resources—a difficult determination. The evaluation process should consider activity priorities, cash flows, and project risk. Projects should then be ranked in order of acceptability. Ranking could be required for both independent and mutually exclusive projects. Ranking independent projects is required to efficiently allocate scarce capital to competing uses. Ranking mutually exclusive projects is required when selecting the best project from the set of alternatives.

LO.7
How do managers rank investment projects?

Ranking Multiple Capital Projects

When managers must make an accept/reject decision for a single asset, all time value of money evaluation techniques normally point to the same decision alternative. A project is acceptable under the NPV method if its net present value is not negative. Acceptability of a capital asset is also indicated by a profitability index of 1.00 or more. Because the PI is an adaptation of the NPV method, these two evaluation techniques always provide the same accept/reject decision. To be acceptable using the IRR model, a project must have an internal rate of return equal to or greater than the specified hurdle rate. The IRR method gives the same accept/reject decision as the NPV and PI methods if the hurdle rate is used as the discount rate.

More often, however, managers must choose among multiple, mutually exclusive projects. Multiple project evaluation decisions require that a ranking be made, generally using net present value, profitability index, and/or internal rate of return techniques. Payback period also can be used to rank multiple projects. However, the payback method does not provide as much useful information as do NPV, PI, and IRR because the payback method ignores both cash flows beyond the payback period and the time value of money.

Managers can use results from the evaluation techniques to rank projects in descending order of acceptability. For the NPV and PI methods, rankings are based on the magnitude of the NPV and PI index, respectively. Although based on the same figures, the NPV and PI methods do not always provide the same rank order because the former is a dollar measure and the latter is a percentage. When the IRR is used, rankings of multiple projects are based on expected rates of return. Rankings provided by the IRR method are not always in the same order as those given by the NPV or PI methods.

Conflicting results arise because of differing underlying reinvestment assumptions among the three methods. The reinvestment assumption focuses on how the cash flows released during a project's life are assumed to be reinvested until the end of that project's life. The NPV and PI techniques assume that released cash flows are reinvested at the discount rate, which is typically the cost of capital rate. The IRR method assumes that released cash flows are reinvested at the expected internal rate of return, which is higher than the COC for projects with positive NPVs. In such a case, the IRR method could provide a misleading indication of project success because additional projects that have such a high return might not be found.

In addition to ranking projects based on financial criteria, managers must evaluate whether there are differences in risks across potential projects.

LO.8
How is risk considered in capital budgeting analyses?

Compensating for Risk in Capital Project Evaluation

When choosing among multiple projects, managers must consider the risk or uncertainty associated with each project. In accounting, risk reflects uncertainty about differences between the expected and actual future returns from an investment. For example, the purchase of a $100,000, 5 percent Treasury note would provide a virtually risk-free return of $5,000 annually because such notes are backed by the full faith and credit of the U.S. government. If the same $100,000 were used to purchase stock, the returns could range from −100 percent (losing the entire investment) to an abnormally high return. The potential for extreme variability makes the stock a much riskier investment than the Treasury note.

Managers considering a capital investment should understand and compensate for the degree of risk involved in that investment. There are three approaches to compensate for risk: the judgmental method, the risk-adjusted discount rate method, and sensitivity analysis. These methods do not eliminate risk, but they do help managers understand and evaluate risk in the decision-making process.

Judgmental Method

The judgmental method of risk adjustment allows decision makers to use logic and reasoning when deciding whether a project provides an acceptable rate of return in relation to its risk. The decision maker is presented all available information for each project, including the payback period, NPV, PI, and IRR. After reviewing the information, the decision maker chooses from among acceptable projects based on personal judgment of the risk-to-return relationship. The judgmental approach provides no formal process for adjusting data for the risk element. Although such a method sounds unorthodox, experienced business managers are generally able to use this method with a high level of reliability.

Risk-Adjusted Discount Rate Method

A more formal method of considering risk requires making adjustments to the discount or hurdle rate. Under the risk-adjusted discount rate method, the decision maker increases the rate used for discounting future cash inflows and decreases the rate used for discounting future cash outflows to compensate for increased risk. As the discount rate is increased (or decreased), the PVs of the cash flows are reduced (or increased). Therefore, larger cash inflows are required to "cover" the investment and provide an acceptable rate of return. Changes in the discount rate should reflect the degree of cash flow variability and timing, other investment opportunities, and corporate objectives. If the internal rate of return were used for higher-risk project evaluation, the risk-adjusted discount rate method would increase the hurdle rate to which the IRR is compared.

Assume that Parker Stores' management is considering the purchase of an automated product-ordering system. The $1,500,000 system would be used for 10 years and then would be sold for $50,000. Exhibit 15–10 provides estimates of the development cost and annual cash savings for the automated ordering system. Parker Stores' management generally uses its 10 percent cost of capital as the discount rate in evaluating capital projects under the NPV method. However, Soloman Klatz, a capital projects committee member, believes that this project has substantially above-normal risk. First, the cost savings realized from the system could be significantly less than planned. Second, the system's salvage value in 10 years could vary substantially from the $50,000 estimate. Klatz wants to compensate for these risk factors by using a 14 percent discount rate rather than the 10 percent rate. Determining the adjustment of the discount rate (from 10 to 14 percent, for example) is most commonly an arbitrary one. Thus, even though a formal process is used to compensate for risk, the process still involves a degree of judgment on the part of the project evaluators. Exhibit 15–10 shows the NPV computations using both discount rates. When the discount rate is raised to 14 percent, the project's NPV is reduced and shows the project to be unacceptable.

The same type of risk adjustment can be used for payback period or accounting rate of return (ARR, which is discussed in appendix 2 of this chapter). If the payback method is used, managers can choose to shorten the maximum allowable payback period to compensate for increased risk. This adjustment assumes that cash flows occurring in the more distant periods are riskier than those occurring sooner. If the ARR method is used, managers can increase the hurdle rate against which the ARR is compared to compensate for risk. Another way in which risk can be included in the decision process is through the use of sensitivity analysis.

Sensitivity Analysis

Sensitivity analysis is a process of determining the amount of change that must occur in a variable before a different decision would be made. In a capital budgeting situation, sensitivity analysis can be conducted for the discount rate, annual net cash flows, or project life. Sensitivity analysis examines what happens if a variable is different from that originally expected. Except for the initial purchase price, all information used in capital budgeting is estimated. Use of estimates creates the possibility of introducing errors, and sensitivity analysis identifies an "error range" for the various estimated

EXHIBIT 15–10
Automated Ordering System Analyses

Initial installation cost	$1,500,000
After-tax net cash flows	
Years 1–5	260,000
Years 6–10	220,000
Year 10 (sale)	50,000

NPV USING 10% DISCOUNT RATE

Cash Flow	Time	Amount	Discount Factor	Present Value
Investment	t_0	$(1,500,000)	1.0000	$(1,500,000)
Annual inflows	t_1-t_5	260,000	3.7908	985,608
Annual inflows	t_6-t_{10}	220,000	2.3538[a]	517,836
Final inflow	t_{10}	50,000	0.3855	19,275
Net present value				$ 22,719

NPV USING 14% DISCOUNT RATE

Cash Flow	Time	Amount	Discount Factor	Present Value
Investment	t_0	$(1,500,000)	1.0000	$(1,500,000)
Annual inflows	t_1-t_5	260,000	3.4331	892,606
Annual inflows	t_6-t_{10}	220,000	1.7830[b]	392,260
Final inflow	t_{10}	50,000	0.2697	13,485
Net present value				$ (201,649)

[a]Factor at 10 Periods at 10% − Factor at 5 Periods at 10% = Factor for Periods 6–10 at 10%
6.1446 − 3.7908 = 2.3538
[b]Factor at 10 Periods at 14% − Factor at 5 Periods at 14% = Factor for Periods 6–10 at 14%
5.2161 − 3.4331 = 1.7830

values over which the project will still be acceptable. The following sections consider how sensitivity analysis relates to the discount rate, cash flows, and asset life.

Range of the Discount Rate

A capital project providing a rate of return equal to or greater than the discount or hurdle rate is considered an acceptable investment. A project's NPV will change, however, if the discount rate changes. Because the discount and hurdle rates should be set minimally at the organization's cost of capital, an increase in the COC would cause an increase in the discount rate—and a corresponding decrease in the NPV of the project's cash flows. The COC, for instance, can increase because of increases in interest rates on new issues of debt.

Sensitivity analysis allows a company to determine how much the estimated COC (and, therefore, the related discount rate) could increase before a project becomes unacceptable. The upper limit of increase in the discount rate (COC) is the project's internal rate of return. At the IRR, a project's NPV is zero; therefore, the PV of the cash inflows equals the PV of cash outflows. As long as the IRR for a project is equal to or greater than the COC, the project is acceptable.

To illustrate the use of sensitivity analysis, assume that Parker Stores has an opportunity to invest $340,000 in new delivery equipment that has a 10-year life and will generate cost savings of $75,000 per year. Using a 10 percent cost of capital rate for Parker Stores, the machinery's NPV is computed as follows:

After-tax cash flows for 10 years
discounted at 10% ($75,000 × 6.1446) $460,845
Initial investment   (340,000)
     Net present value $120,845

The project provides a positive NPV and is considered an acceptable investment candidate.

Parker Stores' management wants to know how high the discount rate can rise before the project would become unacceptable. To find the upper limit of the discount rate, the PV factor for an annuity of 10 periods at the unknown interest rate is computed as follows:

$$\text{Cash flow} \times \text{PV factor} = \text{Investment}$$
$$\$75,000 \times \text{PV factor} = \$340,000$$
$$\text{PV factor} = 4.5333$$

Using the PV factor, the IRR is found to be between 17 and 18 percent. As long as Parker Stores' COC is less than or equal to approximately 17.5 percent, this project is acceptable. As the discount rate increases and approaches the project's IRR, the project becomes less desirable. These calculations assume that the cash flows and project life have been properly estimated.

Range of the Cash Flows

Another factor sensitive to changes in estimation is the investment's projected cash flows. Parker Stores' data for the delivery equipment investment project are also used to illustrate how to determine the range of acceptable cash flows. Company management wants to know how small the net cash inflows could be and still have the project remain desirable. This determination requires that the present value of the cash flows for 10 periods, discounted at 10 percent, be equal to or greater than the investment cost. The PV factor for 10 periods at 10 percent is 6.1446. The equation from the preceding section can be used to find the lowest acceptable annuity:

$$\text{Cash flow} \times \text{PV factor} = \text{Investment}$$
$$\text{Cash flow} \times 6.1446 = \$340,000$$
$$\text{Cash flow} = \$340,000 \div 6.1446$$
$$\text{Cash flow} = \$55,333$$

As long as the net annual after-tax cash flow equals or exceeds $55,333, the delivery equipment project will be financially acceptable.

Range of the Life of the Asset

Asset life is related to many factors, some of which (such as the amount and timing of maintenance and equipment) are controllable. Other factors, such as technological advances and actions of competitors, are noncontrollable. Misestimating the project's life will change the number of periods from which cash flows are to be derived. This change could affect the accept/reject decision for a project. The Parker Stores' delivery equipment example is used to demonstrate how to find the minimum length of time the cash flows must be received from the project for it to be acceptable. The solution requires setting the present value of the cash flows discounted at 10 percent equal to the investment. This computation yields the PV factor for an unknown number of periods:

$$\text{Cash flow} \times \text{PV factor} = \text{Investment}$$
$$\$75,000 \times \text{PV factor} = \$340,000$$
$$\text{PV factor} = 4.5333$$

Review the present value of an annuity table in Appendix A under the 10 percent interest column to find the 4.5333 factor. The project life is between six and seven years. If the project cash flows were to stop at any point before approximately 6.5 years, the project would be unacceptable.

Sensitivity analysis does not reduce the uncertainty surrounding the estimate of each variable. It does, however, provide management a sense of the tolerance for estimation errors by providing upper and lower ranges for selected variables. The preceding presentation simplistically focuses on single changes in each of the variables. If all factors change simultaneously, this type of sensitivity analysis is useless. More advanced treatments of sensitivity analysis, which allow for simultaneous ranging of all variables, can be found under the topic of simulation in an advanced mathematical modeling text.

LO.9
How and why should management conduct a postinvestment audit of a capital project?

Postinvestment Audit

In a **postinvestment audit** of a capital project, information on actual project results is gathered and compared to expected results. This process provides a feedback or control feature to both the persons who submitted the original project information and those who approved it. Comparisons should be made using the same technique or techniques used originally to determine project acceptance. Actual data should be extrapolated to future periods in which such information would be appropriate. For cases in which significant learning or training is necessary, start-up costs of the first year may not be appropriate indicators of future costs. Such projects should be given a chance to stabilize before making the project audit.

As the size of the capital expenditure increases, a postinvestment audit becomes more crucial. Although an audit cannot change a past investment decision, it can pinpoint areas of project operations that are out of line with expectations so that problems can possibly be corrected before they get out of hand.

An audit can also provide feedback on the accuracy of the original estimates for project cash flows. Sometimes project sponsors are biased in favor of their own projects and provide overly optimistic forecasts of future revenues or cost savings. Project sponsors should be required to explain all major variances. Knowing that postinvestment audits will be made could cause project sponsors to provide realistic cash flow forecasts in their capital requests.

Performing a postinvestment audit is not an easy task. The actual information might be in a different form from the original estimates, and some project benefits could be difficult to quantify. Project returns fluctuate considerably over time, so results gathered at a single point might not be representative of the project. Regardless of the difficulties involved, however, postinvestment audits provide management information that can help to make better capital investment decisions in the future.

LO.10
How are present values calculated?

Appendix 1

Time Value of Money

The time value of money can be discussed in relation to either its future or its present value. **Future value (FV)** refers to the amount to which a sum of money invested at a specified interest rate will grow over a specified number of time periods. Alternatively, present value is the amount that future cash flows are worth currently given a specified rate of interest.[9] Thus, FVs and PVs depend on three things: (1) amount of the cash flow, (2) rate of interest, and (3) timing of the cash flow. Future and present values are related: a PV is a FV discounted to time 0. The rate of return used in PV computations is called the discount rate.

In computing FVs and PVs, simple or compound interest is used. **Simple interest** means that interest is earned only on the original investment or principal amount. **Compound interest** means that interest earned in prior periods is added to the original investment so that, in each successive period, interest is earned on both principal and interest. The time between each interest computation is called the **compounding period**. The more often interest is compounded, the higher the actual rate of interest being received relative to the stated rate. The following discussion is based on the use of compound interest because most analyses use this method. Additionally, only PVs are discussed because they are more relevant to the types of management decisions discussed in this text.

Interest rates are typically stated in annual terms and compounding is assumed to occur annually. To compensate for more frequent compounding periods, the number of years is multiplied by the number of compounding periods per year, and the annual interest rate is divided by the number of compounding periods per year.

---

[9]Interest can be earned or owed, received or paid. To simplify the discussion, the topic of interest is viewed only from the inflow standpoint.

Present Value of a Single Cash Flow

Assume that Doug Wong's bank pays interest at 10 percent per year, compounded annually. He wants to accumulate $50,000 in five years to attend graduate school and needs to know what amount to invest now to achieve that goal. The formula to solve for the present value is

$$PV = FV \div (1 + i)^n$$

where PV = present value of a future amount
   FV = future value of a current investment
     i = interest rate per compounding period
     n = number of compounding periods

Substituting known values into the formula gives the following:

$$PV = \$50,000 \div (1 + 0.10)^5$$
$$PV = \$50,000 \div 1.61051$$
$$PV = \$31,046$$

In capital budgeting analyses, many future value amounts must be converted to present values. Rather than using the formula $[1 \div (1 + i)^n]$ to find PVs, a table of factors for the PV of $1 (Table 1) for a variety of "i" and "n" values is provided in Appendix A at the end of the text for ease of computation. Such factors are also available in programmable calculators, making the use of tables unnecessary.

Present Value of an Annuity

An annuity is a cash flow (either positive or negative) that is repeated over consecutive periods. In an *ordinary annuity*, the cash flows occur at the end of each period. In contrast, the cash flows for an *annuity due* occur at the beginning of each period.

To illustrate the computation of the PV of an annuity, consider the following situation. Billy and Billie Bigwell are planning for their daughter's college education. Their daughter, Bobbie, will need $25,000 per year for the next four years. The Bigwells want to know how much to invest currently at 8 percent so that Bobbie can withdraw $25,000 per year. The following diagram presents the situation:

Time period	t_0	t_1	t_2	t_3	t_4
Future value		$25,000	$25,000	$25,000	$25,000
Present value	?				

The present value of each single cash flow can be found using 8 percent factors in Table 1 of Appendix A as follows:

PV of first receipt: $25,000 × 0.9259	$23,148
PV of second receipt: $25,000 × 0.8573	21,433
PV of third receipt: $25,000 × 0.7938	19,845
PV of fourth receipt: $25,000 × 0.7350	18,375
Total present value of future cash flows	$82,801

The PV factor for an ordinary annuity can also be determined by adding the PV factors for all periods having a future cash flow. Table 2 in Appendix A provides PV of ordinary annuity factors for various interest rates and time periods. From this table, the factor of 3.3121 can be obtained and multiplied by $25,000 to yield $82,803, or approximately the same result as just calculated. (The difference is caused by decimal-fraction rounding.)

Appendix 2

Accounting Rate of Return

The **accounting rate of return (ARR)** measures the rate of earnings obtained on the average capital investment over a project's life. This evaluation method is consistent with the accounting model and

LO.11
What are the advantages and disadvantages of the accounting rate of return method?

uses profits shown on accrual-based financial statements. It is the one evaluation technique that is not based on cash flows. The formula for computing the accounting rate of return is

$$\text{ARR} = \text{Average Annual Profits from Project} \div \text{Average Investment in Project}$$

Investment in project refers to project cost and any other costs needed for working capital items (such as inventory) to support the project. Investment cost, salvage value, and working capital released at the end of the project's life are summed and divided by 2 to obtain the average investment over the life of the project.[10] The cost and working capital needed represent the initial investment, and the salvage value and working capital released represent the ending investment. The following information pertains to a new vitamin line being considered by Parker Stores. The information is used to illustrate after-tax calculation of the ARR.

Beginning investment	
Initial cost of equipment and software	$4,000,000
Additional working capital needed for the product line	2,000,000
Return over life of project	
Average increase in profits after taxes	1,000,000
Return at end of project	
Salvage value of investment in 10 years (end of life of product line)	1,000,000
Working capital released at the end of 10 years	2,000,000

Solving the formula for the accounting rate of return gives

$$\begin{aligned} \text{ARR} &= \$1,000,000 \div [(\$6,000,000 + \$3,000,000) \div 2] \\ &= \$1,000,000 \div \$4,500,000 \\ &= 22.22\% \end{aligned}$$

The 22.22 percent ARR on this product line investment can be compared with a preestablished hurdle rate set by management. This hurdle rate need not be the same as the desired discount rate because the data used in calculating the ARR do not represent cash flow information. The ARR hurdle rate can be set higher than the discount rate because the discount rate automatically compensates for the time value of money. In addition, the 22.22 percent ARR for this project should be compared with ARRs on other projects under investment consideration by Parker Stores to see which projects have the higher accounting rates of return.

[10]Sometimes ARR is computed using initial cost rather than average investment as the denominator. Such a computation ignores the return of funds at the end of the project's life and is less appropriate than the computation shown.

Comprehensive Review Module

Chapter Summary

1. Most capital budgeting techniques focus on cash flows because

    •   evaluation of capital projects requires comparing the return on such projects with the cost of capital, which is calculated using actual net cash flows rather than accounting accruals. Investors

    are ultimately interested in cash flows rather than accounting earnings.

    •   cash flows from a capital project can be compared with the cash returns provided from debt investments (in the form of interest) and stock investments (in the form of dividends).

2. The payback period

- is computed by summing the annual net cash flows until they total the original investment.

- is the length of time required for cash inflows to recoup the initial cost of a capital project.

3. Net present value (NPV) and profitability index (PI) use discounted cash flows to measure the expected returns on potential capital projects.

   - NPV is the present value (PV) of cash inflows minus the PV of cash outflows.

     ➢ To be acceptable, a project must generate an NPV of $0 or more.

   - PI is the PV of cash inflows divided by the PV of cash outflows.

     ➢ To be acceptable, a project must generate a PI of at least 1.

4. The internal rate of return (IRR) of a project is the discount rate that causes the NPV to equal zero.

   - IRR can be calculated by trial and error. Using the NPV framework, a discount rate can be arbitrarily selected and an NPV calculated.

     ➢ If the resulting NPV is positive, select a higher discount rate and again calculate the NPV.

     ➢ If the resulting NPV is negative, select a lower discount rate and again calculate the NPV.

     ➢ Repeat the process until the discount rate selected causes the NPV to equal zero.

   - IRR can also be calculated by many handheld calculators and computers.

   - If the only cash inflow is an annuity, the IRR can be found by using the PV of an ordinary annuity table.

5. Taxation and depreciation impact a project's cash flows because

   - operating income is subject to income tax, which reduces the cash inflows from the capital project.

   - depreciation reduces the amount of taxes paid because depreciation is deducted in determining the taxable income from a project.

6. Each capital project evaluation method has certain underlying assumptions and limitations.

   - Payback method

     ➢ Assumptions

       ❖ The speed of investment recovery is the most important investment criterion.

       ❖ The timing and amounts of cash flows can be accurately predicted.

       ❖ The risk is lower for projects with shorter paybacks.

     ➢ Limitations

       ❖ Cash flows occurring after payback are ignored.

       ❖ All cash flows are treated as deterministic.

       ❖ The time value of money is ignored.

       ❖ Any managerial preferences in the pattern of cash flows are ignored.

       ❖ This method should be used in conjunction with another method because it ignores both the cash flows after the payback period is reached and the time value of money.

- NPV method

  ➢ Assumptions

    ❖ The discount rate used is valid for that project.

    ❖ The timing and amounts of cash flows can be accurately predicted.

    ❖ Cash flows received from projects can be reinvested at the discount rate for the life of the project. When comparing projects with unequal lives, the NPV method assumes that the cash inflows from the shorter project can be reinvested at the discount rate for the life of the longer project.

  ➢ Limitations

    ❖ All cash flows are treated as deterministic.

    ❖ The actual rate of return for projects is not revealed.

    ❖ Any managerial preferences in the pattern of cash flows are ignored.

- PI method

  ➢ Assumptions

    ❖ The discount rate used is valid for that project.

    ❖ The timing and amounts of cash flows can be accurately predicted.

- ❖ Cash flows received from projects can be reinvested at the discount rate for the life of the project. When comparing projects with unequal lives, the NPV method assumes that the cash inflows from the shorter project can be reinvested at the discount rate for the life of the longer project.

- ❖ The present value of cash inflows relative to the present value of the investment measures an efficient use of capital.

  - ➤ Limitations

    - ❖ All cash flows are treated as deterministic.

    - ❖ The actual rate of return for projects is not revealed.

    - ❖ Any managerial preferences in the pattern of cash flows are ignored.

    - ❖ Actual dollars of net present value are ignored.

- • IRR method

  - ➤ Assumptions

    - ❖ The hurdle rate used is a valid return benchmark.

    - ❖ The timing and amounts of cash flows can be accurately predicted.

    - ❖ The life of the project can be accurately predicted.

    - ❖ Cash flows received from projects can be reinvested at the internal rate of return for the life of the project. When comparing projects with unequal lives, the IRR method assumes that the cash inflows from the shorter project can be reinvested at the internal rate of return for the life of the longer project.

  - ➤ Limitations

    - ❖ All cash flows are treated as deterministic.

    - ❖ The actual rate of return for projects is not revealed.

    - ❖ Any managerial preferences in the pattern of cash flows are ignored.

    - ❖ The dollar magnitude of return on a project is ignored.

    - ❖ Multiple IRRs can be generated on the same project.

7. Managers can rank capital projects using the following guidelines:
   - • Shorter payback period is preferred to longer payback period.
   - • Higher NPV is preferred to lower NPV.
   - • Higher PI is preferred to lower PI.
   - • Higher IRR is preferred to lower IRR.

8. Capital budgeting analysis considers risk by
   - • requiring a shorter payback period for riskier projects.
   - • applying a higher discount rate for riskier projects when the NPV or PI method is used.
   - • applying a higher discount rate for riskier cash flows when the NPV or PI method is used.
   - • requiring a higher IRR for riskier projects.
   - • applying sensitivity analysis to the original project assumptions and estimates.

9. Postinvestment audits of projects should be conducted
   - • after the project has stabilized rather than shortly after start-up.
   - • to compare actual project performance against expected performance to
     - ➤ evaluate the accuracy of original projections.
     - ➤ diagnose problems with implementation.
     - ➤ assess credibility of project sponsors' information.
   - • in greater depth for high-value investment projects.
   - • using the same technique or techniques originally used to determine project acceptance.

10. Calculation of present values relies on discounted cash flow techniques
    - • which converts future values to present values by separating return on capital from return of capital (discounting).
    - • that can apply to a single cash flow or cash flows that behave as annuities.

11. The accounting rate of return is calculated
    - • using accounting data rather than cash flows.
    - • in a manner that ignores the time value of money.

Potential Ethical Issues

1. Using only financial criteria to evaluate projects that enhance employee safety or reduce detrimental environmental impact

2. Changing assumptions or estimates for projects solely so that they will meet required criteria for investment approval

3. Using an inappropriately low discount rate relative to the risk of a project so that the project will generate a positive NPV and be acceptable

4. Failing to conduct postinvestment audits to hold project sponsors accountable for differences between the investment proposal and actual results achieved by projects

5. Choosing projects based only on their impact on accounting earnings and not on discounted cash flow analyses ▲

Solution Strategies

Prepare a time line to illustrate all moments in time when cash flows are expected. The minimum discount rate used should be the cost of capital.

Payback Period

1. For projects with an equal annual cash flow:

$$\text{Payback Period} = \text{Investment} \div \text{Annuity}$$

2. For projects with unequal annual cash flows:

Sum the annual cash flows until investment is reached to find the payback period.

If the payback period is equal to or less than a preestablished maximum number of years, the project is acceptable.

Net Present Value

$$
\begin{aligned}
&- \text{Investment made currently (no discounting required)}\\
&+ \text{PV of future cash inflows or cost savings}\\
&\underline{- \text{PV of future cash outflows}}\\
&= \text{NPV}
\end{aligned}
$$

If NPV is equal to or greater than zero, the project is expected to return a rate equal to or greater than the discount rate, and it is acceptable.

Profitability Index

$$
\begin{aligned}
&+ \text{PV of future cash inflows or cost savings}\\
&\underline{- \text{PV of future cash outflows}}\\
&= \text{PV of net cash flows}
\end{aligned}
$$

$$\text{PI} = \text{PV of Net Cash Flows} \div \text{Net Investment}$$

If PI is 1.00 or higher, the project is expected to return a rate equal to or greater than the discount rate, and the project is acceptable.

Internal Rate of Return

1. For projects with equal annual cash flows:

$$\text{PV Factor} = \text{Net Investment} \div \text{Annuity}$$

Find the PV factor (or the one closest to it) in the table on the row for the number of periods of the cash flows. The percentage at the top of the column where this factor is found will approximate the IRR. (*Note*: For projects with equal annual cash flows, this factor also equals the payback period.)

2. **For projects with unequal annual cash flows:**

    Make an estimate of the rate provided by the project; compute NPV. If NPV is positive (negative), try a higher (lower) rate until the NPV is zero. Compare IRR to the preestablished hurdle rate. If the IRR equals or is greater than the hurdle rate, the project is acceptable.

Tax Benefit of Depreciation

$$\text{Tax Benefit} = \text{Depreciation Amount} \times \text{Tax Rate}$$

Accounting Rate of Return

$$\text{ARR} = \text{Average Annual Profits from Project} \div \text{Average Investment in Project}$$

$$\text{Average Investment} = (\text{Beginning Investment} + \text{Recovery of Investment at End of Project Life}) \div 2$$

Compare calculated ARR to hurdle ARR. If the calculated ARR is equal to or greater than the hurdle ARR, the project is acceptable.

Basic Concepts of Capital Budgeting Techniques

	Payback	NPV	PI	IRR	ARR
Uses time value of money?	No	Yes	Yes	Yes	No
Indicates a specific rate of return?	No	No	No	Yes	Yes
Uses cash flow?	Yes	Yes	Yes	Yes	No
Considers returns during life of project?	No	Yes	Yes	Yes	Yes
Uses discount rate in calculation?	No	Yes	Yes	No*	No*

*Discount rate is not used in the calculation, but it can be used as the hurdle rate.

Demonstration Problem

Missoula Manufacturing is considering an investment in a B2B system for purchasing office supplies and nonoperating inputs. The project would require an initial investment of $400,000 and have an expected life of six years with no salvage value. At the end of the fourth year, the firm anticipates spending $70,000 to update some hardware and software. This amount would be fully deductible for tax purposes in the year incurred.

Management requires that investments of this type be recouped in five years or less. The pre-tax increase in income, resulting from cost savings, is expected to be $95,000 in each of the first four years and $80,000 in each of the next two years. The company's discount rate is 8 percent, its tax rate is 30 percent, and the investment would be depreciated for tax purposes using the straight-line method with no consideration of salvage value over a five-year period.

Required:

a. Prepare a time line for displaying cash flows. Be certain to consider the effects of taxes.

b. Calculate the after-tax payback period.

c. Calculate the after-tax NPV on the project.

d. Discuss whether this is an acceptable investment.

Solution to Demonstration Problem

a.

End of period	0	1	2	3	4	5	6
Investment	$(400,000)						
Operating inflows[a]		$66,500	$66,500	$66,500	$66,500	$56,000	$56,000
Depreciation tax benefit[b]		24,000	24,000	24,000	24,000	24,000	
Operating outflows[c]					(49,000)		
Total cash flows	$(400,000)	$90,500	$90,500	$90,500	$41,500	$80,000	$56,000

^a$95,000 × (1 − 0.30) = $66,500
$80,000 × (1 − 0.30) = $56,000
^b($400,000 ÷ 5) × 0.30 = $24,000
^c$70,000 × (1 − 0.30) = $49,000

b.

Year	Annual Flow	Cumulative Flow
0	$(400,000)	$(400,000)
1	90,500	(309,500)
2	90,500	(219,000)
3	90,500	(128,500)
4	41,500	(87,000)
5	80,000	(7,000)
6	56,000	49,000

The payback is complete in 5.125 years or in the middle of February in the last year. The portion of the sixth year (0.125) required to complete the payback equals $7,000 ÷ $56,000.

c.

Cash Flow	Time	Amount	Discount Factor	Present Value
Investment	t_0	$(400,000)	1.0000	$(400,000)
Annual flow	t_1-t_3	90,500	2.5771	233,228
Annual flow	t_4	41,500	0.7350	30,503
Annual flow	t_5	80,000	0.6806	54,448
Annual flow	t_6	56,000	0.6302	35,291
Net present value				$ (46,530)

d. The project is unacceptable based on the payback period and fails to qualify based on the NPV criterion as well. Accordingly, from strictly a financial perspective, the project is not acceptable. However, nonquantitative factors, such as effects on competitive position and ability to adopt future technological advances, must be considered.

Key Terms

accounting rate of return (ARR), **p. 573**
annuity, **p. 555**
annuity due, **p. 573**
capital asset, **p. 552**
capital budgeting, **p. 552**
cash flows, **p. 553**
compound interest, **p. 572**
compounding period, **p. 572**
cost of capital (COC), **p. 556**
discounting, **p. 556**
discount rate, **p. 556**
financing decision, **p. 553**
future value (FV), **p. 572**
hurdle rate, **p. 560**
independent project, **p. 566**
internal rate of return (IRR), **p. 559**
investment decision, **p. 553**
judgmental method (of risk adjustment), **p. 569**
mutually exclusive project, **p. 566**
mutually inclusive project, **p. 566**

net present value (NPV), **p. 556**
net present value method, **p. 556**
ordinary annuity, **p. 573**
payback period, **p. 555**
postinvestment audit, **p. 572**
preference decision, **p. 565**
present value (PV), **p. 556**
profitability index (PI), **p. 558**
reinvestment assumption, **p. 568**
return of capital, **p. 556**
return on capital, **p. 556**
risk, **p. 568**
risk-adjusted discount rate method, **p. 569**
screening decision, **p. 565**
sensitivity analysis, **p. 569**
simple interest, **p. 572**
tax benefit (of depreciation), **p. 561**
tax shield (of depreciation), **p. 561**
time line, **p. 554**

Questions

1. What is a capital asset? How is it distinguished from other assets?
2. Why do capital budgeting evaluation methods use cash flows rather than accounting income?
3. How are time lines helpful in evaluating capital projects?
4. What does the payback method measure? What are its major weaknesses?
5. What is the distinction between a return *of* capital and a return *on* capital?
6. What is measured by the net present value (NPV) of a potential project? If the NPV of a project equals zero, is it an acceptable project? Explain.
7. Will the NPV amount determined in the capital budgeting process be the same amount as that which actually occurs after a project is undertaken? Why or why not?
8. How is the profitability index (PI) related to the NPV method? What does the PI measure?
9. What is measured by the internal rate of return? When is a project considered acceptable using this method?
10. Because depreciation is not a cash flow, why is it important in capital budgeting evaluation techniques that use discounted cash flows?
11. What four questions should managers ask when choosing the investment proposals to fund?
12. How is risk defined in capital budgeting analysis? List several aspects of a project in which risk is involved and how risk can affect a project's net present value.
13. How is sensitivity analysis used in capital budgeting?
14. Why are postinvestment audits performed? When should they be performed?
15. (Appendix 1) What is meant by the term *time value of money*? Why is a present value always less than the future value to which it relates?
16. (Appendix 2) How is the accounting rate of return computed? How does this rate differ from the discount rate and the internal rate of return?

Exercises

17. LO.1 (Cash flows vs. accounting accruals) In discussing your cost accounting class with friends, you explained that you were currently studying methods of evaluating capital investments. You mentioned that most of these methods rely upon cash flow analysis. One particularly sophisticated friend was surprised to hear that these analyses used cash flows rather than accounting earnings. He said, "It seems to me that investors are only interested in accounting earnings and don't pay much attention to cash flows. In fact, you never hear market commentators talk about cash flows; they always talk about a firm's income and whether earnings will match investor and analyst expectations."

    Provide a written explanation to your friend that provides the rationale for capital budgeting techniques to focus on cash flows rather than accounting earnings.

18. LO.1 (Cash flows vs. accounting accruals) Burdick Industrial is considering the purchase of a robotic machine that would replace a manual labor production task. This project would require an upfront cash commitment of $1,000,000 to purchase and install the equipment. The equipment would have an expected life of five years and generate annual labor cost savings of $325,000. Assume the equipment would be depreciated over five years with no salvage value. Prepare a time line for this project that shows both the cash flow and accounting earnings effects for the project's five year life. Ignore taxes.

19. LO.1 (Application of discounting methods) Several capital budgeting techniques depend on discounted cash flow concepts, which are applied in business in a variety of settings. Select a business that relies on discounted cash flow analysis, such as a bond investment company, and prepare a brief report on how the firm applies discounting methods to manage the business.

20. LO.1 (Application of discounting methods) In recent years, stock price averages (e.g., the Dow Jones Industrial Average) have shown sensitivity to changes in interest rates. Based on your understanding of the factors that determine stock prices and of how future cash flows are discounted, prepare a brief report in which you explain why stock prices should be sensitive to changes in interest rates.

21. LO.2 (Payback period) Houston Hydraulic is considering the purchase of new production technology that would require an initial investment of $750,000 and have an expected life of 10 years. At the end of its life, the equipment would have no salvage value. By installing the new equipment, the firm's annual labor and quality costs would decline by $150,000.

a. Compute the payback period for this investment.

b. Assume instead that the annual cost savings would vary according to the following schedule:

Years	Annual Cost Savings
1–5	$ 75,000
6–10	100,000

Compute the payback period under the revised circumstances.

22. **LO.2 (Payback period)** Parkwood Automotive is considering a new product line that would require an investment of $160,000 in equipment and $180,000 in working capital. Store managers expect the following pattern of net cash inflows from the new product line over the life of the investment.

Year	Amount
1	$70,000
2	78,000
3	72,000
4	56,000
5	50,000
6	48,000
7	44,000

a. Compute the payback period for the proposed new product line. If Parkwood requires a four-year pre-tax payback period on its investments, should the company invest in the new product line? Explain.

b. Should Parkwood use any other capital project evaluation method(s) before making an investment decision? Explain.

23. **LO.3 (NPV)** LA Pipe Co is considering the installation of a $1,600,000 production conveyor system that would generate the following labor cost savings over its 10-year life:

Years	Annual Labor Cost Savings
1–2	$280,000
3–5	340,000
6–8	288,800
9–10	260,000

The system will have no salvage at the end of its 10-year life, and the company uses a discount rate of 12 percent. What is the pre-tax net present value of this potential investment?

24. **LO.3 (NPV)** Fresno Fasteners has been approached by one of its customers about producing 400,000 special-purpose parts for a new home product. The parts would be produced at a rate of 50,000 per year for eight years. To provide these parts, Fresno would need to acquire new production machines costing a total of $500,000. The new machinery would have no salvage value at the end of its 8-year life.

The customer has offered to pay Fresno $15 per unit for the parts. Fresno's managers have estimated that, in addition to the new machines, the company would incur the following costs to produce each part:

Direct labor	$ 4
Direct material	5
Variable overhead	4
Total	$13

In addition, annual fixed out-of-pocket costs would be $20,000.

a. Compute the net present value of the machinery investment, assuming that the company uses a discount rate of 9 percent to evaluate capital projects.

b. Based on the NPV computed in part (a), is the machinery a worthwhile investment? Explain.

c. In addition to the NPV, what other factors should Fresno's managers consider when making the investment decision?

25. **LO.3 (PI)** The manager at Callie's Carpet is interested in purchasing a computer and software that would allow company salespeople to demonstrate to customers how a finished carpet installation would appear. The total cost of the computer, software, and peripheral equipment has been estimated at $60,000. Based on this cost, the manager has determined that the net present value of the investment is $6,000. Compute the investment's profitability index.

26. **LO.3 (PI)** Miami Tours is considering adding a new bus route. To do so, the company would be required to purchase a new bus, which would cost $600,000, have a 10-year life, and have no salvage value. If the new bus

is purchased, Miami Tours' managers expect that net cash inflows from bus ridership would rise by $89,000 per year for the life of the new bus. Miami Tours uses a 9 percent required rate of return for evaluating capital projects.

a. Compute the profitability index of the bus investment.

b. Should Miami Tours buy the new bus?

c. What is the minimum acceptable value for the profitability index for an investment to be acceptable? Explain.

27. LO.4 (IRR; sensitivity analysis) Port Aransas Municipal Marina is considering adding a new dock to accommodate larger yachts. The dock would cost $680,000 and would generate $144,000 annually in new cash inflows. Its expected life would be eight years, and it would have no salvage value. The organization's cost of capital and discount rate are 7 percent.

a. Calculate the internal rate of return for the proposed dock addition (round to the nearest whole percent).

b. Based on your answer to part (a), should the marina add the new dock?

c. How much annual cash inflow would be required for the project to be minimally acceptable?

28. LO.4 (IRR) Wholesome Foods is considering the purchase of new food processing technology, which would cost $1,800,000 and would generate $300,000 in annual cost savings. No salvage is expected on the technology at the end of its 10-year life. The firm's cost of capital and discount rate is 12 percent.

a. Calculate the internal rate of return for the project. Does the IRR indicate the project is acceptable?

b. What qualitative factors should the company consider in evaluating the investment?

29. LO.3 & LO.4 (NPV; IRR) Joe Johnson recently purchased an annuity contract that will pay him $250,000 per year for the next seven years. According to Johnson's calculations, the estimated internal rate of return on this investment is 14%. If Johnson's cost of capital is 10 percent, what is the estimated NPV of the annuity investment?

30. LO.5 (Depreciation; PV) Pittsburgh Freight provides truck freight services throughout the northeast United States. The firm is considering an investment in a new mainframe computer and communications software, which would cost $2,000,000 and have an expected life of eight years. For tax purposes, the investment will be depreciated using the straight-line method over eight years, with no salvage value expected at the end of its life. The company's cost of capital and tax rates are 8 percent and 30 percent, respectively.

a. Compute the present value of the depreciation tax benefit.

b. Assume instead that Pittsburgh Freight uses the double-declining-balance method of depreciation with a five-year life. Compute the present value of the depreciation tax benefit.

c. Why is the depreciation tax benefit computed in part (b) larger than that computed in part (a)?

31. LO.3 & LO.5 (Alternative depreciation methods; NPV; sensitivity analysis) Modern Equipment Co. is considering an investment in computer-based production technology as part of a business reengineering process. The necessary equipment, installation, and training will cost $30,000,000, have a life of eight years, and generate annual net before-tax cash flows of $6,200,000 from operations. The technology will have no salvage value at the end of its eight-year estimated life. The company's tax rate is 30 percent, and its cost of capital is 6 percent.

a. If Modern Equipment uses straight-line depreciation for tax purposes, is the project acceptable using the net present value method?

b. Assume that the tax law allows the company to take accelerated annual depreciation on this asset in the following manner:

Years 1–2	23% of cost
Years 3–8	9% of cost

What is the net present value of the project? Is it acceptable?

c. Recompute parts (a) and (b), assuming the tax rate is increased to 40 percent.

32. LO.5 (Tax effects of asset sale) Three years ago, Joe Dirt Co. purchased a material conveyor system. The company has decided to sell the system and acquire more advanced technology. Data relating to the existing system follow:

Current market value	$ 74,000
Original cost	190,000
Current book value for tax purposes	36,000
Current book value for financial accounting purposes	70,000
Corporate tax rate	30%

a. How much depreciation has been taken on the conveyor system for (1) tax and (2) financial accounting purposes?

b. What will be the after-tax cash flow from the sale of this asset?

c. What will be the after-tax cash flow from the sale of the asset if its market value is $18,000 rather than $74,000?

33. **LO.6 & LO.11 (Assumptions of capital budgeting methods)** For each of the following assumptions that underlie the capital project evaluation methods, indicate to which method, or methods, the assumption applies. Consider all of the following methods: payback, NPV, PI, IRR, and ARR (accounting rate of return).

a. Speed of investment recovery is a key investment criterion.

b. Cash inflows can be reinvested at the hurdle rate.

c. Cash inflows can be reinvested at the IRR.

d. Timing and size of cash flows can be accurately predicted.

e. Life of project can be accurately predicted.

f. Risk is higher for cash flows in the more distant future.

g. Key consideration in evaluating projects is their effects on accounting earnings.

34. **LO.6 & LO.11 (Limitations of capital budgeting methods)** For each of the following limitations of the capital project evaluation methods, indicate to which method, or methods, the limitation applies. Consider all of the following methods: payback, NPV, PI, IRR, and ARR (accounting rate of return).

a. Cash flows are treated as deterministic.

b. Ignores some cash flows.

c. Ignores cash flows.

d. Ignores the time value of money.

e. Ignores effects on accounting earnings.

f. Does not specifically consider cash flow preferences.

g. Can provide multiple rates of return for the same project.

h. Ignores dollar value of project benefits.

35. **LO.7 (Capital rationing)** Management of California Films is considering the following capital projects:

Project	Cost	Annual After-Tax Cash Flows	Number of Years
New film studios	$20,000,000	$3,100,000	15
Cameras and equipment	3,200,000	800,000	8
Land improvement	5,000,000	1,180,000	10
Motion picture #1	17,800,000	4,970,000	5
Motion picture #2	11,400,000	3,920,000	4
Motion picture #3	8,000,000	2,300,000	7
Corporate aircraft	2,400,000	770,000	5

Assume that all projects have no salvage value and that the firm uses a discount rate of 10 percent. Management has decided that only $25,000,000 can be spent in the current year for capital projects.

a. Determine the net present value, profitability index, and internal rate of return for each of the seven projects.

b. Rank the seven projects according to each method used in part (a).

c. Indicate how you would suggest to the management of California Films that the money be spent. What would be the total net present value of your selected investments?

36. **LO.2 & LO.8 (Uncertain annual cash flow)** KBC Services is considering the installation of a new system for electronically filing tax returns. The system has an initial cost of $120,000 and an expected life of five years.

a. If the company's cost of capital is 12 percent, how much annual increase in cash flows is necessary to minimally justify the investment?

b. Based on your answer to part (a), what would be the payback period for this investment?

37. **LO.3 & LO.8 (NPV; uncertain cost of capital)** Alabama Apiaries is considering the purchase of new honey processing equipment. The equipment would cost $50,000, have an expected life of seven years, and save the firm $14,000 annually in maintenance, operating, and cleanup costs. The firm's cost of capital is estimated to be 12%.

a. Calculate the NPV of the proposed project.

b. Because this is a small firm, the CEO is uncertain about her firm's actual cost of capital. To the nearest whole percent, what is the maximum the firm's cost of capital could be for this project to be acceptable?

38. **LO.10 (Appendix 1)** You have just invested $30,000 in a bank account that guarantees to pay you 6 percent interest, compounded annually. At the end of five years, how much money will have accumulated in your investment account? (Ignore taxes.)

39. **LO.10 (Appendix 1)** You have just purchased a new car, making a down payment of $8,000 and financing the balance of the purchase cost on an installment credit plan. According to the credit agreement, you will pay

$800 per month for a period of 60 months. If the credit agreement is based on a monthly interest rate of 1 percent, what is the cost of the car?

40. **LO.10 (Appendix 1)** Use the tables in Appendix A to determine the answers to the following questions. Ignore taxes in all circumstances.
   a. Owen wishes to have $60,000 in six years. He can make an investment today that will earn 7 percent each year, compounded annually. What amount of investment should he make today to achieve his goal?
   b. Elli is going to receive $300,000 on her 50th birthday, 20 years from today. She has the opportunity to invest money today in a government-backed security paying 5 percent compounded annually. How much would she be willing to receive today instead of the $300,000 in 20 years?
   c. Jason has $60,000 today that he intends to use as a down payment on a house. How much money did Jason invest 20 years ago to have $60,000 now if his investment earned 8 percent compounded annually?
   d. Matt is the host of a television game show that gives away thousands of dollars each day. One prize on the show is an annuity, paid to the winner, in equal installments of $100,000 at the end of each year for the next five years. If a winner has an investment opportunity to earn 8 percent, annually, what present amount would he or she take in exchange for the annuity?
   e. Keri is going to be paid modeling fees for the next 10 years as follows: year 1, $50,000; year 2, $55,000; year 3, $60,000; years 4–8, $100,000; year 9, $70,000; and year 10, $45,000. She can invest her money at 7 percent compounded annually. What is the present value of her future modeling fees?
   f. Jen has just won the lottery that will pay her $200,000 per year for the next five years. If this is the only asset Jen owns, is she a millionaire (one who has a net worth of $1,000,000 or more)? Explain.

41. **LO.11 (Appendix 2)** Dudley's Dredging creates and maintains shipping channels at various ports around the world. The company is considering the purchase of a $36,000,000 ocean-going dredge that has a five-year life and no salvage value. The company depreciates assets on a straight-line basis. The expected annual cash flow on a before-tax basis for this equipment is $10,000,000. Dudley's requires that an investment be recouped in less than five years and have a pre-tax accounting rate of return of at least 18 percent.
   a. Compute the payback period and accounting rate of return for this equipment.
   b. Is the equipment an acceptable investment for Dudley's? Explain.

42. **LO.2 & LO.11 (Appendix 2; comprehensive)** Curley's Copy Korner is evaluating the purchase of a state-of-the-art desktop publishing system that costs $20,000, has a six-year life, and has no salvage value at the end of its life. The company's controller estimates that the system will annually generate $7,000 of cash receipts and create $1,000 of cash operating costs. The company's tax rate is expected to be 30 percent during the life of the asset, and the company uses straight-line depreciation.
   a. Determine the annual after-tax cash flows from the project.
   b. Determine the after-tax payback period for the project.
   c. Determine the after-tax accounting rate of return for the project. (Assume tax and financial accounting depreciation are equal.)

Problems

43. **LO.1 (Financing decision)** Although they should be considered independently, often the investing and financing decisions are considered together. Consider the following quote from personal finance guru Suze Orman:

> *It drives me nuts to see all the money wasted on car leases. In my opinion, leases are a drug for status-conscious people who need the rush of driving a "nicer" car than they can really afford. The auto-financing folks have basically perfected a way to let you think you can have your cake and eat it too. Can't afford to buy a BMW or Lexus? No problem, just lease it!*

Source: Suze Orman, "The Buy vs. Lease Decision (You Auto Think Twice About Leasing a Car)," http://biz.yahoo.com/pfg/e16buylease/ (last accessed 7/30/07).

Complex lease contracts combined with hidden costs complicate the decision to lease or buy. Only recently have key lease terms such as the cost of the car been disclosed to consumers. Laws in a handful of states, as well as Federal Reserve Board Regulation M (effective in October 1997), and leasing data available on the Internet are prompting dealers to make increased disclosures. Unfortunately, some fees, including the interest rate the dealer uses to calculate the lease payment, known in the industry as the *money factor*, still remain unknown to the consumer.

a. Discuss why some consumers might find leasing a car to be more appealing than purchasing one.

b. Even if not required by law, is the practice of not disclosing lease information ethical? Discuss.

c. As an accountant, how could you aid a client in a car-buying situation? ▲

44. **LO.1 (Ethics; qualitative information)** Jody Myers was reprimanded by the home office for recommending a pollution abatement project because the project did not meet the standard financial criterion of a 12 percent rate of return. However, Myers had concluded that the $300,000 piece of equipment was necessary to prevent small amounts of arsenic from seeping into the city's water system. No EPA warnings have been issued to the company.

a. Discuss the company requirement of a 12 percent rate of return on all projects.

b. What might be the ultimate consequence to Myers' employer if it fails to prevent future arsenic seepage into the water system?

c. How should Myers justify the purchase of the equipment to the home office? ▲

45. **LO.2 & LO.3 (Time line; payback; NPV)** Reno Retail is considering expanding its building so it can stock additional merchandise for travelers and tourists. Store manager Bill Duram anticipates that building expansion costs would be $380,000. Duram's suppliers are willing to provide inventory on a consignment basis so he would have no additional working capital needs upon expansion. Annual incremental fixed cash costs for the store expansion are expected to be as follows:

Year	Amount
1	$40,000
2	54,000
3	54,000
4	54,000
5	60,000
6	60,000
7	60,000
8	66,000

Duram estimates that annual cash inflows could be increased by $120,000 from the additional merchandise sales. The firm's contribution margin is typically 25 percent of sales. Because of uncertainty about the future, Duram does not want to consider any cash flows after eight years. The firm uses an 8 percent discount rate.

a. Construct a time line for the investment.

b. Determine the payback period. (Ignore taxes.)

c. Calculate the net present value of the project. (Ignore taxes.)

46. **LO.2 & LO.3 (Time line; payback; NPV)** Local Freight Co. is considering the purchase of a new delivery truck to replace an existing unit. The truck would cost $45,000 and would have a life of seven years with no salvage value. The existing truck could be sold currently for $4,000, but, if it is kept, it will have a remaining life of seven years with no salvage value. By purchasing the truck, Local Freight's managers would anticipate operating cost savings as follows:

Year	Amount
1	$7,900
2	8,100
3	8,300
4	8,000
5	8,000
6	8,300
7	9,200

Local Freight's cost of capital and capital project evaluation rate is 10 percent.

a. Construct a time line for the purchase of the truck.

b. Determine the payback period. (Ignore taxes.)

c. Calculate the net present value of the truck. (Ignore taxes.)

47. **LO.2 & LO.3 (NPV; PI; sensitivity analysis)** Newport Shipyard is considering reengineering some ship production operations with automated equipment. The new equipment would have an initial cost of $10,000,000 including installation. The vendor has indicated that the equipment has an expected life of seven years with an estimated salvage value of $800,000. Estimates of annual labor savings and incremental costs associated with operating the new equipment follow:

Annual labor cost savings (14 workers)	$1,900,000
Annual maintenance costs	80,000
Annual property taxes	56,000
Annual insurance costs	88,000

a. Assuming the company's cost of capital is 7 percent, compute the NPV of the investment in the automated equipment. (Ignore taxes.)

b. Based on the NPV, should the company invest in the new equipment?

c. Compute the profitability index for this potential investment. (Ignore taxes.)

d. Assume that of the estimates its management has made, Newport Shipyard's managers are least confident of the labor cost savings. Calculate the minimum annual labor savings that must be realized for the project to be financially acceptable.

e. What other qualitative factors should the company consider in evaluating this investment?

48. LO.2 & LO.4 (Payback; IRR) Spokane Financial Services prepares tax returns for individuals and small businesses. The firm employs four tax professionals. Currently, all tax returns are prepared on a manual basis. The firm's owner, John Dorak, is considering purchasing a computer system that would allow the firm to service all its existing clients with only three employees. To evaluate the feasibility of the computerized system, Dorak has gathered the following information:

Initial cost of the hardware and software	$120,000
Expected salvage value in 4 years	$0
Annual depreciation	$30,000
Incremental annual operating costs	$8,500
Incremental annual labor savings	$52,500
Expected life of the computer system	4 years

Dorak has determined that he will invest in the computer system if its pre-tax payback period is less than 3.5 years and its pre-tax IRR exceeds 12 percent.

a. Compute the payback period for this investment. Does the payback meet Dorak's criterion? Explain.

b. Compute the IRR for this project to the nearest percentage. Based on the computed IRR, is this project acceptable to Dorak? Explain.

c. What qualitative factors should Dorak consider in evaluating the project?

49. LO.2–LO.4 (NPV; PI; payback; IRR) Dave's Concrete provides custom paving of sidewalks and driveways. One of the most labor-intensive aspects of the paving operation is preparing and mixing materials. Deuce Bigelow, corporate engineer, has found new computerized equipment to mix (and monitor the mixing of) materials. According to information received by Bigelow, the equipment's cost is $580,000 and has an expected life of eight years. If purchased, the new equipment would replace manually operated equipment. Data relating to the old and new mixing equipment follow:

Old Equipment	
Original cost	$56,000
Present book value	$32,000
Annual cash operating costs	$150,000
Current market value	$12,000
Market value in 8 years	$0
Remaining useful life	8 years

New Equipment	
Cost	$580,000
Annual cash operating costs	$30,000
Market value in 8 years	$0
Useful life	8 years

a. Assume that the company's cost of capital is 11 percent, which is to be used in discounted cash flow analysis. Compute the net present value and profitability index of investing in the new equipment. Should Dave's Concrete purchase the machine? Why or why not? (Ignore taxes.)

b. Compute the payback period for the investment in the new machine. (Ignore taxes.)

c. Rounding to the nearest whole percentage, compute the internal rate of return for the equipment investment.

50. LO.3 & LO.5 (NPV; taxes; sensitivity analysis) The owner of Roy's Refrigeration is considering a $195,000 installation of a new refrigerated storage room. The storage room has an expected life of 20 years with no salvage value. The storage room is expected to generate net annual cash revenues (before tax, labor, utility, and maintenance costs) of $43,500 and would increase annual labor, utility, and maintenance costs by $18,500. The firm's cost of capital is 9 percent, and its tax rate is 30 percent.

a. Using straight-line depreciation, calculate the after-tax net present value of the storage room.

b. Based on your answer to part (a), is this investment financially acceptable? Explain.

c. What is the minimum amount by which net annual cash revenues must increase to make this an acceptable investment?

51. **LO.2–LO.5 (After-tax cash flows; payback; NPV; PI; IRR)** Spectra Fashions is considering the purchase of computerized clothes-designing software. The software is expected to cost $320,000, have a useful life of five years, and have no salvage value at the end of its useful life. Assume that tax regulations permit the following depreciation patterns for this software:

Year	Percent Deductible
1	20
2	32
3	19
4	15
5	14

The company's tax rate is 35 percent, and its cost of capital is 7 percent. The software is expected to generate the following cash savings and cash expenses:

Year	Cash Savings	Cash Expenses
1	$122,000	$18,000
2	134,000	16,000
3	144,000	26,000
4	120,000	18,000
5	96,000	10,000

a. Prepare a time line presenting the after-tax operating cash flows.

b. Determine the following on an after-tax basis: payback period, net present value, profitability index, and internal rate of return.

52. **LO.3, LO.7 & LO.8 (NPV; project ranking; risk)** Bosworth Property Management is expanding operations, and the firm's president, Bill Bosworth, is trying to make a decision about new office space. The following are Bosworth's options:

Maple Commercial Plaza	5,000 square feet; cost, $800,000; investment period, 10 years; salvage, $400,000
High Tower	20,000 square feet; cost, $3,400,000; investment period, 10 years; salvage, $1,500,000

If Maple Commercial Plaza is purchased, Bosworth Property Management will occupy all of the space. If High Tower is purchased, Bosworth Property Management will rent the extra space for $620,000 per year. Both buildings will be depreciated on a straight-line basis for tax purposes using a 25-year life. Purchasing either building will save the company $210,000 annually in rental payments. All other costs of the two options (such as land cost) are expected to be the same. The firm's tax rate is 40 percent. Either building would be sold after 10 years.

a. Determine the before-tax net cash flows from each project for each year.

b. Determine the after-tax cash flows from each project for each year.

c. Determine the net present value for each project if Bosworth's cost of capital is 11 percent. Which purchase is the better investment based on the NPV method?

d. Bosworth questions whether the excess space in High Tower can be rented for the entire 10-year period. To compute the NPV for that portion of the project's cash flows, he has decided to use a discount rate of 20 percent to compensate for risk. Compute the NPV and determine which investment is more acceptable.

53. **LO.2, LO.5 & LO.8 (NPV; taxes; sensitivity analysis)** Kelly Properties is considering a 50-room motel for sale outside of Atlanta as an investment. The current owners state that the motel's occupancy rate averages 80 percent each of the 300 days per year the motel is open. Each room rents for $60 per day, and variable cash operating costs are $10 per occupancy day. Fixed annual cash operating costs are $250,000.

Tina Kelly, the company's owner, is considering acquiring the motel for an acquisition price of $1,500,000. The company would keep the motel for 14 years and then dispose of it. Because the market for motels is difficult to predict, Kelly estimates a zero salvage value at the time of disposal. Depreciation will be taken on a straight-line basis for tax purposes. Kelly's tax rate is estimated at 25 percent for all years.

a. Determine the after-tax net present value of the motel to Kelly, assuming a cost of capital rate of 11 percent.

b. What is the highest discount rate that will allow this project to be considered acceptable to Kelly?

c. What is the minimum amount the net after-tax cash flows must be to allow the project to be considered acceptable by Kelly, assuming a cost of capital rate of 11 percent?

d. What is the fewest number of years for which the net after-tax cash flows can be received and the project still be considered acceptable?

54. LO.2 & LO.5 (NPV; taxes) Roe Oil Field Drills is considering the acquisition of new manufacturing equipment that has the same capacity as the current equipment. The new equipment will provide $150,000 of annual operating efficiencies in direct and indirect labor, direct material usage, indirect supplies, and power during its estimated four-year life.

The new equipment costs $300,000 and would be purchased at the beginning of the year. Given the time of installation and training, the equipment will not be fully operational until the second quarter of the year it is purchased. Thus, only 60 percent of the estimated annual savings can be obtained in the year of purchase. Roe Oil Field Drills will incur a one-time expense of $30,000 to transfer the production activities from the old equipment to the new. No loss of sales will occur, however, because the plant is large enough to install the new equipment without disrupting operations of the current equipment.

Although the current equipment is fully depreciated and carried at zero book value, its condition is such that it could be used an additional four years. A salvage dealer will remove the old equipment and pay Roe Oil Field Drills $5,000 for it.

Roe Oil Field Drills currently leases its manufacturing plant for $60,000 per year. The lease, which will have four years remaining when the equipment installation would begin, is not renewable. The company must remove any equipment in the plant at the end of the lease term. Cost of equipment removal is expected to equal the salvage value of either the old or the new equipment at the time of removal.

The company uses the sum-of-the-years'-digits depreciation method for tax purposes. A full-year's depreciation is taken in the first year an asset is put into use. The company is subject to a 40 percent income tax rate and requires an after-tax return of at least 12 percent on an investment.

a. Calculate the annual incremental after-tax cash flows for Roe Oil Field Drills's proposal to acquire the new manufacturing equipment.

b. Calculate the net present value of Roe Oil Field Drills's proposal to acquire the new manufacturing equipment using the cash flows calculated in part (a) and indicate what action Roe Oil Field Drills's management should take. Assume all recurring cash flows occur at the end of the year.

(CMA adapted)

55. LO.7 (Postinvestment audit) Galveston Group has formal policies and procedures to screen and approve capital projects. Proposed capital projects are classified as one of the following types:

1. expansion requiring new plant and equipment
2. expansion by replacement of present equipment with more productive equipment
3. replacement of old equipment with new equipment of similar quality

All expansion and replacement projects that will cost more than $50,000 must be submitted to the top management capital investment committee for approval. The investment committee evaluates proposed projects considering the costs and benefits outlined in the supporting proposal and the long-range effects on the company.

The projected revenue and/or expense effects of the projects, once operational, are included in the proposal. After the committee accepts a project, it approves an expenditure budget from the project's inception until it becomes operational. The expenditures required each year for the expansions or replacements are also incorporated into Galveston Group's annual budget procedure. The budgeted revenue and/or cost effects of the projects for the periods in which they become operational are incorporated into the five-year forecast.

Galveston Group does not have a procedure for evaluating projects once they have been implemented and become operational. The vice president of finance has recommended that Galveston establish a postinvestment audit program to evaluate its capital expenditure projects.

a. Discuss the benefits a company could derive from a postinvestment audit program for capital expenditure projects.

b. Discuss the practical difficulties in collecting and accumulating information that would be used to evaluate a capital project once it becomes operational.

(CMA adapted)

56. LO.3 & LO.9 (Postinvestment audit) Ten years ago, based on a before-tax NPV analysis, Gainesville Sporting Goods decided to add a new product line. The data used in the analysis were as follows:

Discount rate	10%
Life of product line	10 years
Annual sales increase:	
Years 1–4	$125,000
Years 5–8	$175,000
Years 9–10	$100,000
Annual fixed cash costs	$20,000
Contribution margin ratio	40%
Cost of production equipment	$135,000
Investment in working capital	$10,000
Salvage value	$0

Because the product line was discontinued this year, corporate managers decided to conduct a postinvestment audit to assess the accuracy of their planning process. Actual cash flows generated from the product line were found to be as follows:

Actual Investment

Production equipment	$120,000
Working capital	17,500
Total	$137,500

Actual Revenues

Years 1–4	$120,000
Years 5–8	200,000
Years 9–10	103,000

Actual Fixed Cash Costs

Years 1–4	$15,000
Years 5–8	17,500
Years 9–10	25,000

Actual contribution margin ratio	35%
Actual salvage value	$6,000
Actual cost of capital	12%

a. Determine the original projected NPV on the product line investment.
b. Determine the actual NPV of the project based on the postinvestment audit.
c. Identify the factors that are most responsible for the differences between the projected NPV and the actual postinvestment audit NPV.

57. LO.2, LO.3 & LO.11 (Payback; NPV; Appendix 2) Maine Manufacturing is considering adding a new product line that has an expected life of eight years. The product manufacturer would require the firm to incur setup costs of $6,400,000 to handle the new product line. All product line revenues will be collected as earned. Variable costs will average 35 percent of revenues. All expenses, except for the amount of straight-line depreciation, will be paid in cash when incurred. Following is a schedule of annual revenues and fixed operating expenses (including $800,000 of annual depreciation on the investment) associated with the new product line.

Year	Revenues	Fixed Expenses
1	$3,000,000	$1,480,000
2	3,200,000	1,280,000
3	3,720,000	1,280,000
4	5,120,000	1,440,000
5	6,400,000	1,280,000
6	6,400,000	1,280,000
7	4,480,000	1,280,000
8	2,720,000	1,120,000

The company's cost of capital is 9 percent. Management uses this rate in discounting cash flows for evaluating capital projects.

a. Calculate the payback period. (Ignore taxes.)
b. Calculate the net present value. (Ignore taxes.)
c. Calculate the accounting rate of return. (Ignore taxes.)
d. Should Maine Manufacturing invest in this product line? Discuss the rationale, including any qualitative factors, for your answer.

58. **LO.2–LO.4 & LO.11 (Comprehensive; Appendix 2)** The management of Minnesota Metal is evaluating a proposal to buy a new turning lathe as a replacement for a less efficient piece of similar equipment that would then be sold. The new lathe's cost, including delivery and installation, is $1,420,000. If the lathe is purchased, Minnesota Metal will incur $40,000 to remove the present equipment and revamp service facilities. The present equipment has a book value of $800,000 and a remaining useful life of 10 years. Technical advancements have made this equipment outdated, so its current resale value is only $340,000.

The following comparative manufacturing cost tabulation is available:

	Current Equipment	New Equipment
Annual production in units	780,000	1,000,000
Cash revenue from each unit	$1.20	$1.20
Annual costs		
Labor	$160,000	$100,000
Depreciation (10% of asset book value or cost)	$80,000	$142,000
Other cash operating costs	$192,000	$80,000

Management believes that if it does not replace the equipment now, the company will have to wait seven years before the replacement is justified. The company uses a 10 percent discount or hurdle rate in evaluating capital projects and expects all capital project investments to recoup their costs within five years.

Both pieces of equipment are expected to have a negligible salvage value at the end of 10 years.

a. Determine the net present value of the new equipment. (Ignore taxes.)
b. Determine the internal rate of return on the new equipment. (Ignore taxes.)
c. Determine the payback period for the new equipment. (Ignore taxes.)
d. Determine the accounting rate of return for the new equipment. (Ignore taxes.)
e. Determine whether the company should keep the present equipment or purchase the new lathe. Provide discussion of your conclusion.

16 | Managing Costs and Uncertainty

Objectives

After completing this chapter, you should be able to answer the following questions:

LO.1 What are the functions of a cost control system?

LO.2 What factors cause costs to change from period to period or to deviate from expectations?

LO.3 What are the generic approaches to cost control?

LO.4 What are the two primary types of fixed costs, and what are the characteristics of each?

LO.5 What are the typical approaches to controlling discretionary fixed costs?

LO.6 What are the objectives managers strive to achieve in managing cash?

LO.7 How is technology reducing costs of supply chain transactions?

LO.8 Why is uncertainty greater in dealing with future events than with past events?

LO.9 What are the four generic approaches to managing uncertainty?

Introduction

This chapter presents a variety of topics that explain some of the key contributions of accounting and finance personnel to business organizations. The discussion begins with a description of cost control systems and general cost management strategies. Then the discussion turns to the responsibilities and tools of the treasury function including cash management, financial risk management, and supply-chain management. The chapter concludes with a presentation of methods and tools for dealing with uncertainty in budgeting and cost management.

LO.1

What are the functions of a cost control system?

Cost Control Systems

An integral part of the overall organizational decision support system is the cost control system, which is the formal and/or informal tools and methods designed to manage organizational costs. This system focuses on intraorganizational information and contains the detector, assessor, effector, and network components discussed in Chapter 12. Relative to the cost management system, the cost control system provides information for planning and for determining the efficiency of activities while they are being planned and after they are performed, as indicated in Exhibit 16–1.

The general planning and control model in Exhibit 16–2 illustrates that control is part of a management cycle that begins with planning. Without first preparing organizational plans (such as those discussed in Chapter 8), control cannot be achieved because no operational targets and objectives have been established. The planning phase establishes performance targets that become the inputs to the control phase.

Exhibit 16–3 depicts a more specific cost control model. A good control system encompasses not only the managerial functions shown in Exhibit 16–2 but also the ideas about cost consciousness shown in Exhibit 16–3. Cost consciousness refers to a companywide employee attitude toward the topics of understanding cost changes, cost containment, cost avoidance, and cost reduction. Each of these topics is important for a particular stage of cost control.

Managers alone cannot control costs. An organization is composed of many individuals whose attitudes and efforts affect how an organization's costs are controlled. Cost control is a continual process that requires the support and involvement of all employees at all times.

EXHIBIT 16–1
Functions of an Effective Cost Control System

Control Point	Reason	Cost Control Method
Before an event	Preventive; reflects planning	Budgets; standards; policies concerning approval for deviations; expressions of quantitative and qualitative objectives; ethical guidelines
During an event	Corrective; ensures that the event is being pursued according to plans; allows management to correct problems as they occur	Periodic monitoring of ongoing activities; comparison of activities and costs against budgets and standards; avoidance of excessive expenditures
After an event	Diagnostic; guides future actions	Feedback; variance analysis; responsibility reports (discussed in Chapter 13)

EXHIBIT 16–2
General Planning and Control Model

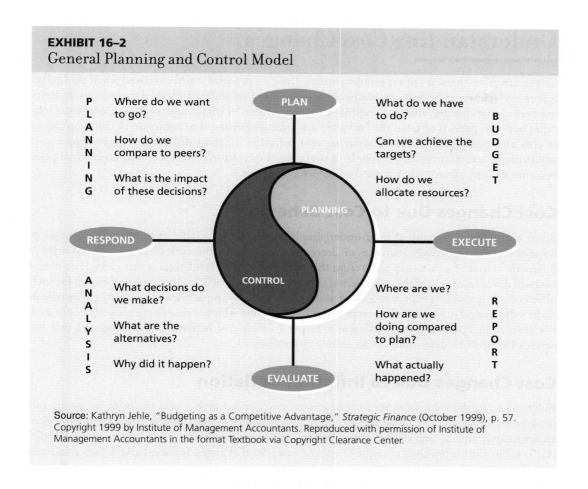

PLANNING

P L A N N I N G

Where do we want to go?

How do we compare to peers?

What is the impact of these decisions?

PLAN

What do we have to do?

Can we achieve the targets?

How do we allocate resources?

B U D G E T

RESPOND

PLANNING

CONTROL

EXECUTE

A N A L Y S I S

What decisions do we make?

What are the alternatives?

Why did it happen?

EVALUATE

Where are we?

How are we doing compared to plan?

What actually happened?

R E P O R T

Source: Kathryn Jehle, "Budgeting as a Competitive Advantage," *Strategic Finance* (October 1999), p. 57. Copyright 1999 by Institute of Management Accountants. Reproduced with permission of Institute of Management Accountants in the format Textbook via Copyright Clearance Center.

EXHIBIT 16–3
Cost Control System

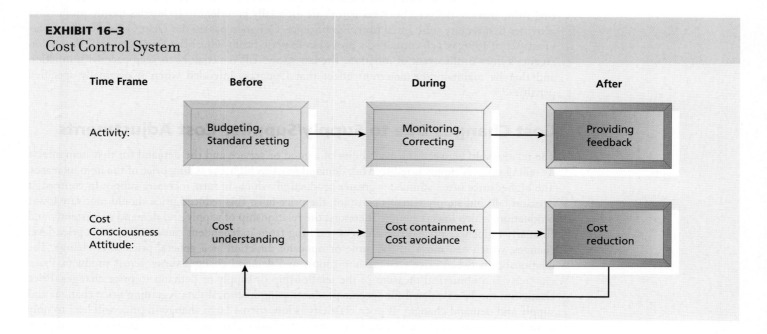

Time Frame	Before	During	After
Activity:	Budgeting, Standard setting	Monitoring, Correcting	Providing feedback
Cost Consciousness Attitude:	Cost understanding	Cost containment, Cost avoidance	Cost reduction

LO.2
What factors cause costs to change from period to period or to deviate from expectations?

Understanding Cost Changes

Control requires that a set of expectations exists. Thus, cost control is first exercised when the budget is prepared. However, budgets cannot be prepared without an understanding of the reasons underlying period cost changes, and cost control cannot be achieved without understanding why costs may differ between periods or from the budgeted amounts. Following is a discussion of common causes of cost changes, which include underlying cost behavior, inflation/deflation, supply/supplier cost adjustments, and quantity purchased. In considering these factors, remember that an external price becomes an internal cost when a good or service is acquired.

Cost Changes Due to Cost Behavior

Some costs change because of their underlying behavior. Total variable or mixed cost increases or decreases with, respectively, increases or decreases in activity. If the current period's actual activity differs from that of a prior period or from the budgeted activity level, total actual variable or mixed cost will differ from that of the prior period or the budget. A flexible budget can compensate for such differences by providing expected costs at any activity level. By using a flexible budget, managers can make valid budget-to-actual cost comparisons to determine whether costs were properly controlled. For costs to be controlled most effectively relative to their cost behaviors, it is important that the driver of the cost be determined as accurately as possible.

Cost Changes Due to Inflation/Deflation

Fluctuations in the value of money, called *general price-level changes*, cause the prices of goods and services to change. If all other factors are constant, general price-level changes affect almost all prices approximately equally and in the same direction. In the United States, the Consumer Price Index (CPI) is the most often cited measure of general price-level changes. Inflation and deflation indexes by industry or commodity can be examined to obtain more accurate information about inflation/deflation effects on prices of particular inputs, such as energy sources.

Some companies include price-escalation clauses in sales contracts to cover the inflation occurring from order to delivery. Such escalators are especially prevalent in industries having production activities that require substantial time. For instance, Congress passed the Debt Collection Improvement Act of 1996, which contained a provision to periodically adjust the Environmental Protection Agency's fines in the event of inflation. The law allows EPA's penalties to keep pace with inflation and thereby maintain the deterrent effect that Congress intended when it originally specified penalties.[1]

Cost Changes Due to Supply/Supplier Cost Adjustments

The relationship between the availability of a good or service and the demand for that item affects its selling price. If supply is reduced but demand remains high, the selling price of the item increases. The higher price often stimulates greater production, which, in turn, increases supply. In contrast, if demand falls but supply remains constant, the price falls. This reduced price should motivate lower production, which lowers supply. Therefore, the relationship of supply and demand consistently and circularly influences price. Price changes resulting from independent causes are specific price-level changes, which can move in the same or opposite direction as a general price-level change. The relationship between price changes and supply and demand changes varies across products. Price elasticity is a numerical measure of the relationship of supply or demand to price changes. Price elasticities can be calculated for specific products using historical data regarding price changes and supply and demand changes. If price elasticity is low, then a large change in price will lead to only a small change in supply or demand; alternatively, if price elasticity is high, a large change in price leads to a large change in supply or demand.

[1]http://www.dol.gov/ocfo/media/regs/DCIA.pdf (last accessed 8/22/07).

Specific price-level changes are also caused by advances in technology. As a general rule, as suppliers advance the technology of producing a good or performing a service, the cost of that product or service to producing firms declines. Assuming competitive market conditions, such cost declines are often passed along to consumers of that product or service in the form of lower prices. Consider that an inexpensive greeting card that plays "Happy Birthday" contains more computer processing power than existed in the entire world before 1950.[2] This simple example illustrates the interaction of increasing technology and decreasing selling prices and costs.

Alternatively, additional production or performance costs are typically passed on by suppliers to their customers as part of specific price-level changes. Such costs can be within or outside the supplier's control. For example, the increase in demand for corn to develop ethanol fuel caused corn prices to rise dramatically in 2006 and 2007. As a result, the cost of many food products using inputs derived from corn (such as corn syrup) increased.

The number of suppliers of a product or service can also affect selling prices. As the number of suppliers increases in a competitive environment, price tends to fall. Likewise, a reduction in the number of suppliers will, all else remaining equal, cause prices to increase. A change in the number of suppliers is not the same as a change in the quantity of supply. If the supply of an item is large, one normally expects a low price; however, if there is only one supplier, the price can remain high because of supplier control of the market. For example, when drugs are first introduced under patent, the supply can be readily available, but the selling price is high because the prescription drug comes from only a single source. As patents expire and generic drugs become available, selling prices decline because more suppliers compete to produce and market the medication.

Sometimes, cost increases are caused by higher taxes or additional regulatory requirements. For example, airlines continually face more stringent noise abatement and safety legislation. Complying with these regulations increases airline costs. The companies can (1) pass along the costs to customers as price increases to maintain the same income level, (2) decrease other costs to maintain the same income level, or (3) experience a decline in net income.

Cost Changes Due to Quantity Purchased

Suppliers normally give customers quantity discounts, up to some maximum level, when bulk purchases are made. Therefore, a cost per unit can change because quantities are purchased in lot sizes differing from those of previous periods or from the lot sizes projected. Involvement in group purchasing arrangements can make quantity discounts easier to obtain.

The preceding discussion indicates why costs change. Next, the discussion addresses actions firms can take to contain (control) costs.

Cost Containment

To the extent possible, period-by-period increases in per-unit variable and total fixed costs should be minimized through a process of **cost containment**. Cost containment is not possible for inflation adjustments, tax and regulatory changes, and supply and demand adjustments because these forces occur outside the organization.

In some circumstances, a significant exchange of information occurs among members of the supply chain, and members of one organization can actually be involved in activities designed to reduce costs of another organization. For example, Ford built a facility called the Total Cost Management Center at which the company conducts workshops and offers training to employees and suppliers to optimize the value customers receive from Ford products. The concepts generated from this training help suppliers "transform their practices to keep up with the fast-changing consumer marketplace."[3]

Costs that rise because of reduced supplier competition, seasonality, and quantities purchased are, however, subject to cost containment activities. A company should look for ways to cap the upward changes in these costs. For example, purchasing agents should be aware of new suppliers for

LO.3
What are the generic approaches to cost control?

[2]John Huey, "Waking Up to the New Economy," *Fortune* (June 27, 1994), p. 37.
[3]Anonymous, "Ford teams with suppliers, sharing best practices and learnings to drive efficiency," http://www.autoworld.com/news/Ford/TCM.htm (last accessed 8/17/07).

goods and services and determine which, if any, of those suppliers can provide items in the quantity, quality, and time desired. Comparing costs and finding new sources of supply can increase buying power and reduce costs.

If bids are used to select suppliers, the purchasing agent should remember that a bid is merely the first step in the negotiation process. Although a low bid may eliminate some competition from consideration, additional negotiations between the purchasing agent and the remaining suppliers could result in a purchase price even lower than the bid amount or concessions (such as faster and more reliable delivery). Purchasing agents must also remember that the supplier offering the lowest bid is not necessarily the best supplier to choose. Other factors such as quality, service, and reliability are important.

A company can circumvent seasonal cost changes by postponing or advancing purchases of goods and services. However, such purchasing changes should not mean buying irresponsibly or incurring excessive carrying costs. Economic order quantities, safety stock levels, and materials requirements planning as well as the just-in-time philosophy should be considered when making purchases.

As to services, it is often possible for employees to repair rather than to replace items that have seasonal cost changes. For example, maintenance workers might find that a broken heat pump can be repaired and used during spring and replaced in summer when the purchase cost is lower.

Cost Avoidance and Reduction

Cost containment can prove very effective if it can be implemented. Sometimes, when cost containment is not possible, cost avoidance might be. Cost avoidance involves finding acceptable alternatives to high-cost items and/or not spending money for unnecessary goods and services. Avoiding one cost may require incurring an alternative, lower cost. For example, some public health agencies advocate increasing taxes on cigarettes to decrease consumption. However, in a recent study, it was discovered that to avoid the higher prices of highly taxed cigarettes, 59 percent of smokers developed a price avoidance strategy that involved purchasing cigarettes from low or untaxed venues or using manufacturer coupons to reduce price.[4] The upshot is that the avoidance strategy adopted by most smokers is not cessation of smoking, but avoidance of higher prices!

Closely related to cost avoidance, cost reduction refers to lowering costs. Benchmarking is especially important in this area so that companies can become aware of costs that are excessive. Companies can reduce costs by outsourcing rather than by maintaining internal departments. Data processing and the financial and legal functions are prime targets for outsourcing in many companies. Distribution is also becoming a highly viable candidate for outsourcing.

Sometimes money must be spent to generate cost savings. For example, in 2005 Baxter International Inc., a global medical products and services company, hired a director of energy management to develop a comprehensive strategy for managing energy costs.[5] In another example, some of the large accounting firms (such as PricewaterhouseCoopers) have their own in-house studios and staffs and provide customized Web-based training to new employees. Although the cost of producing an online presentation is high, the firms believe the cost is justified because the presentation can be played over and over at very low cost.

Some companies are also beginning to look outside for information about how and where to cut costs. Consulting firms, such as Dallas-based Ryan & Company, review files for overpayment of state and local taxes. This firm often works on a contingent fee basis and gets paid only if tax overpayments are found.

Managers can adopt the five-step method of implementing a cost control system shown in Exhibit 16–4. First, the type of costs incurred by an organization must be understood. Are the costs under consideration fixed or variable, product or period? What are the drivers of those costs? Second, the need for cost consciousness must be communicated to all employees for the control process to be effective. Employees must be aware of which costs need to be better controlled and why cost control

---

[4]A. Hyland, J.E. Bauer, Q. Li, S. M. Abrams, C. Higbee, L. Peppone, and K.M. Cummings, "Higher Cigarette Prices Influence Cigarette Purchase Patterns," *TC Online*; http://tobaccocontrol.bmj.com/cgi/content/abstract/14/2/86 (last accessed 8/17/07).
[5]Anonymous, "Energy Usage and Cost Management," *Baxter 2006 Sustainability Report*; http://sustainability.baxter.com/EHS/2006_environmental _performance/energy.html (last accessed 8/17/07).

is important to both themselves and the company. Third, employees must be educated in cost control techniques, encouraged to suggest ways to control costs, and motivated by incentives to embrace the concepts. Incentives can range from simple verbal recognition to monetary rewards to time off with pay. Managers must also be flexible enough to allow for changes from the current method of operation. Fourth, reports that indicate actual results, budget-to-actual comparisons, and variances must be generated. Management must evaluate these costs to determine why costs were or were not controlled in the past. Such analysis can provide insight about cost drivers so that activities driving costs can be better controlled in the future. Last, the cost control system should be viewed as a long-run process, not a short-run solution. "To be successful, organizations must avoid the illusion of short-term, highly simplified cost-cutting procedures. Instead, they must carefully evaluate proposed solutions to ensure that these are practical, workable, and measure changes based on realities, not illusions."[6]

Following these five steps will provide an atmosphere conducive to controlling costs as effectively as possible and to deriving the most benefit from the costs that are incurred. A cost–benefit analysis should be performed before a commitment is made to incur the cost. Costs should also be incorporated into the budgeting system because costs cannot be controlled after they have been incurred. Future costs, on the other hand, can be controlled based on information learned about past costs. Cost control should not cease at the end of a fiscal period or because costs were reduced or controlled during the current period. However, distinct differences exist in the cost control system between committed and discretionary costs. Managers are charged with planning and controlling

LO.4
What are the two primary types of fixed costs, and what are the characteristics of each?

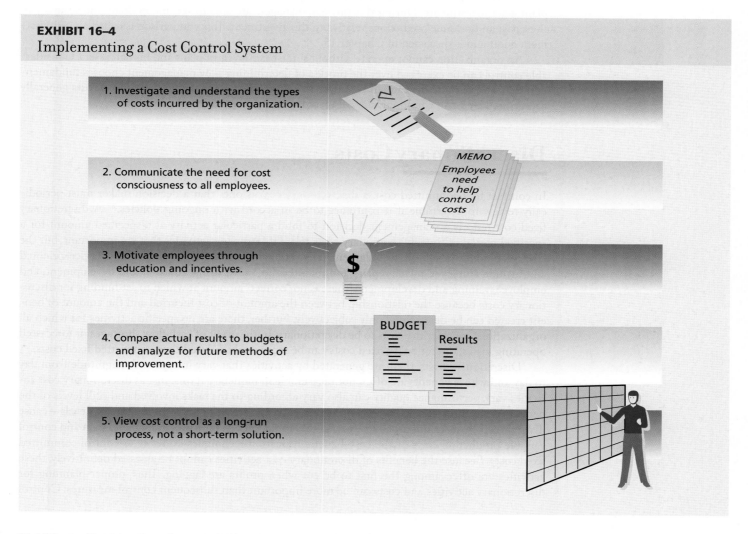

EXHIBIT 16–4
Implementing a Cost Control System

1. Investigate and understand the types of costs incurred by the organization.

2. Communicate the need for cost consciousness to all employees.

MEMO
Employees need to help control costs

3. Motivate employees through education and incentives.

$

4. Compare actual results to budgets and analyze for future methods of improvement.

BUDGET
Results

5. View cost control as a long-run process, not a short-term solution.

[6]Mark D. Lutchen, "Cost Cutting Illusions," *Today's CPA* (May/June 1989), p. 46.

the types and amounts of costs necessary to conduct business activities. Many activities required to achieve business objectives involve fixed costs. All fixed costs (and the activities that create them) can be categorized as either committed or discretionary. The difference between the two categories is primarily the time period for which management obligates itself to the activity and its cost.

Committed Fixed Costs

Costs associated with plant assets and the human resources structure that an organization must have to operate are known as **committed costs**. The amount of committed costs is normally dictated by long-run management decisions involving the desired scale and scope of operations. Committed costs include depreciation, lease rentals, property taxes, and staff salaries, all of which cannot be reduced easily even during temporarily diminished activity.

One method of controlling committed costs is to compare expected benefits of plant assets (or human resources) with expected costs of such investments. Managers must identify activities necessary to attain company objectives and what (and how many) assets are needed to support those activities. Once assets are acquired, managers are committed to both the activities and their related costs for the long run. But managers must understand how committed fixed costs could affect income in the event of changes in operations.

A second method of controlling committed costs is to compare actual and expected results from plant asset investments. During this process, managers are able to see and evaluate the accuracy of their cost and revenue predictions relative to the investment. This comparison is called a postinvestment audit and is discussed in Chapter 15.

An organization cannot operate without some basic levels of plant and human assets. Considerable control can be exercised over the process of determining how management chooses fundamental assets and designs the human resources structure. The benefits from committed costs generally can be predicted and commonly are compared with actual results in the future.

Discretionary Costs

In contrast to a committed cost, a **discretionary cost** is one "that a decision maker must periodically review to determine if it continues to be in accord with ongoing policies."[7] A discretionary fixed cost reflects a management decision to fund a particular activity at a specified amount for a specified period of time. Discretionary costs relate to company activities that are important, but the level of funding is subject to judgment. Discretionary cost activities are usually service-oriented and include employee travel, repairs and maintenance, advertising, research and development, and employee training and development. There is no "correct" amount at which to set funding for discretionary costs because the relationship between the amount of cost incurred and the amount of benefit created can be determined only subjectively. Further, there are no specific activities for which all organizations consider the costs to be discretionary. In the event of cash flow shortages or forecasted operating losses, discretionary fixed costs can be more easily reduced than committed fixed costs.

Discretionary costs, then, are generated by activities that vary in type and magnitude from day to day and whose benefits are often not measurable in monetary terms. Just as discretionary cost activities vary, performance quality can also vary according to the tasks involved and skill levels of the persons performing them. These two factors—varying activities and varying quality levels—cause discretionary costs to not usually be susceptible to the precise measures available to plan and control variable production costs or the cost–benefit evaluation techniques available to control committed fixed costs. Because the benefits of discretionary cost activities cannot be assessed definitively, these activities are often among the first to be cut when profits are lagging. Thus, proper planning for discretionary activities and costs can be more important than subsequent control measures. Control

---

[7]Institute of Management Accountants (formerly National Association of Accountants), *Statements on Management Accounting Number 2: Management Accounting Terminology* (Montvale, N.J.: June 1, 1983), p. 35.

after the planning stage is often restricted to monitoring expenditures to ensure conformity with budget classifications and preventing managers from overspending budgets.

Controlling Discretionary Costs

Described in Chapter 8 as both planning and controlling devices, budgets serve to officially communicate a manager's authority to spend up to a predetermined amount (**appropriation**) or rate for each budget item. Budget appropriations serve as a baseline for comparison with actual costs. Accumulated expenditures in each budgetary category are periodically compared with appropriated amounts to determine whether funds have been under- or overexpended.

Budgeting Discretionary Costs

Before top management can address the control of discretionary costs, it must translate company goals into specific objectives and policies that management believes will contribute to organizational success. Management must then budget the types and funding levels of discretionary activities that will accomplish those objectives. Funding levels should be set only after both discretionary cost activities have been prioritized and cash flow and income expectations for the coming period have been reviewed. Management tends to be more generous about making discretionary cost appropriations when the economic outlook for the organization is strong rather than weak.

Discretionary costs are generally budgeted on the basis of three factors: (1) the related activity's perceived significance to achieving goals and objectives, (2) the upcoming period's expected level of operations, and (3) the ability of managers to effectively negotiate during the budgetary process. For some discretionary costs, managers are expected to spend the full amount of their appropriations within the specified time frame. For other discretionary cost activities, the "less-is-better" adage is appropriate.

As an example of "less is *not* better," consider the cost of preventive maintenance. This cost can be viewed as discretionary, but reducing it could result in diminished quality, production breakdowns, or machine inefficiency. Although the benefits of maintenance expenditures cannot be precisely quantified, most managers believe that incurring less maintenance cost than budgeted is not desired cost control. In fact, spending (with supervisory approval) more than originally appropriated could be necessary or even commendable—assuming that positive results (such as a decline in quality defects) are obtained. Such a perspective illustrates the perception mentioned earlier that cost control should be a long-run process rather than a short-run concern.

Alternatively, spending less than the amount budgeted on travel and entertainment (while achieving the desired results) would probably be considered positive performance, but requesting travel and entertainment funds in excess of budget appropriations might be considered irresponsible.

If revenues, profits, or cash flows are reduced, funding for discretionary expenditures should be evaluated, not simply in reference to reduced operations but also relative to activity priorities. Eliminating the funding for one or more discretionary activities altogether could be possible if other funding levels are maintained at the previously determined amounts. For instance, faced with a downturn in product demand, a company often reduces its discretionary advertising budget—a potentially illogical reaction. Instead, increasing the advertising budget and reducing the corporate executives' travel budget might be more appropriate.

The difference in management attitude between committed and discretionary costs has to do with the ability to measure the benefits provided by those costs. Whereas benefits of committed fixed costs can be measured on a "before" and "after" basis (through the capital budgeting and postinvestment audit processes), the benefits from discretionary fixed costs are often not distinctly measurable in monetary terms, or they may not even be identifiable.

Measuring Benefits from Discretionary Costs

Because benefits from some activities traditionally classified as discretionary cannot be adequately measured, companies often assume that the benefits—and, thus, the related activities—are unimportant. However, many of the activities previously described as discretionary (repairs, maintenance, R&D, and employee training) are critical to survival in a world-class environment. In the long run, these activities produce quality products and services; therefore, before reducing or eliminating expenditures in these areas, managers should attempt to more appropriately recognize and measure the benefits of these activities.

Funds are spent on discretionary activities to provide some desired output, but the value of discretionary costs must often be judged using nonmonetary, surrogate measures. Devising such measures sometimes requires substantial time and creativity. Exhibit 16–5 presents some useful surrogate measures for determining the effectiveness of various types of discretionary costs. Some of these measures are verifiable and can be gathered quickly and easily; others are abstract and require a longer time horizon before they can be obtained.

Comparing input costs and output results can help determine whether there is a reasonable cost–benefit relationship. Managers can judge this cost–benefit relationship by how efficiently inputs (costs) were used and how effectively incurrence of the costs achieved the intended results. These relationships can be seen in the following model:

EXHIBIT 16–5
Examples of Nonmonetary Measures of Output from Discretionary Costs

Discretionary Cost Activity	Surrogate Measure of Results
Preventive maintenance	• Reduction in number of equipment failures • Reduction in unplanned downtime • Reduction in frequency of production interruptions caused by preventive maintenance activities
Advertising	• Increase in unit sales in the two weeks after an advertising effort relative to the sales two weeks prior to the effort • Number of customers referring to the ad • Number of coupons clipped from the ad and redeemed
University admissions recruiting trip	• Percentage of students met who requested an application • Number of students from area visited who requested to have ACT/SAT scores sent to the university • Number of admissions that year from that area
Prevention and appraisal quality activities	• Reduction in number of customer complaints • Reduction in number of warranty claims • Reduction in number of product defects discovered by customers
Staffing law school indigent clinic	• Number of clients served • Percentage of cases effectively resolved • Percentage of cases won
Executive retreat	• Proportion of participants still there at end of retreat • Number of useful suggestions made • Values tabulated from an exit survey

The degree to which a satisfactory relationship occurs when comparing outputs to inputs reflects the activity's efficiency. Efficiency is a yield concept and is usually measured by a ratio of output to input. For instance, one measure of automobile efficiency is miles driven (output) per gallon of fuel consumed (input). The higher the number of miles per gallon, the greater the car's fuel efficiency.

Comparing actual output results to desired results indicates the effectiveness of an activity or how well the activity's objectives were achieved. When a valid output measure is available, efficiency and effectiveness can be determined as follows:

Actual Result $\longrightarrow$ compared to $\longrightarrow$ **Desired Result**

$$\text{Efficiency} = \frac{\text{Actual Output}}{\text{Actual Input}} \longrightarrow \frac{\text{Planned Output}}{\text{Planned Input}}$$

or, alternatively

$$\text{Efficiency} = \frac{\text{Actual Input}}{\text{Actual Output}} \longrightarrow \frac{\text{Planned Input}}{\text{Planned Output}}$$

$$\text{Effectiveness} = \frac{\text{Actual Output}}{\text{Planned Output}} \longrightarrow \text{Preestablished Standard}$$

A reasonable measure of efficiency can exist only when inputs and outputs can be matched in the same period and when a credible causal relationship exists between them. These two requirements make measuring the efficiency of discretionary costs very difficult. First, several years could pass before output occurs from some discretionary cost expenditures. Consider, for example, the length of time between expenditures made for research and development or a drug rehabilitation program and the time at which results of these expenditures are visible. Second, there is frequently a dubious cause-and-effect relationship between discretionary inputs and resulting outputs. For instance, assume that you clip and use a cents-off coupon for breakfast cereal from a magazine advertisement. Can the manufacturer be certain that it was the advertising coupon that caused you to buy the product, or might you have purchased the cereal without the coupon?

Effectiveness, on the other hand, is determined for a particular period by comparing results achieved with results desired. Determination of an activity's effectiveness is unaffected by whether the designated output measure is stated in monetary or nonmonetary terms. Management can only subjectively attribute some or all of the effectiveness of the cost incurrence to the results. Subjectivity is required because comparison of actual to planned output does not indicate a perfect causal relationship between activities and output results. Measurement of effectiveness does not require the consideration of inputs, but measurement of efficiency does.

Assume that last month Atlanta Air increased its customer service training expenditures and, during that period, customer satisfaction ratings improved by 12 percent. The planned increase in customer satisfaction was 15 percent. Although management was 80 percent effective (0.12 ÷ 0.15) in achieving its goal of increased customer satisfaction, that result was not necessarily related to the customer service training expenditures. The increase in customer satisfaction could have resulted partially or entirely from other effects such as a reduction in fares or fewer occurrences of severe weather that disrupted flight service through arrival and departure delays. Therefore, management does not know for certain whether the customer service training program was the most effective way in which to increase customer satisfaction.

The relationship between discretionary costs and desired results is inconclusive at best, and the effectiveness of such costs can only be inferred from the relationship of actual to desired output. Because many discretionary costs result in benefits that must be measured on a nondefinitive and nonmonetary basis, exercising control of these costs during activities is difficult. Therefore, planning for discretionary costs can be more important than subsequent control measures. Control after the planning stage is often limited to monitoring discretionary expenditures for conformity with budget classifications and budgetary amounts.

Control Using Engineered Costs

Some discretionary activities are repetitive enough to allow the development of standards similar to those for manufacturing costs. Such activities result in engineered costs, which are costs that have been found to bear observable and known relationships to a quantifiable activity base. Such costs can be treated as either variable or fixed. Discretionary cost activities that can fit into the engineered cost category are usually geared to a performance measure related to work accomplished. Budget appropriations for engineered costs are based on the static master budget. However, control can be exerted through the use of flexible budgets if the expected level of activity is not achieved.

To illustrate the use of engineered costs, assume that Atlanta Air has found that routine daily aircraft inspections can be treated as an engineered cost. Because Atlanta Air flies only one type of aircraft, inspections are similar enough to allow management to develop a standard inspection time. Atlanta Air managers have found that inspection of each plane averages slightly less than 30 minutes. Thus, each inspector is expected to perform approximately two inspections per hour. From this information, the company can obtain a fairly valid estimate of what inspection costs should be based on the inspection activity level and can compare actual cost against the standard cost each period. The activity base of this engineered cost is the number of inspections performed.

In May, Atlanta Air management predicts that 7,000 inspections will be performed and, thus, 3,500 hours is the expected total inspection time. If the standard average hourly pay rate for inspectors is $60, the May budget for this activity is $210,000. In May, 6,770 inspections are made at a cost of $193,800 for 3,400 actual hours (or $57 per hour). Using the generalized cost analysis model for variance analysis presented in Chapter 7, the following calculations can be made:

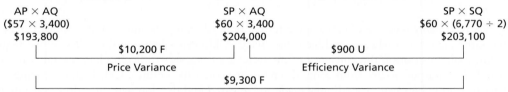

The price variance shows that, on average, Atlanta Air paid $3 less per hour [$60 − $57] for inspectors during May than was planned. The unfavorable efficiency variance results from using 15 hours more than standard [(6,770 ÷ 2) − 3,400] for May.

The preceding analysis is predicated on the company's willingness and ability to hire the exact number of inspection hours needed and a continual availability of planes to inspect. If Atlanta Air can employ only full-time employees on a salary basis, analyzing inspection costs in the preceding manner is not very useful. In this instance, quality inspection cost becomes a discretionary fixed cost, and Atlanta Air might prefer the following type of fixed overhead variance analysis:

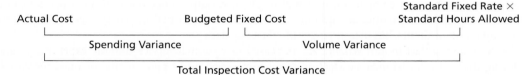

The method of variance analysis and, thus, cost control must be appropriate to the cost category and management information needs. Regardless of the variance levels or the explanations provided, managers should always consider whether the activity itself and, therefore, its cost incurrence were sufficiently justified. Postincurrence audits of discretionary costs are often important in determining an expenditure's value.

Control Using the Budget

After discretionary cost budget appropriations have been made, monetary control is provided through the use of budget-to-actual comparisons in the same manner as for other budgeted costs. Actual results are compared to expected results, and explanations should be provided for variances. Such explanations can often be found by recognizing cost consciousness attitudes. The following illustration involving two discretionary cost activities provides a budget-to-actual comparison that demonstrates employee cost consciousness.

Assume that Atlanta Air is one of many companies that outsources payroll processing activities to Payroll Financial Services (PFS). PFS has prepared the condensed budget shown in Exhibit 16–6 for the first quarter of 2009. Allison James, the controller for PFS, estimates 1,200,000 paychecks will be processed during that period; the company charges clients $0.75 per check processed.

In pursuing a strategy of total quality management and continuous improvement, PFS's management has chosen to fund employee training to improve employee and customer satisfaction. The company also considers maintenance a discretionary cost, and it is budgeted at $1.20 per 50 checks processed. Office costs include utilities, phone service, supplies, and delivery. These costs are variable and are budgeted at $100 per office hour. PFS expects to operate at 600 office hours in the budget quarter. Wages are for 10 employees, who are paid an average wage of $30 per hour. Salaries and fringe benefits are for management level personnel and, like depreciation, are fixed costs.

James collected the revenue and expense data shown in Exhibit 16–7 during the first quarter of 2009. Because of computer downtime during the quarter, PFS worked five extra hours on four different workdays. Additional contracts were responsible for the majority of the increase in checks processed.

After reviewing the actual results, PFS's board of directors requested a budget-to-actual comparison from James and explanations for the cost variances. Because most costs were higher than

---

EXHIBIT 16–6
Payroll Financial Services Budget—First Quarter 2009

Revenues		
Processing fees (1,200,000 × $0.75)		$ 900,000
Expenses		
Employee training	$ 80,000	
Maintenance	28,800	
Office	60,000	
Wages and fringe benefits	180,000	
Salaries and fringe benefits	120,000	
Depreciation	75,000	(543,800)
Operating income before tax		$ 356,200

EXHIBIT 16–7
Payroll Financial Services Actual Results—First Quarter 2009

Revenues		
Processing fees (1,300,000 × $0.75)		$ 975,000
Expenses		
Employee training	$ 70,000	
Maintenance	26,300	
Office	63,860	
Wages and fringe benefits	192,200	
Salaries and fringe benefits	116,450	
Depreciation	85,000	(553,810)
Operating income before tax		$ 421,190

budgeted, the board questioned whether costs had been properly controlled. James prepared the comparison presented in Exhibit 16–8 and provided the following explanations for the variances. Each explanation is preceded by the related budget item number.

1. The discretionary cost for employee training decreased because the vendor providing training services announced a new, higher price for its services. PFS chose to decrease training services while researching the pricing structure of other training service vendors. *Comment: This explanation reflects a cost containment approach to short-term management of training costs. In the long term, the company must provide at least the original level of training to avoid an eventual decline in quality and customer service. If a lower-cost source of training services cannot be identified, the company may consider raising prices to maintain profitability.*

2. Maintenance cost decreased because managers obtained a favorable price on maintenance supplies obtained from a new Internet vendor. *Comment: This explanation reflects an understanding of how to reduce costs without adversely affecting quality. The company has found a way to reduce costs without decreasing levels of maintenance or the quality of service delivered to clients. Costs have been reduced by obtaining the maintenance inputs at a lower unit cost.*

3. Office expenses were influenced by two factors: the additional 20 hours of operation and an increase in local utility rates, which caused PFS's costs to rise $3 per operating hour. *Comment: The first part of the explanation reflects an understanding of the nature of variable costs—working additional hours caused additional costs to be incurred. The second part of the explanation reflects an understanding of the nature of specific price-level adjustments. The increase in utility rates was caused by an increase in fuel prices paid by the utility company and passed along to customers through a higher rate.*

4. The increase in wages was caused by two factors: 20 additional operating hours, and a $1 increase in the hourly cost of fringe benefits because of an increase in health insurance premiums.

10 employees × 620 hours × $30 per hour	$186,000
Increase in cost of fringe benefits (10 × 620 × $1.00)	6,200
Total wages cost	$192,200

Comment: These cost changes reflect the nature of variable costs and an unavoidable increase caused by a vendor cost adjustment.

EXHIBIT 16–8
Payroll Financial Services Budget-to-Actual Comparison for First Quarter 2009

	Budget Item No.	Original Budget	Budget for Actual Results	Actual	Variances
Revenues					
Processing fees		$900,000	$975,000	$975,000	$ 0
Expenses					
Training	(1)	$ 80,000	$ 80,000	$ 70,000	$10,000
Maintenance	(2)	28,800	29,760	26,300	3,460
Office	(3)	60,000	63,860*	63,860	0
Wages and fringe benefits	(4)	180,000	186,000	192,200	(6,200)
Salaries and fringe benefits	(5)	120,000	120,000	116,450	3,550
Depreciation	(6)	75,000	75,000	85,000	(10,000)
Total expenses		$543,800	$554,620	$553,810	$ 810
Operating income before tax		$356,200	$420,380	$421,190	

*This amount is based on the assumption that the higher hourly rate was attributable to an unforeseen utility rate increase: 620 hours × $103 = $63,860

5. A new purchasing agent, hired at the beginning of the quarter, is being paid $14,200 less per year than the previous agent. *Comment: Salaries are usually higher for more experienced managers. Because the new manager is less experienced than the previous manager, the new manager is paid a lower salary.*

6. The depreciation increase was related to the purchase and installation of a new EDI system. The purchase was made with board approval when a competitor went bankrupt during the quarter and had a distress liquidation sale. The purchase of this technology had been included in the capital budget for the end of 2009, not during the first quarter of 2009. *Comment: Acquiring the EDI technology is a good example of the cost containment concept. PFS wanted to buy the software and equipment and had an opportunity to buy it at a substantial savings but earlier than anticipated. This purchase created an unfavorable cost variance for depreciation in the first quarter, but it shows an instance of planning, foresight, and flexibility. The long-run benefits of this purchase are twofold. First, the capital budget will show a favorable variance when the cost of this equipment is compared to the expected cost. Second, in future periods, the budgeted committed cost for depreciation will be less than it would have been had the purchase not been made at this time.*

Note that the variance computations in Exhibit 16–8 are based on comparisons between a revised budget that uses actual checks processed as the cost driver and the actual revenues and costs incurred. When comparing budgeted and actual expenditures, managers must be careful to analyze variances using an equitable basis of comparison. These variance computations illustrate the use of flexible budgeting. Comparisons between the original budget and actual results for the variable cost items would not have been useful for control purposes because variable costs automatically change with changes in cost driver activity.

In addition to effectively controlling costs, management also must develop tools that are effective in managing a resource that is crucial to the survival of any organization: cash.

Cash Management

LO.6
What are the objectives managers strive to achieve in managing cash?

Of all organizational resources, cash is one of the most important and challenging to manage. Cash is the organizational resource that is the medium of exchange in most business transactions. Two key cash management tools were introduced in Chapter 8: the cash budget and budgeted (pro forma) cash flow statement. This section provides an overview of cash management objectives and tools.

An organization's liquidity depends on having enough cash available to retire debts and other obligations as they come due. However, holding too much cash reduces a firm's profitability because the return on idle cash is below both the return that can be earned on other productive assets and the cost of capital.

Firms hold cash to liquidate transactions, to cover unexpected events, and for speculation. Objectives of managing cash are similar to objectives of managing inventories. Cash levels should be sufficient to cover all needs but low enough to constrain opportunity costs associated with alternative uses of the cash. Models useful in managing inventory (discussed in Chapter 18) are also useful for managing cash levels. Optimal cash management requires answers to the three questions posed in the following sections.

What Variables Influence the Optimal Level of Cash?

The cash budget and pro forma cash flow statement provide managers information about the amounts and timing of cash flows. These data are the primary inputs to the determination of the "inventory" of cash that should be available at a specific point in the budget year. However, the actual level of cash maintained can differ from that necessary to meet the cash flow requirements in the cash budget.

The level of confidence that managers have in the cash budget is a nonquantitative factor that influences the desired cash balance. For example, the less certain managers are of either the amount or the timing of cash inflows or outflows, the higher the amount of cash that managers will hold. If actual cash flows fail to match budgetary amounts, more cash could be required to satisfy transactions. Similarly, the greater the variability in cash requirements throughout the year, the more conservative managers must be in managing cash. To avoid liquidity problems, managers of firms with high variability in the operating cycle must hold a greater amount of cash than managers of firms with very stable, predictable operating cycles. Firms that would have difficulty arranging for short-term credit to cover unexpected cash shortages are forced to hold higher amounts of cash to cover contingencies.

Also, securities ratings (particularly bond ratings) can induce firms to hold larger cash balances than is justified based on all other considerations. A favorable bond rating is contingent on the organization's having the ability to pay interest and principal when these amounts are due. Security rating agencies encourage organizations to demonstrate conservative practices in managing cash. Related to bond ratings, firms with debt may be obligated by loan covenants to maintain minimum levels of cash.

What Are the Sources of Cash?

There are three usual sources for cash. First, cash is generated by the sale of equity or debt securities and other shorter-term instruments. Second, assets no longer necessary or productive are liquidated to provide cash. Last, cash is generated in the normal operating cycle assuming goods are sold above their production costs. The capital budget is the key control tool for the first two sources of cash (as discussed in Chapter 15).

Management of cash consumed by and derived from the operating cycle is integral to the management of working capital. **Working capital** equals total current assets minus total current liabilities. In the operating cycle, cash is first invested in material and conversion costs, then in finished goods inventory, followed by (or concurrently with) marketing and administrative activities, and finally in accounts receivable. The cycle is completed when the accounts receivable are collected. Exhibit 16–9 illustrates the cash collection cycle.

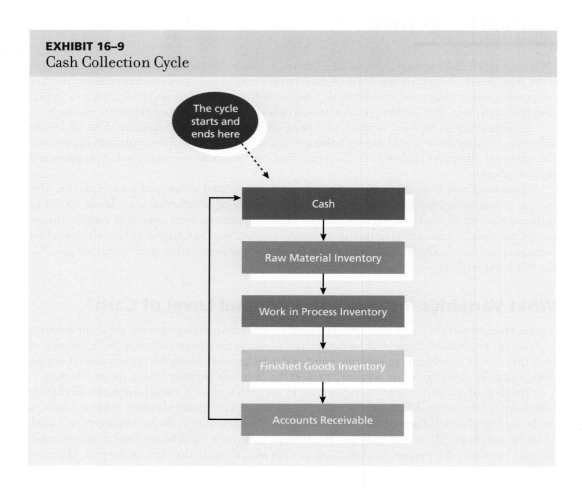

EXHIBIT 16–9
Cash Collection Cycle

Effective management of the cash collection cycle can both reduce the demand for cash and increase its supply. For example, if cash invested during the operating cycle (such as in inventories and receivables) can be reduced by accelerating the cycle, the cash balance will increase. In the utopian case, raw material would be instantly obtained when a customer placed an order. That material would then be instantly converted into a finished product that would instantly be transferred to the customer who would instantly pay in cash. Even without achieving the utopian ideal, any reduction in the length of the operating cycle will reduce inventory and accounts receivable balances and increase the cash balance. A late 2003 survey of corporate treasurers by Treasury Strategies Inc. indicated that liquidity was the most significant issue facing corporate treasurers.[8]

Managers can take explicit measures to accelerate inventory turnover. For example, inventory levels can be reduced if products can be manufactured more quickly after customer orders are received. Just-in-time and other inventory management practices that serve this objective are discussed in Chapter 18.

In addition to reducing inventory, cash collections can be accelerated to increase cash levels. Accounts receivable turnover can be directly influenced by terms given on credit sales, policies governing credit approval, discounts given for early payment, and use of the services of financial intermediaries that specialize in purchasing (or "factoring") accounts receivable. Other practices can be implemented to accelerate customer payments including using electronic funds transfers, customer debit cards, lock boxes, and bank courier services. Centralizing cash collection functions also allows accounts receivable to be converted to cash more quickly.

Alternatively, the cash balance can be increased by slowing down payments for inputs. Managers can search among alternative vendors for the most desirable credit terms and policies. Credit cards rather than cash can be used to purchase inputs. Rather than paying factory employees weekly, a bimonthly or monthly pay plan can be instituted. Also, decentralizing cash disbursement functions can increase the interval from when a check is issued until it clears the financial banking system.

What Variables Influence the Cost of Carrying Cash?

The cost of carrying cash varies over time and there are two classes of costs to manage: the cost of borrowing and the cost of issuing equity capital. For example, short-term borrowing costs will rise and fall with changes in inflation rates, creditworthiness of the borrower, and availability of funds for lending. The higher these costs, the greater the incentive to minimize idle cash balances.

Second, there is the opportunity cost of holding cash. Excess cash can be invested in productive projects or returned to investors. As more investment opportunities become available to a firm, there is a greater incentive to convert idle cash to other assets. Even if few investment opportunities are available, managers can always return cash to investors by reducing debt or repurchasing shares of stock. The higher a firm's cost of capital, the greater the opportunity cost of holding idle cash.

Banking Relationships

Managers depend on banks for much of their short-term liquidity and long-term loans. In turn, bankers depend on financial information from creditors to measure risk and determine eligibility for loans. Accounting and cash flow information are key determinants of loan eligibility, loan limits, and credit terms.

From the bank's perspective, credit risk is a primary concern in determining whether, and how much, a bank will lend to an entity. Credit risk also is a key input in determining the borrower's interest rate. To assess credit risk, banks examine the borrower's credit history, ability to generate cash flow, quality of collateral, character of senior officers, and operational plans and strategies. The loan agreement will include covenants or restrictions that prescribe minimal financial thresholds that the borrower must maintain for the life of the loan. For instance, covenants can stipulate minimum acceptable ratios for debt to assets, current assets to current liabilities, and interest coverage.

Accountants must monitor the firm's compliance with loan agreement covenants. By projecting revenues, expenses, and cash flows, accountants can identify potential problems before they are

---

[8]Mark Prysock, "Top Issues Facing Corporate Treasurers Today," *Financial Executive* (November 2003), p. 60.

encountered and help develop plans to avoid covenant violations. If a covenant violation is inevitable, accountants can work with the bank to negotiate a solution to the situation. Furthermore, accountants should understand the bank's standard lending policies, such as margin requirements for short-term assets, and manage the firm's compliance with those policies.

Trust is an important element of a good relationship between a bank and a borrower. The development of trust depends on accountants providing accurate, conservative financial data to the bank as well as timely information about operating results. Accountants have the responsibility of preparing the reports provided to the bank and of providing interpretations of the data to help bank personnel understand the financial and operating results.

Bankers abhor surprises. If a firm is facing bad news, such as the potential for bankruptcy, the bank should be kept informed about the circumstances and efforts being made to overcome the challenge. By maintaining a trusting relationship with a bank and its officers, a firm will have a valuable partner in weathering financial storms.

In addition to building relationships with banks and other lenders, the trend is to build stronger ties to suppliers and providers of other necessary inputs as well.

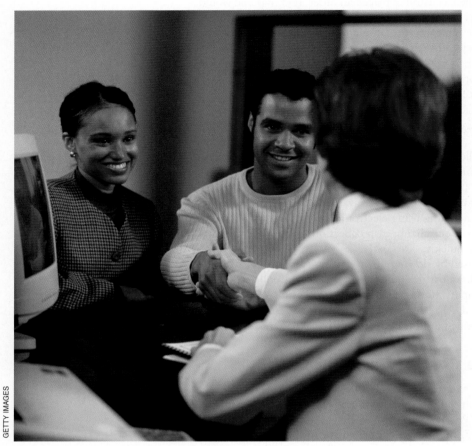

GETTY IMAGES

Mutual trust is key to a good relationship between banker and borrowers.

Supply-Chain Management

Today, competition in markets is as much between supply chains as between individual firms; thus, there is greater joint dependency among firms and their suppliers than previously existed. This dependency creates an incentive to share information and to manage costs across customers and suppliers. Exhibit 16–10 depicts three significant supply chain interactions and dependencies. The most obvious interaction is the downstream flow of goods and services. However, many supply chain costs are associated with the other two arrows: the upstream flow of information and the upstream flow of payments.

LO.7
How is technology reducing costs of supply chain transactions?

Information Technology and Purchasing

Until recently, a significant amount of time and other resources was spent ordering parts and materials from suppliers and issuing payments for those inputs. The downstream firm typically prepared a material requisition form, purchase order, and receiving report. The upstream firm issued documents to control the production, shipping, and billing of the ordered goods. Collectively, these control processes and documents created significant supply chain costs.

Today, firms increasingly use electronic exchanges of information and payments to reduce purchasing transaction costs. These exchanges are generally of two types. First, the exchange can involve the acquisition of significant operating needs, such as direct materials. These acquisitions can be governed by long-term supply agreements that involve major negotiations and a detailed exchange of product specifications and engineering data. For these transactions, documents such as purchase orders, invoices, and payments are transferred electronically through electronic data interchange (EDI) systems. The second type is discussed in the next section.

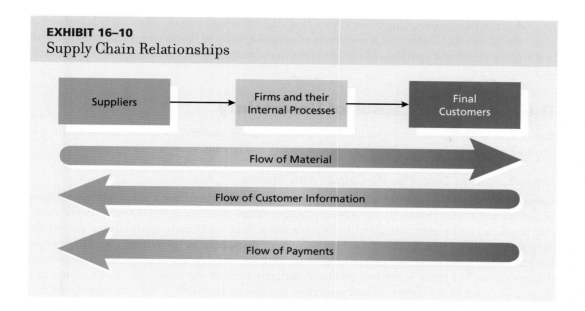

EXHIBIT 16–10
Supply Chain Relationships

Advances in Authorizing and Empowering Purchases

The second general type of purchasing involves indirect materials or nonoperating inputs such as office supplies. In a traditional purchasing system, buying a box of paper clips might require the same set of documents and procedures as required for buying $1,000,000 of raw materials. However, firms are increasingly using e-procurement systems to purchase nonoperating inputs. Such systems are electronic B2B (business-to-business) buy-side applications controlling the requisitioning, ordering, and payment functions for inputs.

One common configuration of such a system involves a large purchaser or a consortium of smaller purchasers, creating an electronic marketplace. Typically, the purchasing organization allows suppliers to make their electronic catalogs of products and materials available online. The e-procurement system then allows authorized personnel to order inputs from those catalogs and pay for the purchases electronically. Other systems allow competing vendors to bid for the right to sell inputs to the purchasing firm. Although the early versions of e-procurement systems were unable to support the interfirm collaboration that is often necessary for operating inputs such as direct materials, the latest editions are including more collaborative functionality. Future versions of these systems will facilitate the exchange of information, such as product specifications or drawings, with an expanded group of potential suppliers to increase competition for both operating (direct materials) and nonoperating (supplies) inputs.

Coping with Uncertainty

LO.8
Why is uncertainty greater in dealing with future events than with past events?

The world of the management and cost accountant is split into two spheres separated by time. The first sphere is the historical, in which the accountant is concerned with accounting accurately and fairly for events and activities that have already occurred; examples include determining the cost of production for the period, determining the cost of equipment purchased, and ascertaining the cost of operating a department or division. The focus of financial accounting is accurately reporting historical accounting data.

The second sphere is futuristic, in which accountants deal with events and activities yet to unfold; examples include budgeting cost of goods to be produced, estimating the cost of equipment to be purchased, and projecting the impact of future events on costs and revenues for departments and divisions. Effectiveness of accountants in this second realm is determined in part by their abilities to cope with and manage uncertainty. Uncertainty reflects the doubt or lack of precision in specifying future outcomes. Uncertainty arises from lack of complete knowledge about future events and is the reason accountants are less accurate in assigning costs to future events and activities than to historical events and activities. Much of the activity of management accountants involves dealing with uncertainty.

The Nature and Causes of Uncertainty

Before discussing specific strategies for dealing with effects of uncertainty in cost management, it is first necessary to understand the nature of uncertainty and its causes.

Understanding Uncertainty Causes and Effects

Uncertainty in cost management has two main sources. First, it arises from a lack of identification or understanding of cost drivers. To estimate and budget future costs, accountants exploit the relationship between a cost and its cost driver. In a simple and perfect world, each organizational cost would have a single driver that would perfectly explain every fluctuation in the related cost. However, in the real world, some costs may be predicted with accuracy based on the relationship of the cost to the cost driver, but rarely is the cost predicted perfectly because the entire cost is not related to a single cost driver. In the context of cost prediction and cost understanding, random refers to the fact that some portion of the cost is not predictable based on the cost driver or that the cost is stochastically, rather than deterministically, related to the cost driver.

For example, a factory controller may use machine hours as the basis for predicting factory utility costs. Although changes in volume of machine hours may account for nearly all of the change in factory utility cost, other factors, such as weather and number of employees, may account for another portion of the cost. If machine hours alone are used as the basis for predicting utility costs, the prediction might be close to the actual cost, but the prediction will contain some error. This error is evidence that part of the utility cost is only randomly related to the machine hour cost driver. Furthermore, logic suggests that whereas machine hours may explain with relative accuracy the quantity of kilowatt-hours of electricity consumed, machine hours may have no relationship to the price the utility company charges for each kilowatt-hour consumed.

Occurrence of Unforeseen Events

A second source of uncertainty is unforeseen events. For example, the events of September 11, 2001, dealt a severe economic blow to most industries in the United States but, for the airline industry, the impact of 9/11 was nearly fatal. This industry is characterized by high fixed operating costs and this situation is a source of significant risk for airlines. In the immediate aftermath of 9/11, the airlines lost 100 percent of their revenues for a brief period and a large portion of revenues for an extended period. Without significant aid from the U.S. government, this entire industry, at least as it existed prior to 9/11, may have been lost from the economy along with thousands of jobs and total disruption of the U.S. transportation system.

When firms plan for unforeseen events, it is impossible to know the severity of all contingencies that could occur. Accordingly, no reasonable plan to deal with unforeseen events will provide solutions for all possible occurrences. Even so, managers must develop strategies for reducing the level of uncertainty to which their firms are exposed.

LO.9
What are the four generic approaches to managing uncertainty?

Four Strategies for Dealing with Uncertainty

There are four generic strategies applicable to cost management in the face of uncertainty. First, uncertainty can be explicitly factored into estimates of future costs. Second, costs can be structured to automatically adjust to uncertain outcomes. Third, options and forward contracts can be used to mitigate effects of uncertainty. Fourth, insurance can be purchased to reimburse the firm in the event of unexpected occurrences.

Explicitly Considering Uncertainty when Estimating Future Costs

Typically the historical relationship between a cost and its cost driver is used as a basis for assessing the extent to which the cost is only randomly related to the cost driver. Statistical tools are often used in this type of analysis. In Chapter 3, ordinary least squares regression was introduced as a statistical tool to predict costs. In the following equation, *y* is the cost or other item to be predicted (dependent variable); *a* and *b* are, respectively, the intercept and slope in the prediction equation; and *X* is the predictor variable (independent variable). The least squares method is used to develop estimates of the values for *a* and *b* in the following prediction equation.

$$y = a + bX$$

When alternative independent variables exist, least squares regression can help select the independent variable that is the best predictor of the dependent variable. For example, managers can use least squares to decide whether machine hours, ambient temperature, factory production hours, or another variable best explains and predicts changes in factory utility expense.

Statistical software packages are often used to develop ordinary least squares estimates of the *a* and *b* values. These packages typically produce a variety of statistical information in addition to the estimates of *a* and *b*. For example, nearly all statistical packages as well as spreadsheet software produce a statistic called the **coefficient of determination**, which is the portion of the variance in the dependent variable (cost) explained by the variance in the independent variable (cost driver). The value of this statistic ranges between 0 and 1. A value of 0 indicates the relationship between the predictor variable and the dependent variable is completely random. A value of 1 signifies that the variance of the independent variable explains completely the variance of the dependent variable. More important, a coefficient of determination value of 0 means the predictor variable is of no value in predicting the dependent variable, and a value of 1 means the predictor variable is ideal.

Although the calculation of the coefficient of determination is beyond the scope of this text, the use of this measure in selecting predictor variables is straightforward and is readily available with even elementary statistical packages. Exhibit 16–11 illustrates the hypothetical relationship of factory utility costs to the possible predictor variable of machine hours or plant production hours. The exhibit features the relationships between dependent and independent variables based on six months of recent data. Ordinary least squares has been used to estimate the regression lines that appear in the exhibit. If the coefficient of determination is 1, all data points will fall on the ordinary least squares regression line. Given the relationships, neither of the candidate predictor variables

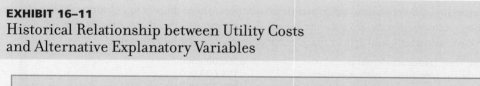

EXHIBIT 16–11

Historical Relationship between Utility Costs and Alternative Explanatory Variables

would provide a coefficient of determination of 1. However, the data points for the machine hours regression are much closer to the line than are the data points for the plant production hours regression. The calculated coefficient of determination reflects the proximity of the data points to the fitted regression line and it follows that the coefficient of determination is higher for the machine hours regression (0.91) than for the plant production hours regression (0.59).

Using the coefficient of determination as a tool to select the best among candidate predictor variables will reduce the uncertainty regarding estimated costs or revenues. All other things being equal, the higher the coefficient of determination, the lower the uncertainty regarding the resulting prediction or forecast.

Other statistical techniques such as computer simulations and more elaborate regression models, which can include multiple independent variables as well as nonlinear relationships between independent and dependent variables, can also be used to select predictor variables. The goal in using more elaborate models is to reduce the prediction error and thereby the effects of uncertainty on accuracy of predictions.

The alternative approach to explicitly considering the effects of uncertainty in cost estimates is to examine the sensitivity of costs and/or revenues to estimation errors. Because tools such as ordinary least squares regression provide predictions of a single value, it is useful to examine effects of errors in estimates. Sensitivity analysis, introduced in Chapter 15, is a tool commonly used for this purpose. To illustrate, assume that Atlanta Air predicts its airline maintenance costs (y) as a function of air miles flown (X) and that the annual estimation equation is as follows:

$$\text{Annual airline maintenance cost function: } y = \$60,000,000 + \$50X$$

If Atlanta Air expects to fly 2,000,000 air miles in the coming year, the predicted cost of airline maintenance would be $\$60,000,000 + \$50(2,000,000) = \$160,000,000$. Further assume that, although Atlanta Air expects to fly 2,000,000 air miles, the possible range of activity is 1,900,000 to 2,100,000. Inserting the minimum and maximum values of X into the airline maintenance equation yields a range for the cost of airline maintenance.

$$\text{Minimum expected airline maintenance cost} = \$60,000,000 + \$50(1,900,000)$$
$$= \$155,000,000$$

$$\text{Maximum expected airline maintenance cost} = \$60,000,000 + \$50(2,100,000)$$
$$= \$165,000,000$$

This approach yields very useful information in instances where there is uncertainty about volume of operations, perhaps because of customer demand. For example, the three Atlanta Air airline maintenance cost estimates could reflect three possible levels of customer demand:

Most likely customer demand	$160,000,000
Pessimistic scenario of customer demand	155,000,000
Optimistic scenario of customer demand	165,000,000

If Atlanta Air's managers are confident of the relationship between air miles flown and airline maintenance costs, as well as their estimates of customer demand, the managers can be relatively confident that airline maintenance cost will fall between $155,000,000 and $165,000,000 for the coming year.

Structuring Costs to Adjust to Uncertain Outcomes

As discussed earlier in the chapter, the events of 9/11/01 were disastrous for the airline industry. There are few other industries that could be harmed as dramatically by a drop in service/product demand. The airline industry is characterized by very high levels of fixed costs and, in the short run, the level of costs is very insensitive to the level of customer demand. Consequently, if demand spikes, profits soar, and if demand falters, profits plummet and losses are quickly experienced. The greater the uncertainty about demand, the greater the risk of allowing fixed costs to comprise a high proportion of total costs. In addition to experiencing revenue losses following 9/11, the airline industry also was dealt a blow by an increase in fuel prices (a variable operating cost) a few years later.

Consider the cost and revenue graphs that are shown in Exhibit 16–12 for Companies A and B. Company A has a cost structure that is entirely variable, and Company B has a cost structure that is entirely fixed. The space between the revenue and total cost lines in the graphs represents

EXHIBIT 16–12
Relationship between Uncertainty and Cost Structure

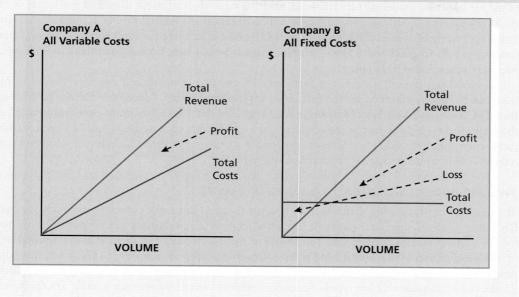

profits or losses. Note how the amount of profit varies greatly with small changes in volume for Company B. Alternatively, Company A's profits change slowly as volume changes. Accordingly, Company A's profits are less exposed to the effects of uncertainty. General relationships between cost structure and profits are discussed in detail in Chapter 9 with regard to cost-volume-profit analysis.

Although fixed and variable costs are not completely substitutable, most companies have substantial opportunities to change their cost structures. For example, in the airline industry, managers could choose to lease rather than to purchase airplanes. The shorter the term of the lease, the more the cost of airplanes can approximate a variable cost. Thus, as demand changes, airplane leases can be added or cancelled.

Using Options and Forward Contracts to Mitigate Price Risk

Uncertainty about the cost of inputs arises from two sources: the quantity and the costs of inputs consumed. Although the quantity of inputs consumed is typically highly correlated with customer demand and production volume, the price of inputs can be influenced by many other factors. Accordingly, even though machine hours may, on a long-term basis, prove to be highly correlated with utility cost, machine hours are more highly correlated with the quantity component of cost rather than the price component. Thus, although the uncertainty surrounding quantity of input usage may be best resolved by an improved understanding of volume drivers, other strategies will be necessary to deal with price uncertainty.

Some companies operate in industries that are intensely competitive, and if prices of inputs unexpectedly increase, the companies may be unable to increase prices sufficiently to cover the increase in costs. These companies in particular need effective strategies for dealing with input price uncertainty. Two tools used in such strategies are options and forward contracts.

Options and forward contracts are agreements that give the holder the right to purchase a given quantity of a specific input at a specific price at a specific time. Generically, the use of options and forward contracts to manage price risk is known as hedging. To illustrate, according to the CPI, gasoline prices increased 146 percent from July 1997 to July 2007. Companies, such as airlines, that are heavily exposed to risks of price changes for fuel can use options and forward contracts as protection against such price increases. The extent to which specific companies in the airline industry used these tools has varied widely in recent years. Southwest Airlines has hedged more of its fuel requirements than other airlines. For example, Southwest Airlines has recently hedged the price of as much as 85 percent of its annual fuel needs. In 2004, Southwest paid the equivalent of $25 per barrel of oil for its jet fuel whereas other airlines paid the equivalent of more than $40 per barrel of oil. As a consequence, Southwest was the only airline to report substantial profits in 2004.[9] Even with industry-leading hedges in place, the substantial increase in jet fuel prices still harmed the company's financial results in 2005 and 2006—but the company would have been substantially more harmed had the hedges not been in effect.

Forward contracts or options can be executed between a company and a specific vendor, or options can be purchased on organized exchanges such as the Chicago Mercantile Exchange, Chicago Board of Trade, and New York Mercantile Exchange. Exhibit 16–13 lists items commonly traded on the organized exchanges. Just as the consumer of a commodity such as diesel fuel can use a forward contract or option to hedge against cost uncertainty, a producer of diesel fuel can use a forward contract or option to hedge against revenue uncertainty.

Insuring against Occurrences of Specific Events

The final strategy for coping with uncertainty involves use of insurance contracts, in which one party (an insurer) in exchange for a payment (premium) agrees to reimburse a second party (an insured) for the costs of certain occurrences. The nature of the occurrences can include events limited only by the imagination of the contracting parties. Common types of occurrences for which insurance protection is sought include events often described as "acts of nature" such as tornados, hail storms, floods, and earthquakes. Other types of common events covered by insurance include fire, theft, vandalism, accidental death of a key employee, and product failure. Companies can also obtain D&O (directors' and officers') insurance that can protect the members of the board and corporate officers from being personally liable while they are acting on behalf of the company. However, D&O insurance does not typically protect directors and officers when they engage in dishonest, fraudulent, or illegal actions.

Whereas the other strategies for dealing with uncertainty largely address uncertainty about costs deriving from quantity and price variability, insurance is purchased to cope with uncertainty about occurrences of specific events. Events usually insured against are those that, in the absence of insurance, would dramatically increase costs (e.g., to rebuild a factory following a fire) or decrease revenues (e.g., business is interrupted by a labor strike in a company's only factory).

EXHIBIT 16–13
Examples of Items Commonly Hedged

Energy	Metals	Interest Rates
heating oil	gold	short-term
crude oil	silver	long-term
gasoline	copper	
natural gas	aluminum	**Agricultural**
electricity	platinum	livestock
coal		meats
propane	**Currencies**	grains
		cotton

[9]Chris Walsh, "Airlines Getting Creative in Saving on Fuel," *Scripps Howard News*; http://www.atca.org/singlenews.asp?item_id=2408&comm=0 (last accessed 8/18/07).

Comprehensive Review Module

Chapter Summary

1. An effective cost control system helps manage costs

    - prior to an event through

        ➢ establishment of budgets and standards or

        ➢ other stated expectations of performance outcomes.

    - during an event by

        ➢ identifying deviations from plans or budgets or

        ➢ monitoring other aspects of operations relative to expectations.

    - following an event by providing feedback on performance.

2. Three generic approaches to cost control include

    - cost containment, which is an approach to minimize cost increases;

    - cost avoidance, which means finding ways to avoid high cost inputs by substituting lower cost inputs; and

    - cost reduction, which involves finding ways to alter operations to lower costs.

3. Costs can change from one period to the next, or deviate from expectations, as a result of

    - variable costs moving with changes in volume.

    - inflation or deflation of prices.

    - supplier-changed prices

        ➢ in response to changes in demand or

        ➢ due to changes in cost of production.

    - purchase volume changes, which affect purchase discounts related to volume.

4. Two primary types of fixed cost are

    - committed fixed costs, which are associated with an organization's basic infrastructure and are determined by long-run strategy (examples include depreciation, lease payments, and property taxes), and

    - discretionary fixed costs, which are incurred for activities for which the level and nature are determined by management judgment (examples include research and development, advertising, and employee training).

5. Control of discretionary costs can occur

    - before an event by the use of budgets or by treating them as engineered costs if they are associated with repetitive activities;

    - during an event by comparing budgets to actual expenditures; and

    - after an event by calculating variances for engineered costs.

6. The objectives in managing cash are to

    - maintain an organization's liquidity by making certain there is enough cash to cover cash expenses and to retire debt and

    - invest any idle cash so that a return is generated on cash balances exceeding liquidity needs.

7. Technology is reducing costs within supply chains by

    - reducing the need to generate paper documents for purchasing transactions;

    - automating payment transactions;

    - enhancing the exchange of information within the value chain; and

    - enhancing competition among alternative suppliers.

8. Uncertainty is greater for future events than for past events because

    - cause-and-effect relationships are incompletely understood.

    - events that are unforeseen can alter outcomes.

9. Four generic strategies for dealing with uncertainty are to

- explicitly consider uncertainty when estimates are generated by

  ➢ using best predictor variables in generating estimates and

  ➢ analyzing effects of estimation errors on estimates using sensitivity analysis;

- structure costs to adjust to uncertain outcomes;

- use options and forward contracts to manage price risks; and

- use insurance to indemnify against occurrences of specific events such as

  ➢ acts of nature or

  ➢ fire, theft, and liability risks.

Potential Ethical Issues

1. Including price escalation clauses in sales contracts but refusing to grant sales price decreases in the event of substantial downturns in costs

2. Artificially reducing the supply of a product or service to force an increase in price (or maintain an artificially high price) to customers

3. Acquiring raw material inputs in excessively high quantities to obtain a low price merely to generate a favorable variance for an individual manager or responsibility center (especially if that manager is primarily evaluated on the basis of price variances) while simultaneously ignoring the related non-value-added carrying costs related to the purchase

4. Engaging in cost avoidance by acquiring counterfeit goods at a lower price than their name-brand counterparts

5. Outsourcing production or procurement activities to companies that violate acceptable (as perceived from the firm's domicile country) labor or environmental laws

6. Slowing down payments to creditors simply to generate larger investment returns on cash balances, especially when those creditors do a high, or the highest, percentage of their business with the company

7. Manipulating or falsifying financial statements to obtain additional credit or lower interest rates on borrowings ▲

Solution Strategies

Efficiency: Relationship of input and output

$$\text{Actual Yield Ratio} = \text{Actual Output} \div \text{Actual Input}$$

or

$$\text{Actual Input} \div \text{Actual Output}$$

$$\text{Desired Yield Ratio} = \text{Planned Output} \div \text{Planned Input}$$

or

$$\text{Planned Input} \div \text{Planned Output}$$

Effectiveness: Relationship of actual output and desired output

Efficiency + Effectiveness = Performance

Cost Variances

Comparison of actual costs with budgeted costs: allows management to compare discrepancies from the original plan

Comparison of actual costs with budgeted costs at actual activity level: allows management to determine how well costs were controlled; uses a flexible budget

Variance analysis using standards for discretionary costs: allows management to compute variances for routine, structured discretionary costs

For discretionary costs susceptible to engineered cost treatment:

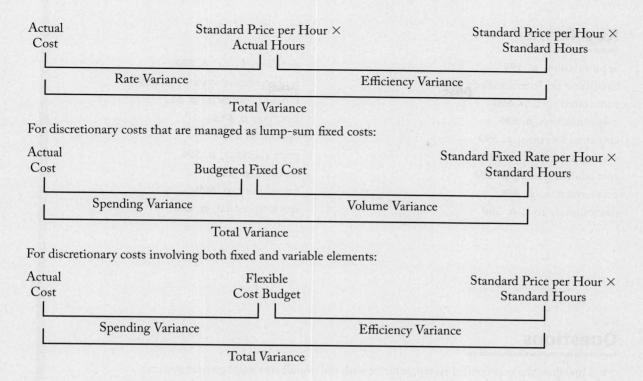

For discretionary costs that are managed as lump-sum fixed costs:

For discretionary costs involving both fixed and variable elements:

Demonstration Problem

TransPacific Services, a firm with global operations, has developed a training program for compliance with company policy and international laws regarding hiring practices. The company believes it can treat the cost of this training as an engineered cost. The following data were extracted from documents addressing the training plan and from records regarding actual performance:

Planned volume of training	10,800 employees
Total budgeted trainer days	120
Actual volume of training	12,400 employees
Actual trainer days	130

Required:

a. Calculate the degree of effectiveness of the training relative to number of employees trained.
b. Calculate planned efficiency for the trainers.
c. Calculate the actual efficiency of the trainers.
d. Comment on the performance of the trainers.

Solution to Demonstration Problem

a. Degree of effectiveness = Actual employees trained ÷ Budgeted employees trained

    = 12,400 ÷ 10,800

    = 1.148, or 115 percent (rounded)

b. Planned efficiency = Planned output ÷ Planned input

    = 10,800 employees ÷ 120 trainer days

    = 90 employees per trainer day

c. Actual efficiency = Actual output ÷ Actual input

    = 12,400 employees ÷ 130 trainer days

    = 95 employees per trainer day (rounded)

d. The performance of the trainers exceeded both effectiveness and efficiency expectations.

Key Terms

appropriation, **p. 599**	engineered cost, **p. 602**
coefficient of determination, **p. 611**	e-procurement system, **p. 609**
committed cost, **p. 598**	forward contracts, **p. 613**
cost avoidance, **p. 596**	hedging, **p. 613**
cost consciousness, **p. 592**	option, **p. 613**
cost containment, **p. 595**	price elasticity, **p. 594**
cost control system, **p. 592**	random, **p. 610**
cost reduction, **p. 596**	uncertainty, **p. 609**
discretionary cost, **p. 598**	working capital, **p. 606**

Questions

1. How does the cost control system interact with the overall cost management system?
2. Why does the general control model begin with planning activities?
3. At what points in time is cost control for any specific organizational activity exercised? Why are these points of cost control important?
4. What factors can cause costs to change? Which of these factors are subject to cost containment and which are not? What creates the difference in controllability?
5. Differentiate between committed and discretionary costs. Could a cost be considered discretionary by one firm and committed by another? If so, discuss and give an example. If not, discuss why not.
6. Why is it often difficult to measure the output of activities funded by discretionary costs?
7. Define the terms *efficiency* and *effectiveness* and distinguish one from the other. Why is measuring the efficiency of discretionary costs often difficult? Explain how the effectiveness of discretionary cost activities can be measured.
8. What types of discretionary costs are subject to control as engineered costs? Provide several examples.
9. Why do firms hold cash balances? Why do some firms require larger cash balances than other firms?
10. How is technology affecting supply chain purchasing practices and transaction costs?
11. What are the four generic approaches to reducing uncertainty?
12. What factors create uncertainty when estimating future costs and revenues?

Exercises

13. **LO.1 (Cost control systems)** Jill Madden, the CEO of Arkadelphia Manufacturing was concerned about the amount the firm had spent on fuel and energy costs in the previous quarter. Madden called the CFO, Alice Briggs, and expressed her concern, "Alice, according to our latest 10-Q, we spent $10 million on fuel and energy costs. Isn't that way too much?"

    As an intern working for Briggs, how would you proceed to answer this query about control of quarterly fuel and energy costs at Arkadelphia?

14. **LO.1 & LO.2 (Cost control; financial records)** Montana Industrial is a medium-size manufacturing corporation in a capital-intensive industry. Its profitability is currently very low. As a result, investment funds are limited and hiring is restricted. These consequences of the corporation's problems have placed a strain on the plant's repair and maintenance program. The result has been a reduction in work efficiency and cost control effectiveness in the repair and maintenance area.

The assistant controller proposes the installation of a maintenance work order system to overcome these problems. This system would require a work order be prepared for each repair request and for each regular maintenance activity. The maintenance superintendent would record the estimated time to complete a job and send one copy of the work order to the department in which the work would be done. The work order would also serve as a cost sheet for a job. Actual cost of parts and supplies used on the job as well as actual labor costs incurred in completing the job would be recorded directly on the work order. A copy of the completed work order would be the basis for the charge to the department in which the repair or maintenance activity occurred.

The maintenance superintendent opposes the program because the added paperwork will be costly and non-productive. The superintendent states that the departmental clerk who now schedules repairs and maintenance activities is doing a good job without all the extra forms the new system would require. The real problem, in the superintendent's opinion, is that the department is understaffed.

a. Discuss how such a maintenance work order system would aid in cost control.

b. Explain how a maintenance work order system might assist the maintenance superintendent in getting authorization to hire more staff.

(CMA adapted)

15. **LO.2 (Cost control activities)** The firm of Xtreme Accountants hires full- and part-time professional employees. Full-time experienced staff can be hired for $57,000 per year; fringe benefit costs for each full-time employee amount to 20 percent of base salary. Xtreme Accountants pays part-time professional employees $40 per hour but does not provide any fringe benefits. If a part-time employee has worked for the firm for more than 1,600 hours by year-end, he or she receives a $4,000 bonus.

a. Does the firm's policy of hiring part-time professional staff represent an example of cost containment, cost avoidance, or cost reduction? Explain.

b. For a given professional position, at what level of annual hours worked should the firm consider hiring full-time rather than part-time professional staff?

16. **LO.2 (Cost consciousness; team activity)** All organizations seek to be aware of and control costs. In a three- or four-person team, choose one of the following industries and do Web research to identify methods that have been used to control costs.

- Internet e-tailers
- Automobile manufacturers
- Hospitals
- Software companies
- Government entities

Prepare a written presentation that discusses the various methods of cost control, dollars of costs saved (if available), and your perceptions of the positive and negative implications of each of the cost control methodologies. You may choose a particular company within the industry should you so desire.

17. **LO.1 & LO.2 (Cost control activities)** Sallie Swoop has just been appointed the new director of Youth Hot-Line, a not-for-profit organization that operates a phone bank for individuals experiencing emotional difficulties. The phones are staffed by qualified social workers and psychologists who are paid on an hourly basis. Swoop took the following actions in the first week on her new job. Indicate whether the actions represent cost understanding, cost containment, cost avoidance, or cost reduction. Some actions may have more than one implication; if they do, indicate the reason.

a. Increased the advertising budget appropriation for the hotline.

b. Exchanged the more expensive push-button, cream-colored, designer telephones for regular push-button desk telephones.

c. Eliminated the call-forwarding feature installed on all telephones because Youth Hot-Line will now be staffed 24 hours a day.

d. Eliminated two paid clerical positions and replaced these individuals with volunteers.

e. Ordered blank notepads for the counselors to keep by their phones; the old notepads (stock now depleted) had the Youth Hot-Line logo and address printed on them.

f. Negotiated a new contract with the telephone company. Youth Hot-Line will now pay a flat rate of $100 per month regardless of the number of telephones installed. The previous contract charged the organization $10 for every telephone. At the time that contract was signed, Youth Hot-Line had only 10 telephones. With the increased staff, Swoop plans to install at least five additional telephones.

18. **LO.3 (Causes of cost changes)** Identify in the following scenarios whether the cost change is attributable to effects of cost behavior, inflation/deflation, supplier cost adjustment, or quantity purchased. Defend your answer.
    a. Allison Mfg. experienced an increase in fuel costs following an increase in crude oil prices by members of OPEC.
    b. Foremost Plastics experienced an increase in the cost of plastic resins when its main supplier merged with one of its competitors.
    c. The amount Kimball Co. spent on raw materials declined when its sales volume dropped by 20 percent because of diminished overseas demand for its products.
    d. Minerva Industrial reduced the price it paid for fasteners when it consolidated the purchases made from five vendors to just one vendor.
    e. The price of corn syrup purchased by California Confectionary increased when the demand for corn-based ethanol jumped dramatically.
    f. The amount Madison Beef Processing expended for direct labor jumped 25 percent when demand for the company's products jumped following Japan's removal of its U.S. beef import restrictions.
    g. The price Vilanova Steel paid for its metal products increased when it adopted JIT manufacturing practices and began purchasing steel in small lot sizes.
    h. The cost of executive travel at Hudson Financial Services dropped by 20 percent when two new airlines began providing services at the airport nearest the firm's headquarters.

19. **LO.4 (Committed vs. discretionary costs)** A list of committed and discretionary costs follows:

Annual audit fees	Internal audit salaries
Annual report preparation and printing	Marketing research
Building flood insurance	Preventive maintenance
Charitable contributions	Property taxes
Corporate advertising	Quality control inspection
Employee continuing education	Research and development salaries
Equipment depreciation	Research and development supplies
Interest on bonds payable	Secretarial pool salaries

    a. Classify each of these costs as normally being either committed (C) or discretionary (D).
    b. Which of these costs can be either committed or discretionary based on management philosophy?
    c. For the expenses marked discretionary in part (a), provide a monetary or nonmonetary surrogate output measure. For each output measure, briefly discuss any objections that could be raised to it.

20. **LO.4 (Committed vs. discretionary costs)** Choose letter C (for committed cost) or D (for discretionary cost) to indicate the type of each of the following described costs. Explain the rationale for your choice.
    a. Control is first provided during the capital budgeting process.
    b. Typical examples include advertising, research and development, and employee training.
    c. This type of cost cannot be easily reduced even during temporary slowdowns in activity.
    d. There is usually no "correct" amount at which to set funding levels.
    e. Typical examples include depreciation, lease rentals, and property taxes.
    f. This type of cost often provides benefits that are not monetarily measurable.
    g. Temporary reductions can usually be made without impairing the firm's long-range capacity or profitability.
    h. This cost is primarily affected by long-run decisions regarding desired capacity levels.
    i. It is often difficult to ascribe outcomes as being closely correlated with this type of cost.
    j. This cost usually relates to service-type activities.

21. **LO.5 (Effectiveness measures)** Williams Wellness Clinic has used funds during 2008 for the following purposes.
    a. Sent two cost accounting staff members to seminars on activity-based costing.
    b. Purchased a kidney dialysis machine.
    c. Built an attached parking garage for the clinic.
    d. Redecorated the main lobby.
    e. Placed a full-page advertisement in the local Yellow Pages.
    f. Acquired new software to track patient charges and prepare itemized billings.

Provide nonmonetary, surrogate measures that would help evaluate the effectiveness of the monies spent.

22. **LO.5 (Effectiveness and efficiency measures)** The president at Southeast University has formed a new department to recruit top out-of-state students. The department's funding for 2008 is $800,000, and the department was given the goal of recruiting 300 new nonresident students. By year-end 2008, the department had been credited with recruiting 330 new students. The department actually consumed $936,600 in its recruiting efforts.
    a. How effective was the newly formed department? Show calculations.
    b. How efficient was the department? Show calculations.

23. **LO.5 (Engineered cost variances)** Floyd's Transport employs three drivers who are paid $16 per hour for regular time and $24 for overtime. A single pickup and delivery requires, on average, one hour of driver time. Drivers are paid for a 40-hour week because they must be on call all day. One driver stands by for after-hour deliveries. Analyze the labor costs for one week in which the company made 105 daytime deliveries and 12 after-hour deliveries. The payroll for drivers for that week was $2,280. The employees worked 120 hours of regular time and 15 hours of overtime.

24. **LO.5 (Engineered cost variances)** Management at Texas Technology Inc. has estimated that each quality control inspector should be able to make an average of 24 inspections per hour. Retired factory supervisors are excellent quality control inspectors because of their familiarity with the products and processes in the plant. Texas Technology management has decided to staff the quality control program with these individuals and has set $18 as the standard hourly rate. During the first month of the new program, 25,020 inspections were made, and the total pay to the inspectors was $20,928 for 1,030 hours of work.
    a. Perform a variance analysis for management on the quality control labor cost.
    b. Assume that management could hire four full-time inspectors for a monthly salary of $5,000 each and hire part-timers for the overflow. Each full-time inspector would work 170 hours per month. How would the total cost of this alternative compare to the cost of a 1,030-hour month at the standard rate of $18 per hour?

25. **LO.5 (Variance analysis; ethics)** Cost control in the Human Resources Office of Warren Grocery Warehouse is evaluated based on engineered cost concepts. The office incurs both variable and fixed costs. The variable costs are largely driven by the amount of employee turnover. For 2008, budgeted costs in the Human Resources Office were:

| Fixed | $200,000 |
| Variable | 400,000 (based on projected turnover of 1,000 employees) |

For 2008, actual costs in the Human Resources Office were:

| Fixed | $220,000 |
| Variable | 450,000 (actual turnover of 1,050 employees) |

Using traditional variance analysis, evaluate the control of fixed and variable costs in the Human Resources Office. Does this method of evaluation encourage the Human Resources Office managers to hire low-quality workers? Explain. ▲

26. **LO.6 (Cash management)** Big Plains Auto Parts manufactures after-market automobile parts that are sold in a variety of outlets including auto parts stores and discount retailers. The following account data (in millions) have been taken from a recent balance sheet.

Current Assets

Cash	$ 10
Accounts Receivable	140
Finished Goods Inventory	25
Work in Process Inventory	170
Raw Material Inventory	90

Current Liabilities

| Accounts Payable | $ 22 |
| Other | 7 |

Discuss recommendations that Big Plains Auto Parts managers could use to improve its cash position. Focus your discussion on the operating cycle rather than on other means of raising cash.

27. **LO.7 (e-Procurement)** You are employed by a firm engaging in heavy manufacturing. Its direct materials are sourced globally, but its nonoperating inputs are sourced from a variety of U.S. vendors. You have been charged with making a presentation to the CFO about the benefits of e-procurement for nonoperating inputs. Outline the benefits your firm could expect to realize if it replaced its paper controls with a state-of-the-art e-procurement system.

28. **LO.8 & LO.9 (Coping with uncertainty)** You have been assigned the task of projecting the cost of 2009 employee fringe benefits for your firm and have identified number of employees, total labor hours, and total labor cost as candidate independent variables for use in the estimation equation. Using historical data and ordinary least squares regression, you calculate the coefficient of determination for each of the candidate variables. You get the following results:

Variable	Coefficient of Determination
Number of employees	0.87
Total labor hours	0.95
Total labor cost	0.81

   a. Discuss how you would use the coefficient of determination to select the best predictor variable.

   b. What are the highest and lowest possible values for the coefficient of determination? Explain.

29. **LO.8 & LO.9 (Coping with uncertainty)** Galveston Fabricators manufactures a variety of industrial products from stock metal components. The firm is engaged in its annual process of budgeting costs and revenues for the coming year. The cost of metal consumes approximately 50 percent of total revenues. Discuss which strategies for dealing with uncertainty would be appropriate for Galveston Fabricators to use in estimating and managing its metal costs for the coming year.

30. **LO.8 & LO.9 (Coping with uncertainty)** Callahan Corp. operates in an industry in which the demand for products is cyclical and often unpredictable. Discuss a strategy for dealing with uncertainty associated with the cycles that would be appropriate for Callahan Corp. to employ to maintain its profitability throughout the cycles.

Problems

31. **LO.1 (Cost control)** Thurston Mfg. produces a variety of consumer goods including lamps, home office desks, storage cabinets, etc. Many products sold by the company are purchased disassembled and are assembled by the customer. To assist the customer with assembly, Thurston provides a free hotline staffed 24 hours daily and provides an assembly manual with each item sold. The firm produces the assembly manuals in-house and maintains very tight control over the production costs of the manuals. For the latest year, the company spent $9,000,000 writing, publishing, and packaging assembly manuals for its products. The manager tasked with managing the production of assembly manuals was speaking with the CEO and noted that "our actual production cost of $9,000,000 for assembly manuals was $500,000 under budget. I am very proud of my employees and their efforts to control costs for the company."

   The CEO pondered the statement for a moment and then responded, "According to survey results that reached my desk only this morning, 65 percent of our customers use the hotline for assistance with product assembly; only 7 percent ever open their manual."

   a. In light of the survey results, did the company effectively control costs of assembly manuals? Explain.

   b. In the long term, why must cost control efforts be viewed through the eyes of the customer rather than through the accounting system only?

32. **LO.1 (Cost control)** The following graph indicates where each part of the dollar that a student pays for a new college textbook goes.

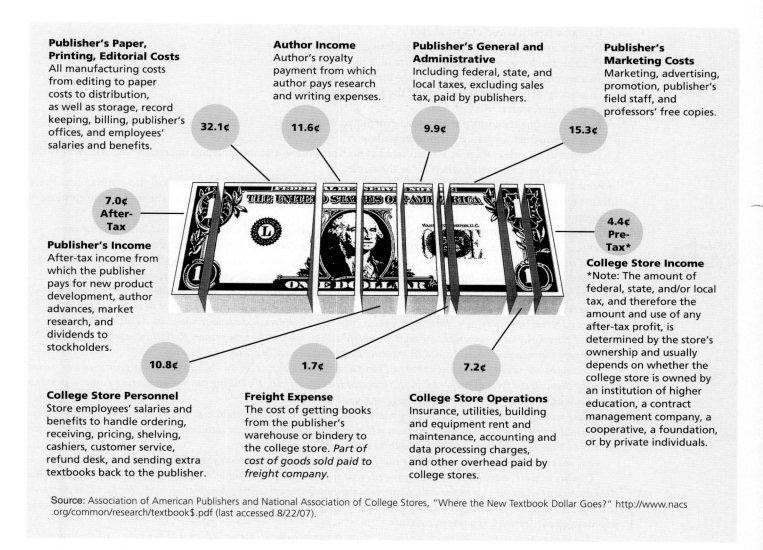

Publisher's Paper, Printing, Editorial Costs
All manufacturing costs from editing to paper costs to distribution, as well as storage, record keeping, billing, publisher's offices, and employees' salaries and benefits.

32.1¢

Author Income
Author's royalty payment from which author pays research and writing expenses.

11.6¢

Publisher's General and Administrative
Including federal, state, and local taxes, excluding sales tax, paid by publishers.

9.9¢

Publisher's Marketing Costs
Marketing, advertising, promotion, publisher's field staff, and professors' free copies.

15.3¢

7.0¢ After-Tax

Publisher's Income
After-tax income from which the publisher pays for new product development, author advances, market research, and dividends to stockholders.

4.4¢ Pre-Tax*

College Store Income
*Note: The amount of federal, state, and/or local tax, and therefore the amount and use of any after-tax profit, is determined by the store's ownership and usually depends on whether the college store is owned by an institution of higher education, a contract management company, a cooperative, a foundation, or by private individuals.

10.8¢

College Store Personnel
Store employees' salaries and benefits to handle ordering, receiving, pricing, shelving, cashiers, customer service, refund desk, and sending extra textbooks back to the publisher.

1.7¢

Freight Expense
The cost of getting books from the publisher's warehouse or bindery to the college store. *Part of cost of goods sold paid to freight company.*

7.2¢

College Store Operations
Insurance, utilities, building and equipment rent and maintenance, accounting and data processing charges, and other overhead paid by college stores.

Source: Association of American Publishers and National Association of College Stores, "Where the New Textbook Dollar Goes?" http://www.nacs .org/common/research/textbook$.pdf (last accessed 8/22/07).

Students are frustrated with the cost of their textbooks, but most publishers would say that the selling prices have merely kept pace with inflation. Buying used books is an option, but publishers say that used books simply drive up the cost of future texts: if the publisher cannot sell as many of the new edition as are printed, the price is raised "to compensate for decreased sales volume, and the cycle starts again." Publishers also must cover the costs of many nonsalable faculty supplements such as instructor manuals, solutions manuals, transparency acetates, videos, and test banks (hard copy and electronic). Additionally, as the books become "fancier" with multiple colors, photographs, and periodical cites, costs also increase. Write a paper that does the following:

a. Provides suggestions for ways the college/university bookstore could control costs.
b. Provides suggestions for ways the publisher could control costs.
c. Provides suggestions for ways students can legally control textbook expenditures (remember that substantial reproduction of the text is illegal).
d. Talk to someone who went to college 20 years ago and discuss how today's college textbooks differ from the textbooks he or she used. Are the current differences cost beneficial from your perspective?

33. **LO.1 (Cost control)** Temporary or part-time employees may be used rather than full-time employees in each of the following situations:
a. To teach undergraduate accounting courses at a university.
b. To serve as security guards.

c. To staff a health clinic in a rural area.

d. To write articles for a monthly technical magazine.

e. To clean the house when the regular maid is ill.

f. To answer questions on a tax help-line during tax season.

g. To work in department stores during the Christmas rush.

h. To do legal research in a law firm.

i. To perform quality control work in a car manufacturing plant.

j. To do seamstress work in a custom dress shop.

k. To work as a clerk/cashier in a small retail store. The store is a mom-and-pop operation, and the clerk is the only employee in the store when he or she works.

Indicate the potential advantages and disadvantages of the use of temporaries in each of these situations. These advantages and disadvantages can be viewed from the standpoint of the employer or the user of the employer's products or services.

34. **LO.1 & LO.2 (Cost control; ethics)** *The managers and partners [who] were interviewed listed reduced manpower costs as the major advantage for utilizing paraprofessionals [in CPA firms]. It seems that these savings were realized in a number of ways. First, there were significant savings in the salaries of paraprofessionals when compared with new staff professionals. Furthermore, since a large number of paraprofessionals were employed for less than 40 hours, many firms were realizing a significant savings in fringe benefit cost. As one manager indicated, "When we want to review inventory, we always try to get our paraprofessional because of his experience in the use of the audit guide, insights on inventory procedures, and level of training." Partners and managers indicated that the part-time nature of the employment agreement for most paraprofessionals offered the firm greater flexibility in scheduling work around peak business periods and aided in reducing hours that cannot be billed.*

Certainly, the savings discussed above can have a significant impact on dwindling profit margins or can be passed on to the client in the form of reduced fees. As indicated [in this article], the billing rate for accounting paraprofessionals seems to be around $60 per hour (for both large and small firms).

Most managers reported that the billing rate for accounting paraprofessionals was 10–15 percent below that of new professional staff personnel. One manager from a [large] firm indicated that the standard billing rate for paraprofessionals was $68 per hour and up to $115 per hour for those with more experience.

For the same firm, the standard billing rate for beginning staff professionals was $115 per hour.

Quality of work, especially on job assignments that require a large amount of detailed and repetitive tasks, was also cited on several occasions as a major consideration when employing accounting paraprofessionals. The fact that paraprofessionals are able to spend longer periods of time on jobs and their willingness to do repetitive tasks may explain the improved quality of work of paraprofessionals.

As one manager stated, "The quality of work of our paraprofessionals far exceeds that of our new staff professionals." Some of the practitioners who were interviewed still expressed concerns about utilizing paraprofessionals and the legal implications of using "less than qualified" individuals on audits. When considering using paraprofessionals on audit engagements, an argument could be advanced that the use of "less than competent audit personnel" is a violation of auditing standards. Of course the basic question is: Do these individuals possess the technical attributes one would normally expect of individuals working in that capacity?

Source: The billing rates and wages stated in this exercise are historical and example data only. Adapted from Ted R. Compton, "Staffing Issues for the New Millennium—The Emerging Role of the Accounting Paraprofessional," *Ohio CPA Journal* (July–September 2000), pp. 56ff.

a. Discuss the use of part-timers and paraprofessionals from the perspective of controlling costs.

b. How could the use of part-timers and paraprofessionals impair the quality of work performed by public accounting firms?

c. Is it ethical for a CPA firm to bill the time of paraprofessionals at the same rate as fully qualified professionals? Discuss.

d. How could the use of part-timers and paraprofessionals affect the effectiveness and efficiency of work performed in public accounting firms? ▲

35. **LO.2 (Cost consciousness)** Betty and Bill Johnson are preparing their household financial budget for December. They have started with their November budget and are adjusting it to reflect the difference between November and December in planned activities. The Johnsons are expecting out-of-town guests for two weeks over the holiday season. The following list describes the budgetary changes from November to December that are contemplated by the Johnson family:

a. Increase the grocery budget by $135.

b. Decrease the commuter transportation budget by $50 to reflect the days off from work.

c. Change food budget to reflect serving pizza rather than steak and lobster each weekend.

d. Budget an extra $70 for utilities.

e. Reduce household maintenance budget by $60 to reflect the fact that outside maid services will not be used over the holiday period.

f. Buy generic breakfast cereal rather than name brand due to the quantity the guests will consume.

g. Use paper plates so as not to need to run the dishwasher as often.

h. Buy the institutional-size packages of paper plates rather than smaller size packages.

i. Budget the long-distance phone bill at $50 less because there will be no need to call the relatives who will be visiting.

j. Budget movie costs at $3 per DVD rather than $9 per person to go to the movies.

k. Postpone purchasing needed work clothes until the January sales.

l. Budget funds to repair the car. Betty plans to use part of her vacation time to make the repairs herself rather than take the car to a garage in January.

Indicate whether each of these items indicates cost understanding (CU), cost containment (CC), cost avoidance (CA), or cost reduction (CR). Some items may have more than one answer.

36. **LO.5 (Efficiency standards)** Keen Eyes has been asked to monitor the efficiency and effectiveness of a newly installed machine. The specialized machine has been guaranteed by the manufacturer to package 4,000 engine gaskets per kilowatt hour (kWh). The rate of defects on production is estimated at 2 percent. The machine is equipped with a device to measure the number of kWhs used. During the first month of use, the machine packaged 700,000 gaskets, of which 10,000 were flawed, and it used 180 kWhs.

a. What is the efficiency standard for flawless output?

b. Calculate the achieved efficiency for the first month and briefly comment on it.

c. Determine the achieved effectiveness and briefly comment on it.

d. Assume that the company was charged $4.50 per kWh during the first month this machine was in service. Estimate the company's savings or loss in power costs because of the machine's efficiency level in the first month of operations.

e. If you were a customer buying this company's gaskets for use in automobile production, what level of quality control would you want the company to have and why?

37. **LO.5 (Effectiveness/efficiency; ethics)** Top management of Bostwick Retail Stores observed that the budget for the EDP department had been growing far beyond what was anticipated for the past several years. Each year, the EDP manager would demonstrate that increased usage by the company's non-EDP departments would justify the enlarged appropriations. The administrative vice president commented that she was not surprised because user departments were not charged for the EDP department services and EDP department personnel were creative and eager to continue expanding services. A review of the current year's statistics of the EDP department revealed the following:

Budgetary appropriation	$1,000,000, based on 2,000 hours of run time; $800,000 of this appropriation is related to fixed costs
Actual department expenses	Variable, $185,250 (incurred for 1,950 hours of run time) Fixed, $815,000

a. Did the EDP manager stay within his appropriation? Show calculations.

b. Was the EDP department effective? Show calculations. Comment.

c. Was the EDP department efficient? Show calculations. (*Hint:* Treat variable and fixed expenses separately.)

d. Using the formulas for analyzing variable and fixed costs, calculate the variances incurred by the EDP department.

e. Propose a rate per hour to charge user departments for EDP services. Do you think charging users will affect the demand for services by user departments? Why or why not?

f. Discuss whether it would be ethical to evaluate the EDP department manager based only on comparing budgeted versus actual costs and ignoring differences between budgeted and actual volume. ▲

38. **LO.5 (Effectiveness vs. efficiency)** *The founder and president of the Institute for Healthcare Improvement, Donald Berwick, is convinced that the U.S. health care system can reduce costs by 30 percent while improving overall quality—just by getting health care professionals to adopt improvements others already have discovered.*

   ■ *Many children, possibly up to 30 percent, are being treated with new, broad spectrum, expensive, and potentially unsafe antibiotics despite national research and expert guidelines urging use of simple, inexpensive antibiotics as far better initial treatment.*

- *MRI scans in the first week of back pain rarely produce useful information compared with "watchful waiting," but many doctors order MRIs for such patients.*
- *Simple, inexpensive medications such as aspirin and beta blocker drugs can significantly reduce the likelihood of dying from heart attacks, but only one in five eligible patients currently receives such medications.*
- *Inhaled steroid medications can prevent disability and complications among asthmatic patients, but fewer than one-third of eligible patients receive such medication.*
- *One HMO-based study showed an 80 percent decrease in hospital days and emergency room visits for asthma care among patients trained to avoid asthma triggers, measure their own lung function, follow a consistent treatment plan, and make adjustments in their own medications.*

Source: Ed Egger, "Best Outcomes May Be Salvation for Shriveling Managed Care Cost Savings," *Health Care Strategic Management* (March 1999), pp. 12–13.

Indicate whether each selected finding mentioned represents effectiveness, efficiency, or both. If the finding represents either efficiency or both, indicate whether you consider it to be primarily cost understanding, cost containment, cost avoidance, or cost reduction. Justify each of your answers.

39. **LO.5 (Budget-to-actual comparison)** Pop and Fizz Beverages evaluates performance in part through the use of flexible budgets. The selling expense budgets at three activity levels within the relevant range follow:

Activity Measures

Unit sales volume	15,000	17,500	20,000
Dollar sales volume	$15,000,000	$17,500,000	$20,000,000
Number of orders processed	1,500	1,750	2,000
Number of salespersons	100	100	100

Monthly Expenses

Advertising and promotion	$1,500,000	$1,500,000	$1,500,000
Administrative salaries	75,000	75,000	75,000
Sales salaries	90,000	90,000	90,000
Sales commissions	450,000	525,000	600,000
Salesperson travel	200,000	225,000	250,000
Sales office expense	445,000	452,500	460,000
Shipping expense	650,000	675,000	700,000
Total	$3,410,000	$3,542,500	$3,675,000

The following assumptions were used to develop the selling expense flexible budgets:
- The average size of the company's sales force during the year was planned to be 100 people.
- Salespersons are paid a monthly salary plus commission on gross dollar sales.
- The travel costs have both a fixed and a variable element. The fixed portion is related to the number of salespersons, and the variable portion tends to fluctuate with gross dollars of sales.
- Sales office expense is a mixed cost with the variable portion related to the number of orders processed.
- Shipping expense is a mixed cost with the variable portion related to the number of units sold. (An order consists of 10 units.)

A sales force of 90 persons generated a total of 1,600 orders, resulting in a sales volume of 16,000 units during November. The gross dollar sales amounted to $14.9 million. The selling expenses incurred for November were as follows:

Advertising and promotion	$1,450,000
Administrative salaries	80,000
Sales salaries	92,000
Sales commissions	460,000
Salesperson travel	185,000
Sales office expense	500,000
Shipping expense	640,000
Total	$3,407,000

a. Explain why the selling expense flexible budget would not be appropriate for evaluating the company's November selling expense, and indicate how the flexible budget would have to be revised.
b. Determine the budgeted variable cost per salesperson and variable cost per sales order for the company.
c. Prepare a selling expense report for November that the company can use to evaluate its control over selling expenses. The report should have a line for each selling expense item showing the appropriate budgeted amount, the actual selling expense, and the monthly dollar variation.

d. Determine the actual variable cost per salesperson and variable cost per sales order processed for the company.

e. Comment on the effectiveness and efficiency of the salespersons during November.

(CMA adapted)

40. **LO.6 (Cash management; research)** Multinational firms domiciled in the United States don't have to pay U.S. income taxes on foreign earnings . . . unless they bring those earnings back to the United States. Accordingly, the U.S. income tax system acts as a deterrent to firms to bring cash earned abroad back to the United States. In 2004, the U.S. Congress passed the American Jobs Creation Act. One of the stated objectives of the act was to induce U.S. multinational firms to bring cash back to the United States to support growth of the domestic economy. Research the American Jobs Creation Act of 2004 and answer the following questions.

a. What was the incentive included in the Act to induce firms to bring cash earned abroad back to the United States?

b. Approximately how much cash was repatriated during the incentive period of the Act?

41. **LO.6 (Cash management)** As the economy entered the new millennium, Internet companies were competing head-to-head in many markets with established, traditional retailers for the consumer's dollar. In comparing the financial statements of "e-tailers" relative to traditional retailing firms such as Wal-Mart, one interesting difference is the comparatively large amount of cash held by the Internet firms. Using concepts presented in this chapter, discuss the most plausible explanations for the Internet companies holding such large sums of cash.

42. **LO.6 (Cash management)** Colin Martin founded a firm that manufactures innovative toys. Since its founding in 1995, the firm has experienced steady growth. However, in the past six months the firm's products were featured on two major network television shows. As a result of that exposure, the demand for the firm's products jumped dramatically. To meet demand, the firm ramped up production by adding a second shift of workers. With the added production capacity, the firm has been producing at 80 percent above levels in the prior year. One of the surprising side effects of this growth has been a severe cash crunch. Just this morning, Martin obtained the following balance sheet information from his CFO.

Current assets

Cash	$ 100,000
Accounts receivable	900,000
Inventory	3,700,000

Current liabilities

Accounts payable	$2,900,000
Wages payable	800,000
Taxes payable	200,000

a. Discuss how the high rate of growth has created the cash crunch Martin's firm is currently experiencing.

b. What strategies would you propose to Martin to deal with the cash shortage?

43. **LO.3–LO.5 (Comprehensive; analyzing cost control)** The financial results for the Continuing Education Department of BusEd Corporation for November 2008 are presented in the schedule at the end of this problem. Mary Ross, president of BusEd, is pleased with the final results but has observed that the revenue and most of the costs and expenses of this department exceeded the budgeted amounts. Barry Stein, vice president of the Continuing Education Department, has been requested to provide an explanation for any amount that exceeded the budget by 5 percent or more.

Stein has accumulated the following facts to assist in his analysis of the November results:

■ The budget for calendar year 2008 was finalized in December 2007, and at that time, a full program of continuing education courses was scheduled to be held in Chicago during the first week of November 2008. The schedule allowed eight courses to be run on each of the five days during the week. The budget assumed that there would be 425 participants in the program and 1,000 participant days for the week.

■ BusEd charges a flat fee of $150 per day of course instruction, so the fee for a three-day course is $450. BusEd grants a 10 percent discount to persons who subscribe to its publications. The 10 percent discount is also granted to second and subsequent registrants for the same course from the same organization. However, only one discount per registration is allowed.

Historically, 70 percent of the participant day registrations is at the full fee of $150 per day, and 30 percent of the participant day registrations receives the discounted fee of $135 per day. These percentages were used in developing the November 2008 budgeted revenue.

■ The following estimates were used to develop the budgeted figures for course-related expenses.

Food charges per participant day (lunch/coffee breaks)	$ 27
Course materials per participant	8
Instructor fee per day	1,000

■ A total of 530 individuals participated in the Chicago courses in November 2008, accounting for 1,280 participant days. This number included 20 persons who took a new, two-day course on pension accounting that was not on the original schedule; thus, on two of the days, nine courses were offered, and an additional instructor was hired to cover the new course. The breakdown of the course registrations was as follows:

Full fee registrations	704
Discounted fees	
Current periodical subscribers	128
New periodical subscribers	128
Second registration from the same organization	320
Total participant day registrations	1,280

■ A combined promotional mailing was used to advertise the Chicago program and a program in Cincinnati that was scheduled for December 2008. The incremental costs of the combined promotion were $5,000, but none of the promotional expenses ($20,000) budgeted for the Cincinnati program in December will have to be incurred. This earlier-than-normal promotion for the Cincinnati program has resulted in early registration fees collected in November as follows (in terms of participant days):

Full fee registrations	140
Discounted registrations	60
Total participant day registrations	200

■ BusEd, which continually updates and adds new courses, includes $2,000 in each monthly budget for this purpose. The additional amount spent on course development during November was for an unscheduled course that will be offered in February for the first time.

Stein has prepared the following quantitative analysis of the November 2008 variances:

BusEd Corporation
Statement of Operations
Continuing Education Department
For the Month Ended November 30, 2008

	Budget	Actual	Favorable (Unfavorable) Dollars	Favorable (Unfavorable) Percent
Revenue: Course fees	$145,500	$212,460	$ 66,960	46.0
Expenses				
Food charges	$ 27,000	$ 32,000	$ (5,000)	(18.5)
Course materials	3,400	4,770	(1,370)	(40.3)
Instructor fees	40,000	42,000	(2,000)	(5.0)
Instructor travel	9,600	9,885	(285)	(3.0)
Staff salaries and benefits	12,000	12,250	(250)	(2.1)
Staff travel	2,500	2,400	100	4.0
Promotion	20,000	25,000	(5,000)	(25.0)
Course development	2,000	5,000	(3,000)	(150.0)
Total expenses	$116,500	$133,305	$(16,805)	(14.4)
Revenue over expenses	$ 29,000	$ 79,155	$ 50,155	172.9

BusEd Corporation
Analysis of November 2008 Variances

Budgeted revenue		$145,500
Variances		
Quantity variance [(1,280 − 1,000) × $145.50]	$40,740 F	
Mix variance [($143.25 − $145.50) × 1,280]	2,880 U	
Timing difference ($145.50 × 200)	29,100 F	66,960 F
Actual revenue		$212,460
Budgeted expenses		$116,500
Quantity variances		
Food charges [(1,000 − 1,280) × $27]	$ 7,560 U	
Course materials [(425 − 530) × $8]	840 U	
Instructor fees (2 × $1,000)	2,000 U	10,400 U
Price variances		
Food charges [($27 − $25) × 1,280]	$ 2,560 F	
Course materials [($8 − $9) × 530]	530 U	2,030 F
Timing differences		
Promotion	$ 5,000 U	
Course development	3,000 U	8,000 U
Variances not analyzed (5% or less)		
Instructor travel	$ 285 U	
Staff salaries and benefits	250 U	
Staff travel	100 F	435 U
Actual expenses		$133,305

After reviewing Stein's quantitative analysis of the November variances, prepare a memorandum addressed to Ross explaining the following:

a. The cause of the revenue mix variance.

b. The implication of the revenue mix variance.

c. The cause of the revenue timing difference.

d. The significance of the revenue timing difference.

e. The primary cause of the unfavorable total expense variance.

f. How the favorable food price variance was determined.

g. The impact of the promotion timing difference on future revenues and expenses.

h. Whether or not the course development variance has an unfavorable impact on the company.

(CMA adapted)

44. **LO.7 (Supply-chain management)** Your employer, Maine Mechanical, implemented an e-procurement system last year for purchasing nonoperating inputs. The installation has been such a success that the firm is now considering using the same system to acquire operating inputs (e.g., direct material and product components).

However, some executives in the firm are reluctant to implement such a system for operating inputs because it does not support the rich collaboration that is necessary for effective supply chain cost management. Current systems support exchange of only basic transactional information: price, product availability, shipping terms and dates, and routine transaction processing including electronic ordering and electronic payments.

a. Assume that you are the firm's controller. Would you support the use of the e-procurement system for purchasing operating inputs? Why or why not?

b. Assume that you are vice president of product development. Would you support installation of the e-procurement system? Why or why not?

45. **LO.8 & LO.9 (Coping with uncertainty)** As an accounting intern working for your local police department, you learn that the department is considering starting a citizen's police academy. In recent years, there have been events that have created friction between the police department and the citizens. The police academy is intended to create goodwill within the community and increase communication between the department and the community. You have been invited to advise the departmental management about managing the financial risk associated with the academy. You have learned that there is a federal program that provides grants to fund citizen police academies and that the program provides a reimbursement of costs up to $500 per participant. Following are estimated costs of the academy as determined by the departmental sponsors of the academy.

Variable costs	
Supplies	$100
Meals	80
Equipment	150
Fixed costs	
Rental for training facilities	$25,000

Although the chief of police is very supportive of the police academy proposal, he is adamant that there is no slack in the department's budget to cover unreimbursed costs; thus, he has asked for assurance that the costs of the police academy will be covered by the federal grant program.

a. How many citizens must participate in the program to reach the breakeven point?

b. Is there financial risk in the proposed police academy for the police department? Explain.

c. What advice would you offer the proponents of the police academy to minimize losses the department could incur in offering the police academy?

46. **LO.8 & LO.9 (Coping with uncertainty)** After reviewing financial results for 2008, Midtown Industrial's President sent the following e-mail to his CFO and Controller, Jason Sharp.

Dear Jason:

I'm disappointed in the financial results for the year just completed. As you know, profits were $2 million below budget. In comparing the actual results to the budget, I note that the cost of natural gas exceeded budget by almost $1.3 million, and that cost alone accounts for 65 percent of the profit deficiency. This is the second year in a row that energy costs have dramatically reduced profits. I am calling a meeting on Tuesday to review our financial results, and I would like you to offer a presentation on the following topics:

1. *Why our estimates of energy costs have been dramatically below actual costs.*
2. *What actions you intend to take to improve our ability to estimate these costs.*
3. *What actions the company could take to better manage these costs.*

As the most recent hire in the Financial Department of Midtown Industrial, Sharp has asked you for help.

a. What suggestions will you give Sharp to improve the estimates of energy costs for future budgeting cycles?

b. What suggestions will you give Sharp to improve the management of energy costs in the future?

47. **LO.8 & LO.9 (Coping with uncertainty)** North Pole Industries manufactures holiday ornaments in its sole plant located in Wisconsin. Because the demand for the company's products is very seasonal, the company builds inventory throughout the first nine months of the year and draws down inventory the last three months of the year as demand in those months greatly exceeds production capacity. The company recently designated a member of management to be Chief Risk Officer (CRO). This individual has been charged with developing strategies to manage the effects of uncertainty on the business. The CRO has identified the following major sources of uncertainty:

1. Financing costs of inventory.
2. The cost of resin, which is the main material used in production.
3. "Acts of Nature" which could harm or destroy the production facility.
4. The price to be realized for products.
5. The level of demand for the company's products.

As a risk consultant, you have been retained by the CRO to develop strategies to deal with each of these major sources of uncertainty. In a report, outline your recommendations for each of the five major sources of uncertainty.

17 | Implementing Quality Concepts

Objectives

After completing this chapter, you should be able to answer the following questions:

LO.1 What is quality, and from whose viewpoint should it be evaluated?

LO.2 What is benchmarking, and why do companies engage in it?

LO.3 What constitutes the total quality management philosophy?

LO.4 How is the Baldrige Award related to quality?

LO.5 What are the types of quality costs, and how are those types related?

LO.6 How is cost of quality measured?

LO.7 How are the balanced scorecard and a cost management system used to provide information on quality in an organization?

LO.8 How is quality instilled as part of an organization's culture?

LO.9 (*Appendix*) What international quality standards exist?

Introduction

Managers recognize that pursuit of high quality is a fundamental organizational strategy for competing in a global economy. Businesses, both domestic and foreign, compete to attract customers by offering more choices to satisfy customer wants and needs. Competition elicits the best in companies, and international competition has evoked even higher quality products and services.

Consumers desire a variety of product choices but companies, having resource constraints, must make trade-offs among price, quality, service, and promptness of delivery—providing customers with a limited set of purchase options. However, customers' ready access to multinational vendors, which has accelerated through the Internet marketplace, has motivated producers to improve quality and customer service. Vendors are continuously adopting more dynamic approaches to improve products, processes, and customer service interactions.

This chapter discusses the issues of quality, benchmarking, total quality management, and quality costs and their measurement, as well as how a balanced scorecard (BSC) and cost management system (CMS) are used to support quality initiatives. Many managers realize that current expenditures on quality improvements can be more than recouped through future material, labor, and overhead cost reductions and sales volume increases. Thus, regardless of how they are treated for financial accounting purposes, quality improvement costs should not be viewed as expenses or losses but as recoverable investments with the potential for profit generation. Because of the potential financial consequences, accountants must understand the short- and long-run implications of the choice between higher and lower product/service quality.

LO.1
What is quality, and from whose viewpoint should it be evaluated?

What Is Quality?

Before an organization can improve its product or service quality, the term *quality* must be defined. After the Industrial Revolution helped manufacturers to increase output and decrease costs, quality was defined as conformity to designated specifications; determination of conformity became the task of quality control inspectors. Philip Crosby provides a more contemporary definition of quality as "conformity to requirements." This definition was adopted by the American Society for Quality Control, which defines requirements as measurable written or verbal "specifications, product descriptions, procedures, policies, job descriptions, instructions, purchase/service orders, etc."[1] An alternative viewpoint is that of Joseph Juran who defines quality as "fitness for use" and, by doing so, allows the user rather than the producer to judge quality. Other noted quality experts define quality in different ways, but a fairly inclusive definition of quality is the summation of all characteristics of a product or service that influence its ability to meet the stated or implied needs of the person acquiring it.

Quality is seen as not simply a production issue but also an organizational profitability and longevity issue. All entity processes (such as production, procurement, distribution, finance, and promotion) are involved in quality improvement efforts. Therefore, two related perspectives of quality are (1) the totality of internal processes that generate a product or service and (2) customer satisfaction with that product or service.

Production View of Quality

Productivity is measured by the quantity of good output generated from a specific amount of input during a time period. Any factor that either hinders (or stops) a production process or causes unnecessary work reduces productivity. Activity analysis can be used to highlight such factors. As discussed in Chapter 4, the various repetitive actions performed in making a product or providing a service can be classified in value-added (VA) and non-value-added (NVA) categories. VA activities increase the worth of the product or service to the customer; NVA activities consume time

[1]American Society for Quality Control, *Finance, Accounting and Quality* (Milwaukee, WI: ASQC, 1990), p. 3.

and generate costs but add no value for the consumer. Minimizing or eliminating NVA activities increases productivity and reduces costs.

Three important NVA process activities include storing products for which there is little immediate demand, moving materials unnecessarily, and experiencing unscheduled production interruptions. Inspecting incoming components, another NVA activity, is caused by potential quality problems of the supplier. To minimize or eliminate this NVA activity, some companies have contracts that require suppliers to provide only zero-defect components. To ensure compliance with this requirement, companies often perform quality audits of their vendors.

Costs incurred to reprocess, rework, replace, and repair those items that do not conform to specifications create production redundancies that can be reduced through quality product design, use of conforming materials, and VA production processes. These efforts will both reduce the product's failure rate and breakage tendencies and increase product longevity. Furthermore, the elimination of redundancies generated by production efforts—such as rework, waste, and scrap—enhances production process quality.

Production technology, worker skill and training, and management programs also help control production process quality. If the impediments to good production are reduced or eliminated, then managers can expect to realize increases in productivity and higher quality products. Some techniques that increase productivity and enhance quality include having suppliers preinspect materials for conformity to specifications, having employees monitor and be responsible for their work output, and fitting machinery for mistake-proof operations.

Many companies focus on a six sigma production view of quality, which means that a process produces no more than 3.4 defects per million "opportunities" (meaning chances for failure or not meeting required specifications). Another way to view six sigma is that its purpose is to generate error-free products 99.9997 percent of the time. According to Bain & Company, a global consulting firm, the average company operates at approximately three sigma or 66,800 errors per million.[2] Although Motorola and Allied Signal were the early pioneers of six sigma, General Electric has been one of the most successful users with estimated benefits of about $10 billion during the first five years the process was used.[3]

All attempts to reduce variability and product defects reflect the implementation of quality control (QC). QC places the primary responsibility for product or service quality at the source: the maker or provider. Many companies use statistical process control (SPC) techniques to analyze where fluctuations or variations occur in the process. SPC is based on the theory that a process has natural (common cause) variations over time and that these variations can cause "errors" resulting in defective goods or poor service. These errors are typically produced at points of uncommon (nonrandom or special-cause) variations. Often these variations are eliminated after the installation of computer-integrated manufacturing systems, which have internal controls to evaluate deviations and detect production problems.

To analyze the process variations, various types of control charts are developed to record the occurrence of specified measure(s) of performance at preselected points in a process. Control charts, such as the one in Exhibit 17–1, graph actual process results and indicate upper and lower control limits. For example, a process is considered either "in" or "out of" control (that is, stable or unstable) depending on whether the results are within established limits and whether there are patterns that reflect some nonrandom or special-cause variation. In effect, control charts use the management-by-exception principle by requiring that workers respond to occurrences that are outside of some predetermined limit or that form nonrandom, telltale patterns.

Control charts must be prepared consistently and accurately for a useful analysis of out-of-control conditions to be made. Although the development and use of such charts is outside the scope of this text, accountants can be directly involved in selecting appropriate performance measures and helping to interpret the charts. Often the measures selected to prepare control charts are nonfinancial, such as number of defective parts, quantity of waste created, and time consumed for task completion. Selection of performance measures to assess quality is discussed in Chapter 14.

[2]Bain & Company, *Management Tools 2007, An Executive's Guide* (http://www.bain.com/management_tools/tools_six_sigma.asp?groupCode=2; last accessed 8/18/07).
[3]iSix Sigma.com, *What is Six Sigma?*; http://www.isixsigma.com/sixsigma/six_sigma.asp (last accessed 8/18/07).

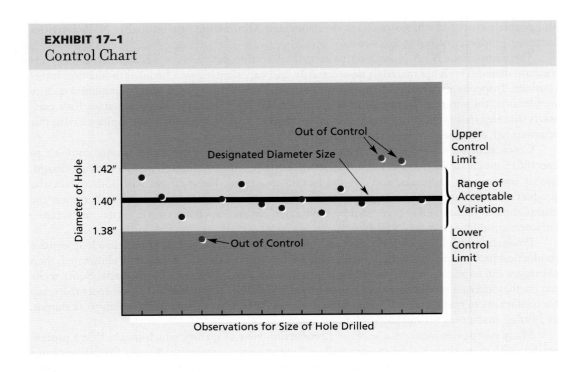

EXHIBIT 17–1
Control Chart

In effect, using SPC causes a process to "talk" to workers about what is occurring in the process. If workers "listen," potential product defects and process malfunctions can be prevented.

Consumer View of Quality

Every customer who acquires a product or service obtains a set of characteristics that includes product/service features, warranty, and packaging as well as organizational characteristics such as convenience of access, timeliness of delivery and service, reputation, and credit availability. The consumer's view of quality reflects more than whether the product or service delivers what was intended or the probability of purchasing a defective unit. The customer perceives quality as the ability of a product or service to meet and satisfy all specified needs at a reasonable cost: in other words, from a customer's perspective, quality relates to both performance and value. This quality perspective derives from increased competition, public interest in product safety, and litigation relative to products and product safety. When high-quality producers dominate a market, successful entering companies must understand both their own customers' quality expectations and their competitors' quality standards.

Exhibit 17–2 lists eight characteristics that are commonly included in a customer's definition of product quality. An important difference between the first six and the last two characteristics is level of objectivity. Characteristics A through F can be reasonably evaluated through objective methods, whereas G and H are strictly subjective. Thus, the first six are much more susceptible to control by an organization than are the other two. Most, if not all, of the quality characteristics in Exhibit 17–2 apply equally to companies that make tangible products and those that provide services. For example, a hotel might consider the provision of in-room high-speed Internet access and luxury spas as "features" and low noise levels in guest rooms as high "performance." In the exhibit, illustrative examples are given for Ritz-Carlton, an up-scale hotel chain dedicated to service quality.

Service quality reflects the manner in which an output is delivered to a customer. Some firms use outside "secret shoppers" to assess the level of service provided. For example, an undercover hotel "guest" could put a nonperforming light bulb in a room lamp at an exclusive hotel to determine whether housekeeping immediately detects the bulb outage and replaces that bulb. Other companies simply reward customers for observations about service conditions: stores of one large discount club pay customers $1 if the cashier does not address them by the name shown on their membership cards.

EXHIBIT 17–2
Characteristics of Quality

A. **Performance** refers to the operating features and relative importance of multiple characteristics such as ease of use and speed. Performance at The Ritz-Carlton might include comfortable beds, fax machines, and speedy Internet connections within each room.

B. **Features** are the extras needed to customize a product. The Ritz-Carlton might include flowers and a fruit basket in a customer's room at check-in and provide guests with spacious hotel rooms and fully equipped health club facilities.

C. **Reliability** refers to the likelihood that a product/service will perform on time as expected without a glitch. Ritz-Carlton customers expect on-time room cleanups and evening turn-down service with quality chocolates on the pillows.

D. **Conformance** is the extent to which products comply with prespecified standards. Ritz-Carlton guests may expect granite countertops on vanities and bathtubs with spa jets.

E. **Durability** refers to expected product life before deterioration and the need for replacement. Ritz-Carlton guests might expect hotel rooms to be refurbished every five years or a fresh fruit basket to be placed in their room every third day of their stay.

F. **Serviceability and Responsiveness** reflect the convenience, ease, and speed with which courteous and competent service staff complete work. Ritz-Carlton customers expect prompt responses to room service and maintenance requests.

G. **Aesthetics** refers to the environmental ambiance required of the discerning customer. The Ritz-Carlton might provide designer towels in the bathrooms and robes and slippers for in-room use.

H. **Perceived Value** is a customer's opinion of the product based on perceptions formed from advertising or product/service reputation. When customers stay at The Ritz-Carlton, they generally expect "royal" treatment.

Source: Adapted from David Garvin, "Eight Dimensions of Product Quality," http://www.1000ventures.com/business_guide/crosscuttings/bizsys_customer.html (last accessed 8/18/07); and David Garvin, "What Does 'Product Quality' Really Mean?" *Sloan Management Review* (Fall 1984), pp. 25–43.

In addition to Exhibit 17–2's list of quality characteristics that apply to all organizations, the following additional quality characteristics apply to service organizations:

■ **assurance: customers expect employees to be knowledgeable, courteous, and trustworthy;**

■ **tangibles: customers expect quality physical facilities, equipment, and appearance of personnel; and**

■ **empathy: customers expect a high degree of caring and attention from employees.**

Not all customers can afford the same grade of product or service. Grade is the quality level that a product or service has relative to the inclusion or exclusion of characteristics, especially price, to satisfy customer needs. Customers try to maximize their satisfaction within the context of their willingness and ability to pay. They view a product or service as a value when it meets the highest number of their needs at the lowest possible total cost (which includes an item's purchase price plus its operating, maintenance, and disposal costs). Thus, although customers may have a collective vision of what constitutes "high quality," some of them may choose to accept a lower grade of product or service because it satisfies their functional needs at a lower cost. Note that "high quality" is a more encompassing concept than "high grade." Someone with 20 minutes left for lunch can find more "value" in a fast-food hamburger than a sit-down restaurant's sirloin steak.

To illustrate the difference between quality and grade, assume that Ron Reeves is in the market for a new car for traveling to and from work, running errands, and going on vacation. He has determined that reliability, gas mileage, safety, and comfort are the most important features to him. He may believe the Lexus is the highest quality car available, but his additional needs are that the car's price be within his budget and that repair and maintenance services be readily available and at a reasonable cost. Thus, he will search for the highest quality product that maximizes his set of quality-characteristic preferences within the grade of car he can afford.

Customers often make quality determinations by comparing a product or service to an ideal rather than to an actual product or service of the same type or in the same industry. For example, Linda Schneider frequently stays at Ritz-Carlton hotels on business trips; the hotel company has received all major awards from the hospitality industry and leading consumer groups as well as twice winning the U.S. Baldrige Award (discussed later in the chapter). On a recent trip, she called a car rental agency to arrange for a car. Schneider could compare the quality of service she received from the car rental agency with the high-quality service she typically receives from The Ritz-Carlton rather than how well the current car rental company served her in comparison to the service from companies she previously used. Schneider is unconcerned that car rental agency employees may not have received the same customer satisfaction training as Ritz-Carlton employees or that The Ritz-Carlton corporate culture is dedicated to high quality whereas the car rental agency may not have yet made such a quality commitment. When formalized, the process of comparing quality levels of one organization to another's is called *competitive benchmarking.*

LO.2
What is benchmarking, and why do companies engage in it?

Benchmarking

Benchmarking involves investigating, comparing, and evaluating a company's products, processes, and/or services against those of either competitors or companies believed to be the "best in class." Such comparisons allow a company to understand another's production and performance methods so that the interested company can identify its strengths and weaknesses. Exhibit 17–3 notes some motivations for benchmarking.

Because each company has its own unique philosophy, products, and people, "copying" such elements is neither appropriate nor feasible. Therefore, a company should attempt to imitate those ideas that are readily transferable but, more importantly, to upgrade its own effectiveness and efficiency by improving on methods used by others. The American Productivity and Quality Center has established a code of conduct for benchmarking activities. The code addresses issues such as equal exchange of information, confidentiality, avoidance of antitrust issues and illegalities, and interorganizational courtesy; the code can be found at http://www.orau.gov/pbm/pbmhandbook/apqc .pdf (last accessed 8/18/07).

The four types of benchmarking (Exhibit 17–4) are internal, results (or performance), process, and strategic. Internal benchmarking directs its focus onto how and why one organizational unit is performing better than another. The techniques of the higher performing unit are then implemented, to the extent possible, in the lower performing units. The primary difficulty with internal benchmarking is that none of the organizational units may be performing on a quality level attained by external parties.

EXHIBIT 17–3
Reasons to Benchmark

1. To increase awareness of the competition
2. To understand competitors' production and performance methods
3. To identify areas of competitors' internal strengths and weaknesses
4. To identify external and internal threats and opportunities
5. To justify and accelerare a plan for continuous process improvement and change
6. To create a framework for program and process assessment and evaluation
7. To establish a focus for mission, goals, and objectives
8. To establish performance improvement targets
9. To understand customers' needs and expectations
10. To encourage creative thinking
11. To identify state-of-the-art business practices and new technologies

EXHIBIT 17–4
Types of Benchmarking

Type	Description	Advantages	Disadvantages
Internal	An approach to benchmarking that allows organizations to learn from "sister" companies, divisions, or operating units. Performance improvement may be 10 percent.	- Provides highest degree of process detail and simplified access to process information - Provides rapid and easy-to-adopt improvements - Is low cost - Provides a deeper understanding of in-house process	- Gives an internal focus that tends to be operational rather than strategic and bound by the organization's cultural norms - Creates an internal bias - Is not much of a stretch - May not find best-in-class practices
Results	An approach to benchmarking that targets specific product designs, process capabilities, or administrative methods used by one's direct competitors. Performance improvement may be 20 percent or better.	- Provides a strategic insight into marketplace competitiveness and can provide a "wake-up" call to action - Prioritizes areas of improvement according to competition - May create a possible partnership - Can show similar regulatory issues	- May generate legal issues regarding business relations between competitors - May provide study data that are insufficient for diagnosis - Could be threatening
Process	An approach to benchmarking that seeks information from the same functional area within a particular application or industry. Performance improvement may be 35 percent or better.	- Takes advantage of functional and professional networks to develop detailed process understanding - Provides industry trend information - Provides quantitative comparisons - Can review common business functions	- Tends to best support operational studies - Takes more time than internal or competitive studies, although it uses an external perspective - May be difficult to find common functions
Strategic	An approach to benchmarking that seeks process performance information from outside one's own industry. Enablers are translated from one organization to another through the interpretation of their analogous relationship. Performance improvement may be 35 percent or better.	- Provides the greatest opportunity for process breakthroughs - Generates reliable, detailed data because noncompeting organizations are used - Is innovative - Has high potential for discovery	- Is difficult to develop an analogy between dissimilar businesses - Is hard to determine which companies to benchmark - Has a high cost - Takes a long time to plan

Source: Adapted from U.S. Patent and Trademark Office, Office of Quality Management, *Benchmarking Workbook* (September 2000), p. 15; http://www.uspto.gov/web/offices/com/oqm-old/benchmarking_workbook_9_00.pdf (last accessed 8/18/07).

In **results benchmarking**, the end product or service is examined using a process called *reverse engineering*. The focus is on product/service specifications and performance results. Results benchmarking helps companies determine which other companies are "best in class" in a particular category. For example, companies such as Cyrix Corp. and Advanced Micro Devices Inc. have successfully reverse-engineered Intel Corp. microprocessors to make less expensive Intel-compatible chips.[4] However, if benchmarking leads to making an exact replica of another's product, serious ethical and legal considerations exist. ▲

[4]Mathew Schwartz, "Reverse Engineering," *Computerworld* (November 12, 2001), http://www.computerworld.com/softwaretopics/software/appdev/story/0,10801,65532,00.html (last accessed 8/18/07).

Although benchmarking against direct competitors is necessary, it can also create the risk of becoming stagnant. To illustrate: historically, General Motors, Chrysler, and Ford competitively benchmarked among themselves and, over time, their processes became similar. When foreign competitors such as Toyota entered the U.S. market, their totally different, and better, processes forced U.S. automotive companies to change and improve their quality systems. In the recent past, however, Toyota faced quality problems because rapid growth had "spread thin the company's famed Japanese quality gurus"; thus, Toyota launched a global campaign to simplify its production systems.[5]

Because of the potential for stagnation, comparisons should also be made against companies that are the best in a specific characteristic rather than just the best in a specific industry. Focusing on how best-in-class companies achieve their results is called process benchmarking. It is in this arena that noncompetitor benchmarking is extremely valuable. For example, many different types of companies have benchmarked L. L. Bean's world-class warehousing and distribution operations. Company call centers often process benchmark against the six Ritz-Carlton call centers that strive for an average answer time of 20 seconds, and use humans to answer calls rather than interactive voice response systems.[6] The widespread applicability of process benchmarking is no better illustrated than when employees from a General Mills plant in California decided to go to a NASCAR track, videotape pit crews, study the tapes, and apply the principles of that process to reduce production changeover processes. Doing so enabled GM to reduce changeover processes from 3 hours to 17 minutes![7]

Strategic benchmarking is also non–industry specific and focuses on strategy and how companies compete. This type of benchmarking is most important at many Japanese companies because their

Disney has long been viewed as "best-in-class" in equipment maintenance. Other organizations, regardless of the industry they are in, can use process benchmarking to compare their maintenance activities against this world-class leader.

[5]Norihiko Shirouzu and Sebastian Moffett, "As Toyota Closes in on GM, It Develops a Big Three Problem," *Wall Street Journal* (August 4, 2004), pp. A1, A2.

[6]Jennifer O'Herron, "Paving the Road for Travellers," *Call Center Magazine* (July 14, 2000); http://www.callcentermagazine.com/shared/printable Article.jhtml?articleID=8701613 (last accessed 8/18/07).

[7]John Hackl, "New Beginnings: Change Is Here to Stay," *Quality Progress* (February 1998), p. 5.

managers focus more on long-run performance than on the short-run benefits that can be gained from process and results benchmarking.

Benchmarking steps are detailed in Exhibit 17–5. Some companies have more steps and others have fewer but all have a structured approach. After the negative gap analysis (step 6) is completed, everyone in the firm is expected to work toward both closing that gap and becoming a best-in-class organization. Through benchmarking, companies are working to improve their abilities to deliver high-quality products from the perspectives of how products are made and how customers perceive those products. Integrating these two perspectives requires involvement of all organizational members in the implementation of a total quality management system.

Total Quality Management

LO.3
What constitutes the total quality management philosophy?

Total quality management (TQM) is a "management approach of an organization, centered on quality, based on the participation of all its members and aiming at long-term success through customer satisfaction, and benefits to all members of the organization and to society."[8] Thus, TQM has four important tenets:

1. to dictate continuous improvement for an internal managerial system of planning, controlling, and decision making,
2. to require participation by everyone in the organization,
3. to focus on improving goods and services from the customer's point of view, and
4. to value long-term partnerships with suppliers.

EXHIBIT 17–5
Steps in Benchmarking

1. Determine the specific area in which improvements are desired and/or needed.

2. Select the characteristic that will be used to measure quality performance.

3. Identify the best-in-class companies based on quality characteristics. Remember that these companies do not have to be industry, product, or service specific.

4. Ask for cooperation from the best-in-class companies. This may be handled directly or through a consulting firm. Be prepared to share information and respect requests for confidentiality.

5. Have the people who are associated with the specific area being analyzed collect the needed information.

6. Analyze the "negative gap" between the company's product, process, or service and that of the best-in-class firm.

7. Act on the negative gap analysis and make improvements.

8. Do not become complacent. Strive for continuous improvement.

---

[8]ISO 8402, *Total Quality Management* (Geneva: ISO, 1994), definition 3.7.

Quality System

Effective quality management requires the implementation of a system that provides information about process quality so managers can plan, control, evaluate performance, and make decisions for continuous improvement. Consideration of quality historically has not been part of the planning process. More often, it involved an after-the-fact measurement of errors because a certain level of defects was tolerated as part of the "natural" business process. Action was not triggered until a predetermined error threshold was exceeded.

In contrast, a total quality system should be designed to promote a reorientation of thinking from an emphasis on inspection to an emphasis on prevention, continuous improvement, and building quality into every process and product. This reorientation should indicate any existing quality problems so that managers can set goals and identify methods for quality improvements. The system should also be capable (often through the use of statistical methods) of measuring quality and providing feedback on quality improvements. Last, the system should encourage teamwork in the quality improvement process and move the organization away from product inspection (finding and correcting problems at the end of the process) to proactive quality assurance (building quality into the process so that problems do not occur).

Employee Involvement

TQM recognizes that all organizational levels share the responsibility for product/service quality. Interactions among employee levels have changed the way managers do their jobs. Upper-level management must be involved in the quality process, develop an atmosphere that is conducive to quality improvements, set an example of commitment to TQM, provide constructive feedback about opportunities for improvement, and provide positive feedback when improvements are made. Workers should be viewed as effectors of success, not creators of problems. Training workers to handle multiple job functions helps improve efficiency and quality.

Encouraging employee suggestions can produce substantial cost savings and increase productivity in all types and sizes of organizations. For example, suggestions at an Amoco plant in Texas City, Texas, saved the company $18.8 million in two years.[9] Britain's Ministry of Defense saved approximately £21 million (or about $40 million) in one year from employee suggestions.[10] In three years at Production Control Units of Dayton, Ohio, over 450 employee ideas were submitted that saved over $275,000.[11] An important attribute of employee suggestions is that the savings they generate typically continue for more than one year.

Product/Service Improvement

Total quality management focuses attention on the relationship between the internal production/service process and the external customer. Satisfying consumer expectations is the ultimate evidence of success. Therefore, TQM requires that companies first know who their customers are.

In analyzing their customers, companies must recognize that they may need to stop serving some groups of customers based on the results of cost–benefit analyses. Some customers simply cost more than they add in revenues and/or other benefits. Each revenue dollar does not contribute equally to organizational profitability because the cost to serve customers varies. The concept that shedding one or more sets of customers would be good for business is difficult to believe at first, but most organizations have some clients who drain, rather than improve, those organizations' ability to provide quality products and service. Managers should be attuned to customers that are not cost beneficial and first attempt to find a way to make them profitable. If no solution is found, "nonperforming" customers should be sent to do business elsewhere so that the company can focus its attention on its current profitable customers and make itself attractive to new profitable customers. Organizations must recognize that customer loyalty and customer profitability are not the same thing.

---

[9]Bob Nelson, "Listen Up! Recognition Works!," Meetings Net, http://meetingsnet.com/corporatemeetingsincentives/meetings_listen_recognition
_works/index.html (last accessed 8/18/07).
[10]Andy Beddows, "Suggestion Schemes for the Future," *Management Services* (February 2001), pp. 14ff.
[11]Robert Marshall, John Talbott, and David Bukovinsky, "Employee Empowerment Works at Small Companies, Too," *Strategic Finance* (September 2006), pp. 34ff.

After identifying its value-adding customers, a company must then understand what those customers want. The primary characteristics currently desired by customers are quality, value, and good service. "Good" service is an intangible; it means different things to different people. But most customers would agree that "good" service reflects the interaction between themselves and organizational employees. Frequently, only service quality separates one product from its competition.

The need for customer satisfaction information is essential to organizations embracing TQM because poor service can be disastrous. Data indicate that most businesses lose 68 percent of their customers because of an employee's "attitude of indifference" versus only 14 percent because of product or service dissatisfaction.[12]

Instituting customer service programs often produces valuable information; for example, many hotel chains have databases that record information on "loyalty" customers. These systems typically contain recency/frequency of use (by hotel and in total); lifetime purchases; customer likes/dislikes; personal and family interests; preferred credit cards; and any previous difficulties encountered by a customer at a hotel. Such data can be used to sort customers and to decide whether a customer relationship merits additional investment. However, customer service programs should not be taken to the extreme: some customers, such as those that demand exorbitant service but are not willing to pay the related price, are not cost beneficial to an organization.

Long-Term Supplier Relationships

Adopting TQM encourages companies to review their supply chain and establish long-term relationships with preferred suppliers. The TQM philosophy sees suppliers as a distinct part of a company's ability to either satisfy customers or create extreme dissatisfaction. Consider, for example, the problems faced by Microsoft in 2007 when widespread problems with the Xbox 360s required that the product warranty be extended to maintain customer satisfaction. Even though the Xboxes are actually made by Flextronics International Ltd., Microsoft accepted the responsibility and took a $1 billion charge against earnings—enough to fix 2.5 million units. However, Microsoft stated that it would not "be seeking to replace [Flextronics]."[13]

Given the extent to which outsourcing is being used today, companies must be certain that they are "linking up" with suppliers that enhance product quality and customer satisfaction. Many of these relationships result in single sourcing or certification of suppliers. For example, the Boeing Company had a Preferred Supplier Certification program that evaluated and rated suppliers in three categories: advanced quality system implementation, business processes, and performance. Suppliers were then placed into bronze, silver, and gold "categories" that entitled them to benefits in the areas of selection preference, reduced inspections, industry recognition, and additional business opportunities.[14] In October 2006, Boeing instituted a new supplier program (the Performance Excellence Award) that still focuses on high-quality performance and supplier recognition, but the company believes that the new program will be more inclusive for suppliers.

Additionally, although suppliers can indirectly enhance customer satisfaction, some companies look for more direct ways to accommodate customers. For instance, in 2002, The Ritz-Carlton launched a marketing agreement with Mercedes-Benz USA so that selected locations could offer guests the use of a new Mercedes vehicle during their stays. The two companies saw this agreement as "a perfect fit because both companies' customers share the same high expectation of service and quality."[15]

The Baldrige Award

LO.4
How is the Baldrige Award related to quality?

The embodiment of TQM in the United States is the Malcolm Baldrige National Quality Award (MBNQA or Baldrige Award), which focuses attention on management systems, processes,

[12] *CBP Knowledge Management Newsletter* (February 1998, Issue 2); http://www.som.cranfield.ac.uk/som/research/centres/cbp/whatsnew/knowled2.htm (last accessed 8/18/07).
[13] Dina Bass, "Xbox Fixes Will Cost Microsoft $1 Billion," *Austin American-Statesman* (July 6, 2007), p. D2.
[14] Boeing Preferred Supplier Certification, http://active.boeing.com/companyoffices/doingbiz/best/psc/Index.cfm (last accessed 8/18/07).
[15] "Mercedes and The Ritz-Carlton Sign Three-Year Marketing Agreement," *Benz World News* (October 28, 2002); http://benzworld.org/news .html?id=181 (last accessed 8/18/07).

consumer satisfaction, and business results as the tools required to achieve product and service excellence. There are three versions of Baldrige criteria: business and not-for-profit, education, and health care. To win the award, applicants must show excellence in seven categories:

1. *Leadership* requires that the organization's senior managers value, communicate, and inspire employees to serve customers and achieve quality goals ethically, given adequate systems and knowledge resources. The ethics would be documented in the organization's corporate governance, social responsibility, and "tone at the top." This section also addresses the performance measures that are used to ascertain movement toward goals and objectives. ▲

2. *Strategic planning* requires that the organization develop strategic objectives and plans that are constantly monitored for progress toward achievement.

3. *Customer and market focus* requires that the organization set requirements, expectations, and preferences for its customers and markets. This category includes building customer relationships, establishing key factors that lead to customer acquisition, satisfaction, and loyalty, and developing business expansion.

4. *Measurement, analysis, and knowledge management* requires that the organization select, collect, analyze, manage, and continuously improve its information system and intellectual capital. Performance measurement and analysis are important aspects of this section as well as data management and integrity, which could reflect on the internal control elements contained in the Sarbanes-Oxley Act of 2002.

5. *Workforce focus* requires that the organization empower and develop its employees and utilize their full potential in establishing and implementing organizational goals and objectives. This section requires a work environment that promotes high morale, job enrichment, and job satisfaction among employees. Employee performance measurement, compensation, and rewards are also addressed in this section.

6. *Process management* requires that organizations examine their core competencies and key components of their product/service and business processes. These elements must be reviewed for conformity with generating customer value, and processes must be assessed as to emergency readiness.

7. *Results* require that organizations improve their key business areas including customer satisfaction, product/service performance, workforce results, financial and marketplace performance, operations performance, corporate governance, and social responsibility. Moreover, organizations should benchmark and compare their performance to that of competitors.

    Exhibit 17–6 illustrates the relationships among the Baldrige performance criteria categories. To achieve at least 70 percent of the points allocated within a category, the National Institute of Standards and Technology (which manages the Baldrige Award) must determine that the organization is effective and systematic in deploying and achieving the multiple requirements within each category and is innovative in continuously seeking improvement.

    Corporate America has accepted the Baldrige Award because it represents excellence. Products and services of companies winning the Award are regarded as some of the best in the world. Such recognition invigorates workers, pleases all stakeholders, and has caused the entire national economy to be strengthened by the enhanced awareness of and attention to quality and its benefits. Winning companies are asked to provide information about their performance excellence strategies so that other organizations can benchmark those strategies and adapt them to suit their own needs.

    Some critics of TQM have called it nothing more than a management fad that does not work when practical attempts are made to implement its concepts. One rebuttal to such criticisms follows: "poor management, not poor ideas, may be responsible for the inconsistency of TQM or other managerial interventions."[16] Most companies using TQM have cited many positive outcomes and benefits, such as those included in Exhibit 17–7.

    Putting TQM into practice in an organization can be very costly given the length of time needed to introduce and teach the philosophy and concepts throughout the company. Evidence indicates, however, that firms' operating performances during the process of implementing TQM are comparable to those of other companies. A 2001 study of quality award-winning firms found that, on average, it takes about five years for a company to implement TQM and another five years

---

[16]David Lemak, Neal Mero, and Richard Reed, "When Quality Works: A Premature Post-Mortem on TQM," *Journal of Business and Management* (Fall 2002), pp. 391ff.

EXHIBIT 17–6
2007 Baldrige Award Criteria

Baldrige Criteria for Performance Excellence Framework: A Systems Perspective

Source: Baldrige National Quality Program, National Institute of Standards and Technology, and United States Department of Commerce's Technology Administration, *2007 Criteria for Performance Excellence* (Gaithersburg, MD: 2007) p. 5; http://www.quality.nist.gov/PDF_files/2007_Business _Nonprofit_Criteria.pdf (last accessed 8/18/07).

EXHIBIT 17–7
Benefits of TQM

Internal

- Improved response time to change
- Increased ability to compete profitably in the marketplace
- Decreased cost through reduction/elimination of non-value-added activities and waste
- Increased profitability through reduced costs
- Improved products, services, and customer relations
- Increased employee morale, motivation, and retention
- Improved internal communications and organizational focus
- Enhanced employee decision-making abilities and teamwork
- Increased innovation and acceptance of new ideas
- Reduced number of errors
- Increased benchmarks for evaluating employee performance

External

- Increased customer trust and loyalty
- Enhanced customer satisfaction
- Improved response time to customer requests
- Decreased prices resulting from reduced internal costs

before its benefits are fully realized. As shown in Exhibit 17–8, Baldrige companies experienced a 20 percent increase in average stock prices compared to a 25 percent decrease in stock price for the benchmarked firms, meaning that stock price increases can be tracked to the operating performance of the TQM firms during five years after the initial implementation of TQM. The study traced these stock price changes to such operating performance measures as operating income, sales, total assets, number of employees, return on sales, and return on assets.[17] All of these performance measures were higher for the Baldrige winners during the five years after receiving the Baldrige Award than for those of the control sample firms.

Japan's equivalent of the Baldrige Award is the Deming Prize, named for the late Dr. W. Edwards Deming. There are three categories of the Deming Prize: (1) the Deming Application Prize, which is for companies or company divisions that have achieved distinctive TQM performance in a particular year; (2) the Deming Prize for Individuals, which is for people who have made great contributions to the field of TQM (or its dissemination) or statistical methodology; and (3) the Quality Control Award for Operations, which is for organizational business units that have achieved distinctive operational improvements using TQM in a particular year.[18] Although the Baldrige Award and the Deming Prize are both designed to recognize quality achievements and increase awareness of TQM, the Baldrige Award is more focused on results and the importance of sharing information.

Other international standards are discussed in the appendix to this chapter.

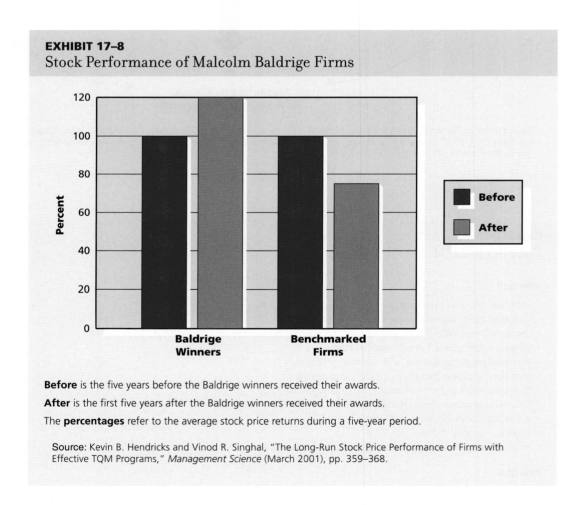

EXHIBIT 17–8
Stock Performance of Malcolm Baldrige Firms

Before is the five years before the Baldrige winners received their awards.

After is the first five years after the Baldrige winners received their awards.

The **percentages** refer to the average stock price returns during a five-year period.

Source: Kevin B. Hendricks and Vinod R. Singhal, "The Long-Run Stock Price Performance of Firms with Effective TQM Programs," *Management Science* (March 2001), pp. 359–368.

---

[17]Kevin B. Hendricks and Vinod R. Singhal, "Don't Count TQM Out," *Quality Progress* (April 1999), pp. 35–42.
[18]More information about the Deming Prize and its winners can be found at http://www.deming.org/demingprize (last accessed 8/18/07).

Types of Quality Costs

LO.5
What are the types of quality costs, and how are those types related?

Instituting TQM in an organization causes a different focus on costs and their incurrence. A company can increase its product and service quality by incurring prevention costs for activities that preclude product defects resulting from dysfunctional processing. For instance, amounts spent on improved production equipment, training, and engineering and product modeling are considered prevention costs. Appraisal costs are incurred to monitor and compensate for mistakes not eliminated through prevention activities. Organizational spending for prevention and appraisal activities will reduce failure costs.

There are two types of failure costs: internal and external. Internal failure costs are expenditures, such as scrap or rework, incurred to remedy defective units before they are shipped to customers. External failure costs are expenditures for items, such as warranty work, customer complaints, litigation, and defective product recalls that are incurred after a faulty unit of product has been shipped to the customer. Although both types of failure costs can be expensive, an organization would prefer to incur internal, rather than external, failure costs.

The results of TQM indicate that increasing the amounts spent on prevention decreases the amounts spent on or incurred for appraisal and failure costs—resulting in an overall decline in costs. Also, eliminating NVA activities and installing technologically advanced equipment should increase productivity and quality. Lower costs mean that the company can contain (or reduce) selling prices; customers, pleased with the higher quality at the same (or lower) price, perceive they have received value and will buy more. These results create higher company profits that can be reinvested in research and development or customer service to generate new high-quality products or services. The profits also can be used to train workers to provide even higher quality products and services than are currently available. This cycle of benefit will continue in a company that is profitable and secure in its market share—two primary goals of any organization.

Thus, the TQM philosophy indicates that total costs decline, rather than increase, as an organization makes quality improvements. It seems that it is the *lack* of high quality, rather than the *pursuit* of high quality, that is expensive. Understanding the types and causes of quality costs helps managers prioritize improvement projects and provide feedback that supports and justifies improvement efforts.

Total quality costs can also be classified into two categories: (1) cost of compliance (or assurance) and (2) cost of noncompliance (or quality failure). The cost of compliance equals the sum of prevention and appraisal costs. Compliance cost expenditures are incurred to reduce or eliminate the present and future costs of failure; thus, they are proactive expenditures. Furthermore, effective investments in prevention activities can even minimize the costs of appraisal. The cost of noncompliance results from production imperfections and is equal to internal and external failure costs. Exhibit 17–9 provides specific examples of each type of quality cost.

Inspection reports, SPC control charts, and customer returns or complaints contain information about production quality or lack thereof. Information about quality costs, on the other hand, is only partially contained in the accounting records and supporting documentation. Historically, quality costs have not been reported separately in the accounting system. For example, the effects and costs of customer complaints that are overheard by potential customers are unknown.

In most instances, the cost of quality is "buried" in a variety of general ledger accounts. For instance, Work in Process Inventory and Finished Goods Inventory contain expenditures for rework, scrap, preventive maintenance, and other overhead items; marketing and advertising expenses contain costs for product recalls, image improvements after poor products were sold, and surveys to obtain customer information; salaries and wages expense include training costs; and engineering department costs include funds spent for engineering design change orders and redesign. When quality costs are not reflected specifically in the accounting records, managers have no idea how large or pervasive these costs are and, therefore, have little incentive to reduce them.

Because accounting records are commonly kept primarily to serve the requirements of financial accounting, the behavior of quality costs relative to changes in activity as well as the appropriate drivers for these costs must be separately developed or estimated for quality management purposes. The need to estimate quality costs makes it essential for accountants to be involved in all activities from system design to accumulation of quality costs. A system in which quality costs are readily available

EXHIBIT 17–9
Types of Quality Costs

COSTS OF COMPLIANCE		COSTS OF NONCOMPLIANCE	
Prevention Costs	**Appraisal Costs**	**Internal Failure Costs**	**External Failure Costs**
Employees:	*Before Production:*	*Product:*	*Organization:*
• Hiring for quality	• Inspecting at receipt	• Reworking	• Staffing complaint
• Providing training and	*Production Process:*	• Creating waste	departments
awareness	• Monitoring and inspecting	• Storing and disposing of	• Staffing warranty claims
• Establishing participation	• Keeping the process	waste	departments
programs	consistent, stable, and	• Reinspecting rework	*Customer:*
Customers:	reliable	*Production Process:*	• Losing future sales
• Surveying needs	• Using procedure	• Reprocessing	• Losing reputation
• Researching needs	verification	• Creating unscheduled	• Losing goodwill
• Conducting field trials	• Automating	interruptions	*Product:*
Machinery:	*During and After Production:*	• Experiencing unplanned	• Repairing
• Designing to detect defects	• Conducting quality audits	downtime	• Replacing
• Arranging for efficient flow	*Information Process:*		• Reimbursing
• Arranging for monitoring	• Recording and reporting		• Recalling
• Incurring preventive	defects		• Litigating
maintenance	• Measuring performance		*Service:*
• Testing and adjusting	*Organization:*		• Providing unplanned
equipment	• Administering quality		service
• Fitting machinery for	control department		• Expediting
mistake-proof operations			• Serving after purchase
Suppliers:			
• Assessing for quality			
• Educating suppliers			
• Involving suppliers			
Product Design:			
• Developing specifications			
• Engineering and modeling			
• Testing and adjusting for			
conformity, effective and			
efficient performance,			
durability, ease of use,			
safety, comfort, appeal,			
and cost			

or easily determined provides useful information to managers trying to make spending decisions by pinpointing areas having the highest cost–benefit relationships. Additionally, quality cost information will indicate how a shift in one or more curves will affect the others.

Exhibit 17–10 indicates points in the production–sales cycle at which quality costs are usually incurred. An information feedback loop should be in effect to link the types and causes of failure costs to future prevention costs. Alert managers and employees continuously monitor failures to discover their causes and adjust prevention activities to close the gaps that allowed the failures to occur. These continuous rounds of action, reaction, and action are essential to continuous improvement initiatives for products currently in production and related products in the design stage.

LO.6
How is cost of quality measured?

Measuring the Cost of Quality

Theoretically, if prevention and appraisal costs were prudently incurred, failure costs would become $0. However, because prevention and appraisal costs must still be incurred to identify and reduce

EXHIBIT 17–10
Time-Phased Model for Quality Costs

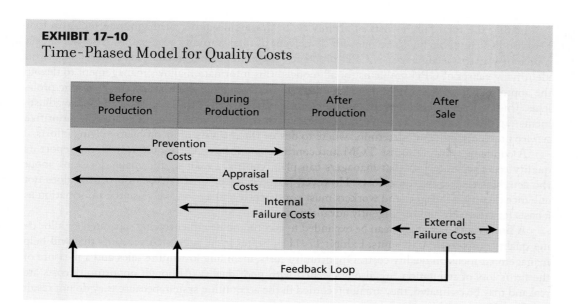

failures, total quality costs can never actually be zero. Then why would quality guru Philip Crosby write a book titled *Quality Is Free*?[19] He is, in essence, correct if the organizational benefits from increased sales and greater efficiency exceed the compliance costs in excess of failure costs. Assume, for instance, that Umber Corp. spent $450,000 on prevention and $250,000 on appraisal activities, which together completely eliminated organizational product failures. At this point, Umber Corp. has incurred $700,000 of quality costs. If, though, $1,000,000 of failure costs were eliminated, then Umber Corp. would be better off by $300,000—making the cost of quality not only "free," but profit-enhancing! Management should analyze the quality cost relationships and spend money for quality in ways that balance costs and benefits. Such an analysis requires measuring the cost of quality to the extent possible and practical and estimating the benefits of quality costs.

As discussed in Chapter 4, Pareto analysis is used to separate the "vital few" from the "trivial many." This technique has repeatedly shown that approximately 20 to 30 percent of the population (regardless of whether that population is inventory items, number of donors resulting from participants at a charity event, or sources of defects) accounts for 70 to 80 percent of the cost or values. Pareto analysis is also one technique that management can use to decide where to concentrate its quality prevention budget. This technique classifies the causes of process problems according to impact on an objective. For example, a company that makes computers might subclassify its warranty claim costs for the past year according to the type of product failure as follows:

Warranty Cost by Type of Failure

Model	Monitor	CPU	Printer	Keyboard	Total Dollars
Desktop PCs	$15,000	$16,000	$12,000	$ 2,760	$ 45,760
Notebooks	10,360	15,000	7,000	3,000	35,360
All others	6,000	8,880	3,000	5,000	22,880
Total	$31,360	$39,880	$22,000	$10,760	$104,000
Percent (rounded)	30%	38%	21%	11%	100%

Model	Dollars	Percent of Total	Cumulative Percent of Total
Desktop PCs	$ 45,760	44%	44%
Notebooks	35,360	34	78
All others	22,880	22	100
Total	$104,000	100%	

[19]Philip Crosby, *Quality Is Free* (New York: Signet, 1979).

Listing the total failure costs of all models in descending order of magnitude indicates that Desktop PCs and Notebooks account for 78 percent of total warranty cost claims. Also, the largest source of warranty claims cost is CPU problems. Therefore, management should focus efforts on identifying causes of CPU problems for all models. This information allows management to devote the appropriate portion of its prevention efforts to minimizing or eliminating these specific problems. This analysis should be conducted sufficiently often to detect trends quickly and make adjustments rapidly. As another example, a large restaurant chain could use Pareto analysis to prioritize service problems and, thus, determine where to devote the majority of its problem-solving efforts.

A company wanting to use TQM and continuous improvement should record and report its quality costs separately so that managers can plan, control, evaluate, and make decisions about the activities that cause those costs. However, just generating quality cost information does not enhance quality. Managers and workers must consistently and aggressively use the information as a basis for creatively and intelligently advancing quality.

A firm's chart of accounts can be expanded to accommodate either tracing separately or allocating quality costs to new accounts. Exhibit 17–11 indicates some suggested accounts that will help management focus on quality costs. Opportunity costs, including lost future sales and a measure of the firm's loss of reputation, are also associated with poor quality. Although opportunity costs are real and may be estimated, they are not recorded in the accounting system because they do not result from specific transactions.

If a firm has a database management system, transactions can be coded so that reports can be generated without expanding the chart of accounts. Coding permits quality transaction types and amounts to be accessible and the generation of a cost of quality report such as the one shown in Exhibit 17–12 (which uses assumed numbers). Two important assumptions underlie this report: stable production and a monthly reporting system. If wide fluctuations in production or service levels occur, period-to-period comparisons of absolute amounts may not be appropriate. Amounts might need to be converted to percentages to have valid meaning. Additionally, in some settings (such as the just-in-time environment discussed in Chapter 18), a weekly reporting system is more appropriate because of the need for continuous monitoring.

Exhibit 17–13 (page 650) provides formulas for calculating an organization's total quality cost, using the prevention, appraisal, and failure categories. Some amounts used in these computations are, by necessity, estimates. It is more appropriate for businesses to use reasonable estimates of quality costs than to ignore such costs because of a lack of verifiable or precise amounts. Consider the following April 2008 operating information for Torantino Company:

EXHIBIT 17–11
New Quality Accounts

Prevention Costs	Appraisal Costs
Quality Training	Quality Inspections
Quality Participation	Procedure Verifications
Quality Market Research	Measurement Equipment
Quality Technology	Test Equipment
Quality Product Design	

Internal Failure Costs	External Failure Costs
Reworking Products	Complaint Handling
Scrap and Waste	Warranty Handling
Storing and Disposing of Waste	Repairing or Replacing Returns
Reprocessing	Customer Reimbursements
Rescheduling and Setup	Expediting

EXHIBIT 17–12
Cost of Quality Report

	Cost of Current Period	Cost of Prior Period	Percent Change from Prior Period	Current Period Budget	Percent Change from Budget
Prevention Costs					
Quality training	$ 5,800	$ 5,600	+4	$ 6,000	−3
Quality participation	8,200	8,400	−2	8,000	+3
Quality market research	9,900	7,700	+29	11,000	−10
Quality technology	9,600	10,800	−11	15,000	−36
Quality product design	16,600	12,200	+36	16,500	+1
Total	$ 50,100	$ 44,700	+12	$56,500	−11
Appraisal Costs					
Quality inspections	$ 3,300	$ 3,500	−6	$ 3,000	+10
Procedure verifications	1,200	1,400	−14	1,500	−20
Measurement equipment	2,700	3,000	−10	3,200	−16
Test equipment	1,500	1,200	+25	1,500	0
Total	$ 8,700	$ 9,100	−4	$ 9,200	−5
Internal Failure Costs					
Reworking products	$ 8,500	$ 8,300	+2	N/A*	
Scrap and waste	2,200	2,400	−8	N/A	
Storing and disposing of waste	4,400	5,700	−23	N/A	
Reprocessing	1,800	1,600	+13	N/A	
Rescheduling and setup	900	1,200	−25	N/A	
Total	$ 17,800	$ 19,200	−7		
External Failure Costs					
Complaint handling	$ 5,800	$ 6,200	−6	N/A	
Warranty handling	10,700	9,300	+15	N/A	
Repairing or replacing returns	27,000	29,200	−8	N/A	
Customer reimbursements	12,000	10,700	+12	N/A	
Expediting	1,100	1,300	−15	N/A	
Total	$ 56,600	$ 56,700	0		
Total quality costs	$133,200	$129,700	+3	$65,700	+103

*TQM advocates planning for zero defects; therefore, zero failure costs would be included in the budget.

Defective units (D)	5,000	Units reworked (Y)	2,400
Profit for good unit (P_1)	$50	Profit for defective unit (P_2)	$30
Cost to rework defective unit (r)	$10	Units returned (Dr)	800
Cost of return (w)	$15	Prevention cost (K)	$80,000
Appraisal cost (A)	$14,400		

Substituting these values into the cost of quality formulas provided in Exhibit 17–13 gives the following results:

$$Z = (D - Y)(P_1 - P_2) = (5,000 - 2,400)(\$50 - \$30) = 2,600 \times \$20 = \$52,000$$
$$R = (Y)(r) = (2,400)(\$10) = \$24,000$$
$$W = (D_r)(w) = (800)(\$15) = \$12,000$$
$$F = Z + R + W = \$52,000 + \$24,000 + \$12,000 = \$88,000 \text{ total failure cost}$$
$$T = K + A + F = \$80,000 + \$14,400 + \$88,000 = \$182,400 \text{ total quality cost}$$

Of the $182,400 total quality cost, Torantino Company managers need to identify the causes of the $88,000 failure costs and work to eliminate those causes. Eliminating the failure cause should also affect the planned amounts of prevention and appraisal costs for future periods.

High quality allows a company to improve current profits, either through lower costs or, if the market will bear them, higher prices. Management should, though, also be interested in business objectives other than short-run profits. An example of an alternative, competing objective is that of

EXHIBIT 17–13
Formulas for Calculating Total Quality Cost

Calculating Lost Profits

Profit Lost by Selling Units as Defects = (Total Defective Units − Number of Units Reworked) × (Profit for Good Unit − Profit for Defective Unit)

$$Z = (D - Y)(P_1 - P_2)$$

Calculating Total Internal Costs of Failure

Rework Cost = Number of Units Reworked × Cost to Rework Defective Unit

$$R = (Y)(r)$$

Calculating Total External Costs of Failure

Cost of Processing Customer Returns = Number of Units Returned × Cost of a Return

$$W = (D_r)(w)$$

Total Failure Cost = Profit Lost by Selling Units as Defects + Rework Cost + Cost of Processing Customer Returns + Cost of Warranty Work + Cost of Product Recalls + Cost of Litigation Related to Products + Opportunity Cost of Lost Customers

$$F = Z + R + W + PR + L + O$$

Calculating the Total Quality Cost

Total Quality Cost = Total Compliance Cost + Total Failure Cost

$$T = (\text{Prevention Cost} + \text{Appraisal Cost}) + \text{Total Failure Cost}$$

$$T = K + A + F$$

Prevention and appraisal costs are total estimated amounts; no formulas are appropriate. As the cost of prevention rises, the number of defective units should decline. Additionally, as the cost of prevention rises, the cost of appraisal should decline; however, appraisal cost should never become zero.

Source: Adapted from James T. Godfrey and William R. Pasewark, "Controlling Quality Costs," *Management Accounting* (March 1988), p. 50. Copyright 1988 by Institute of Management Accountants. Reproduced with permission of Institute of Management Accountants in the format Textbook via Copyright Clearance Center.

increasing the company's market share. Indeed, if increasing market share were an objective, management could combine the strategies of increasing quality and lowering prices to obtain a larger market share. Giving more attention to prevention and appraisal activities increases quality, which should result in a reduction of overall costs and an increase in productivity. These changes will, in turn, support lower prices that often stimulate demand and provide both a higher market share and higher long-run profits.

LO.7
How are the balanced scorecard and a cost management system used to provide information on quality in an organization?

Obtaining Information about Quality from the BSC and CMS

Today's business strategy of focusing on customers and quality requires a firm to manage costs so that a reasonable value-to-price relationship can be achieved. Although prices are commonly set in reference to the competitive market rather than to costs, companies lacking appropriate cost management skills cannot expect to succeed in the long run. Thus, organizations need to engage in cost management.

As discussed in Chapter 12, cost management can be viewed as the use of management accounting information for the purpose(s) of setting and communicating organizational strategies; establishing, implementing, and monitoring the success of methods to accomplish the strategies; and assessing the level of success in meeting the promulgated strategies. An organization's cost management system should accumulate and report information related to organizational success in meeting or exceeding customer needs and expectations as well as quality-related goals and objectives. Managers can analyze and interpret such information to plan and control current activities and to make decisions about current and future courses of action.

One management accounting tool that is useful in implementing strategy is the balanced scorecard, which can be used to view the total quality management strategy from four perspectives: learning and growth, internal business, customers, and financial. These perspectives can be integrated with the seven categories of the MBNQA. For example, the learning and growth perspective of the BSC is compatible with, and reflective of, information shown in the MBNQA workforce focus category. The internal business perspective is compatible with the process management category. The customer perspective reflects the MBNQA's customer and market focus category. The financial perspective can be seen in the results category. Also, both the BSC and the MBNQA criteria emphasize the use of nonfinancial performance measurements as indicators of progress toward organizational goals.

To illustrate the potential use of the balanced scorecard in providing information on quality, the Telecommunications Products Division (TPD) of DalTEX, an illustrative company, is used. Assume that TPD wants to fully automate its fiber-optic production line by year-end to reduce the number of product defects. The BSC's learning and growth perspective focuses on using TPD's intellectual capital to adapt to changing customer needs through automated production. Employees would be trained to use new technologies and then be evaluated on their success while managers focus on employee satisfaction, retention, and productivity. The BSC's internal business perspective addresses empowering employees so that they learn how to troubleshoot production problems and manage quality. For example, TPD might allow production line employees to stop the assembly line to correct a newly evolving production process problem. This empowerment reduces wait time because employees can fix problems without taking the time to seek supervisor approval. The BSC's customer value perspective addresses how well the organization is doing relative to important customer criteria such as speed (lead time), quality, service, and price (both original and after-purchase amounts). TPD may allow its sales staff to satisfy customers by offering discounts and allowances when production time is longer than expected or by servicing a product for a short time after the warranty period ends. This sales staff and employee empowerment allows for some delays in lead time and some product defects without resulting in customer complaints. Finally, the BSC's financial perspective addresses the perceptions held by stockholders and other stakeholders as to issues of profitability and organizational growth. TPD seeks to increase customer loyalty through quality production. If customers are more satisfied with TPD's products after the automation change is made, those customers are more likely to be retained and, thus, increase divisional and corporate revenues and market share. Goals and measurements for the BSC perspectives are shown in Exhibit 17–14; Chapter 14 provides more discussion of the BSC.

In designing a CMS, consideration must be given to cost accumulation and process measurement activities. Cost accumulation for financial accounting purposes can be inadequate for strategy-based decisions. For instance, financial accounting requires that research and development (R&D) costs be expensed as incurred, but a product's cost is largely determined during the design stage. Design has implications for perceived product value, necessary production technology, ease of product manufacturability, product durability, and likelihood of product failure. Consequently, a CMS should accumulate design costs as part of product cost. This cost need not appear on the financial accounting statements, but it must exist for decision-making purposes in the management accounting system.

In contrast to its treatment of R&D costs, financial accounting requires all production costs to be inventoried and does not distinguish whether they add customer value or not. A useful CMS differentiates between costs that add value and those that do not so that managers and employees can work to reduce the NVA costs and enhance continuous improvement.

Another CMS function relates to the production process. Financial accounting is monetarily based and, therefore, does not directly measure nonfinancial organizational activities. For example, the percent of automated production, percent of reworked units, number of customer complaints, and percent of repeat customers are not recorded in financial accounting. Additionally, many activities critical to success in a quality-oriented, global marketplace are related to time—a nonmonetary characteristic. A truly useful CMS ensures the availability of information related to nonmonetary occurrences (such as late deliveries or defect rates) and incorporates that information into a BSC so that management can achieve TQM and profitability goals.

EXHIBIT 17–14
Quality Measures of a Balanced Scorecard

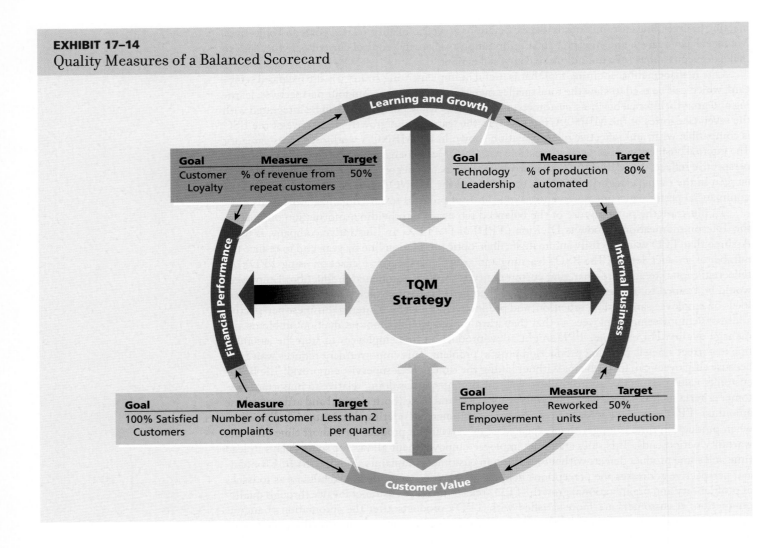

Finally, financial accounting reflects a short-term perspective of operating activity. Continuous improvement is a long-term, rather than a short-term, organizational goal. Gathering monetary information and forcing it into a specific twelve-month period does not clearly indicate to managers how today's decisions will affect the organization's long-run financial success. For instance, not investing in R&D would cause a company's short-run profitability to improve but could be disastrous in the long run.

Thus, a CMS should report more of the costs and benefits of organizational activities than do financial accounting reports. Having strategy-based information included in a BSC allows managers to make informed assessments of the company's performance in the value chain, its position of competitive advantage (or disadvantage), and its progress toward achieving the organization's mission.

LO.8
How is quality instilled as part of an organization's culture?

Quality as an Organizational Culture

Quality, propelled by changing customer needs and better competition, must be viewed as a moving target; thus, TQM is inseparable from the concept of continuous improvement. Continually higher performance standards must be set for everyone in the organization (not just for people in the production area) to provide the sense of working toward a common goal. This philosophy provides a new focus. In the future, it will not be the company with the "best" products or the

EXHIBIT 17-15
Moving toward True Quality

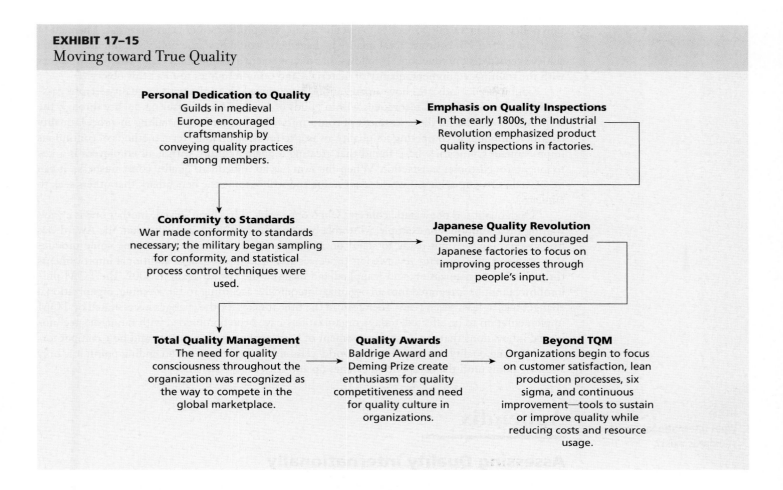

Personal Dedication to Quality
Guilds in medieval Europe encouraged craftsmanship by conveying quality practices among members.

Emphasis on Quality Inspections
In the early 1800s, the Industrial Revolution emphasized product quality inspections in factories.

Conformity to Standards
War made conformity to standards necessary; the military began sampling for conformity, and statistical process control techniques were used.

Japanese Quality Revolution
Deming and Juran encouraged Japanese factories to focus on improving processes through people's input.

Total Quality Management
The need for quality consciousness throughout the organization was recognized as the way to compete in the global marketplace.

Quality Awards
Baldrige Award and Deming Prize create enthusiasm for quality competitiveness and need for quality culture in organizations.

Beyond TQM
Organizations begin to focus on customer satisfaction, lean production processes, six sigma, and continuous improvement—tools to sustain or improve quality while reducing costs and resource usage.

"lowest" costs that will be successful; it will be the company that is the best at learning to do things better.[20]

The behavior of managers and employees composes the basis for TQM. Consistent and committed top management leadership is the catalyst for moving the company culture toward an esprit de corps in which all individuals, regardless of rank or position, are obsessed with exceeding customer expectations. Such an attitude should also permeate everything a company does, including customer relations, marketing, research and development, product design, production, distribution, and information processing. Management can effectively induce change in its organizational culture by providing an environment in which employees know that the company cares about them, is responsive to their needs, and will appreciate and reward excellent results. This knowledge goes a long way in motivating employees to increase cooperation and making them feel trusted, respected, and comfortable. Such employees are more likely to treat customers in a similar manner.

The firm must empower employees to participate fully in the quest for excellence by providing the means by which employees gain pride, satisfaction, and substantive involvement. Managers must provide encouragement, training, job enhancement, and the proper working environment and tools. The new corporate work environment involves the effective and appropriate use of teams. Employees should be recognized with praise and rewarded for being involved in team problem solving, contributing ideas for improvement, monitoring their own work, and sharing their knowledge and enthusiastic attitudes with their colleagues.

With its focus on process and customers, TQM is founded on one very obvious and simple principle: do the right things right the first time, all the time, on time, and continuously improve. The heart of this principle is zero defects now and in the future. For example, a non-TQM produc-

[20]Tom Richman, "What Does Business Really Want from Government?" *The State of Small Business* (1995), p. 96.

tion policy statement might read: "Do not allow defective production to be greater than 1 percent of total production." In contrast, total quality management would have the policy statement: "We will achieve zero-defect production." It follows that management's responsibility is to provide employees with the training, equipment, quality of materials, and other resources to meet this objective.

Exhibit 17–15 indicates how organizations have moved along the path to quality—from passing information on "good" techniques within guilds of craftspeople to assuring quality through the inspection of goods and the assessment of conformity with standards to installing in-process quality control techniques to competing for quality awards to focusing on long-term methods of continuous improvement. Companies have found that creating a quality culture within all employees is a key to long-term customer satisfaction. When the firm has an imbedded "quality consciousness," it can be viewed as having achieved world-class status and will become the benchmark that others seek to emulate.

"High quality" is not a static concept; when one problem has been solved, another one is always waiting for a solution. For example, Motorola received the MBNQA in 1988, when the Award was first given. However, not ready to stand on its laurels especially after experiencing some production problems, the company reviewed its processes and procedures, sought additional improvements throughout the organization, and reapplied and received the Award again in 2002. The TQM philosophy cannot be integrated into an organization quickly; according to Dr. Deming, organizational changes take at least seven years. Therefore, in the time it takes for the changes necessitated by TQM implementation to be effected, today's organizations have been bombarded with numerous technological innovations that require a reassessment of how customers view quality and how competitors are addressing quality issues. Achieving world-class status does not mark an ending point; it is only a resting point until the competition catches up and tries to race ahead.

LO.9
What international quality standards exist?

Appendix

Assessing Quality Internationally

Most large companies view their markets on an international rather than a domestic basis. To compete effectively in a global environment, companies must recognize the need for, and be willing to initiate, compliance with a variety of international standards. Standards are essentially the international language of trade; they are formalized agreements that define the various contractual, functional, and technical requirements to assure customers that products, services, processes, and/or systems do what they are expected to do.

ISO

A primary international guideline for quality standards is the ISO 9000 series. In 1987, the International Organization for Standardization, based in Geneva, Switzerland, developed a comprehensive list of quality standards known as the ISO 9000 series. The series of three compliance standards (ISO 9001, 9002, and 9003) and two guidance standards (ISO 9000 and 9004) were integrated into ISO 9001:2000. As of December 2005, almost 800,000 ISO 9001:2000 certificates had been issued in 161 countries.[21] Exhibit 17–16 shows the ten countries having the most certificates.

The standard is written in a general manner and prescribes the generic design, material procurement, production, quality control, and delivery procedures necessary to achieve quality assurance. The directive is not a product standard and does not imply that companies certified under it have better products than competitors. The standard articulates what must be done to ensure quality, but management must decide how to meet the standards. The eight principles contained in the ISO standard address the following topics: customer focus, leadership, involvement of people, process approach, system approach to management, continual improvement, factual approach to decision making, and mutually beneficial supplier relationships.

Compliance with ISO standards is required for regulated products sold in the European Union; however, there is no international organization that administers the program. Thus, companies seek-

---

[21]International Organization for Standardization, http://www.iso.ch/iso/en/iso9000-14000/pdf/survey 2005.pdf (last accessed 8/18/07).

EXHIBIT 17–16
ISO 9001:2000 Certificates

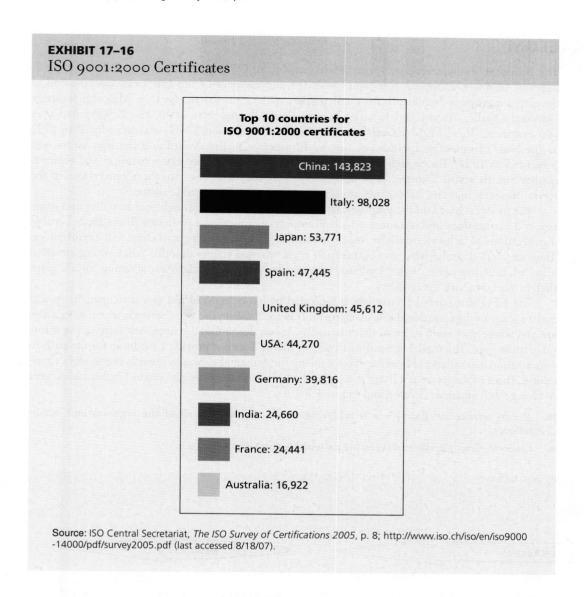

Top 10 countries for
ISO 9001:2000 certificates

China: 143,823
Italy: 98,028
Japan: 53,771
Spain: 47,445
United Kingdom: 45,612
USA: 44,270
Germany: 39,816
India: 24,660
France: 24,441
Australia: 16,922

Source: ISO Central Secretariat, *The ISO Survey of Certifications 2005*, p. 8; http://www.iso.ch/iso/en/iso9000
-14000/pdf/survey2005.pdf (last accessed 8/18/07).

ing ISO certification must qualify under an internationally accepted registration program that is administered by a national registrar. Examples of such registrars in the United States and Great Britain are, respectively, Underwriters Laboratories and the British Standards Institution.

After an internal review, a company deciding that it can meet the standards may apply for ISO registration. To be registered, a company must first submit to a **quality audit** by a third-party reviewer that encompasses a review of product design activities, manufacturing processes and controls, quality documentation and records, and management quality policy and philosophy. After registration, teams visit the company biannually to monitor compliance.

Although registration costs are high, certified companies believe the benefits are even higher. Internally, certification helps ensure higher process consistency and quality and should help to reduce costs. Externally, ISO certified companies have an important distinguishing characteristic from their noncertified competitors. Additionally, certified companies are listed in a registry of "approved" suppliers, which should increase business opportunities. The cost–benefit relationships of the quality system must be measured, documented, and reported under ISO requirements—all jobs for accountants.

ISO certification is not required for doing business in the United States, but many U.S. companies are ISO certified because of international sales. Even companies that do not sell overseas may seek ISO certification because of the operational and competitive benefits. If a company's competitors are in compliance with and registered under ISO standards, good business sense would recognize the necessity of becoming ISO certified.

EFQM

The European Foundation for Quality Management (EFQM) was founded in 1988 by the presidents of 14 major European companies with the endorsement of the European Commission to develop a European framework for quality improvement similar to the U.S. Malcolm Baldrige National Quality Award and Japan's Deming Prize. By the year 2000, the EFQM had over 700 members. The EFQM Excellence Model (shown in Exhibit 17–17) was introduced in 1991 as the basis of assessing applications for the European Quality Award and the first award was presented in 1992. The model has also become the framework for many national and regional quality awards across Europe. As of 2007, there were four trophies: two for organizations in the for-profit sector and two for organizations in the not-for-profit or public sector.[22]

The model is based on the premise that leadership is delivered through people, policy and strategy, and partnerships and resources, which all impact organizational processes. These factors enable organizations to achieve excellent results relative to people, customers, society, and performance. Thus, enablers describe what an organization does, whereas results describe what an organization achieves. Enablers cause results; feedback from results allows innovation and learning to take place that, in turn, improve the enablers.

The EFQM model's effectiveness is indicated by its widespread use as a management system and a means of organizational self-assessment. It helps indicate the gaps between where companies are and where they want to be so that management can determine the necessary activities to minimize those gaps. The model is nonprescriptive in that it does not provide a roadmap for the path to organizational excellence. However, the following fundamental concepts provide the model's foundation. These concepts are not listed in a particular order, and the listing is seen as flexible and subject to change as companies develop and improve.[23]

■   *Results orientation:* **Excellence is achieving results that delight all of the organization's stakeholders.**

■   *Customer focus:* **Excellence is creating sustainable customer value.**

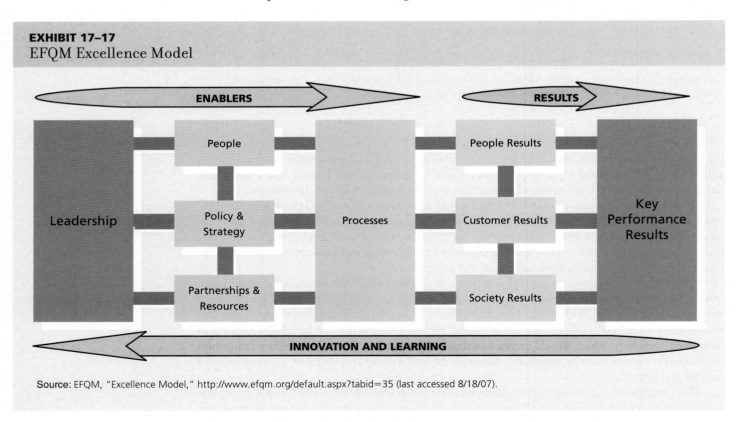

EXHIBIT 17–17
EFQM Excellence Model

Source: EFQM, "Excellence Model," http://www.efqm.org/default.aspx?tabid=35 (last accessed 8/18/07).

[22]Past winners of awards can be found at http://www.efqm.org/Portals/0/History%20of%20past%20winners.pdf (last accessed 8/18/07).
[23]"EFQM Excellence Model," http://www.efqm.org/Default.aspx?tabid=36 (last accessed 8/18/07).

- *Leadership and constancy of purpose:* Excellence is visionary and inspirational leadership, coupled with constancy of purpose.

- *Management by processes and facts:* Excellence is managing the organization through a set of inter-dependent and interrelated systems, processes, and facts.

- *People development and involvement:* Excellence is maximizing the contribution of employees through their development and involvement.

- *Continuous learning, innovation, and improvement:* Excellence is challenging the status quo and effecting change by utilizing learning to create innovation and improvement opportunities.

- *Partnership development:* Excellence is developing and maintaining value-adding partnerships.

- *Corporate social responsibility:* Excellence is exceeding the minimum regulatory framework in which the organization operates and striving to understand and respond to the expectations of its stakeholders in society.

These underpinnings of the model can be seen to relate to both the Baldrige criteria and the balanced scorecard perspectives.

Comprehensive Review Module

Chapter Summary

1. Quality

   - is the sum of all characteristics of a product or service that influence its ability to meet the needs of the person acquiring that product or service.

   - is defined, from a production viewpoint, as conformity with requirements and, from this viewpoint, can be improved by

     ➢ increasing the good output generated from a specific amount of input during a period.

     ➢ reducing variability, often by adding automation in the process.

     ➢ reducing the product's or service's failure rate.

   - is defined, from a consumer viewpoint, as the ability to meet and satisfy all specified needs at a reasonable cost; a consumer viewpoint is typically seen as the better perspective and should encompass

     ➢ making certain that the product or service delivers what was intended.

     ➢ ascertaining that the product or service fulfills consumer needs relative to a grade versus value perspective.

2. Benchmarking

   - refers to investigating, comparing, and evaluating a company's products, processes, and/or services against those of competitors or companies believed to be "best in class."

   - is engaged in by a company to obtain an understanding of another's production and performance methods so that the company can identify its strengths and weaknesses.

   - may be one of four types:

     ➢ internal benchmarking, in which organizational units are compared to each other, with the lower performers "learning" from the higher performers.

     ➢ results benchmarking, in which an end product or service is examined using reverse engineering to focus on product/service specifications and performance results; this type of benchmarking is performed on competitors' products or services.

     ➢ process benchmarking, in which a specific process is examined to determine how a "best-in-class" company achieves its results; this type of benchmarking is often performed on noncompetitors although competitors may also be used.

- ➤ strategic benchmarking, in which the focus is on understanding how successful companies compete.

3. Total quality management

- is a significant management philosophy because it involves all organizational employees and places the customer at the center of focus.

- is defined as seeking continuous improvement in processes so as to meet or exceed customer expectations.

- requires the following conditions to yield full benefits:

  - ➤ sharing planning and decision making among personnel;

  - ➤ eliminating non-value-added activities;

  - ➤ enhancing technology in hardware, production processes, and management systems that increase productivity;

  - ➤ increasing consumer awareness of the numerous types and grades of products available; and

  - ➤ using competitive benchmarking to close any performance gaps.

- may lead a U.S. company to pursue attainment of the Malcolm Baldrige National Quality Award.

4. Quality costs

- include costs of compliance (or assurance), which are expenditures incurred to reduce or eliminate the current costs of quality failure and to continuously improve in the future. Compliance costs include

  - ➤ prevention costs that are incurred to minimize or eliminate the production of nonconforming products and services. The incurrence of prevention costs tend to reduce the costs of appraisal and failure.

  - ➤ appraisal costs that are incurred to identity units of output that do not conform to product specifications. The incurrence of appraisal costs tend to reduce the costs of external failure.

- include the costs of noncompliance (or quality failure), which include

  - ➤ internal failure costs that are incurred to remediate a nonconforming product that is detected through appraisal activities before that product is shipped to a customer. Incurrence of internal failure costs tends to reduce external failure costs.

  - ➤ external failure costs that are incurred to remediate a nonconforming product that is not detected until after being shipped to the customer.

- of compliance and noncompliance are inversely related.

5. The cost of quality is measured as the sum of the

- total cost of prevention,

- total cost of appraisal, and

- total cost of failure, which reflects the following:

  - ➤ cost of profits lost by selling units as defects,

  - ➤ cost of rework for defective goods,

  - ➤ cost of processing customer returns,

  - ➤ cost of warranty work,

  - ➤ cost of product recalls,

  - ➤ cost of litigation related to products, and

  - ➤ opportunity cost of lost customers.

6. Information on the quality of an organization's products and services can be obtained from the

- balanced scorecard through the computation of

  - ➤ manufacturing cycle efficiency,

  - ➤ time to market for new products,

  - ➤ customer satisfaction levels,

  - ➤ on-time deliveries,

  - ➤ defect rates, and/or

  - ➤ success rates of research and development activities.

- cost management system through the computation of

  - ➤ quality costs incurred for production/service activities,

  - ➤ costs of non-value-added activities,

  - ➤ product/service life cycle costs, and/or

  - ➤ rework costs.

7. Quality can be instilled as part of an organization's culture by

- having committed and consistent top management leadership.

- developing an esprit de corps among all employees so that they are eager to meet and exceed customer expectations.

- making certain that a work environment is provided in which employees know that the company cares about and will reward efforts to achieve high quality.

- empowering employees.

- providing job and quality training.

- encouraging the pursuit of quality awards.

8. (Appendix) International assessments about quality can be made using the

- ISO 9001:2000 standard.

  ➤ Registration requires a quality audit conducted by a third-party reviewer.

  ➤ Registration under ISO 9001:2000 is required to sell products in the European Union.

- EFQM model.

  ➤ The model has widespread use as a means of organizational self-assessment.

  ➤ The concepts underlying the model are consistent with those of the Baldrige Award.

Potential Ethical Issues

1. Ignoring the actual range of acceptable variation on control charts to accept a higher level of defects than allowed and, thus, creating a higher possibility of external failure costs

2. Using lower grade raw material and components than specified for production activities to reduce costs while continuing to promote the company's high-quality products

3. Using the benchmarking process as an opportunity to illegally gain information or product designs from competitors

4. Creating a set of preferred supplier characteristics that fosters discrimination against minority suppliers

5. Consciously choosing to discount internal information about product defects and failures that could result in significant consumer or environmental harm

6. Minimizing estimates of internal and external failure costs to justify retaining current practices rather than engaging in expenditures that would, in the long run, be cost beneficial

7. Communicating the importance of implementing total quality management within the firm while simultaneously encouraging practices that will cause TQM to fail (i.e., talking the talk, but not walking the walk)

8. "Low-ball" pricing a product to encourage consumer purchases, only to charge exorbitant repair costs when the product breaks after the warranty period (which the company was aware would happen given internal testing) ▲

Solution Strategies

Total Cost of Quality = Cost of Compliance + Cost of Noncompliance

| Prevention Costs | Appraisal Costs | Internal Failure Costs | External Failure Costs |

Costs of noncompliance are inversely related to the costs of compliance and are a direct result of the number of defects.

Dimensions of product quality include
- Conformity to specifications
- Effective and efficient performance

- Durability
- Ease of use
- Safety
- Comfort of use
- Appeal

Cost of Quality Formulas

Profit Lost by Selling Units as Defects = (Total Defective Units − Number of Units Reworked) × (Profit for Good Unit − Profit for Defective Unit)

$$Z = (D - Y)(P_1 - P_2)$$

Rework Cost = Number of Units Reworked × Cost to Rework Defective Unit

$$R = (Y)(r)$$

Cost of Processing Customer Returns = Number of Defective Units Returned × Cost of a Return

$$W = (D_r)(w)$$

Total Failure Cost = Profit Lost by Selling Units as Defects + Rework Cost + Cost of Processing Customer Returns + Cost of Warranty Work + Cost of Product Recalls + Cost of Litigation Related to Products + Opportunity Cost of Lost Customers

$$F = Z + R + W + PR + L + O$$

Total Quality Cost = Total Compliance Cost + Total Failure Cost

$$T = (\text{Prevention Cost} + \text{Appraisal Cost}) + \text{Total Failure Cost}$$
$$T = K + A + F$$

Demonstration Problem

Kismet Corner's quality report for October 2008 showed the following information:

Profit for a good unit	$76
Profit for a defective unit	$44
Cost to rework a defective unit	$14
Cost to process a returned unit	$20
Total prevention cost	$54,000
Total appraisal cost	$32,000
Litigation related to product failure	$140,000
Opportunity cost of lost customers while litigation is being settled	$100,000
Total defective units	4,000
Number of units reworked	2,800
Number of customer units returned	1,300

Required:

Compute the following:

a. Profit lost by selling unreworked defects
b. Total rework cost
c. Cost of processing customer returns
d. Total failure cost
e. Total quality cost

Solution to Demonstration Problem

a. $Z = (D - Y)(P_1 - P_2) = (4,000 - 2,800)(\$76 - \$44) = 1,200(\$32) = \underline{\$38,400}$

b. $R = (Y)(r) = (2,800)(\$14) = \underline{\$39,200}$

c. $W = (D_r)(w) = (1,300)(\$20) = \underline{\$26,000}$

d. $F = (Z + R + W + L + O) = \$38,400 + \$39,200 + \$26,000 + \$140,000 + \$100,000 = \underline{\$343,600}$

e. $T = (K + A + F) = \$54,000 + \$32,000 + \$343,600 = \underline{\$429,600}$

Key Terms

appraisal cost, **p. 645**

benchmarking, **p. 636**

control chart, **p. 633**

cost of compliance, **p. 645**

cost of noncompliance, **p. 645**

external failure cost, **p. 645**

grade, **p. 635**

internal benchmarking, **p. 636**

internal failure cost, **p. 645**

ISO 9000 series, **p. 654**

prevention cost, **p. 645**

process benchmarking, **p. 638**

quality, **p. 632**

quality audit, **p. 655**

quality control (QC), **p. 633**

results benchmarking, **p. 637**

six sigma, **p. 633**

statistical process control (SPC), **p. 633**

strategic benchmarking, **p. 638**

total quality management (TQM), **p. 639**

value, **p. 635**

Questions

1. What is meant by the term *quality*? In defining quality, from what two perspectives can a definition be formulated? Why are both important?

2. In conducting activity analyses, the presence of certain activities indicates low production process quality. List five of these activities.

3. Compare and contrast the eight characteristics that compose overall quality from the customer's perspective with the three additional characteristics that compose service quality from the customer's perspective.

4. Locate a well-described product on the Internet. Discuss how that product exemplifies the eight overall quality characteristics. Prepare a balanced scorecard for this product assuming that its manufacturer has a total quality management strategy.

5. Describe four types of benchmarking. Use the Internet to find a company that has engaged in benchmarking. Describe the type of benchmarking used and the benefits and costs of the company's experience.

6. What is TQM? What are the four important tenets of TQM, and why are they important?

7. What is the Malcolm Baldrige National Quality Award? Why would an organization apply for that award?

8. In the production-sales cycle, what are the four time phases in which quality costs are incurred? How are these costs interrelated through the phases?

9. How can Pareto analysis help focus managerial efforts on reducing the costs of quality-related problems?

10. How does strategic cost management link information to corporate strategies?

11. (Appendix) Why might a common set of global quality standards be needed or desirable?

12. (Appendix) What is a quality audit?

13. (Appendix) Compare and contrast the EFQM Excellence Model with the Malcolm Baldrige National Quality Award criteria.

Exercises

14. **LO.1 (Quality definition; research; essay)** Use the Internet to find four definitions of quality.
    a. Compare and contrast each of the four definitions with specific emphasis on whether the definition includes conformity or customer orientation.
    b. Assume that you are the manager of (1) a copy store and (2) a kitchen blender manufacturer. Prepare definitions of quality to distribute to your employees and discuss how you would measure service/product adherence to those definitions.

15. **LO.1, LO.2, & LO.5 (True/False)** Mark each of the following statements as true or false and explain why the false statements are incorrect.
    a. SPC control charts are used to plot the costs of quality over time.
    b. Results benchmarking relies only on comparisons to firms within the same industry.
    c. Total quality management focuses on production processes rather than on customer satisfaction.
    d. The total quality cost is the sum of prevention cost plus failure cost.
    e. Appraisal cost is used to monitor and correct mistakes.
    f. Traditional accounting systems have separate accounts to capture quality costs.
    g. Pareto analysis is used to help managers identify areas in which to focus quality-improvement efforts.
    h. As the number of defective products manufactured rises, internal failure costs also rise but external failure costs are expected to decline.
    i. Higher quality yields lower profits but higher productivity.
    j. Quality is free.

16. **LO.1 (Essay; statistical process control)** Find the Web page for Western Digital Corporation in Santa Clara, California.
    a. What products does this company make?
    b. Using the information at *http://www.nwasoft.com/press/mag_westdig.htm* (last accessed 8/18/07), prepare an explanation of how the company uses statistical process controls to manage the quality of its output.

17. **LO.1 (Product defects)** According to the 2007 J.D. Power and Associates Reports, Mercedes-Benz S-Class and Audi A8 models have the fewest quality problems in the industry, with just 72 problems per 100 vehicles.

    Source: *J.D. Power and Associates Reports: Ford Motor Company Captures Most Awards in 2007 Initial Quality Study* (June 6, 2007); http://www.jdpower.com/press-releases/pressrelease.aspx?id=2007088 (last accessed 8/18/07).

    a. Calculate the yield and the process sigma using the calculator at http://www.isixsigma.com/library/content/c021223a.asp (last accessed 8/18/07).
    b. Calculate the yield to sigma using the calculator at http://www.isixsigma.com/library/content/sigma_table.asp (last accessed 8/18/07).
    c. Why is the information provided by these calculations not totally helpful?

18. **LO.1 (Control chart)** Francis Zammillo, owner of Zammillo's Pizza, has a policy to put 36 slices of pepperoni on a large pizza. Zammillo recently hired two college students to work part-time making pizzas and decided to observe them at their jobs for a few days. Zammillo gathered the following data on number of pepperoni slices being used on the pizzas:

    11:00 A.M. to 5:00 P.M.
       13 pizzas were made containing the following number of pepperoni slices: 35, 37, 41, 33, 36, 36, 35, 39, 44, 37, 36, 36, 35

    5:00 P.M. to 11:00 P.M.
       25 pizzas were made containing the following number of pepperoni slices: 35, 37, 41, 42, 36, 39, 44, 43, 44, 37, 48, 36, 35, 40, 39, 41, 29, 36, 36, 42, 45, 44, 37, 36, 36

    a. Prepare a control chart for pepperoni slices.
    b. What information does the chart provide to Zammillo?

19. **LO.1 (Quality characteristics)** Choose one product and one service with which you are well acquainted. Indicate how the product and service each meet (or do not meet) the eight overall quality characteristics. For the service, indicate how it meets (or does not meet) the three additional characteristics for service quality.

20. **LO.1 (Definition of quality; quality characteristics)** In a three-person team, role-play the following individuals who are visiting a car dealership in your community: (1) a 19-year-old college student, (2) a young married couple with two children, and (3) a retired person. Each person is interested in purchasing a new automobile.

a. How does each customer define quality in an automobile? Explain the reasons for the differences.

b. What vehicle characteristics are important to each type of buyer? Which vehicle characteristics are unique to each buyer?

21. **LO.2 (Benchmarks; research)** In 2002, a green engineering case study about automobile emissions and saving energy was performed. The study generated designs for both gasoline- and diesel-powered automobiles with the following characteristics: a mid-size sedan that would get 52 miles per gallon when equipped with a gasoline engine and 68 miles per gallon when equipped with a diesel engine. The automobiles were also designed to be capable of achieving a "Five-Star" crash safety rating based on the anticipated 2004 safety standards, and would cost no more to build than traditionally engineered mid-size sedans.

Source: William Obenchain, Marcel van Schaik, and Pete Peterson, "Green Engineering Case Study: Reducing Automobile Emissions and Saving Energy" (April 11, 2002); http://www.epa.gov/oppt/greenengineering/pubs/ulsab-avc.pdf (last accessed 8/18/07).

a. Obtain miles per gallon and crash test ratings for five new automobiles (either gasoline or diesel). How do these automobiles compare to the benchmarks of the 2002 case study?

b. What might cause the differences between the ratings for the automobiles selected and the benchmarks?

22. **LO.2 & LO.5 (Benchmarks; quality costs)** For a benchmark, assume that the average firm incurs quality costs in the following proportions:

Prevention	25%
Appraisal	25%
Internal failure	25%
External failure	25%
Total costs	100%

Why might each of the following industries be inclined to have a spending pattern on quality costs that differs from the benchmark?

a. Pharmaceutical company

b. Department store

c. Computer manufacturer

d. Used-car retailer

e. Lawn service company

23. **LO.3 (Essay; cost and benefit of TQM)** Colleges and universities have a variety of internal and external customers. Use a team of three or four individuals to answer the following.

a. Who are three internal and two external customers of a college or university?

b. How would each of the customers from part (a) define product or service quality at a college or university? Do any of these views conflict and, if so, how?

c. Are a college or university's internal customers as important as external customers? Explain the rationale for your answer.

24. **LO.3 (Research; supplier relationships)** Find a company's Web site that provides information on the characteristics that are desired for that company when establishing long-term/preferred supplier relationships.

a. What characteristics are listed? Why do you think each of these is important?

b. Did the characteristics within the list or elsewhere on the Web site address supplier diversity? Do you believe that supplier diversity is necessary? Why or why not?

25. **LO.3 (Supplier quality; essay)** Assume that Honda Motor Co. Ltd. paid for a full-page advertisement in *The Wall Street Journal.* The ad neither discussed any Honda products nor referred to year-end earnings or a new stock issuance. Instead, the ad informed readers that "buying quality parts is important to this company." The ad named Honda suppliers and identified their locations. Prepare a brief essay to answer the following questions.

a. Why would Honda want newspaper readers to know what suppliers it uses?

b. Do you think this advertisement would have any benefit for Honda itself? Discuss the rationale for your answer.

26. **LO.5 (Quality costs; essay)** eFrame Computers is evaluating its quality control costs for 2008 and preparing plans and budgets for 2009. The 2008 quality costs incurred in the CPU Division follow:

Prevention costs	$300,000
Appraisal costs	100,000
Internal failure costs	350,000
External failure costs	100,000
Total	$850,000

Prepare a memo to the company president on the following issues:
a. Which categories of quality costs would be affected by the decision to spend $1,500,000 on new computer chip–making equipment that would replace older equipment? Why?
b. If projected external failure costs for 2009 can be reduced 60 percent (relative to 2008 levels) by spending either $50,000 more on appraisal or $80,000 more on prevention, why might the firm opt to spend the $80,000 on prevention rather than the $50,000 on appraisal?

27. **LO.5 (Quality costs)** Windsor House Furniture Manufacturing has prepared the following summary quality cost report for 2008:

Prevention costs	$1,300,000
Appraisal costs	1,500,000
Internal failure costs	1,900,000
External failure costs	1,400,000
Total quality costs	$6,100,000

The company is actively striving to reduce total quality costs. Its current strategy is to increase spending in one or more quality cost categories in the hope of achieving greater spending cuts in other quality cost categories. Prepare a presentation that answers the following questions.
a. Which spending categories are most susceptible to control by managers? Why?
b. Why is it more logical for the company to increase spending in the prevention cost and appraisal cost categories than in the failure cost categories?
c. Which cost category is the most likely target for spending reductions? Explain.
d. How would the adoption of a TQM philosophy affect the focus in reducing quality costs?

28. **LO.5 & LO.6 (Quality costs)** Electronica Components' accounting system reflected the following costs related to quality for 2008 and 2009:

	2008	2009
Customer refunds for poor product quality	$ 48,000	$ 36,000
Fitting machines for mistake-proof operations	18,800	27,600
Supply-line management	16,000	20,000
Disposal of waste	88,000	72,000
Quality training	56,000	60,000
Litigation claims	144,000	112,000

a. Which of these are costs of compliance, and which are costs of noncompliance?
b. Calculate the percentage change in each cost and for each category.
c. Discuss the pattern of the changes in the two categories.

29. **LO.5 (Quality costs)** Jessica's Accessories has gathered the following data on its quality costs for 2008 and 2009:

Defect Prevention Costs	2008	2009
Quality training	$ 9,000	$10,500
Quality technology	7,500	10,000
Quality production design	4,000	9,000

External Failure Costs		
Warranty handling	$15,000	$10,000
Customer reimbursements	11,000	7,200
Customer returns handling	7,000	4,000

a. Compute the percentage change in the two quality cost categories from 2008 to 2009.
b. Write a brief explanation for the pattern of change in the two categories.

30. **LO.5 (Quality costs; essay)** Sometimes a company, in its efforts to reduce costs, might also reduce quality.
a. What kinds of costs could an organization reduce that would almost automatically lower product/service quality?
b. If quality improvements create cost reductions, why would cost reductions not create quality improvements?
c. Are there instances in which cost reductions would create quality improvements? Explain.

31. LO.5 (Quality costs; essay; ethics) By building quality into a process rather than having quality inspections at the end of the process, certain job functions (such as that of quality control inspector) can be eliminated. Additionally, the installation of automated equipment to monitor product processing could eliminate some line worker jobs.

In a nation with fairly high unemployment, would employers attempting to implement valid quality improvements that resulted in employee terminations be appreciated or condemned? Discuss your answer from the standpoint of a variety of concerned constituencies, including the consumers who purchase the company's products. ▲

32. LO.6 (Cost of quality) Managers at Silvoso's Chemicals want to determine the company's cost of quality. The following information has been gathered from the records for August 2008:

Defective units	12,000
Units reworked	2,400
Defective units returned	800
Appraisal costs	$27,200
Cost per unit for rework	$25
Prevention costs	$170,000
Profit per good unit produced and sold	$80
Profit per defective unit sold	$50
Cost per unit for customer returns	$20
Cost of warranty work	$18,000

Compute the following:
a. Lost profits from selling defective work
b. Total costs of failure
c. Total quality cost

33. LO.6 (Cost of quality) The accountant at Bright Eyes Inc. has gathered the following June 2008 information about quality costs for the production of heavy-duty sunglasses:

Total defective units	1,160
Number of units reworked	760
Number of units returned	200
Total prevention cost	$48,000
Total appraisal cost	$17,000
Per-unit profit for defective units	$40
Per-unit profit for good units	$112
Cost to rework defective units	$32
Cost to handle returned units	$20

Using these data, calculate the following:
a. Total cost to rework
b. Profit lost from not reworking all defective units
c. Cost of processing customer returns
d. Total failure costs
e. Total quality cost

34. LO.7 (Quality information system; team activity) Your company is interested in developing information about quality but has a traditional accounting system that does not provide such information directly. In a three- or four-person team, prepare a set of recommendations about how to improve the company's information system to eliminate or reduce this deficiency. In your recommendations, also explain in what areas management would have the most difficulty satisfying its desire for more information about quality and why these areas were chosen.

35. LO.7 (Balanced scorecard; essay) Find The Benchmarking Exchange on the Internet. What are five business processes that are currently the focus of its members? Why do you think benchmarking processes related to managing human resources rank highly on the benchmarking interest list of companies? Explain how benchmarking can be used to implement balanced scorecard goals and targets for each of its four perspectives for a company with a total quality management strategy.

Problems

36. LO.1 (Quality problems; research; essay; ethics) In mid-2007, numerous findings of unsafe products produced in China were disclosed, including pet food, fish, toothpaste, toys, and fireworks. China was quick to address the issues: first with "defiance and denial," followed quickly by "acknowledging problems and cracking down on errant factories."

Source: Neil King, Jr. and Rebecca Blumenstein, "China Launches Public Response to Safety Fears," *Wall Street Journal* (June 30–July 1, 2007), p. A1.

a. Research problems with Chinese products and write a short summary that identifies what products were involved in 2007 (or products that may be currently in the news) and the problems experienced with those products.
b. What conditions in China might have contributed to the quality problems?
c. Do you think that all Chinese products of a similar type should be banned if significant quality problems are found in several like products? Explain the rationale for your answer. ▲

37. LO.1 & LO.2 (Quality problems; benchmarking; essay; ethics) In 2006, pharmaceutical company Pfizer discontinued trials for its new cholesterol drug torcetrapib because of an unexpected number of deaths and cardiovascular problems in patients who used it.

Source: "Pfizer Ends Cholesterol Drug Development," *ABC News* (December 2, 2006), http://abcnews.go.com/Health/wireStory?id=2696392&CMP=OTC-RSSFeeds0312 (last accessed 8/18/07).

a. Find information on the Web about problems in the pharmaceutical industry, including those of Pfizer. Be certain to review annual report footnote information related to contingencies for the company. Discuss your findings.
b. Compare Pfizer's profits with those of other firms in the industry for 2006 until now.
c. Discuss why a total quality management system would be more important in pharmaceutical companies than in most companies. ▲

38. LO.1 (Quality and strategy; essay) Three possible goals for a business are to (1) maximize profits, (2) maximize shareholder wealth, and (3) satisfy customer wants and needs. If goals (1) or (2) are chosen, the primary measurements of "success" are organizational profitability or stock price.
a. Do you believe that one of these three goals can be chosen to the exclusion of the others? Discuss the rationale for your answer.
b. How can total quality management help an organization meet all of these goals?
c. How might the selection of goals (1) or (2) lead to quality problems in an organization? Would the selection of goal (3) be likely to lead to quality problems? Explain.

39. LO.4 (Baldrige Award; research; essay) Go to the Web site for the Malcolm Baldrige National Quality Award and find the answers to the following questions.
a. When and why were the health and education categories established?
b. How do the criteria for the health, education, and manufacturing categories differ? Why are such differences necessary?
c. Choose one of the education recipients and review its profile and application summary. Consider the category of student/stakeholder satisfaction and relationships. Compare your educational institution with the winner and discuss similarities and differences.

40. LO.4 (Baldrige Award) Go to the Web site for the Malcolm Baldrige National Quality Award and find the questionnaire titled "Are We Making Progress?"
a. Download the questionnaire and answer the questions relative to your place of employment or university. Ask four of your colleagues to independently do the same.
b. Compare and contrast the five sets of answers. How would you rank your organization's "progress" solely based on the information from these questionnaires?

41. LO.5 (Quality costs; Pareto analysis) Sowanee Computers identified the following failure costs during 2008:

COST OF FAILURE BY TYPE

Model	CPU	Internal Drive	External Drive	All Other	Total Dollars
Laptop	$ 8,000	$ 7,000	$ 5,120	$ 3,000	$23,120
Desktop	7,000	6,000	14,000	5,640	32,640
Mini	1,000	980	8,000	2,260	12,240
Total	$16,000	$13,980	$27,120	$10,900	$68,000

a. Rearrange the rows in descending order of magnitude based on the Total Dollars column, and prepare a table using Pareto analysis with the following headings:

Model	Dollars	% of Total	Cumulative % of Total

b. Which models account for almost 80 percent of all failure costs?

c. Focusing on the models identified in part (b), prepare a table using Pareto analysis to identify the types of failure causing the majority of failure costs. (Hint: Rearrange the cost of failure types in descending order of magnitude.) Use the following headings for your table:

Failure Type	Dollars	% of Total	Cumulative % of Total

d. Describe the problem areas for which to seek preventive measures first. How, if at all, does this answer reflect the concept of leveraging expenditures?

42. LO.5 (Quality costs; Pareto analysis) Altazar Appliances has identified the following 2008 warranty costs for one of the company products. The information has been categorized according to the type of product failure.

Model	Electrical	Motor	Structural	Mechanical	Total Dollars
Chic	$22,680	$25,000	$13,380	$ 5,600	$ 66,660
Elegant	28,820	32,000	26,100	6,000	92,920
Others	8,830	16,590	6,180	10,820	42,420
Total	$60,330	$73,590	$45,660	$22,420	$202,000

a. Rearrange the rows in descending order of magnitude based on the Total Dollars column, and prepare a table using Pareto analysis with the following headings:

Model	Dollars	% of Total	Cumulative % of Total

b. Which model(s) account for the vast proportion of all failure costs? Discuss.

c. Devise a plan for Altazar Appliances to address the prioritization of preventive measures based on the findings in the Pareto analysis.

43. LO.5 (Quality costs; research; essay) Nanotechnology may be the future of manufacturing. The term refers to any area of research that deals with objects one-tenth the size of an atom. According to the Center for Responsible Nanotechnology and given the current rate of development, general-purpose molecular manufacturing might become a reality by 2010, is likely by 2015, and almost certainly will be achieved by 2020. The last stage of nanoengineering is the ability to create "assemblers" (a device with a submicroscopic arm that is controlled by a computer) that can build consumer goods. For the new technology to become a reality, the assemblers need to be able to self-replicate.

a. What implications would the introduction of nanotechnology and molecular manufacturing have on the four types of quality costs within the manufacturing process? Outside the manufacturing process?

b. What implications would the introduction of nanotechnology and molecular manufacturing have on non-quality costs?

44. LO.5 (External failure cost; research; essay) Many companies' products have had flaws; some of these companies have been more forthcoming than others in publicly acknowledging such flaws.

a. Do you think admitting that a product is defective hurts or helps a company's reputation? Explain the rationale for your answer.

b. Discuss the costs and benefits of halting sales when product flaws are discovered.

c. Use the Internet to find an example of a company that has continued to sell its product in spite of complaints and other negative feedback about quality. What have been the results?

45. LO.6 (Cost of quality) Burtram Ltd. manufactures handheld organizers. The firm produced 30,000 organizers during its first year of operation. At year-end, it had no inventory of finished goods. Burtram sold 28,200 units through regular market channels, but 300 of the units produced were so defective that they had to be sold as scrap. The remaining units were reworked and sold as seconds. For the year, the firm spent $160,000 on prevention costs and $80,000 on quality appraisal. There were no customer returns. An income statement for the year follows:

Sales		
Regular channel	$5,640,000	
Seconds	142,500	
Scrap	10,500	$5,793,000
Cost of goods sold		
Original production costs	$1,917,600	
Rework costs	42,000	
Quality prevention and appraisal	240,000	(2,199,600)
Gross margin		$3,593,400
Selling and administrative expenses (all fixed)		(980,000)
Profit before income taxes		$2,613,400

a. Compute the total pre-tax profit lost by the company in its first year of operations by selling defective units as seconds or as scrap rather than selling the units through regular channels.

b. Compute the total failure cost for the company in its first year.

c. Compute total quality cost incurred by the company in its first year.

d. What evidence indicates that the firm is dedicated to manufacturing and selling high-quality products?

46. LO.6 (Cost of quality) During 2008 (the first year of operations), Sorkowski Company produced 19,900 portable navigation systems; of these, 500 were found defective by quality appraisers. Three hundred of the defective units were reworked and sold through regular channels at the original price; the rest were sold as seconds without rework. (The uncorrected defect did not pose a hazard to customers; it was a "voice flaw" which made the units sometimes sound as if they were yelling at the users.) The navigation systems are sold with a two-year warranty; seconds have a six-month warranty.

In 2008, Sorkowski Company spent $225,000 for prevention measures and $98,000 on appraisal. Following is the partnership's 2008 income statement, which appropriately does not reflect any income taxes:

SORKOWSKI COMPANY
Income Statement
For Year Ended December 31, 2008

Regular sales (19,700 units)	$5,122,000	
Sales of seconds (200 units)	28,000	$5,150,000
Cost of goods sold		
Original production costs	$1,600,000	
Rework costs (300 units)	10,500	
Prevention and appraisal costs	323,000	(1,933,500)
Gross margin		$3,216,500
Selling and administrative expenses (all fixed)		(1,200,000)
Net income		$2,016,500

a. Compute the total profit lost by Sorkowski Company in its first year of operation by selling defective units as seconds rather than reworking them and selling them at the regular price.

b. Compute the company's total failure cost in 2008.

c. Compute the company's total quality cost in 2008.

d. Assume that selling and administrative expenses include $150,000 to operate a customer complaint center. How should this cost be categorized relative to quality costs?

e. Are the costs included in the 2008 income statement completely reflective of Sorkowski's quality costs?

47. LO.6 (Cost of quality) Golf courses are demanding in their quest for high-quality carts because of the critical need for lawn maintenance. Richfield Corp. manufactures golf carts and is a recognized leader in the industry for quality products. In recent months, company managers have become more interested in trying to quantify the company's cost of quality. As an initial effort, the company identified the following 2008 costs by categories that are associated with quality:

Prevention Costs

Quality training	$15,000
Quality technology	50,000
Quality circles	32,000

Appraisal Costs

Quality inspections	$18,000
Test equipment	14,000
Procedure verifications	9,000

Internal Failure Costs

Scrap and waste	$ 6,500
Waste disposal	2,100

External Failure Costs

Warranty handling	$ 9,500
Customer reimbursements/returns	7,600

Managers were also aware that in 2008, 250 of the 8,000 carts produced had to be sold as seconds. These 250 carts were sold for $80 less profit per unit than "good" carts. Also, the company incurred rework costs amounting to $6,000 to sell 200 other carts through regular market channels.

a. Using these data, calculate Richfield Corp.'s 2008 expense for the following:
   1. Lost profit from the 250 units
   2. Total failure cost
   3. Total quality cost

b. Assume that the company is considering expanding its existing 5-year warranty to a 7-year warranty in 2009. How would such a change be reflected in quality costs?

48. LO.6 (Cost of quality) Smooth Sailing is very aware that its scuba diving tanks must be of high quality to maintain its reputation of excellence and safety. The company has retained you as a consultant and you have suggested that quantifying the costs would be important to the understanding and management of quality. Your experience as a cost accountant helped you determine year 2008 costs of quality from the company's accounting records as follows:

Prevention Costs

Foolproofing machinery	$10,000
Quality training	30,000
Educating suppliers	22,000

Appraisal Costs

Quality inspections	$12,000
Recording defects	9,000
Procedure verifications	6,000

Internal Failure Costs

Waste disposal	$ 4,500
Unplanned downtime	1,400

External Failure Costs

Warranty handling	$ 6,400
Customer reimbursements/returns	5,100

You also determined that 1,200 of the 100,000 tanks made in 2008 had to be sold as scrap for $70 less profit per tank than the nondefective tanks. Smooth Sailing also incurred $4,000 of rework costs that had been buried in overhead (in addition to the failure costs listed) in producing the tanks sold at the regular price.

a. Smooth Sailing's management has asked you to determine the 2008 "costs" of the following:
   1. Lost profit from scrapping the 1,200 units
   2. Total failure cost
   3. Total quality cost

b. Assume that the company is considering expanding its existing full 2-year warranty to a full 3-year warranty in 2009. How would such a change be reflected in quality costs?

49. LO.7 (Balanced scorecard; essay; ethics) Assume that you are in charge of Physicians Social Service Agency, which provides counseling services to low-income families. The agency's costs have been increasing with no corresponding increase in funding. In an effort to implement some cost reductions, you took the following actions:

- Empowered counselors to make their own decisions about the legitimacy of all low-income claims.
- Told counselors not to review processed claims a second time to emphasize the concept of "do it right the first time."
- Set an upper and lower control limit of 5 minutes on a standard 15-minute time for consultations to discourage "out-of-control" conditions.

a. Discuss the ethics as well as the positive and negative effects of each of the ideas listed.
b. Develop a balanced scorecard for Physicians Social Service Agency that incorporates the three changes listed. ▲

50. LO.7 (Balanced scorecard; essay) In mid-2004, a study of German accident data indicated that vehicles made by Porsche AG broke down twice as often during 2003 as cars made by Mazda. The top European performer was Volkswagen AG unit Audi.

Source: Chris Reiter and Stephen Power, "Data Show Porsches Broke Down Twice as Much as Mazda Vehicles," *Wall Street Journal* (June 1, 2004), p. D2.

a. What do you perceive to be Porsche's strategy relative to value and grade of its automobiles? How might Porsche modify its strategy to compete better against Japanese vehicles? Do you think such a change in strategy would be profitable for Porsche? Explain.
b. If Porsche were to change its strategy, develop a balanced scorecard that would provide measurements of the new strategy.

51. LO.9 (Appendix; ISO) Many companies are becoming ISO certified because of customer requests and because of the need to compete in the global marketplace.

a. Why do you think customers are insisting that suppliers meet ISO 9001:2000 standards?
b. Does meeting ISO 9001:2000 standards mean that a supplier's products or services are superior to those of competitors? Elaborate on what conformance to the standards means.
c. Why would the fact that a supplier's industry is moving toward ISO 9001:2000 motivate the supplier to seek registration?
d. How would complying with ISO 9001:2000 help a company improve quality?

52. LO.9 (Appendix; EFQM Award) Go to the EFQM Web site and find the case studies archive. Choose one of the companies listed for the past two years. Prepare a synopsis of the company, and gather additional information about it to make a brief presentation on why it received an award or was a finalist.

18 | Inventory and Production Management

Objectives

After completing this chapter, you should be able to answer the following questions:

LO.1 What costs are associated with inventory, and why is inventory management important to manufacturing firms?

LO.2 How do push and pull systems control production?

LO.3 Why do product life cycles affect profitability?

LO.4 What is target costing, and how does it influence production cost management?

LO.5 What is the just-in-time philosophy? What modifications does JIT require in accounting systems?

LO.6 What are flexible manufacturing systems?

LO.7 How can the theory of constraints help in determining production flow?

LO.8 (*Appendix*) How are economic order quantity, order point, and safety stock determined and used?

Introduction

Manufacturing and retail firms face two significant challenges in managing inventory. First, these firms must have the inventory available to match the demand from their customers. To meet this challenge, firms must produce or order the right products at the right price and have them available when customers want those products. Second, to avoid excessive costs and remain competitive, firms must avoid producing or ordering products that are not demanded by their customers. No longer do firms hold inventory until a customer decides to make a purchase; they ardently strive to avoid investing cash in inventory until customers actually place orders. Efforts to avoid inventory investment are captured in the following quote.

> *People who believe you can't have too much of a good thing obviously haven't worked with inventory! Operations managers know inventory dispels this adage and face the constant challenge of keeping inventory levels as low as possible without increasing overall costs or negatively impacting product availability. This isn't an easy job, especially since inventory rears its head throughout any organization—from raw materials, to work-in-process, to finished goods.*[1]

Other than plant assets and development of human resources, inventory is often the largest investment a company makes—although this investment yields no return until the inventory is sold. This chapter deals with ways companies minimize their monetary commitments to inventory while still satisfying customer demands. The chapter appendix covers the concepts of economic order quantity (EOQ), order point, safety stock, and Pareto inventory analysis.

Important Relationships in the Value Chain

Every company has a set of upstream suppliers and a set of downstream customers. In a one-on-one context, these parties can be depicted by the following model:

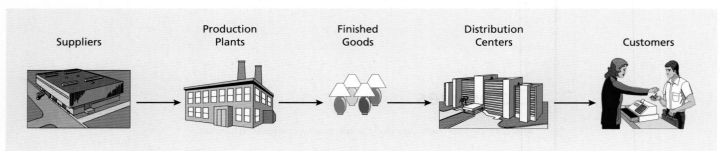

| Suppliers | Production Plants | Finished Goods | Distribution Centers | Customers |

The points at which these relationships interface indicate the real opportunities for inventory cost management. By building improved cooperation, communication, and integration, entities within a value chain can treat each other as extensions of themselves and, thereby, obtain gains in quality, throughput, and cost efficiency. Entities can share expertise and engage in problem solving to reduce or eliminate non-value-added (NVA) activities and enhance value-added activities. Firms can provide products and services faster and with fewer defects as well as perform activities more effectively and reliably with fewer errors and less redundancy. Consider the following areas in which opportunities for improvement between entities exist:

- communicating requirements and specifications,
- clarifying requests for products or services,
- providing feedback about unsatisfactory products or services,
- planning, controlling, and problem solving, and
- sharing managerial and technical expertise, supervision, and training.

[1] Scott W. Hadley, "A Modern View of Inventory," *Strategic Finance* (July 2004), pp. 31–35.

These opportunities are also available to individuals and groups within an organization. Each employee or group of employees has both an upstream supplier and a downstream customer that form an intraorganizational value chain. When employees see their internal suppliers and customers as extensions of themselves and work to exploit the opportunities for improvement, teamwork is significantly enhanced. Improved teamwork helps companies implement just-in-time systems, which are discussed later in the chapter. Increased productivity benefits all company stakeholders by

- reducing investment in inventory,
- improving cash-to-cash cycle time,
- generating higher asset turnover,
- generating higher inventory turnover, and
- reducing inventory risk.

Buying or Producing and Carrying Inventory

In manufacturing organizations, production begins with the acquisition of raw material. Although not always the largest production cost, raw material purchases cause a continuous cash outflow. Similarly, retailers make significant investments in merchandise purchased for sale to customers. Profit margins in both types of organizations can benefit from reducing or minimizing inventory investments, assuming that the demand for products can still be met. The term *inventory* is used in this chapter to refer to raw material, work in process, finished goods, indirect material (supplies), and merchandise inventory.

Efficient inventory management relies largely on cost-minimization strategies. As indicated in Exhibit 18–1, the primary costs associated with inventory are (1) purchasing/production, (2) ordering/setup, and (3) carrying/not carrying goods in stock. The purchasing cost for inventory is the quoted purchase price minus any discounts allowed, plus shipping charges. For a manufacturer, production cost refers to the costs associated with purchasing direct material, paying for direct labor, incurring traceable overhead, and absorbing allocated fixed manufacturing overhead. Of these production costs, fixed manufacturing overhead is the least susceptible to cost minimization in the short run. An exception is that management is able to somewhat control the fixed component of unit product cost by managing production capacity utilization relative to demand in the short run. Most efforts to minimize fixed manufacturing overhead costs involve long-run measures.

The two theoretical approaches to producing inventory are push systems and pull systems. In a traditional approach, production is conducted in anticipation of customer orders. In this approach, known as a push system (illustrated in Exhibit 18–2), work centers buy or produce inventory not currently needed because of lead time, economic order size, or production quantity requirements. This excess inventory is stored until it is needed by other work centers. To reduce the cost of carrying inventory until needed at some point in the future, many firms have implemented pull systems of production control (depicted in Exhibit 18–3). In these systems, inventory is delivered or produced only as it is needed by the next work center in the value chain. Although some minimal storage must exist by necessity, work centers do not produce in order to compensate for lead times or to meet some economic production run model. Matters such as managing inventory levels and optimum order size are discussed in the chapter appendix.

Understanding and Managing Production Activities and Costs

Managing production activities and costs requires an understanding of product life cycles and the various management and accounting models and approaches to effectively and efficiently engage in production planning, controlling, decision making, and evaluating performance.

LO.1
What costs are associated with inventory, and why is inventory management important to manufacturing firms?

LO.2
How do push and pull systems control production?

EXHIBIT 18–1
Categories of Inventory Costs

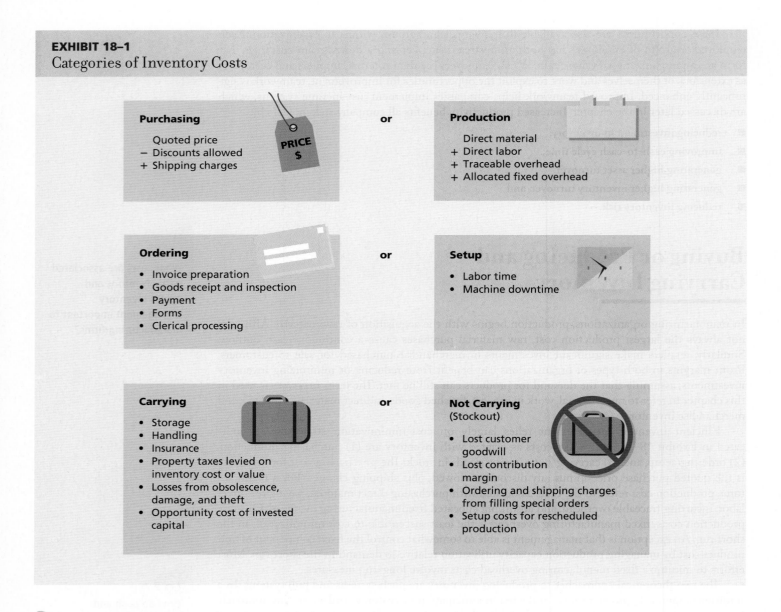

Purchasing

   Quoted price
  − Discounts allowed
  + Shipping charges

or

Production

   Direct material
  + Direct labor
  + Traceable overhead
  + Allocated fixed overhead

Ordering

- Invoice preparation
- Goods receipt and inspection
- Payment
- Forms
- Clerical processing

or

Setup

- Labor time
- Machine downtime

Carrying

- Storage
- Handling
- Insurance
- Property taxes levied on inventory cost or value
- Losses from obsolescence, damage, and theft
- Opportunity cost of invested capital

or

Not Carrying
(Stockout)

- Lost customer goodwill
- Lost contribution margin
- Ordering and shipping charges from filling special orders
- Setup costs for rescheduled production

LO.3
Why do product life cycles affect profitability?

Product Life Cycles

Product profit margins are typically judged on a period-by-period basis without consideration of the product life cycle. However, products, like people, go through a series of sequential life cycle stages. The **product life cycle** is a model depicting the stages through which a product class (not each product) passes from the time that an idea is conceived until production is discontinued. Those stages are development (which includes design), introduction, growth, maturity, and decline. Exhibit 18–4 illustrates a conventional sales trend line as the product class passes through each life cycle stage. Companies must be aware of where products are in their life cycles because, in addition to the sales effects, the life cycle stage can have a tremendous impact on costs and profits.

During the product introduction stage, costs can be substantial and are typically related to engineering change orders, market research, advertising, and promotion. Sales are usually low and prices are often set in relationship to the market price of similar or substitute goods if such goods are available.

The growth stage begins when the product has been accepted by the market and starts to show increased sales. Product quality also can improve during this life cycle stage, especially if competitors have improved on original production designs. Prices are fairly stable during the growth stage either

EXHIBIT 18–2
Push System of Production Control

Purchases and production are constantly *pushed* down into storage locations until need arises.

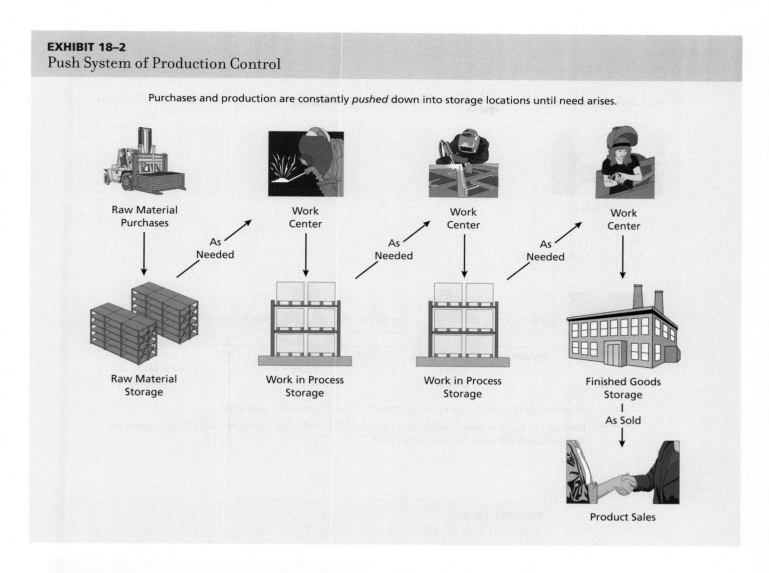

because many substitutes exist or because consumers have become "attached" to the product and are willing to pay a particular price for it rather than buy a substitute.

In the maturity stage, sales begin to stabilize or slowly decline and firms often compete on the basis of selling price. Costs are often at their lowest level during this period, so profits can be high. Some products remain at this stage for a very long time.

The decline stage reflects waning sales. Prices can be cut dramatically to stimulate business. Production cost per unit generally increases during this stage because fixed overhead is spread over a smaller production volume.

Life Cycle and Target Costing

From a cost standpoint, the development stage is an extremely important stage that the traditional financial accounting model almost ignores. Financial accounting requires that development costs be expensed as incurred—even though most studies indicate that decisions made during this stage determine approximately 80 to 90 percent of a product's total life cycle costs. The material and manufacturing process specifications made during development generally affect production costs for the remainder of the product's life cycle.

Although technology and competition have tremendously shortened the time spent in the development stage, effective development efforts are critical to a product's profitability over its entire life cycle. Time spent in the planning and development process typically reduces production and life

LO.4
What is target costing, and how does it influence production cost management?

EXHIBIT 18–3
Pull System of Production Control

Product sales dictate total production. Purchases and production are *pulled* through the system on an as-needed basis.

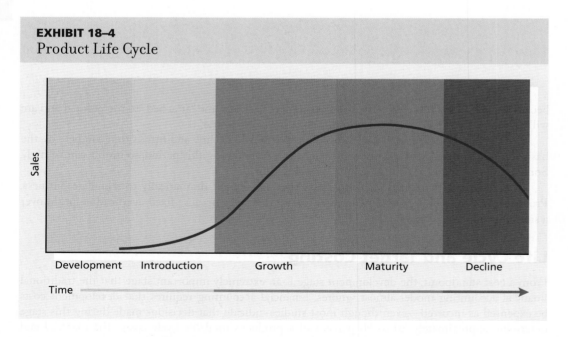

Product Sales

(4)   I
FG   request for FG

Work Center	II request for WIP	Work Center	III request for WIP	Work Center	IV request for RM	Raw Material Purchases
	(3) WIP		(2) WIP		(1) RM	

⟶ Information flow that creates (pulls) demand at each successive operation

⟵ Physical production flow in which raw material (RM) and work in process (WIP) flow successively through work centers until completed (FG)

EXHIBIT 18–4
Product Life Cycle

Sales

| Development | Introduction | Growth | Maturity | Decline |

Time

cycle costs, shortens manufacturing time, increases quality, and adds more flexibility. All manufacturers are acutely aware of the need to focus attention on the product development stage, and the performance measure of time-to-market is becoming more critical.

One technology that is increasingly used in the design stage is virtual reality. **Virtual reality** is an artificial, computer-generated environment in which the user is a "part" of that environment and has the ability to navigate and manipulate objects (such as products) that behave like real-world objects. With virtual reality, much of the new product testing can focus on a virtual, rather than a real, prototype.

Once a product or service idea is formulated, the market is typically researched to determine the features that customers desire. Because many products can now be built to specification, companies can further develop a product to meet customer tastes once it is in the market. Alternatively, flexible manufacturing systems allow rapid changeovers to other designs.

After a product is designed, manufacturers have traditionally determined product costs and set a selling price based, to some extent, on costs. If the market will not bear the resulting selling price (possibly because competitors' prices are lower), the firm either makes less profit than desired or attempts to lower production costs. Because of intensified competition in many product markets, companies often have less discretion in setting prices now than in the past.

Today, most products are designed to be sold at a particular price point that is associated with the preferences of a particular product market segment. To keep production costs in line with the price point, some companies (especially Japanese ones) use a technique called target costing. As expressed in the following formula, target costing develops an "allowable" product cost by analyzing market research to estimate what the market will pay (price point) for a product with specific characteristics.

$$TC = ESP - APM$$

where   TC = target cost
        ESP = estimated selling price
        APM = acceptable profit margin

Subtracting an acceptable profit margin from the estimated selling price leaves an implied maximum per-unit target product cost, which is compared to an expected product cost.

If the expected cost is higher than the target cost, the company has several alternatives. First, the product design and/or production process can be changed to reduce costs. Cost tables help determine how to make such adjustments. Cost tables are databases that provide information about the impact on product costs of using different input resources, manufacturing processes, and design specifications. Second, a less-than-desired profit margin can be accepted. Third, the company can decide not to enter this particular product market at the current time because it cannot make the profit margin it desires. If, for example, the target costing system used by Eastman-Kodak indicated that a product's life cycle costs were too high to make an acceptable profit, the product would be abandoned unless it were strategically necessary to maintain a comprehensive product line or to create a "flagship" product.

An important step in successful product development is the process of value engineering (VE), which involves a disciplined search for various feasible combinations of resources and methods that will increase product functionality and reduce costs. Multidisciplinary teams using various problem-solving tools such as brainstorming, Pareto analysis, and engineering tools seek an improved product cost-performance ratio considering such factors as reliability, conformity, and durability. Cost reduction, shortened production cycles, and increased quality are the major reasons to engage in VE.

Target costing can be applied to services if they are sufficiently uniform to justify the modeling effort required. Assume that a print shop wants to offer customers the opportunity to buy a variety of items personalized with photographs. A market survey indicates that the metropolitan area could sustain an annual 500-order volume and that customers believe $18 is a reasonable fee per service. The print shop manager believes that a reasonable profit for this service is $8 per customer order. Thus, the allowable target cost is $10 per order ($18 − $8). The manager will invest in the equipment necessary to provide the new service if he or she believes that the indicated volume suggested by market research is sufficient to support the cost.

In designing a product to meet an allowable cost, engineers strive to eliminate all NVA activities from the production process. Such reductions in activities will, in turn, reduce costs. The production process and types of components to be used should be discussed among appropriate parties (including engineering, management, accounting, and marketing) in recognition of the product quality and cost desired. Suppliers also can participate in the design phase by making suggestions for modifications that would allow standard components to be used rather than more costly special order items.

Properly designed products should require only minimal engineering change orders (ECOs) after being released to production. Each time an ECO is issued, one or more of the following problems can occur and create additional costs: production documents must be reprinted, workers must relearn tasks, machine dies or setups must be changed, and parts in stock or currently ordered can be made obsolete. If costs are to be affected significantly, any design changes must be made early in the process—preferably before production begins.

Target costing requires a shift in the way managers think about the relationships among cost, selling price, and profitability. The traditional attitude has been that a product is developed, production cost is identified and measured, a selling price is set (or a market price is met), and profits or losses result. Target costing takes a different perspective: a product is developed, a selling price and desired profit amount are determined, and maximum allowable costs are calculated. When allowable costs are constrained by selling price, all costs must be justified. Unnecessary costs should be eliminated without reducing quality. The target costing process is depicted in Exhibit 18–5.

If a company decides to enter a market, the target cost computed at the beginning of the product life cycle does not remain the final focus. Over the product's life, the target cost is continuously reduced in an effort to spur a process of continuous improvement in actual production cost. **Kaizen costing** involves ongoing efforts for continuous improvement to reduce product costs,

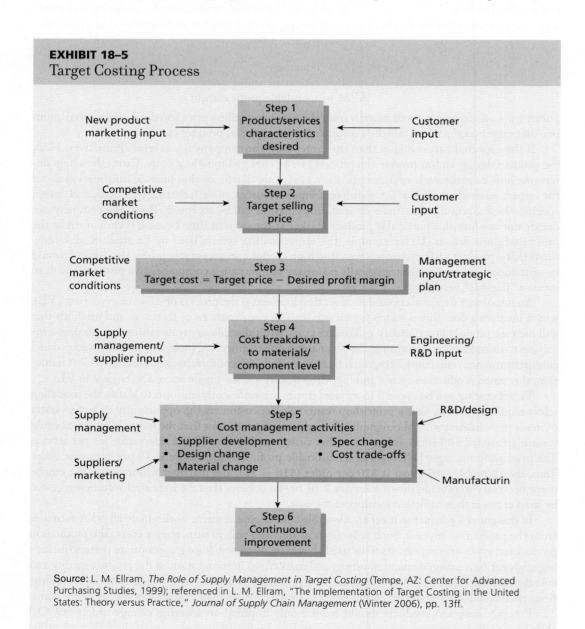

EXHIBIT 18–5
Target Costing Process

Step 1 — Product/services characteristics desired
(New product marketing input; Customer input)

Step 2 — Target selling price
(Competitive market conditions; Customer input)

Step 3 — Target cost = Target price − Desired profit margin
(Competitive market conditions; Management input/strategic plan)

Step 4 — Cost breakdown to materials/component level
(Supply management/supplier input; Engineering/R&D input)

Step 5 — Cost management activities
• Supplier development
• Design change
• Material change
• Spec change
• Cost trade-offs
(Supply management; Suppliers/marketing; R&D/design; Manufacturin)

Step 6 — Continuous improvement

Source: L. M. Ellram, *The Role of Supply Management in Target Costing* (Tempe, AZ: Center for Advanced Purchasing Studies, 1999); referenced in L. M. Ellram, "The Implementation of Target Costing in the United States: Theory versus Practice," *Journal of Supply Chain Management* (Winter 2006), pp. 13ff.

increase product quality, and/or improve the production process *after* manufacturing activities have begun. These cost reductions are designed to keep the profit margin relatively stable as the product price is reduced over the product life cycle. Exhibit 18–6 compares target and kaizen costing. Kaizen initiatives often involve multifunctional teams that study specific production issues to lower costs or improve quality. For example, at Gems Sensors Inc., based in Connecticut, employees conduct two or three kaizen initiatives each month. Each initiative involves a team of up to 15 employees with diverse expertise.[2] Kaizen methods are also being used by companies to reduce energy consumption and the environmental impacts of operations.

Just-In-Time Systems

Just-in-time (JIT) is a philosophy about when to do something. The "when" is as needed and the "something" is a production, purchasing, or delivery activity. The JIT philosophy is applicable in all departments of all types of organizations. JIT's three primary goals follow:

1. eliminating any production process or operation that does not add value to the product/service,
2. continuously improving production/performance efficiency, and
3. reducing the total cost of production/performance while increasing quality.

LO.5
What is the just-in-time philosophy? What modifications does JIT require in accounting systems?

EXHIBIT 18–6
Comparison of Target and Kaizen Costing

	Target Costing	Kaizen Costing
What?	A procedural approach for determining a maximum allowable cost for an identifiable, proposed product, assuming a given target profit margin	A mandate to reduce costs, increase product quality, and/or improve production processes through continuous improvement efforts
Used for?	New products	Existing products
When?	Development stage (includes design)	Primary production stages (introduction and growth); possibly, but not probably, maturity
How?	Works best by aiming at a specified cost reduction objective; used to set original production standards	Works best by aiming at a specified cost reduction objective; reductions are integrated into original production standards to sustain improvements and provide new challenges
Why?	Extremely large potential for cost reduction because 80% to 90% of a product's lifelong costs are embedded in the product during the design and development stages	Limited potential for reducing cost of existing products, but may provide useful information for future target costing efforts
Focus?	All product inputs (material, labor, and overhead elements) as well as production processes and supplier components	Depends on where efforts will be most effective in reducing production costs; generally begins with the most costly component and (in more mature companies) ends with overhead components

[2]Nancy Syverson, *Kaizen: Continuing to Improve,* http://www.impomag.com/scripts/ShowPR.asp?RID=2090&CommonCount=0 (last accessed 8/27/07).

These goals are totally consistent with and supportive of the total quality management (TQM) program discussed in Chapter 17. The elements of the JIT philosophy are outlined in Exhibit 18–7. Because JIT is most commonly discussed with regard to manufacturing or production activities, this is a logical starting point. JIT manufacturing originated in Japan where a card, or *kanban* (pronounced "kahn-bahn"), was used to communicate between work centers to control the flow of in-process products. A *just-in-time manufacturing system* attempts to acquire components and produce inventory units only as they are needed, minimize product defects, and reduce cycle/setup times for acquisition and production.

Production has traditionally been dictated by the need to smooth operating activities over time. Although allowing a company to maintain a steady workforce and continuous machine utilization, smooth production often creates products that must be stored until they are sold. Traditionally, companies filled warehouses with products that were not currently in demand, often while failing to meet promised customer delivery dates on other products. One cause of this dysfunctional behavior was management's preoccupation with spreading overhead over a maximum number of products being produced. This obsession unwittingly resulted in much unwanted inventory, huge inventory carrying costs, and other operating problems to be discussed subsequently.

Thus, raw material and work in process inventories were historically maintained at levels considered sufficient to compensate for inefficiencies in acquisition and/or production. Exhibit 18–8 depicts these inefficiencies or problems as "rocks" in a stream of "water" that represents inventory. The traditional philosophy is that the water level (inventory) should be kept high enough for the rocks to be so deeply submerged that there will be "smooth sailing" in production activity. The intent of this technique is to avoid the original problems, but in fact, it creates a new one. By obscuring the problems, the excess "water" adds to the difficulty of making corrections. The JIT manufacturing philosophy is to lower the water level, expose the rocks, and eliminate them to the extent possible. The shallower stream will then flow more smoothly and rapidly than the deep river.

Changes Needed to Implement JIT Manufacturing

Implementation of a just-in-time system requires a long-term commitment. Toyota invested more than 20 years to develop the system and realize significant benefits from it. JIT techniques are

EXHIBIT 18–7
Elements of a JIT Philosophy

- Quality is essential at all times; work to eliminate defects and scrap.
- Employees often have the best knowledge of ways to improve operations; listen to them.
- Employees generally have more talents than are being used; train them to be multiskilled and increase their productivity.
- Ways to improve operations are always available; constantly look for them, being certain to make fundamental changes rather than superficial ones.
- Creative thinking doesn't cost anything; use it to find ways to reduce costs before making expenditures for additional resources.
- Suppliers are essential to operations; establish and cultivate good relationships with suppliers and, if possible, use long-term contracts.
- Inventory is an asset that generates no revenue while it is held in stock so it can be viewed as a "liability"; eliminate it to the extent possible.
- Storage space is directly related to inventories; eliminate it in response to the elimination of inventories.
- Long cycle times cause inventory buildup; keep cycle times as short as possible by using frequent deliveries.

EXHIBIT 18–8
Depiction of Traditional and JIT Production Philosophies

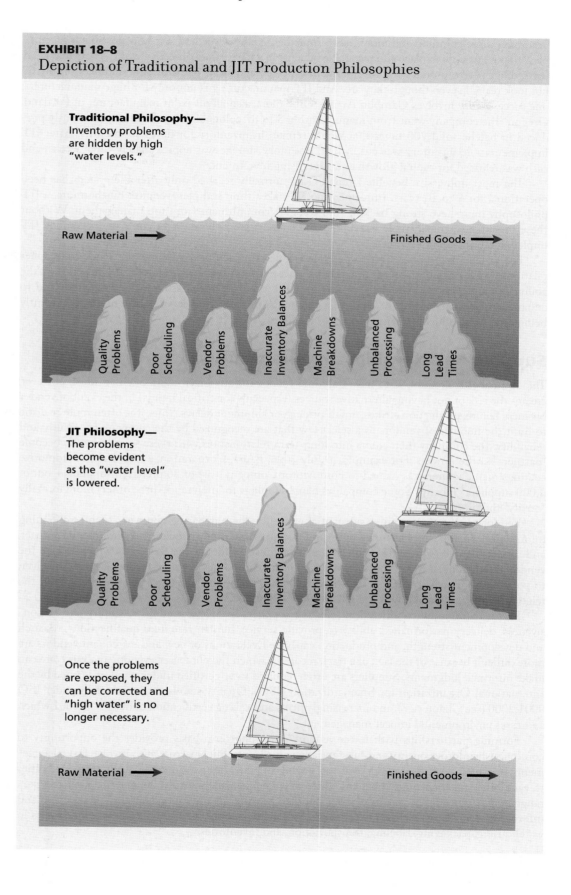

Traditional Philosophy—
Inventory problems
are hidden by high
"water levels."

Raw Material →

Finished Goods →

Quality Problems
Poor Scheduling
Vendor Problems
Inaccurate Inventory Balances
Machine Breakdowns
Unbalanced Processing
Long Lead Times

JIT Philosophy—
The problems
become evident
as the "water level"
is lowered.

Quality Problems
Poor Scheduling
Vendor Problems
Inaccurate Inventory Balances
Machine Breakdowns
Unbalanced Processing
Long Lead Times

Once the problems
are exposed, they
can be corrected and
"high water" is no
longer necessary.

Raw Material →

Finished Goods →

becoming more common and more easily implemented, however, and it is now possible for a company to put a system in place and recognize benefits in a fairly short time. In a world where managers work diligently to produce improvements of a percentage point or two, some numbers simply do not look realistic even though they are. And JIT manufacturing is not only for huge manufacturers: one success story involves Gamblin Artist's Oil Colors, a small oil-paint manufacturer in Portland, Oregon. The company went from manufacturing 3 to 87 colors of paint. Paint was previously produced in batches of 1,200 tubes that would remain in inventory for up to six months. After JIT implementation, inventory was cut in half; inventory storage was approximately three weeks; and cash was released for capital growth and advertising investment.[3]

The most impressive benefits from JIT are normally reached only after the system has been operational for 5 to 10 years. Implementing JIT takes time and perseverance. Furthermore, a JIT philosophy must have strong backing and resource commitment from top management. Without these ingredients, considerable retraining, and support from all levels of company personnel, JIT implementation will not succeed.

For just-in-time production to be effective, certain modifications must be made to supplier relationships, distribution, product design, product processing, and plant layout. JIT depends on the ability of employees and suppliers to compress the time, distance, resources, and activities and to enhance interactions needed to produce a company's products and services. The methods currently being used successfully by many companies are discussed next.

Supplier Relationships and Distribution

The optimal JIT situation is to have only one vendor for any given item. Such an ideal, however, creates the risk of not having alternative sources (especially for critical inputs) in the event of vendor business failure, production strikes, unfair pricing, or shipment delays. Thus, it is often more realistic to limit the number of vendors to a select few that are recognized by the company for quality and reliability. The company then enters into long-term relationships with these suppliers, who become "partners" in the process. For example, in July 2006, BASF Corporation, a world-class automotive coatings manufacturer, was named to Ford Motor Company's list of 36 preferred suppliers—out of 2,000 suppliers globally.[4] Some companies name suppliers to "preference" lists; others more formally "certify" the suppliers.

Vendor certification requires substantial efforts by the purchasing company, such as obtaining information on the supplier's operating philosophy, costs, product quality, environmental impact, and service. People from various functional areas must decide on the factors by which to rate the vendor and then must weigh those factors as to relative importance. Rapid feedback should be given to potential vendors/suppliers so that they can, if necessary, make changes prior to the start of the relationship or understand why the relationship will not occur.

Factors commonly considered in selecting suppliers include a vendor's reliability and responsiveness, delivery performance, ability to provide service, human resources qualifications, research and development strength, and production capacity. Evaluations of new and infrequent vendors are more difficult because of the lack of a track record by which the purchaser's vendor analysis team can make informed judgments. Suppliers are often required to be certified under standards issued by the International Organization for Standardization (ISO). Quality standards are specified under ISO 9001:2000 (see Chapter 17), and increasingly firms are seeking certification under ISO 14001 which addresses environmental impact management.

Forming partnerships with fewer vendors on a long-term basis provides the opportunity to continuously improve quality and substantially reduce costs. Such partnerships involve formal agreements in which both the vendor and the buying organization commit to specific responsibilities to each other for their mutual benefit. These agreements usually involve long-term purchasing arrangements according to specified terms and can provide for the mutual sharing of expertise and information. Such partnerships permit members of the supply chain to eliminate redundancies in warehousing, packaging, labeling, transportation, and inventories.

---

[3]Jane Applegate, "Just-in-time Manufacturing," Entrepreneur.com (May 30, 2001); http://www.entrepreneur.com/management/operations/inventory/article40850.html (last accessed 8/27/07).

[4]Anonymous, "BASF Named by Ford as Preferred Supplier of Automotive Products and Services," WebWire (July 18, 2006); http://www.webwire.com/ViewPressRel.asp?aId=16884 (last accessed 8/27/07).

Product Design

Products should be designed to use the fewest number of dissimilar parts and to minimize production steps and risks. For example, one company found that it used 29 different types of screws to manufacture a single product. Downtime was excessive because screwdrivers were continuously being passed among workers. Changing to one type of screw significantly reduced production time. In another example, a restaurant chain found that it spent an inordinate amount of time washing fresh lettuce because of the safety hazards posed if the lettuce were improperly washed. Buying prewashed, precut lettuce solved the problem by simplifying in-house operations and reducing contaminant threats.[5]

Parts standardization does not necessarily result in identical finished products. Many companies are finding that they can produce a larger number of variations in finished products from just a few basic models. The production process is designed so that the vast proportion of parts and tasks can be standardized and added or performed prior to beginning variation work, which comes near the end of the process. Such differentiation is aided by flexible manufacturing systems and computer-integrated manufacturing, which are discussed later in this chapter.

Products should be designed for the quality desired and should require zero, or a minimal number of, engineering changes (ECOs) after the design is released for production. As mentioned earlier, approximately 80 to 90 percent of all product costs have been established by the time the production design team has completed only 25 to 50 percent of its work. An effective arrangement for a vendor–purchaser partnership is to have the vendor's engineers participate in the design phase of the purchasing company's product; an alternative is to provide product specifications and allow the vendor company to draft the design for approval.

If costs are to be significantly affected, design changes must be made early in the process. As discussed in Chapter 4, ECOs create significant costs for NVA activities. Regardless of whether a company embraces JIT, time that is spent doing work that adds no value to the production process should be viewed as wasted time. Effective activity analysis eliminates such NVA work and its unnecessary cost.

From another point of view, good product design should address all concerns of the intended consumers, even product recyclability. For example, an automobile plant can be equipped to receive and take apart used-up models, remanufacture various parts, and then send them back into the marketplace. Thus, companies are considering remanufacturing as part of their design and processing capabilities. The environmental impact of products can be dramatically altered if products are designed to be remanufactured or recycled at the end of their useful lives.

Product Processing

In the production processing stage, one primary JIT consideration is the reduction of machine setup time so that processing can shift between products more often and at a lower cost. Costs of reducing setup time are more than recovered by the savings derived from reducing downtime, in-process inventory, and material handling as well as by increasing safety, flexibility, and ease of operation. The following quote captures the value of reduced setup times. The quote doesn't derive from Toyota or a twenty-first century management guru; it is from Henry Ford in 1926.

> *One of the most noteworthy accomplishments in keeping the price of (our) products low is the gradual shortening of the production cycle. The longer an article is in the process of manufacture and the more it is moved about, the greater is its ultimate cost.*[6]

Most companies implementing rapid tool-setting procedures have been able to obtain setup times of 10 minutes or less. Such companies use a large number of low-cost setups rather than the traditional approach of a small number of more expensive setups. Under JIT, setup cost is considered almost purely variable rather than fixed as it was in the traditional manufacturing environment. One way to reduce machine setup time is to have workers perform as many setup tasks as possible while

[5]Nancy Backus, "The Changing Face of Fast Food," *Food Product Design* (June 2004), http://www.foodproductdesign.com/current/0604FFOC.html (last accessed 8/27/07).
[6]Anonymous, *Reducing Setup Times: A Foundation for Lean Manufacturing*, http://www.imec.org/imec.nsf/All/Solutions_Source_Reducing_Setup_Times?OpenDocument (last accessed 8/27/07).

the machine is online and running. All unnecessary movements by workers or of material should be eliminated. Teams similar to pit-stop crews at auto races can be used to perform setup operations, with each team member handling a specialized task. Based on past results, it appears that with planning and education, setup times can be reduced by 50 percent or more.

Another essential part of product processing is the institution of high-quality standards because JIT has the goal of zero defects. Under JIT systems, quality is determined on a continual basis rather than at quality control checkpoints. Continuous quality is achieved by first ensuring the quality of vendors' products at purchase. Workers and machines (such as optical scanners) monitor quality during production. Controlling quality on an ongoing basis significantly reduces the assessment cost of obtaining high quality. The JIT philosophy recognizes that it is less costly *not* to make mistakes than to correct them after they have been made. Unfortunately, quality control and scrap costs are often buried in production cost standards, making such costs hard to identify.

The ability to standardize work so that every worker performs according to stated procedures without variation, on time, every time is important in any process. Standard procedures indicate the most efficient way to conduct a particular task as well as allow planning, supervising, and training tasks to be more efficiently and effectively conducted. Standardization also provides the ability

Building in quality checks, such as optical scanners, into product processing helps reduce the costs of obtaining high quality.

to improve processes because tasks are performed with consistency. It is nearly impossible to improve an unstable process because the high level of variation makes the cause-and-effect relationships hard to identify so that modifications can be made.

Plant Layout

Traditionally, manufacturing plants were designed to conform with functional areas; similar machines and workers with similar specialized skills were placed together. For JIT to work effectively, the physical plant must be conducive to the flow of goods and the location of workers and to increasing the value added per square foot of plant space. Manufacturing plants should be designed to minimize material handling time, lead time, and movement of goods from raw material input to completion of the finished product. This goal often requires that machines or workers be arranged in S- or U-shaped production groupings, commonly referred to as manufacturing cells (see Exhibit 18–9), to generate the most efficient and effective production process for a particular product type. This streamlined design allows for more visual controls to be instituted for problems such as excess inventory, production defects, equipment malfunctions, and out-of-place tools. It also allows for greater teamwork and quicker exchange of vital information.

The informational arrows in Exhibit 18–9 indicate how production is "pulled" through the system as successive downstream work centers issue their kanbans to acquire the goods or services from their upstream suppliers needed to produce the goods or services demanded by their downstream customers. Many pull systems today use electronic methods such as computer networks (rather than cards) to send requests for goods or services to upstream workstations.

Exhibit 18–10 (page 686) illustrates the flow of three products through a factory before and after the redesign of factory floor space. In the "before" diagram, processes were grouped together by function, and products flowed through the plant depending on the type of processing needed to be performed. If the company uses JIT and a cellular design, the storage space requirements are substantially reduced because goods should be ordered only as needed. Products also flow through the plant more rapidly. Products 1 and 2 use the same flow, except that Product 2 skips the assembly

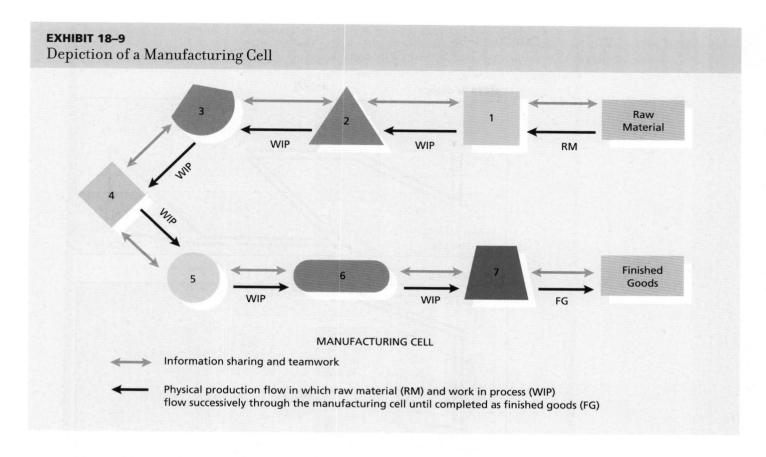

EXHIBIT 18–9
Depiction of a Manufacturing Cell

MANUFACTURING CELL

⟷ Information sharing and teamwork

⟵ Physical production flow in which raw material (RM) and work in process (WIP) flow successively through the manufacturing cell until completed as finished goods (FG)

process. When plant layout is redesigned to incorporate manufacturing cells, workers have the opportunity to broaden their skills and deepen their involvement in the process because of multiprocess handling. Workers are multiskilled, trained to monitor numerous machines, more flexible, and less bored because they are performing a variety of tasks. The ability to oversee an entire process can prompt employee suggestions on improvement techniques that would not have been visible had the employee been working on a single facet of the process.[7]

Although highly automated equipment can run without direct labor involvement, it still requires monitoring. Employees must be available for oversight if an automated piece of equipment is programmed to stop when a given situation arises. The "situation" can be positive (a specified quantity of production has been reached) or negative (a quality defect has been indicated). Use of preprogrammed factory equipment is referred to as autonomation to distinguish it from automated factories in which the machinery is not programmed to stop when specified situations arise. Autonomation derives from the principle of "jidoka" in Toyota's lean manufacturing philosophy, which calls for production to halt when there is a malfunction in the production process. Because machines "know" the certain conditions they are expected to sense, one worker is able to oversee several machines in a single manufacturing cell concurrently.

Logistics of the JIT Environment

In a JIT environment, a certain degree of logistical assistance is developing in the areas of information technology (IT), new support services, and new value-chain relationships. Such advancements

[7]The average U.S. company receives about one suggestion per year from every six eligible employees. On the other hand, Japanese companies receive an average of 32 suggestions. See John Tschohl, "Be Bad: Employee Suggestion Program Cuts Costs, Increases Profit," *The Canadian Manager* (Winter 1998), pp. 23–24.

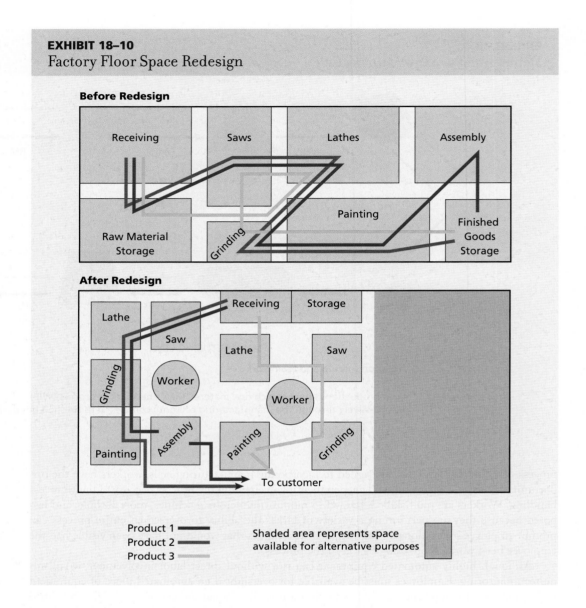

EXHIBIT 18–10
Factory Floor Space Redesign

can enhance the effectiveness and efficiency of companies employing JIT in the preproduction stage, during production, and after production.

JIT can be employed within the context of more comprehensive management models such as TQM and the six-sigma method. As discussed in Chapter 17, six-sigma is a high-performance, data-driven approach to analyzing and solving the root causes of business problems. There are five steps for a successful application of the six-sigma method:

Define ——→ Measure ——→ Analyze ——→ Improve ——→ Control

First, the company defines the projects and processes that need improvement; second, appropriate measurements for success are identified; third, data are gathered and analyzed to ascertain how the organization is working to achieve its goals; fourth, improvement projects are designed and instituted; and, fifth, control measures are implemented to sustain performance. It may not be possible to achieve the control step of the six-sigma cycle process in a single iteration; the middle three steps may require multiple iterations.

The **Internet business model** has become the new orthodoxy, transforming cost and service equations across the corporate landscape. This model refers to a business with (1) few physical assets, (2) little management hierarchy, and (3) a direct pipeline to customers. In this environment, electronic commerce has transformed supply-chain integration and delivered substantial cost savings. This model's benefits are cited in the following quote:

> *Web-based technology allows the sharing of information, not just one-to-one—but one-to-many—and even many-to-many. . . . It is not simply a case of providing access to a Web site, but creating "extranets" where key customers and suppliers have access to "virtual private networks" that enable collaborative planning, forecasting, and replenishment. It is like traditional one-to-one customer/supplier scheduling, but now it has gone to one-to-many—and the supplier can turn around and do the same thing with all of its suppliers. It is basically linking the entire supply chain.*[8]

Supply-chain management is the cooperative strategic planning, controlling, and problem-solving activities conducted by a company and its vendors and customers to generate efficient and effective transfers of goods and services within the supply chain. Three levels of business-to-business (B2B) relationships exist in e-commerce: transactional, information sharing, and collaboration:

> *Transactional relationships include the use of EDI [electronic data interchange] to automate such things as purchase orders and invoices. At the information-sharing level, firms might exchange production schedules or details on the status of orders. At the highest level—collaboration—information is not just exchanged and transmitted, but the buyer and seller also jointly develop it. Generally this information deals with future product plans and needs. . . . However, unlike an information-sharing relationship, information is not shared on an FYI-basis, since either trading partner may change it until both parties agree.*[9]

The use of e-commerce has advanced more rapidly for the acquisition of certain types of inputs than for others. For example, travel arrangements and office supplies and equipment are acquired much more frequently than manufacturing inputs, which are still most frequently acquired through traditional long-term supplier relationships.[10]

In addition to the IT improvements in product design for manufacturability, simulation software is available for developing production systems that can enhance financial performance. The software can be used to observe the important interactions and dependencies that exist in organizational systems and allow the testing of equipment reconfigurations, distribution channel changes, and quality enhancement programs. Benefits from such simulations include greater and faster throughput, reduced inventory levels, reduced waste or spoilage, minimization of errors, and cost savings from reduced run time, setup time, or transportation time.

JIT companies often adopt focused factory arrangements that allow a closer connection between production operations and vendors. The vendors often supply a limited number of specified products or perform a limited number of unique services for the JIT company. Vendors can be other divisions of the same organization or separate, nonrelated companies. Focused factory arrangements can also involve relocation or plant modernization by a vendor, and financial assistance from the JIT manufacturer can be available to recoup such investments. In addition, the vendor benefits from long-term supply contracts. One downside, especially for small vendors, of focused factory arrangements is that they could create overreliance on a single customer. A decline in the business of the primary customer or demands by that customer for lower prices can be disastrous for the focused factory.

Accounting Implications of JIT

Companies adopting a JIT inventory and/or flexible manufacturing system must be aware of the significant accounting implications such a system creates. A primary accounting impact occurs in variance analysis. Because the traditional standard cost accounting system discussed in Chapter 7 is

---

[8]John H. Sheridan, "Pushing Production to New Heights," *Industry Week* (September 21, 1998), pp. 43ff. Reprinted with permission from *Industry Week*. Copyright Penton Media, Inc., Cleveland, Ohio.
[9]Ibid.
[10]Kip R. Krumwiede, Monte R. Swain, and Kevin D. Stocks, "10 Ways E-Business Can Reduce Costs," *Strategic Finance* (July 2003), pp. 25–29.

primarily historical in nature, its main goal is variance reporting so that variances can be analyzed for cause-and-effect relationships to eliminate similar problems in the future.

In JIT systems, variance reporting and analysis essentially disappear because such information is untimely. Variances first appear physically (rather than financially); thus, JIT mandates immediate recognition of variances so that causes can be ascertained and, if possible, promptly remedied if unfavorable or exploited if favorable. JIT workers are trained to monitor quality and efficiency during, rather than at the end of, production. Further, if the firm is using statistical process controls, workers can predict the potential for production defects and take measures to prevent the defects from occurring. Therefore, the number and monetary significance of end-of-period variances being reported for managerial control should be limited.

Under a JIT system, long-term price agreements have been made with vendors, so material price variances should be minimal. The JIT accounting system should be designed so that purchase orders cannot be issued without manager approval for an amount higher than the designated price.[11] This practice assures that the variance amount and its cause be known in advance, providing an opportunity to eliminate the excess expenditure before it occurs. Calls can be made to the vendor to negotiate the price, or other vendors can be contacted for quotes.

The ongoing use of specified or certified vendors also provides the ability to control material quality. It is becoming relatively common for companies to require that their vendors, regardless of global location, maintain quality standards and submit to quality assurance audits. Because better control of raw material quality is expected, few if any material quantity variances should be caused by substandard material. If usage standards are accurate based on established machine-paced efficiency, there should be virtually no favorable usage variance of material during production. Unfavorable use of material should be promptly detected because of the ongoing observation of processing by machines and/or humans. When an unfavorable variance occurs, the manufacturing process is stopped to correct the error causing the unfavorable material usage variance to be minimized.

One type of quantity variance is not caused by errors but by engineering change orders made to the product specifications. A JIT system has two comparison standards: an annual standard and a current standard. Design modifications would change the current standard but not the annual one. The annual standard is one of the bases for the preparation and execution of the company's master budget, and it is ordinarily kept intact because all of the financial plans and arrangements for the year that are covered by the master budget are predicated on the standards and plans used to prepare it.

Such a procedure allows comparisons to be made that indicate the cost effects of ECOs implemented after a product has begun to be manufactured. Exhibit 18–11 shows the calculation of a material quantity variance caused by an ECO. The portion of the total quantity variance caused by the ECO ($2,700 U) is shown separately from that caused by efficiency ($540 F). Labor, overhead, and/or conversion can also have ECO variances.

Labor variances in an automated just-in-time system should be minimal if standard rates and times have been set appropriately. Labor time standards should be carefully evaluated after the implementation of a JIT production system. If the plant is not entirely automated, redesigning the physical layout and minimizing any NVA labor activities should decrease the direct labor time component.

An accounting alternative that could occur in a JIT system is the use of a conversion cost category for purposes of cost control rather than the use of separate labor and overhead categories. This category becomes more useful as factories reduce the direct labor cost component through continuous improvements and automation. A standard departmental or manufacturing cell conversion cost per unit of product (or per hour of production time per manufacturing cell) can be calculated rather than individual standards for labor and overhead. Denominators in each case would be practical or theoretical capacity measured by an appropriate activity base.[12] If time were used as the base, the conversion cost for a day's production would equal the number of units produced multiplied by the standard number of production hours multiplied by the standard cost per hour. Variances would be determined by comparing actual cost to the designated standard. However, direct labor is a very

[11]This same procedure can be implemented under a traditional standard cost system as well as under a JIT system. However, whereas it is less commonly found in a traditional system, it is a requirement under JIT.
[12]Practical or theoretical capacity is the appropriate measure because the goal of JIT is virtually continuous processing. In a highly automated plant, these capacities more closely reflect world-class status than does expected annual capacity.

EXHIBIT 18–11

Material Variances under a JIT System

Annual standard		
8 feet of material M × $3.05	$ 24.40	
5 feet of material N × $3.35	16.75	
	$ 41.15	
Current standard		
7 feet of material M × $3.05	$ 21.35	
6 feet of material N × $3.35	20.10	
	$ 41.45	
Production during month	9,000 units	
Usage during month		
64,800 feet of material M × $3.05	$197,640	
52,200 feet of material N × $3.35	174,870	
Total cost of material used	$372,510	
Material quantity variance		
9,000 × 7 × $3.05	$192,150	
9,000 × 6 × $3.35	180,900	
Material cost at current standard	$373,050	
Actual material cost	(372,510)	
Material quantity variance	$ 540	F
Engineering change variance for material		
9,000 × 8 × $3.05	$219,600	
9,000 × 5 × $3.35	150,750	
Material cost at annual standard	$370,350	
Material cost at current standard	(373,050)	
ECO variance	$ 2,700	U

small part of production in a JIT environment. Use of efficiency variances to evaluate workers can cause excess inventory because these workers are trying to "keep busy" to minimize this variance. Therefore, direct labor efficiency variances in a "cell" setting could be counterproductive.

In addition to minimizing and adjusting the variance calculations, a JIT system can have a major impact on inventory accounting. Companies employing JIT production processes would no longer require a separate raw material inventory classification because material would be acquired only when and as production occurs. Instead, JIT companies could use a Raw and In-Process (RIP) Inventory account.

The focus of accounting in a JIT system is on the plant's output to the customer.[13] Each sequential activity in a production process depends on the previous activity; thus, any problems will quickly cause the system to stop the production process. Individual daily accounting for the costs of production will no longer be necessary because all costs should be at standard, and variations will be observed and corrected almost immediately.

Additionally, fewer costs need to be allocated to products because more costs can be traced directly to their related output in a JIT system. Costs are incurred in specified cells on a time (per hour or per minute) or per-unit basis. In a comprehensive JIT system, energy is considered a direct production cost because there should be a minimum of machine downtime or unplanned idle time for workers. Virtually the only costs that need to be allocated are costs associated with the structure (building depreciation, rent, taxes, and insurance) and machinery depreciation.[14] The reduction of

[13] A company may wish to measure output of each manufacturing cell or work center rather than plant output. Such measurements can indicate problems in a given area but do not correlate with the JIT philosophy of the team approach, plantwide attitude, and total cost picture.

[14] A company using activity-based costing may not even need to allocate these costs because, under ABC, they would be considered nonallocable, organizational-level costs.

allocations provides more useful measures of cost control and performance evaluation than have been traditionally available.

Backflush costing is a streamlined cost accounting method that speeds up, simplifies, and minimizes accounting effort in an environment that minimizes inventory balances, requires few allocations, uses standard costs, and has few variances from standard. During the period, this costing method records purchases of raw material and accumulates actual conversion costs. Then, at a predetermined trigger point such as (1) at completion of production or (2) upon the sale of goods, an entry is made to allocate the total costs incurred to Cost of Goods Sold or to Finished Goods Inventory using standard production costs.

Information for Eastern Manufacturing, a ceramics producer, is used to illustrate JIT system backflush entries. To establish a foundation set of transactions from which to illustrate subsequent alternative recordings in a backflush costing system, entries for one of Eastern's products are presented in Exhibit 18–12. The product's standard production cost is $65.25. A long-term contract with Eastern Manufacturing's direct material supplier indicates a cost of $19.25 per unit, so no material price variance exists at the point of purchase. Beginning inventories for July are assumed to be zero. Standard conversion cost per unit is $46.00.

The following selected T-accounts summarize the activity presented in Exhibit 18–12.

Raw and In-Process Inventory					Conversion Cost Control			
(1)	392,500	(4)	1,305,000	(2)	921,750	(3)		920,000
(3)	920,000							
Bal.	7,500							

Finished Goods Inventory					Cost of Goods Sold		
(4)	1,305,000	(5)	1,291,950	(5)	1,291,950		
Bal.	13,050						

Accounts Receivable			Sales		
(5)	2,178,000			(5)	2,178,000

Four alternatives to the entries presented in Exhibit 18–12 follow. First, if production time were extremely short, Eastern Manufacturing might not journalize raw material purchases until completion of production. In such a case, and in addition to recording entries (2) and (5) in Exhibit 18–12, the entry to replace entries (1), (3), and (4) follows. Completion of the finished goods is the trigger point for this entry.

Raw and In-Process Inventory	7,500	
Finished Goods Inventory (20,000 × $65.25)	1,305,000	
Accounts Payable		392,500
Conversion Cost Control (20,000 × $46.00)		920,000
To record completed production and accounts payable,		
and adjust RIP inventory account valuation		

Second, if goods were shipped immediately to customers on completion, Eastern Manufacturing could use another alternative in which the entries to complete and sell products would be combined. Doing so would replace entries (3), (4), and the first element in (5) in Exhibit 18–12. Entries (1), (2), and the second element in (5) in Exhibit 18–12 would still be needed. Sale of the products is the trigger point for this entry.

Finished Goods Inventory (200 × $65.25)	13,050	
Cost of Goods Sold (19,800 × $65.25)	1,291,950	
Raw and In-Process Inventory (20,000 × $19.25)		385,000
Conversion Cost Control (20,000 × $46.00)		920,000
To record sale of products and adjust RIP		
and FG inventory account valuations		

The third alternative reflects the ultimate JIT system, in which only one entry is made—other than recording entry (2) in Exhibit 18–12. Sale of the products is the trigger point for this entry. For Eastern Manufacturing, this entry would be

---

EXHIBIT 18–12

Basic Entries Used to Illustrate Backflush Costing

Eastern Manufacturing's standard production cost per unit:

Direct material	$19.25
Conversion	46.00
Total cost	$65.25

No beginning inventories exist.

(1) Purchased $392,500 of direct material in July:

Raw and In-Process Inventory	392,500	
Accounts Payable		392,500
To record material purchased at standard cost under a long-term agreement with supplier		

(2) Incurred $921,750 of conversion costs in July:

Conversion Costs	921,750	
Various accounts		921,750
To record conversion costs; various accounts include Wages Payable for direct and indirect labor, Accumulated Depreciation, Supplies, etc.		

(3) Applied conversion costs to RIP for 20,000 units completed:

Raw and In-Process Inventory (20,000 × $46.00)	920,000	
Conversion Costs		920,000
To apply labor and overhead to units completed		

(4) Transferred 20,000 units of production in July:

Finished Goods Inventory (20,000 × $65.25)	1,305,000	
Raw and In-Process Inventory		1,305,000
To transfer completed goods from WIP		

(5) Sold 19,800 units on account in July for $110 each:

Accounts Receivable (19,800 × $110)	2,178,000	
Sales		2,178,000
To record goods sold on account		

Cost of Goods Sold (19,800 × $65.25)	1,291,950	
Finished Goods Inventory		1,291,950
To record cost of goods sold		

Ending inventories:

Raw and In-Process Inventory ($1,312,500 − $1,305,000)	$7,500
Finished Goods Inventory ($1,305,000 − $1,291,950)	$13,050

In addition, there are underapplied conversion costs of $1,750 ($921,750 − $920,000).

Raw and In-Process Inventory (minimal overpurchases)	7,500	
Finished Goods Inventory (minimal overproduction)	13,050	
Cost of Goods Sold	1,291,950	
Accounts Payable		392,500
Conversion Cost Control		920,000
To adjust inventory account valuations and record accounts payable		

A fourth alternative charges all costs to the Cost of Goods Sold account, with a subsequent backflush of costs to the Raw and In-Process Inventory and the Finished Goods Inventory accounts at the end of the period. The following entries replace entries (1), (3), (4), and (5) shown in Exhibit 18–12. Entry (2) in Exhibit 18–12 would still be made at the product sale trigger point.

Cost of Goods Sold	1,312,500	
Accounts Payable		392,500
Conversion Cost Control		920,000
To charge all material, labor, and overhead costs to CGS		
Raw and In-Process Inventory	7,500	
Finished Goods Inventory	13,050	
Cost of Goods Sold		20,550
To adjust inventory account valuations		

Implementation of the JIT philosophy can cause significant cost reductions and productivity improvements. Management should consider the costs of, and benefits provided by, the inventory control alternatives before choosing a system. One qualitative benefit that must be quantified in the decision process is that the use of JIT allows workers as well as managers to concentrate on providing quality service to customers.

LO.6

What are flexible manufacturing systems?

Flexible Manufacturing Systems and Computer-Integrated Manufacturing

Many manufacturers have changed their manufacturing philosophy in the past few decades. Causes of change include (1) automated equipment, (2) a cellular plant layout, (3) computer hardware and software technology, and (4) new manufacturing systems and philosophies such as JIT and activity-based management.

Traditionally, most manufacturing firms employed long production runs to make thousands of identical models of the same products; this process was encouraged by the idea of economies of scale. After each run, the machines would be stopped and a slow and expensive setup would be made to prepare for the next massive production run. Now, many companies are using a new generation of manufacturing known as **flexible manufacturing systems (FMSs)**. An FMS involves a network of robots and material conveyance devices monitored and controlled by computers that allows for rapid production and responsiveness to changes in production needs. Exhibit 18–13 contrasts the dimensions of a traditional manufacturing system with an FMS.

EXHIBIT 18–13

Comparison of Traditional Manufacturing and Flexible Manufacturing System

Factor	Traditional Manufacturing	Flexible Manufacturing System
Product variety	Limited	Extensive
Response time to market needs	Slow	Rapid
Worker tasks	Specialized	Diverse
Production runs	Long	Short
Lot sizes	Massive	Small
Performance rewards basis	Individual	Team
Setups	Slow and expensive	Fast and inexpensive
Product life cycle expectations	Long	Short
Work area control	Centralized	Decentralized
Production activity	Labor intensive	Technology intensive
Information requirements	Batch-based	Online, real-time
Worker knowledge of technology	Low to medium	High

FMSs are used in modular factories and can customize output upon request by customers because the systems have the ability to introduce new products quickly, produce in small lot sizes, make rapid machine and tool setups, and communicate and process large amounts of information. Information is transferred through an electronic network to computers that control the robots performing most of the production activities. The system functions with online, real-time production flow control using fiber optics and local-area networks. Companies are able to operate at high speeds and can quickly and inexpensively stop producing one item and start producing another, making it possible to minimize product costs while building a large assortment of high-quality products to offer customers.

The system can operate in a "lights-out" environment and never tire; thus, the need for direct labor is diminished. However, because workers perform a greater variety of tasks than the narrowly specialized workers of earlier manufacturing eras, workers in a company employing an FMS must be more highly trained than those working in traditional manufacturing environments. Managing manufacturing cells requires that workers have greater authority and responsibility because production and production scheduling changes happen so rapidly on the shop floor that an FMS relies on immediate decisions by persons who "live there" and have a grasp of the underlying facts and conditions.

Two or more FMSs connected via a host computer and an information networking system are generally referred to as **computer-integrated manufacturing (CIM)**. Although an FMS is typically associated with short-volume production runs, many companies (such as Campbell Soup Co., General Motors, and Cummins Engine) use CIM for high-volume lines.

Lean Enterprises

Lean manufacturing refers to making only those items in demand by customers and making those items without waste. Lean manufacturing originated in post-World War II Japan, when Japanese production managers were compelled to develop practices that minimized waste and consumption of resources because access to material, factory equipment, and warehouse space was limited. Lean enterprises use many of the management tools discussed earlier in this chapter such as cellular manufacturing, JIT, six sigma, and autonomation. One of the major themes in lean enterprises is the same as that of JIT: inventory needs to be eliminated to the extent possible because it hides production problems and wastes resources.

Lean enterprises, such as Toyota and Rockwell Automation Power Systems, put pressure on the entire value chain to minimize waste, maximize quality, eliminate activities that add costs but not value to products, and shorten the lead time for delivering products and services. Central to the success of the lean enterprise and its value chain are leveraging technology and training employees. Technology allows for short cycle times, high-quality products, and quick changeovers of production lines. Well-trained employees manage the technology, identify ways to become more efficient, and focus on satisfying the needs of customers. Lean enterprises have raised the competitive bar in many industries through their abilities to quickly develop and sell high-quality products having minimal defects. For some industries, these competitive pressures have led to reduced product life cycles and dramatically reduced time to market for new products. Some of the performance benefits from implementing lean practices are shown in Exhibit 18–14.

The theory of constraints is another important production management tool that is used by lean enterprises.

Theory of Constraints

The **theory of constraints (TOC)** can help management reduce cycle time. This theory indicates that the flow of goods through a production process cannot be at a rate faster than the slowest constraint in the process.[15] A **constraint** is anything that confines or limits the ability of a person or machine to perform a project or function.

Production limitations in a manufacturing environment are caused by human, material, and machine constraints. Some constraints relate to process speed, whereas others relate to absolute

LO.7
How can the theory of constraints help in determining production flow?

---

[15]The theory of constraints was introduced to business environments by Eliyahu Goldratt and Jeff Cox in the book *The Goal* (New Haven, CT: North River Press, Inc./Spectrum Publishing Company, 1986).

EXHIBIT 18–14
Benefits of Being "Lean"

Performance results accomplished by the implementation of lean principles

Business Process Transaction Cycle Time	50 to 90% reduction
Manufacturing Cycle Time	0 to 95% reduction
Inventory	40 to 80% reduction
Manufacturing Floor Space/Office Area	30 to 60% reduction
Productivity	25 to 60% improvement
New Product Development Lead-Time	0 to 50% improvement
Manufacturing/Operating Costs	15 to 25% reduction
Cost of Poor Quality	30 to 50% reduction

Source: UCSD Extension, "Lean Enterprise: A Specialized Certificate Program," http://extension.ucsd.edu/programs/eng/lean.html (last accessed 8/27/07).

production limits such as availability of material or machine time. Still other constraints relate to people and any limitations those people have on their ability to understand, react, or perform at some particular rate of speed. These constraints cannot be totally overcome (because people will never be able to work at the speed of an automated machine) but can be reduced through proper hiring and training. Because the labor content contained in products is declining rapidly as automation increases, constraints caused by machines are often of more concern than human constraints in reducing cycle time.

Constraints, also called **bottlenecks**, are points at which the processing levels are sufficiently slow to cause the other processing mechanisms in the network to experience idle time. Bottlenecks cause the processing of an activity to be impeded. Even a totally automated, "lights-out" process will have some constraints because all machines do not operate at the same speed or handle the same capacity. Therefore, the constraints must be identified and corrected to the extent possible.

Exhibit 18–15 provides a simplistic illustration of a production process constraint. Although Machine 1 can process 90,000 pounds of raw material in an hour, Machine 2 can handle only 40,000 pounds. Of the 70,000 pounds of input, 30,000 pounds of processed material must wait at the constraining machine after an hour of processing. The constraint's effect on production is obvious, but the implications are not quite as clear. Managers have a tendency to want to see machines working, not sitting idle. Consider what this tendency would mean if the desired output were 450,000 pounds rather than 70,000. If Machine 1 were kept in continual use, all 450,000 pounds would be processed through Machine 1 in five hours. However, a backlog of 250,000 pounds [450,000 − 5(40,000)] of processed material would now be waiting at Machine 2! All of this material would require storage space and create additional NVA costs.

Machine constraints also impact quality control. Managers normally choose quality control points to follow the completion of some particular process. When constraint points are known, quality control points should *always* be placed in front of constrained processes. "If you scrap a part before it reaches the bottleneck, all you have lost is a scrapped part. But if you scrap the part after it's passed through the bottleneck, you have lost time that cannot be recovered."[16]

As soon as constraints are known, a company should make the best use of the time or productive capacity the constrained processes provide and limit the constraints' impacts on performance. Options to reduce limitations, such as adding more machines to perform the constrained activity or processing material through other machines, should be investigated. Managing constraints is a process of continuous improvement.

[16]Ibid., p. 156.

EXHIBIT 18–15
Production Constraint

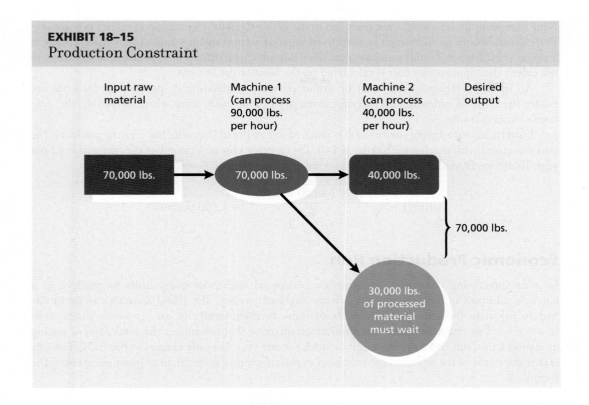

LO.8
How are economic order quantity, order point, and safety stock determined and used?

Appendix

Economic Order Quantity and Related Issues

The concepts of economic order quantity and economic production run are used, respectively, for purchasing and manufacturing decisions.

Economic Order Quantity

Companies making purchasing (rather than production) decisions often compute the **economic order quantity (EOQ)**, which represents the least costly number of units to order. EOQ indicates the optimal balance between ordering and carrying costs by mathematically equating total ordering costs to total carrying costs. EOQ is a tool that is used in conjunction with traditional "push" production and inventory management systems. Because EOQ implies acquiring and holding inventory before it is needed, it is incompatible with "pull" systems such as JIT.

Purchasing managers should first determine which supplier can offer the appropriate quality of goods at the best price in the most reliable manner. After the supplier is selected, the most economical inventory quantity to order—at a single time—is determined. The EOQ formula is

$$EOQ = \sqrt{\frac{(2QO)}{C}}$$

where EOQ = economic order quantity in units
Q = estimated annual quantity used in units
(can be found in the annual purchases budget)
O = estimated cost of placing one order
C = estimated cost to carry 1 unit in stock for one year

Note that unit purchase cost is not included in the EOQ formula. Purchase cost relates to the question of from whom to buy, which is considered separately from the question of how many to buy at a single time. Inventory unit purchase cost does not affect the other EOQ formula costs except to the extent that opportunity cost is calculated on the basis of investment.

All inventory-related costs must be evaluated when purchasing or production decisions are made. The costs of ordering and carrying inventory oppose each other when estimating the economic order quantity.

Eastern Manufacturing uses 64,000 pounds of one material in producing ceramic products. The cost associated with placing each order is $40. The carrying cost of 1 pound of the material is $2 per year. Therefore, Eastern's EOQ for this material is calculated as follows:

$$\text{EOQ} = \sqrt{\frac{(2 \times 64{,}000 \times \$40)}{\$2}} = 1{,}600 \text{ pounds}$$

Economic Production Run

In a manufacturing company, managers are concerned with how many units to produce in a batch in addition to how many units (of raw material) to buy. The EOQ formula can be modified to calculate the appropriate number of units to manufacture in an **economic production run (EPR)**. This estimate reflects the production quantity that minimizes the total costs of setting up a production run and carrying a unit in stock for one year. The only change in the EOQ formula is that the terms of the equation are redefined as manufacturing rather than as purchasing costs. The formula is

$$\text{EPR} = \sqrt{\frac{(2QS)}{C}}$$

where   EPR = economic production run quantity
   Q = estimated annual quantity to be produced in units
       (can be found in annual production budget)
   S = estimated cost of setting up a production run
   C = estimated cost to carry 1 unit in stock for one year

One product manufactured by Eastern Manufacturing is a ceramic sink. A total of 183,750 units of this product are made each year. The setup cost for a ceramic sink run is $240, and the annual carrying cost for each sink is $5. The economic production run quantity of 4,200 sinks is determined as

$$\text{EPR} = \sqrt{\frac{(2 \times 183{,}750 \times \$240)}{\$5}} = 4{,}200 \text{ sinks}$$

The cost differences among various run sizes around the EPR might not be significant. If such costs were insignificant, management would have a range of acceptable, economical production run quantities.

The critical element in using either an EOQ or an EPR model is to properly identify costs, especially carrying costs. This process is often very difficult, and some costs (such as those for facilities, operations, administration, and accounting) that were traditionally viewed as irrelevant fixed costs could, in actuality, be long-term relevant variable costs. Also, the EOQ model does not provide any direction for managers attempting to control all of the separate costs that collectively compose ordering and carrying costs. By considering only the trade-off between ordering and carrying costs, the EOQ model does not lead managers to consider inventory management alternatives that can simultaneously reduce both categories of costs.

Additionally, as companies significantly reduce the necessary setup time (and thus cost) for operations and move toward a "stockless" inventory policy, a more comprehensive cost perspective will indicate a substantially smaller cost per setup and a substantially larger annual carrying cost. These changes will reduce the EOQ and EPR.

Order Point and Safety Stock

The economic order quantity or production run model indicates how many units to order or produce, respectively. Managers are also concerned with the order point, which reflects the level of inventory that triggers the placement of an order for additional units. Determination of the order point is based on three factors: usage, lead time, and safety stock. Usage refers to the quantity of inventory used or sold each day. The lead time for an order is the time in days it takes from placing an order to obtaining or producing the goods. Many times companies can project a constant, average figure for both usage and lead time. The quantity of inventory kept on hand by a company in the event of fluctuating usage or unusual delays in lead time is called safety stock.

If usage is entirely constant and lead time is known with certainty, the order point equals daily usage multiplied by lead time:

$$\text{Order Point} = \text{Daily Usage} \times \text{Lead Time}$$

As an example, assume that Eastern Manufacturing produces ceramic art objects for sale to a chain of department stores. Eastern uses 5,000 pounds of silica sand per day, and the supplier can have the material to Eastern in 2 days. When the stock of silica sand reaches 10,000 pounds, Eastern should order additional sand.

The order point formula minimizes the dollars a company has invested in its inventory. Orders would arrive at precisely the time the inventory reached zero. This formula, however, does not take into consideration unusual events such as variations in production schedules, defective products being provided by suppliers, erratic shipping schedules of the supplier, and late arrival of units shipped. To provide for such events, managers carry a "buffer" safety stock of inventory to protect the company from being out of stock. When a safety stock is maintained, the order point formula becomes:

$$\text{Order Point} = (\text{Daily Usage} \times \text{Lead Time}) + \text{Safety Stock}$$

Safety stock size should be determined based on how crucial the item is to production or to retail sales, the item's purchase cost, and the amount of uncertainty related to both usage and lead time.

One way to estimate the quantity of safety stock is to allow one factor to vary from the norm. For example, either excess usage during normal lead time or normal usage during an excess lead time can be considered in the safety stock calculation. Assume that Eastern Manufacturing never uses more than 8,000 pounds of silica sand in one day. One estimate of the necessary safety stock is 6,000 pounds, computed as follows:

Maximum daily usage	8,000 pounds
Normal daily usage	(5,000) pounds
Excess usage	3,000 pounds
Lead time	× 2 days
Safety stock	6,000 pounds

Using this estimate of safety stock, Eastern Manufacturing would order silica sand when 16,000 pounds (10,000 original order point + 6,000 safety stock) were on hand.

Pareto Inventory Analysis

Unit cost commonly affects the degree of control that should be maintained over an inventory item. As unit cost increases, internal controls (such as inventory access) are typically tightened and a perpetual inventory system is more often used. Recognition of cost–benefit relationships can result in a Pareto inventory analysis, which separates inventory into three groups based on annual cost-to-volume usage.

Items having the highest value are referred to as A items; C items represent the lowest dollar volume of usage. All other inventory items are designated as B items. Exhibit 18–16 illustrates the results of a typical Pareto inventory analysis: 20 percent of the inventory items (A items) accounts for 80 percent of the cost; an additional 30 percent of the items (B items), taken together with the first 20 percent (the A items), accounts for 90 percent of the cost; and the remaining 50 percent of the items (C items) accounts for the remaining 10 percent of the cost.

Once inventory is categorized as A, B, or C, management can determine the best inventory control method for items in each category. A-type inventory should require a perpetual inventory system and would be a likely candidate for JIT purchasing techniques that minimize the funds tied up in inventory investment. The highest control procedures would be assigned to these items. Such a treatment reflects the financial accounting concept of materiality.

Items falling into the C category need only periodic inventory control procedures and can use a two-bin or red-line system. Under a two-bin system, two containers (or stacks) of inventory are available for production needs. When production begins to consume materials in the second container, a purchase order is placed to refill the first container. In a red-line system, a red line is painted on the inventory container at a level representing the order point. Both systems require that production needs and estimates of receipt time from suppliers be fairly accurate.

Having the additional container or stack of inventory on hand is considered to be reasonable based on the insignificant dollar amount of investment involved with C category items. The control placed on C items is probably minimal also because of the lack of materiality of the inventory cost. The type of inventory system (perpetual or periodic) and the level of internal control associated with items in the B category depend on management's judgment. Such judgment is based on the significance of the item to the production process, speed of response time of suppliers, and estimates of benefits to be gained by increased accounting or access controls. Computers have made additional controls over inventory easier and more cost beneficial.

EXHIBIT 18–16
Pareto Inventory Analysis

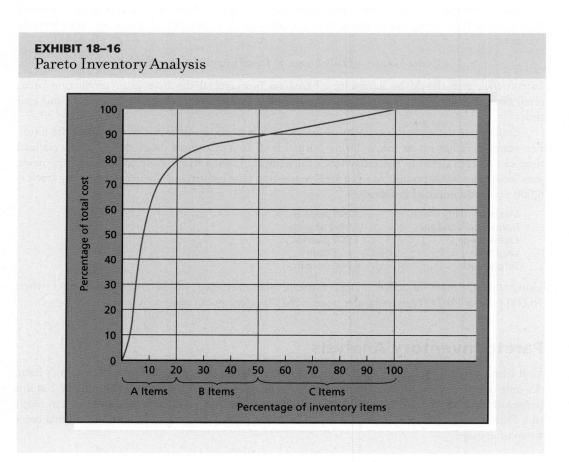

Comprehensive Review Module

Chapter Summary

1. Important value chain relationships for a firm are those

   - with suppliers—to get the highest quality inputs, on time, at a competitive price.

   - with customers—to deliver the features, quality, and value that lead to customer satisfaction.

   - within the firm—to coordinate production activities.

2. Managing inventory costs is important to the firm because inventory

   - produces no value for the firm until it is sold.

   - can hide inefficiencies in production activities.

   - is a significant investment.

3. Two systems for managing inventory and controlling production are called push and pull systems:

   - push systems produce goods to satisfy a production schedule based on economic production run concepts.

   - pull systems produce goods only in response to current customer demand.

4. Product life cycles affect profitability because

   - costs vary across the product life cycles, although most costs are determined in the development stage of the life cycle.

   - sales volume and prices vary across the life cycle stages.

5. Target costing

   - is calculated as estimated selling price minus acceptable profit margin.

   - is a tool to manage production costs

     ➤ in the development stage of the product life cycle.

     ➤ by developing an estimate of an "allowable" production cost (target cost) based on the estimated sales price of the product.

   - forces managers to align the expected production cost with the target cost.

   - is continually reduced over a product's life cycle to spur continuous improvement.

6. Just-in-time (JIT) is a philosophy that states production should not occur until a customer demands the product.

   - Successful implementation of JIT requires

     ➤ elimination of non-value-added activities.

     ➤ a focus on continuous improvement.

     ➤ persistent efforts to reduce inventory.

     ➤ a focus on improving quality of processes.

     ➤ high-quality inputs from vendors.

   - JIT can cause modifications to the accounting system to recognize

     ➤ variances immediately upon occurrence rather than at period-end.

     ➤ that inventories can be sufficiently small to no longer justify separate accounting for raw, in-process, and finished goods. Simpler systems, such as backflush costing, can be adopted.

7. Flexible manufacturing systems

   - integrate computer systems with automated production equipment.

   - are often used in plants organized for cellular manufacturing.

   - minimize the time required to set up for production.

   - are ideal for low-volume, high-quality products.

8. The theory of constraints is a tool for reducing cycle time by

   - maximizing the flow of products through production bottlenecks.

   - overcoming constraints in the flow of goods through a production system.

9. (Appendix) EOQ, EPR, order points, and safety stock are used in purchasing and manufacturing decisions.

*   EOQ

    ➤   is the order quantity that minimizes the sum of ordering and carrying costs for purchased items.

    ➤   is determined based only on variable ordering and carrying costs.

*   EPR

    ➤   is the production quantity that minimizes the sum of the setup and carrying costs for manufactured items.

    ➤   is determined based only on variable setup and carrying costs.

*   Order point

    ➤   is the inventory level of an item that triggers an order for more of that item.

    ➤   is determined in traditional systems using a red-line or two-bin system.

*   Safety stock

    ➤   is a quantity of inventory that buffers a firm from a stock outage during the lead time to replenish the inventory.

    ➤   increases the order point.

Potential Ethical Issues

1. Producing inventory that is not needed relative to current sales demand to increase reported operating profits

2. Avoiding the adoption of innovative production and inventory management methods because of short-run negative effects on profits

3. Blaming suppliers for inventory problems that are, in actuality, artifacts of in-house inventory management mistakes

4. Failing to write-down obsolete or spoiled inventory as soon as information regarding these conditions becomes known

5. Using coercion to force suppliers to yield price concessions so that the cost of manufacturing a product is kept in line with the product's market price

6. Using the adoption of evolving production and inventory management methods as a justification to dismiss workers ▲

Solution Strategies

Target Costing

$$\text{Target Cost} = \text{Expected Long-Range Selling Price} - \text{Desired Profit}$$

Compare predicted total life cycle cost to target cost; if life cycle cost is higher, determine ways to reduce it.

Material and Labor Variances under JIT

Two standards can exist:

1. an annual standard (set and held constant for the year) and

2. a current standard (based on design modifications or engineering change orders).

Generally, firms have minimal, if any, material price variances because prices are set by long-term contracts. A labor rate variance can exist and is calculated in the traditional manner.

Material Quantity Variance

      Actual material cost
    − Material cost at current standard
      Material quantity variance

Engineering Change Variance for Material

      Material cost at annual standard
    − Material cost at current standard
      ECO variance

Labor Efficiency Variance

(Actual labor hours × current standard rate)
− (Standard labor hours × current standard rate)
  Labor efficiency variance

Engineering Change Variance for Labor
(Exists only if a change occurs in the mix of labor used to manufacture the product or through the automation of processes.)

(Standard labor hours × annual standard rate)
− (Standard labor hours × current standard rate)
  ECO variance

(*Appendix*) Economic Order Quantity

$$EOQ = \sqrt{\frac{(2QO)}{C}}$$

where   EOQ = economic order quantity in units
          Q = estimated annual quantity to be used in units
          O = estimated cost of placing one order
          C = estimated cost to carry one unit in stock for one year

(*Appendix*) Economic Production Run

$$EPR = \sqrt{\frac{(2QS)}{C}}$$

where   EPR = economic production run quantity
          Q = estimated annual quantity to be produced in units
          S = estimated cost of setting up a production run
          C = estimated cost to carry one unit in stock for one year

(*Appendix*) Order Point

$$Order\ Point = (Daily\ Usage \times Lead\ Time) + Safety\ Stock$$

Demonstration Problem 1

RotoWax has designed a new consumer product, a floor cleaner and wax, that is expected to have a five-year life cycle. Based on its market research, RotoWax's management has determined that the new product should be packaged in 32-ounce containers, with a selling price of $6 in the first three years and $4 during the last two years. Unit sales are expected as follows:

Year 1	300,000
Year 2	400,000
Year 3	600,000
Year 4	400,000
Year 5	250,000
Total	1,950,000

Variable selling costs are expected to be $1 per package throughout the product's life. Annual fixed selling and administrative costs are estimated to be $500,000. RotoWax management desires a 25 percent profit margin on selling price.

Required:

a. Compute the life cycle target cost to manufacture the product. (Round to the nearest cent.)

b. If RotoWax anticipates the new product will cost $3 per unit to manufacture in the first year, what is the maximum that manufacturing cost can be in the following four years? (Round to the nearest cent.)

c. Suppose that RotoWax engineers determine that expected manufacturing cost per unit over the product life cycle is $2.25. What actions might the company take to reduce this cost?

Solution to the Demonstration Problem 1

a. Step 1—Determine total product life cycle revenue:

Year 1	300,000 × $6 =	$ 1,800,000
Year 2	400,000 × $6 =	2,400,000
Year 3	600,000 × $6 =	3,600,000
Year 4	400,000 × $4 =	1,600,000
Year 5	250,000 × $4 =	1,000,000
Total revenue		$10,400,000

Step 2—Determine average unit revenue during product life (AR):

$$AR = \text{Total Revenue} \div \text{Total Product Life Cycle Units}$$
$$= \$10,400,000 \div 1,950,000 \text{ units}$$
$$= \$5.33 \text{ (rounded)}$$

Step 3—Determine average total fixed selling and administrative cost (ATFS&A):

$$ATFS\&A = (5 \text{ years} \times \$500,000) \div 1,950,000 \text{ units}$$
$$= \$2,500,000 \div 1,950,000$$
$$= \$1.28 \text{ (rounded)}$$

Step 4—Determine unit selling and administrative cost (US&AC):

$$US\&AC = ATFS\&A + \text{Variable Selling Cost}$$
$$= \$1.28 + \$1.00$$
$$= \$2.28$$

Step 5—Calculate target cost (TC):

$$TC = AR - 0.25(AR) - US\&AC$$
$$= \$5.33 - (0.25 \times \$5.33) - \$2.28$$
$$= \$5.33 - \$1.33 - \$2.28$$
$$= \$1.72$$

b. Step 1—Determine total allowable cost over product life:

$$1,950,000 \text{ units} \times \$1.72 = \$3,354,000$$

Step 2—Determine expected total production cost in first year:

$$\$3 \times 300,000 \text{ units} = \$900,000$$

Step 3—Determine allowable unit cost in last four years:

$$(\$3,354,000 - \$900,000) \div 1,650,000 \text{ units} = \$1.49 \text{ (rounded)}$$

c. The following actions are potential options for the company:

- Product design and/or production processes can be changed to reduce costs. Cost tables can be used to provide information on the impact of using different input resources, processes, or design specifications.

■ The 25 percent acceptable profit margin can be reduced.
■ RotoWax can suspend consideration of the project at the present time.

Demonstration Problem 2

DIY Inc. manufactures home-improvement products in a JIT environment. The annual and current material standards for one of the company's products follows.

Annual Material Standards

4 pounds of material 1 × $3.75	$15.00
12 pounds of material 2 × $2.25	27.00
	$42.00

Current Material Standards

8 pounds of material 1 × $3.75	$30.00
8 pounds of material 2 × $2.25	18.00
	$48.00

The current material standards differ from the original because an engineering change order was made near the end of August. During September, the company manufactured 1,000 units of product and used 7,500 pounds of Material 1 and 8,200 pounds of Material 2. All material is acquired at the standard cost per pound.

Required:

a. Calculate the material variance and the ECO material variance.
b. Explain the effect of the ECO on product cost.

Solution to Demonstration Problem 2

a. **Actual Material Usage**

Material 1: 7,500 × $3.75	$28,125
Material 2: 8,200 × $2.25	18,450
Total material cost	$46,575

Material Cost at Current Standards

Material 1: 1,000 × 8 × $3.75	$30,000
Material 2: 1,000 × 8 × $2.25	18,000
Total material cost	$48,000

Material Cost at Annual Standards

Material 1: 1,000 × 4 × $3.75	$15,000
Material 2: 1,000 × 12 × $2.25	27,000
Total material cost	$42,000

Material cost at current standard	$48,000
Actual material cost	(46,575)
Material quantity variance	$ 1,425 F

Material cost at annual standard	$42,000
Material cost at current standard	(48,000)
ECO variance	$ (6,000) U

b. The effect of the ECO was to substitute the higher-priced material 1 for the lower-priced material 2. The financial effect of this change was to increase expected production cost for August by $6,000. However, the cost increase could have been offset by an increase in price, assuming the change in mix of materials increased product quality.

Key Terms

autonomation, **p. 685**

backflush costing, **p. 690**

bottleneck, **p. 694**

computer-integrated manufacturing (CIM), **p. 693**

constraint, **p. 693**

cost table, **p. 677**

economic order quantity (EOQ), **p. 695**

economic production run (EPR), **p. 696**

flexible manufacturing system (FMS), **p. 692**

focused factory arrangement, **p. 687**

Internet business model, **p. 686**

just-in-time (JIT), **p. 679**

just-in-time manufacturing system, **p. 680**

kaizen costing, **p. 678**

kanban, **p. 680**

lead time, **p. 697**

lean manufacturing, **p. 693**

manufacturing cell, **p. 684**

order point, **p. 697**

Pareto inventory analysis, **p. 697**

product life cycle, **p. 674**

pull system, **p. 673**

purchasing cost, **p. 673**

push system, **p. 673**

red-line system, **p. 698**

safety stock, **p. 697**

supply-chain management, **p. 687**

target costing, **p. 677**

theory of constraints (TOC), **p. 693**

two-bin system, **p. 698**

usage, **p. 697**

value engineering, **p. 677**

virtual reality, **p. 676**

Questions

1. What are the three costs associated with inventory? Explain each and give examples.
2. Differentiate between the push and pull systems of production. Is JIT a push or a pull system?
3. How does a product's life cycle stage influence production cost management?
4. What is target costing, and how is it useful in assessing a product's total life cycle cost?
5. Why does the development stage have such a significant influence on a product's profitability over its life cycle?
6. What is kaizen costing, and how does it differ from target costing?
7. What are the primary goals of the JIT philosophy, and how does JIT attempt to achieve these goals?
8. What changes need to occur in a production environment to effectively implement JIT? Why are these changes necessary?
9. How would switching from a traditional manufacturing system to a flexible manufacturing system affect a firm's inventory and production control systems?
10. What is the theory of constraints? How is this concept appropriate for manufacturing and service companies?
11. (Appendix) How are ordering costs and carrying costs related?
12. (Appendix) What is Pareto inventory analysis? Why do A items and C items warrant different inventory control methods? What are some methods that can be employed to control C items?

Exercises

13. **LO.1 (Inventory cost management)** Randomly select annual reports for ten publicly traded manufacturing companies. On the balance sheet, or in the related footnotes, for each firm, find the amounts for the three inventory accounts: raw material, work in process, and finished goods. Then, calculate the following for each firm, and the average for the 10 firms:

    Ratio of Raw Material Inventory to total assets
    Ratio of Work in Process Inventory to total assets
    Ratio of Finished Goods Inventory to total assets
    Ratio of total inventory to total assets

    a. On average, how large is total inventory as a percentage of total assets for your ten firms?
    b. On average, which inventory component comprises the largest percentage of total inventory?

c. Do your answers to parts (a) and (b) suggest that effective inventory management is crucial to the success of these 10 firms? Discuss.

14. **LO.1 (Inventory cost management)** Indicate whether each of the following costs would be considered an ordering cost (O), a carrying cost (C), or a cost of not carrying (N) inventory. For any costs that do not fit these categories, indicate N/A for "not applicable."

   a. Telephone call to supplier
   b. Stationery and purchase order forms
   c. Purchasing agent's salary
   d. Purchase price of product
   e. Goodwill of customer lost due to unavailability of product
   f. Postage on purchase order
   g. Freight-in cost on product
   h. Insurance for products in inventory
   i. Wages of receiving clerks
   j. Preparing and issuing checks to suppliers
   k. Contribution margin lost due to unavailability of product
   l. Storage costs for products on hand
   m. Quantity discounts on products ordered
   n. Opportunity cost of funds invested in inventory
   o. Property taxes on warehouses
   p. Handling costs for products on hand
   q. Excess ordering and shipping charges for rush orders of standard product lines
   r. Spoilage of products awaiting use

15. **LO.1 & LO.9 (Inventory cost management; EOQ)** A plant manager and her controller were discussing the plant's inventory control policies one day. The controller suggested to the plant manager that the ordering policies needed to be reviewed because new technology had been implemented in the plant, including installation of (1) computerized inventory tracking, (2) electronic data interchange capabilities with the plant's major suppliers, and (3) in-house facilities for electronic fund transfers.

   a. As technology changes, why should managers update ordering policies for inventory?
   b. Write a memo to the plant manager describing the likely impact of the changes made in this plant on the economic order quantity of material input.

16. **LO.1 (Inventory cost management)** The supply management director at Tennessee Tool & Die has contracted to purchase $1 million of spare parts that are currently unneeded. His rationale for the contract was that the parts were currently available at a significantly reduced price from the standard price. The company just hired a new president who, on learning about the contracts, stated that the parts contracts should be canceled because the parts would not be needed for at least a year. The supply management director informed the president that the penalties for canceling the contracts would cost more than letting the orders go through. How would you respond to this situation from the standpoint of the president? From the standpoint of the supply management director?

17. **LO.2 (Push vs. pull systems)** Tonight you are going to dine at the restaurant of your choice. To choose the restaurant, you are going to consider the fact that some manage their food production on a push basis and others manage food production on a pull basis.

   a. Discuss the difference between managing food production in a restaurant on a push versus a pull basis.
   b. Are there any circumstances in which you would prefer to dine at a restaurant that uses a push model of food production? Discuss.
   c. Are there any circumstances in which you would prefer to dine at a restaurant that uses a pull model of food production? Discuss.

18. **LO.2 (Push vs. pull systems)** Everyone in your company seems excited about the suggestion that the firm implement a JIT system. Being a cautious person, however, your company president has asked you to write a report describing situations in which JIT will not work. Prepare such a report.

19. **LO.3 (Product life cycle)** Recently you read an article regarding a new product introduced late last year by 3G Inc., a consumer products company. The article's author, although praising 3G Inc. for providing the marketplace this innovative product, simultaneously criticized the company because the product had generated a $50 million loss for the year due to low unit sales. The author concluded the article suggesting that company management had "missed the boat" with this product and should "dump it" as soon as possible. After reading

this article you recall the concept of product life cycle and after contemplating how sales volume behaves over the product life cycle, you believe you can rebut the author of the 3G Inc. story. Write the rebuttal.

20. **LO.3 (Product life cycle)** Tom Ames is a product engineer for a firm that makes various home and office electronic gadgets. Some of this company's products have long product life cycles and others have life cycles that are as short as 9 months. Ames' company uses both target costing and kaizen techniques to manage costs relative to the product life cycle of the firm's products. As an intern with the company you recall a conversation in which Ames stated that the use of kaizen cost management strategies was much more effective for products with longer life cycles than products with shorter life cycles, and that target costing techniques including value engineering were much more critical to products with short life cycles than to products with long life cycles. Do you agree with Ames? Why or why not?

21. **LO.4 (Target costing)** Taurus Tools has developed a new kitchen utensil. The firm has conducted significant market research and estimated the following pattern for sales of the new product:

Year	Expected Volume	Expected Price per Unit
1	38,000 units	$19
2	48,000 units	18
3	90,000 units	16
4	40,000 units	12

If the firm desires to net $4.50 per unit in profit over the life of the product, what is the target cost to produce the new utensil?

22. **LO.3 & LO.4 (Target costing)** The marketing department at Pittsburgh Production Company has an idea for a new product that is expected to have a six-year life cycle. After conducting market research, the company found that the product could sell for $700 per unit in the first four years of life and for $550 per unit for the last two years. Unit sales are expected as follows:

Year 1	4,000
Year 2	3,600
Year 3	4,700
Year 4	5,000
Year 5	1,500
Year 6	1,000

Per-unit variable selling costs are estimated at $160 throughout the product's life; total fixed selling and administrative costs over the six years are expected to be $3,500,000. Pittsburgh Production Company desires a profit margin of 20 percent of selling price per unit.
a. Compute the life cycle target cost to manufacture the product. (Round to the nearest cent.)
b. If the company expects the product to cost $450 to manufacture in the first year, what is the maximum that manufacturing cost can be in the following five years? (Round to the nearest cent.)
c. Assume that Pittsburgh Production Company engineers indicate that the expected manufacturing cost per unit is $270. What actions might the company take to reduce this cost?

23. **LO.4 (Target costing)** Zipper Zapper is developing a propane-powered mosquito zapper for campers. Market research has indicated that potential purchasers would be willing to pay $115 per unit for this product. Company engineers have estimated that first-year production costs would amount to $120 per unit. On this type of product, Zipper Zapper would normally expect to earn $10 per unit in profits. Using the concept of target costing, write a memo that (1) analyzes the prospects for this product and (2) discusses possible organizational strategies.

24. **LO.6 (Value engineering)** Research the topic of value engineering on the Internet, and write a brief report on a company or an organization's experiences using this technique.

25. **LO.5 (Backflush costing)** Consider the following data pertaining to March 2009 for a firm that has adopted JIT.

Production	8,000 units
Sales ($40 per unit)	7,900 units
Standard production costs	
Direct material	$ 8
Conversion costs	16

Assume that there were no cost or usage variances for March, and the quantity of material used equaled the quantity purchased. All material is purchased on account, and all units started were completed.

a. Assuming that the company uses a traditional costing system, record the journal entries to recognize the following:
 1. purchase of material.
 2. incurrence of conversion costs.
 3. completion of the month's production.
 4. sale of the month's production.
b. Assuming that the company initially charges all costs to Cost of Goods Sold and then uses backflush costing to assign costs to inventories at the end of the period, record the journal entries to recognize the following:
 1. incurrence of conversion costs.
 2. completion of production.
 3. backflushing of costs to inventories.

26. **LO.5 (Backflush costing)** Fashion Fabrics uses backflush costing to account for production costs of its clothing line. During August 2008, the firm produced 160,000 garments and sold 159,000. The standard cost for each garment is

EXCEL

Direct material	$2
Conversion costs	4
Total cost	$6

The firm had no inventory on August 1. The following events took place in August:
- Purchased $322,000 of direct material.
- Incurred $648,000 of conversion costs.
- Applied $640,000 of conversion costs to Raw and In-Process Inventory.
- Finished 160,000 garments.
- Sold 159,000 garments for $10 each.

a. Prepare journal entries using backflush costing with a minimum number of entries.
b. Post the amounts in part (a) to T-accounts.
c. Explain any inventory account balances.

27. **LO.5 (JIT variances)** Lazlow Company uses a JIT system. The following standards are related to Materials A and B, which are used to make one unit of the company's final product:

Annual Material Standards

3 pounds of material A × $2.25	$ 6.75
4 pounds of material B × $3.40	13.60
	$20.35

Current Material Standards

2 pounds of material A × $2.25	$ 4.50
5 pounds of material B × $3.40	17.00
	$21.50

Current material standards differ from the original because of an engineering change order made near the end of June. During July, the company produced 3,000 units of its final product and used 11,000 pounds of Material A and 10,000 pounds of Material B. All material is acquired at the standard cost per pound.
a. Calculate the material variance and the ECO material variance.
b. Explain the effect of the ECO on product cost.

28. **LO.5 (JIT variances)** Pretty Pots makes pots for plants and uses JIT to manage inventories and production. The following are standards for a typical 1 gallon pot:

Annual Material Standards

32 ounces of Component X × $0.01	$0.32
2 ounces of Component Y × $0.05	0.10
	$0.42

Current Material Standards

22 ounces of Component X × $0.01	$0.22
4 ounces of Component Y × $0.05	0.20
	$0.42

In-house experiments indicated that changing the material standard would make the pots stronger, so the company issued an engineering change order for the product in February; this ECO established the current material standards. March production was 8,000 pots. Usage of raw material (all purchased at standard price) was 184,000 ounces of Component X and 31,000 ounces of Component Y.

a. Calculate the material quantity variance.

b. Calculate the engineering change order variance.

c. Summarize the company's effectiveness in managing March production costs.

d. Comment on the circumstances in which a company would institute an ECO that results in the expected product cost being unchanged.

29. **LO.5 (JIT implementation)** William Manufacturing Company began implementing a just-in-time inventory system several months ago. The production and purchasing managers, however, have not seen any dramatic improvements in throughput. They have decided that the problems are related to their suppliers. The company's three suppliers seem to send the wrong materials at the wrong times. Prepare a discussion of the problems that might exist in this situation. Be certain to address the following items: internal and external communications; possible engineering changes and their impacts; number, quality, and location of suppliers; and length of system implementation.

30. **LO.6 (Flexible manufacturing systems)** On the Internet, research the topic of manufacturing cells, and write a brief report on company experiences using them.

31. **LO.6 (Flexible manufacturing systems)** The installation of a flexible manufacturing system allows firms to produce a variety of products in small batches. Assume MegaMetal, a metal fabricating company, is considering switching from a traditional assembly line production process to an FMS. Provide answers to the following questions.

a. How would the adoption of an FMS likely affect the inventory levels?

b. How would the adoption of an FMS likely affect the level of employment for production employees?

c. Would the adoption of an FMS require employees to be retrained? Explain.

32. **LO.7 (Production constraints)** Xcaliber manufactures high-end flatware. One of the crucial processes in flatware production is polishing. The company normally operates three polishing machines to maintain pace with the upstream and downstream production operations. However, one of the polishing machines broke yesterday, and management has been informed that the machine will not be back in operation until repairs are completed in three weeks. Two machines cannot keep pace with the volume of product flowing to the polishing operation. You have been hired as a consultant to improve the throughput of the polishing operation. Discuss the tactics you would recommend Xcaliber employ to handle the capacity limitation.

33. **LO.7 (Production constraints)** Office Provisions produces commercial calendars in a two-department operation: Department 1 is labor intensive and Department 2 is automated. The average output of Department 1 is 45 units per hour. Units from Department 1 are transferred to Department 2 to be completed by a robot. The robot can finish a maximum of 45 units per hour. Office Provisions needs to complete 180 units this afternoon for an order that has been backlogged for four months. The production manager has informed the people in Department 1 that they are to work on nothing else except this order from 1 P.M. until 5 P.M. The supervisor in Department 2 has scheduled the same times for the robot to work on the order. Department 1's activity for each hour of the afternoon follows:

Time	1:00–2:00 P.M.	2:00–3:00 P.M.	3:00–4:00 P.M.	4:00–4:58 P.M.
Production	44 units	40 units	49 units	47 units

Each unit moves directly from Department 1 to Department 2 with no lag time. Did Office Provisions complete the 180 units by 5 P.M.? If not, explain and provide detailed computations.

34. **LO.8 (Appendix: carrying cost)** Gidget Gourmet manufactures a variety of animal food products from alfalfa "pellets." The firm has determined that its EOQ is 40,000 pounds of pellets. Based on the EOQ, the firm's annual ordering cost for pellets is $6,700. Given this information, what is the firm's annual carrying cost of pellets? Explain.

35. **LO.8 (Appendix: carrying costs)** Determine the carrying costs for an item costing $6.80, given the following per-unit cost information:

Storage cost	$0.12
Handling cost	0.14
Production labor cost	0.85
Insurance cost	0.22
Opportunity cost	8% of investment

36. **LO.8 (Appendix: multiproduct EOQs)** A retail cosmetics chain carries three types of skin products: face cream, lotion, and powder. Determine the economic order quantity for each, given the following information:

Product	Order Cost	Carrying Cost	Demand
Face cream	$2.25	$2.00	2,000 units
Lotion	3.25	1.45	1,000 units
Powder	1.70	1.25	900 units

37. LO.8 (Appendix: product demand) Compute annual estimated demand for a product if the economic order quantity is 800 units, carrying cost is $0.35 per unit, and ordering cost is $140.00 per order.

38. LO.8 (Appendix: EPR) UpTown Mfg. custom manufactures machine parts used by other companies. The following data relate to production of Part 23:

Annual quantity produced in units	1,600
Cost of setting up a production run	$400
Cost of carrying one unit in stock for a year	$2

Calculate the economic production run for Part 23.

39. LO.8 (Appendix: EPR) Daniellia Steele has taken a job as production superintendent in a plant that makes, among other products, jewelry cases. She is trying to determine how many cases to produce on each production run (EPR). Discussions reveal that last year the plant made 7,500 such cases, and this level of demand is expected for the coming year. The setup cost of each run is $400, and the cost of carrying a case in inventory for a year is estimated at $2.50.

a. Calculate the EPR and the total cost associated with it.
b. Recalculate the EPR and total cost if the annual cost of carrying a case in inventory is $10 and the setup cost is $100.
c. Based on your answer to part (a), how many production runs should Steele expect for the coming year?
d. Based on your answers to parts (a) and (c), estimate the total setup costs to be incurred for the year.

Problems

40. LO.1 (Inventory cost management) In early 2007, Burger King, under pressure from animal rights activists including People for Ethical Treatment of Animals (PETA), announced it would start purchasing pork and eggs from suppliers that use cage-free animal management methods. In its announcement, Burger King stated it would also give purchasing preference to poultry suppliers that use or switch to "controlled atmosphere stunning," which is regarded by some to be a more humane method of slaughtering poultry.

Source: http://www.cbsnews.com/stories/2007/03/28/business/main2618928.shtml (last accessed 8/27/07).

a. Discuss how the change in Burger King's pork and egg supplier policy is likely to affect the prices Burger King pays for pork and eggs.
b. Evaluate the ethics of the new supplier policy from the point of view of a Burger King patron assuming that the new supplier policy will likely increase prices charged for pork and egg food products.
c. Evaluate the ethics of the new policy from the point of view of a supplier who will now face higher costs in providing Burger King with pork or egg products. ▲

41. LO.1 (Inventory cost management) DataPro manufactures various electronic assemblies that it sells primarily to computer manufacturers. DataPro's reputation has been built on quality, timely delivery, and products that are consistently on the cutting edge of technology. DataPro's typical product has a short life; products are in development for about a year and in the growth stage, with sometimes spectacular growth, for about a year. Each product then experiences a rapid decline in sales as new products become available.

DataPro's competitive strategy requires a reliable stream of new products to be developed each year, which is the only way that the company can overcome the threat of product obsolescence. DataPro's products go through the first half of the product life cycle similar to products in other industries; however, differences occur in the second half of the products' life cycles. DataPro's products never reach the mature product or declining product stage. Near the end of the growth stage, products just "die" as new ones are introduced.

a. In the competitive market facing DataPro, what would be key considerations in production and inventory control?
b. How would the threat of immediate product obsolescence affect DataPro's practices in purchasing product components and materials?
c. How would the threat of product obsolescence affect the inventory carrying costs for a typical product produced by DataPro?

(CMA adapted)

42. **LO.1 (Identification of inventory costs)** Orlando Steel's management has been evaluating company policies with respect to control of costs of metal tubing, one of the firm's major component materials. The firm's controller has gathered the following financial data, which may be pertinent to controlling costs associated with the metal tubing:

Ordering Costs

Annual salary of purchasing department manager	$41,500
Depreciation of equipment in purchasing department	22,300
Cost per order for purchasing department supplies	0.30
Typical phone expense per order placed	3.02
Monthly expense for heat and light in purchasing department	400

Carrying Costs

Annual depreciation on materials storage building	$15,000
Annual inventory insurance premium (per dollar of inventory value)	0.05
Annual property tax on materials storage building	2,500
Obsolescence cost per dollar of average annual inventory	0.07
Annual salary of security officer assigned to the materials storage building	18,000

a. Which of the ordering costs should Orlando Steel's controller consider in performing short-run decision analysis? Explain.

b. Which of the carrying costs should Orlando Steel's controller consider in performing short-run decision analysis? Explain.

43. **LO.2 (Push vs. pull systems)** Assume that you are a management consultant who advises manufacturing firms regarding production technologies. One of the hot issues you often discuss with management is whether a pull system or a push system is superior in a particular situation. Consider the following circumstances and discuss whether you would recommend a push system or a pull system in each particular case.

a. The firm manufactures two consumer products; 75 percent of annual sales are made during the year-end holiday sales cycle.

b. The firm manufactures a variety of goods for the petroleum industry; most products are sold in low volume and have a high unit cost.

c. The firm manufactures products subject to rapid obsolescence and that have relatively short product life cycles.

d. The firm manufactures products that have a limited shelf life.

e. The firm manufactures a limited line of products for which there is predictable, but seasonal, demand and the products have long life cycles.

44. **LO.2 (Push vs. pull systems)** Koss Corp. makes high quality headphones for a variety of applications. Koss is a Milwaukee-based company but has significant manufacturing operations in China. When manufacturing operations were moved to China, CEO Michael Koss was a strong proponent of just-in-time inventory management. Although the company maintained significant orders of component parts, finished goods were produced only to satisfy customer orders. Accordingly, work in process and finished goods inventories were small. However, moving production offshore significantly increased the complexity of the firm's logistics. Unexpected changes in product mix and fluctuating demand for products caused the firm's backlog of orders to rise significantly. Mr. Koss responded by scrapping the JIT production and stacking finished goods on the factory floor pending receipt of customer orders.

Source: Paulette Thomas, "Case Study: Electronics Firm Ends Practice Just In Time," *Wall Street Journal* (October 29, 2002), p. B9.

a. Why does globalization of a firm's production operations increase the challenges in controlling inventories using the JIT philosophy (pull system)?

b. After scrapping JIT, Mr. Koss reported that his total investment in inventories dropped from $15 million to $8 million. How could this occur?

c. From the perspective of managing the risk of a stock outage, is Mr. Koss better off holding mostly finished goods inventory, or mostly component parts inventories? Explain.

45. LO.3 (Product life cycles) Assume you are the CFO of a firm that manufactures electronics. Your firm is about to launch an extremely innovative new product. The product planning team has estimated life cycle sales of the product to be as follows (in thousands):

Year 1	35,000
Year 2	75,000
Year 3	125,000
Year 4	90,000
Year 5	15,000

The life cycle average sales price is projected by the product planning team to be $40. The team has recommended to top management and the marketing team that the introductory price for the product be set at $30.

a. As CFO, what is your reaction to the suggested introductory price of $30 relative to the expected life cycle price of $40?

b. Most of the profit of consumer electronic products is realized early in the product life cycle. How would this fact influence your recommendation about where the price for this product should be set for year 1?

c. As CFO, are you concerned that a significant portion of the forecasted life cycle volume for this product is assigned to years 3 and 4? Explain.

46. LO.3 (Product life cycles) Sony Corp. launched its PlayStation 3 in late 2006. It was introduced at a price point of $599 for the top model. At the time of introduction, a California technology firm performed a tear down of the PlayStation and estimated its cost of production to be $839. Based on this cost estimate, the California tech firm estimated Sony was losing as much as $240 per unit sold.

Source: Lee Gomes, "Talking Tech: A Peek Under PlayStation 3's Hood Shows Sony Is Selling Units at a Loss," *Wall Street Journal* (November 21, 2006), p. B4.

a. Assume that Sony generates more profit on royalties from the games played on PlayStation than on the sales of PlayStation itself. In light of this explanation, is it rational for Sony to sell the PlayStation at a $240 loss? Explain.

b. How would setting the price of the PlayStation at $599, rather than the break-even price of $839, likely affect (1) early life cycle sales and (2) total life cycle sales of PlayStation 3?

c. Is Sony's pricing strategy (i.e., introductory price below production cost) more beneficial if the product's life cycle is long or short? Explain.

47. LO.3 & LO.4 (Target costing) The Products Development Division of Family Feasts has just completed its work on a new microwave entrée. After consumer research was conducted, the marketing group has estimated the following quantities of the product can be sold at the following prices over its life cycle:

EXCEL

Year	Quantity	Selling Price	Year	Quantity	Selling Price
1	100,000	$2.50	5	600,000	$2.00
2	250,000	2.40	6	450,000	2.00
3	350,000	2.30	7	200,000	1.90
4	500,000	2.10	8	130,000	1.90

Initial engineering estimates of direct material and direct labor costs are $0.85 and $0.20, respectively, per unit. Variable overhead per unit is expected to be $0.25, and fixed overhead is expected to be $100,000 per year. Family Feasts' management strives to earn a 20 percent gross margin on products of this type.

a. Estimate the target cost for the new entrée.

b. Compare the estimated production cost to the target cost. Discuss this comparison and how management might use the comparison to manage costs.

c. Based on your answer in part (b), should Family Feasts begin production of the new entrée? Explain.

48. O.4 (Target costing) Ben There has just been presented the following market and production estimates on Product Ninja-Z that has been under development in his company.

Projected market price of Ninja-Z	$430 (based on 180,000 life cycle unit sales over 5-year life)
Projected profit per unit	70
Estimated selling and administrative costs per unit	80

Estimated production costs	
Direct material	$140
Direct labor	80
Variable overhead	30
Fixed overhead	$10,000 annually

Use the concept of target costing to integrate the marketing and engineering information and interpret the results for Ben There.

49. **LO.5 (JIT features)** Indicate by letter which of the three categories apply to the following features of just-in-time systems. Use as many letters as appropriate.

D = desired intermediate result of using JIT
U = ultimate goal of JIT
T = technique associated with JIT

a. Reducing setup time
b. Reducing total cost of producing and carrying inventory
c. Using focused factory arrangements
d. Designing products to minimize design changes after production starts
e. Monitoring quality on a continuous basis
f. Using manufacturing cells
g. Minimizing inventory stored
h. Measuring variances caused by an engineering change order
i. Using autonomation processes
j. Pulling purchases and production through the system based on sales demand

50. **LO.5 (JIT journal entries)** iTech Industries recorded the following transactions for its first month of operations.

(1)	Direct Material Inventory	12,000	
	Accounts Payable		12,000
	To record purchase of direct material		
(2)	Work in Process Inventory	12,000	
	Direct Material Inventory		12,000
	To record distribution of material to production		
(3)	Conversion Cost Control	20,000	
	Various accounts		20,000
	To record incurrence of conversion costs		
(4)	Work in Process Inventory	20,000	
	Conversion Cost Control		20,000
	To assign conversion cost to WIP		
(5)	Finished Goods Inventory	32,000	
	Work in Process Inventory		32,000
	To record completion of products		
(6)	Accounts Receivable	58,000	
	Sales		58,000
	To record sale of products		
	Cost of Goods Sold	31,000	
	Finished Goods Inventory		31,000
	To record cost of goods sold		

Because iTechIndustries employs JIT, the company's CEO has asked how the accounting system could be simplified.

a. Prepare the journal entries, assuming that no transactions are recognized until goods are completed.
b. Prepare the journal entries, assuming that goods are shipped to customers as soon as they are completed and that no journal entries are recorded until goods are completed.
c. Prepare the journal entries, assuming that sale of product is the trigger point for journal entries.
d. Prepare the journal entries, assuming that sale of product is the trigger point for journal entries and that the firm uses backflush costing.

51. **LO.5 (JIT journal entries; advanced)** ProLand Products has implemented a just-in-time inventory system for the production of its insulated wire. Inventories of raw material and work in process are so small that Pro-Land uses a Raw and In-Process account. In addition, almost all labor operations are automated, and ProLand has chosen to cost products using standards for direct material and conversion costs. The following production standards are applicable at the beginning of 2008 for one roll of insulated wire:

Direct material (100 yards × $2.00)	$200
Conversion (4 machine hours × $35)	140
Total cost	$340

The conversion cost of $35 per machine hour was estimated on the basis of 500,000 machine hours for the year and $17,500,000 of conversion costs. The following activities took place during 2008:

1. Raw material purchased and placed into production totaled 12,452,000 yards. All except 8,000 yards were purchased at the standard price of $2.00 per yard. The other 8,000 yards were purchased at a cost of $2.06 per yard due to the placement of a rush order. The order was approved in advance by management. All purchases are on account.

2. From January 1 to February 28, ProLand manufactured 20,800 rolls of insulated wire. Conversion costs incurred to date totaled $3,000,000. Of this amount, $600,000 was for depreciation, $2,200,000 was paid in cash, and $200,000 was on account.

3. Conversion costs are applied to the Raw and In-Process account from January 1 to February 28 on the basis of the annual standard.

4. The Engineering Department issued a change order (ECO) to the operations flow document effective March 1, 2008. The change decreased the machine time to manufacture one roll of wire by 5 minutes per roll. However, the standard raised the amount of direct material to 100.4 yards per roll. The Accounting Department requires that the annual standard be continued for costing the Raw and In-Process Inventory for the remainder of 2008. The effects of the engineering change orders should be shown in two accounts: Material Quantity ECO Variance and Machine Hours ECO Variance.

5. Total production for the remainder of 2008 was 103,200 rolls of wire. Total conversion costs for the remaining 10 months of 2008 were $14,442,000. Of this amount, $4,000,000 was depreciation, $9,325,000 was paid in cash, and $1,117,000 was on account.

6. The standard amount of conversion cost is applied to the Raw and In-Process Inventory for the remainder of the year.

Note: Some of the journal entries for the following items are not explicitly covered in the chapter. This problem challenges students regarding the accounting effects of the implementation of a JIT system.

a. Prepare entries for items 1, 2, 3, 5, and 6.

b. Determine the increase in material cost due to the ECO related to direct material.

c. Prepare a journal entry to adjust the Raw and In-Process Inventory account for the ECO cost found in part (b).

d. Determine the reduction in conversion cost due to the ECO related to machine time.

e. Prepare a journal entry to reclassify the actual conversion costs by the savings found in part (d).

f. Making the entry in part (e) raises conversion costs to what they would have been if the ECO related to machine time had not been made. Are conversion costs under- or overapplied and by what amount?

g. Assume that the reduction in machine time could not have been made without the corresponding increase in material usage. Is the net effect of these ECOs cost beneficial? Why?

52. **LO.6 & LO.7 (Lean manufacturing; TOC)** Recent years have been characterized by high, and volatile, energy prices. Some critics of the energy industry suggest that the oil companies' use of JIT inventory management has contributed to the volatility in prices and the supply constraints. Further, oil and natural gas products are crucial inputs to other industrial products such as chemicals and plastics. These industries also have been rocked by the volatility in energy prices and by the availability of the oil- and gas-derived inputs to their products. To illustrate one of the negative outcomes of the supply volatility, Citigroup cut its stock rating of Lear Corp. in late 2005 because of fears of adverse effects on profits from shortages of materials and higher prices of materials derived from inputs produced by the oil and gas industry.

Source: Mary Ellen Lloyd, "Hurricanes' Effects on Oil, Gas Trickle Down to Other Products," *Wall Street Journal* (October 6, 2005), p. A2.

a. Is JIT management of inventories an ethical practice by the oil industry if it is true that JIT practices increase the volatility in energy prices for energy consumers?

b. How could application of the theory of constraints help alleviate the effects of material shortages experienced by firms that consume products derived from the oil and gas industry?

c. What actions could firms that are dependent on inputs from the oil and gas industry take to reduce supply chain risks?

d. In the United States, both federal and state governments increase the price of energy (particularly automotive fuels) to the consumer by assessing taxes on energy sold at the consumer level. Do governments have an ethical responsibility to reduce taxes on energy when prices spike upward? Discuss. ▲

53. LO.8 (Appendix: EOQ) Frank Chone operates a health food bakery that uses a special type of ground flour in its products. The bakery operates 365 days a year. Chone finds that he seems to order either too much or too little flour and asks for your help. After some discussion, you find that he has no idea of when or how much to order. An examination of his records and answers to further questions reveal the following information:

Annual usage of flour	14,000 pounds
Average number of days delay between initiating and receiving an order	12
Estimated cost per order	$16.00
Estimated annual cost of carrying a pound of flour in inventory	$0.50

a. Calculate the economic order quantity for flour.

b. Assume that Chone desires a safety stock cushion of seven days' usage. Calculate the appropriate order point.

54. LO.8 (Appendix: EPR) Herb's Herbs grows and sells a variety of indoor and outdoor plants and garden vegetables. One of the firm's more popular vegetables is a red onion, which has an annual sales quantity of approximately 30,000 pounds. Two of the major inputs in the growing of onions are seeds and fertilizer. Due to the poor germination rate, two seeds must be purchased for each onion plant grown (a mature onion plant provides 0.5 pound of onion). Also, 0.25 pound of fertilizer is required for each pound of onion produced. The following information summarizes costs for onions, seeds, and fertilizer. Carrying costs for onions are expressed per pound of onion; carrying costs for seeds are expressed per seed; and for fertilizer, carrying costs are expressed per pound of fertilizer. To plant onions, the company incurs a cost of $50 to set up the planter and the fertilizing equipment.

	Onions	Seeds	Fertilizer
Carrying cost	$ 0.25	$0.01	$0.05
Ordering cost	—	$4.25	$8.80
Setup cost	$50.00	—	—

a. What is the economic production run for onions?

b. How many production runs will Herb's Herbs make for onions annually?

c. What are the economic order quantities for seeds and fertilizer?

d. How many orders will be placed for seeds? For fertilizer?

e. What is the total annual cost of ordering, carrying, and setting up for onion production?

f. How is the planting of onions similar to and different from a typical factory production run?

g. Are there any inconsistencies in your answers to parts (a) through (c) that need to be addressed? Explain.

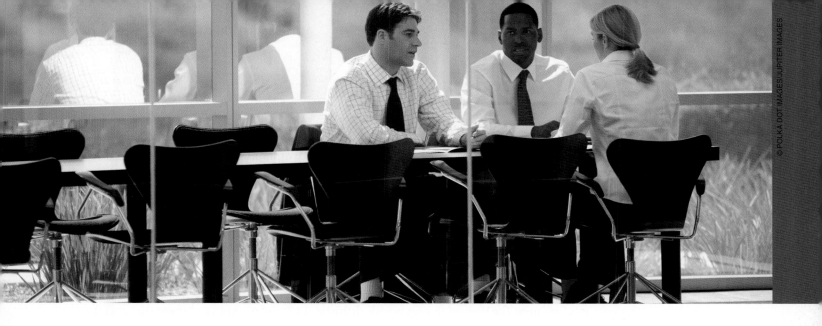

19 | Emerging Management Practices

Objectives

After reading this chapter, you should be able to answer the following questions:

LO.1 How does business process reengineering cause radical changes in the way firms execute processes?

LO.2 How are competitive forces driving decisions to downsize and restructure operations?

LO.3 In what ways, and why, are operations of many firms becoming more diverse? How does the increasing diversity affect the roles of the firms' accounting systems?

LO.4 Why are firms adopting enterprise resource planning systems, and what are their purposes?

LO.5 What are strategic alliances, what forms do they take, and why do firms engage in them?

LO.6 What are the characteristics of open-book management, and why does its adoption require changes in accounting methods and practices?

LO.7 What are the three generic approaches that firms can take in controlling environmental costs?

Introduction

Firms are presently decentralizing information, authority, and responsibility to make decisions. This trend has created opportunities and challenges for the accounting functions. To be effective, decision makers must have the skills to interpret a variety of information, including financial reports. However, not all employees are adequately trained to understand financial information. This circumstance has created some innovative approaches to developing the information skills used by managers.

This chapter discusses innovation in management practices and the impact of innovation on accounting. The "age of change" is an apt description for the current environment in which managers and financial professionals must function. Although some changes have been driven by the fast pace of evolution in management practices and techniques, many changes have been driven by the even faster evolution of technology. These evolving management methods unite around a theme of focusing organizational resources on customers and maximizing the value that the firm delivers to its customers. The discussion begins with dramatic structural workplace changes that are affecting many employers and employees.

The Changing Workplace

The forces of global competition and technological advancements have caused profound changes in business organizations. To survive, managers must develop ways to achieve the competitive changes needed in organizations. Change may occur either immediately or gradually. Managers use both time frames to effect change.

Some overriding principles that managers should follow when implementing changes are presented in Exhibit 19–1. Note that principles 5 through 8 involve major roles for financial professionals within the firm. These roles are explained further as the chapter unfolds. When major operational improvements are mandated, managers completely revise the way activities are performed. Business process reengineering is one tool with which to achieve large, quick gains in effectiveness or efficiency through redesigning the execution of specific business functions.

LO.1
How does business process reengineering cause radical changes in the way firms execute processes?

Business Process Reengineering

Business process reengineering (BPR) is a method of examining processes to identify and then eliminate, reduce, or replace functions and processes that add little customer value to products or services. The focus of BPR is on discrete initiatives to improve specific processes. Process examples include handling or storing purchased materials and components, issuing checks to pay labor and other production expenses, packaging finished products for shipment to customers, recording journal entries, and developing an organizational strategic plan. BPR initiatives in a global enterprise could encompass the entire firm or only a single subunit. Thus, the initiatives can originate with managers at different organizational levels.

BPR is designed to bring radical changes to operations and is often associated with employee layoffs, outsourcing initiatives, and technology acquisition. Three major business trends are promoting the increased use of BPR in the twenty-first century. The first trend is the advancement of technology. Neither the electronic remittance for accounts payable nor the use of robotic equipment to move and assemble components in a manufacturing facility were possible 50 years ago. Both of these practices are common today, even in small companies. Because BPR focuses on alternative ways to execute required organizational functions, it is useful in automating processes that cannot be eliminated. Technology advancements have improved efficiencies throughout the supply chain. The feasibility of automating processes is constantly changing because technology is constantly evolving. For example, in mid-2004, the Federal Reserve announced that its Boston check-processing facil-

EXHIBIT 19–1

Managerial Principles for Successfully Managing Change

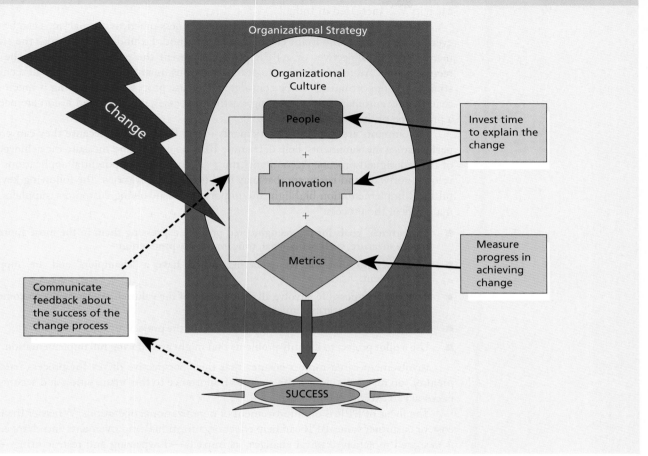

ity would transfer or lay off more than 100 employees. The staff reductions were attributed to the reduction in check-clearing volume, following the increased use of credit and debit cards for store purchases.[1]

The second trend leading toward increased use of BPR is the pursuit of increased quality. As discussed in Chapter 17, global competition allows consumers to purchase products and services from the highest quality providers regardless of their geographical location. In many product and service markets, quality has become one of the most important criteria applied by consumers in purchasing decisions. Because of its attention on processes associated with poor quality, BPR can help indicate ways in which quality can be improved by replacing, changing, or eliminating those processes.

The third trend resulting in expanded BPR usage is the increase in price competition caused by globalization. To successfully compete on the basis of price, firms must identify ways to become more efficient and, thus, reduce costs. BPR can be used to improve efficiency, particularly when a process needs a major overhaul or a new generation of technology is needed. For example, in early 2007, Circuit City replaced 3,400 highly paid workers with lower paid workers. This restructuring

[1]Robert Gavin, "Fed to Cut Hub Jobs as Fewer Use Checks [Third Edition]," *Boston Globe* (August 3, 2004), p. D1.

was driven purely by the necessity of reducing costs to remain competitive.[2] In another example, soon after the turn of the twenty-first century and to increase its cost competitiveness, EDS, the giant IT outsourcing firm, laid off 5,000 employees in the United States as the company's service capacity was increased in India.[3]

Because BPR methodically revolutionizes business practices, formal steps can be defined; however, creativity is an important element of the method. Exhibit 19–2 provides the steps for implementing BPR. Objectives of a BPR project represent the potential benefits to be realized from reengineering. All relevant technological innovations must be known so that all technological constraints and opportunities can be considered. Because process reengineering is much more involved than merely automating or upgrading existing processes, creativity and vision are needed to design a prototype of the revised process.

Accountants are important participants in the BPR process because they can provide baseline performance measurements, help determine BPR objectives, and measure the achieved performance of the redesigned process. Accountants must also be aware of potential applications for newly developed software and hardware that may lead to BPR innovations. The following keys to a successful BPR implementation highlight the importance of involving customers, suppliers, and top-level managers in the process:

- Set "stretch" goals for the reengineered process, expressing them in the most appropriate performance measure, such as financial, time, or quality production.

- Make certain that the reengineering efforts have a "champion" and are supported by top management.

- To the extent possible, involve all constituents of the value chain, especially customers and suppliers, in the reengineering project.

- Assign both the authority and responsibility for the project to a single person.

- Use a pilot project to identify problems that might arise during full implementation.[4]

Involvement of customers ensures that their perspective drives the process redesign. Involvement of top managers signals the project's importance to the organization and secures the resources necessary to execute the project.

The focus of BPR is on improvement of organizational operations. Whether the issue is quality, cost, or customer value, BPR can help effect organizational improvements and change. Because BPR is designed to achieve radical changes, its impacts—downsizing and restructuring—on employees are potentially profound.

EXHIBIT 19–2
Steps to Business Process Reengineering

1. Define the objectives of the BPR project.

2. Identify the processes that are to be reengineered.

3. Determine a baseline for measuring the success of the BPR project.

4. Identify the technology levers. These are the potential sources of innovation, increased quality, increased output, and decreased costs.

5. Develop initial prototypes of the reengineered processes and then, through subsequent iterations, develop incremental improvements to the prototypes until satisfactory results are achieved.

Source: Adapted from Yogesh Malhotra, "Business Process Redesign: An Overview," *IEEE Engineering Management Review* (Vol. 26, no. 3, Fall 1998); http://www.kmbook.com/bpr.htm (last accessed 8/23/07).

---

[2]Ylan Q. Mui, "Circuit City Cuts 3,400 'Overpaid' Workers," *Washington Post* (March 29, 2007), p. D01.
[3]Carolyn A. April, Rick Whiting, and Michele Pepe, "VARBusiness 500 Profiles: The Cream of the Crop," *VARBusiness* (June 11, 2007); http://www.crn.com/article/printableArticle.jhtml?articleId=99703029 (last accessed 8/20/07).
[4]Gene Hall, Jim Rosenthal, and Judy Wade, "How to Make Reengineering Really Work," *Harvard Business Review* (November–December 1993), pp. 119–131.

Downsizing, Layoffs, and Restructuring

LO.2
How are competitive forces driving decisions to downsize and restructure operations?

Global competition is a fact of life in many industries, and survival requires firms to continually improve product quality while maintaining competitive prices. Not all firms are able to adapt and survive under the pressures of global competition. Just as global competition has driven firms to higher levels of quality and efficiency, competitive pressures drive some businesses out of competition altogether. Firms are now forced to evaluate which business operations they want to defend and which they are willing to sacrifice to the competition.

Many methods discussed in this chapter, including the use of automated technology to replace manual labor or equipment run by humans, have proven useful in improving process efficiency and effectiveness as well as product quality. However, in realizing improvements, firms also realize additional problems. Foremost among these problems is the handling of excess personnel. Both businesses that are striving to remain viable and those that are retreating from the competition are forced into restructuring operations and reducing the workforce.

One of the grim realities of ever-improving efficiency is that fewer and fewer workers are required to achieve a given level of output. Using business practices such as BPR, firms are constantly restructuring operations to maintain or gain competitive advantages. Each successful restructuring leverages the work of employees into more output. At higher levels of efficiency, fewer workers are needed and a reduction in workforce is required. Downsizing is any management action that reduces employment upon restructuring operations in response to competitive pressures.

Whether downsizing is an appropriate response to cost pressures depends, in part, on the importance of human capital to an organization's success. Shedding employees is much more hazardous for a firm that relies heavily on its human capital as a competitive advantage than for a firm that relies more on financial capital for competitive advantage. Exhibit 19–3 provides a ranking of industries based on the employee-to-capital cost ratio. The employee-to-capital cost ratio measures the relative importance of human and financial capital to the industry. The higher the ratio, the greater the relative importance of human capital. For firms in industries with high values of the ratio, downsizing and layoffs are potentially much more detrimental because the people who are dismissed take with them knowledge and skills that may be crucial to the competitive position of their employers.

EXHIBIT 19–3
Importance of Human Capital Management by Industry

Industry	Employee-to-capital cost ratio
Software	4.7
Pharmaceuticals	3.3
Consumer goods	3.0
Retail	3.0
Communication equipment	2.6
Airlines	1.9
Chemicals	1.7
Automotive	1.1
Telco services	0.8
Oil	0.4

Source: Felix Barber and J. David Campbell, "Layoffs: Creating or Destroying Shareholder Value?" *Ivey Business Journal* (September/October 2001), p. 14. Reprinted with permission of Ivey Management Services (September 9, 2007).

Even though downsizing has greater risks for firms in some industries than in others, all firms face some risk. For example, firms can find that layoffs have depleted the in-house talent pool. The collective workforce knowledge or **organizational memory** (the aggregation of data, facts, experiences, and lessons learned that is important to an organization's existence) may have been reduced to the point that the ability to solve problems creatively and generate innovative ideas for growth has been greatly diminished. Also, after downsizing, many firms have found positions that once served as feeder pools for future top management talent have been eliminated.

To survive in the presence of global competition, trust and effective communication must exist between workers and managers. Successive rounds of layoffs diminish worker morale, cause worker trust in managers to wane, and lead to a decrease in communication between workers and managers. Workers often fear that sharing information could provide insights to management about how to further increase productivity and reduce costs by eliminating more of the workforce. Many management methods discussed in this chapter depend heavily on cooperation among all employees of a firm. Firms that are downsizing should not concurrently attempt to implement other innovative practices.

Downsizing can destroy a corporate culture that embraced lifetime employment as a key factor in attracting new employees or that was perceived as "nurturing" by employees. Significant negative change in an organization's culture is likely to have a similar negative impact on employee morale and trust.

Downsizing is an accounting issue because of its implications for financial reporting and its role in cost management. The financial consequences of downsizing can be highly significant. When restructuring and downsizing occur in the same year, the firm often reports in that year a large, one-time loss caused by sales of unprofitable assets and severance costs connected with employee layoffs. From a cost management perspective, accountants must understand the full consequences, both monetary and nonmonetary, of downsizing. Before recommending downsizing to improve organizational efficiency, accountants should examine the likely impacts on customer service, employee morale and loyalty, and future growth opportunities.

Exhibit 19–4 demonstrates that strategic decisions affect the manner in which inputs, such as labor, technology, purchased material, and services, are converted into outputs for customers. Downsizing changes the mix of inputs used to produce outputs, increases the emphasis on technology-based conversion processes, and reduces the emphasis on manual conversion processes and, thus, the labor requirement. The two-directional arrow shows increased outsourcing from suppliers and increased dependence on technology as substitutes for labor. As suggested by the data in Ex-

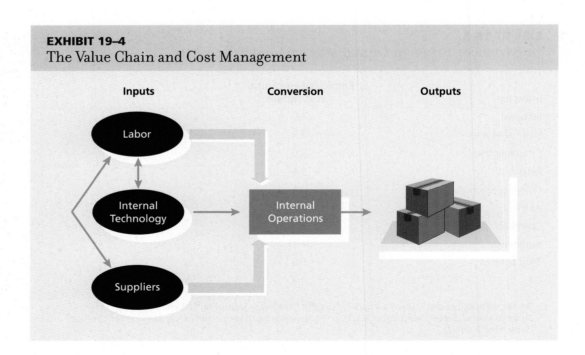

EXHIBIT 19–4
The Value Chain and Cost Management

hibit 19–3, the substitutions among labor and capital (technology) hold much more peril for some firms than others.

Financial analysis of the downsizing decision is complex. The decision relies on comparing cost savings from reduced labor costs realized in the future to the current outlay for restructuring and acquiring additional technology. The capital budgeting methods discussed in Chapter 15 should be applied to this decision. If downsizing involves asset sales, the financial analysis must compare the cash to be realized from such sales to the annual net revenues or net cash flows that will *not* be realized in the future because of the reduced asset base. Capital budgeting tools provide managers information about how downsizing is likely to affect profitability and the return on invested capital.

Workforce Diversity

LO.3
In what ways, and why, are operations of many firms becoming more diverse? How does the increasing diversity affect the roles of the firms' accounting systems?

Under the pressure of global competition, many firms have expanded operations geographically. By sourcing and marketing worldwide, firms are able to develop new markets, reduce input costs, and manage the effects of peaks and valleys in local economies. The globalization of operations presents managers with new opportunities and challenges.

With widespread manufacturing and other operations, companies find that their employees have divergent religions, races, values, work habits, cultures, political ideologies, and education levels. The diversity across countries is evident within companies that operate globally. Corporate policies and information systems must adapt to the changing workforce and greater diversity of operations, which often result in the accounting function having a larger role in managing operations. Although different languages and cultures can impede communications within globally dispersed operations, accounting information can be a powerful coordinating mechanism. The interpretation of accounting information need not depend on local culture or language.

Accounting concepts, tools, and measurements can be the medium through which people of diverse languages and cultures communicate. Accounting provides an ideal international technical language because it is a basic application of another universal language—mathematics. Managing a global business, as opposed to one that operates in a single country, involves many considerations in addition to coordinating employees. Global businesses must consider country differences in currency values, labor practices, political risks, tax rates, commercial laws, and infrastructure such as ports, airports, and highways. These considerations require development of new systems and controls with which to manage risks and exploit opportunities.

Within the United States, there is a trend toward increasing workplace diversity. The trend is driven partly by legal requirements and business initiatives to increase opportunities for minorities and partly by organizational self-interest. Refer to Exhibit 19–5 for reasons, other than legal requirements, that firms may seek a more diverse workforce. Unfortunately, this trend can be problematic in light of other business practices discussed in this chapter. BPR and downsizing diminish the opportunity to diversify and become more responsive to the marketplace.

Technology plays a major role in the communications that are necessary to harmonize employee actions to manufacture products and serve customers. Often the integration of information systems is accomplished with enterprise systems.

As companies become more global, diversity becomes more evident.

GETTY IMAGES

EXHIBIT 19–5
Why Self-Interested Firms Seek a Diverse Group of Employees

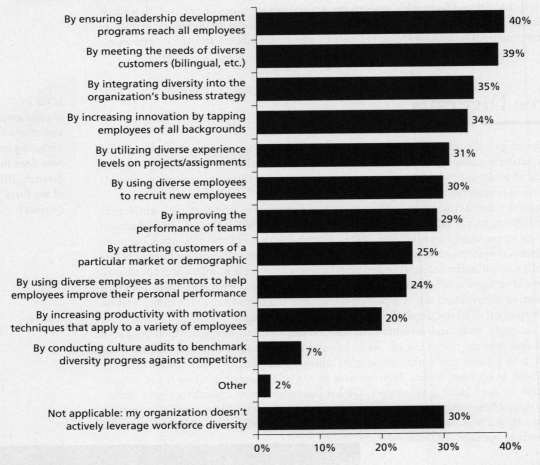

In what ways does your organization actively leverage the diversity of employees for the purpose of increasing competitive advantage? (Number of Respondents = 310)

By ensuring leadership development programs reach all employees	40%
By meeting the needs of diverse customers (bilingual, etc.)	39%
By integrating diversity into the organization's business strategy	35%
By increasing innovation by tapping employees of all backgrounds	34%
By utilizing diverse experience levels on projects/assignments	31%
By using diverse employees to recruit new employees	30%
By improving the performance of teams	29%
By attracting customers of a particular market or demographic	25%
By using diverse employees as mentors to help employees improve their personal performance	24%
By increasing productivity with motivation techniques that apply to a variety of employees	20%
By conducting culture audits to benchmark diversity progress against competitors	7%
Other	2%
Not applicable: my organization doesn't actively leverage workforce diversity	30%

Source: Nancy R. Lockwood, "Workplace Diversity: Leveraging the Power of Difference for Competitive Advantage," *Society for Human Resource Management*; http://www.shrm.org/research/quarterly/2005/0605RQuart_essay.asp (last accessed 8/22/07).

LO.4
Why are firms adopting enterprise resource planning systems, and what are their purposes?

Enterprise Resource Planning Systems

Firms commonly use networked personal computers (PCs) and minicomputers to handle the information management requirements of specific business functions, such as finance, marketing, and manufacturing. PCs allow maximum user flexibility in accessing and manipulating data in real time. However, the increased use of PCs and local-area networks has resulted in the decentralization of information. As data management and storage have become more decentralized, firms have often lost the ability to integrate information across functions and to quickly access information that spans multiple functions. Exhibit 19–6 shows how internal processes and functions are distributed across the supply chain and the types of information that may reside in isolated databases.

Enterprise resource planning (ERP) systems are packaged software programs that allow companies to (1) automate and integrate the majority of their business processes, (2) share common

EXHIBIT 19–6
Internal Supply Chain and Traditional Information Management

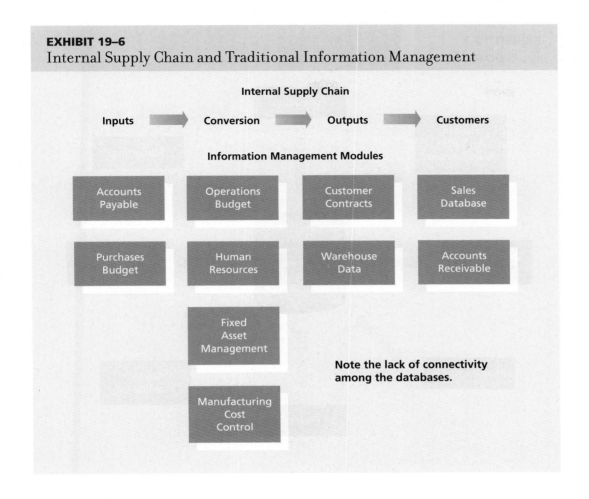

Internal Supply Chain

Inputs → Conversion → Outputs → Customers

Information Management Modules

| Accounts Payable | Operations Budget | Customer Contracts | Sales Database |

| Purchases Budget | Human Resources | Warehouse Data | Accounts Receivable |

Fixed Asset Management

Note the lack of connectivity among the databases.

Manufacturing Cost Control

data and practices across the entire enterprise, and (3) produce and access information in a real-time environment.[5] Implementing an ERP system should help a company to provide customers the highest quality products and best possible service; Exhibit 19–7 illustrates an integrated, centralized information system. In theory, the ERP system should link the customer end of the supply chain with all functional areas responsible for the production and delivery of a product or service—all the way upstream to suppliers. Increasingly, businesses will allow customers to access all necessary data about their orders through the Internet.

The following quote describes the benefits from ERP implementation for the whole business, its marketing function, and its customers:

> *The benefits of an ERP package to a business are in reduced overheads, improved customer service and better quality, and more timely management information. Reduced overheads should be achieved through the elimination of duplication of effort in duplicate keying and reconciliation of independent systems. Better management information becomes available when all company information is held in one database which can be queried to provide quality reports on margins broken down by customer, product, rep, area, etc. E-commerce has the potential to offer a quantum leap in customer service by giving the customer direct access to your systems.*[6]

ERP's key concept is a central repository for all organizational data so that they are accessible in real time by and in an appropriate format for a decision maker. Data are entered into the central depository through a series of modules. Usually 30 or more modules are required to complete an

[5]Win G. Jordan and Kip R. Krumwiede, "ERP Implementers Beware!" *Cost Management Update* (March 1999), p. 1.
[6]Paddy White, "ERP: The Big Company Solution for Small Companies," *Accountancy Ireland* (August 1999), p.4. Reprinted with permission.

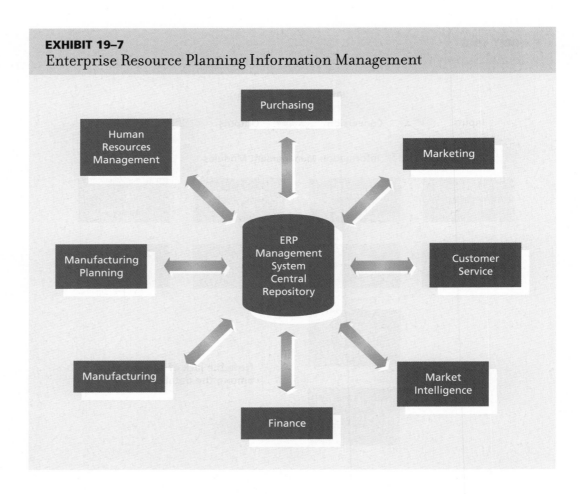

EXHIBIT 19–7
Enterprise Resource Planning Information Management

ERP installation.[7] Exhibit 19–8 provides a list of typical modules included in a manufacturing company's ERP system.

Results from a survey of international company managers about their motivations for implementing an ERP system and the perceived benefits gained from the implementation are shown in Exhibit 19–9 (page 726). Timeliness of information and having information to support decision making are the two most commonly cited reasons for implementing an ERP system. The perceived benefits of implementing ERP appear to align with these motivations.

Installation of an ERP system impacts the financial function in three significant ways. First, financial and system specialists become responsible for selecting and installing the software. ERP software includes brand names such as SAP, Oracle, PeopleSoft, i2, Great Plains, and Invensys. Installing an ERP system in a large company involves thousands of hours of labor and millions of dollars of capital.

Second, financial specialists will be responsible for analyzing the data repository to support management decisions. Data analysis often involves "drilling down" from aggregate data (such as total sales for the firm) to detailed data (such as sales by store or sales by customer type) to identify market opportunities and to better manage costs. Such analysis can explain why a certain product moves well at some stores but not at others.

Analysis can also use **data mining**, which involves statistical techniques to uncover answers to important questions about business operations.[8] Data mining is useful to uncover quality problems,

[7]Ibid.
[8]Ibid.

> **EXHIBIT 19–8**
> ## Typical Modules in an ERP Installation
>
> **Finance** (accounting-related tasks)
>
> *General ledger*: Maintains charts of accounts and corporate finance balances
>
> *Accounts receivable*: Tracks amounts owed to company
>
> *Accounts payable*: Tracks amounts owed by company and schedules bill payments
>
> *Fixed assets*: Manages costs and depreciation schedules related to property, plant, and equipment
>
> *Treasury management*: Monitors and manages cash holdings and investment risks
>
> *Cost control*: Analyzes costs related to overhead, products, and customers
>
> **Human Resources Management** (personnel-related tasks)
>
> *Human resources*: Automates processes such as recruitment, business travel management, vacation allotments, and absences
>
> *Payroll*: Handles accounting and preparation of checks for employees for salary and bonuses
>
> *Training*: Tracks training activities, both provided and needed
>
> *Self-service HR*: Lets workers select benefits and manage personal information
>
> **Manufacturing and Logistics** (production and distribution tasks)
>
> *Production planning*: Performs capacity planning and creates a daily production schedule
>
> *Materials management*: Maintains bills of materials, controls materials purchasing, and manages inventory
>
> *Order entry and processing*: Tracks customer orders and their status
>
> *Warehouse management*: Maintains inventory records and tracks flow of inventory through warehouses and production operations
>
> *Distribution management*: Arranges, schedules, and monitors delivery of products to customers
>
> *Project management*: Monitors costs and work schedules on a project-by-project basis
>
> *Plant maintenance*: Sets plans and oversees upkeep of facilities
>
> *Customer service management*: Administers service agreements and checks contracts and warranties when customers contact the company
>
> **Customer Relationship Management** (customer-related tasks)
>
> *Customer portals*: Allows customers to post service issues, place new orders, and view order histories
>
> *Commissions*: Tracks salespersons commissions from customers' orders
>
> *Contact center support*: Tracks type and resolution of contact items
>
> *Marketing*: Tracks promotions and related customer impacts
>
> *Service support*: Administers service agreements and checks contracts and warranties when customers contact the company

study customer retention, determine which marketing promotions generate the greatest sales impact, and identify cost drivers.

ERP installation places a burden on financial specialists to maintain the integrity of the data depository. Fulfilling this obligation requires accountants and other specialists to monitor the ERP modules and be confident that the system successfully converts raw data into the standardized format required for the main repository.

Also, finance specialists are accountable for integrating externally purchased data (such as industry sales data and other external intelligence) with internally generated data. ERP systems represent a generational leap in the gathering, processing, and analysis of information. As ERP systems become increasingly integrated into Internet-based technology, customers will have ease of access to a worldwide marketplace.

EXHIBIT 19–9
Survey of Reasons for Adopting ERP
and Perceived Benefits from Adoption

Reasons for Adopting ERP Systems	Percentage of Respondents Answering Affirmatively
Increased demand for real-time information	96
Information for decision making	92
Integration of applications	77
Business process reengineering	54
Cost reduction	50
Taxation requirements	35
Increase sales	31
Application of new business plan	27

Perceived Benefits of ERP Implementation in Rank Order

Increased flexibility in information generation

Increased integration of accounting applications

Improved quality of [financial] reports

Improved decisions based on timely and reliable accounting information

Reduction of time for annual closing of books

Improved decision making process

Increased use of financial ratio analysis

Reduction in time for issuance of [financial] reports

Improved internal audit function

Reduction of time for transaction processing

Improved working capital control

Source: Charalambos Spathis and Sylvia Constantinides, "Enterprise Resource Planning Systems' Impact on Accounting Processes," *Business Process Management Journal* 10, no. 2 (2004), pp. 234–247. Published by Emerald Group Publishing Limited.

In turn, customer-driven competition will cause firms to continually seek innovative ways to attract potential customers. These innovations are often obtained through strategic efforts that combine the talents and capabilities of two or more firms.

Strategic Alliances

LO.5
What are strategic alliances, what forms do they take, and why do firms engage in them?

The traditional supply chain structure has clear distinctions between supplier and customer firms—there are no "fuzzy boundaries" that create an inability to determine where one firm ends its contribution to the supply chain and another begins its contribution. In some instances, however, companies have incentives to develop interorganizational agreements that go beyond normal supplier/customer arrangements. Generically, these agreements are called strategic alliances: agreements involving two or more firms with complementary core competencies to jointly contribute to the supply chain.

Strategic alliances can take many forms including joint ventures, equity investments, licensing, joint R&D arrangements, technology swaps, and exclusive buyer/seller agreements. A strategic alliance differs from the usual interactions among independent firms in that the output produced reflects a joint effort between (or among) the firms and the rewards of that effort are split between (or among) the allied firms. An unusual illustration of a strategic alliance is a recent agreement between the Georgia Ports Authority and the Panama Canal Authority. In the agreement, the two parties committed to jointly promote shipping routes between Asia and the Port of Savannah. The agreement also calls for sharing data, technology, and information as well as executing a joint marketing program.[9]

The strategic alliance is typical of many other business arrangements: it involves the exploitation of partner knowledge, includes partners with access to different markets, and allows sharing of risks and rewards. The use of strategic alliances to exploit or create business opportunities is pervasive and economically significant, although the following quote indicates the challenges in measuring the frequency in use of alliances.

> *In Hollywood and Silicon Valley, alliances are old hat: in a sense, almost every movie is an ad-hoc alliance, as is the development of every new computer chip. But, as in so much else, these two fashionable places are proving models for older industries. The most obvious change is in the sheer number of alliances.*
>
> *Mergers, like marriages, can be legally defined and therefore readily counted. Alliances are more like love affairs: they take many forms, may be transient or lasting, and live beyond the easy reach of statisticians.*[10]

A typical strategic alliance involves the creation of a new entity. In structuring the new entity, the contributions required of the parent organizations must be determined. Beyond simply contributing cash, many new ventures will require inputs of human capital, technology, access to distribution channels, patents, and supply contracts. Furthermore, a governing board or set of directors must be established for the entity, and agreement must be reached as to how many directors can be appointed by each parent. Composition of the governing board determines which of the parent entities is more influential in managing the new entity. Simultaneous agreements must be executed to express the rights of the parent organizations in sharing gains and to specify obligations for bearing losses. Such agreements will have significant implications for the risks borne by the parent organizations.

An overriding concern in designing a strategic alliance is aligning the interests of the parent organizations with the new entity. The alliance is likely to work only if both parent organizations believe they are receiving adequate value for their contributions. This caveat is especially true today when many strategic alliances involve agreements between competitors.

Establishing strategic alliances involves a series of complex decisions that are based on inputs from many specialists. For example, financial professionals must assess risk and develop strategies for parent company management. These experts must also design a financial structure, develop management control systems, and install accounting and other information systems. The execution of a strategic alliance is as involved as the establishment of any new business. The process of managing an alliance requires the use of virtually every tool and concept discussed in this text including cost management systems, product costing systems, cost allocation, inventory management, decision making, and performance evaluation.

The technology evolution has been shown to have a significant impact on management practices and the activities of the financial professional. The next section discusses how technological and other organizational changes affect nonprofessional workers and how financial professionals have been pressured to develop ways in which to convey information to those without technical finance and accounting expertise.

Open-Book Management

Open-book management is a philosophy about increasing a firm's performance by involving all workers and by ensuring that all workers have access to operational and financial information necessary to achieve performance improvements. Although no specific definition of open-book management exists, it has some defined principles, as shown in Exhibit 19–10. Firms practicing

[9]"Georgia Ports Authority, Panama Canal Sign Agreement," *Journal of Commerce* (June 20, 2003), p. 1.
[10]"Mergers and Alliances," *The Economist* (May 15, 1999), p. 73.

LO.6
What are the characteristics of open-book management, and why does its adoption require changes in accounting methods and practices?

EXHIBIT 19–10

Ten Common Principles of Open-Book Management

1. Turn the management of a business into a game that employees can win.
2. Open the books and share financial and operating information with employees.
3. Teach employees to understand the company's financial statements.
4. Show employees how their work influences financial results.
5. Link nonfinancial measures to financial results.
6. Target priority areas and empower employees to make improvements.
7. Review results together and keep employees accountable. Regularly hold performance review meetings.
8. Post results and celebrate successes.
9. Distribute bonus awards based on employee contributions to financial outcomes.
10. Share the ownership of the company with employees. Employee stock ownership plans (ESOPs) are routinely established in firms that practice open-book management.

Source: Tim Davis, "Open-Book Management: Its Promises and Pitfalls," *Organizational Dynamics* (Winter 1997), pp. 6–20. Copyright 1997 by Elsevier Science & Technology Journals. Reproduced with permission of Elsevier Science & Technology Journals in the format Textbook via Copyright Clearance Center.

open-book management typically disclose detailed financial information to employees, train them to interpret and use the information, empower them to make decisions, and tie a portion of their pay to the company's bottom line.[11] Application of this philosophy is appropriate in decentralized organizations that have empowered employees to make decisions. Proponents of open-book management argue that the approach helps employees understand how their work activities affect the firm's costs and revenues. With this understanding, employees can adopt or change work practices to either increase revenues or decrease costs.

However, merely opening the financial records to a firm's employees will not necessarily solve any problems or improve anyone's performance. Most employees, particularly nonmanagerial workers, neither have developed skills to interpret business financial information nor understand accounting concepts and methods. Even many highly educated functional specialists have little knowledge of how profits are generated and performance is measured in financial terms. The key to understanding is training. Springfield Remanufacturing, a recession-era spin-off of General Motors, first introduced the concept of open-book management. Gary Brown, human resources director at Springfield Remanufacturing, provides some insights about the learning curve for non-financial workers to become financially literate.

> *Brown estimates that it generally takes two years for people to become financially literate (two iterations of the planning cycle). However, formal financial education and training is not the major expense, nor does training consume the most time, according to Brown. He emphasizes that the most valuable learning takes place in the "huddles" and when employees study the figures by themselves. An exceptionally motivated employee who does a great deal of self-study may become financially literate in six months.*[12]

If financial information is to be the basis of employee decision making, the information must be structured with the level of sophistication of the decision maker in mind. Providing such information requires accountants to become much more creative in the methods used to compile and present financial data.

Effective open-book management requires sharing accounting and financial information with employees who have little knowledge of accounting concepts. Games can be used to teach these concepts to financially unsophisticated employees.

---

[11]Edward J. Stendardi and Thomas Tyson, "Maverick Thinking in Open-Book Firms: The Challenge for Financial Executives," *Business Horizons* (September–October 1997), p. 35.
[12]Tim Davis, "Open Book Management: Its Promises and Pitfalls," *Organizational Dynamics* (Winter 1997), p. 13.

Games People Play

Games make learning both fun and competitive and can motivate employees to understand complex financial practices. To illustrate how games can be used in open-book management, assume that Mobile Manufacturing, a manufacturer of robotic equipment, has decided to implement open-book management concepts. One of its key departments is Assembly, which is responsible for combining mechanical and electronic components of various models into finished products. Most components that are required for assembly are purchased from other manufacturers.

Assembly staff include one manager and 10 workers. Although highly skilled in the technical aspects of assembling electronic and mechanical components, workers know little about financial management or accounting techniques. For these workers, the game must begin with very simple accounting principles. Outcomes of the game, as determined by financial and nonfinancial performance measurements, must be both easy to comprehend and easily related to the motivation for establishing the game—for example, to maximize firm profit, customer satisfaction, and shareholder value.

Data in Exhibit 19–11 pertain to a major component of a production-line robotic welder. These data have been gathered from the most recent month's production and accounting records and have been provided by Mobile's controller.

The starting point in designing a system for providing information to Assembly employees is to determine the system's objectives. Reasonable initial design objectives include the following:

■ enabling Assembly employees to understand how their work affects the achievement of corporate objectives; to this end, it is important to measure what you want employees to do well;

■ helping Assembly workers understand how their work affects upstream and downstream departments; and

■ generating demand from the employees for information and training that leads to improvements in performance in Assembly.

Because overhead cost is more difficult to comprehend than direct material and direct labor cost, information on overhead costs can be excluded from the initial system developed for Assembly

EXHIBIT 19–11
Mobile Manufacturing Assembly Department Cost Data
for Robotic Welder

Item	Quantity	Unit Cost	Total Cost
Continuous Rotation Servo	2	$25.00	$ 50.00
IR Receiver	2	11.00	22.00
Standard Servo	2	19.00	38.00
Wire harness	1	90.00	90.00
Microcontroller	8	17.00	136.00
Chassis	1	48.00	48.00
Mini Sensors	8	7.00	56.00
Ultrasonic Range Finder	1	25.00	25.00
High Current Motor Drivers	3	31.00	93.00
Fasteners	1 package	5.00	5.00
Total direct material cost			$563.00
Direct labor cost	6 hours	25.00	150.00
Total direct cost			$713.00

employees. Direct material and direct labor will be the information focus. Furthermore, employees cannot exert control over the price paid for material or labor, thus these data could be presented as budgeted or standard, rather than actual, cost. If actual costs are used, variations in purchase prices occurring throughout the year could disguise other more important information from the financially unsophisticated workers (such as quantities of materials consumed). If desirable, a more sophisticated system can be developed once the workers fully understand the initial system.

One motivation for providing information to Assembly workers is to cause them to understand how their actions affect achievement of the overall corporate objectives. To initiate this understanding, management can establish a sales (or transfer) price for Assembly's output so that a measure of that department's contribution to corporate profits can be established. Assume that the initial price for the robot assembly is set at $950; it is not necessary for the established sales price to represent actual market value. The per-unit profit calculation for Assembly workers follows:

Sales price	$ 950.00
Total direct cost (from Exhibit 19–11)	(713.00)
Profit contribution	$ 237.00

Total profit equals per-unit profit multiplied by the number of units produced. By analyzing this simple profit calculation, workers quickly realize that they can increase profits by decreasing costs or increasing the units produced. However, some elementary quality information should be added so that the implication of defective production can be seen. For example, quality defect costs could be charged to Assembly for products that are not of the quality specified. An income statement for the Assembly Department for a period would then appear as follows:

Sales	$ XXXXXX
Total direct cost	(XXXXXX)
Rework and defects	(XXXX)
Profit contribution	$ XXXX

With this profit calculation, workers will see that profit maximization requires maximization of output, minimization of direct costs, and minimization of quality defects.

One Japanese company, Higashimaru Shoyu, a maker of soy sauce, went so far as to create its own internal bank and currency.[13] Each department purchased its required inputs from other internal, upstream departments using the currency and established transfer prices. In turn, each department was paid in currency for its outputs. The flow of currency reinforced the profit calculations applying to each department.

To exploit the financial information they are given, workers should be trained in ways to improve profits. The "game" of trying to increase profits serves as motivation for workers to learn about cost and operational management methods. Relating training to the game allows workers to see the relevance of training, and they will seek training to better understand how to read and comprehend a simple income statement and to identify approaches that can be used to improve results.

Motivating Employees

It cannot be assumed that the Assembly workers at Mobile are internally motivated to play the game well. Instead, upper management should promote the game. The obvious way to motivate workers to use the game information to improve profits is to link their compensation to profits. Assembly workers could be paid bonuses if profits are above a target level. Alternatively, the workers could be paid a percentage of profits as a bonus. In either case, linking compensation to profits is a necessary step in motivating workers to have an interest in the game and to improve their performance. The positive effects of a good bonus program are described as follows:

> *Open-book management works only if it is accompanied by adequate incentives. "People start to back away if they don't have some sort of reward. In effect, you are asking people to*

---

[13]Robin Cooper, *When Lean Enterprises Collide* (Boston: Harvard Business School Press, 1995).

take on ownership behaviors, but not treating them like owners. That's like getting to smell lunch, but not being allowed to taste it," says [Corey] Rosen of the National Center for Employee Ownership. "If people don't have a stake in the company, why should they care?"[14]

Some companies offer performance-based bonuses to motivate employees and some offer employee stock ownership plans (ESOPs). Other companies, such as Album Inc., do both. Pay and performance links can also be based on more specific data. For example, measures can be devised for on-time delivery rates (to the next downstream department), defect rates, output per labor hour, and other performance dimensions to make workers aware of how their inputs and outputs affect other departments and financial outcomes. All critical dimensions of performance, including cost, quality, and investment management, can be captured in performance measurements.

As soon as workers have become accustomed to receiving financial and other information to manage their departments, more elaborate information systems can be developed as the sophistication of the information consumers (workers) evolves. For example, once the direct material, direct labor, and quality costs are understood, workers in Mobile's Assembly Department can learn to evaluate overhead cost information.

Implementation Challenges

Open-book management can be difficult to implement. Characteristics of firms that are best suited to a successful implementation include small size, decentralized management, a history of employee empowerment, and the presence of trust between employees and managers. In small firms, employees can more easily understand how their contributions influence the organization's bottom line. Firms with decentralized structures and empowered employees have workers who are accustomed to making decisions. Trust among employees and managers is necessary for games to be devised that result in higher pay and greater job satisfaction for all employees.

Accountants face unique challenges in implementing open-book management in even the most favorable environments. The challenges are present in both the obstacles to be overcome and reporting innovations that need to be designed and implemented. One significant organizational obstacle in many firms is a history of carefully guarding financial information. Even in publicly owned companies that are required to release certain financial information to the general public, top managers have historically limited employee access to financial data that the top managers regard as sensitive. Accountants have typically viewed themselves as the custodians of this sensitive information rather than its conveyors. To successfully implement open-book management, accountants must develop an attitude about information sharing that is as enthusiastic as the traditional attitude of information guarding.

Having been grounded in higher education courses and other appropriate training, accountants have generally operated under the assumption that financial information users have an adequate understanding of the rules used to compile financial data. However, open-book management requires the provision of accounting data to users who have little understanding of accounting conventions and rules. Thus, accountants must develop ways to convey accounting information so that unsophisticated users will understand it. Furthermore, by teaching users to have a better understanding of financial data, accountants help facilitate better organizational decision making.

Accountants must also be innovative when implementing open-book management. One significant requirement is the development of information systems that are capable of generating information for an organizational segment in a format that the segment's employees can understand. Thus, the information system must be designed to be sensitive to the user's financial sophistication.

Similarly, performance measures that employees can understand must be devised. Measures must capture the actual performance relative to the objectives of organizational segments and the organization as a whole. Objectives can be stated in terms of competitors' performance or industry

[14]Julie Carrick Dalton, "Between the Lines," *CFO* (March 1999), p. 61. © 1999 CFO Publishing Corporation. Reprinted with permission.

norms. For example, a firm's objective can be to surpass the average product quality level of the industry. Measurement of actual achievement relative to this objective requires accountants to develop information systems that are focused on gathering nontraditional types of information—in this instance, quality level of output in the industry. The primary principle of measurement is to measure what is important. "The 'what' to measure comes from your mission statement, strategic business plan and the things that drive your business. If customer satisfaction is vital, measure customer satisfaction. If profit is vital, measure profit."[15]

Finally, because principles of open-book management include involving all employees and evaluating and rewarding their performance, measures that can be integrated across segments and functional areas must be devised. For instance, if one of a firm's major objectives is to increase profitability, performance measures must be devised for engineers, accountants, production workers, administrators, janitors, and so forth that cause all of these functional groups to work toward a common end: increased profits.

An emerging area of concern for managers in nearly all entities is the impact of their operations on the environment. The concerns have arisen as a result of an increased consciousness of environmental issues and new governmental regulations enacted to protect the environment.

LO.7
What are the three generic approaches that firms can take in controlling environmental costs?

Environmental Management Systems

The environmental impact of businesses is of increasing concern to governments, citizens, investors, and managers. Accountants are increasingly concerned with both measuring business performance in regard to environmental issues and managing environmental costs. In the future, investors are likely to evaluate a company's environmental track record along with its financial record when making investment decisions.

Management of environmental costs requires the consideration of environmental issues in every aspect of operations. For example, environmental effects are related to the amount of scrap and by-product produced in manufacturing operations, materials selected for product components (recyclable or not), actions of suppliers that produce necessary inputs, and habits of customers in consuming and disposing of products and packaging. In short, environmental issues span the entire value chain. In addition to voluntary intentions to reduce pollution, under the 1997 Kyoto Protocol, many countries (not including the United States) agreed to reduce the pollution (particularly greenhouse gases) generated by their industries. The Kyoto Protocol would go into effect only if two conditions were met. The first was that at least 55 countries ratify the agreement and the second was that the ratifying countries had to account for at least 55 percent of 1990 carbon dioxide emissions. Based on meeting these criteria, the Kyoto Protocol went into effect on February 16, 2005. This agreement calls for reduction in six specific greenhouse gases including carbon dioxide, methane, nitrous oxide, sulfur hexafluoride, HFCs and PFCs. Kyoto Protocol provisions are legally binding on the ratifying nations and stipulate target reductions in emissions for each industrialized nation, but the Protocol does not set targets for developing countries. The goal of enacting the Kyoto Protocol is to reduce worldwide greenhouse gas emissions to 5.2 percent below 1990 levels between 2008 and 2012.[16]

Although some companies are striving to voluntarily reduce pollution because of a social consciousness, other companies are trying to do so to reduce the financial risks associated with generation of pollution. By avoiding these risks, companies may lower their cost of capital as suggested in the following quote.

> *A group of analysts at Innovest contend that a company's strategic response to environmental risk is a window into the company's management ability. The more "eco-efficient" a company is, the better its stock performance is likely to be compared with others in its industry—and that's true, apparently, whether the industry is oil, mining, or solar energy.*[17]

---

[15]Matt Plaskoff, "Measure What You Want to Improve," *Professional Builder* (June 2003), p. 93.
[16]Larry West, "Should the United States Ratify the Kyoto Protocol?" *About.com: Environmental Issues*, http://environment.about.com/od/kyotoprotocol/i/kyotoprotocol.htm (last accessed 8/23/07).
[17]Abrahm Lustgarten, "Lean, Mean and Green?" *Fortune* (July 26, 2004), p. 210.

There are three generic strategies for dealing with environmental effects of operations, and each has unique financial implications. First, an "end-of-pipe strategy" may be employed. With this approach, managers "produce the waste, or pollutant, and then find a way to clean it up."[18] Common tools used in this approach are wastewater cleaning systems and smokestack scrubbers, but this strategy can be ineffective in reducing the generation of greenhouse gases. A second strategy involves process improvements, which include changes to "recycle wastes internally, reduce the production of wastes, or adopt production processes that generate no waste."[19] A popular variant of this strategy is the purchase of renewable energy certificates or "carbon offsets." To illustrate, in late July 2007, PepsiCo announced that its three largest bottlers in the United States would purchase $1.1 million of renewable energy certificates annually through 2009 for the equivalent of 630 million kilowatt-hours of energy. The amount of this expenditure is equivalent to the amount of electricity the bottlers use in their U.S. operations each year.[20] A third strategy is pollution prevention, which involves "complete avoidance of pollution by not producing any pollutants in the first place."[21]

Although minimizing the environmental impact of operations can be a reasonable goal, some impact on the environment is unavoidable. For example, energy must be consumed to manufacture products; similarly, material must be consumed as goods are produced. Without energy and material consumption, no goods can be manufactured.[22] In the management of environmental costs, accountants must analyze the environmental dimensions of investment decisions:

> *In the capital investment area, accountants can help managers by including quality and environmental benefits in the analysis. If a proposed project is more energy efficient or produces less pollution than an alternative, those factors should be included in the analysis. The financial data should include any cost savings from lower energy usage. If the company must control pollution, the financial impact should be recognized.*[23]

Other managerial concerns related to environmental costs include managing quality, research and development, and technology acquisition. Although the relationship between quality costs and environmental costs is not fully understood, many examples can be cited suggesting that quality and environmental costs are highly related. For instance, the reduction in scrap and waste production (quality improvements) serves to reduce environmental costs and concerns (waste disposal).

Research and development identifies new products and new production processes, and develops new materials. New product design influences the (1) types and quantities of materials used, (2) types and quantities of waste, scrap, and by-products produced, (3) amount of energy consumed in the production process, and (4) potential for gathering and recycling products when they reach obsolescence. For example, recently Xerox developed a new "green" paper that requires half as many trees, fewer chemicals and less energy to manufacture than traditional 20-pound copy paper. Further, the new paper weighs less, which should reduce trucking and freight costs that customers must pay.[24]

Technology acquisition also has many environmental impacts. For instance, technology affects energy consumption and conservation; environmental emissions; the quantity, types, and characteristics of future obsolete equipment (for instance, whether it is made of recyclable materials); the rate of defective output produced; the quantities of scrap, waste, and by-products produced; and the nature and extent of support activities necessary to keep the technology operating.

Exhibit 19–12 lists considerations for the financial professional to evaluate when determining whether a firm's information systems provide relevant information for managing environmental costs. An analysis of the checklist shows that the financial professional must effectively gather both quantitative and nonquantitative data both within and outside of the firm.

[18]Germain Böer, Margaret Curtin, and Louis Hoyt, "Environmental Cost Management," *Management Accounting* (September 1998), p. 28ff.
[19]Ibid.
[20]Ibid.
[21]Betsy McKay, "Pepsi Bottlers to Buy Energy Subsidy Vouchers," *Wall Street Journal* (July 30, 2007), p. A9.
[22]For more information on this concept, see Frances Cairncross, *Costing the Earth* (Boston: Harvard Business School Press, 1992), p. 26.
[23]Harold P. Roth and Carl E. Keller, Jr., "Quality, Profits, and the Environment: Diverse Goals or Common Objectives?" *Management Accounting* (July 1997), pp. 50–55.
[24]William M. Bulkeley, "Xerox Develops a 'Green' Paper, But Will Firms Add It to Fold?" *Wall Street Journal* (July 30, 2007), p. B3.

> **EXHIBIT 19–12**
> Considerations for Environmental Cost Control
>
> **Cost Management Systems**
>
> How much does each of our divisions spend on environmental management?
>
> Do we have consistent and reliable systems in place for measuring environmental costs?
>
> How does our cost management system support good environmental management decisions?
>
> How do we track compliance costs?
>
> How do we connect line management decisions to the environmental costs they create?
>
> Which divisions best manage environmental costs?
>
> How do we compare with competitors in managing environmental costs?
>
> What kinds of waste do we produce?
>
> What are the proposed regulations that will affect our company?
>
> **Cost Reporting Systems**
>
> Who receives reports on environmental costs in our company?
>
> Does our bonus plan explicitly consider environmental costs?
>
> How do we charge internal environmental costs to managers?
>
> How does the financial system capture environmental cost data?
>
> Do our managers have all necessary tools to measure total costs of the wastes generated?
>
> Do our systems identify environmental cost reduction opportunities?
>
> **Source:** Germain Böer, Margaret Curtin, and Louis Hoyt, "Environmental Cost Management," *Management Accounting* (September 1998), p. 32.

Comprehensive Review Module

Chapter Summary

1. Business process reengineering causes radical changes in ways firms execute processes by

   - using fewer employees.

   - making better use of technology.

2. Global competition is forcing firms to downsize and restructure operations to

   - defend core competencies.

   - remain cost competitive.

3. Many organizations are becoming more diverse

   - as measured by the religion, race, values, work habits, cultures, political ideologies, and education level of employees.

   - because of globalization and proactive diversification programs.

   - and are placing more pressure on the accounting system for

     ➢ communicating among employees and

     ➢ measuring performance.

4. Many firms are adopting enterprise resource planning (ERP) systems

   - which consist of a number of modules (such as payroll, fixed assets, accounts receivable, and cash management), each of which accounts for specific activities.

   - which facilitate data mining and the integration of financial and nonfinancial information across functional areas of the business.

- to automate accounting processes.
- to share data across the enterprise.
- to provide real-time access to company data.

5. Strategic alliances
   - are agreements involving two or more firms to jointly contribute to the supply chain.
   - often blur traditional boundaries between supplier/customer.
   - take many different forms such as
     - ➤ joint ventures,
     - ➤ equity investments,
     - ➤ licensing arrangements,
     - ➤ joint R&D arrangements,
     - ➤ technology swaps, and
     - ➤ exclusive buy/sell agreements.
   - allow the sharing of risks and rewards between/among firms.

6. Open-book management

- increases the transparency of information within an organization, which often requires accountants to change from a mind-set of guarding to sharing information.
- creates challenges and opportunities for accountants to make information understandable to financially unsophisticated employees, which frequently involves the creation of games and meetings.
- decentralizes both authority to make decisions and responsibility for decision results, which can be implemented by tying rewards to performance.

7. The three generic approaches to controlling environmental costs include
   - cleaning up pollutants after they are produced (end-of-pipe strategy);
   - improving processes to reduce the amount of waste produced; and
   - preventing pollution by never producing polluting materials.

Potential Ethical Issues

1. Allowing executives to collect large bonuses and other perquisites while firing ordinary workers for the sake of remaining cost competitive

2. Firing highly paid long-term employees while hiring new, lower-paid employees to perform identical or similar work

3. Developing data repositories in ERP systems that contain sensitive data on employees, customers, and other stakeholders but not installing adequate systems to protect the privacy and integrity of that information

4. Adopting open-book management principles and holding employees accountable for financial results without first providing them training to understand financial reports

5. Making business decisions by considering only the costs of pollution that are borne by the company and ignoring the costs borne by society

6. Minimizing environmental costs by moving high-impact operations to countries that have lax environmental regulations ▲

Key Terms

business process reengineering (BPR), *p. 716*

data mining, *p. 724*

downsizing, *p. 719*

employee-to-capital cost ratio, *p. 719*

enterprise resource planning (ERP) system, *p. 722*

open-book management, *p. 727*

organizational memory, *p. 720*

strategic alliance, *p. 726*

Questions

1. What is business process reengineering? Does it lead to radical or modest changes in business practices? Discuss.
2. Business process reengineering and downsizing often occur together. Why?
3. Describe "downsizing," its causes, and its primary risks.
4. How has the globalization of firms affected the diversity of their employees? Why has increased diversity put an additional burden on accounting systems?
5. Besides increasing globalization, what trends within the United States are causing firms to seek more diversified workforces?
6. What is an enterprise resource planning (ERP) system? How do ERP systems improve on prior generations of information systems?
7. New strategic alliances are formed every day. What are they, and why are they increasingly being used by businesses?
8. Open-book management is a relatively new philosophy about the use of information in organizations. Describe open-book management and how it differs philosophically from the traditional view of the management of financial information in an organization.
9. How does the implementation of open-book management require an organization's accountants to change their traditional practices?
10. Describe the three generic strategies for dealing with the environmental effects of operations. Is one of the strategies always preferred to the others? Discuss.

Exercises

11. **LO.1 (Technology acquisition)** Acquisition of new technology is often a perilous event for firms. The successful acquisition and implementation of new systems require much more than merely purchasing hardware and software. For example, costs are likely to be incurred for the following:
    - research and consulting to select software and hardware vendor
    - software training
    - upgrading IT infrastructure to operate new hardware and software
    - continuing hardware and software support
    - implementation of the new system
    a. Why should training be included as a cost of technology acquisition?
    b. How can the financial function of a business improve the internal process of technology acquisition?
12. **LO.1 (Technological change)** Financial professionals are at the forefront in adopting new technologies, many of which are at the core of business strategies. Discuss how the increasing reliance of business on technology coupled with the responsibility of the financial professional to manage technology has changed the skills required of corporate accountants.

13. **LO.1 (Business process reengineering)** Business process reengineering (BPR) can be an effective tool to aid in achieving breakthroughs in quality improvement and cost management. Total quality management (TQM) is another philosophy about achieving organizational change. Conduct a library or Internet search to identify articles that discuss BPR and TQM, and write a report in which you compare and contrast the two methodologies.
14. **LO.1 (Business process reengineering)** Process mapping and value analysis are tools often used in business process reengineering. As discussed in Chapter 4, a process map is a flowchart of the set of activities that compose a process. Value (or activity) analysis examines each of the activities identified in the flowchart and determines to what extent it provides "value" to the customer. Those activities that add no value are targets to be designed out of the process.

    Select a process at your college or university such as admissions or enrollment. Prepare a process map, and conduct a value analysis of the process map. Then develop a plan (using Exhibit 19–2 as a guide) to design out of the process activities that add no value to the student customer.

15. **LO.2 (Downsizing)** In the past decade, the Japanese economy has fallen from its lofty levels of the 1980s. As a consequence, many Japanese companies have been forced to downsize. In most companies, one of two strategies can be pursued in downsizing. First, a company can lay off employees. Second, a company can cut employment through natural attrition and by reducing future hiring.

Conduct a library or Internet search of "Japanese management culture" to identify attitudes of Japanese managers about employees. Then prepare a report in which you explain why Japanese companies might prefer one of these downsizing strategies to the other.

16. **LO.2 (Downsizing)** In recent years, the financial press reported story after story regarding downsizing and layoffs in the U.S. auto industry. Often the stories discussed multiple rounds of downsizing events.

    Assume that you are a stock market analyst and are responsible for interpreting the economic significance of corporate layoffs. In general, would you interpret the auto industry layoffs as good news or bad news? Explain the rationale for your answer.

17. **LO.3 (Diversity)** The issue of whether diversity is positive or negative for an organization has been hotly debated for many years. Some people argue that, because of its homogeneous workforce, Japan has an inherent advantage in competing with the United States. The benefits of a homogeneous workforce result from a common language, religion, work ethic, and so forth. Prepare a two-minute oral report in which you take a position and persuasively present an argument on whether diversity aids or hinders an organization.

18. **LO.3 (Diversity and discrimination)** In 2007, Nike settled a class action lawsuit filed on behalf of 400 African American employees of the company's Niketown store in Chicago. One of the allegations in the suit was that the store segregated African American employees into lower-paying jobs including cashiers and stockroom workers rather than sales positions. The settlement cost Nike $7.6 million to resolve the financial claims.

    Discuss the contributions that can be made by the accounting and finance professionals in an organization to actively promote diversification of the workforce while managing real and perceived discrimination in treatment of workers and managers.

19. **LO.4 (Enterprise resource planning)** With an ERP system, a company can develop a "storefront" on the Internet. Through its storefront connection with customers, the company can gather much information about the market and the demand for specific products.

    Assume that you are employed by an automaker. How could you use the Internet storefront and data mining to learn more about the purchasers of your vehicles to improve the market share of future generations of your company's autos?

20. **LO.4 (Enterprise resource planning)** ERP software programs allow tighter linkages within a supply chain than were possible with earlier generations of software. Consider the possibility of a tighter link between the marketing and engineering functions within a firm that makes consumer electronics. Discuss how the link between these two functions could improve the following:
    a. customer satisfaction.
    b. time to bring new products to market.
    c. cost management.

21. **LO.4 (Enterprise resource planning)** ERP software can facilitate the sharing of information throughout the supply chain. For example, an Internet storefront can be used to interact downstream with the final customer. Sales data gathered from the storefront can then be used as a basis for determining the quantity and mix of products to be produced. From this information, a production schedule can be prepared. Discuss how posting the production schedule on the Internet could result in improved coordination with the upstream (vendor) side of the supply chain.

22. **LO.5 (Strategic alliances)** In their annual reports, companies provide brief descriptions of their most important contracts, including strategic alliances. Select a large publicly traded company and obtain a copy of its most recent annual report (in hard copy, on the company's Web site, or on the EDGAR portion of the SEC's Web site). Review the portions of the annual report that discuss strategic alliances. Based on your review, prepare an oral report in which you discuss the following points:
    a. motivations for establishing strategic alliances.
    b. extent to which strategic alliances are used to conduct business.
    c. relative financial success of the strategic alliances.

23. **LO.5 (Strategic alliances)** Assume you are employed by a technology company that is considering entering into a strategic alliance with a communications company to provide certain innovative services delivered via the Internet. As a financial professional, how could you contribute to the organization and management of the strategic alliance?

24. **LO.6 (Open-book management)** MONOPOLY by Parker Brothers has been a popular board game for many years. Assume that you have just been hired by a company in the steel industry. The company manufactures a variety of products from stock steel components. The management of your new employer is examining the potential use of open-book management techniques. Prepare a written report for the top managers in your

company discussing your recommendations for implementing open-book management. In your report, discuss how you would use MONOPOLY as a training tool for workers who have little knowledge of accounting concepts.

25. **LO.6 (Open-book management)** You have been hired as a consultant by a company that manufactures plastic and resin toys. Company management is presently discussing ways to improve product quality. Evidence of quality problems is everywhere: high rates of product defects, many product returns from customers, poor rate of customer retention, and high warranty costs. Top management has traced virtually all quality-related problems to the production department.

    Production workers in the company are paid a flat hourly rate. No bonuses are paid based on corporate profits or departmental performance measures. As the outside consultant, prepare an oral report to present to your client's top management discussing how open-book management could be applied to address the quality problems. At a minimum, include in your report how quality information would be conveyed to workers, how workers would be trained to understand the information, and how incentives would be established for improved quality performance.

26. **LO.7 (Environmental costs)** Following are descriptions of environmental waste situations. Identify the environmental strategy you would select to deal with each situation and discuss your logic.
    a. A relatively small amount of low toxicity waste is produced. This waste is not easily recycled, nor is technology available to avoid its production. Disposal costs are relatively modest.
    b. The waste produced is highly toxic and is associated with several lethal diseases in humans. The cost of disposal is extraordinarily high.
    c. A moderate amount of waste, which is nearly identical to a chemical purchased and used in an etching operation, is produced. The waste differs from the purchased chemical only because of a small amount of contaminants introduced in the production process.

27. **LO.7 (Environmental costs)** Calvert Chemicals produces a variety of chemicals that are used in an array of commercial applications. One popular product, a chemical solvent, contains two very caustic acids: A and B, each of which can present a very serious environmental hazard if not disposed of properly. For every ton of chemical produced, 500 pounds of acid A and 300 pounds of acid B are required. Inefficiencies in the current production process allow 40 pounds of acid A and 20 pounds of acid B to remain as waste from each ton of chemical manufactured. Because of impurities in the waste acids, they cannot be used in the production of future batches of product. The company incurs a cost of $2 per pound to dispose of the waste acid produced.

    Recently, the company has become aware of new technology that reduces the amount of waste acids produced. This technology would generate only 1 pound of acid A and 5 pounds of acid B as waste from each ton of chemical manufactured. Corporate management has estimated that the new technology could be acquired and installed at a cost of $500,000. The technology would have a life expectancy of six years. The new technology would not otherwise affect the cost of producing the chemical solvent.
    a. Which environmental cost management strategy is Calvert Chemicals considering in this example?
    b. Why would the application of discounted cash flow methods (see Chapter 15) be appropriate for evaluating the new technology?

28. **LO.7 (Environmental cost management)** Firms' increasing awareness of their impacts on the environment has led to the establishment of companies that specialize in all aspects of managing the environmental effects of operations. Search the Internet using the term "environmental cost management." Review the Web pages of the vendors of environmental services identified by the search, and then write a brief report in which you describe the types of services that can be purchased to manage environmental costs.

Problems

29. **LO.1 (Business process reengineering)** In 2007, Cerberus Capital Management hired the former boss of Home Depot, Bob Nardelli, to run Chrysler. Earlier in the year Cerberus Capital Management had purchased a majority stake in Chrysler from DaimlerChrysler. Mr. Nardelli, while CEO of Home Depot, implemented the six-sigma philosophy. The essence of this philosophy is to identify causes of variability in processes and reduce the variability—thereby increasing the quality of the process. Critics of Mr. Nardelli suggest that the implementation of six-sigma at Home Depot proved that six-sigma methodologies are inapplicable to widely distributed retail stores and that the attempted implementation was a flop.

Source: Anonymous, "Nardelli's Approach May Not Translate Well at Chrysler," *Wall Street Journal* (August 7, 2007), http://onlinewsj.com/article/SB118643255010789576.html (last accessed 8/20/07).

Conduct research to follow the changes Nardelli implemented at Chrysler and whether six-sigma was implemented as a driver of the changes.

30. **LO.1 & LO.2 (Accounting; downsizing; BPR)** Most accounting professionals would agree that the accounting profession has developed effective tools for measuring and reporting events involving tangible assets. Most might also agree that the profession has miles to travel to report as effectively on events involving intangible assets. Examples of intangible assets are patents developed rather than purchased; customer and supplier relationships; and employee knowledge, skills, and abilities.

Assume that a U.S.-based manufacturing company implemented a BPR that resulted in the layoff of 20 percent of production workers.

a. How would the layoff impact the company's intangible assets?

b. How would the BPR event be reflected in the company's financial statements?

c. Given your answer to part (a), do you think the financial reports reflect all significant effects of the layoffs? Explain.

31. **LO.1 & LO.2 (Downsizing; outsourcing)** One of the key drivers of downsizing and outsourcing is globalization. Recently, the Organization for Economic Cooperation and Development (OECD) acknowledged "growing unease about globalization." The organization expressed concerns that in some countries there may be a backlash against globalization because some workers have been victims of the globalization trend. The conventional wisdom that globalization could be likened to a rising tide that would lift all boats is apparently not true. Particularly, many workers with low skills in developed countries are having difficulty finding work because of the offshoring of jobs to developing countries and the increased use of technology in the manufacturing sector.

Source: Marcus Walker, "Free-Trade Alert: A Warning on Globalization Backlash," *Wall Street Journal* (June 20, 2007) p. A4.

a. Discuss the extent to which accounting systems capture the cost of downsizing incurred in a particular country. Do you think decisions to downsize would be different if all of the costs of downsizing borne by a society were captured by the accounting system of the reporting entity?

b. What ethical obligation, if any, do developed countries have to supply a safety net to workers who are displaced by effects of global competition? Explain. ▲

32. **LO.2 (Downsizing)** *"Most experienced CEOs have seen command-and-control management come and go. They've been through downsizing and rightsizing. Now they're seeing most companies (their own included) working to recast themselves as 'high-performing' organizations, with streamlined, non-hierarchical, fast moving teams of 'knowledge workers' trying to generate the greatest possible return on 'human capital.' The New Economy has put that capital in high demand and short supply, particularly in IT and other high-tech fields. As a result, CEOs and their top executives find themselves facing a broad spectrum of new challenges: competing for top talent, designing jobs consistent with business goals, communicating strategy, sharing information, earning employees' trust and commitment, measuring and improving employee performance, moving them up and leading them onward."*

Source: Hannele Rubin, "How CEOs Get Results," *Chief Executive* (February 2001), p. 8ff.

What can the accounting function in an organization do to help identify potential top management talent from internal operations?

33. **LO.2 (Restructuring and outsourcing; ethics)** Automakers provide an interesting study in cost management strategies. General Motors often provides a contrast to other U.S. manufacturers. For example, DaimlerChrysler and Ford opted to outsource many product components, but GM continues to manufacture a much higher percentage of the parts needed to produce its cars. One of the variables driving GM's strategy is its high level of unionization. The unions have resisted attempts made by General Motors to restructure operations and outsource more components.

a. From the perspective of price-based competition, why would GM want the flexibility to outsource more of its parts and components?

b. From the perspective of managing quality, how could outsourcing positively or negatively affect GM's ability to manage quality relative to its competitors?

c. What ethical responsibility does GM bear to the union in seeking to restructure and outsource more of its parts manufacturing? ▲

34. **LO.1, LO.2 & LO.6 (Various)** Karen Krackle, CEO of Kar Komponents, sat dejected in her chair after reviewing the 2009 first-quarter financial reports on one of the company's core products: a standard, five-speed transmission (product #2122) used in the heavy equipment industry in the manufacture of earth-moving equipment. Some of the information in the report follows:

MARKET REPORT, PRODUCT #2122, QUARTER 1, 2009

Sales Data	
Total sales (dollars), Quarter 1, 2009	$4,657,500
Total sales (dollars), Quarter 1, 2008	$6,405,000
Total sales (units), Quarter 1, 2009	3,450
Total sales (units), Quarter 1, 2008	4,200

Market Data	
Industry unit sales, Quarter 1, 2009	40,000
Industry unit sales, Quarter 1, 2008	32,000
Industry average sales price, Quarter 1, 2009	$1,310
Industry average sales price, Quarter 1, 2008	$1,640

Profit Data	
Kar Komponents average gross profit per unit, Quarter 1, 2009	$ 45
Kar Komponents average gross profit per unit, Quarter 1, 2008	160
Industry average gross profit per unit, Quarter 1, 2009	75
Industry average gross profit per unit, Quarter 1, 2008	140

Kar Komponents' strategy for this transmission is to compete on the basis of price. The transmission offers no features that allow it to be differentiated from those of major competitors. Kar Komponents' level of quality is similar to the average of the industry.

Also on Krackle's desk was a report from her business intelligence unit, on which she underlined the following key pieces of information.

- Commodity transmission components (nuts, bolts, etc.), which all major transmission producers acquire from specialty vendors, decreased in price by approximately 5 percent from January 2008 to January 2009.
- Two major competitors moved their main assembly operations from the United States to China in early 2008. These competitors are believed to have the lowest unit production cost in the industry.
- A third major competitor ceased manufacturing major gear components and began outsourcing these parts from a Mexican firm in mid-2008. This firm increased its market share in 2008 from 10 to 14 percent following a major decrease in sales price.
- Kar Komponents' production operations did not change in any material respect from 2008 to 2009.
- Kar Komponents manufactures approximately 83 percent of the components used in the heavy industrial transmission. The industry norm is to make 57 percent of the components.
- For the balance of 2009, industry experts agree that quarterly demand for the heavy industrial transmission will be even higher than the levels posted for the first quarter of 2009.

a. Examine the information Krackle has gathered. Analyze the data to identify as specifically as possible the problems that have led to Kar Komponents' loss of profit and market share in the heavy industrial transmission market.

b. Based on your analysis in part (a) and the information given to Krackle, suggest specific alternatives that she should consider in making her firm more competitive in its market. Use concepts presented in the chapter as the basis of your recommendations.

35. **LO.4 (Enterprise resource management)** Borders and Amazon.com are competitors in vending books and other consumer items. The two are differentiated to an extent by their marketing strategies. Although Amazon.com relies exclusively on Internet marketing, Borders operates both retail stores and an Internet outlet.

Assume that you work for a financial services firm that specializes in ERP installations. Your personal specialty involves ERP solutions that link the marketing function to the "back end" of businesses. Write a report in which you discuss the benefits that could be realized by Borders and Amazon.com from purchasing ERP software from you. In your report, discuss how the ERP solution that you would design for Borders would differ from the solution you design for Amazon.com.

36. LO.2 & LO.6 (Ethics) *Employees expect that all parties will honor their explicit and implicit obligations. Distrust occurs when these obligations are not met or when the parties have different expectations regarding the obligations. When downsizing is employed as an organizational strategy, it focuses on economic goals over the promotion of commitment, and, as a result, the employees view the strategy with distrust.*

John A. Challenger notes, "It may be unrealistic to expect intense loyalty on the part of the worker when in many instances the employer cannot promise loyalty in return. The current spate of mergers in the banking, media, utilities, and other industries, major re-engineering efforts, and downsizings all have weakened the ties that spur employee commitment and productivity." Frederick Reichheld states, "The great betrayal of American workers is the failure of companies to let them know how much value they are creating, versus how much they are costing."

Source: Adapted from Larry Gross, "Downsizing: Are Employers Reneging on Their Social Promise?" *CPCU Journal* (Summer 2001), p. 112ff.

   a. In your opinion, does the achievement of high-quality operations mandate that a firm treat its employees ethically? Discuss.
   b. Discuss how employee perceptions of their employers mesh with the open-book management requirement to have honest exchanges of information between employees and managers. ▲

37. LO.5 (Strategic alliances) Strategic alliances and joint ventures are being used with increasing frequency to exploit market opportunities. Virtually all larger firms are involved in several-to-many strategic alliances.
   a. From the perspective of controlling the quality of production, discuss how a strategic alliance is significantly different from a typical vendor/customer relationship.
   b. How can the accounting function contribute to the management of quality for strategic alliances?

38. LO.6 (Open-book management) In many large business organizations today, it is common that the financial experts are physically located separately from operational personnel. One effect of this isolation is that the people with financial expertise often lack understanding of important facets of operations. At SC Johnson, financial experts intermingle in teams with production experts and much decision authority is delegated to cross-functional teams. Individuals with responsibilities for cost management, quality, safety, etc., rotate duties to learn about staffing, quality management, production processing, and production scheduling. Top management takes the view that every employee is essential to the success of the company—and the company has 12,000 employees in 70 countries and has never had a layoff!

Source: Staff, "Springfield Remanufacturing, Behlen, and SC Johnson Deliver Outstanding 'Return on Individuals,'" *Manufacturing Business Technology* (April 1, 2006); http://www.mbtmag.com/article/CA6320636.html (last accessed 8/20/07).

   a. How could a financial specialist who is charged with designing an open-book management system benefit from serving a rotation in production, quality management, and other functional areas?
   b. Discuss how open-book management implementation would be affected by including, on cross-functional teams, a specialist in cost management.

39. LO.6 (Open-book management; transparency) Open-book management is consistent with another, larger trend in accounting—increased transparency of financial results. This trend follows a period in which many U.S. firms were guilty of generating misleading financial reports and hiding pertinent facts about financial performance. These practices led to the Sarbanes-Oxley Act of 2002 and other corporate reporting reforms such as the establishment of the Public Company Accounting Oversight Board (PCAOB). Research on the topic of financial reporting transparency to address the following items:

   a. Discuss what is meant by the term "transparency" in the context of financial reporting.
   b. Discuss how open-book management is consistent with increased reporting transparency.

40. LO.6 (Open-book management) Kathy Townsend, Technical Instruments Division manager of Bigelow Electronics, attended a 30-minute seminar on open-book management recently. As a result of the seminar, she decided to implement some open-book management practices in her division. She began the process today when she received the latest quarterly results for her division.

Gary Robinson, the production supervisor of the finishing department in Townsend's division, was surprised to receive the following note in his afternoon mail.

Dear Gary:

I've just finished reviewing the financial results for the last quarter. I am including some data from the financial reports below. Because our firm must identify ways to become more cost competitive, I intend to share data from the financial reports with you each quarter. I want you to use the information as the basis for making your department more efficient. By early in the coming year, I intend to put in place an incentive pay system that will replace your current salary. Accordingly, your income in the future will depend on your ability to manage the costs of your department.

To begin reducing costs, I suggest you concentrate on the cost items which I have circled below. Please give me a call if you have any questions.

Regards,

KT

FINISHING DEPARTMENT COST ANALYSIS

	This Quarter	This Quarter Last Year	Last Quarter
Direct material	$ 95,000	$ 75,000	$ 90,000
Direct labor	925,000	840,000	940,000
Material-based overhead	27,000	22,000	23,000
Labor-based overhead	(413,000)	382,700	396,500
Machine-based overhead	(657,000)	589,000	617,000

As corporate controller of Bigelow Electronics, you are surprised when Robinson calls your office and asks to meet with your staff to discuss the financial report and to discuss the meaning of "overhead." As you consider how to deal with him, you begin to contemplate the memo that you are going to write to Townsend. Before any decisions are implemented, you realize that she can use your expertise to design and implement open-book management practices. As you write the memo, you know that your suggestions must be specific, positive, and informative. Write the memo to Ms. Townsend.

41. **LO.7 (Environmental cost management)** Classic Plastics has experienced serious problems as a result of attempts to manage its impacts on the environment. To illustrate the problems, consider the following events, which occurred during the past five years:

 ■ Classic was assessed $75 million in fines and penalties for toxic emissions. These amounts related to several separate regulatory investigations.
 ■ Classic received reprimands from several regulatory bodies for failing to maintain required records regarding hazardous waste.
 ■ Classic is currently facing a class-action lawsuit filed by former employees of a subsidiary in Mexico alleging that management failed to disclose information to employees about the toxicity of certain materials. As a consequence, the health of the former employees has been permanently harmed.
 ■ Classic must submit bids to obtain most of its business. Managers have casually observed that the company is successful more frequently when it bids on jobs that require handling the most toxic chemicals.
 ■ Classic has a very basic accounting system that tracks costs on a job order basis but is not sensitive to quality or environmental costs.

Assume that you are an employee of the consulting firm that Classic has hired to improve the management of all environmental effects. As the financial expert on the consulting team, you are expected to make recommendations as to how the information systems should be modified to reduce environmental costs. Prepare a report discussing your recommendations for Classic.

42. **LO.7 (Environmental management; ethics)** The chapter discusses three approaches to managing environmental costs. Some strategies deal with hazardous waste only after it has been produced.

 a. Does a firm have any ethical obligations *not* to produce hazardous waste regardless of how successfully it is dealt with by the firm?
 b. Assume that you are a key financial adviser in a firm that produces a large amount of toxic waste and that faces severe financial pressures and risks bankruptcy. By improperly disposing of certain waste materials, your firm could save millions of dollars, avoid bankruptcy, and preserve 10,000 local jobs. What action would you recommend your firm take? Explain the rationale for your answer. ▲

Appendix A

Present Value Tables

TABLE 1 *Present Value of $1*

Period	1.00%	2.00%	3.00%	4.00%	5.00%	6.00%	7.00%	8.00%	9.00%	9.50%	10.00%	10.50%	11.00%
1	0.9901	0.9804	0.9709	0.9615	0.9524	0.9434	0.9346	0.9259	0.9174	0.9132	0.9091	0.9050	0.9009
2	0.9803	0.9612	0.9426	0.9246	0.9070	0.8900	0.8734	0.8573	0.8417	0.8340	0.8265	0.8190	0.8116
3	0.9706	0.9423	0.9151	0.8890	0.8638	0.8396	0.8163	0.7938	0.7722	0.7617	0.7513	0.7412	0.7312
4	0.9610	0.9239	0.8885	0.8548	0.8227	0.7921	0.7629	0.7350	0.7084	0.6956	0.6830	0.6707	0.6587
5	0.9515	0.9057	0.8626	0.8219	0.7835	0.7473	0.7130	0.6806	0.6499	0.6352	0.6209	0.6070	0.5935
6	0.9421	0.8880	0.8375	0.7903	0.7462	0.7050	0.6663	0.6302	0.5963	0.5801	0.5645	0.5493	0.5346
7	0.9327	0.8706	0.8131	0.7599	0.7107	0.6651	0.6228	0.5835	0.5470	0.5298	0.5132	0.4971	0.4817
8	0.9235	0.8535	0.7894	0.7307	0.6768	0.6274	0.5820	0.5403	0.5019	0.4838	0.4665	0.4499	0.4339
9	0.9143	0.8368	0.7664	0.7026	0.6446	0.5919	0.5439	0.5003	0.4604	0.4419	0.4241	0.4071	0.3909
10	0.9053	0.8204	0.7441	0.6756	0.6139	0.5584	0.5084	0.4632	0.4224	0.4035	0.3855	0.3685	0.3522
11	0.8963	0.8043	0.7224	0.6496	0.5847	0.5268	0.4751	0.4289	0.3875	0.3685	0.3505	0.3334	0.3173
12	0.8875	0.7885	0.7014	0.6246	0.5568	0.4970	0.4440	0.3971	0.3555	0.3365	0.3186	0.3018	0.2858
13	0.8787	0.7730	0.6810	0.6006	0.5303	0.4688	0.4150	0.3677	0.3262	0.3073	0.2897	0.2731	0.2575
14	0.8700	0.7579	0.6611	0.5775	0.5051	0.4423	0.3878	0.3405	0.2993	0.2807	0.2633	0.2471	0.2320
15	0.8614	0.7430	0.6419	0.5553	0.4810	0.4173	0.3625	0.3152	0.2745	0.2563	0.2394	0.2237	0.2090
16	0.8528	0.7285	0.6232	0.5339	0.4581	0.3937	0.3387	0.2919	0.2519	0.2341	0.2176	0.2024	0.1883
17	0.8444	0.7142	0.6050	0.5134	0.4363	0.3714	0.3166	0.2703	0.2311	0.2138	0.1978	0.1832	0.1696
18	0.8360	0.7002	0.5874	0.4936	0.4155	0.3503	0.2959	0.2503	0.2120	0.1952	0.1799	0.1658	0.1528
19	0.8277	0.6864	0.5703	0.4746	0.3957	0.3305	0.2765	0.2317	0.1945	0.1783	0.1635	0.1500	0.1377
20	0.8195	0.6730	0.5537	0.4564	0.3769	0.3118	0.2584	0.2146	0.1784	0.1628	0.1486	0.1358	0.1240
21	0.8114	0.6598	0.5376	0.4388	0.3589	0.2942	0.2415	0.1987	0.1637	0.1487	0.1351	0.1229	0.1117
22	0.8034	0.6468	0.5219	0.4220	0.3419	0.2775	0.2257	0.1839	0.1502	0.1358	0.1229	0.1112	0.1007
23	0.7954	0.6342	0.5067	0.4057	0.3256	0.2618	0.2110	0.1703	0.1378	0.1240	0.1117	0.1006	0.0907
24	0.7876	0.6217	0.4919	0.3901	0.3101	0.2470	0.1972	0.1577	0.1264	0.1133	0.1015	0.0911	0.0817
25	0.7798	0.6095	0.4776	0.3751	0.2953	0.2330	0.1843	0.1460	0.1160	0.1034	0.0923	0.0824	0.0736
26	0.7721	0.5976	0.4637	0.3607	0.2812	0.2198	0.1722	0.1352	0.1064	0.0945	0.0839	0.0746	0.0663
27	0.7644	0.5859	0.4502	0.3468	0.2679	0.2074	0.1609	0.1252	0.0976	0.0863	0.0763	0.0675	0.0597
28	0.7568	0.5744	0.4371	0.3335	0.2551	0.1956	0.1504	0.1159	0.0896	0.0788	0.0693	0.0611	0.0538
29	0.7493	0.5631	0.4244	0.3207	0.2430	0.1846	0.1406	0.1073	0.0822	0.0719	0.0630	0.0553	0.0485
30	0.7419	0.5521	0.4120	0.3083	0.2314	0.1741	0.1314	0.0994	0.0754	0.0657	0.0573	0.0500	0.0437
31	0.7346	0.5413	0.4000	0.2965	0.2204	0.1643	0.1228	0.0920	0.0692	0.0600	0.0521	0.0453	0.0394
32	0.7273	0.5306	0.3883	0.2851	0.2099	0.1550	0.1147	0.0852	0.0634	0.0058	0.0474	0.0410	0.0355
33	0.7201	0.5202	0.3770	0.2741	0.1999	0.1462	0.1072	0.0789	0.0582	0.0500	0.0431	0.0371	0.0319
34	0.7130	0.5100	0.3660	0.2636	0.1904	0.1379	0.1002	0.0731	0.0534	0.0457	0.0391	0.0336	0.0288
35	0.7059	0.5000	0.3554	0.2534	0.1813	0.1301	0.0937	0.0676	0.0490	0.0417	0.0356	0.0304	0.0259
36	0.6989	0.4902	0.3450	0.2437	0.1727	0.1227	0.0875	0.0626	0.0449	0.0381	0.0324	0.0275	0.0234
37	0.6920	0.4806	0.3350	0.2343	0.1644	0.1158	0.0818	0.0580	0.0412	0.0348	0.0294	0.0249	0.0210
38	0.6852	0.4712	0.3252	0.2253	0.1566	0.1092	0.0765	0.0537	0.0378	0.0318	0.0267	0.0225	0.0190
39	0.6784	0.4620	0.3158	0.2166	0.1492	0.1031	0.0715	0.0497	0.0347	0.0290	0.0243	0.0204	0.0171
40	0.6717	0.4529	0.3066	0.2083	0.1421	0.0972	0.0668	0.0460	0.0318	0.0265	0.0221	0.0184	0.0154
41	0.6650	0.4440	0.2976	0.2003	0.1353	0.0917	0.0624	0.0426	0.0292	0.0242	0.0201	0.0167	0.0139
42	0.6584	0.4353	0.2890	0.1926	0.1288	0.0865	0.0583	0.0395	0.0268	0.0221	0.0183	0.0151	0.0125
43	0.6519	0.4268	0.2805	0.1852	0.1227	0.0816	0.0545	0.0365	0.0246	0.0202	0.0166	0.0137	0.0113
44	0.6455	0.4184	0.2724	0.1781	0.1169	0.0770	0.0510	0.0338	0.0226	0.0184	0.0151	0.0124	0.0101
45	0.6391	0.4102	0.2644	0.1712	0.1113	0.0727	0.0476	0.0313	0.0207	0.0168	0.0137	0.0112	0.0091
46	0.6327	0.4022	0.2567	0.1646	0.1060	0.0685	0.0445	0.0290	0.0190	0.0154	0.0125	0.0101	0.0082
47	0.6265	0.3943	0.2493	0.1583	0.1010	0.0647	0.0416	0.0269	0.0174	0.0141	0.0113	0.0092	0.0074
48	0.6203	0.3865	0.2420	0.1522	0.0961	0.0610	0.0389	0.0249	0.0160	0.0128	0.0103	0.0083	0.0067
49	0.6141	0.3790	0.2350	0.1463	0.0916	0.0576	0.0363	0.0230	0.0147	0.0117	0.0094	0.0075	0.0060
50	0.6080	0.3715	0.2281	0.1407	0.0872	0.0543	0.0340	0.0213	0.0135	0.0107	0.0085	0.0068	0.0054

Period	11.50%	12.00%	12.50%	13.00%	13.50%	14.00%	14.50%	15.00%	15.50%	16.00%	17.00%	18.00%	19.00%	20.00%
1	0.8969	0.8929	0.8889	0.8850	0.8811	0.8772	0.8734	0.8696	0.8658	0.8621	0.8547	0.8475	0.8403	0.8333
2	0.8044	0.7972	0.7901	0.7832	0.7763	0.7695	0.7628	0.7561	0.7496	0.7432	0.7305	0.7182	0.7062	0.6944
3	0.7214	0.7118	0.7023	0.6931	0.6839	0.6750	0.6662	0.6575	0.6490	0.6407	0.6244	0.6086	0.5934	0.5787
4	0.6470	0.6355	0.6243	0.6133	0.6026	0.5921	0.5818	0.5718	0.5619	0.5523	0.5337	0.5158	0.4987	0.4823
5	0.5803	0.5674	0.5549	0.5428	0.5309	0.5194	0.5081	0.4972	0.4865	0.4761	0.4561	0.4371	0.4191	0.4019
6	0.5204	0.5066	0.4933	0.4803	0.4678	0.4556	0.4438	0.4323	0.4212	0.4104	0.3898	0.3704	0.3521	0.3349
7	0.4667	0.4524	0.4385	0.4251	0.4121	0.3996	0.3876	0.3759	0.3647	0.3538	0.3332	0.3139	0.2959	0.2791
8	0.4186	0.4039	0.3897	0.3762	0.3631	0.3506	0.3385	0.3269	0.3158	0.3050	0.2848	0.2660	0.2487	0.2326
9	0.3754	0.3606	0.3464	0.3329	0.3199	0.3075	0.2956	0.2843	0.2734	0.2630	0.2434	0.2255	0.2090	0.1938
10	0.3367	0.3220	0.3080	0.2946	0.2819	0.2697	0.2582	0.2472	0.2367	0.2267	0.2080	0.1911	0.1756	0.1615
11	0.3020	0.2875	0.2737	0.2607	0.2483	0.2366	0.2255	0.2149	0.2049	0.1954	0.1778	0.1619	0.1476	0.1346
12	0.2708	0.2567	0.2433	0.2307	0.2188	0.2076	0.1969	0.1869	0.1774	0.1685	0.1520	0.1372	0.1240	0.1122
13	0.2429	0.2292	0.2163	0.2042	0.1928	0.1821	0.1720	0.1625	0.1536	0.1452	0.1299	0.1163	0.1042	0.0935
14	0.2179	0.2046	0.1923	0.1807	0.1699	0.1597	0.1502	0.1413	0.1330	0.1252	0.1110	0.0986	0.0876	0.0779
15	0.1954	0.1827	0.1709	0.1599	0.1496	0.1401	0.1312	0.1229	0.1152	0.1079	0.0949	0.0835	0.0736	0.0649
16	0.1752	0.1631	0.1519	0.1415	0.1319	0.1229	0.1146	0.1069	0.0997	0.0930	0.0811	0.0708	0.0618	0.0541
17	0.1572	0.1456	0.1350	0.1252	0.1162	0.1078	0.1001	0.0929	0.0863	0.0802	0.0693	0.0600	0.0520	0.0451
18	0.1410	0.1300	0.1200	0.1108	0.1024	0.0946	0.0874	0.0808	0.0747	0.0691	0.0593	0.0508	0.0437	0.0376
19	0.1264	0.1161	0.1067	0.0981	0.0902	0.0830	0.0763	0.0703	0.0647	0.0596	0.0506	0.0431	0.0367	0.0313
20	0.1134	0.1037	0.0948	0.0868	0.0795	0.0728	0.0667	0.0611	0.0560	0.0514	0.0433	0.0365	0.0308	0.0261
21	0.1017	0.0926	0.0843	0.0768	0.0700	0.0638	0.0582	0.0531	0.0485	0.0443	0.0370	0.0309	0.0259	0.0217
22	0.0912	0.0826	0.0749	0.0680	0.0617	0.0560	0.0509	0.0462	0.0420	0.0382	0.0316	0.0262	0.0218	0.0181
23	0.0818	0.0738	0.0666	0.0601	0.0543	0.0491	0.0444	0.0402	0.0364	0.0329	0.0270	0.0222	0.0183	0.0151
24	0.0734	0.0659	0.0592	0.0532	0.0479	0.0431	0.0388	0.0349	0.0315	0.0284	0.0231	0.0188	0.0154	0.0126
25	0.0658	0.0588	0.0526	0.0471	0.0422	0.0378	0.0339	0.0304	0.0273	0.0245	0.0197	0.0160	0.0129	0.0105
26	0.0590	0.0525	0.0468	0.0417	0.0372	0.0332	0.0296	0.0264	0.0236	0.0211	0.0169	0.0135	0.0109	0.0087
27	0.0529	0.0469	0.0416	0.0369	0.0327	0.0291	0.0258	0.0230	0.0204	0.0182	0.0144	0.0115	0.0091	0.0073
28	0.0475	0.0419	0.0370	0.0326	0.0289	0.0255	0.0226	0.0200	0.0177	0.0157	0.0123	0.0097	0.0077	0.0061
29	0.0426	0.0374	0.0329	0.0289	0.0254	0.0224	0.0197	0.0174	0.0153	0.0135	0.0105	0.0082	0.0064	0.0051
30	0.0382	0.0334	0.0292	0.0256	0.0224	0.0196	0.0172	0.0151	0.0133	0.0117	0.0090	0.0070	0.0054	0.0042
31	0.0342	0.0298	0.0260	0.0226	0.0197	0.0172	0.0150	0.0131	0.0115	0.0100	0.0077	0.0059	0.0046	0.0035
32	0.0307	0.0266	0.0231	0.0200	0.0174	0.0151	0.0131	0.0114	0.0099	0.0087	0.0066	0.0050	0.0038	0.0029
33	0.0275	0.0238	0.0205	0.0177	0.0153	0.0133	0.0115	0.0099	0.0086	0.0075	0.0056	0.0043	0.0032	0.0024
34	0.0247	0.0212	0.0182	0.0157	0.0135	0.0116	0.0100	0.0088	0.0075	0.0064	0.0048	0.0036	0.0027	0.0020
35	0.0222	0.0189	0.0162	0.0139	0.0119	0.0102	0.0088	0.0075	0.0065	0.0056	0.0041	0.0031	0.0023	0.0017
36	0.0199	0.0169	0.0144	0.0123	0.0105	0.0089	0.0076	0.0065	0.0056	0.0048	0.0035	0.0026	0.0019	0.0014
37	0.0178	0.0151	0.0128	0.0109	0.0092	0.0078	0.0067	0.0057	0.0048	0.0041	0.0030	0.0022	0.0016	0.0012
38	0.0160	0.0135	0.0114	0.0096	0.0081	0.0069	0.0058	0.0049	0.0042	0.0036	0.0026	0.0019	0.0014	0.0010
39	0.0143	0.0120	0.0101	0.0085	0.0072	0.0060	0.0051	0.0043	0.0036	0.0031	0.0022	0.0016	0.0011	0.0008
40	0.0129	0.0108	0.0090	0.0075	0.0063	0.0053	0.0044	0.0037	0.0031	0.0026	0.0019	0.0013	0.0010	0.0007
41	0.0115	0.0096	0.0080	0.0067	0.0056	0.0046	0.0039	0.0033	0.0027	0.0023	0.0016	0.0011	0.0008	0.0006
42	0.0103	0.0086	0.0077	0.0059	0.0049	0.0041	0.0034	0.0028	0.0024	0.0020	0.0014	0.0010	0.0007	0.0005
43	0.0093	0.0077	0.0063	0.0052	0.0043	0.0036	0.0030	0.0025	0.0020	0.0017	0.0012	0.0008	0.0006	0.0004
44	0.0083	0.0068	0.0056	0.0046	0.0038	0.0031	0.0026	0.0021	0.0018	0.0015	0.0010	0.0007	0.0005	0.0003
45	0.0075	0.0061	0.0050	0.0041	0.0034	0.0028	0.0023	0.0019	0.0015	0.0013	0.0009	0.0006	0.0004	0.0003
46	0.0067	0.0054	0.0044	0.0036	0.0030	0.0024	0.0020	0.0016	0.0013	0.0011	0.0007	0.0005	0.0003	0.0002
47	0.0060	0.0049	0.0039	0.0032	0.0026	0.0021	0.0017	0.0014	0.0011	0.0009	0.0006	0.0004	0.0003	0.0002
48	0.0054	0.0043	0.0035	0.0028	0.0023	0.0019	0.0015	0.0012	0.0010	0.0008	0.0005	0.0004	0.0002	0.0002
49	0.0048	0.0039	0.0031	0.0025	0.0020	0.0016	0.0013	0.0011	0.0009	0.0007	0.0005	0.0003	0.0002	0.0001
50	0.0043	0.0035	0.0028	0.0022	0.0018	0.0014	0.0012	0.0009	0.0007	0.0006	0.0004	0.0003	0.0002	0.0001

TABLE 2 *Present Value of an Ordinary Annuity of $1*

Period	1.00%	2.00%	3.00%	4.00%	5.00%	6.00%	7.00%	8.00%	9.00%	9.50%	10.00%	10.50%	11.00%
1	0.9901	0.9804	0.9709	0.9615	0.0524	0.9434	0.9346	0.9259	0.9174	0.9132	0.9091	0.9050	0.9009
2	1.9704	1.9416	1.9135	1.8861	1.8594	1.8334	1.8080	1.7833	1.7591	1.7473	1.7355	1.7240	1.7125
3	2.9410	2.8839	2.8286	2.7751	2.7233	2.6730	2.6243	2.5771	2.5313	2.5089	2.4869	2.4651	2.4437
4	3.9020	3.8077	3.7171	3.6299	3.5460	3.4651	3.3872	3.3121	3.2397	3.2045	3.1699	3.1359	3.1025
5	4.8534	4.7135	4.5797	4.4518	4.3295	4.2124	4.1002	3.9927	3.8897	3.8397	3.7908	3.7429	3.6959
6	5.7955	5.6014	5.4172	5.2421	5.0757	4.9173	4.7665	4.6229	4.4859	4.4198	4.3553	4.2922	4.2305
7	6.7282	6.4720	6.2303	6.0021	5.7864	5.5824	5.3893	5.2064	5.0330	4.9496	4.8684	4.7893	4.7122
8	7.6517	7.3255	7.0197	6.7327	6.4632	6.2098	5.9713	5.7466	5.5348	5.4334	5.3349	5.2392	5.1461
9	8.5660	8.1622	7.7861	7.4353	7.1078	6.8017	6.5152	6.2469	5.9953	5.8753	5.7590	5.6463	5.5371
10	9.4713	8.9826	8.5302	8.1109	7.7217	7.3601	7.0236	6.7101	6.4177	6.2788	6.1446	6.0148	5.8892
11	10.3676	9.7869	9.2526	8.7605	8.3064	7.8869	7.4987	7.1390	6.8052	6.6473	6.4951	6.3482	6.2065
12	11.2551	10.5753	9.9540	9.3851	8.8633	8.3838	7.9427	7.5361	7.1607	6.9838	6.8137	6.6500	6.4924
13	12.1337	11.3484	10.6350	9.9857	9.3936	8.8527	8.3577	7.9038	7.4869	7.2912	7.1034	6.9230	6.7499
14	13.0037	12.1063	11.2961	10.5631	9.8986	9.2950	8.7455	8.2442	7.7862	7.5719	7.3667	7.1702	6.9819
15	13.8651	12.8493	11.9379	11.1184	10.3797	9.7123	9.1079	8.5595	8.0607	7.8282	7.6061	7.3938	7.1909
16	14.7179	13.5777	12.5611	11.6523	10.8378	10.1059	9.4467	8.8514	8.3126	8.0623	7.8237	7.5962	7.3792
17	15.5623	14.2919	13.1661	12.1657	11.2741	10.4773	9.7632	9.1216	8.5436	8.2760	8.0216	7.7794	7.5488
18	16.3983	14.9920	13.7535	12.6593	11.6896	10.8276	10.0591	9.3719	8.7556	8.4713	8.2014	7.9452	7.7016
19	17.2260	15.6785	14.3238	13.1339	12.0853	11.1581	10.3356	9.6036	8.9501	8.6496	8.3649	8.0952	7.8393
20	18.0456	16.3514	14.8775	13.5903	12.4622	11.4699	10.5940	9.8182	9.1286	8.8124	8.5136	8.2309	7.9633
21	18.8570	17.0112	15.4150	14.0292	12.8212	11.7641	10.8355	10.0168	9.2922	8.9611	8.6487	8.3538	8.0751
22	19.6604	17.6581	15.9369	14.4511	13.1630	12.0416	11.0612	10.2007	9.4424	9.0969	8.7715	8.4649	8.1757
23	20.4558	18.2922	16.4436	14.8568	13.4886	12.3034	11.2722	10.3711	9.5802	9.2209	8.8832	8.5656	8.2664
24	21.2434	18.9139	16.9355	15.2470	13.7986	12.5504	11.4693	10.5288	9.7066	9.3342	8.9847	8.6566	8.3481
25	22.0232	19.5235	17.4132	15.6221	14.0939	12.7834	11.6536	10.6748	9.8226	9.4376	9.0770	8.7390	8.4217
26	22.7952	20.1210	17.8768	15.9828	14.3752	13.0032	11.8258	10.8100	9.9290	9.5320	9.1610	8.8136	8.4881
27	23.5596	20.7069	18.3270	16.3296	14.6430	13.2105	11.9867	10.9352	10.0266	9.6183	9.2372	8.8811	8.5478
28	24.3164	21.2813	18.7641	16.6631	14.8981	13.4062	12.1371	11.0511	10.1161	9.6971	9.3066	8.9422	8.6016
29	25.0658	21.8444	19.1885	16.9837	15.1411	13.5907	12.2777	11.1584	10.1983	9.7690	9.3696	8.9974	8.6501
30	25.8077	22.3965	19.6004	17.2920	15.3725	13.7648	12.4090	11.2578	10.2737	9.8347	9.4269	9.0474	8.6938
31	26.5423	22.9377	20.0004	17.5885	15.5928	13.9291	12.5318	11.3498	10.3428	9.8947	9.4790	9.0927	8.7332
32	27.2696	23.4683	20.3888	17.8736	15.8027	14.0840	12.6466	11.4350	10.4062	9.9495	9.5264	9.1337	8.7686
33	27.9897	23.9886	20.7658	18.1477	16.0026	14.2302	12.7538	11.5139	10.4664	9.9996	9.5694	9.1707	8.8005
34	28.7027	24.4986	21.1318	18.4112	16.1929	14.3681	12.8540	11.5869	10.5178	10.0453	9.6086	9.2043	8.8293
35	29.4086	24.9986	21.4872	18.6646	16.3742	14.4983	12.9477	11.6546	10.5668	10.0870	9.6442	9.2347	8.8552
36	30.1075	25.4888	21.8323	18.9083	16.5469	14.6210	13.0352	11.7172	10.6118	10.1251	9.6765	9.2621	8.8786
37	30.7995	25.9695	22.1672	19.1426	16.7113	14.7368	13.1170	11.7752	10.6530	10.1599	9.7059	9.2870	8.8996
38	31.4847	26.4406	22.4925	19.3679	16.8679	14.8460	13.1935	11.8289	10.6908	10.1917	9.7327	9.3095	8.9186
39	32.1630	26.9026	22.8082	19.5845	17.0170	14.9491	13.2649	11.8786	10.7255	10.2207	9.7570	9.3299	8.9357
40	32.8347	27.3555	23.1148	19.7928	17.1591	15.0463	13.3317	11.9246	10.7574	10.2473	9.7791	9.3483	8.9511
41	33.4997	27.7995	23.4124	19.9931	17.2944	15.1380	13.3941	11.9672	10.7866	10.2715	9.7991	9.3650	8.9649
42	34.1581	28.2348	23.7014	20.1856	17.4232	15.2245	13.4525	12.0067	10.8134	10.2936	9.8174	9.3801	8.9774
43	34.8100	28.6616	23.9819	20.3708	17.5459	15.3062	13.5070	12.0432	10.8380	10.3138	9.8340	9.3937	8.9887
44	35.4555	29.0800	24.2543	20.5488	17.6628	15.3832	13.5579	12.0771	10.8605	10.3322	9.8491	9.4061	8.9988
45	36.0945	29.4902	24.5187	20.7200	17.7741	15.4558	13.6055	12.1084	10.8812	10.3490	9.8628	9.4163	9.0079
46	36.7272	29.8923	24.7755	20.8847	17.8801	15.5244	13.6500	12.1374	10.9002	10.3644	9.8753	9.4274	9.0161
47	37.3537	30.2866	25.0247	21.0429	17.9810	15.5890	13.6916	12.1643	10.9176	10.3785	9.8866	9.4366	9.0236
48	37.9740	30.6731	25.2667	21.1951	18.0772	15.6500	13.7305	12.1891	10.9336	10.3913	9.8969	9.4449	9.0302
49	38.5881	31.0521	25.5017	21.3415	18.1687	15.7076	13.7668	12.2122	10.9482	10.4030	9.9063	9.4524	9.0362
50	39.1961	31.4236	25.7298	21.4822	18.2559	15.7619	13.8008	12.2335	10.9617	10.4137	9.9148	9.4591	9.0417

Period	11.50%	12.00%	12.50%	13.00%	13.50%	14.00%	14.50%	15.00%	15.50%	16.00%	17.00%	18.00%	19.00%	20.00%
1	0.8969	0.8929	0.8889	0.8850	0.8811	0.8772	0.8734	0.8696	0.8658	0.8621	0.8547	0.8475	0.8403	0.8333
2	1.7012	1.6901	1.6790	1.6681	1.6573	1.6467	1.6361	1.6257	1.6154	1.6052	1.5852	1.5656	1.5465	1.5278
3	2.4226	2.4018	2.3813	2.3612	2.3413	2.3216	2.3023	2.2832	2.2644	2.2459	2.2096	2.1743	2.1399	2.1065
4	3.0696	3.0374	3.0056	2.9745	2.9438	2.9137	2.8841	2.8850	2.8263	2.7982	2.7432	2.6901	2.6386	2.5887
5	3.6499	3.6048	3.5606	3.5172	3.4747	3.4331	3.3922	3.3522	3.3129	3.2743	3.1994	3.1272	3.0576	2.9906
6	4.1703	4.1114	4.0538	3.9976	3.9425	3.8887	3.8360	3.7845	3.7341	3.6847	3.5892	3.4976	3.4098	3.3255
7	4.6370	4.5638	4.4923	4.4226	4.3546	4.2883	4.2236	4.1604	4.0988	4.0386	3.9224	3.8115	3.7057	3.6046
8	5.0556	4.9676	4.8821	4.7988	4.7177	4.6389	4.5621	4.4873	4.4145	4.3436	4.2072	4.0776	3.9544	3.8372
9	5.4311	5.3283	5.2285	5.1317	5.0377	4.9464	4.8577	4.7716	4.6879	4.6065	4.4506	4.3030	4.1633	4.0310
10	5.7678	5.6502	5.5364	5.4262	5.3195	5.2161	5.1159	5.0188	4.9246	4.8332	4.6586	4.4941	4.3389	4.1925
11	6.0698	5.9377	5.8102	5.6869	5.5679	5.4527	5.3414	5.2337	5.1295	5.0286	4.8364	4.6560	4.4865	4.3271
12	6.3406	6.1944	6.0535	5.9177	5.7867	5.6603	5.5383	5.4206	5.3069	5.1971	4.9884	4.7932	4.6105	4.4392
13	6.5835	6.4236	6.2698	6.1218	5.9794	5.8424	5.7103	5.5832	5.4606	5.3423	5.1183	4.9095	4.7147	4.5327
14	6.8013	6.6282	6.4620	6.3025	6.1493	6.0021	5.8606	5.7245	5.5936	5.4675	5.2293	5.0081	4.8023	4.6106
15	6.9967	6.8109	6.6329	6.4624	6.2989	6.1422	5.9918	5.8474	5.7087	5.5755	5.3242	5.0916	4.8759	4.6755
16	7.1719	6.9740	6.7848	6.6039	6.4308	6.2651	6.1063	5.9542	5.8084	5.6685	5.4053	5.1624	4.9377	4.7296
17	7.3291	7.1196	6.9198	6.7291	6.5469	6.3729	6.2064	6.0472	5.8947	5.7487	5.4746	5.2223	4.9897	4.7746
18	7.4700	7.2497	7.0398	6.8399	6.6493	6.4674	6.2938	6.1280	5.9695	5.8179	5.5339	5.2732	5.0333	4.8122
19	7.5964	7.3658	7.1465	6.9380	6.7395	6.5504	6.3701	6.1982	6.0342	5.8775	5.5845	5.3162	5.0700	4.8435
20	7.7098	7.4694	7.2414	7.0248	6.8189	6.6231	6.4368	6.2593	6.0902	5.9288	5.6278	5.3528	5.1009	4.8696
21	7.8115	7.5620	7.3257	7.1016	6.8889	6.6870	6.4950	6.3125	6.1387	5.9731	5.6648	5.3837	5.1268	4.8913
22	7.9027	7.6447	7.4006	7.1695	6.9506	6.7429	6.5459	6.3587	6.1807	6.0113	5.6964	5.4099	5.1486	4.9094
23	7.9845	7.7184	7.4672	7.2297	7.0049	6.7921	6.5903	6.3988	6.2170	6.0443	5.7234	5.4321	5.1669	4.9245
24	8.0578	7.7843	7.5264	7.2829	7.0528	6.8351	6.6291	6.4338	6.2485	6.0726	5.7465	5.4510	5.1822	4.9371
25	8.1236	7.8431	7.5790	7.3300	7.0950	6.8729	6.6629	6.4642	6.2758	6.0971	5.7662	5.4669	5.1952	4.9476
26	8.1826	7.8957	7.6258	7.3717	7.1321	6.9061	6.6925	6.4906	6.2994	6.1182	5.7831	5.4804	5.2060	4.9563
27	8.2355	7.9426	7.6674	7.4086	7.1649	6.9352	6.7184	6.5135	6.3198	6.1364	5.7975	5.4919	5.2151	4.9636
28	8.2830	7.9844	7.7043	7.4412	7.1937	6.9607	6.7409	6.5335	6.3375	6.1520	5.8099	5.5016	5.2228	4.9697
29	8.3255	8.0218	7.7372	7.4701	7.2191	6.9830	6.7606	6.5509	6.3528	6.1656	5.8204	5.5098	5.2292	4.9747
30	8.3637	8.0552	7.7664	7.4957	7.2415	7.0027	6.7779	6.5660	6.3661	6.1772	5.8294	5.5168	5.2347	4.9789
31	8.3980	8.0850	7.7923	7.5183	7.2613	7.0199	6.7929	6.5791	6.3776	6.1872	5.8371	5.5227	5.2392	4.9825
32	8.4287	8.1116	7.8154	7.5383	7.2786	7.0350	6.8060	6.5905	6.3875	6.1959	5.8437	5.5277	5.2430	4.9854
33	8.4562	8.1354	7.8359	7.5560	7.2940	7.0482	6.8175	6.6005	6.3961	6.2034	5.8493	5.5320	5.2463	4.9878
34	8.4809	8.1566	7.8542	7.5717	7.3075	7.0599	6.8275	6.6091	6.4035	6.2098	5.8541	5.5356	5.2490	4.9898
35	8.5030	8.1755	7.8704	7.5856	7.3193	7.0701	6.8362	6.6166	6.4100	6.2153	5.8582	5.5386	5.2512	4.9930
36	8.5229	8.1924	7.8848	7.5979	7.3298	7.0790	6.8439	6.6231	6.4156	6.2201	5.8617	5.5412	5.2531	4.9930
37	8.5407	8.2075	7.8976	7.6087	7.3390	7.0868	6.8505	6.6288	6.4204	6.2242	5.8647	5.5434	5.2547	4.9941
38	8.5567	8.2210	7.9090	7.6183	7.3472	7.0937	6.8564	6.6338	6.4246	6.2278	5.8673	5.5453	5.2561	4.9951
39	8.5710	8.2330	7.9191	7.6268	7.3543	7.0998	6.8615	6.6381	6.4282	6.2309	5.8695	5.5468	5.2572	4.9959
40	8.5839	8.2438	7.9281	7.6344	7.3607	7.1050	6.8659	6.6418	6.4314	6.2335	5.8713	5.5482	5.2582	4.9966
41	8.5954	8.2534	7.9361	7.6410	7.3662	7.1097	6.8698	6.6450	6.4341	6.2358	5.8729	5.5493	5.2590	4.9972
42	8.6058	8.2619	7.9432	7.6469	7.3711	7.1138	6.8732	6.6479	6.4364	6.2377	5.8743	5.5502	5.2596	4.9976
43	8.6150	8.2696	7.9495	7.6522	7.3754	7.1173	6.8761	6.6503	6.4385	6.2394	5.8755	5.5511	5.2602	4.9980
44	8.6233	8.2764	7.9551	7.6568	7.3792	7.1205	6.8787	6.6524	6.4402	6.2409	5.8765	5.5517	5.2607	4.9984
45	8.6308	8.2825	7.9601	7.6609	7.3826	7.1232	6.8810	6.6543	6.4418	6.2421	5.8773	5.5523	5.2611	4.9986
46	8.6375	8.2880	7.9645	7.6645	7.3855	7.1256	6.8830	6.6559	6.4431	6.2432	5.8781	5.5528	5.2614	4.9989
47	8.6435	8.2928	7.9685	7.6677	7.3881	7.1277	6.8847	6.6573	6.4442	6.2442	5.8787	5.5532	5.2617	4.9991
48	8.6489	8.2972	7.9720	7.6705	7.3904	7.1296	6.8862	6.6585	6.4452	6.2450	5.8792	5.5536	5.2619	4.9992
49	8.6537	8.3010	7.9751	7.6730	7.3925	7.1312	6.8875	6.6596	6.4461	6.2457	5.8797	5.5539	5.2621	4.9992
50	8.6580	8.3045	7.9779	7.6752	7.3942	7.1327	6.8886	6.6605	6.4468	6.2463	5.8801	5.5541	5.2623	4.9995

Glossary

ABC see activity-based costing

ABM see activity-based management

abnormal loss a decline in units in excess of expectations during a production process

absorption costing a cost accumulation and reporting method that treats the costs of all manufacturing components (direct material, direct labor, variable overhead, and fixed overhead) as inventoriable or product costs; the traditional approach to product costing; must be used for external financial statements and tax reporting

accounting rate of return (ARR) the rate of earnings obtained on the average capital investment over the life of a capital project; computed as average annual profits divided by average investment; not based on cash flow

activity a repetitive action performed in fulfillment of business functions

activity analysis the process of detailing the various repetitive actions that are performed in making a product or providing a service, classifying them as value-added and non-value-added, and devising ways of minimizing or eliminating non-value-added activities

activity-based costing (ABC) a process using multiple cost drivers to predict and allocate costs to products and services; an accounting system collecting financial and operational data on the basis of the underlying nature and extent of business activities; an accounting information and costing system that identifies the various activities performed in an organization, collects costs on the basis of the underlying nature and extent of those activities, and assigns costs to products and services based on consumption of those activities by the products and services

activity-based management (ABM) a discipline that focuses on the activities incurred during the production/performance process as the way to improve the value received by a customer and the resulting profit achieved by providing this value

activity center a segment of the production or service process for which management wants to separately report the costs of the activities performed

activity driver a measure of the demands on activities and, thus, the resources consumed by products and services; often indicates an activity's output

actual cost system a valuation method that uses actual direct material, direct labor, and overhead charges in determining the cost of Work in Process Inventory

ad hoc discount a price concession made under competitive pressure (real or imagined) that does not relate to quantity purchased

administrative department an organizational unit that performs management activities benefiting the entire organization; includes top management personnel and organization headquarters

advance pricing agreement (APA) a binding contract between a company and one or more national tax authorities that provides details of how a transfer price is to be set and establishes that no adjustments or penalties will be made if the agreed-upon methodology is used

algebraic method a process of support department cost allocation that considers all interrelationships of the departments and reflects these relationships in simultaneous equations

algorithm a logical step-by-step problem-solving technique (generally requiring the use of a computer) that continuously searches for an improved solution from the one previously computed until the best answer is determined

allocate assign cost based on the use of a cost driver, a cost predictor, or an arbitrary method

allocation the systematic assignment of an amount to a recipient set of categories

annuity a series of equal cash flows (either positive or negative) per period

annuity due a series of equal cash flows being received or paid at the beginning of a period

applied overhead the amount of overhead that has been allocated to Work in Process Inventory as a result of productive activity; credits for this amount are to an overhead account

appraisal cost a quality control cost incurred for monitoring or inspection; compensates for mistakes not eliminated through prevention activities

appropriation a budgeted maximum allowable expenditure

approximated net realizable value at split-off allocation a method of allocating joint cost to joint products using a simulated net realizable value at the split-off point; computed as final sales price minus incremental separate costs

asset turnover a ratio measuring asset productivity and showing the number of sales dollars generated by each dollar of assets

authority the right (usually by virtue of position or rank) to use resources to accomplish a task or achieve an objective

autonomation the use of equipment that has been programmed to sense certain conditions

backflush costing a streamlined cost accounting method that speeds up, simplifies, and reduces accounting effort in an environment that minimizes inventory balances, requires few allocations, uses standard costs, and has minimal variances from standard

balanced scorecard (BSC) an approach to performance measurement that uses performance measures from four perspectives: financial, internal business, customer, and innovation and learning

batch-level cost a cost that is caused by a group of things being made, handled, or processed at a single time

benchmarking the process of investigating how others do something better so that the investigating company can imitate, and possibly improve upon, its techniques

benefits-provided ranking a listing of support departments in an order that begins with the one providing the most support to all other corporate areas and ends with the support department providing support primarily to revenue-producing areas

bill of materials a source document that contains information about the product material components and their specifications (including quality and quantities needed)

black box a term for a management control system whose exact nature of operation cannot be observed

bottleneck any object or facility having a processing speed sufficiently slow to cause the other processing mechanisms in its network to experience idle time

break-even chart a graph that depicts the relationships among revenues, variable costs, fixed costs, and profits (or losses)

break-even point (BEP) the level of activity, in units or dollars, at which total revenues equal total costs

budget a financial plan for the future based on a single level of activity; the quantitative expression of a company's commitment to planned activities and resource acquisition and use

budgeting the process of formalizing plans and committing them to written, financial terms

budget manual a detailed set of documents that provides descriptive information and guidelines about the budgetary process

budget slack an intentional underestimation of revenues and/or overestimation of expenses in a budgeting process for the purpose of including deviations that are likely to occur so that results will meet expectations

budget variance the difference between total actual overhead and budgeted overhead based on standard hours allowed for the production achieved during the period; computed as part of two-variance overhead analysis; also referred to as the controllable variance

build mission a mission of increasing market share even at the expense of short-term profits and cash flow; typically pursued by a business unit that has a small market share in a high-growth industry; appropriate for products that are in the early stages of the product life cycle

business process reengineering (BPR) the process of combining information technology to create new and more effective business processes to lower costs, eliminate unnecessary work, upgrade customer service, and increase speed to market

business-value-added activity an activity that is necessary for the operation of the business but for which a customer would not want to pay; a non-value-adding activity

by-product an incidental output of a joint process; is salable, but its sales value is not substantial enough for management to justify undertaking the joint process; has a higher sales value than scrap

capacity a measure of production volume or some other activity base

capital asset an asset used to generate revenues or cost savings by providing production, distribution, or service capabilities for more than one year

capital budgeting a process of evaluating an entity's proposed long-range projects or courses of future activity for the purpose of allocating limited resources to desirable projects

capital rationing a process that allocates scarce or constrained monetary resources to capital asset acquisitions

carrying cost the total variable cost of carrying one unit of inventory in stock for one year; includes the opportunity cost of capital invested in inventory

cash flow the receipt or disbursement of cash; when related to capital budgeting, cash flows arise from the purchase, operation, and disposition of a capital asset

centralization a management style that exists when top management makes most decisions and controls most activities of the organizational units from the company's central headquarters

coefficient of determination a measure of dispersion that indicates the "goodness of fit" of the actual observations to the least squares regression line; indicates what proportion of the total variation in Y is explained by the regression model

committed cost a cost related either to the long-term investment in plant and equipment of a business or to the organizational personnel deemed permanent by top management; cannot be changed without long-run detriment to the organization

compensation strategy a foundation for the compensation plan that addresses the role compensation should play in the organization

competence the notion that individuals will develop and maintain the skills necessary to practice their profession

compounding period the time between each interest computation

compound interest a method of determining interest in which interest that was earned in prior periods is added to the original investment so that, in each successive period, interest is earned on both principal and interest

computer-integrated manufacturing (CIM) the integration of two or more flexible manufacturing systems through the use of a host computer and an information networking system

confidentiality the notion that individuals will refrain from disclosing company information to inappropriate parties, such as competitors; is often specifically defined or referred to in the company's code of ethics

confrontation strategy an organizational strategy in which company management decides to confront, rather than avoid, competition; an organizational strategy in which company management still attempts to differentiate company products through new features or to develop a price leadership position by dropping prices, even though management recognizes that competitors will rapidly bring out similar products and match price changes; an organizational strategy in which company management identifies and exploits current opportunities for competitive advantage in recognition of the fact that those opportunities are transitory

constraint a restriction inhibiting the achievement of an objective

continuous budget a plan in which there is a rolling twelve-month budget; a new budget month (twelve months into the future) is added as each current month expires

continuous improvement an ongoing process of enhancing employee task performance, level of product quality, and level of company service through (1) eliminating non-value-added activities to reduce lead time, (2) making products (performing services) with zero defects, (3) reducing product costs on an ongoing basis, and/or (4) simplifying products and processes

continuous loss any reduction in units that occurs uniformly throughout a production process

contribution margin (CM) the difference between selling price and variable cost per unit or between total revenue and total variable cost at a specific level of activity; the amount of each revenue dollar remaining after variable costs have been covered that goes toward coverage of fixed costs and generation of profits

contribution margin ratio (CM%) the proportion of each revenue dollar remaining after variable costs have been covered; computed as contribution margin divided by sales

control chart a graphical presentation of the results of a specified activity; indicates the upper and lower control limits and those results that are out of control

controllable cost a cost over which a manager has the ability to authorize incurrence or directly influence magnitude

controllable variance the budget variance of the two-variance approach to analyzing overhead variances

conversion cost the sum of direct labor and overhead cost; the cost necessary to transform direct material into a finished good or service

core competency a higher proficiency relative to competitors in a critical function or activity; a root of competitiveness and competitive advantage; anything that is not a core competency is a viable candidate for outsourcing

cost the cash or cash equivalent value necessary to attain an objective such as acquiring goods and services, complying with a contract, performing a function, or producing and distributing a product

cost accounting a discipline that focuses on techniques or methods for determining the cost of a project, process, or thing through direct measurement, arbitrary assignment, or systematic and rational allocation

Cost Accounting Standards Board (CASB) a body established by Congress in 1970 to promulgate cost accounting standards for defense contractors and federal agencies; disbanded in 1980 and reestablished in 1988

cost allocation the assignment, using some reasonable basis, of any indirect cost to one or more cost objects

cost avoidance the practice of finding acceptable alternatives to high-cost items and/or not spending money for unnecessary goods or services

cost-benefit analysis the analytical process of comparing the relative costs and benefits that result from a specific course of action (such as providing information or investing in a project)

cost center a responsibility center in which the manager has the authority to incur costs and is evaluated on the basis of how well costs are controlled

cost consciousness a company-wide attitude about the topics of cost understanding, cost containment, cost avoidance, and cost reduction

cost containment the practice of minimizing, to the extent possible, period-by-period increases in per-unit variable and total fixed costs

cost control system a logical structure of formal and/or informal activities designed to analyze and evaluate how well expenditures are managed during a period

cost driver a factor that has a direct cause-effect relationship to a cost; an activity creating a cost

cost driver analysis the process of investigating, quantifying, and explaining the relationships of cost drivers and their related costs

cost leadership a company's ability to maintain its competitive edge by undercutting competitor prices

cost management system (CMS) a set of formal methods developed for planning and controlling an organization's cost-generating activities relative to its goals and objectives

cost object anything to which costs attach or are related

cost of capital (COC) the weighted average cost of the various sources of funds (debt and stock) that comprise a firm's financial structure

cost of compliance the sum of prevention and appraisal costs

cost of goods manufactured (CGM) the total cost of the goods completed and transferred to Finished Goods Inventory during the period

cost of noncompliance the cost of production imperfections that is equal to the sum of internal and external failure costs

cost of production report a process costing document that details all operating and cost information, shows the computation of cost per equivalent unit, and indicates cost assignment to goods produced during the period

cost-plus contract a contract in which the customer agrees to reimburse the producer for the cost of the job plus a specified profit margin over cost

cost reduction the practice of lowering current costs, especially those that may be in excess of what is necessary

cost structure the relative composition of an organization's fixed and variable costs

cost table a database providing information about the impact on product costs of using different input resources, manufacturing processes, and design specifications

cost-volume-profit (CVP) analysis a procedure that examines changes in costs and volume levels and the resulting effects on net income (profits)

credibility the belief that individuals will provide full, fair, and timely disclosure of all relevant information

critical success factor (CSF) any operational dimension (such as quality, customer service, efficiency, cost control, or responsiveness to change) so important that failure in that area could cause the organization to fail

customer value perspective a balanced scorecard perspective that addresses how well an organization is doing relative to important customer criteria such as speed (lead time), quality, service, and price (both purchases and after purchase)

CVP see cost-volume-profit analysis

cycle (lead) time the time elapsed between the placement of an order and the time the goods arrive for usage or are produced by the company; the sum of value-added time and non-value-added time

data mining a form of analysis in which statistical techniques are used to uncover answers to important questions about business operations

decentralization a management style that exists when top management grants subordinate managers a significant degree of autonomy and independence in operating and making decisions for their organizational units

decision variable an unknown item for which a linear programming problem is being solved

defect a unit that has been rejected at inspection for failure to meet appropriate quality standards or designated product specifications but that can be reworked and sold

degree of operating leverage (DOL) a factor that indicates how a percentage change in sales, from the existing or current level, will affect company profits; calculated as contribution margin divided by net income; equal to (1 ÷ margin of safety percentage)

dependent variable an unknown variable that is to be predicted using one or more independent variables

differential cost a cost that differs in amount among the alternatives being considered

differential revenue a revenue that differs in amount among alternatives

direct cost a cost that is distinctly traceable to a particular cost object

direct costing see variable costing

direct labor the individuals who work specifically on manufacturing a product or performing a service; the time of individuals who work specifically on manufacturing a product or performing a service; the cost of such time

direct material a readily identifiable part of a product; the cost of such a part

direct method a support department cost allocation approach that assigns support department costs directly to revenue-producing areas with only one set of intermediate cost pools or allocations

discounting the process of reducing future cash flows to present value amounts

discount rate the rate of return used to discount future cash flows to their present value amounts; should equal or exceed an organization's weighted average cost of capital

discrete loss a reduction in units that occurs at a specific point in a production process

discretionary cost a cost that is periodically reviewed by a decision maker in a process of determining whether it continues to be in accord with ongoing policies; arises from a management decision to fund an activity at a specified cost amount for a specified period of time, generally one year; can be reduced to zero in the short run if necessity so dictates

distribution cost a cost incurred to warehouse, transport, or deliver a product or service

downsizing any management action that reduces employment upon restructuring operations in response to competitive pressures

downstream cost a cost related to marketing, distribution, or customer service

dual pricing arrangement a transfer pricing system that allows a selling division to record the transfer of goods or services at one price (e.g., a market or negotiated market price) and a buying division to record the transfer at another price (e.g., a cost-based amount)

Du Pont model a model that indicates the return on investment as it is affected by profit margin and asset turnover

earnings management any accounting method or practice used by managers or accountants to deliberately "adjust" a company's profit amount to meet a predetermined internal or external target

economic order quantity (EOQ) an estimate of the number of units per order that will be the least costly and provide the optimal balance between the costs of ordering and the costs of carrying inventory

economic production run (EPR) an estimate of the number of units to produce at one time that minimizes the total costs of setting up production runs and the costs of carrying inventory

economic value added (EVA®) a measure of the extent to which income exceeds the dollar cost of capital; calculated as income minus (invested capital times the cost of capital percentage)

employee stock ownership plan (ESOP) a profit-sharing compensation program in which investments are made in the securities of the employer

employee time sheet a source document that indicates, for each employee, what jobs were worked on during a time period and for what amount of time

employee-to-capital cost ratio a ratio that measures the relative importance of human and financial capital to the industry

engineered cost a cost that has been found to bear an observable and known relationship to a quantifiable activity base

engineering change order (ECO) a business mandate that changes the way in which a product is manufactured or a service is performed by modifying the design, parts, process, or quality of the product or service

enterprise resource planning (ERP) system a packaged software program that allows a company to (1) automate and integrate the majority of its business processes, (2) share common data and practices across the entire enterprise, and (3) produce and access information in a real-time environment